The Documentary History
of the
First Federal Elections
1788–1790

VOLUME   I

The
Documentary History
of the
First Federal Elections
1788–1790

VOLUME I

EDITED BY

Merrill Jensen
Robert A. Becker

The University of Wisconsin Press

Published 1976

The University of Wisconsin Press
Box 1379, Madison, Wisconsin 53701

The University of Wisconsin Press, Ltd.
70 Great Russell Street, London

Copyright © 1976
The Regents of the University of Wisconsin System
All rights reserved

First printing

Printed in the United States of America

For LC CIP information see the colophon

ISBN 0-299-06690-8

Publication of this book was made possible
in part by grants from the
National Historical Publications and Records Commission
and the Trustees of the William F. Vilas Trust Estate

Contents

General Introduction

The first federal elections in 1788, 1789, and 1790 receive little more than passing mention, if any mention at all, in most of the books and monographs on the writing and ratification of the Constitution and the establishment of the new government. Yet the political leaders at the time looked upon those elections as crucial in the establishment of the new government and the implementation of the principles of the Constitution. Furthermore, one of the major issues they debated in the elections was an issue that Americans had begun debating long before independence.

Americans had argued that each colonial legislature had the right to govern the internal affairs of each colony without outside interference. Great Britain replied in the Declaratory Act of 1766 that Parliament had the right to make laws to bind the colonies and people of America in "all cases whatsoever." The Declaration of Independence was the American answer to Britain, but it did not settle the argument within America.

The first constitution of the United States, the Articles of Confederation, was, in part, a logical outcome of the debate with Great Britain. It was an outcome too of one of the basic convictions of many Revolutionary leaders: that unchecked power in government and in the hands of officeholders was dangerous to liberty.

The Articles created a strictly federal government in which each state retained its equality with the other states and had one vote in Congress. Members of Congress were elected annually by the state legislatures and were subject to recall at any time. Furthermore, no man could serve in Congress more than three years in any six. Congress was given specific powers, and specific restraints were laid upon the states, but all powers not delegated to Congress were retained by the states. Article II declared that "Each State retains its sovereignty, freedom and independence, and every power, jurisdiction, and right, which is not by this confederation expressly delegated to the United States, in Congress assembled."

The state governments, created by the first state constitutions, also reflected the disputes and the ideology of the times. The power of governors and courts to check legislatures was almost entirely abolished, and ultimate political power was placed in the hands of legislative majorities.

Nevertheless, there were American political leaders who, from the beginning of the American Revolution, believed that the central government needed more power than the Articles of Confederation granted to it. They tried to create such a government when the Articles were written, and they tried to add powers to Congress by various "constitutional interpretations" before the Articles were ratified. Once the Articles received the required unanimous ratification of the states in March 1781, these men attempted to amend the Articles to give Congress coercive power over the states, an independent income, and the power to regulate trade. In addition, every year from 1780 onwards, proposals were made for calling a convention which would revise the structure and increase the power of the central government.

Attempts to amend the Articles of Confederation were blocked by the real or imagined interests of various states and by the conflict of interest between the Northern and Southern states. Proposals for a convention were opposed by men who were concerned only with their own states and who wanted no outside interference. Conventions were also opposed by men who, while they agreed that Congress needed more power, insisted that any additional power be carefully and specifically defined. They believed that a federal government was best for a nation of such social, economic, and geographic diversity as the United States, and they feared that a convention might undo what they believed to be the achievements of the Revolution. Such men were soon to be known as "Antifederalists." Meanwhile, the men who wanted what they came to call a national government eventually gave up their efforts to amend the Articles and pinned their hopes on a constitutional convention. In 1787 these men took the name "Federalists." The names "Federalist" and "Antifederalist" thus did not represent the basic convictions of the two groups, but the reverse, as people at the time knew.

The events which led to the meeting of a convention began in January 1786 when Virginia invited the states to send delegates to Annapolis, Maryland, to consider the question of uniform trade regulations for the United States. Twelve delegates from five states met at Annapolis in September and issued a report which suggested that uniform trade regulations would require adjustments in other parts of the federal system. Therefore, the report proposed, the states should appoint commissioners to meet in Philadelphia in May 1787 "to devise such further provisions as shall appear to them necessary to render the constitution of the Foederal Government adequate to the exigencies of the Union," and to prepare an act which, when approved by Congress and all the state legislatures, "will effectually provide for the same." The Confederation Congress took no action until 21 February 1787, when it resolved that a convention should meet "for the sole and express purpose of revising the Articles of Confederation. . . ."

The Constitutional Convention abandoned the basic concept of the Articles almost at once. Governor Edmund Randolph of Virginia opened the debate on 29 May with a speech describing the defects of the Confederation and then offered fifteen resolutions. According to the notes of one delegate, "he pointed out the various defects of the federal system, the necessity of transforming it into a national efficient Government. . . ." According to another "he candidly confessed" that his resolutions "were not intended for a federal government—he meant a strong *consolidated* union, in which the idea of states should be nearly annihilated."

In the months that followed, the delegates debated most of the issues that Americans had been debating ever since 1774. A minority of delegates wanted to retain the federal structure of the Articles of Confederation. Delegates from states with large populations wanted representation in both houses of Congress based on population, but the small states won equality in the Senate. Northern and Southern delegates fought long and hard over such issues as the regulation of trade, western expansion, and the slave population as a basis for representation in the House of Representatives.

Despite such disputes, which at times threatened to disrupt the Convention, the delegates wrote a constitution fundamentally altering the structure of the central government. While the Constitution retained some of the federal features and even some of the language of the Articles of Confederation, it transferred sovereignty from the states to the central government. The Constitution itself, the laws of the United States, and treaties made by the United States were declared "the supreme Law of the Land" and judges in every state "shall be bound thereby, any Thing in the Constitution or Laws of any State to the Contrary notwithstanding." Furthermore, the Constitution declared that "the judicial Power [of the United States] shall extend to all Cases, in Law and Equity, arising under this Constitution, the Laws of the United States, and Treaties made, or which shall be made, under their Authority. . . ." The Convention also abandoned the method of constitutional change prescribed by the Articles of Confederation: proposal of amendments by Congress and unanimous approval by the state legislatures. The Constitution provided that it should go into effect when ratified by conventions of nine states.

When the Convention finished its work on 17 September 1787, it sent the Constitution to the Confederation Congress with the suggestion that Congress submit it to the states for consideration. Congress transmitted the Constitution to the states on 28 September 1787, and nine state conventions had ratified by 21 June 1788. On 13 September, after a two and a half month debate over where the new government should meet for the first time, the Confederation Congress adopted an election ordinance which set the dates for the election of presidential Electors, for the Electors to vote for the President, and for the new government to meet. The method of electing presidential Electors and members of Congress was the constitutional responsibility of the states.

Political leaders were concerned about the first federal elections even before nine states had ratified the Constitution and long before Congress adopted the Election Ordinance. They realized that the Constitution provided only the skeleton of a government, and that the first Congress would play a crucial role in giving meaning to the Constitution by legislation. Therefore, both the supporters and the opponents of the Constitution turned from the struggle over ratification to the elections without any break in the continuity of political action.

Of the many issues raised in newspapers, pamphlets, and state conventions, none was more intensely debated than the demand that the Constitution be amended. Nearly 200 amendments were proposed by the state conventions, and ratification was achieved in Massachusetts and Virginia only after the Federalists agreed to support amendments. In New York, ratification was not achieved until the Federalists agreed to support amendments and a call for a second constitutional convention to write them.

Most Antifederalists agreed to support the Constitution if amended, although they differed as to how it should be done. Some demanded a second convention to consider amendments before the new government began operations. Alarmed Federalists feared that such a convention would undo the work of the first one and insisted that if amendments were needed, they should be proposed by Congress after the new government was under way.

The amendments proposed by the state conventions were of two kinds: structural amendments and amendments guaranteeing the civil liberties of the people of the United States. The demand for a bill of rights had a widespread appeal among the voters, but Federalist and Antifederalist leaders alike were far more concerned with the structural amendments designed to limit the power of the central government. They recognized, as most ordinary voters probably did not, that the Constitution proposed a revolutionary transfer of power from the states to the central government. Even so, many Federalists thought that the powers set forth in the Constitution were inadequate at best and wanted to increase them if possible. The Antifederalists insisted that too much power had been granted to the central government and that some of it should be returned to the states; and they insisted too that the powers of Congress, the executive, and the judiciary should be far more precisely defined than they were in the Constitution.

Thus amendments were a major campaign issue in such states as Pennsylvania, Massachusetts, Virginia, and New York. Men continued to debate about them as they had during the campaign for ratification and to back or attack candidates for the Senate and the House of Representatives because of their stand on amendments. In addition, the campaigns in several states also reflected old political issues and divisions; that is, voters tended to line up in the federal elections as they had in previous state elections. And as in political campaigns before 1788, and ever since, personalities, past records, and the supposed ambitions of candidates and their supporters were involved. Men were charged with having been Tories or lukewarm patriots in 1776, with being willing to sell the country back to the British, with corruption in and out of office, with aristocratic ambitions and contempt for the people, with narrow vision and lack of concern for the welfare of the nation as a whole, and with other characteristics and attitudes even less desirable.

The Constitution provided that the state legislatures should elect United States Senators. In some states such as South Carolina, Senators were elected with no apparent clash between the House and the Senate. In Pennsylvania, with a single-house legislature, the only contest was among Federalist candidates; but in Massachusetts there was a short but intense struggle between the House and the Senate, both controlled by the Federalists. In New York, the struggle between the Federalist Senate and the Antifederalist House was so prolonged that the state did not elect Senators until July 1789 and did not elect presidential Electors at all.

The enactment of legislation to provide for the election of members of the House of Representatives generally attracted far more attention than the election of Senators. The main issue in most states was whether to hold statewide elections or divide the state into districts. Federalists and Antifederalists supported one method or the other according to their estimate of how it would affect their prospect of winning the elections. Thus the Federalist-dominated Pennsylvania legislature provided for statewide elections, for district elections would have meant the election of Antifederalists in certain backcountry districts. The Federalist-dominated South Carolina legislature provided for district elections, apparently because it feared that a statewide election would mean the election of a five-man Antifederalist delegation. Virginia created districts, and the legislature, dominated by Patrick Henry, engaged in what was later to be called "gerrymandering" in an attempt to prevent the election of James Madison to the House of Representatives. In Massachusetts, the state was divided into eight districts, and the main argument was whether the districts should follow county lines or whether the state should be divided so that each district had approximately equal population.

The states made various provisions for the election of presidential Electors. Four states had popular elections; two had a combination of popular nominations and legislative elections; three provided for election by the legislatures; and in New Jersey the Governor and Council chose the Electors. New York, because of the quarrel between the House and the Senate, did not take part in the election of the President, nor did North Carolina and Rhode Island, because they had not yet ratified the Constitution.

So far as the Presidency was concerned, there was no contest: George Washington was the unanimous choice long before the Electors cast their ballots on 4 February 1789. The major concern of political leaders throughout the country was with the Vice Presidency. The Constitution offered little guidance as to the precise role of the Vice President, but there were willing and even eager candidates for the office. The election of the first Vice President, therefore, involved much of the kind of political maneuvering that was to become common in the election of the President after George Washington retired.

The chapters of this documentary history are arranged in a chronological order determined by the dates of elections to the United States House of Representatives. Although six states had elected United States Senators before any state elected Representatives, the Senators were elected by state legislatures; and, with certain exceptions, little public attention was paid to the choice of Senators before they were elected. In electing Senators, the state legislatures, in effect, were continuing the procedures they had followed ever since 1776 in electing delegates to the Continental and Confederation congresses.

The great legislative innovation of the Constitution was the creation of a House of Representatives to be elected by the voters of the states. It was therefore necessary for each state to create a new electoral process. In contrast to the lack of attention paid to the election of Senators, the passage of the state laws providing for the elections of Representatives was often accompanied by newspaper discussion and legislative debates. Furthermore, campaigns for seats in the House of Representatives attracted widespread newspaper attention, and the outcome of the elections was regarded by political leaders everywhere as crucial in determining the success or failure of the new government. It is for such reasons that we have used the dates of the elections of members of the House of Representatives as the basis for the organization of this documentary history.

We have not attempted to write the history of the first federal elections, but we have provided sketches of the political events of the time in introductions, headnotes, and editorial notes in order to place the documents in their historical context.

We have included the official documents, such as legislative journals, debates, and laws relating to the elections, and material from letters, diaries, newspapers, and other sources.

Approximately 100 newspapers were published in the United States during this period. Several newspapers were published in each of the major northern cities of Philadelphia, New York, and Boston; and complete runs of most of them are still extant, as well as fairly complete runs of newspapers published in smaller northern towns. Far fewer newspapers were published in the states south of Pennsylvania, and in many cases complete runs are no longer extant.

The newspapers are invaluable for both factual information and opinion. The sheer bulk of such material is so great, however, that it is impossible to print more than a sample. The point is illustrated by the fact that on election day in Massachusetts, 18 December 1788, one of Boston's five newspapers contained eleven articles supporting the election of Samuel Adams to the House of Representatives.

Newspaper writers tended to discuss only a few themes, which they repeated over and over. There are endless articles attacking and defending amendments to the Constitution, and in the case of Samuel Adams, praising his services in achieving independence. We have selected what we think are representative examples of such items.

Although there are gaps which the documents do not fill, we believe that the documents printed in these volumes provide the material for an understanding of the fundamental political acts required to establish the Constitution once nine states had ratified it: the election of Representatives, Senators, Electors, and a President, the men who would give shape and meaning to the government created by the Constitution.

ACKNOWLEDGMENTS

The collecting of documents for what has become the Documentary History of the First Federal Elections began in 1952 when the National Historical Publications Commission started gathering material for the Documentary History of the Ratification of the Constitution. Searchers were instructed to collect copies of all contemporary documents relating to the ratification of the Constitution, the first federal elections, the first federal Congress, and the ratification of the Bill of Rights.

In 1966 the Commission sponsored the establishment of two editorial projects in addition to the Documentary History of the Ratification of the Constitution: the Documentary History of the First Federal Elections at the University of Wisconsin and the Documentary History of the First Federal Congress at George Washington University. The process of dividing the documents collected by the Commission was begun at that time.

Much valuable material had been collected before 1966, but much searching remained to be done. The staff of the Ratification project at the National Archives, under the direction of the editor, Dr. Robert E. Cushman, continued to search as time and money permitted, and members of the Elections project undertook to search the libraries west of the Appalachian Mountains for all three projects. When that task was completed, members of the Elections staff began the search of Eastern libraries that had not been searched before or that needed additional searching.

Without such comprehensive searching, no editorial project can hope for success. The Ratification, Elections, and First Congress projects owe much to the searches of the Commission staff before 1966: to James R. Masterson, Philip M. Hamer, Marion Tinling, Leonard C. Faber, and H. B. Fant. A particular debt is owed to Leonard Rapport, who continued to search as long as he was connected with the Ratification project, and to Gaspare J. Saladino, who not only searched but also undertook to organize and distribute the materials to the three closely related editorial projects.

The searchers on the staff of the Elections project who located thousands of new documents for all three projects over a four-year period were Kenneth R. Bowling, David E. Maas, and John P. Kaminski. In addition, two graduate students at the University of Wisconsin—Thomas D. Caulfield and Richard Leffler—looked for materials while doing research for their own theses. Former graduate students at Wisconsin who volunteered their services in searching were Joseph A. Ernst, Richard H. Kohn, Van Beck Hall, and Jerome Nadelhaft.

In the preparation of these documents, the editors have had the invaluable help of graduate students who have worked as part-time research assistants. They are Le Grand Baker, Steven Boyd, Douglas Clanin, and Gordon DenBoer. Finally, we owe a major obligation to the people who have read eighteenth-century handwriting and newsprint and then typed the material for printer's copy. Without the skill and patience of Virginia Fiedler, Carole Foster, Gail Walter, Judy Marberry, Sylvia Sheridan, Ellen Story, and Joan Westgate, a project such as this could not have been undertaken, much less completed.

Financial assistance has come from various sources: from the National Historical Publications Commission, which provided the money to pay most of the staff from 1966 to 1970; from the Research Committee of the University of Wisconsin Graduate School, which provided the funds for a part-time research assistant; and from the Trustees of the Vilas Estate, who provided money for a research assistant, for books, and for travel. Finally, this project, as so many other projects sponsored by the National Historical Publications Commission, owes much to Dr. Oliver W. Holmes, Executive Director of the Commission until his retirement in February 1972, and to his staff. The debt to him is so great that it can only be stated, not reckoned nor paid.

Grateful acknowledgments are also due to hundreds of librarians and custodians of manuscript collections in the United States and Europe. They have willingly answered letters, helped searchers who worked in their libraries, and given permission to print materials from their collections. A list of such libraries is included in the introduction to each volume. Last, but by no means least, we owe a very great debt indeed to the staff of the library of the State Historical Society of Wisconsin, who have willingly helped us in our use of the resources of that great library, resources without which this project could not have been carried on.

Certain libraries and archives require specific permission to print items from their collections. Such permission has been given freely. The letters of Pierce Butler are printed by courtesy of the Trustees of the British Museum; the Archives Nationales of France has given permission to print the correspondence of French consuls in America contained in Affaires Étrangères, Series B, Correspondance Consulaires; the Archives du Ministère des Affaires Étrangères has given permission to print the dispatches of its representatives contained in Correspondance Politique, États-Unis. We have also received permission to print manuscripts in private hands: from members of the Shippen family to print letters of Dr. William Shippen, Jr., from the Shippen family papers on deposit in the Library of Congress; from the Adams Manuscript Trust to print materials from the Adams family papers.

EDITORIAL POLICIES AND PROCEDURES

Literal Reproduction of Official Documents

Official documents such as laws, proclamations, notifications of election to office, and credentials of men elected are reproduced as literally as possible. A few other documents, because of their character or importance, are also reproduced as literally as possible. The literal reproduction of such documents is indicated by the symbol LT (i.e., literal transcript) in the note citation to the source.

Reproduction of Newspaper, Pamphlet, and Broadside Material

Eighteenth-century printers sometimes used several varieties of type in a single item—large capitals, small capitals, and italics, as well as ordinary type. No attempt is made to reproduce varieties of type except when capital letters and italics were evidently used for emphasis by the author or the printer. In a few cases we have reproduced, so far as possible, the format of newspaper items because of the importance the printers or the public apparently attached to such items (for examples, see the *New York Journal*, 26 June, Chapter II, and the *Boston Gazette*, 25 August, Chapter V).

Newspaper items are usually printed as separate documents, but occasionally more than one item from a single issue is printed under the name and date of the newspaper. In such cases the items are separated by a line in the center of the page.

Salutations, Closings, etc., of Letters

Endorsements, addresses, salutations, and complimentary closings of letters are omitted, except in cases where they provide information important for the understanding or identification of a letter. In such cases they are included in the editorial notes.

Excerpts and Elisions

Many documents, particularly letters, contain material such as family news, business affairs, and the like, which in the judgment of the editors is not relevant to the first federal elections. Hence, such material has been omitted. However, when longer excerpts or entire documents have been printed elsewhere, this fact is noted.

Headings for Documents

All headings are supplied by the editors. They are as follows:

(1) Letters: Headings include the names of the writer and the recipient, and the place and date of writing.

(2) Newspaper essays, broadsides, and pamphlets: Headings are usually shortened versions of the full titles, which are given in editorial notes.

(3) Pseudonymous essays: Headings contain the pseudonym, title or short title of the essay, and the source if the essay was printed in a newspaper. Information and conjectures about the authors of such essays and full titles are placed in editorial notes.

(4) Untitled newspaper items: A short form of the name of the newspaper and the date are used.

(5) Reports of public meetings: The headings consist of the name and date of such meetings, with the source given in editorial notes.

Descriptive Symbols for Manuscripts

In citing various kinds of manuscripts and, in particular, letters, the following symbols are used: MS for manuscript; RC for recipient's copy; FC for file copy; Dft for draft; AD for autograph document; ADS for autograph document signed; DS for document signed; and ALS for autograph letter signed.

Capitalization, Punctuation, and Italics in Manuscript Materials

Capital letters are used to begin sentences. Random capitals and italics are removed except when they are evidently used by the author for emphasis. Periods are used at the ends of sentences in place of dashes, colons, or no punctuation at all. Punctuation is added within sentences if needed to clarify meaning.

Spelling

With one exception, spelling is made to conform to present-day practice. For example, "labour" and "foederal" are spelled "labor" and "federal." The exception to this rule is the spelling of names of individuals. While it is easy enough to correct the spelling of the names of a "Madison" or a "Washington," there are hundreds of legislators and other men whose names are spelled in various ways in document after document, and sometimes in the same document. The editors therefore follow the practice of the editors of such modern publications as the papers of Thomas Jefferson, John Adams, and Benjamin Franklin and print the names as they are spelled in the documents.

Abbreviations, Contractions, Superscripts, Numbers, Crossed-out Words

Abbreviations such as those for place names ("Phila." for Philadelphia, for example) and military titles are spelled out. Contractions, such as "can't," "don't," and "altho," for example, are retained. Superscripts are lowered to the line. Archaic forms such as "yt" and "ye" are spelled out, "&c." is printed "etc.," and "&" is printed "and." Numbers are printed as they appear in the documents. Crossed-out words in documents, if they are significant, are placed in editorial notes. Otherwise they are generally not reproduced.

Brackets

Brackets are used for the following purposes:

(1) Editorial insertions are enclosed in brackets: [Senator].

(2) Conjectural readings, followed by a question mark, are enclosed in brackets: [Senator?].

(3) Illegible and missing words are indicated by dashes enclosed in brackets: [———].

Legislative Proceedings

The actions of state legislatures relating to the first federal elections are printed under the headings "House Proceedings," "Senate Proceedings," or whatever the name of the "upper" or "lower" house may be, and are followed by the day and date. These proceedings consist primarily of excerpts from the journals of state legislatures but are supplemented by other sources.

When both houses acted on the same day upon matters relating to the first federal elections, their journals are placed under the heading: "House and Senate Proceedings." In such cases the journals are arranged in the order of action by the two houses so that the progress of a report, a resolution, or a bill through the two houses can be followed in the order it occurred.

Messages, resolutions, reports, and other actions adopted by one house and sent to the other are often copied in the journals of the house to which they were sent. To avoid duplication in such cases, editorial notes enclosed in brackets are placed at appropriate places in the journals.

No attempt has been made to reproduce exactly the form of printed or manuscript journals. Lists of names of members of committees which appear in column form, for example, are printed as paragraphs, and each motion and resolution is set off as a paragraph.

We have included in the House and Senate Proceedings only those actions relating to the first federal elections. But it should be remembered that the legislatures that enacted election laws and chose United States Senators also carried on the regular business of legislatures during the same sessions, and usually spent far more time on such business than they did on the first federal elections.

Cross-references

Cross-references to documents within the same chapter are indicated in editorial notes by "printed above" or "printed below" with further information provided when needed. Cross-references to documents in different chapters are indicated in editorial notes by "printed, Chapter II," or whatever the chapter may be.

Identification of Individuals

At the end of each state chapter we have included sketches of the political careers of candidates for office in the first federal elections. Other people, such as the writers and recipients of letters, are usually identified, where identification is possible, in the editorial notes to the documents in which their names first appear. Where the documents indicate the positions of political figures, such as governors and state legislators, no further identification has been provided.

Only a few of the hundreds of men involved in the first federal elections have had full-scale biographies. The *Dictionary of American Biography* contains accounts of many of the men who ran for office in the first federal elections, but some men are not included, even though they were elected to the Senate and the House of Representatives. Moreover, some of the accounts in the *Dictionary* are imprecise and even erroneous as to the offices men held and the times they held them. The *Biographical Congressional Directory* contains brief sketches of the men elected to Congress but is often inaccurate about the extent of their political careers and their political affiliations. Clifford K. Shipton's *Biographical Sketches of Those Who Attended Harvard College* and Franklin B. Dexter's *Biographical Sketches of the Graduates of Yale College* are invaluable for the graduates of the two colleges involved in politics. However, it is necessary to go beyond such sources for information about many other men important at the time but forgotten today.

The legislative journals and civil lists of state officers contain information about men who held political office, as do the contemporary newspapers. The reminiscences of participants in the Revolution and nineteenth-century biographies about such men are useful but are sometimes romantic. Genealogies are particularly important for identifying many men, as are church records and collections of vital statistics. The collective biographies, mostly published in the nineteenth century, of military men, clergymen, doctors, lawyers, and judges of the various states contain useful material. The published records and magazines of local historical societies and the multitude of nineteenth-century town and county histories are invaluable for information about local leaders that cannot be found elsewhere. Even so, there are men whom we have not been able to identify with any precision, if at all, even though it is evident that as political leaders they were either admired and followed or loathed and opposed by their fellow citizens.

SHORT TITLE LIST OF SOURCES CITED

Boyd
> Julian P. Boyd, ed., *The Papers of Thomas Jefferson* (Princeton, N.J., 1950——).

Brunhouse, *Counter-Revolution*
> Robert L. Brunhouse, *The Counter-Revolution in Pennsylvania, 1776-1790* (Harrisburg, Pa., 1942).

Butterfield
> Lyman H. Butterfield, ed., *Letters of Benjamin Rush . . .* (2 vols., Princeton, N.J., 1951).

Convention, *Debates*
> *Debates and Proceedings in the Convention of the Commonwealth of Massachusetts Held in the Year 1788 . . .* (Boston, Mass., 1856).

DHOC
> United States Department of State, *Documentary History of the Constitution of the United States of America, 1786-1870 . . .* (5 vols., Washington, D.C., 1894-1905).

Elliot, *Debates*
> Jonathan Elliot, ed., *The Debates in the Several State Conventions, on the Adoption of the Federal Constitution . . .* (reprint of 3rd edition [4 vols., 1836] and supplemental volume [1845], 5 vols., Philadelphia, Pa., and Washington, D.C., 1866).

Ferguson, *Power of the Purse*
> E. James Ferguson, *The Power of the Purse: A History of American Public Finance, 1776-1790* (Chapel Hill, N.C., 1961).

Fitzpatrick
> John C. Fitzpatrick, ed., *The Writings of George Washington from the Original Manuscript Sources, 1745-1799* (39 vols., Washington, D.C., 1931-1944).

Gardiner, *Warren-Gerry Letters*
> C. Harvey Gardiner, ed., *A Study in Dissent: The Warren-Gerry Correspondence, 1776-1792* (Carbondale, Ill., 1968).

Hiltzheimer, *Diary*
> Jacob C. Parsons, ed., *Extracts from the Diary of Jacob Hiltzheimer, of Philadelphia, 1765-1798* (Philadelphia, Pa., 1893).

Historical Magazine
> Henry B. Dawson et al., eds., *The Historical Magazine, and Notes and Queries Concerning the Antiquities, History, and Biography of America* (23 vols., 1857-1875).

Hunt
> Gaillard Hunt, ed., *The Writings of James Madison . . .* (9 vols., New York, N.Y., and London, 1900-1910).

JCC
> Worthington C. Ford et al., eds., *Journals of the Continental Congress, 1774-1789 . . .* (34 vols., Washington, D.C., 1904-1937).

King, *Life*
> Charles R. King, ed., *Life and Correspondence of Rufus King . . .* (6 vols., New York, N.Y., 1894-1900).

Lloyd, *Debates*
> Thomas Lloyd, comp., *Debates of the General Assembly of Pennsylvania ... Volume the Fourth* [2 September–4 October 1788] (Philadelphia, Pa., 1788).

LMCC
> Edmund C. Burnett, ed., *Letters of Members of the Continental Congress* (8 vols., Washington D.C., 1921-1936).

McMaster and Stone
> John B. McMaster and Frederick D. Stone, eds., *Pennsylvania and the Federal Constitution, 1787-1788* ([Philadelphia, Pa.], 1888).

McRee, *Iredell*
> Griffith J. McRee, ed., *Life and Correspondence of James Iredell ...* (2 vols., New York, N.Y., 1857-1858).

N.H. *State Papers*
> Albert S. Batchellor, ed., *Early State Papers of New Hampshire ...* (Vol. XXI of *Documents and Records Relating to the Province and State of New Hampshire*, Nathaniel Bouton et al., eds. [40 vols., Concord, N.H., and elsewhere, 1867-1943]).

Pa. *Archives*
> Samuel Hazard et al., eds., *Pennsylvania Archives. Selected and Arranged from Original Documents in the Office of the Secretary of the Commonwealth ...* (9 series, 122 vols., Philadelphia, Pa., and Harrisburg, Pa., 1852-1935).

Pa. *Statutes*
> James T. Mitchell and Henry Flanders, comps., *The Statutes at Large of Pennsylvania from 1682 to 1801* (16 vols., Harrisburg, Pa., 1896-1911).

PCC
> Papers of the Continental Congress (Record Group 360, National Archives).

PMHB
> *The Pennsylvania Magazine of History and Biography* (1877——).

Ramsay, *Writings*
> Robert L. Brunhouse, ed., "David Ramsay, 1749-1815: Selections from His Writings," *Transactions of the American Philosophical Society*, new series, LV, part 4 (Philadelphia, Pa., 1965).

RG 46
> Records of the United States Senate (National Archives).

Rogers, *Smith*
> George C. Rogers, Jr., *Evolution of a Federalist: William Loughton Smith of Charleston (1758-1812)* (Columbia, S.C., 1962).

S.C. *Statutes*
> Thomas Cooper and David J. McCord, eds., *The Statutes at Large of South Carolina ...* (10 vols., Columbia, S.C., 1836-1841).

Syrett
> Harold C. Syrett, ed., *The Papers of Alexander Hamilton* (New York, N.Y., and London, 1961——).

Taylor, *Western Massachusetts*
> Robert J. Taylor, *Western Massachusetts in the Revolution* (Providence, R.I., 1954).

Thorpe
> Francis N. Thorpe, comp. and ed., *The Federal and State Constitutions, Colonial Charters, and Other Organic Laws of the States, Territories, and Colonies Now or Heretofore Forming the United States of America* (7 vols., Washington, D.C., 1909).

Van Schaack, *Memoirs*
> Henry C. Van Schaack, *Memoirs of the Life of Henry Van Schaack* ... (Chicago, Ill., 1892).

Walker, *Burd*
> Lewis B. Walker, ed., *The Burd Papers: Selections from Letters Written by Edward Burd, 1763-1828* (n.p., 1899).

Wingate, *Wingate*
> Charles E. L. Wingate, *Life and Letters of Paine Wingate* ... (2 vols., Medford, Mass., 1930).

LIST OF SYMBOLS
FOR MANUSCRIPT DEPOSITORIES

CtHC	Hartford Seminary Foundation, Hartford, Connecticut
CtHi	Connecticut Historical Society, Hartford
CtY	Yale University, New Haven, Connecticut
DLC	Library of Congress, Washington, D.C.
DNA	National Archives, Washington, D.C.
ICarbS	Southern Illinois University, Carbondale
M-Ar	Archives Division, Secretary of State, Boston
MB	Boston Public Library
MeHi	Maine Historical Society, Portland
MH	Harvard University, Cambridge, Massachusetts
MHi	Massachusetts Historical Society, Boston
MiU-C	William L. Clements Library, University of Michigan, Ann Arbor
MNF	Forbes Library, Northampton, Massachusetts
MSaE	Essex Institute, Salem, Massachusetts
MWA	American Antiquarian Society, Worcester, Massachusetts
N	New York State Library, Albany
NcD	Duke University, Durham, North Carolina
NcU	University of North Carolina, Chapel Hill
Nh	New Hampshire State Library, Concord
Nh-Ar	New Hampshire State Archives, Concord
NhD	Dartmouth College, Hanover, New Hampshire
NhHi	New Hampshire Historical Society, Concord
NHi	New-York Historical Society, New York City
NjR	Rutgers—The State University, New Brunswick, New Jersey
NN	New York Public Library
NNC	Columbia University, New York City
NNS	New York Society Library, New York City
PHarH	Pennsylvania Historical and Museum Commission, Harrisburg
PHi	Historical Society of Pennsylvania, Philadelphia
PP	Free Library of Philadelphia
PPAmP	American Philosophical Society, Philadelphia
PPL	Library Company of Philadelphia
RHi	Rhode Island Historical Society, Providence
Sc-Ar	South Carolina Department of Archives and History, Columbia
ScU	University of South Carolina, Columbia
ViU	University of Virginia, Charlottesville
ViW	College of William and Mary, Williamsburg, Virginia
WHi	State Historical Society of Wisconsin, Madison

The symbols are those adopted by the Library of Congress, *Symbols of American Libraries* (10th ed., Washington, 1969).

POPULATION AND REPRESENTATION, 1787, 1792

One of the central issues in the Constitutional Convention, in many of the state conventions, and to an extent in the first federal elections, was the balance of power between the Northern and the Southern states. In the Constitutional Convention, the settlement of the dispute over the basis of representation and the apportionment of delegates among the states in the House of Representatives was a compromise embodied in Article I, Section 2, of the Constitution. It provides that Representatives shall be apportioned "by adding to the whole Number of free Persons, including those bound to Service for a Term of Years, and excluding Indians not taxed, three fifths of all other Persons." The "other Persons" were the slaves. In addition, the Southern delegates, convinced that the South and Southwest would grow faster than the North, insisted upon placing in the Constitution the requirement that a national census be taken every ten years and that the House be reapportioned after each census.

The Constitution provided for sixty-five members of the first House of Representatives and apportioned them among the states, but the records of the Convention contain only scattered references to population estimates. The only specific figures that have been located are in a speech by Charles Cotesworth Pinckney to the South Carolina House of Representatives, 17 January 1788, in which he gave the population estimates which he said the Convention had used. His speech was published in the Charleston *City Gazette*, 24 January. On 5 February the New York *Daily Advertiser*, without referring to the source, published the estimates with the statement that "the numbers in the different states, according to the most accurate accounts which could be obtained by the late Federal Convention were as follow." By May 1788 Pinckney's estimates had been published in at least two dozen newspapers throughout the United States.

The first census act became law on 1 March 1790, and the census was completed by February 1792. In the meantime, North Carolina ceded the Southwest Territory (Tennessee) to the United States in 1790; in February 1791 Congress admitted Vermont to statehood as of 4 March 1791 and Kentucky to statehood as of 1 June 1792. In February 1791 Congress also assigned each state two Representatives, pending the completion of the census.

The first reapportionment act became law on 14 April 1792. It provided that after 3 March 1793 the House of Representatives would consist of one member for every 33,000 persons in each state "computed according to the rule prescribed by the Constitution. . . ."

The table below consists of five columns. Column I contains the estimates of population which, according to Charles Cotesworth Pinckney, were used by the Constitutional Convention in assigning Representatives to the states. Column II gives the number of Representatives apportioned by the Constitution of 1787. Column III is derived from the Census of 1790. Subcolumn III-A gives "the whole Number of free Persons, including those bound to Service for a Term of Years, and excluding Indians not taxed . . ." (The Constitution, Article I, Section 2). Column III-B gives the total slave population. Column IV was obtained by adding to the non-slave population given in Column III-A, "three fifths of all other Persons" (The Constitution, Article I, Section 2), that is, the slave population in Column III-B. Column V contains the number of Representatives assigned each state by the Reapportionment Act of 1792.

ORIGINAL STATES

State	I Population estimates used by Convention*	II Number of Repre-sentatives	III Census of 1790 (A) Non-slave Population	(B) Slave Population	IV Population base for reapportion-ment (non-slave population plus 3/5ths slave population)	V Number of Repre-sentatives
New Hampshire	102,000	3	141,727	158	141,822	4
Massachusetts	360,000	8	475,327	0	475,327	14
Rhode Island	58,000	1	67,877	948	68,446	2
Connecticut	202,000	5	235,182	2,764	236,840	7
New York	238,000	6	318,796	21,324	331,590	10
New Jersey	138,000	4	172,716	11,423	179,570	5
Pennsylvania	360,000	8	430,636	3,737	432,878	13
Delaware	37,000	1	50,209	8,887	55,541	1
Maryland	218,000 (80,000)	6	216,692	103,036	278,514	8
Virginia	420,000 (280,000)	10	454,983	292,627	630,559	19
North Carolina	200,000 (60,000)	5	293,179	100,572	353,522	10
South Carolina	150,000 (80,000)	5	141,979	107,094	206,235	6
Georgia	90,000 (20,000)	3	53,284	29,264	70,842	2
Totals	2,573,000	65	3,052,587	681,834	3,461,686	101

NEW STATES AND TERRITORIES

Kentucky	–	0	61,247	12,430	68,705	2
Vermont	–	0	85,539	no data	85,539	2
Northwest Territory	–	0	no data	–	no data	0
Southwest Territory	–	0	32,274	3,417	34,324	0
Totals	–	0	179,060	15,847	188,568	4

*Estimates of the number of slaves in Maryland, Virginia, North Carolina, South Carolina, and Georgia, three-fifths of which were included in the population estimates for those states, are given in parentheses.

CHRONOLOGY OF THE ELECTIONS
WITH NAMES OF MEN ELECTED

Date	State	Office	Men Elected
1788			
30 September	Pennsylvania	Senators	Robert Morris, William Maclay
15 October	Connecticut	Senators	Oliver Ellsworth, William S. Johnson
25 October	Delaware	Senators	George Read, Richart Bassett
8 November	Virginia	Senators	Richard Henry Lee, William Grayson
11 November	New Hampshire	Senators	John Langdon (Josiah Bartlett declined)
21-24 November	Massachusetts	Senators	Caleb Strong, Tristram Dalton
24-25 November	South Carolina	Representatives (Five districts)	Aedanus Burke, Daniel Huger, William Loughton Smith, Thomas Sumter, Thomas Tudor Tucker
25 November	New Jersey	Senators	Philemon Dickinson, William Paterson
26 November	Pennsylvania	Representatives (Statewide)	George Clymer, Thomas FitzSimons, Thomas Hartley, Daniel Hiester, Frederick A. Muhlenberg, John Peter Muhlenberg, Thomas Scott, Henry Wynkoop
9-10 December	Maryland	Senators	Charles Carroll, John Henry
15 December	New Hampshire	Representatives (Statewide)	No decision.
18 December	Massachusetts	Representatives (Eight Districts)	Fisher Ames (Suffolk), George Partridge (Plymouth and Barnstable), George Thacher (York, Cumberland, and Lincoln), George Leonard (Bristol, Dukes, and Nantucket). No decision in four districts.
22 December	Connecticut	Representatives (Statewide)	Benjamin Huntington, Roger Sherman, Jonathan Sturges, Jonathan Trumbull, Jeremiah Wadsworth
1789			
1 January	New Hampshire	Senator	Paine Wingate
7 January	Delaware	Representative (Statewide)	John Vining
7 January	All states (except R.I., N.C., N.Y.)	Presidential Electors	72 men elected.
7-11 January	Maryland	Representatives (Statewide)	Daniel Carroll, Benjamin Contee, George Gale, Joshua Seney, William Smith, Michael Jenifer Stone

17 January	Georgia	Senators	William Few, James Gunn
22 January	South Carolina	Senators	Pierce Butler, Ralph Izard
29 January	Massachusetts	Representatives (Second election)	Elbridge Gerry (Middlesex), Benjamin Goodhue (Essex). No decision in two districts.
2 February	New Hampshire	Representatives (Second election)	Nicholas Gilman, Samuel Livermore (Benjamin West declined)
2 February	Virginia	Representatives (Ten districts)	Theodorick Bland, John Brown, Isaac Coles, Samuel Griffin, Richard Bland Lee, James Madison, Andrew Moore, John Page, Josiah Parker, Alexander White
4 February	All states (except N.Y., R.I., N.C.)	President and Vice President	George Washington, John Adams
9 February	Georgia	Representatives (Statewide)	Abraham Baldwin, James Jackson, George Mathews
11 February– 18 March	New Jersey	Representatives (Statewide)	Elias Boudinot, Lambert Cadwalader, James Schureman, Thomas Sinnickson
2 March	Massachusetts	Representatives (Third election)	Jonathan Grout (Worcester). No decision in Hampshire-Berkshire District.
3-4 March	New York	Representatives (Six districts)	Egbert Benson, William Floyd, John Hathorn, John Laurance, Jeremiah Van Rensselaer, Peter Silvester
30 March	Massachusetts	Representatives (Fourth election)	No decision in Hampshire-Berkshire District.
11 May	Massachusetts	Representatives (Fifth election)	Theodore Sedgwick (Hampshire-Berkshire)
22 June	New Hampshire	Representatives (Third election)	Abiel Foster
8-16 July	New York	Senators	Rufus King, Philip Schuyler
24 November– 9 December	North Carolina	Senators	Benjamin Hawkins, Samuel Johnston

1790

4-5 February	North Carolina	Representatives (Five districts)	John Baptista Ashe, Timothy Bloodworth, John Sevier, John Steele, Hugh Williamson
12 June	Rhode Island	Senators	Theodore Foster, Joseph Stanton
31 August	Rhode Island	Representative (Statewide)	Benjamin Bourne

PRESIDENTIAL ELECTORS AND THEIR VOTES, 4 FEBRUARY 1789

New Hampshire

Benjamin Bellows
John Pickering
Ebenezer Thompson
John Sullivan
John Parker

George Washington   5 votes
John Adams   5 votes

Massachusetts

Caleb Davis
Samuel Phillips
Francis Dana
Samuel Henshaw
William Sever
David Sewall
Walter Spooner
Moses Gill
William Cushing
William Shepard

George Washington   10 votes
John Adams   10 votes

Connecticut

Samuel Huntington
Richard Law
Matthew Griswold
Erastus Wolcott
Thaddeus Burr
Jedidiah Huntington
Oliver Wolcott, Sr.

George Washington   7 votes
John Adams   5 votes
Samuel Huntington   2 votes

New Jersey

David Brearley
James Kinsey
John Neilson
David Moore
John Rutherfurd
Matthias Ogden

George Washington   6 votes
John Jay   5 votes
John Adams   1 vote

Delaware

Gunning Bedford	George Washington	3 votes
George Mitchell	John Jay	3 votes
John Baning		

Pennsylvania

James Wilson		
John O'Hara		
David Grier		
Samuel Potts	George Washington	10 votes
Alexander Graydon	John Adams	8 votes
Collinson Read	John Hancock	2 votes
Edward Hand		
George Gibson		
John Arndt		
Laurence Keene		

Maryland

John Rogers		
William Tilghman		
Alexander Hanson		
Philip Thomas	George Washington	6 votes
Robert Smith	Robert H. Harrison	6 votes
William Matthews		
George Plater*		
William Richardson*		

Virginia

John Pride		
John Harvie		
Zachariah Johnston		
John Roane	George Washington	10 votes
David Stuart	John Adams	5 votes
William Fitzhugh	George Clinton	3 votes
Anthony Walke	John Hancock	1 vote
Patrick Henry	John Jay	1 vote
Edward Stevens		
Warner Lewis*		
James Wood		

*Did not attend

South Carolina

Christopher Gadsden		
Henry Laurens		
Edward Rutledge	George Washington	7 votes
Charles Cotesworth Pinckney	John Rutledge	6 votes
John F. Grimké	John Hancock	1 vote
Thomas Heyward, Jr.		
Arthur Simkins		

Georgia

George Handley	George Washington	5 votes
John King	John Milton	2 votes
George Walton	James Armstrong	1 vote
Henry Osborne	Edward Telfair	1 vote
John Milton	Benjamin Lincoln	1 vote

CALENDAR FOR THE YEARS 1788–1790

1788

JANUARY	FEBRUARY	MARCH	APRIL
1 2 3 4 5	1 2	1	1 2 3 4 5
6 7 8 9 10 11 12	3 4 5 6 7 8 9	2 3 4 5 6 7 8	6 7 8 9 10 11 12
13 14 15 16 17 18 19	10 11 12 13 14 15 16	9 10 11 12 13 14 15	13 14 15 16 17 18 19
20 21 22 23 24 25 26	17 18 19 20 21 22 23	16 17 18 19 20 21 22	20 21 22 23 24 25 26
27 28 29 30 31	24 25 26 27 28 29	23 24 25 26 27 28 29	27 28 29 30
		30 31	

MAY	JUNE	JULY	AUGUST
1 2 3	1 2 3 4 5 6 7	1 2 3 4 5	1 2
4 5 6 7 8 9 10	8 9 10 11 12 13 14	6 7 8 9 10 11 12	3 4 5 6 7 8 9
11 12 13 14 15 16 17	15 16 17 18 19 20 21	13 14 15 16 17 18 19	10 11 12 13 14 15 16
18 19 20 21 22 23 24	22 23 24 25 26 27 28	20 21 22 23 24 25 26	17 18 19 20 21 22 23
25 26 27 28 29 30 31	29 30	27 28 29 30 31	24 25 26 27 28 29 30
			31

SEPTEMBER	OCTOBER	NOVEMBER	DECEMBER
1 2 3 4 5 6	1 2 3 4	1	1 2 3 4 5 6
7 8 9 10 11 12 13	5 6 7 8 9 10 11	2 3 4 5 6 7 8	7 8 9 10 11 12 13
14 15 16 17 18 19 20	12 13 14 15 16 17 18	9 10 11 12 13 14 15	14 15 16 17 18 19 20
21 22 23 24 25 26 27	19 20 21 22 23 24 25	16 17 18 19 20 21 22	21 22 23 24 25 26 27
28 29 30	26 27 28 29 30 31	23 24 25 26 27 28 29	28 29 30 31
		30	

1789

JANUARY	FEBRUARY	MARCH	APRIL
1 2 3	1 2 3 4 5 6 7	1 2 3 4 5 6 7	1 2 3 4
4 5 6 7 8 9 10	8 9 10 11 12 13 14	8 9 10 11 12 13 14	5 6 7 8 9 10 11
11 12 13 14 15 16 17	15 16 17 18 19 20 21	15 16 17 18 19 20 21	12 13 14 15 16 17 18
18 19 20 21 22 23 24	22 23 24 25 26 27 28	22 23 24 25 26 27 28	19 20 21 22 23 24 25
25 26 27 28 29 30 31		29 30 31	26 27 28 29 30

MAY	JUNE	JULY	AUGUST
1 2	1 2 3 4 5 6	1 2 3 4	1
3 4 5 6 7 8 9	7 8 9 10 11 12 13	5 6 7 8 9 10 11	2 3 4 5 6 7 8
10 11 12 13 14 15 16	14 15 16 17 18 19 20	12 13 14 15 16 17 18	9 10 11 12 13 14 15
17 18 19 20 21 22 23	21 22 23 24 25 26 27	19 20 21 22 23 24 25	16 17 18 19 20 21 22
24 25 26 27 28 29 30	28 29 30	26 27 28 29 30 31	23 24 25 26 27 28 29
31			

SEPTEMBER	OCTOBER	NOVEMBER	DECEMBER
1 2 3 4 5	1 2 3	1 2 3 4 5 6 7	1 2 3 4 5
6 7 8 9 10 11 12	4 5 6 7 8 9 10	8 9 10 11 12 13 14	6 7 8 9 10 11 12
13 14 15 16 17 18 19	11 12 13 14 15 16 17	15 16 17 18 19 20 21	13 14 15 16 17 18 19
20 21 22 23 24 25 26	18 19 20 21 22 23 24	22 23 24 25 26 27 28	20 21 22 23 24 25 26
27 28 29 30	25 26 27 28 29 30 31	29 30	27 28 29 30 31

1790

JANUARY	FEBRUARY	MARCH	APRIL
1 2	1 2 3 4 5 6	1 2 3 4 5 6	1 2 3
3 4 5 6 7 8 9	7 8 9 10 11 12 13	7 8 9 10 11 12 13	4 5 6 7 8 9 10
10 11 12 13 14 15 16	14 15 16 17 18 19 20	14 15 16 17 18 19 20	11 12 13 14 15 16 17
17 18 19 20 21 22 23	21 22 23 24 25 26 27	21 22 23 24 25 26 27	18 19 20 21 22 23 24
24 25 26 27 28 29 30	28	28 29 30 31	25 26 27 28 29 30
31			

MAY	JUNE	JULY	AUGUST
1	1 2 3 4 5	1 2 3	1 2 3 4 5 6 7
2 3 4 5 6 7 8	6 7 8 9 10 11 12	4 5 6 7 8 9 10	8 9 10 11 12 13 14
9 10 11 12 13 14 15	13 14 15 16 17 18 19	11 12 13 14 15 16 17	15 16 17 18 19 20 21
16 17 18 19 20 21 22	20 21 22 23 24 25 26	18 19 20 21 22 23 24	22 23 24 25 26 27 28
23 24 25 26 27 28 29	27 28 29 30	25 26 27 28 29 30 31	29 30 31
30 31			

SEPTEMBER	OCTOBER	NOVEMBER	DECEMBER
1 2 3 4	1 2	1 2 3 4 5 6	1 2 3 4
5 6 7 8 9 10 11	3 4 5 6 7 8 9	7 8 9 10 11 12 13	5 6 7 8 9 10 11
12 13 14 15 16 17 18	10 11 12 13 14 15 16	14 15 16 17 18 19 20	12 13 14 15 16 17 18
19 20 21 22 23 24 25	17 18 19 20 21 22 23	21 22 23 24 25 26 27	19 20 21 22 23 24 25
26 27 28 29 30	24 25 26 27 28 29 30	28 29 30	26 27 28 29 30 31
	31		

CHAPTER I

The Constitution, the Confederation Congress, and Federal Elections

INTRODUCTION

The Congress of the United States under the Articles of Confederation was the supreme constitutional authority in the United States from 1 March 1781, when the Articles were ratified by the thirteenth state, until the government created by the Constitution of 1787 went into effect on 4 March 1789. The Confederation Congress was therefore responsible for overseeing the ratification of the Constitution of 1787 and for calling the first federal elections under the new Constitution.

On 21 February 1787 the Confederation Congress in New York authorized a convention to meet in Philadelphia for "the sole and express purpose" of revising and amending the Articles of Confederation. However, instead of offering amendments to the Articles of Confederation, which would have required unanimous ratification by the thirteen states, the Convention wrote a new constitution and proposed that it go into effect when ratified by any nine of the states in special state conventions.

The members of the Constitutional Convention were doubtful of the attitude of the Confederation Congress, but there was no political alternative to submitting the Constitution to the Congress. One of the last actions of the Convention on 17 September, the day it adjourned, was the adoption of two resolutions. The first called for laying the Constitution before "the United States in Congress assembled" and gave it as the "opinion" of the Convention that the Constitution should afterwards be submitted to state conventions which should report their decisions to "the United States in Congress assembled."

The Constitution was laid before Congress on 20 September, only three days after the Convention adjourned. James Madison and other members of the Convention who were also members of Congress hastened to New York and urged Congress to approve the Constitution and send it to the states with a request to ratify it as soon as possible.

Richard Henry Lee led a minority of the members of Congress who insisted that Congress could not approve a document "which had for its object the subversion of the constitution under which they acted." In the course of the debate the supporters of the Constitution admitted that Congress had the right to offer amendments. Lee therefore prepared amendments in the form of a "bill of rights" and others altering the structural details in the Constitution.

The majority of Congress rejected the amendments but did not vote for a motion to approve the Constitution. To achieve unanimity, Congress on 28 September simply resolved to send the Constitution to the state legislatures. It was, as Richard Henry Lee wrote to Samuel Adams on 5 October, "a bare transmission of the Convention plan, without a syllable of approbation or disapprobation on the part of Congress."

State conventions were called, and ratification began with Delaware on 7 December 1787. New Hampshire, the ninth state, ratified on 21 June 1788, and the way was thus cleared for the Confederation Congress to take the next step in setting up the new government.

The second resolution adopted by the Constitutional Convention on the last day it met suggested a procedure for Congress to follow, once nine states had ratified. It declared that in the "opinion" of the Convention, Congress should set the date for each state to choose presidential Electors, the date for the Electors to meet and vote for President, and the time and place for the beginning of the new government.

The Confederation Congress followed this procedure exactly between 2 July 1788, when the official notice of New Hampshire's ratification was laid before Congress, and 13 September 1788, when Congress adopted an ordinance setting the time for the election of Electors, the time for the Electors to meet and vote, and the time and place for the new government to meet.

The Constitutional Convention had disputed at length such issues as the age, citizenship, and terms of office for members of Congress, and the qualifications of voters for members of the House of Representatives. There was so great a diversity of opinion on such questions that in the end the Constitution contained only a few simple provisions concerning the age, citizenship, and residence of Senators and Representatives. Voters for Representatives were to have the same qualifications as the voters for members of the "most numerous" branch of the legislature in each of the states. The time, place, and manner of electing Senators and Representatives were to "be prescribed in each State by the Legislature thereof; but the Congress may at any time by Law make or alter such Regulations, except as to the Places of chusing Senators."

The Convention spent even more time debating the method of electing the President and wrote elaborate provisions into the Constitution for that purpose. However, the Constitution did not require the Electors to cast separate ballots for President and Vice President. This led to the political crisis in the presidential election of 1800 and to the adoption in 1804 of the Twelfth Amendment, which required the casting of separate ballots.

Thus, once the Confederation Congress had set the date for the choice of presidential Electors by the states and the date on which they were to vote for President, the responsibility for establishing the mechanisms by which Electors, Senators, and Representatives were to be chosen was left to the several state legislatures.

The provisions of the Constitution relating to the election of Representatives, Senators, and the President, and the resolutions of the Constitutional Convention suggesting the procedure to be followed by the Confederation Congress in providing for ratification of the Constitution and in calling the new government into being are printed below.

Provisions of the Constitution Relating to Federal Elections and the Qualifications of Candidates

Article I, Section 2. The House of Representatives shall be composed of Members chosen every second Year by the People of the several States, and the Electors in each State shall have the Qualifications requisite for Electors of the most numerous Branch of the State Legislature.

No Person shall be a Representative who shall not have attained to the Age of twenty five Years, and been seven Years a Citizen of the United States, and who shall not, when elected, be an Inhabitant of that State in which he shall be chosen.

Representatives and direct Taxes shall be apportioned among the several States which may be included within this Union, according to their respective Numbers, which shall be determined by adding to the whole Number of free Persons, including those bound to Service for a Term of Years, and excluding Indians not taxed, three fifths of all other Persons. The actual Enumeration shall be made within three Years after the first Meeting of the Congress of the United States, and within every subsequent Term of ten Years, in such Manner as they shall by Law direct. The Number of Representatives shall not exceed one for every thirty Thousand, but each State shall have at Least one Representative; and until such enumeration shall be made, the State of New Hampshire shall be entitled to chuse three, Massachusetts eight, Rhode Island and Providence Plantations one, Connecticut five, New York six, New Jersey four, Pennsylvania eight, Delaware one, Maryland six, Virginia ten, North Carolina five, South Carolina five, and Georgia three.

. . . .

Article I, Section 3. The Senate of the United States shall be composed of two Senators from each State, chosen by the Legislature thereof, for six Years; and each Senator shall have one Vote.

Immediately after they shall be assembled in Consequence of the first Election, they shall be divided as equally as may be into three Classes. The Seats of the Senators of the first Class shall be vacated at the Expiration of the second year, of the second Class at the Expiration of the fourth Year, and of the third Class at the Expiration of the sixth Year, so that one third may be chosen every second Year; and if Vacancies happen by Resignation, or otherwise, during the Recess of the Legislature of any State, the Executive thereof may make temporary Appointments until the next Meeting of the Legislature, which shall then fill such Vacancies.

No Person shall be a Senator who shall not have attained to the Age of thirty Years, and been nine Years a Citizen of the United States, and who shall not, when elected, be an Inhabitant of that State for which he shall be chosen.

. . . .

Article I, Section 4. The Times, Places and Manner of holding Elections for Senators and Representatives, shall be prescribed in each State by the Legislature thereof; but the Congress may at any time by Law make or alter such Regulations, except as to the Places of chusing Senators.

The Congress shall assemble at least once in every Year, and such Meeting shall be on the first Monday in December, unless they shall by Law appoint a different Day.

. . . .

Article II, Section 1. The executive Power shall be vested in a President of the United States of America. He shall hold his Office during the Term of four Years, and, together with the Vice President, chosen for the same Term, be elected, as follows

Each State shall appoint, in such Manner as the Legislature thereof may direct, a Number of Electors, equal to the whole Number of Senators and Representatives to which the State may be entitled in the Congress: but no Senator or Representative, or Person holding an Office of Trust or Profit under the United States, shall be appointed an Elector.

The Electors shall meet in their respective States and vote by Ballot for two Persons, of whom one at least shall not be an Inhabitant of the same State with themselves. And they shall make a List of all the Persons voted for, and of the Number of Votes for each; which List they shall sign and certify, and transmit sealed to the Seat of the Government of the United States, directed to the President of the Senate. The President of the Senate shall, in the Presence of the Senate and House of Representatives, open all the Certificates, and the Votes shall then be counted. The Person having the greatest Number of Votes shall be the President, if such Number be a Majority of the whole Number of Electors appointed; and if there be more than one who have such Majority, and have an equal Number of Votes, then the House of Representatives shall immediately chuse by Ballot one of them for President; and if no Person have a Majority, then from the five highest on the List the said House shall in like Manner chuse the President. But in chusing the President, the Votes shall be taken by States, the Representation from each State having one Vote; A quorum for this Purpose shall consist of a Member or Members from two thirds of the States, and a Majority of all the States shall be necessary to a Choice. In every Case, after the Choice of the President, the Person having the greatest Number of Votes of the Electors shall be the Vice President. But if there should remain two or more who have equal Votes, the Senate shall chuse from them by Ballot the Vice President.

The Congress may determine the Time of chusing the Electors, and the Day on which they shall give their Votes; which Day shall be the same throughout the United States.

No Person except a natural born Citizen, or a Citizen of the United States, at the time of the Adoption of this Constitution, shall be eligible to the Office of President; neither shall any Person be eligible to that Office who shall not have attained to the Age of thirty five Years, and been fourteen Years a Resident within the United States.

Resolutions of the Convention Submitting the Constitution to the Confederation Congress, 17 September 1787[1]

Present The States of New Hampshire, Massachusetts, Connecticut, Mr. Hamilton from New York, New Jersey, Pennsylvania, Delaware, Maryland, Virginia, North Carolina, South Carolina and Georgia.

Resolved, That the preceeding Constitution be laid before the United States in Congress assembled, and that it is the Opinion of this Convention, that it should afterwards be submitted to a Convention of Delegates, chosen in each State by the People thereof, under the Recommendation of its Legislature, for their Assent and Ratification; and that each Convention assenting to, and ratifying the Same, should give Notice thereof to the United States in Congress assembled.

Resolved, That it is the Opinion of this Convention, that as soon as the Conventions of nine States shall have ratified this Constitution, the United States in Congress assembled should fix a Day on which Electors should be appointed by the States which shall have ratified the same, and a Day on which the Electors should assemble to vote for the President, and the Time and Place for commencing Proceedings under this Constitution. That after such Publication the Electors should be appointed, and the Senators and Representatives elected: That the Electors should meet on the Day fixed for the Election of the President, and should transmit their Votes certified, signed, sealed and directed, as the Constitution requires, to the Secretary of the United States in Congress assembled, that the

Senators and Representatives should convene at the Time and Place assigned; that the Senators should appoint a President of the Senate, for the sole Purpose of receiving, opening and counting the Votes for President; and, that after he shall be chosen, the Congress, together with the President, should, without Delay, proceed to execute this Constitution.

By the Unanimous Order of the Convention

[s] W. Jackson   Secretary.   [s] Go: Washington   Presidt.

1. Engrossed Resolution (LT), DNA.

CHAPTER II

The Confederation Congress and the First Federal Election Ordinance of 13 September 1788

INTRODUCTION

Beginning in late September and on through the winter of 1787-1788, the attention of most politically conscious Americans was focused upon the flood of materials in newspapers and pamphlets defending and attacking the new Constitution, and upon the state conventions. Three state conventions ratified the Constitution unanimously by the end of 1787: Delaware on 7 December, New Jersey on 18 December, and Georgia on 31 December. Pennsylvania ratified 46 to 23 on 12 December and Connecticut 128 to 40 on 9 January 1788. Nevertheless tension mounted, for there was so much opposition to the Constitution in such important states as Massachusetts, New York, and Virginia that the outcome was uncertain. Massachusetts did ratify by a narrow margin of 187 to 168 on 6 February, but a few days later the New Hampshire Convention adjourned after the Constitution's supporters realized that it would be rejected if brought to a vote. On 24 March the voters of Rhode Island, in a popular referendum, rejected the Constitution 10 to 1, and the next state convention, Maryland, would not meet until 21 April.

Very few people indeed, including its members, paid much attention to the Confederation Congress whose task it would be to set the new government in operation once nine states had ratified the Constitution. The Articles of Confederation established the beginning of the "federal year" as the first Monday in November, but the required minimum of seven state delegations needed to conduct the ordinary business of Congress did not assemble in New York until 21 January 1788. Attendance soon fell off, and by April not enough states were represented for Congress to function. As one delegate, Samuel A. Otis, reported to James Warren on 26 April: "To your demand to know what we are doing in Congress, I answer—Nothing. To your enquiry what we have done? I answer—almost nothing. . . . The states have been in such a flutter about the new, that they have hardly paid attention to the old government."

As more states ratified, however, members of the Confederation Congress, many of whom had been members of state conventions, began converging on New York; and by July they were commenting that the states were more fully represented than at any time since 1776. Such representation made it possible for Congress to take up the regular business of the "federal year"—and some unusual matters as well.

Thus while it waited for nine states to ratify, and during the two and a half months from 2 July to 13 September while it haggled over an election ordinance, Congress approved the budget for the year 1789 and furthered the settlement of accounts between the states and the central government for expenses incurred during the War for Independence. Congress also concerned itself with the affairs of the Northwest Territory: its government, the land survey, and Indian relations. Georgia's cession of western lands to the United States was considered and rejected. The most unusual issue before Congress was that of statehood for Kentucky. Virginia had agreed to separation, and in September 1787 a Kentucky convention petitioned Congress for statehood. The petition was laid before Congress on the last day of February 1788.

Whatever Congress decided might cause trouble. What effect would Kentucky statehood have on the balance of power between the North and the South, which had been a fundamental issue in the abortive Jay-Gardoqui treaty negotiations in 1786 and in the Constitutional Convention in 1787? Some thought that Vermont should be admitted to the Union to balance Kentucky, but that would raise the issue of New York and New Hampshire claims to Vermont lands. Then too it was known that many Kentuckians opposed the new Constitution, and there were those who did not want to admit such a state to the Union when the fate of the Constitution was still uncertain. But if Kentucky were not admitted, might not its people yield to Spanish blandishments and declare their independence?

On 2 June Congress decided that Kentucky should be created as an independent state and chose a committee of one member from each state to prepare an act for that purpose. By 25 June the committee had concluded that Congress did not have the power to admit new states and that the Articles of Confederation should be amended to give it the power. On 2 July the committee asked to be discharged, whereupon the Virginia delegates moved that Congress ratify the compact between Virginia and Kentucky. The motion was rejected the next day, and Congress declared that the question of Kentucky statehood should be left to the new government.

This evasion was possible because on 2 July Congress received the official document of ratification by the ninth state, New Hampshire. Congress at once chose a committee "for putting the said Constitution into operation in pursuance of the resolutions of the late Federal Convention." The committee reported on 9 July that presidential Electors should be chosen on the first Wednesday in December, that Electors should meet to elect a President on the first Wednesday in January, and that the new Congress should meet on the first Wednesday in February.

On 14 July Congress considered the committee report but did not take it up again officially until 28 July. Most Northerners supported the dates proposed, but several Southern delegates insisted that their states needed more time to prepare for elections. The result was an agreement to put off by one month the election of Electors and the President and the meeting of the new Congress. This agreement was officially accepted by Congress on 28 July.

But there was no agreement whatever about the place the new government should meet. For years the location of the seat of government had been an issue of great concern to political leaders in most of the states. Congress met in Philadelphia from 1774 (except when it fled from the British) until June 1783, when it left for Princeton, New Jersey, after Pennsylvania soldiers surrounded the Pennsylvania State House and demanded a redress of grievances.

Congress was soon involved in the question of a permanent residence. In October 1783 it resolved to settle permanently at the falls of the Delaware River. Then a few days later, to satisfy the Southern States, Congress resolved that there should be a second residence at the lower falls of the Potomac River. The members agreed that until the two places could be made ready, they would move about, residing a year or less at Annapolis, Maryland, and then a similar time at Trenton, New Jersey.

Congress spent the winter of 1783-1784 in Annapolis and then moved to Trenton for the beginning of the federal year in November 1784. As soon as the members convened, they began debating whether to spend the rest of the winter in New York or Philadelphia. After voting once more that a permanent residence should be established and after considerable skirmishing as to whether it should be on the Delaware or the Potomac River, Congress decided on 24 December to adjourn to New York until a permanent home could be erected, wherever it might be.

The dispute subsided after Congress began meeting in New York in January 1785, but it revived in full force by 1788. Philadelphians had never given up hope that Congress would return to their city. Virginians, with George Washington at their head, were equally determined to locate the capital on the Potomac River.

Congress delayed action on the election ordinance throughout July 1788 because it was waiting for the decision of the New York Convention, which had been in session since 17 June. Everyone knew that a substantial majority in it was opposed to ratification, and that if New York did not ratify, the new government could not meet in New York City. However, if New York did ratify, the city where Congress had met since 1785 would be a strong contender for the first meeting place of the new government. The great value New Yorkers such as Alexander Hamilton placed on retaining the government was demonstrated when the Federalist minority in the New York Convention, in order to secure unconditional ratification, agreed to a call for a second constitutional convention.

Men recognized, of course, that the Confederation Congress could not establish a permanent capital: that would be the obligation of the new Congress. The Constitution gave Congress the power "To exercise exclusive legislation in all cases whatsoever, over such district (not exceeding ten miles square) as may, by cession of particular states, and the acceptance of Congress, become the seat of government of the United States. . . ." All the Confederation Congress could do, therefore, was to decide upon the place where the new government would meet for the first time. Nevertheless, men in and out of the Confederation Congress believed that the place, however temporary, would have a decided impact upon the choice of a permanent capital. Therefore, congressmen and their supporters lobbied, wrote propaganda for the newspapers, proposed political deals, and even came close to offering bribes.

Various places were considered and voted upon, including Wilmington, Delaware; Lancaster, Pennsylvania; and Baltimore and Annapolis, Maryland; but the main contest in Congress was between New York and Philadelphia. On 4 August Congress decided upon Baltimore. Two days later it voted for New York. Thereafter, the vote of the necessary seven states could not be obtained to pass the election ordinance with New York as the meeting place, nor could seven votes be obtained for any other location.

The deadlock continued throughout August and on into September. Then on 12 September Congress made the gesture of substituting the words "the present seat of Congress" for "New York" as the meeting place, and the next day nine of the ten states represented adopted the Election Ordinance and sent it to the states.

The struggle over the meeting place of the new government pitted such Federalist leaders as James Madison and Alexander Hamilton against one another to the very last, even though they realized that the delay in calling the elections might endanger the success of the new government. As the deadlock continued, newspaper articles and letters written by Federalist leaders in various states predicted that the delay was playing into the hands of opponents of the Constitution in their continuing demand for amendments and for a second constitutional convention. Furthermore, continued delay might mean that many Antifederalists would be elected to the new Congress. Above all, Federalist leaders such as James Madison feared that a second constitutional convention might remove from the Constitution powers which they thought essential to the success of the new government.

In 1787 when the Constitutional Convention debated the issue of how to provide for amending the Constitution, Madison strenuously opposed a provision that Congress should be required to call a constitutional convention at the request of two-thirds of the state legislatures. He argued that the only safe method was for Congress to have the sole power of proposing amendments to be ratified by the states. Madison was overridden, and Article V of the Constitution embodied both methods of amendment.

The movement for a second convention began at the Constitutional Convention itself. During the final days at Philadelphia in September 1787, the Convention rejected George Mason's proposals for the addition of a declaration of rights. Then, on the last day of the Convention, Governor Edmund Randolph of Virginia declared that he would not sign the Constitution unless the Convention agreed to call a second convention to consider amendments that might be offered by state conventions. Mason of Virginia and Elbridge Gerry of Massachusetts supported Randolph; and when the Convention rejected the idea, the three men refused to sign the Constitution.

When the Constitution was laid before the Confederation Congress in New York, Richard Henry Lee tried to attach amendments to it before sending it to the states. He was defeated, but he and his supporters won a victory of sorts in that the Constitution was transmitted to the states without the approbation of Congress. Immediately thereafter Lee began to urge the necessity of a second convention to adopt amendments.

The proposal for a second convention won the decisive support of the Virginia legislature in the fall of 1787. It agreed to call a state convention to meet in June 1788 to consider the proposed Constitution. Then, in drafting a bill to pay its expenses, the legislature provided money to pay the expenses of Virginia delegates to a second convention. The act, as adopted on 12 December, phrased the idea in general terms, but an earlier draft specifically provided for an "allowance to be made to the deputys to a second federal convention" if such a convention was judged necessary by the Virginia Convention. On 27 December Governor Randolph sent the act to the governors of the other states and their legislatures.

The Massachusetts Convention met on 9 January 1788, but if Governor John Hancock received Randolph's letter during the Convention, he did not notify the delegates. However, there was so much opposition to the Constitution in Massachusetts that the Federalists were convinced that they could not secure ratification without agreeing to amendments. They therefore drafted nine amendments and persuaded Governor Hancock to present them. The Massachusetts Convention then ratified the Constitution by a vote of 187 to 168 on 6 February. The New Hampshire Convention met a week later but adjourned after the Federalist leaders realized that the Constitution would be rejected with or without amendments.

Governor Randolph's letter and the Virginia act providing financial support for Virginia delegates to a second convention did not get to Governor George Clinton of New York until 7 March. Clinton laid the letter before the legislature on 10 March, but it took no action because it had passed a resolution calling a state convention some weeks earlier. Clinton replied to Randolph on 8 May expressing his personal support for "communications" among the states and said that he assumed the Virginia Convention would take the lead since it would meet before that of New York.

Although Governor Clinton took no apparent steps to further the Virginia proposal, his friend and political ally, John Lamb (a one-time leader of the Sons of Liberty), did so almost at once. Ten days after Clinton replied to Randolph, Lamb began writing letters to men throughout the states in an attempt to create an organization to secure amendments to the Constitution. Signing the letters "in behalf of the federal republican committee," Lamb wrote to such men as Aedanus Burke, Rawlins Lowndes, and Thomas Sumter in South Carolina; Timothy Blood-worth, Thomas Person (the former Regulator leader), and Willie Jones in North Carolina; William Grayson, Patrick Henry, Richard Henry Lee, and George Mason in Virginia; Samuel Chase in Maryland; either Samuel or George Bryan in Pennsylvania; and Nathaniel Peabody and Joshua Atherton in New Hampshire. All of these men were prominent opponents of the Constitution, at least in the form presented by the Constitutional Convention.

By 18 May, when Lamb began sending out letters, seven states had ratified, the Rhode Island towns had rejected the Constitution, and, although South Carolina ratified on 23 May, it was uncertain what the remaining states would do. Lamb proposed that supporters of amendments in the Virginia, New Hampshire, and New York conventions communicate with one another and, as he put it in his letter to Richard Henry Lee, "use our best endeavors to procure amendments to the system previous to its adoption."

When the New Hampshire Convention reassembled on 18 June, amendments were proposed; and Joshua Atherton, one of Lamb's correspondents, moved to ratify the Constitution with the amendments, but with the proviso that the Constitution would not take effect in New Hampshire until the amendments had been adopted. His motion was postponed, and then, he wrote to John Lamb, "the gilded pill was swallowed by a majority of ten out of one hundred and four members present."

In the Virginia Convention the demand that amendments be adopted prior to final ratification had so much support that the outcome was in doubt until almost the last day. However, on 25 June the Federalists defeated a motion for the adoption of prior amendments by a vote of 88 to 80 only by agreeing to recommend amendments to the new Congress. The Convention adopted a twenty-section bill of rights and twenty structural amendments, some of which would have sharply limited the powers of the new government. Even so, unconditional ratification carried by a vote of only 89 to 79.

The outcome of the New York Convention was far more uncertain since the great majority of the delegates were initially opposed to ratification, or at least to ratification without prior amendments. In the end the Federalist minority secured unconditional ratification only by agreeing to a list of amendments and to a circular letter requesting the states to require the new Congress to call a constitutional convention. The Convention approved the Circular Letter without opposition, but the act of ratification was adopted by a vote of only 30 to 27 on 26 July.

Most political leaders assumed that North Carolina would ratify. However, on 1 August the North Carolina Convention resolved that "a declaration of rights, asserting and securing from encroachment the great principles of civil and religious liberty, and the unalienable rights of the people, together with amendments to the most ambiguous and exceptionable parts of the said Constitution of government, ought to be laid before Congress, and the convention of the states that shall or may be called for the purpose of amending the said Constitution for their consideration, previous to the ratification of the Constitution aforesaid on the part of the State of North Carolina."

The Convention then agreed to a twenty-section declaration of rights and twenty-six amendments to be added to the Constitution, and adjourned on 4 August, after voting on 2 August by a "large majority . . . neither to ratify nor reject" the Constitution. The amendments proposed by North Carolina brought to a total of nearly 200 the amendments proposed by state conventions and by various groups within the states.

The ratification by ten states by the end of June meant that the new government would go into operation. But the supporters of amendments did not give up hope, and they were encouraged by the New York Circular Letter calling for a second convention. Early in November, John Lamb, again writing for the "federal republican committee," sent a circular letter to the "several states" notifying them that a "society for the purpose of procuring the general convention" had been organized in New York City.

In Virginia, Governor Randolph, who had refused to sign the Constitution and then had supported ratification, welcomed the New York Circular Letter, and so did the majority in the Virginia legislature. On 30 October the House of Delegates resolved that the amendments proposed by the Virginia Convention were needed and that the new Congress, as soon as it met, should call a convention of the states to propose amendments. When the Federalists moved instead that Congress should be asked to adopt and send to the state legislatures a bill of rights and certain of the amendments proposed by the Virginia Convention, the motion was rejected 85 to 39. The Virginia letter of 20 November to Congress and the other states requesting a second convention commented that "the slow forms of congressional discussion and recommendation, if indeed they should ever agree to any change, would, we fear, be less certain of success."

Meanwhile, the Antifederalists were planning for the coming elections. There were those like Joshua Atherton of New Hampshire and Thomas Person of North Carolina who suggested that the state legislatures might refuse to hold federal elections until amendments were assured. However, they realized that if the states did postpone elections, they would have no influence in Congress. Atherton decided that "if a new Congress can be obtained which shall contain a majority for stopping the operation of the new system until the amendments are incorporated, we shall have immediate redress."

Most Antifederalists displayed no interest in trying to prevent the new government from going into effect. They proposed to work for the election of men who would further the cause of amendments. Thus on 8 November the Virginia legislature elected two Senators, Richard Henry Lee and William Grayson, leading Antifederalists who were committed to securing amendments. The next week in New York, shortly after Governor Clinton called the legislature to meet in December to prepare for the first federal elections in that state, "the federal republican committee" sent out another circular letter to the states. It declared that it was of great importance to elect a Vice President "who will be zealously engaged in promoting such amendments to the new Constitution as will render the liberties of the country secure under it." The committee had consulted with "some gentlemen in Virginia" who reported that "they have it in view in that state" to vote for Governor Clinton and that if the other states would unite with Virginia and New York, Clinton could be elected.

The Federalists were fully aware of their opponents' plans. As early as 27 June, the last day of the Virginia Convention, James Madison wrote to George Washington that he suspected that "the plan will be to engage two-thirds of the legislatures in the task of undoing the work; or to get a Congress appointed in the first instance that will commit suicide on its own authority."

The Federalists grew more fearful as the summer of 1788 wore on. The narrow victories in New Hampshire, Virginia, and New York, the refusal of North Carolina to ratify, the widespread publication of the New York Circular Letter, and the meeting of Pennsylvania Antifederalists at Harrisburg in September convinced such men as James Madison, George Washington, and other Federalists that ratification of the Constitution was only a beginning. They declared that they must win the first federal elections or the new government would be destroyed and anarchy would follow. The Antifederalists were equally convinced that they must win and that the Constitution must be amended, or the liberties of the people would be destroyed. Such were the thoughts and feelings expressed privately and publicly while Congress debated the Election Ordinance and before the states enacted legislation providing for the first federal elections.*

NOTE ON SOURCES

The extensive collection of manuscripts long known as "Papers of the Continental Congress" is the principal source for the history of the Continental and Confederation congresses from 1774 to 1789. These consist of the journals, motions, resolutions, letters, and other documents accumulated by Charles Thomson, secretary of Congress from its first meeting in 1774 until the beginning of the government under the Constitution in 1789. Thomson turned the papers over to President George Washington in the summer of 1789. They were then deposited with the Secretary of State and remained in the State Department until the major portion was turned over to the Manuscript Division of the Library of Congress in 1903. These papers and other related documents were transferred to the National Archives in 1952 (Carl L. Lokke, "The Continental Congress Papers: Their History, 1789-1952," *National Archives Accessions* No. 51 [June, 1954], 1-19).

The Library of Congress maintained the papers as they had been arranged and numbered by a clerk in the State Department in 1834. The *Handbook of Manuscripts in the Library of Congress* (Washington, 1918) gives the collection the title, "Papers of the Continental Congress," and describes each of the 196 "numbers," some of which contain many volumes. "No. 1," for instance, consists of thirty-nine volumes of the "Rough Journals" of Congress from 1774 to 1789. The year after the Library of Congress received the Papers of the Continental Congress from the

---

*The foregoing introduction outlines the demand for amendments and the movement for a second constitutional convention, but only one group of documents directly relating to the issue—the New York Circular Letter of 26 July and examples of responses to it—is printed below. The full documentation relating to amendments and a second constitutional convention will be printed in Merrill Jensen, ed., *The Documentary History of the Ratification of the Constitution.*

State Department, it began publishing the Journals, a task not completed until 1937 (W. C. Ford, et al., eds., *Journals of the Continental Congress 1774-1789* [34 vols., Washington, 1904-1937]).

There have been some changes in nomenclature since the Papers were transferred to the National Archives. The Archives has substituted the term "Item" for the "No." used by the Library of Congress for each section of the Papers. The Papers are now a part of Record Group 360 with the title: "Records of the Continental and Confederation Congresses and the Constitutional Convention."

In 1961 the National Archives microfilmed the Papers on 204 reels (*Pamphlet Accompanying Microcopy No. 247: Papers of the Continental Congress, 1774-89*) and in 1962 microfilmed nine additional reels of miscellaneous Papers (*Pamphlet Accompanying Microcopy No. 332: Miscellaneous Papers of the Continental Congress, 1774-89*). The pamphlets contain a somewhat fuller description of the Papers than that in the Library of Congress *Handbook*.

The sections of the Journals printed in this chapter have been transcribed from the Rough Journals, which record many but not all of the actions of Congress. Only the demand by a member for a roll-call vote guaranteed that a motion would be included in the Journals on any given day. Hence it is often necessary to search elsewhere in the Papers for clues to what happened. Particularly useful in this respect are the Reports of Committees Relating Particularly to Congress, the Establishment of the Household of the President, and the Qualifications of Members, 1775-1788 (Item 23) and the Register of Reports from Boards, Offices, and Committees of Congress, 1785-1788 (Item 190). Sometimes information cannot be found in any of the official documents and therefore the letters written by and to members of Congress are invaluable, as are letters written by people outside Congress commenting about what happened in it. Some, but by no means all, of the letters written by members of Congress have been published in Edmund C. Burnett, ed., *Letters of Members of the Continental Congress* (8 vols., Washington, 1921-1937).

The newspapers of the time are useful for following the public debate over the location of the new government and for an indication of the pressure on Congress to come to a decision. The newspapers often published detailed accounts of actions taken by Congress, including the Journals. However, newspaper accounts were often out of date by the time they appeared, especially at a distance from New York.

NOTE ON PROCEDURE IN THE CONFEDERATION CONGRESS

Under the Articles of Confederation each state had one vote, and the votes of nine states were necessary to pass such measures as a declaration of war, the ratification of a treaty, the issuance of paper money, and the like. The votes of seven states were required for the passage of lesser measures. The only exception was that when fewer than seven states were represented, they could pass a motion to adjourn.

While each state had one vote, at least two delegates had to be present and voting for the vote of a state to be counted. When a state delegation divided evenly on a vote, the delegates' votes are given in the Journals but the state's vote was not counted. Such divided votes are indicated by a "d" following the vote of the delegation. If only one delegate was present he could vote and the vote is given in the Journals but, like a divided vote, was not counted. Such votes are followed by an asterisk.

MEMBERS ATTENDING THE CONFEDERATION CONGRESS, 1788[1]

New Hampshire

Nicholas Gilman (21 January—26 August; 4 September—1 November)
Paine Wingate (11 February—13 September)

Massachusetts

Nathan Dane (21 February—13 September or later)
Samuel Alleyne Otis (21 January—13 August; 10 October or earlier—1 November; 30 December)
Theodore Sedgwick (31 July—3 September)
George Thacher (21 January—25 March; 6 August—1 November)

Rhode Island

Peleg Arnold (6 May—7 August; 8 September—1 November)
Jonathan J. Hazard (2 June—24 July; 4-7 August)

Connecticut

Joseph Platt Cooke (29 February—31 March)
Pierpont Edwards (9 June—2 July; 10 July—6 August or later; 28 August—12 September; 10 October or earlier—1 November)
Benjamin Huntington (1 July—1 November)
Jeremiah Wadsworth (21 January—31 March; 10 July—26 August; 12 September or earlier—2 October or later)

New York

Egbert Benson (14 July—13 August or later)
Leonard Gansevoort (25 February—30 April or later; 25 August—10 October)
Alexander Hamilton (25 February—4 March; 30 July—10 October)
Ezra L'Hommedieu (16 June—13 August or later)
Abraham Yates, Jr. (26 May—5 September or later)

New Jersey

Abraham Clark (21 January—15 October)
Jonathan Dayton (22 January—1 November or later; 11 December)
Jonathan Elmer (21 January—9 February; 1 July—14 August)

Delaware

Dyre Kearney (21 January—17 June; 10 July—14 October)
Nathaniel Mitchell (21 January—19 March; 13-20 April; 20 May—13 June; 10
    July—13 September)

Pennsylvania

John Armstrong, Jr. (21 January—29 February or later; 28 July—13 August or
    later; 3-13 September or later)
William Bingham (20 May—7 August or later; 25 August or earlier—5 September or
    later)
William Irvine (21 January—20 May or later; 14 July—1 November)
Samuel Meredith (29 July—13 September or later)
James Randolph Reid (21 January—7 August or later; 26 August—10 October)

Maryland

Benjamin Contee (23 January—29 February; 13 June—13 August; 6 October—3
    November)
John Eager Howard (21 January—29 February; 7-18 July or later)
David Ross (10 March—28 May; 16 July—8 September)
Joshua Seney (28 April—30 May; 14 July—8 September)

Virginia

John Brown (21 January—9 July or later; 4 August or earlier—12 August)
Edward Carrington (6 May or earlier—10 October)
John Dawson (1 December)
Cyrus Griffin (21 January—15 November)
Henry Lee (29 July—13 September or later)
James Madison (21 January—29 February or later; 17 July—15 October)

North Carolina

John Swann (29 May—26 August or later)

John White (21 January—26 April; 10 October or earlier)
Hugh Williamson (16 May—3 November)

South Carolina

Nicholas Eveleigh (6 December)
Daniel Huger (21 January—12 September or later; 15 October or earlier—1 November)
John Parker (21 January—1 November)
Thomas Tudor Tucker (21 January—1 November or later; 15 December)

Georgia

Abraham Baldwin (21 January—9 February; 5 May—18 September)
William Few (26 May—18 September)

1. This list is based on the list in Burnett, ed., *Letters of the Members of the Continental Congress*, VIII, lxxxiii-xcviii, with corrections derived from the Journals, letters, and other sources.

CONFEDERATION CONGRESS CHRONOLOGY, 1788

21 June	New Hampshire Convention ratifies the Constitution.
25 June	News of New Hampshire ratification reaches Congress in New York City.
25 June	Virginia Convention ratifies the Constitution.
2 July	New Hampshire act of ratification laid before Congress and Congress appoints committee to draft ordinance putting the new Constitution into effect.
2 July	News of Virginia ratification reaches New York City.
9 July	Committee reports election ordinance with the meeting place of the new government left blank.
14 July	Congress considers committee report.
15-28 July	Congress suspends consideration of election ordinance pending decision of New York Convention.
25 July	New York Convention votes to ratify the Constitution.
26 July	New York Convention approves formal document of ratification and circular letter to the states proposing a second constitutional convention.
26 July	News of New York Convention's vote of 25 July reaches New York City.
28 July	Debate on election ordinance resumes: Philadelphia proposed and rejected as the meeting place of the new government.

2 August	North Carolina Convention refuses to ratify the Constitution.
4 August	Debate on election ordinance continues: Lancaster, Pa., proposed and rejected as seat of government and Baltimore approved.
5 August	Debate continues: Baltimore reconsidered and rejected; New York City approved.
13 August	Debate continues: New York City rejected.
14 August	News of North Carolina's refusal to ratify the Constitution reaches New York City.
26 August	Debate over election ordinance continues: Wilmington, Del., proposed and rejected and New York City rejected again.
2 September	Debate continues: Lancaster, Pa., proposed and rejected.
3 September	Debate continues: Annapolis, Md., proposed and rejected.
13 September	Election Ordinance adopted: Electors to be chosen on 7 January; to cast their ballots for President on 4 February; and the new government to "commence proceedings" at "the present seat of Congress" on 4 March 1789.

THE DOCUMENTS

News of New Hampshire Ratification Reaches Congress, Wednesday, 25 June 1788

By 9 January 1788, five of the nine states necessary for adoption of the Constitution had ratified unconditionally. The Massachusetts Convention ratified on 6 February, but the Federalists secured ratification only by promising to support amendments. Despite this setback, Federalists were confident that New Hampshire would ratify with little difficulty. The Newburyport *Essex Journal* stated on 2 January "that its being adopted in that state by a great majority, does not admit of a doubt," and the day before the Convention assembled, Jeremy Belknap predicted, "there is *no doubt* of their acceptance of the Constitution" (to Benjamin Rush, Boston, 12 February, RC, Rush Papers, PPL). After the Convention opened, however, the Federalists discovered to their surprise that they did not have enough votes. A majority of the delegates either were opposed to ratification or had received instructions from their towns to vote against the Constitution. Faced with the prospect of almost certain defeat, the Federalists moved to adjourn the Convention until June. After a heated debate on 23 February, the vote for adjournment was carried by five votes.

By the end of May eight states had voted to ratify the Constitution. Three state conventions were scheduled to open in June: Virginia on the 2nd, New York on the 17th, and the adjourned New Hampshire Convention on the 21st. It was widely known that a great majority of the delegates in New York were opposed to ratification, that there was no agreement on the outcome in Virginia, and that a majority of the New Hampshire delegates had been opposed to ratification in February. Federalist leaders were intensely aware that the rapid communication of news from the three conventions would be of the utmost importance. As early as April, Edward Carrington reported that if New Hampshire were the ninth state to ratify it would have a great effect on Virginia (to Thomas Jefferson, New York, 24 April, Boyd, XIII, 101). In May, Alexander Hamilton wrote James Madison that since the New York and Virginia conventions were meeting at almost the same time, "it will be of vast importance that an exact communication should be kept up between us," and that "the moment *any decisive* question is taken, if favorable," Madison should send an express "with pointed orders to make all possible diligence, by changing horses, etc. All expenses shall be thankfully and liberally paid" (New York, 19 May, Syrett, IV, 649-50). Early in June Hamilton wrote John Sullivan, president of the New Hampshire Convention, that since the "Antifederal Party" in New York had a "large majority," a speedy decision by New Hampshire and prompt communication of it was of great importance. Hamilton requested that "the instant you have taken a decisive vote in favor of the Constitution, you send an express to me at Poughkeepsie. Let him take the *shortest route* to that place, change horses on the road, and use all possible diligence. I shall with pleasure defray all expenses, and give a liberal reward to the person" (New York, 6 June, Syrett, V, 2). Rufus King reported to Hamilton from Boston a few days later that he had made arrangements to forward the results from New Hampshire to Springfield, Massachusetts, and that General Henry Knox had arranged to send the news from Springfield to Poughkeepsie (12 June, Syrett, V,

5). Whether or not this was a separate arrangement is unknown, but John Sullivan later informed Hamilton that he had followed Hamilton's instructions and paid the rider the balance of his bill in cash. Sullivan added seven shillings for the discount and postage, and enclosed the bill for payment (Durham, 10 July, Syrett, V, 148-49).

New Hampshire ratified at one o'clock on Saturday afternoon, 21 June (Tobias Lear to George Washington, Portsmouth, 22 June, DHOC, IV, 744-45). Later that day, John Langdon wrote Hamilton that "by the desire of our mutual friend, Rufus King, Esqr." he was sending the news express to William Smith at Springfield (Concord, 21 June, Syrett, V, 34). The letter got to Hamilton in the New York Convention on Tuesday, 24 June. Hamilton gave it to his father-in-law, Philip Schuyler, and asked him to send the news to James Madison. Schuyler wrote to Madison at once, with a copy of Langdon's letter at the end (DHOC, IV, 753-54). Schuyler sent the letter express to New York.

Newspaper Report of the Arrival of the News, 25 June[1]

By EXPRESS

Yesterday, at 12 h.noon, Mr. Kelsey arrived in this city in *ten hours* from Poughkeepsie, with the important intelligence of the RATIFICATION of the CONSTITUTION, by the state of NEW-HAMPSHIRE.

This intelligence was received at Poughkeepsie, by express, under the signature of his excellency *John Langdon*, president of the state of New-Hampshire, and purports, that the Convention, of that state RATIFIED the CONSTITUTION on the 21st instant, by a majority of ELEVEN, yeas 57, nays 46.

At half after twelve this letter was read in Congress. At one o'clock Col. Henley sat off, *express*, for Virginia, with the *joyful tidings*.

At 2 h. the bells in this city were sat a ringing, which incessantly rang until 7 in the evening.

Many citizens were rejoiced on this occasion; to testify which bottles of choice *nectar* were *quaffed—and, at that hour, the guns fired*.

1. *New York Journal*, 26 June.

Abraham Yates, Jr., to Abraham G. Lansing, New York, 25 June (excerpt)[1]

Whilst I am writing advice is brought (I write this in Congress) that New Hampshire had adopted the new Constitution, which bred such an inattention to the business, the Southern members to write letters to Virginia,[2] and others talking the matter over (it being the ninth state), that we adjourned.

I was addressed by several of the members: what would the state of New York do now? I tell them the same they would have done if New Hampshire had not adopted it. They will adopt but I hoped not without previous amendments, that my mind was made up that if all the twelve states were to come in that New York ought not, and I trusted they would not. Whilst I am writing this the bells are set ringing for joy upon this occasion.

1. RC, Yates Papers, NN. Lansing, brother of John Lansing, was an Antifederalist leader in Albany.

2. At this point Yates added the following marginal note: "The Virginia legislature meet the twenty third and by that time it is supposed the Convention will have come to a decision so that by next Saturday it is expected that we will hear the event."

Edward Carrington, John Brown, and Cyrus Griffin to James Madison, New York, 25 June[1]

½ after 12. June 25 1788

The enclosed* this moment came to hand. Contemplating the critical state of the subject it concerns in Virginia we thought it best to dispatch it by express, rather than depend on the progress of the post.[2]

*Letter from Ph. Schuyler to Madison & from Pres. Langdon to A Hamilton [Carrington's footnote].

1. RC (LT), Madison Papers, DLC. This letter, from three of Virginia's delegates to the Confederation Congress, was addressed: "The Honble James Madison, in his absence, Governor Randolph in Convention Richmond." Madison had been reelected to Congress in 1786 and 1787, but had gone to Virginia to take part in the Virginia Convention. He returned to Congress by 16 July.

2. The letter was carried by Colonel David Henley, who had commanded a Continental regiment from 1777 to 1779. During the period of ratification he served as a messenger on several occasions. On Friday, 27 June, the Philadelphia *Pennsylvania Packet* printed an "Extract from a paper in the hands of Colonel Henly, who yesterday passed through this city, express to Mr. Maddison of Virginia, from the President of Congress." The extract reported the vote of New Hampshire. Henley arrived in Alexandria, Va., Friday night, the 27th, a few hours after news of Virginia's ratification reached there (George Washington to Tobias Lear, Mount Vernon, 29 June, Fitzpatrick, XXXVII, 569-70). Henley returned to New York with the news of Virginia's ratification while another express rider carried the letter to Madison in Richmond, where he received it 30 June (Madison to Alexander Hamilton, 30 June, Syrett, V, 137).

Paine Wingate to Mrs. Paine Wingate, New York, 25 June (excerpt)[1]

I am very happy at this moment having within the hour past received the good news of New Hampshire adopting the new Constitution. This is an event of great consequence and diffuses universal joy. The nine pillars are now erected, upon which the new building will stand, even if there should be no more props added; but we hope yet for all thirteen states in due time, which will add stability and beauty to the fabric. You will excuse my filling any part of my letter with politics to a lady. I write from the fullness of my heart and what possesses my mind at this juncture. I also know that you are a mighty political madam, and a staunch Federalist.

1. RC, Wingate Papers, MH, Printed: Wingate, *Wingate*, I, 184-86. Wingate was a New Hampshire delegate to Congress.

Paine Wingate to Samuel Lane, New York, 26 June (excerpt)[1]

I now sir with particular satisfaction, congratulate upon the adoption of the new Constitution in your state, and which has ensured its taking place. The latest news we have from Virginia is dated the 18 instant. By a letter from Governor [Edmund] Randolph we are told that then there had no question been taken to decide the sense of the Convention, but his calculation was that there were 82 for, 76 against and 10 doubtful. Another letter which is from an Antifederalist of the same date says that there are reckoned 80 on each side as certain and 8 as doubtful. The event therefore is yet very dubious. It is supposed that they would come to a determination on Saturday or Wednesday last. Of New York Convention you will have as good an account as I am able to give you by the newspaper which I enclose. I hope that the spirit of lying and controversy upon this important subject will soon be done away, and that harmony and prosperity will attend the United States. . . . The Congress will, I suppose, pretty soon take up the new system and prepare to put [it] in motion. I hope that by the latter end of August we shall be able to adjourn.[2] For my own part I am not for tarrying here any longer than is indispensable. I have my health and find my situation more agreeable than I expected.

1. RC, Wingate Papers, MH. Printed: Wingate, *Wingate*, I, 232. Lane was a New Hampshire farmer, tanner, and shoemaker, and a neighbor of Wingate's.
2. An extract from a letter from New York, dated 26 June, that appeared in the Portland, Me., *Cumberland Gazette* on 10 July expressed similar optimism: "Congress will proceed," it predicted, "to put the new government in operation about the first of August, or at the furthest the 10th." Charles Pinckney was even more sanguine, expecting congressional provisions for organizing the new government to be complete by the end of July (to Rufus King, Charleston, 16 June, RC, King Papers, NHi).

Thomas Willing to William Bingham, Philadelphia, 29 June (excerpt)[1]

I thank you for the good news from New Hampshire which had reached us by Colonel [David] Henly about two hours before the post got in; yet your letter gave me an agreeable confirmation of it. I hope by this time he has got to the end of his journey, and by his intelligence given fresh courage to our friends at Richmond. By post yesterday, Dr. [Benjamin] Rush received a line of the 23d from Mr. [Francis] Corbin. He says "no material change has taken place since my last; tomorrow a question will be put for the adoption with *previous* amendments. This will be rejected by a majority of four or five. The question for ratification generally will then be put, and will be carried by a majority of twenty or thirty"—thus for Mr. Corbin. Dr. [James] Hutchinson says that Mr. C[orbin] is mistaken: that he, Hutchinson, has got the intended amendments sent him, that they were to be offered on Tuesday, would take a long debate, and that no determination would be had on them before Wednesday. Which account is most to be depended on, you may guess. We can do no more at present. For my part I wish the whole may be postponed till Colonel Henly reaches them; for his news must, I think, change the question very materially. The question then need not be whether the Constitution is a good one, or the best possible; it will be, in short, will Virginia form a part of the Union, or not? God grant they may join hands with us, and try to do the best with it. As Number One, I am quite content to take it as it is, with all its *supposed* imperfections; for real or essential ones, I have not sense or skill enough to discover yet.

. . . .

[P.S.] I give this a chance by the stage as being earlier than the post. Did the letter I wrote by the stage last Wednesday morning get to you that evening or not? Great preparations are making for the procession on Friday. It will be a true *gala* day, in which every heart, *almost* will be united. The accession of New Hampshire has wrought a perfect change with some of the most warm Anties. We have heard that the Congress have adjourned to meet here. Is this true or not?

1. RC, Gratz Collection, PHi. Willing, president of the Bank of North America, was Bingham's father-in-law. Bingham was a delegate to Congress from Pennsylvania.

Charles Thomson to John Dickinson, New York, 30 June[1]

I have the pleasure to inform you that authentic accounts have been received of New Hampshire having ratified the new Constitution, so that now nine states have adopted it. It is hoped that Virginia will also adopt it and that we shall soon receive the agreeable intelligence from that state. There are now present seven of the adopting states and a delegate is hourly expected from Maryland. On his arrival eight of the states which have adopted the Constitution will be represented in Congress. As Delaware is absent, I wish you could by any means hasten on the delegates, as I think it of importance that all the states which adopt the Constitution should be present when Congress proceed on the measures necessary for putting it in operation.[2]

1. RC, Dickinson Papers, PPL. The letter was addressed to Dickinson at Wilmington, Del.
2. See Dickinson to George Read, 5 July, printed below. The two Delaware delegates, Dyre Kearney and Nathaniel Mitchell, appeared in Congress on 10 July.

News of Virginia Ratification Reaches New York City, 2 July

New York Journal, 4 A.M., 2 July[1]

NEWS from VIRGINIA!

What this news is, could not be ascertained last evening, but we shall doubtless hear this day by express. It is pretty well authenticated, that the bells rang at Philadelphia Monday evening— and it is *supposed*, that the cause was, the RATIFI-CATION of the Constitution, by Virginia!

The express above referred to, arrived, of which particularly tomorrow. 4 o'clock, A.M.

Henry Knox to Jeremiah Wadsworth, New York, 5 A.M., 2 July (excerpt)[2]

Rejoice—Heaven has influenced the Virginia Convention to adopt the Constitution by a majority of *ten*. This great event took place on Wednesday the 25th of June. Some amendments will be stated in the manner of Massachusetts.

Colonel [David] Henley who went express from this city on Wednesday last with the adoption of New Hampshire met the express from Richmond at Alexandria on Saturday the 28th. He stayed there that day and dined in company with the General and returned here about three hours ago.

An express will be at Poughkeepsie about two o'clock this day.

New York Journal, 3 July

Convention of Virginia.

YESTERDAY morning Col. Henley returned from Virginia, to which place he was expedited on Wednesday last with the intelligence of the ratification of the new Constitution by New Hampshire.

Immediately on the arrival of Col. Henley, William Livingston, Esq. sat off for Poughkeepsie with the intelligence.

Colonel Henley, having arrived at Alexandria, met an express bound to New York, with the intelligence of the RATIFICATION of the new Constitution by the state of VIRGINIA. This interesting circumstance rendered Colonel Henley's further pursuit fruitless; he therefore returned, with the same zealous expedition he went, to bring the tidings to the anxious expectants in New York, and arrived here, at THREE o'CLOCK yesterday morning.

On this occasion the bells of the city were set a ringing immediately, and at FIVE o'clock TEN guns were fired in honor of the ten states which have adopted the Constitution.

The purport of the Virginia intelligence, is, that after a session of eighteen days, in which the merits of the Constitution were fully investigated, clause by clause, both parties being equally zealous in the cause, speaking freely, and discussing (sometimes) dispassionately, on the TWENTY-FOURTH instant, viz. Tuesday sennight, the *decisive* question was put, whether the Convention would RATIFY the Constitution, when there appeared—YEAS 88, and NAYS, 78,[3] giving a MAJORITY of TEN. *Thus have* TEN STATES RATIFIED *the* CONSTITUTION *proposed by the* GENERAL CONVENTION, *who sat at Philadelphia in September last.*

1. Type was being set when the first rumor reached the printing shop. Higher up in column 2, page 3, is printed an extract of a letter from Richmond, dated 10 P.M. 23 June, predicting that a vote would be taken in a day or two with a majority of two or three for ratification. The first paragraph printed above was inserted with a hand pointing to it. The second paragraph, in smaller type, was evidently inserted later.

2. RC, Wadsworth Papers, CtHi. Knox headed the letter "New York 5 oClock Morning of the 2d July 1788." Wadsworth wrote on the cover: "favored by Mr. Base with the glorious news of the adoption by Virginia." Knox was Secretary at War for the Confederation Congress. Wadsworth was a delegate to Congress from Connecticut. He returned to Congress on 10 July.

3. The correct vote was 89 to 79.

Journals of Congress, Wednesday, 2 July[1]

Congress assembled. Present New Hampshire, Massachusetts, Rhode Island, Connecticut, New York, New Jersey, Pennsylvania, Virginia, North Carolina, South Carolina and Georgia, and from Maryland, Mr. Contee.

. . . .

The State of New Hampshire having ratified the Constitution transmitted to them by the act of the 28 of September last and transmitted to Congress their ratification and the same being read, the President [Cyrus Griffin] reminded Congress that this was the ninth ratification transmitted and laid before them.[2]

Whereupon, on motion of Mr. Clarke, seconded by Mr. Edwards,

Ordered, that the ratifications of the Constitution of the United States transmitted to Congress be referred to a committee to examine the same and report an act to Congress for putting the said Constitution into operation in pursuance of the resolutions of the late Federal Convention.[3]

On the question to agree to this order, the yeas and nays being required by Mr. Yates:

New Hampshire			Pennsylvania		
Gilman	ay	ay	Bingham	ay	ay
Wingate	ay		Reid	ay	
Massachusetts			Maryland		
Dane	ay	ay	Contee	ay*	
Otis	ay		Virginia		
Rhode Island			Griffin	ay	
Arnold		excused[4]	Carrington	ay	ay
Hazard			Brown	ay	
Connecticut			South Carolina		
Huntington	ay	ay	Huger	ay	
Edwards	ay		Parker	ay	ay
New York			Tucker	ay	
L'Hommedieu	ay	d	Georgia		
Yates	no		Few	ay	ay
New Jersey			Baldwin	ay	
Clarke	ay				
Elmer	ay	ay			
Dayton	ay				

So it passed in the affirmative.[5]

1. The Journals of Congress printed in this chapter have been transcribed from the Rough Journals, 1774-1789 (PCC, Item 1), XXXIX (June 23, 1788—March 2, 1789). The volume is unpaginated and citations hereafter are by date only.

2. The New Hampshire act of ratification, transmitted by President John Langdon on 25 June to the New Hampshire delegates in Congress, did not reach New York until the evening of 1 July. The delegates submitted it to Congress the next day.

3. The motion is in Reports of Committees Relating Particularly to Congress, the Establishment of the Household of the President, and the Qualifications of Members 1775-1788 (PCC, Item 23, p. 331). This Item contains many but not all of the various drafts of motions made by delegates between 2 July and 13 September. Any wording of the draft motions which is significantly different in meaning from the wording in the Journals will be indicated in the notes. The drafts of motions with alterations and the relevant portions of the Journals of Congress are printed in DHOC, II, 161-73, 204-65.

4. New York, Rhode Island, and North Carolina had not yet ratified. The New York delegates voted. The Rhode Island and North Carolina delegates refused, but later they did vote (see the Journals for 4, 5, and 6 August printed below).

5. The Journals do not mention the appointment of a committee. However, Edward Carrington, Pierpont Edwards, Abraham Baldwin, Samuel A. Otis, and Thomas Tudor Tucker were appointed. Their names are given in The Register of Reports from Boards, Offices, and Committees of the Congress, 1785-1788 (PCC, Item 190, p. 197).

New Hampshire Delegates to President John Langdon, New York, 2 July[1]

We were honored last evening with the letter of the 25th of June, enclosing the ratification of the new Federal Constitution by the State of New Hampshire, and had the honor of laying it before Congress this day; upon which a committee was appointed to report to Congress the necessary arrangements in order to carry into effect the new system of government according to the recommendation of the General Convention of the states.

We have the additional pleasure to inform you that by authentic letters received this day from Virginia, it appears that their Convention, on the 25th ultimo, determined the question in favor of the new government by a majority of ten members.

1. RC, Emmet Collection, no. 9580, NN. The letter was signed by Paine Wingate and Nicholas Gilman. "President" was the title of the chief executive in New Hampshire.

Thomas Willing to William Bingham, Philadelphia, 2 July (excerpt)[1]

I received yours of the 30th ult. by the post yesterday, and have sent forward the letter for Mr. [Dyre] Kearney by a near neighbor of his. I saw Colonel [John Eager] Howard[2] pass by last night and don't hear that he is about to leave town before our gala day is over.

From my heart I congratulate you on the news from Virginia. Their ratification has put an end to the dying faction here, and will totally extinguish the flame which a few only of this city had kindled in the western country.

. . . .

I write this only to send you a copy of Mr. Madison's letter to T[ench] Coxe; it is pleasing of [sic] see that the great business has been conducted with so much regularity. Other letters say "that the greater part of the minority at Richmond have declared their intentions to assist the federal government, now that a majority have agreed to accept it, and say that their votes in many instances were given in compliance with their instructions, tho contrary to their own private inclinations and judgment."

. . . .

Adieu! I am truly sorry for your very long detention from us, but remember that an absence now, may cost you and others many long years of the like inconvenience hereafter.

1. RC, Gratz Collection, PHi.
2. Kearney was a Delaware delegate to Congress, and Howard was a Maryland delegate.

John Dickinson to George Read, Wilmington, 5 July[1]

Yesterday and today I have received letters, one from Tench Coxe, the other from Charles Thomson, by which I learn that Congress is very soon to fix upon a place for commencing the operations of the federal government; and that Philadelphia will unquestionably be chosen, if Delaware shall be represented.

There are, besides, many important determinations to be made, that render it in the highest degree necessary that this state should be immediately represented. The absence of *one man* has frequently confused our public affairs. I expect it will be so again, but I am discharging what I esteem a duty, and earnestly request that every measure which shall appear proper may be taken to give this state a vote in the business that is coming on. [2]

1. William T. Read, *Life and Correspondence of George Read...* (Philadelphia, 1870), 466-67. Dickinson and Read had been delegates from Delaware to the Constitutional Convention. Dickinson held no political office thereafter, while Read was elected to the United States Senate.

2. Even before New Hampshire ratified the Constitution, but particularly afterwards, various leaders urged that the states be adequately represented in Congress during the summer of 1788 (see, for example, Nathan Dane to Theodore Sedgwick, New York, 27 April, 17 June, 22 June, RC, Sedgwick Papers, MHi; Benjamin Huntington and Pierpont Edwards to Jeremiah Wadsworth, New York, 1 July, RC, Wadsworth Papers, CtHi).

William Bingham to Benjamin Rush, New York, 7 July[1]

I received your letter of the 3d inst. and shall forward the enclosed letter for Mr. [John] Adams agreeable to your wishes. The point, in favor of which you are solicitous of engaging his interest, will be determined, long before it will reach him, and I hope to your satisfaction. A proper attention to the Massachusetts delegation in Congress has not been wanting on this occasion.[2]

I agree with you in opinion that our prospects are very flattering, but to realize them we must not relax a moment in our exertions. The proper organization of the government, the institution of the necessary departments, the arrangement of the offices, etc., will require much time and consideration and will greatly influence the future operation of the system.

Your federal procession will be a triumph; any of the other states, but an ovation.[3]

1. RC, Alexander Biddle Papers, PHi. Rush, a Philadelphia physician, was an ardent Federalist publicist in 1787-1788.

2. Rush's letter to Bingham has not been found. Rush's letter to John Adams, dated 2 July, left open for Bingham to read, is printed in Chapter XIV. It stated in part that "the citizens of Pennsylvania will joyfully concur in this measure [making Adams Vice President] especially if the Southern and Eastern states should gratify them by fixing the seat of Congress on the Delaware. This must be the compensation for their placing a citizen of Virginia in the President's chair and a citizen of New England in the chair of the Senate" (RC, Adams Papers, MHi).

3. Beginning late in 1787, Federalists started to celebrate ratifications of the Constitution by the states with festivities and processions. The Fourth of July procession in Philadelphia,

planned in anticipation of ratification by the ninth state, was particularly spectacular. See Whitfield J. Bell, Jr., "The Federal Processions of 1788," *The New-York Historical Society Quarterly*, XLVI (1962), 5-39.

Samuel A. Otis to John Adams, New York, 7 July (excerpt)[1]

At all events the experiment will soon be tried. Ten states have acceded. Congress, feeling an obligation to call upon the people to elect their President, etc., have chosen a committee who will in a day or two report the time for operations to commence under the new government, and which I think will probably be in January or February 1789.[2] New York are indeed opposed, but the last accounts from their Convention from the leaders in favor of the question "lead us hope" [*sic*]. Of North Carolina there can be little doubt. Rhode Island you will be pleased to form your own judgment upon. They are a kind of comet.

1. RC, Adams Papers, MHi. Otis was a delegate to Congress from Massachusetts.
2. John Swann, the North Carolina congressman, wrote to James Iredell the same day that "the arrangements for putting the new government into action have been committed for some days and in all probability will be reported on this week" (RC, Emmet Collection, no. 1197, NN).

Journals of Congress, Wednesday, 9 July

Congress assembled. Present as before.[1]

1. All the states were represented except Delaware, and only one delegate from Connecticut was present. Congress conducted a great deal of business during the day. The report of the committee on putting the Constitution into operation, printed immediately below, was read to Congress this day, but it is not mentioned in the Journals.

Report of the Committee on Putting the Constitution into Operation, Wednesday, 9 July[1]

The committee consisting of Mr. Carrington, Mr. Edwards, Mr. Baldwin, Mr. Otis and Mr. Tucker, to whom were referred the ratifications of the new Constitution which have been transmitted to Congress by the several ratifying states, report as follows:

"Resolved, that whereas the Federal Convention assembled in Philadelphia, pursuant to the resolution of Congress of the 21st of February 1787, did on the 17th of September, in the same year, report to the United States in Congress assembled, in the words following, viz., 'We the People etc.'

"Whereupon, Congress on the 28th of the same September did resolve unanimously, 'that the said report, with the resolutions and letter accompanying the same, be transmitted to the several legislatures in order to be submitted to a convention of delegates chosen in each state, by the people thereof, in conformity to the resolves of the Convention made and provided in that case.' And whereas the states of New Hampshire, Massachusetts, Connecticut, New Jersey, Pennsylvania, Delaware, Maryland, South Carolina and Georgia, have duly ratified the aforesaid Constitution, as appears by the several ratifications of the said states, returned to Congress, and filed in the office of the secretary; and it is expedient that proceedings do commence thereon as early as may be, therefore,

"Resolved, that the first Wednesday in December next be the day for appointing Electors in the several states which have, or shall, before the said day, have, ratified the said Constitution; that the first Wednesday in January next be the day for the Electors to assemble in their respective states and vote for a President, and that the first Wednesday in February next be the time, and _____ the place for commencing proceedings under the said Constitution."

1. PCC, Item 23, pp. 333-35. This committee report was not placed in the Rough Journals. The Library of Congress edition of the *Journals* prints the report in the *Journals* for 8 July (XXXIV, 303-4), presumably because Charles Thomson endorsed it as "read 8 July 1788 Order the day for Thursday 9th" (PCC, Item 23, pp. 333-35). However, Thomson's own entries in Registers of Reports from Boards, Offices, and Committees of the Congress 1786-1788 (PCC, Item 189, p. 36) and Register of Reports from Boards, Offices and Committees of the Congress 1785-1788 (PCC, Item 190, p. 197) indicate that the report was presented on the 9th. The report, then, became the order of the day on Thursday, the 10th. The Journals record no action until 14 July, but for evidence that the report was considered on the 10th, see Samuel Osgood to Melancton Smith and Samuel Jones, 11 July, printed below.

John Brown to John Smith, New York, 9 July (excerpt)[1]

Congress on the 3d. instant came to a final determination upon the subject of the Kentucky address which was to refer the application to the new government and to recommend it to the State of Virginia and the district to make the necessary alterations in these acts and resolutions upon that subject. The great change which has taken place in the general government of the Union in some measure justified the decision, which was contrary to the expectations which I at first entertained; but had it not been for the opposition of the Eastern States, Kentucky might have been admitted into the Union before the new Constitution had been adopted by nine states. I hope this disappointment will not be productive of any bad consequences to the district but that unanimity and good order will still prevail. In my opinion their interest requires that they should assume their independence, frame a constitution, and proceed to the exercise of government and when the new government is in motion then to make application to be admitted into the Union if it should appear advisable.

I thank you for the journal of the Virginia Convention containing the ratification of and proposed amendments to the new Constitution. The proceedings of that body were received here with every possible mark of joy. This state is still in session; what the result of their deliberations will be is as yet very uncertain. North Carolina will doubtless adopt it. Congress are now engaged in taking measures for setting it in motion. The elections are to be held in January next and the new Congress to meet in February—I expect at Philadelphia.

I am as yet uncertain which route I shall take to Kentucky, tho I expect to be governed by the state of the river. I propose to leave this about the tenth of August and hope to be at Danville the 1st. of September in order to attend court at that term. In the mean I propose to pay the Eastern States a visit and shall set out in company with General [Henry] Knox for Boston tomorrow morning. I expect to continue my journey as far as New Hampshire and to return through Connecticut. I promise myself much pleasure in this excursion as I shall go part of the way by sea, a mode of travelling new to me. I [am] happy to hear of the welfare of my father's family and of my other relations. Am much pleased to find that you still entertain hopes of becoming an inhabitant of Kentucky, together with your father's family. Nothing [would] add more to my happiness than this. [E——?] [——ard?] and family I expect will remove to that [country?] this fall. We shall all be there yet. My hopes respecting the future importance of that country are sanguine. I have engaged in foreign negotiations which, if successful, will be of great consequence to Kentucky. Am not at liberty to inform you of particulars at present.[2]

1. RC, Brown Papers, CtY. Brown, of Kentucky, was a Virginia delegate to Congress. The recipient was probably John Smith of Frederick County, Va. He served in the House of Delegates, 1777-1779 and 1786-1787, and ran unsuccessfully for election to the Virginia Convention. He was elected to Congress in 1801 and served until 1815.
2. For the "Spanish conspiracy" in Kentucky and Brown's connection with it, see Patricia Watlington, *The Partisan Spirit: Kentucky Politics, 1779-1792* (New York, 1972).

Extract of a Letter from New York, 9 July[1]

The committee appointed by Congress to begin the organization of the new government have brought in a report, fixing the time, etc., for choosing the Electors for the choice of the President, and fixing on your city for Congress to sit in.[2]

1. *Pennsylvania Packet*, 11 July.
2. This false report that Congress had decided upon Philadelphia was reprinted at least a dozen times. See, in addition to the numerous Philadelphia printings, the *New York Morning Post*, 14 July; *Salem Mercury*, 22 July; and Augusta *Georgia State Gazette*, 16 August.

Peleg Arnold to Welcome Arnold, New York, 11 July[1]

We have this day thirteen states on the floor of Congress which has not been until the present case since the year 1776.

Ten states having ratified the new Constitution, Congress are now deliberating on the time for the states to appoint Electors, to choose a President and when proceedings shall commence under said Constitution. In this important business, from the peculiar situation of our state, the delegation have declined to act. From the present appearance this is the last year that Congress will assemble under the old Confederation. The time reported by the committee to assemble under the new government is the first Monday in February next. The question has not yet been determined on; but I believe it will not exceed that time.

The information from this state's Convention has generally been that they would not adopt the new Constitution; but the last reports say that the Federal Party gain strength and it is generally believed here that it will be adopted. I presume the amendments by the Virginia Convention have had considerable influence on the minds of the members of this state Convention which has occasioned this change.

1. RC, Gratz Collection, PHi. Peleg Arnold was a Rhode Island delegate to Congress. Welcome Arnold was a Providence merchant and a Federalist.

Samuel Osgood to Melancton Smith and Samuel Jones, New York, 11 July (excerpt)[1]

I am this moment informed that Judge [Peter] Ogilvie sets off in a few hours for Poughkeepsie.

Since I wrote Mr. Smith nothing material has occurred here excepting that the thirteen states are now represented, and that the committee appointed in Congress for the purpose of organizing the new government have reported. The report fixes the first Wednesday in February next for convening the members of the new government. Yesterday the report was called up, and I understand was postponed without much objection.[2] The reason for postponing was that New York would in all probability determine in a few days in favor or against the new Constitution. When this should be known, the question about place would be more properly before the House.

The anxiety of the citizens, is probably greater than you would imagine. Both parties seem to me equally to share in this solicitude. If New York should come in, I am not sure that the seat of the general legislature will be New York; yet from the best information we can get, it is almost reduced to a certainty. If New York should hold out, the opposition will have all the blame laid at their door for forcing Congress to leave this city. The topic will be a feeling and a popular one. Philadelphia, I have no doubt, is desirous New York may not come in, for the purpose of getting Congress removed. Whatever may be your sentiments of the advantage of Congress staying in New York, whether any real benefit results from it or not, yet the universal opinion is such now, that it is intimately connected with the rejection of the plan.[3]

1. RC, Federal Hall National Memorial, New York City. Osgood, from Massachusetts, was a member of the Board of Treasury. Smith and Jones were members of the New York Convention.

2. Congress assembled on 10 July, but the Journals are blank for that day.

3. The New York Convention had been in session since 17 June. On 12 July several delegates in the Convention noted the question then pending in Congress. John Jay stated that the government would be organized and that New York would have no part in it, that Congress and the Treasury could not be in the state if it did not ratify, that the presence of Congress was worth "100,000 a year," that it was beneficial to a certain branch of commerce, and that it provided all the hard money which came into the city. Chancellor Robert R. Livingston noted that agents were active at New York trying to get Congress to adjourn to Philadelphia and that New York's present position outside of the Union aided them. Alexander Hamilton also referred to this question in a similar vein (see John McKesson, Notes on Debates, McKesson Papers, NHi, and Melancton Smith, Notes on Debates, Smith Papers, N).

According to an extract from a letter from Poughkeepsie dated 11 July in the New York *Daily Advertiser*, 14 July, the opponents of the Constitution still insisted on amendments and treated "as a feint" the report that Congress had postponed action to make possible the establishment of the new government in New York.

Nathan Dane to Caleb Strong, New York, 13 July (excerpt)[1]

We now have thirteen states on the floor of Congress—a circumstance which has not happened before for several years past. The committee appointed to report an act for putting the Constitution of the United States into operation reported last week and Congress have spent one day in considering the report. The states appear to be very unanimous in this business except as to the place where Congress under the Constitution shall meet. Whether it shall meet at New York or Philadelphia will be a matter much contested. There will not be more than one state majority, I think, for either place, but this you will understand will be a question only in case New York shall adopt the Constitution. If she does not there will, I presume, be no question as it will generally be thought to be improper for Congress to assemble in a nonratifying state. If she shall adopt, from present appearances, it is probable that a majority of the states will prefer this city (New York) for the meeting of the new Congress. This question will probably be decided in a few days. The Convention of this state is every day now expected to finish its business, and it is hoped it will adopt. I think we shall fix the meeting of the new government to be about the first Wednesday in February next. The delegates of Massachusetts and of some other states wish it to be at an earlier period as the states they represent can with ease assemble sooner, but it is said to be impossible for Virginia, North Carolina, etc., from their great extent sooner to make their elections and attend. In the enclosed paper you will see the amendments recommended in Virginia.

1. RC, Strong Papers, MNF. Dane was a Massachusetts delegate to Congress. Strong was a member of the Massachusetts Senate and was elected to the United States Senate.

Samuel B. Webb to Catherine Hogeboom, New York, 13 July (excerpt)[1]

The adoption of the new Constitution by Virginia gave me very great pleasure, and we fondly hoped it would be a sufficient inducement for this state to give up all further opposition; but the accounts by last evening's post are very unfavorable, and you can have no idea of the rage of the inhabitants of this city. Should they not adopt it in a few days, a resolution will pass for the new Congress to meet at Philadelphia, which will be a fatal stroke to our commerce, and where it will end God only knows. The southern district[2] are determined on a separation to join the Union, and I do not believe the life of the Governor [George Clinton] and his party would be safe in this place. I hope they will prevent this gloomy prospect, by acting like rational beings, have the public weal and not private emolument at heart. You must excuse my mentioning this subject; it is a serious one and gives us much uneasiness, however let us hope for the best.

1. RC, Webb Papers, CtY. Webb, a native of Connecticut, had been an aide to George Washington during the American Revolution. He married Catherine Hogeboom in 1790.

2. The "southern district" was one of the senatorial districts established by the New York Constitution of 1777. It consisted of the City and County of New York, Suffolk, Westchester, Kings, Queens, and Richmond counties.

Journals of Congress, Monday, 14 July

Congress assembled. Present New Hampshire, Massachusetts, Connecticut, New York, New Jersey, Pennsylvania, Delaware, Maryland, Virginia, North Carolina, South Carolina and Georgia, and from Rhode Island, Mr. Arnold.

Mr. Egbert Benson, a delegate for New York, attended and took his seat.

The committee consisting of Mr. Carrington, Mr. Edwards, Mr. Baldwin, Mr. Otis and Mr. Tucker to which were referred the acts of the several states ratifying the Constitution, which have been transmitted to Congress, having reported an act for putting the said Constitution into operation, and the following clause in the act being under debate, viz., "That the first Wednesday in December next be the day for appointing Electors in the several states which have or shall, before the said day have ratified the said Constitution," a motion was made by Mr. Edwards,[1] seconded by Mr. Dane, to postpone that clause in order to take up the following: "That the fourth Wednesday[2] in December next be the day for appointing Electors in the several states of New Hampshire, Connecticut, New Jersey, Delaware, Maryland and South Carolina, and that the same day be the day for appointing Electors in the state of Rhode Island provided the said state shall before that day have ratified the said Constitution; and that the third Wednesday[3] in said December be the day for appointing Electors in the states of Massachusetts, Pennsylvania and Georgia, and that the same day be the day for appointing Electors in the state of New York provided that state shall before that day have ratified the said Constitution; and that the first Wednesday in said December be the day for appointing Electors in the state of Virginia and that the same be the day for appointing Electors in North Carolina, provided the said state shall before that day have ratified said Constitution."

On the question to postpone for the purpose above mentioned, the yeas and nays being required by Mr. Kearny:

New Hampshire			New Jersey		
Gilman	no	no	Clarke	no	no
Wingate	no		Elmer	no	
Massachusetts			Pennsylvania		
Dane	ay	d	Irvine	no	
Otis	no		Bingham	ay	no
Connecticut			Reid	no	
Huntington	ay		Delaware		
Wadsworth	ay	ay	Kearny	no	no
Edwards	ay		Mitchell	no	
New York					
L'Hommedieu	ay				
Benson	ay	ay			
Yates	no				

Maryland			South Carolina		
Howard	no		Huger	no	
Seney	no	no	Tucker	no	no
Contee	no		Georgia		
Virginia			Few	ay	
Griffin	no		Baldwin	ay	ay
Carrington	no	no			
North Carolina					
Swann	no*				

So it passed in the negative.[4]

1. A draft of this motion is in PCC, Item 23, pp. 337-[38].
2. The draft of the motion originally read "the last Wednesday save two."
3. Originally "the last Wednesday save three."
4. No evidence has been found to indicate why Edwards offered his motion or why it was supported and opposed.

Clement Biddle to Henry Knox, Philadelphia, 14 July (excerpt)[1]

We are fondly hoping that Congress will determine to form the new government at this place, in which case I expect we shall have the pleasure of your and Mrs. Knox's company. I understand you are going on a visit to Boston and you may perhaps think it advisable to engage a house here. In that case or any other in which I can be any ways useful, I beg to be favored with your command.[2]

1. RC, Knox Papers, MHi. Biddle had been an officer during the American Revolution. He was a Philadelphia merchant and George Washington's agent during the 1780s. Washington appointed him United States marshal for Pennsylvania in 1789.
2. Knox replied on 21 July that "when this event shall take place, I shall with great pleasure avail myself of your friendship" (New York, FC, Knox Papers, MHi).

Ebenezer Hazard to Mathew Carey, New York, 15 July (excerpt)[1]

What New York will do is still uncertain: present appearances lead to an apprehension that she will stipulate for certain amendments as the *condition* of her continuing in the Union. If she should, she will throw herself out of it. Congress have treated her with politeness by postponing the consideration of the report of their committee for organizing the new government, but regard for the dignity of the Union will not let them wait very long; and if this state does not soon determine as she ought to do, the blank for the place at which the new Congress are to meet will be filled with Philadelphia.

1. RC, Lea and Febiger Collection, PHi. This excerpt was printed in the Philadelphia *Pennsylvania Mercury*, 19 July. Hazard was Postmaster General of the United States from 1782 to 1789. Carey was the publisher of the Philadelphia *American Museum*.

Caleb S. Riggs to John Fitch, New York, 15 July (excerpt)[1]

Politics to be or not to be is now the question, time is pregnant with something which must soon appear, but in what shape or color is left at present at best but to conjecture. By the last accounts from the Convention, it is yet a doubt whether they will follow the example of Virginia by adopting and recommending amendments, or have the amendments to precede, which I call rejecting it; the Federalists by their writings from Poughkeepsie express great doubts, though some of the opposition have actually come over, and those of popular characters too. The Antifederalists in this city, very few excepted, expect and seem to hope for its adoption and recommend amendments as the least evil of the two. If it should not be adopted, and that without previous amendments, Congress will certainly remove from hence, and Philadelphia probably will be their place of abode; and we shall not only lose them, but I think, have riot, confusion, and bloodshed introduced amongst us. I have only to add that my prayer is heaven give them wisdom and avert the impending danger.

1. RC, Fitch Papers, DLC. Fitch was the designer of the first successful steamboat in America. He had written to Riggs about the possibility of a congressional subsidy for his experiments. Elsewhere in the letter, Riggs reported "no prospects remaining of any thing being done" unless "some change may take place in government to your advantage."

James Madison to Edmund Randolph, New York, 16 July[1]

The enclosed papers will give you the latest intelligence from Poughkeepsie. It seems by no means certain what the result there will be. Some of the most sanguine calculate on a ratification. The best informed apprehend some clog that will amount to a condition. The question is made peculiarly interesting in this place by its connection with the question relative to the place to be recommended for the meeting of the first Congress under the new government.

Thirteen states are at present represented. A plan for setting this new machine in motion has been reported some days, but will not be hurried to a conclusion. Having been but a little time here, I am not yet fully in the politics of Congress. I had on the road several returns of a bilious lax which made my journey more tedious and less agreeable than it would otherwise have been. At present I am pretty well again.

1. RC, Madison Papers, DLC. Randolph was governor of Virginia from November 1786 to November 1788, when he declined to run for a third term.

Samuel A. Otis to George Thacher, New York, 17 July (excerpt)[1]

... I inform you that we have had thirteen states frequently upon the floor and have been very industrious. What have you been about? Look at the [*New York*] *Journal*. One thing seems to be agreed: that [the] new government is to take place about midwinter. Next week perhaps the time will be agreed upon. The *place* will be a bone of contention. Southern people are opposed to New York, and I think the Yorkers hang back in such manner [I] am rather of opinion it will not be here. For my own part I am in present sentiment for New York, but we are all in suspense for the doings of Convention. Probably the question will this day be taken therein. I am of opinion it will not be a favorable decision. [Governor George] Clinton is popular, has a majority at command, and is very violent. They may possibly adjourn which is the best expectation I form. The Yorkers are determined however to have their frolic, and I don't know but we are in danger of running into excess in regard to processions. Perhaps my gravity and aversion to parade may have induced this opinion. It is an implied triumph over minority which always irritates. I think the movements of the new government should be mild, discreet, and attended with great circumspection.

Enclosed is Greenleaf's[2] which details pretty fairly. . . .

1. *Historical Magazine*, XVI, 349 (excerpt). Thacher, from Maine, was a Massachusetts delegate to Congress. He had left Congress on 25 March and did not return until 6 August.
2. Thomas Greenleaf's *New York Journal*.

Paine Wingate to John Pickering, New York, 17 July (excerpt)[1]

We have now a full representation in Congress from all the states. Have not yet made the arrangements for the new Congress. The first Wednesday in December is proposed for choosing Electors of President and the last Wednesday of that month for the choice of President. The beginning of February it is probable Congress will meet, and it is yet mere conjecture that Philadelphia will be the place. A few days will now determine all those points. We have waited this week to know the determination of the New York Convention. Our intelligence last evening was not favorable from Poughkeepsie. We expect hourly to hear the final result.

There is too much, I suspect, of personal animosity among some members of the Convention, which will be a detriment to that condescension which at this time is very necessary. This city will be exceedingly enraged against the Antifederal Party if they should reject the Constitution as it will necessitate the removal of Congress, which they much fear. Nineteen out of twenty are said to be Federal in the city. Next Wednesday is the day appointed for the procession in New York celebrating the new Constitution, which is to be with extraordinary pomp. I believe the late principal transactions of Congress will be in your newspapers and needless here to mention.

1. Wingate, *Wingate*, I, 235-36. Pickering, a leading New Hampshire lawyer and legislator, was a presidential Elector in 1789.

William Bingham to Benjamin Rush, New York, 18 July[1]

I received the letter you inclosed concerning the effects of the federal procession on the various descriptions of persons that participated in the festive enjoyment, and was much pleased with the perusal.

I have no occasion for a stimulus to increase the force of my exertions to fix the seat of federal government at Philadelphia. I have devoted myself solely to that object for a considerable time past, and have the most flattering prospect of succeeding. But it is far from being certain, for the competition is very great, and there are as many cities contending for this advantage, as there were for the honor of Homer's birth. Our city has so great a start on the others, that many are desirous of depriving us of this benefit, from the operation of low-minded jealousy and envy.

You will please to keep this letter secret, as a strong expectation of success would rather tend to defeat our views.

1. RC, Alexander Biddle Papers, PHi.

Robert Morris to Silas Talbot, New York, 19 July (excerpt)[1]

We are very anxious in this city for the fate of the Federal Constitution in the Poughkeepsie Convention. The procession and rejoicing for the Virginia adoption was postponed, as was the question in Congress for appointing the place for the meeting of the first legislature under the Constitution, in the expectation that New York might make the eleventh adopting state. Our last accounts are rather against this, but are such as to keep expectation anxiously alive. We shall have a number of long faces here if it is rejected. In my own instance I frequently ejaculate my gratitude to Heaven that I have yet a retreat in the bosom of my old state, if the circumstances of this renders living here ineligible.

1. RC, Talbot Papers, Mystic Marine Historical Association Collection, Mystic, Conn. Morris, a New Brunswick, N.J., lawyer, was a former chief justice of that state. During the American Revolution Talbot served as a colonel in the Continental Army and a captain in the Continental Navy.

Nathan Dane to Theodore Sedgwick, New York, 20 July (excerpt)[1]

The enclosed is the report of the committee on the subject of putting the Constitution of the United States of America into operation (our reports you know are not made public till [ac] ted upon).[2] The report some days ago was agreed to in part, that is Congress have fixed the first Wednesday in December for the appointment of the Electors of the President, and the last Wednesday [i]n the same month for them to assemble and vote for him. The majority of the states appear to be for fixing the first Wednesday in February for the government to assemble.[3] The Eastern and Middle states could be much more expeditious in this business, but it is stated by the Southern delegates, that it is impossible for their states to be prepared to elect, etc., sooner than the times mentioned. The principal point in dispute is where shall Congress assemble under the Constitution; should this state adopt, I think from present appearances a majority of the states will be for this city. Those who contended for Philadelphia about ten days ago urged vehemently for the decision of the question, but finding Congress not in a disposition to decide until after this state's Convention shall have acted upon the subject, nothing has been said about it since as every member, I imagine, has made up his mind on the residue of the report; it is probable, we shall finish it in one day's time after we hear the result of the proceedings of the New York Convention. You see by the report we make a simple piece of business of it, nor has it caused much debate or delay. Having thirteen states on the floor we took up this business sooner than was expected.

We now expect every day to hear this state has decided as to the adoption, but there seems to be no certainty what their decision will be, tho I think the probability is in favor of their acceding to the new confederacy.

I propose to stay in New York till the enclosed report shall be acted upon and that I rather expect will be this week. I shall then make a short tour to Massachusetts. There is considerable of business to be done by the present Congress to clear the files, etc., but none of it very important.

1. RC, Sedgwick Papers, MHi. Sedgwick was a Massachusetts delegate to Congress. He arrived on 31 July.
2. See the report of 9 July printed above.
3. Pierse Long wrote to Nicholas Gilman from Portsmouth, N.H., on 22 July that he regretted the decision for Congress to meet in February: "I could have wished them to convene in December. A procrastination can work no good" (RC, Fogg Autograph Collection, MeHi).

James Madison to George Washington, New York, 21 July[1]

I have deferred writing since my arrival here in the hourly hope of being enabled to communicate the final news from Poughkeepsie. By a letter from [Alexander] Hamilton dated the day before yesterday,[2] I find that it is equally uncertain when the business will be closed, and what will be its definitive form. The enclosed gazettes state the form which the depending proposition bears. It is not a little strange that the Antifederal Party should be reduced to such an expedient, and yet be able to keep their members together in the opposition. Nor is it less strange that the other party, as appears to be the case, should hesitate in deciding that the expedient as effectually keeps the state for the present out of the new Union as the most unqualified rejection could do. The intelligent citizens here see clearly that this would be its operation and are agitated by the double motives of Federalism and a zeal to give this city a fair chance for the first meeting of the new government.

Congress have deliberated in part on the arrangements for putting the new machine into operation, but have concluded on nothing but the times for choosing Electors, etc. Those who wish to make New York the place of meeting studiously promote delay. Others who are not swayed by this consideration do not urge dispatch. They think it would be well to let as many states as possible have an opportunity of deciding on the Constitution; and what is of more consequence, they wish to give opportunities where they can take place for as many elections of state legislatures as can precede a reasonable time for making the appointments and arrangements referred to them. If there be too great an interval between the acts of Congress on this subject and the next election or next meeting of a state legislature, it may afford a pretext for an intermediate summoning of the existing members who are everywhere less Federal than their successors hereafter to be elected will probably be. This is particularly the case in Maryland, where the Antifederal temper of the executive [William Smallwood] would render an intermediate and extraordinary meeting of the Assembly of that state the more likely to be called. On my way thro Maryland I found such an event to be much feared by the friends, and wished by the adversaries, of the Constitution. We have no late news from Europe, nor anything from North Carolina.

1. RC, Washington Papers, DLC. The next day Madison wrote a similar letter to Edmund Randolph (RC, Madison Papers, DLC).
2. 19 July. Printed: Syrett, V, 177-78. Hamilton asked Madison if New York could ratify with the condition that it would withdraw from the Union within a number of years if amendments were not considered. Madison replied the next day that New York must ratify unconditionally or it could not become a member of the Union (New York, 20 July, Syrett, V, 184-85).

William Bingham to Tench Coxe, New York, 21 July[1]

I should [not] have suffered your favor of the 9th inst. to have remained so long unreplied to, if I had not been in daily expectation of communicating some pleasing intelligence concerning the subject of that letter.

But from various circumstances the question has been delayed, and I cannot say with certainty when it will be determined.

A competition from different quarters has arisen, which divides the suffrages into as many parties; but however they may vibrate from one side to the other, they must at last come to rest in the center, which is Pennsylvania. Our rising importance in the political scale has caused great jealousy, and is one reason of our not uniting all the votes of Congress in our favor; for in every sense, we have the fittest place to assemble the new Congress in, and it is generally acknowledged. I wish little may be said on this subject, for in proportion as we make exertions to establish our pretensions, there are envious characters that will endeavor to oppose them.

The Convention of New York is still in session. There are faint hopes entertained of an unconditional ratification, or an adjournment which will be tantamount.

1. RC, Coxe Papers, Tench Coxe Section, PHi. Tench Coxe of Pennsylvania had been an active Federalist publicist during the ratification of the Constitution and played a significant role in Pennsylvania politics and in the efforts to remove the seat of government from New York to Philadelphia.

Pennsylvania Gazette, 23 July

Serious apprehensions, says a correspondent, have begun to take place in the minds of many of the friends of the federal government, at the great delay in putting the new government in motion, and fixing the time, etc. of commencing proceedings under its authorities. This circumstance is more alarming, as it appears that on the 2d July Congress appointed a committee to report an act for that purpose, and notwithstanding the recommendation of the Convention, that as soon as nine states had assented, an efficient league should be formed betwixt them, yet we find some obstacle prevents the operation of the intended arrangements, and the Federalists throughout the Union are kept in a state of anxious suspense. But a point of most essential consequence to attend to, is, that there are many hundred families, we are told, in different parts of Europe, who are now waiting with much impatience to hear of measures being taken to assemble the states under the operation of this government, in order to embark for this country, and their correspondents are desirous of imparting the important intelligence.[1]

1. This article was widely reprinted during the summer of 1788 (see, for example, the New York *Daily Advertiser*, 26 July; Hartford *Connecticut Courant*, 28 July; Boston *Massachusetts Gazette*, 1 August; and Charleston *Columbian Herald*, 7 August).

Paine Wingate to President John Langdon, New York, 26 July (excerpt)[1]

Congress have omitted making the necessary arrangements for putting the new government into effect, out of delicacy to the situation of New York, whose decision upon the proposed Constitution has been expected daily for some time. I have now the pleasure of congratulating Your Excellency upon their adoption, which we have just received the news of. The particulars are not yet come to hand, only that there was a majority of five in favor of an unconditional ratification.[2] The new Congress cannot meet so early as most expected, and many wished for, owing to the situation of some of the Southern States. I hope however that there will be no necessity of Congress meeting under the present Confederation after November next. We have now all the states represented in Congress and considerable business which requires the attention of that body, but expect that, as soon as the principal matters are dispatched, the delegates will many of them return home.

1. RC, State Papers Relating to the Revolution, II (1785-1789), Nh-Ar. Printed: LMCC, VIII, 766-67.
2. According to the *New York Packet* of 29 July, the news of New York's ratification reached the city about nine o'clock Saturday evening, 26 July. The news was of the vote on Friday, when the Convention voted 30 to 25 to ratify. The next day the Convention adopted the formal act of ratification by only a three-vote margin, 30 to 27.

Ratification had been achieved only because the Federalists had proposed that the Convention send a circular letter to the other states calling a second constitutional convention to propose amendments to the Constitution. The Circular Letter was adopted unanimously immediately after the final vote on ratification. It is printed immediately below.

Circular Letter of the New York Convention, 26 July[1]

In Convention at Poughkeepsie State of New York July 26th: 1788
(Circular)

We, the Members of the Convention of this State, have deliberately and maturely considered the Constitution proposed for the United States. Several Articles in it appear so exceptionable to a majority of us that nothing but the fullest Confidence of obtaining a revision of them by a General Convention, and an invincible Reluctance to separating from our Sister States, could have prevailed upon a sufficient Number to ratify it, without stipulating for previous Amendments. We all unite in opinion; that such a Revision will be necessary to recommend it to the Approbation and Support of a numerous Body of our Constituents. We observe, that Amendments have been proposed, and are anxiously desired by several of the States, as well as by this; and we think it of great Importance that effectual Measures be immediately taken for calling a Convention to meet at a Period not far remote; for we are convinced, that the Apprehensions and Discontents which those Articles occasion, cannot be removed or allayed, unless an Act to provide for it, be among the first that shall be passed by the new Congress. As it is essential, that an Application for the purpose should be made to them, by two thirds of the States, We earnestly exhort and request, the Legislature of your State (or Commonwealth) to take the earliest Opportunity of making it. We are persuaded that a similar one will be made by our Legislature at their next Session; and we ardently wish and desire, that the other States may concur in adopting and promoting the measure. It cannot be necessary to observe, that no Government, however constructed, can operate well, unless it possesses the Confidence and Good-Will of the great Body of the People; and as we desire nothing more, than that the Amendments proposed by this or other States be submitted to the Consideration and Decision of a General Convention, We flatter ourselves, that motives of mutual Affection and Conciliation, will conspire with the obvious Dictates of sound Policy, to induce even such of the States as may be content with every Article in the Constitution, to gratify the reasonable Desires of that numerous Class of American Citizens who are anxious to obtain Amendments of some of them.

Our Amendments will manifest, that none of them originated in local Views, as they are such, as if acceded to, must equally affect every State in the Union. Our attachment to our Sister States, and the Confidence we repose in them, cannot be more forcibly demonstrated, than by acceding to a Government, which many of us think very imperfect, and devolving the power of determining, whether that Government shall be rendered perpetual in it's present Form, or altered agreeable to our Wishes, on a Minority of the States, with whom we unite.

We request the favor of your Excellency to lay this Letter before the Legislature of your State (or Commonwealth), and we are persuaded, that your Regard for our national Harmony and good Government will induce you to promote a Measure, which we are unanimous in thinking, very conducive to those interesting Objects.

By the unanimous Order of the Convention

1. DS (LT) Journal of the Proceedings of the Convention of the State of New York . . . , N. There are two manuscript versions of the Circular Letter in the Convention journals. The second version, which was signed by forty-seven of the delegates, is printed here.

The New York Circular Letter was reprinted in more than forty newspapers from Vermont to Georgia by 1 September. The letter alarmed Federalist leaders (see James Madison to George Washington, 11 August; Washington to Madison, 17 August; Edmund Randolph to Madison, 13 August, all printed below).

For the public reaction see Newspaper Response to New York's Act of Ratification and Circular Letter of 26 July, printed immediately below. For the relationship of the Circular Letter to election politics in such states as Massachusetts and Virginia, see the chapters on those states.

Newspaper Response to New York's Act of Ratification and Circular Letter of 26 July

Pennsylvania Gazette, 6 August[1]

The *alterations* (not amendments) of the Federal Constitution proposed by the Convention of New York, says a correspondent, are so numerous, that if it were possible to admit them, they would annihilate the Constitution, and throw the United States not only back again into anarchy, but introduce poverty, misery, bloodshed and slavery into every state in the Union. The authors of these alterations would do well to put on match coats and associate with the lawless Indians who inhabit the borders of the western lakes. They have not sense enough to frame, or understand a system of government fit for a civilized nation.

Pennsylvania Gazette, 13 August[2]

The *impertinent* letter sent by the late Convention of New York to all the states, urging what they *impudently* call amendments in the new Constitution, merits the severest treatment from all the friends of good government. It holds out the total annihilation of every useful and wise part of the Constitution. The only design of these supposed amendments is to continue a few New York speculators and land-jobbers in office, who have imposed upon an ignorant but well-meaning majority in the Convention. Nothing proves this more than the enmity these official certificate and land-brokers showed to the government *before* it was published. Let the government have a fair trial. If it should be found faulty, the *faults* will soon show themselves, and they may be amended. Fortunately for the United States, *six* states have adopted the Constitution without a wish for a single alteration. If they continue firm, no alteration can be made until an experiment has been tried with the government. This experiment will certainly be favorable to it, for the demands for alterations in a great majority of the disaffected have arisen from *ignorance* only, which the operations of the government will remove in a few years.

X to the Governors of the States, Connecticut Gazette, 15 August[3]

I observe that the late Convention of the State of New York, have requested a new continental convention to be called, in order to take into consideration the proposed amendments, and make a revision of the new Constitution. I have been told by the rules of war, upon the approach of an enemy, it is justifiable in the meanest subject to give the alarm. I can have no conception that those gentlemen who composed that Convention, expected to have any notice taken of their Circular Letter by Your Excellencies, further than a polite answer in the negative; otherwise, though an obscure individual in private life, I should, for myself, view that requisition with that contempt which I think it deserves. I would ever wish to consider New York in that important scale in which they ought to stand; that is, as a very considerable and valuable member: but they must not have the impudence or expectation to dictate to the Union. I observe they conclude that they are the only expositors of the articles in the new Constitution, and that no different construction must hereafter ever be put any of them, by the united wisdom of the continent. May it please Your Excellencies, be ye not deceived, if they mean or expect anything, they certainly mean and expect, from the contrariety of interests, manners, and customs in the different states (which we all know create prejudices that are difficult to be removed) to procure a delay, increase dissensions, and in the end effect a total destruction of the grand system, and thence reap profit to themselves. And should a new convention be called, depend upon it that their delegates will go armed with every art and finesse, to increase the natural difficulties, and if possible render them incurable; and at any rate they will gain something by procrastination: one year's delay will give them a further opportunity to fill their pockets out of their neighbors by their impost; in which time many incidents may arise, that will assist them in obstructing or overthrowing our glorious fabric. The present Constitution has made ample provision for alterations and emendations; and whenever conviction or experience shall point out the necessity, I am fully convinced they will be made, in the mode expressly reserved and provided by the Constitution, without the inconceivable damage of a total stagnation to all the power of government, for at least twelve months, and an expense of at least two hundred thousand pounds, in calling town meetings, general assemblies, etc. all which, if it does no hurt, will certainly, not be productive of one good consequence, unless we send to Europe, or some other quarter of the globe for our men, to make the emendations; as I am fully persuaded we cannot procure better upon this continent, than composed the last Continental Convention; and we may be assured, that no other body of men, we can assemble for the purpose, will be more disposed to make concessions than the last. But when we become firmly united, by an indissoluble union, we shall begin to consider ourselves more and more as one nation and family; our prejudices will gradually remove, wear out and disappear; and the necessary alterations and emendations take place, without all this circumlocution which is meant to overthrow it. I give this hint to the public, in hopes and full expectation, that persons of more leisure, information and abilities, will take up the subject, and do it justice, as I have not yet seen the famous or rather Circular Letter.

Philadelphia Independent Gazetteer, 16 August (excerpt)

The paragraphs, which have appeared in the last two numbers of the *Pennsylvania Gazette*, exhibit in the clearest point of view the dilemma into which our RED-HOT FEDERALISTS are now driven.

If *trial by jury*, the *liberty of the press*, no *capitation tax*, etc. are to be established as fundamental privileges of freemen; then according to the doctrine of RED-HOT FEDERALISM, "these *alterations*, not *amendments*, would annihilate the Constitution, and throw the United States not only back into anarchy, but introduce *poverty, misery, bloodshed,* and *slavery* into every state in the Union."

In one paper all the members of the honorable Convention of New York are told that they should associate with Indians in match-coats preparing them for being burned to death, etc. In another (severity subsiding a little) they are branded with the *gentle* epithets of *impudent, impertinent*, etc. In this we are also informed, that the Convention of North Carolina had rejected the Constitution by a majority of 100, against 76; instead of saying 176 against 76; and thus, by a pitiful quibble, 76 members are hid from the eye of the reader.

But, Mr. Oswald, without making any farther comments, please to let the paragraphs alluded to, have a place in your paper for the use of your readers, and oblige a subscriber.[4]

Republican, Virginia Independent Chronicle, 27 August[5]

Since the publication of my last number, a proposition has been received from the Convention of New York, for a new convention of the states. Thus a new scene is presented; and a mode suggested, which will, I trust, be effectual in satisfying scrupulous minds. As therefore my only object in writing was to answer this purpose, I expect the accomplishment of it rather from the expedient proposed, than any reasoning, which I can use. With a hope, that a second convention will produce harmony, and a general support of the Constitution, I shall not trouble you further.

Solon, Boston Independent Chronicle, 28 August (excerpt)[6]

The Circular Letter from the Convention of New York has had the epithets of *impertinent* and *impudent* bestowed upon it, and probably more will be advanced, as the time draws near. If amendments are necessary, they *claim* an *early consideration*, and measures for the purpose merit your *first* attention. Will it be improper to hint, that in the choice of *Senators* and *Representatives*, this object among others naturally presents itself to your consideration, and that such *instructions* as may be necessary, be *seasonably prepared*; you have hitherto been the peculiar care of a kind Providence, may you, and your posterity after you, be a name and a praise among the nations of the earth, is the ardent wish of SOLON.

1. The New York Act of Ratification with the proposed amendments to the Constitution was published in two Philadelphia newspapers, the *Pennsylvania Packet* and the *Independent Gazetteer*, on 4 August. The above attack upon the document was reprinted in at least thirteen newspapers in Pennsylvania, New Jersey, Maryland, Virginia, Georgia, Massachusetts, Connecticut, and Rhode Island.

2. The New York Circular Letter was published in Philadelphia in the *Independent Gazetteer* on 9 August, and in the *Freeman's Journal* and the *Pennsylvania Packet* on 11 August. The *Pennsylvania Gazette* did not publish the letter, but the above attack upon it was published in at least twelve newspapers from New Hampshire to South Carolina.

3. The full heading of this article is "X to their Excellencies the Governors of the Several United States of America." The article was reprinted in the Hartford *American Mercury*, 18 August; Boston *Massachusetts Centinel*, 23 August; and *Newport Herald*, 28 August.

4. Following the above are the two items from the *Pennsylvania Gazette*, 6 and 13 August (printed above) and an item from the *Gazette*, 13 August, based on a 6 August "letter from Richmond," which concludes that in Rhode Island and North Carolina, "an attachment to paper money and tender laws, appears in both those corrupted and deluded states, to be the cause of their opposition to the new Constitution."

5. The first letter of "Republican" addressed "To the People of Virginia" was published in the Richmond *Virginia Independent Chronicle*, 16 July. The writer argues that the Constitution was necessary, proposes to remove the doubts of those who oppose it, and promises in his second letter, among other things, to discuss "whether it was not better, under the existing circumstances of America, and especially of Virginia, to rely for amendments on some future, more favorable opportunity." The newspaper containing the second letter has not been located. The *Independent Chronicle* published the New York Circular Letter on 13 and 20 August.

6. "Solon" is printed in full in Chapter V.

Hugh Williamson to James Iredell, New York, 26 July[1]

You may be assured that the delegates from North Carolina have not been inattentive to the respect they owe the state whatever may be their private sentiments respecting the new Constitution.[2] When a committee had reported, and the question was taken up for putting the new government into motion and a time was proposed for choosing Electors and Representatives and for the members entering on business, we stated fully the situation of our state and it was immediately agreed that the time should be put off as far as we should allege was absolutely necessary. But no final question is yet taken and we believe that we shall be able to obtain such delay that North Carolina may in the interim take her measures. Everything on this head is at present stationary.

Some days ago there was a large procession here on 10 states having confederated; and Congress were invited to dine with the company, some thousands of them under a particular pavilion in the fields. The other states attended but the North Carolina delegates stayed at home. We conceived it was a respect we owed the state not to celebrate an event in our public characters which the state we represent has not hitherto sanctioned by her approbation.

Hitherto the State of New York in Convention has not taken its measures; it is thought they will be curious, and a species of Delphic Oracle, neither an adoption nor rejection, or both, as parties may be disposed to construe it.

1. RC, Emmet Collection, no. 9509, NN. Williamson was a North Carolina delegate to Congress. Iredell, a North Carolina lawyer, jurist, and political leader, was a Federalist floor leader of the first North Carolina Convention. Washington appointed him associate justice of the United States Supreme Court in 1790.

2. The North Carolina Convention sat from 21 July to 4 August, when it adjourned *sine die* after a "large majority" voted on 2 August "neither to ratify nor reject" the Constitution.

North Carolina Delegates to Governor Samuel Johnston, New York, 27 July[1]

By express last night from Poughkeepsie, we learn that on Friday 25th a motion was made for adopting the new Constitution as recommended by the General Convention on September last. This motion was carried by a majority of five. A previous question had been taken for adopting the Constitution for a limited time, etc. This was lost by a majority of four. The papers we shall forward may contain more particulars.

The inhabitants of this city since the arrival of the above intelligence have hardly been moderate in their expressions of joy. The state of New York had so many arguments of private interest that seemed to tempt her to adhere to the old form of government that we confess the act mentioned was rather unexpected at so early a period. This event is of such importance that we conceive ourselves bound to give you notice of the same by the first conveyance. Captain Chr[istopher?] Clarke who was to sail early on this morning is charged with this intelligence which probably will be forwarded from Edenton by express, but as water passages are more uncertain, we shall forward this by post and request of some gentleman in Petersburg to give it furtherance.

Congress are extremely desirous to fix the time and place where and when proceedings shall commence under the new government. Hitherto they have been restrained, partly as we conceive, from a regard to the feelings of our state; we flatter ourselves however that no time will be lost in letting us know the result after our Convention shall have taken its resolution.

1. RC, North Carolina Papers, DLC. The letter was signed by John Swann and Hugh Williamson.

Journals of Congress, Monday, 28 July

Congress assembled. Present New Hampshire, Massachusetts, Connecticut, New York, New Jersey, Pennsylvania, Delaware, Maryland, Virginia, North Carolina, South Carolina and Georgia.

The committee consisting of Mr. Carrington, Mr. Edwards, Mr. Baldwin, Mr. Otis and Mr. Tucker to whom were referred the acts of the several states which have been transmitted to Congress ratifying the Constitution for the United States of America having reported an act for putting the said Constitution into operation,[1] and the following paragraph having been debated and amended to read as follows:

"That the first Wednesday in January next be the day for appointing Electors in the several states which have or shall before the said day have ratified the said Constitution; that the first Wednesday in February next be the day for the Electors to assemble in their respective states and vote for a President; and that the first Wednesday in March next be the time, and _____ the place for commencing proceedings under the said Constitution."

A motion was made by Mr. Edwards, seconded by Mr. Williamson, to fill the blank with "Philadelphia" and on the question to agree to this, the yeas and nays being required by Mr. Seney:

New Hampshire
    Gilman   ay ⎱ ay
    Wingate   ay ⎰
Massachusetts
    Dane   no ⎱ no
    Otis   no ⎰
Connecticut
    Huntington   ay ⎫
    Wadsworth   no ⎬ ay
    Edwards   ay ⎭
New York
    L'Hommedieu   no ⎫
    Benson   no ⎬ no
    Yates   no ⎭
New Jersey
    Clarke   no ⎫
    Elmer   ay ⎬ no
    Dayton   no ⎭

Pennsylvania
    Irvine   ay ⎫
    Bingham   ay ⎬ ay
    Armstrong   ay ⎪
    Reid   ay ⎭
Delaware
    Kearny   no ⎱ d
    Mitchell   ay ⎰
Maryland
    Seney   ay ⎫
    Contee   ay ⎬ ay
    Ross   ay ⎭
Virginia
    Griffin   ay ⎫
    Madison   ay ⎬ ay
    Carrington   ay ⎭

North Carolina			Georgia		
Williamson	ay	⎱ ay	Few	no	⎱ d
Swann	ay	⎰	Baldwin	ay	⎰
South Carolina					
Huger	no	⎱ no			
Tucker	no	⎰			

So the question was lost.[2]

1. The committee report of 9 July proposed that the states elect Electors on the first Wednesday in December, that the Electors meet the first Wednesday in January, and that the new government begin operations the first Wednesday in February. On 14 July Congress rejected an amendment changing the dates and no further action is recorded in the Journals until the 28th. However, as a result of the insistence of the Southern States, an agreement to put off the time of elections and the meeting of the new government seems to have been reached during that period. The agreement is embodied in the Journals of the 28th. For explanations by members of Congress see Nathan Dane to Theodore Sedgwick, 20 July; James Madison to George Washington, 21 July; Hugh Williamson to James Iredell, 26 July; and North Carolina Delegates to Governor Samuel Johnston, 27 July, all printed above. There seems to have been little objection, either in or out of Congress, to putting off the meeting of the new government to March 1789 (see Samuel Huntington to Benjamin Huntington, Norwich, Conn., 6 August, contemporary copy, Conarroe Autograph Collection, PHi; Paine Wingate to Samuel Lane, 29 July, and Theodore Sedgwick to Benjamin Lincoln, 1 August, printed below).

2. Two quite different stories about the vote emanated from New York the next day. The *New York Packet* reported on the 29th that "we have the pleasure to inform the public, that yesterday Congress proceeded to fill up the blank for the place of holding the sessions of that honorable body, when the words 'New York' were inserted." This false report was reprinted throughout the country (see, for example, the Philadelphia *Pennsylvania Mercury*, 31 July; *Albany Journal*, 4 August; *Boston Gazette*, 4 August; and Charleston *Columbian Herald*, 14 August).

However, an "extract of a letter from New York," also dated the 29th and printed in the Boston *Massachusetts Centinel*, 6 August, and in other New England newspapers, was more accurate and informative. After giving the roll-call vote on 28 July, the article continued:

"So you perceive only half a vote was wanting to effect the motion. All parties are industrious, and it is yet uncertain what the eventual decision will be. South Carolina and Georgia were some equivalent for the loss of two New England States, although one of them was divided. Since the question was taken, Colonel Harry Lee, and Colonel [Alexander] Hamilton, have arrived, who are both against the motion, as I have heard.

"The papers misstate facts in mentioning, that 'New York' is the place agreed upon for the new government to meet at; the blank is not filled up, the question only being determined in the negative, as to Philadelphia."

Some idea of the reaction in Philadelphia to New York's ratification was contained in an "extract" of a letter from Philadelphia dated 2 August in the *New York Packet*, 12 August, which said that "not a man have I heard speak of it, who does not grieve at heart that they adopted it so soon. They were in hopes that they would have delayed the matter till Congress had passed the vote to remove to Philadelphia, which I hope they may not."

Pennsylvanians attributed the defeat of Philadelphia to the divided vote of Delaware, although Georgia too divided. Edward Burd informed Jasper Yeates that "Congress have not yet determined on the place of meeting of the new Congress. Philadelphia lost it by the division of the Delaware state: Dyer Kearney, a silly young man, having weakly supposed that if Philadelphia lost it, Wilmington would be the place" (Philadelphia, 6 August, Walker, *Burd*, 143).

William Shippen, Jr., wrote that Philadelphia "would have been the place if little Dyer Kearney of Delaware had not said no. He expected to make Wilmington the place by preventing Philadelphia—a young politician!" (to Thomas Lee Shippen, Philadelphia, 5 August, RC, Shippen Family Papers, DLC).

For similar comments see Tench Coxe to James Tilghman, Philadelphia, 6 August (RC, William Tilghman Papers, PHi), and L[ambert] C[adwalader] to [Samuel] Meredith, Trenton, 6 August (RC, Read Family Papers, DLC).

Journal of Comte de Moustier, 28 July[1]

The question of knowing where the next Congress will reside has been debated.

The Southern delegates, who realized that the Northern party was much stronger since Congress resides in New York, have been for Philadelphia, a city which is, by its location and the nature of its commercial connections, entirely dedicated to the interests of Virginia. As for Mr. [William] Bingham and other delegates from Pennsylvania who vigorously insist on this measure, they had houses to rent, in expectation of making room for the new government and of speculating in public funds.

The motion having been debated for a long time, the votes on the two sides were found to be equal. Mr. [Dyre] Kearney, a young delegate from Delaware, alone prevented the Southerners from carrying the vote because he wants the new Congress to meet in Wilmington in the state of Delaware.

Other delegates had less patriotic motives. One voted for New York because his wife's family is settled there, another because he courts several young ladies, a third because the air of that city agrees with his health, etc. It is believed that Mr. [James] Madisson has been so strongly in favor of Philadelphia only because he is to marry a woman who holds an annuity there.[2]

1. Extraits du Journal de M. De Moustier, in Extraits des papiers de la Légation de France aux États-Unis, I, Part II (Cahier 3), 23-[24], Benjamin Franklin Collection, CtY. These three volumes contain extracts from reports, journals, letters, and political memoranda prepared by members of the French legation, most of the originals of which were sent to France. Samuel Flagg Bemis describes them as "the original minutes of the French legation in the United States, 1777-1796..." (*Guide to the Diplomatic History of the United States, 1775-1921* [Washington, 1935], 17). Hereafter, items from these volumes will be cited as French Legation Minutes.

The French government appointed the Comte de Moustier Minister Plenipotentiary to the United States in October 1787. He proved unpopular. Madison wrote to Jefferson on 8 December 1788 that *"Mou[s]tier proves a most unlucky appointment. He is unsocial, proud* and *niggardly and betrays a sort of fastidiousness toward this country. He suffers also from his illicit connection with Madame de Brehan which is universally known* and *offensive to American manners. She is perfectly soured toward this country. The ladies of New York (a few within the official circle excepted)* have for some *time withdrawn their attentions from her. She knows the cause,* is *deeply stung by it, views every thing thro the medium of rancor* and *conveys her impressions to her paramour over whom she exercises despotic sway.* Latterly *their time has* [been] chiefly *spent* in [travelling]. *The first vis*[it] *was to an Indian treaty at Fort Schuyler* and *thence to the Oneida town. The next to Boston* and *thence to N. Hampshire. The last to Mount Vernon from which* they but *lately returned. On their journeys* it is *said they often neglect the* most obvious *precautions for veiling their intimacy "* (Boyd, XIV, 340-41). The italicized portions of the letter were originally in code. As a result of Jefferson's efforts, Moustier was later recalled.

2. In January 1789 Tench Coxe's sister wrote him that "I am told, and hope it is true, that your friend Mr. Madison is going on to New York again. Poor Mrs. T. I pity her for having known, and after having known, for losing such a lover" (from Mary Coxe, Philadelphia, RC, Coxe Papers, Tench Coxe Section, PHi).

Paine Wingate to Samuel Lane, New York, 29 July (excerpt)[1]

For the sake of giving you the earliest intelligence I can, I shall now give you a short letter in great hurry. I congratulate you on the favorable and unexpected determination of New York respecting the new Constitution, an account of which I will enclose. This was a most desirable event especially to the Eastern States. North Carolina [Conve]ntion is now in session and we expect to [hear?] of their adoption within a fortnight. Rhode Island yet remain Antifederal. All the states are now represented in Congress, but I expect the members will many of them return home as soon as some necessary business shall be dispatched. I wish to tarry no longer than necessity shall require, out of principle of economy to the state, as well as a fondness for home. I therefore propose to return as soon as the other members are scattering, which probably may be in about a month.

. . . .

I expected this day to have been able to inform you of the place in which the new Congress will meet, but the President [Cyrus Griffin] was so unwell that he could not attend and the business was postponed. Congress have agreed that the Electors of President shall be appointed on the first Wednesday of January, the President be chosen the first Wednesday of February and Congress assemble the first Wednesday of March next. Those periods may be thought by some to be very late, but earlier dates could not suit the situation of some of the Southern States. I believe, notwithstanding the meeting of the new Congress is so late, there will not be necessity of another Congress under the present Confederation after November next. There are great struggles between Philadelphia and New York which shall be the place of Congress. I think the former most likely to prevail, but this is only mere conjecture.

1. RC, Wingate Papers, MH. Printed: Wingate, *Wingate*, I, 239-40.

James Madison to Tench Coxe, New York, 30 July (excerpt)[1]

I have been much obliged by your favor of the 23 instant,[2] which I have delayed to answer in the daily prospect of being able to include the decision of Congress on the place for the first meeting of the new government. This point continues however unfixed. Perhaps it may be brought to an issue today.[3] From the result of the first question taken on it, the pretensions of Philadelphia bade fair for success; and it is very possible may in the end obtain it. Some circumstances which have intervened with the vicissitudes to which such a question in such an assembly as Congress are liable are notwithstanding very proper grounds for doubtful if not adverse calculations.

1. RC, Madison Papers, DLC.

2. Coxe had written "I am extremely anxious (not so much as a Philadelphian) about the first place of meeting of the new government. Tis a subject on which I would not wish to draw you out, as you are situated. Satisfied as I am that the execution of the government, the means of information and our national consequence in Europe would be benefited by coming here, I wish it upon the clearest conviction that it would be for the good of our country" (RC, Madison Papers, DLC).

3. The next day Paine Wingate reported that "the question is not determined and it is so uncertain that I will not give you a conjecture" (to John Pickering, Wingate, *Wingate*, I, 241).

Journals of Congress, Wednesday, 30 July

Congress assembled. Present as yesterday.

The order of the day being called for and the paragraph which was under debate on Monday being read, a motion was made by Mr. Dayton, seconded by Mr. Huger, to fill the blank with the word "the city of New York in the state of New York," thereupon a motion was made by Mr. Lee, seconded by Mr. Clarke, in lieu of this to amend the paragraph so that the last clause be "and at such place as shall hereafter be appointed by Congress," and on the question to agree to this amendment of the paragraph, the yeas and nays being required by Mr. Bingham:

New Hampshire			Delaware		
Gilman	no	d	Kearny	no	no
Wingate	ay		Mitchell	no	
Massachusetts			Maryland		
Dane	ay	ay	Seney	no	
Otis	ay		Contee	no	no
Connecticut			Ross	no	
Huntington	no		Virginia		
Wadsworth	ay	no	Griffin	no	
Edwards	no		Madison	no	
New York			Carrington	no	no
L'Hommedieu	ay		Lee	ay	
Benson	ay	ay	North Carolina		
Hamilton	ay		Williamson	no	no
Yates	ay		Swann	no	
New Jersey			South Carolina		
Clarke	ay		Huger	ay	
Elmer	no	ay	Parker	ay	ay
Dayton	ay		Tucker	no	
Pennsylvania			Georgia		
Irvine	no		Few	no	no
Meredith	no		Baldwin	no	
Armstrong	no	no			
Bingham	no				
Reid	no				

So it passed in the negative.

Journal of Comte de Moustier, 30 July[1]

Colonel He[n]ry Lee, a delegate from Virginia, puts forward exactly the opposite of what his colleagues Messrs. [James] Madisson and [Edward] Carrington had declared relative to the dispositions of the inhabitants of Virginia for Congress to adjourn to Philadelphia, and he asserts that it is in Virginia's interest to attract this assembly to the shores of the Potomac, and that it would be much easier to fix it there in the event that it remained in New York, than if it found itself wrapped in the nets of the Philadelphians, that it was necessary to look for the true motive for this motion (for Philadelphia) in the heart of Mr. [Robert] Morris who was burning with impatience again to attend to all financial operations and to cause the revival of the pernicious stockjobbing which had ruined the states during the war and takes its source from this virtuous city in which patriotism is displayed so pompously. Mr. Lee, accustomed to speaking his mind frankly, has spared no one.

Mr. [Alexander] Hamilton alleged that the delegates from New York were going to lose their popularity if the new Congress did not remain in that state because they had solemnly promised it at the [New York] Convention if the new Constitution were ratified there. Mr. D[——],[2] one of its delegates, has declared that his reputation was lost if Congress changed its residence. It is astonishing that the personal interest of each delegate is so active in attracting Congress to his own state.

1. French Legation Minutes, I, Part II (Cahier 3), [24]-25, CtY.
2. Probably James Duane, mayor of New York City and former congressman. Duane attended the New York Convention and supported the Constitution.

George Washington to James McHenry, Mount Vernon, 31 July[1]

In reply to your recent favor, which has been duly received, I can only observe; that, as I never go from home except when I am obliged by necessary avocations, and as I meddle as little as possible with politics that my interference may not give occasion for impertinent imputations, so I am less likely than almost any person to have been informed of the circumstance to which you allude.[2] That some of the leading characters among the opponents [of] the proposed government have not laid aside their ideas of obtaining great and essential changes, through a constitutional opposition (as they term it) may be collected from their public speeches. That others will use more secret and, perhaps, insidious means to prevent its organization may be presumed from their previous conduct on the subject. In addition to this probability, the casual information received from visitants at my house, would lead me to expect that a considerable effort will be made to procure the election of Antifederalists to the first Congress; in order to bring the subject immediately before the state legislatures, to open an extensive correspondence between the minorities for obtaining alterations, and in short to undo all that has been done. It is reported that a respectable neighbor of mine has said, the Constitution cannot be carried in execution, without great amendments.[3] But I will freely do the opposition with us the justice to declare, that I have heard of no cabals or canvassings respecting the elections. It is said to be otherwise on your side of the river. By letters from the Eastern States[4] I am induced to believe the minorities have acquiesced not only with a good grace, but also with a serious

55

design to give the government a fair chance to discover its operation by being carried into effect. I hope and trust that the same liberal disposition prevails with a large proportion of the same description of men in this state. Still, I think there will be great reason, for those who are well-affected to the government, to use their utmost exertions that the worthiest citizens may be appointed to the two houses of the first Congress and where state elections take place previous to this choice that the same principle govern in these also. For much will doubtless depend on their prudence in conducting business at the beginning; and reconciling discordant dispositions to a reasonable acquiescence with candid and honest measures. At the same time it will be a point of no common delicacy to make provision for effecting such explanations and amendments as might be really proper and generally satisfactory; without producing or at least fostering such a spirit of innovation as will overturn the whole system.

I earnestly pray that the Omnipotent Being who hath not deserted the cause of America in the hour of its extremest hazard, will never yield so fair a heritage of freedom a prey to *anarchy* or *despotism*.

1. FC, Washington Papers, DLC. McHenry was Washington's secretary for a time during the American Revolution, a Maryland delegate to the Confederation Congress and to the Constitutional Convention, and a member of the Maryland Convention which ratified the Constitution.

2. On 27 July McHenry had written to Washington from Baltimore saying that it was whispered there that opponents of the Constitution in Virginia had hatched a secret plan to suspend the organization of the government or defeat it altogether. McHenry's letter is printed in Chapter IX.

3. The reference is probably to George Mason of Fairfax County.

4. See Benjamin Lincoln to Washington, Boston, 3 June, DHOC, IV, 681-83, and Nathaniel Gorham to Washington, Boston, 5 July, RC, Washington Papers, DLC.

Benjamin Contee to Levi Hollingsworth, New York, 1 August[1]

I was favored with yours by last post. The important blank yet remains to be filled up with a place for meeting of the new Congress.

Philadelphia was tried on Monday. New York is at present the place in nomination. The subject is just called up.

Altho Philadelphia was lost, if New York fails also, Philadelphia may again be proposed.[2] The debates beginning.[3]

1. RC, Hollingsworth Papers (supplemental boxes), PHi. Contee was a Maryland delegate to Congress. Hollingsworth was a Philadelphia merchant.

2. Alexander Hamilton wrote to Philip Schuyler on 1 August that "it is still critical but we are the strongest" (quoted in Schuyler to Robert R. Livingston, Albany, 18 August, RC, Robert R. Livingston Papers, NHi).

3. The Journals of Congress do not record any action on the issue between 30 July and 4 August.

Theodore Sedgwick to Benjamin Lincoln, New York, 1 August (excerpt)[1]

Congress have now before them the report of a committee for the organization of the new government. The gentlemen from the Southward were urgent to postpone the assembling of the administration until March. From a principle of conciliation the Northern members have acceded to it, but the same temper doth not prevail with regard to the place. The Southern members, excepting those of South Carolina, are anxious to assemble at Philadelphia. To this measure I feel myself greatly opposed because in the first place I believe should Congress there assemble, that that city will thence become permanently the seat of government; and in the next place I consider it as the most improper of any great town on the continent because it is the greatest commercial place in America, and because it is generally believed that there exists in that town an undue influence inimical to the general good. Now whether this idea is well or ill founded the effect on the public mind will be precisely the same. Besides should the members of the legislature in that state be men of tolerable discernment, they will be able to dictate in all the matters of national concern.

Certainly the government ought not to be permanently established in any great town, nor in any place accessible by water.

1. RC, Lincoln Papers, MHi. Lincoln had been elected lieutenant governor of Massachusetts in May 1788.

James Madison to Edmund Randolph, New York, 2 August (excerpt)[1]

Congress have been some days on the question where the first meeting of the new Congress shall be placed. Philadelphia failed by a single voice from Delaware which ultimately aimed at that place, but wished to bring Wilmington into view. In that vote New Hampshire and Connecticut both concurred. New York is now in nomination and if those states accede, which I think probable, and Rhode Island which has as yet refused to sit in the question can be prevailed on to vote, which I also think probable, the point will be carried.[2] In this event a great handle I fear will be given to those who have opposed the new government on account of the Eastern preponderancy in the federal system.

1. RC, Madison Papers, DLC. Printed: Hunt, V, 236-37. Madison dated the letter "July 2d," but the content indicates that it was written in August. After his signature Madison added: "I enclose a copy of the ratification of New York. What think you of some of the expository articles?"
2. Brockholst Livingston reported the same day that "much depends on one Rhode Island delegate who has not yet consented to vote on the question. If he does, we shall have a majority" (to William Livingston, New York, RC, William Livingston Papers, MHi). The Rhode Island delegate was evidently Jonathan J. Hazard.

Comte de Moustier to Comte de Montmorin, New York, 2 August[1]

The State of New York on the 25th of last month finally acceded to the new Constitution, which finds itself adopted by eleven states. The recommended modifications are so numerous and so important, that if the new Congress takes them into account, this Constitution will scarcely preserve the appearance of its first shape. However a great blow has been dealt to the individual sovereignty of the states taken separately. The phantom of democracy which had seduced the people is about to disappear. The credulous majority, intoxicated by the noblest hopes, which it allowed itself to be fed, has itself forged the bonds by which sooner or later the leaders of the people will be able to subjugate and control it after having appeared to want to obey it. The Constitution is taken on approval until a better one is found. This tendency always to perfect is infinitely favorable to the designs of the ambitious, who, by means of alterations, will manage to weary the American people and make it receive with indifference the yoke which is prepared for it and which it will probably endure much more patiently than expected. The proposed modifications from the first offer a multitude of pretexts even for the reorganization of the government. This path is open to various parties. It is not doubted that each will profit from it according to its views.

The new Constitution appeared to be a remedy for all the evils under which the United States is groaning. The joy of the majority is especially expressed by public rejoicings. Different cities had processions in which all the classes of citizens were represented. That of New York did not even wait for the state Convention, to which it pertained, to give its decision. It had its procession at a time when it was strongly doubted that the state would adopt the Constitution. What was special about this popular festival is that Congress in a way risked sanctioning its purpose, which was to show the particular opinion of the city in opposition to what was assumed to be the opinion of the state, by attending in a body, and consequently officially, a rather ordinary dinner given by the trade associations of the city. I had been invited and I attended this dinner seated to the right of Congress, and was followed in succession by the Minister Plenipotentiary of the States General, the Chargé d'affaires Plenipotentiary of Spain, consuls, and other foreigners of distinction. To the left of Congress were its officers and members of the clergy of the city, Anglicans, Presbyterians, Catholics, Lutherans, Calvinists, Jews, altogether, except that the Anglican Bishop had turned to the others' right and had said the *blessing*. Congress, itself realizing that it was out of place to be in this festival as an official body, next insisted on maintaining that it had not been there as Congress, but I insisted, in part jokingly, in part seriously with different members, that such had been the opinion of everyone, that were it not for that they should have been located among the guests, and that I should have been to the right of the President [Cyrus Griffin].[2] Besides, this entire ceremony can be regarded as without significance [for] although people endeavored to put it everywhere, it still settled nothing; but it is a malady brought to this country from the mother country, where pretensions of this type are created on every occasion. It is to be hoped that this disadvantage will gradually disappear.

One of the purposes of the festival of the citizens of New York was to coax Congress and to urge it to convene the new sovereign body here. For its part Congress appeared to want to postpone its decision in this regard until the time when the Convention would have adopted the Constitution. Some of its members did not neglect to hint that this uncertainty was the only obstacle preventing Congress from adjourning the new one here. This bait had its effect. The Federalists of the Convention even went so far as to assert that there would be no difficulty as soon as the state of New York had entered into the new Union. Now since the pretense is no longer necessary the Pennsylvanians are staking everything in order to obtain a preference in favor of Philadelphia. The entire week has been spent in debate on this subject, in which it seems that personal interest had a much greater part than the public interest.

The question of determining a suitable time and place to which to adjourn has aroused the attention of all the states and consequently delegates from each one are found here; they will probably disperse as soon as these two subjects are decided. The delegates from Rhode Island content themselves with attending the deliberations without giving an opinion on any question which could be regarded as foreign to their state since it has rejected the new Constitution.

As soon as the opinion of North Carolina is known, I will have the honor to send you at the same time, sir, the Constitution as it has been proposed by the General Convention with the comparison of the different modifications proposed by the individual conventions. I will separate this statement from the observations that I propose to have the honor of submitting to you on the influence of the Constitution on the external politics of the United States and on the likelihood of the system which will be able to prevail in this respect.

There was here an example of what is to be expected from the dominant party during changes of government in spite of the beautiful name of liberty which so rarely finds itself corresponding to the facts. An unfortunate printer who last set about to print a gazette in a city where there are too many of them, in order to give a reputation to his paper had contrived to collect small talk and facts which were in opposition to the Federalist Party. A tasteless joke about a mishap which occured in the federal procession, which has been punished by the destruction of his printing press and personal insults, obliged him to flee from his house and to abandon it to the champions of liberty, who often make a bad use of it against the weakest, when the latter have the indiscretion unwarily to make use of what they believe they have on their side.[3]

1. Ministère des Affaires Étrangères, Archives Diplomatiques Correspondance Politique, États-Unis, XXXIII, 238-41. Comte de Montmorin was the French Minister of Foreign Affairs.

2. The procession and dinner were held on 23 July.

3. On 24 July, the day after the procession, Thomas Greenleaf published an irreverent account in his daily newspaper, the Antifederalist *New York Journal*. On Saturday, 26 July, a few hours after news of New York's ratification reached New York City, a mob broke into Greenleaf's house and printing shop, ruined the shop, and scattered the type. Greenleaf resumed publication of the *Journal* as a weekly newspaper on 31 July. His account of the attack is in the issue of 7 August.

George Washington to James Madison, Mount Vernon, 3 August (excerpt)[1]

The place proper for the new Congress to meet at will, unquestionably, undergo (if it has not already done it) much investigation; but there are certain things which are so self evident in their nature as to speak for themselves—this, possibly, may be one. Where the true point lays, I will not undertake to decide, but there can be no hesitation I conceive in pronouncing one thing: that in all societies, if the bond or cement is strong and interesting enough to hold the body together, the several parts should submit to the inconveniences for the benefits which they derive from the conveniences of the compact.

1. RC, in Signers of the Declaration of Independence volume, Amherst College, Amherst, Mass. Printed: Fitzpatrick, XXX, 32-33.

Journals of Congress, Monday, 4 August

Congress assembled. Present the thirteen states.

. . . .

The order of the day being called and the motion [of 30 July] renewed by Mr. Dayton, seconded by Mr. Ross, to fill the blank with the words "city of New York in the state of New York." A motion was made by Mr. Williamson, seconded by Mr. Seney, to postpone the motion in order to admit a motion to fill the blank with the word "Lancaster"[1] and on the question to postpone for the purpose above mentioned, the yeas and nays being required by Mr. Williamson:

New Hampshire
    Gilman   no ⎫ no
    Wingate   no ⎬
Massachusetts
    Sedgwick   ay ⎫
    Dane   no ⎬ no
    Otis   no ⎭
Rhode Island
    Hazard   no ⎫ no
    Arnold   no ⎬
Connecticut
    Huntington   no ⎫
    Wadsworth   no ⎬ no
    Edwards   ay ⎭
New York
    L'Hommedieu   no ⎫
    Benson   no ⎬ no
    Hamilton   no ⎥
    Yates   no ⎭
New Jersey
    Clarke   no ⎫
    Elmer   ay ⎬ no
    Dayton   no ⎭
Pennsylvania
    Irvine   ay ⎫
    Meredith   ay ⎬ ay
    Bingham   ay ⎥
    Reid   ay ⎭

Delaware
    Kearny   ay ⎫ ay
    Mitchell   ay ⎬
Maryland
    Seney   ay ⎫
    Contee   ay ⎬ ay
    Ross   ay ⎭
Virginia
    Griffin   ay ⎫
    Madison   ay ⎥
    Carrington   ay ⎬ ay
    Lee   no ⎥
    Brown   ay ⎭
North Carolina
    Williamson   ay ⎫ ay
    Swann   ay ⎬
South Carolina
    Huger   no ⎫
    Parker   no ⎬ no
    Tucker   no ⎭
Georgia
    Few   ay ⎫ ay
    Baldwin   ay ⎬

So it passed in the negative.

A motion was then made by Mr. Carrington, seconded by Mr. Seney, to postpone the motion for New York in order to admit "Baltimore in the state of Maryland" and on the question to postpone for the purpose above mentioned the yeas and nays being required by Mr. Seney:

New Hampshire			Delaware			
Gilman	no	} no	Kearny	ay	} ay	
Wingate	no		Mitchell	ay		
Massachusetts			Maryland			
Sedgwick	no		Seney	ay		
Dane	no	} no	Contee	ay	} ay	
Otis	no		Ross	ay		
Rhode Island			Virginia			
Hazard	no	} no	Griffin	ay		
Arnold	no		Madison	ay		
Connecticut			Carrington	ay	} ay	
Huntington	no		Lee	ay		
Wadsworth	no	} no	Brown	ay		
Edwards	no		North Carolina			
New York			Williamson	ay	} ay	
L'Hommedieu	no		Swan	ay		
Benson	no	} no	South Carolina			
Hamilton	no		Huger	ay		
Yates	no		Parker	ay	} ay	
New Jersey			Tucker	ay		
Clarke	no		Georgia			
Elmer	no	} no	Few	ay	} ay	
Dayton	no		Baldwin	ay		
Pennsylvania						
Irvine	ay					
Meredith	ay					
Armstrong	no	} ay				
Bingham	ay					
Reid	ay					

So it passed in the affirmative.

On the question to fill the blank with the words "the town of Baltimore in the state of Maryland," the yeas and nays being required by Mr. Carrington:

New Hampshire			Rhode Island			
Gilman	no	} no	Hazard	no	} no	
Wingate	no		Arnold	no		
Massachusetts			Connecticut			
Sedgwick	no		Huntington	no		
Dane	no	} no	Wadsworth	no	} no	
Otis	no		Edwards	no		

New York			Maryland		
L'Hommedieu	no		Seney	ay	
Benson	no	no	Contee	ay	ay
Hamilton	no		Ross	ay	
Yates	no		Virginia		
New Jersey			Griffin	ay	
Clarke	no		Madison	ay	
Elmer	no	no	Carrington	ay	ay
Dayton	no		Lee	ay	
Pennsylvania			Brown	ay	
Irvine	ay		North Carolina		
Meredith	ay		Williamson	ay	ay
Armstrong	no	ay	Swann	ay	
Bingham	ay		South Carolina		
Reid	ay		Huger	ay	
Delaware			Parker	ay	ay
Kearny	ay	ay	Tucker	ay	
Mitchell	ay		Georgia		
			Few	ay	ay
			Baldwin	ay	

So it was resolved in the affirmative.[2]

The preamble reported by the committee was then taken into consideration which is in the words following "Whereas the Convention assembled in Philadelphia pursuant to the resolution of Congress of the 21st of February 1787, did on the 17th of September in the same year report to the United States in Congress Assembled in the words following viz. 'We the people etc.' (here to be inserted the Constitution and resolutions as entered on the Journal of last year September 28th 1787) whereupon Congress on the 28th of the same September, did resolve unanimously, 'That the said Report, with the resolutions and letter accompanying the same, be transmitted to the several Legislatures, in order to be submitted to a Convention of Delegates chosen in each State, by the people thereof, in conformity to the Resolves of the Convention made and provided in that case.' And whereas the states of New Hampshire, Massachusetts, Connecticut, New York, New Jersey, Pennsylvania, Delaware, Maryland, Virginia, South Carolina, and Georgia, have duly ratified the aforesaid Constitution, as appears by the several acts of the said states returned to Congress, and filed in the office of the secretary; and it is expedient that proceedings do commence thereon as early as may be, therefore," etc.[3]

A motion was made by Mr. Tucker,[4] seconded by Mr. Huger, to postpone the said preamble in order to take up the following, viz.,

"Whereas the Constitution proposed by the late General Convention held in the city of Philadelphia has been ratified in the manner therein declared to be sufficient for the establishment of the same; and whereas the ratifications of the several states are to be considered as containing virtual authority and instructions to their delegates in Congress to make the preparatory arrangements recommended by the said Convention to be made by Congress, therefore, resolved."

And on the question to postpone for the purpose abovementioned, the yeas and nays being required by Mr. Tucker:

New Hampshire
 Gilman ay ⎫ ay
 Wingate ay ⎭
Massachusetts
 Sedgewick no ⎫
 Dane ay ⎬ no
 Otis no ⎭
Rhode Island
 Arnold ay*
Connecticut
 Huntington ay ⎫
 Wadsworth ay ⎬ ay
 Edwards no ⎭
New York
 L'Hommedieu no ⎫
 Benson no ⎬ no
 Hamilton no ⎪
 Yates ay ⎭
New Jersey
 Clark ay ⎫
 Elmer ay ⎬ ay
 Dayton no ⎭
Pennsylvania
 Irvine ay ⎫
 Meredith ay ⎪
 Armstrong ay ⎬ ay
 Bingham no ⎪
 Reid ay ⎭

Delaware
 Kearny ay ⎫ ay
 Mitchell ay ⎭
Maryland
 Seney no ⎫
 Contee ay ⎬ ay
 Ross ay ⎭
Virginia
 Griffin ay ⎫
 Madison ay ⎪
 Carrington ay ⎬ ay
 Lee ay ⎪
 Brown ay ⎭
North Carolina
 Williamson no ⎫ d
 Swann ay ⎭
South Carolina
 Huger ay ⎫
 Parker ay ⎬ ay
 Tucker ay ⎭
Georgia
 Few ay ⎫ ay
 Baldwin ay ⎭

So it was resolved in the affirmative.

1. In his draft of the motion Hugh Williamson originally wrote "Philadelphia" (PCC, Item 23, pp. 339-42).

2. The vote for Baltimore "surprised" people in and out of Congress (William Knox to Henry Knox, 4 August, printed below) and was carried largely because of the indignation aroused by the Rhode Island vote on the issue of the seat of government (Mrs. Henry Knox to Henry Knox, 5 August, printed below). On 2 July when Congress appointed the committee to prepare an election ordinance, the Rhode Island delegates were "excused" from voting because their state had rejected the calling of a convention. The North Carolina delegation was present but was not recorded in the roll call, presumably because the North Carolina Convention would not meet until 21 July. The New York delegates displayed no such delicacy on 2 July, and by August, neither did those of Rhode Island and North Carolina. Jonathan J. Hazard of Rhode Island was absent from Congress after 24 July but rejoined his colleague, Peleg Arnold, on the morning of 4 August, when they both helped defeat the motion to substitute Lancaster for New York. Immediately thereafter Baltimore was offered as a substitute. The South Carolina delegation, which usually supported New York, switched its vote and thus carried the motion for Baltimore.

3. With a few minor changes this is the preamble reported on 9 July.

4. A draft of this motion is in PCC, Item 23, pp. 107-8.

William Knox to Henry Knox, New York, 4 August (excerpt)[1]

You will undoubtedly be surprised to hear that this day seven states in Congress were decided upon Baltimore in Maryland as the place of the future residence of the government of the United States.[2] It has surprised everybody out of doors and even the members themselves (several of whom and the President [Cyrus Griffin] I have dined in company with); however, it is a fact which I have had from their own mouths. Colonel [Alexander] Hamilton seems to think it not final. Mr. [William] Bingham says it is impossible for the same members to change their sentiments who have voted for the measure today. Colonel [Edward] Carrington is said to have made the motion. All this is strange enough, but so it is.

1. RC, Knox Papers, MHi. Knox headed this letter "8 o'clock Monday Eveng." William Knox was Henry Knox's brother and a clerk in the Department of War.
2. The spread of the news of the vote for Baltimore resulted in considerable commentary by Pennsylvanians. Tench Coxe reported that "the exertions against Philadelphia were so virulent that Mr. Bingham, and Colonel Carrington of Virginia suddenly surprised them with a proposition of Baltimore, which was carried by seven states, that number being necessary to a quorum, without any blind attachment to this city" (to James Tilghman, Philadelphia, 6 August, RC, William Tilghman Papers, PHi).

Philadelphians also heard that the vote would probably be reconsidered. Edward Burd reported that the vote for Baltimore had "alarmed the Eastern States, and they are about reconsidering their vote" (to Jasper Yeates, Philadelphia, 6 August, Walker, *Burd*, 143). Thomas Willing, who heard about the vote from William Bingham in Congress, replied that "you have acted wisely, in supporting a removal to Baltimore, since you could not prevail in favor of this place; and the Eastern delegates may have reason to regret that they did not at first concur in the vote to come here, instead of a more Southern position; which will be less safe on account of health, and where they can't possibly be so well accommodated. However, the vote it seems has passed for Baltimore, and I hope it may not have been reconsidered as you seem to apprehend. If it should have been again taken up, I fear that the party strong enough to open the business again, will be too strong for you on a fresh vote for New York" (Philadelphia, 7 August, RC, Charles Francis Jenkins Autograph Collection, PHi).

For the response in Maryland see the Baltimore *Maryland Journal*, 12 August, and the Baltimore *Maryland Gazette*, 19 August, both printed below.

Journal of Comte de Moustier, 4 August[1]

One delegate from the South [Edward Carrington] has surprised all the members by the motion to adjourn to Baltimore. The partisans of New York not being prepared to struggle against this new phantom, the motion has been approved by 7 states, but it was proposed that this question be reconsidered tomorrow.

1. French Legation Minutes, I, Part II (Cahier 3), 25, CtY.

George Morgan to George Washington, New York, 5 August (excerpt)[1]

The organization of the new government has been long retarded by a difficulty in uniting seven states to vote for one place. The contest lay between New York and Philadelphia. As both parties could not be indulged, a vote was carried yesterday for Baltimore; so that the ordinance will be completed this morning, unless New York succeeds in their intention to move for a reconsideration of it, as the place is not agreeable to several of the most Southern States, tho they voted for it.

1. RC, Washington Papers, DLC. This is a postscript to a letter dated 31 July. Morgan, a Pennsylvania land speculator and promoter of the Indiana Company, was a leading opponent of Virginia's claims to western lands. He shared with Washington an interest in agricultural improvement. The body of his letter discusses methods of controlling the Hessian fly, which was devastating wheat crops.

Journals of Congress, Tuesday, 5 August

Congress assembled. Present as yesterday.

. . . .

The order of the day being called, the preamble moved by Mr. Tucker, seconded by Mr. Huger, was read in the words following "Whereas the Constitution proposed by the late General Convention held in the city of Philadelphia has been ratified in the manner therein declared to be sufficient for the establishment of the same; and whereas the ratifications of the several states are to be considered as containing virtual authority and instructions to their delegates in Congress to make the preparatory arrangements recommended by the said Convention to be made by Congress, therefore"—

A motion was made by the delegates of North Carolina to amend this proposed preamble by striking out the words "and instructions to their delegates in Congress" and in lieu thereof to insert "to the United States in Congress Assembled."

A motion was thereupon made by Mr. Dane, seconded by Benson, to postpone both the proposed preamble and the amendment; and on the question to postpone, the yeas and nays being required by Mr. Williamson:

New Hampshire			New York		
Gilman	ay	ay	L'Hommedieu	ay	ay
Wingate	ay		Benson	ay	
Massachusetts			Hamilton	ay	
Sedgwick	ay	ay	Yates	no	
Dane	ay		New Jersey		
Otis	ay		Clarke	ay	ay
Rhode Island			Elmer	ay	
Hazard	no	no	Dayton	ay	
Arnold	no		Pennsylvania		
Connecticut			Armstrong	ay	ay
Huntington	ay	ay	Bingham	ay	
Wadsworth	ay		Reid	no	
Edwards	ay		Delaware		
			Kearny	no	no
			Mitchel	no	

Maryland
  Seney   ay ⎫
  Contee   no ⎬ ay
  Ross   ay ⎭
Virginia
  Griffin   ay ⎫
  Madison   ay ⎪
  Carrington   ay ⎬ ay
  Lee   ay ⎪
  Brown   ay ⎭

North Carolina
  Williamson   no ⎫
  Swann   no ⎬ no
South Carolina
  Huger   no ⎫
  Parker   no ⎬ no
  Tucker   no ⎭
Georgia
  Few   ay ⎫
  Baldwin   ay ⎬ ay

So it was resolved in the affirmative.

A new preamble being agreed to,[1] a motion was made by Mr. Hamilton, seconded by Mr. Dane, to reconsider the question for filling the blank in the resolution with the words "The town of Baltimore in the state of Maryland," and on the question for reconsideration, the yeas and nays being required by Mr. Seney:

New Hampshire
  Gilman   ay ⎫ ay
  Wingate   ay ⎭
Massachusetts
  Sedgwick   ay ⎫
  Dane   ay ⎬ ay
  Otis   ay ⎭
Rhode Island
  Hazard   ay ⎫ ay
  Arnold   ay ⎭
Connecticut
  Huntington   ay ⎫
  Wadsworth   ay ⎬ ay
  Edwards   ay ⎭
New York
  L'Hommedieu ay ⎫
  Benson   ay ⎪
  Hamilton   ay ⎬ ay
  Yates   ay ⎭
New Jersey
  Clark   ay ⎫ ay
  Dayton   ay ⎭
Pennsylvania
  Irvine   no ⎫
  Meredith   no ⎪
  Armstrong   no ⎬ no
  Bingham   no ⎪
  Reid   no ⎭

Delaware
  Kearny   no ⎫ no
  Mitchell   no ⎭
Maryland
  Seney   no ⎫
  Contee   no ⎬ no
  Ross   no ⎭
Virginia
  Griffin   no ⎫
  Madison   no ⎪
  Carrington   no ⎬ no
  Lee   ay ⎪
  Brown   no ⎭
North Carolina
  Williamson   no ⎫ no
  Swan   no ⎭
South Carolina
  Huger   ay ⎫
  Parker   no ⎬ no
  Tucker   no ⎭
Georgia
  Few   no ⎫ no
  Baldwin   no ⎭

So it passed in the negative.

1. The new preamble was not entered on the Journals at this point but on the Journals of 6 August, printed below.

William Knox to Henry Knox, New York, 5 August (excerpt)[1]

I informed you yesterday that seven states had voted in favor of Baltimore as the future seat of government; the business however has been resumed this day and it is said the opinions in Congress have taken another turn. It seems to stand thus from the information given me this afternoon by Mr. [Abraham] Baldwin. The proceeding in the first instance was intended to be a resolve but by management is now an ordinance, and therefore the proceedings of yesterday is construed into a first reading; and he says it is still open to final decision. I have not been able to converse with any other members, and as to retailing what passes outdoors would be endless. However, the spirits of the town are vastly raised from the state they were in yesterday.

1. RC, Knox Papers, MHi. At the close of the letter is written: "Tuesday Afternoon—5 oClock Augt. 5th. 1788."

Mrs. Henry Knox to Henry Knox, New York, 5 August (excerpt)[1]

And now what think you of a jaunt to Baltimore? Yesterday Congress formed themselves into a committee of the whole to determine upon a proper place for the seat of government. Coolness and candor seemed to pervade them, when the *phiz* of Mr. [Jonathan J.] Hazard, who appeared ready to vote, threw them up in the wind. They cried collusion and immediately took the question for Baltimore, in which the seven states south of Jersey concurred.[2] This day the question or vote will be taken in form with the President in the chair, but I fear it is a hopeless case. None but Pennsylvania can with any face retract, and they probably think that it will end well for them. I am to dine this day at Mr. [William] Duer's, where I shall hear more upon the subject.

1. RC, Personal Papers Misc., DLC. Mrs. Knox's letter is headed "Tuesday morn 6 of August." It was evidently written on the 5th, which was Tuesday, and it refers to actions in Congress "yesterday," actions which occurred on Monday, the 4th.
2. See Journals of Congress, 4 August, n. 2.

Journals of Congress, Wednesday, 6 August

Congress assembled. Present the thirteen states.

The order of the day being called for and the act as amended for putting the Constitution into operation being read as follows:

"Whereas the Convention assembled in Philadelphia pursuant to the resolution of Congress of the 21 February 1787 did on the 17 of September in the same year report to the United States in Congress Assembled a Constitution for the people of the United States, whereupon Congress on the 28 of the same September did resolve unanimously 'that the said report with the resolutions and letter accompanying the same be transmitted to the several legislatures in order to be submitted to a convention of delegates chosen in each state by the people thereof in conformity to the resolves of the convention made and provided in that case'; and whereas the Constitution so reported by the Convention and by Congress transmitted to the several legislatures has been ratified in the manner therein declared to be sufficient for the establishment of the same and such ratifications duly authenticated have been received by Congress and are filed in the office of the secretary therefore,

"Resolved, that the first Wednesday in January next be the day for appointing Electors in the several states which before the said day shall have ratified the said Constitution, that the first Wednesday in February next be the day for the Electors to assemble in their respective states and vote for a President and that the first Wednesday in March next be the time and the town of Baltimore in the state of Maryland the place for commencing proceedings under the said Constitution."

A motion was made by Mr. Tucker,[1] seconded by Mr. Lee, further to amend the act by striking out the words "and the town of Baltimore in the state of Maryland" and inserting as follows, "And whereas a central situation would be most eligible for the sitting of the legislature of the United States, if such could be found in a condition to furnish in due time the accommodations necessary for facilitating public business, and at the same time free of weighty objections which might render it improper or unlikely to be the seat of government either permanently or until a permanent seat can be agreed on; and whereas the most effectual means of obtaining finally the establishment of the federal government in a convenient central situation is to leave the subject to the deliberate consideration of the future Congress, uninfluenced by undue attachment to any of the places which may stand in competition for preference on so interesting a question, and unembarrassed by want of time and means to fix on and prepare the most proper place for this purpose; and whereas the removal of the public offices must be attended with much expense, danger and inconvenience, which ought not to be incurred but with a well founded expectation of advantages that may fully counterbalance the same; and whereas no such advantages can be expected from a removal to any place now in a condition to receive the federal legislature; and whereas in addition to the before mentioned reasons unnecessary changes of the seat of government would be indicative of instability in the national councils and therefore highly injurious to the interests as well as derogatory to the dignity of the United States, therefore,

"Resolved, that the city of New York in the state of New York be the place for commencing proceedings under the said Constitution."

A motion was then made by Mr. Williamson,[2] seconded by Mr. Reid, to postpone the motion before the house in order to take up the following:

"Whereas it is proper that the seat of the new Congress and of the national government should be placed as near the center of the Union as may consist with present accommodation in order that its influence and benefits may be equally felt by the great body of citizens throughout the United States, that members of Congress and other persons may approach it with equal convenience from the opposite extremes, and that no species of partial favor may seem to have been extended to one extreme, rather than to the other; and whereas the present residence of Congress is far removed from the center of the Union, whether population or distance are considered, since the new Congress is to consist of eight Senators from states to the eastward of New York, and sixteen from states to the southward, and since there are to be only 17 members in the House of Representatives from the Eastern States, though there are to be 42 members from Southern States; and since the distance to the seat of government in the extreme eastern state is hardly equal to one third of the distance to the seat of government in the most southerly state; and whereas it is to be desired that the new Congress may be convened in the same spirit of mutual accommodation which has hitherto appeared in all deliberations respecting the new government, and that proceedings under the said government may commence under the impressions of mutual confidence, without that general irritation and loss of time which must attend the removal from an improper situation, and without those painful apprehensions which will naturally arise from a measure that may seem to have originated in an undue regard to local considerations, therefore,

"Resolved, that the seat of the new Congress ought to be in some place to the southward of New York."

And on the question to postpone for the purpose above mentioned, the yeas and nays being required by Mr. Williamson:

New Hampshire			Delaware		
Gilman	no	no	Kearny	ay	ay
Wingate	no		Mitchell	ay	
Massachusetts			Maryland		
Sedgewick	no		Seney	ay	
Dane	no	no	Contee	ay	ay
Otis	no		Ross	ay	
Thatcher	no		Virginia		
Rhode Island			Griffin	ay	
Hazard	no	no	Madison	ay	
Arnold	no		Carrington	ay	ay
Connecticut			Lee	no	
Huntington	no		Brown	ay	
Wadsworth	no	no	North Carolina		
Edwards	ay		Williamson	ay	ay
New York			Swann	ay	
L'Hommedieu	no		South Carolina		
Benson	no	no	Huger	no	
Hamilton	no		Parker	no	no
Yates	no		Tucker	no	
New Jersey			Georgia		
Clark	no		Few	ay	ay
Elmer	ay	no	Baldwin	ay	
Dayton	no				
Pennsylvania					
Irvine	ay				
Meredith	ay				
Armstrong	ay	ay			
Bingham	ay				
Reid	ay				

So it passed in the negative.

A motion was then made by Mr. Carrington, seconded by Mr. Bingham, to amend the amendment by striking out the words "New York in the state of New York," and in lieu thereof, inserting "Philadelphia" and on the question to agree to the amendment, the yeas and nays being required by Mr. Reid:

New Hampshire
| Gilman | no | } no |
| Wingate | no | |

Massachusetts
Sedgewick	no	
Dane	no	} no
Otis	no	
Thatcher	no	

Rhode Island
| Hazard | no | } no |
| Arnold | no | |

Connecticut
Huntington	no	
Wadsworth	no	} no
Edwards	ay	

New York
L'Hommedieu	no	
Benson	no	} no
Hamilton	no	
Yates	no	

New Jersey
Clark	no	
Elmer	ay	} no
Dayton	no	

Pennsylvania
Irvine	ay	
Meredith	ay	
Armstrong	ay	} ay
Bingham	ay	
Reid	ay	

Delaware
| Kearny | ay | } ay |
| Mitchell | ay | |

Maryland
Seney	ay	
Contee	ay	} ay
Ross	ay	

Virginia
Griffin	ay	
Madison	ay	
Carrington	ay	} ay
Lee	no	
Brown	ay	

North Carolina
| Williamson | ay | } ay |
| Swann | ay | |

South Carolina
Huger	no	
Parker	no	} no
Tucker	no	

Georgia
| Few | no | } d |
| Baldwin | ay | |

So it passed in the negative.

[Congress approved Tucker's motion to substitute New York for Baltimore in the resolving clause.] [3]

A division was then called for and on the question to agree to the resolving clause, the yeas and nays being required by Mr. Lee:

New Hampshire
| Gilman | ay | } ay |
| Wingate | ay | |

Massachusetts
Sedgewick	ay	
Dane	ay	} ay
Otis	ay	
Thatcher	ay	

Rhode Island				Maryland			
Hazard	ay	} ay		Seney	no	} no	
Arnold	ay			Contee	no		
Connecticut				Ross	no		
Huntington	ay			Virginia			
Wadsworth	ay	} ay		Griffin	no		
Edwards	ay			Madison	ay		
New York				Carrington	no	} no	
L'Hommedieu	ay			Lee	ay		
Benson	ay	} ay		Brown	no		
Hamilton	ay			North Carolina			
Yates	ay			Williamson	no	} no	
New Jersey				Swann	no		
Clark	ay			South Carolina			
Elmer	ay	} ay		Huger	ay		
Dayton	ay			Parker	ay	} ay	
Pennsylvania				Tucker	ay		
Irvine	no			Georgia			
Meredith	no			Few	ay	} d	
Armstrong	no	} no		Baldwin	no		
Bingham	no						
Reid	no						
Delaware							
Kearny	no	} no					
Mitchell	no						

So it was resolved in the affirmative.

On the question to agree to the preamble, the yeas and nays being required by Mr. Irvine:

New Hampshire				New York			
Gilman	ay	} ay		L'Hommedieu	ay		
Wingate	ay			Benson	ay	} ay	
Massachusetts				Hamilton	ay		
Sedgewick	ay			Yates	ay		
Dane	ay	} ay		New Jersey			
Otis	ay			Clark	ay		
Thatcher	ay			Elmer	no	} ay	
Rhode Island				Dayton	ay		
Hazard	ay	} ay		Pennsylvania			
Arnold	ay			Irvine	no		
Connecticut				Meredith	no		
Huntington	ay			Armstrong	no	} no	
Wadsworth	ay	} ay		Bingham	no		
Edwards	no			Reid	no		

Delaware			South Carolina		
Kearny	no	} no	Huger	ay	}
Mitchell	no		Parker	ay	} ay
Maryland			Tucker	ay	}
Seney	no	}	Georgia		
Contee	no	} no	Few	ay	} d
Ross	no		Baldwin	no	}
Virginia					
Griffin	no	}			
Madison	no				
Carrington	no	} no			
Lee	ay				
Brown	no	}			
North Carolina					
Williamson	no	} no			
Swann	no				

So it was resolved in the affirmative.

1. A draft of this motion is in PCC, Item 23, pp. 343-[44b].

2. A draft of this motion is in PCC, Item 23, pp. 339-42. The draft, except for the deletion of Lancaster as the place to meet, and some minor revisions, is apparently the same document which Hugh Williamson used as the basis of his motion on 4 August.

3. The Rough Journals of Congress contain no record of a vote to approve Tucker's motion. Nevertheless, at this point in the proceedings, it was still the motion before Congress. Charles Thomson noted on his copy of Tucker's motion to amend the resolving clause: "Passed Aug 6th 1788" (PCC, Item 23, p. 345). Since the following vote was on the resolving clause as a whole, it seems evident that Tucker's motion must have been passed before the vote was taken, and the draft of the ordinance read to Congress on 13 August included Tucker's motion with only slight changes in wording.

William Bingham's Proposed Resolution Concerning the Location of the Government, 6 August[1]

Whereas by the recommendation of the Federal Convention assembled at Philadelphia, Congress are desired (*inter alia*) to fix the place, where proceedings are to commence under the Federal Constitution.

1. And whereas, the states which have parted with all those powers which regulated their national and aggregate interests, and which they have vested in the federal government, have been fully persuaded that in so doing they have consulted their mutual advantage by their consolidating and strengthening the powers of the Union.

2. And whereas, it is essentially necessary to the peace, prosperity and preservation of the Union, that in all the arrangements made by Congress, the respective interests and accommodation of the states be impartially attended to.

And whereas, the dangers that the Union has most to apprehend, arise from the unequal portion of strength, possessed by the Northern and Southern states, which involves the necessity of taking care that the ambition of the powerful members should not be accompanied by the means of degrading the weak, and rendering them subordinate and dependent which might tend to dissolve the Confederacy, as has happened with other political leagues constituted on dissimilar terms.

And whereas, the power of regulating commerce which may confine and monopolize the carrying trade; and establishing such high duties on the importation of foreign articles of consumption (in order to encourage the domestic manufactures of the country) as may operate as a prohibition, may be exercised by the seven navigating and manufacturing states alone, and which may be made the engines of severe oppression to the Southern States, and which renders it their interest to guard against the effects of such a combination.

3. And whereas, the Southern States have been more seriously alarmed on these, than on any other points and have selected them as inducing the strongest objections to the Federal Constitution; should therefore the seat of government be placed amongst the navigating and manufacturing states it must evidently discompose the harmony of the Union by creating strong apprehensions of an influence and cooperation of interests which would engender commercial and fiscal regulations exceedingly oppressive and injurious to them. The government would consequently commence in distrust, proceed with jealousy, and possibly terminate in discord; for if influence, by facilitating the means, gives the opportunity, and a distinct and separate interest forms the impulse, to concert and carry into effect schemes of oppression for any part of the Union, there is nothing to depend upon as an adequate control to check the inducements that will exert to sacrifice the weaker party. That a conjecture concerning the extent of influence is well founded, we need only recollect that most of the officers who will grow out of the necessities of revenue and are an appendage to that system; most of the appointments of the federal judiciary on whose decision will depend the great controversies in which states both foreign and domestic will be parties, as well as those betwixt citizens of the different states; most of the officers in the military establishment of the Union; most of those, superior and subordinate, in the great departments will probably be chosen from the inhabitants of the surrounding district as they will possess the advantage of soliciting and supporting their pretensions by personal application and address.

And whereas, there is great cause of alarm in the facility with which a combined force in the federal legislature, if connected with the adjacent states, may be assembled whenever any great question to which they were attached, was to be agitated, or any great point determined in which it was necessary to outnumber their opponents, and accomplish the secret wishes of an interested majority.

It becomes an object, therefore, deeply affecting the interests of the Union, to determine where the federal government shall be placed to satisfy the general wishes, and consult the mutual convenience of the Union; where it will be the best situated to preserve the Confederacy by suppressing faction, guarding internal tranquillity and repelling external invasion, for, if its influence will be great in the first years of its establishment by the creation of numerous offices and the enjoyment of a most extensive patronage, Congress should so place it that the first fruits of its benefits may circulate as equally as possible, and that it may equally diffuse its animating effects. To answer this salutary purpose it must be placed in the center of the Union, from whence its operation may diverge and be proportionally felt throughout the whole extent of the United States. If it is placed at a distance from this central point, its foundation will be laid in extreme partiality, and a view to local aggrandizement and particular interests, which spirit, if too much cultivated in one part of the Union, must beget so unequal a division of strength as must terminate, when aided by ambitious views, in the extinction of the Confederacy or the degradation of a considerable portion of it.

And whereas, it has been contended by very respectable authority that this government was on too extended a scale and that its movements could not be sufficiently energetic to reach to, and control the extremities, and that the reins of government would consequently be relaxed at a distance from the seat of empire. Now, to obviate this objection as far as possible and to satisfy every part of the Union that there is an equal attention paid to its interests and convenience, its position should be fixed in the midst of the population of the country where, by strengthening the center, the extremities are fortified; where the collective resources of the Confederacy may be drawn into a point and administered with the greatest facility; where the speediest intelligence of hostile preparations and movements may be obtained and a military force to oppose them directed with the greatest dispatch.

By being thus situated the more Southern States which are in the neighborhood of continual danger from their contiguity to the settlements of foreign nations, as well as to hostile tribes of Indians, will feel a confidence by knowing that the government to which they look up for protection is placed as near them as the general interests of the country will permit. Besides, the frequent and necessary communications betwixt the members of the federal legislature and their constituents will be thereby facilitated, as well as those betwixt the officers of the great departments, and their respective dependencies in the different states.

And whereas, the place where Congress resides should be free from danger and not exposed to the predatory naval incursions of an enemy, for without such security the functions of government must be suspended during an alarm of war until a place of refuge can be found where the deliberations of Congress could be free from apprehension, and where its records could be deposited in unmolested security.

And whereas, the objects that will press most on the attention of the first Congress will be those of commerce and revenue; the regulation of the former and establishment of the latter, require the government to be situated in a maritime, opulent, and populous country, as well to promote the success of the great operations of finance, which essentially depend on the confidence of the monied interest, as to profit by the institution of a bank, which is an engine of powerful effect to aid the fiscal administration, by anticipating the revenues of the country, and facilitating the requisite supplies to the treasury.

And whereas, Pennsylvania is not only the middle state that separates the Union into equal divisions but is situated in the very center of the national population as must appear evident from the equal number of Senators and Representatives that the respective states in the Northward and Southward districts, are, by the Constitution, entitled to send to the federal legislature. And whereas, by being thus critically placed in the midst of the Union, it fortunately happens that Pennsylvania is a state of great resource and vigor, inhabited by a frugal and industrious people and is calculated to afford a respectable weight to aid the government in counterposing the undue preponderance of either the Northern or Southern scale, as well as to furnish assistance by a well trained militia to any part of the Union that may require it, altho these circumstances which under the old Confederation might beget a political jealousy in other states must under the Federal Constitution become a cause of congratulation as by the consolidated system of Union, all the states are melted down into one great mass of common undivided interest, and the benefits to be produced by the exertions and local advantages of this state, are proportionally participated of by all the others, more particularly, as the most productive branches of revenue are exclusively appropriated by the general government.

And whereas, from the general expectation throughout the United States that Pennsylvania would be the state where proceedings under the new Constitution would commence, which opinion was founded not only on its various advantages, both local and political, its central and secure situation, but from its having been the place where the united voice of America fixed the first Congress, and where the united voice of America assembled the Federal Convention, the Convention of the State of Pennsylvania have voted for the accommodation of Congress until it has fixed a permanent residence, the use of all their public buildings situate in Philadelphia with an elegant garden as an appendage, occupying an entire square; which buildings, are sufficiently extensive to supply large and commodious rooms for two deliberative assemblies, as well as offices for the secretaries of the different departments.

1. AD, Bancroft Collection, NN. This undated document in Bingham's handwriting is endorsed "A Proposed Resolution to be made in Congress." Apparently the resolution was not introduced in Congress, perhaps because Hugh Williamson introduced a resolution on 6 August which contained similar arguments (see Journals of Congress, printed immediately above). We have assigned the date 6 August to the document because of the similarity between it and Williamson's resolution. Bingham's proposed resolution contains one of the fullest developments of the argument for a centrally located capital city. The arguments in it are more detailed than those in Williamson's resolution and in a newspaper essay Bingham wrote on the same subject ("A Member of the Federal Club," Philadelphia *Pennsylvania Packet*, 22 August, printed below).

Journal of Comte de Moustier, 6 August[1]

The delegates from South Carolina, incapable of making a firm decision and attached to some New York women, by means of being importuned by the New Yorkers, were not able to resist their entreaties and it was proposed to replace the word Baltimore with the word New York, which passed with a majority of seven states, 5 states being opposed to it and Georgia divided.[2]

1. French Legation Minutes, I, Part II (Cahier 3), 25-[26], CtY. Although the extract is dated 5 August in the "Minutes," it refers to the last two roll-call votes on 6 August.
2. In neither of the two letters from the South Carolina delegates to Governor Thomas

Pinckney that have been located (16 August, 6 September, printed below) do they mention their consistent support of New York. However, one delegate, Thomas Tudor Tucker, reported that he feared the "aristocratical influence" of Philadelphia (to St. George Tucker, 26 August, printed below).

Massachusetts Centinel, 6 August

It is yet doubtful at which place the new government will commence proceedings, New York or Philadelphia. The latter cannot much expect the honor—seeing they once permitted a lawless rabble to insult the sovereign power of the Union with impunity.[1]

"Procrastination is the thief of time" and yet the new government, which has been ratified a month, is not to be exercised for seven more.

"Is there not something rotten in the State of Denmark?" asks an old correspondent, or how can Congress answer to our foreign creditors, the loss of several months impost, etc.?

1. This is a reference to the mutinous Pennsylvania troops who surrounded the State House in Philadelphia on 21 June 1783 while Congress was in session. A few days thereafter Congress moved to Princeton, N.J.

Pennsylvania Gazette, 6 August

Should Virginia give a President, and Massachusetts a Vice President to the United States, Pennsylvania should certainly come in for the honor of being the seat of the federal government. Her central situation, her active federal spirit, which set the whole Union in motion in favor of the Constitution upon its first promulgation, her numerous resources for arts and manufactures, and the connection of her name with the original splendor and fame of Congress, all strongly mark her as the most proper state for the new government of the United States.[1]

1. This item was reprinted in at least twelve newspapers: two in Pennsylvania, one in New Jersey, and nine in New England.

Journals of Congress, Thursday, 7 August

Congress assembled. Present as yesterday.[1]

1. The Journals contain only the above line, but it is evident that an intense dispute took place. The previous day Congress had voted approval of various sections of the election ordinance, but it was necessary to vote on the ordinance as a whole. On 4, 5, and 6 August Jonathan J. Hazard and Peleg Arnold of Rhode Island had voted to locate the new government in New York. Now they refused to vote on the ordinance, and, without them, the votes of seven states could not be obtained to pass the ordinance. Alexander Hamilton moved a

resolution providing a theoretical justification for voting by the Rhode Island and North Carolina delegates, even though their states had not ratified the Constitution. The North Carolina delegates moved an amendment to Hamilton's motion disassociating their state from Rhode Island and demanded a roll-call vote. Hamilton then withdrew his motion, the Rhode Islanders left for home the next day, and Congress was deadlocked again.

For the proceedings of Congress on 7 August and comments upon them, see the documents dated 7 August, printed below.

Alexander Hamilton's Motion, Thursday, 7 August[1]

Whereas the Convention assembled at Philadelphia in the Commonwealth of Pensylvania did on the 17th day of September last past resolve as the opinion of that Convention that as soon as the Conventions of nine states should have ratified the Constitution then and there agreed upon by the said Convention the United States in Congress assembled should fix a day on which electors should be appointed by the states which should have ratified the same and a day on which the electors should assemble to vote for the President and the time and place for commencing proceedings under the said constitution. And Whereas the United States in Congress assembled having received the ratifications of the said constitution by eleven states have in conformity to the resolution aforesaid passed an ordinance for the purposes aforesaid. And Whereas although the state of Rhode Island hath not ratified the said Constitution and it is not known that the state of North Carolina hath ratified the same, the Delegates of the two last mentioned states have thought fit to vote upon the said ordinance in virtue of the right of suffrage on all questions taken in Congress vested in them by the Articles of Confederation and perpetual Union.

Resolved as the sense of this Congress that the conduct of the delegates of the said state of Rhode Island in voting concerning the said ordinance [can?] in no wise be construed directly or indirectly to imply either on their part or on the part of the state which they represent an approbation of the Constitution aforesaid or a relinquishment [in?] any manner or kind of obligation on the part of the said state touching the same or the relinquishment of any right heretofore enjoyed claimed or which may be claimed by the said state under the said Articles &c or otherwise, and that all and singular the rights of the said state remain continue and are to all intents and purposes in the same situation as if the said delegates had refrained from voting on the whole or any part of the said ordinance.

1. (LT) PCC, Item 23, pp. 345-[47]. So far as it can be deciphered, this draft motion is printed here as written by Hamilton. Charles Thomson, who took notes of the proceedings, made a copy of Hamilton's motion in which he altered the text and placed the resolving clause at the beginning (PCC, Item 23, pp. 93-[95]). Thereafter, someone, presumably a clerk, lined out sections of Hamilton's draft with a heavy pen and inserted others to make it conform to Thomson's copy. The Library of Congress edition of the *Journals* prints Thomson's copy with an inaccurate text of Hamilton's draft as a footnote (JCC, XXXIV, 403-4 and 403, n. 2). The Syrett edition of Hamilton's *Papers* (V, 197-98) prints a version that attempts to combine Hamilton's insertions and deletions and the clerk's alterations.

2. The document is endorsed "Motion of Mr. Hamilton Aug 7. 1788 Withdrawn." According to Thomson's notes (PCC, Item 23, p. 93) the motion was seconded by "Mr. D." The seconder could have been either Nathan Dane of Massachusetts or Jonathan Dayton of New Jersey.

North Carolina Amendment to Hamilton's Motion, Thursday, 7 August[1]

Motion by delegates of North Carolina to amend the motion by striking out in the preamble "it does not appear that the states of Rhode Island and North Carolina have ratified the said Constitution" and in lieu thereof to insert "the Convention of the State of North Carolina is supposed now to be in session and the state of Rhode Island has rejected the new Constitution."

And in the resolving clause to strike out "the delegate or delegates of any state which hath not ratified the said Constitution," and in lieu thereof to insert "the delegates of the state of Rhode Island which state hath rejected the new Constitution."

1. PCC, Item 23, p. 94. The proposed amendment printed here is as it appears in Charles Thomson's notes on the proceedings, except that abbreviations and contractions are spelled out and quotation marks are substituted for the parentheses Thomson used to indicate quotations. Two scraps of paper in Hugh Williamson's handwriting contain elements of the motion as given by Thomson. One reads: "By the Delegates of the State of Rhode Island which state hath rejected the new Constitution." The second reads: "And whereas the Convention of the State of North Carolina is supposed now to be in Session and the State of Rhode Island has rejected the new Constitution" (PCC, Item 23, p. 96).

Hugh Williamson's Explanation of the North Carolina Amendment of 7 August[1]

By letters from sundry correspondents, it appears that North Carolina has at length thrown herself out of the Union, but she happily is not alone; the large, upright, and respectable state of Rhode Island is her associate. This circumstance however does not, I hope, render it necessary that the delegates from North Carolina should profess a particular affection for the delegates from Rhode Island. That state was some days ago represented by a Mr. [Peleg] Arnold who keeps a little tavern 10 miles out of Providence and a Mr. [Jonathan J.] Hazard, the illiterate quondam skipper of a small coasting vessel and now the very leader of Know Ye justices[2] who officiates at county courts, and receives small fees, not as a lawyer, but agent for suitors. These two respectable delegates with the innate desire of promoting a bad measure lately voted on several questions respecting the organization of the new government in order to fix it in New York, a corner of the Union. But before the final question was taken on the ordinance they caused a member to move in Congress for a vote "that nothing which the delegates from Rhode Island or North Carolina had done or might do in voting on this subject should be construed as in any measure affecting the rights etc. of their constituents." This was to be a bull of absolution. On this motion the delegates from North Carolina moved that the word "North Carolina" should be struck out of the vote of absolution, and thereon we called for the yeas and nays to prove that we did not wish to have North Carolina associated in any vote with Rhode Island, that we did not wish for absolution, being conscious of having pursued our duty. That with respect to the final vote which was to be taken on the ordinance we proposed never to assist in such vote unless North Carolina should confederate for we would not be guilty of parricide by throwing our state out of the Union. On this the motion was withdrawn; the Rhode Island gentlemen missed the promised pleasure of doing wrong and on the next morning they set out homeward.[3]

1. Williamson to James Iredell, New York, 23 August (excerpt). RC, Iredell Papers, NcD. Printed: McRee, *Iredell*, II, 236-38. In the remainder of the letter Williamson refers to an earlier letter he had written to the governor of North Carolina, Samuel Johnston, attacking the delaying tactics of some members of Congress. The letter was read to the North Carolina Convention. It has not been found, but Thomas Person reported that in it Williamson "aristocratically complains" that a New York delegate who was once a shoemaker [Abraham Yates, Jr.] delayed proceedings by calling for yeas and nays, "on which occasions he says he was *obliged to retire*, as representing a non-adopting state" (to John Lamb, Goshen, N.C., 6 August, RC, Lamb Papers, NHi).

2. When creditors refused to accept Rhode Island paper money for debts owed to them, Rhode Island laws after 1786 allowed debtors to pay those debts by depositing the paper money with a court. Newspaper advertisements of such deposits usually began with the words "know ye" and hence the nickname "Know Ye justices" for those who administered the law.

3. The Rhode Island delegates returned home Friday, 8 August (William Knox to Henry Knox, New York, 10 August, RC, Knox Papers, MHi). Thereafter Congress remained deadlocked until September because the votes of seven states could not be obtained to pass the ordinance with New York as the place of meeting. Hamilton offered to finance the return of the Rhode Island delegates in order to break the deadlock (see his letter to Jeremiah Olney, 12 August, printed below).

From William Bingham, New York, 7 August[1]

My last letter informed you that the town of Baltimore had been fixed on by Congress as the place for commencing proceedings under the new government. As this was a Southern position, uniting the suffrages of the seven Southern States, it was expected that it would have been retained, until the Eastern States made overtures to accommodate, by offering Philadelphia as an alternative, in which they would concur. But our expectations were defeated by the defection of South Carolina, which state, on a motion to strike out Baltimore and insert New York, gave an unreserved concurrence, from an idea suggested that Baltimore was only a circuitous route to Philadelphia—so violent are their antipathies to this latter place.

The delegates of Rhode Island, who are strong Antifederalists, and whose state has formally rejected the Constitution, were seduced into a vote (which was requisite to complete the stipulated number to insure success) to put a government in motion, highly inimical to their views. The indecency of such conduct struck even their own partisans with astonishment.

But a determination on the place, is only one part of the ordinance; the periods, on which the Electors and the President are to be chosen etc., constitute very essential objects, which they absolutely declined having any agency in determining; it becomes necessary after the various parts of the ordinance have been individually deliberated on, and assented to, that a question should be taken on the whole, which has no authenticity until it receives the sanction of seven states; a sense of the striking impropriety of concurring in an act of this nature, has determined the delegates of the state of Rhode Island not to vote on this question, more especially as it is clearly evident that they have no right—they have made this declaration in Congress. The consequence will be that seven states will not be found, who will concur in the ordinance, whilst New York continues the destined place for assembling the new Congress. This must stagger the minds of the Eastern delegates, who are convinced that the present arrangement is an act of partiality and oppression to the Southern States, and has a view to local aggrandizement at the expense of a considerable part of the Union.

Thus stand affairs at present—what will be the result, time will discover. The various vicissitudes that have already occurred in the progress of this business, leave no room for probable conjecture. At any rate, there is an appearance of a longer detention, which for several reasons, has become very inconvenient.

P.S. Please to communicate this letter to Dr. [Benjamin] Rush and Mr. T[ench] Coxe, who have wrote to me on this subject, and I have not time to answer their letters.

1. RC, Gratz Collection, PHi. Although no addressee is indicated, the letter was probably written to Thomas Willing.

William Knox to Henry Knox, New York, 7 August (excerpt)[1]

The decisions in Congress yesterday were in favor of New York, seven states for it, viz., New Hampshire, Rhode Island, Connecticut, Massachusetts, New York, New Jersey, and South Carolina. Mr. [James] Maddison and Colonel Harry Lee from Virginia in favor and Mr. [William] Few of Georgia. However today the subject of the whole ordinance being on the carpet Rhode Island either declines voting or is not permitted by the Southern States to vote, so that the final business is still undetermined, and tomorrow may produce another change in the majority of votes.[2]

1. RC, Knox Papers, MHi. Knox headed this letter "New York Thursday afternoon 6 o'clock 7th. Augt 1788."
2. For additional comments on the dispute and on the role of the Rhode Island delegates, see Richard Platt to Winthrop Sargent (New York, 8 August, RC, Sargent Papers, MHi); Samuel Powel to George Washington (Philadelphia, 9 August, RC, Washington Papers, DLC); "Extract" of a letter from New York, 10 August, Portland, Me., *Cumberland Gazette*, 21 August.

Ebenezer Hazard to Jeremy Belknap, New York, 7 August (excerpt)[1]

Congress have been a week debating about the place for the new Congress to *meet* at. Philadelphia was proposed and lost it: Lancaster (in Pennsylvania) too. Baltimore carried it, but lost it on reconsideration. New York was inserted in the blank, having 7½ states in its favor. Today Rhode Island refuses to vote on the *whole ordinance*, and all is undone again for the present. I often meet with proofs of Solomon's wisdom.

1. RC, Belknap Papers, MHi. Printed: Massachusetts Historical Society *Collections*, 5 Ser., III (1877), 57-58. Belknap, pastor of a Boston church, historian, and founder of the Massachusetts Historical Society, corresponded with many leading political figures.

Benjamin Contee to Levi Hollingsworth, New York, 8 August (excerpt)[1]

I wrote you by last post.[2] The ground, with respect to Baltimore is greatly changed since. It is more uncertain what place may succeed. New York is now in the vote of the House [Congress], but it is doubtful what she must not give way to some p[lace?] more south. I almost give Philadelphia up [———] this question, but no opportunity will be spared.

Colonel [John Eager] Howard, if you happen to see him, can explain to you the cause of Baltimore being struck out.

1. RC, Hollingsworth Papers (supplemental boxes), PHi.
2. 6 August, RC, Hollingsworth Papers, PHi.

Agreement between Abraham Yates, Jr., and the Other New York Delegates, 8 August[1]

Being confident that the Constitution for the general government in its present form will be destructive to the liberties of the people, and as such by every means to be avoided as one of the greatest of all evils, and that the Convention of New York in adopting it without express conditional amendments have been mistaken both in their expectations and apprehensions, I intended upon the ordinance to organize the same to preserve to myself the evidence of a dissent on the final question.

But being now called upon by my colleagues and informed that Messrs. [Ezra] Lehommedieu and [Egbert] Benson must leave this place on Wednesday next to meet the Six Nations; that it is not likely that Mr. [Leonard] Gansevoort, altho wrote for, will then be down; that in the meantime the vote of the state may be called for, and if so cannot be carried without me; that the Convention having adopted the Constitution, my vote cannot be attended with any other inconsistency or inconveniency than that of acting against my private judgment; when the loss of the vote of the state might be attended with the removal of Congress to a place less convenient to the citizens of this state, and less promising to obtain the amendments which the Convention have looked upon indispensably necessary for the security of the liberty and freedom of the people.

In this situation, if the question should be put, and as often as the vote of the state cannot be carried without me, I shall join in the vote to complete the ordinance, being assured that should the vote be put before Messrs. Lehommedieu and Benson go of[f] or after Mr. Gansevoort is arrived they will assist me in getting my dissent entered or to avoid voting in a manner most decent and proper.
Done on Friday 8 August 1788   [s] Abm. Yates Junr.

We do certify that Mr. Yates has delivered to us a paper subscribed by him (of which the preceding is a copy) as declarative of the principles on which he will vote in Congress in the affirmative on the final question on the ordinance for putting the new Constitution for the United States into operation.

                                                [s] Ezra L Hommedieu
                                                [s] Egbt. Benson
                                                [s] Alexander Hamilton

1. ADS, Yates Papers, NN. The first part of the document is in Yates's handwriting and signed by him. The second part of the document, in a different hand, is signed by Ezra L'Hommedieu, Egbert Benson, and Alexander Hamilton. Leonard Gansevoort, the absent delegate, wrote to Stephen Van Rensselaer from Albany on 15 August that "I am under the necessity of repairing to New York early in the succeeding week (having received a letter from Mr. Benson requesting my attendance in Congress)" (RC, Fogg Autograph Collection, MeHi). Yates, despite his continuing opposition to the Constitution, kept his agreement. On 3 September, for example, when he was the only New York delegate present, he voted against a motion to locate the new government at Annapolis, Md. The next day he and Gansevoort voted for a motion to locate the government at a place to be decided upon later, or at the seat of Congress if an agreement could not be reached. He left Congress shortly thereafter and therefore did not vote on the final passage of the Election Ordinance on 13 September.

New York Daily Advertiser, 8 August

Yet it is a time of wonders. In Baltimore, it is a wonder why that town should not be the seat of government. In New York, it is a wonder why the government should be removed. The Pennsylvanians wonder that any city should be thought of for the seat of empire but Philadelphia. They wish themselves the arbiters of the continent, and wonder that everybody does not wish so too.

Henry Lee to Richard Henry Lee, New York, 10 August (excerpt)[1]

Congress are yet engaged concerning the temporary residence of the federal government. New York will probably succeed, notwithstanding the ardent love which so many bear to Philadelphia and therefore Potomac will have a good chance for the permanent residence. At all events I think that the ten miles square may be to the south of the Susquehanna which will assist in its consequences very much the trade of the Chesapeake.[2]

1. RC, Lee Family Papers, ViU.
2. William Knox informed Henry Knox the same day that "the different parties in Congress for and against Philadelphia as the seat of government still expect to contest this subject" (New York, RC, Knox Papers, MHi).

James Madison to George Washington, New York, 11 August[1]

I have been duly favored with yours of the 3d. instant.[2] The length of the interval since my last has proceeded from a daily expectation of being able to communicate the final arrangements for introducing the new government. The place of meeting has undergone much discussion as you conjectured and still remains to be fixed. Philadelphia was first named and negatived by a voice from Delaware. New York came forward next. Lancaster was opposed to it and failed. Baltimore was next tried and to the surprise of every one had seven votes. It was easy to see that that ground, had it been free from objections, was not maintainable. Accordingly the next day New York was inserted in the place of it with the aid of the vote of Rhode Island. Rhode Island however has refused to give a final vote in the business and has actually retired from Congress. The question will be resumed between New York and Philadelphia. It was much to be wished that a fit place for a respectable outset to the government could be found more central than either. The former is inadmissible if any regard is to be had to the Southern or Western country. It is so with me for another reason, that it tends to stop the final and permanent seat short of the Potomac certainly, and probably in the state of New Jersey. I *know* this to be one of the views of the advocates for New York. The only chance the Potomac has is to get things in such a train that a coalition may take place between the Southern and Eastern states on the subject and still more that the final seat may be undecided for two or three years, within which period the Western and South Western population will enter more into the estimate. Wherever Congress may be, the choice if speedily made will not be sufficiently influenced by that consideration. In this point of view I am of opinion Baltimore would have been unfriendly to the true object. It would have retained Congress but a moment; so many states being north of it, and dissatisfied with it, and would have produced a coalition among those states and a precipitate election of the permanent seat and an intermediate removal to a more northern position.

You will have seen the Circular Letter from the Convention of this state.[3] It has a most pestilent tendency. If an early general convention cannot be parried, it is seriously to be feared that the system which has resisted so many direct attacks may be at last successfully undermined by its enemies. It is now perhaps to be wished that Rhode Island may not accede till this new crisis of danger be over. Some think it would have been better if even New York had held out till the operation of the government could have dissipated the fears which artifice had created, and the attempts resulting from those fears and artifices. We hear nothing yet from North Carolina more than comes by the way of Petersburg.[4]

1. RC, Washington Papers, DLC. Madison wrote similar letters to Thomas Jefferson, 10 August (Boyd, XIII, 497-99) and to Edmund Randolph, 11 August (RC, Madison Papers, DLC).
2. Printed above.
3. Circular Letter of the New York Convention, 26 July, printed above.
4. Washington's reply of 17 August is printed below.

Alexander Hamilton to Jeremiah Olney, New York, 12 August[1]

We have a question of very great importance depending in Congress, in which the vote of your state would be decisive. It relates to the place of meeting of the future Congress—six states and a half prefer New York five and a half Philadelphia. When your delegates were here they voted with us on the intermediate questions; but when the final question came to be put Mr. [Jonathan J.] Hazard's scruples prevailed over his inclination for New York. He however gave me to hope he would return in a short time. Mr. [Peleg] Arnold would have made no difficulty whatever if his colleague would have gone with him; but he could not be prevailed upon to do it.

This is a matter of such moment not only to this state but to the Northern

States in general that I have taken the liberty to address you on the subject, to request that every effort may be made to induce a representation of your state to come forward without loss of time. I am persuaded that the meeting of Congress here or at Philadelphia would make a difference on your politics and would facilitate or impede, as the one or the other place should obtain, the adoption of the Constitution in your state. The intimate intercourse between us and you makes us look up to you as to a natural ally in this matter.

A doubt might perhaps be raised about your right to a vote under the present circumstances. There is not a member of Congress but one who has even *pretended* to call your right in question. Tis agreed generally that the power of organizing the government is given by the ratifying states to the United States in Congress Assembled, who are mere agents under a special authority and therefore the non-adopting states stand on the same footing with the adopting. Nor can the exercise of that right operate in any manner upon your situation. If the United States should even be considered as a foreign power, you might have a choice in such a question.

Hazard I believe is softening, so that I should not think it politic to make any representation of his conduct which might irritate him. What is here said respecting him must therefore be received in confidence as indeed must be this whole letter.

If any difficulty about expense should arise I will with pleasure accept a draft on me. You will excuse this intimation which arises from my information that your state has not made provision for its delegates and from a knowledge that individuals have been torn to pieces by your tender laws etc.[2]

1. Syrett, V, 199-200. Olney was a Rhode Island merchant and a strong Federalist, who was later appointed collector of the Port of Providence by President Washington.

2. Olney received Hamilton's letter 22 August. He replied that since Hamilton's proposal was "extreme delicate," to avoid "the least suspicion" he would draw on "our friend" Colonel [Levi?] Hall for the money if need be. He told Hamilton to explain to Hall "in person" so that he would honor Olney's drafts (Providence, 23 August, Syrett, V, 203-4). Two days later Olney wrote to Hamilton about a talk with Peleg Arnold. "He is zealous in the matter and assures me he will go forward in one of the New York packets by the last of this week. I have wrote Mr. H[azard] on the subject and warmly urged the necessity of his going on with his colleague Mr. A[rnold] and have made him an offer of a draft for 60 dollars on Colonel Hall, which Mr. A[rnold] says will be sufficient as he himself is not in want. I have hopes that Mr. H[azard] will be prevailed on to go, if not I will immediately see one of the other delegates and push the matter with him. I hope you will be able to keep the question off until we are represented" (Providence, 25 August, Syrett, V, 204-5). Arnold was back in Congress by 8 September. Hazard refused to return until after the October session of the legislature, and another delegate could not be sent without special orders from the legislature (Olney to Hamilton, Providence, 10 September, Syrett, V, 215-16).

Maryland Journal, 12 August

By the latest accounts from New York we learn, that Congress, on Tuesday last, were to reconsider the resolution which fixed the meeting of the first Congress at this town. That reconsideration carried, the question will stand again on its original ground, and the merits of the respective places again come under review. If a nearly central situation; if a good market; if houses fit for the reception of the President, foreign ministers, etc. and, above all, a people animated by the pure spirit of Federalism, could have any weight in the determination, we might yet flatter ourselves that this honor was in reserve for Baltimore.[1]

1. The news that Congress had voted for Baltimore on 4 August reached that city by way of a letter from Philadelphia published in the Baltimore *Maryland Journal*, 8 August. Samuel Chase forwarded the news to Governor William Smallwood (n.d., RC, Etting Collection, PHi).

Journals of Congress, Wednesday, 13 August

Congress assembled. Present as yesterday.[1]

The order of the day being called up for putting the Constitution into operation, and the act as amended being read as follows:

"Whereas the Convention assembled in Philadelphia pursuant to the resolution of Congress of the 21st February 1787, did on the 17th of September in the same year report to the United States in Congress Assembled a Constitution for the people of the United States, whereupon Congress on the 28th of the same September, did resolve unanimously that the said report with the resolutions and letter accompanying the same be transmitted to the several legislatures in order to be submitted to a convention of delegates chosen in each state by the people thereof in conformity to the resolves of the Convention made and provided in that case; and whereas the Constitution so reported by the Convention and by Congress transmitted to the several legislatures has been ratified in the manner therein declared to be sufficient for the establishment of the same and such ratifications duly authenticated have been received by Congress and are filed in the office of the secretary; therefore,

"Resolved, that the first Wednesday in January next be the day for appointing Electors in the several states which before the said day shall have ratified the said Constitution; that the first Wednesday in February next be the day for the Electors to assemble in their states and vote for a President and that the first Wednesday in March next be the time for commencing proceedings under the said Constitution; and whereas a central situation would be most eligible for the sitting of the legislature of the United States, if such could be found in a condition to furnish in due time the accommodations necessary for facilitating public business and at the same time free of weighty objections which might render it improper or unlikely to be the seat of government either permanently or until a permanent seat can be agreed on, and whereas the most effectual means of obtaining finally the establishment of the federal government in a convenient central situation is to leave the subject to the deliberate consideration of the future Congress, uninfluenced by undue attachment to any of the places which may stand in competition for preference on so interesting a question and unembarrassed by want of time and means to fix on and prepare the most proper place for this purpose; and whereas the removal of the public offices must be attended with much expense, danger and inconvenience which ought not to be incurred but with a well founded expectation of advantages that may fully counterbalance the same; and whereas no such advantages can be expected from a removal to any place now in a condition to receive the federal legislature; and whereas in addition to the before mentioned reasons unnecessary changes in the seat of government would be indicative of instability in the national councils and therefore highly injurious to the interests as well as derogatory to the dignity of the United States; therefore,

"Resolved, that the city of New York in the state of New York be the place for commencing proceedings under the said Constitution."[2]

On the question to agree to the said act, the yeas and nays being required by Mr. Sedgwick:

New Hampshire			Delaware		
Gilman	ay	ay	Kearny	no	no
Wingate	ay		Mitchell	no	
Massachusetts			Maryland		
Sedgwick	ay		Seney	no	
Dane	ay	ay	Contee	no	no
Otis	ay		Ross	no	
Thatcher	ay		Virginia		
Connecticut			Griffin	no	
Huntington	ay	ay	Madison	no	no
Wadsworth	ay		Carrington	no	
New York			Lee	ay	
L'Hommedieu	ay	ay	South Carolina		
Hamilton	ay		Huger	ay	
New Jersey			Parker	ay	ay
Elmer	ay*		Tucker	ay	
Pennsylvania			Georgia		
Irvine	no		Few	ay	d
Meredith	no	no	Baldwin	no	
Armstrong	no				

So the question was lost.

An ordinance was then moved by Mr. Kearny, seconded by Mr. Contee, which was read in the words following:

"An ordinance for establishing the times for appointing Electors and choosing a President under the new Constitution, with the time and place for commencing proceedings under the said Constitution, agreeably to the resolves, of the Convention assembled in Philadelphia, of the 17 September 1787.

"Whereas the Convention assembled in Philadelphia pursuant to the resolution of Congress of the 21 of February 1787 did on the 17 day of September in the same year report to the United States in Congress Assembled a Constitution or form of government for the people of the United States, whereupon Congress on the 28 day of the same September did resolve unanimously that the said report with the resolutions and letter accompanying the same be transmitted to the several legislatures in order to be submitted to a convention of delegates chosen in each state by the people thereof in conformity to the resolves of the Convention made and provided in that case and whereas the Constitution so reported by the Convention and by Congress transmitted to the several legislatures has been ratified in the manner therein declared to be sufficient for the establishment of the same and such ratifications duly authenticated have been received by Congress and are filed in the office of the secretary thereof;

"Be it therefore ordained by the United States in Congress Assembled that the first Wednesday in January next be the day for appointing Electors in the several states which before the said day shall have ratified the said Constitution, that the first Wednesday in February next be the day for the Electors to assemble in their respective states and vote for a President and that the first Wednesday in March next be the time and _____ the place for commencing proceedings under the said Constitution. Done etc."[3]

On the question shall this ordinance be read a second time, the yeas and nays being required by Mr. Kearny:

New Hampshire			Maryland		
Gilman	no	} no	Seney	ay	
Wingate	no		Contee	ay	} ay
Massachusetts			Ross	ay	
Sedgwick	no		Virginia		
Dane	no	} no	Griffin	ay	
Otis	no		Madison	ay	} ay
Thatcher	no		Carrington	ay	
Connecticut			Lee	no	
Huntington	no	} no	South Carolina		
Wadsworth	no		Huger	no	} no
New York			Parker	no	
L'Hommedieu	no	} d	Georgia		
Hamilton	ay		Few	no	} d
New Jersey			Baldwin	ay	
Elmer	ay*				
Pennsylvania					
Irvine	ay				
Meredith	ay	} ay			
Armstrong	ay				
Delaware					
Kearny	ay	} ay			
Mitchell	ay				

So the question was lost.[4]

1. Present were New Hampshire, Massachusetts, Connecticut, New York, Pennsylvania, Delaware, Maryland, Virginia, North Carolina, South Carolina, and Georgia, and Jonathan Elmer from New Jersey.

2. A copy of the act as amended is in PCC, Item 23, pp. 101-2.

3. This motion is in PCC, Item 23, pp. 97-[98].

4. This vote of Congress was widely reported in the newspapers. The *New York Journal* on 14 August, after giving the vote, said that "from the present complexion there is the greatest reason to hope that the question will finally be carried in favor of New York." This article was reprinted in at least a dozen newspapers, including the Philadelphia *Independent Gazetteer*, 18 August; Boston *Massachusetts Centinel*, 23 August; and *Pittsburgh Gazette*, 30 August. However, the Philadelphia *Pennsylvania Mercury* on 16 August gave a more accurate version in an "Extract of a letter from New York, dated Wednesday, August 13, 12 o'clock," which stated: "Congress have just rejected the measures as they stood. A new ordinance is introduced leaving the place blank—rejected from a second reading. The subject will hereafter be taken up anew."

Edmund Randolph to James Madison, Richmond, 13 August (excerpt)[1]

Inclosed are the first two numbers of the Republican, according to your request.[2]

Governor [George] Clinton's letter to me for the calling of a convention is this day published by my order.[3] It will give contentment to many, who are now dissatisfied. The problem of a new convention has many difficulties in its solution. But upon the whole, I believe the Assembly of Virginia *perhaps* ought, and probably will concur in urging it. It is not too early; because it will only incorporate the theory of the people with the theory of the convention; and each of these theories is entitled to equal respect. I do indeed fear, that the Constitution may be enervated if some states should prevail in all their amendments; but if such be the will of America, who can withstand it? For my own part, I fear that direct taxation may be too much weakened. But I can only endeavor to avert that particular evil, and cannot persuade myself to thwart a second convention merely from the apprehension of that evil. This letter will probably carry me sooner into the Assembly than I intended. I will prepare a draft upon this subject, and forward a copy to you, as soon as I can. My object will be (if possible) to prevent instructions from being conclusive, if any should be offered, and to leave the conventioners perfectly free.[4]

1. RC, Madison Papers, DLC.
2. "Republican's" first letter "To the People of Virginia" appeared in the Richmond *Virginia Independent Chronicle*, 16 July. In the *Chronicle* of 27 August, "Republican" announced the end of the series (see Newspaper Response to New York's Act of Ratification and Circular Letter of 26 July, printed above).
3. The *Virginia Independent Chronicle* of 13 August is missing, but the issue of 20 August printed the last portion of the New York Circular Letter as "continued from our last."
4. Madison's reply of 22 August is printed below.

William Knox to Henry Knox, New York, 14 August (excerpt)[1]

Congress have undone yesterday all they had heretofore done with respect the ordinance, and nothing today has been transacted on the business so that where they will next meet is uncertain. North Carolina has rejected the Constitution by a great majority.

1. RC, Knox Papers, MHi.

George Clymer to Samuel Meredith, Philadelphia, 14 August (excerpt)[1]

By the way, seeing no other argument in favor of the island of New York than its neighborhood to disaffection, why should you not endeavor for a like reason to carry Congress to the big island on the Susquehanna. It has besides a good prospect and a fine fishery and is less liable to the objection of eccentricity. Another argument too in behalf of the latter island—they have never yet that I have heard of set Columbus on horseback or made such execrable verses as we lately have seen at the former.

1. RC, Berol Collection, NNC. Printed: Frederick R. Kirkland, ed., *Letters on the American Revolution in the Library at "Karolfred"* (Philadelphia, 1941), 91. The letter is addressed to "Dear S," but Kirkland identifies the recipient as Samuel Meredith, who was a member of Congress from Pennsylvania. Another excerpt from this letter is printed in Chapter IV.

Mathew Carey to Ebenezer Hazard, Philadelphia, 14 August (excerpt)[1]

Politics are as dull here as with you. We have, for a long time, chameleon-like, fed ourselves on air; and counted the vast fortunes we were all most assuredly to make, by the return of Congress. Some of us, I believe, had fixed on the places where our estates were to be purchased, and settled on the number of years we were to remain in business, favoring the public with our services; but we have awoke, and found it all a dream. "Blessed are they that expect nothing, for they shall never be disappointed."

1. FC, Carey Letterbooks, PHi.

Pennsylvania Mercury, 14 August

It is truly astonishing (says a correspondent) that Congress should divide, or even hesitate about the most suitable place for the residence of the new Congress. The central situation of Pennsylvania should certainly give her the preference to any other state, while the frugal habits of the citizens of Philadelphia render our city the first in the Union, for the seat of a republican government. It is probably from a dread of the superior energy, dignity, and popularity, that the new government will acquire in our city, that the Antifederalists in general, with Rhode Island at the head of them, wish the new Congress to meet anywhere rather than in Philadelphia.

William Bingham to Samuel Meredith, Philadelphia, 15 August[1]

I am much obliged to you for the communications contained in your letter of the 12th inst. I expected that the ordinance would have been rejected by being put to the vote, which was the policy intended to be pursued, when I left New York.

I am at a loss to determine what effect the accounts from North Carolina will have.

If the delegation from South Carolina, and Mr. [William] Few from Georgia, are not too much warped by their prejudices to Philadelphia, it might be expected that they would now concur in the removal further southward, as these two weak and defenseless states must feel a greater confidence by having the government to which they are to look up for protection, situated as near them as possible.

I shall return to New York in a few days.

1. RC, Clymer-Meredith-Read Papers, NN.

South Carolina Delegates to Governor Thomas Pinckney, New York, 16 August (excerpt)[1]

The ratification of the new Constitution by the State of New Hampshire, making the 9th state, having been received, Congress immediately proceeded to the consideration of the measures recommended by the late General Convention as preparatory to the meeting of the new legislature. It is with regret that we find ourselves yet unable to communicate to Your Excellency the final result of the deliberations on this subject. After much time spent in debate on the several periods to be fixed and the place for the first meeting of the new Congress, a set of resolutions were at length completed, which separately obtained the approbation of the House [Congress], but on taking the question upon the whole, it unfortunately passed in the negative, so that the business remains still undetermined. In the resolutions alluded to, the first Wednesday in January next was fixed for the appointment of Electors, the first Wednesday in February for the Electors to assemble in the respective states and give their votes for a President, the first Wednesday in March for the meeting of the new Congress, and the city of New York for the place of meeting. With respect to the periods just mentioned, we flatter ourselves there will be no farther debate, and we are the more inclined to wish so, as we had much difficulty in getting the first (which is the most important) so well adapted to the convenience of our state. It is indeed not entirely as we would have had it, but it is much better than we had reason to expect, considering the impossibility of avoiding inconvenience to many of the states. Under this arrangement our legislature will be enabled to establish any mode they may think proper for the appointment of Electors, without the necessity of either an extraordinary meeting or a protracted session. A day somewhat later in the same month would probably have been more convenient, but that we were not able to obtain. The difference of opinion with regard to the place of meeting, we apprehend, may still occasion some trouble. On this subject we have only to add, that since the commencement of the proceedings thereon, Congress have received the instruments of ratification by the states of Virginia and New York.

1. RC, Dreer Collection, PHi. Signed by Daniel Huger, John Parker, Thomas Tudor Tucker. Printed: LMCC, VIII, 780-82, from a contemporary copy in the Gratz Collection, PHi.

George Washington to James Madison, Mount Vernon, 17-18 August (excerpt)[1]

That the Circular Letter from the Convention of New York should be handed to the public as the unanimous sense of that body has, I must confess, surprised me. It will, I fear, be attended with pernicious consequences. The decision of North Carolina, unaccountable as it is, is not (in my opinion) more to be regretted.
P.S. August 18th.
I had written this letter but had not dispatched it to the post office when your favor of the 11th[2] was brought to me. I am clearly in sentiment with you, that the longer the question on the permanent seat of Congress is delayed, the greater certainty there will be of a central spot for it. But not having the same means of

information and judging that you have, it would have been [a] moot point with me whether a temporary residence of that body at New York would not have been a less likely means of keeping it ultimately from the center (being farther removed from it) than if it was to be at Philadelphia because in proportion as you draw to the center the inconveniences which are felt by the Southern and Western extremities of the Union will be lessened, and of course their anxieties, and when to these are safe added the acquaintances and connections which naturally will be formed, the expenses which more than probably will be incurred for the accommodation of the public officers, with a long train of etceteras it might be found an arduous task to approach nearer to the axis thereafter.

These, however, are first thoughts, and many [sic] not go to the true principles of policy by which the case is governed.[3]

1. FC, Washington Papers, DLC. Printed: Fitzpatrick, XXX, 52-53.

2. Printed above.

3. Washington, like others, was becoming far more concerned with getting the new government under way than with its location (to Benjamin Lincoln, 28 August, printed below). In September, Washington declared that "the present Congress, by its *great* indecision in fixing on a place at which the new Congress is to convene, have hung the expectations, and patience of the Union on tenter hooks, and thereby (if further evidence had been necessary) given a fresh instance of the unfitness of a body so constituted to regulate with energy and precision the affairs of such an extensive empire" (to Samuel Powel, 15 September, FC, Washington Papers, DLC).

Paine Wingate to Timothy Pickering, New York, 18 August (excerpt)[1]

We have lately had a very full Congress consisting of 40 members from the 13 states, a greater number it is said than has been for 12 years past. There have been great disputes where the meeting of the first Congress should be under the new Constitution. The question is not determined and I view it as uncertain but suppose the probability is in favor of New York. Philadelphia and New York are in competition. There are many considerations of weight on both sides and I think nearly balanced. New Hampshire would have been content with Philadelphia and gave their ay for it, when that place was proposed but when 7 states were not agreed in that by means of some Southern States dissenting, we had no objection to New York as being more convenient to the Eastern States, and accordingly voted for that likewise when proposed.

1. RC, Pickering Papers, MHi. Printed: Wingate, *Wingate*, I, 243-45.

William Irvine to Samuel H. Parsons, New York, 18 August (excerpt)[1]

[All the states?] except Rhode Island and North Carolina have adopted the new government. Accounts have just arrived here that the latter have rejected by 100 of a majority in their Convention. Congress have been employed some time on an ordinance for organizing the government, which was all pretty easily gone through til the place of meeting of the new Congress became a question, since which there has been a stagnation; many places have been proposed and rejected, some agreed to then reconsidered, in short there has been on this subject hitherto little spirit of accommodation shown. At present this business is suspended, in part occasioned by a kind of abdication of the Rhode Island delegates, who did not think themselves at liberty to vote on the final question for organizing the government, as their state had rejected, tho they did on the place of meeting. Some say they are to return with instructions, but I hope on that, a greater degree of harmony will prevail. Should this be the case it is not improbable I think that Lancaster in Pennsylvania will be the place, but if *violent* voting is still adhered to, New York will be the place.

1. Copy, Roberts-Irvine Collection, PHi. Irvine was a Pennsylvania delegate to Congress. Parsons was a Connecticut lawyer who served as a Continental officer during the Revolution. Congress appointed him a land commissioner to deal with Indians in the Old Northwest in 1785, and first judge of the Northwest Territory in 1787. He became a director of the Ohio Company in the same year. In April 1788 he moved to the Ohio frontier.

William Bingham to Benjamin Rush, New York, 19 August[1]

I find that some of the advocates for New York begin to be alarmed at the tendency of their perseverance in supporting the pretensions of a place so very improper for the seat of federal government.

If they could have carried the point by a coup de main the public mind would not have had time to be agitated.

The delay has given room for reflection and the more the object is contemplated, the greater appears the injustice, oppression, and partiality that must arise to the Southern States from such an arrangement.

The friends to the federal government, even in the Eastern States, if they wish the tranquillity of the Union, must deprecate the pernicious consequences that will ensue.

It would have a good effect to let it appear, that the views of those who advocate the claim of New York are known out of the doors of Congress. For this purpose I have hurried over a rough piece, which I would wish inserted in Dunlap's paper tomorrow.[2]

The signature does not involve an expectation of much attention to the style. It must be kept an entire secret that I am the author.

It is plain argument divested of personal reflection, and can give no offense.

Care should be taken to have it inserted in several Philadelphia papers, as well as to introduce it in some of those of New York, which possibly can be accomplished thro the agency of the printers.

It is impossible to determine as yet what will be the issue of this business.

1. RC, Alexander Biddle Papers, PHi. The letter is undated, but at the end Bingham wrote "New York Tuesday Morning." Tuesday was the 19th.
2. The piece was evidently "A Member of the Federal Club" in the Philadelphia *Pennsylvania Packet*, 22 August, printed below.

Maryland Gazette (Baltimore), 19 August

The truly federal spirit, says a correspondent, exhibited in the conduct of the state of Maryland, and the town of Baltimore, extended its influence and forwarded the adoption of the new Constitution. Greater unanimity has not been displayed in any state. Strangers and foreigners beheld the pleasing scene with admiration, and expressed their approbation in the most flattering terms.

That the first meeting of Congress, under the new government, would be at Baltimore, was not in the idea of our citizens. They were not actuated by mercenary motives; but the consistency of their proceedings, their singular firmness, and adherence to the federal plan, justly rendered them adequate in their pretensions to continental attention to any other state in the Union.

To a people, conscious of the sincerity of their views, and animated with an ardent desire for the support and permanency of the proposed Constitution, the resolve of Monday, the 4th inst. was extremely pleasing; but we were somewhat chagrined and felt something like insult, on finding that a motion, on the Wednesday following, obliterated the *federal town* of Baltimore, and gave the preference to New York. Maneuvers, similar to these, frequently overset the most salutary resolves, tend to make the ordinances of government inconsistent and variable; from whence too frequently arises that want of dignity and efficiency in public bodies, which has been, with some reason, the subject of universal complaint! But this might have passed unnoticed, if a contemptuous paragraph had not appeared in a New York paper, signifying that the foreign ministers, etc. would not take a pilgrimage to Baltimore after Congress, if they resolved to go thither.[1]

To discover the author of this insignificant paragraph, is not worth the pains of an investigation; the state in which it originated, indicates sufficient to teach us, how offensive Federalism is to some men, and that their exertions are unremitted to destroy it in every stage of its progress. But whatever this scribbler may insinuate against Baltimore, it is beyond his ability to point out any satisfactory reasons, why foreign ministers, etc. should be averse to make a pilgrimage after Congress to a town so truly respectable. There are many cities in Europe, that cannot boast of its advantages, and there are not many in America, more distinguished for their rapid progress and improvements. Its principal streets are well paved, and the appearance of Market Street, and several others, is remarkably elegant. Its prospect from Federal Hill, and other eminences, is equal, if not superior, to most on the continent. The amphitheatrical form of its basin, the perspective of Fell's Point, and many other of its natural beauties, have been justly admired by travelers; but above all, inhospitality was never the characteristic of its inhabitants, which can be proven by the testimony of the first men amongst us, and by the Congress who resided here sometime during the late war. Foreigners have always been treated with delicacy, kindness and attention—witness that friend of our country, the Marquis De la Fayette, and the officers of the French army. The public prints attest the truth. But enough on this subject. Congress may resolve and re-resolve, and not meliorate their choice.

1. No New York printing of the article has been located, but an article in the Elizabethtown *New Jersey Journal*, 6 August, and in other newspapers stated: "Congress we hear, passed a vote on Monday for fixing their temporary residence at Baltimore in the state of Maryland. This measure has given great disgust to the foreign ministers, who, in their dudgeon, declare they will not attend that august body in their pilgrimage to Maryland."

James R. Reid to Tench Coxe, New York, 20 August[1]

On my arrival I made some inquiries into the relative views and strength of the parties on the question lately agitated with so much violent intemperance in Congress. I found them nearly as I had left them, with wounds still smarting and the *cicatrice* unformed; and indeed at present they have the appearance of two fortified camps within view of each other, neither of whom wish to come out of their stronghold. What will be the probable consequence is mere conjecture. The Eastern States seem more anxious (though not more interested) to give immediate operation to the new government than the people of the South. The late rebellion in Massachusetts urges to an immediate transition from this to a better government. The powerful Antifederal influence in this state will not weaken by delay.

We can pretend that the Southern States will be very well accommodated if the new government shall [not] be put in motion until next fall coming a year and in a particular manner the state of Pennsylvania who can lay up a private purse out of her impost. Virginia is also a state of great internal resources and can better her funds by delay. What those arguments may produce depends upon the experiment. This, my dear friend, is a jesuitical policy which grows out of necessity, and is the only weapon with which we can combat an enemy with similar weapons and on similar grounds. Honesty is certainly the best policy but it cannot always be brought fairly into view.

As soon as opinion takes any form, I shall send it to you, if it has but one feature. At present there is no such thing by which we can judge of the event.

1. RC, Coxe Papers, Tench Coxe Section, PHi. The salutation is "My Dear Sir" and no addressee is indicated, but evidently the letter was written to Coxe. Reid was a Pennsylvania delegate to Congress.

From Thomas FitzSimons, Philadelphia, 20 August (excerpt)[1]

I would have wrote to you sometime ago if I had not expected your return, but if you mean to stay till Congress agree where their successors are to meet, I am afraid I shall be deprived for a good while of the pleasure of seeing you.

Without knowing more than any person out of Congress can know it would be impertinent to offer an opinion as to what is best to be done under present circumstances; but on the other hand, those without are better informed of the opinions of people abroad than Congress are. It seems to be a very general one here, that their delaying to make the recommendation pointed out by the new Constitution till the adoption by New York was improper and laid the foundation of all the subsequent cabal, intrigue, and final disappointm[ent], but the delay now is considered by many (and I confess I am one of them) as highly injurious to the common cause. There are moments in public as well as private affairs, which if not improved, are never to be recovered. I fear you are losing that time and giving an opportunity to artful and industrious enemies to counteract all that has been done.

. . . .

I will say nothing as to place. I suppose it must be New York tho I confess I think them least entitled to that honor. I think too Pennsylvania may have it in her power to retaliate severely in some of those who have so rancorously opposed her; but at any rate let us not lose the fruit of all our former exertions and remain the scoff of every other country.

1. RC, John Read, Jr., Papers, PPL. No addressee is indicated and there is no signature, for the end of the letter is missing. The handwriting is that of Thomas FitzSimons. The letter was written to a member of Congress, probably Samuel Meredith, for other letters to Meredith are in the Read Papers. Other portions of this letter are printed in Chapter IV.

Robert Morris to Samuel Meredith, Philadelphia, 20 August (excerpt)[1]

If Congress permit the ordinance for the new government to sleep much longer they will probably meet the reproaches of the major part of the people of America. The sole consideration that ought to influence the determination of place for the meeting of the new government should be which is the properest place for them, not which is most agreeable to the interest or humor of the members of the present Congress. However, I don't care much how this question is determined but I think it ought to be soon *determined*.

1. RC, Clymer-Meredith-Read Papers, NN.

Massachusetts Centinel, 20 August

"Great bodies move slow"—or it would seem, says a correspondent, that Congress have had time sufficient, since the ratification by nine states, of framing an act for putting the new government into operation. The delay does not give satisfaction to the masters of Congress, The People, who scruple not to attribute it to motives, which it is to be hoped do not exist.[1]

1. This piece was reprinted several times (see, for example, the Hartford *Connecticut Courant*, 25 August; *New York Morning Post*, 28 August; and Philadelphia *Pennsylvania Gazette*, 3 September).

Thomas B. Wait to George Thacher, Portland, Maine, 21 August (excerpt)[1]

Why, my friend, do you contend so warmly for New York, as the seat of government? Do you, in this, act the part of a *true Federal Philosopher*? We should remember the question is not, what will be most convenient or best suit the interest of New England, but what does the interest of the Union require? How shall that be accommodated? But this last I suppose would be an odd question in Congress. There, it is the *Southern* interest, or the *Northern*; and every man of them ranges himself upon one side or the other, and contends with as much earnestness and warmth as if at an Olympic game.

Well, fight it out; and I will have the pleasure of standing aloof, looking on and making *now and then* an observation on the squabble. One remark now, if you please, or rather a query: will not this clashing of interest produce a creation of *new* and a division, and subdivision of the *old* states? A *diminution* of state influence will follow in exact proportion to *which* the power and consequence of Congress will be increased. Curse on the prospect. It does not please me, so I will say no more about it.

1. RC, Thacher Papers, MB. Printed: *Historical Magazine*, XVI, 350. Wait was the publisher of the Portland, Me., *Cumberland Gazette*.

James Madison to Edmund Randolph, New York, 22 August[1]

I have your favor of the 13th. The effect of [Governor George] Clinton's Circular Letter in Virginia does not surprise me. It is a signal of concord and hope to the enemies of the Constitution everywhere, and will I fear prove extremely dangerous. Notwithstanding your remarks on the subject I cannot but think that an *early* convention will be an unadvised measure. It will evidently be the offspring of party and passion, and will probably for that reason alone be the parent of error and public injury. It is pretty clear that a majority of the people of the Union are in favor of the Constitution as it stands, or at least are not dissatisfied with it in that form; or if this be not the case it is at least clear that a greater proportion unite in that system than are likely to unite in any other theory. Should radical alterations take place therefore they will not result from the deliberate sense of the people, but will be obtained by management, or extorted by menaces, and will be a real sacrifice of the public will as well as of the public good, to the views of individuals and perhaps the ambition of the state legislatures.

Congress have come to no final decision as to the place for convening the new government. It is unfortunately become a question now between North and South, and notwithstanding the palpable unreasonableness of the thing, an adherence to New York in preference to any more central position seems to grow stronger and stronger, and upon grounds which tend to keep Congress here till a permanent seat be established. In this point of view I own the business has a serious aspect considering the injustice and oppression to the Southwestern and Western parts of the Union.[2]

1. RC, Madison Papers, DLC. No addressee is indicated, but the letter is clearly a reply to Randolph's letter of 13 August, printed above.
2. Randolph's reply of 3 September is printed below.

James Sullivan to George Thacher, Boston, 22 August (excerpt)[1]

We are generally attentive in this town to the question where the seat of the federal government is to be. The general opinion is that you ought by no means to agree upon Philadelphia for the first meeting of the new arranged Congress, because the government if it meets in a large city will take a style instead of giving one. If it meets there it will not be easily removed to a more central and convenient place, but if it meets at New York a removing will be easily effected. When we cast our eye on the map of the Union and consider the extent westward we should, I think, conceive the Potomac the central place. A river navigable into the country two hundred miles including the Chesapeake will, I believe, invite to the building a metropolis where packets may have access and where an army or fleet cannot reach in hostility before the whole country is subdued. Why the members of the Southern States vote for Philadelphia unless they intend to fix Congress finally there I do not conceive.

1. RC, Fogg Autograph Collection, MeHi. Printed: *Historical Magazine*, XVI, 350. Sullivan, a Boston lawyer, was prominent in Massachusetts politics.

A Member of the Federal Club, Pennsylvania Packet, 22 August

I am a plain unlettered man, but a good Federalist,[1] and strongly attached to the Constitution and form of government established by the Convention.

I belong to a club that meet every evening, where none but federal liquors are introduced, such as Hare's porter, Haines's beer, or Jones's cider.

It is said that it requires some previous tuition to make a cobbler, but that every man thinks himself born a politician; this is literally the case with our club. But although we freely discuss all subjects of a public nature, we admit no crooked or eccentric paths in our politics. We endeavor to square our opinions by the straight lines of plain reason.

We have been lately much agitated with the question, concerning the place where the federal government is to be convened, which we think ought to have been determined as soon as nine states had ratified, but which we find is not as yet decided. This delay has given a great alarm, and has begun to create a very considerable clamor through the country.

Our first conjecture was, that an attempt was made to arrest the progress of this business, and that Congress was not willing to sign its own death warrant, or if it must die, like Macheath in the opera, it would die hard, and not part with its existence without a struggle. This was soon found to be an Antifederal report.

However, we have since been informed, that the contest in Congress is concerning the place where the new government is to be convened.

The dictates of common sense induced us to believe, that Philadelphia being the place where the first Congress was assembled, and where the Federal Convention was appointed to meet, would be preferred, until a permanent residence was fixed by Congress, more particularly, as we never heard that any state had expressed a dissatisfaction with this arrangement.

But we find that the city of New York claims a preference over Philadelphia, Lancaster, and Baltimore, which places, we understand, have been successively in nomination. We have examined the pretensions of this city, and the causes that could lead its friends to advocate them.

Some of our club, Messrs. Printers, are mechanics, who are in the habit of rearing their superstructures on solid foundations; they therefore require that arguments addressed to them, must be well supported.

We began with an examination of the letter addressed to Congress, by the President of the Convention, when the Constitution was transmitted, in which he informs them that a spirit of amity and of mutual deference and concession alone induced so unanimous a concurrence to this plan of government, which the diversity of state interests seemed rather calculated to preclude. It was but a reasonable expectation, that the same spirit would actuate Congress, and that the first act of government would indicate a disposition to impart equal advantages and accommodations to every part of the Union, that consequently the government would be assembled to commence proceedings in the place, nearest the center of national population.

The Convention has furnished a rule by which the relative situation of each state, in this respect, may be determined, which is, by the number of Representatives, that it is entitled to send to the federal legislature. We examined the pretensions of New York by this scale, and found that there were but 17 Representatives from the states to the northward, and as many as forty-two from those to the southward, which calculated by 40,000^2 to each Representative makes 680,000 inhabitants on one side, and 1,980,000^3 on the other. We found likewise that the extreme part of the district from which the 168,000 are to come, amount to above 1000 miles and on the opposite side to about 350 miles. Such an arrangement militates against every principle of republican government, and of the Federal Constitution, which was instituted for the purpose of promoting the general welfare, and of securing equal rights to the people. It must involve the Southern States in the greatest inconvenience, from the number of persons that will have business to transact with the federal government, and the federal judiciary, who must travel such a great distance beyond the central point.

Besides, the more Southern States, which are in the neighborhood of continual danger from their contiguity to hostile tribes of Indians, as well as to foreign nations, and which are so weak and defenseless, must complain at having the power of that government exercised at such a distance, whose protection alone can insure them tranquility; and in case of domestic insurrections, or external invasions, the necessary assistance must be delayed, in proportion to the time it will take in soliciting it. The essential communications betwixt the Southern members of the federal legislature and their constituents will be greatly obstructed by placing Congress in such an eccentric position; and these communications will be required with the greater solicitude, as the states, having resigned such considerable powers in favor of the federal government, will be impatient to know in what manner they will be affected by the exercise of them, in the organization of the new system. The great and complicated interests of the Western Country, where new settlements are forming that will soon rise into independent states, demand a pointed attention, and require Congress to be placed in a central situation.

We know, Messrs. Printers, that the Southern and Northern parts of the Union have interests and pursuits essentially different. The former, consisting chiefly of planters and consumers, and the latter of agricultural, commercial, and manufacturing people.

We have been told, that the Southern delegates in the Convention, with great reluctance yielded to a bare majority the powers of regulating commerce, from an apprehension that a combination of states that had similar interests might be easily formed, which by partial operations of government, could greatly oppress the Southern district of the Union.

We find, that this has been the popular topic of declamation, to work on the passions of the people, in the Southern conventions, and we discover that Virginia has founded one of her proposed amendments on her fears on this subject. We are likewise told, that Patrick Henry so much deprecated the pernicious effects that might arise to Virginia from the exercise of this power, that he concluded a most eloquent harangue, by saying, that he would narrowly watch its tendency, with the eye of an eagle, watching its prey.

If the strength and connection of the Northern members of the Confederacy have already created such great alarm in the Southern States, why should it be increased by placing Congress in the midst of this district, thereby throwing all the influence of government in the scale that is already thought to be preponderant.

This local influence must be immense when it is considered that the numerous appointments of officers under government will be generally confined to the inhabitants of the surrounding district, they being on the spot to solicit, and by personal application and address to enforce their pretensions.

The revenues of the Confederacy, drawn from all parts of the Union, will be mostly expended in the adjacent country, to the great benefit and emolument of those states, which approach nearest to the seat of government; and in the discussion of great points which involve peculiar advantages to the Northern parts of the Union, the ease of obtaining a full representation of their members, so as to insure a decided majority, is certainly a cause of serious apprehension to the Southern States.

I have been told, Messrs. Printers, that the kings of England have much increased the powers of the executive authority, since they have been compelled to exchange the stern voice of prerogative, for the more persuasive accents of influence; this influence must exist in every government, in proportion to the extent of its powers and of its revenue system; and its effects must be greatly felt in the districts which approach the place where the government is administered.

To prevent the appearances of local aggrandizement operating at the expense of public interests, it becomes absolutely necessary to place the government in the center of the Union, that its benefits and advantages may be equally diffused.

I cannot expect, Messrs. Printers, that the sentiments of a plain man, like myself, can have any effect on the opinions of those great statesmen in Congress that hold the reins of government. But it certainly would be expedient at this critical period of our affairs, to sacrifice points of lesser magnitude, to preserve the Union.

How can the Northern States expect a ready concurrence of the Southern, in granting a monopoly of the carrying trade, in establishing high duties on the importation of such articles from Europe, as they manufacture and can supply the Southern States with, in the attainment of great advantages in commercial treaties, when their first agency in an act of government that has a view to the new system involves partiality and injustice as it regards the Southern States, and must create in them, a spirit of discord and disunion, instead of a temper of harmony and conciliation, and which must necessarily operate in the formation of the first acts of legislation.

It will be said that the delegates from a Southern State, acquiesce in the obnoxious derangement; individuals may err but the people can never be mistaken, for their language is always governed by their interests; and what the interests of that state are, viewing its local position, taking into consideration its surrender of powers to the general government, will not admit of a moment's hesitation to decide.

It is really time this important question was determined. Every Federalist throughout the Union laments and deprecates the consequences of delay. Every Antifederalist rejoices in it, as most conducive to the purposes of confusion.

It will not be surprising that New York obstinately adheres to her pretensions; but it is to be expected that the other states, less interested in the event, will possess a more accommodating spirit, and put an end to a contest that has disgraced the councils of the nation, and must terminate, if longer pursued, in the most dreadful consequences to the Union.

1. William Bingham was evidently the author (see Bingham to Benjamin Rush, 19 August, printed above, and Thomas Willing to Bingham, 27 August, printed below). The essay was reprinted in the *New York Journal*, 4 September. An article using similar arguments appeared in the Philadelphia *Pennsylvania Packet*, 25 August.

2. The constitutional provision was one Representative for each 30,000 inhabitants, not 40,000. This error was repeated in later newspaper pieces (see, for example, the *Pennsylvania Packet*, 1 September, printed below).

3. The correct figure here and in the next line as well should be 1,680,000.

James Madison to George Washington, New York, 24 August[1]

I was yesterday favored with yours of the 17th, 18th,[2] under the same cover with the papers from Mr. Pleasants. The Circular Letter from this state is certainly a matter of as much regret, as the unanimity with which it passed is matter of surprise.[3] I find it is everywhere, and particularly in Virginia, laid hold of as the signal for united exertions in pursuit of early amendments. In Pennsylvania the Antifederal leaders are, I understand, soon to have a meeting at Harrisburg in order to concert proper arrangements on the part of that state.[4] I begin now to accede to the opinion, which has been avowed for some time by many: that the circumstances involved in the ratification of New York will prove more injurious than a rejection would have done. The latter would have rather alarmed the well-meaning Antifederalists elsewhere, would have had no ill effect on the other party, would have excited the indignation of the neighboring states, and would have been necessarily followed by a speedy reconsideration of the subject. I am not able to account for the concurrence of the Federal part of the Convention in the circular address, on any other principle than the determination to purchase an immediate ratification in any form and at any price, rather than disappoint this city of a chance for the new Congress. This solution is sufficiently justified by the eagerness displayed on this point, and the evident disposition to risk and sacrifice everything to it. Unfortunately the disagreeable question continues to be undecided and is now in a state more perplexing than ever. By the last vote taken, the whole arrangement was thrown out, and the departure of Rhode Island, and the refusal of North Carolina to participate further in the business, has left eleven states only to take it up anew. In this number there are not seven states for any place, and the disposition to relax, as usually happens, decreases with the progress of the contest. What and when the issue is to be is really more than I can foresee. It is truly mortifying that the outset of the new government should be immediately preceded by such a display of locality as portends the continuance of an evil which has dishonored the old, and gives countenance to some of the most popular arguments which have been inculcated by the Southern Antifederalists.

New York has appeared to me extremely objectionable on the following grounds. It violates too palpably the simple and obvious principle that the seat of public business should be made as equally convenient to every part of the public as the requisite accommodations for executing the business will permit. This consideration has the more weight, as well on account of the catholic spirit professed by the Constitution, as of the increased resort which it will require from every quarter of the continent. It seems to be particularly essential that an eye should be had in all our public arrangements to the accommodation of the Western Country, which perhaps cannot be sufficiently gratified at any rate, but which might be furnished with new fuel to its jealousy by being summoned to the seashore, and almost at one end of the continent. There are reasons, but of too confidential a nature for any other than verbal communication, which make it of critical importance that neither cause nor pretext should be given for distrusts in that quarter of the policy towards it in this. I have apprehended also that a preference so favorable to the Eastern States would be represented in the Southern as a decisive proof of the preponderance of that scale, and a justification of all the Antifederal arguments drawn from that danger. Adding to all this the recollection that the first year or two will produce all the great arrangements under the new system, and which may fix its tone for a long time to come, it seems of real importance that the temporary residence of the new Congress, apart from its relation to the final residence, should not be thrown too much towards one extremity of the Union. It may, perhaps, be the more necessary to guard against suspicions of partiality in this case, as the early measures of the new government, including a navigation act, will of course be most favorable to this extremity.

But I own that I am much influenced by a view to the final residence, which I conceive more likely to be properly chosen in Philadelphia than in New York. The extreme eccentricity of the latter will certainly, in my opinion, bring on a premature, and consequently an improper choice. This policy is avowed by some of the sticklers for this place, and is known to prevail with the bulk of them. People from the interior parts of Georgia, South Carolina, North Carolina, and Virginia, and Kentucky will never patiently repeat their trips to this remote situation, especially as the legislative sessions will be held in the winter season. Should no other consequence take place than a frequent or early agitation of this contentious subject, it would form a strong objection against New York.

Were there reason to fear a repugnance to the establishment of a final seat, or a choice of a commercial city for the purpose, I should be strongly tempted to shun Philadelphia at all events. But my only fear on the first head is of a precipitancy in carrying that part of the Federal Constitution into effect, and on the second the public sentiment, as well as other considerations, is so fixedly opposed as to banish the danger from my apprehensions. Judging from my own experience on this subject I conclude that from motives of one sort or another ten states at least (that is 5 from each end of the Union) to say nothing of the Western States, will, at any proper time, be ready to remove from Philadelphia. The only difficulty that can arise will be that of agreeing on the place to be finally removed to, and it is from that difficulty alone, and the delay incident to it, that I derive my hope in favor of the banks of the Potomac. There are some other combinations on this subject into which the discussion of it has led me, but I have already troubled you with more I fear than may deserve your attention.

The newspapers herewith inclosed contain the European intelligence brought by the last packets from England.

1. RC, Washington Papers, DLC. The previous day Madison had written in a similar vein to Thomas Jefferson (Boyd, XIII, 539-41).
2. Printed above.
3. The New York Circular Letter, 26 July, is printed above.
4. Documents relating to the Harrisburg Convention, 3-6 September, are printed in Chapter IV. This meeting of leading Pennsylvania Antifederalists created alarm in the minds of such men as James Madison, who looked upon it as further proof of the mischief created by the Circular Letter of the New York Convention (to Washington, 14 September, printed below).

William Bingham to Tench Coxe, New York, 25 August[1]

The spirit which now exists in Congress is of such a nature, as to require reasons more forcible than the strength of personal or party views, to eradicate it.

Nothing can more effectually induce the advocates for New York to abandon the pretensions of this place, than to find the public mind agitated on the subject of the delay, and the public voice clamorous for a more equitable and impartial arrangement.

The only method to answer this purpose is to awaken the people in the Eastern States and in South Carolina to a sense of the unjust views of their delegates in Congress, and to the pernicious consequences that may result to the Union, from the pursuit of such measures.

You have an extensive correspondence, and will have the means of answering such views, without the appearance of design.

The legislature of Jersey is to meet this week. It is an essential object to induce them to instruct their delegates to vote in favor of a more central and southern position that they may no longer concur in the support of a measure, which has in view local aggrandizement, at the expense of general interests.

From the attachment that exists in Jersey to the Federal Constitution, much is expected from their legislature. What they will decide on will give the *ton* to the other states, when delegates have voted for New York; which renders it an object of essential consequence, to gain their suffrages in our favor.

As Dunlap's paper [*Pennsylvania Packet*] and Hall's [*Pennsylvania Gazette*] have an extensive circulation, it would be very politic to insert paragraphs on this subject, which would be transposed into other gazettes, and have an excellent tendency. I have wrote a few, which I enclose you for the purpose, and would recommend that whenever anything of this nature is published, the papers should be transmitted to all the states.[2]

But these arrangements must be kept secret, or they will lose their effect.

1. RC, Coxe Papers, Tench Coxe Section, PHi. The salutation is "Dear Sir" and no addressee is indicated, but the letter was evidently written to Coxe.
2. For an earlier publication by Bingham, see "A Member of the Federal Club," *Pennsylvania Packet*, 22 August, printed above. No further publications by Bingham can be positively identified, but see the *Pennsylvania Packet*, 1 September, printed below, for items using the same arguments Bingham had used previously.

William Ellery to Benjamin Huntington, Newport, 25 August (excerpt)[1]

The little sister left you in the lurch. New York influenced our delegates to vote that the new Congress should meet there, and Pennsylvania I suppose persuaded them to leave Congress before a vote was taken on the whole ordinance.

Mr. [Jonathan J.] Hazard I am informed has said that if they had tarried they should not have voted on the ordinance. Indeed our delegates voting at all in a matter that regarded the new Constitution has exposed them to the censure of the Antifederalists, and Hazard has had recourse to leasing [i.e., lying] to justify his conduct.

He has said that he objected to voting with respect to the place of the meeting of the new Congress, and that Mr. [Alexander] Hamilton got that part of the ordinance altered so that the question respected only the present Congress.

He declared on his arrival, in our main street before a number of people, that if the new Congress would sit here for three years, he would be for the new Constitution; and the country people he has told that the adoption of it would be the destruction of the state, that the New England delegates have allowed that the Eastern States have been taken in by the Southern States, and that they repent their having embraced the new Constitution.

That this state by standing out may derive great benefits in point of trade, that he can procure as many British bottoms as the merchants may want, that out ports may be free, that this state has been imposed upon, that we have been called upon for a fiftieth part of the expense of the war, when in fact we ought not to pay more than a two hundredths part, etc. etc. etc. It is said that when he was at New York he was frequently with Mr. [John] Temple.[2]

If you expect that this state will join you in endeavoring to put an end to any dispute about the new Constitution you will be deceived. They had at present much rather foment, than conciliate. What they may do hereafter I cannot positively say, but I think they will be compelled to come in, and make a part of the federal government. If the determination on the place for the meeting of the Congress under the new government, could establish their future residence I should not wonder that a dispute about the place should run high; but as the new Congress, after they are organized, may adjourn to what place they please, I hope that the obstinacy of competitors will not delay the organization beyond the period which was candidly and accommodatingly agreed to. It is of the utmost importance that the new government should be organized as soon as possible. It is high time that we had an efficient government. We are all afloat, trade almost at an end, fraud and injustice triumph over truth and honesty, and discord and confusion have taken the place in some states, of peace and good order. There must be an accommodation with regard to place as well as time. The interest of the United States must not be sacrificed to the obstinacy of any two ratifying states. You may perhaps agree in a third place where it is probable the new government will not fix, and thus it may be left with them to decide between Pennsylvania and New York.

Suppose this should be the place of the first meeting of the new Congress. Neither of those states could be jealous of the little W--h--r--.

1. RC, Thomas C. Bright Autograph Collection, Jervis Library, Rome, N.Y. Ellery, a Rhode Island lawyer and signer of the Declaration of Independence, served several times in the Confederation Congress, and in 1788 was commissioner of the Continental Loan Office in

Rhode Island. In 1790 President Washington appointed him collector of the Port of Newport, a post he held until he died in 1820. Huntington, a Connecticut delegate to the Confederation Congress, was elected to the first House of Representatives in 1788.

2. John Temple, a member of the American Board of Customs Commissioners before the Revolution and a son-in-law of James Bowdoin of Massachusetts, was appointed British Consul General in 1785.

Journals of Congress, Tuesday, 26 August

Congress assembled. Present New Hampshire, Massachusetts, Connecticut, New York, New Jersey, Pennsylvania, Delaware, Maryland, Virginia, North Carolina, South Carolina and Georgia.

A motion being made by Mr. Sedgwick,[1] seconded by Mr. Clark, in the words following:

"Whereas the Federal Convention assembled in Philadelphia, pursuant to a resolution of Congress of the 21st of February 1787, did on the 17th of September last report to the United States in Congress Assembled, a form of government; and whereas the said form of government hath been adopted in the manner therein declared necessary for the ratification thereof, and thereby become the Constitution of the states adopting the same,

"Resolved, that the city of New York in the state of New York being the seat of the present federal government, be the place for commencing proceedings under the said Constitution.

"Resolved, that the first Wednesday in January next be the day for appointing Electors in the several states, which before that time shall have adopted the said Constitution; that the first Wednesday in February next be the day for the said Electors to assemble in their respective states, and vote for a President; and that the first Wednesday in March next be the time for commencing proceedings under the Constitution aforesaid."

The first resolution being under debate a motion was made by Mr. Kearny, seconded by Mr. Mitchell, to strike out the words "the city of New York in the state of New York, being the seat of the present federal government," and in lieu thereof to insert, "Wilmington in the state of Delaware." And on the question to agree to this amendment, the yeas and nays being required by Mr. Kearny:

New Hampshire			New York		
Gilman	no	} no	Hamilton	no	} no
Wingate	no		Gansevoort	no	
Massachusetts			New Jersey		
Sedgwick	ay		Clark	no	} no
Dane	no	} no	Dayton	no	
Thatcher	no		Pennsylvania		
Connecticut			Irvine	ay	
Huntington	no	} no	Meredith	ay	} ay
Wadsworth	no		Bingham	ay	
			Reid	ay	

Delaware				South Carolina		
Kearny	ay	ay		Huger	no	
Mitchell	ay			Parker	no	no
Maryland				Tucker	no	
Seney	ay	ay		Georgia		
Ross	ay			Few	no	d
Virginia				Baldwin	ay	
Griffin	ay					
Madison	ay	ay				
Carrington	ay					

So the question was lost.

On the question to agree to the resolution as moved, the yeas and nays being required by Mr. Sedgwick:

New Hampshire				Virginia		
Gilman	ay	ay		Griffin	no	
Wingate	ay			Madison	no	no
Massachusetts				Carrington	no	
Sedgwick	ay			South Carolina		
Dane	ay	ay		Huger	ay	
Thatcher	ay			Parker	ay	ay
Connecticut				Tucker	ay	
Huntington	ay	ay		Georgia		
Wadsworth	ay			Few	ay	d
New York				Baldwin	no	
Hamilton	ay	ay				
Gansevoort	ay					
New Jersey						
Clark	ay	ay				
Dayton	ay					
Pennsylvania						
Irvine	no					
Meredith	no					
Bingham	no	no				
Reid	no					
Delaware						
Kearny	no	no				
Mitchell	no					
Maryland						
Seney	no	no				
Ross	no					

So the question was lost.

1. A draft of this motion is in PCC, Item 23, pp. 103-6.

Abraham Clark to Governor William Livingston, New York, 26 August[1]

I am unable to say when the act of Congress for putting the new government into operation will be agreed to. The matter was taken up in Congress as soon as nine states had ratified, but the Convention of New York being then setting, in which two thirds of the members were opposed to the new Constitution, it was thought unadvisable to proceed in the business at that time further than agreeing upon the time to choose Electors, the time for them to meet to elect a President and Vice President, and the time of meeting of the new Congress: but the place of meeting was purposely delayed until the New York Convention should come to some final determination. Two reasons induced Congress to this delay. First that New York could not be fixed upon as the place unless they ratified. Secondly, to appoint any other place while they were deliberating would, in all probability insure a final rejection, to prevent which it was suffered to pass as a very probable event, if not as a matter of certainty, that in case they did adopt, New York would be the place of meeting. This perhaps was one principal cause of their adopting, and without their being led into this opinion I believe they would have rejected the Constitution. In this business I feel no particular attachment in favor of New York, nor as they have adopted the new Constitution whereby all former grounds of complaint are removed, ought I as a member from New Jersey to retain any resentment. I am influenced by other motives; for as it was a very important and desirable object to have this state become a member of the new government, so it is necessary for Congress to act in such a manner as to avoid the charge of deceiving the state in what I consider well-grounded expectations. Besides, all our public offices are here and cannot be removed without a great expense which our treasury cannot conveniently defray; and after all we might go to a place the new Congress might disapprove of as a temporary residence. New Jersey laying between New York and Philadelphia are equally contiguous to each and at this time in that point of view ought not to give a preference to either, such as a removal from one to the other. The same reason would hold good against removing to New York were Congress at Philadelphia; to which I may add, that a removal to Philadelphia would be losing all chance of having the permanent seat of government fixed near the falls of Delaware as formerly agreed to, which is an object New Jersey ought not to lose sight of so long as a probable chance remains.[2] To go to Philadelphia before the future seat of government is fixed on, will be giving up all prospects of this kind, as there will not be a probability of obtaining it to the northward of the place Congress shall be in at the time. They may go from hence to the Delaware near Trenton, Pennsylvania may as formerly join in such a measure, but never will if Congress are at Philadelphia. These are reasons that induced me to give New York the preference. Should the delegation of New Jersey join in favor of Philadelphia, it would be of no avail; it would only make an equal division of the states. There would in that case be five states and a half for New York, and the same number for Philadelphia, as eleven only vote upon the occasion, and no more can be expected unless Rhode Island comes forward in favor of New York as is expected. The delegation of North Carolina will not vote on the question.

As there may be different opinions in the legislature respecting the conduct of their delegates on this question, I have taken the liberty to request Your Excellency to communicate to both houses this statement of the principal reasons that influenced my conduct, which I trust will be satisfactory. The several votes will appear in the Journals of Congress sent forward by the secretary.

In order to accommodate all the states we were obliged to place the times for electing etc. at periods much more distant than were necessary for New Jersey. Some legislatures could not be convened earlier than November, none except the present meeting in New Jersey will be before some time in October. Should the business be delayed some time longer in Congress (which it is wished may not be long) no inconvenience will happen, provided the same go to the states by the time they meet in October.

1. RC, William Livingston Papers, MHi. Clark was a New Jersey delegate to Congress.

2. Speaker Ephraim Harris called a special session of the New Jersey legislature which met from 27 August to 9 September. Both Philadelphia and New York interests exerted pressure on the legislature to instruct the state's delegation to favor one city or the other. The journal of the session contains no reference to instructions, but Nathan Dane in a letter to Theodore Sedgwick, 13 September (printed below) said that the legislature approved the conduct of the delegation which had been supporting New York (see also Alexander Hamilton to William Livingston, 29 August; Thomas Willing to William Bingham, 29 August; and Abraham Ogden to Nicholas Low, 7 September, printed below). Although the New Jersey delegates in Congress and political leaders in the state supported New York, their hope was to locate the permanent seat of government in New Jersey. Between 6 and 9 September the New Jersey legislature agreed unanimously to an act granting a ten-mile square to the United States.

James R. Reid to Tench Coxe, New York, 3 o'clock, 26 August[1]

At 12 o'clock this day the advocates for New York came into the field with many whereas's and took a question for the city of New York as the residence for the new Congress. They lost it. They will lick their sores till tomorrow. We are firm and redoubtable, nor have we come out of our works.

I will write you more particularly tomorrow. The opposition seem very *anxious* to give immediate operation, etc.

1. RC, Coxe Papers, Tench Coxe Section, PHi.

Thomas Tudor Tucker to St. George Tucker, New York, 26 August (excerpt)[1]

I am in appointment for as much of the next federal year as will run out the present Constitution, which probably will expire in the beginning of March, for that is the time which has long been agreed on in Congress for the meeting of the new legislature, but being very much divided concerning the place no act on the subject has yet obtained final approbation. The contest at present seems to be betwixt this city and Philadelphia, and the parties are so tenacious that nothing can be done. I am for several reasons averse to Philadelphia. I fear the aristocratical influence of that city.

1. RC, Tucker-Coleman Papers, ViW. Thomas Tudor Tucker was a South Carolina delegate to Congress. His brother, St. George Tucker, a lawyer in Virginia, became a judge of the Virginia General Court in 1788.

Thomas Willing to William Bingham, Philadelphia, 27 August (excerpt)[1]

Your favors of the 20th and 25th have been received. . . .

Your reflections and animadversions on the very critical situation of our public affairs are just and truly alarming. The conduct of Congress is certainly unbecoming the representatives of all America. Local prejudices and private interest may very naturally influence the individuals of New York, as well as those of Philadelphia, but that these causes should govern the votes of other states is extraordinary. The Member of the Federal Club[2] has wrote well on the subject and the truth of every argument he has adduced can most certainly be supported. But had I been at his elbow, I would have quoted an old saying to him: "the truth is not always to be spoken, tho he ought never to say anything which is not true." *He* says (I had like to have said *you* say) too much about the advantages which will be obtained by those who are nearest to the seat of the new government. In saying this to the people at New York, you are just as wrong, as you would be to talk of a halter in the house of a man whose father had been hanged. *Hinc ille lachrymy*: they well know what they are to lose by the removal of Congress, and of course what we are to gain by it, if, as their rival, the new Congress should here be fixed.

However, as this is the only error, and even this error is a truth too, I forgive you or him, whoever he is that wrote the piece to which I allude. I have just seen the proceedings of your great body published in Dunlap's paper. The introduction is well hit off and worth reading.[3] I wish I could say as much of the proceedings of Congress which follow it. I have heard many a good text from the pulpit, followed by a wretched sermon. In this instance, your employment is not quite as innocent as the Battle of [Sequist?] where no man is killed, and no man is hurt. For I fear we shall all of us be hurt, and terribly too, unless you act more like wise men and settle this long and now perplexed business. If you don't soon do it, the white boys, or wild boys, or some other mischievous boys, will do it for you and us too. But enough of all this; you are a parcel of froward children, and my advice will be thrown away upon you.

. . . .

[P.S.] Some such boys as I have mentioned above are to meet at Harrisburg. B[lair] M[Clenach]an was named by a meeting of 4 or 5 at Germantown to go for the county; and G[eorge] B[rya]n, C[harles] P[etti]t, Dr. Ja[mes] [Hutchinso]n appointed by themselves, I believe, for there has been no public meeting or even one called, to give any body such appointment, are going from this city to cooperate with other Antis, to take advantage of your tedious delay.[4]

1. RC, Gratz Collection, PHi.

2. Philadelphia *Pennsylvania Packet*, 22 August, printed above.

3. The reference is to an article in the *Pennsylvania Packet*, 25 August, which is similar to Bingham's article in the *Packet* on 22 August. The article is followed by excerpts from the Journals of Congress giving the roll-call votes on 28 and 30 July, and 4, 5, and 6 August.

4. Documents relating to the Harrisburg Convention, 3-6 September, are printed in Chapter IV.

Lambert Cadwalader to Samuel Meredith, Trenton, 28 August (excerpt)[1]

I have received your favor of the 25 inst. and wish it was in my power to promote your views here, but having resolved the whole business in my mind, I fear there is greater danger in the attempt than prospect of success.

I have taken into view the interests of the different counties and stated them fully to [William] Bingham to whom I refer you.

You cannot imagine how impatient the people are everywhere for your determination, the delay the cause of which is everywhere known has lowered the dignity of your honorable body [ex]ceedingly. They consider the object [of?] the contest as unworthy of so much [w]armth, when others of much greater importance and even necessity requir[e] your coming to a speedy conclusion.

You do not say how the votes now stand. Have the North Carolina members withdrawn? How does Virginia appear after the adjournment sine die of their Convention? Do let me know the history of it if you can and what prospect there is in that country.

I shrewdly suspect the disappointed Virginia Antifeds have been very busy in North Carolina. I have so little charity towards them that this opinion will prevail till I have demonstration to the contrary.

[P.S.] I just now received yours of the 27th. [Abraham] Clark has written to several of the member[s] of the legislature that his reason for voting against Pennsylvania is that[2]

1. RC, Clymer-Meredith-Read Papers, NN. The letter is signed L. C., and it is in the handwriting of Lambert Cadwalader, a former New Jersey delegate to Congress (1784-1787), who was elected to the House of Representatives in the first federal elections.

2. The remainder of this letter is missing.

George Washington to Benjamin Lincoln, Mount Vernon, 28 August (excerpt)[1]

The public appears to be anxiously waiting for the decision of Congress respecting the *place* for convening the National Assembly under the new government, and the ordinance for its organization. Methinks it is a great misfortune that local interests should involve themselves with federal concerns at this moment.

So far as I am able to learn, federal principles are gaining ground considerably. The declaration of some of the most respectable characters in this state (I mean of those who were opposed to the government) is now explicit that they will give the Constitution (as it has been fairly discussed) a fair chance, by affording it all the support in their power. Even in Pennsylvania, the minority, who were more violent than in any other place, say they will only seek for amendments in the mode pointed out by the Constitution itself.

I will, however, just mention by way of *caveat*, there are suggestions that attempts will be made to procure the election of a number of Antifederal characters to the first Congress, in order to embarrass the wheels of government and produce premature alterations in the Constitution. How far these hints, which have come through different channels, may be well or ill founded, I know not: but, it will be advisable, I should think, for the Federalists to be on their guard so far as not to suffer any secret machinations to prevail, without taking measures to frustrate them. That many amendments and explanations might and should take place, I have no difficulty in conceding; but, I will confess, that my apprehensions that the New York Circular Letter is intended to bring on a general convention at too early a period, and in short, by referring the subject to the legislatures, to set everything afloat again. I wish I may be mistaken in imagining, that there are persons, who, upon finding they could not carry their point by an open attack against the Constitution, have some sinister designs to be silently effected if possible. But I trust in that Providence which has saved us in six troubles, yea in seven, to rescue us again from any imminent, though unseen, dangers. Nothing, however, on our part ought to be left undone. I conceive it to be of unspeakable importance, that whatever there be of wisdom, and prudence, and patriotism on the continent, should be concentered in the public councils, at the first outset.

Our habits of intimacy will render an apology unnecessary. Heaven is my witness, that an inextinguishable desire the felicity of my country may be promoted is my only motive in making these observations.

1. RC, George Washington to Benjamin Lincoln Letters, 1777-1799, MH. Printed: Fitzpatrick, XXX, 62-63.

Alexander Hamilton to Governor William Livingston, New York, 29 August (excerpt)[1]

We are informed here that there is some probability that your legislature will instruct your delegates to vote for Philadelphia as the place of the meeting of the first Congress under the new government. I presume this information can hardly be well founded, as upon my calculations, there is not a state in the Union so much interested in having the temporary residence at New York as New Jersey. As between Philadelphia and New York, I am mistaken if a greater proportion of your state will not be benefited by having the seat of the government at the latter than at the former place. If at the latter too, its exposed and eccentric position will necessitate the early establishment of a permanent seat; and in passing south it is highly probable the government would light upon the Delaware in New Jersey. The Northern States do not wish to increase Pennsylvania by an accession of all the wealth and population of the federal city. Pennsylvania herself when not seduced by *immediate possession* will be glad to concur in a situation on the Jersey side of Delaware. Here are at once a majority of the states. But place the government once down in Philadelphia, Pennsylvania will of course hold fast. The state of Delaware will do the same. All the states south looking forward to the time when the balance of population will enable them to carry the government farther south, (say to the Potomac) and being accommodated in the meantime as well as they wish, will concur in no change. The government from the delay will take root in Philadelphia, and Jersey will lose all prospect of the federal city within her limits. These appear to me calculations so obvious, that I cannot persuade myself New Jersey will so much oversee her interest as to fall in the present instance in the snares of Pennsylvania.

1. RC, William Livingston Papers, MHi. Printed: Syrett, V, 208-9. See also Abraham Clark to Livingston, 26 August, printed above.

Thomas Willing to William Bingham, Philadelphia, 29 August (excerpt)[1]

I thank you for your letter of 27th. inst. I rejoice to see that out opponents have again been foiled. I hear that every exertion will be made at Trenton to procure a change in the vote of the delegates from Jersey; but I fear it will be an uphill work to change the conduct of Mr. [Abraham] Clark, and his eastern colleague [Jonathan Dayton].

Your exertions are very pleasing to most folks here, and your constant attention in giving such regular information will not be forgot soon. Where so much is at stake, it's natural to feel great anxiety; and tho we may not be finally gratified in the extent of our wishes, yet we read with pleasure an account of the daily proceedings and steps taken by our friends to bring it about.

Your reasons are well founded, and your sentiments are conveyed in language clear and intelligible; and some handsome things frequently drop from those I communicate your letters to.

1. RC, Gratz Collection, PHi.

New York Independent Journal, 30 August

A correspondent observes, with real concern, that notwithstanding it is more than two months since the ratification of the Constitution by the *ninth* state was transmitted to Congress, yet, to the grief and astonishment of all true Federalists, no steps whatever are taken by that honorable body towards putting it in operation. After the various obstacles and impediments that attended its adoption in different states had been happily overcome, and the insidious arts of its adversaries frustrated, they had good reason to hope no difficulty would occur in that body, whose province it was only to set it in motion.

The question on the place for commencing proceedings under the new government, it appears, has been the cause of this extraordinary delay; and the proposed ordinance rejected because the blank had been filled up with the city of New York. Can any impartial American admit, that this was a point of sufficient magnitude to authorize so disagreeable a measure, at a time when unanimity and energy in the federal council is particularly necessary! We have surprised all Europe by an unprecedented example of patriotism; we are now about to give them another cause for wonder and astonishment, but of a *very* different nature. A majority of the states in Congress (though not a sufficient number, according to the rules of their proceedings, to pass an ordinance) are in favor of New York; can or ought the minority then to expect that they will give up their opinion on a subject which they have an equal right to decide upon? It would be highly dishonorable to suppose it; and the gentleman from the southward who has it in his power to determine the question, must be sensible of the truth of the observation. Though the citizens of New York may not extol the advantages she possesses, or feel inclined to become the *arbitress of the Union*, nor like some states boast of the *purity of their morals*, yet her consequence to the Union will appear as great to the unprejudiced mind, as those who, publican-like, make a parade of their justice and virtue, and profess to hold in contempt all who do not acknowledge their imaginary superiority. As to situation, New York appears at present to be as eligible for the seat of government as Philadelphia; the intercourse between the states to the southward of Maryland, and both places is principally by water, and the navigation of the former is seldom or ever impeded, whilst the port of the latter is generally shut up three or four months in the year. But independent of all other considerations which might be urged in her favor, the city of New York has undoubtedly a just claim to all the benefits which may arise from its being the residence of Congress. No city on the continent has suffered so much by the ravages of war as she has; nearly one-third has been destroyed by fire; and her inhabitants, returned from a painful exile of seven years, are yet unable to rebuild what has been so unfortunately laid waste. Her merchants too are many of them nearly ruined by the depreciation of the continental currency, and other losses, sustained in common with the rest of their fellow citizens. These considerations alone (without the additional one of expense which must attend the removal of the public offices, etc.) appear sufficient to satisfy the mind of every candid friend to the federal government in the United States.[1]

1. This article was reprinted at least eight times and in newspapers as far apart as the Boston *Massachusetts Centinel*, 6 September, and the Charleston *Columbian Herald*, 18 September. For a reply see the Philadelphia *Pennsylvania Packet*, 6 September, printed below.

William Ellery to Benjamin Huntington, Newport, 31 August (excerpt)[1]

I am grieved to find that you cannot yet agree upon the place where the new Congress are to meet; and should be very unhappy if the time of their meeting should be postponed one week beyond the time proposed in the ordinance which failed; because the sooner the new government is organized the better it will be for this, and other states, for then the mouth of opposition will be stopped, and we shall have a head to look to, and a center to attract, and draw and bind us together.

I hope soon to hear that you have somehow or other, I had like to have said I don't care how, accommodated, and that the time of election, and the place of the new Congress are fixed.

The Feds here think it very strange, that after all the struggle there has been about the new Constitution, that now, when eleven states have agreed to it, Congress should not agree to do what is necessary on their part towards its operation. The Antifeds are pleased, and probably the same sentiment and sensation may take place, if they should not have already taken place, in some other states. Accommodate. Accommodate.

1. Typescript, Huntington Autograph Collection, Jervis Library, Rome, N.Y.

Pennsylvania Packet, 1 September

A correspondent remarks, that if the new government should be summoned to assemble in a *northern* situation, remote from the center of population, it must create a very alarming effect on the minds of the Southern citizens of the United States; for whenever there is a call of both houses of legislature, on important questions, the Northern States being in the vicinity, and their members having but a small distance to travel, will be enabled to appear with all their force, and *outvote* their opponents, some of whom will have to come upwards of a thousand miles, through bad roads.

Since the publication of the journals of Congress respecting the question on the place where the federal government should assemble, a correspondent has favored us with the respective pretensions of those places which have been in nomination, according as they regard centrality and population.

New York has 17 Representatives to be sent from the northward, which multiplied by 40,000 [*sic*] (being the number of inhabitants for each Representative, as settled by the Convention) makes 680,000 inhabitants.

	42 Representatives from the southward,	
	at the same rate, makes	1,680,000
Philadelphia,	27 on one side, makes	1,080,000
	30 on the other side	1,200,000
Baltimore,	23 on one side, makes	920,000
	36 on the other	1,440,000

So that, by this scale, New York has the worst pretensions to centrality and population, and is proportionally much further removed from the centrality of local situation. The center of the population of the Union evidently falls in some part of Pennsylvania—why then are measures necessary to the existence of the Union delayed, to carry the government from this central position?

These are characteristic evidences of difference of pretensions, which require no refinement of policy to discover, and which the people at large throughout the Union can determine, as well as the great council of the nation.[1]

1. One or both articles were reprinted in at least eighteen other newspapers including four in Philadelphia; the Trenton *Federal Post*, 9 September; Winchester *Virginia Centinel*, 10 September; *New Haven Gazette*, 11 September; and Augusta *Georgia State Gazette*, 11 October.

Journals of Congress, Tuesday, 2 September

Congress assembled. Present as yesterday.[1]

A motion was made by Mr. Clark, seconded by Mr. Sedgwick, in the words following, viz.:

"Whereas the Convention assembled in Philadelphia pursuant to the resolution of Congress of the 21st of February 1787, did on the 17th day of September in the same year report to the United States in Congress Assembled a Constitution or form of government for the people of the United States, whereupon Congress on the 28th of the same September did resolve, unanimously, that the said report with the resolutions and letter accompanying the same be transmitted to the several legislatures in order to be submitted to a convention of delegates chosen in each state by the people thereof, in conformity to the resolves of the Convention made and provided in that case. And whereas the Constitution so reported by the Convention, and by Congress transmitted to the several legislatures has been ratified in the manner therein declared to be sufficient for the establishment of the same, and such ratifications duly authenticated have been received by Congress and are filed in the office of the secretary thereof, therefore,

"Resolved, that the first Wednesday in January next be the day for appointing Electors in the several states which before the said day shall have ratified the said Constitution, that the first Wednesday in February next be the day for the Electors to assemble in their respective states to vote for a President and that the first Wednesday in March next be the time and the seat of the federal government at that time, the place for commencing proceedings under the said Constitution."[2]

On the question to agree to this resolution, the yeas and nays being required by Mr. Sedgwick:

New Hampshire			Delaware		
Wingate	ay*		Kearny	no	no
Massachusetts			Mitchell	no	
Sedgwick	ay		Maryland		
Dane	ay	ay	Seney	no	no
Thatcher	ay		Ross	no	
Connecticut			Virginia		
Huntington	ay	d	Griffin	no	
Edwards	no		Madison	no	no
New York			Carrington	no	
Hamilton	ay	ay	South Carolina		
Gansevoort	ay		Huger	ay	
New Jersey			Parker	ay	ay
Clarke	ay	ay	Tucker	ay	
Dayton	ay		Georgia		
Pennsylvania			Few	ay	d
Irvine	no		Baldwin	no	
Meredith	no	no			
Bingham	no				
Reid	no				

So the question was lost.

A motion was then made by Mr. Edwards, seconded by Mr. Sedgwick, in the words following:

"Whereas the Convention assembled in Philadelphia pursuant to the resolution of Congress of the 21st of February 1787 did on the 17 day of September in the same year report to the United States in Congress Assembled a Constitution or form of government for the people of the United States, whereupon Congress on the 28th day of the same September did resolve unanimously that the said report with the resolutions and letter accompanying the same be transmitted to the several legislatures in order to be submitted to a convention of delegates chosen in each state by the people thereof in conformity to the resolves of the Convention made and provided in that case. And whereas the Constitution so reported by the Convention and by Congress transmitted to the several legislatures has been ratified in the manner therein declared to be sufficient for the establishment of the same and such ratifications duly authenticated have been received by Congress and are filed in the office of the secretary thereof, therefore,

"Resolved, that the first Wednesday in January next be the day for appointing Electors in the several states, which before the said day shall have ratified the said Constitution; that the first Wednesday in February next be the day for the Electors to assemble in their respective states to vote for a President and that the first Wednesday in March next be the time for commencing proceedings under the said Constitution."[3]

A motion was made by Mr. Irvine, seconded by Mr. Bingham, to amend the motion before the house by inserting after the word "time" the following words viz., "and that Lancaster be the place" and on the question to agree to this amendment, the yeas and nays being required by Mr. Bingham:

Massachusetts
  Sedgwick ~~ay~~ no ⎫
  Dane no ⎬ ~~ay~~ no
  Thatcher ay ⎭
Connecticut
  Huntington no ⎫ d
  Edwards ay ⎭
New York
  Hamilton no ⎫ no
  Gansevoort no ⎭
New Jersey
  Clarke no ⎫ no
  Dayton no ⎭
Pennsylvania
  Irvine ay ⎫
  Meredith ay ⎬ ay
  Bingham ay ⎪
  Reid ay ⎭

Delaware
  Kearney ay ⎫ ay
  Mitchell ay ⎭
Maryland
  Seney ay ⎫ ay
  Ross ay ⎭
Virginia
  Griffin ay ⎫
  Madison ay ⎬ ay
  Carrington ay ⎪
  Lee ay ⎭
South Carolina
  Huger no ⎫
  Parker no ⎬ no
  Tucker no ⎭
Georgia
  Few no ⎫ d
  Baldwin ay ⎭

So ~~it passed in~~ the question was lost.[4]

1. Present were Massachusetts, Connecticut, New York, New Jersey, Pennsylvania, Delaware, Maryland, Virginia, North Carolina, South Carolina, and Georgia, and from New Hampshire, Paine Wingate.

2. This motion is in PCC, Item 23, pp. 109-10.

3. This motion differs from Clark's only in that the phrase "and the seat of federal government at that time, the place" is omitted.

4. It would appear from the deletions in the manuscript journals that on the roll call the initial vote was 5 to 3 for Lancaster and then Sedgwick switched his vote from "ay" to "no" and changed the vote of Massachusetts.

Pennsylvania Packet, 2 September

A gentleman of deep investigation in the relative value of the commerce carried on betwixt the different states calculates, that there is six times more connection in trade betwixt Philadelphia and the Southern States, than betwixt them and New York; that consequently the revenues of the country drawn into Philadelphia would have comparatively a far better chance of returning to them by circulation, than if they centered at New York.

Now, as the Southern States manufacture nothing, but from the immense value of their exports consume largely, they will be the great contributors to swell the amount of the impost on imported articles. They should therefore have an opportunity of drawing back in trade a part of the money they supply in revenue, or they will be soon exhausted, and be exposed to the most unreasonable hardships.

Several of the legislatures will meet in a short time, expecting to receive the act of Congress, announcing the manner how, and the time when, the federal government is to be put in operation. But unfortunately this important arrangement is not as yet decided on, though Congress was recommended to determine it, as soon as nine states had ratified the Constitution. The pernicious effects arising from this delay must be felt most sensibly in all parts of the Union; and all our advices from the southward deplore the unfortunate circumstance.

It is devoutly to be wished, that all the legislatures of the states who have ratified the Federal Constitution will, at their first meeting, call their delegates in Congress to a strict account, with respect to their particular conduct in prolonging the determination of this important business, which has created such serious apprehensions; and if the tendency of any of their votes was to defer the decision, by having a view to obtain partial advantages for one part of the Union, at the expense of the other, and in which the other states, in justice to their constituents could not possibly concur, that they will meet with the severest censure of their respective states; as this conduct is so diametrically opposed to that spirit of perfect equality in point of rights, advantages and convenience, which formed the new government, and which alone ought to continue to regulate its administration.

It is remarked, that there is an amendment which now appears necessary in the new Constitution, which has never been in the contemplation of a single state, and of which recent experience in Congress dictates the necessity. It is permission for the Senate to vote by proxy; otherwise the Southern States, being at such a distance, and consequently more exposed to have their members frequently absent, may be oppressed by the operation of laws, which could never have passed, if they had had a full representation.

The suspension of the Federal Constitution by North Carolina, if it should be followed by a rejection, would be a most alarming circumstance to the states of South Carolina and Georgia, who would then be cut off from a connection with the other parts of the Union, by the intervention of a disaffected state; more especially, as they are in the neighborhood of the British and Spanish settlements, as well as to hostile tribes of Indians, whose enmity to one of these states [Georgia] seems to be implacable. In case of any disturbances, internal or external, in that quarter of the

Union, it is somewhat doubtful in what manner military assistance could be afforded, as North Carolina might probably oppose the passage of troops, from an apprehension that she will naturally entertain, of an attempt to compel her to enter into the Union. These, and many other important considerations, *loudly call* for a speedy meeting of the new government.

Journals of Congress, Wednesday, 3 September

Congress assembled. Present Massachusetts, Connecticut, New Jersey, Pennsylvania, Delaware, Maryland, Virginia, North Carolina, South Carolina and Georgia, and from New Hampshire, Mr. Wingate and from New York, Mr. Yates.

. . . .

The motion which was yesterday made by Mr. Edwards, seconded by Mr. Sedgwick, being again moved and read,

A motion was made by Mr. Seney, seconded by Mr. Ross, to amend the same by inserting the words "and that the city of Annapolis in the state of Maryland be the place" immediately after the words "be the time," and on the question to agree to this amendment, the yeas and nays being required by Mr. Seney:

New Hampshire			Maryland			
Wingate	no*		Seney	ay	}	ay
Massachusetts			Ross	ay		
Sedgwick	no	} no	Virginia			
Dane	no		Griffin	no	}	
Connecticut			Madison	no	} no	
Huntington	no	} no	Carrington	no		
Edwards	no		South Carolina			
New York			Huger	no	}	
Yates	no*		Parker	no	} no	
New Jersey			Tucker	no		
Clarke	no	} no	Georgia			
Dayton	no		Few	ay	} d	
Pennsylvania			Baldwin	no		
Meredith	ay	} ay				
Armstrong	ay					
Bingham	ay					
Reid	no					
Delaware						
Kearny	no	} d				
Mitchell	ay					

So the question was lost.

Edmund Randolph to James Madison, Richmond, 3 September (excerpt)[1]

I am much obliged to you for your favor of the 25th ult.[2] Being in Williamsburg when I received it, I imparted it to our friend, the president, who espouses with warmth an early convention.[3] I sincerely wish, that the valuable parts of the Constitution may suffer no ill from the temper with which such a body will probably assemble. But is there no danger, that, if the respect, which the large minorities at present command should be effaced by delay, the spirit of amendment will hereafter be treated as heretical? I confess to you without reserve, that I feel great distrust of some of those who will certainly be influential agents in the government, and whom I suspect to be capable of making a wicked use of its defects. Do not charge me with undue suspicion; but indeed the management in some stages of the [Constitutional] Convention created a disgustful apprehension of the views of some particular characters. I reverence [Alexander] Hamilton, because he was honest and open in his views.

Perhaps the states may not concur in any particular correction of the new theory. But if dissensions in opinion should prevent an amendment, the Constitution remains as it is. If on the other hand they should be in unison as to even one amendment, it will satisfy, and bear down all malcontents.[4]

1. RC, Madison Papers, DLC.
2. Randolph is probably referring to Madison's letter of 22 August, printed above.
3. The "president" referred to is the Reverend James Madison, president of the College of William and Mary and a cousin of James Madison.
4. Madison's reply of 14 September is printed below.

Pennsylvania Gazette, 3 September

A friend to cool reason and public good has favored us with some remarks on the present posture of affairs in the honorable Congress. Certainly, he observes, the sessions of several state legislatures, Pennsylvania, Jersey, etc., rendered it desirable that the ordinance for arranging and putting into motion the new government should be passed and promulgated. The late unquiet situation of Massachusetts, and the countenance given to the insurgents by Rhode Island, seems to render this procrastination an object of just uneasiness and apprehension at the eastward. The Indian disturbances in the western parts of Georgia must make this delay very dangerous to that state and South Carolina. One of the most immediate and most desirable effects of the new government was to put us on a footing sufficiently respectable to induce Great Britain to withdraw her intruding troops from our western posts. She will be encouraged in this conduct, rather than deterred by what has happened on this occasion. Connecticut, New Hampshire, New Jersey, Delaware, South Carolina, and Georgia are justly expecting a participation of the great imposts of Massachusetts, New York, Pennsylvania, and Virginia. But if time is permitted to fly away after this manner, the year 1789 will yield them no more than 1787 and 1788. But whence arises this delay? Is it to convene the new government in a place where the archives of Congress may be burned or taken by a single ship of war, by which means our affairs must be thrown into irretrievable confusion, or the secrets of our public councils and our allies be laid open to an enemy? This is not an unimportant matter. The city of New York is not tenable without a large fleet. We see their own government has determined to remove its treasury and public papers from it, and it is said the fort is to be sold as not defensible in the present situation of our affairs without great hazard to the city.

Shall, then, vouchers of all our unsettled public accounts, and the federal treasury, be placed in so hazardous a situation? The judicious citizens of the United States, it is said, with all due respect and deference, cannot approve the position as a safe one. But is it probable the people of South Carolina will be satisfied to send their delegates 900 miles, or those of Georgia 1,000, when they find the Massachusetts delegates will only come 250 miles, and those of New Hampshire little more than 300? Is it prudent or generous to put such an hardship upon them? Nor is New York the center of population of the United States. The people on the south of that state are more than double the people on the north, so that an undue inconvenience is imposed upon two thirds, to give an accommodation to the remaining third, which they are too just and generous to desire.

A correspondent deplores the peculiar distress of the United States of America, from the declining state of commerce, the failure of the funds of the United States, and of each of the single states, the Antifederalism of North Carolina, and above all from the *New Yorkism* of the present Congress, which deprives us, by its delays, of the only remedy that exists for all the other evils which have been mentioned. The partiality discovered for that oblique corner of the United States by a few interested men, to the great injury of the Union, which requires a central situation, suggests a most alarming hint of the future views of the Eastern States. It is high time for Virginia, South Carolina, and Georgia to take care of themselves.

Journals of Congress, Thursday, 4 September

Congress assembled. Present New Hampshire, Massachusetts, Connecticut, New York, New Jersey, Pennsylvania, Delaware, Maryland, Virginia, North Carolina, South Carolina and Georgia.

The motion made by Mr. Edwards, seconded by Mr. Sedgwick, being again moved and read, a motion was made by Mr. Tucker, seconded by Mr. Huger, that the same be postponed in order to take up the following, viz.:

"Whereas after long deliberation on the subject of the new Constitution so far as the agency of Congress is required to give it effect, there appears to be a diversity of sentiment with respect to the place for commencing proceedings under the said Constitution, which may prevent a speedy and definite decision thereon; and whereas a farther delay of the other essential parts of this business might be productive of much national inconvenience, therefore,

"Resolved, that the first Wednesday in January next be the time for appointing Electors in the several states, which before the said day shall have ratified the said Constitution; that the first Wednesday in February next be the day for the Electors to assemble in their respective states, and vote for a President, and that the first Wednesday in March next be the time for commencing proceedings under the said Constitution, at such place as Congress shall hereafter appoint, or failing such appointment, at the place which shall immediately before the last mentioned day, be the seat of Congress."[1]

On the question to postpone for the purpose above-mentioned, the yeas and nays being required by Mr. Tucker:

New Hampshire
  Gilman   ay ⎰ ay
  Wingate ay ⎱

Massachusetts
  Dane   ay ⎰ ay
  Thatcher ay ⎱

Connecticut
  Huntington ay ⎰ ay
  Edwards   ay ⎱

New York
  Gansevoort ay ⎰ ay
  Yates   ay ⎱

New Jersey
  Clarke ay ⎰ ay
  Dayton ay ⎱

Pennsylvania
  Irvine   no ⎫
  Meredith no ⎬ no
  Bingham no ⎪
  Reid   no ⎭

Delaware
  Kearny no ⎰ no
  Mitchell no ⎱

Maryland
  Seney no ⎰ no
  Ross   no ⎱

Virginia
  Griffin   no ⎫
  Madison no ⎬ no
  Carrington no ⎪
  Lee   ay ⎭

South Carolina
  Huger ay ⎫
  Parker ay ⎬ ay
  Tucker ay ⎭

Georgia
  Few   ay ⎰ d
  Baldwin no ⎱

So the question was lost.

On the question to agree to the motion of Mr. Edwards as entered on the Journal of Tuesday last, the yeas and nays being required by Mr. Gilman and Mr. Huger:

New Hampshire
  Gilman   ay ⎰ ay
  Wingate ay ⎱

Massachusetts
  Dane   ay ⎰ ay
  Thatcher ay ⎱

Connecticut
  Huntington ay ⎰ ay
  Edwards   ay ⎱

New York
  Gansevoort ay ⎰ ay
  Yates   ay ⎱

New Jersey
  Clarke ay ⎰ ay
  Dayton ay ⎱

Pennsylvania
  Irvine   no ⎫
  Meredith no ⎬ no
  Bingham no ⎪
  Reid   no ⎭

Delaware
  Kearny no ⎰ no
  Mitchel no ⎱

Maryland
  Seney no ⎰ no
  Ross   no ⎱

Virginia
  Griffin   no ⎫
  Madison no ⎬ no
  Carrington no ⎪
  Lee   ay ⎭

South Carolina
Huger	ay	
Parker	ay	} ay
Tucker	ay	

Georgia
Few	no	
Baldwin	no	} no

So the question was lost.

1. This motion is in PCC, Item 23, pp. 349-50.

From William Few, New York, 4 September[1]

Parson Boyd will this day sail from here for Georgia, and go immediately to Augusta, which is so direct an opportunity, that I cannot resist the propensity of dropping you a few lines, altho we have little news that is worth communicating.

Congress have not yet agreed on the place for the first meeting of the legislature under the new Constitution. Several places have been proposed among which are Annapolis, Baltimore and Lancaster, but the competition at present lies between Philadelphia and New York, and on this question there is a diversity of opinion. It is said by the advocates for Philadelphia that it is more central and possess[es] other advantages in an equal degree and ought therefore to be the place of residence of the national government. To this it is objected and said that the national legislature ought not to reside in a large commercial city where the members would be subject to the undue influence of the local policy of the place; and that such [a] large city would derive such advantages as would be injurious to the equal rights and privileges of the other members of the Union; and contrary to the genius and principles of republican government and will evidently tend to facilitate the growth of that aristocracy or monarchy, so hateful to Americans, and to which there is too much reason to apprehend the new government will have a tendency; that the place for the permanent residence of the new Congress is an object of much importance and highly interesting to those states which are so situate as to stand in competition for that advantage, and they will be induced by their own interest to make advantageous offers to the United States to establish the federal town in their respective limits. If Congress in the first instance does not give any partial advantage, and therefore they say the first Congress under the new Constitution ought to meet in New York where all the officers and documents of government are and from whence the new legislature may with more impartiality determine where the permanent residence of the National Legislature ought to be.

These considerations divide Congress on the question, and I cannot at present conjecture what may be the result. For news I must refer you to the enclosed papers.

1. RC, Few Papers, NcD. The bottom of the last page, which probably contained the name of the addressee, is missing.

Nicholas Gilman to President John Langdon, New York, 5 September[1]

I have to acknowledge the honor of Your Excellency's obliging favor of the 25th ultimo,[2] and it is with real regret that I am again constrained to inform you that the ordinance for the organization of the new government remains incomplete owing to the absence of the delegates of Rhode Island and to a want of that spirit of accommodation which has hitherto confessedly marked the conduct of New Hampshire on this subject. The ordinance has once been completed in all its parts and when the final question was about to be taken the delegates of Rhode Island left the hall and the city.

The time for choosing Electors, of their meeting and the assembling of the new Congress was fixed at later periods than could meet the wishes of the Eastern States in order to accommodate the Southern.

The question on the place for commencing proceedings under the new government was first taken for Philadelphia when the delegates of New Hampshire and Connecticut (conceiving it to be the wish of the Southern States, and being actuated by that spirit of accommodation and conciliation which it is their ardent desire to see operating in the general government of the states, and on which our national prosperity so greatly depends) gave their assent. But to their surprise the question was lost by the negative of South Carolina and the division of Delaware and Georgia among the Southern States. The question was afterwards taken for New York in a full representation of all the states and carried, South Carolina voting in the affirmative and Georgia divided. But as the final question did not obtain, owing to the circumstance above related, an attempt has since been made to send out the ordinance without inserting the place, leaving it for the new Congress to assemble where the old Congress should be sitting at the time, but without success. Thus has the business passed on from day to day waiting the return of the delegates from Rhode Island.

As it seems to be the general opinion that New York or Philadelphia must be the place for the first Congress to assemble in and as seven states and an half are in favor of the former and half the delegation of Delaware, in addition, pointedly opposed to the latter, it appears to be the effect of unwarrantable obstinacy that the minority will not concede the point in question without further delay.

I hope however that we shall be able to finish this business within a few days when I shall do myself the honor to give Your Excellency the earliest notice.

1. RC, State Papers Relating to the Revolution, II (1785-1789), Nh-Ar.
2. Langdon had written Gilman from Portsmouth on 25 August that "I am not going to find fault, as I am not possessed of all the reasons; but I lament exceedingly that so much time has elapsed without completing the ordinance for arranging the new government. This delay in my opinion is not only injurious; but very dangerous. Not a moment should be lost *in fixing* the government. The trifling consideration where the new Congress should first meet should not be made an objection. Rhode Island have acted like themselves. I feel indignant at their conduct" (RC, Personal Papers Misc., DLC).

Extract of a Letter from New York, 5 September[1]

What engrosses conversation principally now is the difficulty in getting out the ordinance of Congress respecting the organization of the new government. To people, out of doors, there appears to be the most shameful *party spirit* in that august body—perpetual jarrings—no convictions, nor conciliating temper. The place in which the new Congress shall meet is the only bone of contention. New York, Philadelphia, Wilmington, Baltimore, and Annapolis have all had their advocates, and attempts in their favor. Mr. [Pierpont] Edwards, Mr. [Alexander] Hamilton, and Mr. [Theodore] Sedgwick have been extremely busy in the matter, and brought forward their respective motions. We see no prospect of any determination on the subject, except that of pertinaciously adhering to sentiments suggested by local interests or attachments.

1. Litchfield *Weekly Monitor*, 15 September.

South Carolina Delegates to Governor Thomas Pinckney, New York, 6 September (excerpt)[1]

We are sorry to inform Your Excellency that no act is yet passed by Congress respecting the arrangements for the new Constitution, every plan that has hitherto been brought forward for the accomplishment of that business having failed to receive the final approbation of the House. We, however, cannot but flatter ourselves that before the meeting of our legislature we shall be enabled to communicate to Your Excellency some definitive measure on that subject.

1. RC, Gratz Collection, PHi. Printed: LMCC, VIII, 791-92. The letter was signed by Daniel Huger, John Parker, and Thomas Tudor Tucker.

New York Independent Journal, 6 September

Our brethren of the type in Philadelphia seem to be laboring very hard to persuade Congress that *their* city is the only place in the United States fit for the seat of government; indeed they have magnified and praised this *metropolis of America* to such an excess, that it appears the honor will be conferred on Congress (by permitting them to reside there) instead of Congress conferring it upon them. What pity it is, that the *New Yorkism* of that honorable body should make them so blind to their real interest, as not to prefer the *first* city, on the *finest* river, in the *most respectable* state in America, to a *parcel of buildings*, confusedly situated on a *pitiful* island, which has neither *ice* in winter to protect it, nor *force* in summer sufficient to prevent Congress and all their papers being carried off by pirates. It appears wonderful that men of sense should hesitate in their choice of two places so *very* different; yet it has been the case and what is most surprising is that a majority have approved of the one hardly fit for a *gentleman*, much more a *Pennsylvanian* to live in.[1]

1. For reprints see the Philadelphia *Pennsylvania Packet*, 16 September; Richmond *Virginia Independent Chronicle*, 17 September; and *Pittsburgh Gazette*, 4 October. The New York printers complained about anti-New York City propaganda in the Philadelphia newspapers but reprinted very little of it.

Pennsylvania Packet, 6 September

It seems a great hardship upon the people of the United States, says a correspondent, that so great a majority as voted for Philadelphia should not determine the residence of Congress. New Hampshire, Connecticut, Pennsylvania, Maryland, Virginia, and North Carolina having 1,480,000 people, according to the statement of the Federal Convention, voted for Philadelphia; and Massachusetts, New York, New Jersey, and South Carolina, having only 920,000 people, were for New York. Delaware and Georgia were divided.

We cannot, says a correspondent, but wonder at the want of reflection in the writer of a New York paragraph of August 30,[1] who complains that Congress have not determined the question of the residence of the new government, though a ninth state has adopted the Constitution above two months. Surely this gentleman will not complain *as a New Yorker*, that Congress delayed *for many weeks* to determine the matter, when New York was not in a capacity to be fixed on, or even put in nomination. How indelicate is the personal part relative to the Southern delegate! This writer tells us, that *the sufferings* of New York ought to influence Congress to fix the government there. Upon that principle it should go to New Jersey. But does he remember, that half the ships and cargoes belonging to Philadelphia, that were captured in the war, would rebuild all they lost. Our greater proportion of voluntary public loans, now reduced three-fourths in value, would also rebuild it. But they have been amply repaid for this loss, by the confiscation of a great number of the most capital city estates. Pennsylvania, he says, wishes to become the arbitress of the United States. This we deny and despise. Let New York remember, how firmly she refused to make *common cause* even with her sister states, by refusing the impost; and let the worthy citizens of Connecticut and New Jersey remember, how safe it would be for New York, with such an unjust spirit, to become the arbitress of America. The dispositions of this state are, and *always* have been, national. When Boston suffered before the war, Pennsylvania subscribed to their relief. When the South Carolinians were exiled, Pennsylvania subscribed for their poor, and lent to their rich citizens. How much did New York do on these two occasions? They did not furnish in gifts, or loans, a tenth penny. When our Philosophical Society, our bank, our Manufacturing Society, etc., were established, all America were publicly and heartily invited to partake. Our little societies have offered premiums for inventions, improvements, and new articles of produce to the citizens of the most distant states. Our spirit has always been federal, both before and since the Revolution, as is well known.

Let it not be supposed we wish to take up a contention with New York. We know there is and ever will be a jealousy. Let us, however, rather make it *a generous emulation* than a little comtemptible jealousy, unworthy of the good citizens of that metropolis, and unworthy of us. The meeting of the new Congress must rest upon solid arguments, of which *the people at large* are able to judge, and will think for themselves. Our correspondent would only humbly observe to the gentlemen of the present Congress, that it will be an unpleasant thing to any patriot, and an unhappy thing for *the new Union*, if their determination should not coincide with *the sentiments and wishes of the people*.

1. See the New York *Independent Journal*, 30 August, printed above. The author of that piece replied in the *Independent Journal*, 13 September, asserting that only Pennsylvanians wanted the seat of government moved and that they should be censured for delaying action by Congress.

Abraham Ogden to Nicholas Low, Narrows, New Jersey, 7 September (excerpt)[1]

I am sorry that indisposition has yet prevented my personal attention to the subject of your letter of the last week. On Tuesday I flatter myself with the hopes of reaching Trenton. If not then too late I shall personally aid the solicitations of my friends in averting the evil which you have but too much reason to dread. Immediately after receipt of your letter, I wrote to all my acquaintance who had influence with the legislature. Their united efforts, I hope, have been abundantly sufficient to defeat the schemes of the Pennsylvanians. Mr. [Elias?] Boudinot and many others of the Eastern gentlemen have entered very heartily into the interests of New York.

1. RC, Low Papers, NjR. The letter is undated but is endorsed "Abraham Ogden Narrows 6 Sept. 1788." However, Ogden concluded the letter "Narrows Sunday." Sunday was 7 September. Low was a New York merchant, a land speculator, and a Federalist representative from New York City at the state Convention. Low had engaged Ogden to lobby for New York as the seat of the new government (Richard P. McCormick, *Experiment in Independence: New Jersey in the Critical Period, 1781-1789* [New Brunswick, 1950], 250).

Jeremiah Hill to George Thacher, Biddeford, Maine, 9-10 September (excerpt)[1]

Have just arrived from Boston, kissed Mam and set down to peruse yours of the 26th ult. Am mad, that is, politically disordered in mind, to find the Congress so obstinate, as to keep that government the *people*, their constituents, have adopted out of motion. They ought to show their exordiums on less momentous occasions, not when their best friends have their eyes lifted to heaven, their hearts sending forth ejaculations, and heaving, with every shoulder while their petitions are ascending, for their spirited exertions, when the wheels of government are, as it were, stuck in the mud.

The friends of the new government are alarmed to find Congress so dilatory, they say one party (that is, the smallest) ought upon every political principle to give way to the great object in view, the good of the whole: for while they are dallying along in this way the enemy is sowing tares among the wheat. Antifederalism is a common enemy we ought all to guard against and obstinacy is a *ditto*. But true genuine political qualities are an open mind, a clear head, and an honest heart. This minute (September 10th 10 o'clock) the post has arrived and brought me yours of the 2d inst. Went immediately to see Mrs. Thacher, delivered your enclosed letter, kissed Madame and returned by the by all well. Janey laughed, Sally smiled, Rachel seemed pleased and Samuel wanted me to praise his little wheel carriage etc. Am now at home, my harp's upon the willows, lamenting the imprisonment of the new Constitution.

1. RC, Thacher Papers, MB. Printed: *Historical Magazine*, XVI, 351-52. Hill had been an officer during the Revolution and was town clerk of Biddeford in 1788. He was appointed a United States collector of customs in Maine in 1789.

New York Packet, 9 September

The Philadelphians appear to be exceedingly solicitous that the United States in Congress Assembled should fix upon their city as the place of holding the sessions of that honorable body. We have had Philadelphia represented to us as the center of population, the mistress of arts and sciences, the emporium of commerce, and the *arbitress* of America. Quere, is not this *great Babylon*, which *they* have built?

Pennsylvania Mercury, 9 September

A correspondent asks, why is the almost unanimous voice of the people treated with neglect? Why are the dearest interests of America, and the wishes of her best citizens, disregarded? In fine, why have not Congress complied with the recommendation of the Federal Convention, in organizing the new government, when adopted by *nine* states? The plan proposed by that august body has been re-echoed by *eleven* states, a considerable while since; yet, strange to tell, (in a republican government) the great voice of the people has not been respected by our rulers; and the impending ruin which has long threatened to overwhelm the United States, instead of rousing them to action, seems to have thrown them into a lethargy fatal to the prosperity of their country. But we are told, forsooth, that they cannot agree in appointing a place of meeting for the new Congress. This, to say the best of it, is but a childish tale. Surely they cannot fix upon any permanent place of residence for their successors, who will have the power of determining for themselves. This being the case, would it not be prudent in them to avoid the trouble and expense of moving from New York at present, which they must do, should they appoint any other place for the first meeting of the federal government. It is to be hoped, that they will immediately awake to a sense of their duty, to a sense of their own dignity, and not suffer uninteresting and trivial debates to engage their attention, at this alarming, this important crisis. Let the place of meeting be New York, Philadelphia, or Baltimore, nay, the banks of the Potomac, Ohio, or Mississippi, let it be anywhere; but for Heaven's sake, let the *vox populi* prevail, let the government be put in motion.

Morgan Lewis to Tench Coxe, New York, 10 September (excerpt)[1]

The question *"Where shall the new legislature meet"* is still undecided in Congress; but I think appearances in favor of New York. There are, no doubt, great jealousies on the subject; and the endeavor to run the question, while our [New York] Convention was in session, and on the eve of ratification, did not tend a little to excite them. They have, however, so far subsided, that all parties are at least in appearance in perfect good humor, a few hot and disappointed excepted.

You and I can hardly give an impartial opinion on the question as it relates to Philadelphia and New York. A temporary residence being all they have at present in view, I cannot conceive the interests of the continent materially affected, be the determination in favor of either. I do not consider a central situation for the seat of government so important an object as tis generally thought. Kingdoms, states etc. have long subsisted independent of it; nor do I recollect an instance, where any national calamity has been ascribed to the want of it. Circumstanced as we are, perhaps in determining this question, if of such importance, policy would dictate the propriety of looking forward to the da[y] when our government will embrace vast tracts of country at present un[in]habited, and others in possession of foreig[n] powers. However visionary it may be, [I] do not view the day far distant when all the northern parts of this continent shall compose a part of confederated America. Should it take place, it will doubtless add to the grandeur of our country; but I question its adding one particle to the happiness of your obliged friend.

1. RC, Coxe Papers, Tench Coxe Section, PHi. The letter is signed "M. Lewis." The handwriting is that of Morgan Lewis, a New York lawyer who was elected to the state legislature in 1789.

William Bingham to William Irvine, Philadelphia, 10 September (excerpt)[1]

I observe by the letter you were so obliging as to favor me with, that our hopes will be defeated by the arrival of the Rhode Island delegation. I am not fully convinced that they will presume to vote. Tho there is great reason to apprehend it.

We are very anxious for the ordinance, but if there was any prospect of gaining the point by a little delay, it would perhaps be advisable.

The present session of Assembly will terminate about the end of the month.

I observe that Maryland has abandoned you,[2] which I am fearful will raise the hopes of our opponents. I shall be thankful to you, for a detail of occurrences on this and every other important point.

1. RC, William Irvine Papers, PHi.
2. The two Maryland delegates, Joshua Seney and David Ross, left Congress after the session of 8 September "in a temper" according to James Madison (to Edmund Randolph, 14 September, printed below).

Lambert Cadwalader to Samuel Meredith, Trenton, 10 September (excerpt)[1]

I saw [William] Bingham in his way to Philadelphia. He informed that matters relative to the fixing the place where the new legislature shall convene remained in status quo. I suppose the troops are marshaled according to their several state interests, whenever a motion is preferred on this important business. The arguments are clearly and incontrovertibly in favor of the Southern States and I have no doubt they will steadfastly adhere to their point. But if the question stands connected with the ordinance and it cannot be carried, what is to become of the ordinance? This is a most serious consideration and requires the particular attention of Congress.

I observed by the Journals of Congress that on the 6th August it was determined on a motion of [Thomas Tudor] Tucker, seconded by H[enry] Lee, that the "city of New York in the state of New York be the place for commencing proceedings under the said Constitution" and that the preamble to said resolve was also agreed to. So, however, I apprehend it. This is quite new to me.

I wish you would make the proposition which I recommended in my letter to Bingham for Princeton, rather than this place or Burlington, which being situate on the waters communicating with Philadelphia, are more liable to objections in the House [Congress]. The other being more central may be more plausibly maintained and who knows but a motion of the kind which carries with it the appearance of concession on your part may meet the approbation of some of the members who are now against you. It will certainly have this effect at least that it must draw off New Jersey from the Northern Party and add their weight to yours.

1. RC, George Clymer Papers, PPAmP. The letter is signed L. C. It is in the handwriting of Lambert Cadwalader.

Tench Coxe to James Madison, Philadelphia, 10 September (excerpt)[1]

The question about the place of first meeting is likely to issue I find in favor of New York. I confess I wish Philadelphia may not any longer procrastinate the issuing of the ordinance. Tis much to be lamented that so much time has been spent, and that the most favorable and proper position has not been taken, but tis too serious a matter to hazard the government by delay for any such consideration.

1. RC, Madison Papers, DLC. Printed: DHOC, V, 47-48. Another excerpt from this letter is printed in Chapter IV.

Massachusetts Centinel, 10 September

SHIP NEWS—EXTRA: The ship Federal Constitution, after experiencing a long and dangerous voyage, having suffered much from the gales of faction, and on the quicksands of jealousy the Scyllas and Charybdies of our coasts, and after, through the firmness of her crew, who were superior to all embarrassments and storms, doubling the Cape, in Good Hope of having speedily made an end of the voyage, notwithstanding she has long been in sight, has not yet been moored in the harbor of permanency, owing to the bickerings of the branch pilots, to whose direction she was two months since submitted, who cannot agree on what particular ground to cast anchor. Thereby depriving the owners of the benefit of her cargo, exposing the property of the people to the dangers of the ocean of uncertainty, and suffering the revenue rats of individual states to devour the rightful income of the continent.

Pennsylvania Gazette, 10 September

As the new Congress under the Federal Constitution will be *a complete representation* of the Union, a correspondent earnestly wishes they may be called to meet in Princeton, from whence they could adjourn to such place as, in their wisdom, shall seem proper.

A correspondent, well acquainted with the public opinions of Pennsylvania, assures us, that he is convinced the people at large, and particularly the citizens of Philadelphia, wish their pretensions to the seat of federal government may be waived, and that even their rival, New York, may be the place of first meeting, rather than have one hour's delay of putting the government in motion, which is so necessary to the happiness and honor of the United States.

Paine Wingate to President John Langdon, New York, 11 September (excerpt)[1]

My colleague has informed Your Excellency of the reasons which actuated our conduct in the late endeavors to organize the new government.[2] They were such as we supposed ought to influence us, and would vindicate us from any blame in the past delay. Nothing has been further attempted in this business since Mr. [Nicholas] Gilman wrote, but we have reason to think it will be completed in a few days. I do not imagine that the delay as yet has put off the time when the operation of the new government would commence, or has been injurious, further than a waste of time in Congress, and keeping the public in a painful suspense and some little irritation of the parties. These it is true, tho I think they will be attended with no very disagreeable consequences, are evils which I wish had been avoided, and that the government had commenced with a perfect harmony of sentiment. Had all parties been as disinterested as the delegates of New Hampshire in this affair, it might have been the case; but the rivalship of Philadelphia and New York would not admit of it.

1. RC, State Papers Relating to the Revolution, II (1785-1789), Nh-Ar. Printed: LMCC, VIII, 792-93.
2. See Nicholas Gilman to Langdon, 5 September, printed above.

Journals of Congress, Friday, 12 September

Congress assembled. Present as before.[1]

. . . .

A motion being made by Mr. Lee, seconded by Mr. Gilman, in the words following:

"Whereas longer delay in executing the previous arrangements necessary to put into operation the federal government may produce national injury,

"Resolved, that the first Wednesday in January next be the time for appointing Electors in the several states which before the said day shall have ratified the said Constitution and that the first Wednesday in February next be the day for the Electors to assemble in their respective states and vote for a President and that the first Wednesday in March next be the time and the present seat of Congress the place for commencing proceedings under the said Constitution."

A motion was made by Mr. Carrington, seconded by Mr. Madison, to amend the proposition by striking out the words "and the present seat of Congress be the place" and by adding "and whereas it is of great importance, that a government founded on the principles of conciliation and impartial regard to the interests and accommodation of the several parts of the Union should commence in a spirit corresponding with these principles, and under every circumstance calculated to prevent jealousies in one part of the Union, of undue bias in the public councils or measures towards another part, and it is conceived that these desirable purposes will be much favored by the appointment of some place for the meeting of the new government more central than the present seat of Congress, and which will at the same time be more likely to obviate disagreeable and injurious dissensions concerning the place most fit for the seat of federal business until a permanent seat be established as provided for by the new Constitution.

"Resolved, that _____ be the place for commencing proceedings under the new Constitution."

On the question to agree to this amendment, the yeas and nays being required by Mr. Gilman:

New Hampshire			Delaware		
Gilman	no	no	Kearney	ay	ay
Wingate	no		Mitchell	ay	
Massachusetts			Virginia		
Dane	no	no	Griffin	ay	
Thatcher	no		Madison	ay	ay
Connecticut			Carrington	ay	
Huntington	no		Lee	no	
Wadsworth	no	no	South Carolina		
Edwards	ay		Huger	no	
New York			Parker	no	no
Hamilton	no	no	Tucker	no	
Gansevoort	no		Georgia		
New Jersey			Few	no	d
Clark	no	no	Baldwin	ay	
Dayton	no				
Pennsylvania					
Irvine	ay				
Meredith	ay	ay			
Reid	ay				

So the question was lost.

A motion was then made by Mr. Kearny seconded by Mr. Mitchell to strike out the words "and the present seat of Congress the place,"[2] and on the question shall those words stand, the yeas and nays being required by Mr. Mitchell:

New Hampshire			Massachusetts		
Gilman	ay	ay	Dane	ay	ay
Wingate	ay		Thatcher	ay	

Connecticut			Delaware		
Huntington	ay	} ay	Kearny	no	} no
Wadsworth	ay		Mitchell	no	
Edwards	ay		Virginia		
New York			Griffin	ay	} ay
Hamilton	ay	} ay	Madison	ay	
Gansevoort	ay		Carrington	ay	
New Jersey			Lee	ay	
Clark	ay	} ay	South Carolina		
Dayton	ay		Huger	ay	} ay
Pennsylvania			Parker	ay	
Irvine	ay		Tucker	ay	
Meredith	ay	} ay	Georgia		
Armstrong	ay		Few	ay	} ay
Reid	no		Baldwin	ay	

So it was resolved in the affirmative.

The motion being then amended to read as follows:

"Whereas the Convention assembled in Philadelphia pursuant to the resolution of Congress of the 21st February 1787, did on the 17th of September in the same year, report to the United States in Congress Assembled a Constitution for the people of the United States, whereupon Congress on the 28th of the same September did resolve unanimously, 'that the said report with the resolutions and letter accompanying the same, be transmitted to the several legislatures in order to be submitted to a convention of delegates chosen in each state by the people thereof, in conformity to the resolves of the Convention made and provided in that case.' And whereas the Constitution so reported by the Convention, and by Congress transmitted to the several legislatures, has been ratified in the manner therein declared to be sufficient for the establishment of the same, and such ratifications duly authenticated have been received by Congress, and are filed in the office of the secretary, therefore,

"Resolved, that the first Wednesday in January next be the day for appointing Electors in the several states, which before the said day shall have ratified the said Constitution; that the first Wednesday in February next be the day for the Electors to assemble in their respective states, and vote for a President; and that the first Wednesday in March next be the time, and the present seat of Congress the place for commencing proceedings under the said Constitution."

When the question was about to be put, the determination thereof was postponed till tomorrow by the State of Delaware.

1. Present were New Hampshire, Massachusetts, Connecticut, New York, New Jersey, Pennsylvania, Delaware, Virginia, North Carolina, South Carolina, and Georgia, and from Rhode Island, Peleg Arnold.

2. A motion by Kearny, endorsed by Charles Thomson as "Motion Mr. Kearny respecting the Constitution Sep. 12, 1788" and "Mr. Kearny Mitchel to" is in PCC, Item 23, pp. 111-12. The motion consists of a revised preamble and a resolve that the new government should meet "at such place as Congress shall hereafter appoint." The motion is not included in the Rough Journals.

Journals of Congress, Saturday, 13 September

Congress assembled. Present New Hampshire, Massachusetts, Connecticut, New York, New Jersey, Pennsylvania, Virginia, North Carolina, South Carolina and Georgia, and from Rhode Island, Mr. Arnold and from Delaware, Mr. Kearny.

On the question to agree to the proposition which was yesterday postponed by the State of Delaware, the yeas and nays being required by Mr. Gilman:

New Hampshire			Virginia		
Gilman	ay	} ay	Griffin	ay	
Wingate	ay		Madison	ay	} ay
Massachusetts			Carrington	ay	
Dane	ay	} ay	Lee	ay	
Thatcher	ay		South Carolina		
Connecticut			Parker	ay	} ay
Huntington	ay	} ay	Tucker	ay	
Wadsworth	ay		Georgia		
New York			Few	ay	} ay
Hamilton	ay	} ay	Baldwin	ay	
Gansevoort	ay				
New Jersey					
Clarke	ay	} ay			
Dayton	ay				
Pennsylvania					
Irvine	ay				
Meredith	ay	} ay			
Armstrong	ay				
Reid	ay				

So it was resolved as follows.[1]

1. For the Ordinance see the Journals for 12 September, printed immediately above, and the Election Ordinance, 13 September, printed below.

Election Ordinance, 13 September[1]

By the United States in Congress assembled
SEPTEMBER 13, 1788

WHEREAS the Convention assembled in Philadelphia, pursuant to the Resolution of Congress of the 21st February, 1787, did, on the 17th of September in the same year, report to the United States in Congress assembled, a Constitution for the People of the United States; whereupon Congress, on the 28th of the same September, did resolve unanimously, "That the said report, with the Resolutions and Letter accompanying the same, be transmitted to the several Legislatures, in order to be submitted to a Convention of Delegates chosen in each State by the people thereof, in conformity to the Resolves of the Convention made and provided in that case:" And whereas the Constitution so reported by the Convention, and by Congress transmitted to the several Legislatures, has been ratified in the manner therein declared to be sufficient for the establishment of the same, and such Ratifications duly authenticated have been received by Congress, and are filed in the Office of the Secretary—therefore,

RESOLVED, That the first Wednesday in January next, be the day for appointing Electors in the several States, which before the said day shall have ratified the said Constitution; that the first Wednesday in February next, be the day for the Electors to assemble in their respective States, and vote for a President; and that the first Wednesday in March next, be the time, and the present Seat of Congress the place for commencing Proceedings under the said Constitution.

1. Broadside (LT) signed by Charles Thomson, PCC, Miscellaneous Papers: Broadsides Issued by the Continental Congress 1775-1788, Reel 9.

The Election Ordinance of 13 September 1788 was the last one passed by the Confederation Congress, and 200 copies were ordered printed. Charles Thomson signed those sent to the governors as well as some others. The dates the governors received the Election Ordinance are known for only two states. The Virginia copy was endorsed as received on 22 September. The Minutes of the Privy Council of South Carolina, 27 September (printed, Chapter III) indicate that the letter reached Charleston on 26 September.

Members of Congress sent copies of the Election Ordinance to state officials and to friends. John Jay, Secretary for Foreign Affairs, sent one to Thomas Jefferson in Paris (New York, 23 September, Boyd, XIII, 630-31) and one to William Carmichael in London (New York, 23 September, FC, Jay Collection, NNC). William Knox in the War Office sent one to General Josiah Harmar in the Northwest Territory (New York, 15 September, RC, Harmar Collection, MiU-C).

At least fifty newspapers printed the Election Ordinance, beginning with the New York *Daily Advertiser* on Monday, 15 September. North and east of New York City it was printed in the New Haven *Connecticut Journal* on the 17th and the *New Haven Gazette* on the 18th; in the Litchfield *Weekly Monitor* and Hartford *American Mercury* on the 22nd; in the Poughkeepsie *Country Journal* and the *Salem Mercury* on the 23rd; and in the Worcester *American Herald*, the *Norwich Packet*, the Portsmouth *New Hampshire Gazette*, and the Portland, Me., *Cumberland Gazette* on the 25th.

South of New York City it appeared in the Elizabethtown *New Jersey Journal* on the 17th; in five Philadelphia newspapers on the 17th and 18th (and in German translation in the *Gemeinnützige Philadelphische Correspondenz* on the 23rd); in the Baltimore *Maryland Journal* on the 19th; in the *Carlisle Gazette*, the German *Neue Unpartheyische Lancaster Zeitung*, and the Richmond *Virginia Independent Chronicle* on the 24th; in the Annapolis *Maryland Gazette* and the Fredericksburg *Virginia Herald* on the 25th; in the *Norfolk and Portsmouth Journal* on 1 October; in the Savannah *Gazette of the State of Georgia* on the 9th; in the Charleston *State Gazette of South Carolina* on the 16th; and in the Lexington *Kentucky Gazette* on 1 November.

Pennsylvania Delegates to Thomas Mifflin, Speaker of the Pennsylvania Assembly, New York, 13 September[1]

This letter will be accompanied by an act of Congress of this morning, which Mr. Secretary Thomson will have the honor of transmitting.[2]

The public interest and expectation excited by the subject of it, the time employed in its discussion, and the temper in which it has been advocated by some states and opposed by others, make it not less necessary, than respectful, that we should state the facts under which we gave the assent of Pennsylvania to the decision which has been taken. These are:

1st. That some states who invariably contended with us for giving a more central residence to the national government withdrew themselves from Congress while the dispute was depending, leaving the minority extremely small and without a hope of succeeding, but such as grew out of the bare possibility of a change of sentiment or relaxation of obstinacy in the majority.

And 2d. That others of the same description, believing that the organization of the new government could not be longer suspended without risking consequences more disagreeable than any that could result from the mere circumstance of the place at which the government might be convened, determined to yield the objections they had made and acquiesce in the appointment of New York.

Under these facts the delegates of Pennsylvania were left to choose between opposing alone and unsuccessfully, or submitting to the predetermined sense of the Union. We did not hesitate in choosing the latter, persuaded that of the two alternatives, this was at once the most dignified and wise.

1. *Minutes of the Third Session of the Twelfth General Assembly of the Commonwealth of Pennsylvania* (Philadelphia, 1788), 238. The letter was signed by William Irvine, Samuel Meredith, John Armstrong, Jr., and James R. Reid.

2. Speaker Thomas Mifflin received a copy of the Election Ordinance on the evening of 16 September (Clement Biddle to George Washington, Philadelphia, 17 September, RC, Washington Papers, DLC).

Nathan Dane to Theodore Sedgwick, New York, 13 September (excerpt)[1]

The question about the place of the new government meeting is finally well settled. The day after you went away some person on our part moved a resolution for fixing the times of the elections etc. and leaving the place to be determined hereafter. This resolution for myself I did not like. However those who advocated New York voted for it and the advocates of Philadelphia against it, and the question was lost. Soon after they proposed to move a like resolution, but gave it up. Last Tuesday [Peleg] Arnold arrived from Rhode Island and informed that his colleague would be on in a few days. New Jersey assembled approved of the conduct of her delegates and information was received that the people of Charleston did the same as to the South Carolina delegates. There is a federal legislature now in session in Pennsylvania. A new one is soon to be chosen and in this the Federalists I understand are apprehensive the other party will prevail. Considering all these circumstances the advocates for Philadelphia concluded that it was best to give up their opposition and this day the resolves were unanimously passed and with New York for the place of meeting etc.

1. RC, Sedgwick Papers, MHi.

Henry Lee to George Washington, New York, 13 September (excerpt)[1]

At length the new government has received the last act necessary to its existence. This day Congress passed the requisite previous arrangements. The first

Wednesday in January the ratifying states are to appoint Electors, on the first Wednesday in February the President is to be chosen, and the first Wednesday in March is the time, and this city the place for commencing proceedings.

Some delay has attended this business from a difference in opinion respecting the place of meeting, but this delay has not in the least affected the sooner or later operation of the Constitution. The Southern gentlemen did not accord in the place of temporary residence, from a discordance in sentiment, of its effect on the establishment of the permanent seat of government. Some considered this city, others a more southern position, as the most favorable theater to negotiate the determination of the ten miles square. Many plausible and some cogent reasons are adducible in support of either opinion and time only can show which is founded in propriety.

1. RC, Washington Papers, DLC. Printed: DHOC, V, 48-51. The remainder of Lee's letter urging Washington to accept the Presidency and Washington's reply of 22 September are printed in Chapter XIV.

Louis-Guillaume Otto to Comte de Montmorin, New York, 13 September[1]

The United States never has found itself so completely represented as about six weeks ago; this was neither to wait for the issue of the debates on the new government nor to conclude the important treaties, nor to decide on some altercation between different states, but it was to determine the residence of the new Congress. If one had need of proof to demonstrate that the states are hardly disposed to forming only a *consolidated* empire, in the same way as the new Constitution implies it, the passion of the debates which have taken place on this occasion would provide many convincing proofs for it. The party of the South and that of the North equally wanted to locate the assembly in a city which is devoted to them. New York, Philadelphia, Baltimore, Annapolis were proposed and rejected alternately and it had come to the point of not wanting to grant the elections for the new government, because they could not agree on a residence. The candor with which the members of Congress express themselves often in public in their debates has augmented the scandal which this singular discussion had occasioned, and even the newspapermen began to throw some ridicule on one assembly which, from the beginning, obstructed the formation of the new government, which they had had so much trouble ratifying. The party of the South, or the minority, failed, however, to show plausible arguments for insisting on the transference of the residence of Congress from New York to a city more centralized. The delegates of Virginia and of Pennsylvania observed that it was indispensable for pacifying their constituents to transfer this residence to a place, any whatsoever, between Delaware and the Potomac, that this measure has caused much anxiety in the states of the North and it would rather make the present Congress carry the blame than to begin the new government with some discussions that would be so much more passionate than the respective delegates would have had time to receive instructions on and to prepare debates for. The minority has, however, yielded, and the Congress has just passed an ordinance, by which, without naming the city of New York, it will convoke the new government *in the present residence of Congress*. It set the first Wednesday of the following January for the nomination of the Electors, the first Wednesday of February for the assembly of Electors to choose a President of the United States, and the first Wednesday of March for the assembly of all the members of the new government.

This important affair is finally terminated and it remains with us to see what the effect of this revolution will be, for which so much trouble has been taken to make the people of the interior assent to, and to which they still only grudgingly assent.

As for the residence, Monseigneur, it is not doubted that the new Congress, where the party of the South will have a decided majority in the lower chamber, will leave the city of New York to establish itself in a more central place. This city is almost entirely English with regard to prejudices, to habits, to commerce, to correspondence, and as far as the Congress will reside in the Northern part of the United States, the principal places of government will be given to the men of the North, generally less disposed to favor us. These two motives cause me to strongly desire the transference of the residence and it would have still more value if the party of the South had triumphed from this moment on. Many delegates have never lived in the great cities; upon arriving in New York they go out into society and from there they draw prejudices unfavorable to our liaisons with the United States. We have many more partisans in the Middle States and in those of the South and if one has reason to hope the new government becomes settled in Pennsylvania or Maryland, the system of commerce will feel the effects of the spirit of these two states who are interested in treating us kindly.

The relative question of the residence decided for the moment, the members of Congress are beginning to disperse again and they find themselves with hardly seven states represented.

1. Ministère des Affaires Étrangères, Archives Diplomatiques, Correspondance Politique, États-Unis, XXXIII, 263-65. Louis-Guillaume Otto served in the French legation in the United States during the American Revolution. In 1785 he returned to the United States as chargé d'affaires, a post he held until 1792.

Nathan Dane to Governor John Hancock, New York, 14 September (excerpt)[1]

I have the pleasure, after a long and somewhat disagreeable discussion relative to the place of the new government assembling, to transmit to Your Excellency the act of Congress passed yesterday for putting the Constitution into operation. As the Secretary of Congress will, no doubt, by this or the next post transmit to Your Excellency an authenticated copy, the delegates of the state think it unnecessary to send one formally. This act finally passed by a unanimous vote, nine states being present, Rhode Island, Delaware, Maryland, and North Carolina being absent. A considerable majority has all along preferred New York to any other place for the new Congress to meet at, though not a majority sufficient to pass a constitutional vote without Rhode Island till yesterday. When gentlemen gave the preference to this city, considerations respecting the early establishment of a federal town or district had their weight as well as present circumstances, and from what I hear from the different parts of the country, I believe the pretty general opinion is that the assembling of the new government at New York will be for the interest of the Union at large.

. . . .

P.S. I did not get the inclosed signed by Mr. Thompson meaning it as well as this letter only for Your Excellency's private information. The delegates of Massachusetts and most of the Eastern delegates wished the new government to meet at a much earlier period, but the Southern members said it was impracticable for them in their extensive states to make their elections and meet sooner, and as the Eastern members had their choice as to the place of meeting, and the Southern gentlemen were many of them disappointed in this, it was thought advisable not to press them very hard as to the time of meeting.

1. RC, Federal Hall National Memorial, New York City.

James Madison to Edmund Randolph, New York, 14 September[1]

Your favor of the 3d instant[2] would have been acknowledged two days ago but for the approaching completion of the arrangement for the new government which I wished to give you the earliest notice of. This subject has long employed Congress and has in its progress assumed a variety of shapes, some of them not a little perplexing. The times as finally settled are January, for the choice of Electors, February for the choice of a President, and March for the meeting of the Congress, the place, the present seat of the federal government. The last point was carried by the yielding of the smaller to the inflexibility of the greater number. I have myself been ready for bringing it to this issue for some time, perceiving that further delay could only discredit Congress and injure the object in view. Those who had opposed New York along with me could not overcome their repugnance so soon. Maryland went away before the question was decided in a temper which I believe would never have yielded. Delaware was equally inflexible. Previous to our final assent, a motion was made which tendered a blank for any place the majority would choose between the North River and the Potomac. This being rejected the alternative remaining was to agree to New York or to strangle the government in its birth. The former as the lesser evil was of course preferred and must now be made the best of. I acknowledge at the same time that I anticipate serious inconveniences from it. It will, I fear, be regarded as at once a proof of a preponderancy in the Eastern scale and of a disposition to profit of that advantage. It is but just, however, to remark that the event is in great degree to be charged on the Southern States which went into that scale. It will certainly entail the discussion on the new government, which ought if possible to be exempt from such an additional cause of ferment in its councils. New York will never be patiently suffered to remain even the temporary seat of government by those who will be obliged to resort to it from the Western and Southern parts of the Union. This temporary period must continue for several years, perhaps seven or eight, and within that period all the great business of the Union will be settled. I take it for granted that the first session will not pass without a renewal of the question, and that it will be attended with all the unpleasing circumstances which have just been experienced. In the last place, I consider the decision in favor of New York as in a manner fatal to the just pretensions of the Potomac to the permanent seat of the government. This is unquestionably the light in which many of the advocates for New York view the

137

matter. The legislature of New Jersey which lately met approved of the part taken by her delegates on the principle that the first meeting of the government at New York would give the best possible chance for an early choice of the permanent seat, as this would do for a preference of Trenton. As the case now stands, the Susquehanna is probably the most that can be hoped for with no small danger of being stopped on the Delaware. Had any place south of the Delaware been obtained, the Susquehanna at least would have been secured with a favorable chance for the Potomac.

The result of the meeting at Harrisburg is I am told in the press and will of course be soon before the public. I am not acquainted with the particulars, or indeed with the general complexion of it. It has been said here that the meeting was so thin as to disappoint much the patrons of the scheme.

I am glad to hear that Mazzei's book is likely to be vendible. The copies allotted for this and several other markets will not I fear be so fortunate.[3]

1. RC, Madison Papers, DLC.
2. Printed above.
3. The reference is presumably to Philip Mazzei's *Recherches historiques et politiques sur les États-Unis de l'Amerique Septentrionale . . . 1788* (4 vols., Paris, 1788).

James Madison to George Washington, New York, 14 September[1]

The delay in providing for the commencement of the government was terminated yesterday by an aquiescence of the minor number in the persevering demands of the major. The time for choosing the Electors is the first Wednesday in January, and for choosing the President, the first Wednesday in February. The meeting of the government is to be the first Wednesday in March, and in the city of New York. The times were adjusted to the meetings of the state legislatures. The place was the result of the dilemma to which the opponents of New York were reduced, of yielding to its advocates or strangling the government in its birth. The necessity of yielding and the impropriety of further delay has been for some time obvious to me, but others did not view the matter in the same light. Maryland and Delaware were absolutely inflexible. It has, indeed, been too apparent that local and state considerations have very improperly predominated in this question, and that something more is aimed at than merely the first session of the government at this place. Every circumstance has shown that the policy is to keep Congress here till a permanent seat be chosen, and to obtain a permanent seat, at farthest, not beyond the Susquehanna. New Jersey, by its legislature, as well as its delegation in Congress, has clearly discovered her view to be a temporary appointment of New York, as affording the best chance of a permanent establishment at Trenton. I have been made so fully sensible of these views in the course of the business, as well as of the impropriety of so eccentric a position as New York, that I could have finally concurred in any place more southward to which the Eastern States would have acceded; and, previous to the definitive vote, a motion was made tendering a blank for that purpose. At any place south of the Delaware, the Susquehanna, at least, would have been secured, and a hope given to the Potomac. As the case is, I conceive the Susquehanna to be the utmost to be hoped for, with no small danger of being stopped at the Delaware. Besides this consequence, the decision will, I fear, be regarded as at once a proof of the preponderancy of the Eastern strength, and of a disposition to make an unfair use of it; and it cannot but happen that the question will be entailed on the new government, which will have enough of other causes of agitation in its councils.

The meeting at Harrisburg is represented by its friends as having been conducted with much harmony and moderation. Its proceedings are said to be in the press, and will, of course, soon be before the public. I find that all the mischief apprehended from [Governor George] Clinton's Circular Letter in Virginia will be verified. The Antifederalists lay hold of it with eagerness as the harbinger of a second convention, and as the Governor [Edmund Randolph] espouses the project, it will certainly have the cooperation of our Assembly.[2]

I enclose a sensible little pamphlet, which falls within the plan of investigating and comparing the languages of the aboriginal Americans.

1. RC, Washington Papers, DLC. Madison wrote to Thomas Jefferson later, summarizing what he wrote to Washington (21 September, Boyd, XIII, 624-27). For other letters from New York discussing the final passage of the Ordinance, see A. R. C. M. de la Forest to Comte de la Luzerne, 14 September, DeWitt Clinton to Dr. Charles Clinton, 19 September, and St. John de Crèvecoeur to Thomas Jefferson, 20 October, all printed below; Edward Carrington to James Monroe, 15 September, and Hugh Williamson to James Iredell, 22 September, LMCC, VIII, 796, 800-801; James Madison to Edmund Pendleton, 20 October, Hunt, V, 428-29.

2. The proceedings of the Harrisburg Convention were published in the Philadelphia *Pennsylvania Packet* on 15 September (printed, Chapter IV). Compare Madison's comments in this letter with those in his letter to Governor Edmund Randolph, printed immediately above.

Antoine R. C. M. de la Forest to Comte de la Luzerne, New York, 14 September[1]

After three months of debate Congress yesterday passed the Ordinance which brings about the operation of the new Constitution. This measure, which should have been adopted immediately after the ratification of New Hampshire, was suspended for so long only because of the difficulty of fixing the place where the general government is to reside. Congress had been divided into two parties on this question, which supported their respective opinions with a passion of which there have been few examples until now. Each of them seemed disposed to jeopardize the fate of the new Constitution rather than to yield, and for some time people feared to see the slightest incident stop a system of government which the most happy circumstances had combined to bring so far. The subject of the debates was all the more complicated since in the state where the finances of the United States are located, it is not only a question of finding the central point among the representation, population, wealth, and maritime and interior parts of the dominion, but it is also necessary to have a convenient place of provisional residence while waiting for Congress to have the federal city built. Philadelphia and Baltimore challenge this advantage [of] New York; the five Southern States want to entice Congress there; the Northern States want it to move as little as possible; each side fears that the [state] which has Congress nearest it will have too much influence on national affairs. On the other hand each state which because of its position could claim to have Congress, clings to it all the more fervently since it supposes that reasons of convenience will cause preference to be given to its citizens for public jobs and that it counts on having a special influence in this manner. But all the intrigues which originated from this clash of interests having been exhausted in vain, Pennsylvania finally voted with the party for New York, so that the new government will begin its operations in the latter city on the first Wednesday of March of next year. It is very likely that after having won this difficult point, New York will continue to be the residence of the general government until one is built in the central point which Congress is to be occupied with determining. The motive for this unforeseen compromise on the part of the delegates of Pennsylvania, must be attributed to the advantage which the Antifederalists have drawn from the delays of Congress, in order to manage to make sure of the election of members of their party in the individual legislatures and in the general government. The danger had become alarming and the Federalists whispered loudly about seeing the public good sacrificed to secondary viewpoints. The latter prevail in most of the present legislatures and will perhaps be the minority in those that will follow. It was essential for the success of their cause that Congress immediately ask the legislatures to appoint the two Senators which each of the states are to send and to order the election of the delegates and of the President. In effect, if all these officers were appointed through the influence of the Antifederalists, they would assist themselves in the attempts that their party must make to reduce the powers of the new government. Pennsylvania in particular has just had a conference among the Antifederalists of all the counties of the state under specious pretexts, and they have secretly agreed to the list of officers whom their party must appoint; the Ordinance of Congress appears to be in time to permit the legislature currently seated at least to assure itself of Federalist Senators. It is because of this circumstance that that state had to vote in favor of the New York residence.

1. Archives Nationales, Affaires Étrangères, Series BI, Volume 910, Correspondance Consulaires, New York: II (1788-1792), 65-66. Antoine-René-Charles-Mathurin de la Forest had served in the French legation in the United States during the Revolution. After serving as Vice-Consul in Georgia and South Carolina, he moved to New York in 1785 where he served as Consul-General from 1786 until 1793.

DeWitt Clinton to Dr. Charles Clinton, New York, 19 September (excerpt)[1]

I suppose you have heard that North Carolina has rejected the Constitution by a majority of 102. This step is imputed to letters from this state giving reason to suppose that our Convention would set the example. I imagine P[atrick] Henry's mighty influence in that state has assisted in bringing about the measure. A meeting of delegates from every county in Pennsylvania was held the 3d instant at Harrisburg. The ostensible design is this: that the opponents to the new Constitution may concenter their endeavors in the election of Antifeds to the new Congress. Some suppose it was intended to prevent the operation of the government in that state, but the result of their proceedings evinces the contrary.

After a great struggle between the Northern and Southern members in Congress as to the place of the meeting of the first Congress under the new Constitution, it is finally determined by an ordinance that this city shall be the place, the first

Wednesday of January next the time of appointing Electors throughout the several states, the first Wednesday of February next the day of electing the President, and the first Wednesday of March the day of putting the government in operation. I always supposed that subsequent amendments were never the serious design of the great friends of the new government and that the idea was only a political maneuver to lead the people to its adoption. In some of the Philadelphia and Boston newspapers, emendations to the government are evidently reprobated, the Circular Letter and proposed amendments of our Convention styled impertinent and destructive, and an attempt to procure alterations, until the government is tried, called high treason against the majesty of the people.[2] Messieurs Samuel Adams and [Elbridge] Gerry are nominated in the Massachusetts newspapers as Senators for that state. The first is earnest for amendments and the second was a member of the General Convention and refused to subscribe to the Constitution. By a cooperation of influence, it is supposed they may get in.[3]

1. RC, Washington's Headquarters Museum, Newburgh, N.Y. DeWitt Clinton was a nephew and personal secretary of Governor George Clinton of New York. Dr. Charles Clinton was DeWitt Clinton's great-uncle.

2. See Newspaper Response to New York's Act of Ratification and Circular Letter of 26 July, printed above.

3. Documents describing Adams' and Gerry's involvement in the election are printed in Chapter V.

George Washington to James Madison, Mount Vernon, 23 September[1]

I duly received your letter of the 24th of last month,[2] but as we had no intelligence or circumstance in this quarter worthy of your acceptance, I postponed even the acknowledgment until I was gratified by the receipt of your subsequent favor of the 14th instant.[3] Indeed I have now little more to give you in return, than this information to prevent your apprehension of miscarriage; and my thanks for your illustration of the subject which has lately engaged the attention of Congress.

Upon mature reflection, I think the reasons you offer in favor of Philadelphia as the place for the first meeting of Congress are conclusive: especially when the farther agitation of the question respecting its permanent residence is taken into consideration. But I cannot, however, avoid being satisfied that the minority should have acquiesced in any place, rather than to have prevented the system from being carried into effect. The delay had already become the source of clamors and might have given advantages to the Antifederalists. Their expedient will now probably be an attempt to procure the election of so many of their own junto under the new government, as, by the introduction of local and embarrassing disputes, to impede or frustrate its operation.

In the meantime it behooves all the advocates of the Constitution, forgetting partial and smaller considerations, to combine their exertions for collecting the wisdom and virtue of the continent to one center; in order that the Republic may avail itself of the opportunity for escaping from anarchy, division, and the other great national calamities that impended. To be shipwrecked in sight of the port would be the severest of all possible aggravations to our misery; and I assure you I am under painful apprehensions from the single circumstance of Mr. [Patrick]

H[enry]'s having the whole game to play in the Assembly of this state, and the effect it may have on others; it should be counteracted if possible.

1. RC, Lee-Kohns Collection, NN. In a postscript Washington asked Madison "to forward the letters under cover with this by a favorable conveyance."
2. Printed above.
3. Printed above.

St. John de Crèvecoeur to Thomas Jefferson, New York, 20 October 1788 (excerpt)[1]

After a long and melancholy interval there are at last well-grounded hopes, that the new Constitution will take place and bind every part of this continent into a firm and solid political compact; I shall greatly rejoice to see this auspicious event. The murmurs of partial discontent, cloaked under what is called here Antifederalism, seem now greatly to abate; there remains but one wish, which is, that those country parties may not preponderate in the choice of federal Senators, and Delegates; if a majority of Federalists can be obtained in those two bodies, everything will go smoothly on. Their first session, which is to begin in March, will put the finishing hand to the great organization: but an amazing task when one considers the extent of all the departments. What a cool and exploring [sa]gacity will be wanted in the discussion and acceptation of those numberless amendments which a few of the states insist upon in order to please everybody; and yet to discriminate the useful from the needless, etc. In contemplating this great event I see with pleasure the happy and immediate consequences which will result to this country from this achievement of reason, for hitherto no other weapon has been made use of, if the natural order of causes and effects is not interrupted by untoward circumstances, by those fatal accidents which are so apt to start up, the transient evils which this country labors under, will gradually disappear to lead the people to gradual and substantial happiness. Experience will prevent and correct past errors; the inhabitants of this country will awake from their delusive dreams of credit, of unlimited trade, from those motley expedients which have been so often made use of by several of the states, in which dignity, national honor, justice and law have been perverted; the destructive jealousy, the fatal influence of local prepossessions, will be partly extinguished, one great national prevailing sentiment will operate throughout the whole. Never was so great a change in the opinion of the best people, as has happened these five years, almost everybody feels the necessity of coercive laws, government, union, industry and labor. I hope the small differences, entertained by some people about the mode of regeneration, will no longer be a barrier. Such will be the foundations of America's future peace, opulence and power. The exports of this country have singularly increased within these two years, and the imports have decreased in proportion. Manufactures of the most useful kind are establishing in Pennsylvania, Connecticut, and Massachusetts; in the South they begin to cultivate cotton; and in the North, they are erecting engines to spin it. Nails, canvass, cordages, glass, woolens, linens are now making, as good of their kind as any in Europe. Bridges are building everywhere, new communications are opening, new settlements forming, the fisheries have been singularly prosperous this year. Even here a singular spirit of improvement is conspicuous, they are paving all their streets in *dos d'âne* with elegant footpaths on each side; towards the North River, immense docks are filling up, with the adjacent banks, over which, a beautiful street 60 feet wide is already laid out, which begins at the Battery, and is to extend two miles, a considerable part of which is already done and paved. 4,000 pounds have been subscribed for embellishing, and enlarging the City Hall, in order to accommodate the new federal corps with more decency, and Major [Pierre] l'Enfant has been appointed to preside over these works, which he has planned himself. This country, once consolidated, will easily pay all its debts, by a wise system of commercial laws, encourage the industry of its inhabitants, and draw forth all this genius. The Transappalachian country is filling apace, there lies the embryo of new connections, a vast political field which I dare not explore.

1. RC, Jefferson Papers, DLC. Printed: Boyd, XIV, 28-31. According to the *Dictionary of American Biography*, Crèvecoeur's full name was Michel-Guillaume Jean de Crèvecoeur, although this letter was signed "St. Jno. de Crèvecoeur." Crèvecoeur was born in France and served for a time in the French army in Canada during the Seven Years War. He came to New York in 1759, travelled widely, and then became a citizen in 1765 and settled on a farm. Because of his opposition to certain aspects of the American Revolution, he went to France in 1780, leaving his wife and family behind. He published his *Letters from an American Farmer* in 1782 and returned in 1783 to New York, where he served as French Consul until his final return to France in 1790.

CHAPTER III

The Elections in South Carolina

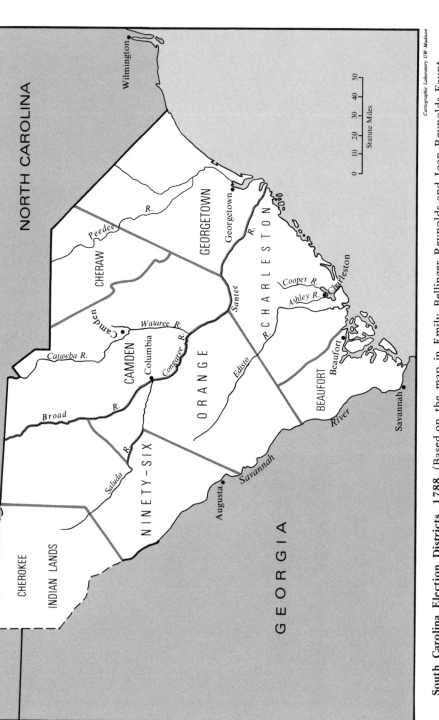

South Carolina Election Districts, 1788. (Based on the map in Emily Bellinger Reynolds and Joan Reynolds Faunt, compilers, *Biographical Directory of the Senate of the State of South Carolina 1776-1964* [South Carolina Archives Department, Columbia, 1964], n.p.)

INTRODUCTION

The first federal elections in South Carolina took place in a context of continuing demands by backcountry residents for a greater share of political power, and of resistance by planters, merchants, and lawyers in and around Charleston and other tidewater areas to those demands.

By 1770 the backcountry contained at least half of the legal voters in the colony but had only three representatives, whereas the lowcountry parishes had forty-five. The tidewater magnates who dominated the political life of the colony were forced to yield in part, however, when they wrote South Carolina's first constitution in March 1776, for they needed backcountry support in the struggle with Great Britain. The new constitution created a 202-member lower house which included seventy-six backcountry representatives, but lowcountry members still retained a substantial numerical edge. Charleston District received ninety-six representatives (with thirty from Charleston itself) and Beaufort and Georgetown districts received a combined total of thirty. Furthermore, the upper house or Legislative Council was elected by the lower house from among its own members, and the governor, also chosen by the legislature, had absolute power to veto legislation.

Demands for revision of the constitution began before it was a year old. In March 1778 the legislature approved a new constitution which abolished the veto power of the governor. Apportionment in the lower house remained unchanged, and although the new Senate which replaced the old Legislative Council was popularly elected, it too was heavily weighted in favor of the tidewater parishes. Charleston District got thirteen senators, Beaufort and Georgetown five, and the backcountry areas eleven.

The disparity between population and representation continued to grow during the 1780s. By the end of the decade, only about 20 percent of a total white population of about 140,000 lived in the three lowcountry districts, while about 80 percent lived in the backcountry, which pressed continuously for more representation in the legislature, for removal of the capital away from Charleston, and for a new constitution.

The South Carolina delegation in the Constitutional Convention at Philadelphia in 1787 consisted of John Rutledge, General Charles Cotesworth Pinckney, Charles Pinckney, and Pierce Butler, all of whom represented the lowcountry. They fought vigorously in the Convention for the election of federal Representatives as well as Senators by the state legislatures rather than by popular vote. John Rutledge reflected a central issue in South Carolina politics when he told the Convention that if "this convention had been chosen by the people in districts it is not to be supposed that such proper characters would have been preferred."

South Carolina, in effect, had two debates over the ratification of the proposed Federal Constitution. The Constitution was read to the South Carolina House of Representatives on Wednesday, 16 January 1788, and then debated for three days, with lowcountry delegates favoring and backcountry delegates attacking it. The legislature then unanimously agreed to call a convention to consider ratification, but the question of where it would meet divided the members along sectional lines. By a vote of 76 to 75 the Convention was called to sit at Charleston on 12 May. Lowcountry delegates strongly supported the motion, while backcountry representatives just as strongly opposed it.

The South Carolina Convention ratified the Constitution on 23 May by a vote of 149 to 73. The 137 delegates from the three lowcountry districts (representing about 20 percent of the white population) voted 121 to 16 to ratify. The 85 delegates from the middle and backcountry districts (representing nearly 80 percent of the white population) voted 57 to 28 against ratification.

South Carolina was entitled to five Representatives according to the Constitution. In writing its election law, the South Carolina legislature rejected the recommendations of a joint committee of both houses that federal Representatives be chosen at large, and voted instead for election by districts. Scarcely more than half the members of the lower house, 113 out of 202, were present for the vote. Lowcountry representatives supported the district plan 56 to 18, while backcountry representatives divided almost evenly, 21 in favor and 18 opposed. In the Senate, the four backcountry senators present voted for district elections, while the senators from the lowcountry and adjoining districts divided almost evenly. It is perhaps fair to speculate that the lowcountry representatives, knowing that the backcountry was overwhelmingly opposed to the Constitution, feared that statewide elections would mean the election of five Antifederalists to the House of Representatives. And as it turned out, three of the five districts elected Antifederalists in the first federal elections.

The election law of 4 November 1788 divided the state into five election districts based on the seven judicial districts established before the Revolution. The Charleston, Camden, and Ninety-Six districts were assigned one Representative each. The Beaufort and Orangeburg districts were combined to elect a Representative, as were the Georgetown and Cheraws districts. The candidates were not required to reside in the districts. The law provided that the election be held at the same time as the regular state election prescribed in the state constitution, which in 1788 was to be on 24 and 25 November. The state Senate proposed to elect United States Senators as soon as the election law passed, but the state House of Representatives insisted on delaying until the following January.

The one election contest that can be documented was in the Charleston District, and it was a clash of personalities and political ambitions rather than of political philosophies. The three candidates, Dr. David Ramsay, Commodore Alexander Gillon, and William Smith, had all supported ratification of the Constitution.

Gillon had acquired a popular following after the War for Independence by leading the opposition to British merchants in South Carolina, but little was said about him during the campaign. The contest, fought out in newspapers and broadsides in the few days before the election, was between David Ramsay and William Smith. Ramsay charged that Smith was not a citizen because he had lived in England during most of the Revolution and had not returned to South Carolina until 1783. Ramsay was charged with opposition to slavery, and, having been born in Pennsylvania, had the additional handicap of being a "foreigner." Smith won the three-way contest and became an ardent Federalist leader in Congress.

Since the Governor and Council announced only the votes received by the winning candidates in the other four districts, it is unknown how much opposition, if any, they had, except that the newspapers reported that Robert Barnwell carried Prince William Parish in the combined Beaufort-Orangeburg District. Daniel Huger, a native Carolinian, was elected in the combined Georgetown-Cheraws District and served two terms in the House of Representatives. He was evidently a Federalist but played no particular role in Congress. The other three candidates, all born outside the state, had opposed ratification of the Constitution, and two of them became important Republican leaders. Aedanus Burke, born in Ireland, was elected in the combined Beaufort-Orangeburg District and served one term in Congress. Thomas Sumter, born in Virginia, was elected from Camden District, and as a Representative, and later as a Senator, was a supporter of Thomas Jefferson. Thomas Tudor Tucker, born in Bermuda, was elected in Ninety-Six District, served two terms, and then was defeated. Thomas Jefferson appointed him Treasurer of the United States in 1801.

Almost nothing is known about the election of United States Senators, and it is uncertain how many candidates there were. Charles Pinckney later said that he could have been elected but that he refused for personal reasons. Rawlins Lowndes was asked to be a candidate but refused on grounds of age and health. On 22 January 1789 the legislature chose Pierce Butler and Ralph Izard. Butler, born in Ireland, was elected as a Federalist although there was some doubt about him. He later opposed Federalist policies and resigned in 1796 because of the Jay Treaty. For a time he supported the Republicans and was reelected to the Senate but resigned once more in protest against Republican policies. Izard, perhaps the wealthiest planter in South Carolina, was a Federalist and retired after one term in the Senate.

NOTE ON SOURCES

The principal sources for legislative proceedings in South Carolina in this period are the unpublished manuscript journals for the House and Senate in the South Carolina Department of Archives and History, Columbia. The journals give only the barest outline of actions taken and very few roll-call votes. An indispensable publication for editing these documents is the *Biographical Directory of the Senate of the State of South Carolina 1776-1964* (South Carolina Department of Archives and History, Columbia, 1964), compiled by Emily Bellinger Reynolds and Joan Reynolds Faunt. The book contains, in addition to the names and terms of office of the state senators, the names and terms of office of governors, lieutenant governors, councillors, and other state officials, and useful maps of election districts.

The election law of 1788 required that the votes of the districts for members of the United States House of Representatives be sent to the Governor and Privy Council for counting, and then be deposited with the Secretary of State. However, the Governor and Council reported only the votes for the successful candidates. The actual vote tallies in each of the districts forwarded to the Secretary of State have apparently been lost. Therefore, except for the Charleston District, where the newspapers reported the votes for the rival candidates, there is almost no evidence that the men elected in the other four districts had much if any opposition.

Very few private letters have been found concerning the election of members to the first federal Congress. Because of the scarcity of such letters, newspapers and broadsides are particularly important sources. Three newspapers were published in South Carolina, all of them in Charleston. They were John Markland and John M'Iver's *The City Gazette, or the Daily Advertiser*; Thomas B. Bowen and James Vandle's *The Columbian Herald, or the Independent Courier of North America*, a semi-weekly; and Ann Timothy's *The State Gazette of South Carolina*, a semi-weekly. The *City Gazette* is the best of the three. It printed items written by candidates and their allies, voting returns, and reports of legislative debates. The State Historical Society of Wisconsin has the most complete collection of the issues of the *City Gazette* for this period, and in addition, several important election broadsides that are available nowhere else. Nevertheless, many questions concerning the first federal elections in South Carolina will have to remain unanswered until, if ever, new materials are found.

SOUTH CAROLINA CHRONOLOGY, 1788–1789

1788

26 September	Election Ordinance of 13 September delivered to Governor Thomas Pinckney.
27 September	Governor Pinckney issues proclamation urging legislature to meet punctually on 7 October.
7 October	Legislative session begins.
9 October	Election Ordinance of 13 September transmitted to House of Representatives and referred to committee to report thereon.
14 October	House of Representatives and Senate appoint joint committee to consider Election Ordinance.
17 October	Joint committee recommends at-large election of Representatives and election of Senators in the present session of legislature. House postpones consideration of report to 20 October.
18 October	Senate approves joint committee report after rejecting proposal for division of state into five districts for election of Representatives.
20 October	House approves joint committee report and bill ordered brought in.
23 October	Bill for electing Representatives and Electors brought in and read first time in House.
27 October	House amends bill to provide for elections of Representatives in five districts instead of at-large elections and sends bill to Senate.
28 October	Senate reads bill first time.
30 October	Motion in Senate to restore at-large elections is defeated and bill returned to House.

31 October	House passes election law and sends it to Senate.
3 November	Senate proposes and House accepts minor amendments and act is ordered engrossed. Senate proposes to elect United States Senators that afternoon but House refuses.
4 November	Engrossed copy of election law approved; legislative session ends.
8 November	Newspaper nominations of candidates for House of Representatives published in *City Gazette*.
22-25 November	Newspaper and broadside campaign in Charleston District between David Ramsay and William Smith.
24-25 November	Election of United States Representatives and South Carolina state senators and representatives.
1 December	Election returns for Charleston District printed in *State Gazette*.

1789

6 January	Privy Council counts votes for members of House of Representatives.
7 January	Governor Thomas Pinckney issues proclamation announcing election of William Smith, Aedanus Burke, Daniel Huger, Thomas Sumter, and Thomas Tudor Tucker to United States House of Representatives.
7 January	Legislative session begins; legislators choose presidential Electors: Christopher Gadsden, Henry Laurens, Arthur Simkins, Edward Rutledge, Charles Cotesworth Pinckney, Thomas Heyward, John Faucheraud Grimké.
22 January	Joint legislative session elects Pierce Butler and Ralph Izard United States Senators.
4 February	South Carolina Electors vote for George Washington (7), John Rutledge (6), and John Hancock (1).

THE DOCUMENTS

Privy Council Proceedings, Saturday, 27 September 1788[1]

Present: His Excellency the Governor, His Honor the Lieutenant Governor, Honorable Mr. R. Izard, Mr. Pinckney, Mr. Washington, Mr. Gervais, Mr. Rutledge.

Read the act of Congress of the 13th September 1788 for putting into operation the Constitution ratified by eleven states and received by government on yesterday. His Excellency desired the opinion of Council upon the necessity of notifying to the representatives the above act in order to have a full representation and in what manner that notification should be given. Agreed and recommended that His Excellency do issue his proclamation for the punctual attendance of the legislature to the time of their adjournment and that it should be sent by express and that three hundred proclamations should be struck off.

1. Rough Minute Book of the Privy Council, 1783-1789, Sc-Ar. The smooth journals for 1783-1786 and the rough minute book for 1786-1789 are published in Adele S. Edwards, ed., *Journals of the Privy Council 1783-1789* (Columbia, 1971).

Proclamation by Governor Thomas Pinckney, Saturday, 27 September[1]

Whereas the United States in Congress assembled by their act passed the thirteenth day of September one thousand seven hundred and eighty eight resolved "That the first Wednesday in January next be the day for appointing electors in the several states which before the said day shall have ratified the said constitution That the first Wednesday in February next be the day for the electors to assemble in their respective states and vote for a President And that the first Wednesday in March next be the time and the present seat of Congress the place for commencing proceedings under the said Constituion" And whereas the times places and manner of holding elections for senators and representatives under the constitution of the United States are to be prescribed in each state by the legislature thereof I do therefore issue this proclamation giving authentic information of the above act of Congress as an additional inducement to the punctual attendance of the members of the legislature on the seventh day of October next being the day to which they stand adjourned. Given under my hand and the great seal of the State in the city of Charleston this 27th. day of September in the year of our Lord one thousand seven hundred and eighty eight and of the sovereignty and Independence of the United States of America the thirteenth.

1. (LT), Miscellaneous Record Book, XX, 406-7, Sc-Ar. Of the 300 copies ordered printed, none has been located. The proclamation was published in the *City Gazette*, 29 September.

David Ramsay to Benjamin Rush, Charleston, 29 September (excerpt)[1]

If my country should confer on me a seat in the federal House of Repesentatives I would not refuse it but this only *inter nos*. I shall not seek for it nor shall I be disappointed if I do not obtain it. If it comes at all it shall come unsolicited by me. There are some circumstances unfavorable to the scheme. Of late some jealousy of offices being conferred on men who were not natives has showed itself among a few leading characters. Our narrow minded politicians say that the Southern States will be made tributary to the Northern by the new Constitution. Some may and probably will object the impolicy of trusting the legislative part of that business in the hands of a Northern man by birth. The bulk of our people are candid and liberal but they are not exempt from some prejudices which will be unfavorable to me. I shall be indifferent about the event. If I should not be appointed my business of superintending the printing of my book[2] being over I shall return to the practice of physic. Should the appointment take place I can both afford and would be willing to sacrifice my profession to public service. You are the only person in the world to whom I have hinted this matter.

1. RC, Rush Papers, PPL. Printed: Ramsay, *Writings*, 122-23.
2. *The History of the American Revolution* (2 vols., Philadelphia, 1789).

House Proceedings, Thursday, 9 October[1]

[The House received the following message from the Governor.]

Events which have taken place during your recess have evinced the propriety of your adjournment to the present period.

Eleven states having acceded to the Constitution proposed for the government of the United States by the Federal Convention, Congress have taken measures pursuant to the recommendation of the Convention for carrying it into effect. Their resolutions for this purpose are herewith transmitted to you.

The Convention of this state met for the purpose of considering and of ratifying or rejecting the Federal Constitution, after twelve days spent in deliberation thereon, finally ratified the same on the 24th day of May last. A copy of the ratification is by their direction lodged in the office of the secretary of the state; having had the honor of being elected president of that body I shall direct the journal of their proceedings to be laid before you for your information.

The other dispatches now submitted to your consideration were received subsequent to your last adjournment.

Thomas Pinckney, Charleston,
Thursday, 9 October 1788

Ordered, that the following letters and papers accompanying the above message be referred to committees, viz.,

. . . .

An act of Congress of the 13th September last, for putting into operation the Constitution ratified by eleven states referred to Mr. Chancellor Rutledge, General Pinckney, Mr. Charles Pinckney, Major Butler, Mr. Bee, Mr. Chancellor Mathews, Mr. Justice Burke, Mr. Lincoln, Commodore Gillon, Mr. Cudworth, Mr.

Craig, Mr. Izard, Mr. Justice Heyward who are directed to report thereon as speedy as possible.

1. Journals of the House of Representatives of the State of South Carolina, Sc-Ar. Hereafter, the proceedings of the House and the Senate, unless otherwise indicated, are from the manuscript journals, and will be cited by date only. The working papers of the South Carolina House of Representatives and Senate, including messages between the two houses, are in Legislative Records and Papers, Sc-Ar.

Newpaper Report of House Proceedings on Thursday, 9 October[1]

On a committee being named to consider the resolve of Congress relative to election of members for the new government, Dr. [David] Ramsay observed, that as this was the only business the House had met to accomplish, the committee might sit immediately, bring up a report, which if the House agreed to, then they might all go home.

1. *City Gazette*, 10 October.

House and Senate Proceedings, Tuesday, 14 October

The House

A motion was made and seconded that a message be prepared and sent to the Senate requesting that they would appoint a committee to join a committee of this House to take into consideration "an act of Congress of the 13th September 1788 for putting into operation the Constitution ratified by eleven states" and to report thereon as speedily as possible, which being agreed to, the following message was accordingly prepared, viz.,

In the House of Representatives, October 14th 1788

Honorable Gentlemen: This House having appointed a committee to take into consideration "an act of Congress of the 13th September 1788 for putting into operation the Constitution ratified by eleven states and to report thereon as speedily as possible," this House request that your House will appoint a committee to join the committee of this House for the foregoing purpose. Our committee are Mr. Chancellor Rutledge, General Pinckney, Mr. Charles Pinckney, Major Butler, Commodore Gillon, Mr. Cudworth, Mr. Craig, Mr. Chancellor Mathews, Mr. Justice Burke, Mr. Lincoln, Mr. Izard, Mr. Bee, Mr. Justice Heyward.

By order of the House, John Julius Pringle, Speaker.

Ordered, that the message be sent to the Senate, and that General Pinckney and Mr. William Smith do carry the same.

The Senate

[The Senate received the Governor's message of 9 October. For text see House Proceedings, 9 October.]

Read the act of Congress for putting into operation the Constitution ratified by eleven states dated the 13th September 1788.

Ordered, that the said message and act of Congress be referred to a committee, and a committee was appointed accordingly, viz., General Moultrie, General Barnwell, Colonel Vanderhorst, Colonel Huger, Mr. Desausure.

. . . .

[The Senate received the message from the House of Representatives asking for the appointment of a joint committee to consider the act of Congress of 13 September.]

The House [Senate] having taken the said message into consideration agreed thereto, and appointed a committee accordingly, viz., General Moultrie, General Barnwell, Colonel Vanderhorst, Colonel Huger, Mr. DeSaussure.

Ordered, that a message be prepared and sent to the House of Representatives to inform them that this House, agreeable to their request, have appointed a committee to join their committee for the purposes mentioned in their said message.

Pursuant to order a message was prepared which being read was agreed to as followeth, viz.,

Mr. Speaker and Gentlemen: In answer to your message just received, this House inform your House, that this House agreeable to your request, have appointed a committee to join the committee of your House "to take into consideration an act of Congress of the 13th September 1788 for putting into operation the Constitution ratified by eleven states, and to report thereon as speedily as possible." Our committee are General Moultrie, General Barnwell, Colonel Vanderhorst, Colonel Huger, Mr. DeSaussure.

Ordered, that Mr. President do sign the message and that the clerk do carry the same to the House of Representatives.

House and Senate Proceedings, Friday, 17 October

The House

Mr. Chancellor Rutledge reported from the committee appointed to join a committee of the Senate to take into consideration an act of Congress of the 13th day of September last, which he read in his place and afterward delivered it in at the clerk's table where it was again read for information.

Ordered, that it be taken into consideration on Monday next, the 20th instant.

The Senate

General Moultrie, from the committee appointed to join a committee of the House of Representatives to take into consideration an act of Congress of the 13th September 1788 for putting into operation the Constitution ratified by eleven states, informed the House that the committee had prepared a report which they had directed him to report to the House. He read the said report in his place, and afterwards delivered it in at the clerk's table where the same was again read and is as followeth, viz.,

That your committee joined the committee of the House of Representatives for the above purposes and agreed to report the following resolutions, viz.,

Resolved, that the election for the House of Representatives shall be chosen by the people at large in the several parishes and districts of this state and that the last Monday and Tuesday in November next, shall be the days for the said election to be held at the same time and places where the general election for members of the legislature of this state shall be held.

Resolved, that the Senators shall be chosen by the legislature at this present sitting.[1]

Resolved, that seven Electors be appointed by the Governor and Council in case the legislature should not be sitting on the first Wednesday in January next for the purpose of choosing a President.

Ordered, that the said report be taken into consideration tomorrow.

1. The election of United States Senators by a joint session of the two houses of the legislature was based on this resolution, which did not become a part of the election law. Apparently there was no controversy over the method of electing Senators, as there was in such states as New York and Massachusetts.

Senate Proceedings, Saturday, 18 October

Ordered, that the order of the day to take into consideration the report of the committee appointed to join a committee of the House of Representatives to whom was referred an act of Congress of the 13th September last for putting into operation the Constitution ratified by eleven states, be now read. And the same was read accordingly. The House then proceeded to debate the report, and after having spent some time therein,

A motion was made and the question being put that the first resolution be amended by striking out the following words, viz., "in the several parishes and districts of this state and that the last Monday and Tuesday in November next shall be the days for the said election to be held at the same time and places where the general election for members of the legislature of this state shall be held," and to insert in lieu thereof, "and for that purpose the state shall be divided into five districts, and that each district shall elect one member as a Representative to the general government."

It passed in the negative.

It was moved that this House do concur with the remainder of the report, which was agreed to. The report being debated and gone through,

Resolved, that this House do agree with the said report and resolutions.

Ordered, that the clerk do sign and carry the same to the House of Representatives for their concurrence.

It was moved and seconded, that leave be given to bring in a bill to carry into effect the foregoing resolutions, which was agreed to, and leave was given accordingly.

Ordered, that the same committee do prepare and bring in the said bill.

Ordered, that a message be prepared and sent to the House of Representatives to inform them that this House have agreed to the report of the committee appointed to join a committee of their House to take into consideration an act of Congress of the 13th September last, for putting into operation the Constitution ratified by eleven states, and to request their concurrence thereto.

Pursuant to order, a message was prepared, which being read was agreed to as followeth, viz.,

Mr. Speaker and Gentlemen: This House having taken into consideration the report of the joint committee of both house[s] respecting the act of Congress of the 13th of September last, for putting into operation the Constitution ratified by eleven states, agreed thereto, and have herewith sent your House the said report and resolutions, to which this House request your concurrence.

Ordered, that Mr. President do sign the message, and that the clerk do carry the same to the House of Representatives.

House Proceedings, Monday, 20 October

[The House received the Senate message of 18 October approving the resolutions of the joint committee.]

. . . .

Agreeably to the order of the day, the House took into consideration the report of the committee appointed to join a committee of the Senate to take into consideration an act of Congress of the 13th September last, which being read through, was agreed to and is as follows, viz.,

Report, that your committee have met the committee of the Senate and taken into consideration the said act of Congress. And the said committee and your committee concurred in opinion that Senators be chosen by the legislature at this session, that elections for members of the House of Representatives be held at the times and places for choosing members of the next legislature of this state, that five members be chosen at each of those places, and that the five persons who have the highest numbers of votes of all the electors be the members.

And that seven Electors of a President be appointed on the first Wednesday in January next by the legislature if then sitting, and if not, by the Governor and Council.

Ordered, that the report be referred back to the same committee to bring in a bill agreeably thereto.

House Proceedings, Thursday, 23 October

Mr. Chancellor Rutledge from the committee appointed to bring in a bill prescribing on the part of this state, the times, places and manner of holding elections for Representatives in the Congress, and the manner of appointing Electors of a President of the United States, reported a bill for that purpose which was received and read a first time.[1]

Ordered, that the bill be read a second time tomorrow.

1. The original draft of this bill has not been located.

House Proceedings, Friday, 24 October

On motion, ordered, that Monday next be appointed for the second reading of the bill for prescribing on the part of this state, the times, places and manner of holding elections for Representatives in the Congress, and the manner of appointing Electors of a President of the United States, and that there be a call of the House on that day.

House Proceedings, Monday, 27 October

Agreeably to the order of the day the House proceeded to the second reading of a bill for prescribing on the part of this state the times, places and manner of holding elections for Representatives in the Congress and the manner of appointing Electors of a President of the United States. On reading the first clause a motion was made and seconded that it be struck out and another clause inserted in its place.[1] On the question being put, the yeas and nays were required by Mr. Justice Pendleton and seconded by Mr. Cudworth are as follows, viz.,

Saint Philip and St. Michaels Parishes, Charleston

Edward Rutledge	ay
David Ramsay	ay
William Johnson	ay
Charles C. Pinckney	ay
Edward Darrell	ay
Thomas Jones	ay
Isaac Motte	ay
John Matthews	ay
Daniel Stevens	ay
John Blake	no
Anthony Toomer	ay
John F. Grimké	ay
Thomas Heyward, Jr.	no
Richard Lushington	ay
Francis Kinloch	ay
Jacob Read	ay
Edward Blake	no
John Budd	ay
Rawlins Lowndes	ay
Thomas Bee	ay
Aedanus Burke	ay
Edward Lightwood	ay

Christ Church Parish

Charles Pinckney	no
Plowden Weston	ay
Joseph Manigault	ay

St. John's Parish, Berkeley County

Thomas Simons	ay

Saint Andrew's Parish

John Rivers	ay
William Scott, Jr.	ay
James Ladson	ay
Ralph Izard, Jr.	ay

St. George's Parish, Dorchester

Matthias Hutchinson	ay
William Postell	ay
John Bell	no
Thomas Waring	ay

St. James's Parish, Goose-Creek

Ralph Izard	ay
John Deas, Jr.	ay
Gabriel Manigault	ay
William Smith	ay
Peter Smith	ay

St. Thomas and St. Dennis's Parish

Thomas Screven	ay
Lewis Fogartie	ay
Isaac Parker	no

Saint Paul's Parish

George Haig	ay
William Washington	ay
Roger P. Saunders	ay
Paul Hamilton	ay
Joseph Slann	ay

St. Bartholomew's Parish

William Clay Snipes	no
John North	ay
Daniel Doyley	ay
William Fishburne	ay
Benjamin Postell	no

Saint Helena's Parish

William H. Wigg	no
John Jenkins	ay
Robert Barnwell	no
Benjamin Reynolds	ay
Bernard Elliott	no

St. James's Parish, Santee

Thomas Horry	ay
John Bowman	no

Prince George's Parish, Winyah

James Withers	ay
Thomas Waties	no
Matthew Irvine	no

All Saints Parish

Robert Heriot	ay

Prince Frederick's Parish

Benjamin Porter	ay

St. John's Parish, Colleton County

Isaac Jenkins	ay
Isaac Holmes	ay
William Smelie	ay
Hugh Wilson	ay

Saint Peter's Parish

John Chisholm	ay

Prince William's Parish

Pierce Butler	no
John McPherson	no
William Murray	no

Saint Stephen's Parish

Peter Sinkler	no
Thomas Cordes	ay

District to the Eastward of Wateree River

John Chesnut	no
Thomas Sumter	ay
Joseph Lee	ay
Thomas McFadden	ay
George Cooper	ay
Benjamin Cudworth	ay
Samuel Dunlap	ay

District of Ninety Six

Arthur Simpkins	no
Robert Anderson	no
James Lincoln	no
Adam Crain Jones	no
William Butler	no

District of Saxe Gotha

    Henry Pendleton   no

Lower District between Broad and Saluda rivers

    Philemon Waters   ay
    George Ruff   ay

Little River District

    Angus Campbell   ay
    James Mayson   no

Upper or Spartan District

    Thomas Brandon   no
    Samuel McJunkin   no
    William Kennedy   no

District between Broad and Catawba rivers

    Minor Winn   ay
    James Craig   no
    Thomas Baker   ay
    Aromanus Lyles   no
    John Cook   ay
    James Pedian   ay

District called the New Acquisition

    William Fergus   ay
    William Bratton   ay
    James Ramsay   ay
    John Dunnan   ay
    James Martin   no
    Joseph Palmer   no

Saint Mathew's Parish

    John Frierson   no

Orange Parish

    John Dantignac   no
    Lewis Lesterjette   no

Saint David's Parish

    William Strother   ay
    Calvin Spencer   ay
    Andrew Hunter   ay

District between Savannah River and the North Fork of Edisto

    Isaac Bush   ay

             Ayes 77   Nays 36[2]

So it was resolved in the affirmative.

The bill being then read through, and some amendments made therein, it was agreed to.

Ordered, that the bill be sent to the Senate and that Mr. Kinloch and Mr. Cordes do carry the same.

1. No copy of the motion which carried has been located, but it evidently proposed striking out the committee's proposal for the at-large election of Representatives and substituting election by districts. This is indicated by the fact that when the bill reached the Senate an effort was made to strike out the first clause and substitute a clause calling for at-large elections (see Senate Proceedings, 30 October, printed below).

2. The manuscript journal reads "Nays 38," but only 36 negative votes are recorded in the roll call.

Senate Proceedings, Tuesday, 28 October

A verbal message from the House of Representatives by Mr. Kinloch and Mr. Cordes, viz.,

Honorable Gentlemen: The House of Representatives have read a second time a bill prescribing on the part of this state, the times, places and manner of holding elections for Representatives in the Congress and the manner of appointing Electors of a President of the United States, and have sent the said bill to this House.

Read a first time, the bill prescribing on the part of this state, the times, places and manner of holding elections for Representatives in the Congress, and the manner of appointing Electors of a President of the United States.

A motion was made and the question being put, that the bill be read a second time tomorrow. It passed in the negative.

Ordered, that the bill be read a second time on Thursday morning next, precisely at 11 o'clock, and that the messenger do summon the members to attend the service of the House at that hour.

Senate Proceedings, Thursday, 30 October

Pursuant to the order of the day, read a second time, the bill for prescribing on the part of this state, the times, places and manner of holding elections for Representatives in the Congress, and the manner of appointing Electors of a President of the United States.

The House then proceeded to debate the bill.

A motion was made and the question being put, that the first enacting clause be struck out, and to insert in the room thereof the following clause, viz.,

And be it enacted by the honorable the Senate and House of Representatives now met and sitting in General Assembly, and by the authority of the same, "that the election for the House of Representatives shall be chosen by the people at large in the several parishes and districts of this state, and that the last Monday and Tuesday in November next shall be the days for the said election to be held at the same time and places where the general election for members of the legislature of this state shall be held."

It passed in the negative.

The yeas and nays being required by Colonel Vanderhorst and Colonel Taylor are as followeth, viz.,

Yeas [9]

Mr. Bourdeaux	[St. Philip's and St. Michael's]
Mr. Middleton	[Prince William's]
Colonel Scott	[St. Andrew's]
Colonel Huger	[St. Thomas' and St. Dennis']
Colonel Vanderhorst	[Christ Church]
General Barnwell	[St. Helena's]
General Moultrie	[St. John's, Berkeley]
Mr. Simons	[St. James', Santee]
Major Smith	[St. James', Goose Creek]

Nays [11]

Mr. DeSaussure	[St. Philip's and St. Michael's]
Mr. Dunbar	[District between Savannah and North Fork of Edisto]
Major Hampton	[Lower District between Broad and Saluda rivers]
Major Jenkins	[St. John's, Colleton]
Mr. Garner	[St. Paul's]
Colonel Taylor	[District between Broad and Catawba rivers]
Colonel Hill	[New Acquisition District]
Colonel Thomson	[St. Mathew's and Orange]
Colonel Maham	[St. Stephen's]
Captain Allston	[Prince George's, Winyah, and All Saints']
Mr. Tucker	[Prince Frederick's]

A motion was made and the question being put, that after the word—"case"—in the fourth line of the last enacting clause be inserted "appoint one Elector out of each circuit court district and shall,"

It passed in the negative.

The bill being debated, amended and gone through,

Ordered, that the clerk do carry the bill to the House of Representatives.

House Proceedings, Friday, 31 October

[The House received the election bill from the Senate on 30 October.]

The House proceeded to the third reading of a bill for prescribing on the part of this state, the time, places and manner of holding elections for Representatives in the Congress and the manner of appointing Electors of a President of the United States, which being read through and some amendments made thereto was agreed to.

Resolved, that the bill do pass and that the title thereof be an act ["An Act prescribing on the part of this State the times places and manner of holding Elections for Representatives in the Congress and the manner of appointing Electors of a President of the United States"].[1]

Ordered, that the act be sent to the Senate and that Mr. Cuthbert and Mr. Kaltiesen do carry the same.

1. The journals do not include the title of the act, which is supplied from the Election Law, 4 November, printed below.

Senate Proceedings, Saturday, 1 November

[The Senate received the election bill from the House on 31 October.]

A motion was made and the question being put, that this House do proceed to read a third time the bill prescribing on the part of this state, the times, places and manner of holding elections for Representatives in the Congress, and the manner of appointing Electors of a President of the United States. It passed in the negative.

House and Senate Proceedings, Monday, 3 November

The Senate

Read a third time the bill prescribing on the part of this state, the times, places and manner of holding elections for Representatives in the Congress, and the manner of appointing Electors of a President of the United States.

The House then proceeded to debate the bill. It was moved and seconded that this House do propose by message to the House of Representatives the following amendments, viz.,

To insert between the words "conducted" and "shall" in the second line of the 2nd enacting clause, the words, "and who shall be the same persons as shall conduct the elections for members of the legislature, and they."

Which was agreed to. The bill being debated and gone through,

Ordered, that a message be prepared and sent to the House of Representatives to request that they will be pleased to permit this House to make the foregoing amendment to the said bill. . . .

Pursuant to order, a message was prepared which being read was agreed to as followeth, viz.,

Mr. Speaker and Gentlemen: This House are of opinion that the bill which your House have entitled "an Act, prescribing on the part of this State, the Times, places and manner of holding Elections for Representatives in the Congress, and the manner of appointing Electors of a President of the United States," should be amended by inserting between the words "conducted" and "shall" in the 2nd line of the 2nd enacting clause the following words—"and who shall be the same persons as shall conduct the elections for members of the legislature, and they" to which this House, request your concurrence, and that you will be pleased to permit this House to amend the bill entitled "an act" accordingly.

Ordered, that Mr. President do sign the message and that the clerk do carry the same to the House of Representatives.

The House

[The House received the Senate message.]

Ordered, that a message be prepared and sent to the Senate in answer thereto and that Mr. Speaker [do sign?] the same, the following message was accordingly prepared, viz.,

In the House of Representatives, 3rd November 1788

Honorable Gentlemen: This House having considered your message of this day respecting the amendment proposed by your House to be made to the bill intitled "An Act prescribing on the part of this State the times, [places] and manner of holding Elections for Representatives in the Congress and the manner of appointing Electors for a President of the United States" have agreed to the same and request that your House will amend the bill accordingly.

By order of the House, John Julius Pringle, Speaker

Ordered, that the message be sent to the Senate and that Colonel Motte and Mr. Gabriel Manigault do carry the same.

The Senate

[The Senate received the message from the House.]

The House [Senate] having amended the said bill agreeably to the request of the House of Representatives,

Resolved, that the bill do pass. . . .

Ordered, that the clerk do carry the act to the House of Representatives.

The House

The Senate returned to this House by their clerk a bill intitled "An Act prescribing on the part of this State the times, places and manner of holding elections for Representatives in the Congress and the manner of appointing Electors for a President of the United States" which had been read a third time in that House and passed.

Resolved, that the act be engrossed.

The Senate

On motion, ordered that a message be prepared and sent to the House of Representatives to inform them that this House are desirous of proceeding to the election of Senators to the Congress of the United States, and propose to meet this evening at 6 o'clock *for that purpose only*, and to request their concurrence thereto.

Pursuant to order, a message was prepared, which being read was agreed to as followeth, viz.,

Mr. Speaker and Gentlemen: This House are desirous of proceeding to the election of Senators to the Congress of the United States, and propose to meet this evening at 6 o'clock, *for that purpose only*, and to which this House request your concurrence.

Ordered, that Mr. President do sign the message and that the clerk do carry the same to the House of Representatives.

The House

This House took into consideration the clause of the report of the committee of this House appointed to join a committee of the Senate to take into consideration an act of Congress of the 13th September last, recommending that Senators be chosen by the legislature at this session,[1] and the question being put to agree to the same, the House divided. The yeas went forth:

Teller for the yeas, Major Snipes; votes 56.

Teller for the nays, Colonel Lushington; votes 61.

So it passed in the negative.

[The House then received the Senate's message calling for the election of Senators at six o'clock that evening.]

Ordered, that a message be prepared and sent to the Senate in answer to the above message and that Mr. Speaker do sign the same, the following message was accordingly prepared, viz.,

In the House of Representatives, 3rd November 1788

Honorable Gentlemen: In answer to your message just received relative to the proceeding to the election of Senators to the Congress of the United States, this House inform your House that having taken the same into consideration have disagreed thereto.

By order of the House, John Julius Pringle, Speaker

Ordered, that the message be sent to the Senate and that Colonel Motte and Mr. Gabriel Manigault do carry the same.

The Senate

[The Senate received the House message.]

On motion, ordered that a message be prepared, and sent to the House of Representatives to request that they will inform this House when they propose to proceed to the election of Senators to the Congress of the United States.

Pursuant to order, a message was prepared which being read was agreed to as followeth, viz.,

Mr. Speaker and Gentlemen: This House request that your House will inform this House when you propose to proceed to the election of Senators to the Congress of the United States.

Ordered, that Mr. President do sign the message and that the clerk do carry the same to the House of Representatives.

1. For the report, see Senate Proceedings, 17 October, printed above.

House and Senate Proceedings, Tuesday, 4 November

The House

[The House received the Senate's message of the previous day.]

Ordered, that a message be prepared and sent to the Senate in answer to the above, and that Mr. Speaker do sign the same. The following message was accordingly prepared, viz.,

In the House of Representatives, 4th November 1788

Honorable Gentlemen: In answer to your message of yesterday requesting that this House will inform your House, when this House propose to proceed to the election of Senators to the Congress of the United States, this House inform your House that this House have postponed the election till the next session of the legislature in January next.

By order of the House, John Julius Pringle, Speaker

Ordered, that the message be sent to the Senate and that Colonel Anderson and Mr. Lincoln do carry the same.

The Senate

[The Senate received the House message and took no further action on the election of Senators at this session.]

Joint Session of House and Senate, Tuesday, 4 November

At the end of each session, the legislature met in joint session to ratify acts passed during the session. Accordingly on the afternoon of 4 November, the election law was ratified by a joint session of both houses meeting in the Senate chambers, signed by the President of the Senate and the Speaker of the House, and sealed with the Great Seal of the State of South Carolina.

The South Carolina Election Law, 4 November[1]

State of South Carolina

At a General Assembly begun and holden at Charleston on Monday the first day of January in the year of our Lord one thousand Seven hundred and eighty Seven and in the eleventh Year of the Independence of the United States of America and from thence continued by divers adjournments to the fourth day of November in the year of our Lord one thousand seven hundred and eighty eight

An Act prescribing on the part of this State the times places and manner of holding Elections for Representatives in the Congress and the manner of appointing Electors of a President of the United States

In order to carry into effect on the part of this State the Constitution for the United States of America Be it Enacted by the honorable the Senate and the House of Representatives now met and sitting in General Assembly and by the authority of the same that the Elections in this State for Members of the House of Representatives in the Congress of the United States Shall be had in the manner following that is to say this State shall be and is hereby declared to be divided into five Districts of which for the present Charleston District shall form one Beaufort and Orangeburgh Districts united another Georgetown and Cheraw Districts united another Camden District another and Ninety Six District another[2] and each of the said five Districts shall Send one Member from this State to the House of Representatives in the Congress of the United States to be chosen by the persons qualified to vote for Members of the House of Representatives of this State And the said Elections shall be holden at the times and places and regulated and conducted in the same manner as the Elections for the Members of the House of Representatives of this State at the next general Election[3] And the person who at the said Election shall have the greatest number of votes in the District of Charleston and the person who shall have the greatest number of votes in the United Districts of Beaufort and Orangeburgh and the person who shall have the greatest number of votes in the United Districts of Georgetown and Cheraw and the person who shall have the greatest number of votes in Camden District and the person who shall the greatest number of votes in Ninety Six District shall be the Members from this State to the House of Representatives in the Congress of the United States.

And be it further Enacted by the authority aforesaid That the Officers or persons by whom each of the said Elections shall be conducted and who shall be the same persons as shall conduct the Elections for Members of the Legislature shall Make a true return within twenty days thereafter to the Governor or Commander in Chief of this State of the names of the persons voting and of the Candidates or persons voted for at the said Election and of the number of votes given thereat for each of the said Persons And that on the fifth day of January next or as soon thereafter as the Council can be convened the Governor shall cause the said returns to be examined in Council in a public manner and ascertain the number of votes given at the said Elections for every person and what five persons have respectively the greatest number of votes in the said Districts And having ascertained who are the said five persons duly elected in manner aforesaid to be Members of the House of Representatives in the Congress of the United States the Governor or Commander in Chief for the time being shall cause the same to be immediately notified by proclamation and notice of Such Election to be given to each Member And that the Governor or Commander in Chief shall deposit the original poll of each District in the Secretarys Office of the State.

And be it further Enacted by the authority aforesaid that in case the same person shall be returned for two or more of the said Districts he may chuse within twenty days after due notice shall be given him thereof for which District he will serve and on his making such choice or neglecting so to do within the said term the Governor or Commander in Chief for the time being shall direct another Election to be held within twenty days thereafter for the vacant District or Districts to be conducted and regulated in like manner as before prescribed And the Governor or the Commander in Chief shall proceed in the same manner where the Member elected in any of the said five Districts refuses to serve or omits to signify to the Governor or Commander in Chief his intention of serving within twenty days after he has received due notice of his Election and in case of the death of any person Elected or if his seat shall become vacated by any other means or if two or more persons shall have equal votes for any District the Governor shall order a new Election as the case may require to be conducted as near as may be in manner before prescribed.

And be it further Enacted by the authority aforesaid that Electors of a president of the United States shall be appointed by the Legislature of this State on the first Wednesday in January next or by such persons as shall be returned Members thereof and shall attend on that day and the said Electors previous to executing their appointment shall before his Excellency the Governor or Commander in Chief for the time being take the following Oath or Affirmation viz. I A.B do solemnly swear or affirm that I will faithfully and conscientiously discharge my duty as an Elector of a President of the United States So help me God.—

> In the Senate House the fourth day of November in the year of our Lord one thousand Seven hundred

and eighty eight and in the thirteenth year of the
Independence of the united States of America
John Lloyd president of the Senate
John J. Pringle, Speaker of the House
of Representatives

{ State of South Carolina
{ Secretary's Office—I hereby Certify that the foregoing
is a true Copy from the Original Act
of Record in this Office, compared
therewith by me this tenth day of
February 1789
[s] Peter Freneau
Secretary

1. (LT), RG 46, DNA. The engrossed copy of the law has not been located. The law is
transcribed from the two certified copies enclosed in a letter from Charles Cotesworth
Pinckney to Charles Thomson, secretary of the Confederation Congress, on 13 February
1789 (printed below). Both certified copies are mutilated. Missing words are supplied from
the earliest printed version in *Acts and Ordinances of the General Assembly of the State of
South Carolina; Passed in October and November 1788* (Charleston, 1789), 3-4.

2. The districts into which the state was divided for the election of United States Representatives were based on the seven circuit court districts created by the colonial legislature in
an act of 29 July 1769 (*Acts of the General Assembly of South Carolina, Passed in the Year
1769* [Charleston, 1769], 3-18). Those districts were retained essentially unchanged until at
least 1790.

3. Under the South Carolina Constitution of 1778 (Articles XII and XIII) state senators
were elected annually and state representatives every two years. The elections were held on
the last Monday of November and the day following (Thorpe, VI, 3250-51). In 1788 the
elections for both state senators and representatives came on 24 and 25 November.

Official Notice of Polling Places for State and Federal Elections,
7 November[1]

The general election for members to represent this state, in the Senate and
House of Representatives [of South Carolina] will take place on Monday and
Tuesday the 24th and 25th instant, viz.,

For the Parishes of Saint Philip and Saint Michael, Charleston, at Saint
Michael's Church. Managers—The Church-Wardens of both parishes.

For Christ-church Parish, at the house of Mr. James Eden. Managers—The
Church-Wardens.

For Saint John's Parish, Berkeley County, at the Club-House near the church.
Managers—Theodore Gourdine and John Broughton, esquires.

For Saint Andrew's Parish, at the parish church. Managers—The Church-
Wardens.

For Saint George's Parish, Dorchester, at the village of Dorchester. Managers—
The Church-Wardens.

For Saint James, Goose-Creek, at the parish church. Managers—The Church-
Wardens.

For Saint Thomas and Saint Dennis, at the parish church. Managers—The
Church-Wardens.

For Saint Paul, at the Parsonage-House. Managers—The Church-Wardens.

For Saint Bartholomew, at the Calvinist church, near Pon Pon church. Managers—Henry Hyrne and Artemas Ferguson, esquires.

For Saint Helena, at Beaufort church. Managers—The Church-Wardens.

For Saint James, Santee, at the parish church. Managers—Messrs. Samuel Dupre and Benjamin Webb.

For Prince George, Winyah, at the town on George-Town. Managers—The Church-Wardens.

For All Saints, at the west end of Long Bay, at Peak's Old Place. Managers—Thomas Sterritt and James Bolin, esquires.

For Prince Frederick, viz. At the house of Nathan Savage; managers—John Erwin and William James Cooper. At the house of George White; managers—Robert McCotterry and John James, jun. At King's Tree; managers—John Fulton and John Erwin. (The ballots to be drawn on Wednesday following, at the house of George White.)

For Saint John, Colleton County. At the Rock Landing, on Wadmelaw [Island]. Managers—The Church-Wardens.

For Saint Peter. At the house of Captain William Maner, on Black Swamp. Managers—Joseph Brailsford and William Page, esquires.

For Saint Stephen. At the parish church. Managers—The Church-Wardens.

For the District Eastward of the Wateree, viz. At Stateburgh; managers—Henry Maxwell and William Murrell, esquires. At Camden; managers—Burwell Boykin and William Lang, esquires. At Lancaster court-house; managers—Eleazer Alexander and John Simpson, esquires. (The ballots to be drawn on Wednesday following, at Camden.)

For the District of Ninety-Six, viz. At Abbeville court-house; managers—Andrew Hamilton, Richard Andrews Rapley, and Samuel Watt, esquires. At Edgefield court-house; managers—Arthur Simkins and John Martin, esquires; Captain William Butler. (The ballots to be drawn on Wednesday following at the town of Cambridge.)

For the District of Saxe-Gotha. At the house of John Burkett. Managers—Joseph Culpeper, John James Haig, and William Fitzpatrick, esquires.

For the District between Broad and Saluda Rivers, viz. Lower district, at the Dutch church, near the Block-house; managers—Hon. John Hampton, Esquire, and Jeremiah Williams, Esquire. Little-River district, at Hammond's Old Store; managers—James Caldwell and Geo. Ross, esquires.

Upper or Spartan District, viz. At Spartanburgh court-house; managers—William Benson and Richard Harrison, esquires. At Union court-house; managers—William Kennedy and Adam Potter, esquires. (Ballots to be drawn on Wednesday following, at the house of Robert Harris.)

For the District between Broad and Catawba Rivers, viz. At Chester court-house; managers—Edward Lacey and Hugh Knox, esquires. At Winnsborough; managers—Hugh Milling and John Pearson, esquires. At Richland court-house; managers—Joel McLemore and Jesse Baker, esquires. (The ballots to be drawn on Wednesday following, at the town of Winnsborough.)

For the district called the New Acquisition, at York court-house. Managers—John Drennan, James Martin, William Fergus, and Alexander Moore, esquires.

For Saint Matthew. At the house of Captain William Watts. Managers—William Russell Thomson and William Heatley, esquires.

For Orange District. At the town of Orangeburgh. Managers—John Sally and Samuel Rowe, esquires.

For Saint David's Parish, viz. At Chesterfield court-house; managers—William Pegues and Alexander Craig, esquires. At Marlborough court-house; managers—Colonel George Hicks and William Thomas, esquires. At Darlington court-house; managers—Lamuel Benton and William DeWitt, esquires. (Ballots to be drawn on Wednesday following, at Cheraw court-house.)

For the District between Savannah River and the North Fork of Edisto, viz. At the plantation of Charles Brown, on the Lower Three Runs; managers—Aaron Smith and Thomas Wyld, esquires. At Kelley's Cow-Pen; managers—Daniel Greene and Nathaniel Walker, esquires. (The ballots to be drawn on Wednesday following, at the house of Benjamin Odom.)[2]

John Sandford Dart, Clerk of the House of Representatives.
Charleston, Nov. 7, 1788.

1. (LT), *State Gazette*, 13 November.
2. At least one polling place, Prince William's Parish in Beaufort District, was not included in the above list. Results for that parish were printed in the *City Gazette* on 1 December, which reported that Robert Barnwell carried the election for Congress.

Official Election Notice for St. Michael's Parish, 7 November[1]

By virtue of a Writ of Election to us directed, *Notice is hereby given*, To such persons as are qualified to vote for Representatives of the General Assembly, that an election for the purpose of choosing one suitable person, to serve in Congress, and two Senators for this state, and thirty Members for the General Assembly of the same, will be held at the parish church of St. Michael, Charleston, of Monday and Tuesday the 24th and 25th days of November, from the hours of 9 to 12 in the morning, and from two to four in the afternoon of each respective day.

[Signed] John Folker, Edward Trescot, Robert Dewer, Geo. Banfield, Church-Wardens.

N. B. All persons who are qualified to vote, will please to observe, that no more than one name can be for Member of Congress on one paper, and 2 names for [state] Senators, and 30 for the General Assembly.

Nov. 7, 1788.

1. (LT), *State Gazette*, 10 November.

City Gazette, 8 November

Messrs. Markland and M'Iver. As the names of several of the candidates to represent this state in Congress have been announced, I think it proper they should be published in the *Daily Advertiser*,[1] that we may know whom to elect.

For Charleston District: Commodore [Alexander] Gillon; William Smith, Esq.; Dr. David Ramsay.

For Beaufort and Orangeburgh District: John Bull, Esq.; John Barnwell, Esq.; Aedanus Burke, Esq.; John Kean, Esq.

For Ninety-Six District: Thomas T[udor] Tucker, Esq.; Daniel Huger, Esq.; Henry Pendleton,[2] Esq.

For Camden District: General [Thomas] Sumpter;[3] Daniel Huger,[4] Esq.

For Cheraw and Georgetown Districts: William Smith, Esq.[5]

1. The full name of the *City Gazette* at this time was *The City Gazette, or the Daily Advertiser*. John Markland and John M'Iver were the publishers.

2. See note 5.

3. Later Sumter said he sent letters to the election managers in Camden District and to friends, denying his candidacy and warning that he could not serve if elected (Sumter to Governor Charles Pinckney, 27 January 1789, printed below).

4. On 15 November the *City Gazette* reported that "the name of the Hon. Daniel Huger, Esq. was published in our paper, on the 8th instant, for the districts of Ninety-Six and Camden, to represent this state in the federal government; we think it our duty to say, that the publication proceeded from misrepresentations, that we are now authorized to declare him a candidate for the united districts of Georgetown and Cheraw only." The correction was repeated on 18, 21, and 22 November.

5. On 14 November the *City Gazette* reported that "there were two mistakes in the list of candidates for the representation of this state in the federal government, inserted in Saturday's paper. Judge Pendleton declined serving for Ninety-Six, and the Hon. William Smith, Esq. is a candidate for the suffrages of the electors of Charleston District only."

From Alexander Gillon, Ashley Hill, 17 November[1]

For this three months past, have I intended visiting your neighborhood, but one matter or another has detained me, however next week [I] think to get under way for it. My friends have applied to me to go to Congress for Charleston District and they flatter me, with the idea of being elected, as they wish a commercial character to be in Congress. My reply has been, that if elected I will go *next* April, as I wish to assist in our legislature next January to complete the installment law, by obtaining a further issue of paper medium, to open our inland navigation, and to fix Columbia at once.[2]

Who are to be our members for Saxe-Gotha? Some say I have been a naughty boy and therefore you all are determined not to elect me for the House of Representatives. My reply is, you all know whether I can be of service or not—to you then do I leave it.

. . . .

[P.S.] Petitions to the next House of Assembly to issue paper will be useful.

1. RC, Robert Wilson Gibbes Autograph Book of the American Revolution, South Caroliniana Library, ScU. The name of the addressee is missing but the letter is headed "Dear Colonel." It was probably written to Colonel Richard Hampton, state senator from Saxe-Gotha District, which Gillon represented in the lower house.

2. Proposed revisions of the state's laws providing for the payment of debts in installments, paper money emissions, improvement of transportation within the state, and proposals to move the state capital out of Charleston were all important issues in state politics at the time of the first federal elections.

William Thomson to Richard Hampton, 21 November[1]

I never knew that Judge [Aedanus] Burk would serve in the new Congress until [Monday?] last by letter from Commodore [Alexander] Gellion which I am exceedingly happy to hear. And if you think as I do there will be no doubt of his being elected.

1. RC, Robert Wilson Gibbes Autograph Book of the American Revolution, South Caroliniana Library, ScU. The writer was probably the William Thomson who represented the combined St. Matthew's and Orange parishes in the state Senate from 1778 to 1796. As a delegate from St. Matthew's Parish in the state Convention, he voted to ratify the Constitution.

The David Ramsay—William Smith Controversy in the Charleston District, 22-25 November

The election for the South Carolina House and Senate and for the federal House of Representatives was held on Monday and Tuesday, 24 and 25 November. On Saturday, 22 November, an anonymous newspaper article in the *City Gazette* denied that one of the candidates, Dr. David Ramsay, would work for the emancipation of the slaves if elected to Congress. The same issue of the *Gazette* also contained a piece titled "An Elector for Charleston District to the Public," which challenged William Smith's eligibility for a seat in Congress. The author was Dr. Ramsay, who argued that because Smith had been in Europe during the War for Independence he had not been a citizen for the seven years required by Article I, Section 2, of the Constitution. He warned that if Smith were elected his seat would probably be vacated and the Charleston District deprived of representation.

Smith immediately responded in a broadside ("To the Citizens of Charleston District," 22 November), stressing his native birth and his contributions to the war effort despite his absence in England and Europe. Smith also challenged Ramsay's motives for publishing his objections only two days before the election and raised the issue of Ramsay's Northern birth and opposition to slavery.

A second broadside ("Another Elector for Charleston District," 22 November), probably by Ralph Izard, Smith's father-in-law, attacked Ramsay for his Northern birth and his insensitivity to the interests of the state. Izard warned that while Ramsay was constrained by the Constitution from promoting the emancipation of Negroes for twenty years, he was an opponent of slavery and had distributed antislavery pamphlets in the state.

Smith's and Izard's broadsides were circulated in Charleston on Monday, 24 November, the first day of the election (William Mason to William Bentley, 3 December).

Ramsay replied to each broadside. In "A Short Reply to a Long Piece Signed William Smith" (24 November) Ramsay restated his argument that Smith was ineligible to serve in Congress: Smith had chosen to remain in England for two years after he became of age and did not return to South Carolina until 1783. Therefore he had been a citizen of South Carolina for only five years, and his election could result in a "chasm in our representation" in the first Congress.

In "A Calm Reply" (24 November) Ramsay responded to Izard's charges. He reiterated that the reason for publishing his objections was solely a disinterested concern for the state's representation, and he repeated his charge that Smith had not been a citizen for the requisite seven years. He also declared his opposition to the emancipation of the slaves and denied circulating antislavery pamphlets knowingly.

Other remarks on Smith's eligibility were published in both the *City Gazette* and the *State Gazette* on Monday, the 24th. Additional comments were published in the *City Gazette* on Tuesday, the 25th, the second day of the election, as was Smith's broadside, "A Dose for the Doctor." Smith again asserted that he was a citizen and that Ramsay's charges were groundless. He pointed out that Ramsay had acknowledged Smith's citizenship in 1785 when Ramsay voted for Smith's election to the Privy Council. Ramsay's objections were, Smith charged, solely the result of personal ambition. Smith was, however, willing to forgive Ramsay for his ignoble conduct, a pledge he later repeated in an election-day victory speech given at St. Michael's Church (*City Gazette*, 27 November).

The campaign in the Charleston District is the only one that can be documented. The extant issues of the *City Gazette* and the *State Gazette of South Carolina*, together with the broadsides, illustrate the clash between two of the candidates, while Alexander Gillon, the third candidate, was ignored, although he received twice as many votes as Ramsay. The above-cited documents and others illustrating the Charleston contest are printed immediately below.

City Gazette, 22 November

A report having been industriously inculcated, to the prejudice of one of the candidates for representing Charleston District, in Congress, that he would if elected, use his endeavors to promote an emancipation of the Negroes in this state, we have authority to contradict the assertion, and to declare, that he never entertained any such design. Indeed the new Constitution by the 9th section of the first article, puts it out of the power not only of the individual members of Congress, but of the Congress itself, to interfere in any manner respecting the Negro property of this country for twenty years to come.[1]

1. Apparently rumors had been circulating before this piece appeared that David Ramsay favored the abolition of slavery. After the election Ramsay attributed his defeat to the fact that he was a Northerner and to his being represented as opposed to slavery (to John Eliot, 26 November, printed below). A few days later William Mason commented that it was supposed that Ramsay had an equal chance until the above piece appeared (to William Bentley, 3 December, printed below).

An Elector for Charleston District to the Public, City Gazette, 22 November[1]

By the third paragraph of the new Constitution it is declared "That no person shall be a Representative in the proposed Congress, who should not have attained to the age of 25 years, and been *seven years a citizen of the United States*." One of the candidates to represent Charleston District left this country when a British province, and continued in Europe until the year 1783. He could not be a citizen of the United States at the time of his going to England, for then there were no citizens; the states were not in existence. He could not be a citizen of the United States during his 13 years residence in Europe, for during the whole of that time he owed allegiance to George the Third, who was at war with the United States; for it is absurd to suppose that the same individual can owe two contradictory allegiances at the same time. His citizenship, therefore, cannot have commenced prior to his return to America. He at present and for two years to come will be therefore ineligible to be a Representative in Congress. It will be to no purpose to object that the aforesaid candidate was a virtual citizen in right of his father; for his father never was a citizen, but lived and died a British subject. Neither can it be inferred that as aforesaid candidate is received as a member of Assembly here he will of course be received at New York, as a qualified citizen to represent us in Congress, for the qualifications are totally different. By our state constitution citizenship is not mentioned. A *residence for three years in the state* is substituted in lieu of *citizenship for seven years* in the Federal Constitution. The case will not be decided by our citizens, nor by our laws or instances; for each house of Congress, by the 5th section of the first article of the new Constitution, is to judge of the qualifications of its own members, agreeably to the principles therein laid down. It will also be determined by men who will be under no bias, to explain away the letter of the Constitution by a liberal or lax interpretation. For they deem a foreign education a political evil, and will say that these guards were placed round the new Constitution on purpose to exclude men, who from the circumstances of birth or education might be supposed to have a partiality for European customs, manners, or forms of government.

When we separated from Great Britain, every American had his choice to remain a British subject, or join our new political society. Soon after the Declaration of Independence the line was drawn, and every free man was called upon to take an oath of allegiance to this state.[2] Several natives refused, and went to England. The circumstance of birth in the country by no means made a citizen. This high privilege was not a thing of course, nor could it be acquired, but by some positive act of individuals obtaining it, and on their giving some test of their attachment to the cause of independence. The state also called on all absentees, to come home, and particularly on all young men, who were abroad for their education, to return within one year after they were of age.[3] The aforesaid candidate, notwithstanding this call, continued in Europe for three or four years after he was of age. He was therefore a voluntary British subject, long after he was a free agent. On the whole, for the first 25 years of his life the aforesaid candidate was by birth—by the political condition of his father,[4] and especially by his voluntary continuance in his British allegiance, to all intents and purposes a British subject. Nor did he become a citizen of the United States until December, 1783, when he arrived in Carolina; nor even then unless he took the oath of allegiance to the state immediately on his return.

Should a candidate circumstanced as aforesaid be returned as duly elected, his seat will be liable to be vacated, and in that case Charleston District would for some months lose the advantage of representation, to the great injury of its political interests.

1. This article attacking William Smith's eligibility was written by David Ramsay (see "William Smith to the Citizens of Charleston District," 22 November, printed immediately below). A correspondent sent the article to the *New York Daily Gazette* and asked that it be reprinted because "the questions agitated in Charleston, respecting the eligibility of a candidate for a seat among the representatives of the Union, being a common concern, ought to be well understood. . . . " The *Daily Gazette*, which republished much of the debate over Smith's eligibility, reprinted this article on 13 January 1789.

2. See "An Act to oblige every free male inhabitant of this State, above a certain age, to give assurance of Fidelity and Allegiance to the same, and for other purposes therein mentioned," S.C. *Statutes*, I, 147-51. The act was passed on 28 March 1778.

3. A tax law in March 1778 provided that "all persons holding estates in this state who are absent from the United States, shall be double taxed," but it specifically exempted "minors and those not yet twenty-two years old, who shall be allowed one year after their coming of age to return to this state . . ." (S.C. *Statutes*, IV, 414).

4. Smith's father, Benjamin Smith, died in 1770. For a sketch of his life and politics, see Rogers, *Smith,* Chapters II-IV.

William Smith to the Citizens of Charleston District, Charleston, 22 November[1]

Having seen some observations in the *Morning Post*,[2] which I am informed by the printer, are the productions of *my competitor, Dr. Ramsay*, respecting my supposed ineligibility to Congress, on the ground of my not having been seven years a citizen of the United States of America, I think it my duty to counteract him in his designs, and shield myself from the effects of his pitiful electioneering maneuver.

It is now upwards of three weeks since I have been announced to the public as a candidate to represent this district in Congress, and yet the idea of my being ineligible never occurred to any of my fellow citizens, till the ingenuity of a gentleman (who could as a financier, gravely declare in the legislature that *two* and *two* made *five*, and as a politician, that slavery was not necessary to this state) first made this wonderful discovery.

To his prodigious sagacity must be attributed that objection to me, which all the men of abilities in Carolina were too ignorant to find out, and which would never have occurred to the Doctor himself, had he not been my competitor upon this occasion.

But it seems, after trying other expedients to win the free suffrages of the citizens of this district, and finding that he was not likely to be the man of their choice, he has had recourse to this his last expedient. That he can reconcile it to his feelings thus to *intrude* himself upon the citizens of the district, by an uncandid and unfair attempt to disqualify his opponent, is, I confess, surprising. For my part, I envy him no honors obtained by such means. Painful as it is to speak of myself upon this occasion, yet the Doctor's disingenuous attempt to deprive me of my *birth right* in the minds of my countrymen, compels me to inform the public, that my ancestors were amongst the very first settlers in South Carolina—that I was born in this city, and was sent by my father to Europe for my education in my twelfth year—in my sixteenth I was sent by Colonel [Henry] Laurens and Colonel [Isaac] Motte, from London, to finish my education at

Geneva, *one of the freest republics* at that time in the world. I there studied near five years, and after making some excursions to other countries, I went to France, where, as an American, I waited on Dr. Franklin, Mr. [John] Adams, and Mr. [Arthur] Lee, the ministers from America to the Court of France. I was invited to their houses, entertained and considered by them *as an American citizen*, which right I certainly acquired with the rest of my countrymen by the Declaration of Independence, tho at Geneva, as much as if I had been in America.

Having stayed two months at Paris, in the character of an American citizen, I went to London, and being then a minor, immediately requested of the gentleman (who had been appointed my guardian in England by my father) to furnish me with the means of embarking for America—this I could not obtain. Soon after South Carolina fell into the hands of the enemy, and I was then advised by my friends in this country to remain in England and prosecute my studies. I accordingly studied the law at the Temple, and altho qualified for the English bar, and strongly urged by some acquaintances, to get admitted with promises of support, yet as I could not have been admitted without taking the oath of allegiance to the British government, I positively refused, and left England in October, 1782, to come to this country. After having been shipwrecked and meeting with a variety of difficulties, I did not arrive here till the end of November, 1783. On my arrival I found that my property had been greatly reduced in consequence of my friends having placed the monies of my father's estate in the treasury: between £30,000 and £40,000 sterling of that estate was deposited in the treasury of South Carolina. My fortune, such as it was, was lent to the public of our country, and it was made use of to carry on the operations of war. Not long after my arrival,[3] I was admitted at the bar: in less than a year after my arrival, I was elected a member of the Assembly, where I have had the honor of a seat four years. I was elected a privy councillor (and the Doctor himself gave me his vote on the occasion). I have been twice elected to the office of warden of the city, and yet the Doctor suffers himself to be so far warped in his judgment, by his great inclination to go to the northward in a *public character*, that he has (tho without putting his name to it) published in the papers that I was not a citizen till I took the oaths of allegiance. If that is the sole criterion of citizenship, half of the natives of this country are not citizens. The oath of allegiance is a test of fidelity, administered to a person before he enters upon the execution of an office. There are now thousands of young people in America, who have come of age since the peace, who vote at elections and are deemed citizens without having ever taken the oath, and probably never will, unless elected to some office. A person cannot take the oath of allegiance till he is of age; according to the doctrine laid down by Dr. R. he is not therefore a citizen till he is of age, consequently as the new Constitution requires that a person should be a citizen seven years before he is eligible, adding seven to twenty-one, a candidate ought not to be eligible till he is twenty-eight, and yet the Constitution allows him to be eligible at twenty-five. Probably the ingenuity of the Doctor can reconcile this absurdity by the same rule of arithmetic by which he proved that two and two made five. Again, to draw an instance from Maryland (a country with which the Doctor has some acquaintance, and for which he once in Congress, though a member from South Carolina, gave a striking instance of partiality, which is pretty generally known) that state did not accede to the Confederation till the first day of March, 1781, consequently, according to the Doctor's mode of reasoning, a Marylander could not be a citizen of the United States till the 1st of March, 1781—and therefore ineligible to a seat in the House of Representatives till seven years after, viz., 1st of March 1788, and yet the delegates of Maryland signed this new Constitution in September 1787. Now it is not to be supposed they would have been so blind to their own interests as to have signed a constitution which, if put in immediate operation, would have precluded all her own inhabitants from being Senators or Representatives in the Federal Congress.

Indeed, according to *his* construction, no citizen of Maryland can be a Senator to the federal government till the 1st of March, 1790, because he must have been *nine years a citizen of the United States*, and Maryland was not one of the United States till the 1st of March, 1781.

The Doctor says that during my 13 years *residence in Europe*, I owed allegiance to George the IIId. This I deny—and it is the first time I ever heard that a residence *in Europe* made a man *a subject of the King of Great Britain*. If so, his Britannic majesty is indebted to the Doctor for a gift of all the inhabitants of Europe. Why, during a residence of five years did I not owe allegiance to the republic of Geneva? Why, during my occasional tours in Switzerland, Savoy, France, the Low Countries, etc., did not I become a citizen of those respective countries. During all that time, all my property was in Carolina, paying a tax to the support of the American government, all my relations were here, the bones of all my ancestors were deposited in this state, in short every thing I held dear and valuable to me in the world was here, and had not a fond parent (whose death soon after left me an orphan at the age of eleven) thought that I could better qualify myself to serve my country hereafter by receiving my education abroad, I should have been here myself. The Doctor dislikes a foreign education—he says *They* deem a foreign education a political evil. *Who deem it?* Those men, he says, who will be under no biases—not *our citizens*, No! The question will be determined *not by our citizens* nor *by our laws or instances*; why did not the Doctor speak *plainly* out at once, and give us a proof of the *biases of birth and education*, and convince us that, if a person by receiving an European education, will, from the circumstances of *birth and education*, have a partiality for *European customs and manners*, so will a person *educated* or *born* anywhere else have a predilection for the customs and manners of the country where he was born and educated. Now, the Doctor admits that *birth* and *education* create a partiality for the country in which a person was born and educated, and although I received my education abroad, yet *I was born here*, and consequently according to the Doctor's own position, I ought to have a greater attachment to this state than himself—For he, if I am not misinformed, was neither born nor bred here.

The Doctor says the circumstance of birth does not make a citizen—This I also deny. Vattel says, *"The country of the father is that of the children, and these become citizens merely by their tacit consent."*[4] I was born a *Carolinian*, and I defy the Doctor with all his ingenuity, arithmetical or political, to say at what moment I was *disfranchised*—at what moment I lost my citizenship. The revolution which took place in America made me a citizen of America under the new government, though then resident at Geneva. I never by any act disqualified myself. *There never was a moment when I became a citizen of any other country*. I never took an oath of any kind in my life, till I was admitted at the bar in Carolina. I never paid any tax to any other country—therefore, unless I was a citizen of South Carolina, I should be glad the Doctor's great ingenuity in discoveries would inform me what country I was a citizen of. Surely he, who is a citizen of the thirteen United States won't refuse me the advantage of being a citizen of some country! He does not mean to make me an outcast of society altogether; his disappointment and mortification will not lead him that length. *But how happens it that the Doctor never discovered this important secret sooner?* He has well thumbed the Constitution, and knows every part of it, I dare say, by heart; he was also well acquainted with my history. Why did it occur to him only *at the very moment of the election?* I will inform the public. The Doctor thinking himself a very *popular* man and having no doubt that his being named a candidate was sufficient to carry his election throughout the district, when he found that he stood no chance of being elected by *his own merits*, he thought he would try what he could obtain by the *demerit* of his opponent. Not finding any thing in his *character or morals*, which he dared attack, he was driven to this expedient: he attacked his *right of citizenship, his birth right—the inheritance of his ancestors*—that, which at the age of eleven, when an orphan, was left him by his father! Mortified at the prospect of not succeeding in his favorite object, the Doctor first went about under the hypocritical cloak of candor and secrecy, suggesting to my friends that such an objection had just occurred to him, and assuring them that he meant to take no advantage of it, *prior to the election*, that he had nothing in view but to put me on my guard, that I might not be surprised *after the election*. He afterwards mentioned the matter under the veil of secrecy, to a friend of mine, and drew from him some loose expressions, which fell from my worthy friend, without considering the subject, *while his attention was occupied by a pamphlet which he was then reading*—delighted with having extorted something like an opinion favorable to him, he informed several of his friends, that the honorable gentleman above alluded to, had declared himself of opinion, that I was ineligible. As soon as my friend heard the report, he wrote to the Doctor, and assured him that what he had said to him was without reflection or thought, and that *so far from his being of opinion* that I was ineligible, *he intended to give me his vote*,—thereby sufficiently showing, that at all events, *he* did not think *the Doctor himself an eligible person*. But notwithstanding the Doctor *declared that he should not avail himself of this objection before the election*, yet finding himself *pinched*, he could no longer refrain, and published in this day's paper an unfair state of facts, *for the sole purpose of promoting his election at my expense.*

My fellow citizens will easily see the object of the publication, and that it was sent abroad at *a late period, when it was thought no time or opportunity would be afforded me of giving it an answer*. But I should be unworthy of the good opinion of my fellow citizens, were I, for an instant, to suffer their minds to be biased by such attempts, or a reflection to be thrown on those who have, at various times, since my return to Carolina, given me their votes for public offices. When it is recollected that my ancestors came into Carolina upwards of a hundred years ago—that *I was born in this very city*—that every thing I hold most dear in the world is in Carolina, nay, in *this very district*; I trust, my countrymen, will not suffer themselves to be duped with the artifices which have been made use of, and will not think that my having been a few years in Europe for my education, *with the public consent*, should deprive me of my right of citizenship. That I should have been left an orphan at the age of eleven, that I should have lost a considerable estate in Carolina, by the attachment of my friends to the country, who placed large sums in the treasury, was a sufficient misfortune, without endeavoring to deprive me of my right of citizenship! The Doctor says that the state called on all young men to come home, and particularly to young men who were abroad for their education, to return within one year after they came of age. So far from this being true, the legislature of this country were so well convinced of the utility of a good foreign education, that they expressly allowed all young men who were abroad for their education, to stay till a year after they were of age, and although remittances were generally prohibited at that time to England, yet an *exception was made by the legislature of South Carolina for remittances intended for the support of the youth who were abroad for their education.*[5] The Doctor then says that for *two years* to come I shall be ineligible: he will then have no objection to my going! He will then have *printed his book*[6] and having no other *personal* object to answer, will be willing to return here; I am indeed much obliged to him for his kindness, and the citizens of this country not less so, for his public spirit.

The Doctor is greatly alarmed at the influence foreign education may have on my conduct; but I should be glad to ask him whether a person *whose property and connections are in this state, who can have nothing in this world to attach him to any other country,* could possibly be influenced to any thing prejudicial to its true interests, merely because he was some years in Europe for his education. If so, *some of the men of the greatest abilities in America ought to be excluded from her councils.*

This is the first instance in this country of one candidate publishing to the world in the newspaper the ineligibility of his competitor. In general, *gentlemen* wait the event of the election and trust to the good sense of the electors that they will not elect improper men. But the Doctor affects *singularity* and does things which *no gentleman* ever did before.

Had he consulted a real friend on this occasion, I apprehend the answer would have been nearly as follows: "Doctor you are about to do a very imprudent thing, which will hurt Mr. Smith but little and will unquestionably injure you much. For the sole purpose of carrying your election you are endeavoring to deprive of the right of citizenship your antagonist, because *you are conscious that you stand on bad ground yourself.* If your fellow citizens think you are the *fittest* man to represent them, *they will elect you*; if not, no artifices, no maneuvers, no publication in the newspapers will induce them to do it. Therefore *act like a man* upon this occasion, and stand the contest like a man."

But it seems the Doctor is apprehensive that my seat may be vacated, if I am elected; and that this district may for some months lose the advantage of a representation to the great injury of its *political* interests. Does he think his *presence* in Congress would greatly promote the *true political interests of South Carolina?*

I would rather submit it to the good sense of the electors whether it is not better that the district should be unrepresented than represented by a man who is *principled against* the true political interests of this country. The Doctor however declares that he *will not, if elected, endeavor to procure the emancipation of slaves*; but then he must act *contrary to his principles and sentiments*, and surely he would not wish the citizens of the district should impose so painful a burden upon him as to require him to thwart perpetually his own sentiments and principles. It is very well known that *he is principled against slavery*, and it is idle for him to contradict *what is so universally known*. People can see, hear, and recollect as well as the Doctor and his handing about *pamphlets* imported from the northward *against slavery, is a strong proof of his inclination to abolish it.*

But it is not sufficient that he should barely not endeavor to promote emancipation; has he declared to the public that he will endeavor *to reconcile the Northern States, to slavery*, to convince them that *without slavery, this district must be abandoned and rendered a mere wilderness*; that the slaves of this country are well treated, and live more happy than the white peasantry in Europe? No, he is silent on that head—in short—one of these two things must happen; either the Doctor must act according to his principles and injure the country, or he must to serve the country thwart and oppose his own sentiments and principles; and I am sure I would never trust a man to do my business, whose inclination it was to injure me.

I ask pardon of my fellow citizens for this long intrusion on their patience, which I should never have been guilty of under any other circumstances: but the very unjust and unwarrantable attack of this morning required on my part an immediate reply. I therefore trust that the candid public after perusing this answer will be convinced that the said publication of the Doctor's was calculated solely for *electioneering purposes*, with a view of imposing on the public and robbing me of the votes of my friends.

1. Broadside, South Carolina, Portfolio 172, no. 12, Rare Book Room, DLC. Republished in the *State Gazette of South Carolina*, 24 November, and in the *New York Daily Gazette*, 6 and 7 January 1789. The Miscellaneous Manuscript Collection, DLC, contains a manuscript dated Charleston, 22 November, and signed by William Smith. It is endorsed "To the Electors of the Parish of St. Bartholomew." It covers the same ground as the published broadside in shorter form.

2. Smith's reference is to Ramsay's "An Elector for Charleston District" in the *City Gazette*, 22 November, printed above. Although Smith called it the *Morning Post*, the name of that paper had been changed to *The City Gazette, and the Daily Advertiser* on 6 November 1787.

3. Smith did not arrive back in South Carolina until late in 1783. His efforts to reach America during the war appear to have been considerably less ardent than this and subsequent campaign broadsides made them appear. See Rogers, *Smith*, Chapter V.

4. See Emerich de Vattel, *The Law of Nations; or Principles of the Law of Nature Applied to the Conduct and Affairs of Nations and Sovereigns* (Joseph Chitty, trans., Philadelphia, 1835), 101.

5. S.C. *Statutes*, IV, 413-22; South Carolina House Journals, 11 October 1776, Peter Force, ed., *American Archives* (5th series, 3 vols., Washington, 1848-1853), III, 59.

6. The reference is to Ramsay's *History of the American Revolution*, which was published in Philadelphia in 1789.

Another Elector for Charleston District, Charleston, 22 November[1]

The feelings of every honest citizen must be deeply affected upon reading a publication in the *City Gazette* of this day, written for the purpose of imposing upon the understandings of the electors of this district,[2] and probably by a person who has been endeavoring to obtrude himself as a Representative to Congress, contrary to the opinion of a majority of the inhabitants who are qualified to vote. The base and ungentlemanlike conduct of the writer is so apparent to every man of common understanding, that his letter has already produced, and will continue to produce very different effects from those which were intended. He knew that his assertions were false, and that they would not bear the test of examination, and therefore like an assassin, who uses his dagger in the dark, that the intended victim may be deprived of the means of defense, he has postponed the publication of his letter to the last day on which a newspaper is printed, previous to the election; hoping thus to give full operation to his poison, before the antidote could be applied. The writer of the letter is known to possess an uncommon volubility of tongue; but although he may in some instances be compared to the Devil in Milton, who is represented as possessing the power of making the "worse appear the better part," yet on the present occasion he appears more to resemble those wicked ones "who have dug a pit for others, and have fallen into the midst of it themselves." To enter into a serious discussion of the point, whether the gentleman whose citizenship is called in question by the letter writer, is qualified, or not, to represent the state in Congress, would be an idle waste of time. It is a matter about which there cannot be the smallest doubt; and I do not believe that there is a man in the world so absurd as to think that a gentleman born in this country, whose whole property and connections are in this country, and who never did any act to forfeit his citizenship, should on account of his having resided in Europe for his education during the war, be now looked upon to have been an alien during that period. Especially as he has been continually employed since his return in the most confidential offices in the state, and has upon all occasions met with the approbation of his fellow citizens. The most detestable productions have frequently been known to proceed from envy and disappointed ambition. But, for the honor of human kind, I hope that many instances cannot be produced, of so complete a depravity of the heart, as is apparent in that of the letter writer. He has added to those qualities the basest ingratitude to this country. When the discrimination between citizen and citizen was nearly buried in oblivion, he has called upon the public to revive those distinctions, and to keep alive those animosities with which they have been so long distracted. When the wounds, occasioned by the last war, were upon the point of being healed, he with a savage hand has endeavored to tear them open, and to set them bleeding afresh. He who came a stranger into this country, and was taken in, and who by the patronage and kindness of some gentlemen here has been placed in a situation to make them repent of their partiality to him. Possessed now of affluence, by adventitious circumstances, and by the unaccountable revolutions of the wheel of fortune, like most other successful adventurers, he is no longer satisfied to walk in the path of equality with those by whom he has been adopted. But stimulated by ambition, he aims at preeminence; and not contented with endeavoring to obtain it by justifiable means, he is not ashamed to make use of any other which afford him hopes of being gratified. The opinions of this state, he informs us, are not to be consulted. The question is to be determined, he says, by men who will pay no regard to our laws, and who will not put a *liberal* interpretation on the Constitution. I shall take the liberty of differing with the letter writer on this point. Whatever may have hitherto been looked upon as citizenship, by the respective states, will certainly be acknowledged as such by the new Congress. They are to make no ex post facto laws, but they may determine what shall be the qualification of citizens in future. Such opinions propagated of the tyrannical proceedings of the new government, are calculated to inspire disgust; and although I believe them to be totally unfounded, it behooves the citizens of this country, to consider whether they can, with propriety, trust the management of their interests in the hands of a man who holds such opinions. The letter writer deals in bold assertions, and pretends to be possessed of a prophetic spirit; for he not only affects to know who the future members of Congress are to be, but seems to be already let into their secrets. "They deem," he says, "a foreign education a political evil, and will say that these guards were placed round the new Constitution, on purpose to exclude men, who from the circumstances of birth or education, might be supposed to have a partiality for European customs, manners, or forms of government." How does the letter writer know that Congress in this instance, as well as in the other I have quoted, are to be illiberal, and to deem a foreign education a political evil? If there be any truth in the speculation of this profound letter writer, the citizens of this country will, I hope, avail themselves of it, and exclude a man from every office of trust or confidence, who has shown that either *from the circumstances of his birth or education*, or from any other circumstance whatever, he is an enemy to that policy which the wisdom of more than a century has adopted for this country. The writer in the paragraph immediately preceding his letter to the public, informs us, that if he is elected a member to Congress, he will not use his endeavors to promote an emancipation of the Negroes in this state. And he himself gives a good reason why he will not. For says he, "indeed the new Constitution puts it out of the power, not only of the individual members of Congress, but of the Congress itself, to interfere in any manner respecting the Negro property of this country for twenty years to come."[3] But will the letter writer say, that he has never declared that he thought slavery ought to be abolished, or that he never distributed pamphlets which were intended to render the inhabitants of this state odious in the eyes of the world. If he should have the effrontery to do so, proofs of this fact, upon oath, shall be given to the public.[4]

1. Broadside bound with the *City Gazette*, WHi. The author was probably Ralph Izard, William Smith's father-in-law (see William Mason to William Bentley, 3 December, printed below). The broadside was also published in the *City Gazette* on 24 November.
2. Ramsay's "An Elector for Charleston District," *City Gazette*, 22 November, printed above.
3. See *City Gazette*, 22 November, printed above.
4. For Ramsay's answer see his "A Calm Reply," 24 November, printed below.

An Enemy to Quibblers, City Gazette, 24 November

Gentlemen, Please to insert the following observations in your paper.

Extract from the Federal Constitution.

Qualification[s] of the President of the United States.

"No person except a *natural born citizen*, or a citizen of the United States, at the time of the adoption of this Constitution, shall be eligible to the office of President; neither shall any person be eligible to that office who shall not have attained to the age of 35 years, and *been* 14 *years a resident within the United States*."

Observations upon that clause—A *natural born citizen* here clearly means *a person born in the American colonies*, while they were under the British government. This is abundantly evident from what immediately follows. The candidate for the presidentship must have been a resident *within the United States* 14 years; now, unless the words, United States, mean that part of America which is now called the United States, no person is qualified to be President, because the United States have only been in existence since the 4th July, 1776, and consequently no person can be said to be a resident *within the United States* (according to the letter writer's construction of the Constitution)[1] until 14 years after the 4th July, 1776; viz., until the 4th July, 1790. To obviate the absurdity of this construction, the framers of the Constitution wisely declared that a *natural born citizen* should be eligible, provided he had been a resident 14 years in America. Now, Mr. W. Smith, being a *natural born citizen*, and having been a resident 14 years in America, would certainly, under this clause, be eligible to the office of President of the United States, were he 35 years of age; and it would be highly absurd to admit, that he should be eligible to that eminent station, and at the same time declare him ineligible to the House of Representatives. To place in a still stronger light, the absurdity of the argument employed by Mr. Smith's opponents: the Confederation formed the act of union; 12 of the states ratified it in 1778. *Maryland* absolutely refused to ratify it, they wished for some alterations, but as they could not obtain them, they at last ratified it on the first November,[2] 1781. From that moment, and not before, Maryland was constitutionally, *one of the United States*. Consequently an inhabitant of Maryland, and a resident of that state, cannot be deemed a resident within the United States, for 14 years, until the first March, 1795; no resident of Maryland can therefore be eligible to the office of President, till the first March, 1795. Nay, General Washington himself, is not now eligible to the office of President, according to the letter writer's construction, because if the words United States, are construed to mean the states of America, as formed into a new government, on the 4th July, 1776; General Washington has certainly not been a resident within the United States, for the term of 14 years, because the United States have not yet been in existence 14 years.

1. Ramsay's "An Elector for Charleston District," *City Gazette*, 22 November, printed above.

2. Maryland ratified the Articles of Confederation on 1 March 1781.

A Bye Stander, State Gazette, 24 November

I am sorry to see so much heat excited among us by a publication in the *Daily Advertiser* of Saturday last.[1] It is not *who* but *what*. Whether Dr. Ramsay, or any other, be the author. Let Mr. Smith show, to the satisfaction of the public, that he was a citizen previous to his return here, and his work is done—he will not lose a single vote. But if he was no citizen, the whole community are indebted to the author of that address to the public, ascribed to the Doctor, as it may be the means of securing a full representation in Congress at a very critical period.

1. See Ramsay's "An Elector for Charleston District," *City Gazette*, 22 November, printed above.

A Short Reply to a Long Piece Signed William Smith, Charleston, 24 November[1]

Well might the framers of the new Constitution exclude from a seat in Congress those who had not been citizens of the United States for seven years. Mr. S——'s performance proves the wisdom of this measure. He has therein shown himself to be unacquainted with the legal history and the principles of the Revolution to a degree that can only be palliated by his short residence in these free states. He says that "the oath of allegiance is a test of fidelity administered to a person before he enters upon the execution of an office." Had he been here during the war, he would have known that on the recommendation of General Washington and of Congress, a law was passed, obliging every freeman to take an oath of allegiance to the state, and that taking that oath was an indispensable criterion of citizenship not confined to public officers, but extending to every overseer in the state.[2] He says farther, "that a person cannot take the oath of allegiance till he is of age." This is English law, but to be a ruler of the United States a man ought to be long enough a citizen of them to know their laws on this subject. Our test oath was by our law tendered to every boy above sixteen. Take another instance of the wisdom of the Convention in excluding those from Congress who from too short a term of citizenship cannot be supposed to know the principles of our republican governments. He says, "Maryland did not accede to the Confederation till March, 1781, and therefore, he infers that according to my mode of reasoning it follows that a Marylander could not be a citizen of the United States till the 1st of March, 1788." No man could make this assertion who had ever read the Declaration of Independence with attention. That though passed on July 4th, 1776, concludes with this strong declaration, "These United Colonies are, and of right ought to be free and independent states." In this declaration Maryland as well as the other twelve states concurred. Every American who personally or representatively was a party to this declaration, was in that moment virtually transformed from a subject to a citizen. I will go farther and say into a confederated citizen or citizen of the United States. To prove this,

I refer to the circular letter of Congress, dated September 13th, 1779, eighteen months before the formal accession of Maryland to the present Articles of Confederation. "For every purpose essential to the defence of these states in the progress of the present war, and necessary to the attainment of the objects of it, these states now are as fully, legally, and absolutely confederated, as it is possible for them to be."[3] If at the Declaration of Independence Mr. S—— was a party, I give up the argument. Younger men than he then was, were parties by being in our armies. Every man who voted primarily or secondarily for a member of Congress was a party.

But Mr. S—— was not interested in that solemn transaction either personally or representatively. This state did not long rest on this virtual citizenship, but founded that privilege on the personal act of every freeman above sixteen. I have examined the act passed on this occasion,[4] and there is no day of grace extended therein to minors abroad. The language of the act is, "He that is not for us is against us." It is true in the year 1778, an indulgence to the age of twenty-two was given to minors in foreign countries, for the purpose of their returning home. The country called on all her sons to come to her help, and generously allowed them sufficient time for that purpose, and thereby virtually promised them equal rights with those who had borne the heat and burden of the day, if they closed with this offer. Mr. S——, by delaying in Europe till he was 25, and till the war was ended, cut himself off from the proffered generosity of his country with regard to any right to virtual citizenship while he resided in Europe.

We are told that Mr. S—— has been an assemblyman, councillor, etc. He has been so, and he was qualified so to be, for no other qualification was required for those offices but residence and property. The case is different with respect to our new Congress. Membership there requires higher qualifications, of which he is not possessed. I allow him to be a resident for fifteen years, but a citizen only for five.

Birth will make citizens by tacit consent of those who have been born since 1776, and also of those who are daily growing of age: but this does not apply to those who were grown up at the time of the Revolution, and especially when they resided abroad as British subjects. Their personal consent was necessary. I state my argument thus. No Carolinian who was above the age of sixteen in the year 1778, could, by a law passed in that year, become a citizen, without taking the oath of allegiance to the state. Mr. S—— was above 16 in that year, and therefore must have taken the oath of allegiance before he could become a citizen. This he did not do till 1783, or 1784. This then must be the date of his citizenship. His birthright, of which he talks of being deprived is that of being a British subject. He says he never disqualified himself from being a citizen. I reply he never qualified himself to obtain that new and high privilege, till the period above mentioned. By the laws of this state a positive act on his part was necessary. Till seven years have elapsed subsequent to his adoption into our new political society which was *formed* while he was in Europe, he is not eligible to a seat in Congress. The consequence of his election therefore would be a chasm in our representation.

1. Broadside bound with the *City Gazette*, WHi. It is signed "An Elector of Charleston District." David Ramsay is identified as the author by "A Friend to Justice" (*State Gazette of South Carolina*, 1 December, printed below). The broadside was printed in the *State Gazette*, 27 November, and in the *New York Daily Gazette*, 8 January 1789.

2. See *City Gazette*, 22 November, n. 3, printed above.
3. JCC, XV, 1052-62.
4. S.C. *Statutes*, I, 147-51.

A Calm Reply, Charleston, 24 November[1]

The delay of publishing my objections to the eligibility of a certain candidate, for representing Charleston District in Congress, till Saturday, was occasioned by the following circumstances: the reasons militating against his eligibility, did not occur till Thursday last. On that very day two of his friends were informed of these reasons, and requested to communicate them to the gentleman, whose eligibility was questioned. Had the proper steps been taken, in consequence of this candid procedure, the public would never have heard more of the matter. The delay arose from this candor. Is this like an assassin? Nor was there any design to poison the minds of the public. My duty to my country, made it necessary for me to warn the electors of the danger of losing their representation, to which they were exposed by the perseverance of the candidate, in seeking for a place to which he was ineligible. I had a real respect for the gentleman, and have on all occasions acknowledged his ability, and nothing but a superior respect for the good of the state, could have induced me to declare my sentiments.

Instead of answering the arguments brought to prove the ineligibility of the candidate, a strong assertion is made, that no man, considering his circumstances, can suppose he was an alien during the war. To this, I reply, that by the generosity of this country he had the advantage of aliens so far, that at any time, on application, he might be admitted to citizenship. It is also granted, that the gentleman has not forfeited his citizenship, since he acquired it, and that he has since been highly trusted, and acted with propriety; but it is contended, that he never was a citizen at all till 1783, and that, therefore, he though eligible to offices in this state, must wait two years before he is qualified to be a member of Congress, agreeably to the new Constitution, which requires a citizenship of seven years in its members. This is so tenable a position, that, I think, I may safely defy the learned gentleman to support his eligibility by any mode of reasoning which may not easily be confuted. The question at issue may be thus stated: is he a citizen of seven years standing? Uncontroverted facts prove the contrary. Seven years ago he was an adult of sufficient age to choose his side, and he chose for two subsequent years to continue in his native character of a British subject, though this country called on him to return to its defense. He was not born a citizen, nor did he acquire that adventitious character till his return to this country. That an adult, who five years ago was by voluntary choice a British subject, and had always been a British subject, should be a citizen of the United States of seven years standing, is contrary to reason and common sense.

I declare, that I never approved of the emancipation of the Negroes of this country, and I hold, that the adoption of such a measure would be ruinous both to masters and slaves.[2] Experience proves, that those who have grown up in the habits of slavery are incapable of enjoying the blessings of freedom.

I can recollect nothing more about the distribution of pamphlets on the subject of slavery, than that a number of packets, containing (as I afterwards learned) Clarkson's essays,[3] were left at my house, in my absence, by some unknown person, and without any letter to me. Those were sealed and addressed to particular gentlemen. I forwarded them as letters, without knowing their contents till after they were opened. My own copy I never read nor circulated.

1. Broadside bound with the *City Gazette*, WHi. The full title is "A Calm Reply To all that is *material*, in an *angry* publication, signed 'Another Elector for Charleston District.' " It was signed "An Elector for Charleston District," but the text makes it clear that David Ramsay was the author. The broadside is undated, but we have given it the same date as Ramsay's reply to William Smith, printed immediately above.
2. Cf. Ramsay to Benjamin Rush, 31 January 1785. "I trust the day will arrive when the test laws and slavery will both be abolished" (Ramsay, *Writings*, 87).
3. The reference is probably to two antislavery tracts written by British abolitionist Thomas Clarkson: *An Essay on the Slavery and Commerce of the Human Species, Particularly the African* (Philadelphia, 1786) and *An Essay on the Impolity of the African Slave Trade* (Philadelphia, 1788).

David Ramsay to the Printers, 24 November[1]

Had the friends of a particular competitor, at the present election used no improper means to oppose my election, I was determined to leave the issue to the free voice of the people; but the falsehoods they have circulated, and the low artifices they have practiced, have at last imposed the necessity of self-defense, which I am sure the candid public will justify, when they know all the base methods which have been taken to injure me in the opinion of my fellow citizens.

1. *City Gazette*, 25 November.

Epaminondas to the Public, City Gazette, 25 November

In the *City Gazette* of the 22d inst. I find some sentiments addressed to the public on the subject of the ineligibility of one of the candidates for the new government;[1] and I confess that they struck me in a manner which I thought deserved consideration, and surely if the electing of that gentleman as delegate may expose the state to a temporary chasm in her representation, it is worthy the consideration of every constituent. We are to remember that the Southern interest will at best be but feebly represented on the floor of Congress, seeing North Carolina is not in the scale; and we are to remember also, that those interests may be materially affected by the first arrangements to be made by Congress. The only question necessary to be decided appears to be at what time is the date of his citizenship to be fixed; or in other words—*when* did he become a citizen of the United States? For that he is a citizen now we may well admit, altho it may be denied by that principle of the British constitution, which says, "that the natural born subject of one prince cannot by swearing allegiance to another prince put off or discharge him from that natural allegiance, and that it cannot be deserted without the concurrent act of that prince to whom it was first due."[2] But being now an independent nation we make no appeals to the British constitution, but to the general laws of nations, which must decide this point, should his allegiance ever be claimed by the Crown of Great Britain, what then do these laws say? They say, "that the first founders of states, and all those who afterwards became members thereof, are supposed to have stipulated, that their children and descendants should at their first coming into the world have the right of enjoying those advantages which are common to all the members of the state; provided nevertheless, that those descendants, when they attain to the use of reason, be on their part *willing* to submit to the government and to acknowledge the authority of the sovereign; but the stipulation of the parents cannot in its own nature have the force of subjecting the children against their will to an authority to which they would not themselves choose to submit. Hence the authority of the sovereign over the children of the members of the state, and the right on the other hand which these children have to the protection of the sovereign and to the advantages of the government, are founded on mutual consent. Nor if the children of members of the state upon attaining to the years of discretion are *willing to live* in the place of their parentage, or in their native country, they are by *this very* act supposed to submit themselves to the power that governs the state." From this account of the matter, I think, two corollaries may be drawn: 1st. That no person does or can by *birth* become the absolute subject of any state; there is indeed an obligation on the sovereign of that state where he is born, to *admit him* as a subject, should such be his election, when he arrives at the age of discretion, but no obligation on his part so to elect. 2d. That a voluntary residence in the country where one is born, after he arrives to years of discretion; (and *a fortiori* to years of *maturity*) completes his part of the contract, and establishes his civil connection with that state. This cannot be destroyed but by some overt act of a higher and stronger nature, *either on the part of the sovereign, or on his own part.* In the one case it may be a withdrawing of common protection, or a banishment of his person; in the other case a voluntary removal from that state, and the swearing of allegiance to and settling of himself in another. When either of these take place the connection is dissolved. If the first of these inferences be not true, then it remains that the honorable gentleman now offering as a candidate inherited an unqualified allegiance to the Crown of England, from his father, who died a British subject. If so, nothing could change this allegiance but the taking a part in the Revolution, and the Declaration of Independence; or the acquiring an allegiance by oath, after they were completed and established. The former of these was not his case, for he was at the time in England, where he carried his natural allegiance before the war, where he exercised it during the war, and where he left it when he left the kingdom. It will follow therefore that he acquired his allegiance and citizenship together, when he came into the United States, and took the oath. Since which seven years have not elapsed. If the second inference be just, it puts his disqualification in a still stronger and more unanswerable point of view; for there he completed the imperfect allegiance imparted to him by his birth, by a voluntary acquiescence in and residence under the British government, after arriving not only to the years of *maturity* but to years of *discretion*. This, if I may be allowed the expression, *sealed the contract* between him and the Crown of Great Britain—a contract which nothing could supersede but his subsequent transfer of allegiance to the United States, when and when only he became a citizen; a period however which was less than seven years ago. It would be very easy to push this disquisition farther, and present the reasons on this subject (drawn from many other topics) in various points of view. I shall content myself however with submitting to the public what I have already said, trusting that they will be no cause of offense, either to the honorable gentleman, to whom they immediately relate, and whose abilities and character I very much respect, or to any who may be zealous in his interest. It is exercising, I hope, with decency, the rights of a free man—and how far these remarks and the subject in general merit the scrutiny and attention of the public they will best judge, after reflecting upon the probability there may be of Congress vacating the seat, and the serious consequences which may result to this state from such an event. Nothing less than the dearest and most important interests of this country may be agitated and concluded upon in Congress, while not only the Southern States are feebly represented, but our own representation incomplete. That Congress will declare the seat is vacant is more than I can say; but that they will not is more than anybody else can say. Should a party desirous of carrying a favorite point, to which they might apprehend an opposition from the Southern representation, seize this opportunity of weakening such opposition, they would have as good reason to expect success, as we have to apprehend such an event.

1. Ramsay's piece signed "An Elector for Charleston District," *City Gazette*, 22 November, is printed above.

2. The quotation is from Blackstone's *Commentaries*. See Robert Malcolm Kerr, ed., *The Commentaries on the Laws of England of Sir William Blackstone, Knt.* (4 vols., London, 1876), I, 336.

A. B. to An Enemy to Quibblers, City Gazette, 25 November

A natural born citizen in the new Constitution, means one born after the Declaration of Independence. They who were born before were naturally born British subjects. There is no fear notwithstanding of being without a President, for the next clause gives room enough for choice, by extending eligibility to every citizen of the United States, at the time of the adoption of the new Constitution; but this again is guarded, to prevent new citizens from intruding into the office, by limiting the choice to those only who have been 13 years resident in the United States. Here the distinction is well kept up between residents and citizens, and a strong argument may be drawn from it, that birth in the country did not make citizens of those who were adults at the commencement or early stages of the late Revolution; especially if they resided abroad under their native allegiance.

A Native of South Carolina to the Public, City Gazette, 25 November

An illiberal attack having been made in the *City Gazette*, of Saturday last, on one of the candidates to represent this state in the general government; I think it right, that any improper impression which it might create, should be prevented. I call it an illiberal attack, because it is made at a time entirely favorable to its own success, and calculated to preclude that information which is necessary for the satisfaction of unprejudiced minds. The elector, if that be his true description, ought, agreeable to the principles of candor and justice, to have published his sentiments at a more early period, if the real object he had in view was the good of the country, by preventing an illegal election; but a conviction forces itself upon my mind, that he has not been actuated by the proper feelings of an elector, but instigated by the alluring prospect of a candidate, to raise his fortune at the expense of another, who has at least as much merit as himself. It is not to be supposed that an elector would endeavor to impress his opinion with respect to the eligibility of a candidate, on the minds of his countrymen, with the prompt decision remarkable in the publication alluded to, but he would with that modesty, which is becoming in all men, state his doubts, if he should have any, in order that they might be either confirmed or removed. This would have been acting in a manner worthy an elector for Charleston District. But how difficult is it for self-interest, to mark itself in such a manner as to avoid detection! The gentleman attacked is a native of this country, and in every respect deserving of the confidence of his countrymen. Whether he is capable of a seat in the general government, agreeable to the third paragraph of the Constitution, which declares that every Representative shall be a citizen of the United States seven years previous to his election, is the question to be deduced. It is natural to suppose, that this clause related only to foreigners, in consequence of the inconvenience which would arise from their being admitted in a shorter period, to all the rights of citizenship, subject as they must be, to the opinions and prejudices prevalent in their native country. The Constitution therefore with great propriety, makes citizenship necessary, in order that strangers in that time may be in some measure weaned of their local prejudices. Can any man in his senses imagine that this meant to effect natives of the soil. Persons who are attached to it by the most powerful interests, such as birth, property, connections, and in short every thing which can most forcible engage the affections of the human heart? The idea is big with absurdity. Every reasonable man must allow that seven years citizenship, which the Constitution requires, cannot purge a man so effectually of all improper ingredients, as to render him a fit object of comparison with a native citizen. The candidate therefore by the right of birth, which is by all nations considered as sacred, and conferring great privileges, is a citizen of the state. But it is said that it cannot be seven years since he has taken the oaths of allegiance to the state. If this argument has any force, I believe some of our oldest inhabitants who have neglected to observe this ceremony, would be deprived of the rights of citizenship, and be put on the footing of strangers. It must be readily allowed, that this right, when acquired by birth, is of a more transcendent nature than when acquired by any other means. *Omne majus continet in se minus*, is a maxim founded on common sense. I put a case: a doctor is sent to for an emetic for one of his patients; he sends Hippo instead of Tartar; the patient disputes the bill because he disapproved of the doctor's choice; I make no doubt but that in such a case the learned son of Esculapius would tell him, that Hippo is a safer medicine, that it fully answered the intended effect; in reality I think the doctor's bill ought to be paid if it were not too exorbitant. It is further said, that as the candidate went to Europe before the union of the thirteen states, and did not return until the year 1783, he could not in the intermediate space of time between his going and returning, have been a citizen of the United States. By what criterion is this fact to be established? Certainly by the circumstance of nativity. When he was at school, it is not to be supposed he took any oaths of allegiance to any foreign power. After he arrived to years of manhood, I believe he was in a transient state, travelling from one country to another, for his improvement. In this case he must be considered as a citizen of South Carolina, where he was born, or a vagrant in Europe, and subject to no power; besides, if he had the inclination, he had not the power of throwing off the natural allegiance he owed to his native country, and this is laid down in Blackstone's *Commentaries*, and other writers upon the subject; with no propriety then can it be implied, that because he did not come over to this country to assert his right of citizenship, that he thereby virtually lost it, especially when it is considered that he did not during his absence from this state, expressly subject himself to any foreign power whatever. Some of the British subjects in this city have, notwithstanding the allegiance they owe to the King of Great Britain, become citizens of this state, and I am warranted in saying that they are still considered as English subjects, in England; and that in case they should be found in arms against their sovereign, they would be liable to capital punishment. So that if the candidate did owe allegiance to his native country, which he certainly did, if not from birth yet from acquiescence, and from his declining to become the subject of any foreign power, he could not at this time shake it off. It is also remarked, that during his absence from this country, there was a change in the political situation of America; or in other words, that a new sovereignty commenced, independent of the preexisting one, and that therefore he could not be subject to this power, whatever he might have been to the old one. I lay it down as an axiom, that men owe obedience to whatever power is predominant in their native country, and notwithstanding any changes which may take place in the government. The circumstance of absence can make no difference, for an Englishman in the East Indies, is still an English subject. When the House of Lancaster, contrary to the rules of descent and the rights of blood, seized upon the Crown of Great Britain, was not obedience due by all English subject to the usurped power. Had not this been the case, would not the whole English nation have been guilty of treason, and the kingdom deluged with blood, when the House of York afterwards established its right to the throne? When the monarchy of England was changed into a republic by Cromwell, was not a ready obedience paid to this monster of blood and iniquity, and shall it be said that the same tribute is not due to the sovereignty of America, although reared on the noblest foundation? The whole property of the candidate was within the jurisdiction of the United States. Could Great Britain protect it for him? Certainly not, nay, if he had been one of her subjects, it would have been long since forfeited and applied to the purposes of government. But his country very rationally thought, that so long as he did not disclaim his allegiance to her, that he continued her subject, and accordingly protected his property from all invasions.

Thus I think I have removed every objection to the eligibility of the candidate. I hope the elector will upon more reflection, retract the too hasty opinion which he has formed. It may be necessary to declare, that I have not been actuated by any motive of friendship or attachment, being a perfect stranger to the gentleman attacked, but solely from a love of justice, which I trust nature has planted in my breast. There is one observation more, which I beg leave to submit to the serious consideration of my countrymen. It is this—that they should be very cautious to elect such persons only as have a fellow feeling with themselves, in all matters which touch the happiness and welfare of their country. Who can be so likely to answer this description as men united to them by the tie which binds countrymen together. The history of the proceedings of the federal government it has been truly said, will be a narrative of the conflicts of local prejudices. Should they elect men cold in their interests—whose minds have received from foreign causes a bent unfavorable to their good—feeble must be their exertions in the general struggle, and hurled along in a vortex of irresistible force, this country will soon have to lament its folly, and imprudence.

William Smith, A Dose for the Doctor, Charleston, 25 November[1]

Ecce iterum Crispinus! or in plain English, the Doctor has again intruded himself on the patience of the public. Finding that arguments have failed him, he is obliged to have recourse to misquotations, quibbles, distinctions without a difference, and to laws made to answer temporary purposes, which by no means apply to the present question. What have we, for example, to do with *virtual citizenship*, when I am in possession of, and never have been deprived of *actual citizenship*? May not the Doctor with propriety be compared to a certain cunning animal, who when hard run, and all his windings, artifices and tricks have availed him nothing, steeps his tail in an unsavory liquor, and endeavors to whisk it into the eyes of his pursuers.

The Doctor asserts that by the generosity of this country I had the advantage of aliens so far, that at any time on application I might be admitted to citizenship. Here then is a new class of men never known in society before!—not aliens—not citizens—but an intermediate set of beings, who neither aliens nor citizens, partake of the nature of both, and may be compared to what is very well understood by the Doctor under the name of a *tertium quid*.

I think it unnecessary to follow the Doctor through all his subterfuges, but shall attach myself to the main point, to which I flatter myself I shall give a satisfactory answer, by condemning him out of his own mouth. The Doctor has declared, that *I was*, at the time of my election, *qualified to be a privy councillor*. Let us examine then the qualification of a privy councillor—the following are the words of the constitution: "The members of the privy council shall have been *residents in this state five years preceding their election*." I arrived here from Europe in *November* 1783—I qualified as a privy councillor in *August* 1785, *the short space of* 21 *months*. The Doctor however *admits* that *I had a qualification*: what then was my qualification? If my residence here, during my minority, and previous to my going to Europe, was not considered as part of the residence of five years required by the constitution, how could I have possibly been qualified, or what does the Doctor conceive could have been my qualification? Had I arrived here in November 1783, *an alien, a British subject*, could I have been elected a privy councillor and qualified in August 1785? *Will the Doctor say I could*? The Doctor we know is fond of *paradoxes*: a stronger proof than the following cannot be adduced. In *his Calm Reply*,[2] he says I was, in November 1783, *a British subject*; in *his Short Reply*,[3] he says I was in August

1785 eligible to the office of privy councillor, and in October 1785, I actually had *his* vote for that office. Let him reconcile this monstrous absurdity! Should the Doctor favor us with another reply, whether it be *calm* or *short*, I hope he will be able to extricate himself from this difficulty. I shall conclude with a word of advice to the Doctor. He frequently speaks of his *candor* and *his regard for the good of the state*; these expressions have been so hackneyed, that every person who has had any transactions in public life, must now be sickened with them; they have been often made use of as a *stepladder*, to mount into popularity, or a *mask* to conceal the most ambitious designs.

The Doctor says *he had a regard for me*: the public will not be imposed upon [by] his words, but will judge from his actions. I am conscious of never having injured him in the course of my life; and yet when he found that I was likely to obtain the suffrages of my fellow citizens, his regard vanished: malevolence, and detraction were substituted in the room of it, and one single object seemed to engross his attention, namely, the gratification of his ambition. He has confessed that if at the Declaration of Independence I was a party to it, either personally *or representatively, he gives up the argument*. That I was so, must be now apparent, even to the most prejudiced of his friends, and therefore I hope he will adhere to his word.

He must, I believe, not only give up the argument, but likewise the good opinion which has hitherto been entertained of him by many worthy citizens of this country. Nothing but *repentance* for the insult which he has offered by his unjustifiable conduct, can be an atonement to them, and reinstate him in their good opinion. As far as depends upon myself, I shall be ready to forgive him. Though the shaft was aimed at my heart, and at the same time could not fail to wound every native of this country! yet my forgiveness shall not be the last obtained, as implacability forms no part of my character.

Doctor farewell.

1. Broadside, South Carolina, Portfolio 172, no. 13, Rare Book Room, DLC. This broadside was republished in the *State Gazette of South Carolina*, 1 December, along with a post-election commentary by "A Friend to Justice," printed below.

2. 24 November, printed above.

3. 24 November, printed above.

Speech by William Smith, 25 November[1]

On declaring the number of voters for a member in the federal House of Representatives, in the church of St. Michael, a correspondent whose remembrance is memory's dear reward, has favored us with the following address, delivered by William Smith, Esq.:

Gentlemen,

And I may now add,

My Fellow Citizens!

Give me leave to return you my acknowledgements for the high mark of your approbation and confidence.

You have on this day inculcated as moral a lesson perhaps as was ever delivered in this church, for you have shown to the world that candor, fairness, and liberality of conduct, are the surest means to obtain your applause; and that you will at all times discountenance every proceeding which is uncandid, unfair, or illiberal.

Although one of my opponents has endeavored to prejudice you against me by disingenuous insinuations, yet, standing under this sacred roof, having before my eyes that place from which we are taught principles of mutual forbearance and benevolence, ill would it become me, upon this occasion, to add to his depression. Indeed, not only the place where I address you, but a sentiment of compassion forbid it. I shall leave him to his own feelings, and when he lays his head on his pillow tonight, his conscience, I am sure, will sufficiently reprove him for the unprovoked injury he intended me.

When it is known that I drew my first breath within sight of this very spot, that my property was placed in that treasury to carry on the war, your astonishment at the attack made upon me, could only be surpassed by the just indignation which it roused in your breasts. But even if birth, property, connections, friends, everything that can attach a man to a country, were insufficient to endear South Carolina to me, this extraordinary proof of your esteem and regard must rivet me to it forever. Should my fellow citizens in the other parishes of Charleston District, concur in sentiment with you in choosing me their Representative, gratitude will be superadded to other ties, and must forcibly prompt me to promote to the best of my ability, the prosperity, honor, and happiness of the district.

1. *City Gazette*, 27 November.

David Ramsay to John Eliot, Charleston, 26 November (excerpt)[1]

We have just finished our election for Representatives to Congress. I was a candidate and lost my election on two grounds. One was that I was a Northward man and the other that I was represented as favoring the abolition of slavery. Such is the temper of our people here that it is unpopular to be unfriendly to the further importations of slaves. That would be certainly wrong on every principle.[2]

1. RC, Andrews and Eliot Papers, MHi. Printed: Ramsay, *Writings,* 123-24. Eliot was pastor of the New North Church in Boston.
2. Ramsay did not let the matter of William Smith's eligibility drop after the election ended with Smith's victory. He petitioned the House of Representatives on 15 April 1789 to deny Smith his seat and wrote to several congressmen, among them Elias Boudinot of New Jersey, who was himself involved in a contested election, and James Madison, asking them to support his petition (to Boudinot, Charleston, 31 March 1789, Ramsay, *Writings,* 124; and to Madison, Charleston, 4 April 1789, RC, Madison Papers, DLC). Ramsay also prepared a new anti-Smith tract, *A Dissertation on the Manner of Acquiring the Character and Privileges of A Citizen of the United States* (n.p., 1789), which he planned to have printed and distributed to every member of Congress. The printing was delayed, however, until after Congress had decided the issue.
This contested election was particularly important because it was the first one dealt with by the new Congress, whose members were acutely aware that their actions would set important precedents. Thomas Tudor Tucker, a bitter political rival of Ralph Izard and William Smith, managed Ramsay's case. The House of Representatives debated Ramsay's

petition and rejected it by a vote of 36 to 1 on 22 May 1789. Jonathan Grout, a Massachusetts Antifederalist, stood alone in the minority. Even after this defeat, Ramsay would not let the matter rest, and he published another tract attacking Smith, *Observations on the Decision of the House of Representatives of the United States, on the 22d Day of May, 1789 . . .* (New York, 1789). Congressional action on the petition, including Smith's speech in his own defense, is in M. St. Clair Clarke and David A. Hall, eds., *Cases of Contested Elections in Congress, from the Year 1789 to 1834, Inclusive* (Washington, 1834), 23-37.

City Gazette, 26 November

Yesterday afternoon ended the election of a member for Charleston District to the House of Representatives in Congress; 30 members of the [state] House of Representatives, and two senators for Charleston District, in the General Assembly. Owing to the uncommon number of voters at this election, it is probable it will be several days before the favored candidates can be declared.

Election Returns for the Charleston District[1]

We are favored with the following returns for members of Congress.

	W. Smith	C. Gillon	Dr. Ramsay
Charleston	349	169	146
Goose-Creek	34	3	4
Christ-Church	17	6	18
St. Andrew's	28	24	8
St. John, Berkeley	12	11	10
St. John, Colleton	32	4	5
St. Bartholemew's	70	150	0
St. Thomas and St. Dennis	28	0	0
St. Paul's	30	19	0
	600	386	191

1. *State Gazette,* 1 December. The Charleston newspapers began reporting election results on 27 November, but the reports consist only of the names of the winners in scattered parishes. The names of opponents and the number of votes cast are not given. The above list of the votes cast in each parish of the Charleston District is the only one of its kind that has been located. Apparently type for this issue of the *State Gazette* was being set as the returns came in. On page 2 there is the drawing of a hand pointing to the following item: "At the election of member of Congress for Charleston District, the votes of the city of Charleston were as follows: William Smith, 349 Com. Gillon—169 Dr. Ramsay—146."

This item was followed by foreign news and by news stories about the reaction in North Carolina to the failure of that state's Convention to ratify the Constitution. These items are followed on page 3 by the complete returns for the Charleston District, printed above.

A Friend to Justice, State Gazette, 1 December

I was much displeased at seeing in your paper of Thursday last, a publication entitled "a reply to a piece signed William Smith."[1] The election being over, the publication of that piece in your paper could have no other tendency than to prevent that reconciliation and harmony taking place, which must be the wish of every good citizen. After the electors of Charleston had so plainly declared their opinion against the Doctor, and had, by a very large majority, convinced him that they deemed Mr. Smith worthy of their choice, was there not more of ill-nature, spleen, and disappointed ambition in republishing that reply than of good sense or policy? Was it not a disrespect to the electors of Charleston, and an insult on their understanding? Or did the Doctor suppose that, having failed in convincing the citizens of Charleston, he could, by circulating his reply (through the channel of your newspaper) into the different parts of the country, render them contemptible to the rest of their fellow citizens? The gentleman, whose political conduct is impeached in that publication, and his friends are averse to a further prosecution of this business. Whatever the Doctor's designs might have been, Mr. S—— is satisfied at their having been rendered abortive, by the good sense and judgment of his countrymen, and although HE wishes to rest the matter here, yet some of his friends think YOU ought, in justice to him, to publish in your paper the answer which he gave to the abovementioned piece.

[Smith's broadside of 25 November, "A Dose for the Doctor," was reprinted at this point in the article.]

1. The reference is to David Ramsay's broadside of 24 November, "A Short Reply," which was republished in the *State Gazette* on 27 November, two days after the election.

William Mason to William Bentley, Charleston, 3 December (excerpt)[1]

Our election for member for Congress has caused great commotion among the candidates. Commodore [Alexander] Gillon, Dr. [David] Ramsay and William Smith were competitors for Charleston District. Ramsay it was supposed stood an equal chance with either of the others when a piece appeared in the *Gazette* of the 22d November which you have enclosed.[2]

On Sunday morning a handbill was put at the corners desiring a suspicion [suspension] of the opinion of the public till his answer should appear on Monday, one by Ralph Izard the same day, the rest followed according to the dates.

Votes in Charleston   146 Ramsay
                                  349 Smith
                                  169 Gillon

There are not returns from all the parishes but it is settled that Smith is the man by a remarkable majority.

1. RC, Bentley Papers, MWA. Mason graduated from Harvard in 1787, and in 1788 he was teaching in an academy in Charleston. Bentley taught at Harvard until he became pastor of a church in Salem in 1783.

2. The reference is to a story in the *City Gazette*, 22 November, printed above, denying a rumor that one of the candidates, if elected, would work for the emancipation of the slaves.

The *City Gazette* of 22 November also contained an article by Ramsay attacking Smith's eligibility, and it is probable that Bentley turned both Mason's letter and the newspaper over to the *Salem Mercury*. On 13 January 1789, the *Mercury* published the following item:

"We have received late Charleston papers, by which it appears, that William Smith, Esq., is chosen Representative to Congress for Charleston District. This gentleman, Commodore

Gillon, and Dr. Ramsay were competitors. The latter was supposed to stand an equal chance with either of the others, when a piece appeared in the gazette, representing Mr. Smith as an ineligible candidate. This produced a warm contention in the public papers, which so weakened the Doctor's interest, that Mr. Smith carried the election, he having 600 votes—Commodore Gillon 386—Dr. Ramsay 191."

The figures for the vote in Charleston District in the above item are those given in the *State Gazette*, 1 December, printed above.

Official Notice to the Legislature of the Date for Electing Electors, 20 December[1]

Mrs. Timothy, Please to insert in your next paper the undermentioned clause of an act, intitled, "An Act prescribing on the part of this state the time, places, and manner of holding Elections for Representatives in the Congress, and the manner of appointing Electors of a President of the United States," passed November 4, 1788, for the information of the members of the legislature, who agreeably to the constitution of this state, are to meet in Charleston on Monday the 5th day of January next, being the first Monday in the said month.

John S. Dart.
[Clerk of the House of Representatives]
December 20, 1788.

"And be it further enacted by the authority aforesaid, That Electors of a President of the United States shall be appointed by the Legislature of this State on *the first Wednesday in January next*, or by such persons as shall be returned members thereof, and shall attend on that day; and the said Electors, previous to executing their appointment, shall, before his Excellency the Governor or Commander in Chief for the time being, take the following oath or affirmation, viz., *I A. B. do solemnly swear or affirm, that I will faithfully and conscientiously discharge my duty as an Elector of a President of the United States.* SO HELP ME GOD."

1. (LT), *State Gazette,* 22 December.

Privy Council Proceedings, Tuesday, 6 January 1789[1]

Present: His Excellency the Governor, His Honor the Lieutenant Governor, the Honorable R. Izard, Charles Pinckney, Edward Rutledge, Thos. Waties, Pierce Butler.

His Excellency the Governor and the honorable the Council proceeded to examine the district returns of elections for five members to represent this state in the federal House of Representatives in the following order:

The parishes of St. Philips and St. Michaels, Charleston; Christ Church; St. Johns, Berkeley; St. Andrew, St. George, Dorchester; St. James, Goose Creek; St. Thomas and St. Dennis; St. Paul; St. Bartholomew; St. James, Santee; St. John, Colleton; and St. Stephens; composing Charleston District. Majority for Wm. Smith (653 votes).

The parishes of St. Helena, St. Peters, Prince Williams, Saxe Gotha, Lower

District between Broad and Saluda Rivers, St. Mathews, Orange District between Savannah River and the North Fork of Edisto, composing the United District of Beaufort and Orangeburgh. Majority of votes for Aedanus Burke (422 votes).

Parishes of Prince George, Winyah; All Saints; Prince Fredrick and St. Davids; composing the United Districts of Georgetown and Cheraw. Majority of votes for Daniel Huger, Esquire (496 votes).

The districts: Eastward of the Wateree, between Broad and Catawba Rivers; the New Acquisition; and the County of Chester (which made no return); composing the District of Camden. Majority of votes for Thos. Sumter (507 votes).

The District of 96, Little River and Upper or Spartan, composing Ninety Six District. The majority of votes for Thos. Tudor Tucker (759 votes).

And accordingly His Excellency declared the following gentlemen duly elected to serve in the House of Representatives, to wit, Willm. Smith at the election held for Charleston District. In the United Districts of Beaufort and Orangeburgh, Aedanus Burke, Esqr. In the United Districts of Georgetown and Cheraw, Daniel Huger, Esqr. In Camden District, Thos. Sumter, Esqr. and in the District of Ninety Six, T. T. Tucker, Esqr. and they were accordingly proclaimed and their election likewise notified to them in the following letter, to wit,

"Sir, In conformity to the Act of the Genl. Assembly prescribing on the part of the State the times, places and manner of holding the Election for Representatives in the Congress of the United States, I hereby transmit to you official Information that you are Elected a Member from this State to the House of Representatives in the Congress of the United States by a Majority of the suffrages of the Electors in   District

Signed, Thomas Pinckney"[2]

The managers of the election for the District between Savannah and the North Fork of Edisto have not made a return of the names of the persons voting for members to the House of Representatives of Congress or of the ballots. But Daniel Green, Esq., who was one of the managers, did yesterday deliver to His Excellency the Governor a paper signed by himself certifying that the Honorable Aedanus Burke had 199 votes, John Bull 2, Robt. Barnwell 1, and Judge [Henry] Pendleton 1. Upon which His Excellency asked the opinion of Council, whether altho it might otherways be a true return it could be admitted under such circumstances—when the Council were of opinion as it was not agreeable to the act, "Regulating the time, place and Manner of holding the Elections" the return made by Mr. Greene was inadmissible.

The County of Chester which is in Camden District made no return of their election.

S. Drayton

1. Rough Minute Book of the Privy Council, 1783-1789, Sc-Ar.
2. (LT). A copy dated 7 January is in the Thomas Pinckney Letterbook, 1787-1789, Pinckney Family Papers, DLC, with the following endorsement: "The above letter was wrote to W. Smith, Adanus Burke, Dl. Huger, Thos. Sumter, and T. T. Tucker, esqres., each."

Proclamation by Governor Thomas Pinckney, 7 January[1]

State of South Carolina

By His Excellency Thomas Pinckney Esqr
Governor and Commander in Chief in and over the State aforesaid—
Proclamation.

Whereas, Elections for representatives in the Legislature of the United States were held on the Twenty-fifth and twenty-Sixth days of November last in the Several Districts of this State pursuant to the directions of An Act entitled "An Act prescribing on the part of this State the Times Places and Manner of holding Elections for Representatives in the Congress and the manner of appointing Electors of a President of the United States dated the fourth day of November A D. 1788 and in the thirteenth year of the Independence of the United States of America" And whereas I have caused the returns transmitted from the said Election Districts respectively to be examined in Council in a Public Manner and the five Persons who had respectively the greatest number of Votes in the said Districts have been thereby ascertained—I do therefore in Conformity to the above mentioned Act issue this Proclamation hereby notifying that William Smith Esqr. had at the said Election the greatest number of Votes in the District of Charleston The Honble Aedanus Burke had the Greatest number of Votes in the United Districts of Beaufort and Orangeburgh. Daniel Huger Esqr. had the Greatest number of Votes in the United Districts of George Town and Cheraw, Thomas Sumter Esqr. had the greatest number of Votes in Camden District and Thomas Tudor Tucker Esqr. had the greatest number of Votes in the District of Ninety Six Whereby the said William Smith Aedanus Burke Daniel Huger Thomas Sumter and Thomas Tudor Tucker Esqrs. are duly elected Members from this State to the House of Representatives in the Congress of the United States— Given under my hand and the Great Seal of the State in the City of Charleston this Seventh day of January in the year of our Lord One thousand Seven hundred and eighty Nine and of the Sovereignty and Independence of the United States of America the thirteenth

By His Excellency's Command—   Thomas ([LHS?]) Pinckney.
    Peter Freneau Secretary   Recorded 7th January 1789

1. (LT), Miscellaneous Record Book, XX, Sc-Ar. The following day the *City Gazette* reported that "General Sumter, Judge Burke, Dr. Tucker, D. Huger, and William Smith, esquires, are elected Representatives for this state in the House of Representatives of the United States." Results of the election were reprinted in newspapers throughout the states (see, for example, the Savannah *Georgia Gazette*, 22 January; Baltimore *Maryland Journal*, 17 February; Philadelphia *Pennsylvania Gazette*, 18 February; New London *Connecticut Gazette*, 20 February; *New York Packet*, 24 February; Northampton *Hampshire Gazette*, 25 February; Boston *Independent Chronicle*, 26 February; and *Pittsburgh Gazette*, 7 March). Several papers carried brief descriptions of the winners' political affiliations, pointing out that Sumter and Burke had voted against ratification of the Constitution and that Burke had been a zealous opponent of the Society of Cincinnati (see, for example, the Portland, Me., *Cumberland Gazette*, 26 February; *Providence Gazette*, 28 February; *New York Daily Gazette*, 2 March; and Philadelphia *Pennsylvania Packet*, 5 March).

City Gazette, 7 January

The members of the legislature, now in Charleston, are requested to attend in the House of Representatives this morning, at ten o'clock, in order to proceed to the choice of seven persons as Electors for this republic, to meet on the first Wednesday in February next, for the purpose of voting, by ballot, for a President and Vice President of the United States.

House and Senate Proceedings, Wednesday, 7 January

The House

The House met according to adjournment, there being a sufficient number of members present to make a House, whose names are here undermentioned: [72 members were listed] respectively took the Oath of Qualification as directed by law, and the Oath of Allegiance and Fidelity agreeably to the constitution, and having signed their names to the roll of the House, when there appeared there was no House, the members then present made choice of the Honorable Rawlins Lowndes, Esquire, to be their chairman, he by desire of the rest adjourned the meeting of the House 'till 10 o'clock tomorrow morning.[1]

The Senate

A verbal message from the chairman appointed by the members of the House of Representatives by Mr. Izard and Mr. E. Rutledge, requesting that the members of the Senate would be pleased to attend in the House of Representatives, and join with the members thereof in balloting for seven Electors of a President of the United States.

The members present having taken the said message into consideration agreed thereto, and appointed Mr. Desaussure as chairman, who with the said members proceeded to the House of Representatives, where they joined with the members of that House in balloting for seven Electors of a President of the United States, agreeably to the last clause of an act, entitled "An Act prescribing on the part of this State, the times, places and manner of holding Elections for Representatives in the Congress and the manner of appointing Electors of a President of the United States," passed the 4th day of November 1788.

Joint Session of House and Senate Members

In pursuance of the last enacting clause of an act entitled "An Act prescribing on the part of this State the Times, Places, and Manner, of holding Elections for Representatives in the Congress, and the Manner of appointing Electors of a President of the United States," this being the first Wednesday in January—the undermentioned members of the legislature met in the House of Representatives, viz.,

Senators: Honorable John Parker, Honorable William Moultrie, Honorable Melcher Garner, Honorable John Collins, Honorable Thomas Horry, Honorable Arnoldus Vanderhorst, Honorable Daniel DeSaussure, Honorable Robert Pringle, Honorable John Huger, Honorable John Glaze.

House of Representatives: Edward Rutledge, John F. Grimké, Edward Darrell, John Blake, Thomas Jones, Hugh Rutledge, Edward Blake, Rawlins Lowndes,

Daniel Cannon, Michael Kalteisen, Anthony Toomer, John Budd, Peter Fayssoux, Henry Laurens, Junior, Richard Hutson, John Hume, William Frierson, Thomas O. Elliott, Charles Drayton, Mathias Hutchinson, John Postell, Thomas Waring, Peter Smith, Ralph Izard, John Deas, Junior, Gabriel Manigault, William Smith, Peter Gray, John Elias Moore, George Haig, William Washington, Roger Parker Saunders, Daniel Wilson, John Sanders, Obrien Smith, Benjamin Postell, Benjamin Reynolds, William Douxsaint, John Mayrant, George Simmons, Henry Patrick, Alexander Gillon, Thomas Sumter, Richard Lushington, William Johnson, Francis Kinloch, David Ramsay, Nathaniel Russell, Thomas Corbett, William Drayton, Jacob Read, John Julius Pringle, Charles Pinckney, William Scott, Junior, Joseph Manigault, William Harleston, Thomas Simons, Thomas Waties, Cleland Kinloch, Patrick Dollard, John Burgess, Joshua Ward, Nathaniel Heyward, Peter Porcher, Junior, Benjamin Cudworth, Andrew Baskin, Arthur Simkins, Joseph Culpeper, William Fitzpatrick, Jacob Brown, John Cooke, William Bratton, John Drennan, Robert Patton, John Linton, Jacob Rumph, Christian Rumph, Henry Cannon, C. C. Pinckney, Daniel Greene, Richard Tradaway, Robert Brown, Levin Collins, William Melwee, Joshua Saxon, Samuel Saxon, esquires.

The Honorable Rawlins Lowndes, Esquire, being chosen chairman, the members present proceeded to the election of seven Electors of a President of the United States of America.

On casting up the ballots it appeared that the following gentlemen were duly elected, viz.: Christopher Gadsden, Henry Laurens, Arthur Simkins, esquires; Honorable Edward Rutledge, Esquire; Charles Cotesworth Pinckney, Esquire; Honorable Thomas Heyward, Honorable John Faucheraud Grimké, esquires.

Mr. Chairman thereupon declared the said gentlemen to be duly elected.

On motion, ordered that Mr. Chairman do sign a certificate, and send to each of the Electors informing them of their election, and to desire of them to proceed on the duties of their office agreeable to the resolves of the Congress of the United States of America, in that case made and provided.

Mr. Chairman then left the chair.

The Senate

The members being returned, Mr. Chairman reported that upon casting up the votes, it appeared that the following gentlemen were declared Electors of a President of the United States, viz.: General Gadsden, Colonel Laurens, Mr. Simpkins, Mr. E. Rutledge, General Pinckney, Judge Heyward, Judge Grimké.

And then adjourned until tomorrow morning 11 o'clock.

1. The House met on the 5th and 6th of January but did not have a quorum until the 7th, when 72 members appeared, took their qualifying oaths, and signed the House roll. At that point, according to the *City Gazette*, the House learned that the Senate could not form a quorum for two or three days. Therefore, the two bodies could not meet as a legislature to choose Electors on the day set in the Election Ordinance adopted by the Confederation Congress on 13 September. However, the South Carolina Election Law provided that Electors could be chosen either by members sitting as a legislature or by members voting as individuals. It was probably for this reason that the Journals state "there was no House." The "members then present" elected a chairman who adjourned the meeting to the 8th, and a verbal message was sent to the senators requesting their presence in the House chambers to choose Electors. This procedure was explained in the *City Gazette* on 8 January, printed immediately below.

Newspaper Report of House Proceedings on Wednesday, 7 January[1]

Yesterday a sufficient number of members attended in the House of Representatives to make a quorum.

The Intendant [Rawlins Lowndes] observed, that the immediate business of the day was, to ballot for seven Electors to choose a President for the United States. It was stated in the law passed last session for this purpose, "That electors of a president of the United States should be appointed by the legislature of this state on the first Wednesday in January next, or by such persons as shall be returned members thereof, and shall attend on that day." Altho' there was a sufficient number of members on the floor to make a House, yet it being necessary the Senate should join them to constitute the legislature, and as there was not a prospect that that body would make a house in less time than two or three days, the second mode must of course be resorted to, and they must ballot as individuals; he therefore moved that a chairman should be appointed.

Mr. E[dward] Rutledge seconded the motion, and named the Intendant who took the chair.

A message was sent to the Senate chamber to request the attendance of such members as might be there, when ten attended, and gave in their ballots.

On casting up the votes there appeared to be a majority in favor of General [Christopher] Gadsden, Colonel [Henry] Laurens, General [Charles C.] Pinckney, Mr. Justice [Thomas] Heyward, Mr. Justice [John F.] Grimké, E[dward] Rutledge, and A[rthur] Simkins, esquires, who were declared duly elected.[2]

After which such members as were present took the Oath of Qualification.

1. *City Gazette*, 8 January.
2. Reports of the South Carolina choice of Electors were reprinted in newspapers throughout the states (see, for example, the Baltimore *Maryland Journal*, 17 February; Philadelphia *Pennsylvania Journal*, 18 February; and *Newport Mercury*, 27 February).

Aedanus Burke to Governor Thomas Pinckney, Charleston, 9 January[1]

I have received Your Excellency's letter containing official information that I have been elected a Representative to Congress; and I beg leave to inform Your Excellency in answer to it, that although I have very great reluctance to absent myself from the duties of my office as a judge of the state;[2] yet I conceive that I cannot with propriety frustrate the expectations of the very respectable number of citizens who did me the honor of electing me, particularly as it is not without a precedent for a judge to serve in Congress. I trust that the gentlemen in the commission, will be able during the short intervals of my absence, to do the business of the department. It was generally done by Mr. [Henry] Pendleton and myself in the years 1778 and 1779, when two of our associates, one in each year, were appointed to Congress.

1. Copy, Legislative Records and Papers, Sc-Ar. Governor Thomas Pinckney sent a copy of the letter to the House on 20 January.
2. Burke was an associate justice of the Court of Sessions and Common Pleas.

William Smith to Governor Thomas Pinckney, Charleston, 10 January[1]

In answer to Your Excellency's letter of the 7th[2] instant notifying my election as a member from this state to the House of Representatives of the United States, for the District of Charleston, I beg leave to inform Your Excellency that I accept the appointment which my countrymen have honored me with, and shall endeavor to prove myself worthy of so important a trust.

1. Copy, Legislative Records and Papers, Sc-Ar. Governor Thomas Pinckney sent a copy to the South Carolina House on 20 January.
2. See Privy Council Proceedings, 6 January, printed above.

House Proceedings, Wednesday, 14 January

On motion, resolved, that the Electors who have been appointed by this state pursuant to law for the purpose of electing a President of the United States be convened at the Exchange in Charleston at 12 o'clock in the forenoon of Wednesday the fourth day of February next.

Ordered, that the resolution be sent to the Senate for their concurrence, and that Colonel Lushington and Mr. Hume do carry the same.

House and Senate Proceedings, Thursday, 15 January

The Senate

[The Senate received the House's message of the previous day.]

The House [Senate] having taken the said report into consideration agreed thereto.

Resolved, that this House do concur with the House of Representatives in the said resolution.

Ordered, that the clerk do sign, and carry the resolutions to the House of Representatives.

The House

The Senate returned to this House by their clerk a resolution of the 14 inst. respecting the election of a President of the United States, with their concurrence thereto.[1]

1. On 16 January the *City Gazette* reported that "The Intendant [Rawlins Lowndes] informed the House that he had received information from those gentlemen who were chosen Electors for President, that they accepted the appointment, and intended to meet according to law."

Rawlins Lowndes Refuses To Be a Candidate for United States Senate, 15 January[1]

The Intendant said, that several worthy, respectable members had done him the honor to request he would become a candidate for the office of Senator in Congress. It gave him peculiar pleasure to understand that he possessed the good opinion of that House, and as it had always been his greatest ambition to devote his labors to the public service whenever called upon so to do, on the present occasion he sincerely wished it was in his power to comply, but his time of life and infirmities required repose, nor did his age permit those exertions which would be found indispensably necessary to discharge with fidelity the duty of a Senator. He hoped the House would not consider what he had taken the liberty to trouble them as resulting from ostentatious vanity, his only object being to prevent splitting of votes.

1. *City Gazette*, 16 January.

John F. Grimké to Henry William Harrington, Charleston, 16 January (excerpt)[1]

Our Representatives to Congress are for 96 [District], Dr. [Thomas Tudor] Tucker; for Orangeburgh and Beaufort, Adanus Burke; for Camden, General [Thomas] Sumpter. These 3 are clearly Antifederal.[2] For Georgetown and Cheraws, Danl. Huger, doubtful; for Charleston District, Wm. Smith, Federal. What a black list. We must endeavor to mend it by our election of Senators which will come on next Wednesday and which I hope will prove a Federal one.[3]

I send you a few of the latest newspapers.

1. RC, Henry W. Harrington Papers, NcU. The letter was addressed to "General Harrington on the Pedee North Carolina." This was probably Henry William Harrington, who had been a brigadier general in the North Carolina militia during the Revolution.

2. Jean-Baptiste Petry, the French Consul in Charleston, reported on 20 December that "four Antifederalists are counted" among the five Representatives elected. He said they owed their election "not to the number of inhabitants opposed to the new government but to the pains they have taken to obtain votes" (to Comte de la Luzerne, Ministère des Affaires Étrangères, Archives Diplomatiques, Correspondance Politique, États-Unis, Supplément, IV, 395).

3. A few weeks earlier, John Brown Cutting, in reporting to Thomas Jefferson on the results of senatorial elections in other states, remarked that the senatorial candidates in South Carolina were Ralph Izard, "Federal," Thomas Sumter, "Antifederal," and Pierce Butler, "dubious" (Charleston, 27 December, Boyd, XIV, 394).

Timothy Ford to Robert Morris, Charleston, 17 January (excerpt)[1]

Of news our place is at present very barren and we are turning our eyes to your city [New York] as the fountain of interesting intelligence. The legislature will in a few days proceed to the election of Senators. The Electors for the President are already appointed; as are also our Representatives in the lower house. In the last we do not anticipate as much respectability on the floor of Congress as this state could have entitled herself to by a different election. Our men of first abilities uniformly declined and the people much straitened in their choice resorted to those who offered themselves as candidates.

1. RC, Robert Morris Papers, NjR. Ford, a native of New Jersey, had moved to South Carolina after the Revolution and had begun the practice of law. Morris was a former chief justice of New Jersey.

House Proceedings, Monday, 19 January

A motion was made and seconded, that a message be prepared and sent to His Excellency the Governor requesting of him to inform this House whether Mr. Justice Burke, elected a Representative to represent this state in the House of Representatives of the United States, intended to take his seat, which being agreed to, the following message was accordingly prepared, viz.,

In the House of Representatives, January 19th, 1789

This House request of Your Excellency to inform them whether Mr. Justice Burke, elected one of the Representatives to represent this state in the House of Representatives of the United States, had communicated to Your Excellency his intention of taking his seat.

By order of the House
Jacob Read, Speaker

Ordered, that Mr. Laurens and Mr. Cleland Kinloch do wait on His Excellency the Governor with the said message.

House Proceedings, Tuesday, 20 January

A message from His Excellency the Governor by his secretary in the following words, viz.,

Mr. Speaker and Gentlemen of the House of Representatives,

Gentlemen: In answer to your message of this morning,[1] I herewith transmit to you copies of the only two letters I have received from the gentlemen elected members of the House of Representatives in Congress.[2]

Thomas Pinckney
Charleston, 20 January 1789

1. The House's message of "this morning" was prepared on the 19th and is printed under the House Proceedings for that date.
2. The message Pinckney sent is in Legislative Records and Papers, Sc-Ar. It is endorsed: "1789 Jany 20 Messe. from Governor with two Letters—one from Mr. Justice Burke and the other from Mr Wm Smith." They were no doubt the letters dated 9 and 10 January respectively, both of which are printed above.

House and Senate Proceedings, Thursday, 22 January

The House

A motion was made and seconded that a message be sent to the Senate requesting their attendance in this House in order to proceed to the election of two Senators to represent this state in the Senate of the United States.

A message was accordingly sent.

The Senate

A verbal message from the House of Representatives by Colonel Lushington and Dr. Irvine, viz.,

Honorable Gentlemen: The House of Representatives inform this honorable House that they are ready to proceed to the election of two Senators to represent this state in the Congress of the United States and request that this House would be pleased to join with them in the said election.

The House having taken the said message into consideration, agreed thereto.

Ordered, that Dr. Pringle and Major Jenkins be a committee to remain in the House of Representatives, and report the said election to this House.

Mr. President, with the Senate, attended in the House of Representatives accordingly where they joined with that House in balloting for two Senators to represent this state in the Congress of the United States.

The House

The Senate attended in this House and voted with this House for two Senators to represent this state in the Senate of the United States.

On casting up the ballots it appeared that Pierce Butler, Esquire, was the only gentleman in nomination that had a majority of votes of the members present.

Mr. Speaker thereupon declared Pierce Butler, Esquire, to be duly elected a Senator to represent this state in the Senate of the United States.[1]

The Senate

The committee appointed to remain in the House of Representatives and report the said election to this House, reported, that upon casting up the votes it appeared that only the Honorable Major Pierce Butler was duly elected a Senator to represent this state in the Congress of the United States.

The House

A motion was made and seconded that a message be sent to the Senate requesting their attendance in this House, in order to proceed to the election of a Senator to represent this state in the Senate of the United States, there being but one Senator elected on the first election.

The Senate

A verbal message from the House of Representatives by Mr. P. Smith and Mr. Freer, viz.,

Honorable Gentlemen: The House of Representatives inform this honorable House, that upon casting up the votes for two Senators to represent this state in the Congress of the United States, it appeared that only one Senator was duly elected. They therefore request that this House would be pleased to join with them in balloting for the other Senator.

The House having taken the said message into consideration, agreed thereto.

Ordered, that the same committee do remain in the House of Representatives and report the said election to this House.

Mr. President with the Senate attended in the House of Representatives accordingly, where they joined with that House in balloting for a Senator to represent this state in the Congress of the United States.

The House

The Senate accordingly attended and voted with this House for a Senator to represent this state in the Senate of the United States.

On casting up the ballots it appeared that Ralph Izard, Esquire, had a majority of the votes of the members present.

Mr. Speaker thereupon declared Ralph Izard, Esquire, to be duly elected a Senator to represent this state in the Senate of the United States.[2]

The Senate

The committee appointed to remain in the House of Representatives and report the said election to this House, reported, that upon casting up the votes, the Honorable Ralph Izard, Esquire, was duly elected a Senator to represent this state in the Congress of the United States.

1. John Brown Cutting, in a letter introducing Butler to Vice President John Adams, reported that Butler was elected "almost unanimously" (Charleston, 8 April, RC, Adams Papers, MHi).

2. Results of the South Carolina Senate election were widely reported in newspapers throughout the states (see, for example, the Savannah *Georgia Gazette,* 5 February; *New York Daily Gazette,* 9 February; Philadelphia *Pennsylvania Packet,* 17 February; Boston *Independent Chronicle,* 26 February; and Baltimore *Maryland Journal,* 10 March).

Both Izard and Butler were given leave to remain in the state until April, ostensibly to settle their affairs (House Journals, 22, 24 January). However, both were members of the legislature, and very important matters were expected to be raised during the spring session, including proposals for electing a convention to draft a new state constitution. Alexander Gillon, had he won his campaign for election to Congress, intended to delay his departure for Congress until April for purely political reasons (from Alexander Gillon, 17 November, printed above).

Aedanus Burke to Daniel DeSaussure, President of the Senate, Charleston, 22 January[1]

On the 7th inst. I received official information from His Excellency the Governor, that I was elected a member of the House of Representatives in Congress and as the appointment was without any solicitation of mine, it was not my wish to frustrate the expectations of the respectable number of citizens who elected me; and I informed His Excellency that I would serve. It did not then occur to me that any doubt could arise respecting the propriety of going without permission of your House, or else I would, as a servant of the people, and from the duty and respect I owe their representatives, have previously applied for leave, which I do now sir, through Your Honor, take the liberty of requesting.

1. RC, Burke Papers, ScU. Burke's letter was placed before the House and Senate the day it was written. His request for leave raised the question of whether or not he should continue receiving pay as a justice of the Court of Sessions and Common Pleas during his term as a member of Congress. The issue was apparently resolved on 27 January when both houses agreed to grant him leave of absence "provided nevertheless that the salary and fees of one of the justices aforesaid shall cease during the time he shall continue a member of the Congress of the United States." However, two weeks later, on 12 February, the House attempted to revise the agreement so that Burke's pay would be stopped "during the time he shall or may be absent from the state and no longer," a revision the Senate adamantly refused to allow (see the House and Senate Journals for 12 and 17-19 February). The report of a joint conference committee (which failed to reach a compromise settlement) appears in the Senate Journals for 3 March.

Charles Pinckney to Rufus King, Charleston, 26 January[1]

I am much obliged to you for your friendly letter which I received some days since and for the information it contains respecting our new federal system, a system you well know I am much attached to, not so much I trust from that fondness which men sometimes feel for a performance in which they have been concerned, as from a conviction of its intrinsic worth and that it is now almost our only refuge.

I am flattered by your wish that I might be one of the Senators of this state in Congress, and I should in all probability have been one, had not considerations of a private nature prevented me from becoming a candidate. These were the advanced age and infirmities of Mr. [Henry] Laurens and my mother, the latter of whom was extremely averse to my leaving Carolina for two or three years, and a purchase I had made in this city which I wished to complete. Besides, I expect Madam will favor me in March with a son, an event so pleasing, that I would not on any account have been absent. Indeed the considerations I have stated, appeared when combined to be so forcible that I yielded without hesitation to the propriety of remaining some time longer at home. This being once determined, my too partial friends requested me to say that if I was elected, I would accept the appointment of governor as successor to my kinsman [Thomas Pinckney]. I agreed to this and being very generally elected, on Monday last, I was qualified.

Our Senators were on Thursday chosen. They are Pierce Butler and Ralph Izard, esquires—both strong Federalists, and will I trust do credit to their appointment. Our members are for the other branch, William Smith and Daniel Huger, esquires, Federalists; Aedanus Burke and Thomas Sumpter, esquires, who opposed the Constitution; and Dr. [Thomas Tudor] Tucker, who is with you and whose sentiments I am unacquainted with.

You know I always preferred the election by the legislature to that of the people, and I will now venture to pronounce that the mode which you and [James] Madison and some others so strenuously contended for and ultimately carried is the greatest blot in the Constitution—of this however more hereafter.

I take it for granted you will be in the federal legislature. If your state knows her interest, and she is not in general blind to it, I am sure you will be there. My present office requires more particular attention to political inquiries than any other and as our state, if not now the first in exports, stands high in the commercial line, it will become me to be very punctual and exact in receiving the earliest information of what may be done upon this subject by Congress. Be therefore liberal in your favors and write me often and fully.

Tell Madison I wrote him lately but have not heard from him since. As soon however as I know he is in New York he will hear from me, if nothing should prevent.

If I am well in April I set off on a tour into our upper districts to review the different brigades of militia there and expect to return by the beginning of May. Direct for me in Charleston.

. . . .

[P.S.] Remember me to [William] Duer, Livingston, and our other acquaintances. Mr. [John] Jay I am told is going into a consumption. Mention me to [Alexander] Hamilton and C[harles] Thomson.

1. RC, King Papers, NHi. See also Pinckney's letter to Madison, 28 March, printed below.

Thomas Sumter to Governor Charles Pinckney, Charleston, 27 January[1]

Since I had the honor of receiving His Excellency's the late Governor's letter announcing my appointment as a member of the House of Representatives in Congress, I could not well before now give a decisive answer. So far was the appointment from my choice or solicitation, that previous to the election, I wrote circular letters to the managers throughout Camden District and also to several of my friends assuring them I could not serve if they made choice of me. Reflecting, however, on the great inconvenience the people of the district will be put to, in attending another election and the displeasure I might incur, were I to decline the appointment of so respectable a majority of my fellow citizens, I will reconcile myself to it, and will serve accordingly.

1. Copy, Legislative Records and Papers, Sc-Ar.

John Huger to Governor Charles Pinckney, Charleston, 29 January[1]

As my brother Daniel is absent from the town, I take the liberty to acquaint Your Excellency (in his behalf) that it is his intention to accept of the honorable, and important, office of a delegate to Congress by qualifying as a member of the House of Representatives, in consequence of his being elected by a majority of the inhabitants, of the United Districts of Georgetown and Cheraw to represent them, in that capacity in the new federal government.

1. Copy, Legislative Records and Papers, Sc-Ar. The letter was transmitted to the legislature on 17 February. Six days later, Governor Pinckney sent the legislature a letter from Daniel Huger confirming his acceptance of the post.

Votes of the South Carolina Presidential Electors, 4 February[1]

City of Charleston State of South Carolina.

We the Subscribers being duly appointed in the manner directed by the Legislature of the State of South Carolina Electors for the purpose of chusing a President of the United States of America agreeable to the Federal Constitution, did meet at twelve oClock on this fourth day of February at the Exchange of the City of Charleston in the State of South Carolina, and being first duly sworn before his Excellency the Governor agreeably to an Act intitled "an Act prescribing on the part of this State, the times places and manner of holding Elections for Representatives in the Congress and the manner of appointing Electors of a President of the United States" and having also taken the Oath of Allegiance and Abjuration agreable to the 36th Clause of the Constitution of the State of South Carolina did vote by ballot for two Persons accordingly, and on opening the said ballots, We found that the Honorable George Washington Esqr. of Virginia and the Honble John Rutledge Esqr. of South Carolina and the Honble John Hancock Esqr. of Massachusetts —— were voted for, and that George Washington —— had Seven-votes and John Rutledge —— had Six-votes and John Hancock had one vote—

all which We do Certify, and in Testimony thereof have signed our Names and affixed our Seals this fourth day of February in the year of our Lord One thousand seven hundred and Eighty nine, and in the thirteenth year of the Independence of the United States of America.

	Christ Gadsden	Edward Rutledge
[Signed:]	Henry Laurens	Charles Cotesworth Pinckney
		Thos Heyward Jr.
	Arthur Simkins	John Fauchereaud Grimké

1. (LT), RG 46, DNA. This official report of the votes of the South Carolina Electors was sent to Charles Thomson, secretary of the Confederation Congress, by Charles Cotesworth Pinckney, one of the Electors, on 13 February. Pinckney's covering letter is printed below.

Pierce Butler to Weeden Butler, Charleston, 8 February (excerpt)[1]

In future, please to direct your letters to me to New York as I shall shortly go there to remain some time. You will please to send either by the packet or merchant vessels. When you write by the packet, I believe it will be necessary to pay some trifle at the office on putting the letter in. I beg to hear from you by every packet. Direct your letters to Pierce Butler, Senator from the State of South Carolina to the Federal Government. The legislature of this state elected me in so handsome a manner tho absent, to represent them in the Senate of the United States that I could not well refuse, however inconvenient to my private affairs, to go for a short time. I am willing to give my feeble aid to get the new government well underway. That accomplished I purpose returning here.

1. RC, Letters of Major Pierce Butler of South Carolina, British Museum Additional Manuscripts 16,603.

Thomas Tudor Tucker to Governor Thomas Pinckney, New York, 10 February[1]

I have had the honor of receiving Your Excellency's letter of the 7th of January giving me official information of my election by the District of Ninety Six to the House of Representatives of the United States. I am very sensible of the honor done me by my fellow citizens and shall endeavor to merit their confidence by a conscientious discharge of the duties of the appointment to the best of my ability.

1. Copy, Legislative Records and Papers, Sc-Ar. Tucker was in New York serving as a member of the Confederation Congress. Governor Pinckney's letter is included in Proceedings of the Privy Council, 6 January, printed above.

Governor Charles Pinckney to Secretary Peter Freneau, February[1]

The Governor presents his compliments to Mr. Freneau and will thank him to prepare an authenticated copy of the act of election—and a certificate of the appointments and of the Electors having taken the oath before him agreeable to the acts. The Governor is anxious to have it as soon as possible as General Pinckney wishes to transmit it today or tomorrow.[2]

1. RC, n.d., Charles Pinckney Papers, ScU.
2. Charles Cotesworth Pinckney, one of the South Carolina Electors (who was frequently referred to as General Pinckney), sent the results of the election to Charles Thomson, secretary of the Confederation Congress, on 13 February.

Certificate of Qualification for South Carolina Electors, 11 February[1]

State of South Carolina

By His Excellency Charles Pinckney Esquire, Governor and Commander in chief in and over the State aforesaid.

To all to Whom these Presents shall come, Greeting.

Be it Known, That on the fourth day of this Instant February before me personally came Christopher Gadsden, Henry Laurens Charles Cotesworth Pinckney, Edward Rutledge Arthur Simkins Thomas Heyward Junior and John Fauchereaud Grimke Esquires being the Electors chosen in the manner directed by the Legislature of this State to elect a President and Vice President of the United States of America and did then take in my presence the Oath of Qualification prescribed in the Law hereunto annexed and the Oath of Office and Trust prescribed by the Constitution of this State, And I further make known That Peter Freneau Esquire who hath certified the writing hereunto annexed to be a true Copy of an Act of the Legislature of this State entitled "An Act prescribing on the part of this State, the Times, Places and manner of holding Elections for Representatives in the Congress and the manner of appointing Electors of a President of the United States passed the fourth day of November last, is Secretary of the said State in whose Office the Original Laws thereof are deposited and to whose Certificate full Faith and Credit is and ought to be had and given.

In Testimony whereof I have hereunto Set my hand and caused to be affixed the Great Seal of the State in the City of Charleston this eleventh day of February in the year of Our Lord One thousand Seven hundred and eighty nine and of the Sovereignty and Independence of the United States of America the thirteenth.

By His Excellency's Command.
[s] Peter Freneau
Secretary

1. (LT), RG 46, DNA. A copy is in Miscellaneous Record Book A, 123-24, Sc-Ar.

Charles Cotesworth Pinckney to Secretary Charles Thomson, Charleston, 13 February[1]

I have the honor of transmitting to you the return made by the Electors chosen by this state to elect a President of the United States, and will be much obliged to you to acknowledge the receipt of it.

1. RC, RG 46, DNA. In addition to the votes of the South Carolina Electors, Pinckney also enclosed a copy of the South Carolina election law of 4 November 1788 and a certificate of qualification for the South Carolina Electors, 11 February 1789, both printed above.

John Brown Cutting to John Rutledge, Jr., Charleston, 21 February (excerpt)[1]

I have already repeated to you again and again my sincere thanks for the social pleasure which through your instrumentality I have continually enjoyed here from the first day of my arrival. And to evince my gratitude I have from time to time informed you of the anecdotes of the city and the politics of the state, so far as they have been disclosed to me, supposing that this sort of intelligence must be pleasant, as it reminds you of objects dear and familiar.

You are informed of all the new appointments to office on the part of South Carolina—whether of domestic or federal complexion, excepting only the late appointment of two new associate judges in the places of Mr. [Henry] Pendleton deceased and Mr. [Thomas] Heyward resigned. On the first vacancy the two candidates were Mr. [Thomas] Waities and Mr. [William] Drayton (father of him whom we knew in London). The whole back country interest supported the former—most of your friends the latter. Waities carried the election by a small majority—about twelve votes. A few days afterwards, namely last week, Mr. Heyward resigned whereupon Mr. Drayton was almost unanimously elected. It is not yet known whether Mr. Drayton accepts. Rumor says that he will, provided Mr. Waities yields him that precedence on the bench to which his years, maturity of experience, and legal knowledge so justly entitle him. I have heretofore told you that Charles Pinckney is governor and Commodore [Alexander] Gillon lieutenant governor.[2] But I did not tell you that the latter was married to Miss Nancy Purcel, daughter of the clergyman of that name *aetat* 20. Nor did I mention to you that I believed one reason why the Commodore obtained his

213

election was the belief on the part of some persons skillful in political management here, that his *nominal honor* would be less troublesome in the executive than *his real power* in the legislative department. Whether it be owing to accident or system I know not—but it would seem that all those political personages in the legislature of South Carolina who *are* or *seem* hostile to the measures of your family and that of the Pinckney's—and in short to the most able and respectable description of men in this country—are lately appointed to offices which remove them from the legislature. For instance, Major [Pierce] Butler is a federal Senator, General [Thomas] Sumpter and Judge [Aedanus] Burke are federal Representatives, Commodore Gillon, lieutenant governor, etc., etc. These gentlemen and a few others you know are the leaders of that fierce column of rural representation which when influenced by any popular passion rushes to whatsoever may be the object of the hour with an irresistible impetuosity.

A committee of both houses is appointed to take into consideration the propriety of calling a convention this year to alter and amend the constitution. It is proposed, I find, to lessen the enormous representation which now prevails, and in a word to diminish the expense of the civil list and establish a constitution for South Carolina more conformable to that of the Union than the present. Meanwhile there is a vote of the Senate, to which it is thought the other house will accede, for removing the next session of the legislature to the new town of Columbia one hundred and forty miles from Charleston.

Both branches seem determined to abide by the last installment law, and to reject the further emission of paper money, and all future legislative interferences between debtor and creditor. Some gentlemen however are of opinion that when the federal judiciary is organized and the government of the Union becomes strong and stable, the last installment law will be set aside.

1. RC, John Rutledge Papers, NcU. Cutting had come to South Carolina as agent for the Chevalier Luxembourg and was trying to collect from Alexander Gillon and the state of South Carolina for the ship *South Carolina*, which Luxembourg had leased to the state in 1780 (see below, South Carolina Candidates: Gillon).

2. Gillon was elected in January and told the legislature he would qualify before the end of the session, but in March he refused the post on the grounds of health.

Commissions of the South Carolina Senators, 4 March[1]

STATE of SOUTH CAROLINA
By His Excellency Charles Pinckney Esqr
Governor and Commander in Chief in
and over the State aforesaid—

To The Honorable Pierce Butler Esqr. Greeting

Whereas it is declared by the Constitution of the United States that the Senate of the United States shall be composed of Two Members from each State Chosen by the Legislature thereof and whereas in pursuance of the said Constitution the Legislature of this State did on the Twenty-Second day of January One Thousand Seven hundred and Eighty nine proceed to the Election of Two Senators and upon casting up the Votes it appeared that the Honorable Pierce Butler and Ralph Izard Esquires were duly elected I do therefore by Virtue of the Power and Authority in me Vested commission you the said Pierce Butler as a Senator to Represent this State in the Senate of the United States.

By His Excellency's Command

[s] Peter Freneau
Secretary

Given under my hand and the Great Seal of the State in the City of Charleston this fourth xxxxx day of March in the Year of our Lord one Thousand Seven hundred and Eighty nine and of the sovereignty and Independence of the United States of America the Thirteenth.

[s] Charles Pinckney

1. (LT), RG 46, DNA. A commission of the same tenor and date was made out for Ralph Izard. On 23 February, Governor Pinckney asked the legislature to determine "in what manner and by whom proper credentials of their appointment shall be given, to the gentlemen who are elected to represent this state in both branches of the federal legislature." Both houses appointed committees to make recommendations on the subject, and after some initial disagreement over how many copies of each commission should be prepared, both houses agreed that "proper credentials" should consist of "a commission under the Great Seal of the State, signed by the Governor and directed to each Senator and Representative" (see the House Journals for 23 and 27 February and 11 March, and the Senate Journals for 7 and 11 March). However, the commissions printed here were dated 4 March.

Commissions of the South Carolina Representatives, 4 March[1]

State of South Carolina

By His Excellency Charles Pinckney Esquire Governor and Commander in Chief in and over the State aforesaid—

To William Smith Esquire. Greeting—

Whereas it is declared by the Constitution of the United States that the House of Representatives in the Legislature of the United States shall be composed of Members chosen every Second Year by the People of the Several States and that the Times Places and Manner of holding Elections for Representatives shall be prescribed in each State by the Legislature thereof. And Whereas in pursuance of the said Constitution the Legislature of this State did on the fourth day of November One thousand Seven hundred and eighty eight pass an Act prescribing the Time Places and manner of Holding Elections in this State by declaring that the same should be conducted by Districts and that the Inhabitants qualified by Law to Vote for Members in the State Legislature in the District of Charleston in the United Districts of Beaufort and Orangeburgh in the United Districts of George Town and Cheraw in the District of Camden and in the District of Ninety Six should be entitled to elect one Member for each of the said Districts to represent this State in the House of Representatives of the United States and Whereas an Election has been duly held in pursuance of the above mentioned Act on the twenty fourth and twenty fifth days of November last for the District of Charleston and on examining and collecting the Votes in the Manner directed by the said Law it appeared that William Smith Esqr. was duly elected by the Return of the District of Charleston as a Member of the said House of Representatives By Virtue of the Power and Authority in me vested I do therefore Commission you the said William Smith as a Member to represent this State in the House of Representatives of the United States—This Commission to continue in force for two Years—

Given under my hand and the Great Seal of the State in the City of Charleston this fourth day of March in the Year of Our Lord One thousand Seven hundred and eighty nine, and of the Sovereignty and Independence of the United States of America the thirteenth.—

Charles (LHS) Pinckney.

By His Excellency's Command.

Peter Freneau Secretary.—

Four other Commissions of the same Tenor and Date were made out at the same Time, One for the Honorable Aedanus Burke Esqr. for the United Districts of Beaufort and Orangeburgh. One other for Daniel Huger Esqr. for the United Districts of George Town and Cheraw, One other for Thomas Sumter Esquire for the District of Camden and One other for Thomas Tudor Tucker Esqr. for the District of Ninety Six.—

1. Copy (LT), Miscellaneous Record Book A, 131-32, Sc-Ar.

Charles Pinckney to James Madison, Charleston, 28 March 1789[1]

It is not often I am deficient in attention to my friends, particularly those whose friendship I think worth cultivating—but I will confess that to you I have been almost inexcusably and to myself unaccountably inattentive. There are however some excuses to be made for me. I have not been sure of ever finding you either in New York, Philadelphia or in Virginia—for being in Congress, in our unsettled state of public affairs, and there seldom being a quorum, and if so, no question of any importance to interest your attention, I took it for granted you were seldom there. Besides I have had a great deal upon my own hands—enough most surely to excuse me in the opinion of a bachelor and a *young man.* Although it is not more than sixteen months since I saw you I have done a great deal of business—sometimes in public and more frequently of a private nature. But what is more than all I have become a husband and a father—and you know, *or ought* by this time to know, and I trust for your character's sake *will soon* know that a wife and a son are although pleasing, yet serious concerns. Let these therefore atone for my seeming inattention and let us commence a correspondence as if no such chasm had existed, but as if I had been as punctual as I ought.

I will begin by saying what I am sure you will believe, that I am much pleased to find you in the federal legislature. I did expect you would have been in the Senate and think your state was blind to its interests in not placing you there, but where you are may in the event prove the most important situation—for as most of the acts which are to affect the revenue of the Union must originate with your House, and as they are the most numerous body, a greater scope will be afforded for the display of legislative talents than in the other branch, whose radical defect is the smallness of their numbers and whose doors must be always shut during their most interesting deliberations.

It will be some time perhaps before I hear of you, but when you write, answer me candidly as I am sure you will the following queries without suffering any little disappointment to yourself to warp your opinion.

Are you not, to use a full expression, abundantly convinced that the theoretical nonsense of an election of the members of Congress by the people in the first instance, is clearly and practically wrong—that it will in the end be the means of bringing our councils into contempt and that the legislature are the only proper judges of who ought to be elected?

Are you not fully convinced that the Senate ought at least to be double their number to make them of consequence and to prevent their falling into the same comparative state of insignificance that the state senates have, merely from their smallness?

Do you not suppose that giving to the federal judicial *retrospective jurisdiction in any case whatsoever*, from the difficulty of determining to what periods to look back—from its being an ex post facto provision, and from the confusion and opposition it will give rise to, will be the surest and speediest mode to subvert our present system and give its adversaries the majority?

Do not suffer these and other queries I may hereafter put to you to startle your opinion with respect to my principles. I am more than ever a friend to the Federal Constitution, not I trust from that fondness which men sometimes feel for a performance in which they have been concerned but from a conviction of its intrinsic worth—from a conviction that on its efficacy our political welfare depends. My wish is to see it divested of those improprieties which I am sure will sooner or later subvert, or what is worse bring it into contempt.

Although I am persuaded motives of friendship will always induce you to attend as far as you can with convenience to my requests I must apologize to you for the trouble I give in requesting you after the impost has passed to mention to your friends in the Senate Mr. George Abbott Hall our present collector, as the collector of the impost for this state. It is upwards of twelve years since he held this post and has discharged its duties with such diligence and fidelity, that I am well warranted in not only privately but officially recommending him.

Mr. [William] Smith will deliver you this. He goes tomorrow to New York as one of the members for this state in the House of Representatives. He is a near relation of mine—but it is not only on this account that I recommend him to your particular notice and attention. You will find him a valuable acquaintance, with a mind highly cultivated and accomplished and an attention to public business which when he comes to be acquainted with the affairs of the Union will render him an useful member of your House. Present him if you please in my name to [John] Henry, [William] Grayson[2] and all our quondam acquaintances and be assured that any civilities he receives from you will be gratefully remembered by me.

You may perhaps be surprised at not seeing me a member. I think there is no doubt I could if I had pleased have been a member of the Senate. My friends were sufficiently numerous and powerful both among the members of the upper and lower country to have, in all probability insured my election and I was for a considerable time talked of as one—but the situation of my wife just on the point of giving me a son and the advanced age and infirmities of my mother and some others whom I did not wish to leave, and the large purchase of a house determined me not to leave Carolina for a time—but to stay at home at least for a few years and place myself in a situation [———] after to do and go where I please if alive and well. In the interim I am placed in an office where although I have a great deal of trouble I have the pleasure to reflect that my former endeavors have been so far approved as to give me the confidence and respect of my country. I have only to get well through this and I think the next two or three years I will struggle to be my *own master* or rather the master *of my own time*—in other words, to enjoy the *luxury of doing as I please*.

If you are still at Elsworth's give my compliments to Mrs. E. and Mrs. H. and tell them that I still keep my opinion about Charleston—that I think the house I have lately bought is not only a handsomer and better house than any in New York (which it might very easily be) but that the situation is as easy and the prospect as fine as any they have—that in short I like Charleston so well at present that I cannot consent to exchange it for any other place and that it will be with very great reluctance I shall ever leave it again for any length of time, except for a trip to Europe, to which as my wife is from her education almost an European I am the more than ever inclined, but which must still be subordinate to my more important pursuits.

Write me frequently and fully and give me as much political intelligence as you can.

. . . .

[P.S.] Excuse the blots and scrawl of this letter. I am writing in an astonishing hurry and my secretary is so much engaged in copying public, that he has no time to devote to private letters—and my *female secretary* is at present in *the straw* with a young gentleman who sends his compliments to you.

1. RC, Madison Papers, DLC.
2. In 1785 and 1786 Pinckney had served in the Confederation Congress with Grayson of Virginia and Henry of Maryland. Both men were United States Senators in the first Congress.

SOUTH CAROLINA CANDIDATES

Barnwell, Robert (1761-1814), Candidate for Representative, Beaufort-Orangeburg District

Born in St. Helena's Parish, where he became a planter, Barnwell served in the South Carolina militia throughout the War for Independence and was captured at the fall of Charleston in May 1780. He was elected to the South Carolina House in 1787 and to the Confederation Congress in January 1788 but did not attend. He voted for ratification of the Constitution in the state Convention and carried Prince William's Parish against Aedanus Burke in the election for Representative. He was elected to the second Congress in 1792 and served one term. He represented St. Helena's Parish in either the state House of Representatives or state Senate from 1794 to 1806.

Burke, Aedanus (1743-1802), Elected Representative, Beaufort-Orangeburg District

Born in Galway, Ireland, Burke was studying law in Virginia by 1769. Thereafter he moved to South Carolina. In 1778 he resigned a commission in the Continental Army to accept appointment as associate justice of the Court of Sessions and Common Pleas. He was a member of the state House of Representatives from 1781 to 1789. In 1783 he wrote pamphlets defending amnesty for Loyalists and attacking the Society of the Cincinnati. Elected to the state Convention from the Lower District between the Broad and Saluda rivers, he and the five other delegates from that district voted against ratification of the Constitution. In the first Congress he opposed most Federalist policies except the payment of the national debt at face value and the assumption of state debts. Apparently he did not run for reelection, and he spent the remainder of his life as a judge of the state courts.

Butler, Pierce (1744-1822), Elected Senator

Born in County Carlow, Ireland, the son of Sir Richard Butler, Butler became a major in a British regiment. In 1771 he married a daughter of Thomas Middleton of Prince William's Parish, South Carolina. He lived in South Carolina thereafter and resigned his British commission in 1773. He was adjutant general of the state for a time during the War for Independence. He served in the state House of Representatives from 1778 to 1789 and supported backcountry demands for increased representation and for the removal of the capital from Charleston. He was elected to the Confederation Congress and to the Constitutional Convention in March 1787. He supported a strong central government in the Constitutional Convention and in the South Carolina Convention, but as a Senator he opposed many Federalist policies. He was reelected to the Senate in 1792 but resigned in 1796 after opposing the Jay Treaty. Elected to the Senate again in 1802, he resigned in 1806 after accusing the Republicans, as he had accused the Federalists, of abuse of power.

Gadsden, Christopher (1724-1805), Presidental Elector

Born in Charleston, Gadsden was educated in England and in a Philadelphia counting house and served for a time as purser on a British naval vessel. After his marriage in 1746, he became a Charleston merchant and a plantation owner. As a member of the colonial assembly from 1757 to the Revolution, he was one of its most aggressive leaders in opposition to British policies. Outside the assembly he was the spokesman and hero of the Charleston artisans. He attended the Stamp Act Congress, the first and second Continental congresses, and in February 1776 argued for independence in the South Carolina provincial congress. From 1776 until 1778, when he resigned, he was first a colonel in the South Carolina military forces and then a brigadier general in the Continental Army. Elected to the House of Representatives in 1778, he helped write the second South Carolina constitution, which some thought too democratic. His opponents then removed him from House leadership by electing him vice president of the state. He was captured by the British when Charleston fell in May 1780 and was imprisoned at St. Augustine, Florida. He refused to accept the governorship in 1782 but remained in the House until 1784. By then he had lost his popularity with the artisans because he opposed drastic measures against Loyalists and British merchants. His only political services thereafter were in the state Convention in 1788, when he voted to ratify the Constitution; as presidential Elector in 1789; and as a member of the state convention which wrote a new constitution in 1790.

Gillon, Alexander (1741-1794), Candidate for Representative, Charleston District

Born in Rotterdam, Holland, Gillon had settled in Charleston by 1766 and by 1776 was a wealthy merchant and landowner. He joined the militia, was elected to the provincial congress in 1775, and began importing war supplies. In 1778 he was appointed commodore of the South Carolina navy and was instructed to procure ships in Europe. In 1780 he leased a ship for the state for three years from the Chevalier Luxembourg, agreeing to pay a share of the profits from the sales of captured enemy vessels. After some successful privateering, the *South Carolina* was captured by the British late in 1782. Gillon's financial loss was great, and the claims of Luxembourg and his heirs against the state were not settled until the mid-nineteenth century.

By 1783 Gillon was a member of the state House of Representatives. He led the Charleston artisans and others in often violent opposition to returning Loyalists and British merchants. He was also a spokesman for the backcountry and a leader in the struggle for a new state constitution and the removal of the capital from Charleston.

He lost the election for intendant (i.e., mayor) of Charleston in 1784 but was elected to the House. In 1786 he was elected from both Charleston and the backcountry district of Saxe Gotha and qualified for the latter seat. He was reelected again from Saxe Gotha in 1788 at the same time that he was defeated for election to the United States House of Representatives. His opponents tried repeatedly to remove him from the legislature by electing him to other offices. He refused the lieutenant governorship in 1783 and a seat in the Confederation Congress in 1784. In January 1789 he was elected lieutenant governor. He notified the legislature that he would qualify before the end of the session, but, near the end of the session, he informed the House that he could not accept because of ill health. He was elected to the third Congress in 1792 and served there until his death, which ended the state's lawsuit against him and his insolvent estate.

Grimké, John Faucheraud (1752-1819), Presidential Elector

Born in Charleston, Grimké graduated from Cambridge University in 1774, studied law at the Middle Temple, and returned to Charleston in September 1775. He became an officer in the South Carolina artillery in 1776 and was captured by the British at the surrender of Charleston in May 1780. He became a judge in 1783, and in 1799 he became, in effect, chief justice of the state. He was a member of the state House of Repesentatives from 1784 to 1789, was speaker of the House in 1785 and 1786, and was elected intendant (i.e., mayor) of Charleston in October 1787. He was a member of the state Convention in 1788 and voted to ratify the Constitution.

Heyward, Thomas, Jr. (1746-1809), Presidential Elector

Born in St. Helena's Parish, South Carolina, Heyward was admitted to the Middle Temple in 1765 and to the South Carolina bar in 1771. Elected to the assembly from St. Helena's Parish in 1772, he was a member of the provincial congresses between 1774 and 1776 and was a member of the committee that wrote the first state constitution in the spring of 1776. He was elected to the second Continental Congress in 1776, signed the Declaration of Independence, and remained in Congress until 1778, when he was appointed a circuit judge. He was captured by the British at the surrender of Charleston in May 1780 and was imprisoned at St. Augustine, Florida, until 1781. He represented Charleston in the state House of Representatives from 1782 to 1784 and was a circuit judge from 1782 until he resigned in 1789.

Huger, Daniel (1741-1799), Elected Representative, Georgetown-Cheraws District

Born in South Carolina, Huger had three brothers who played important roles in winning independence. He was elected to the legislature in 1778, and in 1780 he was a member of the Privy Council. When the British army approached Charleston in the spring in 1780, Huger fled from the city with Governor John Rutledge, Colonel Charles Pinckney, and John L. Gervais. After military resistance to the British collapsed, Huger and Pinckney returned to Charleston and took an oath of loyalty to Great Britain, but after the war Huger escaped confiscation of his property by the South Carolina government. In 1784 he was elected to the state Senate and in 1786 to the Confederation Congress, where he served until the fall of 1788. He served two terms in the federal House of Representatives from 1789 to 1793.

Izard, Ralph (1742-1804), Elected Senator

Born in South Carolina, Izard was probably the wealthiest planter in the colony. Sent to England to school at the age of twelve, he returned to South Carolina in 1764, married Alice De Lancey of New York, and in 1771 returned to England, planning to live there permanently. After the Declaration of Independence, he moved to France, and in 1777 Congress appointed him minister to Tuscany. He was embroiled in the quarrels between Arthur Lee and Silas Deane and became a bitter enemy of Benjamin Franklin. Following his recall in 1779, Izard served in the Confederation Congress in 1782 and 1783 and thereafter in the South Carolina House of Representatives until he was elected to the United States Senate in 1789. He retired from the Senate in 1795.

Laurens, Henry (1724-1792), Presidential Elector

Born in Charleston, the descendant of Huguenot refugees, Laurens received commercial training in England, became a leading Charleston merchant by 1763, and in the years that followed acquired several plantations. Except for one year, he served continuously in the colonial assembly from 1757 to the Revolution, although he lived in England from 1771 to 1774. When he returned, he served in the provincial congresses from 1774 to 1776 and helped write the first state constitution in the spring of 1776. He was elected to the Continental Congress in January 1777 and was its president from November 1777 until December 1778, when he resigned. He left Congress in November 1779 after he was elected to negotiate a loan in Holland. He left for Holland in August 1780 but was captured by the British and imprisoned in the Tower of London from October 1780 until December 1781. Congress elected him one of the peace commissioners, but he did not arrive in Paris until two days before the signing of the preliminary treaty. He stayed in Europe until 1784, and upon his return, he retired. He was elected to the Constitutional Convention but did not attend. His last public service was as a presidential Elector.

Lowndes, Rawlins (1721-1800), Candidate for Senator

Born in the West Indies, Lowndes was brought to Charleston by his family in 1730. When his father died, his mother returned to the West Indies, leaving him with Robert Hall, provost-marshal of the colony. He studied law and succeeded Hall as provost-marshal when Hall died in 1740. He sat in the colonial assembly almost continuously from 1749 to the Revolution, and was speaker of the assembly from 1763 to 1765 and from 1772 to 1775. He was appointed associate justice of the Court of Common Pleas in 1766 and was a member until removed in 1773. He was a member of the provincial congresses in 1774, 1775, and 1776 and helped write the first state constitution in the spring of 1776, but he opposed independence. In 1778 he was elected president of the state despite his opposition to the second state constitution adopted that year. He was attacked for Loyalist sympathies and refused a second term as president. He represented Charleston in the state House of Representatives from 1786 until 1790 and was elected intendant (i.e., mayor) of Charleston in October 1788. In January 1788 he opposed the Constitution in the legislative session that called the state convention, and he refused to serve in the Convention. Despite his opposition to the Constitution, his prestige was so great that he was proposed for United States Senator, but he refused to be considered.

Pinckney, Charles Cotesworth (1746-1825), Presidential Elector

Born in Charleston, Pinckney was taken to England in 1753, was educated at Oxford, the Middle Temple, and in France, and was admitted to the English bar in 1769. He returned to Charleston that year, was elected to the colonial assembly, and began the practice of law. He served in the provincial congress in 1775 and 1776 and was chairman of the committee that drafted the first state constitution in the spring of 1776. He was an officer in South Carolina military forces, served as an aide to George Washington, and was captured by the British at the fall of Charleston in May 1780. He was not exchanged until November 1782, when he rejoined the Continental Army and was promoted to brigadier general. He resumed his law practice after the war and was a member of the state House of Representatives, of the Constitutional Convention, and of the state Convention that ratified the Constitution. He was a strong Federalist, and President Washington asked him to serve as an associate justice of the Supreme Court, as Secretary of War, and as Secretary of State. He refused to accept these posts but accepted appointment as minister to France in 1796. The next year President John Adams appointed Pinckney, Elbridge Gerry, and John Marshall as special commissioners to France (the X.Y.Z. mission), and in 1798 he was appointed major general in charge of all military operations south of Maryland, in anticipation of a war with France. He was the Federalist candidate for Vice President in 1800 and for President in 1804 and 1808.

Ramsay, David (1749-1815), Candidate for Representative, Charleston District

Born in Lancaster County, Pennsylvania, Ramsay graduated from the College of New Jersey (Princeton) in 1765 and studied medicine with Dr. Benjamin Rush. He received a medical degree from the College of Philadelphia in 1772, practiced a year in Maryland, and moved to South Carolina in 1773. He was soon involved in politics. He represented Charleston in the House of Representatives from 1776 to 1782, was captured by the British at the fall of Charleston in May 1780, and was imprisoned at St. Augustine, Florida, for one year. He was a member of the Confederation Congress from 1782 to 1785, represented Charleston in the state House of Representatives from 1784 to 1790, and voted for the adoption of the Constitution in the South Carolina Convention. After his defeat in the election to the United States House of Representatives, he was elected to the state Senate in 1792, 1794, and 1796, serving as president of the Senate in each term. He retired from politics in 1796 and became a bankrupt in 1798 as a result of his land speculations. In addition to his work as a doctor and as a politician, he wrote medical treatises and histories. Among the latter are the *History of the Revolution in South Carolina* (1785), *History of the American Revolution* (1789), *Life of George Washington* (1807), *History of South Carolina* (1809), and *History of the United States* (1816-1817).

Rutledge, Edward (1749-1800), Presidential Elector

Born in Charleston, the younger brother of John Rutledge, Rutledge began the study of law at the Middle Temple in 1767 and was admitted to the English bar in 1772. He returned to Charleston in 1773 and began the practice of law. He was a member of the first and second Continental congresses and of the South Carolina provincial congresses in 1775 and 1776. He signed the Declaration of Independence, after initially opposing it, and left Congress in November 1776 to become a captain of artillery. In 1778 he was elected to the state House of Representatives and in 1779 to the Continental Congress. Rutledge was captured by the British at the fall of Charleston in May 1780 and was imprisoned at St. Augustine, Florida, for a year. He was a member of the state Convention in 1788 and voted to ratify the Constitution. A Federalist leader in the state, he was a presidential Elector in 1789 and 1792. Rutledge, like many other South Carolina Federalists, was outraged by the Jay Treaty, and in 1796 he headed the list of presidential Electors committed to Thomas Jefferson and Thomas Pinckney. He represented Charleston in the state House of Representatives from 1782 to 1796, was elected to the state Senate in 1796 and 1798, and was elected governor in 1798. He died while holding that office.

Simkins, Arthur (1742-1826), Presidential Elector

Born in Virginia, Simkins moved to South Carolina in 1772 and by 1776 was living in Ninety-Six District. He was elected to the provincial congress from the district in 1775 and to the first state House of Representatives in 1776. He served as a militia captain during the war and represented Ninety-Six District in the House of Representatives from 1781 to 1790. In January 1788 he voted against Charleston as the meeting place for the state Convention to consider the Constitution. The state constitution of 1790 divided Ninety-Six into Abbeville and Edgefield districts, and Simkins represented the latter district in the state legislature from 1790 to 1806.

Smith, William (1758?-1812), Elected Representative,
Charleston District

Born in Charleston, the son of a wealthy merchant, Smith was sent to Europe for an education in 1770. He did not return to South Carolina until the end of 1783, despite the pleas of friends and the orders of the government for all South Carolinians to return home. From 1779 to 1783 he studied law and lived the life of a gentleman in England. Smith had politically powerful friends in the state, and within weeks after his return he was admitted to the bar and before the end of 1784 was elected to the legislature. In 1786 he married the daughter of Ralph Izard, one of the wealthiest and most powerful men in the state. Smith served five terms in the federal House of Representatives, where he was an influential supporter of the policies of the Washington administration. In 1797 he was appointed minister to Portugal, but he was removed from the post after the election of Thomas Jefferson to the Presidency. When he returned to Charleston in 1803, he was defeated for election to the House of Representatives.

Sumter, Thomas (1734-1832), Elected Representative,
Camden District

Born to a poor family near Charlottesville, Virginia, Sumter fought on the frontier during the Seven Years War. In 1765 he was jailed for debt but escaped to South Carolina, acquired land near Eutaw Springs, and became a justice of the peace. He was a member of the provincial congresses in 1775 and 1776, a captain in the campaign against the Cherokee Indians, and then an officer in the Continental Army. He resigned in 1778, but after the British conquest of the state in 1780 he became a brigadier general of state militia and such an effective guerrilla leader that the British offered rewards for his betrayal. In 1782 he quarreled with General Nathanael Greene of the Continental Army, resigned from the militia, and was elected to the state House of Representatives from the District Eastward of Wateree River. He represented that district until he was elected to the United States House of Representatives. He was a representative of the district in the state Convention in 1788 and voted against ratification of the Constitution. He served two terms in Congress and opposed most Federalist policies. He was defeated in 1792 for the third Congress but was reelected to the House of Representatives in 1796 and served there until elected United States Senator in 1801. A supporter of Thomas Jefferson, he remained in the Senate until he resigned in 1810.

Tucker, Thomas Tudor (1745-1828), Elected Representative,
Ninety-Six District

Born in Bermuda, Tucker studied medicine at the University of Edinburgh and in 1771 moved from Bermuda to Virginia with his brother St. George Tucker. Later he moved to South Carolina to practice medicine and served as a doctor in the army during the Revolution. He was elected to the South Carolina House in 1784. In 1785 William Smith defeated him in an election for the Privy

Council. The next year Ralph Izard campaigned against Tucker for the state House of Representatives, and the two men then fought a duel in which Tucker was badly wounded. Shortly thereafter Tucker was elected to replace a representative who had died. He was elected to the Confederation Congress in 1787 and was serving in Congress when elected to the House of Representatives. He served two terms in the House and was an ardent opponent of the program of the Washington administration. He was defeated for a third term in October 1792 when he ran for election in Charleston District. In 1801 President Thomas Jefferson appointed Tucker Treasurer of the United States, a post which he held until his death.

CHAPTER IV

The Elections in Pennsylvania

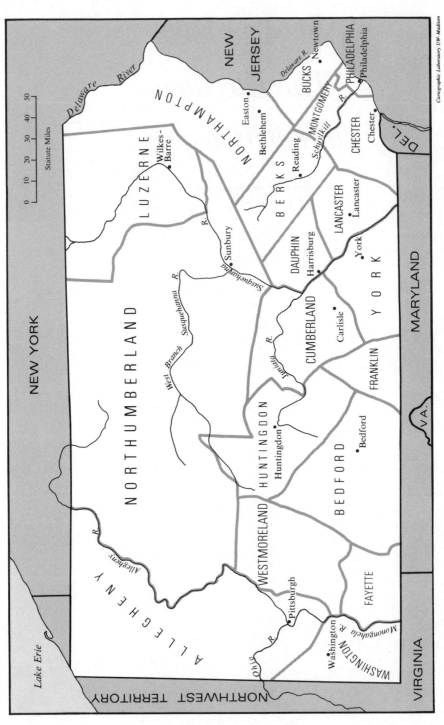

Pennsylvania Counties, 1788-1789. (Based on a map published in the Philadelphia *Columbian Magazine*, January 1788.)

INTRODUCTION

The first federal elections in Pennsylvania were in large measure the continuation of a struggle between two well-defined political parties which began forming within weeks after the writing of the Pennsylvania Constitution of 1776. By the end of the War for Independence, the parties were commonly known as the Constitutionalists and the Republicans. The principal supporters of the Constitutionalists were backcountry farmers and their leaders—such as William Findley, Robert Whitehill, and John Smilie—but the party also had support in the eastern counties, where one of its best known leaders was George Bryan of Philadelphia. Philadelphians—such as Robert Morris, Thomas Willing, and James Wilson—led the Republicans, and while their principal support came from the city and the three eastern counties, they, like the Constitutionalists, had allies scattered throughout the state.

In 1776 most of Pennsylvania's colonial leaders opposed independence, either openly or covertly, and because they did, they lost control of the state. In the summer of 1776, new men, with far more radical ideas than the colonial leaders, seized power and wrote a state constitution that promised, in terms of ideas and specific provisions, a political revolution within Pennsylvania.

The Declaration of Rights prefacing the constitution proclaimed that "all power being originally inherent in, and consequently derived from, the people; therefore all officers of government, whether legislative or executive, are their trustees and servants, and at all times accountable to them."

This principle was spelled out in one specific provision after another. The constitution abolished property qualifications for voting and gave all taxpayers, and the non-taxpaying sons of freeholders, the right to vote. The old grievance of inadequate representation for the backcountry counties was more than redressed. In 1775 the three eastern counties and Philadelphia had twenty-six representatives in the colonial assembly; the eight western counties, with about half the population, had but fifteen. The constitution provided that representation should be according to the number of taxable inhabitants, but that until a census could be taken, each county and Philadelphia would have six representatives, thus giving the "West" forty-eight and the "East" twenty-four.

The constitution retained the single-house legislature of colonial times but replaced the governor and his veto power with a Supreme Executive Council consisting of a delegate from each county and the city of Philadelphia elected for three-year terms. The Council was given certain appointive and administrative powers, but no legislative authority whatever.

The votes and proceedings of the Assembly were to be published weekly. All public bills were to be printed for the "consideration of the people," and except in case of "sudden necessity," could not be enacted into law until the session of the Assembly following the one in which they were introduced. Furthermore, the public was free to attend all sessions of the Assembly "except only when the welfare of this state may require the doors to be shut."

The distrust of men in power and the fear of power-seekers so characteristic of the political thought of the age were spelled out by requiring rotation in office. The purpose, declared the constitution, was to train men for public business, "and moreover the danger of establishing an inconvenient aristocracy will be effectually prevented." Assemblymen could not serve more than four years in seven; members of the Council and county sheriffs could not hold office more than three years in seven; and Pennsylvania delegates in Congress who served two consecutive years could not be reelected for three years thereafter.

The legislature was forbidden to tamper with the constitution in any way. Only the Council of Censors, to be elected for the first time in October 1783, could call a constitutional convention. And even if the Censors did call a convention, proposed changes in the constitution had to be published for the consideration of the people at least six months before they elected and instructed delegates.

The convention completed the constitution on 16 September 1776. It horrified political leaders in eastern Pennsylvania, and within a month they met in Philadelphia and adopted thirty-two resolutions condemning it. When the first state elections were held in November 1776, they elected enough delegates to prevent the state government from functioning until March 1777. The Philadelphians continued to oppose the constitution and to demand a new one. In March 1779 they organized the Republican Society, which published a statement denouncing the constitution as a "monster," the Council of Censors as a "jubilee of tyranny," and the oath to support the constitution as a daring infringement of the rights of freemen to judge and determine for themselves. They demanded a two-house legislature and the appointment of judges during good behavior, rather than election for limited terms. The statement was signed by eighty-one men, including such Philadelphians as James Wilson, Dr. Benjamin Rush, Thomas Fitz-Simons, Robert Morris, and George Clymer. These "Republicans," almost to a man, were the leaders of the Federalist Party in 1787 and 1788.

They worked continuously to get control of the Assembly, and, after partial success in the elections of 1780 and 1781, they won clear majorities in 1782 and 1783. They elected a majority of the Council of Censors in 1783 but could not muster the two-thirds vote necessary to call a constitutional convention. The Constitutionalists won the elections in 1784 and 1785 and revoked the charter of the Bank of North America, which Robert Morris and his allies had secured from the Assembly in 1782. They issued paper money to loan to farmers, and they assumed the national debt owed to Pennsylvanians.

The Republicans regained control of the Assembly in October 1786. The next year they rechartered the Bank of North America, and in 1789-1790 they achieved the goal which they had sought for a decade: a state convention which wrote a new state constitution more in keeping with their ideas.

Party divisions within the state were reflected in national affairs throughout the 1780s. The Republicans, led by Robert Morris when he was Superintendent of Finance for the Confederation Congress between 1781 and 1784, did everything they could to strengthen the central government. The Constitutionalists usually opposed any infringement on Pennsylvania's power to govern itself, and opposed grants of power to the central government.

The Republicans controlled the Assembly which elected the delegates to the Constitutional Convention of 1787. The delegation consisted exclusively of Philadelphia Republicans: Robert Morris, Thomas FitzSimons, Thomas Mifflin, George Clymer, Jared Ingersoll, James Wilson, and Gouverneur Morris (a New Yorker who had spent some years in Philadelphia). Benjamin Franklin, courted by Republicans and Constitutionalists alike, was elected just as the Convention began.

In Pennsylvania, most Republicans became Federalists, while most Constitutionalists became Antifederalists. The Constitution was read to the Assembly on 18 September, the day after the Constitutional Convention adjourned. On 29 September the Republican majority proposed to call elections for a state convention, but enough Constitutionalist members stayed away to prevent a legal quorum. A mob seized and brought to the Assembly chamber two absent members, and the Assembly then voted 43 to 19 to hold elections for delegates on 6 November. The Pennsylvania Convention met in Philadelphia on 20 November and on 12 December ratified the Constitution by a vote of 46 to 23.

The controversy over the Constitution grew in intensity after ratification. The twenty-three men who voted against ratification at once issued "The Address and Reasons of Dissent of the Minority of the Convention of the State of Pennsylvania to their Constituents." In it they attacked the Constitutional Convention for its secrecy and the Assembly for its haste and use of force in calling the state Convention. They decried the lack of a bill of rights and the rejection of such a bill by the Pennsylvania Convention. They criticized many aspects of the Constitution but declared they would accept it if amendments were adopted.

Shortly thereafter, Antifederalist leaders began a petition campaign against the Constitution. The petition asked the Assembly to bring to account the Pennsylvania delegates to the Constitutional Convention for exceeding their powers and for their "reprehensible" conduct, and demanded that the Assembly reject the ratification of the Constitution by the Pennsylvania Convention. The petition was first printed in the *Carlisle Gazette* on 30 January 1788, and in March copies containing more than 6,000 signatures were laid before the Assembly, which ignored them.

Meanwhile, continued opposition to the Constitution was expressed in sporadic violence in some of the backcountry counties. Nevertheless, as more and more states ratified the Constitution, moderate Antifederalist leaders came to the conclusion that they would have to accept the Constitution, but at the same time they did not give up their conviction that it must be amended.

Both the conclusion and the conviction were made clear when the Antifederalist leaders in Cumberland County learned on 30 June that Virginia had ratified the Constitution. They sent out letters at once calling a convention to meet at Harrisburg in September to propose amendments to the Constitution and to nominate for Congress a slate of candidates who would support amendments.

Some Federalist leaders began looking forward to the first federal elections as early as May, and discussion of a state election law began in July, months before it was known when elections would be held. However, Pennsylvanians, like the citizens of other states, had to wait until 13 September, when Congress settled the dispute over the location of the new government and adopted an election ordinance.

The Republicans who controlled the Assembly which was elected in October 1787 were fearful that the Constitutionalists might win the state elections in October 1788, and they were determined to write an election law and elect Pennsylvania's two United States Senators before those elections. The fear of a Constitutionalist victory in those state elections was one of the principal reasons the Pennsylvania delegates in Congress gave up their struggle to locate the new government in Philadelphia.

The Pennsylvania Assembly was in session when the Election Ordinance of 13 September 1788 arrived in Philadelphia. The Republican majority at once began drafting an election law calling for the statewide election of Representatives. The demand of the Constitutionalists for district elections was rejected outright. On 29 September the Assembly approved the election law without a roll call. The law provided for the election of Representatives on 26 November and for the popular election of presidential Electors on 7 January 1789.

Speculation about candidates for the two Senate seats had been going on ever since March 1788. Among the names mentioned were John Armstrong, Jr., William Irvine, and William Bingham (Pennsylvania delegates in the Confederation Congress), and Robert Morris, George Clymer, and William Maclay. All of them were Republicans. Constitutionalist William Findley was mentioned, but the only real issue was which Republicans would be chosen. Political deals were made and broken but finally, on 29 September, an agreement was reached that the two Senators would be William Maclay and Robert Morris; and the next day they were elected.

Almost no public attention was paid to the election of Pennsylvania's two Senators until after the event. However, the election of Pennsylvania's eight Representatives came after a bitter two-month campaign in the newspapers about the merits of the candidates nominated by the Federalists and Antifederalists, and the issue of whether or not the Constitution needed amendments.

The Harrisburg Convention, 3-6 September, had drafted amendments to the Constitution but did not overtly nominate candidates. However, what was known as the "Harrisburg" or "Amendments" ticket was soon circulating about the state, although it was not published in a newspaper until 7 November. Five men on the ticket were Constitutionalists in state politics: Robert Whitehill, William Findley, Charles Pettit, William Montgomery, and Blair M'Clenachan. During the 1790s these men were Jeffersonians in state and national politics, and some of them were important leaders on both levels. Two of the Republicans were placed on the ticket because they were Germans and popular with the German voters. One of them, Peter Muhlenberg, was an opponent of Federalist policies from the beginning and became an important Jeffersonian. The other German, Daniel Hiester, voted against some Federalist policies from the start and was considered a Jeffersonian by the middle 1790s. The third Republican, William Irvine, who had been narrowly defeated for the Senate by Robert Morris, soon became an important Jeffersonian leader in state politics.

Pennsylvania Republicans learned about the Harrisburg Convention in mid-August, but they did not have specific information until the publication of the Cumberland County Circular Letter of 3 July in the *Pennsylvania Gazette* on 10 September. The next day a group of Philadelphia Republicans sent out circular letters calling for action to meet what they declared to be a threat. However, nothing was done until the day after the election of the Senators. On 1 October a group of Republicans, mostly members of the Assembly, called a conference which met at Lancaster on 3 November and nominated candidates for the House of Representatives and for presidential Electors. The men nominated for the House were Thomas Hartley, George Clymer, Henry Wynkoop, Thomas Scott, Stephen Chambers, Thomas FitzSimons, John Allison, and Frederick Muhlenberg. The candidates were all Republicans and, with the exception of Frederick Muhlenberg, loyal members of the Federalist Party during the 1790s.

The Harrisburg ticket was published for the first time on 7 November and the Lancaster ticket on 8 November. A few days later an anonymous broadside declared that the Germans were not adequately represented and presented a revision of the two tickets. Frederick Muhlenberg from the Lancaster ticket was substituted for Robert Whitehill on the Harrisburg ticket. Daniel Hiester and Peter Muhlenberg from the Harrisburg ticket were substituted for John Allison and Stephen Chambers on the Lancaster ticket. An anonymous newspaper writer created further confusion by suggesting a ticket made up of six men from the two tickets and two men not on either one. Alarmed Republicans, fearful of losing, urged all supporters of the Constitution to vote for the Lancaster ticket.

The campaign for the House of Representatives was in part a continuation of the debate over the Constitution. The Constitutionalists (Antifederalists) demanded amendments and, above all, a bill of rights. The Republicans (Federalists) denied that amendments were necessary, or argued that they could wait until the new government got under way and experience revealed their need.

Newspaper writers went over the history of Pennsylvania ever since 1776 and attacked the measures, motives, and achievements, or lack thereof, of the parties and their leaders. A major issue in the campaign was Robert Morris—"Bobby the Cofferer"—who was charged with corruption during the War for Independence. Much was made of the fact that he had not settled his wartime accounts with the United States and, furthermore, that several men on the Lancaster ticket were involved in his dealings. The Republicans, including Morris himself, defended themselves in the newspapers.

The voting for the two tickets, aside from the votes for the three Germans, followed rigid party lines. In Cumberland County, a center of opposition to the Constitution, the vote for the Lancaster ticket ranged from 271 to 287 and for the Harrisburg from 1,559 to 1,588. In Republican-dominated York County just to the south, the vote for the Lancaster ticket ranged from 1,475 to 1,497, while the vote for the Harrisburg ticket ranged from 193 to 209. In his home county of Washington, Thomas Scott received only 44 votes, while the votes for the other seven men on the Lancaster ticket ranged from 28 to 35. The vote for the Harrisburg ticket ranged from 298 to 308.

When the returns were in, it was evident that the German vote had been decisive. Peter Muhlenberg and Daniel Hiester on the original Harrisburg ticket and Frederick Muhlenberg on the original Lancaster ticket were elected, with the latter receiving more votes than any other candidate. John Allison and Stephen Chambers on the Lancaster ticket were defeated, but the other five men were elected: Thomas Hartley, George Clymer, Henry Wynkoop, Thomas Scott, and Thomas FitzSimons.

The election of presidential Electors on 7 January 1789 aroused little interest, although there were Lancaster and Harrisburg tickets for Electors. The Federalists, however, professed alarm. They warned of conspiracies to prevent the election of George Washington as President; published attacks on Patrick Henry and George Clinton, the alleged Antifederalist candidates; and exhorted the voters to turn out on election day. The Antifederalists showed little interest, and on election day most of the "real friends of liberty and republicanism" chose not to vote.

The completion of the elections was delayed by Thomas Scott's announcement that he wished to resign as United States Representative. The Federalists feared that if Scott from Washington County did resign, he might be replaced by Antifederalist William Findley from Westmoreland County. Scott apparently did not want to give up his post as prothonotary of Washington County, but an agreement was made whereby his son was appointed to the post in March 1789; and Scott agreed to serve as Representative.

NOTE ON SOURCES

The manuscript minutes of the Supreme Executive Council, in both rough and smooth form, are in the Pennsylvania State Archives at Harrisburg. They were printed as *Minutes of the Supreme Executive Council of Pennsylvania, From its Organization to the Termination of the Revolution* (vols. XI-XVI, Harrisburg, 1852-1853). Volume XV contains the minutes from 4 July 1786 to 6 February 1789 and volume XVI the minutes from 7 February 1789 to 20 December 1790.

The original manuscript journals of the House of Representatives are not extant. However, the journals were published at the end of each session, and it is these contemporary printed journals that we have used.

Pennsylvania is unique among the states during this period in that the debates in the legislature were reported and published. Thomas Lloyd began taking short-hand notes of the debates in September 1787 and continued to do so until 4 October 1788. These debates were published by Lloyd as *Proceedings and Debates of the General Assembly of Pennsylvania . . .* (4 vols., Philadelphia, 1787-1788). The fourth volume, which contains the debates on the passage of the election law, is entitled *Debates of the General Assembly of Pennsylvania. . . .*

The printed and manuscript letters of political leaders and others throw considerable light on men and issues. The most helpful are the papers of Tench Coxe, Albert Gallatin, William Irvine, John Nicholson, Timothy Pickering, and the Shippen family.

The thirteen Pennsylvania newspapers which were published during the elections provide invaluable materials. Eight newspapers, including three dailies and one German-language weekly, were published in Philadelphia. The three dailies were Andrew Brown's *The Federal Gazette and Philadelphia Evening Post*; Eleazer Oswald's *The Independent Gazetteer; or, the Chronicle of Freedom*; and John Dunlap and David C. Claypoole's *The Pennsylvania Packet, and Daily Advertiser*. Brown's paper was ardently Federalist and Oswald's paper ardently Antifederalist. Daniel Humphreys' *The Pennsylvania Mercury and Universal Advertiser* was published tri-weekly. Thomas Bradford's *The Pennsylvania Journal and the Weekly Advertiser* was published semi-weekly until the end of 1788 and as a weekly thereafter except during legislative sessions, when it was printed more frequently. The weekly newspapers were William Hall, David Hall, and William Sellers' *The Pennsylvania Gazette* and Francis Bailey's *The Freeman's Journal; or, The North American Intelligencer*. The German-language weekly was Melchior Steiner's *Gemeinnützige Philadelphische Correspondenz*.

Two German-language weeklies were published outside Philadelphia: Michael Billmeyer's *Die Germantauner Zeitung* and Johann Albrecht and Jacob Lahn's *Neue Unpartheyische Lancaster Zeitung, und Anzeigs-Nachrichten*. The three English-language weeklies published outside Philadelphia were John Scull and

John Boyd's *The Pittsburgh Gazette;* George Kline and George Reynolds' *The Carlisle Gazette, and the Western Repository of Knowledge;* and James Edie, John Edie, and Henry Willcocks' *The Pennsylvania Herald, and York General Advertiser,* which began publication 7 January 1789.

York County was a center of Federalism and its newspaper represented that fact. The Carlisle and Pittsburgh papers were Federalist in the midst of two centers of strong and even violent Antifederalist activity, but neither newspaper reflected the political realities of the area in which it was published.

PENNSYLVANIA CHRONOLOGY, 1788–1789

1788

30 June	News of Virginia's ratification reaches Cumberland County, Pennsylvania.
3 July	Cumberland County Circular Letter calls convention to meet at Harrisburg, 3 September, to propose amendments to the Constitution and nominate candidates for Congress.
16 July	Article by "Numa" in *Pennsylvania Gazette* begins public debate over district vs. at-large elections for the House of Representatives.
5 August	Westmoreland County meeting proposes amendments to the Constitution.
6 August	Supreme Executive Council receives New York ratification of the Constitution and the New York Circular Letter calling for a second constitutional convention.
18 August	Fayette County elects delegates to Harrisburg Convention.
20 August	News of convention at Harrisburg reported in *Pennsylvania Gazette.*
20 August	Huntingdon County elects delegates to Harrisburg Convention.
25 August	Bucks County elects delegates to Harrisburg Convention.
2 September	Legislative session begins.
3-6 September	Harrisburg Convention meets.
6 September	Supreme Executive Council transmits to Assembly the Virginia, South Carolina, and New York ratifications of the Constitution and a letter from the president of the North Carolina Convention.
13 September	Confederation Congress adopts Election Ordinance.
16 September	Supreme Executive Council receives Election Ordinance from Congress.
17 September	Supreme Executive Council transmits Election Ordinance to Assembly.
18 September	Assembly appoints committee to draft election bill.

23 September	Committee reports election bill, which is read first time.
24 September	Election bill read second time and debated by paragraphs. Ordered printed for public consideration.
24 September	Assembly approves resolution to elect United States Senators on 30 September.
27 September	Election bill read third time. Further consideration postponed until Monday, 29 September.
29 September	Election bill read, debated, and ordered engrossed.
30 September	Assembly elects Robert Morris and William Maclay United States Senators.
1 October	Philadelphia Federalists call conference at Lancaster to nominate candidates for Congress.
4 October	Engrossed election law, providing for at-large election of Representatives on 26 November, and at-large election of Electors on 7 January, is approved.
4 October	Assembly defeats a motion that the Massachusetts, New York, and Virginia acts of ratification, and the letter from North Carolina, be "specially recommended to the succeeding House of Assembly."
4 October	Legislative session ends.
10 October	Philadelphia County appoints delegates to Lancaster Conference.
14 October	Annual election of members of state Assembly and Supreme Executive Council.
18 October	City of Philadelphia elects delegates to Lancaster Conference.
23 October	Cumberland County elects delegates to Lancaster Conference.
25 October	Philadelphia town meeting nominates candidates to represent the city in the House of Representatives and as presidential Electors.
27 October	Legislative session begins.
3 November	Lancaster Conference nominates Federalist candidates for the House of Representatives and presidential Electors.
7 November	Harrisburg ticket for Representatives printed in the *Federal Gazette*.
8 November	Lancaster ticket for Representatives and Electors printed in *Pennsylvania Packet*.
13 November	German broadside adds the two Germans on Harrisburg ticket to Lancaster ticket, and the one German on Lancaster ticket to Harrisburg ticket.
18 November	Mixed Federal-Antifederal ticket printed in the *Independent Gazetteer*.
22 November	Legislative session ends.

24 November   Harrisburg ticket for Electors printed in the *Independent Gazetteer.*

26 November   Election of members of the House of Representatives.

1789

5 January   Supreme Executive Council issues proclamation announcing election of members of the House of Representatives: Frederick A. Muhlenberg, Henry Wynkoop, Thomas Hartley, Thomas Fitz-Simons, Thomas Scott, Peter Muhlenberg, Daniel Hiester.

7 January   Election day for presidential Electors.

3 February   Supreme Executive Council issues proclamation announcing election of presidential Electors: Edward Hand, George Gibson, John Arndt, Collinson Read, Lawrence Keene, James Wilson, James O'Hara, David Grier, Samuel Potts, Alexander Graydon.

4 February   Electors meet at Reading and vote for George Washington (10), John Adams (8), and John Hancock (2).

THE DOCUMENTS

John Armstrong, Jr., to Horatio Gates, New York, 30 May 1788 (excerpt)[1]

There's no part of my conduct on which I would not wish your approbation and I have yet no reason to think the resignation of my judicial appointment an improper step.[2] On the contrary I think with you it was right and that a little in society is much more desirable than a great deal in a desert. The career however which the new government opened I'm far from thinking flattering to men of any age or character, for tho a friend and advocate of the system (as a step towards common sense and practicable government) yet it falls so far short of what I know to be the situation and believe to be the character of this country that I despair at once of both the stability and convenience of the edifice. The fact is my dear General that my creed as to popular governments is very much changed under a little experience of their operation, and I suspect that shape them as you will, you must find them on experiment both foolish and feeble. The philosophy that teaches the equality of mankind and the dignity of human nature is founded in vanity and addressed to it alone. In my opinion, tho there be less consolation, there is infinitely more truth in the opposite doctrine, that the many were made for the few, and that we are better governed by rods than by reason. These ideas I wish you to consider, however, as merely speculative and such as I would express only to a tried and bosom friend; they convey my fears, not my wishes, and will ever be more a matter of opinion than a rule of conduct. What particular part I'm destined to play in this new drama I know not? My standing at present, considering my age, and that I have been obliged to make my way thro very narrow and hostile politics, is as forward as I had any right to expect, and more so perhaps, when I consider how many with better pretensions, because with more collateral supports, I have left behind me. This consideration will not however induce me to push myself forward for other or greater distinctions. I will neither conceal myself from view, nor obtrude myself upon it, and then if appointments come, they will sit easy. My friends in Pennsylvania have I hear already tho't of a place for me, and mean to try their force in sending me to the new Senate; but as they will have but two seats of that kind to fill, I need hardly say that they will be seats of much competition.[3] The rich and the aged (as the natural representatives of property and wisdom and the true counterbalance to the cormorants of the lower house), will expect, and most probably get them, and indeed so little am I set upon success in the trial, that I scarcely feel a wish to cross them. My leading wish is to see them *well* filled.[4]

1. RC, Gates Papers, NHi. General Gates was living in retirement in Virginia.

2. The Confederation Congress elected Armstrong, who was a member of Congress, one of the three judges for the Northwest Territory on 16 October 1787 (JCC, XXXIII, 686). He declined the appointment in January 1788 (JCC, XXXIV, 9).

3. See James McLene to William Irvine, 12 September, printed below, in which McLene assumes that Armstrong will be one of the Senators, and Tench Coxe to James Madison, 26 September, printed below, where he is listed as one of several candidates for the post.

4. For Armstrong's opinion of the Federalist nominations for the House of Representatives and of the results of the election, see his letter to Robert McPherson, Election Day Appeals and Commentaries, 26 November, printed below.

Proceedings of a Cumberland County Meeting, 3 July[1]

At Mr. James Bell's, in a meeting of delegates from the several townships of the beforesaid county, Benjn. Blyth in the chair, called for the purpose of advising the most eligible mode of obtaining such amendments in the Constitution, proposed by the General Convention for the government of these United States, as may remove the causes of jealousy and fears of a tyrannical aristocracy the foundation of which appears to be in many parts of the said Constitution, and secure and hand down to posterity the blessings of dear bought freedom; and thereby most cordially engage each state and every citizen, not only for wrath but conscience sake, to aid and support the officers of the government in the due execution thereof; after seriously considering the importance of the subject and the duty of citizens, have come to the following resolutions, viz.,

Resolved, that it is the opinion of this meeting that the Constitution proposed by the General Convention of the United States is in several parts destructive of that liberty for which so much blood and treasure has been spent, and subversive of the several state governments by which the rights and liberties of the people have been guarded and secured; that it is the indispensable duty of every citizen to use all lawful means to obtain such amendments in the said Constitution or take such measures as shall be necessary for the security of religion and liberty. Resolved, that it is the opinion of the members of this meeting that it will be expedient to collect as soon and as accurately as possible the sentiments of the citizens of this state touching such amendments and such mode of obtaining them as shall be to said citizens most agreeable.

Resolved, that in order to effectuate the foregoing resolution, that a circular letter be written, signed by the chairman and addressed to such societies in each county as have already been formed for political purposes, and to such as shall be formed in any county where none is yet formed or to such persons as shall be judged fit, requesting that measures be taken to call a meeting of delegates from each township within the respective counties to meet as soon as conveniently may be and take into consideration the necessity and propriety of amending the Constitution of the United States. And for that purpose to appoint delegates to meet in a general conference of the state at Harrisburg on the third day of September 1788, then and there to consider and devise a plan the most likely to succeed in obtaining the desired amendments. Resolved by the meeting, that five members be chosen by the county Cumberland or three out of the five to represent said county in the conference to be held at Harrisburg the 3d day of September 1788; the place and time aforesaid.

1. RC, Pennsylvania Papers, Harrisburg Convention, NN. The proceedings are undated but are contained in a letter from Benjamin Blyth to John Nicholson, 3 July, printed below. Presumably the meeting was held after the news of Virginia's ratification reached Cumberland County by way of Baltimore on Monday, 30 June (*Carlisle Gazette*, 2 July). The Circular Letter authorized by the meeting is printed below.

On 14 July the New York *Daily Advertiser* published an "extract" from a letter from Philadelphia dated 11 July which stated: "I am informed from good authority, that in consequence of the 9th state having adopted the new Constitution, the Antifederalists of Cumberland County in this state held a meeting near Carlisle; the result was, that they were determined to support it, and give it a fair trail, and solicit amendments in a constitutional way. Only three at the meeting were opposed to it." This item was reprinted in the *Boston*

Gazette, 21 July; Poughkeepsie *Country Journal*, 22 July; *Salem Mercury*, 22 July; Boston *Massachusetts Centinel*, 23 July; Providence *United States Chronicle*, 24 July; and Portsmouth *New Hampshire Spy*, 26 July, but no reprinting has been located in a Pennsylvania newspaper.

Cumberland County Circular Letter, 3 July[1]

That ten states have already, unexpectedly, without amending, ratified the Constitution proposed for the government of these United States, cannot have escaped the notice of the friends of liberty. That the way is prepared for the full organization of the government, with all its foreseen and consequent dangers, is too evident, and unless prudent steps be taken to combine the friends to amendments in some place in which they may confidently draw together and exert their power in unison, the liberty of the American citizens must lie at the discretion of Congress, and most probably, posterity become slaves to the officers of government.

The means adopted and proposed by a meeting of delegates from the townships of this county for preventing the alleged evils and also the calamities of a civil war, are, as may be observed in perusing the proceedings of the said meeting herewith transmitted to request such persons as shall be judged fit within the counties respectively, to use their influence to obtain a meeting of delegates from each township to take into consideration, the necessity of amending the Constitution of these United States, and for that purpose to nominate and appoint a number of delegates to represent the county, in a general conference of the counties of this commonwealth, to be held at Harrisburg on the third day of September next, then and there, to devise such amendments, and such mode of obtaining them, as in the wisdom of the delegates shall be judged most satisfactory and expedient.

A law will no doubt be soon enacted by the General Assembly for electing eight members to represent this state in the new Congress. It will therefore be expedient to have proper persons put in nomination by the delegates in conference, being the most likely method of directing the views of the electors to the same object and of obtaining the desired end.

The society of which you are chairman is requested to call a meeting agreeably to the foregoing designs, and lay before the delegates the proceeding of this county, to the intent that the state may unite in casting off the yoke of slavery and once more establish union and liberty.

1. RC, Pennsylvania Miscellany, DLC. The circular was signed by "Benjamin Blyth Chairman" and was headed "East Pennsborough, Cumberland Co. 3d July 1788." Although only one copy of the Circular Letter has been found, it was evidently sent to Antifederalist leaders throughout the state and provided the impetus for meetings to elect delegates to the convention at Harrisburg on 3 September (see George Clymer to Samuel Meredith, 14 August; James Hanna to John Vandegrift et al., 15 August; Certificate of Election for Fayette County, 18 August; and Proceedings of a Bucks County Meeting, 25 August, all printed below).

A meeting at Greensburg in Westmoreland County on 5 August did not refer to the Circular Letter, but it appointed a committee to correspond with committees in other counties as to the best means of securing amendments to the Constitution. The committee drafted proposed amendments to the Constitution (Proceedings of a Westmoreland County Meeting, 5 August, printed below), but the county did not sent delegates to Harrisburg.

The Cumberland County Circular Letter was not printed in a newspaper until after the Harrisburg Convention was over ("A Freeman," *Pennsylvania Gazette*, 10 September, printed below), but the Federalists knew about it by mid-August (anonymous to Francis Hopkinson, 17 August, and *Pennsylvania Gazette,* 20 August, both printed below).

Benjamin Blyth to John Nicholson, Cumberland County, 3 July[1]

You are earnestly requested to call a meeting of some of the best informed men of your county, from each township, with design to consider of the necessity of sending delegates from the counties to represent you in a general conference of the state in order to conclude upon such amendments and such mode of obtaining them as the conference in their wisdom may judge proper. The time and place of meeting is as you will see by our resolutions. The necessity of the measure need not be urged. Confiding in your friendship and integrity, we hope you will exert yourself for the good of mankind.

1. RC, Pennsylvania Papers, Harrisburg Convention, NN. Immediately after Blyth's signature is the account of the proceedings of the Cumberland County meeting on 3 July, printed above. Presumably, Blyth also sent Nicholson a copy of the Circular Letter of 3 July, printed above. The endorsement on the letter in Nicholson's handwriting states that it was received 20 August and answered 26 August. He evidently sent the letter to an unknown correspondent. A note on it, not in his handwriting, reads: "You will be punctual in laying these resolutions before your committee, if there are any such in the city, and use your endeavors that they comply with the same." Nicholson, comptroller general of the state, was a leading Antifederalist, and his office seems to have been a communications center for the Antifederalists (see William Petrikin to Nicholson, 23 March 1789, printed below).

James Wilson's Fourth of July Oration, 1788 (excerpt)[1]

Allow me to direct your attention, in a very particular manner, to a momentous part, which, by this Constitution every citizen will frequently be called to act. All those in places of power and trust will be elected either immediately by the people; or in such a manner that their appointment will depend ultimately on such immediate election. All the derivative movements of government must spring from the original movement of the people at large. If, to this, they give a sufficient force and a just direction, all the others will be governed by its controlling power. To speak without a metaphor; if the people, at their elections, take care to choose none but representatives that are wise and good; their representatives will take care, in their turn, to choose or appoint none but such as are wise and good also. The remark applies to every succeeding election and appointment. Thus the characters proper for public officers will be diffused from the immediate elections of the people over the remotest parts of administration. Of what immense consequence is it, then, that this primary duty should be faithfully and skilfully discharged? On the faithful and skilful discharge of it the public happiness or infelicity, under this and every other constitution, must, in a very great measure, depend. For, believe me, no government, even the best, can be happily administered by ignorant or vicious men. You will forgive me, I am sure, for endeavoring to impress upon your minds, in the strongest manner, the importance of this great duty. It is the first concoction in politics; and if an error is committed here, it can never be corrected in any subsequent process. The certain consequence must be disease. Let no one say that he is but a single citizen; and that his ticket will be but one in the box. That one ticket may turn the election. In battle, every soldier should consider the public safety as depending on his single arm. At an election, every citizen should consider the public happiness as depending on his single vote.

1. *Pennsylvania Gazette*, 9 July (supplement). Wilson's speech was reprinted in several other states (see, for example, the *New York Journal*, 18 July; Charleston *Columbian Herald*, 28 July; and *Norwich Packet*, 7 August).

Antifederalists Celebrate the 4th of July at Carlisle

The Federalists and the Antifederalists celebrated the 4th of July at two different meetings in Carlisle. On 9 July, the *Carlisle Gazette*, a Federalist newspaper, reported both celebrations without any political commentary. The next week, on 16 July, the York *Pennsylvania Chronicle* published a widely reprinted satire on the Antifederalist celebration. The two accounts are published below to illustrate the political methods of newspaper publishers.

Carlisle Gazette, 9 July

On Friday the 4th July instant, being the anniversary of the 13th year of American independence, a number of the respectable inhabitants of the borough of Carlisle, and the adjacent townships, together with the volunteer company of militia, and detachments from other militia companies, convened in the public square of this borough. After attending a discourse suitable on the occasion, delivered by the Reverend Dr. Robert Davidson, they marched from thence to the Meetinghouse Springs, to celebrate the day, when a genteel repast was prepared; after partaking of which, the following toasts were drank, each accompanied with a discharge of musketry.

1. May the thirteen American states forever remain united, on real federal principles.

2. May such amendments be speedily framed, and unanimously adopted, as may render the proposed Constitution for the United States truly democratical.

3. May agriculture, manufactures and commerce forever flourish in America.

4. May America continue the asylum of civil and religous liberty to the latest ages.

5. May the example of America, in the late Revolution, be copied by every enslaved people throughout the world.

6. May the fate of Great Britain in the late contest be the fate of all tyrants.

7. The memory of the heroes who fell in support of American independence.

8. The virtuous minority of the late Convention of Pennsylvania.

9. The minorities of our sister state conventions.

10. The constitution of Pennsylvania.

11. Our friends in Europe.

12. May the designs of such as endeavor to enslave the citizens of America prove abortive.

13. May America remain forever free from tryanny, anarchy, and consolidation.

After which they marched in order to the public square, from thence to the commons south of town, where after firing three volleys they repaired again to the public square, and dispersed. We are happy to announce to the public, that joy, peace, and good order pervaded the whole scene.

Pennsylvania Chronicle, 16 July[1]

At a meeting of the Anties, on the fourth of July, at the Meetinghouse Springs, near Carlisle, for the purpose of a general condolence, at the success of the friends to good government. The entertainment began in a prayer, by an elder from Stony Ridge,[2] to the Daemon of Anarchy, as follows:

"O thou who ridest in the whirlwind, and directest the storm of intestine broil; who dwelleth in darkness, impenetrable and full of mystery; whose throne is built on licentiousness, and supported by ignorance and discontent; from whose presents the restraints of religion, society and government fly, and leave free agency in full perfection—attend to the last speech and dying works of a poor, miserable, disconsolate group, and grant that peace, with her insipid train of arts, science, order and equal justice, may be exiled this country. Reach forth thy ebon wand of defamation, and blacken the infant Constitution of this country, lest it sink us from the zenith of political eminence to the abyss of private life; lest it destroy our *"dearest right,"* the right to do wrong; lest it shut the door of civil dissension, and thereby rob us of our only anchor of hope, convulsion, as we are placed below the reach of the mild and milk and water medicines of frugality and industry; lest it compel us to pay taxes, that worse than Egyptian cruelty, for thou knowest we have no money; lest an experiment of it give the lie to our soothsayers; lest it furnish talents and political integrity, with an opportunity to supplant the ignorance, bigotry and solemn nonsense of our ruling demagogues. In fine, we humble ourselves before thee, in whom we live, move, and have all our consequence, we pray that thou mayest visit this land in all thy terrors, to prevent a general, permanent, efficient government, let loose the dogs of civil war, and hunt the proposed system to death, to the great affliction of every honest man, and the no little satisfaction of your very humble servants."

A buzz, very like that of drones, marked the approbation of the swarm. After having devoured some solids, thirteen libations of *whuskey* were poured to the following toasts:

1. Margery.[3]

2. David [i.e., Daniel] Shays.

3. John Franklin and our brethren on the east branch.[4]

4. Felix Makckintosh.

5. General Po——er and preemption rights.[5]

6. Lu[th]er Mar[ti]n, not forgetting the speech he *was* to have made in the Maryland Convention.

7. Paper money and legal tender.

8. Funding system and mobocracy.

9. The 19 runaways of the Assembly of 1787.[6]

10. The minorities of our sister states, except Rhode Island.

11. That perfection of politics, the constitution of Pennsylvania.

12. Liberty of conscience.

13. The still—lasting honors to the inventor.

The table exhibited in the most manifest light that truly republican virtue, FRUGALITY, while full bellies and empty dishes marked nicety of calculation. The whiskey was remarkably free from verdigris, having been duly *fined* by the filings of a horse's hoof. A fast was proposed and agreed to, when it was recommended to every man to be clothed in sackcloth, and sit upon a bank of ashes, and try if possible to avert the impending curses of good order, and the administration of justice. After this they marched to town and fired! Ye Gods how they fired! Their evolutions would have astonished the reviewing generals of Prussia. The great misfortune that attended them was, they could not muster *cash* for more than three rounds! Oh poverty! thou curse of curses!

1. The *Pennsylvania Chronicle* for 16 July is not extant. This item is from the reprint in the *Pennsylvania Mercury*, 29 July. It was also reprinted in at least nine other newspapers, including the *New York Morning Post*, 31 July; Hartford *Connecticut Courant*, 11 August; Boston *Massachusetts Gazette*, 19 August; Winchester *Virginia Gazette*, 20 August; *Newport Herald*, 21 August; Portsmouth *New Hampshire Spy*, 26 August; and Charleston *City Gazette*, 20 September.

2. Stony Ridge was on the estate of Antifederalist leader Robert Whitehill.

3. George Bryan, Antifederalist leader and a justice of the Pennsylvania Supreme Court, was satirized as "Margery" (see the *Pennsylvania Mercury* 8 July, n. 1, printed below).

4. Franklin was a leader of the Connecticut settlers in the Wyoming Valley in northeastern Pennsylvania.

5. This is probably a reference to General James Potter, an Antifederalist leader from Northumberland County.

6. The reference is to the members of the Assembly who in September 1787 refused to attend the Assembly, in an unsuccessful attempt to prevent the calling of a state convention to consider the Constitution.

Pennsylvania Mercury, 5 July

TO BE SEEN, near the Jersey Market, price Two Coppers, a strange sort of an ANIMAL, half Man, half Quadruped, has the properties of a Snapping Tortoise, spitefully snapping and growling at his best friends and benefactors, whenever he hears the words, Federalist, New Government, &c. &c. &c. mentioned, but happily his bite is not venomous, as his teeth are now worn out; he roves about from place to place, and is thought will soon run mad. The public are cautioned to be aware of him. Tis supposed he will endeavour shortly to make his escape to Carlisle, as tis said, at that place, there is a Nursery of a few more Animals of the same Species.[1]

1. When this article was reprinted in the New York *Daily Advertiser*, 10 July, "A Correspondent" commented that the "Semi-beast" had been seen in New York City. It was also "reported that the monster has his Eye upon either Shrewsbury or Burlington in New-Jersey

as the Place of his future Residence:—it is hoped that our friends in that State will be particularly careful lest they should be bitten by him, for their Federalism will certainly excite his venom to an uncommon Degree."

Pennsylvania Mercury, 8 July

The adoption of the new form of government, by the ten United States, has inspired the most lively joy in every patriotic and rational mind; and must serve to convince its mistaken and deluded enemies and opponents, that their conjectures were altogether groundless and visionary in the commencement, as well as events. Nothing (continues our correspondent) is now wanting, but an active cultivation of political harmony, unison, and concord, to fulfil the designs of heaven, which were calculated to make us a great and happy people.

Respected by all the nations abroad, and contented, heartfeltedly contented at home, America has every felicity at her command, which any young rising empire could expect or desire. What hath she to fear, but her God? Yet in vain do we view our blessed situation, without it tends to make the people better men and good citizens. The best government is of no consequence, when it falls to the fatal management of bad ministers and indifferent rulers. Nor are laws, the most salutary, any security in themselves, when they are inverted and abused. This we have mournful evidence of, every day, and in no instance more striking, than the oppressions of the trading magistrates of this city, and their man-catchers, the constables.

Let it, therefore, be our inflexible aim, to trust our federal affairs to men of approved probity and talents, upon whose skill we may rely with safety. For virtuous and intelligent representation is the mainspring of social happiness, and the only proper path of American glory.

It must also give pleasure (observes our correspondent) that as the chief part of legislative and executive business will be conducted by Congress, so far as respects federal points, there cannot be any longer reason for that surprising length of sessions in the Assembly, which has always been attended with heavy expenses, fleeced our pockets severely, and seldom answered any purpose, except diffusing the execrable spirit of party and faction. Nor will the same necessity urge the Executive Council to retain so full a board of members, nor to sit constantly as heretofore. Such considerations will naturally lead to strict frugality, savingness and economy, in public expenditures; and, of course, the citizens will be eased at large, in a considerable measure, from their embarrassments.

It will not be extraordinary, under these prospects, to see all salaries, from the President downwards, lessened and reduced, and the superfluous officers of the state demolished, of every degree. Even Margery (concludes our correspondent) will not take it hard, if she participates of the common sufferings, and the old red cloak itself, tattered and worn out in the solicitations of public favor and pity, can no longer recommend her.[1]

1. Between 21 February and 20 March 1788 the *Pennsylvania Mercury* printed eight satirical essays attacking George Bryan as "Margery" who wore an "old red cloak." The satirist assumed that Bryan rather than his son Samuel had written "Centinel" essays (for the authorship of "Centinel," see "Centinel" XIX, *Independent Gazetteer*, 7 October, n. 1, printed below).

Numa to the Inhabitants of the States That Have Adopted the New Constitution, Pennsylvania Gazette, 16 July

You will soon be called upon to enact laws for choosing members of the House of Representatives in the new federal legislature. The following mode of electing them is hereby recommended to such of the states as choose more than one Representative. Divide the state into as many districts as there are members to be chosen, and direct the electors to fix upon a member from *each* district, and then let the whole state vote for the whole number of members. By these means a knowledge of the local interests of every part of the state will be carried to Congress, but in such a manner, as not to interfere with the *general* interest of the whole state. When members are chosen by the *whole* state, they will consider themselves as the servants of the *whole* state, and not suffer themselves to be misled by the local prejudices or interests of a few men who often govern counties and districts. By these means the agriculture and commerce of the states will always be kept in friendship with each other, for the farmer and the merchant will mutually vote for the same rulers. By these means likewise, none but men of real character and abilities will be returned, for such men are generally best known throughout every part of a state. A House of Representatives, thus chosen, cannot fail of being truly respectable. The members of each state will be a band of brothers. No local considerations, no sacrifice of the general interests to the customs of a store, or a mill, will ever divide or influence them. In every vote they will have their eyes fixed upon the commerce, agriculture, manufactures, and upon the interest of every county, town, and individual of the whole state.[1]

1. "Numa" was reprinted at least eight times (see, for example, the Baltimore *Maryland Gazette*, 22 July; Winchester *Virginia Centinel*, 6 August; Elizabethtown *New Jersey Journal*, 20 August; and *Boston Gazette*, 29 September). The widespread reprinting indicates the interest in what was to become a crucial issue in drafting election laws in several states. Federalist and Antifederalist leaders alike strove for either statewide or district elections of Representatives according to their estimate of the method that would further their political goals.
   "Pompilius" (*Pennsylvania Gazette*, 23 July) supported "Numa," and in a reply to both articles "A Friend to Agriculture, Trade, and Good Laws" applied their arguments specifically to Pennsylvania (*Pennsylvania Gazette*, 30 July, printed immediately below).

A Friend to Agriculture, Trade, and Good Laws to Numa and Pompilius, Pennsylvania Gazette, 30 July

The plan you propose for electing the eight federal Representatives for Pennsylvania has some good qualities, but has others which I do not approve, and which cannot be executed without real injury to the public interests.

The new Constitution allots to Pennsylvania eight Representatives, to take care of her interests and those of *the whole body of her people* in the federal House. Your plan would narrow them down from representatives of Pennsylvania to representatives of districts, and would reduce me from an elector for a confederated state, to an elector for a part of a state. I think this is contrary to the spirit of the new confederation, and to the true nature of confederacies in general. The new Constitution gives me a right to choose as a Pennsylvanian, and to elect any Pennsylvanian, and I am certain our legislature will not lessen my rights and privileges. Besides, if we adopt your plan, I think, though you may not have adverted to it, that it will tend *to destroy and undermine the state governments.* It is theirs to have elections in and for *parts* of states. We have no right to encroach upon them, by dangerous arrangements of any of the federal elections. I therefore freely profess, that I think every Pennsylvanian should be permitted to repair to *his proper election district*, as by the *state election laws they are laid out*, and *there* to give his vote for such eight men (being Pennsylvanians) as he thinks best qualified to perform the trusts and duties of a federal Representative.[1]

And now, as I have taken notice of this matter, I beg leave to add a thought concerning the execution of the mode herein proposed. It is clear to every man, that the farming or landed interest in Pennsylvania is *the most numerous* and *the most important.* It appears absolutely necessary to our safety therefore, that we should have it in our power to prevent any vote of our eight members that would injure the farming interest or body of citizens. We must therefore have *at least four* out of the eight of that body sincerely attached to them, so we can prevent any vote that will hurt them, and have a complete check on the vote of Pennsylvania on every occasion. We shall also find it proper, perhaps, to have *two* men who understand foreign and domestic trade, which is necessary to the well being of the landed interest, and of the state in general. A considerable share of mercantile knowledge and abilities will be particularly necessary in the first federal legislature or new Congress, because that subject is to be taken up for the first time upon general national principles, and it will require more knowledge of trade, and more certainty, than we can safely trust to or expect from *any one man.* Some of the states do not carry on any trade, and have no manufactures, so that it will be incumbent *on us* to do our best to have the commercial interest well represented.

The great importance of taking up the execution of the government in due form, will render some law knowledge very useful, and as the federal judiciary is to be constructed from the foundation, *two* learned and judicious law characters appear absolutely necessary, and may be chosen from the country as well as from the city, as there are men of excellent character, extensive knowledge and sound judgment in that profession, in several parts of the state.

1. "A Citizen of Franklin County," writing in the *Carlisle Gazette* of 13 August, raised further objections to district elections. He warned that "to divide the state into eight equal districts, which is the number of Representatives we are to send from this state, would be impossible, unless counties were also divided; and to divide counties in this case, would produce such a scene of confusion, as must inevitably terminate in the destruction of that harmony which ought, and hope always will characterize our elections."

Tench Coxe to Robert Smith, Philadelphia, 5 August (excerpt)[1]

I am favored with your letter of 31st ultimo. . . .[2]

· · · · · · ·

I am of opinion you are very judiciously employed in Maryland in securing sincere, firm, and intelligent Federalists for state representatives. Very much will depend upon the legislatures chosen this year on the score of amendments. I also saw Mr. M[adison] several times on his way through this city and found him strongly impressed with the opinions you mention, and I have since heard from him. I find appearances and information at New York have heightened his belief and strengthened his opinion of the necessity of exertions on our parts. His words are somewhat particular: "The combination against direct taxes is *more extensive & more formidable* than some gentlemen suspect. It is clearly seen by the Enemies to the Constitution, that an abolition of that power will reestablish the Supremacy of the state legislatures, *the real object* of all their Zeal in opposing the System."[3]

I have observed, from the adoption of Virginia till this time, a strong *profession* of acquiescence in some very cool and artful men, who till then were in the opposition; and it [is] striking that they never enumerate their points of amendment without taking in direct taxes, which they say will be impracticable sometimes, and sometimes improper. The persons I allude to are of weight in our general politics and in our western counties but here are lost. They however are formidable for their talents, information, and especially for their political industry.

A combination was taken up in the back parts and center of Pennsylvania for the purpose of obtaining amendments in concert with the opposition in New York, who were then supposed to have an absolute command in that state. They proposed to meet at Harrisburg and meant to term themselves a convention. The unexpected adoption by the Convention of New York has staggered them a good deal, but I do not think they will drop their measures, tho they may be less extravagant and assuming for that check.

A fact of a very curious nature occurred to me about the time Virginia was determining. Some little question arose in conversation between a strong and sensible opponent and myself on the probable nature of the Virginia amendments, as they would be proposed to Congress. We thought differently on them when he made this remark. "It is not worth making a question about the amendments for I have *a copy of them in my pocket.*" It is but a single fact, but it comes in confirmation of the many symptoms of *concert* in this plan, which are daily presenting themselves.

On the whole, sir, I am clearly of opinion that the fixed aversion of some to the government and the pliancy of temper and want of sufficient apprehension and perception of danger in many, who are disposed to favor it, render it necessary to keep up a vigilant attention, a strong and constant exertion, and to observe a firm and decided, tho a mild, deportment towards the opposition. I would do everything that could be done and trust nothing to the chapter of accidents. Above all things, I would not think too favorably of the views of the opposition nor too lightly of their exertions or their strength. Put in only such men as will not swerve, under any temptations, from maintaining the energy of the government.

The enclosed paper addressed to our western inhabitants is calculated to remove some very gross errors and prejudices. From Harford [County] back it may have some effect in Maryland, and I find the last argument about the representation thought well of in many places. Tis a simple style, calculated to be understood, where education blesses but few and in a small degree. I wish you may think it worth republishing.[4] Our principal inducement to it was to show the opposition that, tho we were successful, we were not disposed to cease from exertion, while a prejudice remained to be done away.

1. FC, Coxe Papers, Tench Coxe Section, PHi. Smith, a prominent Baltimore attorney, was an Elector in 1789. He served as Secretary of the Navy and Secretary of State in the administrations of Jefferson and Madison.
2. Printed in Chapter IX.
3. James Madison to Tench Coxe, 30 July. Printed: LMCC, VIII, 723.
4. "A Friend of Society and Liberty," "To the Inhabitants of the Western Counties of Pennsylvania," *Pennsylvania Gazette*, 23 July. The essay was reprinted in the Baltimore *Maryland Journal,* 12 August.

Proceedings of a Westmoreland County Meeting, Greensburg, 5 August[1]

At a meeting of a number of freemen, inhabitants of the different townships in the County of Westmoreland, held at Greensburg the 5th day of August, 1788, John Moore, Esquire, was unanimously chosen to the chair.

Upon motion being made, it was resolved unanimously, that it is the duty of this meeting, to endeavor to procure several amendments to the plan proposed for the general government of the United States, by the late Federal Convention, and now adopted by the conventions of ten states.

Resolved unanimously, that a committee, consisting of seven persons, be chosen by this meeting to correspond with the different counties of this state, respecting the most proper method of procuring those amendments, in connection with other states, and according to the method laid down in the said plan of general government.

Resolved, that Captain Thomas Morton; Christopher Truby, Esq.; William Jack, Esq.; Christopher Lovinguire; Colonel John Shields; Charles Campbell, Esq.; and James Brison, be a standing committee of correspondence for the aforesaid purpose.

Resolved, that the aforesaid committee, with the chairman, be requested to receive and take charge of the proceedings of this meeting. John Moore, Chairman.

1. *Pittsburgh Gazette*, 9 August. The account of the meeting was reprinted in the *Carlisle Gazette*, 20 August; *Pennsylvania Mercury*, 23 August; Baltimore *Maryland Gazette*, 2 September; and Fredericksburg *Virginia Herald*, 4 September. For the report of the committee appointed, see Amendments Proposed by Westmoreland County Committee, *Pittsburgh Gazette*, 20 September, printed below.

George Clymer to Samuel Meredith, Philadelphia, 14 August (excerpt)[1]

My purpose is little else than to thank you for the letters you have wrote and for those I know you will yet write while you stay at New York. This anticipation will save both of us some future trouble of writing and reading.

At a yellow whig convention the other day in Dauphin [County][2] on the question to resist or submit [to the new Constitution], it was carried to submit in order the better to oppose, thinking that as the family compact could not be prevented from taking place it might be afterwards more effectually broke up by getting into the house. Pray who has the first honor of this ingenious device, [George] Clinton or [Robert] Whitehill? For this purpose the said yellow whigs are to push every means to return an assembly that will provide the proper Senators. As for the other House they are to depend on their strictly uniting in the same ticket.

1. RC, Berol Collection, NNC. Printed: Frederick R. Kirkland, ed., *Letters on the American Revolution in the Library at "Karolfred"* (Philadelphia, 1941), 91. The letter is addressed to "Dear S." Kirkland identifies the recipient as Samuel Meredith. Another excerpt from this letter is printed in Chapter II.
2. The "yellow whig convention" was probably a meeting called to prepare for the Harrisburg Convention. No other record of the meeting has been located.

James Hanna to John Vandegrift, Nathan Vansant, and Jacob Vandegrift, Newtown, 15 August[1]

The important crisis now approaching (confident I am you will think with me) demands the most serious attention of every friend of American liberty. The Constitution of the United States is now adopted by eleven states in the Union, and no doubt the other two will follow their example; for, however just the sentiments of the opposition may be, I do conceive it would be the height of madness and folly, and in fact a crime of very detrimental consequence to our country, to refuse to acquiesce in a measure received in form by so great a majority of our country; not only to ourselves individually, but to the community at large. For the worst that we can expect from a bad form of government is anarchy and confusion, with all its common train of grievances, and by an opposition in the present situation of affairs, we are sure of it. On the other hand, by a sullen and inactive conduct, it will give the promoters and warm advocates of the plan an opportunity (if any such design they have) to shackle us with those manacles that we fear may be formed under color of law, and we be led to know it is constitutional, when it is too late to extricate ourselves and posterity from a lasting bondage.

To you it is not worth while to animadvert on the plain and pointed tendency the Constitution has to this effect, and how easily it may be accomplished in power under its influence. That virtue is not the standard which has principally animated the adoption of the Constitution in this state I believe is too true. Let us, therefore, as we wish to serve our country, and show the world that those only who wished amendments were truly Federal, adopt the conduct of our fellow citizens in the back counties. Let us, as freemen, call a meeting of those citizens who wish for amendments, in a committee of the county, delegated from each township, for the purpose expressed in a copy of the (circular) inclosed.[2] In promoting a scheme of this kind, I hope we shall not only have the satisfaction of seeing the minds and exertions of all who wish for amendments center in this object, which will swallow others more injurious, but that we will enjoy the supreme felicity of having assisted in snatching from slavery a once happy and worthy people.

I therefore hope you will undertake to call together your township, have delegates chosen to represent them in a committee to be held at the house of George Piper, on Monday the 21st inst. at nine o'clock in the forenoon, for the purpose of appointing delegates to represent them in the state conference, and for giving them instructions, etc.

If you should apprehend the people will not call a town meeting for the purpose, that you will, as we intend here, write or call on a few of the most respectable people of your township, to attend at the general meeting, as they intend to do at Philadelphia, if they cannot accomplish their purpose in the other way.

Your usual public spirit on occasions of this kind, I am sure, needs no spur. We shall, therefore, rest assured that we will meet a representation of the township *committed to your charge* on the day appointed.

1. *Pennsylvania Gazette,* 10 September. Newtown was the county seat of Bucks County. The letter was addressed to the three men at Bensalem, a township in the extreme southern corner of Bucks County. None of the three men attended the county meeting (see Proceedings of Bucks County Meeting, 25 August, printed below).
2. Presumably the Cumberland County Circular Letter of 3 July, printed above.

To Francis Hopkinson, 17 August[1]

An alarm!

I have a sincere love for my country and therefore cannot be silent and torpid when I see danger approaching. There is an old adage, i.e. a spoonful of water will put out a fire at the beginning which if suffered to increase into a flame an ocean may prove inadequate to extinguish its raging violence. But I will come to the point without further procrastination. Last Friday morn [15 August] I stopped with a friend at the public school near Germantown when Colonel Dunning the master informed us that Mr. Ashurst had prevailed on him the evening before to go to a public meeting at Nises's Tavern and that they happened to be the first in the room, soon after which Dr. [Henry Fraly?], Colonel [Engle?], and two others entered the apartment, when one of them took a writing out of his pocket and handed it to Mr. Ashurst to read which he attempted, but the writing being bad and much interlined he found it too difficult and therefore handed it to Colonel Dunning who read it aloud to the company; but ere he had perused it a second time with hope of fully developing its real intentions (the which the company appeared ignorant of) Mr. Blare McClanegan seated himself opposite and instantly declared his disapprobation of any persons being in that private meeting (as he called it) except those of their own society. This caused Dunning to lay down the paper which was instantly pocketed by McClanegan and an altercation succeeded. Dunning contended that no meetings of a public nature ought to be under the rose and that he evidently saw from the tenor of what he has read there was evil at the root. This Circular Letter was wrote from Cumberland County[2] where patriotic meetings (as they term em) are established in all the towns and to meet in Harrisburg the 3 day of September as well for *wrath* as conscience sake to consider of amendments to the proposed government previous to its organization. Similar letters it seems are forwarded to all states to ascertain the numbers and strength of the Antifederalists and if found sufficient to make effectual opposition, then to stand forth boldly in the cause. There are, I'm informed, very alarming expressions in the waiting. Blood and slaughter seem unavoidable unless speedily counteracted by sufficient authority. We have in Pennsylvania a wise Council and President and their wisdom will direct them to pursue the proper measures. Perhaps they may see the necessity of issuing a proclamation suitable to the occasion without loss of time, stating the iniquity of these proceedings, the danger of perservering and the humiliating fate of the ring[leader?] Shay in his vain opposition to the government of Massachusetts and the necessity of sending a sufficient body of militia instantly to remove the sinews of war from Carlisle [and] Philadelphia as likewise to take effectual measures to secure the insurgents their papers at their meeting on Thursday evening at the same tavern.[3]

At the instance of Mr. Ashurst a letter was wrote to General [Thomas] Mifflin on the above [———] subject, signed by him, who declares himself ready to give every particular, when [———] upon by proper authority; but the General being in New York the hope of [———] secretary was lost thro his means. However it may yet be revived thro [your?] means as the happiness of America is near your heart. Should the matter be conducted with due secrecy and prudence in those appointed to go to the tavern, great discoveries may be made. Mr. Ashurst was the next day informed by [some?] in the secret that Dr. Fraley was selected to go over Schuylkill to sound people. Mr. McClanegan to the Northern Liberties of the city and others to [various?] parts of the country for the like purpose; there appears to be a firm plan to defeat the government if they possibly can and without speedy spirited [———], perhaps a civil war will be unavoidable, the horrors of which none [———] imagine but those who have unhappily experienced its dreadful conseque[nces] which may God in his infinite goodness preserve us from.

1. RC, Franklin Papers, PP. Hopkinson, a Federalist publicist, was a lawyer, a musician, and a poet. In 1788 he was judge of the Pennsylvania Admiralty Court.

2. See the Cumberland County Circular Letter, 3 July, printed above.

3. Presumably, Hopkinson sent this letter to Franklin, president of the Supreme Executive Council. No proclamation was issued, and no militia force was sent against the "insurgents" at Germantown.

Certificate of Election for Fayette County Delegates to the Harrisburg Convention, 18 August [1]

We whose names are hereunto subscribed, at a conference held at Union Town for the County of Fayette, being appointed a committee, do certify that the Honorable John Smilie and Mr. Albert Galattin were chosen by the people then convened, to represent them in a general conference of the state to be held at Harrisburg the third day of September, in order to conclude upon such amendments and such mode of obtaining them as the conference in their wisdom may judge proper: Given under our hands at Union Town August the eighteenth Anno Domini 1788.

[Signed:] Nathanial Breading, James Finley, Daniel Cannon, Zadok Springer, Joseph Torrence

1. DS, Gallatin Papers, NHi.

Thomas FitzSimons to Samuel Meredith, Philadelphia, 20 August (excerpt)[1]

There are moments in public as well as private affairs which, if not improved, are never to be recovered. I fear you are losing that time and giving an opportunity to artful and industrious enemies to counteract all that has been done. You know the indefatigable perseverance of a party in this state and how deficient their opponents are in these necessary qualities. They are at this moment using every means in their power. The principle one will be to delay any measure that relates to the general government till the meeting of the new Assembly, in which they hope to have more influence than in the present.[2] Whether that will be the case or not, it is not easy to determine, but it would at least be safer to take advantage of the present which I suppose may be done if your ordinance comes out.[3] It must occur to you that the representation of this state in the new Congress will in a great measure depend upon the plan that may be adopted for choosing them. A good mode might now, I believe, be obtained, which in another Assembly would not be practicable. This perhaps may exist more in my fears than in reality, but I see such a supineness in many that I confess I have my fears.

There is one circumstance which gives weight to my opinion: that is the number of people concerned in public securities and who will make their interest in that respect the Pole Star of their direction. At present they receive interest from the state, which tho depreciated is important.[4] This interest arises from impost and excise both of which they foresee will immediately fall into the hands of the new government and as it will not be possible for them to make any arrangement immediately of the domestic debt, of course a suspension must take place. Some men's fears go further and suggest the possibility of a composition in that debt, and from hence numbers advocating the alteration of that part [of the Constitution] that respects direct taxation. They say: make requisition, and if not complied with, then let Congress have the power. In case of requisition they would levy the tax and set off the interest paid on Continental certificates.

There are so many people interested in this arrangement that you may depend upon it, the friends of the new government will divide upon it, and those so circumstanced will endeavor to push in men that will promote their views. You know moreover that the Constitutionalist Party in Pennsylvania foresee their annihilation if they cannot get into the general legislature [i.e., Congress] where they may combine with men of like views from the other states. I am persuaded the more time they have, the more formidable they will appear and that nothing can happen so injurious to the common cause as the delay of Congress.

1. RC, John Read, Jr., Papers, PPL. Another excerpt from this letter is printed in Chapter II, where the writer and recipient are identified.

2. The Pennsylvania Assembly elected in October 1787 was predominantly Republican. FitzSimons, like other Federalists, feared that the Constitutionalists would win control in the state elections in October 1788.

3. See Chapter II for the Election Ordinance which Congress adopted on 13 September.

4. Between 1785 and 1787, Pennsylvania assumed the national debt held by its citizens. The plan was vigorously opposed by such Pennsylvania leaders as Robert Morris, because it included the issuance of £150,000 in state bills of credit, and because they believed that state assumption of the national debt would be a serious blow to their efforts to strengthen the central government. For a discussion of Pennsylvania funding, and its relation to state political factions and the movement for a new national constitution, see Ferguson, *Power of the Purse*, Chapter XI, and Brunhouse, *Counter-Revolution*, Chapter VI.

Pennsylvania Gazette, 20 August

Circular letters, it is confidently asserted, have been sent to most of the counties and many townships from Cumberland to request persons to meet at Harrisburg in September, for the purpose of procuring certain alterations in the federal government.[1] Though we cannot think any citizen in the smallest degree censurable for pursuing measures which he may think necessary or proper, yet the secrecy of this measure, and the omission of such circular letters to the townships in our vicinity and to Philadelphia has a very improper appearance.[2] There is *a fear of open discussion*, and *a depth of maneuvering*, which we hope will have *a serious effect* upon the minds of the good people of Pennsylvania. It is evidently calculated to affect the ensuing election. Let the friends of just government and of the peace and happiness of Pennsylvania *not sleep upon the watch*.

1. See the Cumberland County Circular Letter of 3 July, printed above.

2. John Nicholson received the Circular Letter on 20 August (Blyth to Nicholson, 3 July, printed above).

Robert Galbraith et al. to President Benjamin Franklin, Huntingdon, 23 August [1]

With the utmost regret we find ourselves once more under the disagreeable necessity of informing Your Excellency that our part of the state is still torn and distracted by the machinations of wicked and evil disposed persons. A few days after our last letter to your honorable board from Messrs. Smith and Henderson,[2] a party armed with bludgeons, about twenty in number, headed by Abraham Smith, William M'Cune and Samuel Clinton, the latter of them a most notorious rioter, came into the town and violently beat Mr. Alexander Irwin, one of our citizens. Some of the same riotous party, whose names and persons we have not been able properly to ascertain, have frequently, at night, assaulted our houses with showers of stones. Threats have been sent from all parts of the county that death—or what is to a man of feeling worse—cropping, tarring, etc., should be inflicted on us or any other officer of the county who should attempt to put the laws in force. On Wednesday last [20 August] about one hundred and eighty men collected from different parts of the county—some few of the townsmen among them—paraded the streets, not with muskets, as before, altho we have reason to believe they had a number secreted. They were headed by William M'Elroy, Abraham Smith, John Smith and John Little, Esq., one of the county justices. What their intentions were we know not, but hearing from many different quarters that they were determined to destroy some of us, we collected a few friends of government and some arms and met at the house of Benjamin Elliot, Esq., our sheriff, resolved, if any attack was made, to repel force with force, and to the utmost defend our own lives. This salutary precaution, of which we are satisfied, their spies had given them information, was without doubt, the reason of their not committing any violence that day. After marching with colors flying and fifes playing thro the town, they held, what they called an election, at the house of William Kerr, for members to meet in convention at Louisburg [Harrisburg], as we have been informed. At this election they excluded from voting everyone who did not march with them, and admitted promiscuously everyone who did. A number of insults were thrown out against the government, but no personal injury done.

To your honorable board, as the supreme executive power of the state, we apply for such assistance in support of government, as to your wisdoms shall deem proper.

1. *Pa. Archives,* 1 ser., XI, 379-380. The letter was signed by Robert Galbraith, Thomas Duncan Smith, Andrew Henderson, and Benjamin Elliot.

2. Thomas Duncan Smith and Andrew Henderson to President Benjamin Franklin, Huntingdon, 5 June, *Pa. Archives,* 1 ser., XI, 305-7.

Proceedings of a Bucks County Meeting, 25 August[1]

The ratification of the Federal Constitution and its expected operation forming a new era in the American world, and giving cause of hope to some and fear to others; it has been thought proper that the freemen of the state, or delegates chosen by them, should meet together and deliberate on the subject. Accordingly it has been proposed that a meeting of deputies from the different counties be held at Harrisburg the third day of September next. A Circular Letter, bearing the above proposition was sent to this county,[2] and in pursuance thereof there met this day at Piper's Tavern, in Bedminster Township, the following gentlemen from the townships annexed to their names respectively:

Newtown: James Hanna, Esquire.

Warwick: John Crawford, Hugh Ramsey, Captain William Walker, Benjamin Snodgrass, Samuel Flack.

New Britain: James Snodgrass, Thomas Stewart, David Thomas.

Bedminster: Jacob Utt, Alexander Hughes, George Piper, Daniel Soliday.

Haycock: Captain Manus Yost, John Keller.

Rockbill: Samuel Smith, Esquire.

Millford: Henry Blilaz, Henry Hoover.

Springfield: Colonel John Smith, Charles Fleming.

Durham: Richard Backhouse, Esquire.

Tinicum: John Thompson, Jacob Weaver, George Bennet.

Nockamixon: Samuel Wilson, George Vogle.

Richland: Benjamin Seagle.

Plumstead: Thomas Wright, Thomas Gibson, James Ruckman, Major John Shaw, James Farres, Thomas Henry, Moses Kelly, Henry Geddis.

Warrington: Reverend Nathaniel Erwin, Captain William Walker.

Buckingham: Captain Samuel Smith.

Solesbury: Henry Seabring.

Hilltown: Joseph Grier.

Samuel Smith, Esquire, chosen chairman, and James Hanna, Esquire, secretary. After some time spent in discussing the business of the meeting, Resolved, that the Reverend Nathaniel Erwin, Richard Backhouse, Samuel Smith, John Crawford, and James Hanna, esquires, be a committee to draw up resolves expressive of the sense of this meeting on the subject before them.

In a short time thereafter the following were presented by the gentlemen appointed, and unanimously approved.

Resolved I. That it is the opinion of this meeting that the plan of government for the United States, formed by the General Convention, having been adopted by eleven of the states, ought, in conformity to the resolves of said Convention, to come into operation, and have force until altered in a constitutional way.

2. That as we mean to act the part of peaceable citizens ourselves, so we will support the said plan of government and those who act under it against all illegal violence.

3. That the said plan of government will admit of very considerable amendments, which ought to be made in the mode pointed out in the Constitution itself.

4. That as few governments once established have ever been altered in favor of liberty without confusion and bloodshed, the requisite amendments in said Constitution ought to be attempted as soon as possible.

5. That we will use our utmost endeavors in a pacific way to procure such alterations in the Federal Constitution as may be necessary to secure the rights and liberties of ourselves and posterity.

6. That we approve of a state meeting being held at Harrisburg the third day of September next, on the subject of the above resolves.

7. That four persons ought to be delegated from this county to attend said meeting, and join with the deputies from other counties who may meet with them (in a recommendation to the citizens of this state) of a suitable set of men to represent them in the new Congress, and generally to acquiesce and assist in the promotion of such plan or plans as may be designed by the said state conferees for the purpose of obtaining the necessary amendments of said Constitution, as far as is consistent with our views, expressed in the foregoing resolves.

Agreeably to the resolve last past the Reverend Nathaniel Erwin, Richard Backhouse, John Crawford, and James Hanna, esquires, or any two of them, were appointed to represent us in said conference to be held at Harrisburg.

Resolved, that James Hanna, Esquire be requested to hand the foregoing proceedings to the press for publication.[3]

Samuel Smith, Chairman.

1. *Pennsylvania Packet*, 2 September.
2. Presumably the Cumberland County Circular Letter of 3 July, printed above.
3. In addition to four other Philadelphia newspapers, the report was printed in the *Carlisle Gazette*, 17 September; Charleston *City Gazette*, 17 September; *Boston Gazette*, 22 September; and Portland, Me., *Cumberland Gazette*, 2 October.

Thomas McKean to Robert Magaw, Philadelphia, 28 August (excerpt)[1]

It is reported here, that there is to be a convention at Louisburg[Harrisburg] on the 3d. of next month relating to the new Constitution. The motives for this I have not learnt. I have some apprehensions, that such meetings may prove injurious to good order, and therefore wish that they may not be drawn into practice, nor ever had but upon great and necessary occasions. Persons thus assembled are too apt to work themselves up to an opinion that they are a public legal body, instead of so many individuals collected together; and sometimes assume and exercise actual authority, which must always have a tendency to weaken if not disturb the regular government. May their zeal be tempered with prudence.

1. RC, James Hamilton Collection, PHi. McKean was chief justice of the Pennsylvania Supreme Court and had been a member of the Pennsylvania Convention, which ratified the Constitution. Magaw, a lawyer and an officer in the War for Independence, was a resident of Carlisle.

Extract of a Letter from Carlisle, Pennsylvania, 28 August[1]

Our *friends* the *Antifederals* are not yet quiet; a large body of them from the east and west side of the Susquehanna are to assemble next Tuesday at Harrisburg, by private appointment, secretly communicated. Mr. [William] Finley, of Washington County, has just passed through this town, on his way thither, to confer, it is supposed, with Mr. [Robert] Whitehill, who lives near that place. The object of this meeting, it is universally believed, is to devise and adopt, in concert with the Anties throughout the continent, some plan for subverting the federal government. May their clandestine designs be disappointed!

1. Baltimore *Maryland Journal*, 2 September.

William Shippen, Jr., to Thomas Lee Shippen, Philadelphia, 2 September (excerpt)[1]

Congress have been disputing very foolishly where the new Congress shall meet above 5 weeks. The contest is between this city and New York but neither can obtain seven states and the matter remains still *sub judice*. I think Philadelphia must finally be the place. There is a great convention now sitting at Harrisburg on the Susquehanna, composed of Antifederalists from every county. Blair McClenachan is gone from Philadelphia County and George Bryan and Charles Pettit from the city. Their business is to agree upon and recommend such alterations as they may think necessary and there is so respectable a minority in every state that I think one of the first acts of the new government will be to propose a general convention of the people to make these necessary alterations, till when the minds of a great part of the United States will not be easy. To effect this measure I am apt to think at our next election the Constitutionalists will prevail. General [Thomas] Miflin is to be our next president. Our Assembly met this morning and [Thomas] Lloyd takes down their debates in shorthand. I will preserve them for you.

. . . .

Tis proposed that the new government shall meet next March. Tis said Washington will be President, [John] Hancock Vice President. Jno. Adams, Jno. Rutledge, [John] Jay, [James] Wilson and [George] Wythe are all talked of for Chief Justice. I should imagine he will be chosen out of the Middle States.

1. RC, Shippen Family Papers, DLC. Shippen's letters to his son, who was travelling in Europe, were usually written over a period of time. The above excerpt is from a letter written between 21 August and 21 September. The excerpt is dated 2 September because Shippen writes that the Assembly met that morning. The Pennsylvania Assembly met for its fall session on 2 September.

Shippen, a Philadelphia physician, was the son of Dr. William Shippen, Sr., and was married to a sister of Richard Henry Lee and Arthur Lee of Virginia.

Proceedings of the Harrisburg Convention, 3-6 September

Delegates representing thirteen counties and the city of Philadelphia met at Harrisburg on 3 September. The report of the convention, published in Philadelphia on 15 September, gives only an outline of the proceedings. Fragmentary notes in the Albert Gallatin Papers, including a set of draft resolutions and a manuscript copy of the final report, offer some additional insight.

There was evidently considerable difference among the delegates as to policies to be pursued. One group wanted to create an interstate organization of Antifederalists and hold an Antifederalist convention (Albert Gallatin, Draft Resolutions; William Petrikin to John Nicholson, 23 March), but the convention obviously did not agree. Three years later Charles Pettit informed George Washington that he had attended the convention in order to exercise a moderating influence and claimed credit for being "instrumental in restoring harmony in the state" (Philadelphia, 19 March 1791, RC, RG 59: Department of State, Miscellaneous Letters, DNA).

The Cumberland County Circular Letter of 3 July calling the convention suggested that, in addition to proposing amendments to the Constitution, the convention should also nominate eight candidates for the House of Representatives. Although the published proceedings do not mention candidates, there is some indication that a slate was at least discussed, if not agreed upon.

Thomas Hartley, in forwarding a copy of the proceedings to Tench Coxe in Philadelphia (9 September) added: "I dare say they have fixed upon tickets etc." Coxe and other Federalists were convinced that the purpose of the convention was to "influence the elections for state and federal representatives" (Coxe to James Madison, 10 September) and that it was "an election job" (Samuel Miles et al. to Timothy Pickering, 11 September, and Richard Peters to George Washington, 17 September). In New York the French Consul General reported to his government that the Antifederalists had met at Harrisburg under "some specious pretenses" and had "secretly" agreed upon a list of candidates (Antoine R. C. M. de la Forest to Comte de la Luzerne, 14 September, printed, Chapter II).

In mid-October Dr. William Shippen, Jr., in Philadelphia reported that a ticket had been agreed upon at Harrisburg and listed six of the eight names that were first published in a newspaper in early November, a list commonly known as the "Harrisburg" or "Amendments" ticket (to Thomas Lee Shippen, 10-15 October; The Harrisburg Ticket, *Federal Gazette*, 7 November). Long after the election, one delegate declared that the members of the convention did more harm than all their enemies because they had spent all their time canvassing for places in Congress instead of taking decisive action (William Petrikin to John Nicholson, 23 March 1789). "Civis" praised the convention for its moderation (*Pennsylvania Packet*, 19 September), but his was a lone voice. The convention created widespread alarm among Federalists. The convention was denounced for the "clandestine manner" in which it had been called (Extract of a Letter from Carlisle, Pennsylvania, 28 August) and James Madison in Congress expressed his alarm to George Washington (24 August, 14 September, printed, Chapter II).

The convention's demand for amendments to the Constitution was attacked even before the report was published (see, for example, the *Pennsylvania Gazette*, 10 September; *Pennsylvania Mercury*, 13 September; and *Pittsburgh Gazette*, 20 September). The attack continued until the federal election on 26 November and even afterwards (see the Appointment of Delegates to the Lancaster Conference, Philadelphia County, 10 October; *Federal Gazette*, 7, 19 November; and *Pennsylvania Mercury*, 25 November).

The above-cited documents and additional documents printed in this chapter testify to the activity of the Pennsylvania Antifederalists and the alarm created by that activity among their political opponents.

Albert Gallatin, Draft Resolutions[1]

We etc. To expect that [we] are united in opinion that a federal government is the only one that can preserve the liberties and secure the happiness of the inhabitants of such an extensive empire as the United States and experience having taught us that the ties of our Union under the Articles of Confederation were so weak as to deprive us of some of the greatest advantages we had a right to expect from such a government—therefore are fully convinced that a more efficent *government* /one/[2] is absolutely necessary. But at the same time we must declare that altho the Constitution proposed for the United States is likely to obviate most of the inconveniencies we labored under, yet several parts of it appear so exceptionable to us that nothing but the fullest confidence of obtaining a revision of them by a general convention and our reluctance to enter into any *dangerous* /violent/ measures could prevail on us to acquiesce in its organization in this state. We are sensible that a large number of the citizens, both in this and other states, who gave their assent to its being carried in execution previous to any amendments, were actuated more by the fear of the dangers that might arise from any delays than by a conviction of its being perfect. We, therefore, *are convinced* /hope/ they *now* will concur with us in pursuing every peaceable method of obtaining a speedy revision of the Constitution in the mode pointed out by the same and when we reflect on the present situation of the Union we can entertain no doubt that motives of conciliation and the dictates of policy and prudence will conspire to induce every man of true federal principles to give his support to a measure not only calculated to recommend the new Constitution to the approbation and support of a numerous class of American citizens but even necessary to prevent the total defection of some members of the Union. Strongly impressed with those sentiments we have resolved as follows viz.,

1st. Resolved, that in order to prevent a dismemberment of the Union and to secure our liberties and those of our posterity it is necessary that a ~~speedy~~ revision of the Federal Constitution be obtained as soon as possible.

2d. That as few governments once established have ever altered in favor of liberty without confusion and bloodshed, an early attention ought to be given to the business and that the safest manner to obtain such a revision will be in conformity to the request of the state of New York to use our endeavors to have a federal convention called as soon as possible.

Resolved, therefore that a petition be presented to the Assembly of this state requesting them to take the earliest opportunity to make an application for that purpose to the new Congress.

3d. That in order that the friends to amendments of the Federal Constitution, who are inhabitants of this state, may act in concert it is necessary and it is hereby recommended to the several counties in the state to appoint committees who may correspond one with the other and with such similar committees as may be formed in other states.

4th. That the friends to amendments to the Federal Constitution in the several states be invited to meet in a general conference to be held at ——— on ——— and that ——— members be elected by this conference, who or any ——— of them shall meet at said place and time in order to devise in concert with such other delegates from the several states, as may come under similar appointments, on such amendments to the Federal Constitution as to them may seem most necessary and on the most likely way to carry them into effect.

1. Gallatin Papers, NHi. There are several other documents in Gallatin's handwriting in the Gallatin Papers pertaining to the Harrisburg Convention and the movement for a second constitutional convention in 1788: two sheets of paper (one mutilated) with proposed constitutional amendments; a two-page fragment containing Antifederalist arguments that were apparently written before the Harrisburg Convention; and a manuscript copy of the proceedings of the Harrisburg Convention.

2. A few words are written above the line. We have placed them between slant lines after the word they were apparently intended to replace but which Gallatin did not cross out.

Report of the Proceedings[1]

Agreeably to a Circular Letter which originated in the county of Cumberland, inviting to a conference such of the citizens of this state, who conceive that a revision of the federal system, lately proposed for the general government of the United States, is necessary, a number of gentlemen from the city of Philadelphia and counties of Philadelphia, Bucks, Chester, Lancaster, Cumberland, Berks, Northumberland, Bedford, Fayette, Washington, Franklin, Dauphin, and Huntingdon,[2] assembled at this place for the said purpose, viz., Hon. George Bryan, Charles Pettit, Blair M'Clenachan, Richard Backhouse, James Hanna, Joseph Gardner, James Mercer, Benjamin Blyth, Robert Whitehill, John Jordan, William Sterrit, William Rodgers, William Petriken, Jonathan Hoge, John Bishop, Daniel Montgomery, John Lytle, John Dickey, Hon. John Smiley, Albert Gallatin, James Marshall, Benjamin Elliot, Richard Baird, James Crooks, Adam Orth, John Rodgers, Thomas Murray, Robert M'Kee, John Kean, John A. Hanna, Daniel Bradly, Robert Smith, James Anderson.

Blair M'Clenachan, Esquire, was unanimously elected chairman, and John A. Hanna, Esquire, secretary.

After free discussion and mature deliberation had upon the subject before them, the following resolutions and propositions were adopted.

The ratification of the Federal Constitution having formed a new era in the American world highly interesting to all the citizens of the United States, it is no less the duty than the privilege of every citizen to examine with attention the principles and probable effects of a system, on which the happiness or misery of the present as well as future generations so much depend. In the course of such examination many of the good citizens of the state of Pennsylvania have found their apprehensions excited, that the Constitution, in its present form, contains in it some principles which may be perverted to purposes injurious to the rights of free citizens, and some ambiguities which may probably lead to contentions incompatible with order and good government. In order to remedy these inconveniencies and to avert the apprehended dangers, it has been thought expedient that delegates, chosen by those who wish for early amendments in the said Constitution should meet together for the purpose of deliberating on the subject, and uniting in some constitutional plan for obtaining the amendments which they may deem necessary.

We the conferees, assembled for the purpose aforesaid, agree in opinion,

That a federal government only can preserve the liberties and secure the happiness of the inhabitants of a country so extensive as these United States; and experience having taught us that the ties of our Union, under the Articles of Confederation, were so weak as to deprive us of some of the greatest advantages we had a right to expect from it. We are fully convinced that a more efficient government is indispensably necessary; but although the Constitution proposed for the United States is likely to obviate most of the inconveniencies we labored under, yet several parts of it appear so exceptionable to us that we are clearly of opinion considerable amendments are essentially necessary. In full confidence, however, of obtaining a revision of such exceptionable parts, by a general convention, and from a desire to harmonize with our fellow citizens, we are induced to acquiesce in the organization of the said Constitution.

We are sensible that a large number of the citizens, both in this and the other states, who gave their assent to its being carried into execution, previous to any amendments, were actuated more by the fear of the dangers that might arise from delays than by a conviction of its being perfect; we therefore hope they will concur with us in pursuing every peaceable method of obtaining a speedy revision of the Constitution in the mode therein provided; and when we reflect on the present circumstances of the Union, we can entertain no doubt that motives of conciliation and the dictates of policy and prudence will conspire to induce every man of true federal principles to give his support to a measure, which is not only calculated to recommend the new Constitution to the approbation and support of every class of citizens, but even necessary to prevent the total defection of some of the members of the Union.

Strongly impressed with these sentiments, we have agreed to the following resolutions:

I. Resolved, that it be recommended to the people of this state to acquiesce in the organization of the said government; but although we thus accord in its organization, we by no means lose sight of the grand object of obtaining very considerable amendments and alterations, which we consider essential to preserve the peace and harmony of the Union and those invaluable privileges for which so much blood and treasure have been recently expended.

II. Resolved, that it is necessary to obtain a speedy revision of said Constitution by a general convention.

III. Resolved, that in order to effect this desirable end, a petition be presented to the legislature of this state, requesting that honorable body to take the earliest opportunity to make application for that purpose to the new Congress.[3]

The petition proposed is as follows:

To the Honorable Representatives of the Freemen of the Commonwealth of Pennsylvania, in General Assembly met.

The petition and representation of the subscribers humbly show,

That your petitioners possess sentiments completely federal, being convinced that a confederacy of republican states, and no other, can secure political liberty, happiness, and safety throughout a territory so extended as the United States of America. They are well apprised of the necessity of devolving extensive powers to Congress, and of vesting the supreme legislature with every power and resource of a general nature; and consequently they acquiesce in the general system of government framed by the late Federal Convention; in full confidence, however, that the same will be revised without delay: for however worthy of approbation the general principles and outlines of the said system may be, your petitioners conceive that amendments in some parts of the plan are essential, not only to the preservation of such rights and privileges as ought to be reserved in the respective states, and in the citizens thereof, but to the fair and unembarrassed operation of the government in its various departments. And as provision is made in the Constitution itself for the making of such amendments as may be deemed necessary; and your petitioners are desirous of obtaining the amendments which occur to them as more immediately desirable and necessary, in the mode admitted by such provision,

They pray that your honorable House, as the representatives of the people in this commonwealth, will, in the course of your present session, take such measures as you in your wisdom shall deem most effectual and proper to obtain a revision and amendment of the Constitution of the United States, in such parts and in such manner as have been or shall be pointed out by the conventions or assemblies of the respective states; and that such revision be by a general convention of representatives from the several states in the Union.

Your petitioners consider the amendments pointed out in the propositions hereto subjoined as essentially necessary, and as such they suggest them to your notice, submitting to your wisdom the order in which they shall be presented to the consideration of the United States.

The amendments proposed are as follow, viz.,

I. That Congress shall not exercise any powers whatsoever, but such as are expressly given to that body by the Constitution of the United States: nor shall any authority, power or jurisdiction be assumed or exercised by the executive or judiciary departments of the Union under color or pretense of construction or fiction: But all the rights of sovereignty which are not by the said Constitution expressly and plainly vested in the Congress shall be deemed to remain with, and shall be exercised by the several states in the Union according to their respective constitutions: And that every reserve of the rights of individuals made by the several constitutions of the states in Union to the citizens and inhabitants of each state respectively, shall remain inviolate, except so far as they are expressly and manifestly yielded or narrowed by the national Constitution.

II. That the number of Representatives be for the present, one for every twenty thousand inhabitants according to the present estimated numbers in the several states, and continue in that proportion till the whole number of Representatives shall amount to two hundred; and then to be so proportioned and modified as not to exceed that number till the proportion of one Representative for every thirty thousand inhabitants shall amount to the said number of two hundred. (Article I, Section 2, Paragraph 3.)

III. That Senators, tho chosen for six years, shall be liable to be recalled, or superseded by other appointments, by the respective legislatures of the states at any time. (Section 3.)

IV. That Congress shall not have power, to make or alter regulations concerning the time, place and manner of electing Senators and Representatives except in case of neglect or refusal by the state, to make regulations for the purpose: and then only for such time as such neglect or refusal shall continue. (Section 4.)

V. That when Congress shall require supplies which are to be raised by direct taxes, they shall demand from the several states their respective quotas thereof, giving a reasonable time to each state to procure and pay the same; and if any state shall refuse, neglect or omit to raise and pay the same within such limited time, then Congress shall have power to assess, levy and collect the quota of such state, together with interest for the same from the time of such delinquency, upon the inhabitants and estates therein, in such manner as they shall by law direct, provided that no poll tax be imposed. (Section 8.)

VI. That no standing army of regular troops shall be raised or kept up in time of peace, without the consent of two-thirds of both houses in Congress. (Section 8.)

VII. That the clause respecting the exclusive legislation over a district not exceeding ten miles square, be qualified by a proviso that such right of legislation extend only to such regulations as respect the police and good order thereof. (Section 8.)

VIII. That each state respectively shall have power to provide for organizing, arming and disciplining the militia thereof, whensoever Congress shall omit or neglect to provide for the same. That the militia shall not be subject to martial law, but when in actual service in time of war, invasion or rebellion: and when not in the actual service of the United States, shall be subject to such fines, penalties, and punishments only, as shall be directed or inflicted by the laws of its own state: nor shall the militia of any state be continued in actual service longer than two months under any call of Congress, without the consent of the legislature of such state, or, in their recess, the executive thereof. (Article I, Section 8.)

IX. That the clause respecting vessels bound to or from any one of the states be explained. (Section 9.)

X. That Congress establish no courts other than the Supreme Court except such as shall be necessary, for determining causes of admiralty jurisdiction. (Article 3, Section 1.)

XI. That a proviso be added at the end of the second clause of the second section of the third article to the following effect, viz. Provided that such appellate jurisdiction, in all cases of common law cognizance, be by writ of error, and confined to matters of law only, and that no such writ of error shall be admitted except in revenue cases, unless the matter in controversy exceed the value of three thousand dollars. (Section 2, Paragraph 2.)

XII. That to article 6, clause 2, be added the following proviso, viz. Provided always, that no treaty which shall hereafter be made, shall be deemed or construed to alter or effect any law of the United States, or of any particular state, until such treaty shall have been laid before, and assented to by the House of Representatives in Congress. (Article 6, Paragraph 2.)

Resolved, that the foregoing proceedings be committed to the chairman for publication.

Blair M'Clenachan, Chairman

Attest: John A. Hanna, Secretary

1. *Pennsylvania Packet,* 15 September. A manuscript version of the proceedings, in Albert Gallatin's handwriting, is in the Gallatin Papers, NHi. Henry Adams suggested that Gallatin was probably given the task of drafting the convention's final report and the petition and proposed amendments (*The Life of Albert Gallatin* [Philadelphia, 1879], 77).

The Federalists had a "trusty friend" at Harrisburg, but who he was or whether he was a member of the convention is unknown. Thomas Hartley at York sent the "transcript" he had received to Tench Coxe in Philadelphia (Hartley to Coxe, 9 September, printed below).

The proceedings were reprinted at least twenty-nine times in Pennsylvania newspapers and newspapers throughout the United States (see, for example, the New York *Independent Journal* and New York *Daily Advertiser,* 17 September; Baltimore *Maryland Journal,* 23 and 26 September; Richmond *Virginia Independent Chronicle,* 24 September; Boston *Massachusetts Gazette,* 26 September; Providence *United States Chronicle,* 2 October; and Edenton *State Gazette of North Carolina,* 13 October).

2. The counties not sending delegates were Northampton, Montgomery, York, Westmoreland, and Luzerne.

3. No evidence has been found to indicate that the petition was delivered to the Pennsylvania legislature.

Pennsylvania Gazette, 3 September

We hear that the principal design of the proposed Antifederal conference at Harrisburg is to oppose direct taxation by the new government, and thereby to preserve the present funding system of Pennsylvania.[1]

A correspondent has furnished us with the following curious paragraph, extracted from a letter which was forwarded to three gentlemen in a respectable township, by a very active promoter of *the Antifederal conclave* intended to meet this day (3d September) at Harrisburg:

"If you should *apprehend* the people *will not* call a town meeting for the purpose, that you will, *as we intend here*, write or call on *a few* of the most *respectable* people of your township to attend at *this general* meeting, as they *intend* to do at Philadelphia, *if they cannot accomplish their purpose* the other way."[2]

Thus we see that these kind gentlemen, knowing *the people at large* are opposed to their scheme, intend that *"a few* respectable" *wellborn* people shall carry it on for them. Our correspondent observes further, that it appears this *"general* meeting" is to be made up of *"a few"* particular persons. The circular letter, which was enclosed in the abovementioned, plainly talks of *"a civil war,"* and proposes that the eight federal Representatives for Pennsylvania shall be put in nomination by *the conclave* of *"the respectable few"* at Harrisburg. These obliging volunteers, we presume, mean to save all the trouble of *free elections* in future; for it seems, if the people do not come into their scheme, they intend to accomplish their purpose in another way.

1. See Thomas FitzSimons to Samuel Meredith, 20 August, n. 4, printed above.
2. The excerpts quoted in the above piece are from a letter of James Hanna to John Vandegrift et al., written on 15 August and printed above under that date, although the entire letter was not published until it appeared in the *Pennsylvania Gazette* on 10 September.

Alexander Graydon to Lambert Cadwalader, Louisburg, 7 September (excerpt)[1]

We have had a meeting of the Antifederal Party in this town consisting of deputies from most of the counties in the state. They have fixed upon several amendments which they propose offering to Congress thro the medium of the Assembly. These amendments are extremely moderate indeed and by no means such as would justify the violent opposition given by these gentlemen to the Constitution. But tho the ostensible motive for meeting was to propose amendments, the real one seems to be to let themselves down as easy as possible and to come in for a share of the good things the new government may have to bestow. You will probably see their proceedings published.

1. RC, Cadwalader Papers, PHi. When Dauphin County was established in 1785, Harris's Ferry on the Susquehanna River was made the county seat. The commissions issued to county officers named the place "Louisburg," although most contemporaries called it Harrisburg, which became the official name in 1791.

Thomas Hartley to Tench Coxe, York, 9 September[1]

By a trusty friend whom we had at Harrisburg, I have a transcript of their proceedings there. The obvious intention of those men is to distract this country and embarrass the new Constitution.

Their sentiments are known to you and all of us.

They like no part of the system because it operates against their power, but for the moment they wish to appear under the plausible pretensions of amendments.

Their proceedings will probably be published early in the city, but I thought it prudent to send you a copy as early as possible to be communicated to our friends.

Besides this, I dare say they have fixed upon tickets etc.

I can add no more than that I am in great haste.

1. RC, Coxe Papers, Tench Coxe Section, PHi.

Tench Coxe to James Madison, Philadelphia, 10 September (excerpt)[1]

We have been made uneasy here by an effort of our opposition, promoted by some of their friends in the adjacent states, to influence the elections for state and federal representatives, not only in Pennsylvania but in those states also who elect about this season of the year. The paper enclosed will show you how the matter has been conducted. It is probable it may be of use to republish it, as the facts are carefully stated, and it is addressed to the Union at large. From the temper of a part of the New York opposition it may have some effect there, and indeed there has been such a run upon amendments that a little from the friends of the Constitution may not be malapropos. I mean the paper signed a Federal Centinel.[2]

Our present legislature, whose time expires on the 2d Tuesday of October will proceed to elect the Senators, if the ordinance[3] comes forward, which I presume will be the case from a hint of Mr. [Thomas] Fitzsimons hastily this morning. The next house I hope will be Federal, but the present are certainly so. Mr. [Robert] Morris will be one of our Senators, and is certainly an able man in commerce, finance, and some other very important matters. The other is uncertain. On the Federal side are several candidates; but one of them in my opinion has any pretensions to the appointment, and he has very respectable qualifications. I do not know that his election is certain as I could wish.[4]

1. RC, Madison Papers, DLC.
2. See "A Federal Centinel," *Pennsylvania Gazette*, 10 September, printed immediately below.
3. Congress passed the Election Ordinance on 13 September.
4. This is possibly a reference to George Clymer, who was among the most talked-about candidates for the Senate. See, for example, James McLene to William Irvine, 12 September, printed below. On the other hand, Coxe in a letter to Madison, 26 September, printed below, does not mention Clymer in connection with the Senate but does mention William Bingham.

A Federal Centinel, Pennsylvania Gazette, 10 September[1]

The appearance of an important movement in this state, the present meeting at the town of Harrisburg, renders a little information on the subject absolutely necessary, to prevent your being deceived and misled. The account of the proceedings of a few persons in the county of Bucks, published in our late gazettes,[2] in which a studied moderation is observed, and an appearance of acting on the public sentiments and feelings is industriously displayed, require some explanation, which will lead to further remarks on the nature and objects of the Harrisburg meeting.

The opposition to the general government in this state, finding that the minorities of the other conventions, after full and fair discussion, had determined to acquiesce in and even to support a Federal Constitution, which appeared to them necessary to preserve our Union, and which was sanctioned by *the supreme authority of the majority of a free people*, determined to assume also, at least to the other states, the appearance of moderation and acquiescence. They knew that the conduct, which the dispositions of some of their leaders prompted them to pursue, could not be acceptable to the great body of the opposition, either north or south. Their declarations therefore have been that they would support the government, till altered according to the forms provided, and such is the language of the Bucks County publication referred to above. But at the moment of these declarations, AMENDMENTS and CIVIL WAR were held forth as the alternatives, by which the friends of peace were to be alarmed, and *a large majority* of the independent freemen of Pennsylvania were to be overawed. This is no loose unfounded suggestion, no phantom of the heated brain of a jealous partyman, but is an existing fact, contained in the letters which invited the townships of Bucks County to the meeting at Harrisburg.[3] Submission to the minority, then, or the sword, is their meaning.

It is necessary that you should be informed of the manner in which this meeting has been collected, and let every friend to peace and every lover of free government mark the extraordinary proceedings. In Philadelphia, Lancaster, and York, are printed weekly twenty-three newspapers at ten presses. In not one of these was ever published a single notification to the freemen of the state, that such a measure was in contemplation, nor any call to the freemen of the neighborhood to meet for the purpose of electing persons to assemble at Harrisburg. In York and Lancaster, and many other places, the matter was discovered or suspected by the enemies to the measure, but nothing was said to *the public* by its *friends*. Some secret whispers, symptoms of the nature of the proceedings, were passed about among those in whom they thought they could confide. In the city of Philadelphia it was not known who meant to assume to represent them, till after their departure. In the county of Philadelphia, where a meeting was discovered, the tenth man of those assembled was not in favor of sending a deputation. In some of the townships of Bucks, the measure was rejected unanimously, but of this not a word is said in the proceedings; in others not more than three of four attended, and yet they undertook to appoint out of their number. So secret have the movements been in some places, that even in Dauphin County, of which Harrisburg is the seat of justice, the matter was carefully concealed, and gentlemen of the first intelligence, now holding the highest public offices *by the voice of the people*, were unacquainted with the intended meeting. But improper as these measures must appear to every genuine commonwealth's man, they have been shockingly exceeded in some parts of the state. The most respectable proofs are now in this city, of the people in several places having been informed, that the Harrisburg meeting was to be held *by order of Congress*, that they must therefore elect their deputies as to a lawful and constitutional body, and that it was expected they would be able to procure *a deduction of taxes for three years!* Such has been the abuse of the honest unsuspecting people of the remote counties.

Reflect, my countrymen, on such proceedings. Are these open *republican* measures, *seeking the face of day*, or oligarchic stratagems and wicked deceptions, calculated to cheat the electors of this state. Are these the men, who called the Convention of the United States *a conclave*, and the conventions of the people, their constitutional legislators, our Franklin and our Washington, dark conspirators. Ye virtuous patriots of *the Connecticut minority*, who first set the example of acquiescence, who, tho dissentient yourselves, first pledged your endeavors to support the measures of the majority of that body of freemen to which you belong,[4] ye genuine republicans among the minorities of the other states, who, waiving prejudice, magnanimously followed that noble example, can you approve of measures such as these, or can you hope the happiness of your country will result from such proceedings. Measures of this nature are seriously alarming. We cannot but apprehend the worst consequences to *liberty and happiness* from this violence, precipitancy, secrecy, and deception in the business of amendments. The objects before the people of America are the most important and the most arduous that ever engaged the attention of mankind. *To perfect a republican system* for each state in the Union, and *to balance on general laws the affairs of an extensive confederacy of many members*, is a work of so great difficulty, that no human genius, however profound and comprehensive, can be able by mere force of reason and reflection to effect it at once. Let us then, in such a work, beware of passion. Tis a serious task for the coolest minds, and the judgments of many must unite in the work. None must be thus excluded, or shamefully deceived. Experience and observation must guide our labors. We have already acquired great political light in the progress of the American Revolution, of which every philosopher and politician must deem this measure a principal part. Time will advance us further, and can alone bring us to perfection. The experience of inconveniencies must correct the mistakes we may have fallen into. In the course of our deliberations, let the wise and good of each opinion remember the duty and indispensable necessity of keeping their minds cool, and fit for discussions so important to liberty, and their hearts full of deference towards each other, as brothers embarked in the same cause. Let the government be got into motion. The clauses provided for considering amendments will remain. They will always be of force, and can always be recurred to. We want not irregular meetings produced by self-creation and deception, and fostered in secrecy, to procure a reconsideration of the new government. Our state legislatures, who remain and always will continue our immediate guardians, can apply for and procure them, if they shall be found proper on due consideration.

It is a matter of serious consequence to the freemen of this commonwealth, and not unimportant to the people of the Union, that all the objects of this meeting should be understood. Our state elections are fast approaching. October is the month fixed by the constitution. To affect those elections is a very principal object. Let the independent electors of Pennsylvania be upon their guard. Take care you do not choose the friends of paper tenders,[5] or of oppressive test-laws,[6] which are now no longer necessary in their former extent. Let men of sense, information and good moral characters, at least of competent property and industrious habits, be your choice. With such men you will always be safe. If the new Constitution proves injurious to your liberty, peace and property, it will be equally so to theirs, and they will apply for and ratify the alterations, or call conventions for the purpose. Be not inattentive to the importance of the present moment, for on the ensuing Assembly more will depend, than on any that has been elected since you were an independent people.

Another object, which the secret letters soliciting the Harrisburg meeting plainly express, is the election of the eight federal Representatives. They recommend a plan of concert and union. Let us not then be supine and inactive, when they are thus forward in their operations and united in their plans. A great majority of Pennsylvania is favorable to good government, and sensible that amendments to the new Constitution can always be procured. Let them therefore exert themselves to get into all offices, men whom their judgments and consciences approve. Let them beware of the plan of amendments formed and promoted by the deceitful, dangerous and insulting means abovementioned, means which disgrace those who have stooped to them, would degrade the electors of Pennsylvania from their rank as freemen, and must disgust the honest part of the opposition in all the other states.

1. The full title is "A Federal Centinel to the People of the United States, and Particularly to the Independent Electors of Pennsylvania." Tench Coxe was probably the author (see Coxe to James Madison, 10 September, printed above). Although he suggested to Madison that the essay should be reprinted, no reprinting has been located. In addition to the above essay, this issue of the *Gazette* contained two additional items attacking the Harrisburg Convention. One, signed "A Freeman," and dated Germantown, 4 September (printed below), contained the first printing of the Cumberland County Circular Letter, 3 July (printed above) and a copy of the letter from James Hanna to John Vandegrift et al., 15 August (printed above). "A Freeman" cited the letters as proof that a "secret association" had existed in Pennsylvania for some time and that "the government over the members of this association is a kind of aristocracy."

2. Proceedings of a Bucks County Meeting, 25 August, printed above.

3. Cumberland County Circular Letter, 3 July, printed above.

4. There was considerable newspaper debate concerning the attitude of the Connecticut minority (see the *Independent Gazetteer,* 21 January; *Pennsylvania Mercury,* 22 January; and *New Haven Gazette,* 24 January and 7 February for examples).

5. See Thomas FitzSimons to Samuel Meredith, 20 August, n. 4, printed above.

6. For the conflict from 1777 to 1789 over the laws requiring men over eighteen to renounce their allegiance to George III and swear allegiance to the state, see Brunhouse *Counter-Revolution,* 16-17, 40-41, 154-55, 167-69, 180-81, 197-98.

Pennsylvania Gazette, 10 September

By a gentleman, who passed through Harrisburg a few days ago, we learn that the Antifederal conference had met, and appointed Blair McClenachan chairman of their meeting, and George Bryan and Charles Pettit, with some others, a committee to bring in a *string* of amendments to the new Constitution, that they were much disappointed in meeting no deputies from several of the most respectable counties in the state, and that of the deputies who were there, many of them were so hampered with moderate instructions, that they could do nothing with them, that the whole squad of malcontents was dull and dissatisfied, as there appeared to be no chance of kindling a civil war in the United States—and that the opinion of all the considerate men in the neighborhood of Harrisburg was, that the persons met would be much better employed in mending *themselves*, than in trying to mend a government which was framed by the wisest and best men in America.

A Freeman, Pennsylvania Gazette, 10 September[1]

In a free country, private or *secret* associations for the purpose of taking care of the government are always dangerous, and should be narrowly watched and opposed. The following letters will show that such a secret association has existed for some time in Pennsylvania. The government over the members of this association is a kind of aristocracy. The heads of it are some of the officers of the state government, one of whom has lately got an appointment in Bucks County, viz., Mr. [James] Hanna. It is to be hoped the independent citizens of Pennsylvania will guard their power and offices, hereafter, from men who make politics a private business, and who have no other means of maintaining their families.

P.S. Would it not be proper to obtain the names of the persons to whom the *charge*, or government, of every township in the state is *committed* so that we might know our new masters and obey them accordingly?

[Here followed the Cumberland County Circular Letter of 3 July, and James Hanna's letter to John Vandegrift et al. of 15 August, both printed above.]

1. This item was dated Germantown, 4 September.

Samuel Miles et al. to Timothy Pickering, Philadelphia, 11 September[1]

The present important crisis in the affairs of Pennsylvania having induced a considerable number of respectable inhabitants of this city and neighborhood to meet and consider of such measures as would be most likely to secure to the state a representation of men in the next Assembly, equally known for their firm attachment to the federal government, and real interests of this state as well as for their candor, integrity and good sense, a committee, to communicate their sentiments to, and correspond with their friends in the different counties, was thought essentially necessary.

We therefore as the committee of correspondence,[2] take the liberty to address you on this important subject, being not only well assured of your zeal and regard for the new government, but that you will, on all occasions use your influence with your friends to promote its true interests.

To have persons of the best qualifications elected to represent us in the General Assembly, is at all times an object of very great consequence, but at the present moment, when the new Federal Constitution is to be carried into effect, it is a matter of the utmost importance. The ensuing legislature will not only have the ordinary objects of our state affairs before them, but they will have in charge to complete the arrangements of the general government, so far as the present House shall leave them unfinished. It is probable also that the great subject of amendments may form a part of their deliberations. All those points will require representatives of undoubted integrity and sound judgment. But to revise the new Constitution if that should be brought before them, they should be men of great candor free from prejudices against it, and well disposed to the continuance of an energetic power in our federal head.

The late meeting of the opponents of the new Constitution in the town of Harrisburg must have given serious alarm to its friends, and the election purposes, both with regard to the federal and state representatives, which we conceive it was calculated to promote, should excite our most active exertions, and vigilance, and awaken all our caution. You will see at once that as this measure was confessedly intended, so it may seriously affect the election of the eight federal Representatives, as well as of the state legislature. Their circular letter plainly recommends the nomination of eight persons for that purpose.[3] You will permit us therefore to put you on your guard concerning that election also, and to recommend it equally to your attention in due time, according as the same may be ordered by the present or future Assembly.

As we shall on all occasions be happy to communicate to you every necessary information which we may obtain in this business, so we are desirous to receive the same from you.

1. RC, Pickering Papers, MHi. The letter was signed by Samuel Miles, Walter Stewart, Francis Gurney, Tench Coxe, John Nixon, Benjamin Rush, and Hilary Baker. A draft of this letter is in the Coxe Papers, Tench Coxe Section, PHi.

2. There is no evidence of a meeting to create such a "committee of correspondence." However, at a meeting on 1 October to plan for forthcoming federal elections, these and other men were appointed to a committee to plan for a meeting at Lancaster to nominate Federalist candidates (Federalists Call Conference at Lancaster, 1 October, printed below).

3. This refers to the Cumberland County Circular Letter, 3 July (printed for the first time in the *Pennsylvania Gazette* on 10 September) rather than to the proceedings of the Harrisburg Convention, which were not printed in Philadelphia until 15 September. It is possible, however, that Tench Coxe had received a copy of the proceedings of the Convention by this time (see Thomas Hartley to Coxe, 9 September, printed above).

James McLene to William Irvine, Philadelphia, 12 September[1]

The meeting at Harrisburg has for some time past been a subject of much conversation and great inquiry amongst a certain class of people in this city. Mr. [John] Smiley (who attended the meeting) came to town yesterday; by him we learn that the business was carried on with great harmony and moderation. The proceedings are printing at Lancaster[2] and will be forwarded to you as soon as possible. The bearer Dr. [Samuel?] Jackson, having seen Mr. Smiley, can tell you all that we know about it. G[eorge] Clymer[3] and W[illia]m McClay were talked of for the Senate long before we met. Within this few days the tune is changed. It is said a number of the citizens (not members of the House) waited upon Mr. [Robert] Morris to know if he would consent to serve. He consented and so he and your colleague J[ohn] Armstrong[4] are to be the Senators. A *blessed choice*. A few of us have thought of Dr. Franklin and yourself. McClay is much sha-greened at being long talked of and now dropped. Some of our people begin to think that our best policy will be to take McClay and not the Dr. [Franklin]. We are now told that General Ervin [Irvine] is appointed by Congress to an high office in the department of accounts with an high salary.[5] This I consider as a scheme hatched here and finished in Congress to answer a special purpose. We do not consider this appointment as a bar in the way of your election but believe it will be made use of by the opposite party for that purpose.[6] Let me hear from you on this and as many other subjects as you please with the first conveyance.

1. RC, William Irvine Papers, PHi. Irvine was a member of the Confederation Congress in New York.

2. See the Proceedings of the Harrisburg Convention, 3-6 September, printed above.

3. See note 6 below.

4. See Armstrong to Horatio Gates, 30 May, printed above.

5. On 9 September, Congress chose Irvine as one of the commissioners to settle accounts between the United States and the individual states (JCC, XXXIV, 502). A commissioner's salary was $1,250 a year (JCC, XXXII, 266).

6. Some Federalists began discussing candidates for the Senate and methods of electing Representatives before the Constitution had been ratified by nine states. Thomas Hartley wrote to Tench Coxe from York on 3 March that it was likely the Constitution would be ratified and that "this brings us naturally forward to the administration of it in our own state.

"You speak of Mr. George Clymer as one of the Senate. It is only to know him to agree to the choice amongst a virtuous people.

"So far as my knowledge goes, and I have been acquainted with his character several years, he is a man of virtue, understanding and firmness fit to take a part in this or any other government that is founded on liberty or justice. Among the circle of my acquaintance, he stands high.

"General Irvine has been spoke of as the country Senator. He is a man of prudence, understanding, and steadiness and well affected to the Constitution notwithstanding some insinuations against him upon the latter head.

"When parties run very high in a popular assembly, a person is necessarily obliged to act under one party or another—but when a gentleman is in a distinct body, as Mr. Irvine lately in Congress, and not obliged to give his sentiments officially, his silence to the general world should not be an objection. He stands well with the people beyond the mountains—he lived with them and protected them—he opposed them in the Council of Censors and so he will (if I am not mistaken in the man) again in any improper measures, which they may attempt in any public body of which he may be a member.

"Perhaps at the present sessions of Assembly it would be improper (and indeed the attempt might prove unsuccessful) to make a provisional law (in case nine states should adopt the present Constitution) to choose members of the House of Representatives for the Federal Congress, etc.

"If members were to be chosen out of the state at large, you might possibly elect the best men; but when we find considerable disaffection in the back counties, districts well settled might be more acceptable" (RC, Coxe Papers, Tench Coxe Section, PHi).

A Word to the Wise to the Electors of Pennsylvania, Pennsylvania Mercury, 13 September

The enemies of the new Constitution having failed in their attempts to prevent its establishment, are now busily employed in endeavoring to *overset* it in a constitutional way. For this purpose they have held an electioneering conference at Harrisburg, the design of which is to fill all the elective posts of the state and federal government with Antifederal characters. It becomes the friends of the Constitution to *keep a good look-out*, and thereby prevent any such persons from seizing the helm of our federal barque, in order to run her ashore within sight of the port of liberty and safety. The times are difficult and critical. Let the wisest and best men, therefore, be fixed upon to compose our representatives in Congress and in the Assembly. It is not enough that they should be men of integrity and fair characters. They should be men of abilities, and perfectly acquainted with the principles of government. They should understand, in a particular manner, the *place* and *use* of every peg in the Federal Constitution. Such men will never be imposed upon or surprised by *side motions* or resolves in favor of amendments, which, in the present state of this country, cannot fail of involving us in ruin.

Extract of a Letter from Harrisburg (the Seat of the Self-created Pennsylvania Congress)[1]

Our real design in meeting here, is to make the last arrangement in our power for the next general election, so as, if possible, to keep ourselves and get our friends into the legislature; and what some of us wish much more, is to get into the general government; but we cover our real design, by making the people believe that our intentions are to propose amendments to the new Constitution, and you will see petitions handed about, so soon as any of the worthy gentlemen of your city go down. These petitions were printed, and sent over to us from our good friends in London, as you may see by looking at the stamp on the paper, where our favorite GR and crown, plainly appear. We have been disappointed by not having any representatives from the German counties, viz., Lancaster, York, Berks and Northampton.

1. *Pennsylvania Mercury*, 13 September. This "letter" was evidently a Federalist attempt to discredit both the Harrisburg Convention and the Constitutionalist Party. For additional attacks on the Harrisburg Convention see "A Freeman," "A Correspondent," and "A Friend of Liberty and Government" in the *Pennsylvania Gazette*, 17 September, and "A Doubter," ibid., 24 September; "A Correspondent" in the *Pennsylvania Mercury*, 18 September, and "A Despiser of Demagogues," ibid., 20 September.

Supreme Executive Council Proceedings, Tuesday, 16 September[1]

The Council met at the President's house the same day.[2] Present His Excellency Benjamin Franklin, Esquire, President, the Honorable Peter Muhlenberg, Esquire, Vice President, William Maclay, Henry Hill, Samuel Dean, Nathan

Dennisen, George Ross, Abraham Smith, James Read, John Smilie, Frederick Watt, and Christopher Kucher, esquires.

A letter from Charles Thomson dated the thirteenth instant inclosing the proceedings of Congress of the same date for putting in operation the Constitution for the general government of the United States which has been adopted by eleven of the said states, was received and read, and transmitted to the General Assembly.

1. Unless otherwise indicated, the proceedings of the Supreme Executive Council are printed from the smooth manuscript version of the minutes in the Pennsylvania State Archives and are cited by date only. The proceedings have been printed in *Minutes of the Supreme Executive Council of Pennsylvania* . . . , XV [4 July 1786–6 February 1789] and XVI [7 February 1789–20 December 1790] (Harrisburg, 1853).

2. The Council had met earlier in the day to conduct other business and then "adjourned to meet at the President's house." During the final months of Benjamin Franklin's term as president of the Council, it often met at his house because of his age and frail health.

Pennsylvania Mercury, 16 September

We hear from Massachusetts, that the inhabitants of that state have resolved to choose their eight federal Representatives in such a manner, that each citizen shall have a vote for the whole eight.[1] They claim this mode of voting as a *federal right* given to them by the Federal Constitution, and which the state *cannot* take from them. It is to be hoped the citizens of Pennsylvania will show the same discernment and zeal in preserving their liberties, by their mode of electing Representatives, that have been discovered by the enlightened citizens of Massachusetts. In this mode the characters most noted for wisdom and virtue will be brought forth, local prejudices will be destroyed, and each member of the federal House of Representatives will consider himself as the servant (not of a county or district, or of 2 or 3 electioneering friends) but of the *whole state*, and his eye will be fixed of course in every vote he gives (not upon pleasing a few of his neighbors by bringing a post road near their plantations) but upon the commerce, agriculture, and manufactures of *every part of the state*. The whole state has now become as to Congress, what a county has always been to the state. Let our federal elections be conducted upon the same principles. Let there be but one ticket, let the most suitable men be taken from *any*, or from *every* part of the state, and let the voters be given in at the same places in which the electors have been accustomed to vote for members of Council and Assembly.

1. The Massachusetts election law was not adopted until 20 November, and it provided for district rather than at-large elections (see Chapter V). This false story, which originated in Philadelphia, was reprinted at least nine times, three of them in Massachusetts newspapers.

Assembly Proceedings, Wednesday, 17 September[1]

A letter from His Excellency the President of the Supreme Executive Council was presented to the chair, and read, together with its inclosures, as follows, viz.,

In Council, September 16th, 1788.

Sir: The inclosed letter from our delegates, together with a letter from Charles Thomson, Esquire, inclosing an act of the United States in Congress assembled, for putting into operation the Constitution now ratified by the conventions of eleven states, the Board direct me to transmit to you, the consideration of the General Assembly.

I have the honor to be, with great respect, your most obedient servant, B. Franklin.

A letter directed to His Excellency the President of the Supreme Executive Council, of a similar tenor with the foregoing letter directed to Mr. Speaker, was also transmitted, and read.[2]

1. The Assembly proceedings are reprinted from the *Minutes of the Third Session of the Twelfth General Assembly of the Commonwealth of Pennsylvania* ..., (Philadelphia, 1788) and are cited by date only. The third session met from 2 September to 4 October.

2. The letter from the Pennsylvania delegation to Speaker Thomas Mifflin and the Election Ordinance, dated 13 September, are printed in Chapter II. The Pennsylvania delegation's letter to the Speaker was read to the Assembly before Franklin's letter.

Richard Peters to George Washington, Philadelphia, 17 September (excerpt)[1]

Our Antifederalists have changed their battery. They are now very Federal. They want amendments and they must get into the seats of government to bring them about, or what is better, to share the loaves and fishes. Their Harrisburg Convention have agreed to submit to and support the government, and some of them, like the moderate men and converted Tories formerly, now make up in sound what they want in patriotism. In short their convention was a mere election job and no harm is to be expected from it except they get into the government which in the whole cannot be prevented. When they have got warm in their seats they will, as it always happens in such cases, find it their interest to support a government in which they are sharers tho they may make a little bustle *ad captandum*.

. . . .

[P.S.] We shall take up the federal subject, having received the Ordinance of Congress, and on our parts organize the government. I believe Mr. [Robert] Morris will certainly be a Senator. Who the other will be is not so certain.

1. RC, Washington Papers, DLC. Peters was elected speaker of the Pennsylvania General Assembly after the state elections in October 1788.

Assembly Proceedings, Thursday, 18 September

The letter of His Excellency the President, and the act of Congress for putting into operation the Constitution now ratified by eleven states, read yesterday, were read the second time.

Ordered, that they be referred to Mr. Clymer, Mr. Peters, Mr. Wynkoop, Mr. Findley and Mr. M'Lene, with instructions to report the principles of a bill, if they think proper.

Civis, Pennsylvania Packet, 19 September

The publication of the proceedings of a late meeting at Harrisburg has afforded to me, and probably to many others, an agreeable disappointment. From what we had heard of the disposition of the people who promoted the meeting, there was reason to expect a result widely different from that which their proceedings exhibit. The moderation they have shown on this occasion does honor to those who were assembled, and entitles the measures they have recommended to attention and respect. However widely some of them may have heretofore strayed from the line of sound policy and good citizenship in their conduct concerning the Federal Constitution, they had, or imagined they had, sufficient cause for the opposition they gave. If in the manner of doing it passion should be supposed to have unduly interposed its influence, candid reflection on the occurrences shortly after the promulgation of the plan of government, may extenuate though it may not excuse the fault. But however this may be, they have now made a conciliatory advance, which ought to be met and cherished by those from whom they have differed in opinion, as well for the sake of promoting harmony in the state, as to give fair operation to the plan of confederation. For although in a free government, the *will* of the majority may, and ought to predominate, a wise and prudent majority will nevertheless calculate and conduct their measures in as conciliating a manner as is consistent with the dignity and energy of government, and cautiously avoid giving unnecessary cause of irritation or disgust to the minority. Success naturally produces moderation, complacency and dignity in cultivated minds. These effects are therefore expected to be found in the conduct of a majority; and when it is otherwise they generally diminish their own strength, by adding to that of the minority, and not unfrequently change places with them. I wish, therefore, as one of the majority, to see our public measures so conducted as to leave no ground for prejudice itself to generate alarms upon, and in such manner as may be most likely to improve the *acquiescence* of the minority into *approbation*.

A large proportion, probably a majority of those who have assented to the ratification of the new Constitution in its present form, are desirous that it should be amended in some parts as early as such amendments can be made without impeding its operation, or hazarding its being destroyed, by being wholly submitted to the arbitration of another general convention. The amendments proposed are but few, and pointed to particular parts, which may be subjected to revision by a general convention, without danger to the general principles or vital parts of the Constitution, and without impeding its organization and operation in the meantime. Several of the most considerable of the states have accompanied their adoption with an instruction to procure amendments as early as possible. As the Convention of Pennsylvania omitted this accompaniment to their ratification on a supposition, it is imagined, that their power was limited to the mere adoption or rejection of the instrument laid before them. The Assembly, who are expressly authorized by the Constitution itself to propose amendments, are now requested to do it. Whether they will comply with this request or not, is with them to determine.

May wisdom govern their choice!

Amendments Proposed by Westmoreland County Committee[1]

Report of the Committee: A committee having been chosen, at a meeting held in Greensburg, for the County of Westmoreland on the 5th day of August, and authorized to correspond with other counties of this state, respecting the propriety of joining with other states in endeavoring to procure amendments to the Constitution for the general government of the United States; and the respective citizens present at the said meeting, having unanimously voted that amendments were necessary, and the committee having received letters on the subject, think it their duty to express their own sentiments, and what they believe to be the prevailing sentiments of the people of the County of Westmoreland on this important subject.

They profess to possess sentiments completely federal, and do believe that no other than a federal republican form of government can secure political liberty in an empire so extensive as the United States. They are also fully convinced of the necessity of vesting more extensive powers in Congress, than it could exercise under the Confederation, consequently they heartily approve of vesting the general government with every power and resource which is of a general nature, and which is generally relating to all the states; such as imposts or duties arising from importation, regulation of commerce, treaties of all sorts, armies, navies, coin, post office, etc. etc. But they regret that the general government goes much farther than these federal principles will admit, and vests Congress with such extensive local powers, in addition to the necessary general powers, as must eventually destroy the state governments, and absorb the whole sovereignty [and] consequently prove to be one entire consolidated government, which in our extensive situation must be a despotic one. They therefore wish that it may be expressly stipulated, that Congress shall not assume or exercise any further or other powers than what is expressly defined and clearly vested therein by the express words of the Constitution.

Secondly, they consider the representation to be disproportioned to the powers wherewith the government is vested, not only because the Representatives are too few in number to have that knowledge of and common interest with the people at large, which is essential to political safety, but also because the smallness of the number, together with the greatness of the powers and privileges which the new Congress will possess, will subject the members to the greatest temptation to corruption and undue influence: they therefore [propose] the Representatives to be increased to one to thirty thousand at least, and regularly proportioned to certain districts to be described by the state legislatures; and also that Congress may not be vested with the unnecessary and dangerous powers of lessening their own numbers, and consequently exercising the supreme power, by as few hands as ambition or corruption may see fit.

Thirdly, they further consider the power of regulating elections as vested by the new general government, to be unsafely lodged; they apprehend these powers, especially to the place and manner, to be only competent for the state governments, where the most equal and most responsible representation, in the very nature of things will always be found, and where there can be no interest in abusing the powers to dangerous purposes. They conceive this power is not necessary to the general government for any good purpose, but seems rather calculated to secure and promote a corrupt and dangerous influence in the hands of Congress over the election of its own members, highly dangerous to the essential rights of a free people: therefore, they earnestly wish a revision of this part of the general government.

Fourthly, they also observe, that the extensive and unlimited powers of internal taxation, added to the resources of the general government, must be in their operation entirely subversive of the state governments, and that this vested without any constitutional check or control, are sufficient means of absolute power in the most extensive sense, if those who occupy the government think proper to make use of them for that purpose, and we ought not to trust more than is necessary to future men and future measures. But more particularly they wish that Congress may not be vested with the power of levying internal direct taxes upon the citizens of any state, unless when such state proves obstinately delinquent; nor even then to have the power of levying poll taxes as they are in their nature unequal and always oppressive, as they go to tax not only the poor individuals, but the poor and remote counties equal with the more wealthy and more valuable situations. They wish to have the powers of levying excise defined, so that it may be known what the particulars are the citizens eat, drink or wear, which shall be subject to excise.

Fifthly, they apprehend that the unlimited power of keeping standing armies in time of peace, especially as combined with the power over every source of revenue is inconsistent with the principles of a federal republican government, and the freedom of the citizens. They therefore earnestly recommend, that if keeping standing armies in time of peace should be thought necessary, the power should be put under such checks, as to secure the liberty of the community at large, and the personal safety of individuals; and this they conceive may be accomplished by rendering a majority of three-fourths of the Senate and House of Representatives agreeing to the necessity and propriety of raising a standing army in time of peace necessary, and by keeping the military in due subordination to the civil law.

Sixthly, they conceive that by so imperfect a bill or declaration of rights as the new plan of general government contains, whereby the trial by jury in criminal cases, the habeas corpus act, etc., only is secured; trial by jury in civil cases, and every other essential right of freemen is impliedly given up to the arbitrary will of future men. They therefore wish that such a declaration of rights may be added to the general frame of government as may secure to posterity those privileges which are essential to the proper limiting the extent of sovereign power, and securing those rights which are essential to freemen; and that Congress may not have power to pass any laws which in their effects may infringe on or tend to subvert the constitution of any particular state, except in such cases as are mentioned in the first clause to be of a general nature, and properly belonging to Congress.

Seventhly, they further observe, that the undue mixture of legislative and executive powers in the Senate is highly corrupting in its nature, and dangerous to liberty in its influence; and that the power of putting the militia under the terrors of martial law in time of peace, or of marching them, perhaps, to destroy the freedom of an oppressed sister state, without any check or control from the state governments, stand also in absolute need of revision and amendments.

The foregoing particulars the committee have tho't proper to point out as amongst the most obvious exceptionable powers vested by the new system of general government in the future Congress: at the same time they believe that the people of the County of Westmoreland are willing to concur with such further, or other amendments, as shall render the proposed plan a government of freedom, confidence and energy.

William Jack, Chairman.

1. *Pittsburgh Gazette,* 20 September. The committee was appointed at a Westmoreland County meeting in August (Proceedings of Westmoreland County Meeting, Greensburg, 5 August, printed above). There is no evidence to indicate when the committee prepared its report. After its publication, it was reprinted in the Philadelphia *Freeman's Journal,* 24 September, and the *New York Morning Post,* 1 October.

Observations by a Member of the Convention at Harrisburg, Pittsburgh Gazette, 20 September [1]

This convention had not a Franklin, or a Washington at the head of it, but it had a [Charles] Pettit and [George] Bryan. It may be observed, that in the amendments proposed we have said nothing about a *bill of rights, the liberty of the press, or the trial by jury.* It was found upon examination there was nothing in the Constitution which interfered with any of these. The people might try their causes, advertise their stray colts, and wear their breeches just as they used to do. It may be thought wrong to have made such a noise about these things, when there was no ground for it; more especially to have *run away from a house of assembly,*[2] to have *signed protests,* setting forth the want of these particulars, to have *voted against the Constitution,* and published a *dissent in writing;*[3] by these means setting the whole country in a flame, etc., representing those as traitors who did not raise the same clamor. But the people do not consider that they might not have been all villains and rascals who did this, but some of them actually well-meaning ignorant men, who believed, at least a great deal of what they said.

It is true the amendments now proposed, are a great part of them unnecessary, containing little more than what is in the Constitution already, but it was expedient to do something to satisfy the people; just as a physician who has led a man to believe that he is sick, and to make him think that he is well again, gives him a little warm water, with the powder of a dried leaf in it perhaps; that if it does no good, it can do him no harm.

There is one thing a little different, viz., the power of "recalling the Senators." This is right; and is like a man tying a string to his monkey, or his raccoon, that he is afraid will run away; so that when it climbs up the tree a certain distance, he can at his pleasure bring it back again. It will be perfectly expedient in this state, where there are two parties, for the Senators will be changed, as these alternately prevail; so that like buckets in a well the one goes down, while the other comes up; and the Senate from being the most stable and dangerous body, will become the most fluctuating and absurd. In this case there will be nothing to dread from them and the immediate representatives of the people may do just what they please. Perhaps after all it might have been as well to have proposed lessening the period, for which they are chosen, but make the appointment irrevocable for the time.

It is said the Congress shall not have the power of "altering the places, times and manner of choosing Senators." They have not the power as the case now is. The clause in the Constitution respects only the choice of Representatives in the second house; but this was put into the amendments, either seeming to imply that it was otherwise before, or was a mere blunder and oversight in some of us that drew up the writing.

Take notice that there is to be no *poll tax*, so that the newcomers, the shopkeepers, jobbers, wayfaring men, and bachelors, that *have no land*, are to go free; and the *farmers*, because they are able, pay the whole.

There is to be no standing army, because it is better that people should go out and be shot themselves, than pay others for doing it. The militia are to serve only two months at a time, because there can be no war that can last longer. And if the time should expire just a day before the battle ought to be, it is only to put it off until the recruit comes, and leave the *baggage and artillery standing there as a scarecrow to the enemy*.

There are to be no subordinate courts established, as for instance at Pittsburgh, or in Kentucky, or elsewhere, but must all go to one *supreme court*, at the federal town I suppose, which will help to increase the domilitium [*sic*] of the empire.

As to the proceeding of the convention, you will hear of them in due time. I will mention only some particulars, viz., it was insisted much amongst us, to put in a clause, that all doctors should tell diseases by the water; but it was thought this would be construed into a slur upon the Germans and the Scotch Irish, and so left out. It was [Robert] Whitehill that proposed this. [William] Findly did not come to the convention; he had thrown out such rhapsodies before in speaking and writing, that he was ashamed to appear and support them at this place.

We made a ticket at this meeting for the new Congress. Blair M'Clenachan is one. He may be no conjurer, as the saying is, but he is a good man. Dr. [Joseph] Gardner is also in the ticket; he is a relation by marriage, to the Simpsons in Chester County, and I think will do very well. There is one Simon Drusback pitched upon, I imagine being of the same name with one *Simon, a tanner*, who made good leather in the scriptures, a great while ago. It was right that Findly should be put in nomination,[4] because he can "address the chair," and say, "Myster Spacker," and avoid being "parsenal," and will do great credit to the western country, amongst the orators in the new Congress. I think it would not be amiss to have him sent ambassador to the Barbary states, or some part of the world, where his dialect would be understood as an original language.

I am just thinking with myself, what these [men?] when they first go to the Congress, will propose. I should be glad to get a law passed, "Myster Spacker," to have all Fridays turned into Saturdays, and all Saturdays into Sundays, for I have observed for several years, that all Saturdays are days of rain; when we might as well be going to sermons as anywhere else, but can get no work done.

But we must let these things rest, and in the meantime rejoice, that this convention have, with such unanimity, agreed upon what was of no consequence nor ever will be. However, that is as it takes, and so wishing you all health and happiness, and meaning no ill to any man, I am the public's humble servant.

1. It is evident that this piece was not written by a member of the Harrisburg Convention.

2. On 29 September 1787 enough opponents of calling a convention stayed away from the Assembly to prevent a quorum. Two of these men were taken forcibly from their lodgings to the Assembly, which then called for the election of delegates to the state Convention. See McMaster and Stone, Chapter II.

3. The "Dissent of the Minority" in the Pennsylvania Convention is published in McMaster and Stone, 454-82.

4. Blair M'Clenachan and William Findley's names appeared on the Harrisburg ticket when it was published (The Harrisburg Ticket, *Federal Gazette*, 7 November, printed below) but not the names of Dr. Joseph Gardner and Simon Driesbach. Gardner held various offices in Pennsylvania and had been a delegate to the Confederation Congress in 1784 and 1785. Driesbach had been a member of the Council of Censors in 1783 and 1784 from Northampton County.

Assembly Proceedings, Tuesday, 23 September

The committee appointed September 18th, on the letter from the Honorable the Vice President,[1] with its enclosures, relative to the organization of the Constitution adopted for the government of the United States, reported a bill, entitled "An Act directing the times, places and manner of holding elections for representatives of this state in the foederal government of the United States, and of appointing electors on the part of this state for the choice of a President of the United States, agreeably to the foederal constitution," which was read the first time, and ordered to lie on the table.

1. The letter was from President Benjamin Franklin, not the Vice President.

Assembly Debates, Tuesday, 23 September[1]

Mr. Clymer, from the committee appointed for the purpose of reporting the mode of commencing proceedings under the new Federal Constitution, presented a bill for that purpose; and a resolution that this House would go into the appointment of Senators to the federal government.

1. Lloyd, *Debates*, IV, 131.

Assembly Proceedings, Wednesday, 24 September

The report of the committee, to whom was referred the resolution of Congress relative to the organization of the federal government, and etc. read yesterday, was read the second time: Whereupon,

Resolved, that this House will during this session appoint two Senators by ballot, to take their seats as Senators for this state in the Congress of the United States, agreeably to the Federal Constitution now adopted for the government of such of the United States as have agreed to or shall hereafter adopt the same: Whereupon,

On motion of Mr. M'Lene, seconded by Mr. Hubley, ordered, that Tuesday next be assigned for the election of two Senators conformably to the foregoing resolution, and that nomination take place previous to that day.

. . . .

The bill, entitled "An Act directing the times, places and manner of holding elections for Representatives of this state in the foederal government of the United States, and of appointing Electors on the part of this state for the choice of a President of the United States, agreeably to the foederal constitution," was read the second time, and debated by paragraphs.

Assembly Debates, Wednesday, 24 September[1]

The alien bill being the order of the day, was postponed in order to give place to the bill for originating the federal government. On which Mr. Findley rose and stated some hesitation he had with respect to the general principles on which this bill was constituted; he was of opinion it would be much better if the state was laid out into eight election districts, and each district to elect one member for the House of Representatives in Congress, and this he conceived was the only method which under the new Constitution could any how answer the purposes of representation; it was by this means only that eight men could have a particular knowledge of the local and common interest of their constituents throughout the state, so very necessary to enable them to pursue those ends. He knew some gentlemen were of opinion that this mode was not agreeable to the plan of the general government, but this matter had never been fully discussed. It is true he had stated it on a former occasion as an objection to the Constitution, that this point was not ascertained with accuracy, which he thought it ought to be, though for his own part he had never doubted of the powers of the state governments to do what they thought best in this matter: and he still continued to be of the same opinion. As he conceived it almost impossible in so large a state as Pennsylvania, to have an actual representation in Congress, if the whole state was to be one election district, he could wish the principles of the bill altered, but he was apprehensive the time of the House was too nearly expired to mature a plan congenial with his ideas,[2] but he would endeavor to digest something suitable; but in the mean time if no other person objected but himself he was content to let the bill pass forward for the present. There was another reason also which had considerable weight with him, but he did not know how it affected them. It was very observable that since the counties had been divided into election districts great frauds and much chicanery was used in making up the returns at the county towns. Now if there is to be but one place where the returns for the whole state is to be made up, as it extends the labor and trouble of making up, so also does it extend the opportunity of cheating, which is hereby more encouraged and better screened. Practices of this kind are destructive of the vital principles of representation, which it is the peculiar duty of the legislature to prevent.

Mr. Lewis declared that he thought it inconsistent with his duty to set still on a question of this importance, and he was free to declare that his ideas were very different indeed from those expressed by the gentleman from Westmoreland (Mr. Findley). He took it, that the bill before them went upon ground strictly proper and constitutional, and that the contrary ground which was advocated by that gentleman would be a deviation from the Constitution. This he was of opinion was a subject of great importance, and well worthy of the attention of the House. He took the principles held in the bill to be founded in reason, and on the nature of things, and he would proceed to an enquiry into the construction which was to be put upon the words of the Constitution, and now it corresponded with the practice and usage under the constitution of this state; and further, he meant to consider what were the rights given to the Representatives of the Union. He could not see much room for doubt on this subject; the words of the Constitution are "The House of Representatives shall be composed of Members chosen every second Year by the People of the several States"; again "No Person shall be a Representative who shall not have attained to the Age of twenty five Years, and been seven Years a Citizen of the United States, and who shall not, when elected, be an Inhabitant of that State in which he shall be chosen." Now the gentleman's principles go to narrow down the rights and privileges of the Representative in such a manner, that a person shall not be duly qualified for a Representative of the state of Pennsylvania, altho' he has every requisite mentioned in the Constitution, beside being an inhabitant of the state, yet he shall not be qualified to serve unless he is an inhabitant of that particular district, or part of the state for which it is proposed to choose him. This he thought was sufficient for him to say on this head, he should therefore proceed to the other.

By the Constitution it is ordained that the Representatives be chosen by the people of the several states; and not by the people of this or that district, or any smaller part. The Constitution requires the Representative to be an inhabitant of the state, and not the inhabitant of any particular district, if this is the construction in the one case is it not also the proper construction in the other. Supposing that he lived in the city of Philadelphia, and fixed his eye upon a gentleman residing at Pittsburgh, at Carlisle, or any part of the state as a person the most noted for wisdom and virtue. Should he not be qualified to serve him under the words of the Constitution, because he does not reside in his neighborhood? He thought a sufficient answer would be to say that he is 25 years of age, has been seven years a citizen, and is now an inhabitant of the state. The Constitution requires no more and hence he is capable of being elected. But by whom? Not the people of this or that particular district, but by the people at large, or in the words of the Constitution, by the people of the several states. Does not the people of the several counties of this commonwealth for the state of Pennsylvania, and does not the several states form a similar political body, only on a larger scale, and are not the representatives upon this floor the representatives of their particular counties? Or are they the representatives of those particular districts into which a county for the convenience of its inhabitants are divided, and in which the member happens to reside, or which by its unanimity in voting has placed him on the return? Surely they are the choice of the county at large, and so is it that the people at large choose for the state at large, and the persons so chosen represents the whole state. Surely this is correspondent to the practice and usage of Pennsylvania, under her constitution, which declares, that the members of the House of Representatives shall be chosen by the freemen of every city and county respectively, and no person shall be elected unless he has resided in the city or county, for which he shall be chosen, two years immediately before the election. Thus every individual of a county, notwithstanding his residence being in this or that district, has a right and continually exercises it, of voting for the whole number of representatives to which the proper county is entitled to by law, and whatever alterations may be made as to the time, place or manner of conducting elections, by any act of the legislature, this right and privilege is secured under both constitutions to every citizen of Pennsylvania. There is a small variation indeed in the form of expression used in the constitution of Pennsylvania, and that of the United States; but as to the substance, it is out of the power of ingenuity itself to point out the smallest difference. If the state was divided into eight districts, and each to choose one member, he did not see how any one of them could be called a Representative of Pennsylvania, or how confidence could be reposed in a person disagreeable to 7-8ths of the inhabitants of the state, which was not impossible might be the case. He therefore thought with justice the idea of dividing a state into election districts was repugnant to the Federal Constitution. But, he went further, when persons so chosen should meet the Congress (who are authorized to judge of the qualifications of their own members) it might be urged against them individually, that you are not a Representative of Pennsylvania, because you are elected by only one eighth part of that state, and for this reason your election is irregular and ought to be set aside.

He would add one other observation, which was, that although the citizens at large were to choose eight members, yet it did not follow that they were all to attend at one spot to execute their privilege. He admitted that the choice might be improved if this was the case, but in a state so large as Pennsylvania it was impracticable; therefore the legislature ought to take the next best step for obtaining the unanimous voice of the people, as to the eight persons who they shall approve of to represent them. Upon the whole he concluded that if under the idea of directing the time, place and manner of holding elections, the state extending its jurisdiction to abridge the rights of the citizens by a limitation in the smallest degree of the rights secured to them by the constitution, they might annihilate those rights altogether and deprive the people of a representation in the new Constitution, which was the greatest security they could have to assure to themselves and their posterity, liberty, tranquility and happiness.

As to what the gentleman from Westmoreland had said relative to the frauds occasioned by dividing counties into election districts, he had little to reply, but should just remark that he was no friend to those regulations, in the extent to which they were now carried; but until the election laws were simplified and reduced to a better plan than they were upon at present, he believed the members must content themselves to use them as they are. In short, he saw nothing from the usage in Pennsylvania, or from the Constitution of the United States, that would countenance the principle which the gentleman advocated, and therefore wished the House would go on with the bill.[3]

. . . .

Mr. Findley now proceeded to answer the observations made by the honorable member from the city [Mr. Lewis][4] and said he would beg the House to take no notice of what had been argued against confining to the district for which he should be elected, because he did not contend that this ought to be the case; he knew well that a person who was 25 years of age, who had been 7 years a citizen, and who was an inhabitant of the state, was sufficiently [sic] (at least under the general government) to be a Representative in Congress; and therefore all that had been advanced on this head, by the learned gentleman, did not apply. It was certainly in the recollection of every member of the House, that the practice under the former government of Pennsylvania did not oblige a county to send for a member an inhabitant of the county. Both Cumberland and Berks were frequently represented by gentlemen residing in Philadelphia; and this in his opinion was the plan which the general government seems to have taken up.

But the new Constitution certainly gives the power to the state to elect the Representatives in such manner as shall be thought proper, until the general government chooses to assume it to themselves. In the Convention of this state, it may be recollected that it was objected, that it ought to have been more explicitly pointed out, but it was there answered, that no doubt could be entertained but what the state had full power on this head, and might do as it judged convenient, that such states as approved of it might and would do it, was then agreed upon all hands, and it was matter of admiration that it was now opposed.

Indeed if gentlemen could prove to him that the states had not this power it would alter his opinion of the Constitution very much. It would then appear to him that the legislature, the guardians of the citizens, had no power to secure any of their rights or privileges, or prevent their absolute ruin. But he did not see the Constitution as binding upon the legislature in this respect, and therefore he was not so very apprehensive as he otherwise would be of the effects which it would be productive of; moreover it would be found that his ideas agreed with several states in the Union. He was well informed that the elections in New York and Massachusetts were to be conducted on these principles.[5] Indeed it seemed to him the best if not the only mode that could beget a confidence, among the common people, in the general government. He was far from thinking that his principles were inexpedient or impractical, though he acknowledged some difficulty would occur in completing a system upon the outlines which he had drawn, in so short a space of time as there remained of the session; but as gentlemen seemed to insinuate and argue that they were improper and unconstitutional, he was determined to take the sense of the House upon this point, and should therefore call the yeas and nays on a question of amendment.

Mr. M'Lene enumerated some observations which had been made in the committee, similar to those mentioned by the gentleman who last preceded him, and was of opinion that the legislature had the power to divide the state into election districts, and that it would be the practice pursued by New York; but he was well satisfied upon considering the short time which the House had to set, that the mode pointed out in this bill [at-large elections], was the only mode by which the election for Representatives could be held at present, and therefore, though it was not agreeable to his sentiments of propriety, he should agree to let the bill go on as it was.

Mr. Peters thought the bill had been settled in the committee, and therefore was surprised at gentlemen's objections, because he thought it was generally agreed that the bill should go through without opposition. Though he was clearly of opinion with his worthy friend from the city (Mr. Lewis) that dividing the state into election districts was not agreeable to the Constitution, yet he thought it a subject about which the House might freely differ without affecting the principles of the present bill, for it is clear that if the state has or has not a right to divide itself into districts, it has a right to permit the whole of Pennsylvania to vote for Representatives in the federal government. If gentlemen are concerned to find equivocal terms in the Constitution, let them reflect it is a human performance, though for his part he thought them plain and expressive enough, there might be some parts which wanted some explanation, and so there would be thought if all the wisdom of all the opponents to the system was employed in altering it, but such is the lot of human nature. However in the present case neither alteration or explanation would be an improvement, because it is certain that the people of the state have a right to choose Representatives for the state and that each Representative will be elected by a majority of the citizens.

The worthy member from Westmoreland (Mr. Findley) had stated an objection against numerous election districts, which he alleges have been productive of frauds. He believed the observation to be founded in fact, but what argument is this for increasing election districts on this occasion, unless it be to introduce state cheating as well as county cheating. But he thought that the nature of things required that the House of Representatives should be chosen in this manner, because they were to represent the whole state, and to attend to its general interest and welfare, and not that alone of a particular district, hence state characters (if he might be indulged with the expression) ought to be sought for, instead of local or district men, who are of use only in the small way. Besides he asked, to what inconveniencies would a district election subject us? A man in one district might be chosen a Representative, by having 500 votes, and which are all the votes he has in the state, while the other candidate might have 400 in that district, and 800 in another, and yet be returned in neither; but when this subject comes before Congress, is it not likely they will determine him to be the Representative who has the largest number of the votes of the people of the state, and set aside the district judgment?

As to what gentlemen had said respecting the conduct of other states as to the principles on which they mean to conduct their elections, he had little to remark; he had heard that an idea of the kind just mentioned was entertained some time ago in the state of Massachusetts, but he was well informed that it was now given up, because it was at best a doubtful point with its advocates whether any state has a right to parcel out the people of the several states into lesser portions. But all this was no argument either one way or the other, states as well as men will differ, therefore we must think and act for ourselves. But at all events he should agree to the bill as it stood, unless he meant to do nothing; for he could not help thinking that altering it to the gentleman's principles would be tantamount to doing nothing, inasmuch as it would be impracticable to complete a bill founded on such principles.

Mr. Findley knew there were some things equivocally expressed in the new Constitution, and in this he was supported by the amendments proposed by some of the state conventions, that, of who should choose the Electors was not clear, but whenever the legislature have the power of judging, they ought not out of delicacy decide in their own favor. This would operate with him to vote in favor of that part of the bill which left the choice of Electors to the people at large, but the other point he was not so willing to give up. The gentleman who was last up had stated some difficulty which might result from a Representative being sent into Congress with 500 votes; this might happen to be the case, but he did not think it necessary to enter into a discussion or inquiry of all the inconveniences resulting from electing in the manner proposed in the bill; he should not remark even the advantage arising from taking pains, while three fourths of the state are divided among five or six sets of men, that the other one fourth may carry the election by acting in concert, and holding a correspondence with each other. He could not help thinking that this mode of electing Representatives went to extend the influence of the general government, without taking the proper care to conciliate the minds of the people, if it is meant to give them a representation in Congress, let that representation be had by voting to effect, for a man who has their confidence, who either resides among them, or is well known to them by the common interest and concern which he has with them; how can our Representatives know what is proper in the exercise of the internal power which the general government is authorized to use, unless they are possessed of local and common, as well as general knowledge, and how is this to be obtained so fairly as by dividing the people into districts?

But as he did not design to oppose this bill altogether, he should perhaps eventually be for passing it, though he could not help protesting against the principle; he hoped to be permitted to introduce a clause that should confine it expressly to the next election. If it was agreeable to conciliate upon these terms he should add no more, for he believed that it would at this time be impracticable to pass a law that should make a proper division of the districts [in] time enough for those concerned to have due notice.

Mr. Peters expressed himself willing to meet the gentleman on this ground, but should like to see the clause before he pledged himself; he was disposed tho to concede any thing in his power that might tend to introduce unanimity.

Mr. Fitzsimons believed it really very unimportant what were the principles the bill went upon so far as it is thought to relate to future assemblies. Could this House bind their successors by saying the law should last a given period? Certainly every gentleman knew better; then to what purpose was all this argument? He hoped the House would consider whether the bill was proper, and adapted to our present circumstances; if it was, they would pass it, and leave others to the exercise of their own judgments.

Mr. M'Lene thought it best to go on with the law, and was of opinion that the words of it already confined it to the next election.

Mr. Clymer did not expect a single member would have given the bill opposition, because it was well known to every gentleman that the present House could not direct any other principle of holding the election than was mentioned in the bill; but if it could, he should oppose any other, because it was neither constitutional nor legal, inasmuch as it would prejudice and narrow down the rights and privileges meant to be secured by the great charter or Federal Constitution. But this was not a proper time for argument, and he should therefore decline saying any more, yet would just impress upon the House the necessity there was of having the state of Pennsylvania well represented in the next Congress, and how much more likely a good and respectable representation was to be obtained by being selected from the state at large, and voted for in the same manner, than from district elections. Men in this case would have a proper influence in Congress, as well as more general knowledge and experience of things which in the present situation of affairs is very desirable.

The bill hereupon was gone through without further debate, and ordered to be published for consideration.[6]

A resolution for the purpose of appointing Senators to the federal government was taken up.

Mr. Kennedy did not see any necessity for the present House to make choice of Senators, he thought there would be abundance of time for the next House to go into this measure, as the meeting of Congress was so far distant, and therefore hoped it would be deferred.

Mr. Peters looked upon this as a part of the great subject that they had before them, and did not see what reason there was for transferring a power to the next House, which might be conveniently and laudably exercised by this. He thought prudence would direct the House not to defer that to tomorrow which could be done today.

Mr. Clymer added besides its being as much the equal right of this as any other House, to appoint Senators, another consideration, which is, that the trust reposed in these gentlemen is important and established for a considerable length of time, and therefore it will be necessary that they should have some months to arrange their private affairs, as their duty might probably occasion a very considerable absence from home.

Mr. M'Lene was also for choosing the Senators at this session, because he had a vote and should know the men in whom he reposed his confidence, he might have no such opportunity if it was delayed, and beside he might as a citizen at the next election wish to put in as a Representative the very man whom the legislature shall appoint to the Senate, whereby his vote would be thrown away.

Mr. Peters thought the last reason mentioned by the gentleman from Franklin (Mr. M'Lene) was so striking, that nothing need be added, and he hoped the House would agree to appoint Senators on Tuesday next, which being agreed to, the House adjourned till the afternoon.

1. Lloyd, *Debates,* IV, 179-90.
2. The Pennsylvania Constitution (Section 8) required the annual election of the Assembly on the second Tuesday in October, which in 1788 was 14 October (Thorpe, V, 3084).
3. The House turned to other business for a few moments, before continuing the election-law debate.
4. Lloyd's *Debates* reads "Mr. M'Lene," but this is obviously an error. James McLene represented Franklin County, not the city of Philadelphia. William Lewis, who represented the city, was the only member who had spoken previously (besides Findley himself), and Findley's arguments were directed at points raised in Lewis's speech.
5. The *Pennsylvania Mercury,* 16 September, printed above, falsely reported that Massachusetts had rejected district elections in favor of at-large elections.
6. The Pennsylvania Constitution (Section 15) required that all "bills of public nature" must be published for consideration before final passage (Thorpe, V, 3086). The bill was printed in the *Pennsylvania Packet,* 26 September, and the *Pennsylvania Journal,* 27 September.

Diary of Jacob Hiltzheimer, Thursday, 25 September[1]

After the Assembly adjourned, had to dine with me, General [Thomas] Mifflin, Richard Peters, D. Whelen, Mr. Edward Troxler, with Colonel [Timothy] Pickering, Matthew Clarkson, and Captain Falkner. In the evening about twenty-five members met at Hassell's Tavern to consult on the selection of two Senators to represent this state.

1. Hiltzheimer, *Diary,* 146. Born in Germany, Hiltzheimer came to Pennsylvania in 1748. He represented Philadelphia in the Assembly from 1786 until his death in 1798.

Tench Coxe to James Madison, Philadelphia, 26 September (excerpt)[1]

Enclosed you will find a bill now pending in our legislature for the election of Representatives and Electors, and indeed all our state arrangements in the federal affairs, except the election of Senators, which is fixed for Tuesday 30th inst. The candidates are among the citizens, Mr. R[obert] Morris, and if they take two from hence, Mr. [William] Bingham, but of the latter not much has been said since Mr. Morris's name has been in circulation. From the country Generals [William] Irwin [Irvine], [John] Armstrong, Messrs. [William] Maclay, [Charles] Pettit and [William] Findlay. If the Federal interest act in concert, Morris and McClay will be the men as they have the most votes among the friends of the Constitution. General Armstrong's friends are strenuous and apparently determined. Should the Federal interest divide tis impossible to say what will be the issue, but it must be in part unfavorable. The two last are decided for the resumption by the states of the power of direct taxation, and therefore we must earnestly hope they may not succeed. If elected their efforts will accord with the protest of our minority.

You will observe we are to elect the Representatives and Electors by our general ticket. The latter is given to the people, tho it might have been reserved by this House. To avoid a special session, was one of the reasons; probably to make a general ticket in aid of a general one for the Representatives was another. I think it will be safe in Pennsylvania both as to the Electors and federal Representatives, but it will give a precedent to the other states, where the majority are unfavorable, such as New York etc., which may require the early attention of our friends in those places.

1. RC, Madison Papers, DLC. Printed: DHOC, V, 76-77 (excerpt).

Assembly Proceedings, Saturday, 27 September

The bill, entitled "An Act directing the times, places and manner of holding elections for representatives of this state in the foederal government of the United States, and of appointing electors on the part of this state for the choice of a President of the United States, agreeably to the foederal constitution," was read the third time.

Ordered, that the further consideration thereof be postponed until Monday next, in the afternoon.

Assembly Debates, Saturday, 27 September[1]

The bill for organizing the federal government was resumed, and a long desultory conversation arose upon the time most proper for holding elections for federal Representatives, and federal Electors; but this point was not determined this day, therefore the bill was postponed.

1. Lloyd, *Debates*, IV, 215. Beginning with Saturday, 27 September, the printed debates are misdated. The editors have corrected these errors in dating.

John Simpson to James Potter, Northumberland Town, 27 September (excerpt)[1]

I cannot be silent at such a critical period. I conceive members for the ensuing House is a matter of the greatest moment. As the necessity of measures are well known to you, I shall say no more on that score. But can assure you, your friends has you in view for the House; [———] Dale and Mr. Strawbridge are principally spoke of also. Your acceptance and approbation is requested to be early known. Next Saturday there is to be township meetings, to choose men to send to a county meeting the Wednesday following in order to form a general ticket. Before this time would wish to hear from you, for at that day you must be made known to the people, one way or other. To refuse it, I hope will not be the case.

Captain Robison with a strong party at Pine Creek is for you and against Dale; your old friend B[———]ham is against you; and for Dale [or?] Strabridge; but his interest is little and getting less. It will give me the highest pleasure to hear of you brightening up the old chain.

I am convinced you cannot be silent, nor inactive nor satisfied at this time, when a matter of the highest magnitude are depending for posterity. I hope it is not yet too late to obtain some amendments.

1. RC, Northern, Interior and Western Counties Papers, 1744-1859, PHi. The letter was signed "J. Simpson." The writer was probably John Simpson, who later served as a Jeffersonian leader in Northumberland County. The salutation is "Dr. Genl." Since the writer asks the recipient to present his compliments to "Mrs. Potter," the recipient was probably James Potter, a militia general and a leader of the Constitutionalist Party in Northumberland County. Simpson was obviously concerned with preparing a county ticket of candidates for the Assembly in the state election on 14 October.

Pennsylvania Packet, 27 September

We learn that the honorable the legislature have now before them a bill, by which the ten Electors of the President and Vice President will be chosen *by the people at large* throughout the state. Thus it is that *the power of the people* under the new Constitution is increased and maintained. This popular mode of election furnishes a new argument, that did not occur to us before, in favor of general tickets; for were we to go into district elections, we must have ten districts for Electors of the President, and eight for the federal Representatives, which would oblige us to hold the elections on different days, at the expense of double cost and time, and with a repetition of the confusion that attends an election.[1]

1. This article was widely reprinted in the North (see, for example, the Hartford *Connecticut Courant,* 6 October; Boston *Independent Chronicle,* 16 October; Pittsfield *Berkshire Chronicle,* 23 October; and Portsmouth *New Hampshire Gazette,* 23 October).

Assembly Proceedings, Monday, 29 September

The bill, entitled "An Act directing the times, places and manner of holding elections for representatives of this state in the foederal government of the United States, and of appointing electors, on the part of this state, for the choice of a President of the United States, agreeably to the foederal constitution," was read the third time; and in debating the same,

On motion, it was agreed to postpone the further consideration of the said bill, in order to take a question on the following proposition, viz.,

"Is it the opinion of the House, that the election of Representatives to serve in the federal government should take place on the first Wednesday of January next."[1]

On the question, "will the House agree to the same?" the yeas and nays were called by Mr. Findley and Mr. M'Calmont, and were as follow, viz.,

YEAS.

1. George Clymer
2. Thomas Fitzsimons
3. Jacob Hiltzheimer
4. John Salter
5. George Logan
6. James Moore
7. Richard Thomas
8. Samuel Evans
9. Richard Willing
10. Townsend Whelen
11. Adam Hubley
12. Joseph Lilley
13. Hugh Davison

NAYS.

1. William Lewis
2. William Robinson, Jr.
3. Richard Peters
4. Gerardus Wynkoop
5. John Chapman
6. Samuel Foulke
7. Valentine Upp
8. Robert Ralston
9. Alexander Lowrey
10. Joseph Work
11. James Clemson
12. Jacob Erb
13. John Hopkins
14. Michael Schmyser
15. William Mitchell
16. David M'Clellan
17. Joseph Reed
18. David Mitchell
19. Thomas Beale
20. Thomas Kennedy
21. John Oliver
22. Joseph Heister
23. Gabriel Heister
24. Joseph Sands
25. Philip Kreemer
26. Peter Traxler, Jr.

27. Thomas Mawhorter
28. Peter Burkhalter
29. Peter Ealer
30. John Piper
31. Jacob Saylor
32. Samuel Maclay
33. John White
34. William Findley
35. James Barr
36. John M'Dowell
37. James Allison
38. Alexander Wright
39. John Flenniken

40. Theophilus Philips
41. John Gilchreest
42. James M'Lene
43. James M'Calmont
44. Jacob Reiff
45. Robert Lollar
46. Benjamin Rittenhouse
47. Peter Richards
48. Jacob Miley
49. Robert Clark
50. John Carson
51. John Paul Schott

So it was determined in the negative; and the consideration of the bill being resumed,

It was moved by Mr. Lewis, seconded by Mr. Fitzsimons,

To amend the title, to read in the words following:

"An Act directing the times, places and manner of holding elections for representatives of this state in the Congress of the United States, and for appointing electors, on the part of this state, for choosing a President and Vice President of the United States."

Which was determined in the affirmative.

And the bill having been fully debated by paragraphs,

Ordered, that it be engrossed, for the purpose of being enacted into a law.[2]

1. Brunhouse, *Counter-Revolution,* 216, suggests that the attempt of certain eastern Republicans to put off the election of Representatives until January was to make it difficult for the Constitutionalists to get out the vote when the weather might be bad. Ten of the thirteen men who voted for the delay were from Philadelphia, Philadelphia County, and Chester County, but the rest of the Republican assemblymen refused to support the motion.

2. The engrossed bill was formally approved on 4 October and is printed below under that date.

Assembly Debates, Monday, 29 September [1]

The federal bill was resumed, and the House agreed to appoint two separate days of election, viz., on the motion of Mr. [Richard] Peters, for eight members to the federal House of Representatives, the fourth Wednesday in November next, to be chosen by the people at large, at their usual places of election.

And that conformably to the directions of the Congress of the United States, the first Wednesday in January next is appointed for holding elections throughout this state for ten federal Electors, who are to meet at Reading on the first Wednesday in February, to vote for a President and Vice President for the United States, agreeably to the Federal Constitution.

After having gone through this bill, the House adjourned till tomorrow.

1. Lloyd, *Debates,* IV, 216.

Diary of Jacob Hiltzheimer, Monday, 29 September[1]

From the State House a large number of members went to Hassell's Tavern, when it was determined to run Robert Morris and William Maclay for Senators.

1. Hiltzheimer, *Diary*, 146.

Assembly Proceedings, Tuesday, 30 September

Agreeably to the order of the day, the House proceeded to the election of Senators to represent this state in the Congress of the United States, agreeably to the Constitution adopted for the government of the said states; and the ballots being taken, it appeared that the Honorable William Maclay and Robert Morris, esquires, were duly elected.

Commentaries on the Election of the Pennsylvanian Senators, 1-22 October

The Pennsylvania Senators were the first members elected to the new Congress, and the election attracted nationwide attention. Three Philadelphia newspapers (the *Pennsylvania Journal, Pennsylvania Gazette,* and *Federal Gazette*) reported the news on October 1, and within a month these and other stories about the election were printed in at least thirty other newspapers throughout the United States.

Robert Morris was well known, but William Maclay was virtually unknown outside Pennsylvania, and various Pennsylvanians wrote to friends about him (see, for example, Tench Coxe to James Madison, 22 October, printed below; Benjamin Rush to Jeremy Belknap, Philadelphia, 7 October, and Rush to John Adams, Philadelphia, 22 January 1789, Butterfield, I, 489-91, 498-500). When Thomas Jefferson informed William Short, who was in Rome with John Rutledge, Jr., that Pennsylvania had elected "Robert Morris and a Mr. Mc.lay," Short replied that neither he nor Rutledge could "conceive" who "McLay" could be and that Rutledge thought Jefferson must mean "McKaine [Thomas McKean?] but I am sure you do not" (Jefferson to Short, Paris, 21 November, and Short to Jefferson, Rome, 11 February 1789, Boyd, XIV, 275, 539).

The following excerpts from letters by Pennsylvanians and others discuss issues and personalities involved in the choice of the two Senators.

Benjamin Rush to John Montgomery, Philadelphia, 1 October (excerpt)[1]

The law for electing Representatives, and Electors, and the choice of two Senators give universal satisfaction. A conference will be held in York or Lancaster for setting the tickets. Young General [John] Armstrong was opposed to Mr. [William] Maclay as a Senator, but at a meeting previous to the day of the election he had only 7 out of 33 votes. Maclay's age and steadiness of character were urged against his youth and inexperience in public business. Mr. [William] Bingham was not put in nomination.[2]

. . . .

Our citizens are busy in preparing for the elections, but my state of health does not admit of my attending any of their meetings as they are all held after night, and in crowded rooms.

From all the accounts I can collect, the first and best men in all the states will be chosen to fill the Senate and House of Representatives of the new government. *All will end well.*

George Thacher to Mrs. George Thacher, New York, 1 October (excerpt)[3]

The southern mail arrived today about twelve and brings account of the Pennsylvania election which was yesterday at Philadelphia. Robert Morris and William McClay were chosen federal Senators for that state. The former lives in the city of Philadelphia and is the greatest merchant, perhaps, in all America. He was for several years Financier General of the United States, in which office he acquired immense riches; whether honestly or dishonestly is not for you or me to determine, nor is it of any consequence to us now. And it may be enough to regulate his future conduct for him to know, which I believe he does, that the people in general think pretty independently upon this subject; and three to one don't hesitate to say, in speaking of his wealth, that *ill-gotten riches are of short duration.*

Wm. McClay, the other Senator, was originally a lawyer. He lives now on a large farm upon the River Susquehanna, about one hundred and ten or twenty miles from Philadelphia. He is a member of Council in that state and highly respected by the *landed interest*, as *Morris is by the mercantile.*

I hope to be able, in my next, to give you a more particular detail of these two Senators—their characters, and the views of the parties that choose them. It is an object with me to acquire as accurate a knowledge as possible of the members of the first Congress under the new Constitution.

Ephraim Blaine to William Irvine, Philadelphia, 2 October (excerpt)[4]

The election for Senators is over and Mr. [William] McClay and Mr. [Robert] Morris have been the two fortunate. There had been several meetings of the members of Assembly previous to the election. Your friends, with those of McClay, agreed to run a close ticket but by some means there was jockeying and McClay and his friends are rudely suspected, and indeed I think justly. The prejudice of party carry people amazing lengths in opposition to the best character amongst us; therefore there is nothing in that line certain. The candidates mentioned the morning of the election were Morris, [William] Irvine, McClay, [John] Armstrong and [Frederick] Mullinburgh [Muhlenberg]. The parties withdrew Armstrong and Mullinburgh. The votes stood thus: McClay 66, Morris 37, Irvin[e] 31. From this state of the votes I leave you to judge.

David Redick to William Irvine, Philadelphia, 2 October (excerpt)[5]

I suppose you will receive intelligence from some of your friends of this place in what manner the out-of-doors electioneering business for Senators was conducted. Mr. [William] Maclay's friends deserted our friend in a shameful manner else you would doubtless have been elected.[6] But sir, your Republicans have no faithfulness about them; perhaps you will say neither have my Constitutionalists. In this case they were firm, but unfortunate. General [John] Armstrong is surely in a very awkward situation at present. I feel very sorry for him. Perhaps he rested too much on his unfaithful friends when he resigned his office of one of supreme justices etc.[7]

George Thacher to Nathan Dane, New York, 2 October (excerpt)[8]

Tho tis but two or three days since I wrote you I cannot omit, this post, to inform you of the Pennsylvania election of Senators. This come on this week a Tuesday. The city party strove hard to command the election and held up [Robert] Morris and our *loquacious* [John] Armstrong. The country party was willing the trading interest should have one choice; but they thought the country was entitled to the other. This the city did not like; but held up Armstrong to the country interest. However, after the usual maneuvering, on such occasions, Morris and William McClay on the Susquehanna were chosen. The latter I am told is a good man, much esteemed by the country. He was originally a lawyer, and is now one of their Executive Council, and a man of great landed property.

Andrew Craigie to Daniel Parker, New York, 2 October (excerpt)[9]

Mr. [Robert] Morris and Mr. [William] McClay are appointed Senators for Pennsylvania in the new government, the first appointments which have been made. But he, Morris, is not so popular as he once was and I doubt if his influence will ever again cause much jealousy. It is thought his *Alliance* which arrived lately will produce about 120,000£ Pennsylvania currency. Whether he is sole owner or not is unknown.[10]

Thomas Mifflin to Jeremiah Wadsworth, Schuylkill Falls, 5 October (excerpt)[11]

I agree with you that our friend Reed [James R. Reid?] deserves much from his country and that he would fill the office you hinted at as well as most men in our state. When your letter reached my hand the members had taken their decided parts and the contest lay with [Robert] Morris, [William] McClay, and [William] Irvine. McClay on trial had 66, Morris 37, and Irvine 31 votes.

I gave my vote for Morris and Irvine but did not solicit a vote for either from any member.[12] The representation has gratified one party and the strongest. The minority who are timid *Anti* are exerting themselves to obtain a representation in the first branch who will vote for the New York amendments.

On Saturday a motion was introduced to recommend the letter from Governor [George] Clinton with the amendments of the New York Convention to the succeeding General Assembly but it was negatived by a great majority.[13] Our late House was strongly Federal and there is great probability that the next will be equally so.

John Irvine to William Irvine, Philadelphia, 7 October (excerpt)[14]

Our unsuccessful attempts to carry you for the Senate, will not discourage us from making one other effort to secure you in the federal government; we have therefore determined to run you for Representative in our general ticket. Whatever may be our success, our warmest exertions shall not be wanting. Tomorrow I set out on my journey homewards.

Tench Coxe to James Madison, Philadelphia, 22 October (excerpt)[15]

You will have great satisfaction in hearing that Mr. [William] Maclay, our agricultural Senator is a decided Federalist, of a neat clean landed property, with a law education, a very straight head, of much more reading than the country gentlemen in the Middle States usually are, a man of fair character and great assiduity in business. My own opinion is that he is properest character for the agricultural member in the state, and he was elected by 66 votes out of 67—all the opposition concurring in him, and all our friends but one. I consider this election of Mr. Maclay by all the opposition as of great importance, as a sort of acceptance of the government. They were 31 in the last House, and one absent. Mr. [Robert] Morris you know.

1. RC, Rush Papers, PPL.
2. In a letter to Vice President John Adams, 22 April 1789, Rush said that James Wilson had been considered for the Senate. "Pennsylvania," he told Adams, "looks up with anxious solicitude for the commission of Chief Justice for Mr. Wilson. It was from an expectation of this honor being conferred upon him that he was left out of the Senate, and House of Representatives" (Philadelphia, RC, Adams Papers, MHi).
3. RC, Thacher Papers, MHi.
4. RC, William Irvine Papers, PHi.
5. RC, William Irvine Papers, PHi.
6. According to an extract from a letter from New York (*Independent Gazetteer*, 22 November, printed below), Irvine was one of those responsible for the financial report of a committee of Congress (30 September, JCC, XXXIV, 554-70) which charged fraud and speculation in public monies during the Revolution, and he had therefore been dropped by his fellow Republicans.
7. See John Armstrong, Jr., to Horatio Gates, 30 May, printed above.
8. RC, Dane Papers, DLC.
9. FC, Craigie Papers, MWA.
10. Morris purchased the Continental frigate *Alliance* in 1786. In June 1787, he sent her to Canton, China. The ship arrived back in Philadelphia on 17 September.
11. RC, Wadsworth Papers, CtHi.
12. The Assembly proceedings on 30 September do not record the votes for Senators and perhaps Mifflin, although he was speaker of the Assembly, did vote.
13. On 4 October, the last day of the session, James McLene moved that the letters and proposed amendments sent by the presidents of the Massachusetts, New York, and Virginia conventions, and the letter from the president of the North Carolina Convention, "be specially recommended to the succeeding House of Assembly." The motion was defeated, 38 to 24.
14. RC, William Irvine Papers, PHi. For additional commentary on the Senate election, see the *Federal Gazette*, 25 and 27 October.
15. RC, Madison Papers, DLC.

Federalists Call Conference at Lancaster, 1 October

The Federalists learned of the Harrisburg Convention by mid-August. However, the Cumberland County Circular Letter of 3 July calling the convention for the purpose of proposing amendments to the Constitution and nominating for Congress eight men who would support amendments was not published until 10 September in the *Pennsylvania Gazette*. The next day a group of Federalists in and around Philadelphia declared themselves a "committee of correspondence" and began writing to Federalist leaders throughout the state. They expressed alarm at the Cumberland County letter and the Harrisburg Convention, and urged that plans be made for the coming state and federal elections (Samuel Miles et al. to Timothy Pickering, 11 September, printed above). However no further action seems to have been taken until 1 October, two days after the Pennsylvania election law was ordered engrossed for final passage.

Proceedings of a Philadelphia Meeting, 1 October[1]

At a meeting of a number of gentlemen from the city and county of Philadelphia and from the counties of Berks, Chester, Lancaster, York, Cumberland, Berks,[2] Northumberland, Montgomery, Dauphin and Huntingdon, convened for the purpose of deliberating on the mode of procuring gentlemen to represent this state in the House of Representatives in the new government and to fix on proper persons to elect the President and Vice President:

Resolved, that Henry Wynkoop Esqr. be requested to take the chair and that Mr. James Campbell act as secretary.

Resolved, that it is the opinion of this company, that a conference be held at the borough of Lancaster on the first Monday in November next, in order to fix on tickets for the above purpose.

Resolved, that Samuel Miles, John Nixon, Benjamin Rush, Hilary Baker, Walter Stuart, Henry Kammerer, Francis Gurney, Richard Wells, Tench Coxe, William McClay, William Rawle, Henry Wynkoop and George Latimer, be a committee for the purpose of informing the different counties in the state of the proposed meeting and to request their deputations to it.[3]

Resolved, that this committee meet tomorrow morning at 8 o'clock at the City Tavern for the above purpose.

1. Copy, Timothy Pickering Papers, MHi.
2. The manuscript reads "Berks," but since Berks County had already been listed once, it was probably an error for Bucks.
3. See Federalist Committee to Colonel Nathan Dennison and Timothy Pickering, 2 October, printed immediately below.

Federalist Committee to Colonel Nathan Dennison and Timothy Pickering, Philadelphia, 2 October[1]

The importance of the election for eight federal Representatives, which is now fixed by law to be held on the fourth Wednesday of November next, ought to engage the attention of every well-wisher to his country. Impressed with these sentiments, a number of gentlemen from the different parts of the state, have held a meeting in the city of Philadelphia, the result of which was to propose a meeting of deputies from the different counties of the state at Lancaster on the first Monday of November next, as will appear by the minutes of the same meeting, which we have enclosed to you. You will therefore please to take such measures, as to you shall seem expedient for appointing two deputies (being the number agreed to for each county by the committee) to attend at Lancaster at the time aforesaid.[2] Little need be said to enforce the utility of this measure. As it is evidently just that the federal Representatives should be taken from the different parts of the state, it cannot be expected that every individual will be acquainted with the whole of them. A full and free investigation of character is therefore absolutely necessary. The time, the circumstances of the state require it. We rest satisfied that your attention to this business and your exertions on this occasion, will be equal to the importance of the object now before us.

At the meeting to be held at Lancaster, it is likewise expected that ten suitable persons will be fixed upon as Electors of the President of the United States, who are to be chosen on the first Wednesday of next January, agreeably to the Ordinance of Congress, and the law of the state, to which we beg leave to refer you.

1. RC, Pickering Papers, MHi. This circular letter was signed by the men appointed at a meeting the previous day.
2. See Appointment of the Delegates to the Lancaster Conference, 10-25 October, printed below.

Robert Morris and William Maclay to Speaker Thomas Mifflin, 3 October[1]

A letter from the Honorable Robert Morris and William Maclay, esquires, was presented to the chair, and read, as follows, viz.,

Sir: We have this day been honored with the receipt of your letters, announcing the election which the General Assembly have been pleased to make of us as Senators, to serve this state in the Congress of the United States; and indicating, that it would be agreeable to have our acceptance of the appointment acknowledged in a letter to the Speaker.

Sensible as we are of the distinguished confidence reposed in the persons to whom this important trust is committed, and feeling, as we ought, the honor which the House has conferred on us by that high degree of confidence, we do not hesitate to accept of the appointment. Permit us at the same time to declare, that we do it in the hope of being serviceable to our country. The high station to which we are chosen will afford us the opportunities of meriting the approbation of the General Assembly, and of all our fellow citizens. It shall be our study to avail ourselves of those opportunities, by a faithful discharge of our duty.[2]

1. Assembly Proceedings, Friday, 3 October.
2. Their credentials, dated 28 February 1789, are printed below.

Assembly Proceedings, Saturday, 4 October[1]

An ACT *directing the times, places and manner of holding elections for Representatives of this state in the Congress of the United States, and for appointing Electors, on the part of this state, for choosing a President and Vice-President of the United States.*

On motion, resolved, that one thousand copies of the last mentioned act be printed, and transmitted to the prothonotaries of the respective counties of this commonwealth, for the information of the citizens thereof.

1. Saturday, 4 October, was the last day of the 12th General Assembly, which had been elected in October 1787.

The Pennsylvania Election Law, 4 October[1]

[SEAL]

An Act directing the time, places and manner of holding elections for Representatives of this State in the Congress of the United States and for appointing Electors on the part of this State for chusing a President and Vice-President of the United States.

Section 1st. Whereas the Constitution of the United States declares and directs that "the House of Representatives in the Congress of the United States, shall be composed of Members chosen every second year by the people of the several States, that the electors in each State shall have the requisite qualifications of Electors of the most numerous branch of the State Legislature;" that until the enumeration therein pointed out of the citizens of the United States, shall be made the number of Representatives for this State shall be eight, and That "the times, places and manner of holding elections for Senators and Representatives shall be prescribed in each State by the Legislature thereof." And Whereas it is further declared and directed in and by the said Constitution, that for the purposes of chusing a President and Vice President of the United States, "each State shall appoint in such manner as the Legislature thereof may direct, a number of Electors equal to the whole number of Senators and Representatives to which the State may be entitled in the Congress:" And Whereas the Convention which framed the said Constitution resolved "that as soon as the Conventions of nine States should have ratified the said Constitution the United States in Congress assembled, should fix a day on which Electors should be appointed by the States which should have ratified the same, and a day on which the Electors should assemble to vote for the President and the time and place for commencing proceedings under the said Constitution, and that after such publication the Electors should be appointed and the Senators and Representatives elected; And Whereas the United States in Congress assembled by their Act of the thirteenth day of September in the present year (reciting that the said Constitution had been ratified in the manner therein declared to be sufficient for the establishment of the same) did resolve that the first Wednesday in January next be the day for appointing Electors in the several States ratifying the said Constitution before the said day and that the first Wednesday in February next be the day for the Electors to Assemble in their respective States and Vote for a President.

And whereas a Convention duly appointed by the People of this State did by their Act of the twelfth day of December in the Year of our Lord one thousand seven hundred and eighty seven, in the name of the said People assent to and

299

ratify the said Constitution, in order therefore to carry the said Constitution into effect

Be it enacted and it is hereby enacted by the Representatives of the Freemen of the Commonwealth of Pennsylvania in General Assembly met, and by the authority of the same, That the Election of Representatives agreeably to the said Constitution, and the directions of this Act, to serve in the Congress of the said United States, shall be held by the Citizens thereof, qualified to vote for Members of Assembly on the last Wednesday in November next, and of Electors agreeably to the said Constitution on the first Wednesday of January next, of which elections due Notice shall be given by the Sheriffs of the respective Counties agreeably to the election laws of this State at the places in the City of Philadelphia and in the several Counties of this State prescribed by the election laws aforesaid in like manner, as in and by the said election laws is directed for the election of Members of the General Assembly of this State, and all and every officer and person whose duty it is or may be to attend conduct and regulate according to the Election laws of this State the general election to be held on the second Tuesday in October next are hereby authorised enjoined and and required to attend conduct and regulate the Elections herein directed to be held for the purposes aforesaid in like manner as in and by the said election laws is directed and the several Powers and Authorities to them given by the laws of this State relating to the Election of Members of Assembly of this State are and shall be continued and vested in the said officers and persons respectively for the purposes of holding and conducting the said Elections to be held in pursuance of the directions of this Act as fully and effectually to all intents and purposes as if the Powers and Authorities aforesaid, were herein particularly enumerated and expressed, and in case of the death absence or inability of any of the said officers or persons before the holding the Elections in and by this Act directed to be held others shall be chosen or appointed in their stead according to the directions of the said Election Laws and all and every person and persons who shall or may be guilty of any neglect or abuse of the said Election laws, or of any part thereof at any Election to be held in pursuance of this Act, shall be prosecuted and punished in the same manner as if he or they, was or were guilty of the like neglects, abuses or Breaches of the said Election laws in the Election of Representatives to serve in the General Assembly of this State.

And be it further enacted by the authority aforesaid That every person coming to elect Representatives shall deliver in writing on one ticket or piece of paper the names of Eight persons to be voted for as Representatives, And that every person coming to vote for Electors agreeably to the said Constitution and the directions of this Act shall deliver in writing on one ticket or piece of paper the names of ten persons to be voted for as Electors agreeably to the said Constitution and for the purposes therein mentioned the said Persons so voted for as Representatives and Electors to be selected from the Citizens and Inhabitants of the state at large who are duly qualified according to the said Constitution to serve in the said respective Stations which said tickets or Ballots shall be received and dealt with in like manner with those delivered in at the General Elections for Members of Assembly and Councillors of this State.

And be it further enacted by the authority aforesaid That after the Polls in the several Districts shall be closed and the votes of the Electors cast up in manner and form directed by the laws of this State on that Subject, the names of the several Persons voted for at the several Wards and Districts in the City of Philadelphia and the several counties of this State shall be written on Parchment or paper, and the number of the Votes for each Candidate in the Wards and Districts fairly enumerated and set down which numbers shall be written in Words at length and not in figures only, and the tickets and other papers relating to the elections, shall be sealed up and deposited in manner and form as directed by the election laws of this State; And on such Names and Numbers being so set down and written, the Judges of the several Elections in the City of Philadelphia and in each and every District in all and every county of this State when assembled at the place for that purpose directed shall respectively within the space of three days after the said Election sign and seal the papers or Instrument on which the same are so written and shall make out sign Seal and execute Duplicate Returns thereof one whereof shall be delivered to the Prothonotary of the county to be kept safely, and one other copy thereof shall be delivered to the Sheriff of the proper county to be delivered or safely transmitted by him within ten days after, each respective Election to the Secretary of the Supreme Executive Council of this State for the inspection and examination of the said Supreme Executive Council, And in the City of Philadelphia and in such counties wherein the said Election shall be holden at one place, the said Elections shall be carried on and conducted and the return thereof made in like manner as is herein directed, And the said Supreme Executive Council after having received the returns papers and instruments aforesaid from the said City and each and every of the counties aforesaid shall enumerate and ascertain the numbers of Votes for each and every Candidate and person so as aforesaid chosen as representatives or Electors respectively and shall thereupon declare by proclamation issued by the said Council duly signed by the President, and without delay dispersed thro' the State, the names of the Eight persons highest in Votes of the Electors throughout the State, and in consequence duly elected and chosen as Representatives of and for the State in the Congress of the United States, and the names of the ten persons highest in Votes and therefore elected as Electors agreeably to the Constitution aforesaid.

And the said Supreme Executive Council shall so soon as conveniently may be after such Examination and Declaration transmit the same together with the Documents on which it is founded to the Secretary of the United States in Congress assembled to be by him delivered to the House of Representatives in the Congress of the United States when they shall be assembled at the time and place by the present Congress of the United States directed and fixed on.

And be it further enacted by the authority aforesaid, That the Electors so as aforesaid to be chosen shall assemble on the first Wednesday in February next at the borough of Reading and shall perform the duties enjoined on them by the said Constitution agreeably to the Directions thereof, and the same allowance of Mileage and daily Wages when travelling to, remaining at and returning from the place aforesaid shall be paid them and each and every of them as is by Law allowed and paid to members of Assembly of this Commonwealth, the same to be paid by the Treasurer of this State, or the Treasurer of the counties in which such Electors respectively reside on Warrants signed by the President of the Meeting of such Electors if any they shall choose or by the Majority of such electors exclusive of the Person in whose favour such Warrants may or shall be respectively drawn.

Enacted into a law, at   Signed by order of the House
Philadelphia, on Saturday   [s] Thomas Mifflin
the fourth day of October,   Speaker
in the year of our Lord
One thousand seven hundred
and eighty eight—

[s] Peter Zachary Lloyd, Clerk of the General Assembly—

1. Engrossed Act (LT), PHarH. It is printed, with minor variations, in Pa. *Statutes*, XIII, 140-45. On 13 November the legislature passed a supplementary election law allowing certain voters to vote at county courthouses and in Philadelphia on election day. It is printed below under that date.

Commentaries on the Pennsylvania Election Law, 1-10 October

The question of statewide vs. district elections was an issue in several states. For examples of the discussions in the Pennsylvania newspapers before the passage of the state election law, see "Numa" in the *Pennsylvania Gazette*, 16 July; "A Friend to Agriculture" in the *Pennsylvania Gazette*, 30 July; and an article in the *Pennsylvania Mercury*, 16 September (all printed above). There was very little commentary after the passage of the law, but the four documents below indicate contemporary awareness of the law's significance.

Federal Gazette, 1 October

On Tuesday afternoon,[1] the bill for holding the election for 8 Representatives in Congress, and ten Electors of a President of the United States, was enacted into a law. The election is to be held on the last Wednesday of November. The elections are to be held at the usual places of voting for assemblymen and councillors, and the candidates are to be taken at the option of the voters from every part of the state. This mode of electing the members of the House of Representatives, it was thought was the only one that could have been adopted, without violating the Constitution of the United States.

Benjamin Rush to Jeremy Belknap, Philadelphia, 7 October (excerpt)[2]

Our state has taken the lead in making arrangements for setting the new government in motion. By obliging the whole state to vote in one ticket, it is expected the Federalists will prevail by a majority of two to one in the choice of Representatives for the lower house of Congress.

James Madison to Thomas Jefferson, New York, 8 October (excerpt)[3]

The result of the meeting at Harrisburg was the latest event worthy of notice at the date of my last. Nothing has since taken place in relation to the new government, but the appointment of Mr. Robt. Morris, and a Mr. [William] McClay, to represent Pennsylvania in the Senate. A law has also passed in that state providing for the election of members for the House of Representatives and of Electors of the President. The act proposes that every citizen throughout the state shall vote for the whole number of members allotted to the state. This mode of election will confine the choice to characters of general notoriety, and so far be favorable to merit. It is however liable to some popular objections urged against the tendency of the new system. In Virginia I am inclined to think the state will be divided into as many districts as there are to be members. In other states, as in Connecticut, the Pennsylvania example will probably be followed; and in others again a middle course be taken. It is perhaps to be desired that various modes should be tried, as by that means only the best mode can be ascertained.

Nathan Dane to George Thacher, Boston, 10 October (excerpt)[4]

The legislature of Pennsylvania has done as I expected with regard to the election of Representatives, in making the whole state one district. The city influence has prevailed, but I cannot think this a measure calculated to produce peace and contentment in the state.

1. The bill was approved and ordered engrossed on Monday, 29 September, not Tuesday.
2. RC, Belknap Papers, MHi. Printed: Butterfield, I, 489-91.
3. RC, Madison Papers DLC. Printed: Boyd, XIV, 3-4.
4. RC, Thacher Papers, MHi.

Federal Gazette, 4 October

A correspondent wishes to awake the friends of Federal measures, to a sense of the duty which they owe alike to their country, to posterity, and themselves, in the choice of men to represent them in the federal body. Let no lukewarm patriot, no disguised enemy to their glorious cause, be suffered to have a seat in that honorable house; but let them nobly copy the worthy example of our legislature, who have chosen for Senators, two gentlemen of inviolable attachment to the great cause of liberty and the Union. Should such men be chosen in the different states, the Constitution will have a fair trial, our drooping commerce will revive, and our distressed mechanics be enabled to procure bread. Such men will not mutilate, maim, distort, nor deform that plan of government which has been the result of long experience, mature deliberation, tried integrity, and universally acknowledged abilities—by foisting into it, the absurd doctrines of Martin,[1] Mason,[2] and our other Antifederal ringleaders. In fine, such men will never attempt to make *alterations* in the system, until they appear to be *amendments*.

1. See Luther Martin's *The Genuine Information, delivered to the Legislature of the State of Maryland* . . . (Philadelphia, 1788) and his replies to the "Landholder" which appeared in the Baltimore *Maryland Journal* from 14 to 25 March.
2. George Mason's "Objections" to the Constitution were at first circulated by him in manuscript form, but by the end of 1787 they were being widely printed in newspapers (see, for example, the Boston *Independent Chronicle*, 22 November; *New York Packet*, 30 November; *Pennsylvania Packet*, 3 December; Richmond *Virginia Independent Chronicle*, 5 December; and Charleston *Columbian Herald*, 27 December).

Thomas Hartley to Tench Coxe, York, 6 October[1]

I have received your favor of the 17th. of September past as well as a letter from the committee of correspondence of the 11th. of that month.[2]

The persons who are against the new Constitution are taking all the pains in their power to obtain a majority in the federal legislature; and unless equal exertions are made on the other side, we shall find the government embarrassed and the wheels prevented from moving.

The Antifederalists look forward to such events. I hope they will be disappointed.

The system for a general ticket of members of the House of Representatives in Congress from this state has been adopted by our Assembly in preference to districts etc. On this, as the law is passed, I shall say little.

It has been observed by some gentlemen that by electing out of the state at large you have a better chance of obtaining good men than obliging the electors to vote for separate Representatives in districts. If this principle is right, too much care cannot be used in fixing upon them. They should be men of knowledge and information, well attached to the new plan and should have characters unexceptionable as to their integrity.

I do not know how far it will be proper to determine that the Representatives shall be composed of certain numbers from different professions. It is true you should have men acquainted with trade etc., and they ought to have an adequate knowledge of the police etc. of this country, but if you can find men of acknowledged abilities and virtue, I should not much regard to what profession or interest they belong.

As I have not been lately in the city, I know not what arrangements have been talked of there. However, I think if you can agree upon good men the more they are scattered over the state, the more acceptable it would be at first view to the people.

The city should have her proportion but I confess we shall have much trouble in fixing upon proper members for this side of the [Susquehanna] River. There are but few men who have abilities and leisure and are fit objects for choice, and when you ask me for my opinion of a ticket, I acknowledge my deficiency on that score; tho my knowledge of the state is not very confined.

I would mention a few names out of which some might be selected but not the whole: William Bingham, Tench Cox, James Willson, Henry Wynkoop, Esqr., F[rederick] Augustus Muhlenberg, Esqr., George Clymer, Thomas Fitzimmons, John Cox, Anthony Wayne, Jasper Yeates, Stephen Chambers.

On this side of the river the matter is new. Some gentlemen might be nominated in York and Cumberland; and over the mountain you might have General [John] Nevil. There should be at least two or three on the west side of Susquehanna.

As you take me somewhat by surprise, my list, I dare say, is not so perfect. You must only consider it for yourself.

There is a probability we shall carry a majority of Federalists for our state Assembly in this county. Perhaps I might say more.

We have no news. I therefore conclude with much respect and regard.

1. RC, Coxe Papers, Tench Coxe Section, PHi.
2. See Samuel Miles et al. to Timothy Pickering, 11 September, printed above.

A Freeman to the Citizens of Pennsylvania, Federal Gazette, 6 October

Friends and Fellow Freemen: The time is fast approaching, when you will have an opportunity of exercising that most invaluable privilege of free citizens— the right of election. A prudent but manly exertion of this important trust, was never more necessary than now. That independence for which many of you have sustained the rigors of the summer sun and the nipping frosts of winter, exposed to nakedness and famine, through eight successive years—and for which the frozen regions of the North, and the burning sands of the South, have been deluged with the best blood of our citizens, and strewed with their mangled bodies—that independence, my countrymen, is yet incomplete: one generous effort remains to crown all your past success with glory. The wisdom of America has formed and adopted a Constitution which seems well calculated to secure the freedom and establish the national importance of the United States. But in vain have you struggled for liberty, in vain have you formed a Constitution, to preserve that liberty, and adopted it in *name*, unless you also adopt it in *practice*.

To effect this, however, is no arduous task, it is only necessary that you should be vigilant and active in your choice of eight federal Representatives, whose known abilities, integrity and firm attachment to the Constitution should be their chief recommendation; and without which no man should be entitled to your suffrages. Unhappy, indeed, were our case if men of a different stamp should be suffered to creep into the general government, to clog its wheels and retard its motions, by endeavoring to foist in a train of *amendments* as they are pleased to call their absurd, ill-digested, and contradictory *alterations*, which could not fail to overthrow this hitherto unequalled fabric, and render all your labors abortive.

The liberties of your country can never be endangered but by two things. The first is, an injudicious exercise of this your darling privilege; the second, your total negligence concerning it.

With respect to the first, an injudicious choice changes this blessing into the worst of curses; and, instead of liberty, order, and good government, do not fail to introduce slavery, anarchy and intestine commotions. Be watchful therefore, be steadfast, and let no consideration under heaven warp your integrity, when the safety and happiness of your country, when your life, liberty, and property, when everything that is dear to freemen, is at stake. It has been objected by Luther Martin, that the people at large should not be the electors of federal Representatives, but that they ought to be chosen by the state legislatures:[1] the worthy framers of our new Constitution thought otherwise, and were not afraid to commit this important trust to your charge, relying on your wisdom and firmness for a faithful discharge of it. Consider then, that by every abuse of this privilege you show yourselves unworthy of the trust reposed in you by your Constitution; that by placing unworthy men at the head of affairs, you violate the social compact between you and your fellow citizens, and exercise this right not only to your own but to their destruction.

Our government flowing, from the people, must necessarily be pure while its source remains uncontaminated. But it must also be muddy and impure whenever the fountain becomes corrupted. Let me therefore once more call upon you to guard well your integrity, and act like men of an independent spirit, who will spurn from you with indignation, the wretch who shall dare to insult your understanding, direct your judgment, or bias your choice. Let no electioneering jobber be suffered, with impunity, to lie in wait for the unwary on the day of election with a ticket which he shall have the daring insolence to offer them, without having previously consulted them on the subject. Such treatment is beneath the dignity of freemen; it is only fit to be exercised over stalls of asses. You should therefore consider well whether you are to give up your freedom of election to a wretch, who is not a freeman, but the miserable tool, the drudge of a party. If you wish to preserve this sacred right, you will treat with becoming contempt every endeavor to rob you of it; and will faithfully exercise it to your own, your fellow citizens, and your country's advantage, by electing men of wisdom, and patriotic firmness, to represent you in the general government; bearing in mind, that even a Constitution framed by the creator of the universe himself, would be inadequate to the preservation of your freedom, if it were not well administered: now if you be improperly governed, the fault must be your own, in choosing improper Representatives. May you consider this point with the importance it deserves, and be active in choosing men of worth and integrity.[2]

1. See Max Farrand, ed., *The Records of the Federal Convention of 1787* (rev. ed., 4 vols., New Haven, Conn., 1937), I, 437-43, 444-45; and Luther Martin, "To the People of Maryland," Baltimore *Maryland Journal,* 18 March.

2. The conclusion of this essay, in the *Federal Gazette*, 8 October, is printed below.

James Campbell to Tench Coxe, York, 7 October[1]

I have received your favor by Mr. McClelan and am obliged by the part you acted with respect to my letter. It was the production of half an hour after *supping out* and could not embrace all the points requisite to be touched on in a letter of that nature.

Notwithstanding the partiality which parents feel for their offspring, I had not a moment's hesitation to prefer yours. I hope your complaisance has not got the better of your earnest in so important a case, or in other words I hope the Senator's [William Maclay] letter is not less calculated to promote the purposes of the committee than yours.[2] I acknowledge I thought it improper to have Mr. McClay on the committee and it will be still more improper that the circular letter should go forth as his, for its influence in favor of the new government will not be increased by a discovery that it was written by one of its officers— but it is the letter of the committee. I fancy it will be the disposition of the western and middle deputies to keep the representation of the several interests as distinct as possible and to consider the chief interest of each candidate—but strong arguments may be brought in favor of the man who connects in himself the farmer, the merchant, and the manufacturer—who like the city Senator [Robert Morris] is at once the genius of commerce, the patron of manufactures and an extensive landholder. So much accomodations as will unite your exertions will be absolutely necessary; for tho the opposition cannot outvote, they can and will outcheat you. The number of votes in the western counties will be little short of the number of inhabitants.

I am sure that the deputies of this county will meet on principles of moderation and agreement; that the whole, not parts, will be their object.

1. RC, Coxe Papers, Tench Coxe Section, PHi. Campbell had been secretary of the Pennsylvania Convention and was secretary of the Philadelphia meeting on 1 October which decided to call a conference at Lancaster to nominate Federalist candidates for Congress (see Proceedings of a Philadelphia Meeting, 1 October, printed above).

2. See Federalist Committee to Colonel Nathan Dennison and Timothy Pickering, 2 October, printed above.

Centinel XIX, Independent Gazetteer, 7 October[1]

Friends, Countrymen, and Fellow Citizens: When I last addressed you on the subject of the new Constitution, I had not a doubt of its rejection: the baneful nature and tendency of this system of ambition had been so fully exposed, that its most zealous advocates were constrained to acknowledge many imperfections and dangers, and *seemingly* to acquiesce in the necessity of amendments. However, by the time this general conviction had taken place in the minds of the people, so many states had adopted the Constitution, and the public anxiety was so great to have an efficient government, that the votaries of power and ambition, were enabled, by adapting their language and conduct to the temper of the times, to prevail upon a competent number of the states to establish the Constitution, without previous alteration, upon the implied condition of subsequent amendments, which they assured would certainly be made, as everybody were agreed in their propriety.

My knowledge of the principles and conduct of these men, for many years past, left me no room to doubt of their insincerity on this occasion. I was persuaded that all their professions of moderation, and assurances of future amendments, were founded in deception, that they were but the blind of the moment, the covered way to dominion and empire. Like a barrel thrown to the whale, the people were to be amused with fancied amendments, until the harpoon of power, should secure its prey and render resistance ineffectual. Already the mask of ambition begins to be removed, and its latent features to appear in their genuine hue, disdaining any further veil from policy; the *wellborn*, inebriated with success, and despising the people for their easy credulity, think it unnecessary to dissemble any longer. Almost every newspaper ridicules the idea of amendments, and triumphs over the deluded people. Ye patriots of America, arouse from the dangerous infatuation in which ye are lulled, and, while it is yet time, strain every nerve to rescue your country from the servile yoke of bondage and to preserve that liberty which has been so recently vindicated, at the expense of so much blood and treasure. Upon the improvement of the present moment depends the fate of your country; you have now a constitutional opportunity afforded you, to obtain a safe and a good government, by making choice of such persons to represent you in the new Congress, as have congenial sentiments with yourselves. Suffer not, ye freemen of America, the *wellborn*, or their *servile*

307

minions, to usurp the sacred trust, to impose themselves upon you as your guardians; for whatever professions they may make, or assurances they may give you, depend upon it they will deceive you, like the wolf in sheeps' clothing they will make you their prey.

Treat with contempt the slanderous arts of the wellborn to prejudice you against your true friends, and convince them on this great occasion, by your good sense, union and vigor, that you are not to be duped out of your liberties by all the refinements of *Machiavellian* policy. The future government of these United States will take its tone from the complexion of the first Congress; upon this will greatly depend, whether despotic sway, or the salutary influence of a well regulated government, shall hereafter rule this once happy land. As the legislature of this state have appointed the last Wednesday in November next for the election of 8 Representatives for this state in the new Congress, you ought to be prepared from that *all important* day; and as success is only to be ensured by unanimity among the friends of equal liberty, local and personal predilections and dislikes should give place to the general sentiment; whatever ticket may be agreed to by the majority of the opposition to the new Constitution in its present shape, ought to be supported by all those who are sincere in wishing for amendments. I trust that all prejudices and antipathies arising from the late war, or from difference of religion, will be sacrificed to the great object of the public welfare, and that all good and well-meaning men of whatever description will harmonize on this occasion. For among the various artifices and stratagems of the wellborn, the principal one, and upon which they will the most rely for success, will be the endeavor to divide you, and thus by scattering your suffrages between various candidates to frustrate your object.

From the mode of appointment, the Senate of the general government will be chiefly composed of the *wellborn*, or their minions, and when we consider the great and various powers which they will possess, and their permanancy, it ought to operate as an additional stimulus with you to obtain faithful Representatives in the other branch of legislature, to shield your privileges and property from the machinations of ambition, and the rapacity of power. The Senate, besides their proper share in the legislature, have great executive and judicial powers—their concurrence is made necessary to all the principal appointments in government. What a fruitful source of corruption does not this present! In the capacity of legislators they will have the irresistible temptation to institute lucrative and needless offices, as they will in fact, have the appointment of the *officers*.

When I consider the nature of power and ambition; when I view the numerous swarm of hungry office hunters, and their splendid expectations, anticipation exhibits such a scene of rapacity and oppression, such burdensome establishments to pamper the pride and luxury of a useless herd of officers, such dissipation and profusion of the public treasure, such consequent impoverishment and misery of the people, that I tremble for my country.

Such evils are only to be averted by a vigorous exertion of the freemen of America, to procure a virtuous, disinterested, and patriotic House of Representatives. That you may all view the importance of this election in its true light, and improve the only means which the Constitution affords you for your preservation, is the fervent wish of Centinel.

1. This essay was dated Philadelphia, 3 October. This and the following essays by "Centinel" were addressed either to "the People" or "the Citizens" of Pennsylvania. "Cen-

tinel" was Samuel Bryan, the son of George Bryan, one of the most important leaders of the Constitutionalists. At the time, the "Centinel" essays were sometimes attributed to the father. However, Samuel Bryan stated and implied that he had written them (to Dr. James Hutchinson, n.p., 18 December 1790, copy, Albert Gallatin Papers, NHi; to Thomas Jefferson, Philadelphia, 27 February 1801, and n.p., 24 July 1807, RC, RG 59: Department of State, Applications and Recommendations, Jefferson Administration, 1801-1809, DNA). Some men at the time recognized that George Bryan was not the author. On 25 November 1788, "Detector" in the *Independent Gazetteer* said that there was now proof that he was not. "Detector" pointed out that five numbers had appeared while Judge Bryan was more than 300 miles away attending sessions of the Supreme Court and that "these five numbers are written in the same style and with equal ability as the former."

The first essay appeared on 5 October 1787, and by 9 April 1788 Bryan had published eighteen numbers attacking the Constitution and the Federalists. Most of them were published first in *The Independent Gazetteer; or, the Chronicle of Freedom* and they were frequently reprinted in other newspapers. Bryan resumed publication of "Centinel" at the beginning of the campaign for seats in the House of Representatives. The second series of six essays are numbered consecutively with the first eighteen and are reprinted in full in McMaster and Stone, 670-98.

A Freeman to the Citizens of Pennsylvania, Federal Gazette, 8 October[1]

Friends and Fellow Freemen: Having endeavored to warn you of the dangers attendant on a careless or improper discharge of your elective trust, I now proceed to consider the baneful effects of betraying that trust, by entirely neglecting it.

I call it a trust, committed to each and all of you, because it is the privilege of every citizen, poor as well as rich; and is to be exercised not to his private advantage only, but for the general good. I call it a trust of the greatest importance; because it is the very basis, the soul of a free government, without the faithful discharge of which, the whole must become a foundationless fabric—an unanimated heap of ruins: therefore, every man who is guilty of neglect or omission of this essential duty, is a traitor to freedom and his country—is unworthy the name of freeman, and deserves not to breath[e] the free air of a republic, where "one is made for all, not all for one." No: he deserves not the enjoyment of liberty, whose apathy of soul renders him totally insensible of it. The Constitution of his country may preserve his life, liberty and property but it cannot expand his contracted mind, nor give him the spirit of a freeman. He is forever a miserable dependent on his patriotic fellow citizens, who share with him that liberty of which they are nobly tenacious, and to preserve which this slavish sluggard would scarcely deprive himself of one slothful slumber. What a pity, that the drone should feast luxuriously on the industrious labor of the active bee!

Pardon me, my fellow citizens, if I give vent to those feelings which the enormity of this crime awakes in my soul. Behold all the powers of slavery, anarchy and hell conspired against the peace, order and happiness of our country! Behold them assembled for the diabolical purpose, at Harrisburg, the pandemonium of Pennsylvania! Behold them, under the specious pretext of deliberating on *amendments*, endeavoring to sap and undermine that Constitution, which has hitherto baffled their open attacks, and withstood their collective fury! Behold them in ambuscade, collecting their shattered forces, once more, to try their bankrupt fortune at the approaching elections of state and federal representatives; when they hope, no doubt, to find the friends of union, harmony and order elated with former success, and off their guard!

Behold these things, ye patriotic citizens of Pennsylvania! and say, what punishment is adequate to his crime, who basely or indolently shrinks from his duty, when everything that is dear in life—nay, when liberty, which alone can make life desirable, is at stake? Does he not, at least, merit to be expelled the society of freemen, and to be sent in exile to the dominions of some eastern despot, where he might wear his chains unmolested, without having it in his power to betray the liberties of others?

Let no sneering critic say, that I inveigh against what does not exist: it is notoriously real. The returns from elections in different parts of the state, compared with the lists of taxable inhabitants in those parts, incontrovertibly prove the truth of the fact. In some places one third, in others half the inhabitants have been guilty of this fatal omission of their duty; among these, however, I am willing to believe were many honest men, and sincere friends to their country, who have not been aware of the extent of their crime, or who have mistakenly imagined that activity in politics belonged only to factious men, or to the leaders of a party. What an absurd opinion this, to induce any person to relinquish his dearest privilege!

Far be it from me to foment or wish for the preservation of that party spirit, which has so long distracted the counsels of this state—yet I must confess my belief, that were it not for this, which keeps up a continual ferment among the people, they would long ere this have fallen into a lethargy, which is the most unfortunate situation to which they could be reduced—a situation in which, of all others, they would be most easily enslaved. But is it not strange that our citizens, who are averse to party bickerings, will suffer themselves to be governed agreeably to the will of the leading party, be it right or wrong? Why do they not judge for themselves, and support whatever measures they may approve of, like men who have the good of their country at heart—and decidedly oppose every factious machination which may be inimical to the peace, liberty, or happiness of the community?

It is equally the duty of every honest republican, to give energy to a wise and good government, and to stem the iniquitous torrent of a bad one. Let no freeman neglect to exercise his right of suffrage, under the fatal mistake that his vote would be of little or no importance. Perhaps his single vote might turn the scale, and prove the salvation of his country: should it be otherwise, he will at least have the heart felt satisfaction of having faithfully discharged his duty—and, to an honest man, a self-approving conscience is of much greater value, and affords more real happiness, than he could possibly derive from the possession of all the wealth of the Indies.

It is the indispensable duty of free republicans, at all times, to guard well this *sine qua non*, this necessary source of national liberty, happiness and glory; but more particularly at this critical period, when the great, the important cause of federal unanimity is in the utmost danger, from the insidious machinations of factions and self-interested men. What an eternal disgrace would it reflect on the friends of federal measures, supinely to neglect their duty on the great day of election, and thus suffer the enemies of the Union to elect men of their own principles! I need not point out the ruinous consequences that must inevitably ensue—they are obvious.

Thanks to the genius of freedom, the enemies of order and good government are comparatively few; but let not a sense of this induce a single man among you to conclude, that his vote and exertions are unnecessary. Should such an unfortunate idea influence one individual, why may it not have equal weight with others? And should all, or a greater part of all the sons of liberty be seized with this inglorious lethargy, while their opponents are eagerly watching for such an opportunity, you might in anguish and despair repent your indolence; but its cursed effects must long remain as infamous testimonials of your disgrace.

I am under greater apprehensions that you will betray this important trust by neglecting it altogether, than by discharging it unfaithfully. My apprehensions of the future, are founded on experience of the past. I know that *very few* of my fellow citizens are wicked enough, deliberately to conspire against the happiness of that community, whereof they are a component part. I also know, that *many*, *very many* thoughtlessly omit the discharge of their elective duty, not reflecting, that by such negligence, they are accessary to their own, their fellow citizens, and their country's ruin.

I would therefore conjure you, by all that is precious to freemen, by every patriotic and social tie that can endear you to your country and to each other, and by your tender regard for your beloved offspring, to consider that the common cause demands your united aid. Let not your elective privileges perish in your hands; but may they, like the fires of the vestal virgins, be preserved in all their splendor, and transmitted from generation to generation, till time shall be no more.

1. Continued from the *Federal Gazette*, 6 October, printed above.

Cassius, Federal Gazette, 9 October

The insidious efforts of the Antifederalists, to prevent the adoption of the new Constitution, having failed of success, they have now altered their plan, and are applying their strength to secretly undermine what they could not openly and fairly destroy. All their endeavors are now concentrated in the election of federal Representatives, in hopes, that by introducing into that eminent body, men who may impede its operations and disgrace its character, by their utter incapacity in some instances, or by their concealed treacheries and artful combinations in others; the government may become inefficient, or at least unpopular in its outset; and the people consent to relapse into their former systems of weakness, poverty and domestic tyranny—systems in which the leaders of the few remaining Antifederalists naturally delight, as affording means of supporting that ascendancy which the possession of the best offices and emoluments of the state affords.

There is something in this plan so base and contemptible, that the indignation of every honest elector must rise against it. It is like applying to poison when the generous weapons have failed. It is worse than the Machiavellian policy with which the scribes of the party have affected to designate the conduct of the friends to American prosperity. It is the true dark and deadly system of the two Borgias, who were accustomed to make a feeble attack, in order that by a feigned reconciliation, their adversaries, disarmed of suspicion, might be secretly and safely destroyed.

The meeting at Harrisburg, the affected protestations of submission to the government, are their feigned reconciliation; the proposed amendments, the terms of the fictitious treaty. It is as clear as anything in human events can be, that their aim is not to amend but to destroy. Their object is not a good federal government; it is to have no solid union whatever. Seduced in some instances by visionary notions of existence as unconnected states, terrified from a sense of the tenure by which they hold their own importance, at the possibility of losing anything of the state prerogative in the federal compound, the chief object of their wishes is to render the new government as difficult, expensive, and unsatisfactory as possible.

If the misfortunes of this state should still hang over her so far as to determine the election in their favor, and they should attempt on the one hand to introduce the amendments proposed at Harrisburg, we shall at much expense lose a great deal of that valuable time which ought to be immediately applied to the regulation of our finances, commerce, and internal resources, without a chance that the people will consent to diminish any part of that beautiful combination of strength and liberty which forms the character of the structure. But if on the other hand, in pursuance of that secret plan which it is generally believed was laid at Harrisburg, no farther mention is made of amendments, then will all the well known ingenuity and industry of this sect of people be applied to the introduction of discord and dissension, to the general detriment and final dishonor of America.

This is therefore an occasion which ought to excite our alarm and urge our exertion. Whoever holds his liberty dear, whoever detests anarchy and loves government, peace, and independence, should now press into service all the abilities he possesses. To himself and to his country he now owes all his assiduity and all his labor, till the issue of the election shall have evinced that the good sense of Pennsylvania is incapable of being deceived by the specious assurances and treacherous machinations of her real enemies.

William Shippen, Jr., to Thomas Lee Shippen, Philadelphia, 10-15 October (excerpt)[1]

Our elections for the federal government take place soon. The Senators are chosen by our Assembly who were sitting and are Rob. Morris and Wm. McClay of Sunbury. The other Senators will be chosen as soon as the respective assemblies meet. The Congress is to be elected the first Wednesday in January '89. The President and Vice [President] the first Wednesday in February, and the whole meet at New York in March. The whole state vote for a Federal and Antifederal ticket. The Anti ticket was formed at the Harrisburg Convention and are C[harles] Pettit, B[lair] McClenachan, [William] Findley, [Robert] Whitehil, [Simon] Driesbach, W[illiam] Montgomery, General [William] Irwin [Irvine] and I believe [John] Smilie.[2] The Feds have not yet formed one. There is to be a conference held at Lancaster consisting of two from city and each county to form a ticket. These conferees are to be chosen by a committee of 3 from each ward and to be approved at a town meeting next Saturday. Great power will be in the hands of these conferees. They will, in effect, choose your Representatives. The men talked of for the city are [George] Clymer, [William] Bingham and [Thomas] Fitzsimmons. I am apt to think it will be the first and last for the country. Mr. [Thomas] Hartley of York, [Stephen] Chambers of Lancaster, Mr. [Henry] Wyncoop of Bucks, [John] Nevill of Franklin, a son of General [John] Nevills, General [John] Armstrong, Jr. (very doubtful) and another are talked of. Yesterday was our state election when the old assembly for the county were chosen unanimously except Major [William] McPherson vice somebody whose time is out [Thomas Mifflin].[3] Colonel [Samuel] Miles, councilor for the city. The assemblymen for the city the same as before only Lawce. Sickle, a German, vice [William] Will. T[homas] Mifflin, councilor for the county and to be chosen governor. James Ash is sheriff after a hard struggle with [William] Will. [William] Jackson don't like the conference business at Lancaster; he nor Lewis were consulted and he is very jealous of the peoples' right of suffrage. He spoke badly at a town meeting. T[ench] Coxe answered almost as badly. Watty [i.e., Walter] Stewart made a much better speech than either of them and was loudly applauded and Jackson put on one of his [longa?] looks. Poor fellow is down in the mouth—gets no business nor do I see any place for him. He may possibly be clerk to one of the new houses.[4]

1. RC, Shippen Family Papers, DLC. The letter from which this excerpt is taken was written between 10 and 18 October.

2. If the delegates at the Harrisburg Convention agreed upon a ticket, they did not announce it publicly. It is evident, however, that the Antifederalist leaders began circulating a list of names and that Shippen had either heard about it or seen it. The names he mentions, except those of Simon Driesbach and John Smilie, who were replaced by Daniel Hiester and Peter Muhlenberg, were first published on 7 November (see the Harrisburg Ticket, *Federal Gazette*, 7 November, printed below).

3. Section 8 of the Pennsylvania Constitution of 1776 prohibited anyone from being a member of the legislature for more than four years in any seven (Thorpe, V, 3084).

4. William Jackson, who had been secretary of the Constitutional Convention of 1787, began the practice of law in Pennsylvania in 1788. He sought the post of secretary of the Senate in 1789 but was defeated by Samuel A. Otis of Massachusetts.

Appointment of Delegates to the Lancaster Conference, 10-25 October

After the call for a conference at Lancaster (see Federalists Call Conference at Lancaster: Proceedings of a Philadelphia Meeting, 1 October, and Federalist Committee to Colonel Nathan Dennison and Timothy Pickering, 2 October, printed above) Federalists throughout the state met and appointed delegates. The documents printed below illustrate the methods of appointment and reveal considerable differences of opinion among Federalist leaders.

Western Federalists wanted to make sure that westerners were nominated. Northumberland County proposed that two merchants, a manufacturer, a lawyer, and four farmers make up the ticket, and that at least some of the Representatives should be able to speak German. Philadelphians argued that the city should have more than two Representatives because of its importance, and that men should be nominated who would work for the removal of the capital from New York to Philadelphia, promote commerce, and take care of Pennsylvania's public creditors, who were the "largest" in the Union. Philadelphia nominated six candidates, although at least one Philadelphian thought that number would "alarm" the country. Aside from Northumberland County, none of the documents shows any concern for representation of the large German population, a lack of concern which was to be one of the principal objections to the ticket nominated at Lancaster.

Philadelphia County Meeting, 10 October[1]

We are informed that on Friday, at a very large and respectable meeting of the free electors of the County of Philadelphia, held at Germantown, that George Gray and Enoch Edwards, esqrs., were unanimously appointed to attend the federal conference to be held at Lancaster for the purpose of recommending suitable persons to represent this state in Congress, and also Electors to choose the President of the United States.

It must give pleasure to all honest Federal minds to observe, that this business was done openly, at a very public meeting of the county, publicly advertised, and that men of respectable, established, unequivocal Federalist characters, were appointed to so important a trust. This appointment wears a very different complexion to what the smuggling business which took place in the sending members to Harrisburg did, with the ostensible pretensions of procuring amendments, but in fact to form a ticket for Representatives in Congress. A very curious story indeed, that eight Antifederal men should represent one of the greatest Federal states in the Union!

Instructions to the Northumberland County Delegates, 16 October[2]

At a meeting of a number of freemen at the courthouse in Sunbury, on the 16th of October, 1788, the Honorable William Maclay, Esquire, in the chair, the following instructions to the deputies were drawn up, and after being duly considered, were unanimously agreed to, and ordered to be signed by the chairman.

Gentlemen, in your attendance at the conference to be held at Lancaster on the first Monday in November next, for the purpose of recommending proper persons to represent the state in the new Congress, we desire you to pay attention to the following instructions:

Let integrity and decency of character be considered as the first qualification—industry and application to business as the second. No brilliancy of talents, or show of knowledge, should atone for the want of the above qualities. Thirdly, extensive information, and some degree of practice in agriculture, commerce and manufactures, with a general knowledge of the laws of the land, are necessary. But as it may be objected, that men qualified in all the above respects, cannot easily be found—and that different men adapted to the different interests must be chosen, we recommend something of the following kind.

That two able merchants who may attend to the interest of commerce, one person remarkably attached to the principles of manufactures, and an eminent law character, with four substantial yeomen, should form our representation in Congress.

Although as Pennsylvanians we declare ourselves actuated by one common interest, and abhor every idea of national distinction; yet as a respectable body of our fellow citizens speak the German language, we are of opinion, that a part of the representation should be qualified to do business in that language; and accordingly recommend this subject as a matter worthy of your attention.

W[illiam] Maclay, Chairman

Attest, Charles Smith, Secretary

William Maclay to Benjamin Rush, Sunbury, 18 October[3]

Your letter by Benny Young came to my hands just as we were going to the meeting to appoint the Lancaster conferees. We had made our previous arrangements, and it was too late to make any alterations, or I should with pleasure have attend[ed] at the conference. The men whom we have appointed will, however, attend, and I hope will be useful. They are Colonel [William] Wilson and Chas. Smith.[4] The former is now in Philadelphia and will have an opportunity of learning the sense of the citizens. And it will be well enough that he be spoke to, for I make no doubt but some warm characters about Lancaster will be for pushing matters far in their own favor.

Our common friend Tench Coxe is much talked of, even here, for a Representative in Congress. It will, however, be necessary that he stand well with the conferees from the city.

The call of the gentleman who is to be the bearer of my letter prevents me adding more save that I am, with the highest respect, your sincere friend and humble servant.

Charles Smith to Tench Coxe, Sunbury, 18 October[5]

Enclosed you have a copy of the instructions of a number of the inhabitants of Northumberland County to their deputies appointed to attend at the state conference at Lancaster; which I beg you will commit to the press, for the sole purpose of acquainting our friends and fellow citizens with the decisive measures we have pursued in consequence of the circular letter from Philadelphia. To investigate and fix upon proper characters to form a Federal ticket is surely a matter of considerable moment, and which requires coolness an[d] deliberation. To purge the minds of thousands of our fellow citizens of the poison with which they have been infected will and ought to be an important object with the Representatives of this great commonwealth. Perhaps, indeed, all their fears are vain—but when popular passions are roused, and those passions kept alive by designing and ambitious men, an attempt to reason them down is frequently construed into insult. It seems, therefore, to be the wish of the moderate and reasonable men of all parties that some necessary explanations should take place, in order to quiet the minds of our dissenting fellow citizens, and to introduce union and harmony throughout the state. Attention to this subject ought to be considered as a duty incumbent upon our first federal Representatives.

Amongst the other characters pointed out by our instructions, *two* able merchants has been thought an essential part of our representation. From the local situation and circumstances of Pennsylvania, characters of this description cannot be called, with equal propriety, from any other place than Philadelphia. It must chiefly rest upon the deputation from the city to point out those characters. But it will become our duty to take care that they shall be men (in general) acceptable to the great body of citizens and yeomanry throughout Pennsylvania. If you have leisure, I would thank you for such general information upon the subject as you may think necessary, and which the laborious attention you have paid to it must enable you to give. At the same time I would be glad to be informed if you will suffer your name to be mentioned as a candidate at the conference. Let me hint further, that light inconveniences ought never to excuse the man whom his country calls to deliberate upon subjects of the greatest magnitude, and of most considerable importance to the present age, and the remotest posterity.

The matter contained in this letter, I hope, will be a sufficient apology with you. I will thank you to render my love to my brother Richard. I hope he is attentive to business.

N.B. Colonel [William] Wilson, my colleague in the deputation, is now in the city and will forward any information to this place or Lancaster.

Hints to the Gentlemen of the Philadelphia Ward Committees,
17 October[6]

The trust that is reposed in you by your fellow citizens, to select two proper characters to meet conferees at Lancaster, in order to form a suitable ticket for the federal House of Representatives, is of the most important nature, and must deeply affect the interests of your constituents.

The advantages that are to be expected from the operation of the federal government, will greatly depend on a proper choice of characters to administer its affairs.

The City of Philadelphia should be very careful in the selection, and should examine with the most scrutinizing attention, the respective qualities and qualifications of the candidates.

There are many objects of considerable magnitude that peculiarly relate to the interests of Pennsylvania that must engage the attention of the new Congress.

The removal of that body to Pennsylvania (the center of the national population of the Union) is amongst the number. Considering the partiality of the act that provides for their assembling at New York, so injurious to the rights, and oppressive to the interests of the Southern States, and so opposed to the spirit of the Federal Constitution, which contemplates an equal portion of advantage to every member of the Union, there is no doubt that with proper exertions, the removal may be effected.

Arrangements that relate to commerce, revenue and public credit, are amongst the most important points of discussion that will agitate the councils of Congress, and which are highly interesting to the city of Philadelphia, as well as the state at large.

Your constituents will therefore require of you, that as far as your agency extends you will provide for the choice of characters from the city, who have a deep and accurate knowledge, both practical and theoretical, of the various branches of foreign and domestic commerce, that can involve the interests of the state of Pennsylvania; the most productive sources of revenue must arise from a connection with, and dependence on commerce, which forms an additional argument in favor of those who are in the practice of commercial investigation.

This state is in a predicament, which distinguishes it from every other in the Union—its patriotic citizens, by loans made to the United States in the gloomy periods of the war, being collectively the largest public creditors of the Union.

Interests of such magnitude should be seriously attended to, and every individual in the state must benefit by the favorable result. For, if the public obligations are substantially funded, by sufficient revenues being appropriated for the annual payment of their interests, they will become an available property to the possessors, and proportionally augment the circulating medium of the country, to the great benefit of the agricultural, commercial, and manufacturing professions—for there is no political maxim more true than that the price of property must rise and fall with the increase or decrease of money. These substantial benefits, to be procured for the state, will not be at the expense of taxes, drawn from its citizens, but from a contribution levied on the United States at large, in which the quota of Pennsylvania has hitherto been estimated at about an eighth part. Every citizen in the state is therefore concerned in procuring the most ample justice to the public creditors, and it is expected that in the selection of representatives from the city, such weighty interests will have a due consideration in the choice of the candidates.

City of Philadelphia Meeting, 18 October[7]

At a town meeting held at the State House, on Saturday, October 18, 1788, George Clymer, Esquire, chairman, and George Fox, Esquire, secretary.

Mr. [John] Willcocks, on behalf of the ward's committee, reported, "That that committee, in conformity to their appointment on Saturday last [11 October], had proceeded to consider the subject referred to them, and after due deliberation had agreed to recommend to this meeting James Wilson and George Latimer, esquires, as suitable persons to represent this city in the conference proposed and shortly to be held at Lancaster. Whereupon it was unanimously resolved, that this meeting do authorize and appoint James Wilson and George Latimer, esquires, to meet the conferees from the other counties in this state, for the purpose of forming a ticket for the Representatives of this state in the House of Representatives of the United States.

On motion resolved, that the committee appointed from the several wards of this city at a former meeting be instructed to report on Wednesday evening next at 6 o'clock, to a general meeting to be held at this place, the names of six suitable persons from whom the Representatives for this city in the Congress of the United States may be chosen.

On motion resolved, that the same committee be further instructed to report the names of six suitable persons from whom the Electors for a President of the United States may be chosen.

The thanks of the meeting being given to the chairman, it adjourned to meet at this place on Wednesday evening next [22 October] at 6 o'clock.[8]

Published by order, George Fox, Secretary

Tench Coxe to James Madison, Philadelphia, 22 October (excerpt)[9]

As I know your anxiety upon the subject of the state legislatures, I have great satisfaction in assuring you that by the returns of our new House at least 38 are firmly attached to the Constitution. The whole number is 69, but we have no returns of the greater part of the remainder. I think we have the best ground to believe the House will be 40 to 29 at least and a very able man, Mr. [William] Findley, is out by the [state] constitution.[10] He was a powerful opponent.

The city are conversing about their ticket for the House of Representatives. They have appointed a committee of 36 to report six proper persons here out of whom the number which the country will give to the city interests is to be taken. I have been somewhat surprised to find my name upon the list, as so strong an interest is making for several respectable commercial characters. The persons proposed by the committee to be offered to the town on Saturday evening are Thos. Fitzsimons, Saml. Powel, Wm. Bingham, Geo. Clymer, Benj. Chew and myself. My own opinion is they should strike off mine, and Messrs. Chew and Powel's names and leave the other three or perhaps only two, as it may give alarm to the country to have so many citizens mentioned. We cannot expect they will exceed three. I have therefore determined to withdraw my name.

Cumberland County Meeting, 23 October[11]

On Thursday last at a very respectable meeting of freemen from different parts of this county, held in this town [Carlisle] Thomas Duncan, Esquire, and Colonel George Gibson, were appointed to attend the federal conference, to be held at Lancaster, for the purpose of recommending suitable persons to represent this state in Congress.

Allegheny, Fayette, Washington, and Westmoreland County Meetings[12]

At a meeting of the inhabitants of Pittsburgh on the evening of the 25th instant.

Adamson Tannehill, in the chair.

Mr. [Hugh Henry] Brackenridge. Sir. After our last meeting, at which deputies were appointed to confer at Lancaster on the forming a general ticket of Representatives in Congress, I was present at a meeting at Washington, where it was proposed to elect deputies for the same purpose. But the time being short and the place distant, there was no one to whom it could be convenient to undertake the journey. It was therefore proposed by me, that they should commission the deputies of this county, to act for them also. It was some sacrifice of pride for one county, to delegate the deputies of another; nevertheless, thro the liberality of Thomas Scott, Esq., and other gentlemen, it was done.

Two days after, I was present at a meeting of gentlemen of Fayette County, to whom the same difficulty occurred of finding persons who could immediately set out, and be present at the conference at Lancaster. The same thing was proposed by me as at Washington, and on the same principles the measure was adopted. At a meeting at Greensburgh, testimonials of appointment were procured for our deputies for the same reasons, and putting these testimonials into the hands of our deputies, they became the representatives of the whole western Federalists.

My wish that there should be deputies of the whole western country, was founded on the idea that otherwise we could not reasonably expect a Representative on this side [of] the mountains.

Philadelphia Nominations for Representatives and Electors, 25 October[13]

At a town meeting, held at the State House on Saturday evening, 25th of October 1788.

Colonel [Samuel] Miles in the chair.

The committee appointed from the several wards of this city reported the names of six suitable persons from whom the Representatives for this city in the Congress of the United States may be chosen, and were agreed to as follow, viz.,

Thomas Fitzsimons, George Clymer, Henry Hill, Hilary Baker, William Bingham, and John M. Nesbit, esquires.

The same committee reported the names of six suitable persons from whom Electors may be appointed to represent this city, for the purpose of choosing a President of the United States, and were agreed to as follow, viz.,

Walter Stewart, Thomas Mifflin, Philip Wager, James Wilson, Samuel Howell, Sr., and Thomas M'Kean, esquires.

The thanks of the meeting were given to the chairman, and then adjourned.

Richard Fullerton, Secretary.

John Townes to Tench Coxe, Easton, 30 October[14]

I do myself the honor, by Mr. [Jared] Ingersol, to inclose you our proceedings for the choice of two deputies to attend at Lancaster, which was done in a great hurry; and beg you will be so obliging as to put it in form and give it to some of the printers, and you will very much oblige your friend [John] Arndt and, sir, you[r] most obedient very humble servant.

1. *Pennsylvania Mercury,* 14 October. While the meeting named Enoch Edwards and George Gray delegates to the conference, it also nominated candidates for the Assembly and other offices to be filled in the state election on 14 October (see the *Federal Gazette,* 11 October).

2. *Federal Gazette,* 22 October. The Northumberland County delegates, William Wilson and Charles Smith, had apparently been chosen at an earlier meeting.

3. RC, Coxe Papers, Tench Coxe Section, PHi. Rush probably gave this letter to Coxe because he was mentioned in it.

4. Smith was a son of the Reverend William Smith, provost of the College of Philadelphia before the Revolution. He was a lawyer and a leading figure in the political and legal life of Pennsylvania until his death in 1836.

Wilson, an emigrant from northern Ireland, was an officer in the Continental Army. After the war he became a merchant in Northumberland County and a Federalist leader. He voted to ratify the Constitution in the Pennsylvania Convention.

5. RC, Coxe Papers, Tench Coxe Section, PHi.

6. *Pennsylvania Packet,* 17 October. The essay was signed "A Citizen of Philadelphia." According to the Pennsylvania law regulating state elections, the wards and other political divisions of Philadelphia were required to meet on the Saturday before the annual election (in 1788 this was 11 October before the election on Tuesday, 14 October) to choose election inspectors. At the ward meetings in Philadelphia on 11 October each ward was asked to appoint members of a committee to nominate candidates to go to the Lancaster Conference (see the account of the meeting in Philadelphia, 18 October, printed above).

7. *Pennsylvania Packet,* 20 October.

8. The meeting on Wednesday, 22 October, was adjourned to Saturday, 25 October, because proper notice had not been given to the public (*Pennsylvania Packet,* 24 October).

9. RC, Madison Papers, DLC.

10. Section 8 of the Pennsylvania Constitution of 1776 prohibited anyone from being a member of the legislature for more than four years in any seven (Thorpe, V, 3084).

11. *Carlisle Gazette,* 29 October.

12. *Pittsburgh Gazette,* 29 November (excerpt). Allegheny County was created out of portions of Washington and Westmoreland counties late in September. No other record of

the Pittsburgh meeting to select delegates from the new county to the Lancaster Conference has been located except for the report made by Brackenridge at the meeting on 25 November. The delegates were John Wilkins, Jr., and James O'Hara. For Brackenridge's comments on the Lancaster Conference, see Proceedings of the Lancaster Conference, 3 November, printed below.

13. *Pennsylvania Packet*, 27 October. Philadelphia Federalists did not adopt instructions to their delegates to Lancaster, as did those in Northumberland County. However, their wishes were indicated by their choice of conferees and their nominations, and in such newspaper articles as the "Hints to the Gentlemen of the Ward Committees," 17 October, printed herein, and by "A Few Remarks for the Conference at Lancaster" in the *Pennsylvania Mercury,* 30 October, printed below.

14. RC, Coxe Papers, Tench Coxe Section, PHi. We have not been able to determine the date of the Northampton County meeting, nor locate an account of it in the Philadelphia newspapers.

Centinel XX, Independent Gazetteer, 23 October (excerpt)

Whilst the fate of the new Constitution was doubtful, great was the assumed moderation, specious were the promises of its advocates. The despotic principles and tendency of this system of government were so powerfully demonstrated as to strike conviction in almost every breast, but this was artfully obviated by urging the pressing necessity of having an energetic government and assurances of subsequent amendments. The people were moreover told, "you will have the means in your own power to prevent the oppression of government, viz., the choice of your Representatives in the federal legislature, who will be the guardians of your rights and property, your shield against the machinations of the *well-born*." But how changed the language, how different the conduct of these men, since its establishment? They are taking effectual measures as far as in their power to realize the worst predictions of the opponents to the new Constitution. Having secured the avenue to offices under the new Congress by the appointment of the Senators, they are now exerting all their influence to carry the election of the Representatives in the federal legislature, and thereby get the absolute command of the *purse strings* to confirm their domination; every artifice is practicing to delude the people on this great occasion, which in all probability will be the last opportunity they will have to preserve their liberties, as the new Congress will have it in their power to establish despotism without violating the principles of the Constitution. The proposed meeting at Lancaster is a high game of deception; under the appearance of giving the people an opportunity to nominate their Representatives, the minions of ambition are to be palmed upon them. Ostensible deputies are to be sent from every county for this purpose, who, if we may judge from those already appointed, will take especial care to prevent the nomination of men who have congenial feelings with the people, as such would prove troublesome obstacles in the way of ambition; the intention is to monopolize both branches of the legislature, and make the government harmonize with the aggrandizement of the *well-born* and their minions. The deputies appointed to go from this city characterize the juggle and designate the intention more strikingly than is in the power of language to express, or the ingenuity of artifice to conceal: the man [James Wilson] who confessedly has had a principle share in the framing of a Constitution that is universally allowed to be dangerously despotic; and therefore to require great amendments; the man who in every stage of its adoption has been its greatest advocate; whose views of aggrandizement are founded upon the unqualified execution of this government, whose aristocratic principles, aspiring ambition, and contempt of the common people, have long distinguished; I say this man is now selected as one of that body who are to dictate the choice of the people—to point out *faithful* Representatives who are to check ambition and defend their rights and privileges. If the people suffer themselves to be thus fooled upon so momentous an occasion, they will deserve their fate. But I am persuaded they will discern the fraud and act becoming freemen, that they will give their suffrages to real patriots and genuine Representatives.

John Harris to Tench Coxe, Harrisburg, 28 October[1]

I received your kind letter with the pamphlet and almanac, for which I thank you. We must set up manufactories, be frugal and industrious, and then we shall make the times better. It's all in our own power. If any British vessels are arrived, please to send Mr. [William?] Maclay's two boxes of window glass by the bearer, Christian Flakingar, a wag[one]r, who will be very careful of them. I carried my point with respect of Mr. Carson. The meeting at Lancaster will be by one side of the question. I hope they'll name good men. There will be a party election. If good men are elected as our Representatives, it will answer the public utility. A few amendments will please every honest man to the Constitution, and none called for, but what's reasonable (and necessary) and not a string of them that would destroy the whole Constitution, which might be attended with bad consequences. I hope for the best, and means to be a good subject as I ever has been. A few lines from you with a late paper will be very acceptable to, sir, your most humble servant.

P.S. I write from home with a very bad pen, in haste.

1. RC, Coxe Papers, Tench Coxe Section, PHi. Harris omitted the place from which he was writing, but since the letter was written "from home," it was evidently written at Harrisburg, the town he founded. He was the father-in-law of William Maclay, Senator-elect.

A Few Remarks for the Conference at Lancaster, Pennsylvania Mercury, 30 October[1]

1st. The proportion in the representation of the state of Pennsylvania in the federal Congress, which Philadelphia is entitled to.

This proportion may be best judged of by the quota of the state tax the citizens of Philadelphia pay to the treasury of the United States, the number and respectability of her inhabitants, and the influence of the trade of the city in this state in particular, as well as on the neighboring states. The proportion which the city of Philadelphia pays of the state quota is said to be about one third of the whole, and consequently entitles her a representation from this circumstance only, of two members; but when other reasons are weighed, we conceive a further number will be granted, viz., the revenue raised by excise and by the impost duties will probably be equal to one half or two thirds of the whole state quota, and consequently may entitle Philadelphia to a larger portion in the representation.

2dly. The importance and variety of business which the Congress will have before them, are first, the organization of laws and government under the new Constitution; the revisal of the laws of the several states which may interfere with the constitutional authority of Congress; the general business of the Confederation; the laying out of the new states, and giving them temporary government suitable to their circumstances and local prejudices, until they can form systems for themselves under the federal authority; and thirdly, the regulating the commerce of the United States as well with each other as with foreign powers. The last points appear to be not only the most difficult and arduous in their nature, but the only probable points in which Congress may be defective in her representation. It is presumed that a large proportion of the representation of the United States in Congress, will be composed of gentlemen of legal knowledge and landed property. These two descriptions of men will be fully equal to the several duties required under the second general head, viz., judiciary government, division of districts, and inland or internal regulation in general; but the regulations of trade, commercial treaties, and the maritime affairs which are to be negotiated with most of the nations of Europe, appear to call loudly on the citizens of Philadelphia for the most extensive mercantile knowledge and experience in commercial affairs, which her merchants can afford, on the wisdom of which principally depends the future peace, wealth, and happiness of confederated America. It is also probable that the representation of the United States in Congress will have but few merchants in comparison of the wealth, population, and national consequence of which they are possessed (say Massachusetts 1, New York 1, Pennsylvania 3, and possibly Maryland one, in all not exceeding six, who can be called merchants). It will therefore be a particular part of your duty to obtain as full a representation of this description of men as can be procured. It will be alleged that the forming of treaties, making war and peace, etc., are already lodged in the hands of the President and Senate of the United States by the Constitution, but notwithstanding this is the case, it is presumed the wisdom and experience of Congress will be consulted and may be of great use in their deliberations. Attending to this object, and observing in all cases to preserve federal harmony, it is therefore hoped, that all prejudices and local attachments will be laid aside, and characters fraught with wisdom, virtue, and the fullest knowledge of political and commercial experience, brought forward in the ticket to be offered to the state at large for the general election, to represent Pennsylvania in Congress.

1. The full title of the article is "A Few Remarks for the General Conference chosen by this state, to be held at Lancaster on the 3d of November, submitted to the Conferees."

Official Notice of the Election for the House of Representatives, 1 November[1]

Pursuant to an act of *General Assembly* of the state of Pennsylvania, passed the 4th day of October, 1788, directing the time, places and manner of holding elections for Representatives for this state in the Congress of the United States:

PUBLIC NOTICE is hereby given, to all the *Freemen* of Chester county, qualified to vote for members of Assembly, that an *election* will be held at the several districts of said county, at the same places where the general elections have been hertofore held, on Wednesday, the 26th day of November inst. when and where they are to vote for *Eight persons to represent this state in the Congress of the United States*, at which time and places the Judges, Inspectors and others, officers of the late general election, are notified to attend and take upon themselves their several duties agreeable to law. The election to be opened between the hours of ten o'clock in the morning and one in the afternoon, and to be carried on and conducted agreeably to the election laws of this state.

EZEKIEL LEONARD, Sheriff.

West-Chester, November 1, 1788.

1. (LT), *Pennsylvania Gazette,* 5 November. A notice by James Ash, sheriff of Philadelphia, was published in the *Pennsylvania Packet* on 7 November and ran frequently in the city's papers until 26 November. For notices by the sheriffs of Franklin, Montgomery, and Lancaster counties, see the *Carlisle Gazette, Pennsylvania Gazette,* and *Neue Unpartheyishe Lancaster Zeitung,* 19 November. For a charge that backcountry sheriffs had neglected to publish notices see the *Federal Gazette,* 20 November, printed below.

Proceedings of the Lancaster Conference, 3 November

Delegates representing eighteen counties and the city of Philadelphia assembled on 3 November. Westmoreland, Washington, and Fayette counties were represented by the two delegates from Allegheny County. Only Luzerne County did not send delegates.

The conference's nominations for the House of Representatives and for presidential Electors were published in almost every Pennsylvania newspaper, beginning with the *Pennsylvania Packet* on 8 November, and were frequently reprinted outside the state as well (see, for example, the New York *Daily Advertiser,* 13 November; Baltimore *Maryland Journal,* 14 November; Trenton *Federal Post,* 25 November; and Providence *United States Chronicle,* 4 December).

The official report of the proceedings is only a bare outline and does not indicate any disagreements. However, private correspondence and other documents show that many Federalists were unhappy with the outcome. Charles Smith thought that Stephen Chambers and Thomas Hartley were incompetent to debate great issues with men such as James Madison who would be elected from other states. Tench Coxe's friends felt that he should have been nominated. The major source of discontent was with the fact that only one German, Frederick A. Muhlenberg, was nominated. The result was the publication on 13 November of a broadside addressed "To the German Inhabitants," which revised both the Harrisburg ticket, published on 7 November, and the Lancaster ticket, published on the 8th. The broadside substituted Peter Muhlenberg and Daniel Hiester, two Germans on the Harrisburg ticket, for Stephen Chambers and John Allison on the Lancaster ticket; and a German, Frederick A. Muhlenberg, from the Lancaster ticket for Robert Whitehill on the Harrisburg ticket.

For various views of the Lancaster ticket, see the following documents printed below: Charles Smith to Tench Coxe and William Bradford, Jr., to Elias Boudinot, 14 November; John Arndt to Coxe, 15 November; "A True Federalist," *Federal Gazette,*

18 November; "A German," and "A German Federalist," *Pennsylvania Packet,* 25 November; "A Spectator," *Independent Gazetteer,* 25 November; Major John Clark to John Nicholson, 25 November; John Armstrong, Jr., to Robert McPherson, 26 November; Coxe to Timothy Pickering, 17 December; Thomas McKean to William A. Atlee, 24 December; Benjamin Rush to Coxe, 19 and 25 January 1789; and Stephen Chambers to Coxe, 5 April

Minutes of the Proceedings[1]

At a conference from the several counties in this state, for the purpose of recommending eight suitable persons to serve in the House of Representatives in the Congress of the United States, and ten persons as Electors of the President and Vice President of the United States.

George Gray, Esquire, in the chair.

Present—City of Philadelphia: James Wilson, George Latimer; County of Philadelphia: Enoch Edwards, George Gray; Bucks County: John Barclay, William Dean; Chester County: John Hannum, Thomas Bull; Lancaster County: Edward Hand, Robert Coleman; York County: William Crawford, Henry Miller; Cumberland County: George Gibson, Thomas Duncan; Berks County: James Collins, Peter Filbert; Northampton County: John Arndt, Peter Rhoads; Bedford County: Hugh Barclay; Northumberland County: William Wilson, Charles Smith; for the counties of Westmoreland, Washington, Fayette and Allegheny: James O'Hara, John Wilkins, Jr.; Franklin County: Edward Crawford, Jeremiah Talbot; Montgomery County: James Morris, James Vaux; Dauphin County: John Joseph Henry, John Gloninger; Huntingdon County: Andrew Henderson.

Note. The County of Luzerne not represented.

It was unanimously resolved that the following gentlemen, viz., Thomas Hartley, Henry Wynkoop, Stephen Chambers, John Allison, George Clymer, Thomas Scott, Thomas Fitzsimons, and Fred. Augustus Muhlenberg, esquires, be recommended to be chosen as the Representatives of the citizens of this state in the Congress of the United States.

It was also resolved that the following gentlemen, viz., James Wilson, Collinson Read, Laurence Keene, John Arndt, Edward Hand, James O'Hara, Samuel Potts, George Gibson, David Grier, and Alexander Graydon, esquires, be recommended to be chosen Electors of a President, and Vice President of the United States.

Signed, George Gray, Chairman.

Extract from the minutes, James Campbell, Secretary.

James Wilson's Report of the Proceedings[2]

Last evening, agreeably to advertisement,[3] a large and respectable number of the citizens of Philadelphia met at the Statehouse, for the purpose of receiving the report of their conferees who had attended at Lancaster, to settle a general Federal ticket for Representatives in the Congress of the United States.

J[ohn] Wilcocks, Esquire, being placed in the chair, and Major Fullerton appointed secretary,

Mr. Wilson addressed the meeting.

Gentlemen, at a former meeting held in this place, you did Mr. Latimer and me the honor of appointing us your representatives, to attend a conference purposed to be held at Lancaster.[4] The present meeting has been called in order to receive a report of what has been done on that occasion. That report I shall endeavor to lay before you, comprised in a clear and plain narrative of the transactions which took place.

In discharge of the trust reposed in us, we repaired to Lancaster, and had the pleasure of finding on the afternoon of the day appointed for our meeting, deputies attending from almost every county in the state; on the next forenoon, deputies attended from every county, that of Luzerne excepted. The characters of the gentlemen who were nominated on this business, need not be dwelt upon. Their names have been published. Many of them you are acquainted with. And as to those with whom you are not personally acquainted, it will be satisfactory to you to hear that they were gentlemen of respectability and worth; and when they produced their credentials, it appeared that they were appointed by a numerous and respectable body of the inhabitants of their respective counties. Having satisfied each other on the propriety of the credentials, we next proceeded upon the business for which we were sent. Here we found, as you may naturally expect, some delicacies, difficulties, and embarrassments with regard to the great question, who should represent the citizens of the state in Congress? Many important considerations were to be taken into view: many important interests were to be adjusted, and some prepossessions were necessarily to be consulted.

But this I believe I can say for myself, and on behalf of my colleague; nor do I know a single exception in the whole body of the deputies—that we entered on the business with the best disposition to bring it to a fortunate issue. After conversing with one another in a friendly and candid manner, we endeavored to form a ticket, which so far as we could judge from the instructions we had, and on comparing them with those from every other part of the state, would be the most agreeable to the community at large. When our sentiments on this subject came to be collected to a center, an unanimity surprising, was discovered! We voted in the same proportion as the counties are entitled to vote in the Assembly; and as all the counties were represented but Luzerne, and as Luzerne has but one vote, we were entitled to sixty-eight votes in all. When the tickets were cast up, if my memory serves me right, it appeared that the lowest of the eight gentlemen had fifty-three votes out of the sixty-eight. (My colleague tells me he recollects the same thing.) The whole ticket was then unanimously received; and it was unanimously resolved by the members to support it.

Gentlemen, where a number of people are concerned in the same business, let it be the appointment of officers or any other thing of a public nature, it is not to be expected that the management of it can be, in every respect, agreeable to everyone. When even a few persons meet on matters of but trifling consequence, you seldom find their sentiments strike in perfect unison. These little differences we must lay our account with, so that, if upon the whole, the business is conducted in such a manner as to be useful and generally satisfactory, it is all that can be expected. Had each single conferee been entrusted to make a ticket for his district, it is probable that no one would have been precisely the same with the present. For my own part, I can say, that perhaps in one, or more than one instance, I should not have been dissatisfied if a different nomination had taken place; but could I, or any other expect, that *every other* member should entirely submit his opinion to me or to him? No, gentlemen, mutual deference was necessary.

We had confidence in each other, and were satisfied that one great object was kept steadily in view; the ticket which has been so unanimously produced has strongly marked that object. There is not in it a disputed character, with regard to Federalism.

I have heard, since my return to town, that it was expected more than one German should appear on that ticket.[5] In matters of this kind it is the best way to give a plain and candid account of what happened; when I went on this business, I own that I expected this would be the case. I expected that a German gentleman would have been proposed from Lancaster, a large and important county, where the German citizens are numerous, but such nomination did not take place.

Permit me now (and I shall do it briefly) to make a few observations upon the importance of that duty which we are called upon to discharge the day after tomorrow: citizens of Pennsylvania ye never had a more important part to act! I need not mention that our prosperity, I may go farther, and add, that perhaps our existence as a nation depends on the conduct of the citizens of this and the other states in making a proper choice of the Representatives in the Congress. This consideration is addressed with peculiar propriety to you. The first election to this great office, held by the PEOPLE, will be by the citizens of Pennsylvania; their conduct will have an influence through every part of the United States. If this is the case, and that such is the case there can be no doubt, of what consequence is it that each discharge his duty on that all-important day. Pains have been taken (and I hope not unsuccessfully) to collect the sentiments of the friends of the new Constitution in this state, and to bring them to a point; let us not now divide, for in division is certain destruction.

Gentlemen, I would willingly suppose there could be no source of division on this subject, among the citizens of this state, but I am obliged, and sorry I am to be obliged to mention, that there is cause to apprehend a degree of it.

We know that unfortunately for this state, the sentiments of all its inhabitants have not been unanimous with regard to the Federal Constitution itself. We know, for the period is too recent to be forgot, that a number of citizens, but far from a majority, have expressed themselves unfavorable with regard to it; we know that some have attacked it with the bitterest malignity; and if I am not mistaken, an attempt is now made to bring forward some of those characters in order to administer this very Constitution; this I think appears, from a ticket that has been published and has been named "the amendment ticket."[6] I make no observations that are personal, but I submit it whether some of those, whose names are to be found in that ticket are not the same whom many of you now present heard about twelve months ago, most warm, most earnest, and most anxious to obtain the rejection of that system of government. You will recollect this gentlemen, for you heard the debates within these walls. Now say, is it natural that those who were for the rejection of this system, should be its supporters? Or ought such to be appointed to carry it into execution? I think it is not natural on their part to expect it: but it would certainly be more unnatural for its friends to throw it into their hands.

No doubt, gentlemen, the pretense of amendment is a specious one. It is well known, that everything *human* is *capable* of being amended; it may therefore be said, and said truly, that this system, like every other production of the human mind, is capable of improvement. But let me ask, who is most likely to improve it, its friends or its opposers? This question is easily answered, and upon that answer your votes will be formed. I have no doubt but they will be formed in the same manner throughout the state.

Each will say, let the Constitution be fairly carried into execution, by those who are not its enemies, then such amendments, as experience may discover to be necessary, can be made without tearing the whole to pieces. And the United States may reasonably hope to enjoy that happiness, which, I trust, is destined for them under every administration of their government.

The ticket, gentlemen, recommended on this occasion to your support, contains the names of George Clymer, Thomas Fitzsimons, Henry Wynkoop, Stephen Chambers, Thomas Heartly, John Allison, Thomas Scott, Frederick A. Muhlenberg.

The meeting having received this report with an unanimous plaudit, it was moved, by Colonel Shee, to return the thanks of their fellow citizens to Messrs. Wilson and Latimer, for their cheerful acceptance and able execution of the commission assigned to them: this being unanimously agreed to,

The thanks of the meeting were returned to the chairman and secretary. Adjourned.

Hugh Henry Brackenridge's Report of the Proceedings (excerpt)[7]

At a meeting of the inhabitants of Pittsburgh on the evening of the 25th instant.

Adamson Tannehill, in the chair.

Mr. Brackenridge. Sir.[8]

. . . .

I have in my hand a letter from the two deputies James O'Hara, and John Wilkins, Jr. addressed to gentlemen of this town, with that ticket enclosed which has been the result of their deliberations, and we find that the object has been gained, viz., a Representative from this country.

To read this letter and hand you this ticket, is the object of the present meeting. But let me make one observation and conclude. You are doubly, nay quadruply bound on the principles of contract and of honor to support this ticket. The act of the deputies is your act, and your act in this instance has become the act of the whole four counties. It is to be expected therefore, you will give it your warm and undivided support.

Seconded by Dr. Nathaniel Bedford, and resolved unanimously that the ticket be supported *as to Representatives in Congress.*

Charles Smith to Tench Coxe, Sunbury, 14 November[9]

The hurry of the week at Lancaster, and my anxiety to return early here, in order to prepare for the Court of Nisi Prius now sitting, prevented me from answering and acknowledging your favors of October 21st and 30th. But lest a further delay should be attributed to inattention, I shall take the liberty of writing to you, tho with a head not a little confused with the multiplicity of professional business.

The conference at Lancaster did not, in many respects, turn out to my wish. But lest a division should distract us, the principles of accommodation and unanimity were strongly impressed upon every mind. I did attend, for my own part, to do the best I could, and that done, by an happy union amongst all the members, to endeavor to advance the interests and happiness of our common country. A man with contracted views had no business there, and different opinions obstinately adhered to might have proved fatal to the welfare of Pennsylvania.

I have a pretty strong friendship for [Stephen] Chambers and [Thomas] Hartley. But (to speak confidentially to you) I regret that they were nominated; and if I dared, I would regret still more that they have been agreed upon. But, sir, it is a very hard task to meet both the *prejudices* and *wishes* of a whole country. But I found myself obliged in this instance to submit to the voice of *all* with respect to the latter, and to the voice of a very great majority with respect to the former, to the exclusion of characters who certainly would have reflected greater dignity and luster on the delegation of Pennsylvania. That they are men with good hearts, and firmly attached to the true interests of their country, strictly Federal, with a decent share of plain sense, is their highest commendation. We can surely find thousands of the same description in every place, even amidst the remotest woods and mountains of Pennsylvania. But we have need, upon this great occasion, of more important characters, men of science and of large minds. Our ticket may indeed be called a *good one.* But should great national questions be agitated, which of them, upon subjects of the vastest moment, can step forward upon the floor of Congress? Which of them could vie with a Maddison, a Hamilton, with our Wilson or an Adams? Our sister states will probably send some of their first and ablest characters. I hope their brilliancy may not diminish our splendor, nor their importance decrease our weight in the national scale.

I am sorry since Hartley and Chambers are fixed, that they are lawyers. If they should be looked upon as a specimen of the lawyers of this state, they may impress no very favorable ideas upon the minds of the gentlemen of other states, with respec[t] to us. It is true they are used to the wrangles and jargon of the bar, and are hackneyed in the rules and principles of common law, but they are *not men of science.* They would lose themselves were they once to step out of the confined sphere in which they have been used to range. To speak the truth, I am afraid the education of a very large majority of our lawyers in Pennsylvania is too defective. Without a mind duly cultivated and prepared, a lawyer's office can effect but little. And many of our young men come forward in the world more impressed with notions of amassing wealth from the practice, than with true ideas of a beautiful science, of general utility to mankind, which receives additional splendor from the assistance of the other sciences. The civil law and the laws of nature and nations, which ought to be fundamental, are too often laid aside that we may be hurried into life, by no means the ornaments of genius and learning of our country. This is the reason why we cannot call from every part of the state men of that learning and abilities which are essentially requisite to enable them to fill, with a proper degree of dignity, the most important offices of government.

It will perhaps be satisfactory to you to learn that amongst the members of the conference, tho from every different part of the state, there was not one man who did not know your character and revere you. There was also a very respectable number very anxious to fix your name upon the ticket, but the city seemed desirous to obtain the two names which stand now upon the list. If the country members would have consented to have taken a third from the city, I verily believe your name (even by the gentlemen *from* the city) would have been preferred to the 4 remaining characters who were in nomination from that place. But at that time, it could not be accomplished. Your very *particular* friends were from Northampton, Cumberland, Allegheny, Bucks, Berks, Montgomery and Huntingdon.

It is needless for me to say that I have admired the several papers with which you have favored your country. They have been admired by all who have seen them, who can judge of the propriety and elegancy of language and of the true interests of the United States—in short, by all who are attached to the principles of good government. And I have no doubt, sir, at a period not far distant, that a grateful country will pay a due tribute to merit. She cannot long remain ignorant of her sincere and steady friends; and excuse my enthusiasm, if I say, too, that I hope the period is not far distant when she may with safety call forth some *Mountain-Patriots*, not inferior to the first characters amongst us.[10]

John Arndt to Tench Coxe, Near Easton, 15 November[11]

I've been honored with your favor of the 31st ult. at Lancaster, from which place I was hurried away by company that it was not in my power to write you from there. I delayed myself that pleasure until my return home, and here I find no direct conveyance.

I expect long before this reaches you, that the ticket we framed at Lancaster must have come to your hands. My wonder now is whether it was more satisfactory to you than it was to me. I must confess that I certainly had reason to expect some attention would have been paid to the opinion of the deputies from this county [Northampton]. In that conference I was convinced that my notion was erroneous. In the end I found that in every solicitation, request or representation made by me, must in the opinion of others have been absurd in the highest degree.

My fear is that the ticket will not meet the approbation of the Federalists in general, and the Germans in particular. Should that be the case, the consequences may be disagreeable.

1. *Pennsylvania Packet,* 8 November. The report was brought to the *Packet* by "a gentleman who arrived in town last night from Lancaster. . . ."

2. *Federal Gazette,* 25 November. The report was delivered on 23 November.

3. *Federal Gazette,* 22 November.

4. Appointment of Delegates to the Lancaster Conference, 10-25 October, printed above.

5. See "To the German Inhabitants of the State of Pennsylvania," 13 November, printed below.

6. See The Harrisburg Ticket, *Federal Gazette,* 7 November, printed below.

7. *Pittsburgh Gazette,* 29 November.

8. The omitted portion of Brackenridge's report describes how he persuaded Fayette, Washington, and Westmoreland counties to appoint the two Allegheny County delegates to represent them at Lancaster to ensure the nomination of a Representative "on this side [of] the mountains." It is printed above as a part of Appointment of Delegates to the Lancaster Conference, 10-25 October.

9. RC, Coxe Papers, Tench Coxe Section, PHi.

10. For another criticism of the Lancaster ticket see William Bradford, Jr., to Elias Boudinot, 14 November, printed below.

11. RC, Coxe Papers, Tench Coxe Section, PHi.

Lucullus to the Freemen of Pennsylvania, Pennsylvania Gazette, 5 November[1]

Friends and Countrymen: You will be called upon, on the last Wednesday of the present month, to give your votes for eight persons to represent you in the legislature of the United States.

You never were called upon to exercise the privilege of electing rulers upon a more important occasion. Two tickets will be offered to you. The one will contain men, who will support the new Constitution in its present form; the other ticket will contain men, who will overset the government under the specious idea of *amending* it.

To give you just ideas of the Antifederal ticket, I shall only add, that it was composed and will be supported by persons, who violated the *rights of conscience,* by imposing a wicked and tyrannical test law upon the Quakers, Menonists, and other sects of Christians, who hold war to be unlawful. Who ruined half the widows, orphans and aged citizens in the state, by an unjust and cruel tender law. Who, in the execution of the militia law, ruined and drove from the state many hundred farmers, by seizing and selling cows for nine pence, wagons for three shillings and nine pence, wheat for one shilling a bushel, thereby wasting property to the amount of one hundred pounds in some instances, to pay a fine of only twenty shillings. Who have pocketed or squandered away as much confiscated property as would have paid, if it had been properly disposed of, half the debt of the state. Who have banished specie and credit from the state, by their last emission of paper money. Who have nearly ruined the state by assuming and funding the debts of the United States, whereby they have checked our agriculture, commerce and manufactures, and driven many thousands of our farmers and mechanics to Kentucky and Niagara. Who have burdened the state with expensive establishments and salaries, thereby encouraging idleness, dependence and servility among our citizens. Who have violated the constitution of the state, by sacrilegiously robbing an institution of learning and charity of its charter and funds. Who, by the number and weight of their taxes, have reduced landed property to *one fourth* of its former value, and thereby forced many ancient and respectable farmers and merchants, possessed of large visible estates, to submit to the operation of laws, which have reduced them from a well earned affluence or independence to poverty and misery. Who have opposed the adoption of the federal government by the grossest falsehoods, by the abuse of the best characters in the United States, and by an attempt to excite a CIVIL WAR. Who aim at nothing but power or office—who have nothing to lose, and everything to hope, from a general convulsion. Whose private characters are as profligate, as their public conduct has been oppressive, dishonest and selfish, and who, instead of aiming to share in the honors of the new government, should retire in silent gratitude, for having escaped those punishments to which their numerous frauds, oppressions, and other crimes, have justly exposed them.

Such are the persons who have framed and who are to support the Antifederal ticket.

The Federal ticket will be framed and supported by men, who afforded the supplies in taxes and loans, that fed and often paid the American army during the late war. By men, who repealed the tender and test laws of Pennsylvania, and who sheltered the Quakers, and other sects of Christians, from general banishment or extirpation. By men, who have opened new sources of commerce to the state, and thereby afforded employment to our sailors and a respectable body of our mechanics. By men, who have established profitable manufactories in many parts of the state, which have already given bread to many hundreds of our industrious inhabitants. By men, who have steadily opposed paper money and tender laws. By men, who have no private views to gratify, and who live by their own labor. From such men we have reason to expect a revival of credit and commerce, the protection of manufactures, and the establishment of the order and happiness of the United States, upon a lasting foundation.

Two things are essentially necessary to ensure success to the Federal ticket.

1st. That *every* Federalist in the state should vote for it. Let the old man of eighty and ninety years of age come forward once more with his vote, and place his seal upon the liberties of his country. Let the men who are opposed to the shedding of blood come forward with their votes; for should the Antifederal ticket prevail, we shall probably soon be exposed to all the calamities of a civil war. Let our young men be active in collecting and conducting those of their neighbors, who are indolent or uninformed, to the places of election. Let it be a disgrace that no time can wipe away, for a freeman to neglect to exercise the privilege of constituting the sovereigns of his country, on the day of the election of the federal Representatives.

2d. Let no objection be made to any one or more members of the Federal ticket. Our success will depend upon our union in *every* man that shall compose it. Let no private considerations of friendship or resentment influence a single vote. By striking a single name out of the ticket, we cannot expect to carry the one we shall substitute in its room. On the contrary, we shall give a vote to a member of the Antifederal ticket.[2] Remember, friends and countrymen, that on your success in the ensuing election will depend the liberties of America. Be wise—be active—and you cannot fail of being free and happy.

P.S. The German printers in Germantown and Lancaster, and the English printers in York, Carlisle and Pittsburgh, are requested to republish the above address in their newspapers.[3]

1. "Lucullus" was almost certainly Dr. Benjamin Rush. In the political disputes of the times he was often referred to as "Galen" or "the Doctor," and in his answer to "Lucullus," Samuel Bryan used both terms ("Centinel" XXII, *Independent Gazetteer*, 14 November, printed below). Bryan defended the record of the Constitutionalists in his reply. For an analysis of the various disputed issues see Brunhouse, *Counter-Revolution.*

2. Rush changed his mind when he saw the Lancaster ticket, which was published three days later. See "To the German Inhabitants of the State of Pennsylvania," 13 November, n. 1, printed below.

3. The *Neue Unpartheyische Lancaster Zeitung* republished the article in German on 19 November.

The Harrisburg Ticket, Federal Gazette, 7 November

No manuscript or previously printed version of the address by "A Friend to Liberty and Union" sent to the *Federal Gazette* by "A Friend to Truth and Freedom" has been located, but the address would appear to be authentic. There is uncertainty as to whether or not the Harrisburg Convention agreed upon a ticket (see Proceedings of the Harrisburg Convention, 3-6 September, printed above). The address printed below was probably not written and circulated until after 24 September, when the Assembly ordered the bill providing for statewide elections printed for public consideration.

The address was reprinted several times after it appeared in the *Federal Gazette* (see the *Freeman's Journal* and the *Independent Gazetteer,* 12 November; *Pennsylvania Packet,* 14 November; *Carlisle Gazette* and *Neue Unpartheyische Lancaster Zeitung,* 19 November). None of these papers printed the denunciation of the address by "A Friend to Truth and Freedom."

A Friend to Truth and Freedom

The clandestine manner, in which the enclosed address has been communicated to the inhabitants of the interior counties, furnishes proof, beyond contradiction, that this political poison was intended to operate its baneful effects, in places where the antidotes of truth and information could not be administered. It is the nature of falsehood to shrink from enquiry, and it has been the unvaried practice of the *designing few,* in Pennsylvania, who are opposed to the happiness of Confederated America, to conduct their schemes of political rapine and murder, with the secrecy of thieves and assassins. The dark lanthorn, and the *dagger,* are the means best suited to effect their purpose. But the light of truth, and the arm of freedom, shall watch over and defend the Federal Constitution, against all the attacks of either open or insidious enemies; nor, until the name of *Bryan* shall be more grateful to the ear of a Pennsylvanian than that of the illustrious Washington, will the specious deceptions, set forth in the following address, be permitted to prevail against the moral and political truths contained in the Federal Constitution.

No American, who wishes the prosperity of his country, can think of sending men into the federal House of Representatives, who are the *avowed enemies* of that system on which the duration, dignity, and happiness of the Union, essentially depend. Let no such men be trusted.

A Friend to Liberty and Union to the Freemen of Pennsylvania

Friends and Countrymen: A fellow citizen, who is impressed with real anxiety at the approaching crisis of our public affairs, begs leave to address a few words to you.

Whilst the enterprising and ambitious are pressing forward to the harvest of office and emolument, which they promise themselves under our new Constitution, he freely resigns all hopes of private advantage from the government, and feels no other interest than that which every citizen ought to feel, in the misfortunes or prosperity of his country. He expects no benefit from the administration of public affairs; but that which every individual will share in common with himself. He fears no misfortunes but those, which will equally affect every member of the community. With these views and motives which are alike interesting to every good citizen, he flatters himself he shall be heard with attention.

Liberty was the avowed object of the late glorious Revolution, in search of which we waded with patience and resolution, through all the horrors of a civil war; and the constitutions of the several states were framed with admirable wisdom, according to the best models, and upon the noblest principles of civil liberty. One only defect remained. The general government of the continent, under the late Articles of Confederation, was too feeble to secure the safety of the people. Its defects were evident; and yet, as if by a studied contrivance, they were suffered to remain, with hardly an attempt to remedy them, until the public affairs of the continent had sunk into utter imbecility and ruin. The cry, at length, for a new form of continental government, became loud and universal.

A Continental Convention was called; the hopes of the people were raised to the highest pitch of expectation, and the sun never beheld a more glorious opportunity of establishing a happy form of government. Nothing short of the most glaring defects could have excited any shadow of opposition. But it is to be feared, some selfish and artful men amongst us were but too willing to avail themselves of so favorable an opportunity of consulting the profit and power of the future governors of the continent, at the expense of the liberties of the people. Whether, however, it was the effect of accident or design, most glaring defects appear in the Constitution which they have proposed to the people. These defects have been freely stated by writers in the public papers, throughout the continent, as well as in the debates of the several state conventions. Indeed many of these defects seem now to be generally acknowledged, even by those men who, there is too much reason to fear, would still wish to evade their amendment and to retain them in the system. Some of these defects are very glaring and important: others perhaps, in the heat of contention have been exaggerated. One or two of the most considerable, I shall attempt briefly to lay before you.

The future Congress, if the new Constitution be not amended, will be vested with unlimited powers: the state governments, which have been founded on the most excellent constitutions in the world, will crumble into ruin or dwindle into shadows, and, in their stead, an enormous unwieldy government will be erected, which must speedily fall to pieces by its own weight, and leave us to the wretched alternative of anarchy or tyranny: whereas by a due temperature, the continental government may be clothed with all necessary powers, for the management of foreign affairs, and leave the state governments in possession of such powers, as will enable them to regulate our internal concerns, which a continental government can never effectually reach. It is just as absurd to suppose, that the general government of the whole empire can regulate the internal police of the several states, as to believe that the several states could regulate our foreign trade, and protect us in our intercourse with foreign nations. The latter we have already tried without success: the former will be found equally impracticable.

Another defect in the Federal Constitution is equally alarming. No security is provided for the rights of individuals; no bill of rights is framed, nor is any privilege of freemen secured from the invasion of the governors. Trust me, my fellow citizens! We shall not be more powerful or more respected abroad, for being liable to oppression at home; but on the contrary, the freest states have been ever the most powerful. Yet with us no barriers will remain against slavery, under the new continental government, if it be not amended: the state governments, by the express terms of the Constitution, can afford no protection to their citizens, and not even a single right is defined or stipulated, which the subject may appeal to against the will and pleasure of the moment.

These circumstances and others of a like tendency, have excited great opposition; but the absolute necessity of a continental government of some sort, has silenced the opposition of those, who were dissatisfied with the present constitution [Articles of Confederation], first in the Continental Convention, and afterwards in most of the conventions of the states. The wiser, if not the major, part of the Continental Convention, would have produced to us a much better form of Continental Union, had it been in their power; but they preferred this to none, and, in the different states, the wisest and best of the people have acquiesced in the scheme of adopting it in its present form, from the hope of obtaining those amendments, which the Constitution itself has provided for the attaining: provided two-thirds of Congress, or two-thirds of the state legislatures, shall concur in requiring them. Without such a clause of obtaining amendments, there is little doubt but a majority of the freemen of America, would have spurned at the idea of subjecting themselves to the other terms of the new Constitution: with this clause of obtaining amendments, it has become the duty of good citizens to make a beginning with the Constitution as it is, confiding in the hope of obtaining all essential amendments in a constitutional mode. In this mode which is provided, it is certainly more eligible to reform the Constitution, than by any violent or irregular opposition to attempt to overthrow it. We must have a continental government, or we are an undone people: at the same time, we ought to preserve our liberties, if possible, so far as they may consist with our essential protection. If these two points can be attained, and this extensive continent held together, in the course of a few years, we may, at once, be the greatest and happiest people on earth.

Impressed with these sentiments, and in the hope of reconciling the wishes of all parties, which, on the present question, we trust, when fairly explained, are more nearly the same, than possibly were those of any people, who, by the arts of intriguing men, were ever set at variance; a large number of the freemen of Pennsylvania have, without noise or disturbance, resolved to invite their fellow citizens to accord with their inclinations, which they trust are the inclinations of a great majority of the freemen of this state. They wish most ardently for a Continental Union and a continental government, upon free principles. They wish to set the proposed government in motion: but they wish for amendments. They think that the strength of this great continent may be exerted, without impairing the private and essential rights of the meanest individual. They have therefore opened a communication with the different parts of the state; they have conferred freely together; they have corresponded; and the purpose of their investigation has been to discover men to represent them in Congress, who will give their aid to the effectuating the great object of the late Continental Convention, that of promoting a continental government for the purpose of uniting our strength, and at the same time of securing the liberties of the subject. In a word, of carrying into execution the new government, and at the same time amending it.

In consequence of this communication, it became necessary to think of forming a ticket, to represent this state in Congress, of such men as would concur in carrying these views into effect; and great care has been taken in the choice of such men, as it was supposed, would at once concur in Federal measures and accord with the different particular interests of which this state is composed. However frivolous this latter idea may appear, and however plausibly it may sound, to talk of choosing the best men, without regard to nation or distinction; yet to Pennsylvanians the precaution will appear to be far from being unnecessary. We have great confidence in their abilities and integrity, and we trust that they will all concur in promoting the real interests of this state and the United States. Such as are friends to the new Constitution, and at the same time wish for amendments, it is hoped will unite their suffrages with ours.

The following are the gentlemen whose names will be run in our ticket: William Findley, Charles Pettit, General William Irvine, Robert Whitehill, William Montgomery, Blair M'Clenachan, Daniel Hiester, Peter Muhlenberg.[1]

The friends of this ticket are desired to remember that this election is for the whole state, and that however numerous or few may be its friends in particular districts, every vote will count one, and not one should omit voting who can possibly attend. The liberties of our country are at stake.

1. Years later William Findley said that he had "declined being a candidate and wrote such reasons to my friends in Philadelphia etc. as satisfied them," but that he was placed on the ballot nevertheless (to William Plumer, Washington, D.C., 27 February 1812, PMHB, V, 444-45).

Centinel XXI, Independent Gazetteer, 8 November (excerpt)[1]

Galen [Benjamin Rush] who, in common with those of his party, had experienced the galling mortification of being defeated in every attempt to overthrow our invaluable state constitution, declared in the [Pennsylvania] Convention, "that he rejoiced at the prospect which the establishment of the new Constitution afforded of the state governments being laid at the feet of Congress."[2] This sentiment, which the Doctor had indiscreetly suffered to escape from him in the hour of insolence and triumph, was afterwards ingeniously explained away, lest the people should be apprised of the real object in view by this premature discovery, for James the Caledonian [James Wilson], the principal framer and advocate of the new Constitution, had been obliged to confess, that so extensive a country as the United States include, could not be governed on the principles of freedom by one consolidated government, but that such a one must necessarily be supremely despotic.[3]

My next number will be on the subject of the immense sums of public money unaccounted for, now ascertained by a late investigation of Congress, which perhaps will be the most effectual methods of elucidating the principles of a number of the great advocates of the new Constitution, and enable the public to form a better judgment of one of the men lately appointed by the legislature of this state to a seat in the federal Senate [Robert Morris] and of some of the men proposed as federal Representatives who will be found to be but puppets to this great public defaulter.[4]

1. This essay was dated Philadelphia, 6 November.
2. The *Pennsylvania Packet*, 6 December 1787, reported that on 3 December, Rush, speaking before the Pennsylvania Convention, "insinuated that he saw and rejoiced at the eventual annihilation of the state sovereignties."
3. See Wilson's speech to the state Convention, 24 November 1787, McMaster and Stone, 218-30.

4. In "Centinel" XXII (*Independent Gazetteer*, 14 November, printed below) Bryan answered the "Lucullus" essay of Dr. Benjamin Rush (*Pennsylvania Gazette*, 5 November, printed above). He did not publish the promised attack on Robert Morris until "Centinel" XXIII (*Independent Gazetteer*, 20 November, printed below).

Pennsylvania Packet, 10 November

Every Federalist, says a correspondent, must rejoice at the unanimity of the conference at Lancaster. The eight gentlemen recommended to the people of this state must unite the voices of all who are really and truly attached to the peace and prosperity of the United States. The counties will see, that the utmost impartiality has been observed towards them; for while they have liberally concurred in two characters to promote the interests of foreign and domestic commerce, they will find that no part of the state has escaped the notice of the conferees. From the banks of Delaware they have travelled to the further bank of the Ohio, with wisdom and justice. Two of the gentlemen are of the law, but both reside near the Susquehanna. The German gentleman has been honored with the chair of speaker of the legislature, and was president of the state Convention. A repetition of their names, with their places of abode, may not be useless, or unpleasing.

Thomas Hartley, Esq., of York County, on the west bank of Susquehanna. Henry Wynkoop, Esq., of Bucks County, on Delaware. Stephen Chambers, Esq., of Lancaster County, on the east bank of Susquehanna. John Alison, Esq., of Franklin County, on the center of south side of Pennsylvania, between the Susquehanna and Ohio. George Clymer, Esq., of Philadelphia. Thomas Scott, Esq., of Washington County, on the west bank of the Ohio, and in the southwest angle of the state. Thomas Fitzsimons, Esq., of Philadelphia. Frederick Augustus Muhlenberg, Esq., of Montgomery County, on the river Schuylkill.

It is impossible for a ticket more completely to embrace the various interests of Pennsylvania. It is hoped therefore that it will be run by all good men.

To the Public, Carlisle Gazette, 12 November

The last Wednesday in this month is appointed by the General Assembly of the State of Pennsylvania, for the purpose of choosing eight members to represent us in the new Congress. As amendments in the proposed plan are thought necessary, it therefore behooves every freeman to attend at his respective district, and give his vote to such men as will use their endeavor to procure the same. The following gentlemen are approved of by the friends of equal liberty; and will be run in our ticket:

Robert Whitehill, William Montgomery, Daniel Hiester, Peter Muhlenberg, William Findley, Charles Pettit, Blair M'Clenachan, General William Irvine.[1]

1. On the 19th the *Gazette* reprinted "A Friend to Liberty and Union" (see The Harrisburg Ticket, *Federal Gazette*, 7 November, printed above).

Pennsylvania Gazette, 12 November

It is very remarkable, says a correspondent, that six of the Representatives fixed upon by the conferees at Lancaster were members of the late state Convention, and the remaining two members of the Federal Convention. These men of course must know the construction of every part of the government. They have heard it discussed with abilities, and several of them have distinguished themselves in defending it. It will be impossible to surprise these men by *side motions*, or maneuvers for alterations—*falsely* called amendments. Most of these gentlemen are so well known thro every part of the state, that nothing need be said to recommend them. It will be sufficient only to add in favor of Colonel [Thomas] Scott and Colonel [John] Allison, who live at a distance from us, that they are both respectable and enlightened country gentlemen, of considerable experience in public affairs, and tied to the state by birth, by numerous families of children, and by clear and independent property. Mr. Scott distinguished himself by a plain, sensible speech, which threw light upon a difficult subject, upon the opening of the business of the state Convention, and Colonel Allison's name is upon record, for seconding the judicious and well timed motion of the Hon. Mr. [Thomas] M'Kean, for adopting by *one* vote the *whole* of the Constitution of the United States.[1]

1. On 26 November 1787, the first day of substantive debate at the Pennsylvania Convention, Scott spoke in favor of McKean's motion to have the Convention either accept or reject the Constitution as a whole, rather than article by article. For an attack on this item see "A Reader," *Independent Gazetteer,* 17 November, printed below.

Supplementary Pennsylvania Election Law, 13 November[1]

[SEAL] An Act to enable such persons within this State who are entituled to vote in the Election of Representatives of this State in the House of Representatives of the United States, and who shall be necessarily out of their respective districts at the ensuing election, to give their votes in the several places where public Business shall require their attendance.

Whereas by an Act of Assembly, passed the fourth day of October last past, entituled "An Act for directing the time, places and manner of holding elections for Representatives of this State in the Congress of the United States, and for appointing Electors on the part of this State for chusing a President and Vice President of the United States," the Inhabitants of this State who are or shall be qualified as therein is mentioned are authorized to elect Representatives of and for this State, in the Congress of the United States, at the places of holding the district elections wherein they severally reside.

And Whereas the time of holding the said Election, is the same when the County Courts of Chester and Northumberland Counties are by Law to be held, and those persons who are bound by Recognizance, summoned as Jurymen, Subpoenaed as Witnesses, or have occasion, to attend such Courts as Officers thereof or as parties to suits or otherwise; and the Members of the Supreme Executive Council, and the General Assembly of this Commonwealth cannot go to the several places, appointed for the election aforesaid, and at the same time attend at the other places where their duty requires their appearance—And it is reasonable to allow persons necessarily absent from the places of district Elections, an opportunity of giving their Voices in this General Election.

Be it therefore enacted, and it is hereby enacted by the Representatives of the Freemen of the Commonwealth of Pennsylvania in General Assembly met, and by the Authority of the same, That it shall and may be lawful, for every person, who by Law is or shall be entitled to vote, under the said recited Act of Assembly, in the choice of Representatives of the State of Pennsylvania, in the Congress of the United States who resides in the counties of Chester or Northumberland or who shall attend either of said Courts as an Officer thereof or as parties or Witnesses, or who being a Member of the Supreme Executive Council or General Assembly of this Commonwealth and who at the time of holding such election for Representatives of this State in the Congress of the United States shall attend at the place of holding the said County Courts or either of them or at the City of Philadelphia in prosecution of public Business, to give in his vote or Ballot for the choice of Representatives of this State, in the Congress of the United States at the place of holding such Courts in the said Counties of Chester and Northumberland and in the City of Philadelphia, in the same manner and under the same Regulations, as if he were to deliver such vote or Ballot, at the place or places appointed for holding Elections within the district or districts whereof he is a resident.

Provided always nevertheless that every person who shall offer a vote at any of the places appointed for holding such Elections and not residing within such election district, shall, before such vote shall be received, make Oath or Affirmation (besides other Oaths and Affirmations requisite to entitle him to vote) that he hath not voted in such Election at any other place, for Members of the House of Representatives in the Congress of the United States, and that he will not afterwards vote in any other place, at the election before mentioned.

[s] Signed by order of the House
Richard Peters
Speaker

Enacted into a Law at Philadelphia on Thursday the thirteenth day of September in the year of our Lord, one thousand seven hundred and eighty eight.

[s] Peter Zachary Lloyd, Clerk of the General Assembly—

1. Engrossed Act (LT), PHarH. The act is printed with variations in Pa. *Statutes*, XIII, 171-73.

The occasion for the passage of the supplementary election law was the receipt of a petition signed by twenty men of Chester County stating that the date for election of Representatives (26 November) was the second day of the session of the Chester County court. The petitioners asked to be allowed to vote at the courthouse instead of in their home districts (n.d., John A. McAllister Papers, PPL). The petition was read to the legislature on 3 November and a second time on 4 November, when it was referred to a committee to report. The committee report was read twice on 5 November, and a committee was appointed to bring in a bill allowing members of the Assembly and the Executive Council in Philadelphia on 26 November to vote in the city and allowing the voters in Chester and Northumberland counties attending courts in those counties to vote at the courthouses rather than in the districts in which they resided.

The bill was read the first time on 6 November, a second time on 7 November, and was ordered printed for public consideration. It was read a third time on 12 November, debated by paragraphs, and ordered engrossed. On 13 November the engrossed copy was enacted into law, and the Speaker was directed to sign it (*Minutes of the First Session of the Thirteenth General Assembly of the Commonwealth of Pennsylvania* [Philadelphia, 1788], passim). The first session of the Assembly elected 14 October met from 27 October to 22 November, when it adjourned to 3 February 1789.

To the German Inhabitants of the State of Pennsylvania, Philadelphia, 13 November[1]

The character of the German (at least in Pennsylvania) has never been to demand privileges he is not intitled to. From natural diffidence, he rather steps aside. But when he has cause to believe that others intend to use him as a tool of their pride and ambition, then he knows how to resist in a proper manner. These thoughts have struck those Germans from the country, whose office requests their presence here at this time, and the German inhabitants of this city; and they have made a deep impression upon their minds, when they saw the ticket framed in Lancaster, for the new government. They have therefore, in a full meeting, and after mature deliberation, thought necessary to lay before their German brothers in Pennsylvania the following remarks concerning the present ensuing election.

1. It is known that the State of Pennsylvania has elected two Senators, and that the 26th of this month eight Representatives, and after that ten Electors will be chosen, in all 20 persons.

2. Many of our German brothers have perhaps never taken the trouble to enquire, what might be their number in this state. These may with certainty be assured that the Germans form at least one-third of the inhabitants of this state. The English must allow that the utility of the Germans and their property is not in the least inferior to their own.

3. According to the above proportion, it is easily concluded what might have been the number of Germans in the ensuing election. But what has been done in Lancaster, where the election ticket has been framed? Not six or eight Germans appear as candidates for election! No; but the election ticket clant [*sic*] from political reasons one German on it, and the ticket for the Electors, probably from the same motives, has, very condescendingly, also one German. Two whole Germans, therefore, among eighteen Englishmen. This shows how little intention there is to pay to the industrious and useful Germans their due regard. Is this not degrading the character of the Germans to the lowest degree? And who of our countrymen, that deserves the name of a German can bear such treatment with cold blood? A fine compliance with the great promises made to the Germans, when they are wanted. If this is the proceeding at the first election, what will be the consequence in the new government, when the English believe they can gain their point without the Germans, then they will be totally excluded, and the German nation in Pennsylvania, will be, and remain the hewers of wood and carriers of water.

Rouse, worthy countrymen! Be for the future warm Germans. Be deserving of the honor which this name gives you. Judge for yourselves, and act as brothers should do for each other. Rouse, ye, [to] whom the honor of the German name, and their nation is dear. Muster all your strength in the ensuing election, and neither receive nor give a ticket which has not at least three Germans on it. This is, as you see, by no means the number it should be, but the present circumstances, and the shortness of time, render another proposition impossible; and at the same time may the Englishmen see the yielding modesty of the Germans, and will hardly object one syllable against our proposal. Here are the tickets as we have altered and concluded them. They will be effectually supported from the above mentioned gentlemen from the country, and the German inhabitants of this city. They have promised each other upon their word and honor to give no other but one of the following tickets, and they have the confidential hope that all Germans in Pennsylvania will agree with them herein.

Lancaster: Thomas Fitzsimons, George Clymer, Frederick A. Muhlenberg, Henry Wynkoop, Daniel Hiester, Peter Muhlenberg, Thomas Scott, Thomas Hartley.[2]

Harrisburg: William Findley, Charles Pettit, Blair M'Clenachan, Peter Muhlenberg, Daniel Hiester, William Irvine, Frederick A. Muhlenberg, William Montgomery.[3]

Our dear countrymen will easily see that this address has no design of a political division. They will also easily conceive why just these three, and no other Germans, have been proposed. The time was too short to form a new ticket, if we therefore wish to gain our point, we must keep the three Germans, of whom it is well known that they have separately been proposed by both tickets. Our whole intention is not only to promote the honor, but also the benefit of the Germans in general when we endeavor to have some of our nation in the new government; and who can think it a harm? Will not the Germans have business with the new government as well as others? Is it not known that many of our countrymen are unacquainted with the English language, and will be in need of both interpreters and advocates, if their business shall gain the desired determination? These motives will undoubtedly make a proper impression upon our countrymen, and will induce them not to neglect the ensuing election; else repentance might come too late.

1. It seems evident that Dr. Benjamin Rush either wrote this address or was responsible for having it written. See his letters to Tench Coxe, 19 and 25 January 1789, printed below. The address was published as a broadside, but no copy has been found. It was printed in German in the *Gemeinnützige Philadelphische Correspondenz* on 18 November. The text printed here is from the translation in the *Pennsylvania Packet*, 19 November.

The question of German representation was a major campaign issue (see, for example, "A True Federalist," *Federal Gazette*, 18 November, and "A German Federalist" and "A German," *Pennsylvania Packet*, 25 November, printed below).

2. The names of Peter Muhlenberg and Daniel Hiester were substituted for those of Stephen Chambers and John Allison, who had been nominated at Lancaster. Peter Muhlenberg's and Daniel Hiester's names were taken from the Harrisburg ticket, which was first published on 7 November (see The Harrisburg Ticket, *Federal Gazette*, 7 November, printed above).

3. Frederick A. Muhlenberg's name was substituted for the name of Robert Whitehill on the Harrisburg ticket.

William Bradford, Jr., to Elias Boudinot, Sunbury, 14 November (excerpt)[1]

We have seen since we came here the ticket agreed on by the conference at Lancaster. I suppose you will see it before this reaches you. I am sorry to find that there is no *leading* character among them, no man of a superior mind, or fully capable of managing the business on the *floor* of Congress. They will be overshadowed by the delegates from other states, *in argument,* and Pennsylvania I am apprehensive will not have that weight to which her consequence in the Union entitles her. In every other respect, except that I have mentioned the ticket is a good one. Yet even in point of abilities I fear the Antifederals have got the advantage in their ticket. I wish Mr. [Charles] Pettit had not have gone to Harrisburg. I think he would have been generally chosen by the public creditors and a great part of the state, and would have been a useful man. I shall be glad to learn from you what the state of politics with you at present is, and who it is probable will be chosen in the Senate and Assembly.

1. RC, John William Wallace Collection, PHi. Bradford was attorney general of Pennsylvania. Elias Boudinot of New Jersey was his father-in-law.

Centinel XXII, Independent Gazetteer, 14 November[1]

Friends and Fellow Citizens: It was my intention to appropriate this number to the consideration of the enormous sums of public money unaccounted for by individuals, now ascertained by a late investigation of Congress; but accidentally meeting with an address to the freemen of Pennsylvania, signed *Lucullus,* published in the *Federal Gazette* of November the 6th,[2] I thought no time should be lost in detecting the atrocious falsehoods, and counteracting the baneful poison contained in that address. In a former number[3] I noticed the base policy practiced by the Republicans, as they styled themselves, of imitating and prejudicing that part of the community who were disaffected to our cause in the late war, against the constitutional whigs, by the grossest calumny and misrepresentation of their conduct and principles, and thereby duping the disaffected into the support of measures, which their dispassionate judgment would have reprobated, as highly injurious to the common welfare. That address is a continuation of the same policy, and from characteristic features, is known to be the production of Galen, who has done more to destroy the harmony of Pennsylvania, and forward the vassalage of her citizens to the *rich and aspiring,* than all the other firebrands of party and instruments of ambition.

We are now hastening to a crisis that will determine the fate of this great country, that will decide whether the United States is to be ruled by a free government, or subjected to the supremacy of *a lordly and profligate few.* Hitherto the gratification of party spirit and prejudice was attended with the ruin of the honest whigs and the emolument and aggrandizement of the Republicans at the common expense; but now it would be attended with the loss of all liberty and the establishment of a general thralldom—men of all descriptions, except our rulers, would equally wear the fetters, and experience the evils of despotism; it therefore behooves every man who has any regard for the welfare and happiness of his country, of himself, or his posterity, to endeavor to divest himself of all prejudices that may bias or blind his judgment on this great occasion. In confidence of a dispassionate perusal and consideration, I will now take up the address and expose its fallacy. It begins "you will be called upon, on the last Wednesday of the present month, to give your votes for eight persons to represent you in the legislature of the United States. You never were called upon to exercise the privilege of electing rulers upon a more important occasion. Two tickets will be offered you. The one will contain men who will support the new Constitution *in its present form*; the other ticket will contain men, who will overset the government under the specious pretext of amending it." Here is a plain, explicit avowal that the new Constitution is to be supported in its *present form*; I hope this declaration will open the eyes of those people who have been deluded by the deceitful promises of amendments, and, that being thereby convinced of the fallacy of the reiterated assurances of amendments, they will now embrace the only method left of obtaining them, by giving their suffrages and influence to the other ticket. The bugbear raised to intimidate the people from voting for this ticket, viz., "that the design is to destroy the government under the specious pretext of amending it," I trust will be treated with the deserved contempt, and that this low device will only confirm the people the more in their determination to support men favorable to amendments. The address proceeds, "to give you just ideas of the Antifederal ticket, I shall only add, that it was composed and will be supported by persons, who violated the rights of conscience, by imposing a wicked and tyrannical test law upon the Quakers, Menonists, and other sects of Christians, who hold war to be unlawful." In regard to the test law, I shall only observe that the circumstances of the times justified, nay made it indispensably necessary, that it was a dictate of common sense and agreeable to the great law of self-preservation to draw a line of discrimination, and exclude from our councils and places of power and trust, those persons who were inimical to our cause; and that such has been, and must ever be, from the nature of things, the practice of all nations when engaged in civil war. However, I am clearly of opinion that sound policy dictates the repeal of such laws as soon as it can be done consistent with the public safety, to prevent men of such principles and views as Galen and his party from availing themselves of the irritated feelings of the non-jurors and their friends, to compass designs prejudicial to the public liberties and welfare.

The tender law stands next in the catalogue of crimes. "Who ruined half the widows, orphans and aged citizens in the state, by an unjust and cruel tender law?" In order to form a judgment of the propriety of this law, we must recur to the occasion of making it. When the thirteen late provinces, new states of America, in Congress assembled, came to the resolution of supporting their liberty and independence by the sword, they found it necessary to anticipate the resources of the country by emitting bills of credit, and as the value and efficiency of this mean, depended on their being received in all transactions equal to gold and silver money, of like denominations, a legal compulsion to ensure this currency to them was *then* deemed essentially necessary, and accordingly Congress recommended the measure to the several states, who, in compliance therewith, passed laws making the continental money a legal tender. This paper money was the sinew of the war, and as such was to be cherished—upon its credit depended our political salvation. However, it is my decided opinion that Congress were mistaken in supposing that the credit of paper money could be supported by making it a legal tender: it is adequate funds of redemption being provided, and public confidence only that can stamp the value of money on paper.

But why censure the government of Pennsylvania for laws that were made ministerially, in compliance with the recommendations of Congress? May not every government in the Union be stigmatized on the same principle, as they all passed similar laws? Moreover with what consistency can the Republicans adduce the tender laws as a crime against the Constitutionalists, when the former were the authors of the most oppressive of them, when they renewed these laws, after they had been suspended by the Constitutionalists? A recurrence to the minutes of the Assembly and the laws of the state will fully establish this fact. It will thereby appear that the Assembly elected in October 1779, who were to a man Constitutionalists, suspended the operation of the laws making the continental money a legal tender for three months by their act passed on the 31st May, 1780, which was further continued by their act of the 22d of September following; and by the succeeding Assembly, which were Republicans, it was continued without limitation. Thus the legal tender of the continental money was first suspended by the Constitutionalists; and this same Assembly passed a law, on the 25th March, 1780, for emitting £100,000 in bills of credit, founded on the City Lots and Province Island, without making them a legal tender.

It will also appear by the minutes of Assembly and laws, that the Republicans afterwards, viz., on the 9th April, 1781, emitted the enormous sum of £500,000 in bills of credit, at a time when the public exigencies did not require or justify this oppressive emission of paper money, and could only be accounted for by the scene of profitable speculation that was made on this money by the *Cofferer* [Robert Morris] and his friends, and this paper the Republicans made a legal tender with heavy forfeitures and penalties in case of refusal.

The Republicans moreover made the 100,000 l. island money emitted by the Constitutionalists a legal tender, although the fund of redemption was so abundantly adequate, the consequence of which was a greater depreciation. And these tender laws were not made in pursuance of recommendations of Congress, but were the original acts of the Republicans.

If the tender laws have been so cruel and wicked, so destructive as "to ruin half the widows, orphans and aged citizens in the state," how came the immaculate Republicans to renew them at so late a period in the war, when they must have been fully informed of their operation, and when they had not so good a plea to justify them? What unparalleled impudence to charge the Constitutionalists with the hardships and evils of laws that they the Republicans were instrumental in reviving and continuing! And yet as extravagant and inconsistent as this charge is, the prejudice and credulity of party spirit has implicitly believed it. Although the Republican Party devised and made the last tender laws for their private emolument, although *they* reaped the rich harvest of speculations on the public credit, by means of these laws, yet the Constitutionalists must bear all the odium of them.

The Doctor has exhibited a most exaggerated picture of the grievous consequences of the militia law; he says that wagons have been sold for 3s. 9d. cows for 9d. etc. Whoever reprobates the militia law, must on the same principle reprobate the late glorious contest for liberty; for any person the least acquainted with the transactions of the war, must know that the militia were very instrumental to our success—a law was therefore necessary to form and call forth this militia when requisite. If, in the execution of a general system, hardships have happened to individuals, they are to be considered as private misfortunes, not public oppressions; or if collectors and other officers have prostituted this law to private gain, they are to be stigmatized, not the law, or its framers.

The address continues, "who have pocketed, or squandered away as much confiscated property as would have paid, if it had been properly disposed of, half the debt of the state?" This is a charge easily made, but until the mere assertion of an anonymous writer is deemed sufficient to substantiate the fact, the public will expect better evidence. I call upon the Doctor to name the instances, point out the persons and produce the proof of this peculation on the confiscated property; and in answer to the other part of the charge, viz., "that it was squandered," I will say it is equally groundless, whether as to the appropriation that was made of this property, or as to the premature disposition of it; for if we may judge from the temper and conduct of succeeding houses of assembly, it is evident, that had the sales of this property been postponed, they would never have taken place, as it would have been restored to the original owners.

The address proceeds, "who have banished specie and credit from the state, by their last emission of paper money. Who have nearly ruined the state by assuming and funding the debts of the United States, whereby they have checked our agriculture, commerce and manufactures, and driven many thousands of farmers and mechanics to Kentucky and Niagara." If an honest, just compliance with public engagements, if the support of public credit, so prized by every wise nation and inviolably maintained by the enlightened government of Great Britain, as its great resource in time of need, is considered criminal in Pennsylvania, the funding law and the last emission of paper money cannot be vindicated; but I am persuaded the people of this state have too high a sense of justice and too much discernment to their permanent interests, for this doctrine to become popular.

"Who have burdened the state with expensive establishments and salaries, thereby encouraging idleness, dependence and servility among our citizens." This is a groundless assertion and base calumny.

"Who have violated the constitution of the state, by sacrilegiously robbing an institution of learning and charity of its charter and funds." I refer my readers to the reasons of the majority of the Council of Censors, for a complete refutation of this charge.

"Who by the number and weight of their taxes, have reduced landed property to one fourth of its former value, and thereby forced many ancient and respectable farmers and merchants, possessed of large visible estates, to submit to the operation of laws, which have reduced them from well-earned affluence or independence to poverty and misery." How lost to all sense of truth and decency must the Doctor be to ascribe the evils of the oppressive taxes to the Constitutionalists, when he knows his party were the authors of them? Does he forget the enormous tax of 1782, imposed by his friend Mr. Morris, which vastly exceeded the ability of the people to pay, amounting to £425,000 in specie besides the paper money: a tax that has been productive of more distress and mischief than the aggregate of all the previous and subsequent taxes, and is the efficient cause of our present difficulties in taxation; and does the Doctor forget the other numerous taxes imposed by the same party, some of them to favor their speculations in the paper monies?

"Who have opposed the adoption of the federal government by the grossest falsehoods, by the abuse of the best characters in the United States, and by an attempt to excite a civil war." A review of the discussion of the new Constitution will expose the fallacy of this charge; whilst sound reason and well supported arguments were made use of by the opposition, scurrility and abuse of every person who dared to object to the new Constitution, were lavished by the Federalists, and if there was any danger of a civil war, it arose from their violence and precipitance in forcing down the government without giving the people time or opportunity to examine or judge for themselves.

"Who aim at nothing but power or office—who have nothing to lose, and everything to hope, from a general convulsion." This comes very consistently from a party which abounds in needy office hunters, whose staunch Federalism and obsequious services are founded on, and stimulated by, the ravishing prospect of sharing in the great loaves and fishes of the United States, under the new Constitution.

"Whose private characters are as profligate, as their public conduct has been oppressive, dishonest, and selfish, and who, instead of aiming to share in the honors of the new government, should retire in silent gratitude, for having escaped those punishments to which their numerous frauds, oppressions and other crimes, have justly exposed them." If I was disposed to recriminate, there is an ample field, I would begin with the Cofferer, the head of the other party, and trace his character through the numerous speculations on the public, from his appointment to the c[ontinenta]l a[ssembl]y of the United States, to his resignation as f[inancier]; I would delineate the corrupt principles and conduct of the rest of the party down to the herd of base parasites and minions, the Doctor included, who would make a conspicuous figure in the black picture. On the other hand, I challenge the Doctor or his associates to sully the integrity, the disinterested conduct of the leaders of the Constitutional Party, by any colorable charge of peculation or abuse of the public trusts, so often confided to them. Like the virtuous Fabricius, they retired from offices of the highest eminence and opportunities of embezzling the public treasure, with unpolluted hands and native integrity; so far from growing rich in the public service, they have impaired their own fortunes by their zeal and contributions for the public welfare, and instead of receiving applause for their patriotism, they are loaded with obloquy, are vilified and stigmatized with that poverty which is their greatest glory, and by the very men too who charge them with peculating on the public. How ungenerous and inconsistent! At the same time I must confess, that there have been villains of the Constitutional Party, for perfection is not to be expected on this side eternity. But it has been the good fortune of this party, that the instances have been rare and of an inferior kind; they did not ascend to the principal of the party, to the great influential leading characters, who gave the complexion and tone to the measures of government.

The foregoing remarks upon the first part of the address apply equally to the remainder, and prove the fallacy and turpitude of the whole of it.

1. The article was dated Philadelphia, 12 November.
2. "Lucullus" appeared in the *Pennsylvania Gazette* on 5 November. It is printed above.
3. "Centinel" XIX, *Independent Gazetteer,* 7 October, printed above.

A Reader, Independent Gazetteer, 17 November[1]

In Hall and Sellers's [*Pennsylvania*] *Gazette* of the 12th instant,[2] I observed some remarks of one of their correspondents, who I take to be some foreigner, fond of dabbling in other people's business, though ignorant of it, or some trifling tool of a party. In the name of wonder, how could any man of common sense expect to impose a *title* (and that where it is not nor never was due) instead of a *character*, on the enlightened people of Pennsylvania? "Colonel [Thomas] Scott"–(silly correspondent)–"a plain, sensible speech, which cast light on a difficult subject"–another gentleman "seconded the well-timed motion." Are these traits of character to induce Pennsylvanians to choose men to such high and important trusts as that of their national legislature? The correspondent is ignorant of one of these gentlemen, who he wishes to recommend; and must be a dupe to his own folly, or he would possess himself of better materials before he embarked in a business which the world must and will inspect. I heard, sir, Thomas Scott, Esquire, make the *sensible speech* alluded to—it might have been expected from a lad of 17 years. Mr. Scott did not think it deserved praise, and must despise the wretch who gives it praise. Mr. Scott is a gentleman with whom I am acquainted. I have heard him argue causes at the bar which did him honor as a lawyer, and as a man of an excellent understanding. Has he not represented a respectable county [Washington] of this state in the legislature, and Council heretofore? Did he not fill the chair of a justice of the peace and pleas, before the Revolution with great respectability? And does he not at this moment enjoy the last-mentioned offices through the confidence of the people, together with the office of prothonotary of one of the most respectable counties of the state? These things have not been known to the drivelling correspondent, or else he intended to insult the gentleman. If these relations are not justly founded, he must be a most consummate fool indeed. If Mr. Scott's domestic concerns will permit him to accept a seat in the national assembly, and he should happen to be elected, I am confident he will not be one of the Pennsylvania members who will disgrace the state. And if the ticket in which he is named should succeed, I most religiously wish, for the honor of the state, the others were his equals. And if the advocates for that ticket wish to preserve the little reputation they have left to Pennsylvania, they will erase four or five names, indeed I believe six of them, and substitute others more eligible and agreeable to the people at large. Why not elect Mr. [James] Wilson, who is the only man who has supported the credit of the new government, and who certainly has more real knowledge than the whole *junto* besides—and what is more, Mr. Wilson will not only do honor to the state, but his late disappointment respecting the prothonotary's office of the city and county of Philadelphia makes it necessary that something should be done for him.

I am one of that class of men, Mr. Oswald, who wish for amendments, not the destruction of the federal government. Mr. Scott, I know to be a good man to prevent amendments, and I am persuaded both he and Mr. Wilson have too much wisdom to dare to do it.

1. This item attacking the Lancaster ticket was dated Philadelphia, 15 November.
2. Printed above.

A True Federalist, Federal Gazette, 18 November[1]

I have just been informed, that some very respectable Germans of this city are opposed to the ticket of Representatives returned by the conferees who met at Lancaster.[2] This has given to many of their real friends of the same party, though not of the same society, a great deal of uneasiness. The opinions of so valuable a class of people ought to be attended to. I consider them as the most useful members of society; and it was not without emotion I observed a division of interest, and an animosity at the last election between those who hitherto were always united, and invariably pursued the same object, the public good. I rather think, nay, I am sure, the cause of this difference was accidental. Honesty and goodness of intention have everywhere characterized the Germans: warm in their friendships, and perhaps rather too much so in their enmities, but generally meaning to do what is right themselves, they are apt to place more dependence on those they meet than is prudent, therefore no wonder that they should feel an increased degree of resentment when they find themselves deceived. The gentleman who was put in nomination for councilor by the city [John Nixon], was very obnoxious to them (not as I think, with sufficient reason; on the contrary, it is acknowledged by all who know him best, that few were more capable to perform the duties of that office) but this was not evident at the town meeting; if it had [been], his name most certainly would have been withdrawn, and then no opposition would have ensued. I flatter myself, that this little difference, like the trifling disputes of bosom friends, which eventually connect them closer than before, will teach them both mutual condescension, and convince them how weak they are when divided. But I know that the enemies of our country are sowing the seeds of contention among us, yet I expect their harvest will be blasted. This is always the last resort of men in desperate circumstances, and too often proves successful. Let us therefore beware of it.

The necessity of having one general Federal ticket throughout the state occasioned the meeting at Lancaster. The next measure was to instruct the conferees whom they were to use their interest to have appointed—this was done; the deputies from each county received a list of names for that purpose—they met; eight persons were elected—and then each member returned to inform his constituents of the issue. Now, after this regular proceeding, in which every man had indirectly, though not directly, a voice, is not an opposition, let it come from whatever quarter it may, really dishonorable? I consider it as a most alarming thing. If any other ticket could be agreed on more unanimously, and time enough to serve our purpose, I would give my vote most cheerfully for it. But how are the opinions of the people to be procured in a decisive manner, suppose a new conference should be agreed on? Why, before it could assemble, the time for the election would be past. If two or three counties reject the ticket, and vote for one they like better, the event will prove that they have added just as much weight to the opposite party, as they have taken away from their own. They will therefore do well to consider this matter coolly, and let not their actions be so much influenced by heat and resentment, as by a strict regard for their own interest.

1. The article was dated Philadelphia, 14 November.
2. See "To the German Inhabitants of the State of Pennsylvania," 13 November, printed

above. See also "A German Federalist" and "A German" in the *Pennsylvania Packet,* 25 November, printed below.

A Federalist to the Public, Independent Gazetteer, 18 November[1]

The time is approaching in which you are to exercise one of the greatest privileges of freemen, that of electing Representatives to serve you in Congress. The importance of this appointment ought to induce your greatest deliberation and most dispassionate reasoning. The question is not whether you will have this or that man in Congress who will serve the purposes of party, but who will consider the state as a family of which he is the guardian and protector. The passions and prejudices of a party man ought not to find entrance in the breast of him to whom thousands look up for safety. Let the patriot and honest man meet your appointment, whether he be stigmatized with the odious and party appellation of an Antifederalist, or called by the popular and delusive name of a Federalist. These distinctions are only intended to bias your minds and excite your passions against men who have every claim upon you, and whose bosoms glow with as much patriotic warmth as the most republican spirit could desire. The most zealous advocates for the federal government will admit that it has defects which ought to be remedied, and as it has a remedy in itself, why shall the man who wishes to avail himself of this constitutional redress, be rejected? If it is a perfect system of government (and that it is not no one will deny) I would load the man with the bitterest execrations who attempted an alteration; but if it is not, would it not be consistent with reason and prudence to make such men our choice who would give us the security we desire? None but he who would wade through the filth of party to serve his purposes, would deny the propriety and justice of the measure. No doubt these opinions will be considered by some as flowing from Antifederal principles, but I can declare with the honesty and sincerity of a man of honor, that I feel as much interest in obtaining the operation of the Federal Constitution, as the most zealous advocate for it; but under the impression of the necessity of amendments, I should be glad to see our Representatives in Congress men of moderation, abilities, and zeal for the liberty and happiness of our country. With this view I have suggested the following ticket for your consideration, as being in my estimation superior to any that has hitherto been offered to you: William Bingham, Charles Pettit, John Armstrong, William Findley, Peter Muhlenberg, General William Irvine, William Montgomery, Edward Hand.[2]

In the formation of this ticket, party has not had the smallest influence. I disclaim every connection with party, but in common with my fellow citizens I have something to lose; this something I should wish to entrust with such as knew the full value of it, and I conceive none more proper than the above mentioned gentlemen, many of whom afforded their personal services for the security and happiness of our country.

1. In a covering letter "A Federalist" reported that he had sent his proposed ticket to Andrew Brown, publisher of the *Federal Gazette,* but that Brown had not published it. Brown replied in the *Federal Gazette,* 19 November, that he had not done so because the piece was designed to destroy the characters of three "highly Federal gentlemen" by running

them with members of the Harrisburg ticket. "A Federalist" replied to Brown in the *Independent Gazetteer,* 22 November, that his reason was "as palpable an absurdity and as great an insult as was ever offered to the understandings of men."

2. The proposed substitution of Bingham, Armstrong, and Hand for Daniel Hiester, Robert Whitehill, and Blair M'Clenachan of the Harrisburg ticket alarmed the Federalists, who looked upon the proposal as an Antifederalist plot to divide the votes in the eastern part of the state (see "A Real Patriot to All True Federalists," *Federal Gazette,* 22 November, printed below). For other attacks see several items in the *Federal Gazette,* 19 November. The proposed ticket was supported enthusiastically by writers in the *Independent Gazetteer* (see, for example, "A Friend to Harmony and Federalism," 21 November, and "A Spectator," 25 November).

Federal Gazette, 19 November

A correspondent recommends to the Federalists, *union* and *industry* in supporting the Federal ticket. The establishment of the new Constitution may, perhaps, rest upon the *single* vote of Pennsylvania. The paper money rage has broke out afresh in South Carolina. Nothing but the immediate establishment of the federal government can save us from paper money, tender laws, Indian incursions, mobs, anarchy, poverty, civil war, and finally, from submission to the government of Great Britain, or to some one or more of the demagogues of particular states.

Consistency, Independent Gazetteer, 19 November

It is high time for the whigs to open their eyes. The junto at the helm have thrown off the mask, and tories are openly brought forward to the highest places of trust and profit. Even the man [Tench Coxe] who joined the British armies, who accompanied Cornwallis in his triumphant entrance into this city, and shouted by his side, is now made a delegate to Congress.[1] If these people are not speedily checked, we shall before long find [Joseph] Galloway and [Benedict] Arnold in the list of our principal magistrates, and tory principles and tory chains fixed upon us. Methinks I see the indignant shades of [Joseph] Warren and [Richard] Montgomery, rising and exclaiming at our base desertion of that glorious cause for which they bled and died, and complaining that we already trample upon the blood of our illustrious martyrs. For shame, if not from principle, let us not suffer those men to govern us, who so lately endeavored to enslave us—who joined the arms of a cruel and implacable enemy in the attempt to murder and destroy every friend of his country.

1. On 14 November the Pennsylvania Assembly elected Coxe to serve as a delegate to the Confederation Congress (JCC, XXXIV, 613). For a more detailed attack on Coxe and his war record, see "Civis," *Independent Gazetteer,* 21 November. For a defense of Coxe, see "A Mechanic" and "A True Federalist," *Federal Gazette,* 22 November, printed below. Additional details are given in Jacob E. Cooke, "Tench Coxe: Tory Merchant," PMHB, XCVI, 48-88.

Centinel XXIII, Independent Gazetteer, 20 November[1]

Friends and Fellow Citizens: I have promised a number on the subject of the enormous sums of public monies unaccounted for by individuals, now ascertained by a late investigation of Congress,[2] but find so extensive a field opened, as to require many numbers to treat of the several parts in a proper manner; I shall, therefore, confine my remarks at present to one paragraph of it. This investigation, after being long suppressed, has at length reached the public eye, and is of such magnitude and exhibits such immense peculations on the public treasure, by men who now assume the lead in this and some other of the state governments, and are among the most distinguished patrons of the new Constitution, as to demand the serious attention of the citizens of the United States at this peculiar crisis of public affairs.

Unawed by that power and influence, that false glare of reputation, and by that clamor and partiality of party spirit, which for many years had rendered the characters of the great public defaulters sacred and impervious to public scrutiny, the Centinel, regardless of consequences in such a cause, impeached them at the bar of the public; he charged them with the receipt of millions of public money, for which they had not accounted; and notwithstanding he produced sufficient documents to substantiate the charge, such was the shameless effrontery of these men and their minions, on the one hand, and the confirmed prejudice and partiality of the public on the other hand, that the Centinel was deemed a *libeler*, a *calumniator* of some of the best and most illustrious characters in the United States. So immaculate was the *Cofferer* [Robert Morris] considered, that the epithets of rascal, villain, etc. were lavished upon every person who dared to assert anything to his prejudice, and the cry of a cruel persecution was raised against the Centinel, and others, for endeavoring to compel him to disgorge the public treasure.

Congress have now confirmed the charges adduced by the Centinel against Mr. *Robert Morris*, and the other great public defaulters; so that if any person hereafter advocates the principles and measures of these men, he will thereby acknowledge congenial sentiments, and proclaim his own character—the public will be equally aware of the one as of the other.

In my seventeenth number, there is the following paragraph: "When we consider the immense *sums* of public money taken up by Mr. Morris, as commercial agent, to import military supplies, and even to trade in behalf of the United States, at a time when the risk was so great, that individuals would not venture their property; that all these transactions were conducted under the private firm of *Willing* and *Morris*, which afforded unrestrained scope to peculation and embezzlement of the public property, by enabling Mr. Morris to throw the loss of all captures by the enemy, at that hazardous period, on the public, and converting most of the safe arrivals (which were consequently very valuable) into his private property; and when we add to these considerations, the principles of the *man*, his bankrupt situation at the commencement of the war, and the immense wealth he has dazzled the world with since, can it be thought unreasonable to conclude, that the principal source of his wealth was the commercial agency of the United States, during the war, not that I would derogate from his successful ingenuity in his numerous speculations in the paper monies, Havana monopoly and job, or in the sphere of financiering."[3]

And in a piece which I wrote under the signature of "One of the People," published in the *Independent Gazetteer* of April 17th last, I referred to a report of a committee of Congress of the 11th February, 1779, to prove that Mr. Morris was a member of the secret or commercial committee, and that this committee had authorized and entrusted him *solely* with the purchasing of produce in the different states, and exporting the same on the public account, and that all such contracts were made by him under the private firm of *Willing* and *Morris*.

Mr. Morris being absent in Virginia, when the Centinel made the foregoing charge against him, his friends and minions undertook the vindication of his character; they asserted that he had rendered his accounts as commercial agent and that they were settled; but Mr. Morris, sensible that the ground which his advocates had taken for his justification was not tenable, and that their officious zeal had led them to make assertions that could easily be disproved, was obliged to confess that he had not settled, nor even rendered his accounts as commercial agent, at the distant period of ten years after his transactions in that capacity; but with his usual ingenuity endeavored to apologize for not doing it, as will appear by a recurrence to this address to the public, dated Richmond, March 21st, and published in the *Independent Gazetteer* of April 8th last.

I will make an extract of this address containing Mr. Morris's acknowledgment of receiving the public money and his not settling his accounts. It is as follows, viz., "At an early period of the Revolution, I contracted with the committees to import arms, ammunition and clothing, and was employed to export American produce, and make remittances on account of the United States, for the purpose of lodging funds in Europe. To effect these objects, I received considerable sums of money. The business has been performed, but the accounts are not yet settled."

Having stated the charge formerly made against Mr. Morris and the evidence that was then in my power to establish it, I will now add a quotation from the late investigation made by Congress, extracted from their journals of the 30th September last, viz., "Your committee turning their attention to an act of Congress of the 22d of May last, directing the Board of Treasury to call upon all such persons as had been entrusted with public money, and had neglected to account for the same, and such other persons as had made partial or vague settlements, without producing proper vouchers, were desirous to obtain a particular statement of the accounts which are in the above predicament; but they are sorry to find that such a detail is too lengthy to be here inserted. Some of those accounts are stated in the file of papers marked *papers respecting unsettled accounts*, which is herewith submitted. From the general aspect of those accounts, your committee are constrained to observe, that there are many strong marks of the want of responsibility or attention in the former transactions respecting the public treasures. No less a sum than 2,122,600 dollars has been advanced to the secret committee of Congress, before August 2d, 1777, and a considerable part of this money remains to be accounted for otherwise than by contracts made with individuals of their *own* body, while those individuals neglect to account."

Thus it appears that a considerable part of the enormous sum of two millions, one hundred twenty-two thousand and six hundred dollars, nearly equal to specie, which was advanced to the secret committee of Congress, remains unaccounted for, otherwise than by contracts made with individuals of their *own* body, *while those individuals neglected to account.* And who those individuals are is evident from the report of the committee of Congress of the 11th of February, 1779, before quoted, and from other records of Congress. By them it appears, that after the death of Mr. [Samuel] *Ward,* who was the first chairman and agent of the *secret* committee, which happened very early, before this committee had transacted much business, that Mr. Robert Morris was solely entrusted by the secret committee with the disposition of the public money advanced to them, and that all his transactions as commercial agent, were conducted by him under the private firm of Willing and Morris.

Eleven years have now elapsed since Mr. Morris was entrusted with the disposition of near two millions of specie dollars, and no account of this immense sum has yet been rendered by him. What conclusion must every dispassionate person make of this delinquency? Is it not more than probable that he has converted the public money to his own property, and that, fearful of detection and reluctant to refund, he has, and will as long as he is able, avoid an investigation and settlement of these long standing accounts?

I will ask, did the majority of the late Assembly evince either wisdom or virtue, when they appointed this man to a seat in the *federal Senate,* or will the people evidence any regard to their own interests if they give their suffrages to his creatures, who are now proposed as federal Representatives? Under the administration of such men, is it rational to expect that public defaulters will be called to account, or that future peculation and pocketing of the public money will be discouraged or detected?

I intend in future numbers to notice the other numerous instances of public defaulters, and to show that if it had not been for the immense peculations and pocketing of the public monies by individuals, and those among our most distinguished Federalists, that the people would not have been burdened with above one third of the present national debt and consequent taxes.

The following article of the last report of the committee of Congress on the finances, will be the subject of my next number, viz., "Your committee were desirous to discover in what manner the large sums of money received in France, have been accounted for, but the subject of this inquiry seems to be involved in darkness.

		Livre	s.	d.
The amount of the several receipts is		47,113,859	12	8
Of this sum there has been sent over or drawn for				
and expended in America	26,246,727		5	5
Salaries of foreign ministers	1,160,183			
		27,406,910	5	5
There remains		19,704,949	7	3

"The documents for the expenditures of this balance have never been produced at the treasury. They must be in France if there are any such papers. A full inquiry into the premises now claims the attention of the Board of Treasury. Some time must be expended in making the necessary investigation, but the result may be of important service to the United States."[4]

In the investigation of this article, which informs us of a deficiency of up-wards of nineteen millions of livres specie, however it may offend, I must expose the names of the men who have received this money.[5]

1. The article was dated Philadelphia, 17 November. The *Gazetteer* incorrectly labeled it "Centinel" XXII.

2. The reference is to a report on finances delivered to the Confederation Congress on 30 September 1788 (JCC, XXXIV, 554-70).

Morris defended himself in a letter to the printer of the *Independent Gazetteer* on 22 November and was defended by "Justice" in the *Federal Gazette* on 25 November (both printed below). The attack on Morris continued with an "extract" of a letter from New York (*Independent Gazetteer*, 22 November, printed below) and by Samuel Bryan ("Centinel" XXIV, *Independent Gazetteer*, 24 November, printed below).

The charges against Morris had an impact. On 19 November Edward Fox in Philadelphia wrote to Andrew Craigie in New York that "the report of the committee of Congress on the subject of public money has hurt him here, even with some of his advocates" (RC, Craigie Papers, MWA), and on election day George Clymer published a letter disassociating himself from Morris's wartime activities (*Federal Gazette*, 26 November, printed below). For an account of those activities see E. James Ferguson, "Business, Government, and Congressional Investigation in the Revolution," *William and Mary Quarterly*, 3 ser. XVI, 293-318.

3. See "Centinel" XVII in McMaster and Stone, 660-64.

4. JCC, XXXIV, 563-64.

5. See "Centinel" XXIV, *Independent Gazetteer*, 24 November, printed below.

Federal Gazette, 20 November

A correspondent, of Chester County, asks why the different sheriffs of the interior counties of this state, have declined an obvious duty? An express act of Assembly, enjoins them to give public notice of the ensuing election, on the 26th inst. but the *obedience*, as far as present knowledge extends, paid by these officers, except the respectable Mr. Ash, has been a *contemptuous neglect*.[1] Great as the business of Chester County now is and ever since the Revolution hath been, so as to oblige the present as well as former sheriffs to keep two subs in constant commission, besides bailiffs occasionally, it seems but reasonable to think that a *house* so well supplied with *servants* might easily have performed the service here noticed. On the other hand there has been attention enough paid to the distribution of information respecting the said election by the Antifederalists. Their *runners, emissaries and Jacksnaps*, are sedulously attentive to their *commission*. Their circular letters, messages and *sermons* have buoyed up the expectations of the *turkonians* of this county (generally of this stamp) to such a pitch, that a Federalist, known to be such, mixing in their company, is immediately divested of personal safety! Miserable therefore must the comfort be which results from an association with such overbearing and discordant spirits—wherefore the voice of *reason, common justice, interest, duty,* and *inclination* severally combine to give efficacy to the injunction, *"come ye out and be separate."* Amen.

1. James Ash, sheriff of Philadelphia County, placed an election notice in the *Pennsylvania Packet* on 7 November and several times thereafter. No evidence has been located to indicate whether or not the charges against the backcountry sheriffs were true.

Robert Morris to the Printer, 21 November[1]

In your paper of the 20th day of this month,[2] I find a repetition of the charges against me, which were introduced into the *Independent Gazetteer* last winter whilst I was in Virginia, and to which I made a reply in March that was published in your paper of the 8th of April.

On the repeated slanders of my enemies, so far as they can effect myself, I look down with silent contempt; but as I have been lately honored with a high trust in the federal government, and as an attempt is made to wound the Federal cause by attacks on my reputation and the conduct of those who appointed me to a seat in the Senate, my attachment to that cause, and my respect for my fellow citizens, lead me to inform them that I have lately been in New York for the purpose of bringing forward a settlement of my accounts with the United States, that they are now in the train of investigation, and that I shall do everything in my power to obtain a final settlement of them before the meeting of Congress under the new Constitution.

My enemies seem to expect that the report of a committee of Congress lately published, will give sanction to their assertions and insinuations; but this report cannot make me responsible for one dollar more or less than I received. The largeness of the sums (which however bear but a small proportion to those mentioned in the report) may indeed prove the greatness of the confidence reposed in me; but cannot justify the charge of delinquency. On the contrary, if I render a faithful account of their expenditure, they will prove the extent and vigor of my exertions in the public cause. By the settlement of my accounts the merit or demerit of my conduct, respecting the money put into my hands, will be evinced. Till that settlement shall take place (and nothing has been done or shall be done by me to retard it) no candid citizen will draw an inference against me merely from the importance of the trusts which have been committed to me by my country.

1. *Independent Gazetteer,* 22 November.
2. "Centinel" XXIII, *Independent Gazetteer,* 20 November, printed above.

Extract of a Letter from New York[1]

The late report of the committee of Congress has made much noise here; certainly it opens up an astonishing scene of fraud and peculation on the public monies;[2] and the general cry here is, Make them refund! Bring them to justice! Your General [William] Irvine was the promoter of these useful and important inquiries; for which, I am told, he is much abused in your state by the party called Republicans, and that they have left him out of their ticket for Representatives to the new Congress, and for the same reason (as a friend to his country) I hear, the other party have taken him up, and placed him at the head of their ticket; God grant that this ticket may succeed, as all our hopes of bringing the public defaulters to refund will be ruined if the Republican ticket as formed by lawyer [James] Wilson, at Lancaster, should come forward to Congress, unless we have a majority from the other states, for I perceive that ticket is composed of devoted sticklers for your great defaulters, whereas the Harrisburg ticket we take to be truly enemies to pilfering the public monies, from their repeated attempts in Congress to bring every person trusted with public monies to settlement. We are in hopes of paying off nearly half the national debt, by the monies due from defaulters: and what heavy taxes would be thus taken off the good people of this country, while the widows, etc., who repent their lending the public their monies, would be made to rejoice, and public deficiency, peculation, and fraud prevented by the example of punishment.

How we were astonished at your late appointment of delegates to Congress, and how blind must many of the party among you be if their eyes are not opened by this act of their leaders.[3]

All good Feds as well as Antis in this state call for amendments, and are astonished at some paragraphs against amendments published from your papers; certainly there must be some among you, who would go to any length to carry the new government in its present form, would involve America in all the horrors of a civil war and dissolve the Union, if the people would be led by them into such measures. You know the office hunters would be much sorrowed in their prospects when amendments take place.

None go into Congress from this state except they promise to secure the rights of the people by amendments—and we will admit no lawyers into the House of Representatives or popular part of Congress. How careful should the people be to appoint good men to hold their purse strings, when the great men are always watching to peculate!

Our legislature will take up the business of the Union the first in order, and will, I have no doubt, adopt amendments.

1. *Independent Gazetteer,* 22 November. The extract was headed: "Extract of a letter from a gentleman of information in New York to his friend in this city."

2. JCC, XXXIV, 554-70. See "Centinel" XXIII, *Independent Gazetteer,* 20 November, printed above.

3. The reference is to the election of Tench Coxe.

A Real Patriot to All True Federalists, Federal Gazette, 22 November

Friends and Fellow Citizens: Once more your country calls upon you, to step forth and rescue her from impending ruin—you have already done much. You have waded thro deluges of blood, to stem the torrent of tyranny and purchase freedom to yourselves, and your posterity—you have formed and adopted a Constitution to preserve the blessings of liberty and independence, which you had so dearly purchased. These achievements, my fellow citizens, will be gratefully remembered by millions yet unborn, who will revere the memory of the men, who established their rights on a firm basis, and whose pride it will be, that such were their forefathers.

The cause of virtue, of liberty and your country, again summons you to the field, to complete the great work, and by one generous effort to crown all your past success with happiness and glory: I need not tell you that the enemies to the Federal Constitution in this state, having failed in their base attempts to prevent its adoption, are endeavoring under the show of amendments, to debilitate and destroy its energy, and to make it as wretched a system as that by which we are at present exposed to misery at home, and contempt abroad.

With this view, a ticket formed by the junto at Harrisburg has been industriously circulated through the back counties, with that secrecy and silence, which are ever the concomitants of dark and villainous designs, and which have always characterized the party.

With this ticket, they hope for success, in some of the back counties; but as this alone would be insufficient, they have fallen upon another grand project, to effect a division of the Federal interest, in this part of the state; and to effect this infamous purpose have dared to place some worthy, Federal gentlemen on the ticket, with three members of the Harrisburg ticket.[1]

It requires but a very small share of penetration, to perceive that the Federal gentlemen on this last ticket, are only intended as mere machines to serve their purpose; they will not be run in the back part of the state, but they will be run here, to divide the Federal interest, so that if they should fail of success with the members of the Harrisburg ticket, *in toto,* they may at least ensure the election of such of them as are on both their tickets.

Never was a more artful plan projected than this: but their dark contrivances are now exposed to public view, and it remains with you, to say, whether you are weak enough to be duped, by such base artifices, and thus be led to overthrow that Constitution which you have strenuously endeavored to establish; or whether you will not rather vote for those men, who are firm friends to your cause, and have been nominated by conferees elected by the people at large, throughout the state, and convened for the purpose at Lancaster. I will not, my friends, suppose you mean enough to desert the great cause of America, at this critical juncture; when her fate is to be determined, as it were by one throw. Forbid it Heaven, that ever my fellow citizens should be so lost to all sense of their own, and their country's happiness.

1. See "A Federalist to the Public," *Independent Gazetteer,* 18 November, printed above.

A Mechanic, Federal Gazette, 22 November[1]

The man [Tench Coxe] alluded to in the address signed Consistency, in one of our papers,[2] I am assured, never shouted with Cornwallis upon his entering the city of Philadelphia.

He was driven by the violence and threats of a body of armed men, when a boy, to the British army, but his conduct while with them was uniformly peaceable, and in many instances kind to the friends of the American cause. To this, several worthy officers of the American army can bear ample testimony.

But why this sudden complaint of his being appointed to a seat in Congress? No such objection was made to his taking his seat in the convention at Annapolis. To this infinitely higher and more honorable trust, he was appointed by the present Antifederal Party. He executed the trust with fidelity, and his name stands upon record with some of the first patriots in America, for having laid the foundation of that august Convention, to which America owes her present federal government, and all her prospects of safety and happiness.

The labors of this gentleman in the defense and establishment of the federal government, merit the gratitude of every true Federalist. The letters and addresses generally ascribed to him, have been republished in every state in the Union. They have spread information and begat conviction in the minds of many people. His services in this business, are certainly more than sufficient to cancel *one* youthful indiscretion. If they are not—then, alas! poor human nature! The appointment has been received with general approbation, more especially by the mechanics, and friends to American manufactures, who know the degrees of his zeal and patriotism in serving them.

1. The article, dated New Market Ward, 19 November, was apparently written by Coxe (see Jacob E. Cooke, "Tench Coxe: Tory Merchant," PMHB, XCVI, 48).
2. *Independent Gazetteer,* 19 November, printed above.

A True Federalist, Federal Gazette, 22 November[1]

How long, gentlemen, will you suffer the friends and defenders of our federal government to be offered up, every morning, as sacrifices to the resentment of a disappointed faction? After torturing the characters of Mr. [Robert] Morris, Mr. [James] Wilson, and other gentlemen who have distinguished themselves in establishing the federal government, they have turned with fresh rancor to the character of Mr. Tench Coxe. This gentleman's talents and virtues have, for many years, attracted the attention and esteem of his fellow citizens. He has, in a variety of ways, made himself the servant of the public. His services the Council (consisting at that time of James M'Lene, Esq. and other members of the present Antifederal Party) *first* honored and rewarded, two years ago. Be not deceived. The present attack upon Mr. Coxe is aimed *only* at the federal government. Let us support the appointment, and thereby support OURSELVES.[2]

1. The full title was "A True Federalist to the Friends of the Federal Government."
2. For further comment on the controversy over Tench Coxe see William Shippen, Jr., to Thomas Lee Shippen, 26 November, printed below.

Federal Gazette, 24 November

A correspondent says, that he has no objection to the Federal ticket, formed by the conferees at Lancaster, except one; and that is, that scandal has been silent with respect to the characters of those men who are in nomination. This, continues our correspondent, renders their Federal principles questionable; for it has been a general rule with the opponents of the new Constitution, for want of better argument, to attack the characters of the most distinguished patriots amongst us—from the *disinterested* FABIUS and the venerable SOLON of America, down to the humblest citizen who has embarked in the Federal cause, insomuch that it is an infallible proof of any gentleman's worth and of his patriotic principles, to find him bedaubed with a copious shower of dirt, discharged through the sink of an Antifederal newspaper. Who would wish for a greater honor than to share the same fate with a Washington and a Franklin, and the other chosen patriots of his country, in having his name like theirs recorded in the list of fame; for such undoubtedly is the Antifederal page of scandal, written by men whose praise would be the severest satire and whose censure is the best panegyric! Hence, concludes our correspondent, we obtain an infallible criterion of any gentleman's merit, which we generally find proportioned to the abuse which is teemed forth against him from those registers of scandal, scurrility and falsehood.

Harrisburg Ticket for Presidential Electors, Independent Gazetteer, 24 November

The real friends of American liberty, who wish to carry the Constitution of the United States into execution, and at the same time to procure such amendments, as will secure the liberties of the people, have determined to vote for the following gentlemen as Representatives and Electors.[1]

[The names of the eight men on the Harrisburg ticket for Representatives were printed at this point in the article.]

Electors to be chosen the first Wednesday in January next:

General James Potter
General Walter Stewart
James M'Lean
John Smilie
General Edward Hand
Joseph Hiester
Colonel Thomas Craig
David Rittenhouse
Philip Wager
William Gibbons

1. No evidence has been found to indicate when or by whom this ticket of Electors was prepared.

Centinel XXIV, Independent Gazetteer, 24 November[1]

Friends and Fellow Citizens: This number was appropriated to the investigation of that article of the last report of a committee of Congress, which informs us of a deficiency of nineteen millions of livres specie, in the monies entrusted to our commissioners in France, the principal of whom was the Honorable Benjamin Franklin, the sanction of whose name has given such weight and success to the new Constitution; but I shall be obliged to postpone the discussion of this subject in order to notice Mr. [Robert] Morris's answer published in the *Independent Gazetteer* of this morning to my last number.[2]

Mr. Morris, presuming upon the strength and continuance of those prejudices which his ingenuity and address had so successfully raised, and which for many years had blinded the public to his real principles and conduct, and enabled him to prosecute his schemes of profit and aggrandizement to an immense extent, without detection or jealousy, has now the effrontery to treat the serious, well-founded charges of the Centinel, and a report of a committee of Congress, with supercilious contempt, and to suppose that his unsupported assertions in a matter where he is so deeply interested, will be implicitly believed by that public, whose property to the amount of millions, he was entrusted with above eleven years ago, and for which he has not yet accounted.

Mr. Morris says: "On the repeated slanders of my enemies, so far as they can effect myself, I look down with silent contempt; but as I have been lately honored with a high trust in the federal government, and as an attempt is made to wound the Federal cause by attacks on my reputation and the conduct of those who appointed me to a seat in the Senate, my attachment to that cause, and my respect for my fellow citizens, lead me to inform them, that I have lately been at New York for the purpose of bringing forward a settlement of my accounts with the United States, and they are now in a train of investigation, and that I shall do everything in my power to obtain a final settlement of them before the meeting of Congress under the new Constitution."

Is it slander to call upon a public officer to account for the disposition of millions of public money entrusted to him above eleven years ago? Or is it slander to denominate such a man a public defaulter? Can any reasonable or honest obstacle have so long delayed the settlement of his accounts, especially when we consider the abilities and accuracy of this man in accounts, and his persevering diligence and assiduity to business? Is it now probable that he really means to render his accounts, when we advert to the unsuccessful exertions of a series of the greatest characters in Congress to compel him to account, and who, for more than eleven years, have been baffled in all their virtuous and patriotic attempts by the predominant influence and the machinations of this man and his minions? What have become of the labors of Manheim, where Mr. Morris retired at a gloomy and doubtful crisis of public affairs, under the avowed pretense of preparing these very accounts for settlement? Where is the man besides Mr. Morris, who can thus act and preserve any character or confidence, or who with so serious and weighty a charge against him would continue to be preferred to the highest honors and trusts of his country, with the power of screening past delinquencies, and the opportunity of further speculations; or who would be supported and justified by so numerous and powerful a party?

As an instance of Mr. Morris's dangerous influence, and also of his reluctance to have his accounts, even as Superintendent of Finance, investigated, it may be observed that the public spirited men in Congress on the 21st of June, 1785, procured, with great difficulty against the strenuous opposition and low subterfuges of Mr. Morris's friends and minions, a resolution of that honorable body to this effect, that three commissioners be appointed to examine the receipts and expenditures of the late Superintendent of Finance;[3] but this resolution was the only consequence of this virtuous effort, for Mr. Morris has been able to prevent any commissioners being appointed in pursuance of this resolution entered into above three years since.

It is true that very lately the disinterested part of Congress, strengthened by the attacks made by the Centinel and others upon the great public defaulters, and the consequent clamor of the people, have, against the secret inclination of a majority of Congress, obtained resolutions and appointments of officers to compel the public defaulters to account and restore the public monies: but the efficacy of these resolutions and appointments entirely depends on the complexion of the Congress under the new Constitution; for if the great public defaulters and their minions be elected, it would be ridiculous to suppose that they would countenance a scrutiny into the conduct of themselves and patrons. Mr. Morris, sensible that if he can carry his creatures who are proposed as Representatives in the new Congress,[4] he may laugh at and really condemn any future attempts to call him to account, has, therefore, at the eve of the approaching decisive election, promised to settle and account for the immense sums of public money that he received above eleven years ago, and even assures that he has been at New York lately on this business and that his accounts are in a train of investigation. But like the Manheim investigation, promised as seriously eight or nine years ago, the present will prove to have no other existence than in the deception of the moment—and this train will be found delusive and without end.

My fellow citizens, suffer not yourselves to be thus continually imposed on by a man whose whole career in public life has been so marked by delinquencies in money concerns, but make choice of such men to represent you as will secure your liberties and property. And as you are now well acquainted with the principles and views of Mr. Morris, you are enabled to form a proper opinion of Messrs. [Thomas] Fitzsimons, [George] Clymer, etc. who for ten years past have been the devoted instruments and partisans of Mr. Morris and participators in his numerous speculations.[5]

1. The article was dated Philadelphia, Saturday noon, 22 November.
2. See the *Independent Gazetteer,* 22 November.
3. JCC, XXVIII, 470-71.
4. In "Centinel" XXI (*Independent Gazetteer,* 8 November, printed above), Bryan had charged that "some of the men proposed as federal Representatives" were "but puppets to this great public defaulter."
5. For an election-day attack on Morris see "Public Justice," *Independent Gazetteer,* 26 November. For Clymer's defense, see Election Day Appeals and Commentaries, 26 November, printed below.

John Clark to John Nicholson, York, 25 November (excerpt)[1]

Nothing here but Fed[era]l and Antif[edera]l. Tomorrow will I hope end it. This county never was so roused! And the people are unanimous in favor of the ticket settled at Lancaster and exceedingly incensed at the Philadelphians for deviating from it. I say if the Germans thought they were not represented,[2] why not strike out [Thomas] Fitzsimmons, and [George] Clymer and leave [Stephen] Chambers and [John] Allison? In short there will be the Devil to pay about it yet, and I believe much good will result to the community from the maneuver. There will be about 2000 votes in favor of the [selected?] ticket here.

1. RC, Gratz Collection, PHi. Clark was a York lawyer.
2. See "To the German Inhabitants of the State of Pennsylvania," 13 November, printed above.

Pennsylvania Mercury, 25 November

A friend of peace does not like the ticket for Wednesday made at Harrisburg. That meeting rose from violence. He remembers that same Stoney Ridge Convention which called that meeting, declared that *the blood* of the Federalists would not satisfy them, and they held even their ministers at nought—and therefore thinks it would be prudent to omit at this time electing any of the men first put in nomination by them—such as Robert Whitehill, William Findley, Charles Pettit, etc., besides he objects strongly to the ticket formed here, because it contains several of the members of that meeting—who have therefore elected themselves, as it were. This no free elector can possibly like.

The Lancaster Conference did not propose any of themselves—which looks much more impartial, and our correspondent, who says he is not any way in the secret, likes this much better. Being a plain man, he begs to be indulged with expressing his fears, that the Harrisburg business was a plan to secure their own elections. He thinks therefore it would be more advisable at this time for the city to give their votes to Thomas Fitzsimons and George Clymer, who were not at Lancaster, than to Charles Pettit and Blair M'Clenachan, who were both at Harrisburg.

Justice, Federal Gazette, 25 November

It has been a general practice with the enemies of the Constitution in Pennsylvania, to assert that its leading friends were "public defaulters," "old rogues," "base conspirators," etc. and they have endeavored to deceive the public by telling them that Mr. [Robert] Morris and others were public defaulters, and that they were friends to the Constitution only to evade a settlement or payment of their accounts. Mr. Morris's own candid letter in Oswald's paper of Saturday[1] is sufficient to prove that no such cause of complaint really exists. But, for argument sake, let us suppose that it does. Is it by any means probable that public defaulters would contribute to the establishment of an energetic federal government, which must certainly compel them to settle their accounts to the satisfaction of the people? Is it not more reasonable to expect that such men would rather support our present worthless and impotent system, under which they might be enabled to evade a settlement of their accounts much better than under the scrutinizing eye of the new Constitution which will exact rigorous justice of all men? But the Antifederal scribblers presume to mislead the credulous and unwary, by asserting what they well know to be a glaring falsehood, viz., that public defaulters will be favored by the new government. Is it not evident that the contrary effect must be produced by it; and that it will awake the voice of public as well as private justice throughout the Union; that it will compel knaves to be honest, and consequently cannot fail to revive confidence and credit among us? Most certainly; and if there really are public defaulters who have hitherto been able to evade a settlement of their accounts, for Heaven's sake let us have that government established which will speedily bring them to Justice.

1. *Independent Gazetteer,* 22 November, printed above.

A German Federalist, Pennsylvania Packet, 25 November[1]

It is well known, that the Germans, from every county in the state, are dissatisfied at having so small a representation in the Federal ticket lately agreed upon at Lancaster. The Germans compose at least one third part of the inhabitants of Pennsylvania, and yet they have only two Representatives allowed them out of the twenty persons who compose the Federal tickets. But it has been said, are we not all Americans, or Pennsylvanians, and why should the distinction of nations be kept up among us? To this we answer, that we are differently circumstanced from the natives of Britain and Ireland, in Pennsylvania; from a great proportion of our people being ignorant of the English language, by which means they are deprived of all kinds of information of what is going forward in government, unless they can receive it from German Representatives, who are able to speak to them in their own language. From the want of this only means of knowing the proceedings of our public bodies, our people have been often deceived by bad men to their own ruin, and sometimes to the great distress and danger of the whole state.

It has been said, that we have no men suitable to send to Congress. Then let us take pains to qualify a few for that high trust, by sending them there for instruction in the principles of government, and the forms of business; until this is done, we shall always be unqualified for legislators. But I hope this objection to us is not a true one. Such of our people as have held any part of the power of the state, have, I trust, executed it with faithfulness, and have not dishonored themselves, or the German nation.

Let it be remembered, that we have, notwithstanding the neglect with which we have been treated by the Lancaster conferees, still adhered to the principles of Federalism with which we at first set out.

Federal ticket, as altered by a number of citizens, composed of the following gentlemen: Thomas Fitzsimons, George Clymer, Fred. A. Muhlenberg, Thomas Hartley, Henry Wynkoop, Peter Muhlenberg, Thomas Scott, and David [i.e., Daniel] Heister.[2]

The subscriber has a right to declare, that this ticket will be zealously supported by all the German Federalists in the state. He therefore flatters himself, that all the lovers of union and the federal government, in Pennsylvania, will concur in supporting it.

1. This article, dated 24 November, was addressed "To the Friends of Liberty and of the Federal Government, in Pennsylvania."
2. This revision of the Lancaster ticket was proposed in the broadside "To the German Inhabitants," 13 November, printed above.

A German, Pennsylvania Packet, 25 November

As a German, I have all the national prejudices and partialities which the people of every country have for the place of their nativity. And I have had great pleasure in observing upon many occasions the respect and attention that has been paid to us Germans by the natives and citizens of this country, both before and since the Revolution. My pride has been frequently foolishly elevated.

But this insidious flattery begins now to be too gross and manifest, to be any longer mistaken. I have taken a retrospective view of twenty years past, and find, that whenever all was quiet—no electioneering going forward—no party views in agitation—no public schemes on foot, in which the votes, influence, or contributions of the Germans could be of any service—then, we were *ignorant Germans* etc. But as soon as our numbers can be of use in promoting the political maneuvers of any man or party, the newspapers are filled with—*the respectable body of Germans—the honest and enlightened Germans etc.* And these good souls are much more anxious about our rights, interests and advancement, than we are ourselves.

The present contest between Federalists and Antifederalists has brought us Germans once more into high consideration; and accordingly we see the papers filled with flatteries too absurd, in my opinion, to be digested by any but fools. And I am persuaded, that those who pretend to be so deeply concerned for our privileges, think we are incapable of judging for ourselves, or taking care of our own interests, and only fit to be the tools of their purposes. We are now told, that *the respectable body of Germans* must have a ticket—they must be represented in the federal government—and so on. For my part, I can scarcely imagine a case wherein the interests of the Germans, as such, can come in competition with those of the other citizens of Pennsylvania; much less can partial advantages be expected, or partial oppressions apprehended under the general government of the United States. If any national distinctions can possibly be made in the future laws of the empire, why are not these anxious writers equally concerned for the Scotch and for the Irish? Why are they not desirous that they also should have their due proportion of federal representation? Nay, distinctions of this kind may be carried to any extent; and there seems to me just as much reason that the *tall* citizens should be jealous of the *short*, and that there should be a *fat* ticket in opposition to a *lean* one; or that each should insist upon their proportional share of representation in the great federal assembly.

I think, in matters of government, we should lay aside all national distinctions. I am not ashamed of being a German, far from it, but I boast of being a citizen of Pennsylvania, and of course a citizen of the United States of America. And whilst I enjoy, as I am sure I shall, all the rights and privileges of other citizens, natives or foreigners, I am content. As a German, I neither wish to gain, nor do I fear to lose, any exclusive political advantages. And I cannot help looking on those, who run at these invidious distinctions, rather as enemies than friends, both to us and to the country: and have no doubt but that the same narrow motives which induce them to flatter, would, if it served their purposes better, induce them to abuse the Germans, and give them to the Devil.

I hope, my dear countrymen, you will no longer suffer yourselves to be the dupes of party men and party politics. Think and act for yourselves, as you have a right to do; and consider that your interests, and the *general* interests of the country, are inseparably connected. If you think that the new Federal Constitution will benefit our country, by uniting the strength of the states for the defense of the whole; by the establishing good order, preserving peace, and promoting general justice, dignity and happiness, then do not reject a ticket which you know will be favorable to this purpose, merely because somebody has found out that the Germans, as such, have not their full proportion in it.

If not as *Germans*, we shall be fully represented as *citizens*; and this is by far the most valuable title of the two.

A Spectator, Independent Gazetteer, 25 November

Several tickets have been published for the consideration of the citizens of this state, for the ensuing election, none of which accord so well with my inclination as the last published by *"A Federalist."*[1] His moderation is commendable and worthy of imitation. He has made choice of men whose conduct and talents, during the late war, entitle them to the remembrance and notice of every honest and virtuous American. The man who has endured the fatigues and dangers of war conducted under every disadvantage, who has been scorched by the summer's sun and pierced with the winter's cold to render his country service, is passed by unnoticed by the *conferees*, while he who has kept himself aloof from those trying situations, is to reap the well and dear earned harvest. Ungrateful country! Ungrateful Pennsylvanians, who thus reward your military sons! Suffer your judgments for a moment to operate, throw aside the vile yoke of party spirit, and then say whether you will prefer the man who proposed *Tench Coxe* to be a member of Congress, or he who spurned at the petition of the virtuous public creditors, to the gentlemen proposed by a Federalist. Are the characters of a *Clymer* or a *Fitzsimons*, to bear a preference to a *Hand* or an *Irvine*? Are the abilities of an *Hartley* or a *Chambers* to take the lead of the comprehensive minds of a *Pettit* or a *Findley*? Who do you expect are to defend the rights of Pennsylvania in the *grand diet* of America? Take a survey of the *Lancaster* ticket and answer if there is a man on it who can take a part in a debate, where a *King*, a *Madison*, an *Henry* or an *Hamilton,* is concerned? Are the *mute* arguments of those gentlemen to answer the eloquence and power of the *Virginia* or *Massachusetts* Representatives! Will the blundering of a C[lymer] or the squeaking of a W[ynkoop] serve the purposes of Pennsylvania? Will the heterogeneous ideas of an H[artley] or the circular babbling of a C[hambers] maintain our consequence and defend our interests in Congress? As well might we have no representation—they may serve as centinels to alarm but not as an army to defend—they may serve to make up the number, but not the wisdom of Congress. I could wish an amendment were made to the ticket proposed by a Federalist. It would be in favor of a German—these people have too long been withheld from their proportion in government, and am well pleased to find they have at length become sensible of it, and are asserting their right. The conferees have *condescended* to place *one* German on their ticket, and this more from *policy* than *inclination.* I would gladly admit three, but I think it improper that two gentlemen of one family should go into Congress at once; it looks too much like a monopoly. The *Harrisburg* ticket contains two Germans; those two gentlemen cannot be objected to; I would therefore propose the following ticket: William Bingham, Peter Muhlenberg, Daniel Hiester, Charles Pettit, General William Irvine, John Armstrong, William Findley, Edward Hand.

For the honor and consideration of Pennsylvania, I could wish this ticket were adopted—our state would then be on equality with any in the Union.

1. *Independent Gazetteer,* 18 November, printed above.

Proposed Tickets for Members of the House of Representatives, 26 November

By election day various tickets, including those proposed by anonymous newspaper writers, had been presented to the voters of Pennsylvania. The voters, of course, could pick any eight names they wished in writing out their ballots.

The various tickets offered have been printed above. They are reprinted here in summary form for the convenience of the reader. The dates given are those when the tickets first appeared in print.

The Harrisburg Ticket, *Federal Gazette,* 7 November

Robert Whitehill	William Montgomery
William Findley	Blair M'Clenachan
Charles Pettit	Daniel Hiester
William Irvine	Peter Muhlenberg

The Lancaster Ticket, *Pennsylvania Packet,* 8 November

Thomas Hartley	Stephen Chambers
George Clymer	Thomas FitzSimons
Henry Wynkoop	John Allison
Thomas Scott	Frederick Augustus Muhlenberg

The German Harrisburg Ticket, Broadside, 13 November

William Findley	Daniel Hiester
Charles Pettit	William Irvine
Blair M'Clenachan	Frederick Augustus Muhlenberg
Peter Muhlenberg	William Montgomery

The German Lancaster Ticket, Broadside, 13 November

Thomas FitzSimons	Frederick Augustus Muhlenberg
George Clymer	Peter Muhlenberg
Thomas Hartley	Thomas Scott
Henry Wynkoop	Daniel Hiester

"A Federalist's" "Mixed Ticket," *Independent Gazetteer,* 18 November

William Bingham	Peter Muhlenberg
Charles Pettit	William Irvine
John Armstrong	William Montgomery
William Findley	Edward Hand

"A Spectator's" Ticket, *Independent Gazetteer,* 25 November

William Bingham	Peter Muhlenberg
Daniel Hiester	Charles Pettit
William Irvine	John Armstrong
William Findley	Edward Hand

Election Day Appeals and Commentaries, 26 November

The Philadelphia newspapers published on election day contained various appeals to the voters. Printed below are examples from two Federalist newspapers, the *Pennsylvania Gazette* and the *Federal Gazette,* and from an Antifederalist newspaper, the *Independent Gazetteer.* In addition there is George Clymer's denial of "Centinel's" charge that he was involved in Robert Morris's speculations,

William Shippen's letter to his son commenting on men and issues, and John Armstrong's criticism of the candidates nominated by the Lancaster Conference, written from Livingston Manor in New York.

Pennsylvania Gazette, 26 November

Federalists, remember all your endeavors—all your anxieties. Do not hazard the Constitution you have thus labored to establish, by giving your votes for any person who is known to oppose the Constitution. Virginia, you see, has sent to the federal Senate two gentlemen who are unfriendly to the new Constitution.[1] Look at the reasons of dissent of the Pennsylvania minority in Convention—look at the members of the Harrisburg meeting—all those whose names appear to those papers must be considered as enemies of the Federal Constitution. Let no specious reasoning, or affections, prejudices, or resentments, lead you to vote for any but a Federalist.[2]

Federal Gazette, 26 November

Let the friends of Federalism, says a correspondent, be unanimous on this great, this important day, in support of that ticket, which their conferees at Lancaster unanimously fixed upon, and agreed to support: let them spurn from them, with indignation, the Harrisburg ticket, on which are the names of men, who, in our General Assembly, like the Know Ye gentry of Rhode Island, opposed even the calling of a convention to consider the Constitution. Men who thus endeavored to strangle it at its birth, and who, in our state Convention, were for rejecting it altogether, will most certainly, if it be put in their power, destroy this rock of our political salvation, and deliver us up, an easy prey, to the demon of anarchy.

Beware then, continues our correspondent, ye Federal patriots of Pennsylvania, that ye suffer not yourselves to be divided, by the artful designs of the Antifederal junto. Let not the respectable names of [William] Bingham, [John] Armstrong and [Edward] Hand, induce you to vote for the *five Harrisburg members* who are coupled with them on the new Antifederal ticket.[3] Nay, let no consideration, under Heaven, induce you to vote for any other men than those on the Lancaster ticket, though they should be firmly Federal; for, by a multiplicity of Federal tickets, the Federal interest will be divided, which, of all things, ought to be guarded against; for though the Antifederalists, like chaff before the wind, must ever give way to the Federalists united, yet let us remember, that Antifederalists united must vanquish divided Federalists. Beware then of division, as you would wish to avert the curses of an Antifederal government. In vain did you purchase independence, with the blood of your choicest heroes, in vain have you been taught wisdom in the school of national adversity, and experienced the miseries of a weak and despicable government, and in vain have you formed and struggled for the establishment of an energetic one, if you now suffer yourselves to be divided and vanquished by those very men over whom you have so recently triumphed, and in despite of whom you have adopted the Federal Constitution. But, continues our correspondent, away with the degrading thought! It cannot be, that the freemen of Pennsylvania will suffer their laurels to be tarnished, by basely shrinking from a duty the most important that ever called for their united support! Not even the Declaration of Independence was of more magnitude, for by the establishment of this Constitution only, can independence prove a blessing.

It is hoped the Federalists will THIS DAY be active, and adhere firmly to their cause. It will be in vain that they have discussed and defended the Constitution, if they relinquish it at the important crisis of the election. Let no man stay at home, but let each manfully do his own duty, and exhort his neighbor to the same. An omission cannot be repaired perhaps forever. Not one unfavorable vote will be withheld in the counties which are opposed to the Constitution—not one favorable one should be withheld here. Let us take care we do not rue tomorrow the inactivity of today. With proper exertion we can easily bear up the Constitution on the shoulders of the people, for they are surely on its side.

Independent Gazetteer, 26 November

A correspondent asks the following questions. Who was it that nominated Tench Coxe for a member of Congress? George Clymer. Who was the cause that the petition of the widow and the orphan, in the character of public creditors, was rejected? Thomas Fitzsimons. Who have the conferees proposed for your Representatives in Congress? George Clymer and Thomas Fitzsimons. O tempora! O mores![4]

George Clymer to the Printer, Federal Gazette, 26 November

The Centinel says, that I have shared in Mr. [Robert] Morris's speculations:[5] such participation might be very innocent, for though Mr. Morris may have calculated [very] well for himself, I have never heard that any of his schemes were of a nature to injure the public; some of them, doubtless, have had a contrary effect.

Now it happens that in the whole course of my life I have never had any joint concern, commercial or otherwise, with that gentleman, except in the purchase of some lottery tickets, a few tracts of land in the western country, and in the relief given, during the war, to the distressed inhabitants of Pownalborough, at the earnest solicitation of the delegates of Massachusetts, without profit, but at every risk of loss.

Never having had intimacy or friendship with any other persons supposed to conduct that paper, none of them ought to pretend to the least knowledge of my affairs; this charge then rests upon no authority but the audacity of the Centinel, and is a forgery in his usual way, thrown out to take its chance against the Federal ticket on the election ground.

William Shippen, Jr., to Thomas Lee Shippen, Philadelphia, 26 November (excerpt)[6]

This day our election is held and tis supposed that the Federal ticket which I gave you before will prevail; I wish honest [William] Findley may be one. I believe many Federalists are of my opinion; none of the rest will dare to contend with a [Richard Henry] Lee, a [Patrick] Henry, [James] Madison or a [Rufus] King. The Antifederalists will be numerous in the country but the day is so bad that many will not turn out. Your friend T[ench] Cox is appointed a member of Congress till March which has incensed the good whigs much and he is very severely handled in Oswald's papers. I believe he wishes they had not appointed him; [Thomas] Fitzsimmons and [George] Clymer are much and publicly abused for choosing him and as minions of Robert [Morris] who is also very ably and severely written against by the Centinel as a public defaulter not having as yet accounted for the immense sums put into his hands; if a private opportunity presents I will enclose you the papers. Bobby is very angry and swears vengeance against the Centinel after he has settled his accounts. [Benjamin] Rush fills the *Federal Gazette* with encomiums on T Cox, which always produces new abuse.[7] I think tis too soon for such characters to fill our first places.

John Armstrong, Jr., to Robert McPherson, Manor of Livingston, 26 November[8]

The same post that brought me your letter, brought me others, informing me of the issue of the Lancaster Conference. It was however given abstractedly. The mere fact of the election made, was told—not a syllable of comment—not a reason assigned why this one was chosen, and that one rejected. But for the reasons of a popular choice—who that has lived in a popular government would ask them? Do we not all know them to be matters of compromise and that I'll give you your man if you'll give me mine. As to the ticket I'm far from thinking it ruinous or disgraceful, tho I'm not the less persuaded that it has not a single name upon it that can pretend to much political or other capacity.[9]

[Thomas] Hartley has a good deal of the temper and manners of the deliberative character—that is he is mild and decent—but he wants sense to support and apply them. He wants knowledge too. [Stephen] Chambers has natural capacity but wants the other requisites. [George] Clymer is supposed deep because he refuses to be fathomed. But were his talents and knowledge better and more unequivocal than they are, they would go for nothing, obscured and embarrassed by his monkish shyness off the floor, and his most wretched of all contemptible figures upon it. I predict and you may see it verified that he will but pass for an nought in the political arithmetic of our national Commons. The rest are *herd* and human cattle may be found anywhere. I give you these traits without fearing the imputation of impatience, acrimony or disappointment. My opinions would have been the same under very different circumstances and indeed the truth is that I'm far from being sore upon the subject—for tho not on all occasions a leibnitzian I do not think that this is for the best. The only effect I regret is that it will most probably take me from a state I love and in which I wished to pass my days, and from friends I never wished to change. From these however though it may separate, it can never alienate me and it will always be my pleasure to remember them and my pride to be remembered by them and their number.[10]

1. On 8 November the Virginia legislature elected two Antifederalist Senators: Richard Henry Lee and William Grayson.

2. This article was one of three similar last-minute appeals in this issue of the *Gazette*.

3. See "A Federalist to the Public," *Independent Gazetteer*, 18 November, printed above.

4. This issue of the *Independent Gazetteer* also contained an article by "Public Justice" attacking Robert Morris for his failure to settle his accounts with the United States.

5. "Centinel" XXIV, *Independent Gazetteer*, 24 November, printed above.

6. RC, Shippen Family Papers, DLC.

7. On 22 November the *Federal Gazette* printed several vindications of Coxe, but it is unknown if Rush wrote any of them.

8. RC, Robert McPherson Papers, PHi.

9. On 27 January 1789 Armstrong wrote to George Washington that he believed all the Pennsylvania Representatives were "Federal, but in some of the important respects the choice is not thought so respectable as the state admitted of and the weight of business requires" (Carlisle, RC, Washington Papers, DLC).

10. Later on, Armstrong wrote to Horatio Gates that "last winter" he had married the youngest sister of Chancellor Robert R. Livingston and that it was argued that to elect him would be to elect a citizen of New York, not of Pennsylvania. He added: "Some envy and some prejudice mingled themselves with it, and excluded me from the Senate, where (notwithstanding my nonage) I should have else been seated by an almost unanimous vote. A seat in the other house I would not accept. The Morris junto were the real authors of the opposition given me. By refusing to be their tool I have made myself their enemy. But I have done with them and politics too—perhaps forever" (New York, 7 April 1789, RC, Gates Papers, NHi).

The Reporting of Election Returns

The Philadelphia *Federal Gazette* printed the first election returns on 27 November, the day after the election, and it and other newspapers printed updated returns in almost every issue thereafter. It was soon evident that the Federalists had won, although during the first week in December they were alarmed when the overwhelming votes of the backcountry counties for the Harrisburg ticket began arriving in Philadelphia. By 13 December only the votes of Washington and Fayette counties west of the Alleghenies were missing. By 20 December only Fayette had not been heard from. On 31 December the Supreme Executive Council authorized a public announcement of the votes except those from Fayette County. That county's votes were laid before the Council on 5 January 1789, and it at once issued an official proclamation naming the eight winners. For the votes cast, see Election Returns for Representatives, 5 January, printed below.

Thomas Hartley to Jasper Yeates, York, 29 November[1]

I inclose you a list of the persons voted for and the number of votes in our county [York] on Wednesday last.[2]

The badness of the day prevented many from coming to our district election. In it there were only four Antifederal votes.

The gentlemen here are anxious to know what has happened in your county and elsewhere on the 26th inst. relating to the election so far as you may have been informed. Mr. John Meam goes express. You will be pleased to be as particular as you can and dispatch the messenger as soon as possible.

1. RC, Yeates Papers, PHi. The letter was addressed to Yeates at Lancaster.
2. The votes as given by Hartley were: Thomas Hartley, 1497; Henry Wynkoop, 1494; Thomas FitzSimons, 1488; George Clymer, 1482; Thomas Scott, 1486; John Allison, 1489; Stephen Chambers, 1475; Frederick A. Muhlenberg, 1492; William Findley, 209; William Irvine, 205; Blair M'Clenachan, 195; Peter Muhlenberg, 205; Daniel Hiester, 203; Robert Whitehill, 198; William Montgomery, 193; Charles Pettit, 201; and Thomas Ewing, 1.

James Madison to Henry Lee, Philadelphia, 30 November (excerpt)[1]

The elections of Representatives for Pennsylvania is over, but the result is not yet known from all the counties; little doubt is entertained on one side, that it will prove favorable, though the other side do not renounce its hopes. In the city the majority was nearly as five to one—in Lancaster County still greater I am told, and in one or two others, the proportion not less. The Antifederal counties however are farthest off, and have not yet been heard from. In Berks where unanimity almost prevailed on that side, the badness of the day and the height of the waters reduced the number of voters to about 400—although the county must contain several more. In general a small proportion of the people seemed to have voted. How far this is to be charged on the weather [or?] an indifference to the occasion I am not able to say.

1. Copy, Madison Papers, DLC. Printed: Hunt, V, 306-9. Another excerpt from this letter is printed in Chapter X.

William Shippen, Jr., to Thomas Lee Shippen, Philadelphia, 8 December (excerpt)[1]

On Saturday the Feds by the returns received had 6000 majority and [Dr. James] Hutchinson[2] gave up the matter but this morning the back counties come in so powerfully numerous that they have reduced the 6000 to 2400 and 7 counties are not yet come in. Hutchy's mercury rises and the Feds are a little alarmed.

1. RC, Shippen Family Papers, DLC.
2. Hutchinson, a Philadelphia doctor, was an Antifederalist leader until his death in 1793.

James Madison to Thomas Jefferson, Philadelphia, 12 December (excerpt)[1]

Since mine already in the hands of Mr. Morris further returns have been received from the western counties of this state, which tho not the entire residue, reduced the final result to certainty. There will be seven Representatives of the Federal Party, and one a moderate Antifederalist. I consider this choice as insuring a majority of friends to the Federal Constitution, in both branches of the Congress; as securing the Constitution against the hazardous experiment of a second convention; and if prudence should be the character of the first Congress, as leading to measures which will conciliate the well-meaning of all parties, and put our affairs into an auspicious train.

1. RC, Madison Papers, DLC. Printed: Boyd, XIV, 352-53.

Federal Gazette, 12 December

A correspondent from the westward informs us, that the conduct of many electors, etc., at the election for federal Representatives in Cumberland County was disgraceful, and as contrary to every principle of honor, honesty, and common sense, as that of the writers against the new Constitution in Philadelphia. Our correspondent asserts, that steps were taken to carry the Antifederal ticket, that would dishonor the most perfidious tribe in the savage nation. The particulars of this conduct, he says, will shortly be laid before the public.[1]

1. The "particulars" promised above were not published in later issues of the newspaper.

Tench Coxe to Timothy Pickering, 17 December (excerpt)[1]

I presume you by this time know the fate of the Federal cause at the late election. Six of the Lancaster ticket are carried and two Germans more than the one who was in that list, which gives us eight safe members for Pennsylvania, none of whom will injure and some of whom can essentially serve the Constitution. Had a German been put in the place of Mr. [Stephen] Chambers at Lancaster I believe [John] Alison would have been in. The jealousy of the country prevented a gentleman lately of Massachusetts from being put in nomination, tho no other objection was adduced, and the weight of every argument in his favor admitted.[2] The same jealousy prevented their accepting a third citizen, tho nominated by several counties. He or Mr. [George] Clymer must have given way, and the latter his friends knew he would not think of, could he prescribe the determination of the conference. We have great satisfaction in knowing that of the merchants we have the two ablest—of the Germans the two ablest and three of the most respectable—that among the other landed Representatives [Henry] Wynkoop and [Thomas] Scott are equal to anybody we could send, and in [Thomas] Hartley we have an upright lawyer, beloved by this country. Seven are unquestionably Federal, and I believe also the eighth. Also the gentlemen are pretty good judges what the people of Pennsylvania can do—and what they can be brought to undertake. Some of them are men of experience and resource. I am upon the whole much more than satisfied with the ticket, for five are as good as we could send, the rest are very well, none bad.[3]

1. RC, Pickering Papers, MHi.
2. The reference is evidently to Pickering, who had remained in Pennsylvania after the Revolution. When Pennsylvania created Luzerne County in 1787, Pickering was appointed to organize the county.
3. For additional comments see Thomas McKean to William A. Atlee, 24 December, and Arthur Lee to Nancy Shippen Livingston, December, both printed below.

Pennsylvania Gazette, 17 December

Nothing can better show the prevalence of Federal sentiments in Pennsylvania, than the conduct of the two sides of the question in the late election for Representatives in the new Congress. The conference held at Harrisburg by the opposition brought forward, in the first instance, a ticket with three Federal characters, and five of the opposition; and afterwards dropped the name of one of the latter, and adopted another respectable Federalist. Their ticket then stood with four decided opponents, being afraid to risk more, and four friends of the new Constitution. The Federal interest, when they formed their ticket, took eight Federalists, knowing the sense of the state to be that way. But tho the opposition ticket thus availed themselves of four Federal names, part of whom were two respectable Germans, and tho they appear frequently to have run all three of the Germans, they could not carry *one* of the four Antifederal names which they ran in their ticket. Six of the Federalists in the Federal ticket, and two German Federalists in the Antifederal ticket, are the successful candidates. The two latter gentlemen were put high on the return by the general voice of the Germans, joined by some of the Federalists; and it is a very remarkable proof of the strength of the Federal interest, that the two unsuccessful candidates in the Federal ticket, though thrown out by the two Federal German competitors, were yet above all the remainder, both Federal and Antifederal characters, in the opposition ticket.

The *legislature* and *people* of Pennsylvania, says a correspondent, may be justly considered as having *each* ratified the Constitution of the United States *anew*. The legislature, by having elected two Federalists to represent them in the Senate, and the people, by having chosen eight Federalists to represent them in the House of Representatives. There is not a shadow of doubt but that they will give their voice for a Federal President and Vice President.

The Election of Presidential Electors and the Votes of the Electors, 19 December 1788–4 February 1789

Pennsylvania, Delaware, Maryland, and Virginia provided for the direct popular election of presidential Electors. In accordance with the provisions of the Election Ordinance of the Confederation Congress, the Pennsylvania election law of 1788 set 7 January as the date for the election of Electors, with the elections to be held at the usual polling places throughout the state. The law directed the Electors to meet at Reading on 4 February to cast their ballots.

The Federalist meeting at Lancaster on 3 November nominated a ticket of ten Electors as well as candidates for the House of Representatives. A ticket of Antifederalist candidates was not published until two days before the election of Representatives, when a newspaper republished the names of the men nominated on the Harrisburg ticket and, along with them, the names of the ten electoral nominees (*Independent Gazetteer*, 24 November, printed above).

The official proclamation calling the election, printed immediately below, was published on 19 December. Immediately thereafter, newspaper articles began urging the voters to vote for the Electors nominated on the Lancaster ticket to prevent the election of Patrick Henry as President and Governor George Clinton as Vice President (see the *Federal Gazette*, 20 and 26 December, and the *Pennsylvania Packet*, 7 January 1789, printed below). The Antifederalists seemingly made no campaign for their electoral nominees and cast only a handful of votes on 7 January.

The Supreme Executive Council hired two express riders to collect the votes for Electors in the more distant counties in an effort to prevent the kind of delay which held up the official proclamation of the results of the election for the House of Representatives until 5 January. Nevertheless, there was delay; and the Council could not issue a proclamation announcing the result of the votes for Electors until 3 February, the day before the Electors were required to meet at Reading and cast their ballots.

Public Notice of the Election of Presidential Electors, 19 December[1]

Pursuant and in obedience to an act of general assembly of the commonwealth of Pennsylvania, passed the 4th day of October, 1788, directing the time, places and manner of holding elections for electors for this state, for the purpose of choosing a President of the United States—PUBLIC NOTICE is hereby given to all the freemen of the city and county of Philadelphia, qualified to vote for members of the general assembly of the said commonwealth of Pennsylvania, That an election will be held on Wednesday the 7th day of January next, at the same places where the general elections have been heretofore held, when and where the said freemen are to vote for ten persons, as electors, for the purpose of choosing a President and Vice-President of the United States. And at the said last mentioned time and places, the judges, inspectors, and other officers of the last general election, are hereby notified and requested to attend and discharge their several and respective duties, agreeably to the said act of general assembly, passed the said fourth day of October, 1788, for the purpose aforesaid.

The election will be opened between the hours of ten o'clock in the morning and one in the afternoon, and to be carried on and conducted agreeably to the election laws of this state heretofore made and provided.

JAMES ASH, Sheriff.

Philadelphia, December 19, 1788.

1. (LT), *Federal Gazette,* 20 December. The notice was reprinted several times in Philadelphia. Notices signed by Ezekiel Leonard, sheriff of Chester County, appeared in the *Federal Gazette,* 24 December; by William Perry, sheriff of Westmoreland County, in the *Pittsburgh Gazette,* 27 December; by Francis Swaine, sheriff of Montgomery County, in the *Pennsylvania Gazette,* 31 December.

Federal Gazette, 20 December

It is to be hoped (says a correspondent) that the citizens of Philadelphia will exert themselves in a particular manner, in supporting the ticket for the Federal Electors at the ensuing election. The gentlemen who compose it are worthy men, decided Federalists, and warm friends to General Washington. Many of them have followed him to battle and victory, or shared with him in the distresses of the gloomiest years of the late war. The contest will be between the FIRST BENE-FACTOR of the United States, and an ambitious demagogue in Virginia [Patrick Henry], who has placed himself at the head of the debtors and speculators of that state, and who sees that the establishment of the federal government must forever make him a contemptible state bawler; for he well knows he has not talents to influence a federal assembly of the pitched characters of the United States. It becomes us (adds our correspondent) to oppose George Clinton as Vice President of the United States. His talents are as contemptible as his principles. He possesses neither dignity nor understanding fit for that important station. After inflaming the state of New York by false jealousies, he now calls for a new convention, to *quiet the minds of the people.* Let an [John] Adams, a [John] Rutledge, a [Samuel?] Huntington, or some other patriot of equally respectable Federal character, be chosen the second officer in the United States.[1]

1. See Chapter XIV for the election of the President and the Vice President.

Henry Wynkoop to Reading Beatty, 21 December (excerpt)[1]

The success of the Lancaster ticket for Electors is of the utmost importance to our country; I hope therefore no endeavors will be wanting to induce the people to support it at the ensuing election.

1. RC, Wynkoop Letters, Bucks County Historical Society, Doylestown, Pa. Printed: PMHB, XXXVII, 45-46.

Supreme Executive Council Proceedings, Tuesday, 23 December

On motion, resolved, that the Secretary employ two proper persons to ride to the counties of Washington, Westmoreland, Fayette, Bedford, Huntingdon, Northumberland, Cumberland, Luzerne, Franklin, and Dauphin to bring to Council from those counties the returns of Electors for the choice of President and Vice President of the United States and that he assign to the said expresses their proper counties, give them the necessary instructions, and direct the said expresses to set off on Monday next.[1]

1. Two men, James Dunwoodie and John White, were employed. See Secretary Charles Biddle's instructions to Dunwoodie, 27 December, printed below.

Thomas McKean to William Augustus Atlee, Philadelphia, 24 December (excerpt)[1]

The election for our Representatives in the new Congress is closed, six of the Lancaster ticket are elected, and Messieurs Peter Muhlenberg and Daniel Heister of the Louisburgh [Harrisburg]; Messrs. [John] Alison and [Stephen] Chambers are the next highest, but wanted about 400 votes to be chosen. This has been owing to the nationality of the Germans, and the badness of the day, and in some degree to the too great confidence of the advocates of the new Constitution. And indeed, the Louisburgh ticket was better formed than the other for success, and was very respectable.

1. RC, Atlee Papers, DLC. Atlee had been a judge of the Pennsylvania Supreme Court since 1777.

Federal Gazette, 26 December

Is it not high time, says a correspondent, for the citizens of Philadelphia to form meetings in their respective wards, to concert plans for bringing forth every vote in the city in favor of the Federal ticket, for Electors of a President and Vice President? The Antifederalists are active, and it is said have formed a plan for bringing in [Patrick] Henry and [George] Clinton instead of our beloved Washington, and the great and honest Mr. Adams to fill those great offices. It is hoped the Southern States will unite in John Adams as Vice President, otherwise Governor Clinton will be the man. A division among the Federalists in the choice of this great officer, will give the most votes to Clinton.

If the western counties should be as dilatory in sending returns of the elections for Electors of the President and Vice President as they have been in sending the returns of the federal Representatives, Pennsylvania will have no vote in the election of those great officers; for it will not be known at the time of the election, what persons have a majority of the votes of the state. Should not some steps be taken by Council to prevent the mischief which must arise from such negligence? It may be the means of putting Clinton into the Vice President's chair of the United States, and of lessening the number of votes in favor of General Washington.

Secretary Charles Biddle to James Dunwoodie, 27 December[1]

You are to proceed on Monday next with the letters for the sheriffs of Washington, Westmoreland, Fayette, Bedford, Huntingdon, Cumberland, Franklin and Dauphin, and get from them the returns of the elections for Electors, and bring them to Council as soon as possible. On your way to Fort Pitt try to inform the sheriffs of Cumberland, Franklin, Bedford and Huntingdon that you will call as you come down for their returns and fix upon some convenient place for them to be left at.

As it is of importance the returns should be here soon after the election, if any accident happens to detain you on the road, hire some careful person to perform the business you are sent upon and give him these instructions.

1. FC, Papers of the Supreme Executive Council, PHarH. On the same day the Supreme Executive Council agreed to pay Dunwoodie two dollars and a half in specie per day for his services. No instructions to John White have been located, but he was sent to Luzerne County. Samuel Miles, a member of the Council, wrote to Timothy Pickering that "the bearer, Mr. White is sent to your county to wait for the returns of the Electors, which Council are anxious to receive as soon as possible, in order to give as much time as they can for the gentlemen who may be elected to prepare for the meeting at Reading" (3 January 1789, RC, Pickering Papers, MHi). White was paid £22.3.1 for his services (Proceedings of the Supreme Executive Council, 22 January).

For Dunwoodie's difficulties in Fayette County, see Ephraim Douglass to Secretary Charles Biddle, 17 January, and Sheriff Joseph Torrence to Biddle, 19 January, printed below. For Dunwoodie's account, see his letter to the Supreme Executive Council, 2 February, printed below. Dunwoodie received £34.6.12 for his services (Proceedings of the Supreme Executive Council, 11, 28 February).

Thomas Hartley to Tench Coxe, York, 30 December[1]

After presenting you with the compliments of the season, I acknowledge the receipt of your favors of the 5th and 6th inst., with the inclosures, for which you have my thanks.

Our old printers have been dismissed, but we have established a permanent newspaper under Messrs. Edies and Wilcox. The title will be the York *Herald*, and the first number will appear on Wednesday the 7th January.[2] We shall be happy to publish any essays or pieces for our friends, which may tend to promote the common interest, and hope you will make your communications as frequent as possible.

The Lancaster ticket for members of the House of Representatives in Congress has, it seems, carried as to six members, and the other two express themselves *Federal*. Dr. [Enoch] Edwards or some of your friends may have informed you of what happened at the fixing the ticket at Lancaster. But more of this when I see you.

I congratulate you upon your appointment to New York, and, with many others, hold in contempt the insidious publications which have been offered against you.[3] Nothing better is to be expected from that party. They endeavor (as much as in them lies) to ruin or injure the characters of all the men who attempt to act or think different from them.

Every human good has its certain alloy of evil, and the liberty of the press is sometimes prostituted to the most improper purposes.

It is sufficient for an honest man in a public duty to be sensible that he acts from principle, and according to the best of his judgment; and leave the rest to the winds etc. The good and just part of the community will despise all such dishonorable practices as are attempted against you and several other characters.

My being appointed to Congress will certainly be very injurious to my private interest, but however unfit I may be, I was under the necessity of submitting to the opinion of *many, many* persons whom I considered as my friends.

Our spring circuit courts I must certainly attend, as a number of men have a right and do demand it of me under prior engagements.

I mean, however, to be at New York on the 4th of March, and stay as long as I can. Your friendly correspondence in the meantime will be of use to me, and prepare me for the business which may be brought forward.

The election of Electors comes on the 7th of January. I fear the people may be too supine on this subject, looking upon it as immaterial which of the tickets should carry.

I have just come home but have not been idle. I trust we will have a few votes for our ticket in this county.

1. RC, Coxe Papers, Tench Coxe Section, PHi.
2. *The Pennsylvania Chronicle or the York Weekly Advertiser,* published by Matthias Bartgis and Thomas Roberts, had stopped publication some time in 1788. The title of the new newspaper, published by James Edie, John Edie, and Henry Willcocks, was *The Pennsylvania Herald, and York General Advertiser.*
3. See "Consistency," *Independent Gazetteer,* 19 November, printed above.

Supreme Executive Council Proceedings, Wednesday, 31 December

The return of members to represent this state in the Congress of the United States having been received by Council from the City of Philadelphia and the several counties except the County of Fayette.

Resolved, that for the information of the public the following state of the returns be published: Frederick Augustus Muhlenberg, 8707; Henry Wynkoop, 8246; Thomas Hartly, 8163; George Clymer, 8094; Thomas Fitzimmons, 80[86]; Thomas Scott, 8068; Peter Muhlenberg, 7417; Daniel Hiester, 7403; John Allison, 7067; Stephen Chambers, 7050; William Findley, 6586; William Irvine, 6492; Charles Pettit, 6481; William Montgomery, 6348; Blair McClenachan, 6223; Robert Whitehill, 5850.[1]

1. The information was published in the *Federal Gazette* the next day.

Arthur Lee to Nancy Shippen Livingston, December (excerpt)[1]

By the return of names for the Representative under the new Constitution, the Morrisonian influence I see prevails entirely. There do not exist two more devoted and wicked tools to all his public plundering than the two first on that list.[2] The second has been so from his first dash at the public purse to the last. The object of these men is to renew their depredations in the new system.

1. RC, Shippen Family Papers, DLC. The letter is unsigned and undated, but the handwriting is that of Arthur Lee. It was probably written in December from New York, where Lee was a member of the Board of Treasury. The recipient was his niece.
2. The reference is probably to George Clymer and Thomas FitzSimons, who were most often charged with being associates of Robert Morris.

Samuel Miles to Timothy Pickering, Philadelphia, 3 January 1789 (excerpt)[1]

The returns of the election of federal Representatives, from Fayette County, is not yet come in, which prevents Council issuing a proclamation. Six of the Lancaster ticket, with Mr. Peter Muhlenberg and Danl. Heister in place of Mr. [Stephen] Chambers and Mr. [John] Allison, will undoubtedly be in, but the majority of votes will be much less than I expected. They [*sic*] difference between Federal and Antifederal will not exceed fifteen hundred votes, perhaps not so many.

1. RC, Pickering Papers, MHi.

Election Returns for Representatives, 5 January

The election returns of the votes cast on 26 November are compiled from newspaper reports and are printed in the tables immediately below. The tables are derived from the returns reported in the *Pennsylvania Packet,* 20 December; *Pennsylvania Gazette,* 24 December; and *Freeman's Journal,* 9 January 1789. There are some minor discrepancies between the totals reported by the Supreme Executive Council on 31 December for all the districts except Fayette County and those reported by the *Pennsylvania Gazette* on 24 December for the same districts. In no case, however, is there a difference of more than eleven votes.

LANCASTER TICKET FOR REPRESENTATIVES

County	Thomas Hartley	Henry Wynkoop	Frederick A. Muhlenberg	George Clymer	Thomas FitzSimons	Thomas Scott	Stephen Chambers	John Allison
City of Philadelphia	1726	1743	1774	1699	1714	1718	1217	1214
County of Philadelphia	776	786	812	769	764	766	593	600
Bucks	656	658	682	658	657	651	632	647
Chester	903	904	901	890	900	895	890	896
York	1497	1497	1492	1482	1488	1486	1475	1489
Berks	24	27	187	26	7	5	24	28
Lancaster	655	656	771	642	652	649	651	647
Cumberland	285	283	285	287	268	281	271	271
Northampton	256	271	311	260	267	261	31	23
Montgomery	311	349	367	320	321	308	272	266
Dauphin	96	91	121	85	86	79	76	71
Northumberland	197	198	196	195	199	197	195	197
Franklin	374	375	373	363	363	365	364	380
Huntingdon	134	139	134	131	138	138	133	135
Bedford	91	92	97	93	92	90	51	50
Westmoreland	133	137	145	137	118	118	129	110
Luzerne	17	17	16	17	17	17	17	17
Washington	32	28	33	33	35	44	32	33
Fayette	28	29	29	29	30	28	27	24
Totals	8191	8280	8726	8116	8116	8096	7080	7098

HARRISBURG TICKET FOR REPRESENTATIVES

County	Peter Muhlenberg	Daniel Hiester	William Findley	Charles Pettit	William Irvine	William Montgomery	Blair M'Clenachan	Robert Whitehill
City of Philadelphia	821	796	376	357	333	309	286	272
County of Philadelphia	495	495	346	333	337	329	289	293
Bucks	259	226	231	220	230	230	220	208
Chester	211	209	205	204	198	199	198	199
York	205	203	209	201	205	193	195	198
Berks	450	458	442	440	437	435	430	275
Lancaster	320	348	347	347	344	343	342	223
Cumberland	1553	1559	1569	1563	1588	1560	1560	1562
Northampton	406	419	186	177	176	176	155	128
Montgomery	300	286	246	243	244	232	209	185
Dauphin	486	498	495	494	485	481	480	443
Northumberland	355	355	358	357	355	356	356	353
Franklin	545	541	555	551	552	554	549	545
Huntingdon	70	65	77	66	67	65	66	70
Bedford	214	212	175	173	173	172	172	168
Westmoreland	426	426	466	453	459	425	414	426
Luzerne	1	1	2	1	1	1	1	1
Washington	298	306	302	304	308	299	303	307
Fayette	50	52	51	53	54	50	52	52
Totals	7465	7455	6638	6537	6546	6409	6277	5908

Supreme Executive Council Proceedings, Monday, 5 January

A return from the County of Fayette of members to serve in the Congress of the United States . . . was received and read.

On motion, resolved, that agreeably to the act of General Assembly passed the fourth of October last a proclamation of the members elected to represent this state in the Congress of the United States be now issued under the Great Seal.

A draft of a proclamation being prepared and laid on the table . . . was read and agreed to as follows, viz.,

Pennsylvania ss. [state seal]

By The Supreme Executive Council of the Commonwealth of Pennsylvania.— A Proclamation[1]

Whereas pursuant to an Act of the General Assembly of the said Commonwealth passed on the fourth day of October last intituled "An Act directing the time places and manner of holding Elections for Representatives of this State in the Congress of the United States &ca." Election for such Representatives were held on the last Wednesday in November last in the City of Philadelphia—and in the several Counties of this State and the returns of the said several Elections having been transmitted by the Sheriffs of the said City and Counties respectively to the Secretary of this Council. Now We the Supreme Executive Council of the said Commonwealth having agreeably to the directions of the said Act inspected and examined the said Returns, and enumerated and ascertained the number of votes for each and every Candidate do hereby make known and declare that Frederick Augustus Muhlenberg, Henry Wynkoop, Thomas Hartly, George Clymer, Thomas Fitzimmons Thomas Scott[2] Peter Muhlenberg and Daniel Heister are according to the said Returns highest in votes of the Electors throughout this State and in consequence are duly elected and chosen as Representatives of and for this State in the Congress of the United States.—

Given in Council under the hand of His Excellency Thomas Mifflin Esquire President and the Seal of the State at Philadelphia this fifth day of January, in the year of our Lord one thousand seven hundred and eighty nine

Attest   Thomas Mifflin
        Charles Biddle Secry.

1. (LT). The proclamation was widely reprinted outside the state (see, for example, the Baltimore *Maryland Gazette,* 13 January; Hartford *Connecticut Courant,* 19 January; and *Newport Herald,* 29 January).

2. Shortly after the proclamation by the Supreme Executive Council, Thomas Scott announced that he did not want to serve as a Representative, reputedly because he did not wish to give up his post as prothonotary of Washington County. An arrangement was made whereby Scott agreed to serve in exchange for the appointment of his son as prothonotary (see Supreme Executive Council Proceedings, 5, 17 February, and Assembly Proceedings, 13 February, printed below).

A Federalist, Pennsylvania Packet, 7 January

Federal Electors: James Wilson, Esq.; Joseph Potts, Esq.; General Edward Hand; Alexander Graydon, Esq.; Mr. James O'Harra; Collinson Read, Esq.; General George Gibson; John Arndt, Jr., Esq.; Lawrence Keene, Esq.; David Grier, Esq.[1]

Fellow Citizens: The above is the ticket for Electors, agreed to by the conferees who met at Lancaster; and although it may not come up to the wishes of every Federalist in the state, yet it is the only one that could possibly have been formed upon that occasion which would have been equally satisfactory.

Under this idea of the matter, and it having been reported, that an attempt will be made to appoint as President and Vice President of the United States, Patrick Henry, Esq., of Virginia and Governor [George] Clinton, of New York, it necessarily therefore becomes the duty of every well-wisher to these states, to use his utmost industry and endeavors to counteract this design, and instead of these gentlemen, to bring forward our illustrious Washington, and the learned and patriotic Adams—men, who in the worst of times faithfully served us; the one in the cabinet, and the other in the field; and whose services, under divine Providence preserved this devoted country from the most wretched vassalage.

Tomorrow, then, my fellow citizens, is the great, the important day, for a proper display of your zeal—let every true Federalist turn out, even to a single man, to give his vote and interest for the Federal ticket that these illustrious men, Washington and Adams, may have another glorious opportunity of saving their country from ruin.[2]

1. This item was dated 6 January. Several newspapers printed the Lancaster ticket for Electors on or before election day (see, for example, the *Federal Gazette*, 3 January; *Pennsylvania Mercury*, 6 January; and *Pennsylvania Gazette*, 7 January).

2. The above item aroused the indignation of Walter Stewart, who charged that it was an attack on him and that Dr. Benjamin Rush was responsible for it (Rush to Tench Coxe, 19 January, printed below). On 9 January, the *Packet* contained an item signed "I" which denied that an attack on Stewart was intended if read "unconnected" with what preceded it in the newspaper. That item (not printed here) also praised Washington and Adams and concluded with listing both the Harrisburg and Lancaster tickets for Electors. Stewart was one of the Electors on the Harrisburg ticket, probably because he was a son-in-law of Blair M'Clenachan.

Philadelphia Vote for Presidential Electors, 7 January[1]

At the close of the poll yesterday evening, at the Statehouse in this city, "for ten persons as Electors, for the purpose of choosing a President and Vice President of the United States," the following gentlemen (all truly Federal) stood highest on the returns, viz.,

James Wilson	1530
Collinson Read	1531
Laurence Keen	1531
John Arndt	1532
Edward Hand	1545
Samuel [James] O'Hara	1535
Samuel Potts	1525
George Gibson	1530
David Grier	1530
Alexander Graydon	1533

It is with singular pleasure we inform the public, that the highest number in the Antifederal ticket, opposed to the foregoing, did not exceed sixteen votes: this prodigious majority of 1535 to 16, will appear still the more extraordinary, when we consider, that the Antifederal Party had the audacity to run, in their ticket, three or four worthy and highly Federal gentlemen, with [James] *M'Lene*, [John] *Smilie*, and others of the same unpopular and detested principles. Respect for those "three or four" Federal characters, induces us to omit publishing the Antifederal, and consequently unsuccessful, ticket.[2]

1. *Federal Gazette,* 8 January.
2. The next day the Antifederalist *Independent Gazetteer* commented that "the real friends of liberty and republicanism" had not made any opposition.

Alexander McKeehan and George Logue to John Nicholson, Carlisle, 8 January (excerpt)[1]

There was an election held yesterday for Electors but our party left it to the others and did not vote.[2] We are sorry the last election day proved such a wet day which was much to the advantage of the opposite party. We would wish you to write us the intention of the new Representatives to Congress (if in your power) respecting amendments.

1. RC, Nicholson Papers, PHarH. The first portion of this letter from two Cumberland County commissioners dealt with county business. The portion printed here was marked "private." The letter was carried to Nicholson by William Irvine.
2. Later there were evidently charges of irregularity in one of the districts in Cumberland County. James M'Murray published the following statement, dated 19 January, in the *Carlisle Gazette* on 28 January and in the three succeeding issues: "The subscriber is publicly censured by honorable gentlemen as a judge of an election of Electors for the district of Rye and Greenwood townships, in Cumberland County, by reason of an irregular inordinate ticket having prevailed, but he is able to prove himself unconnected."

Pennsylvania Mercury, 8 January

The severity of the weather, says a correspondent, has been assigned by some as a reason why so few of the freemen in this state have attended the late town meeting for the choice of federal Representatives and Electors. How surprising that a matter so trivial, when put in competition with the object in view, should operate as has been evinced. The chilling frosts of winter, are but trifling compared to the consequences which will result from choosing men to govern us, who are unworthy of our trust and confidence—wherever a choice should not take place, freemen think of these things.

Secretary Charles Biddle to Secretary Charles Thomson, Philadelphia, 9 January[1]

By directions of the Supreme Executive Council I herewith transmit to you the proclamation issued by Council declaring the names of the eight persons duly elected and chosen Representatives of this [state] in the Congress of the United States together with the returns from the city and counties agreeably to the act of General Assembly directing the time, places and manner of holding the said elections.

1. FC, Supreme Executive Council Letterbook, PHarH. The proclamation of 5 January is printed above. The voting returns sent to Charles Thomson, secretary of Congress, have not been located in the National Archives.

Timothy Pickering to Samuel Hodgdon, 11 January (excerpt)[1]

Our election of Electors was better than the last.[2] We had 36 voters. The citizens of Philadelphia would hardly travel from 5 to 100 miles to attend any election whatever: but the people of this county must do it or our elections will be small. They know little about the new government and of course felt little interested in elections. Added to the above circumstances, the weather was bad, which prevented many in the neighborhood from assembling.

1. RC, Pickering Papers, MHi. Hodgdon was Pickering's business partner in Philadelphia.
2. In the election for Representatives in Luzerne County there were only 17 votes for each member of the Lancaster ticket, except Frederick A. Muhlenburg, who received 16, and 1 vote for each member of the Harrisburg ticket, except William Findley, who received 2.

Thomas Hartley to Tench Coxe, York, 12 January (excerpt)[1]

I wrote to you on the 28th ult. but have not had the pleasure of hearing from you since.

So far as we can learn, our ticket for federal Electors will carry. In our county the votes stood 858 Fed. to 1 Anti. Lancaster was also nearly unanimous.

Pray, will there not be some difficulty about the Vice President? Will [John] Hancock or J[ohn] Adams be the man? Which is most agreeable to the people of New England?

As I shall see some of the Electors before the meeting, this information may be of use.

I inclose you one of our newspapers and which contains a piece you wished to have published.[2] We apprehend our [Pennsylvania] Herald will have a pretty general circulation. Some materials from you now and then will be acceptable.

1. RC, Coxe Papers, Tench Coxe Section, PHi.
2. Presumably Coxe's "Thoughts on the Subject of Amendments of the Federal Constitution," signed "An American Citizen," printed in the Herald, 7 January.

Ephraim Douglass to Secretary Charles Biddle, Union Town, 17 January[1]

Understanding from the bearer that a part of his business was to collect the returns of elections in the several counties, and he being denied by circumstances the opportunity of receiving an answer from the sheriff [Joseph Torrence], whose duty it is to make such return, I take the liberty, for the satisfaction of Council to inform you that no election has been held in this county [Fayette] for the election of Electors. The number of persons who attended on that day was not sufficient to have filled the necessary offices of such an election.

1. *Pa. Archives,* 1 ser., XI, 535. For Sheriff Torrence's explanation see his letter to Biddle, 19 January, printed immediately below.

Sheriff Joseph Torrence to Secretary Charles Biddle, Fayette County, 19 January (excerpt)[1]

I have just received yours of 27th December last but had not the pleasure of seeing Mr. [James] Dunwoodie. I would just inform you we had no election for Electors; neither judges, inspectors, electors attended, the people in general thinking it a matter of no consequence to them. For further particulars I refer you to John Smilie Esqr. our councilor who I am informed goes to Philadelphia in a few days. Mr. John Gilchrist Esqr. one of our representatives sets off for Philadelphia tomorrow morning by whom I send this. I am very sorry that I have incurred the displeasure of the Board in not sending the return of Representatives in due time. I assure you it was not inattention to my duty but wishing for an opportunity without expense to the county by express.

1. RC, RG 46, DNA. Biddle sent Sheriff Torrence's letter to Secretary Charles Thomson on 28 February, along with other documents relating to the election of Electors and the votes of the Electors for President.

Benjamin Rush to Tench Coxe, Philadelphia, 19 January[1]

The intelligence contained in your letter was very acceptable, and shall be attended to agreeably to your request.

There has been no systematic opposition in any part of the state to the choice of federal Electors. Mr. [John] Adams will now certainly have *ten* votes for the Vice President's chair from Pennsylvania. This is Mr. [James] Wilson's wish, and his advice, I have no doubt, will be conclusive in that business. I wish Mr. Adams's friends to know how much Mr. Wilson concurs in their views. He will probably have all the votes of the Maryland Electors. The Jersey Federalists are alarmed without reason for the honor and fate of General Washington. Do try to prevent their throwing away their votes.

Mr. Wilson thinks there will be no impropriety in Mr. [George] Clymer and Mr. [Thomas] Fitzsimons retaining their seats in our Assembly till next October. They may help next summer to make the wheels of the two governments roll more easily upon each other. The measure, too, will favor a proper election of suitable successors to them. The clamor about public credit, and the influence of the *postillions* of the *high* varnished coach might at the present juncture defeat the *wishes* of some of the best citizens of Philadelphia.

There is great wrath, I hear, against me in York and Lancaster for favoring the German alterations in the Federal ticket.[2] They do me great honor, for it has saved the state. The *secession* of the Federalists who adopted the two Germans, or even their *neutrality* on the day of the election (one of which events would *certainly* have happened, had not the ticket been altered), would have thrown the six Antifederalists into Congress by a majority of several hundred votes.

I am still a Federalist and a Republican, but I am no longer a *party man*. On the contrary, I despise the conduct and principles of a great part of the men with whom I have so long had the misfortune of being associated in my disinterested endeavors to serve my country.

Many of our friends think that *now* is the time to push for a convention to change our state constitution.[3] The Anties have by their late conduct bequeathed the power of the state to us, to do as we please.

[The?] [pub]lication on the day of the last election reflected on Patrick Henry and Governor [George] Clinton. General [Walter] Stewart supposed it was aimed against *him*, and abused *me* as the author of it in several companies. Mr. R[obert] Morris, who heard his complaints against me, stopped me in the street and asked me if I was the author of the piece. I told him *I was not—nor did I know who was*. At that time I had scarcely read it. Upon looking at it when I came home, I was astonished to find it had not the most *distant* relation to the General, but by the plainest rules of grammar [and?] [c]ommon sense, it alluded wholly to the [gentlem?]en before mentioned. Every citizen [———] who read it, concurred in the same opinion.[4] The General has become an Ishmael—*his hands are against every man*. But he differs from the patriarch's son in this—that *no man's hand is against him*. "*Muscas non captant aquilae.*" Let them alone. They die of themselves.

Have you met with a trusty person going to London in the next packet? The volume of essays has met with a candid reception.[5] A foreigner has applied to me for permission to translate them into German, and to publish them in Germany.

Adieu.

1. RC, Coxe Papers, Tench Coxe Section, PHi.
2. See "To the German Inhabitants of the State of Pennsylvania," 13 November, n. 1, printed above.
3. For the calling of a state constitutional convention in 1789, see Brunhouse, *Counter-Revolution*, 221-27.
4. See "A Federalist," *Pennsylvania Packet,* 7 January, printed above.
5. Benjamin Rush, *Medical Inquiries and Observations* (Philadelphia, 1789).

Benjamin Rush to Tench Coxe, Philadelphia, 25 January (excerpt)[1]

In my account of the manners of the Germans in Pennsylvania, you will perceive that persecution has served only to unite me closer to my German friends.[2] In the year 1781 I undertook three great objects: 1. to enlighten, or divide the Irish Presbyterians by means of a college at Carlisle; 2. to unite the Quakers with the Republicans, by writing down the test law; and lastly to attach the Germans to them both, by diffusing knowledge among them, and inviting them to share with them in the honors and offices of government. Each of these objects after many struggles has been accomplished. The Republicans as a *party* had no share in the difficulties of effecting these objects. They opposed, at one time, the repeal of the test law, and in the late conference at Lancaster they treated the idea of a German representation with indignation and contempt. The happiness of Pennsylvania can only be established upon the basis of a union between the Quakers, Germans, and the virtuous part of the Irish inhabitants of the state. The Germans for some time will be held by a precarious tenure. Their ignorance of our language, and close attachment to the pursuits of agriculture, will render them, for some time to come, easy subjects of popular deception. They must therefore be courted and cherished until they have been taught the means of promoting their own interests as far as government is necessary for that purpose. Had the sensible English gentlemen in New York founded a Low Dutch college at Albany forty years ago, that city would not now have been the theater of the disgrace, and perhaps of the ruin of their state. In every struggle for liberty in New York, the friends of arbitrary power have found their chief support in the wealthy ignorance of the Low Dutch citizens. Of this Governor [James] Delan[c]ey and Governor [William] Tryon had the most successful experience long before Governor [George] Clinton. It will only be, by establishing a seminary of learning in the center of their state, that they will ever place its power upon the basis of reason, and *rescue* their honest but ignorant citizens, from the influence of dishonest, but sensible demagogues.

I am pleased to find that you have written to Colonel [Samuel] Miles. Do enclose a few paragraphs in a *friendly* letter to Mr. Hall under *cover* to me. I find you are doing a great deal of good; but I do not like your *secrecy* in business. You possess too much, I fear, of what General [Charles] Lee used to call the rascally virtue of prudence in politics. I like the *"suaviter in modo"* but the *"fortiter in re"* is equally necessary. What have we to fear from owning ourselves the open friends of Jno Adams—or of the Germans of Pennsylvania? But I forget that you are only a young *racer*—while I am an *old dray horse*. A single fly to you is more than a beehive to me. Under all the slander that I have lately met with from the westward, beginning at the corner of 8th Street, I have not once lifted a foot, moved my tail, or shaken an ear.

1. RC, Coxe Papers, Tench Coxe Section, PHi.
2. "An Account of the Manners of the German Inhabitants of Pennsylvania," *The Columbian Magazine*, III (January 1789), 22-30.

Tench Coxe to Benjamin Rush, New York, 29 January (excerpt)[1]

I have received your favors per the post to which I shall attend. I shall immediately forward Mr. [John] Adams's letter and do what you wish to Colonel [William Stephens] Smith who requested it of me.[2]

It will be proper that Mr. [George] Clymer and Mr. [Thomas] Fitzsimons know that I have discovered that there is some idea of attempting to declare their seats in the state legislature vacant on account of their election to the federal House. This information must not be [extended?] far as coming from me. Mr. [James] Wilson, I think, should be consulted. The argument is clearly in favor of their right to their present seats. They are only Representatives in Congress elect; when sworn in there, their present seats will be vacated.[3]

1. RC, Rush Papers, PPL.
2. Rush's letter to John Adams, 22 January, concerning the Vice Presidency, is printed in Chapter XIV. Rush's letter to Coxe, enclosing the letter to Adams, has not been located.
3. See Rush to Coxe, 19 January, printed above.

Benjamin Rush to Tench Coxe, Philadelphia, 31 January (excerpt)[1]

Sometime ago the Council dispatched a messenger to bring in the returns of the elections for federal Electors from every part of the state—*time* enough to convey notice to each of them to [repair?] to Reading on the first Wednesday of next month. Unfortunately, a man was pitched upon for that purpose who had private business to transact in one of the frontier counties, and he has not yet returned.[2] Of course we shall either have no election or only part of our Electors will meet. Mr. [James] Wilson will attend, and thinks the business may be yet effected by an adjournment. The express who has disappointed, and injured the state so materially, was recommended (Mr. [William] McClay informs me) by Charles Biddle.

1. RC, Coxe Papers, Tench Coxe Section, PHi.
2. See James Dunwoodie to the Supreme Executive Council, 2 February, printed immediately below.

James Dunwoodie to the Honorable Members of Council, 2 February[1]

To give you satisfaction concerning my proceeding in bringing the returns from the western counties and the cause of my delay I hope to give sufficient satisfaction.

First I was stopped at the river Susquehanna for four day[s] before I could cross and then delivering the letters in charge at different places agreeable to direction, could not reach Fort Pitt before the 19th of January. I left that place the next day in return to this place; the returns from Huntingdon was to have been sent to Bedford but was not. I then had to cross through to that place with great difficulty; as the snow was not broken in many places made it difficult and not finding the protho[notary] at home, followed him to Green Castle in Franklin County. I expect before I reached this place calculating the different routes makes near eight hundred and thirty or forty miles; taking this long distance into consideration and the season of the year that I had to accomplish it, I hope your honors will rather give me credit than find any fault in [me].

1. RC, Records of the Supreme Executive Council, PHarH. The letter is undated, but it is endorsed as being read the first time on 9 February. We have dated it 2 February, since Dunwoodie must have delivered the election returns to the Council before it issued its proclamation on 3 February.

Federal Gazette, 2 February

It is to be lamented that the laws of this state are so badly executed, that they are generally treated with the most sovereign contempt. The election returns for federal Representatives, from some of the counties, instead of being made in *ten days*, were kept back *four weeks*. Those for Electors of a President and Vice President of the United States, have not yet been made from all the counties. Quere, as next Wednesday is the day appointed for the meeting of the Electors, in their respective states, is Pennsylvania like New York, to look on as a silent spectator. And shall a few Antifederal sheriffs (or prothonotaries) be suffered, with impunity, thus to trample on the laws, and render the Federal state of Pennsylvania, the scoff of the Union?[1]

1. The *Federal Gazette* was apparently unaware that the Supreme Executive Council had sent two men to collect the returns. For the legislative deadlock in New York that prevented the election of Electors and United States Senators, see Chapter XIII.

Supreme Executive Council Proceedings, Tuesday, 3 February

On motion, resolved, that the several returns of Electors for choosing a President and Vice President of the United States, which have been transmitted to Council, be referred to Mr. Maclay and Mr. Smith to inspect the same, and report to Council the names of the ten persons highest in votes; which being done,
A draft of a proclamation was laid before the board, read, and adopted. . . .

Proclamation by the President and Supreme Executive Council, 3 February[1]

Pennsylvania ss.
[SEAL]
[s]Thomas Mifflin

Whereas pursuant to an Act of the General Assembly of the said Commonwealth passed on the fourth day of October last, entituled "An Act directing the time places and manner of holding elections for Representatives of this State in the Congress of the United States, and for appointing Electors on the part of this State for choosing a President and Vice President of the United States," elections for such Electors were held on the first Wednesday in January Last, in the City of Philadelphia and in the several Counties of this State.—And Whereas it appears from the returns transmitted to the Secretary of this Council, that Edward Hand George Gibson, John Arndt Collinson Read, Lawrence Keene, James Wilson, James O Harra, David Grier, Samuel Potts and Alexander Graydon, are highest in votes as Electors aforesaid. Now We, the Supreme Executive Council of the said Commonwealth, do hereby make known and declare that Edward Hand, George Gibson, John Arndt, Collinson Read Lawrence Keene, James Wilson James O Harra, David Grier, Samuel Potts and Alexander Graydon are according to the said returns highest in Votes, and in consequence are duly elected and chosen as Electors of and for this State for Choosing a President and Vice President of the United States. ————————————

Given in Council under the hand of His Excellency Thomas Mifflin Esquire President and the Seal of the State, at Philadelphia this third day of February, in the Year of our Lord one thousand seven hundred and eighty nine, and of the Commonwealth the thirteenth.————————————————————————

Attest

[s] Cha. Biddle secy

1. (LT), RG 46, DNA. The proclamation was sent to Secretary Charles Thomson by Secretary Charles Biddle on 28 February, along with other papers relating to the election of presidential Electors.

The Votes for Presidential Electors

The manuscript returns of the votes for Electors were sent by city and county officials to the Supreme Executive Council. After the votes were counted, the original returns were sent to Charles Thomson, secretary of the Confederation Congress, by Charles Biddle, secretary of the Council. These original returns are in the National Archives (RG 46).

The first table gives the votes for the Lancaster and Harrisburg tickets and is compiled from the tables which follow it. Those tables are copied from the original manuscript returns for the city of Philadelphia and the counties of the state except for Fayette, where not enough people appeared on election day to hold an election. The names of all the men voted for and the number of votes they received are given as they appear in the original returns except for spelling. County officials often spelled the name of a given individual in various ways, so we have corrected spelling of such names wherever possible.

LANCASTER TICKET: RETURNS FOR ELECTORS

County	Alexander Graydon	Samuel Potts	James O'Hara	James Wilson	Collinson Read	George Gibson	Laurence Keene	David Grier	John Arndt	Edward Hand
City of Philadelphia	1533	1525	1535	1530	1531	1530	1531	1530	1532	1545
County of Philadelphia	642	635	643	640	644	641	644	642	645	647
Bucks	443	443	443	443	443	443	443	443	443	443
Chester	129	492	490	491	490	490	491	491	491	501
York	853	855	851	858	858	857	858	857	842	858
Berks	159	159	159	147	159	158	158	159	158	157
Lancaster	540	498	540	540	540	540	540	540	539	549
Cumberland	158	156	160	160	160	160	158	148	154	155
Northampton	304	311	301	312	312	312	312	258	324	324
Dauphin	215	165	198	197	197	196	196	196	194	369
Montgomery	318	327	322	320	327	324	327	318	323	343
Northumberland	156	157	157	157	157	157	156	157	157	157
Franklin	311	311	301	301	322	313	312	315	315	349
Huntingdon	66	66	66	66	66	65	66	66	66	90
Bedford	62	62	62	62	62	62	62	62	62	62
Westmoreland	5	6	6	15	6	7	4	15	4	105
Luzerne	36	36	36	36	36	36	36	36	36	36
Washington	21	21	9	21	19	21	21	17	21	21
Totals	5951	6225	6279	6296	6329	6312	6315	6250	6306	6711

HARRISBURG TICKET: RETURNS FOR ELECTORS

County	David Rittenhouse	Joseph Hiester	James Potter	Thomas Craig	James McLene	John Smilie	Philip Wager	Walter Stewart	William Gibbons
City of Philadelphia	15	14	15	14	13	13	13	16	13
County of Philadelphia	1	1	1	2	1	1	3	1	1
Bucks	0	0	0	0	0	0	0	0	0
Chester	0	9	10	9	9	9	9	9	378
York	1	1	1	1	1	1	1	1	1
Berks	0	0	0	0	0	0	0	0	0
Lancaster	9	9	9	9	9	9	9	9	9
Cumberland	0	0	0	0	0	0	0	11	0
Northampton	15	16	12	77	12	13	12	12	1
Dauphin	178	178	175	174	173	172	198	142	135
Montgomery	17	16	17	17	16	17	16	17	16
Northumberland	0	0	0	0	0	0	0	0	0
Franklin	80	82	82	80	83	82	79	71	34
Huntingdon	24	0	24	24	24	24	24	24	24
Bedford	0	0	0	0	0	0	0	0	0
Westmoreland	83	76	75	80	72	75	6	69	60
Luzerne	0	0	0	0	0	0	0	0	0
Washington	0	0	0	0	0	0	0	0	0
Totals	423	402	421	487	413	416	370	381	672

CITY OF PHILADELPHIA RETURNS

	New Market Ward	Dock Ward	South Ward	Walnut Ward	Middle Ward	Chesnut Ward	High Street Ward	North Ward	Lower Delaware Ward	South Mulberry Ward	North Mulberry & Upper Delaware Wards	Total
James Wilson	220	171	84	47	186	53	61	199	58	197	254	1530
Collinson Read	221	170	83	47	186	53	61	200	58	197	255	1531
Laurence Keene	221	171	84	47	185	53	61	200	58	197	254	1531
John Arndt	221	170	84	47	185	53	61	200	58	197	256	1532
Edward Hand	221	173	84	47	187	55	62	202	58	198	258	1545
James O'Hara	221	172	84	47	186	52	61	201	58	197	256	1535
Samuel Potts	221	170	83	47	184	53	61	200	58	197	254	1525
George Gibson	220	171	84	47	186	52	61	200	56	196	254	1530
David Grier	221	171	84	47	185	53	61	201	58	197	254	1530
Alexander Graydon	221	171	84	47	186	53	61	201	58	197	254	1533
Walter Stewart	1	2			2	2	1	3		1	4	16
John Smilie		2			2	2	1	2		1	3	13
James Potter		2			2	2	1	3		1	4	15
James McLene		2			2	2	1	2		1	3	13
Joseph Hiester		2			2	2	1	2		1	4	14
Thomas Craig		1			2	2	1	3		1	4	14
David Rittenhouse		2			3	2	1	3		1	3	15
Philip Wager		2			3	1		1		4	2	13
William Gibbons		2			2	2	1	2		1	3	13
James Irwin					1		1					2
William Irvine					1		1	1			1	3

Name								Total
Joseph Potts	1		2			2	1	6
John Steinmetz		1						2
Joseph Montgomery		1						1
George Clymer				1				1
John Nixon				1				1
George Palmer				1				1
Jacob Hiltzheimer				1				1
Lewis Farmer				1				1
Henry Kammerer				1				1
John Wilson				1				1
William Heyshaus				1				1
Robert Hunt				1				1
John Ralston				1				1
John Van Compton				1				1
John Allison				1				1
Charles Pettit	1							1
Francis Mentges	1							1
George Habacker	1							1
Benjamin Penington						1		1
Joseph Montgomery								1
John Karr	1							1

COUNTY OF PHILADELPHIA RETURNS

	First District	Second District	Third District	*Total*
James Wilson	433	155	52	640
Collinson Read	433	159	52	644
Laurence Keene	433	159	52	644
John Arndt	434	159	52	645
Edward Hand	438	157	52	647
James O'Hara	433	158	52	643
George Gibson	433	156	52	641
Samuel Potts	425	158	52	635
David Grier	434	156	52	642
Alexander Graydon	433	157	52	642
Philip Wager	3			3
George Clymer	1			1
Joseph Potts	6			6
Thomas Craig	2			2
James Potter	1			1
Walter Stewart	1			1
James McLene	1			1
John Smilie	1			1
Joseph Hiester	1			1
David Rittenhouse	1			1
William Gibbons	1			1
Adam Hubley		2		2

BUCKS COUNTY RETURNS

				Newton District			Totals	Upper District Totals	Bucks County Totals
Bristol Borough	6	Lower Makefield	34	Middletown	40	Northampton	87			
Bristol Township	8	Wrightown	21	Warwick	4	Southampton	9			
Bensalem	7	Buckingham	20	Warrington	0	Warminister	1			
Falls	12	Upper Makefield	32	Solebury	9	Newtown	41			
	33		107		53*		138*			

							Totals	Totals	Totals
James Wilson	33		107		51		142	333	110	443
Collinson Read	33		107		51		142	333	110	443
Laurence Keene	33		107		51		142	333	110	443
John Arndt	33		107		51		142	333	110	443
Edward Hand	33		107		51		142	333	110	443
James O'Hara	33		107		51		142	333	110	443
Samuel Potts	33		107		51		142	333	110	443
George Gibson	33		107		51		142	333	110	443
David Grier	33		107		51		142	333	110	443
Alexander Graydon	33		107		51*		142*	333	110	443

*The discrepancies between the vote totals for individual towns in the third and fourth columns, and the vote totals for individual candidates given below them, are the discrepancies shown in the official returns sent to the Supreme Executive Council.

395

CHESTER COUNTY
RETURNS

Edward Hand	501
Samuel Potts	492
James Wilson	491
John Arndt	491
David Grier	491
Laurence Keene	491
Collinson Read	490
James O'Hara	490
George Gibson	490
William Gibbons	378
Alexander Graydon	129
James Potter	10
Thomas Mifflin	9
John Smilie	9
James McLene	9
Walter Stewart	9
Joseph Hiester	9
Philip Wager	9
Thomas Craig	9

YORK COUNTY
RETURNS

Edward Hand	858
James Wilson	858
Collinson Read	858
David Grier	857
George Gibson	857
Laurence Keene	858
Alexander Graydon	853
James O'Hara	851
Samuel Potts	855
John Arndt	842
James Arndt	12
John O'Hara	4
Jonathan Arndt	1
Thomas Craig	1
Joseph Hiester	1
Walter Stewart	1
James Potter	1
William Gibbons	1
David Rittenhouse	1
John Smilie	1
James McLene	1
Philip Wager	1

BERKS COUNTY
RETURNS

Collinson Read	159
James O'Hara	159
Samuel Potts	159
David Grier	159
Alexander Graydon	159
Laurence Keene	158
John Arndt	158
George Gibson	158
Edward Hand	157
James Wilson	147
Nicholas Lutz	11

LANCASTER COUNTY
RETURNS

Edward Hand	549
James Wilson	540
Collinson Read	540
Laurence Keene	540
John Arndt	539
James O'Hara	540
Samuel Potts	498
David Grier	540
George Gibson	540
Alexander Graydon	540
John Hannums	42
Walter Stewart	9
David Rittenhouse	9
Philip Wager	9
Thomas Craig	9
Joseph Hiester	9
James Potter	9
James McLene	9
John Smilie	9
William Gibbons	9

CUMBERLAND COUNTY RETURNS

	Hopewell, Newton, & Shippenburgh Township	Carlisle District	Rye, Tyrone, & Teboyn Township	*Total*
James Wilson	59	83	18	160
Laurence Keene	57	83	18	158
Edward Hand	54	83	18	155
Samuel Potts	55	83	18	156
David Grier	47	83	18	148
Collinson Read	59	83	18	160
John Arndt	54	82	18	154
James O'Hara	59	83	18	160
George Gibson	59	83	18	160
Alexander Graydon	57	83	18	158
Walter Stewart	11			11
John Potts	4			4
Adam Hubley	1			1
Alexander McGee	5			5
Matthew Scott	2			2

NORTHAMPTON COUNTY
RETURNS

James Wilson	312
Edward Hand	324
John Arndt	324
Collinson Read	312
Laurence Keene	312
Samuel Potts	311
George Gibson	312
David Grier	258
Alexander Graydon	304
James O'Hara	301
Thomas Craig	77
Joseph Hiester	16
David Rittenhouse	15
John Smilie	13
James Potter	12
James McLene	12
Walter Stewart	12
Philip Wager	12
William Gibbons	1

DAUPHIN COUNTY
RETURNS

Edward Hand	369
Alexander Graydon	215
Philip Wager	198
James O'Hara	198
James Wilson	197
Collinson Read	197
George Gibson	196
Laurence Keene	196
David Grier	196
John Arndt	194
David Rittenhouse	178
Joseph Hiester	178
James Potter	175
Thomas Craig	174
James McLene	173
John Smilie	172
Samuel Potts	165
Walter Stewart	142
William Gibbons	135
William Stewart	34
Joseph Montgomery	26

MONTGOMERY COUNTY RETURNS

Edward Hand	343	David Rittenhouse	17
James Wilson	320	James McLene	16
Collinson Read	327	Joseph Hiester	16
Laurence Keene	327	Philip Wager	16
Samuel Potts	327	William Gibbons	16
George Gibson	324	Isaac [---]	11
John Arndt	323	George Grier	6
James O'Hara	322	Levi Hollingsworth	4
David Grier	318	John O'Hara	3
Alexander Graydon	318	Edward Roberts	1
James Potter	17	Christian Steer	1
Walter Stewart	17	William Dean	1
John Smilie	17	John Cope	1
Thomas Craig	17	Andrew Porter	1

NORTHUMBERLAND COUNTY RETURNS

	First District	Second District	Lycoming District	*Total*
James Wilson	85	51	21	157
Collinson Read	85	51	21	157
John Arndt	85	51	21	157
Edward Hand	85	51	21	157
James O'Hara	85	51	21	157
Samuel Potts	85	51	21	157
George Gibson	85	51	21	157
David Grier	85	51	21	157
Alexander Graydon	84	51	21	156
Laurence Keene	84	51	21	156
Alexander Potts	1			1
John Boyd	1			1
John Mackey		1		1

FRANKLIN COUNTY RETURNS

James Wilson	301	James Potter	82
Collinson Read	322	James McLene	83
Laurence Keene	312	John Smilie	82
Edward Hand	349	James Riddle	1
James O'Hara	301	William Stewart	2
Samuel Potts	311	Alexander Grier	2
George Gibson	313	George Clingan	1
David Grier	315	George Potts	1
Alexander Graydon	311	George Bryan	45
John Arndt	315	James Gibbons	44
Walter Stewart	71	John Allison	2
David Rittenhouse	80	Alexander Grayson	3
Philip Wager	79	John Hiester	1
Thomas Craig	80	James Potts	1
Joseph Hiester	82	William Findley	10
William Gibbons	34	Robert Whitehill	19

HUNTINGDON COUNTY RETURNS

Edward Hand	90
James Wilson	66
Collinson Read	66
Laurence Keene	66
John Arndt	66
James O'Hara	66
Samuel Potts	66
David Grier	66
Alexander Graydon	66
George Gibson	65
James Potter	24
Walter Stewart	24
James McLene	24
John Smilie	24
Thomas Craig	24
David Rittenhouse	24
Philip Wager	24
William Gibbons	24

BEDFORD COUNTY RETURNS

James Wilson	62
Collinson Read	62
Laurence Keene	62
John Arndt	62
Edward Hand	62
James O'Hara	62
Samuel Potts	62
George Gibson	62
David Grier	62
Alexander Graydon	62

WESTMORELAND COUNTY RETURNS

General Edward Hand	105	Alexander Graydon	5
John Woods	94	John Arndt	4
David Rittenhouse	83	Laurence Keene	4
Colonel Thomas Craig	80	Robert Hunter	3
Joseph Hiester	76	Robert Whitehill	3
General James Potter	75	Joseph Cook	3
John Smilie	75	Frederick Rora	3
James McLene	72	Thomas McKean	2
Colonel Walter Stewart	69	General William Irvine	2
William Gibbons	60	William Stuart	2
James Edgar	35	William Todd	2
David Grier	15	John Irwin	2
James Wilson	15	John Parker	2
Jared Ingersoll	15	John Stuart	1
James Gibbons	14	John Young Esq.	1
Daniel Hiester	14	John Bradshaw	1
Samuel Postlewait	13	John Craig	1
Robert Clark	12	Daniel Rittenhouse	1
Moses McLean	12	William McGee	1
Robert Lollar	12	Joseph Sharp	1
James Irwin	13	John Barr	1
William Gibson	8	William Hunter	1
George Gibson	7	James McLauren	1
James O'Hara	6	James Heister	1
Collinson Read	6	John Baird Esq.	1
Samuel Potts	6	James Barr	1
Philip Wager	6		

LUZERNE COUNTY RETURNS

James Wilson	36
Collinson Read	36
Laurence Keene	36
John Arndt	36
Edward Hand	36
James O'Hara	36
Samuel Potts	36
George Gibson	36
David Grier	36
Alexander Graydon	36

WASHINGTON COUNTY RETURNS

James Wilson	21
George Gibson	21
Samuel Potts	21
Edward Hand	21
Alexander Graydon	21
Laurence Keene	21
John Arndt	21
Collinson Read	19
David Grier	17
John Woods	16
James O'Hara	9

Votes of the Pennsylvania Presidential Electors, 4 February[1]

At a Meeting of the Electors appointed by the State of Pennsylvania for choosing a President and Vice President of the United States of America held at the Borough of Reading in the said State on the first Wednesday in February in the Year of Our Lord one thousand seven hundred and eighty nine all the Persons voted for and the Number of Votes for each were as follow Vizt. for

George Washington	ten Votes
John Adams	eight Votes
John Hancock	two Votes

Reading February 4th 1789   Signed and certified by

[Signed:]	James Wilson	Edwd Hand	
	James O'Hara	Geo Gibson	Electors for
	David Grier	John Arndt	the State of
	Saml. Potts	Collinson Read	Pennsylva
	Alex Graydon	Laurence Keene	

To the President of the
Senate of the United States

1. (LT), RG 46, DNA. Secretary Charles Biddle sent his official report of the votes of the Pennsylvania Electors to Secretary Charles Thomson on 28 February (printed below).

Supreme Executive Council Proceedings, Thursday, 5 February

A letter from Thomas Scott, Esquire, elected one of the Representatives of this state in the Congress of the United States, signifying his wish to resign the said office, was received and read, and an order taken that the same be transmitted to the General Assembly.[1]

1. According to the Minutes of the Supreme Executive Council, 17 February, Scott's letter was dated 20 January. The York *Pennsylvania Herald*, 21 January, reported that Scott had resigned, but no other comments about Scott's resignation have been located prior to 5 February.

For official actions on Scott's letter, see Supreme Executive Council Proceedings, 6, 17 February, 28 March, and Assembly Proceedings, 13 February, printed below. For private reactions, see Benjamin Rush to Tench Coxe, 5 February; William Bradford, Jr., to Elias Boudinot, 7 February; Coxe to Benjamin Rush, 12 February; and William Bingham to Coxe, 23 February, all printed below.

Benjamin Rush to Tench Coxe, Philadelphia, 5 February (excerpt)[1]

Mr. [James] Wilson left town on Tuesday for Reading. It is expected *all* the Electors will attend—from mere Federal instinct—for the Council issued their proclamation too late to bring them together. Two or three votes will be thrown away from Mr. [John] Adams, to prevent his being equal in votes to General Washington.[2]

Thos. Scott of Washington has resigned.[3] Our politicians are angry, and at a loss what to do. I have strongly advised to enact a new law immediately, for a new election to be held on the *3rd* of March—before the power for ordering new elections devolves on Congress. The usual inclemency of the weather on that day will confine the votes chiefly to the towns which are all Federal. Presley Nevil will probably be the Representative.[4] The members of the Assembly will form the ticket.

1. RC, Coxe Papers, Tench Coxe Section, PHi.
2. Cf., Rush to Coxe, 31 January, printed above.
3. Scott did not resign but expressed a wish to do so. See Supreme Executive Council Proceedings, 5 February, printed immediately above.
4. Presley Neville was the son of Pittsburgh Federalist John Neville.

Supreme Executive Council Proceedings, Friday, 6 February

The following draft of a message to the General Assembly was laid before Council, read and approved, viz: A Message from the President and the Supreme Executive Council to the General Assembly:

Gentlemen: In pursuance of the act of Assembly passed the fourth day of October last, Frederick Augustus Muhlenberg, Henry Wynkoop, Thomas Hartley, George Clymer, Thomas Fitzsimmons, Thomas Scott, Peter Muhlenberg, and Daniel Hiester, have been duly elected to represent this state in the Congress of the United States, and Edward Hand, George Gibson, John Arndt, Collinson Read, Lawrence Keene, James Wilson, James O'Hara, David Grier, Samuel Potts and Alexander Graydon, have been duly chosen as Electors in behalf of this state to ballot for a President and Vice President of the United States.[1]

1. The remainder of the message reported on accumulated business since the adjournment of the first session of the Assembly on 29 November 1788, recommended various actions to the Assembly, and transmitted letters received by the Council, including Thomas Scott's letter expressing his wish to resign as a Representative from Pennsylvania.

William Bradford, Jr., to Elias Boudinot, Philadelphia, 7 February (excerpt)[1]

One of our delegates-elect, Mr. [Thomas] Scott, of Washington County has sent to the Executive Council a resignation of his appointment. The inconveniences of losing a single voice, on the interesting questions which will early engage the attention of Congress is evident: but our politicians at [are] puzzled how to remedy it and seem perfectly at a fault. One set, think that as the Constitution directs all vacancies to be filled by the executive that the Council should immediately appoint: but to this it is objected that the provision only extends to vacancies which take place after the government is organized. The Council therefore will have nothing to do with it. Another set supposed that as the legislature directed the choice to be made, and it is not *effectively* made, that *they* ought to direct a new election. But the time is too short, and it is conceived by most that it would not be good—that the election has been made and the resignation can only be officially or properly tendered to the body of which he is a member. The last resource seems to be to persuade Mr. Scott to take his seat. His health is the pretense for his resignation, but the real reason is proposed to be a fear that he will lose his office which he at present holds, I mean that of prothonotary of the Common Pleas.[2] Assurances will be sent to him on this subject and it is probable that he may, for one session at least, take a seat in Congress.

1. RC, John William Wallace Collection, PHi. The letter is unsigned, and the addressee is not given. The handwriting is that of William Bradford, Jr., and from the context of this and other letters it was evidently written to his father-in-law, Elias Boudinot.
2. On 24 February the *New York Packet* reported "that the Hon. Thomas Scott, Esq. of Catfish, near Pittsburgh, declines serving as a Representative in Congress, from an opinion that the station would be incompatible with the prothonotaryship of Washington County, in Pennsylvania, which office he now holds, more especially as he was put into nomination, in the Federal ticket, without being previously consulted." The story that Scott had resigned spread throughout New England (see, for example, the Boston *Massachusetts Centinel,* 7 March, and reprints of this item in the Portsmouth *New Hampshire Gazette,* 11 March; Worcester *American Herald,* 12 March; and Portland, Me., *Cumberland Gazette,* 19 March).

Tench Coxe to Benjamin Rush, New York, 12 February (excerpt)[1]

Mr. [Thomas] Scott's resignation is very unfortunate and will probably let in Mr. [William] Finlay unless there is more sense of danger and greater exertion than I hope for.[2] The Federalists alas are men and discover sad proofs of it. Mr. Scott never having been sworn in was only a Representative-elect. I am therefore clear the state legislature is competent without a writ from the federal government. I hope they will proceed in that way.

. . . .

I wish Mr. Scott may be persuaded to serve. His resignation is unfortunate. Tho I think we shall do very well even if Finlay gets in as things now appear.

1. RC, Rush Papers, PPL.
2. There is no evidence to indicate why Coxe thought Findley might replace Scott. Perhaps Coxe assumed that if an election were held, Findley might win, since he was a popular Antifederalist leader and was respected by some Federalists as well. Findley was eleventh among the sixteen candidates in the number of votes received, but he got more than any other candidate on the Harrisburg ticket except for the two Germans, Peter Muhlenberg and Daniel Hiester.

Assembly Proceedings, Friday, 13 February[1]

The committee appointed February 11th, to confer with Council on the subject of the letter from Thomas Scott, Esquire, containing his resignation, made report, which was read; and on motion, and by special order, the same was read the second time, and adopted, as follows, viz.,

The committee appointed to confer with Council on the subject of Mr. Scott's resignation, report,

That having been in conference with a committee of Council, the conferees were of opinion that no authority existing within the state are competent to accept of Mr. Scott's resignation as a Representative to the Congress of the United States. The committee, conceiving that Mr. Scott's letter of resignation communicated to the House should be returned to Council, to be disposed of as they shall think proper, beg leave to offer a resolution,

Resolved, that the Speaker be directed to return the said letter to the Supreme Executive Council.

1. *Minutes of the Thirteenth General Assembly of the Commonwealth of Pennsylvania in their Second Session . . .* (Philadelphia, [1789]), 70.

Supreme Executive Council Proceedings, Tuesday, 17 February

The report of the committee to whom was referred the letter from Thomas Scott, Esquire, with the proceedings of the General Assembly thereon, was read and adopted as follows, viz.,

Resolved, that the letter from Thomas Scott, Esquire, of the twentieth of January last together with the proceedings of the General Assembly on the same be transmitted by the earliest opportunity to the said Thomas Scott with an intimation that it would be agreeable to Council if he would endeavor to serve during the first session of Congress or until his place can be supplied without expense to the state at the next annual election.[1]

1. Evidently an agreement was reached whereby Scott would take his seat and his son would succeed him as prothonotary of Washington County. See Supreme Executive Council Proceedings, 28 March, printed below.

William Bingham to Tench Coxe, Philadelphia, 23 February (excerpt)[1]

You need entertain no apprehensions of the substitution of an Antifederal character in the room of Mr. [Thomas] Scott, as it is expected, from the persuasive arguments of his friends, that he will accept his seat in Congress.

1. RC, Coxe Papers, Tench Coxe Section, PHi.

Assembly Proceedings, Saturday, 28 February

A motion was made by Mr. Lewis, seconded by Mr. Fitzsimons, and adopted, as follows, viz.,

Resolved, that credentials of the following form shall be prepared, and delivered to the Senators chosen by the legislature of this state, to compose, with the Senators of the states who have ratified the Constitution of the United States, the Senate thereof, and that such credentials shall be signed by the Speaker, and attested by the clerk of this House.[1]

1. The proceedings of the Supreme Executive Council on 27 February contain the following item:

"Upon the verbal report of the committee to whom it was referred to consider of and report to Council, on the propriety of granting credentials to the Senators and Representatives of this state in the Congress of the United States,

"Resolved, that no farther order be taken by Council thereon."

There is no record in previous Council proceedings of the appointment of such a committee, nor is there any evidence of negotiations between the Council and the Assembly concerning credentials for Senators and Representatives.

Credentials of the Pennsylvania Senators, 28 February[1]

State of Pennsylvania ss.

By the Representatives of the
Freemen of the Commonwealth of Pennsylvania
in General Assembly met—

Be it known that on the thirtieth Day of September, in the Year of our Lord One thousand seven hundred and eighty eight, The Honourable William Maclay and Robert Morris Esquires were by the General Assembly of this State, being the Legislature thereof, duly elected and chosen at the Time and Place, and in the Manner by the said Legislature prescribed, Senators of and from the said State, to compose with the Senators elected by the Legislatures of the States who have ratified the Constitution for the United States, the Senate of the United States, agreeably to the Constitution thereof—

Signed by Order of the House, this twenty eighth — Day of February — in the Year of our Lord One thousand seven hundred and eighty nine, and in the thirteenth Year of the Independance of the United States ——

Attest ——
[s] Peter Zachary Lloyd
        Clerk of the
    General Assembly

[s] Richard Peters
        Speaker

1. (LT), RG 46, DNA.

Secretary Charles Biddle to Secretary Charles Thomson, Philadelphia, 28 February[1]

I herewith transmit to you the proclamation issued by Council declaring the names of the ten persons duly elected and chosen Electors on the part of this state for choosing a President and Vice President of the United States—together with the returns from the city and several counties of this state agreeably to an act of the General Assembly passed the fourth day of October 1788.

1. RC, RG 46, DNA. A draft of this letter, dated 20 February, is in the Supreme Executive Council records, PHarH. The voting returns under the date 3 February, the proclamation of 3 February, and the votes of the presidential Electors on 4 February are printed above.

William Petrikin to John Nicholson, Carlisle, 23 March[1]

I Recd yours of the 24th of Decr the 9th of March our Printers who is also Post Masters knew your hand and detained it till they Judged what it contained would be antiquated I have no doubt but they also broke it up there is nothing too gross for any of the party to be guilty off. Our being out-voted was no disappointment to one. I repeatedly fortold it befor the Election. I am Clearly of opinion our Harrisburgh conference did more injury to our cause than all the strategems of our advarsaries. Our friends throughout the state expected something decisive from us and we spent our whole time Canvassing for places in Congress (a body we had so often rebrobated according to its present constitution). I expected the intention of our meeting was to unite the opposition in the different parts of the state that they might act in concert—to form commitees and associations and open a Chanel of communication through-out the united states if posible. Had this been done which I think was very practicable the opposition would have appeared so formidable to the Federalists that they durst not have refused us our demands. Had they been so imprudent as still to continue obstonate we could have compeled them to a compliance but the avidity with which some of our leaders courted preferment has defeated every salutary measure and we will perhaps never find the people in the same spirit again. Opportunitys once lost is not easily recovered; however in this place we are determined to die hard. We chose a new commitee of correspondence last friday. Our Volunteer company is very large, well armed and Equipted, parades often and exercises very well while their light-Infantry federal company is retired to the land of forgetfullness. If a party of Feds and anties happens to meet upon any convival or public occasion the feds is sure to get a compleat dressing befor they dissmiss. A saint Patricks night one of our Volunteers almost killed four stout young Feds without receiving the least damage and the night following another volunteer floged six Federal soldiers of a recruting party and left one of them under the care of the docters. They got a state warrant for him next day. He lives in the country. The whole party with a Constable at their head went to take him but he defened himself so gallantly that they returned as they went except a litle of their Blood which adhered to the Volunteers Hickrey Bludgeon. They scared some women with their swords and pistols which was all the damage they did. I am afraid our disturbances here will never cease till the cause is removed, that is till the foedaral government is rectifyed. There is a paragraph in the Federal Gazett respecting you which gives your friends in this place a good deal of uneasiness. We know that Hell will be ransacked by the present Assembly to discover Ostensable causes to remove the friends of liberty and Mankind from every place of trust. We would be happy to hear the patticulars from yourself. A few lines from by [sic] the Bearer will be a very acceptable favor to your sincere friend.

P.S. The assembly is going on with a high hand. It pleases me very well that they dont do it by peicemeals. They:ll soon overdo themselves. There are some brutes who cannot see who perhaps may yet feel.

1. RC, Nicholson Papers, PHarH. This letter is printed as written except for the addition of capital letters at the beginning of sentences and punctuation for clarity.

Nicholson had been comptroller general of Pennsylvania since 1782. As a leading Antifederalist, he was subject to attack by the Federalists (see also Petrikin to Nicholson, 14 April, printed below). In 1790 an attempt to remove him from office failed. In 1793 he was impeached by the state House of Representatives. The state Senate acquitted him, but he resigned his offices and became a partner of Robert Morris in land speculation. In 1800 he was sent to debtor's prison, where he died before the end of the year.

William Petrikin, a native of Scotland, was a tailor and merchant in Carlisle. An aggressive Antifederalist leader, he wrote a pamphlet in Carlisle in April 1788 which Federalist John Montgomery described as "a foolish thing" (to William Irvine, Carlisle, 27 April, RC, William Irvine Papers, PHi). The pamphlet, *The Government of Nature Delineated; or an Exact Picture of the New Federal Constitution,* was a satirical attack on James Wilson and the Constitution. Its tone is indicated by the dedication: "To his serenity the right respectable, most honourable highly renowned J[ame]s W[ilso]n, political hackney writer to the most lucrative order of the bank, patronee of the most illustrious R[ober]t M[orri]s, and principal fabricator of the New Constitution." Petrikin was one of Cumberland County's delegates to the Harrisburg Convention. In 1795 he was appointed a justice of the peace for Cumberland County but removed to Mifflin County, the following year. He was appointed a justice of the peace for Centre County in 1800 and served as register and recorder from 1809 until his death in 1821.

York Pennsylvania Herald, 25 March

By a correspondent from Carlisle, we learn that the spirit of political enmity (like its kindred passion, religious zeal) has begun another persecution. While national and private peace pervade the other parts of Pennsylvania, that town is in a state of civil war. Every man's hand is raised against his neighbor. Bludgeons are walking sticks, and bricks are finger-stones. Neither sex or age are free from the insults of a newly imported rabble, who have scarcely escaped from the offended laws of their own country until they have commenced outrage on ours, who having already forfeited their lives for transatlantic crimes, and playing the desperate game of *nothing to lose.* Conscious of insufficiency to oppose with success a government which promises the restoration of order and law, and afraid to risk a general quarrel, they now resort [to] private lurking assaults on the decent people of that town, (for almost every person of that description, is at political variance with them) and as their "deeds are evil" they "shunning the light" go forth like other prowlers in the silent hours of sleep, and "cover themselves over with darkness as with a mantle." Individuals, and small companies unarmed are watched in their walks of business and pleasures, and assailed in the dark by ruffians who would shrink from single or equal combat. We may however reflect with pleasure that these are the last struggles of a dying party, and in justice to Carlisle, it should be told that most of her respectable inhabitants who opposed the new government before its adoption, now acquiesce in it, so that the present violences must arise from a banditti, who have *little* to do and *less* to lose.

Note.—To be seen in town, at Mr. ——, a Carlisle *walking-stick* and *finger-stone.*—Price, one bowl of *whuskey*-grog.

Supreme Executive Council Proceedings, Saturday, 28 March

Present: His Excellency Thomas Mifflin, Esquire, President; the Honorable George Ross, Esquire, Vice President; James Read, Samuel Miles, Amos Gregg, Frederick Watt, Abraham Smith, John Smilie, David Redick, Richard Willing, Christopher Kucher, Nathan Dennison, and George Woods, esquires.

Whereas Thomas Scott, Esquire, prothonotary of the County of Washington, hath informed this Council by letter that he hath been elected a Representative of this state in the Congress of the United States, and that he is on his way to New York to take his seat as such. And whereas the said Thomas Scott, Esquire, by the acceptance of his appointment as Representative in Congress, is incapable of discharging the duties of prothonotary of the county aforesaid. And it is therefore proper that a prothonotary for the said county should forthwith be appointed in his room and stead.

Resolved, that Alexander Scott, son of the said Thomas Scott, be and he is hereby appointed prothonotary of the County of Washington, in the room and stead of Thomas Scott, Esquire.

Stephen Chambers to Tench Coxe, Lancaster, 5 April[1]

Last Friday I received yours of the 20th ult. with the newspapers inclosed. The pieces signed "A Freeman" have been delivered to the printers, who promised to translate them for publication. They have considerable merit, as the interest of the people (a principal feeling) is addressed by arguments easily understood. My opinion of our present [state] constitution was early known, and I hope I have given no reason to charge me with inconsistency, nor now with being passive. The city has given great offense to Franklin, York and this county by the alteration of the ticket settled here, but no pains will be spared to have that for the present put out of view. I say for the present because I know at the next election of Representatives they will retaliate.

I find by some late publications that the opposition is commenced with indecent violence. I wish our friends would not pursue their example. Cool perseverance will certainly be most agreeable to the active and thinking part of the state. My earnest wishes are for the success of the measure and every person who will be active shall have my hearty thanks.

1. RC, Coxe Papers, Tench Coxe Section, PHi.

William Petrikin to John Nicholson, 14 April 1789[1]

I Recd. your Letter of the 21st ult. with a mixture of pleasure and indignation, pleasure to hear from you, indignation to see how "wicknedness walks on every side when vile Men are high in power". One would think that truth had deserted the habitations of Mankind when those men who are appointed to direct the affairs of a whole state should be so far transported with party rage as to report an egregious falshood, for it is a fact known to every person of intelligence in the state that application to Business has often endangered your health and even the Federals in this place are so candid as to acknowledge that you do Business sufficient for three men to perform. They say farther that instead of a register-General with 500 £ and an host of Clerks, in the present distracted state of our finances had they allowed you another Clerk the Business would be better done and a vast of Money saved to the State. But it is something Ludicurous to See the wretches providing such Lucrative Sinecures for themselves and their favourites, and at the same time Resolving that the expenses of Government can hardly be Born under the Present constitution. Please Sir to inform me in your next what Lattent clause in the constitution our Assembly have discovered which has Laid them under the necessity of creating a Register-General with £ 500 per annum and an unlimited number of Clerks. I am certain were it not in the constitution such economical Spirits never would have dared it; for you know Sir in all their proceedings they religiously adhere to the established rules of the constitution. Nevertheless I find they have recommended to the people to recurr to origional principles and abolish the Government that they may have the making of a new one.[2] But from what I can learn of the disposition of the people in this place if they dont desist from Such Nefarious practices, they will soon reduce them to their origonal principles and mingle their dust with dust and their ashes with ashes. Untill something like this is done they will never cease to distract the state with their Machinations. We are to have a County Meeting at Stonyridge upon this Subject next Wednesday, we will delibirate & hope upon something efectual to stop their progress; perhaps a state meeting will be thought expedient to unite the friends of Liberty in the different countys. Without we act in concert we will still be defeat. It is for want of this that Matters have come to such a Crises in this state as they are at present. I have seen a Copy of a remonstrance which we expect will be sent us in print for the purpose of signing; I like the spirit of it, it is excelently calculated for the Miridian of Cumberland; but I think while we pursue this Measure we ought to prepare something More decisive and Vigirous in case it should be rejected, we ought to convince them that we can apply something beside empty Menaces. I hope you and our other friends in the city will not be remiss in communicating with us on this Ocasion, but beware who you write to, or with; we have Wolves in sheeps Clothing amongst us. Carson, Davidson, Criegh, and Lyons the Prothonater are None of us tho they once were. As your hand is so well know I wish you Would get another to indorse you letters on this subject, because seeing a letter from you Would alure them to Break the Seal should it happen to fall in their hands. The federalists have affect to be displeased with their party in the Assembly respecting the constitution, but their sincerity is very much to be questioned. Your friends here Were very Much alarmed when they read the passage Stating that Strange discoveries were making &c. We knew that Nothing Would be wanting that Malignity could hatch to ruin you, but we now rejoice to find that your invincible integrety has triumphed over the inveterate Malice of Your enemies. From the Miserable Shifts they were oblidged to take to injure you it is obvious they could find nothing that had an appearance of a crime against you or an impeachment would certainly have been prepered. I suppose they intend that this Donaldson shall learn from you the method of doing the Business and then you to turn out; rather as gratify them thus I would resign were I you. But perhaps times May yet take a turn, We may yet have an Assembly that will show Mr. *Register* himself, the way to the door, dismiss him as a useless Federal tool and a nuisance to the public. I Understand 11000 in the city signed a petition for opening the theatre. These names will do very well to the petition for choosing a new convention to tear up the constitution and if every county produce in proportion that will be 154000 signers; this instead of a majority will be 82000 more then the whole number of votables in the state. By this means they leave us poor Anties all that number less than none at all to our remonstrance. I presume when they carry their point (and who dare hinder them to carry it) they'll vote us poor di[vi]ls Back amongst the Indians or to Rhode Island which they Please. God help us. 146000 None-entities is a formidable army officered by 8000 Federal existances [the number of Federal polls at the election for Congress-men][3] all connoissuers in the arts of Finesse. But should some propitious Deity preside over our stars and enable us by some unforseen incident to defeat them we will try to remove the seat of Government from Philadelphia. From such a nursery of corruption nothing but the most pernicious Measures can be expected, it is imposible to purge our Councils while exposed to such contagion, and untill they are purged the people will never be happy or safe. When the Legislature is converted into the tool of a faction and made the instrument of their intrigues, When the rulers treat the most sacred obligations with contemp and Swallow the most Solemn oaths as they would Oysters, when Perjury is Patronized and perpetuated By men in power and high treason hatched in the Mansions of our Ministers, when the school of vice is openly established and the Votaries of Morality Laughed out of Countenance, when honesty is sacrefised to the caprice of faction and to be obnoxious to the prevailing party is a crime sufficient to deprive the most upright of the reward due to their merit and the public of its Best and ablest Servants. In fine when every speceies of inquity that presents it is established by Law, what security can the people enjoy or what happyness can they possess? The truth of these things are obvious and it is as obvious that they are produced by the influence of your overgrown Citizens and the Bank. Many of the country Members are so elated with a nod, a smile, a Bottle of wine or a dinner from some of your Citts, that they begin directly to fancy themselves Men of some consequence when their company is courted by persons of such dignity; and the smalest return they can make their Benefactors is to compliment them with their Vote when required that is to vote as Fitzimons, Clymer or Lewis shall please to direct them. Now these men if left to the derection impulse of their own dispositions might do well enough but they have not fortitude sufficient to withstand the Enchanting alurements of Your Ambrosial city entertainments. A ticket to a play or admittance into the Levee of a Banker are honors too powerfull for human nature to resist. However when any of our county Members happen to be thus fascinated we take care to disolve the Charm the first Election. In my next I will give you an account of the proceedings at Stonyridge. If you are not very much engaged I will expect a letter with the Bearer. If you complain that this Misive is too long all the apologey I shall offer is I had not time to Make it shorter. I intend it also for a precedent for your next. Your friends here are all well as is also your very afft friend and humble servt.

1. RC, Nicholson Papers, PHarH. This letter is printed as written except for the addition of capital letters at the beginning of sentences and punctuation for clarity.

2. The Republicans, whose attempts to revise the Constitution of 1776 had been so often frustrated, renewed the effort in the spring of 1789. On 24 March the Assembly voted to ask the people if they wished a constitutional convention. This appeal turned the attention of local political leaders like Petrikin from concern about the recent federal election to the forthcoming debate over the revision of the state constitution.

3. The square brackets are Petrikin's.

PENNSYLVANIA CANDIDATES

Allison, John (1738-1795), Candidate for Representative (Lancaster Ticket)

Born in Cumberland County to parents who came to Pennsylvania from northern Ireland a few years before his birth, Allison was appointed justice of the peace for the county in 1764. He was active in the politics leading to independence and was a delegate to the provincial conference in June 1776. Later he commanded a county militia battalion in campaigns in 1776 and 1777. He was elected to the Assembly in 1778 and was reelected in 1780 and 1781. Franklin County was created from a portion of Cumberland County in 1782, and he represented the new county in the state Convention in 1787 and seconded the motion to ratify the Constitution. Nothing is known of him after his defeat in the election of 1788.

Armstrong, John, Jr. (1758-1843), Candidate for Senator

Born at Carlisle, Pennsylvania, Armstrong was the son of John Armstrong, an immigrant from Ireland in the 1740s who settled in what became Cumberland County, was a hero in the Seven Years War, and was a major general of Pennsylvania troops during the first years of the War for Independence. Armstrong, Jr., left the College of New Jersey (Princeton) when the war began, became an aide to General Horatio Gates, and served throughout the war. In 1783 he wrote the Newburgh addresses, which threatened that unless Congress met its demands, the army would quit if the war continued, or refuse to disband if the war ended. At the end of the war Armstrong became secretary of the Supreme Executive Council. In 1787 he was elected to the Confederation Congress, and in 1788 Congress elected him one of the judges of the newly created Northwest Territory. Armstrong refused to accept the post, for his supporters thought he could be elected to the Senate. After the election he married the sister of Chancellor Robert R. Livingston of New York and moved to that state. When the Federalist Livingstons switched their support to the Republicans in 1800 and helped to reelect George Clinton governor of New York and to elect Thomas Jefferson President of the United States, Armstrong switched parties too. He was rewarded by election to the United States Senate in 1800, but he resigned in 1802 to allow the Governor's nephew, DeWitt Clinton, to take the seat. When Clinton resigned the next year to become mayor of New York, Governor Clinton appointed Armstrong to the Senate. Armstrong resigned again in 1804 to become minister to France in place of his brother-in-law, Robert R. Livingston. He was contemptuous of his own government and of the French, and he resigned in 1810.

Despite his dislike for President Madison, he supported him for reelection in 1812. Madison named Armstrong brigadier general in charge of New York City's defenses. When the Secretary of War, William Eustis, resigned at the end of 1812, Madison wanted to appoint his Secretary of State, James Monroe, to the post, but he dared not appoint a Southerner, so he reluctantly appointed Armstrong. Armstrong made disastrous decisions as Secretary of War, and he resigned after the British captured Washington in August 1814. He spent the rest of his life farming, writing about agriculture, and defending his wartime record.

Arndt, John (1748-1814), Presidential Elector (Lancaster Ticket)

Born in Bucks County, Arndt moved with his family to Northampton County in 1760. As a captain of Northampton County troops, he was captured at the battle of Long Island in 1776. After his exchange, he returned to Northampton County and held a variety of county and state offices. He represented the county in the state Convention in 1787 and voted to ratify the Constitution. In November 1788 he was a representative from Lancaster County to the Lancaster Conference, where he was nominated for Elector. He held various county offices during the 1790s, was defeated when he ran for the United States House of Representatives in 1796, and, like other local Federalist officeholders, was removed after Thomas McKean, running as a Republican, was elected governor in 1799.

Bingham, William (1752-1804), Candidate for Senator

Born in Philadelphia, the great-grandson of a man who had come from England and established the family in Pennsylvania, Bingham graduated from the College of Philadelphia in 1768. He was appointed British consul in the French West Indies island of Martinique in 1770 and served there until 1776, when the Continental Congress appointed him its agent in the West Indies. As agent, he mingled public duties and private trade with such skill that he returned to Philadelphia in 1780 with one of the largest private fortunes of the times. In 1780 he married Anne Willing, daughter of Thomas Willing, and the next year he was one of the principal founders of the Bank of North America, along with his father-in-law and Robert Morris. He spent the years 1784-1786 in Europe. When he returned, he was elected to the Confederation Congress, where he led the fight for the location of the new government in Philadelphia. While he had support for the Senate, Robert Morris was the choice of most Federalists. Bingham was a member of the Pennsylvania legislature from 1790 to 1795, when he resigned to take Morris's place as United States Senator. In 1801 Bingham was replaced as Senator by Peter Muhlenberg, a Republican. In addition to his financial holdings, Bingham invested heavily in land, including more than two million acres in Maine. His mansion was a center of Federalist society, and his two daughters married two brothers, Henry Baring and Alexander Baring (Lord Ashburton), of the great British banking house.

Chambers, Stephen (1750?-1789), Candidate for Representative (Lancaster Ticket)

Born in northern Ireland, Chambers arrived in Pennsylvania sometime before 1776 and was an attorney in Sunbury, Northumberland County. He received a commission in a Pennsylvania regiment in October 1776 and retired from the army in 1778. Elected to the Assembly from Northumberland County in 1778, he served one year. In 1780 he moved to Lancaster County, where he developed a lucrative law practice. He was an original member of the Republican Society in 1779 and was a delegate from Lancaster County to the Council of Censors in 1783-1784 and to the state Convention in 1787. He voted to ratify the Constitution. He died in May 1789 from wounds received in a duel.

Clymer, George (1739-1813), Elected Representative (Lancaster Ticket)

Born in Philadelphia, Clymer became a prosperous merchant and an active leader in city affairs. He was elected to the Continental Congress 20 July 1776 as one of the replacements for the Pennsylvania delegates who opposed independence, and he signed the Declaration of Independence. In 1775 Congress had appointed him as one of two continental treasurers, and, as a member of Congress, he served on committees dealing with financial and military matters until the Pennsylvania legislature removed him from Congress in September 1777. He was again elected to Congress in November 1780 and reelected in November 1781.

He was a founder of the Republican Society in 1779, represented Philadelphia in the state legislature four terms (1785-1789), and was a delegate to the Constitutional Convention in 1787. He was elected to the first Congress but declined election to the second Congress and was then appointed collector of the excise in Pennsylvania. After serving in that and other posts, he retired from active political life in 1796.

Craig, Thomas (1739-1832), Candidate for Elector (Harrisburg Ticket)

There were several Thomas Craigs in Pennsylvania during this period, and most of them were related to one another. The Thomas Craig who was a presidential Elector was apparently born in 1739 in what later became Northampton County. He was a farmer until 1776, when he received an officer's commission. He served in the army throughout the war and retired as a colonel in 1783. In September 1784, the Supreme Executive Council elected him prothonotary of Montgomery County, which was created from a portion of Philadelphia County that year, and the Council elected him to other county offices as well. Governor Thomas Mifflin reappointed him to the offices in 1791. In 1798 he was appointed a major general of Pennsylvania militia, a post he held until 1814.

Findley, William (1741-1821), Candidate for Representative
(Harrisburg Ticket)

Born in Ulster, Ireland, Findley came to Cumberland County, Pennsylvania, in 1763. After working as a weaver and a school teacher, he bought land and became a farmer. He supported independence enthusiastically and played an important role in county affairs until he moved to Westmoreland County in 1782. There he became a county leader almost at once. He was elected to the Council of Censors in 1783 and to the Assembly in 1784, 1785, 1786, and 1787. He was a delegate to the state Convention, where he was one of the leading opponents of the ratification of the Constitution. In October 1788, despite the constitutional provision that no one could serve in the Assembly more than four years in seven, his constituents elected him to a fifth term. He was elected to the Supreme Executive Council in 1789 and to the state constitutional convention of 1789-1790. He played an important part in writing the new state constitution and was elected to the legislature in 1790. In 1791 he was elected to the United States House of Representatives and was reelected for three consecutive terms. He refused to run in 1798 and was elected to the state Senate in 1799. He was reelected to the House of Representatives in 1802 and served until he retired in 1817. Throughout his personal and political life he was a democrat, enormously popular with his constituents in backcountry Pennsylvania. In state politics and in the United States House of Representatives he was a consistent and powerful supporter of the Jeffersonian Republicans.

FitzSimons, Thomas (1741-1811), Elected Representative (Lancaster Ticket)

Born in Ireland, FitzSimons had arrived in Philadelphia by 1761, the year he married the daughter of a prosperous merchant. Shortly thereafter he formed a partnership with his brother-in-law and became a wealthy merchant himself. He supported independence and commanded troops in several campaigns.

During the war, he was connected with Robert Morris in the export of tobacco and in other ventures. He traded with Martinique and provided supplies for the French navy. In 1781 he was one of the founders and first directors of the Bank of North America, and later he was a founder, director, and president of the Insurance Company of North America.

He was a founder of the Republican Society and was a leader of the Republican Party in state politics. He was elected to the Confederation Congress in October 1782 and served one year. In 1783 he was elected to the Council of Censors. Thereafter, beginning in October 1785, he represented Philadelphia in the Assembly for four successive terms. He was a delegate to the Constitutional Convention of 1787. He served three successive terms in the House of Representatives, where he was a firm supporter of Federalist economic policies and was regarded as a Federalist "boss" in Pennsylvania. His political career ended in 1794, when he was defeated by a fellow merchant, John Swanwick, for a fourth term in the House of Representatives. Later he became a bankrupt because his connection with Robert Morris involved him in the collapse of Morris's projects. Although he regained some of his wealth, he never recovered his prestige and political power.

415

Gibbons, William (1737-1803), Candidate for Elector (Harrisburg Ticket)

Born in Chester County to Quaker parents, Gibbons became a farmer. In 1775 he was disowned by the Quakers when he became an officer in the county militia. In 1773 he was appointed a justice of the peace in the county and in 1783 was elected sheriff. In 1787 he was a delegate to the state Convention, where he voted to ratify the Constitution, and he was a delegate to the convention which wrote a new state constitution in 1789-1790. He was appointed prothonotary of the county in 1791 and served nine years, was a volunteer with the troops sent to suppress the Whiskey Rebellion in 1794, and was elected to the state House of Representatives in 1801. No evidence has been located to indicate why he was nominated on the Harrisburg ticket.

Gibson, George (1747-1791), Presidential Elector (Lancaster Ticket)

Born in Lancaster County, Gibson was apprenticed to a Philadelphia merchant, then joined his brother in the Indian trade at Fort Pitt. In 1772 he became a farmer and a miller in Cumberland County near Carlisle, took part in Dunmore's War in 1774, and raised and commanded a company of frontiersmen in 1775. In 1776 he led an expedition to New Orleans to secure gunpowder, and in 1777 and 1778 he served in campaigns in New York and New Jersey. He was made commander of the American prison camp at York, Pennsylvania, in 1779 and held the position until the end of the war. In November 1788 he represented Cumberland County in the Lancaster Conference, where he was nominated for Elector. He lived on his farm in Cumberland County until 1791, when he commanded a regiment in Arthur St. Clair's campaign against the Indians northwest of the Ohio River. He died of wounds received in a battle near the Wabash River.

Graydon, Alexander (1752-1818), Presidential Elector (Lancaster Ticket)

Born in Bucks County, Graydon was the son of Alexander Graydon, who emigrated from Dublin, Ireland, about 1730 and who became a Philadelphia merchant. Graydon received a captain's commission in 1776, was captured by the British at Fort Washington the same year, and was exchanged in 1778. More interested in literature than politics, he was nevertheless appointed prothonotary of newly created Dauphin County in 1785 and moved to Harrisburg. He was an ardent advocate of the Constitution. He held his office until 1799, when, with other Federalists, he was removed by Governor Thomas McKean. Graydon devoted the rest of his life to writing. His *Memoirs of a Life, Chiefly Passed in Pennsylvania Within the Last Sixty Years* ... were published in 1811.

Grier, David (1742-1790), Presidential Elector (Lancaster Ticket)

Born in York County, Grier studied law and was admitted to practice in 1771. In 1776 he received a captain's commission in a battalion of the Pennsylvania line and became a lieutenant colonel. He retired from the army in 1781 and resumed the practice of law in York County. He was elected to the Assembly in 1783 and to the state Convention in 1787. He voted to ratify the Constitution.

Hand, Edward (1744-1802), Presidential Elector (Lancaster and Harrisburg tickets)

Born in Leinster, Ireland, Hand studied medicine at Trinity College, Dublin, and came to Philadelphia in 1767 as surgeon's mate in an Irish regiment. In 1773 he resigned his commission and began the practice of medicine at Lancaster. He served in the American armies from 1775 to 1783, rising in rank from lieutenant colonel to major general. He resumed the practice of medicine in 1783 and was a member of Congress, 1784-1785, and of the Pennsylvania Assembly, 1785-1786. He represented Lancaster County at the Lancaster Conference in November 1788. He was nominated for Elector by the conference and was also nominated on the Harrisburg ticket. He received more votes than any other candidate. He was a staunch Federalist until his death.

Hartley, Thomas (1748-1800), Elected Representative (Lancaster Ticket)

Born in Berks County, Hartley went to York County to study law, was admitted to the bar in 1769, and developed a lucrative practice. He represented York County at the provincial conferences in 1774 and 1775 and was an officer in the militia. He received a commission from Congress in January 1776, served in the Canadian expedition in 1776 and at Brandywine in 1777, and led a punitive expedition against the Indians in western Pennsylvania in 1778. He resigned from the army in February 1779 and represented York County in the Assembly for one term. As a Republican in state politics, he was a delegate to the Council of Censors in 1783-1784 and in 1787 was a member of the state Convention, where he vigorously supported ratification of the Constitution. From 1789 to 1800 he served in the House of Representatives, where he was an undeviating supporter of Federalist policies. He resigned because of ill health and died shortly thereafter.

Hiester, Daniel (1747-1804), Elected Representative (Harrisburg and German tickets)

Born in Philadelphia County, to which his father had come from Germany ten years earlier, Daniel Hiester took over his father's farm and tannery in 1774. The next year he assumed management of the estate of his father-in-law, Jonathan Hager, founder of Hagerstown, Maryland. Although reluctant to accept independence, Hiester became a militia officer in 1777. He was in the Assembly from 1778 to 1781, and in 1784 he was elected to the Supreme Executive Council from Montgomery County, which had been created from a portion of Philadelphia County in 1784.

Although he was a Republican in state politics, the Constitutionalists nominated him on the Harrisburg ticket, as they had Peter Muhlenberg, because of his popularity with German voters. Like Muhlenberg, he opposed many Federalist policies during his four terms as Representative (1789-1796), although, unlike Muhlenberg, he did not become a leader of the Jeffersonian Republicans. He voted against the assumption of state debts in 1790 and against condemnation of the Democratic societies in 1794. In 1796 he resigned and moved to Maryland, where he had large landholdings. He was elected to the House of Representatives from Maryland in 1800 and served until his death.

Hiester, Joseph (1752-1832), Candidate for Elector (Harrisburg Ticket)

Born in Berks County, the son of immigrants from Germany, Joseph Hiester was first a farmer and then a storekeeper. He attended the provincial conference in Philadelphia in June 1776 and then raised troops in Berks County and was elected a captain. Captured by the British at the Battle of Long Island in August 1776, he was exchanged and rejoined the army in 1777 and served until 1779. He returned to his business as storekeeper and became active in state politics as a Constitutionalist. He served five terms in the Assembly between 1780 and 1790. He represented Berks County in the state Convention in 1787 and voted against ratification of the Constitution. He was a member of the state constitutional convention in 1789-1790 and of the state Senate in 1790-1794. He was a presidential Elector in 1792 and 1796, and supported Thomas Jefferson for the Presidency in the latter year. He was the cousin of Daniel Hiester, who was elected to the United States House of Representatives in 1788. He succeeded Daniel Hiester in the House in 1797, was a member of the House until 1805, and served again from 1815 to 1820. He was defeated for governor in 1817 but won in 1820 as a reformer. He refused to run for a second term because of his belief in the principle of rotation in office.

Irvine, William (1741-1804), Candidate for Senator and for Representative (Harrisburg Ticket)

Born in Ulster, Ireland, Irvine studied medicine, graduated from Dublin University, served as a surgeon in the British navy during the Seven Years War, and settled at Carlisle, Cumberland County, Pennsylvania, in 1764. He was a delegate to the first provincial conference in 1774, and at the beginning of the Revolution he raised a Pennsylvania regiment and became its commander. He was captured while on the Canadian expedition in 1776. When he was exchanged in 1778, he rejoined the Continental Army, and the next year he became a brigadier general. In 1781 he was placed in charge of frontier defense and was stationed at Pittsburgh until the end of the war. After the war, he directed the disposition of lands promised Pennsylvania soldiers. When that task was completed, he was elected to Congress in 1786 and served until the fall of 1788. Although he was a Republican in state politics, he was distrusted because he was a member of the committee of Congress which in September 1788 charged Robert Morris with corruption in the handling of wartime finances. Nevertheless, he received only six votes less than Morris for United States Senator. He was then nominated for Representative on the Harrisburg ticket.

During the 1790s he was an active organizer of the Jeffersonian Republicans. His popularity was such that in 1792 both the Federalists and the Republicans nominated him for Representative in Congress. He was elected and served one term. In 1794 he was the commander of the state troops sent to suppress the Whiskey Rebellion. In 1796 he was one of the principal organizers of the campaign that ended with the election of thirteen presidential Electors committed to Thomas Jefferson, out of a total of fifteen Electors for the state. In March 1801, shortly after Jefferson was elected President, Irvine was appointed superintendent of military stores in Philadelphia, a post he held until his death.

Keene, Laurence (?-1789), Presidential Elector (Lancaster Ticket)

Little is known about Keene except that he was from Sunbury in Northumberland County and that he served as an officer of Pennsylvania troops from 1777 to 1783. In September 1783, the Supreme Executive Council elected him prothonotary of Northumberland County and in January 1784, justice of the Court of Common Pleas in the county. On 27 July 1789 the Council, "occasioned by the death of Lawrence Keene," resolved to appoint a new prothonotary.

Maclay, William (1737-1804), Elected Senator

Born in Chester County, where his father had settled after emigrating from northern Ireland in 1734, Maclay received a classical education, studied law, and served as an officer in the Seven Years War. After the war he went to England, and on his return was a surveyor for the Penn family. In 1769 he married a daughter of John Harris, the founder of Harrisburg. When the new county of Northumberland was organized in 1772, Maclay laid out the town of Sunbury and held several county offices. During the War for Independence, he served in the local militia and as a local commissary. He represented Northumberland County in the Assembly, 1781-1783 and 1785, and in the Council, 1786-1788.

In the political maneuvering prior to the election of Senators, Maclay was at first agreed upon, then dropped, and finally accepted as a candidate the day before the election. He was regarded as a representative of the "agricultural interest" in a state which demanded "interest representation." He served in the Senate only until March 1791 because, in the drawing for terms, he drew the two-year term while Robert Morris drew the full six years. Maclay's successor was not chosen until nearly two years later because the two houses of the state legislature, under the Pennsylvania Constitution of 1790, could not agree. The eastern Federalists in the state Senate insisted that the two houses vote separately. The House of Representatives, in which Antifederalists and westerners had greater influence, insisted upon a joint ballot. The Senate surrendered in February 1793, and the two houses elected Albert Gallatin from Fayette County in the far west, only to have him denied a seat by the Federalist-controlled United States Senate on the grounds that he had not been a citizen for nine years.

During the 1790s, Maclay was an active opponent of the Federalists in the state. He worked to elect a slate of presidential Electors committed to Thomas Jefferson in 1796 and was one of the thirteen elected. He represented Dauphin County in the legislature from time to time. In 1798 he proposed that the state House of Representatives go on record as opposing war in any shape or with any country, particularly with France, on the grounds that the nation could neither benefit from a war nor stand the burdens a war would entail. He was also active in the fight to move the state capital from Philadelphia to Harrisburg.

He was virtually forgotten until nearly a century later when his *Journal* of the debates in the Senate was published. The Senate of the United States did not admit the public, and debates were not recorded; hence Maclay's *Journal*, with its acid comments on men and measures, reveals much about the first two years of government under the Constitution and explains why he supported the Jeffersonian Republicans during the 1790s.

M'Clenachan, Blair (?-1812), Candidate for Representative (Harrisburg Ticket)

Born in Ireland, M'Clenachan came to America sometime before his marriage in Philadelphia in 1762. By 1776 he was reputed to be one of the leading importing merchants in that city. He was a member of a group associated with Robert Morris who received war contracts from the Secret Committee of Congress. He also engaged heavily in privateering, including ventures in partnership with Morris. In 1779 he and Morris were charged with profiteering and were threatened with mob action. The next year he and Morris were the two largest contributors to a "bank" created to buy supplies for the army, and he became a stockholder in the Bank of North America in 1781. When the state assumed the national debt owed to Pennsylvanians, M'Clenachan was one of the two largest holders, although most of his holdings had been obtained as payment for services during the war, rather than by speculation afterwards.

He allied with the Constitutionalists in politics, even though he had economic ties with the Republicans. He was chairman of the Harrisburg Convention in 1788 and was nominated for Congress on the Harrisburg ticket. During the 1790s he was an ardent opponent of the Federalists. He was a member of the Pennsylvania legislature, 1790-1795, and was president of the Pennsylvania Democratic Society. In July 1795 he denounced the Jay Treaty before a Philadelphia mass meeting and told the crowd to "kick it to hell." He then led a mob which burned the treaty before the houses of the French and British envoys, the house of the British consul, and the home of William Bingham, where some windows were broken. In 1796 M'Clenachan was elected to Congress and served one term. He went to debtor's prison after the failure of some of his speculative ventures. After his release, President Thomas Jefferson appointed him Commissioner of Loans, a post he held until his death.

McLene, James (1730-1806), Candidate for Elector (Harrisburg Ticket)

Born in Chester County, McLene settled in Cumberland County in the early 1750s. He was a member of the convention that wrote the Pennsylvania Constitution of 1776; of the Assembly, 1776-1777; of the Supreme Executive Council, 1778-1779; and of the Continental Congress, 1780. Franklin County was created from a portion of Cumberland County in 1784, and McLene represented the new county on the Supreme Executive Council, 1784-1787; in the Assembly, 1787-1789; and in the state constitutional convention, 1789-1790. He was a member of the state House of Representatives in 1790-1791 and 1793-1794.

Montgomery, William (1736-1816), Candidate for Representative (Harrisburg Ticket)

Born in Chester County, Montgomery represented the county in the provincial conferences in 1775 and 1776 and became a colonel of Pennsylvania troops in 1776. In the same year he moved his family to Northumberland County, where he had bought land. As a landowner and investor in business enterprises, he soon became a leading figure in the county. A member of the Constitutionalist Party, he represented Northumberland in the Assembly, 1778-1782, and in the Council of Censors, 1783-1784. The Assembly elected him to Congress in 1784, but he refused to serve. The next year the Supreme Executive Council appointed him a justice of the peace and a justice of the Court of Common Pleas in Northumberland County. In 1790 he was elected to the state Senate and in 1792 to the United States House of Representatives, where he served one term and opposed Federalist policies.

Morris, Robert (1734-1806), Elected Senator

Born in Liverpool, England, Morris was brought to Maryland at the age of thirteen by his father, the Maryland agent of a Liverpool tobacco firm. Morris was sent to Philadelphia to be educated, but after his father's death he was apprenticed to the mercantile house of Charles Willing. In 1751, after Willing's death, his son Thomas and Morris formed a partnership. Willing was elected to the Continental Congress in the spring of 1775 and Morris in November of the same year. Both men opposed independence, and Morris refused to vote for it, although he later signed the Declaration. He continued to serve in Congress until November 1778.

Meanwhile, in 1775 Congress had begun giving Willing and Morris contracts to buy war supplies. Morris was a key member of various secret committees to secure such supplies, and more and more contracts were given to his firm. Morris mingled the public with his private business and developed a network of partnerships throughout the United States and overseas, and he continued to do so after he retired from Congress in 1778. In 1781 Congress appointed Morris Superintendent of Finance and gave him virtually unlimited control over finance. The same year, Morris, Thomas Willing, William Bingham (who made a fortune as Congress's agent in the French island of Martinique between 1776 and 1780), and other merchants founded the Bank of North America, the first private bank in America.

As Superintendent of Finance, Morris developed far-reaching plans to strengthen the government of the United States, economically and politically; plans that were, in most essentials, carried out by the new government after 1789.

Morris's plans were thwarted, partly by the end of the war in 1783, and partly because his business methods and political program aroused so much opposition. Merchants like Henry Laurens of South Carolina and political leaders like the Lees of Virginia and the Adamses of Massachusetts as well as the Pennsylvania Constitutionalists looked upon him as their principal enemy. Color was lent to charges of corruption because he did not settle his accounts with Congress, and he had not done so at the time he was elected United States Senator.

Morris resigned as Superintendent of Finance in 1784 and was elected to the Pennsylvania Assembly in 1785. He was a delegate to the Constitutional Convention in 1787 and served in the United States Senate from 1789 to 1795. By the end of his term, he was on the verge of bankruptcy. At first he made money speculating in land, but he bought more land than he could pay for, including large portions of the newly created District of Columbia. Early in 1798 he was sent to debtor's prison in Philadelphia and was not released until August 1801. During the last years of his life, he lived on money supplied to his family by his one-time assistant in the Office of Finance, Gouverneur Morris of New York.

Muhlenberg, Frederick Augustus Conrad (1750-1801), Elected
Representative (Lancaster and German tickets)

Born in Pennsylvania, the second son of the Reverend Henry Melchior Muhlenberg, Frederick Muhlenberg was sent with his brothers to Germany in 1763 to be educated. He returned to Pennsylvania in 1770, was ordained, and became pastor of a German Lutheran church in New York City. He returned to Pennsylvania in 1776. In 1779 he abandoned the ministry for politics when the Constitutionalist-controlled Assembly elected him to the Continental Congress, where he served until the end of 1780. In that year he joined forces with the Republicans, and in October 1780 he was elected to the Assembly from Philadelphia. He was reelected in 1781 and 1782 and was speaker of the Assembly in 1782 and 1783. In 1783 he was elected to the Council of Censors and was chosen its president.

After Montgomery County was created from a portion of Philadelphia County in 1784, he was appointed to local offices in the county and was elected to the state Convention in 1787. He was chosen president of the Convention over Chief Justice Thomas McKean by a vote of 30 to 29. He received more votes than any other candidate in the election for Representatives. He was reelected to the second, third, and fourth Congresses. He was speaker of the first House of Representatives in 1789, defeated for the post in the second Congress, but was speaker in the third Congress.

As his congressional career progressed, it became evident that Muhlenberg was not a die-hard Federalist because he voted more and more with the opposition. However, in 1796, as presiding officer of the committee of the whole, he broke a tie vote in favor of a resolution recommending that the House of Representatives appropriate money to carry out the Jay Treaty. A few days later he was stabbed by his brother-in-law. Muhlenberg recovered, but he had lost much popularity in Pennsylvania because of his vote for the Jay Treaty. He was never again elected to public office. In 1800 Governor Thomas McKean appointed him receiver-general of the Pennsylvania land office.

Muhlenberg, John Peter Gabriel (1746-1807), Elected Representative (Harrisburg and German tickets)

Born in Pennsylvania four years after his father, the Reverend Henry Melchior Muhlenberg, arrived from Germany, Peter Muhlenberg and his two brothers were sent to Germany in 1763 to be educated. He returned to Pennsylvania in 1767, trained for the ministry, and in 1772 became pastor of a German Lutheran church in Virginia's Shenandoah Valley. He became a local leader there and was a member of the revolutionary conventions in Virginia from 1774 to January 1776, when he was appointed colonel of a German regiment raised in the Shenandoah Valley. He eventually became a major general in the Continental Army and fought throughout the war.

After the war he entered Pennsylvania politics as a Republican. He represented Montgomery County in the Executive Council, 1785-1787, was vice president of the state in 1787, and supported ratification of the Constitution. Although a Republican, he was nominated on the Harrisburg ticket because of his popularity with German voters.

As a member of the United States House of Representatives, he soon became an opponent of Federalist policies. He was defeated for election to the second Congress but was returned to the third Congress, where he continued to oppose the Federalists. After the third Congress ended in March 1795, he was not reelected to the House of Representatives until 1798. Meanwhile, he was active in state politics. He helped organize the German Republican Society, cooperated with the Democratic societies, and condemned the Jay Treaty. The Republicans nominated him for the Senate in 1795, but he was defeated by the Federalist candidate, William Bingham, by a vote of 58 to 35. In 1796 he was one of the slate of fifteen presidential Electors committed to Thomas Jefferson, and he helped elect thirteen of them. In 1797 he was elected to the state House of Representatives, and the next year he returned to Congress. In 1799 he helped manage the election of Thomas McKean, now a Republican, as governor and was described as "the Moses of the German Israelites."

In Congress he voted against the Alien and Sedition Acts and supported Jefferson for the Presidency. Furthermore, Governor McKean placed him in command of the Pennsylvania militia with orders to march them to Washington if the Federalists tried to delay the election of a President beyond inaugural day, 4 March 1801.

Shortly before the end of his term in the House on 3 March 1801, the Pennsylvania legislature elected him to the United States Senate. He resigned within a few weeks, and President Jefferson first appointed him supervisor of United States Customs in the Pennsylvania District, and then, two years later, he was appointed collector of customs in Philadelphia, a post he held until his death.

O'Hara, James (1752-1819), Presidential Elector (Lancaster Ticket)

Born in Ireland, O'Hara arrived in Pennsylvania in 1772. The next year he was employed by a Pittsburgh firm engaged in the Indian trade. O'Hara raised a company of volunteers, was elected captain, and served in George Rogers Clark's campaign in the Illinois Country in 1778-1779. O'Hara was sent east in 1779 to ask General Washington for supplies, became commissary of a hospital at Carlisle, Pennsylvania, and in 1781-1783 was assistant quartermaster for General Nathanael Greene. After the war he made his home in Pittsburgh. In November 1788 he represented Westmoreland, Washington, Fayette, and Allegheny counties at the Lancaster Conference, where he was nominated for Elector. During the 1790s he was quartermaster of the United States army for a time and was an investor in glassworks, shipbuilding, iron works, and Pittsburgh real estate.

Pettit, Charles (1736-1806), Candidate for Representative (Harrisburg Ticket)

Born in New Jersey, the son of a Philadelphia merchant, Pettit held various offices in colonial New Jersey, including that of aide to the last royal governor, Sir William Franklin. In 1776 he became an aide to the first elected governor of the state, William Livingston. In 1778 he was appointed assistant quartermaster general of the Continental Army, a post he held until 1781. At the end of the war he moved to Philadelphia, where he was a merchant and was increasingly involved in the insurance business.

He was elected one of Philadelphia's representatives in the Assembly in October 1784. He was a speculator in the national debt and, as a member of the Assembly, was one of the principal authors of the state law assuming the national debt owed to Pennsylvanians, an act bitterly opposed by Robert Morris and most other Republican leaders. Pettit was defeated for reelection to the Assembly in 1786 and 1787. Meanwhile, he had been elected to Congress in 1785, reelected in 1786, and then replaced by John Armstrong, Jr., in the spring of 1787.

He was defeated in the election of delegates to the Constitutional Convention of 1787, and he was one of the defeated Philadelphia Antifederalist candidates for the Pennsylvania Convention. He attended the Harrisburg Convention in

1788, and he was occasionally proposed for office thereafter but was never elected. He was a supporter of the Jeffersonian Republicans in state and national politics until his death.

Potter, James (1729-1789), Candidate for Elector (Harrisburg Ticket)

Born in Tyrone, Ireland, Potter came to Pennsylvania in 1741. His father settled in what became Cumberland County in 1746 and was its first sheriff. Potter served as a militia officer on the frontier during the Seven Years War and then settled in what became Northumberland County. He was a colonel in the militia in 1775 and was a major general by 1782. A member of the Constitutionalist Party, he was vice president of the state, 1781-1782; was a member of the Council of Censors, 1783-1784; and was a justice of the peace of Northumberland County when he died.

Potts, Samuel (1736-1793), Presidential Elector (Lancaster Ticket)

Born in Pennsylvania, Potts was a member of a family engaged in the iron business and lived in Pottstown from 1752 until his death. By 1764 he and his brother were operating ironworks at Valley Forge, and during the Revolution he cast cannon for the United States. He represented Philadelphia County in the colonial assembly in 1767, 1768, and 1769. He continued his iron business until his death.

Read, Collinson (1753-1815), Presidential Elector (Lancaster Ticket)

Little is known about Read except that he was admitted to practice law in Berks County in 1772, that he opposed the state Constitution of 1776, and that he was appointed county clerk of Berks County in 1783. In 1801 he published a digest of Pennsylvania laws and in 1806 *The American Pleader's Assistant,* a handbook for lawyers.

Rittenhouse, David (1732-1796), Candidate for Elector (Harrisburg Ticket)

Born near Germantown, Pennsylvania, the son of a farmer, Rittenhouse early displayed mechanical and mathematical talent and became in time a distinguished surveyor, astronomer, and builder of astronomical equipment. He was appointed an engineer for the Committee of Safety in 1775 and helped manufacture guns and munitions. In March 1776 he was elected to the colonial assembly as a Philadelphia representative in place of Benjamin Franklin, in May to the Committee of Safety, and on 8 July to the convention that wrote the first state constitution. He was a member of the committee to draft the constitution, chairman of the committee that wrote the bill of rights, and a member of the committee that prepared the final draft. From 1776 onward he was a firm Constitutionalist.

He ran for a seat in the legislature from Philadelphia but was defeated by men who were soon to call themselves Republicans. He was defeated again when he ran for the state Convention in 1787 as an opponent of the Constitution. In 1796 he was a presidential Elector committed to Thomas Jefferson.

During the war and afterwards, he served in various state posts, notably as treasurer from 1777 until he resigned in 1789. He helped plan the first United States Mint and was its director from 1792 to 1795. In addition, he became professor of astronomy and a trustee of the University of Pennsylvania, and he was one of the most active members and officers of the American Philosophical Society. Amidst all such duties, he continued to conduct the scientific experiments and write the papers which won him an international reputation as a scientist.

Scott, Thomas (1739-1796), Elected Representative (Lancaster Ticket)

Born in Lancaster County, by 1770 Scott had moved into the border area on the Monongahela River claimed by both Pennsylvania and Virginia. When Pennsylvania created Westmoreland County in the disputed area in 1774, Scott was appointed a justice of the peace, and in 1776 he was elected to the first state assembly. In 1777 he was elected to the Supreme Executive Council, where he served until 1780. In 1781, a few days after Washington County was created from a part of Westmoreland County, Scott appointed prothonotary and clerk of the courts.

He was a political ally of a group of men in the Pittsburgh area associated with John Neville, a Federalist leader in western Pennsylvania. Scott voted to ratify the Constitution in the state Convention in 1787. The next year he was nominated on the Lancaster ticket as a representative of "the West." However, he was elected by Federalist voters in the East, for the West voted overwhelmingly for the Harrisburg ticket, his own county ten to one. Scott refused to take his seat in the House of Representatives until the Supreme Executive Council agreed to appoint his son in his place as prothonotary of Washington County. He refused to run for the second Congress, because he wanted to retain the post of clerk of the Washington County courts, which he had held since 1781. However, Governor Thomas Mifflin removed him. In 1792 he was elected to the third Congress, but he apparently declined to run for the fourth Congress.

Although he had no formal education, he studied law and in 1791 was admitted to the bar and ended his career as a lawyer in the western counties.

Smilie, John (1742-1813), Candidate for Elector (Harrisburg Ticket)

Born in County Down, Ireland, Smilie came to Pennsylvania with his family and settled in Lancaster County. Smilie was elected to the provincial conferences in 1775 and 1776 and then enlisted as a private in the state militia. He was elected to the Assembly from Lancaster County in 1778 and 1779, and was one of the principal backers of the act of 1780 providing for the gradual abolition of slavery in Pennsylvania. He moved to Westmoreland County in 1781 and represented the county in the Council of Censors, 1783-1784, where he opposed any change in the state Constitution of 1776. After Fayette County was created from a portion of Westmoreland County in 1783, Smilie was elected to the Assembly from the new county in 1784 and 1785 and then to the Supreme Executive Council in 1786, 1787, and 1788. An ardent Constitutionalist in state politics, he voted against ratification of the Constitution in the state Convention in 1787. He was a delegate to the state constitutional convention, 1789-1790, and was a member of the state Senate from 1790 until 1792, when he resigned after he was elected to United States House of Representatives. Defeated for reelection in 1794, he was elected to the state House of Representatives in 1795, 1796, and 1797, and was a presidential Elector in 1796, supporting Thomas Jefferson for the Presidency. He was again elected to the United States House of Representatives in 1798 as a Republican and was reelected in every election thereafter until his death.

Stewart, Walter (1756-1796), Candidate for Elector (Harrisburg Ticket)

Born in Londonderry, Ireland, Stewart came to Pennsylvania sometime before 1776. He received a commission in 1776 as captain of a Pennsylvania battalion in the Continental Army, served throughout the war, and was breveted a brigadier general in 1783. He married a daughter of Blair M'Clenachan and became a Philadelphia merchant. He was probably nominated on the Harrisburg ticket because he was the son-in-law of an Antifederalist leader, but after the election the newspapers announced that he was a supporter of the Constitution. From 1793 until his death he was inspector of the revenue and surveyor of customs of the Port of Philadelphia.

Wager, Philip (1748-1813), Candidate for Elector (Harrisburg Ticket)

Born in Philadelphia, the son of an immigrant from Germany, Wager became a Philadelphia wine merchant. During the war he served as a private in various Philadelphia militia companies. He was a Republican in politics, was an investor in various business enterprises, and was elected a warden of the city in 1786. No evidence has been located to explain why he was placed on the Harrisburg ticket.

Whitehill, Robert (1738-1813), Candidate for Representative (Harrisburg Ticket)

Born in Lancaster County, the son of an immigrant from northern Ireland, Whitehill bought land in Cumberland County in 1770 and lived there the rest of his life. He was an aggressive leader in the revolutionary movement and was an early supporter of independence. He played an important role in writing the Pennsylvania Constitution of 1776 and was one of its leading defenders. He represented Cumberland County in the Assembly, 1776-1778, the Supreme Executive Council, 1779-1781, and the Assembly, 1784-1787. As one of Robert Morris's strongest political opponents, he led a successful fight to revoke the charter of the Bank of North America in 1785.

He was a leading opponent of ratification of the Constitution in the state Convention in 1787, continued to demand amendments afterwards, and was a delegate to the Harrisburg Convention in September 1788. He was a member of the state constitutional convention in 1789-1790 and refused to sign the new constitution because he thought it too undemocratic. He was a member of the state Assembly, 1797-1801, and the state Senate, 1801-1805. In 1805 he was elected to the United States House of Representatives. A firm supporter of the Jeffersonian Republicans, he served in the House until his death in 1813.

Wilson, James (1742-1798), Presidential Elector (Lancaster Ticket)

Born in Scotland and educated at St. Andrews and Edinburgh universities, Wilson arrived in New York in 1765 with letters of introduction to important Pennsylvanians. He became a Latin tutor at the College of Philadelphia in 1766 but quit in order to study law with John Dickinson and was admitted to the bar in November 1767. He began the practice of law at Reading in 1768 and then moved to Carlisle, where he became a prominent lawyer and began the land speculations that were to be his undoing. He was elected to the provincial conferences in 1774-1775 and to the Second Continental Congress in May 1775. He initially opposed independence but finally voted for it on 2 July 1776. He was a bitter opponent of the Pennsylvania Constitution of 1776 and was a principal organizer of and spokesman for the Republican Party, whose purpose was to revise that constitution. In 1778 he moved to Philadelphia, where he served as an attorney for wealthy men such as Robert Morris. He was elected to Congress in 1782 after the Republicans gained control of the Assembly and served in Congress sporadically during the year 1783. He was elected to Congress again in 1785 and attended off and on until mid-1786. As a Pennsylvania delegate to the Constitutional Convention, he was one of the most vigorous supporters of a powerful national government. In the debate over the ratification of the Constitution in Pennsylvania and throughout the United States, Wilson was one of the most important Federalist spokesmen. In November 1788 he represented the city of Philadelphia at the Lancaster Conference, where he was nominated a presidential Elector. His supporters hoped that he would become Chief Justice of the United States Supreme Court, and he wrote to President Washington offering to serve in that post. Instead, the President appointed him an associate justice. In his judicial opinions he anticipated the nationalistic opinions of Chief Justice John Marshall, but while serving on the Court he continued to speculate in land. In 1797 he fled to New Jersey and then to North Carolina to escape imprisonment for debt in Pennsylvania. He died in North Carolina, mentally unbalanced but still a member of the Supreme Court.

Wynkoop, Henry (1727-1812), Elected Representative (Lancaster Ticket)

Born in Bucks County, Wynkoop was active in politics by 1774. He represented the county in the provincial conferences in 1774 and 1775 and became a major in the militia. He held various posts in the state government from 1776 to 1779. He was elected to the Continental Congress in March 1779 and was reelected in 1780 and 1781. In 1780 he was appointed one of the justices of the Court of Common Pleas and Orphan's Court, a post he held until 1789. He was elected to the state Convention in 1787 and voted to ratify the Constitution.

In 1791 the Pennsylvania election law divided the state into districts, placing Philadelphia and Bucks counties in one district. This pitted Wynkoop against Frederick A. Muhlenberg, and the latter won. The Federalists nominated Wynkoop for a seat in the third Congress in 1792, but he lost again. Meanwhile, in August 1791 Governor Thomas Mifflin appointed him an associate judge in Bucks County, a post he held until his death.

CHAPTER V

The Elections in Massachusetts

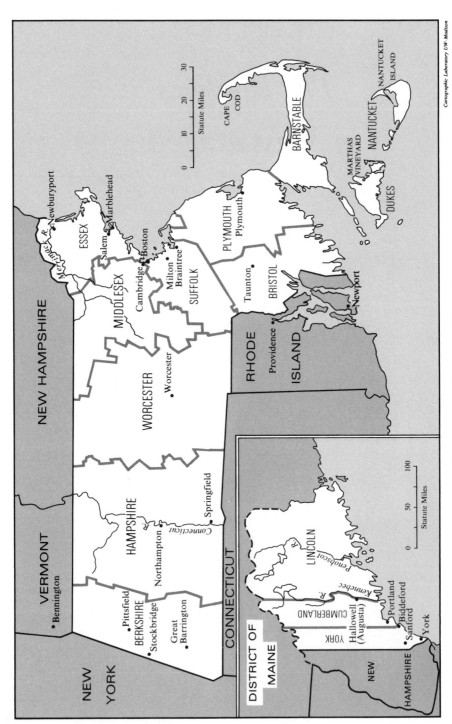

Massachusetts Counties, 1788-1789

INTRODUCTION

Massachusetts politics in the 1780s were dominated by cleavages ranging from political rivalries among a small number of leaders to basic divisions between the urban and rural areas of the state, which in their broadest sense were between the seacoast towns and the backcountry farmers. Some of the cleavages began before independence. In 1763 a small tightly-knit group of men centered around the Hutchinson and Oliver families and their recognized leader, Thomas Hutchinson, dominated the government of the colony. As lieutenant governor, chief justice of the Superior Court, member of the Council, and the holder of several lesser posts, Hutchinson was the most influential man in the colony, far more so than the royal governor.

In the 1760s the power of the Hutchinson-Oliver political alliance was challenged by a rising popular party which attacked Hutchinson's leadership within the colony and led the opposition to British colonial policies. The leaders of the party were the Boston representatives in the colonial legislature. The most conspicuous leader in the early 1760s was James Otis, Jr., but by 1770 Samuel Adams was the leading figure. Associated with him were such Boston merchants as John Hancock and Thomas Cushing; John Adams, a young lawyer from nearby Braintree; Elbridge Gerry, a Marblehead merchant; James Warren of Plymouth, the husband of James Otis's sister, Mercy; and a number of Congregational ministers and Boston artisans, the most conspicuous of whom was the engraver and silversmith Paul Revere. The popular party's influence was limited almost entirely to the seacoast, while the backcountry counties were still controlled by Hutchinson's political supporters.

The popular party achieved its first success on a colony-wide level in the spring elections of 1766, when it gained a narrow majority in the House of Representatives. However, Thomas Hutchinson and his allies retained control of the colony-wide network of appointed justices of the peace and militia officers. In 1771 Hutchinson was appointed governor of the colony, but the destruction of the East India Company's tea at Boston in December 1773 and the parliamentary acts in 1774, which closed the port of Boston and altered the charter of the colony, soon brought about the downfall of royal government. Hutchinson left for England in June 1774 and was replaced as governor by General Thomas Gage, commanding general of the British army in America. Gage, however, never had the power of his predecessor. County conventions throughout the colony overthrew the county courts and took control of the local militia. Hutchinson's political allies fled or retired from office, and by the end of 1774 the government of the colony was in the hands of a provincial congress controlled by leaders of the popular party.

The members of the provincial congress were at odds with one another almost at once. Eastern leaders were determined to avoid hostilities during the winter of 1774-1775, while country leaders, and particularly those from the backcountry counties, wanted to start hostilities immediately. Furthermore, the backcountry counties sent far more delegates to the provincial congress than they had ever sent to the colonial legislature. Despite the efforts of eastern leaders, and of General Gage, hostilities began at Lexington and Concord in April 1775.

Meanwhile, the backcountry counties, as well as some eastern towns, made it plain that they wanted a revolution in the internal government of the colony.

They declared themselves in a "state of nature" and insisted on the right to elect their own officials and govern themselves instead of being ruled by men appointed in Boston. The eastern leaders appealed to the Continental Congress for help in the spring of 1775, and Congress advised them to resume government under the royal charter of 1691. They did so in June 1775, with the Council assuming the executive powers of the royal governor while continuing to serve as the upper house of the legislature.

The attempt to reestablish the old government was defied in the backcountry. The members of a Berkshire County convention in December 1775 demanded the right to elect their own civil officials. As far as they were concerned, the new government was just as corrupt as the old. By the spring of 1776, backcountry people were demanding a "fundamental constitution" to be written by a specially elected convention and approved by a majority of the people. Furthermore, they blocked all efforts to restore the old court system presided over by appointed justices and proceeded instead to elect their own. The backcountry continued its defiance and governed itself during the early years of the War for Independence.

In 1778 the legislature drafted a constitution which was rejected by the voters. Then in 1779 a convention was elected to write a constitution. However, the convention was controlled by men opposed to any basic changes in the structure of the government inherited from colonial times. The Massachusetts governor was given the power to veto legislation (the only state governor who had such power), and he retained the power to appoint local officials. Representation in the Senate was based on taxable wealth, not on population or towns, and the property qualifications for voters were raised over what they had been prior to 1776. The constitution was submitted to a popular vote and then was declared adopted by the convention, a declaration made possible only by miscounting or ignoring the votes against it. Those who had demanded democratic reforms were bitterly discontented, but soon after the "adoption" of the constitution, their anger was directed instead toward the economic policies of the government.

Meanwhile, the leadership of the popular party itself was rent by dissension. Its members had never been a monolithic group, and by 1776 they were quarreling with one another over power and position. Samuel Adams, James Warren, and Elbridge Gerry continued to represent the "old revolutionary" wing of the party, while James Bowdoin became the leader of an eastern mercantile faction. For a time these two factions were united by their enmity to John Hancock and his political ally, Thomas Cushing. Prior to 1776 Hancock had been treated by some as a tool, useful because of his money. But thereafter he developed a popular following and set out to destroy the political influence of Samuel Adams, even in the town of Boston, by accusing him of being an enemy of General Washington, and by hinting that Adams was the leader of a pro-British faction in the Continental Congress.

Hancock was so successful that he was elected the first governor of the state in 1780 and was reelected annually every year until his death in 1793, except in 1785 and 1786 when he did not run. No matter how virulently other leaders publicly and privately denounced him as a fool and an unprincipled demagogue, the majority of voters usually supported him.

The quarrels among such leaders after the adoption of the Constitution of 1780 were not about the fundamental economic policies of the state. They agreed upon most of those policies, which benefited eastern merchants and creditors at the expense of the farmers and poorer people of the state.

During the first years of the Revolution, the state had issued great sums of paper money to finance the war. As soon as the state constitution was adopted in 1780, the legislature abolished paper money as legal tender in the payment of taxes and debts. The legislature then proceeded to refinance the state debt, much of which had been acquired by eastern merchants and speculators for a fraction of its original value. The legislature provided that the old debt, whatever the form, could be exchanged for new "consolidated notes" at the market value of the debt at the time it was created, not at the depreciated value at which most speculators had bought it. This act more than doubled the real value of the debt. Furthermore, the legislature provided that the interest and principal on the new notes be paid in specie, and then levied taxes payable in specie to provide the money.

Between 30 and 40 percent of all the taxes levied by the state between 1780 and 1786 were poll taxes, and these fell heaviest on the poor and the farmers. As specie grew scarcer and scarcer, hundreds of farmers could not secure enough gold or silver in any given year to pay their poll taxes, much less to pay their private debts. Furthermore, the state courts, at the behest of private creditors, collected private debts as rigorously as they did state taxes; and when citizens could not pay, their property was seized and sold, and when their property did not suffice, they were thrown in jail. In 1784 in Worcester County there were more than 2,000 court suits for the collection of private debts, and the next year 94 of the 104 people jailed in the county were imprisoned as debtors.

Farmers everywhere protested against the inequity of the refinancing of the debt, the taxes levied to pay it, and the rigorous collection of private debts. They pled their lack of ready cash and begged that they be allowed to pay taxes and debts with the produce of their farms. The eastern-dominated legislature ignored the plight of the farmers, who began holding county conventions as early as 1782.

Protests mounted, and after the legislature adjourned in July 1786 without making a serious effort to redress grievances, Bristol County held a convention. Shortly thereafter, conventions were held in Middlesex, Worcester, Hampshire, and Berkshire counties. Many of the county conventions demanded the same constitutional reforms demanded in 1776 but denied in the Constitution of 1780, and all of them called for economic relief.

Discontented farmers soon turned to extreme measures. After the Hampshire County convention adjourned in August 1786, a mob of 1,500 men forced the county court at Northampton to adjourn, and other mobs soon terrorized and stopped the courts in Bristol, Middlesex, Worcester, and Berkshire counties. Governor James Bowdoin ordered the sheriffs to call out the militia, but most local militiamen were farmers themselves and could not be depended upon. The Governor then called an emergency session of the legislature to meet on 27 September. The day before the legislature met, a mob prevented the Supreme Judicial Court itself from meeting at Springfield in Hampshire County.

The legislature suspended the collection of private debts in specie for eight months, postponed the sitting of courts in Hampshire and Berkshire counties (which merely legalized what the rebels had achieved), and agreed to pardon those who had stopped the courts if they would take an oath of allegiance. But at the same time the legislature suspended the writ of habeas corpus and empowered the Governor and Council to imprison and hold without bail anyone they declared to be an enemy of the state.

These measures did not discourage the insurgents, and bands of armed men continued to prevent the county courts from sitting. Meanwhile, the legislature agreed that troops should be raised, since most of the militia could not be depended upon, but it did not provide any money. General Benjamin Lincoln, in charge of securing the troops, asked the wealthy men of the state for money, and within a short time he had received over £5,000 from about 130 men, including £250 from Governor Bowdoin.

Lincoln marched west to protect the county court which was to meet at Worcester on 23 January 1787. By the time he got there, General William Shepard with over 1,000 loyal militia had occupied the United States arsenal at Springfield in Hampshire County. Insurgent leaders Luke Day, Eli Parsons, and Daniel Shays gathered near Springfield with bodies of armed men. Shays asked General Lincoln for a cessation of hostilities until the legislature could meet, and when Lincoln refused, Shays marched on Springfield. General Shepard fired on Shays's men and killed four of them. The insurgents then fled and that, in effect, ended what was later known as Shays's Rebellion.

A mop-up operation followed in which a few more "regulators," as they called themselves, were killed. Their leaders had not wanted to fight; they wanted only a redress of grievances. However, when the forces of government demonstrated that they were going to suppress rather than redress, the leaders fled to other states.

When the legislature met at the end of February, it empowered the Governor to pardon the rebels; but it also passed an act disqualifying them, even if pardoned, from voting, holding office, or carrying on business for at least three years. Eleven leaders, including Daniel Shays, were indicted for treason and condemned to death. The attitude of the more hysterical easterners toward the rebels was probably best expressed by the Reverend Jeremy Belknap, who hoped that the state would follow Oliver Cromwell's maxim and "pay well and hang well."

Then in the spring elections there came a political revolution. In February 1785 John Hancock had resigned as governor on the grounds of ill health; and, despite his efforts, he could not secure the election of his ally Thomas Cushing (who had been lieutenant governor since 1780). James Bowdoin, who had been defeated by Hancock every year since 1780, was elected governor by the legislature after no candidate received a majority of popular votes, and he was reelected in 1786 without opposition. In the spring of 1787 Hancock began campaigning for the governorship, and he defeated Bowdoin by a three-to-one margin in April. Furthermore, there was a revolution in the membership of the legislature. Nineteen of the 40 senators elected had not been members of the previous Senate, and 164 of the 221 members of the House of Representatives had not been members of the previous House. So far as many easterners were concerned, the Shaysites had achieved at the polls what they had not achieved in the field.

The new legislature repealed the disqualifying act and reduced the taxes for 1788, while Governor Hancock pardoned everyone, including the leaders who had been condemned to death. Many of the basic grievances of the rebels were not redressed, but the Governor and legislature did enough to head off any further trouble, and Hancock was more popular than ever with the majority of voters.

Entirely aside from its impact on state politics, the uprising of backcountry farmers produced a dramatic change in the attitude of most Massachusetts leaders toward the central government. Between 1781 and 1783 they had been strong opponents of Robert Morris, who, as Superintendent of Finance for the Confederation Congress, had led a movement to strengthen the central government by securing for it sweeping economic and political power. And they rejoiced when he was driven from office in 1784. The Massachusetts leaders did support grants of money to the Confederation Congress, and increasingly they demanded that it be given the power to regulate trade. But they did not support the continuing efforts to revise and amend the Articles of Confederation advocated by the merchants in the Middle States and men like Alexander Hamilton and James Madison. Shays's Rebellion changed the minds of many Massachusetts leaders; and the state sent a delegation to the Constitutional Convention, which, with the exception of Elbridge Gerry, supported the overthrow of the Articles of Confederation and its replacement by the Constitution.

But could the newly proposed Constitution be ratified in Massachusetts? The elections to the state Convention, which opened on 9 January 1788, reflected the internal bitterness that had developed within the state. The Antifederalists probably had a majority, but neither they nor the Federalists dared call for a vote early in the Convention.

The Federalist leaders became convinced that their only hope of securing ratification was to offer amendments to the Constitution, which so many Antifederalists demanded. Governor Hancock, although elected president of the Convention, did not attend because of his health, although his enemies believed that he was waiting to see which way the Convention would go. The Federalists devised the strategy of drafting amendments and then persuading Hancock to appear and offer them as his own. Furthermore, it was said that Hancock was told that Virginia would probably not ratify. If it did not, George Washington could not be elected President, and Hancock would be the obvious man for the position. Samuel Adams, who sincerely opposed the Constitution, was forced into line when Federalist leaders persuaded the Boston artisans to support the Constitution and by the Convention's acceptance of amendments. The result was that Massachusetts ratified the Constitution on 6 February by a vote of 187 to 168.

The struggle continued without letup after ratification. The Antifederalists did not trust the promise of their Federalist opponents to support amendments and began a campaign to win control of the state in the spring elections. If they could win control, they would be in a position to exert pressure for the adoption of amendments to guarantee the powers of the states and protect the liberties of the people. Before the end of February the Antifederalists held a convention in Worcester County and nominated Elbridge Gerry for governor and James Warren for lieutenant governor. Gerry made it clear that he did not want to be governor, and in any case Hancock was unbeatable. Furthermore, the Federalists had apparently agreed that they would not run a candidate against him but contented themselves with running General Benjamin Lincoln for lieutenant governor. In addition, a group of Samuel Adams's supporters ran him for lieutenant governor, thus dividing the votes that might otherwise have gone to Warren.

Hancock won the governorship. No one received a majority for the lieutenant governorship, and the legislature elected Lincoln. In the elections for the legislature, several Antifederalist leaders were defeated. The new Senate was firmly in the hands of the Federalists. It is uncertain which group had a majority in the House of Representatives, but the Federalists had enough strength to elect Theodore Sedgwick, the Federalist leader from Berkshire County, as speaker of the House. This, then, was the legislature that provided for the first federal elections in the state.

The state was divided into eight districts for the election of Representatives. The legislature proclaimed the principle of representation according to population, but the districts established favored the Federalist eastern part of the state over the populous rural and backcountry counties which had voted against ratification of the Constitution.

The voters in each district voted for presidential Electors, but the legislature chose one Elector from the two men receiving the highest number of votes in each district. The legislature was to elect two Electors at large from among those who received no popular votes in the districts. When the legislature learned that more than 200 men had received popular votes (which eliminated virtually all the Federalist leaders), it changed the rules by deciding that it could elect two men as Electors at large even though they had received votes.

The legislature elected two Federalist Senators. The House chose Caleb Strong and Dr. Charles Jarvis. The Senate accepted Strong but rejected Jarvis three times before the House yielded and accepted the Senate's final candidate, Tristram Dalton. Dalton was an unequivocal Federalist whereas Jarvis was an ally of Governor Hancock who had supported amendments to the Constitution in the state Convention and who became a Republican in the 1790s.

NOTE ON SOURCES

The legislative records of the Massachusetts legislature, the General Court, are fairly complete but widely scattered among various manuscript groups in the Massachusetts Archives, Boston. The manuscript journals of the House of Representatives and the Senate provide a general outline but do not contain a complete record of legislative actions. In addition, the Senate clerk often placed subsequent and final actions on a bill in the journal under the date the bill was initiated, not under the date it was passed or rejected. The texts of some resolutions are not given in the journals of either house. The two houses had a practice of writing resolutions on separate sheets and even scraps of paper. Official actions were then entered on such sheets of paper following the resolutions and were signed by the speaker of the House or the president of the Senate as the case might be. When the document was sent to the other house, it in turn usually entered its official action on the same sheet or sheets of paper.

Since the journals are incomplete, documents in the following groups of manuscripts in the Massachusetts Archives are indispensable for tracing the evolution of the Election Resolutions adopted by the two houses on 20 November. Those groups are: Council Records, XXX-XXXI; Miscellaneous Legislative Documents, House Files; Miscellaneous Legislative Documents, Senate Files; Miscellaneous Resolves, 1788, Chapter 10; Miscellaneous Resolves, 1788, Chapter 17; Miscellaneous Resolves, 1788, Chapter 49; Miscellaneous Resolves, 1788, Chapter 85. At the end of each session of the General Court, most of the measures adopted during the session were printed. Two such publications contain materials for the first federal elections: *Resolves of the General Court . . .* [29 October—24 November] (Boston, 1788) and *Resolves of the General Court . . .* (Boston, 1789).

Thirteen newspapers were published in Massachusetts during the first federal elections. Five of them were published in Boston, although, unlike Philadelphia and New York, Boston had no daily newspaper. The *Boston Gazette and the Country Journal* was a continuation of the prewar *Gazette*. Benjamin Edes, who bought the paper in partnership with John Gill in 1755, had been the sole owner since 1775. In 1788 his son Benjamin was associated with him. The *Gazette* was the popular party newspaper before 1776. During the first federal elections it supported such men as Samuel Adams and Elbridge Gerry, as it had before the war, and was a leading supporter of amendments to the Constitution. *The Independent Chronicle: and the Universal Advertiser* had been published since 1784 by Thomas Adams and John Nourse. Like the *Gazette*, it supported the Antifederalists during the first federal elections. Edmund Freeman and Loring Andrews began publishing *The Herald of Freedom, and the Federal Advertiser* as a semi-weekly on 15 September 1788; and as the last part of its title indicated, it was devoted to Federalist candidates and opposed amendments to the Constitution.

The outstanding Federalist newspaper in Boston, and one of the most vigorous in the nation, was *The Massachusetts Centinel*, founded in 1784 by Benjamin Russell. The paper is invaluable for political opinion and for accounts of the debates in the House of Representatives. The fifth Boston newspaper, John Allen's *The Massachusetts Gazette*, stopped publication on 11 November 1788.

Most of the eight weekly newspapers published outside Boston were relatively neutral and uninformative about the elections, at least as compared to the Boston newspapers. Three were published to the east and northeast of Boston. They were John Dabney and Thomas Cushing's *Salem Gazette;* William Hoyt's *The Essex Journal and New Hampshire Packet*, Newburyport; and Thomas B. Wait's *The Cumberland Gazette*, Portland, Maine. In the west two newspapers were published in Worcester. Isaiah Thomas's *The Massachusetts Spy* was moved from Boston to Worcester in 1775. The paper went through several minor changes in name in the 1780s, but during the elections its title was *Thomas's Massachusetts Spy: Or, The Worcester Gazette*. The other Worcester newspaper was *The American Herald; and the Worcester Recorder* published by Edward E. Powars. The newspaper, which Powars moved from Boston in June 1788, was a continuation of the prewar *Boston Evening Post*, which he renamed *The American Herald* in 1784. During ratification of the Constitution it had been a leading Antifederalist newspaper but it was neutral during the elections.

Two newspapers were published in Hampshire County: Ezra W. Weld's *The Hampshire Chronicle* in Springfield and William Butler's *The Hampshire Gazette* in Northampton. In Pittsfield in Berkshire County, Roger Storrs began publishing *The Berkshire Chronicle* on 8 May 1788.

There are many manuscript collections containing information about the elections, although as often as not the information is incomplete or limited to tantalizing hints about men and their actions that are never explained. Particularly useful are the manuscripts of the Adams family, Henry Knox, Rufus King, Elbridge Gerry, and Theodore Sedgwick.

A useful contemporary printed source is Thomas and John Fleet's *Fleet's Pocket Almanac for the Year of Our Lord . . . To Which Is Annexed the Massachusetts Register* for the years 1787, 1788, and 1789. The almanac contains lists of the men elected to the state legislature and of the holders of other public offices such as sheriffs, justices of the peace, and coroners. *Historical Data Relating to Counties, Cities and Towns of Massachusetts* (prepared by Kevin H. White, Secretary of the Commonwealth, n.p., 1966) gives modern spellings of place names and changes in names since the eighteenth century. In addition, the hundreds of town and county histories and published town records are important for political and biographical information.

Samuel B. Harding's *The Contest Over the Ratification of the Federal Constitution in the State of Massachusetts* (New York, 1896) has information about several of the men involved in the elections. Clifford K. Shipton's *Biographical Sketches of Those Who Attended Harvard College* contains detailed information about the Harvard graduates who were candidates. Anson E. Morse's *The Federalist Party in Massachusetts to the Year 1800* (Princeton, 1909) is a useful outline of political events. Robert A. East, "The Massachusetts Conservatives in the Critical Period," in Richard B. Morris, ed., *The Era of the American Revolution* (New York, 1939) gives an account of how Shays's Rebellion changed the attitude of Massachusetts leaders toward the central government. Robert J. Taylor's *Western Massachusetts in the Revolution* (Providence, 1954) is the fullest account of events in the backcountry. Van Beck Hall's *Politics Without Parties: Massachusetts, 1780-1791* (Pittsburgh, 1972) contains a detailed analysis of political and economic divisions and voting patterns in the state. The background of the politics of the 1780s is set forth in Stephen E. Patterson, *Political Parties in Revolutionary Massachusetts* (Madison, Wis., 1973).

MASSACHUSETTS CHRONOLOGY, 1788-1789

1788

20 June	General Court adjourns to await call of Confederation Congress for first federal elections.
2 August	Newspaper nomination of John Adams and James Bowdoin for United States Senate.
25 August	Newspaper nomination of Samuel Adams and Elbridge Gerry for United States Senate.
27 August	"Hortensius" begins newspaper debate on amendments by attacking supporters of amendments to the Constitution.
28 August	"Solon" publishes newspaper essay in behalf of amendments to the Constitution.

19 September	Governor John Hancock lays Election Ordinance of 13 September before the Council.
1 October	Beginning of newspaper debate over method of choosing presidential Electors.
22 October	Beginning of newspaper debate over statewide vs. district election of Representatives.
29 October	General Court reassembles.
1-20 November	General Court debates methods of electing Electors, Senators, and Representatives.
20 November	General Court adopts Election Resolutions.
21-24 November	General Court elects Caleb Strong and Tristram Dalton United States Senators.
24 November	General Court adjourns.
18 December	Elections for Representatives and nominations of presidential Electors.
31 December	General Court reassembles.

1789

6 January	Governor and Council record the votes in the election of Representatives on 18 December; Representatives elected in Suffolk, Plymouth-Barnstable, York-Cumberland-Lincoln, and Bristol-Dukes-Nantucket districts.
6 January	Governor issues precepts for new elections in Essex, Middlesex, Worcester, and Hampshire-Berkshire districts.
7 January	General Court elects ten presidential Electors.
8 January	Governor sends message to General Court recommending amendments to the Constitution.
10 January	General Court adopts additional election resolutions concerning further elections.
29 January	Second election held in four districts.
3 February	Governor transmits to the General Court papers from New York and Virginia calling for a second constitutional convention to write amendments to the Constitution.
4 February	Presidential Electors cast ten votes for George Washington and ten votes for John Adams.
9 February	Governor and Council record the votes in the second election; Benjamin Goodhue elected in Essex and Elbridge Gerry in Middlesex districts.
9 February	Governor issues precepts for third election in Worcester and Hampshire-Berkshire districts.
17 February	General Court directs Governor to notify the governors of New York and Virginia that amendments to the Constitution

	should be proposed by the first Congress under the Constitution.
17 February	General Court adjourns *sine die*.
2 March	Third election in Worcester and Hampshire-Berkshire districts.
16 March	Governor and Council record votes in the third election; Jonathan Grout elected in Worcester District.
16 March	Governor issues precepts for fourth election in Hampshire-Berkshire District.
30 March	Fourth election in Hampshire-Berkshire District.
6 April	John Hancock elected governor and Samuel Adams lieutenant governor.
10 April	Governor and Council record votes in fourth election; no candidate receives a majority in Hampshire-Berkshire District.
10 April	Governor issues precepts for fifth election in Hampshire-Berkshire District.
11 May	Fifth election in Hampshire-Berkshire District.
27 May	Governor and Council record the election of Theodore Sedgwick in Hampshire-Berkshire District.

THE DOCUMENTS

From the Adjournment to the Reconvening of the General Court, 20 June–29 October 1788

On 20 June, the day before the ninth state, New Hampshire, ratified the Constitution, the General Court requested Governor John Hancock to adjourn it and to call it back in session after he received a request from the Confederation Congress to prepare for the first federal elections. For a time after the adjournment, relatively little attention was paid to the forthcoming elections. Occasional newspaper articles discussed the qualifications of desirable candidates; privately a few political leaders began making plans; and one newspaper nominated John Adams and James Bowdoin for the Senate. This surface calm was destroyed by the publication of the New York Act of Ratification in seven Massachusetts newspapers between 6 and 14 August and by the publication of the New York Circular Letter in nine newspapers between 14 and 21 August. These publications and the publication on 20 August of the news of North Carolina's refusal to ratify the Constitution set off a public debate in which the central issue was amendments to the Constitution.

The attack on amendments was begun by "Hortensius" in the *Massachusetts Centinel* on 27 August and the defense of amendments by "Solon" in the *Independent Chronicle* the next day. At the same time, the *Boston Gazette*'s nomination of Samuel Adams and Elbridge Gerry for the Senate on 25 August began a newspaper debate about candidates who would or would not support amendments.

The newspaper debate was in a very real sense a continuation of the debate over the ratification of the Constitution by the state. Federalists insisted that amendments were unnecessary or should be delayed to some future time, while Antifederalists insisted that the Constitution should be amended at once. Candidates for office were denounced or praised for their role in state politics ever since colonial times, the stand they had taken in the ratification debate, and the stand they might take if elected to Congress.

Certain other issues were also debated in the newspapers. Should the state be divided into districts for the election of Representatives or should there be state-wide elections? Should the voters or the legislature elect presidential Electors?

Thus by the time the legislature assembled on 29 October to adopt procedures for the first federal elections, several of the candidates had been mentioned either publicly or privately, and most of the issues involved had been the subject of public debates.

Extract of a Letter from Boston, 17 June[1]

There seems to be a general infatuation here among the *magi*; the vulgar have caught it, so that there is no reasoning with them on the subject, though of the greatest importance. Ask any of them, *high* or *low*, whether they have any ill apprehensions from the adoption of the new system, they answer, without hesitation, *yes*; but they say, Congress will *certainly* make the proposed alterations. Ministers, lawyers, and merchants made a large proportion of our Convention, so that it is no great wonder that the people *at large* are so many of them *deluded*; yet, I believe, could the voice of the people in general be taken, a very large majority would be found in opposition to the proposed plan. Of this I am convinced from the frequent conversations I have had with farmers, etc.

1. *New York Journal,* 26 June.

House and Senate Proceedings, Friday, 20 June[1]

The House, P.M.

Ordered, that Mr. Jones, Mr. Washburn, and Mr. Choate, with such as the honorable Senate may join, be a committee to wait upon His Excellency the Governor and acquaint him that the General Court have passed upon the business which was before them, and to request His Excellency to adjourn the said Court to the first Wednesday in September next; and also to request His Excellency, with advice of Council, to prorogue the General Court from time to time, until he shall receive an application from Congress, for the appointment of Senators and Representatives in order to organize the general government, provided he does not prorogue them to a further day, than the first Wednesday in January next.

Sent up for concurrence.

The Senate, P.M.

[The Senate received the House's message.]

Read and concurred with an amendment, viz., to delete "January" and insert *December* and Ebenr Bridge and Joseph B. Varnum are joined.

Sent down for concurrence.

The House, P.M.

[The House received the Senate's message.]

Read and concurred.

The committee on the part of the House appointed to wait on the Governor reported that they had attended that service.

The Secretary came down and said . . . it was His Excellency's pleasure, by and with the advice and consent of the Council, and at the request of the General Court, that the said Court should be adjourned to the first Wednesday in September next at 9 o'clock in the forenoon, then to meet in the Statehouse at Boston, and that the said Court was adjourned to meet at that time and place accordingly.[2]

1. MS Journals, M-Ar. Unless otherwise indicated, the Massachusetts House and Senate proceedings are transcribed from the manuscript journals of the two houses and hereafter will be cited by date only.

2. On 20 June Governor John Hancock prorogued the legislature to 3 September (*Massachusetts Centinel,* 21 June); on 6 August to 8 October (*Independent Chronicle,* 7 August); and on 9 September to 29 October (*Independent Chronicle,* 11 September).

Theodore Sedgwick to Governor John Hancock, Stockbridge, 18 July[1]

Your Excellency ought to be made acquainted with every fact which may have an effect on the peace and tranquility of the commonwealth. It hath been insinuated very extensively in this part of the country, that the adjournment of the legislature to September was from an intention of excluding the country interest from a voice in organizing the national government; for say those who are themselves jealous of an ill design, or wish to excite jealousy in others, *the great men* will know it would be impossible to procure a representation of the landed interests in the month of September. The suggestion hath in some instances had the intended effect on honest minds. It has been my endeavor to prevent any ill-effect resulting from this impression by assuring all with whom I conversed in the subject that it was not the intention of the General Court to convene at so early a period, unless necessity rendered it indispensable.

At the time the resolution passed the measure appeared to me injudicious. Your Excellency will pardon me for suggesting as my opinion that proroguing the General Court to a period late in October may take place without the smallest inconvenience, because Massachusetts may then be as early as it is possible the Southern States [shall?] be, and it is of infinite importance that no foundation should be given to complaints.

In a very few days I shall be in New York, but considering the business to be transacted at the next session, I hope to have it in my power then to pay my respects to Your Excellency.

A spirit of keen animosity prevails in the Convention of New York. A very great majority is doubtless Antifederal. Yet it is my opinion the Constitution will not at the present session be either ratified or rejected. The leading characters have artfully so inflamed the people that an adoption would at present be dangerous. The popular [passions?] must first subside. Nor do I believe they possess sufficient hardihood to reject. It is therefore probable that an adjournment will be the present result.

1. RC, Miscellaneous Manuscripts, Sedgwick Folder, NHi. Sedgwick had been elected speaker of the Massachusetts House of Representatives in May 1788. He was also a member of the Confederation Congress, which he attended from 31 July to 3 September 1788.

James Warren to Elbridge Gerry, Plymouth, 20 July (excerpt)[1]

We are now to see the operation of the new Constitution with all its splendid advantages. You must prepare yourself for taking a part in the execution in one house or the other. Policy will prevail over malevolence and make your election certain. And your acceptance, I think, must be as certain as your election and will be a choice only of the least evil. I have much to say to you on this and other subjects, which I design to do ere long *viva voce.*[2]

1. RC, Sang Collection, ICarbS. Printed: Gardiner, *Warren-Gerry Letters,* 210-11. Warren, like Gerry, had worked hard for independence before 1776 and, like Gerry, Warren and his wife, Mercy Otis Warren, had opposed ratification of the Constitution without amendments.
2. For Gerry as a reluctant candidate for the House of Representatives, see The Second Election in Middlesex District, 29 January 1789, printed below.

A Federal Elector, Massachusetts Centinel, 23 July

Friends, in the important business of electing your FEDERAL REPRESEN-TATIVES, you will doubtless receive advice from various quarters; and the *motives* of the advisers will be as various. The observations of *truly federal* men, and *real* republicans, will claim a distinguished portion of your attention. They will be easily discerned, breathing a *national* spirit, free from *local* attachments, and party prejudices. They will discover a mind fraught with philanthropy, which while it gives a natural preference in its good wishes to "our dear country," will consider the whole human race as one family. Sentiments like these will do honor to our America, and lay the foundation of its glory deep in the bosom of futurity. AN AMERICAN, upon these principles, will become a more honorable character than ever has graced the annals of mankind.

But, my friends, you will be addressed by very different advisers. There are those who find it for their interest to keep a party spirit alive; these if successful will direct your views in such a medium as will usher their own *dear selves* into public life. Such will endeavor to excite jealousies and fears respecting the most unblemished characters that they imagine *stand in their own way.* They will declaim vehemently against *British influence* and *British connections,* to blast the fairest reputations, when *they know* at the same time that not a *shadow* of such influence exists. They will endeavor to point your attention to particular individuals, whose politics, calculated for a day, have not expanded with the growing importance of the American states.

But you, fellow electors, will easily detect the artifices of such demagogues, and while the confident and able patriots of your country claim a due share of your attention, you will spurn with indignation every attempt to disseminate a spirit of discord and party.

Your political fathers have *proposed,* and you have *adopted,* a form of government adapted to your circumstances. It remains for you to make this instrument a blessing or a curse.

Let your suffrages therefore fall on men of *candor,* VIRTUE, and *abilities,* from THESE we may expect a *wise* and *righteous* administration of the federal government. America, separated from all the world besides, if she is wise in the choice of her FEDERAL RULERS, will keep herself clear from the politics of Europe, and cemented into one FEDERAL BOND OF UNION AND AMITY, will make such arrangements in her *government, manufactures,* and *commerce,* as will be paramount to every unfriendly ordinance and commercial restriction of any foreign power.[1]

1. This item was addressed "to the Federal Electors of this Commonwealth." Throughout the summer and fall of 1788 and into early 1789, Massachusetts newspapers published many essays exhorting voters to elect "good" men and men of "virtuous morals," and to reject "office seekers," "demagogues" and the like. Such essays usually did not mention candidates by name. For other examples, see "A Republican," *Independent Chronicle,* 17 July; essays by unidentified correspondents: *Massachusetts Gazette,* 26 August; *Massachusetts Centinel,* 23 August; *Herald of Freedom,* 25, 29 September, 6 November, and 1 December; "Mount Tom," *Hampshire Gazette,* 21 January 1789; and "Independent Reflector" and "An Old Farmer," *Hampshire Gazette,* 29 April.

A Federal Elector, Massachusetts Centinel, 2 August

While some of our great characters, as I am told, are *privately* sharing among *themselves*, the federal "loaves and fishes," others appear to be aiming at a *monopoly* of all the great offices in the general government for the men of Massachusetts. The first class, in the opinion of many persons, are rather *officious*—the latter *selfish*—and neither federal. As such they must be considered in all the other states, who at least expect to be consulted on the subject.

If the method of proposing candidates for office in the public papers will tend to unite the suffrages of the people and direct to a more proper choice, let us adopt it. But let us at least be *consistent,* and not propose to the people, candidates for offices, the appointment of which they have delegated to Congress.

Proper persons for federal Representatives ought to be the first object of ATTENTION.

With respect to Senators, the legislature will not have a doubt; their eyes have long been, and still are, fixed on a [James] BOWDOIN and a J[ohn] ADAMS.[1]

With such and similar characters in the federal legislature—with a WASHINGTON President, and a HANCOCK, Vice President, America, like the Phoenix, rising from her ashes—the ashes of imbecility and national disgrace—will mount to that station of respectability, dignity, and happiness, which her extensive boundaries, great resources, and the enlightened and liberal ideas of her citizens, justly entitle her to.

1. This was the first of several newspaper "nominations" in Massachusetts newspapers. For the next such nomination, see the *Boston Gazette,* 25 August, printed below.

Christopher Gore to Rufus King, Boston, 10 August (excerpt)[1]

I sincerely congratulate you on the adoption of New York—which was the more pleasing as it was unexpected. Your friends are very desirous of your being in the administration of the new government—but are anxious as to your election, unless you are really an inhabitant of Massachusetts, previous to the time of electing. The Federalists are solicitous that you should be actually a resident in this commonwealth immediately. They wish for your aid and support in administering this Constitution, and very publicly say—you may choose your district—but are fearful that your remaining in New York will be urged as an objection. Unless your coming here is attended with real difficulties, I think the good of your country too loudly demands your removal this autumn, to leave a doubt in your mind. The candidates in this county [Suffolk] are [Charles] Jarvis, [Samuel A.] Otis, [Thomas] Dawes, and [William] Heath. I think Dawes the most likely to succeed, and as far as my little influence can weigh, it will add to his scale, unless there is a probability of our having you for the Representative of Suffolk—which I think is probable if you take your residence in Boston or the vicinity this fall. Let me pray you will consider this subject, and say to me what are your intentions and when they shall be brought into practice. Jarvis, [Benjamin] Hitchborn, and [James] Sullivan, it is said, are busy in attaining influence and votes for the former in serious hopes of introducing Han[cock] into the first seat of the general government. Whether this is the case I will not undertake to determine; but there are many circumstances which evidence a probability of such views in them.

1. RC, King Papers, NHi. Printed: King, *Life,* I, 341-42. Gore and King attended Harvard together and were lifelong friends. King had been elected to the Confederation Congress for the first time in November 1784 and was reelected in 1785 and 1786. After his marriage in March 1786 to the daughter of John Alsop, a wealthy New York merchant, he lived in New York. Gore and some other Federalists wanted King to represent the state in either the Senate or the House of Representatives, but there was evidently considerable opposition because of his "non-residence." Apparently the subject of buying a house came up when King was in Boston as a member of the Massachusetts Convention, for Gore wrote King on 13 February that a house was available and urged: "pray conclude the bargain, and be again a son of Massachusetts" (King, *Life,* I, 323). King returned to Boston in May but was back in New York about the first of August. Gore then resumed the correspondence about the purchase of a house (see also Gore to King, 30 August, printed below).

Gore, a lawyer, served in the Massachusetts Convention in 1788 and was elected to the state House of Representatives the same year. In 1789 he was appointed United States district attorney for Massachusetts. He lived in London from 1796 to 1804 as one of the commissioners provided for by the Jay Treaty. He was elected governor of Massachusetts in 1809 but was defeated by Elbridge Gerry in 1810 and again in 1811. He was a United States Senator from 1813 to 1816, when he retired from public life.

Henry Knox to Rufus King, Boston, 17 August[1]

I was mortified on my arrival here to find that you and Mrs. King had returned to New York.

The deep impressions you have made here on the minds of men are favorable to any political employment within the power of this state. But I learn with chagrin that some persons, whose views may be intercepted by your continuance here, have been but too successful in disseminating the idea that your apparent intentions of making this state your future residence were entirely delusive and calculated only for particular purposes.

You are too well acquainted with human nature to suffer this information to have any injurious effect on your mind.

My object and earnest desire is that you take the earliest measures to counteract the poison. You will be the best judge how this is to be effected.

Mr. [Nathaniel] Gorham's opinion and my own concur that you should instantly demonstrate your intentions either by purchasing or hiring an house in country or town. Mr. Gorham particularly wishes that it might be Lanes at Cambridge.

In any event of your determination, I am persuaded that you will receive this letter with that cordial friendship with which it is written. No person knows that I write but Mr. Gorham.

I neither expect or wish you to reply, as I shall set out for Penobscot in a day or two and shall be absent a month.

1. RC, King Papers, NHi.

Massachusetts Centinel, 20 August

We feel a little mortified in informing our readers, that by papers and letters received in the mails last evening, we learn, that the Convention of North-Carolina has rejected the Federal Constitution by a majority of 100. However, New-York rejected the proceedings, and Georgia refused to send delegates to the *first* Congress, and yet both these states, in two years afterwards, were among the foremost in zeal and activity in supporting the independence of the United States. N. Carolina and R. Island have been permitted to withdraw from the union, on purpose to shew the other States the miseries they have escaped, by adopting the government. An attachment to paper money and tender laws, appears in both those corrupted and deluded states, to be the cause of their opposition to the new constitution.

It were a circumstance rather of *hope* than *expectation*, that the Constitution would be adopted by all the States, in the *first Conventions* that should meet to deliberate and determine upon the important subject—the wisdom and discernment of our country, has however transcended the highest anticipations of the best and greatest patriots of America. Had NORTH-CAROLINA acceded to the union—the secession of RHODE-ISLAND would have left the senatorial ballance against the eastern States—but the *defection* of the former is a counterpoise to the *delinquency* of the latter. Thus in every stage of our political progress as a nation, the hand of Providence is conspicuously evident. The Federal Constitution must eventually appreciate in the minds of our brethren of North-Carolina, as well as those of Rhode-Island, and its final adoption by those States, upon every principle of sound policy, is inevitable.[1]

1. On 16 August the ardently Federalist *Massachusetts Centinel* published the New York Circular Letter calling for a second constitutional convention. In its next issue on 20 August it reprinted attacks on the New York Act of Ratification and the Circular Letter from the Philadelphia *Pennsylvania Gazette* of 6 and 13 August (printed in Newspaper Response to New York's Act of Ratification and Circular Letter of 26 July, Chapter II). On the 20th the *Centinel* also printed two reports of North Carolina's refusal to ratify, in addition to the above "editorial" by publisher Benjamin Russell. The section of the editorial declaring that Rhode Island and North Carolina refused to ratify because of their attachment to paper money and tender laws was copied without acknowledgment from an item in the *Pennsylvania Gazette* of 13 August.

The alarm created among Massachusetts Federalists by the news from New York and North Carolina is described in the following letter from Antifederalist James Winthrop to Antifederalist Mercy Warren: "We have had contradictory accounts from North Carolina. The last week Russell announced in his paper the rejection of the Constitution by a majority of 100 clear. He was so mortified that he could not help mentioning it three or four times in his paper. Now the story is that the Convention voted by that majority to amend the Constitution, and then adjourned to a distant day, and that they had not then heard of the accession of New York. It is impossible to describe the anxiety of the victorious party in this state upon hearing the first report. They immediately begun to vilify that state as being originally peopled by outlaws and convicts, who were driven from the more civilized parts of the world into the wilds of Carolina, where they had formed a settlement but little superior in morals to the infernal world" (Cambridge, 26 August, RC, Warren Papers, MHi).

Boston Gazette, 25 August

A Correspondent says, That the Hearts and the Eyes of the old sound Whigs, the early Revolutionalists, the Men of 1774 and 1775, will be *"turned as one Man,"* towards

The Hon. Samuel Adams, and } Esquires.
Elbridge Gerry,

For their two *Federal Senators*—and what endears them to us the more, is, the Objections against them from the other Side—that they are *Two obstinate Democratics*—therefore, *"we safely trust in them."*[1]

1. For an attack on this "nomination" see "Laco," *Massachusetts Centinel,* 27 August, printed below.

Hortensius, Massachusetts Centinel, 27 August

The general joy which has diffused throughout America, in consequence of the adoption of the new Constitution, is a striking proof of that philanthropic disposition, which has hitherto so eminently distinguished the enlightened patriots of America. Willing to relinquish whatever might be found necessary for the preservation of the whole, they have generously given up all local advantages, with a firm and determined resolution of supporting the Union, and establishing that friendship and reciprocity of interest, which cannot but contribute to the general welfare. Fears and apprehensions have arisen in the minds of some, from the powers vested in the general government by this Constitution. But these, if on trial they are found dangerous to our liberties, will doubtless be removed; for America has yet citizens who have wisdom and circumspection to discern them. But let us be cautious, lest those, who, under the mask of obtaining *amendments,* only wish for such alterations, erasements, or additions, as shall utterly destroy the fair fabric which has caused us so much labor and expense, should get into power, by our own election, to work our ruin. Our first and principal care ought to be, in being watchful of whom we trust, and to choose none but those who are undeniably friends to the rights of human nature. Friends to justice, public faith, and honor, who have adequate ideas of the *present state* of the continent, and stability enough to adopt, and to pursue, such measures as the exigencies of the times may require. Those who wish to preserve their liberty, ought to remember that their dignity, their honor and happiness, rests with those they appoint to represent them. And let the government be what it will, if the representatives are virtuous, the people may live happy. But when the citizens neglect this great and important privilege, and forget that they are freemen, designing men may step into authority—that predominant principle, interest, will most assuredly follow, and anarchy must be the natural consequence.[1]

1. Warnings against electing Antifederalists and the argument that those who demanded amendments really wanted to destroy the Constitution and would do so if elected were major themes in Federalist newspaper essays during the campaign. For examples in addition to the documents printed in this chapter, see the following essays in the *Massachusetts*

Centinel: "Laco," 30 August; "To Federal Electors," 10 September; "A Hint," 13 September; "A Federalist," 20 September; "Antilocalis," 27 December; and "An Elector," 24 January 1789. Additional essays by unidentified correspondents on the same theme are in the *Centinel,* 1, 5, and 8 November, and the *Herald of Freedom,* 15, 18 September, and 27 October.

Laco, Massachusetts Centinel, 27 August[1]

What would your patriots of '74 have said, had a writer in the papers of that era have recommended as persons worthy the choice of the freemen of Massachusetts, a THOMAS HUTCHINSON, and a TIMOTHY RUGGLES,[2] as members to represent them in the first American Congress? Let those answer the question who at this day recommend the appointment of the enemies of a plan of government, to be its guardians.

1. "Laco" was possibly Stephen Higginson, who used that pseudonym in a series of newspaper articles attacking John Hancock in February and March 1789. The articles were published in a pamphlet entitled *The Writings of Laco* (Boston, 1789), but the item printed here was not included (Thomas W. Higginson, *Life and Times of Stephen Higginson* [Boston, 1907], 125-38).
2. Thomas Hutchinson, the last royal governor of Massachusetts (except for General Thomas Gage), and his political ally, Timothy Ruggles, opposed independence and remained loyal to Great Britain.

The Response to Laco, 28 August–1 September

"Laco's" brief paragraph in the *Massachusetts Centinel,* 27 August (printed above), was immediately recognized as an attack on Samuel Adams and Elbridge Gerry, who had been nominated for the Senate in the *Boston Gazette* on 25 August (printed above). The day after "Laco's" attack, two replies appeared in the *Independent Chronicle* ("A Mechanic" and "A Friend to Amendments"), and on 1 September the *Boston Gazette,* a paper that had supported Adams and reflected his politics since the opening years of the American Revolution, printed two more denunciations of "Laco" ("Truth" and "A Republican"). The four replies to "Laco" are printed immediately below.

A Mechanic, Independent Chronicle, 28 August

The piece in yesterday's *Centinel,* designating a gentleman as an enemy to the Federal Constitution, whose signature has been affixed in approbation of it, discovers no less rancor to the object of its abuse, than it betrays a disposition to insult a large majority of the inhabitants of this town, who have lately proved their attachment to Mr. Adams, by their suffrages in his favor, when a candidate for the second office in the government; an office, by the way, out of which he was meanly intrigued by the subtlety of his pretended friends: among which number, we may most probably rank the incendiary Laco.[1] The unwearied malice of the opponents to this steady patriot, however, will be defeated by the zeal of those, who, in sustaining his pretensions, exhibit their own respect for the rights and freedom of the people. It is scarcely possible to conceive a degree of effrontery more detestable than that which gave rise to such infamous publications, and it has been with pleasure I find the authors so universally reprobated. Mr. Adams has his enemies, no doubt, but he has this consolation attending the reflection, that, generally speaking, his enemies are the enemies of liberty, of the Revolution, and of America.

A Friend to Amendments, Independent Chronicle, 28 August

A writer in the Centinel, under the signature of Laco, has given several specimens of his impertinence. His introducing the names of Hutchinson and Ruggles is supposed a reflection on Messrs. Adams and Gerry, recommended in Edes's paper for Senators of this state. The known patriotism of the former of these gentlemen can never be injured by any reflections thrown on him by certain timeserving busybodies, who are now anxious to introduce themselves and party into our new government, and who are eager to share the loaves and fishes among a few of their adherents.

It is not doubted the sentiments of the people will be united in such men as are known to be the friends to our country, independent of sinister motives, and who are advocates for amendments in our Federal Constitution, as a large and respectable majority of the states have earnestly recommended them.

A friend to amendments has now become the criterion of a Federalist, and none but a set of headstrong aristocratics, who will ever disregard the voice of the people, will endeavor to introduce those men into our new government, who are not strenuous advocates for amendments.

As the federal government guarantees a Republican form of government to the several states, it is presumed the people will be so prudent as not to choose any of that party, who already are attempting to destroy this form by recent publications.

Truth, Boston Gazette, 1 September

The distinguished effrontery of the writers, who have lately appeared in the Centinel, in placing the "early" and "decided" friends of the Revolution on the same footing with two of the most execrable traitors which the state of Massachusetts has produced, has met the resentment of the honest and respectable of every denomination. To mention a Gerry and an Adams in the same page with a Ruggles and a Hutchinson, as objects of comparison, is a profanation of freedom, and an insult upon every real whig in the community. The shuffling and contemptible Laco, that—but I forbear personalities, as I detest the authors of those infamous scurrilities with which some of our modern papers are crowded—personalities, Messrs. Edes, which were execrated as long as the open enemies and lukewarm friends of the Revolution were the objects of them, by the same persons who now read them with pleasure when the firmest, wisest, and most resolute supporters of this momentous event are the subjects of their infamous and accumulated slanders. I am sometimes led to question whether this town is the same, or whether its inhabitants or their principles are the same as they were, when the first effort of American heroism disclosed itself in the expulsion of the British regiments after the horrid massacre of our citizens. Would the people then tamely have submitted to the names of Hutchinson and Adams being insolently compared, in order that the reputation of this last and steady patriot should be infamously traduced. But *they* do not now; they feel the insult, and execrate the insidious attempt—to blast the long tried virtues of this hoary patriot, bending with age, venerable with cares, but firm in courage and persevering in his integrity; whose strong marked features denote the soul within—hated for his consistency—hated for the virtues which proclaim his fame and fix his immortality. Yet Laco says he is an enemy to the Federal Constitution, and surely Laco is an "honorable man"; so are they all "honorable" who are his open or concealed enemies, who basely mean to pierce the heart of liberty with a dagger when they appear merely to aim the stroke at the character of Adams.

It is very certain indeed that this sage and enlightened statesman has not "wholly" approved of the Constitution which is now the great political medium by which we are united, and under the influence of which we are to hope that our freedom will be secured and our commerce extended. But is Mr. Adams the only man who is in a similar predicament? Have the public testimonials of a Franklin, a Washington, a Jay, or a Hancock been expressive of the high approbation, of the blind idolatry with which many have affected to contemplate this fancied model of perfection—in saying it is the "greatest single effort of human wisdom"? Does the finished politician of Braintree [John Adams] declare that it is beyond the reach of amendments? Not a character of the first rank throughout America has pretended it.

Where then is the crime of doubting its superlative excellence, when the Convention, which formed the Constitution, declared it to be the result of compromise, and by no means the object of their entire approbation. To suppose the united wisdom of America, after a long and dispassionate enquiry, cannot improve upon the labor of thirty of her citizens, however respectable, is paying a very extravagant compliment to them, at the expense of the rest. Let us be wise and temperate; but in justice to him, let the citizens of Boston respect and revere the man, whose resolution has been invincible, and whose wisdom has been only equalled by his virtue.

A Republican, Boston Gazette, 1 September

The political scene is opened, the canvass is begun, in order to prepare the minds of an enlightened people for the choice of their federal legislators. Much depends upon the wisdom of the first choice. While the citizens of Massachusetts carefully guard against giving their suffrages for such as wish for an inefficient and feeble government, it is to be hoped, that equal caution will be observed towards those persons who are so ardently desirous of erecting a government of an arbitrary, oppressive, and tyrannical complexion. We have many of this last description of men among us; they are violently opposed to any alterations of the new Constitution in favor of the freedom of the people, while they secretly wish for alterations on the side of arbitrary power. But as three-fourths of the people are desirous of amendments not favorable to their views, they dare not hazard their principles in public, and content themselves at present in endeavoring to prevent the amendments already recommended, from being adopted. To effect this, they insist upon our trying the Constitution first, in order, they say, by that means to discover its defects, well knowing, if once put in motion under their administration, no amendments favorable to liberty will ever be obtained thereafter. These aristocratical tyrants are ever insulting and abusing the old patriots and true friends of our country, because they are not as despotically inclined as themselves, and also with the view of raising themselves upon their ruin. They compare the Honorable Mr. Adams with Governor Hutchinson and other traitors to our country. A republican is called a Shayite and a destroyer of all government, if he only wishes the adoption of one alteration recommended; although if it had not been for the expectation of amendments, the Constitution would have been rejected in this state, by a majority of more than two to one of our Convention. Thus notwithstanding it is the wish of the people that the alterations recommended should take place, these arbitrary aristocratics are perpetually scribbling in the little papers to induce the people to neglect the true patriots of our country, that themselves may be chosen into the federal legislature. How absurd and inconsistent will it appear, Messieurs Printers, after having recommended amendments, to elect such men to administer the federal government, as have publicly declared themselves opposed to all amendments which have been recommended? "But as we have hitherto been the care of Divine Providence, we have reason to hope, that our federal councils will be preserved from the direction" of *Recanting Tories*, *British Agents*, and *Aristocratical* and *Monarchical Tyrants*.

1. In the spring of 1788, Adams ran a poor third against Benjamin Lincoln and James Warren for the post of lieutenant governor. No candidate received a majority and the General Court chose Lincoln (Ralph V. Harlow, *Samuel Adams* ... [New York, 1923], 340-41).

Solon, Independent Chronicle, 28 August[1]

Fellow Countrymen and Citizens: Animated by those noble principles of *virtuous freedom*, which are the dignity of human nature, you spurned the idea of dependence and vassalage, asserted your rights, and, under the smiles of Heaven, to the wonder of an admiring world, established your *independence* and sovereignty.

Actuated by sentiments of wisdom and foresight, you have generally adopted a Federal Constitution, which is ere long to be put in practice, and to an eye of reason promises, if well administered, to *confirm* your independence and sovereignty, to render you prosperous and happy at home, and respected abroad. But it has been, and still is the opinion of many, that *certain amendments* are absolutely necessary to render the Constitution still more perfect, and to secure to you, and your posterity, under every administration, the blessings of that liberty you have so dearly purchased, and which it is the duty of enlightened freemen ever to provide. These considerations have induced me to address you at this time, and with all deference to interest, that you do not lose sight of the important object so highly interesting to yourselves and posterity. The amendments which have been proposed by the different state conventions are not local, they equally concern all the states; but whether all that have been mentioned are absolutely necessary is not for me to determine. But in some of them, there is such a general concurrence, that but little, if any doubt can remain of their eligibility. It is not improbable that there will be found some who do not wish for *any* amendments; or that any further *checks* should be provided, than are at present in the Constitution. But I assure myself, that a large majority of you think otherwise, and that you will not be diverted from proper and necessary endeavors to obtain the object by any animadversion, cant, or ridicule that may be thrown out on the subject. It is to be observed, that this is already beginning to discover itself. The Circular Letter from the Convention of New York has had the epithets of *impertinent* and *impudent* bestowed upon it, and probably more will be advanced, as the time draws near. If amendments are necessary, they *claim* an *early consideration*, and measures for the purpose merit your *first* attention. Will it be improper to hint, that in the choice of *Senators* and *Representatives*, this object among others naturally presents itself to your consideration, and that such *instructions* as may be necessary, be *seasonably prepared*; you have hitherto been the peculiar care of a kind Providence, may you, and your posterity after you, be a name and a praise among the nations of the earth, is the ardent wish of SOLON.

1. The article was addressed "to the Respectable Freemen of the United States of America." "A Federalist," in the *Massachusetts Centinel,* 30 August (printed below) implied that "Solon" was William Heath, a candidate for the House of Representatives. Three additional articles by "Solon" arguing for amendments to the Constitution appeared in the *Independent Chronicle,* 4, 25 September, and 30 October.

Christopher Gore to Rufus King, Boston, 30 August (excerpt)[1]

I did not receive your last favor[2] till some posts after it were due, owing to my absence from town. The subject of it is really interesting to me, and I have endeavored to see and converse with Mr. [Nathaniel] Goreham on the contents, but he is gone to the westward on his land purchase. Before the receipt of your letter, we did consult on the propriety of your taking some decisive steps which should evidence to the citizens of Massachusetts that you were really an inhabitant of this state. He was then fully of opinion that it was not only proper but absolutely necessary to the attainment of our wishes. And I assure you, my friend, the more information I attain, and the oftener I reflect on the subject, the more I am convinced of the necessity that you should fix your domicile in this commonwealth—the sooner, the better. Parties begin to run high. It is said the Governor [John Hancock] aims at the Presidency, and disdains a second seat. How far this is true you can determine as well as myself. It is said, and I believe with truth, that Mr. [John] Adams is desirous of being Vice President. The candidates for Senators are [James] Bowdoin, [Caleb] Strong, [Theodore] Sedgwick, [Samuel A.] Otis and yourself, and Sam Adams. The two first I presume would not willingly accede to the choice. Otis and Adams are not likely to be successful. Clearing up the question of inhabitants, I think the friends of the Constitution, and those who wish to see it administered with dignity, would be anxious to give you a decided choice, and that their wishes would be completely gratified. [John] Lowell declines going for this district, and I really believe [Thomas] Dawes the most likely candidate, but this is judging of what appears at present, and these appearances may greatly alter in future.

1. RC, King Papers, NHi. King endorsed the letter: "Answered: 6 September and requested him to purchase for me Cushing's house at 5000 dollars." For Gore's difficulties in purchasing John Cushing's mortgaged house and in persuading Cushing to move out, see

Gore to King, Boston, 14, 23, and 25 September; 5 and 12 October (RC, King Papers, NHi). Gore got possession of the house on 13 October, and King and his wife left New York for Boston on 17 October (John Alsop to Isaac Wharton, New York, 20 October, FC, Alsop Letterbook, NHi).

2. King's letter has not been located.

A Federalist, Massachusetts Centinel, 30 August

It is a well known fact, that the *"proposed amendments,"* as they are called, to the Federal Constitution, took their rise from a variety of causes, very few of which, if impartially considered, will be found *honest* or *praiseworthy*—so far as they were acceded to, by the *real patriots* of our country, the *prompt* and *speedy* advocates for an *unconditional* adoption of the Constitution, a laudable motive may be assigned—that of peace and conciliation.

Let us advert to the conduct of those who are now clamorers for introducing into the federal legislature the sticklers for *alterations* while they were members of the Convention. Particular reference is now had, to the writer whose signature is Solon, in last Thursday's *Chronicle*.[1] The conduct of this man has been uniformly such, both in the *field* and *legislature*, that he may with propriety be called the *doubting* general,[2] and the *doubting* politician. When the proceedings of the Grand Convention, in their excellent system, were first promulgated, the *vague, doubting,* and *inconclusive* lucubrations of this *doubting* statesman, upon the subject, saluted the public eye. Through some *fatality*, he obtained a seat in the state Convention, and there he added fresh laurels to his *doubting* character (see his very extraordinary declamation upon the subject without object, spirit, or decision—an *enemy* to, and an *advocate* for, the *same thing* in the *same speech*).[3] What good fruit can ever be expected from such a non-descriptive soil? While the die spun *doubtful*, this *doubting* orator fluttered upon the wings of uncertainty; but when he found a *clear vote* would be obtained for the adoption of this system, the friends of the Constitution were enabled, and *not before*, to count him in the affirmative. Can it be possible that such a character is ever actuated by *independent* principles? However capable of forming adequate ideas upon any subject, no credit is due to, nor can any reliance be placed upon, so equivocal a character. And yet astonishing as it may appear, THIS MAN is a candidate for a seat in the federal legislature. And what are the methods by which he is now trying to effect his purpose; are they manly, decisive, and patriotic? By no means. Under the appearance of contending for amendments, his design is to draw the public attention to *himself,* and some *other* characters, who, when in Convention, would have effected a total rejection of the Constitution, had not their *secret* machinations been counteracted by those *inflexible* and *able* patriots, who realized and demonstrated that our ALL was suspended on a decisive system of conduct.

Should the plan of this *chameleon* politician succeed; should we be so highly unfortunate as to have persons of *his kidney* introduced into the federal legislature, the blessed effects to be derived from the operation of the new government, which the people so justly and fondly anticipate, will in all probability be procrastinated to a period that shall exhaust the patience of the states;

and may be finally productive of that *despair, anarchy,* and *confusion,* from which we have but *just* escaped.

But, Mr. Russell, our FEDERAL REPRESENTATIVES are to be *instructed*—and such instructions are to be "seasonably prepared"! Blessed proposition! To say nothing of its absurdity, which neither the General himself, nor any of a *similar cut,* could reduce to a *consistent* idea. It has been thought that such a flagellation as *some folks* received from the pen of a very ingenious satirist, for his code of ready *"cut and dried"* instructions, respecting the "annihilation of the order," would have operated a *little* to prevent a like fruitless essay in future. It is devoutly to be wished that this *stepping stone* may fail, as it did on the above occasion. "And as we have hitherto been the care of a kind Providence," we have reason from that circumstance to hope, that our federal councils will be preserved from the direction of *shufflers, shifters, doubters,* and *timeserving politicians.*[4]

1. See "Solon," *Independent Chronicle,* 28 August, printed above.

2. "A Federalist" evidently thought that William Heath was "Solon." In January 1777, Heath, a major general in the Continental Army, had been ordered to secure the surrender or evacuation of the British garrison at Kingsbridge on the mainland across from the northern tip of Manhattan Island. He failed, and Washington reprimanded him in a public letter and virtually called him a coward in a private letter (to Heath, Morristown, N.J., 3, 4 February, Fitzpatrick, VII, 94-96, 99-100). From then until the end of the war Heath did not command troops in the field.

3. The comment about the "extraordinary declamation" is presumably a reference to Heath's speech in the Massachusetts Convention on 31 January, in which he proposed that the first members of Congress from Massachusetts be instructed to secure amendments to the Constitution (Convention, *Debates,* 222-24).

4. "A Correspondent" replied in the *Boston Gazette,* 1 September, that "Solon" had been a firm supporter of the colonial cause "previous to the Revolution, when such characters as the Federalist and his associates dared not risk their lives or fortunes." The General had, he continued, always been "decidedly in favor" of the Constitution, "although he saw some alterations necessary for the security of the people."

Steady, Massachusetts Centinel, 3 September

Among the candidates for appointments in the federal legislature, we may expect many who will make a *stalking horse* of the deceiving term *"amendments."* I shall notice at this time four different classes of these *seekers,* viz.: One description of them will by this device attempt to ingratiate themselves in the favor of many of the good people, whose fears of lurking mischiefs in the Constitution have been excited by the artful misrepresentation of these demagogues. These are totally inadequate in point of abilities to originating or sustaining any amendments, and therefore have no thoughts of exerting themselves to obtain them. Their object is to effect their OWN ELECTION.

Another class may be denominated self-opinionated *system mongers,* who can see no beauty or perfection in anything, but in their own fabrications.

A third class are those whose volatility of disposition leads them to fly from one thing to another, doubting, condemning, and approving by turns as occasion prompts.

But a fourth, and the most *dangerous* class, are those who are *inveterate enemies* to the system itself; it would not do for them *openly* to avow their sentiments—it being the general idea, that the Constitution is now fixed beyond the power of malice or false patriotism to affect its stability—but under the idea of being friendly to what are termed amendments, they mean to get into power, and when *once elected*, they will leave nothing unattempted that may tend to subvert the Constitution.

It is clearly evident that none of the foregoing characters can *consistently* receive the suffrages of the *real, decided* friends to the Constitution, or of their country.

If the Constitution is a *bad one*, let it be proved so by experience. If it is a *good one*, let us not choose men to deface and injure it, by *pretended amendments*.

If an ingenious artist had constructed a machine, upon the best principles, after *severe* investigation and labor, should we not consider him as a MAD MAN for making *alterations*, before he had made a trial to ascertain the goodness of his invention? We certainly should.

Massachusetts Centinel, 6 September

The legislature (thank God *they* choose the Senators) and the freemen of the county of Suffolk, in particular, will undoubtedly fix their eyes upon men of *real* federalism, *consistent, independent* characters, who have judgment to *discern*, and spirit to *pursue*, the best interests of their country. You will not find such men pledging themselves to *alter* the Constitution. The proposition is treason against the majesty of the people. It is their *own Constitution*, by a fairer and better title than any nation under Heaven can boast, having been conceded to in its *present form* by a greater proportion of the free citizens, than we can naturally suppose any alterations ever will, and therefore we may safely repeat, that unconditional promises to support and bring about alterations, previous to a *full trial* and experience of its competency to the great purposes of the Union, is TREASON AGAINST THE MAJESTY OF THE PEOPLE.[1]

1. This is the second of four paragraphs "From Correspondents." For a reply see "A Federal Correspondent," *Independent Chronicle,* 11 September, printed below.

Benjamin Lincoln to Theodore Sedgwick, Boston, 7 September (excerpt)[1]

We are anxious here that any reasons do exist which makes it indispensable to defer an organization of the new government to so late a period. We must, however, submit for there are so many circumstances constantly turning up and so many different interests to be reconciled that much time must be expended in adjusting them. We should, therefore, be quiet though it is difficult to keep all so.

I am sorry that North Carolina has rejected the Constitution. I cannot feel on the occasion as you do. I am very apprehensive (soldiers may have apprehensions, but no fears) that the Anties in Virginia will find aid and support by their brethren in North Carolina. Besides, I think it will have its influence in calling the convention proposed by New York. May Heaven avert the design. Rhode Island, that little trollop of a sister, will take support, be flattered in her wickedness, and encouraged in her obstinacy.

The General Court is prorogued to Wednesday the 29th of October, as it was not probable that the business could be well done in our session. November was thought to be the month which would best accommodate the members. I was of that opinion and think it probable that there will be then a short session. I hope you will attend it for a thousand reasons.

The matter as it relates to the Governor will probably remain as it now stands. He may not think it proper to be explicit. If he should not and suffer himself to be chosen Vice President and decline the trust it will mortify many.[2]

Truly we cannot think seriously of calling a [second] convention. It is a measure of all others to be dreaded. When you say we are pledged not to oppose, who do you mean by *we*. Not surely the *state* that must and, I think, will oppose and continue earnestly in support of the opposite side of the question. If this measure should take place I shall in that moment bid adieu to those pleasing prospects which I have embraced with so much real satisfaction for months past. Do not let us procrastinate. Let us begin as soon as possible to secure ourselves as far as we have proceeded. Would you not think it a very laughable circumstance should a number of gardeners in possession of the most valuable plants, plants necessary to be cultivated for the very existence of the proprietor, quarrel so long respecting that fruit of the garden in which they should be cultivated and so fiercely as to omit the care of them and in the meanwhile the goats should enter and devour them.

1. RC, Sedgwick Papers, MHi. Sedgwick, a Massachusetts delegate in Congress, had left New York before the letter arrived (see Sedgwick to Lincoln, 23 September, printed below).

2. The reference is to Governor John Hancock. For Hancock as a candidate for Vice President, see Chapter XIV.

Federalist to the Printers, Boston Gazette, 8 September

As you profess to be, and have always distinguished yourselves as, impartial Printers, it is expected you will publish the following.

It is too late in the day to effect any very important points by "great swelling words of vanity." Meer *assertions* without proof, and *declamations* without truth, or sentiment for their basis, are become too *trite* and *stale* to mislead the judgment, or impose upon the understandings of the free Electors of this metropolis.

It is an easy thing to disseminate doubts, and conjure up spectres to alarm the unwary—to talk of "Tyranny, Aristocracy, and Daggers in the heart of Liberty," without having *one rational* or *competent* idea upon either of the subjects. For evidence of this, let any dispassionate reader recur to the three speculations in your last.[1] These writers appear to be a *second edition* of the Aristocratick Croakers of '86 and '87—without any additions or amendments.—What, Messrs. Edes, are the *same ideas*, so far as they have any, the *same words* and phrases *always* to *serve* their [own?]? Let the subject be what it will, "Aristocracy, *Tories, British Agents, Small Party,*" form in gross [———] the great Volume of their Essays. Can such Trumpery amuse or instruct the people? Can there possibly be any tastes so vitiated, as to find musick in such Jargon?

These are days of free enquiry, Messrs. Printers—and to strip such false Patriots of their disguises, and expose their nakedness, barrenness, and wickedness, should be the duty of all who love the *peace,* the honor, and the prosperity of their Country.

Thank God, the people of this metropolis are truly *Federal. Federalism* is their polar Star; but these Croakers of Aristocracy, these Sticklers for Amendments to the Constitution, what are *they?* Let a candid retrospect of their conduct declare; not one of them, but what would have rejected the Constitution, if they had possessed the power so to do. —And now, forsooth since we have obtained a Constitution, maugre all their opposition, they have the assurance to put in their claim to be Repairers, Patchers, Alteration Mongers, and finally, *Lords-Directors* of the Federal Government. As it is certain, that the *good offices* of these people would, if successful, have *lost us* the Constitution. The truly Federal Spirit of Massachusetts, and of this *Town* and *Country,* in particular, will effectually prevent such Mar Plots from being the objects of their suffrages for the Federal Government.

1. See "A Republican" and "Truth," *Boston Gazette,* 1 September, printed above.

A Federal Correspondent, Independent Chronicle, 11 September

A *federal* correspondent observes, that howsoever a *correspondent* of the *Centinel* of Saturday last[1] may amuse himself with air, *"thin air,"* the *enlightened* freemen of the United States of America are not so destitute of *common sense,* as not to *see* and *laugh* at any suggestions, direct or implied, that *convey* an *idea,* that it is treason against themselves, to *propose,* and *endeavor* to obtain, in the *constitutional* way, *necessary amendments,* to their *own* Constitution; *"treason against the majesty of the people"* lies on the *other* hand. The *people* of this *commonwealth,* in *particular,* by their *very respectable Convention,* in *February* last, at the ratification of the Federal Constitution, after stating sundry amendments, then enumerated, did, "In the name and in the behalf of the people of this Commonwealth, enjoin it upon their Representatives in Congress, at all times, until the alterations and provisions aforesaid, have been considered, agreeably to the fifth article of the said Constitution, to exert all their influence, and use all reasonable and legal methods to obtain a ratification of the said alterations and provisions, in such manner, as is provided in the said article."[2]

Is it then, this correspondent asks, the *holding* up the *propriety* and *importance,* of *obtaining,* if *possible,* this *enjoined* object of the people; or *sentiments, advanced* in *opposition* to *it,* that *exhibits most,* the complexion of TREASON AGAINST THE MAJESTY OF THE PEOPLE. Of this the enlightened people are fully competent to determine for themselves. But not only the Convention of this commonwealth, but those of several other states (the whole included, being entitled, as fixed by the Constitution, to a majority of Representatives, of those states which have adopted the system) have likewise proposed amendments. And it is highly probable, that if the mode of first adopting the Constitution, and then proposing amendments, had been at first thought of, all the ratifying states, would have pursued nearly the same line of conduct. The *freemen* of *these states*, have a *foresight* to discern, that their liberties *may* be in *danger*, although *not* attacked, if an *avenue* is left open, *through* which they may, at *some future time*, *be* attacked; they will, therefore, naturally be anxious, that any *aperture* in the *barrier* between *powers delegated* and *retained*, be *closed, explicitly defined*, and well understood. To leave matters to a *full trial* of experience, as *some* are *urging*, may perhaps be compared to the loaning a man's money, *untold* and without *proper security* for the payment thereof, in order to *ascertain* his *honor* and *honesty;* or to neglect to *repair* a *breach* in the walls of a city liable to be besieged, in order to discover whether the assailants *would* avail *themselves* of the advantage *offered* them. The *loss* of property, however, in the one case, and a *lodgment gained behind the breach*, in the other, would render *after* precaution *unavailable*.[3]

1. See *Massachusetts Centinel,* 6 September, printed above. For another attack on the *Centinel* article, see "A True Federal Correspondent," *Independent Chronicle,* 11 September.
2. Convention, *Debates,* 84-85.
3. For a reply see "A Federalist," *Massachusetts Centinel,* 20 September.

Executive Council Proceedings, Friday, 19 September[1]

His Excellency communicated a letter from the Honorable Mr. [Nathan] Dane inclosing a resolution of Congress for putting the Constitution determined upon by the United States into operation[2] and requested the Council to consider the expediency of a further prorogation of the General Court. The Council having read the letter and resolution of Congress and considered the expediency of further proroguing the Court,[3] thereupon advised that it would be inexpedient that the Court should be prorogued to a further time. His Excellency being made acquainted with the above advice was pleased to adjourn the Council to Friday the twenty-fourth of October next, and the Secretary adjourned them accordingly.

1. Council Records, XXX, 394-95, M-Ar.
2. On 14 September Dane wrote to Governor John Hancock from New York enclosing a copy of the Election Ordinance for the Governor's private information (Dane to Hancock, printed, Chapter II). Hancock evidently did not wait to receive an official copy of the Ordinance from Charles Thomson but consulted the Council after receiving Dane's letter. Thomson's letter of 13 September and the official copy of the Ordinance are in Miscellaneous Legislative Documents, House Files, M-Ar, but are without endorsement indicating the date received.
3. On 9 September Hancock had prorogued the legislature from 8 to 29 October.

Theodore Sedgwick to Benjamin Lincoln, Springfield, 23 September (excerpt)[1]

Your favor of the 7th arrived in New York just after I left it on my return home, and I have now met it here.

I wish to be understood in regard to what I said with respect to the obligation we are under not to oppose the meeting of a convention. You remember that attendant in the form of our ratification was an instruction to our delegates hereafter to be appointed to use their influence to procure the amendments we proposed. My meaning was that we, the Federal members of the Convention, would do nothing in contradiction of that act. At the same time I am fully in opinion that a convention called at any period not far distant would probably defeat every beneficial effect to be expected from the un[ob]structed operation of the system. It is therefore my opinion that the business should rest on the natural effort and the vote of our Convention and the character of our members so far as respects the agency of Massachusetts.

There were certainly very powerful reasons against convening the government at Philadelphia, that shall be the subject of a conversation when I have the pleasure to see you.

I should be sorry that the General Court should convene at the time to which it now stands prorogued [29 October].[2] The General Court will, I suppose, be disposed to choose the Electors themselves. From the 29th of October until the time appointed for that purpose will be a longer period than the members will choose to continue together. To adjourn for a short period will give a slender representation. It is of importance that the members, with as little inconvenience as possible, should have it in their power generally to attend. Besides the last of October is an inconvenient season for farmers to leave their domestic concerns. But should the General Court be further prorogued until the first of December, the season will be convenient. The whole business of the year can be completed. This will naturally extend the session into January. The attendance will be general and good humor most likely to prevail. Pardon, my dear sir, my thus interfering in the executive.[3]

I hope that every prudent precaution will be taken to [secure?] a good federal representation. The amendment mongers, I trust in Heaven, will be universally excluded. The danger is not that the first operations of the new government will be too rigorous, but too cautious and timid. Nothing however, I hope, will in any part of the state be ultimately decided on until the legislature meets, when characters will be duly balanced.

1. RC, Lincoln Papers, MHi.
2. On 18 July Sedgwick had written to Governor John Hancock urging him to prorogue the meeting of the legislature until the end of October (printed above).
3. Lincoln had been elected lieutenant governor in May 1788.

Jeremiah Hill to George Thacher, Biddeford, 25 September (excerpt)[1]

Congress having unanimously fixed on a place for the new-Congress to convene at, electioneering follows of course, and *mode* is the first thing.

The Democratical Scale is, "the House of Representatives shall be composed of members chosen every second Year by *the people* of the several States," and this Mode, "shall be prescribed in each State by the Legislature thereof"—and as you wish to know the Sentiments of the people here upon this Subject, I will, (errors excepted) endeavor to state them.

Let this State be divided into eight Districts as equal as circumstances will admit—suppose the three eastern Counties to be one District at present. let each Town meet in their respective Towns on an appointed day, & give in their votes in writing, to some body appointed to receive them. let them be sorted & counted & sealed up in the same manner we now choose Senators to the general Court. let the Town then choose a Delegate to meet in District Convention some where in the Center of the District & commit the Towns choice to him with their Instructions (if they see cause to instruct) every Town in the District doing the same, every choise will be convened in the place assigned for said Convention to meet at. these Delegates being duly arranged *de Legibus conventionis* let there votes by the returns from each Town be opened, sorted, & counted: if there appears to be a majority for any one Man, all is well, if not Let these delagates select the *three* highest & by ballot choose one of those *three* to be the Representative—this, they say, will be the nearest the Choise of the people the Circumstances of the Case will admit of, in a reasonable way of reasoning, because, say they, if the Genl. Court should select, when the people are divided, the other Districts in the State will have a voice in saying who shall represent this District &c—besides, they say, it will be throwing a part of the Democratical weight into the Aristocratical Scale, which may in time endanger the nation or rather the Government, & further that every precaution ought to be taken to keep every branch as distinct as possible from each other, while they are as dependent on each other as they are distinct—if any thing here is worthy—may it make a lasting impression on your mind, if you have any illaminations *blaze* them out, they shall be duly noticed by, your Friend.

. . . .

[P.S.] If I had Room in my sheat I would write a short Postscript, and tell you, that I had the Honor & Pleasure of dining yesterday on Roast Beef (Septr. 25) with Mr. G Thatcher &c. in Company with Bro. Cobb & Dr. Porter & chatted over our old roast meat Stories. in turn brought in our friend George & other Acquaintances, talked over congressional Matters, rectified some Mistakes of the general Court, appointed Electors, made choice of a President, Senators & established a mode for choosing Representatives. and I believe in my Soul if the roast beef had not been brought on in ten Minutes we should have compleatly organised the new Congress but the roast Beef, a Glass of Grog & small Beer commanded our Attention another way. Sammy paid great Attention, not only to the roast Beef, but to the soldierlike Appearance of the Company in exercising their Knives & forks. Sammy wished his papa was there, Sally shewed her full Approbation of the several Manoeuvres as well as of the agreeable Conversation which displayed itself in her little risable muscles, & her Mama called her a little dear honey.

1. RC, Thacher Papers, MHi. The original capitalization and spelling of this letter have been retained.

Constitution, Massachusetts Centinel, 1 October

It appears by the Southern papers that the Antifederal junto of Pennsylvania are at their old game [a] gain. Notwithstanding they *profess* to be *Federal* in their late publications, yet by carefully attending to names, we shall find they are the *same set* that opposed the adoption of the Constitution, "and can the Ethiopian change his skin, etc."[1]

There is a select number of similar geniuses in this commonwealth, who never knew what would suit them. When we were destitute of a federal government, and all our continental concerns were at *"loose ends,"* these persons would talk of the necessity of giving powers to Congress, but when the impost was proposed and voted by a majority of the states, oh then we were going to sacrifice our liberties forsooth, and by the utmost *wit* and *cunning* the measure was finally defeated. When the Federal Constitution came upon the carpet, they exerted themselves to nip it in the bud, but THE PEOPLE said they *would* have it adopted, and adopted it was; for they would confide in lying prophets no longer. At present these *Antifederal anarchiads* are trying a new maneuver and under the specious, delusive idea of *amendments* or *alterations* to the federal system, they intend to embarrass the operation of the continental government. *Charity* itself cannot think more favorably of a set of men, let them pretend what they will, who have done nothing but throw impediments in the way, and hang as dead weights upon the business of forwarding the CONSTITUTION.

1. The article presumably refers to the members of Pennsylvania's Harrisburg Convention (see Proceedings, 3-6 September, printed, Chapter IV). Although "Constitution" read the proceedings in one of the "Southern papers" (probably a New York or Philadelphia newspaper), the *Massachusetts Gazette* published them on 26 September. For another essay critical of the Harrisburg Convention, see "Federal Commonwealth," *Massachusetts Centinel,* 27 September.

Debate Over the Mode of Choosing Electors, 1-8 October

The method of electing presidential Electors was a major issue in Massachusetts. Before the legislature assembled on 29 October, newspapers printed articles arguing for popular election and for election by the legislature. The three items printed below present arguments for both methods.

Massachusetts Centinel, 1 October

On the Question,
Whether the Electors of the President are to be chosen by the state legislatures, or by the people of the several states.

The new government is altogether national in regard to its *operation* because it operates upon the people in their *individual* capacities, which seems to be one obvious reason why the people themselves, as individuals, should be concerned as much as possible in the appointment of the President, who is emphatically their great representative. To borrow an idea from the address prefixed to the Massachusetts state constitution, the very reason given for authorizing the governor to object to and revise the laws is because he is the representative of the whole people, being chosen by the people at large.[1] Now as the President of the United States has a similar authority, it seems reasonable that he should be chosen as nearly in the same way as the nature of things will permit. And though from the vastness of the continent, and the number of its inhabitants, it would be almost impossible to appoint the President at large, yet the people of each state may choose Electors at large, who may appoint the President, which is the next best mode, and as near as the nature of things will admit.

Again, as the people at large choose the Representatives only for two years, and as the several bodies politic choose the Senators for six years, which seems to be a strong check upon the democratic branch, perhaps the people will better preserve their balance by choosing Electors for the special and immediate purpose of appointing the President.

If it is asked, do not the people at large choose their state representatives, and may not *they* appoint the Electors, I would answer that there are two objections made: 1st., it is one remove further from the people than if the Electors were chosen by the people; and 2d., it would be very bad policy to oblige the people to choose such representatives to the state assembly as would always appoint Electors agreeable to the people. If the state legislatures are to appoint the Electors, the people must either send such deputies as will appoint the proper Electors, or the people must have no voice at all in the appointment. And if they do choose such deputies as will answer that purpose, they may sacrifice many other benefits in the choice of their deputies; for a man may be a very excellent representative to make laws, and yet not be favorable to the appointment of the same Electors whom the people themselves would elect. The people themselves had better appoint the Electors for the special purpose of choosing such a President as they themselves like; and when they choose their own state representatives, they will choose such men as they think will make the best laws, and not such as perhaps may have no other quality than that of agreeing with the people in the choice of a President.

A third reason why it would be improper for the General Court to choose the Electors is, because that mode would be more liable to the cabals and artifices of any popular man who wanted to be President; for the General Court being of a whole year's standing, there would be much time given for making an interest among the members, whereas no such interest could be made among the Electors, as it is impossible to foresee who the people are to choose. And this seems to be the object of the Constitution, in directing that all the Electors shall sit on the same day, so as to make it impossible for any communications of runners between.

A Citizen of Essex, Salem Mercury, 7 October

Hearing, the other day, that it had become a question with some, whether the Electors, mentioned in our Federal Constitution, could be appointed by the legislatures of each state, I was a little surprised, that no doubt had ever occurred to my mind, in reading the Constitution, on that subject; since which, I have attended a little more particularly to it, and must confess, that to me the case is so plain, that it will not, in a liberal construction, admit of any ambiguity. "Each State shall appoint, in such a manner as the Legislature thereof may direct, a number of Electors, equal to the whole number of Senators and Representatives to which the state may be entitled in the Congress, etc."

I suppose the word, *state,* as used in the foregoing sentence, is by some thought to mean the people at large, inhabiting a territory, in distinction from the legislature thereof; and thence infer, that the authority of the legislature extends only to the prescribing the mode, or manner, whereby the people may make the appointment; whereas, to me, the words, "each state," appear to be used only as a summary mode of expression, and it is the same as though the Constitution had said, New Hampshire, Massachusetts, etc., shall respectively appoint, etc., thus leaving it entirely optional for the appointment to be made by the legislature or the people, as may best suit their convenience. I think, by the late resolution of Congress, it is pretty evidently the sense of that honorable body, that the appointments might be made by the legislatures, and that they expected they would be now so made;[2] and indeed the times, which they have fixed on for that purpose, and the subsequent meeting for the choice of a President, render any other mode, in our local situation, almost impracticable. No one, I conceive, will imagine, if the appointment is to be made by the people, that, from the first Wednesday in January to the first Wednesday in February, the time is sufficient for the votes of the distant counties in this commonwealth to be returned into the secretary's office, in order to ascertain the elections; for the persons chosen then to be notified of their appointment, and afterwards to journey to Boston, for the assembling themselves together for the choice of a President.

If the ideas I have suggested are just, it follows that our legislature must be in session the first Wednesday of January. And I humbly hope, in order that the present legislature may maintain its character of economy, that His Excellency the Governor may see fit still further to adjourn the Court, so that they may be together on the aforementioned day, without the great expense of a tedious and lengthy session.

Massachusetts Centinel, 8 October

It is evident, says a correspondent, that Congress construe the Constitution, that the legislatures of the several states, not the people, are to choose the Electors, as that body has ordered the choice of said Electors to be on the first Wednesday of January, and their meeting for the choice of President, in four weeks after. For, if the people, as hath been asserted, are to choose the Electors, is it possible, that in the large states of Virginia, Massachusetts, etc., the returns can be made of the choice, notice given to the persons chosen, and the persons thus chosen have time to meet together, in the short space of one month? No—it is impossible, and can only be remedied by the legislatures, who, in fact, are *"the states"* making the choice.[3]

1. See "An address of the [Massachusetts] Constitutional Convention, to their Constituents, 1780": "The Governor is emphatically the Representative of the whole People, being chosen not by the Town or County, but by the People at large. We have therefore thought it safest to rest this Power [the veto] in his hands . . ." (Robert J. Taylor, ed., *Massachusetts, Colony to Commonwealth: Documents on the Formation of its Constitution, 1775-1780* [Chapel Hill, 1961], 125-26).

2. The Election Ordinance of 13 September does not support this statement.

3. The newspaper discussion concerning Electors continued with an ambiguous essay in

the *Herald of Freedom,* 10 November. It opposed election by the legislature but concluded that if "the united wisdom of our General Court determine that the Senate and Representatives shall by joint ballot appoint the Electors, our doubts respecting the propriety of such a measure will be hushed to silence."

Alfred I, Massachusetts Spy, 2 October (excerpt)[1]

The time, and place, for the meeting of Congress under the Federal Constitution, are at length established.

It is not of so much importance to the public, who shall appear as Senators and Representatives, as what measures that august assembly shall adopt when they meet in their first session: *At that session* our national concerns will receive a deep impression, and our tender political frame, like that of a young animal, will then, either have those careful and prudent touches which will give uniformity and perfection to all its limbs and features, or attach disproportion to its members, and distortion to its countenance.

The obstinate virulence of party scribblers, the abusive declamation of candidates for places and pensions, and the mistaken zeal of those, who, without inquiry, conceive everything to be stamped with perfection, which has the approbation of certain great characters, seem to be an obstacle to all free and judicious inquiry, in matters of the highest moment to the people and to posterity. But the real friend to his country, the man who loves her freedom, and delights in her happiness, will still pursue the great object of his attention, and, regardless of the illiberal shafts of party rage, or the unprovoked arrows of mistaken zealots, will still point his countrymen to the path of public security.

That a Federal Constitution has long been necessary to the safety of the Union, is well agreed, on all hands. That the present is a very good one, and that it reflects great honor upon the Convention which compiled it, will be acknowledged by all who regard their own reputation. But the idea, that it is a good Constitution, and is without blemishes, because a Franklin and Washington, with other great men, composed the Convention, is too contemptible for the American state of information. We examine into the nature and tendency of systems, before we decide upon them. The education of our country is too liberal to suffer us to be fascinated with the charm of names. We view each proportion with a philosophic eye; and the body of our people, though incapable of exposing their sentiments, in an elegant and pleasing language, decide at all times, where they have opportunity to deliberate, with wisdom and ability.

1. The author of "Alfred" is unknown, although the person who sent the second "Alfred" essay to the Providence *United States Chronicle,* where it was reprinted on 20 November, noted that it was "said to be written by Caleb Strong, Esq., a candidate for Senator to represent the state of Massachusetts in the new government." Strong was elected a Senator on 22 November. An attack on "Alfred" I by "Publius" (*Independent Chronicle,* 16 October) suggested that the author was also the author of "Solon" (*Independent Chronicle,* 25 September, printed above). For a defense of "Alfred" I, see "An Impartial Observer," *Independent Chronicle,* 23 October.

Two more "Alfred" essays were published during the campaign. "Alfred" II appeared in the *Massachusetts Spy,* 16 October. It argued that the Constitution granted Congress "a discretionary, undefined, and unlimited authority" and concluded that amendments were necessary to secure the rights and liberties of the people. "Alfred" III appeared in the *Massachusetts Spy* on 23 October. It argued that the amendments proposed by the Massachusetts Convention were necessary and urged voters to support men committed to obtaining them. Each of the "Alfred" essays was reprinted at least three times (see the *Massachusetts Gazette*, 7, 18 October; *Independent Chronicle*, 9, 30 October; *Hampshire Gazette*, 29 October; *Cumberland Gazette*, 6, 20 November; Philadelphia *Independent Gazetteer*, 20 November, 6 December; and Providence *United States Chronicle*, 20 November).

District vs. Statewide Election of Representatives, 22 October–5 November

The question of whether Massachusetts should be divided into districts for the election of Representatives, or have a statewide election, did not become a subject of public discussion until shortly before the legislature reassembled on 29 October. The article by "Numa" in the Philadelphia *Pennsylvania Gazette,* 16 July, arguing for statewide elections (printed, Chapter IV), was reprinted in the *Massachusetts Centinel,* 23 July. It was reprinted without the signature "Numa" in the *Boston Gazette,* 29 September, and the *Independent Chronicle,* 2 October. The publication in the latter paper was followed by a request from "One of the People" in the *Chronicle* on 9 October for a fuller explanation. "One of the People" assumed that the article had originated in Massachusetts.

The four newspaper articles printed below state both sides of the question. Although there was considerable disagreement about the makeup of districts and the number of Representatives to be allotted to various sections of the state, the legislature approved the idea of district elections from the beginning.

Real Farmer, Hampshire Chronicle, 22 October

The time is now approaching when the new government is to be organized and put into operation in the United States of America. The Constitution has been adopted by the conventions of more than nine states. In several of those conventions, the members have been nearly equally divided. In most of them, a number of amendments have been resolved upon as highly expedient for securing the liberties and welfare of the people, on the one hand, and for preventing the baneful effects of the abuse of power, on the other. In a situation thus critical, it is ardently to be wished, if not confidently expected, that the legislatures in the several states, and the people at large, may proceed in the organization of this government with the highest degree of candor, prudence, and sagacity. In transacting this all-important business, violent parties and venal measures would, probably, produce a corrupt and violent administration of government.

A diversity of interests subsists among the citizens in every state. In order that those interests should be equally secured, it is undeniably necessary that they should be equally represented in that government, to the support of which they are equally held to contribute, and on which they equally depend for protection. The *mercantile* interest may be *nominally* represented by men who are in the *landed* interest; and *vice versa.* But it would be idle to expect, either the one or the other to be *really* represented by any, unless by those whose interests, whose feelings, and whose views, are the same with those whose nominal representatives they are. "The end to be aimed at," says an eminent writer, "in the formation of a representative assembly, seems to be the sense of the people, the public voice: *The perfection of the portrait consists in its likeness.*" A mere nominal representation is of but little advantage. To be entirely unrepresented is more eligible, perhaps, than to be represented by those whose interests, feelings, and views are very diverse from those of their constituents.

The *landed,* is the great, the important interest of this country; and therefore it demands the most careful and particular attention. On the flourishing of this interest, as I conceive, eventually depends, not only the wealth, but the liberties and happiness of the nation. At the same time, this interest, of all others, seems to be the most straitened and distressed. I believe it is found that the liberties of a people have generally vanished, nearly in the same proportion as their landed interest has been depressed. And for this there is a cause, as truly natural, as for any effect whatever. For the sake of the public at large, it is therefore most ardently to be desired, that in the new government, especially when it first begins to operate, the landed interest may be, not only nominally and fully, but *really* represented. The importance of this idea is still enhanced from a consideration that the landed interest is exposed to public burdens vastly beyond any other interest. It is an interest which cannot be concealed, and is *legally* exposed to a congressional, or national, tax, equally with the mercantile interest. It is, at the same time, almost the only permanent resource for paying the debts, or defraying the internal expenses of the individual states.

In order that an equal and *real* representation may, in any measure, be secured, it seems to be necessary that the travel to elections should be rendered as short as may be, and that the circles or districts, in which Representatives shall be chosen, should be as small as the nature of the case, and the Constitution, will admit of. By this means, the citizens will more generally know, and be known by, their Representatives. And this I take to be an object worthy of more attention than at first sight some may imagine.

That the various classes of citizens may be *really* represented in a government, firm as Mount Zion, gentle and mild; that every department thereof may be filled with men of virtue, moderation, and discernment; and the great body of the people feel themselves free, happy and safe, is the ardent wish of a REAL FARMER.

Massachusetts Centinel, 1 November

The method of choosing *federal Representatives* by *districts* is justly to be deprecated, inasmuch as it will deprive the people, in a great degree, of the opportunity of electing such characters as *they* may think are the most *competent.*

On the plan of choosing *federal Representatives* at *large,* the pernicious acts of caballing and influencing will be avoided and the best chance afforded of obtaining the *best men* and *the best abilities.*

Honorius, Herald of Freedom, 3 November

That plan of electing our federal Representatives, which affords the *fairest chance* of selecting the *best* and most *competent* characters *through the commonwealth,* ought in all reason to be preferred and adopted; this sentiment will readily be admitted by all *honest men*; and there is no doubt but the method adopted by some of the states, of electing them *at large,* has the advantage of all others. This plan will naturally expand the views of every ELECTOR; for not being confined to any particular *district,* for one man, but having the superior privilege of giving his vote for the WHOLE NUMBER, his inquisitive and patriotic mind will be on the stretch to do honor to his choice, and benefit his country, by giving his suffrage not merely for his own townsman, but for the man of abilities, honor, and integrity, wherever he may reside, and whatever may be his rank or profession in life. Upon this system, that bane of our country in times past, *local prejudice,* is much more likely to lose its pernicious influence, and men of *narrow, partial,* and *incompetent* understandings will be defeated in their cabals, and miss an election; an event devoutly to be wished by all who feel for the reputation of this commonwealth.

This system is a truly FEDERAL ONE, congenial to the *spirit* and *meaning* of the Constitution; it gives every elector an EIGHT-FOLD CONSEQUENCE; it makes *every one* an active agent in the organization of the federal government; it enhances the importance of the duty which every elector will have to perform, and consequently will inspire a deep sense of the necessity of doing it well. It likewise has a happy tendency to *nationalize* the citizens, and to blend the interests of *towns, districts, counties,* and the *whole commonwealth,* into one *great* and *general* concern; and hence, by an easy and natural transition, to feel the intimate connection and dependence of the great interest of the *United States* with, and upon, that of the *individual* governments. Every real Federalist must be decidedly in favor of those measures that bear the strongest impression of federal features—for whatever plan has a tendency to *socialize* the citizens, to *obliterate jealousies* and *unreasonable local attachments,* to counteract the arts and intrigues of unprincipled men, whose hope is confusion. I say, whatever system is calculated to effect these salutary purposes, must meet the approbation, and find the steady support of the wise, the good, the federal patriots of our country. This is so evidently the case with respect to electing our *federal Representatives* AT LARGE, that it can hardly be supposed that our honored fathers, the legislature of this commonwealth, will think of, or propose any other.

Real Farmer, Hampshire Chronicle, 5 November

Be pleased to insert the following in the *Hampshire Chronicle.*

> LIBERTY is best secured, where the legislative power is lodged in several persons, especially if these persons are of different ranks and interest. For where they are of the same rank, and consequently have an interest to manage peculiar to that rank, it differs but little from a despotical government in a single person. But the greatest security a people can have for their liberty is, when there is no part of the people that has a common interest with at least one part of the legislators.

SPECTATOR

Agreeable to the Federal Constitution, the Representatives in Congress are to be chosen by the people. The legislatures in the several states are, in the first instance, to *prescribe the times, places, and manner of holding the elections.* It is a matter exceedingly important in government, that the great body of the people should be *equally* and *really* represented. It is therefore a matter of no less importance, that in fixing the times, places, and manner, of holding elections, the most effectual provision should be made for securing such representation. In almost every government that has yet been established, the want of an *equal* and *real* representation of the people has, probably, been a principal cause of the rapid, or more gradual and imperceptible loss of their liberty, till in process of time, the *many* have become the real slaves of a *few*. To the want of an *equal* and *real* representation of the people, we are, in a great measure, to attribute that tyranny and oppression under which the world, in every age, has groaned.

The expediency of elections being made by districts will, I believe, be almost universally conceded by candid and distinguished men.

Should they be made at large through a state, situate like that of Massachusetts and some others in the Union, and the highest number of votes, in the first instance of voting, determine the election of a Representative, a few seaport towns might, and probably would, choose the whole number of Representatives for the state. The consequence of this to the landed interest must be too obvious to require a single remark.

Provided the election should be made by *districts,* and the highest number of votes should, in every instance, determine the election of a Representative, it might, and would frequently happen, that such choice would be made by not more than one-third, or one-fourth part of the whole number of actual voters. The local situation of people in the country is such as precludes their agreeing together in what point to center their votes. A gentleman therefore in some particular line of business, whose family or other connections are extensive, and whose interest and views are very diverse from those of the body of the people, by securing a small number of votes in various parts of the district, may obtain the highest number of any one person; and at the same time, be most obnoxious to three-fourths of the actual voters. Should the elections in general be finally carried in this manner (as in many, if not in most cases, they probably will be in the first instance of voting) the following effects will naturally take place. The people will not be *really* represented. Hence, they will be in eminent danger of being cruelly oppressed. They will place no confidence in the administration, consequently the government must be weak, as it respects national protection and defense; and instead of deriving a voluntary and firm support from the affection of the people, must be supported by the mere dint of military force.

The following outlines of a scheme of election, are humbly suggested to the consideration of those by whom this important business is to be adjusted.

Let a state be divided into as many districts as there are Representatives to be chosen in a state. Let the inhabitants of each town, qualified according to the Constitution, to vote for a Representative, meet in their respective towns, and give in their votes for a Representative in the same district. Let these votes be sealed up and sent to a certain office to be instituted for that purpose. In this office, let them be opened, sorted, and counted; and if no one person shall be found to have a majority of the whole number of votes, in that case, let the names of a certain number (say four) who shall stand highest in the nomination, be returned to the several towns in the district, and let the inhabitants, qualified as aforesaid, be again called upon to meet, and out of the number thus returned, to choose one Representative. And if on a second return to the said office, no one person shall be found to have a majority of the whole number of votes, let the person who shall then be found to have the highest number, be the person elected. If on a second return, any two or more persons, who stand highest in the nomination, should be found to have an equal number of votes, let the process, so far as it respects them, be again repeated. By thus repeating the process, I am sensible, an additional expense will be incurred. But this additional expense will be of no weight, when compared to an *equal* and *real* representation of the people.

After all that is said, no provision that can possibly be made by law for an *equal* and *real* representation will be of any avail, unless the people themselves are vigilant and wise enough to unite their suffrages in favor of virtuous and discerning men, and men whose interests and views are the same with those of their constituents at large.

That our government may be firm, equal, and mild, is the fervent wish of a REAL FARMER.

Herald of Freedom, 27 October

The Honorable James Bowdoin and the Honorable John Adams, esquires, it is said, are talked of as Senators from this state, to the new federal Congress. Should our wise legislature, observes a correspondent, fix their choice on these gentlemen, Massachusetts may expect to derive all that benefit she can reasonably hope for from their exertions. The integrity, wisdom, and fidelity discovered by a Bowdoin and an Adams, through every department in which they have been engaged, will doubtless be displayed to the best advantage in the important matters which will command the attention of the new federal Congress.[1]

1. On 2 November Adams wrote Theophilus Parsons that he would not accept election to the Senate. The letter is printed below in The Election of United States Senators, 21, 22, 24 November.

Samuel A. Otis to Nathan Dane, New York, 29 October (excerpt)[1]

In your determination to relinquish political pursuits I am glad to find you have not involved your political friends in the same resolution, which, until your favor 22d came to hand this day I began to apprehend. Be assured I shall omit no opportunity of evincing "my desires to keep up a communication." I presume by this time the Court are assembling, and from various circumstances, I can easily suppose, modes as well as elections are very uncertain. I presume from the circumstance of Mr. [Rufus] King's going post haste to Boston, he is also amongst the candidates. From intimations, that not all the Middle States will vote for Mr. H[ancock] and that some of the Southern will vote for Mr. [Edmund] Rando[l]ph, it remains doubtful who will be Vice President.

Your determination to sit down to your private business I have given you my sentiments upon. Five or six years application will make you more independent, than anything the USA can give you in that time, and when you have a wish for public employment, you may make your own terms. When I see how much more every way independent, the private man is, how much freer from anxiety, toil, and mortification, than the crowded, studious, busy man of the public, at his best state, is, I cannot but wonder at any man's courting public employment who can live without; and in this sentiment I don't speak the language of disappointment; I have been favored by my country beyond my exp[ect]ations, and know I have numerous friends still disposed to push me forward. Neither am I old or sick; yet this truth is long since strongly marked on my mind, and because I cannot use better words, pronounce the pursuits, vanity and vexation. Vain however as they may be, I suspect my friend will plunge anew into them, before the time I have prescribed above; and it will be no surprise to find him engaged in opening the spring campaign.

1. RC, Dane Papers, DLC.

Honestus, Independent Chronicle, 30 October[1]

I have observed in some late publications a disposition to inculcate among the people, an idea, *that those persons who are in favor of the proposed amendments, are not to be trusted in our federal government;* and some have gone even so far as to brand all such persons with the opprobrious epithet of *Antifederalists.* This being the case, I conceive it has now become a serious question to be determined: *Whether the amendments were proposed with an intention of having them adopted, or whether they were artfully introduced to deceive the members of the Convention?* We cannot in candor suppose, that any members of that respectable body (particularly the gentleman who introduced them) meant to betray their constituents, by pretending to adopt a Constitution under the mask of amendments, and then desert them after its ratification. We cannot, in justice to those respectable characters who composed that august assembly, conceive that so much cunning and subtlety should prevail among any individuals; neither ought we to presume, that men possessing so much political wisdom, would have been so *impolitic,* as to introduce the new government, by deceiving the people in its first establishment. Such a mode of conduct, they must be sensible, would have a tendency to raise a jealousy in the minds of the public, which would ever operate as a clog on all the future operations of government. No policy can be more destructive, than to raise a distrust of the *integrity* of those with whom we have intrusted our political concerns. What must be the sentiments of the people with respect to the Convention, if we are now told, *that the amendments are not to be regarded;* and that they were only introduced as a measure to pass the Constitution; and that our members for the federal government should be of that class of men who are *openly opposed* to any amendments whatever. Provided this is the case (but which I conceive was far from the intention of the Convention) would not a distrust naturally prevail among the body of the people? What must be their conjectures? Will they think more favorably of that government, which needs such deception for its adoption? What decisions can they trust to in future, if this solemn form of ratification, signed by a man in whom they have ever confided, is to be treated as words of no signification? If the determinations of a body of men, consisting of characters as respectable for their wisdom and patriotism as any in the commonwealth, are to be considered only as the mere trick of state policy, how will the people be ever able to ascertain the reality of any doings hereafter, however solemnly and deliberately resolved? Surely then if we mean to act consistent with the principles of *common prudence,* or wish to effect a lasting and beneficial government, founded on the CONFIDENCE of the PEOPLE, we ought at least to avoid those persons whom we have reason to believe are opposed to the proposed amendments. As the Convention have pledged to the people, that exertions shall be made to effect the adoption of the propositions, we should be careful to have such members as are disposed to comply with these resolutions; that if the amendments are of any importance, they may be adopted; if not, that they may be set aside, after that decent investigation which is due to the propositions of this commonwealth.

If we attend to the words of the recommendation, we cannot but consider them of some importance, "And the Convention do in the name, and in behalf of the people of this Commonwealth, enjoin it upon their Representatives in Congress, at all times, until the alterations and provisions aforesaid, have been considered, agreeably to the 5th article of the said Constitution, to exert all their influence, and use every reasonable and legal method to obtain a ratification of the said alterations and provisions, in such manner as is provided in the said article."[2]

After reading the form of the ratification, it is the highest reflection on their probity, to doubt of the sentiments of the Convention, with respect to the *importance* of the amendments. How abusive and uncandid then to stigmatize those who are for adhering to them, as Antifederalists? Certainly those who are opposed to them, may with greater propriety be styled such, as they are opposed to the decided voice of the Convention. If we are to *enjoin* upon our Representatives the alterations and provisions mentioned—and they are *bound to exert* all their influence for these purposes—how absurd to think of choosing men, whom we have reason to suppose will rather use their influence to backward any attempts for their adoption? Real Federal men are those who are for the propositions submitted; for REAL FEDERALISM *consists in promoting the harmony and union of all the states.* These happy consequences are most likely to be effected by complying with the decisions of the several states, as far as their proposals can be adopted. But to disregard the several propositions, and pretend to choose men professedly with a view to backward any attempt to gratify the people, must have a direct tendency to destroy that UNION, which must ever be our national support.

Besides, what dependence can we place in men, who arrogantly presume to disregard the almost unanimous voice of the conventions of the several states!

To ascertain the real sentiments of several respectable gentlemen of the Convention, let us attend to a few extracts from the debates.

Judge [Increase] Sumner said: "He sincerely hoped that the propositions would meet with the approbation of the Convention, as it appeared to him to remedy all the difficulties, which gentlemen in the course of the debates had mentioned; and concluded by observing, that the probability was very great, that if the amendments proposed were recommended *that they would be adopted by the general government.*" Judge [Francis] Dana and several other gentlemen spoke in favor of the amendments, and the probability of their being adopted. Dr. [Charles] Jarvis said: "That the propositions are general, and not local; and that they were not calculated for the peculiar situation of this state; but with indiscriminate justice comprehended the circumstances of every individual on the banks of the Savannah, as well as the hardy and industrious husbandman on the margin of the Kennebec, and if they were not ingrafted on the Constitution, *it would be our own faults.*"[3]

From the above quotations, we can judge of the sentiments of some of the gentlemen in the Convention. How greatly arrogant then, it is for writers to abuse those who are in favor of the amendments, after such explicit declarations from gentlemen whose sincerity cannot be doubted.

I am sensible it is rather unfashionable among some circles, to adhere to our old republican principles. A republican and an Antifederalist with them are synonymous. The term Antifederalist has of late been used by such persons to weaken the influence of some of our old tried republicans. But however lightly they may esteem our staunch patriots, or however contemptible our republican principles may appear to *them,* yet the body of this people I doubt not are convinced that those are the *men* who will work out our deliverance, and those are the *principles* which must eventually secure the rights and liberties of those states. This country was founded on those principles; actuated by them, our forefathers secured to themselves and posterity the privileges of freemen against the arbitrary attempts of their enemies. Animated by the same sentiments, we opposed Britain, defeated their armies, and finally established our independence. Surely then at this period, when we are just about to reap the fruits of our perseverance, we will not relinquish those principles which have been our support, from the first settlement of this country to the present day? Neither will we stigmatize our firm, and *aged patriots,* who have helped us in every time of danger.

Let us then, while we are anxious to secure a permanent federal government, continue steadfast in our *first principles.* Let us preserve the spirit of moderation, and carefully avoid the dangerous extremes of *licentiousness* and *inattention.* On our own prudence and wisdom under God depend the salvation of our country. The proceedings of the first Congress will give the leading traits of our future national character; therefore, as we regard the happiness of America, let us give our suffrages for those tried patriots, who early stood forth in the cause of their country. We may then be assured that while we act thus, we act safely.

The objects of our federal government, are not to gratify the vanity of the ambitious, or to provide maintenance for seekers, but to restore our national vigor, and to promote our agriculture, manufactures, and commerce. The *latter* therefore depending so materially on the union of the Southern and Northern states, and the propositions of Virginia and Carolina being so similar with this, we ought particularly to inculcate that harmony which may produce those mutual advantages, so earnestly wished for by every sincere friend to the prosperity and lasting happiness of America.

To accomplish the important purposes of our government, we need those faithful servants of the public, whose zealous patriotism and *stern integrity* early rendered them objects of British vengeance; likewise those whose knowledge in European politics has rendered them competent to defeat the most subtle measures of our enemies. Thus doubly secured by the goodness of our Constitution, and the virtues of our legislators, America, under the smiles of Providence, "shall enjoy without further interruption, that WEIGHT and CONSIDERATION, due to its EXTENT, its POPULATION, and the CHARACTER of its INHABITANTS."[4]

1. "Honestus" was a pseudonym used by Benjamin Austin, Jr., in a series of essays that appeared in the *Independent Chronicle* in the spring of 1786 (published in pamphlet form as *Observations on the Pernicious Practice of the Law*). The style of those essays is similar to the one printed here, and it is probable that Austin was the author. A political ally of Samuel Adams in Boston during the Revolution, he continued to be active in popular politics after the war, and could be found at the head of crowds and demonstrations into the 1790s. He served several scattered terms in the state Senate beginning in 1787, and he remained a critic of Federalism throughout his active political life, opposing the politics of the Washington administration and supporting Thomas Jefferson.

2. This is an excerpt from the Massachusetts Convention's act of ratification agreed to on 4 February (Convention, *Debates,* 84-85).

3. The speeches by Sumner and Jarvis are in Convention, *Debates,* 240, 254-57.

4. Another "Honestus" essay supporting amendments appeared in the *Independent Chronicle,* 6 November.

The Passage of the Massachusetts Election Resolutions, 1-20 November

The legislature reassembled on 29 October, and on 1 November the two houses appointed a joint committee to report on methods of electing Electors, Senators, and Representatives. On 4 November the committee reported to the Senate, which adopted the report without amendment, sent it to the House, and appointed another committee to write a bill based on the report. The House ignored the Senate's proposal and began debating and amending the report, a process which lasted from 6 until 13 November, when the House sent the amended report to the Senate.

The House debates centered around three issues: popular vs. legislative election of presidential Electors, the method of electing United States Senators, and the makeup of legislative districts. There was strong support for popular election of Electors, but eventually a compromise provided for popular nomination, with the legislature choosing as Electors one of the two men receiving the highest number of votes in each district and two Electors from the state at large. The House insisted on electing Senators by a joint ballot as well, but the Senate refused to agree. The result was that the Election Resolutions of 20 November contained no provision for the election of Senators.

The newspapers reported the debates on these two issues in some detail but not on a third issue: the makeup of districts. The report of 4 November proposed that each of the eight districts contain one-eighth of the voters in the state, but that counties should not be divided. However, the report also listed the counties to be contained in each district, and this list had little to do with population. The representatives from Maine and from Hampshire and Berkshire counties tried repeatedly but in vain to secure representation more in accord with population.

The final Election Resolutions included the districts as set forth in the report of 4 November. Thus the three counties in Maine, with over 20 percent of the population of the state, were one district, while Bristol-Dukes-Nantucket counties, with but 8 percent of the population, were another. Suffolk County with 9.5 percent of the population was a district, as was Middlesex County with 9 percent, while Berkshire and Hampshire counties with 19 percent of the population were combined into one district. Thus the four eastern districts, with 35 percent of the population, had four Representatives, to four for Maine and the western counties, with 65 percent of the population.

This division of the state was in part a result of the old struggle between the seacoast and the frontier areas and in part the result of a belief on the part of Federalist leaders that the creation of districts with equal populations might give the Antifederalists an advantage in the election of Representatives.

House and Senate Proceedings, Friday, 31 October

The Senate, A.M.

The Secretary came into the Senate chamber, and informed the Senate, that His Excellency the Governor had directed him to acquaint them, that his ill state of health prevented him from making his communications this day, that he had sent the several papers which he had received in the recess (which papers the Secretary afterwards laid on the table) and should, when his health would permit, address the General Court, if necessary.[1]

Ordered, that the papers which His Excellency the Governor directed the Secretary to communicate, be committed to the committee of both houses, appointed to consider what public business is necessary to be acted on the present session.[2]

Sent down for concurrence.

The House, A.M.

The Secretary came down and said that he was directed by His Excellency the Governor to inform this House that His Excellency intended respectfully to have addressed the legislature, but was prevented by severe sickness and that he had directed such papers as he had received during the recess to be laid before them, which were left with the honorable Senate and that His Excellency would address the legislature in person as soon as his health would admit.

The House, P.M.

The Hon. S. Choate, Esqr., brought down [from the Senate] a resolve of Congress of September 13, 1788, for organizing the new federal government.

. . . .

Also the proposed amendments to the new Federal Constitution of the Convention of the State of Virginia with their ratification thereof.

. . . .

Also a letter from the Convention of the State of New York with their ratification of the Federal Constitution and their proposed amendments.

. . . .

Also a letter from the President of the Convention of North Carolina inclosing a resolve of the said Convention recommending it to the legislature of that state, whenever Congress should pass an impost law, to pass a similar law therein for the benefit of Congress; and another resolve of the said Convention recommending it to the said legislature to redeem their paper currency; also an extract from the journal of their proceedings.

. . . .

Also the following order of Senate of this day, viz., that the foregoing papers which His Excellency the Governor directed the Secretary to communicate, be committed to the committee of both houses, appointed to consider what public business is necessary to be acted on the present session.

. . . .

Read and concurred.

The Senate, P.M.

Came up concurred.[3]

1. The two houses had notified Governor Hancock on 29 October that they were prepared to begin work. He replied to the Senate that "his late indisposition of body has prevented him from making an arrangement of the public business but that as soon as he had done it, he should make his communications" (Senate Journals, 29 October).

Although Governor Hancock did not deliver a speech, there are two drafts of a speech. One draft (Hancock Papers, Smithsonian Institution: Division of Political History) emphasizes the importance of amendments to the Constitution. The other draft (Rosenbach Foundation, Philadelphia) discusses the need for amendments but also emphasizes the importance of the method of elections. This draft points out that two states (Pennsylvania and Connecticut) had already interpreted the Constitution differently so far as the choice of Electors was concerned and expresses the wish that the Constitution had provided for elections "in such technical and unequivocal language as would have given a uniformity of practice in the whole nation. . . ."

2. The joint committee was appointed on 29 October to consider the public business of the session. Samuel Henshaw, Timothy Paine, and Samuel Breck represented the House, and Caleb Strong and Cotton Tufts the Senate.

3. The House concurrence is entered in the Senate Journals for the morning session instead of the Journals for the afternoon session where it belonged.

Newspaper Report of House Proceedings on Friday, 31 October[1]

A message was received from His Excellency the Governor, acquainting the honorable House that he intended to have addressed them this day, but was prevented by indisposition of body—that he had directed the Secretary to lay before the legislature the public papers, received in the recess, and that he would address the Court as soon as his health would admit.

(The papers communicated consisted of several acts and resolves of Congress; the forms of ratification of the Federal Constitution by the conventions of Virginia and New York, and their proposed amendments; the proceedings of that of North Carolina, etc., which being read were committed. Among them is the following half federal resolution:

North Carolina.

In Convention, August 2, 1788.

Whereas this Convention has thought proper neither to reject or ratify the Constitution proposed for the government of the United States; and as Congress will proceed to act under said Constitution, ten states having ratified the same, and will probably lay an impost on goods imported into said ratifying states.

Resolved, that it be recommended to the legislature of this state, that whenever Congress shall pass a law for collecting an impost in the states aforesaid, this state enact a law for collecting a similar impost on goods imported into this state, and appropriating the money arising therefrom to the use of Congress.

Samuel Johnston, President.)

1. *Massachusetts Centinel*, 1 November.

House and Senate Proceedings, Saturday, 1 November

The Senate

Report of committee of both houses, on the papers communicated by the Governor, respecting the organization of the federal government etc., read and accepted.

Sent down for concurrence.

Ordered, that Caleb Strong, Charles Turner, and Nathl. Wells and Phanuel Bishop, Esqr., with such as the honorable House may join, be a committee to take into consideration the Resolve of Congress of the 13 September 1788 relative to the appointment of Electors of the President and Vice President of the United States; and also to consider those parts of the Constitution lately adopted for the people of the United States, which respect the appointment of Senators and Representatives in the federal government, and to report in what particular mode the said Electors, Senators, and Representatives shall be chosen in this commonwealth.

Sent down for concurrence.

The House

[The House received the Senate message appointing a committee to consider an election law.]

Read and concurred, and Mr. Dawes, Mr. Bowdoin, Mr. Russell of Boston, Mr. Gore, and Mr. Heath were joined.

Newspaper Report of House Proceedings on Saturday, 1 November[1]

A short conversation ensued on the question for appointing a committee for considering the mode of federal elections, etc. in which

The honorable General Heath observed, that the subject on which the committee were to report, was of the utmost magnitude to the people of the United States and that probably the committee might want to know the sense of the House on the subject, in order that their report may coincide therewith; and thereby much time—otherwise uselessly spent—might be saved. He wished, therefore, that a conversation might be entered into, in order to ascertain the sentiments of the House on the subject. The worthy General added, that it had been made a question—whether the people at large were to choose the Electors of President, etc., or the legislatures—and whether the state ought to be divided into separate districts, for the purpose of choosing federal Representatives—or to be considered as one great district. These, and other considerations, he said, induced him to wish for the previous discussion.

Mr. Wedgery said, he could not conceive there could be any propriety in the discussion the honorable gentleman wished for at this time as there could be no question in order. The proper time, he said, for the discussion would be when the committee reported, and, therefore, he was in favor of concurring.

Dr. Jarvis agreed with the honorable gentleman from Roxbury [Heath] in the importance of the subject, but was of opinion that any discussion on it at the present time, would be of no avail. The Senate, he said, had already decided on the subject—and unless there were to be a similar discussion in that branch, the committee being a joint one, the determination of the House would probably only tend to procrastinate the report. He was for concurring with the Senate.

The honorable Judge Fuller said, if the committee, when they came together, found themselves so much embarrassed as not to be able to proceed, they could then apply for directions, and might then be instructed. But, perhaps, said he, the committee will not be in any doubt how to proceed. In any case, he said, it would be soon enough to advise him [*sic*] when they wish for the advice. He was therefore against the discussion, and for concurring.

1. *Massachusetts Centinel*, 5 November.

Theodore Sedgwick to Alexander Hamilton, Boston, 2 November[1]

In my last hasty letter,[2] I engaged to write you soon after my arrival in this town. Various questions will be agitated in the legislature (of considerable magnitude) which respect the organization of the government. There is a party of Federalists, who are of opinion that the Electors should [———] by the people, and the Re[presentatives?] not in districts but at large. These [———] be joined by all the Antis probably. I yet hope they will not succeed. We yesterday committed to a committee of both houses the Circular Letter from your Convention. The event is uncertain as a considerable number of Federalists have been brought over to the amendment system, the prospect is notwithstanding that the real friends of the Constitution will prevail. Everything depends upon it, and the exertion will be proportio[nate?] to the magnitude of the object.

Should the Electors be chosen by the legislature, Mr. Adams will probably combine all the votes of Massachusetts. I am very certain that the suggestion that he is unfriendly to General Washington is entirely unfounded. Mr. Hancock has been very explicit in patronizing the doctrine [———] amendments. The other gentleman is for postponing the conduct of that business until it shall be understood from experience.[3]

1. RC, Hamilton Papers, DLC.
2. 16 October (printed, Chapter XIV).
3. On 9 November, Hamilton replied from New York: "I am very sorry for the schism you hint at among the Federalists; but, I have so much confidence in the good management of the fast friends of the Constitution that I hope no ill consequences will ensue from that disagreement. It will however be worthy of great care to avoid suffering a difference of opinion on collateral points to produce any serious division between those who have hitherto drawn together in the great national question. Permit me to add that I do not think you should allow any line to be run between those who wish to trust alterations to future experience and those who are desirous of them at the present juncture. The rage for amend-

ments is in my opinion rather to be parried by address than encountered with open force. And I should therefore be loath to learn that your parties have been arranged professedly upon the distinction I have mentioned. The *mode* in which amendments may best be made and twenty other matters may serve as pretexts for avoiding the evil and securing the good" (Syrett, V, 231).

Joint Committee Report, Tuesday, 4 November[1]

The committee of both houses appointed to consider and report in what particular mode the Electors of the President and Vice President and the Senators and Representatives in the federal government shall be chosen beg leave to report the following propositions expressing their opinion of the mode in which the elections aforesaid shall be made.

1. That the Electors be chosen by the two houses of the General Court, by joint ballot.

2. That the Electors meet on the first Wednesday of February, in the town of Boston, for the purpose of voting for President and Vice President; and for their time and travel receive the same compensation as members of the [state] Senate are entitled to.

3. That the Senators be chosen by the two houses of the legislature, each having a negative upon the other.

4. That the commonwealth be divided into eight districts, the inhabitants of each of which shall be authorized to choose one Representative.

5. That each district be formed in such manner as to comprehend one-eighth part of the polls in the commonwealth, as nearly as may be, without dividing counties.

6. That the county of Suffolk form one district.

The county of Essex, one.

The county of Middlesex, one.

The county of Hampshire and Berkshire, one.

The county of Plymouth and Barnstable, one.

The counties of York, Cumberland, and Lincoln, one.

The counties of Bristol, Dukes County, and Nantucket, one.

The county of Worcester, one.

7. That precepts issue to the towns in the several districts to vote on the ——— day of ———, for their respective Representatives, and to return lists of the votes to the Supreme Executive on or before the ——— day of ———; and if any of the districts shall not have given a majority of votes to any one candidate, the Supreme Executive shall issue new precepts to such district for the choice of a Representative out of the two highest candidates, first voted for, and that a majority of votes in this last instance constitute a choice; but in case the two candidates shall have an equal number of votes, the senators and representatives in the state legislature, from such district, shall determine which of the persons so voted for shall be the Representative.

8. That one Elector be chosen out of each district entitled to elect a Representative and that the two remaining Electors be chosen in any part of the state.

[s] C. Strong per order.

1. Miscellaneous Resolves, 1788, Chapter 49, M-Ar. The report was summarized in the *Massachusetts Centinel,* 5 November, and printed in the *Independent Chronicle,* 6 November. For the report as finally agreed upon, see Final Joint Committee Report, Thursday, A.M., 19 November, printed below.

Senate Proceedings, Tuesday, 4 November[1]

In Senate, November 4, 1788.

Read and accepted and ordered, that Caleb Strong and William Whiting, esquires, with such as the honorable House may join, be a committee to report a bill conformable to the foregoing report.

Sent down for concurrence.

[s] Saml. Phillips, Jr., President.

1. Miscellaneous Resolves, 1788, Chapter 49, M-Ar. The Senate Journals, 4 November, do not record the Senate's acceptance of the report. The Senate action is recorded on the manuscript of the Joint Committee Report, 4 November, printed above, and is in the form of a message to the House. The House ignored the Senate proposal to appoint a joint committee to prepare a bill based on the report. The House then proceeded to debate and amend the report between 5 and 13 November.

House Proceedings, Wednesday, A.M., 5 November

The Hon. D. Sewall, Esqr., brought down a report of the committee appointed to consider and report what particular mode the Electors of the President and Vice President, and the Senators and Representatives in the federal government shall be chosen, containing the following propositions expressing their opinion of the mode in which the elections aforesaid can be made.

[Here follows the text of the Joint Committee Report of 4 November and the Senate resolution of the same date proposing a joint committee to draft an election bill in accordance with the report.]

Read and ordered, that Thursday morning, 10 o'clock, be assigned for considering the said report and that the House will then resolve themselves into a committee of the whole House for that purpose.

Newspaper Report of House Proceedings on Wednesday, 5 November[1]

After some time spent in the consideration of private petitions,

Dr. Jarvis called for the report of the committee raised to report a mode of federal elections, which had come down accepted from the Senate and which was then read. [The newspaper then summarized the Joint Committee Report of 4 November, printed above.]

A desultory conversation ensued the reading of this report on the propriety of assigning a time for its consideration, in which Dr. Jarvis, Mr. Breck, Mr. Choate, and Mr. Gore took a part. A motion for assigning tomorrow (Thursday) morning, 10 o'clock, was at length carried—yeas 82—nays 69.

On motion it was voted, that the House will tomorrow resolve itself into a committee of the whole, for the purpose of more liberally discussing the report of the committee on federal elections.

1. *Massachusetts Centinel*, 8 November.

House Proceedings, Thursday, 6 November

Ordered, that seats be assigned for His Excellency the Governor, His Honor the Lieutenant Governor, the members of the honorable Council, the Hon. John Adams, Rufus King, and Nathan Dane, esquires, if they incline to attend the debates upon the subject of the report of the committee respecting the mode in which the Electors of the President, and Vice President, and Senators and Representatives in the federal government shall be chosen.[1]

A message was sent to the honorable Senate to inform them that the House could not receive any communications at present, they being about to resolve themselves into a committee for the purpose of considering the report above mentioned.

Voted, that the Speaker leave the chair.

The House then resolved themselves into a committee of the whole House for the purpose of considering the subject aforementioned.

Samuel Breck, Esqr., was chosen chairman. After debate it was voted, that the Speaker resume the chair, and that the chairman be directed to report to the House that the committee have proceeded in the consideration of the subject referred to them but have not finished the same, and that they ask leave to sit again.

The Speaker resumed the chair, and the committee made report accordingly, which was accepted.

Adjourned to 3 o'clock, P.M.

Afternoon

Met according to adjournment.

. . . .

Voted, that the Speaker leave the chair.

The House then sat again as a committee for the purpose of considering the report of the committee appointed to report in what particular mode the Electors of the President and Vice President, and the Senators and Representatives in the federal government, shall be chosen. After debate,

Voted, that the chairman report that the committee have proceeded in the consideration of the business reserved to them, but not having finished the same ask leave to sit again.

The Speaker resumed the chair and the committee reported accordingly, which report was accepted.

Adjourned to Friday morning, 9 o'clock.

1. On 12 November, the *Massachusetts Centinel* reported that "the debates in the House of Representatives, on the important subject of organizing the new government" were attended by Lieutenant Governor Benjamin Lincoln, the Governor's Council, John Adams, General Henry Knox, Samuel A. Otis, Rufus King, Nathan Dane, "and several other dis-

tinguished persons." Among the latter might have been Thomas Tudor Tucker of South Carolina and Nicholas Gilman of New Hampshire, members of Congress, who were assigned seats for their use "whenever they may incline to attend the debates of the House" (House Journals, 10 November).

Newspaper Reports of House Proceedings on Thursday, 6 November

Massachusetts Centinel, 8 November

The order of the day, for considering the report of the committee on federal elections, being called for, the House resolved itself into a committee of the whole, Samuel Breck, Esquire in the chair,

When the first article of the report being read, a lengthy debate ensued in which the Honorable Speaker [Theodore Sedgwick], Mr. Parsons, Dr. Jarvis, Mr. Dawes, General Heath, Mr. Ames, Mr. Gore, Mr. Widgery, Judge Fuller, Major Nasson, Mr. Lyman, Mr. Bowdoin, and several other gentlemen took a part. The constitutionality of the legislature's appointing the Electors and the expediency of the measure formed the principal points of the discussion. In support of the former it was alleged, that the Constitution pointed out, in the 1st section of article iii that "each State shall appoint, *in such manner as the Legislature may direct*, a number of electors," etc., and that therefore, the legislature had a right to direct who should appoint the Electors of President, etc., whether the people [———] themselves, or any other body of men. To this it was objected that the direction of the *"manner"* of the choice only, was in the power of the legislature, and that the example of the states who had already proceeded in the organization of the new government, as well as the common acceptation of the word "State," which it was asserted could only mean the people, were clearly in favor of their choosing the Electors. It was further urged by the supporters of the report, that even if the right belonged to the people, they could not, in the present case, understandingly exercise it, from the shortness of time allowed them, and that therefore the general sentiment of the people appeared to be in favor of the legislature's making the present appointment. On the other hand, it was said by gentlemen that there was time sufficient for the people to effect the choice by a majority of votes—but admitting there was not, there certainly was for a choice by a *plurality* of votes—which they contended was a mode preferable to an election by the legislature. They said further, that the people were tenacious of the privileges of election, and that they never would consent to be abridged of them; that precedents would have great weight in influencing elections in future; and that, what might now be adopted from necessity, would hereafter be adduced to warrant a like measure, when no such necessity existed—or which designing men might misrepresent—and thereby the people be curtailed in their privileges. A variety of other reasons were given, both for and against the report, but which neither our time nor capacities will permit us to narrate. We can only generally say, that the debates were learned, ingenious, and animated; and discovered a thorough knowledge of the great principles of government, an ardent desire to explore the truth, and a firm and zealous attachment for the rights of the people, in the several gentlemen who took part in them.

On motion, the Speaker resumed the chair. The chairman then reported progress, and asked leave to sit again, which, being granted, the House adjourned.

New York Journal, 20 November (excerpt)[1]

It became a question of importance with some, whether the Electors should be chosen by the people at large, or by their representatives in some corporate body. The Constitution, with regard to this, seemed to be somewhat ambiguous, and not so full and explicit as to remove all doubts concerning the mode of appointment. Arguments of equal weight were offered on both sides, with much warmth. It was said by some, that as the Constitution was left obscured, the privilege naturally devolved upon the people; and all the power not expressly given up in the Constitution was reserved to them, the exercising of which was an important right which they ought not to be deprived of. This idea was forcibly pursued by Dr. Jarvis, who further added, that he never heard that the people ever complained of being tired with the privilege of electing their governor, lieutenant governor, or any civil officers of the commonwealth, and therefore did not think it very likely they would hesitate in being empowered to elect the Electors of the President, etc., of the United States. Such were the arguments made use of in favor of the people choosing the Electors. It was urged in answer, that the people were debarred from exercising this right (if any they had) in consequence of the time being fixed for the Electors to meet; for should the people meet in their several districts to appoint the Electors, it was very improbable that any choice would be made; and as there was no authority to warrant a second meeting, this mode of procedure would very probably rob the commonwealth of the important privilege of sharing in the appointment of the first magistrates in America. Some seemed inclined to suppose the people might still appoint the Electors, and all difficulties be removed, if the strong attachment of New Englandmen to a majority would give way to a plurality of votes.

1. On 20 November the *New York Journal* printed reports of the proceedings of the Massachusetts House on 4, 6, and 7 November. The account of the proceedings on the 7th was reprinted from the account in the *Massachusetts Centinel* on the 8th, but the *Journal's* report of the debate on the 6th differs significantly from the *Centinel's* account and from the speeches by William Heath and Dr. Daniel Cony on the 6th, both printed below.

William Heath's Speech Supporting Popular Election of Presidential Electors, 6 November[1]

Admitting that the word STATE does not absolutely give it to the people (although this may be contended for), the mode of expression made use of certainly admits of two constructions, and although it may be constitutional for the legislature to make the appointment, yet the construction in favor of the people ought to predominate, for our government being republican, we are to suppose that those powers which have not been expressly delegated are retained. Indeed it is fit and right that the people should do such of their own business as is within their own reach; that which is beyond, must be done by their substitutes, and although the people may not be qualified to do all their important business themselves, they are well qualified to determine and to choose who shall do it for them.

The wisdom conspicuous in the legislature is an evidence that the people have a foresight to select proper persons to represent them, and their discernment is not exhausted, they are still able wisely to elect. But it is said that the general government may become a consolidated government, and that to prevent this we ought to throw as much weight as possible into the scale of the legislature in order to secure the state sovereignty; to this I reply, that there is already sufficient power in the state legislatures to preserve their sovereignty so long as the new Constitution of the United States shall retain its present form, for so long as the state legislatures are to choose the first branch of the legislature of the general government, their sovereignty will remain, but if there is a probability that eventually at some future day the states' sovereignty may be shipwrecked, it will then be fortunate for the people if too much of their invaluable property be not embarked in that bottom, as both might be lost together; the more power the people retain in their own hands the better terms will they be able to stipulate for themselves should there hereafter be a change in the government. If you will allow me to make a military comparison, I will say, that no able general would risk the fate of a battle on an attack with his army in one line; he will reserve some of his best troops for a critical moment, when they may not only secure him from confusion and rout, but perhaps gain him a victory. To apply this in the present case, the reserve of power should ever remain in the hands of the people, the surplus can nowhere be better held than by the original proprietors. I am sorry to hear even an idea advanced, that the people have, or will grow weary in exercising their rights and privileges; these are said to be invaluable; if then they are compared to an inestimable treasure, the holding the key can never be considered as a burden, or the unlocking the casket when necessary a fatigue; the exercise of so important a privilege, will be considered both a pleasure, and an honor, by the proprietor, who will feel an importance in himself in proportion to his independence, and the share of political liberty which he possesses. I am therefore *clearly* and *decidedly* in favor of the appointment of the Electors being made by the *people*.

1. *Independent Chronicle,* 20 November. The newspaper headed the speech: "Summary of General Heath's observations on the right and propriety of the people's appointing the Electors of the President and Vice President, of the United States." The *Chronicle* did not date the speech, but Heath argued for popular election on 6 November (see Newspaper Report of House Proceedings on 6 November, printed above).

Dr. Daniel Cony's Speech Supporting Popular Election of Presidential Electors, 6 November[1]

Mr. Chairman, I will not intrude on the patience of this assembly, but a few moments, as the question under consideration has already been so largely and ingeniously discussed.

I conceive, sir, that although a number of motions have been made by different gentlemen of the Convention, yet the proper question is, whether the people or the legislature shall exercise the important privilege of choosing Electors; whose constitutional business it will be, on the first Wednesday of February next, to give their suffrages, for the President General of the United States.

It has been conceded by almost every gentleman, who has spoke on the question, and I think it is clearly expressed in the Constitution, that this great and interesting privilege may be exercised by either, as the wisdom of the state legislatures shall direct; for my own part, sir, I am decidedly in favor of submitting the choice to the *people*.

Some gentlemen tell us, sir, that the people do not wish to exercise this valuable privilege, but, sir, I am of a very different opinion. I believe that the people wish, and that they ever ought to exercise, every privilege which they can conveniently do, and which they have not expressly delegated to their representatives; and I believe, sir, that my constituents, situated on the margin of the Kennebec, remote from the seat of government, and distant as they are from political information, yet they expect, and have a just right to expect, to be called upon to give their votes, and, in this way, have their share in the choice of Electors.

What, sir, shall I tell my constituents, when I go home, if they should enquire, why the choice of Electors was not submitted to the people? Shall I tell them that the General Court judged themselves more competent to this business, than the people at large? A poor compliment, and, sir, too barefaced an insult to be imposed on the good sense of the free, virtuous, and enlightened citizens of this commonwealth. Did not, sir, the Convention of this state, whose wisdom and integrity cannot be questioned; did not they, sir, solemnly recommend a number of amendments to this national Constitution, one of which, if I recollect, was, that every right, not expressly delegated, was explicitly reserved to the several states, to be exercised by the people thereof?[2] And, sir, in every view of the case, I think the people ought to exercise this important right, and shall at this time only observe, that as the minority at the adoption of the Constitution was very respectable, is it not, sir, an object highly deserving the attention of this Court, to adopt such measures and to provide such regulations for the organization of the new government as shall be most likely to conciliate, most likely to unite the affections, and secure the firmest attachment of the *whole people* to this Constitution, by which they are to be governed? With these impressions on my mind, I consider it my duty, to give my vote in favor of submitting the choice to the *people*.

1. *Independent Chronicle*, 20 November. The newspaper gave Dr. Cony's speech the following heading: "Substance of the observations made by Dr. Cony, member from Hallowell, on the important question respecting the choice of Electors." The *Chronicle* did not date Cony's speech, and the newspaper report of the House proceedings on 6 November (printed above) did not list Cony's name as one of the major participants. It is possible that Cony made the speech the next day, when the House again debated the issue, but we have placed it on the 6th.

Although the newspapers do not report any speeches opposing popular election of Electors, it is evident that the opposition was strong enough to force a compromise that resulted in popular nominations and legislative elections.

2. The first amendment to the Constitution agreed to by the Massachusetts Convention provided "That it be explicitly declared, that all powers not expressly delegated by the aforesaid Constitution are reserved to the several states, to be by them exercised" (Convention, *Debates*, 83).

House Proceedings, Friday, 7 November

The House set again as a committee for the purpose of considering the report of the committee appointed to report in what particular mode the Electors of

President and Vice President, and the Senators and Representatives in the federal government, shall be chosen etc. After debate,

Voted, that the first article in the said report be referred to a subcommittee who shall report a system for the election of the Electors by the people, if the same be practicable; if not, such other mode as shall appear to them to be expedient.

Voted, that the subcommittee consist of a member from each county represented.

The following persons were then appointed on the said subcommittee viz., Mr. Heath, Mr. Parsons, Mr. Rice, Mr. Lyman, Mr. Davis, Mr. Spooner, Mr. Nasson, Mr. Washburn, Mr. Noyes, Dr. Cony, and Mr. Ives.

A motion was made and seconded that the committee report to the House that the third article in the said report be stricken out and that the following be inserted in the room thereof, viz., "That the Senators be chosen by the legislature of the commonwealth, the two branches to proceed to the election in their respective houses separately at the same time, and the majority of the votes in each house meeting in the same person, shall determine the choice; and that this mode be continued, until the election is completed" and the question being put, passed in the negative.

It was then moved, and seconded that the following words in the said article *each having a negative upon the other* be expunged, and the words "by joint ballot in one room assembled" be inserted in the room thereof and the question being put, passed in the affirmative.

Voted, that the chairman leave the chair, and report the progress which the committee have made, and ask leave to sit again.

The Speaker resumed the chair and the chairman reported accordingly. Report accepted.

. . . .
Afternoon

Met according to adjournment.

. . . .

Voted, that the Speaker leave the chair.

The House set again as a committee for the purpose of considering the report of the committee appointed to report in what particular mode the Electors of President and Vice President, and the Senators and Representatives in the federal government, shall be chosen etc.

A motion was made and seconded that the words "who shall be a resident within the district for which he shall be chosen," be added to the 4th article, and the question being put, it passed in the negative, and the said article was passed without amendments.

Ordered, that a committee be appointed to consist of a member from each county represented to consider of dividing the commonwealth into districts, without dividing towns, for the purpose of choosing eight Representatives.

The following gentlemen were chosen, viz., Mr. Bowdoin, Mr. Choate, Mr. Fuller, Mr. Henshaw, Mr. Davis, Mr. Mitchel, Mr. Hays, Mr. Learned, Mr. Fox, Mr. Ludwig, and Mr. Peirce.

Voted, that the chairman leave the chair and report the progress which the committee have made, to the House and ask leave to set again.

The Speaker resumed the chair and the chairman reported accordingly. Report accepted.

Adjourned to Saturday morning, 9 o'clock.

Newspaper Report of House Proceedings on Friday, 7 November[1]

The House being met, it was again resolved into a committee of the whole, and the gentlemen who had taken part in the debates yesterday, again came forward in support of their several opinions. A number of motions were made and superseded, until finally one for submitting the first article of the report (i.e., determining who shall choose the Electors) to a subcommittee consisting of one from each represented county, was carried—yeas 125—nays 38. Committee chosen were General Heath, Mr. Parsons, Mr. Rice (Sudbury), Mr. Washburn, Mr. Lyman, Mr. Ives, Mr. Davis (Plymouth), Major Nasson, Mr. Noyes, Dr. Coney, Mr. Spooner.[2] This committee was enjoined to sit immediately.

The committee of the whole then proceeded to consider the 2d article, directing the Electors to meet in Boston, etc., which was concurred.

The third article, which provides that in the choice of Senators each branch shall have a negative on the other, was then considered, and Mr. Dawes explained the reasons which induced a majority of the reporting committee to agree to [———]. He said, the Federal Constitution had directed that the choice should be by the legislatures of the several states. In order to ascertain what was meant by the term legislature, a recurrence was had to the constitution of this state, and it had there been found, that the legislature consisted of the two branches of the General Court, acting on each other by a negative. The committee therefore could do no other than report as they had. Some conversation on the subject ensued, but the committee in general considering it as prejudicial to the privileges of the House, the motion for concurrence was negatived by a great majority. The sentiments of the committee were in favor of the election by joint ballot of both houses as in the choice of delegates to Congress.

The 4th article of the report was much opposed, upon the principal that in the election of Representatives, the choice in each district ought to be confined to a person resident in such district; but it was urged, on the other hand, that the legislature had the right only of prescribing the time, place, and manner of the choice; and not the qualifications of the persons to be elected, that these qualifications were pointed out in the Constitution, and that the requisition of any other would militate therewith. After considerable debate, the question of concurrence was put and carried—yeas 89—nays 72.

The 5th article (which appoints the districts) next came under debate—and was objected to by the members for the county of Berkshire, York, Cumberland, and Lincoln, who conceived that justice was not done them, in the mode reported. The necessity of the measure, and its temporary nature, were urged in favor of it. The debate [in the appointment?] of a subcommittee, consisting of a member from each county, which is to take the article into consideration and to new-form the districts, having regard only to the boundaries of towns. Adjourned.

1. *Massachusetts Centinel,* 8 November.

2. The printer placed the names of the towns of two members of the committee in parentheses because there was more than one Rice and more than one Davis in the legislature.

House Proceedings, Saturday, A.M., 8 November

Voted, that the Speaker leave the chair.

The House set again as a committee for the purpose of considering the report of the committee appointed to report in what particular mode the Electors of President and Vice President and the Senators and Representatives in the federal government, shall be chosen etc.

The subcommittee appointed yesterday to consider of dividing the commonwealth into districts etc. made report, and the following was made a question, viz., whether the committee will set off districts for the choice of Representatives, without regard to county lines, and the question being put, it passed in the negative.

A motion was then made and seconded, "That the counties of Hampshire and Berkshire be entitled to two Representatives, and the five southern counties be entitled to one only," and the question being put, passed in the negative.

Voted, that the committee report a concurrence of the 6th article.

Voted, that the 7th article in the said report be committed to a committee of five. Mr. Sedgwick, Mr. Dawes, Dr. Cony, Mr. Lyman, and Mr. Spooner, were appointed on the committee.

Voted, that the chairman leave the chair, and report to the House the progress which the committee have made, and ask leave to sit again.

The Speaker resumed the chair, and the chairman made report accordingly. Report accepted.

Newspaper Report of House Proceedings on Saturday, 8 November[1]

After some private business was transacted, the Speaker left the chair, and, in committee of the whole, the report of the committee on the subject of organizing the new government was again discussed (the 8th article under debate).[2] The members from the county of Berkshire, still considering that part of the state as not having justice done it, in the division of districts made in the report, called the attention of the committee to various statements and motions, which they contended, if adopted, would do greater justice. But the sense of the committee being taken, whether in districting the state, regard should be paid to county lines, and this appearing to be their opinion, and a motion for giving to Hampshire and Berkshire two Representatives and the five southern counties but one being negatived, the members from Berkshire ceased in their endeavors, the committee tacitly agreeing to give them an opportunity further to discuss the matter, when the subject came under consideration in the House, and the 6th article of the report was concurred.

The committee proceeded to the discussion of the 7th article (the mode of choosing Representatives), which occasioned much debate and was at last committed to Mr. Sedgwick, Mr. Dawes, Dr. Coney, Mr. Lyman, and Mr. Spooner, to consider at large, and to report.

The chairman left the chair and the House was resumed. The chairman then reported progress, and asked leave to sit again.

1. *Massachusetts Centinel,* 12 November.

2. The House debated the districting provisions of the report, contained in Articles Five and Six, not Article Eight, which dealt solely with Electors.

House Proceedings, Monday, 10 November

Voted, that the Speaker leave the chair.

The House set again as a committee for the purpose of considering the report of the committee appointed to report in what particular mode the Electors of President and Vice President, and the Senators and Representatives in the federal government, shall be chosen etc.

The subcommittee appointed to consider and report a system for the appointment of the Electors of the President and Vice President of the United States by the people if the same be practicable, etc., reported as follows, viz.,

"That when the inhabitants of the several towns and districts qualified to vote for Representatives for the general government shall be assembled for that purpose, they shall also give in their votes for some one person an inhabitant of the district in which such town or district respectively may be, for an Elector of the President and Vice President; or if such district is to choose two Electors the votes shall be given in accordingly. And a list of the votes so given in as aforesaid, shall by the selectmen of the several towns and district, or the major part of them be transmitted to the secretary's office, on or before the first Tuesday in January next, and, on the next day the General Court there in session, shall examine the returns, and from the *three* who shall be found to have the greatest number of votes in their respective districts, the two houses assembled in one room, shall by joint ballot choose one, who shall be considered the Elector for the district to which he belongs observing also to double the number of candidates in those districts which are to choose more than one Elector, and that provision be made in the bill accordingly.

W. Heath per order."

Which report was accepted and voted to report to the House to concur in accepting the report committed, with an amendment, viz., to expunge the first and eighth articles therein, and to insert the foregoing in lieu thereof.

The subcommittee on the 7th article in the report committed, made report as follows, viz.,

"That the selectmen of the several towns and other incorporated places in this commonwealth shall ——— days before the ——— day of ——— next issue their warrants to convene the inhabitants qualified by the constitution to vote in their respective towns and other places incorporated for a representative in the state legislature, at that time to assemble and vote for a Representative of the people of this state in Congress, at which meeting the selectmen shall preside, and a fair record shall in open town meeting, be made by the town clerk, or in his absence by such person as the selectmen shall for that purpose appoint, of the names of persons voted for, and the number of votes for each, and a declaration thereof shall be made by the selectmen in the same meeting: a copy of which record, within ——— days thereafter, certified by the selectmen and attested by the clerk, shall by them be transmitted to the office of a register of deeds within the districts to which they respectively belong.

"That the registers of deeds to whom copies of the said votes shall be transmitted, shall record the same in a book by them severally to be specially kept for that purpose and they shall count the said votes returned as aforesaid, and if it shall appear that any person shall have a majority of all the votes, in such case the register shall transmit within ——— days thereafter to the secretary's office, an account of the names of all the persons voted for in the respective towns and other places incorporated, and which the Secretary shall lay before the Governor and Council, and His Excellency the Governor shall make a certificate under the Seal of the Commonwealth of the election of the person so chosen to be one of the Representatives of the people of this state.

"That if it shall appear, upon the said votes being so counted by any register as aforesaid, that no person hath had a majority of votes, the said register in every such case, shall within ——— days give notice thereof to the selectmen of the several towns and other places incorporated within the district, to which such register belongs and shall therewith transmit the names of all the persons voted for and the number of votes for each, and the said selectmen shall thereupon within ——— days thereafter issue their precepts as aforesaid, for the voters as aforesaid, to assemble and vote in their respective towns, and other places incorporated within ——— days after issuing said precepts, and when so assembled the same proceedings shall be had in recording, declaring and returning the votes as above specified, and the said register shall again examine and record the returns in manner as is aforesaid, and he shall thereupon make return of the state of votes specifying the towns and other incorporated places, and the names of the persons voted for, and the number of each in the respective towns to the secretary's office, and on the second process as above pointed out, the person having the greatest number of votes shall be the Representative of the people of this commonwealth, from such district, and shall receive a certificate from the Governor as aforesaid, that if on the second time of voting two or more persons who have the greatest number of votes shall have an equal number the same proceedings shall be repeated, with this only difference, that information shall be communicated in manner above expressed of the names of the persons who have an equal number of votes as aforesaid, and so until some one person shall have a greater number of votes than any other, whereupon all proceedings in such election shall be transmitted to the secretary's office, and all other above pointed out, be performed as aforesaid.

"The subcommittee are further of opinion that all frauds in conducting this business and all neglects should be severely punished, and that provision should be made for a reasonable recompense to the registers."

Which report was accepted and it was voted that it be reported to the House to concur in accepting the report committed with a further amendment, viz., to expunge the seventh article in the said report and to insert the foregoing in the room thereof.

Voted, that the chairman leave the chair and make report of the proceedings of the committee as soon as may be.

The Speaker then resumed the chair and the House adjourned to 3 o'clock P.M.

. . . .

Afternoon

Met according to adjournment.

. . . .

The committee of the whole House appointed to consider the report of the committee appointed to consider and report in what particular mode the Electors of the President and Vice President and the Senators and Representatives in the federal government shall be chosen etc. made report (see their proceedings entered at large). The House proceeded to consider the same, and after debate,

Adjourned to Tuesday morning 9 o'clock.

Newspaper Report of House Proceedings on Monday, 10 November [1]

The House resolved itself into a committee of the whole. The subcommittee, of which General Heath was chairman, reported, substantially, the following amendment, instead of the 1st and 8th articles (respecting the legislature's choosing the Electors) of the report under consideration, viz., That at the time the people assemble for the choice of federal Representatives, they shall give in their votes, in their several districts, for one Elector of President, etc., or as the case may be, for two Electors—and a list of the votes shall be transmitted to the secretary's office, on or before the first Tuesday of January next, and on the next day, the General Court shall examine the returns, and from the three having the greatest number of votes in each district, the Court, by joint ballot, shall choose one, who shall be considered the Elector for the district to which he belongs; observing to double the number of candidates in those districts which are to choose two.

The subcommittee raised to consider the 7th article reported a mode for choosing Representatives to the general government different from that in the report under consideration, which from its length we are not able to give this day, and as probably we shall give it in the act, when completed, we think it not essential. Its consideration, however, occasioned a lengthy and desultory debate but was finally accepted.

The chairman reported progress and asked leave to sit again.

. . . .

The subject of organizing the new government was taken up in the House [in the afternoon] and debated, and the members from Berkshire County again coming forward in their demands for justice, the consideration was adjourned until tomorrow morning.

1. *Massachusetts Centinel,* 12 November.

House Proceedings, Tuesday, A.M., 11 November

The House proceeded to consider the report of the committee of the whole House upon the subject of the report of the committee appointed to consider and report in what particular mode the Electors of President and Vice President, and the Senators and Representatives in the federal government shall be chosen etc. After debate,[1] it was

Ordered, that a committee consisting of a member from each county represented, be appointed to consider the districts for the choice of Representatives, as assigned by the said report. The following gentlemen were then appointed on the said committee viz., Mr. Clarke, Mr. Sewall, Mr. Curtis, Mr. Smead, Mr. Washburn, Mr. Dean, Mr. Paine, Mr. Bradbury, Mr. Phinney, and Mr. Stanley.

1. On 12 November the *Massachusetts Centinel* reported that "the subject of the districts was again taken into consideration—and after much debate" given to the committee "to report thereon."

House Proceedings, Wednesday, P.M., 12 November

The committee appointed to consider the districts for the choice of federal Representatives as assigned by the report of the committee appointed to consider and report in what particular mode the Electors of President and Vice President, and the Senators and Representatives, in the federal government shall be chosen etc. made report of a new assignment of the said districts, in part, and, on the question whether the committee shall proceed in the said business, it was determined in the affirmative.

Adjourned to Thursday morning, 9 o'clock.

House Proceedings, Thursday, P.M., 13 November

The committee appointed to consider the districts for the choice of federal Representatives, as assigned by the report of the committee, appointed to consider and report in what particular mode the Electors of President and Vice President, and the Senators and Representatives in the federal government shall be chosen etc., reported a division of the commonwealth into districts without regard to county lines.

[Report of the Committee] [1]

"The committee appointed to divide the commonwealth into districts for the purpose of electing eight Representatives, to represent this state in the Congress of the United States, have attended that service, and ask leave to make the following report, viz.,

"1. That the counties of Dukes County, Nantucket, and Barnstable, the towns of Plymouth, Wareham, Rochester, New Bedford, Dartmouth, Westport, Halifax, Middleborough, Plympton, Bridgewater, Kingston, Duxbury, and Marshfield, form one district.

"2. That the towns of Scituate, Pembroke, Hanover, Abington, Berkley, Raynham, Taunton, Freetown, Dighton, Swansea, Rehoboth, Attleboro, Norton, Mansfield, Easton, Braintree, Weymouth, Hingham, Needham, Medfield, Stoughton, Sharon, Wrentham, Walpole, Cohasset, Franklin, Medway, Bellingham, Hull, Foxborough, and Dover, form one district.

"3. That the towns of Boston, Roxbury, Brookline, Dorchester, Milton, Chelsea, Dedham, Charlestown, Medford, Malden, Cambridge, Watertown, Newton, Waltham, Woburn, Concord, Framingham, Weston, Westford, Reading, Billerica, Lexington, Chelmsford, Tewksbury, Carlisle, Dracut, Wilmington, Stoneham, Boxborough, Lincoln, Bedford, and East Sudbury, form one district.

"4. That the several towns in the county of Essex form one district.

"5. That the several towns in the counties of York, Cumberland, and Lincoln, form one district.

"6. That the towns of Marlborough, Sudbury, Hopkinton, Stow, Groton, Shirley, Pepperell, Ashby, Townsend, Holliston, Acton, Dunstable, Littleton, Natick, Sherborn, Worcester, Lancaster, Mendon, Oxford, Charlton, Sutton, Leicester, Rutland, Paxton, Oakham, Hubbardston, Southborough, Westborough, Northborough, Shrewsbury, Boylston, Lunenburg, Fitchburg, Uxbridge, Harvard, Bolton, Upton, Leominster, Douglas, Grafton, Princeton, Northbridge, Ward, Milford, Sterling, Berlin, Holden, and Gardner, form one district.

"7. That the towns of Springfield, Longmeadow, West Springfield, Wilbraham, Northampton, Hadley, South Hadley, Amherst, Granby, Hatfield, Whately, Deerfield, Greenfield, Sunderland, Montague, Northfield, Brimfield, South Brimfield, Monson, Pelham, Greenwich, Palmer, New Salem, Belchertown, Ware, Warwick, Shutesbury, Ludlow, Leverett, Orange, Holland, Easthampton, Petersham, Athol, Hardwick, Western, New Braintree, Sturbridge, Brookfield, Dudley, Barre, Royalston, Winchendon, Ashburnham, Templeton, Gerry, Spencer, and Westminster, form one district.

"8. That the several towns in the county of Berkshire together with the towns of Granville, Blandford, Southwick, Southampton, Westhampton, Montgomery, Chester, Middlefield, Worthington, Cummington, Plainfield, Number Seven, Heath, Buckland, Rowe, Leyden, Norwich, Bernardston, Charlemont, Colrain, Shelburne, Chesterfield, Goshen, Ashfield, Conway, Westfield, and Williamsburg, form one district.

"All which is submitted, Tho. Clarke per order."

And on the question whether the House will accept the said report, it passed in the negative 159 members present, yeas 52 only.

The question was then put whether the House will concur with the honorable Senate in accepting the said report, with the three amendments as reported by the committee of the whole House, and it passed in the affirmative 163 members present, yeas 92 and Mr. Gore, Mr. Parsons, and Mr. Lyman were joined to the committee.

Sent up for concurrence.

In the House of Representatives, November 13, 1788.[2]

Read and concurred with the following amendments: viz., to expunge the first and eighth articles, and insert as in paper marked A; to expunge the following words in the third article viz., *each having a negative upon the other* and to insert "by joint ballot in one room assembled"; to expunge the seventh article and insert as in paper market B;[3] and Mr. Gore, Mr. Parsons, and Mr. Lyman are joined to the committee.

Sent up for concurrence.

[s] Theodore Sedgwick, Speaker

1. The text of this report is from the manuscript in Miscellaneous Legislative Documents, House Files, M-Ar. In making this report the committee had ignored the refusal of the House on 8 November to allow it to disregard county lines.

2. This message is not in the House Journals but is written on the manuscript containing the original committee report of 4 November, immediately after the Senate's approval of that report on 4 November (Miscellaneous Resolves, 1788, Chapter 49, M-Ar).

3. "Paper A" amending Article One, the amendment to Article Three, and "Paper B" amending Article Seven are printed below in the Final Joint Committee Report, Wednesday, A.M., 19 November.

House and Senate Proceedings, Tuesday, 18 November

The Senate[1]

In Senate, November 18, 1788.

Read and concurred in expunging the first and eighth articles and nonconcurred in the proposed amendment on paper marked A, and instead thereof propose the amendment on paper marked D. Nonconcurred in expunging the words in the 3d article "each having a negative on the other" and the Senate propose an addition as on paper marked C at the end of the third article. At E in the 5th article propose to insert "or connecting counties very remote from each other." Nonconcurred in expunging the seventh article and in the proposed amendment marked B. At F in the 7th article they propose dele[te] from F to G and insert "That the selectmen of the towns and districts in the several districts described in this report cause the inhabitants thereof duly qualified, to assemble on the ——— day of ——— to vote for their respective Representatives, such Representative being an inhabitant of the district for which he may be chosen and return lists of the votes to the secretary's office" and at I to dele[te] from I to K and insert "returns thereof to be made as aforesaid, and in case there shall be an equality of votes for the two candidates then voted for another precept shall issue for the Supreme Executive as aforesaid and so [thus?] until one of the candidates shall have a majority of v[otes]."

In the 7th article at L propose to dele[te] "new."

Sent down for concurrence.

[s] Saml. Phillips, Jr., President

The House, P.M.

[The House received the Senate message.]

Read and referred for consideration to the morning.

Adjourned to Wednesday morning, 9 o'clock.

1. The Senate Journals for 18 November do not record this action, but it is written on the manuscript of the Joint Committee Report of 4 November (printed above). For the Senate's revisions and amendments, see the Final Joint Committee Report, Wednesday, A.M., 19 November, printed below.

House and Senate Proceedings, Wednesday, A.M., 19 November

The House

The House proceeded to consider the proposed amendments of the honorable Senate on the report of the committee appointed to consider and report in what particular mode the Electors of President and Vice President and the Senators and Representatives in the federal government shall be chosen etc. and concurred with the said amendments, excepting as to the proposed amendment in the third article [election of Senators] and as to that the House adhered to their own vote, 192 members present.[1]

Sent up.

The Senate

The report respecting the organization of the federal government came up concurred except as to the amendment in the third article. A motion was made for the Senate's concurring with the House and it was determined in the negative.

Adjourned to 3 o'clock P.M.

1. See Newspaper Report of House Proceedings on Wednesday, A.M., 19 November, printed immediately below.

Newspaper Report of House Proceedings on Wednesday, A.M., 19 November[1]

A resolve prescribing the mode of conducting the federal elections, with the amendments proposed thereto by the honorable Senate, was considered, and the amendments concurred in, except the article which gives a negative in each branch in the choice of Electors [i.e., of Senators].[2]

This last article occasioned a long debate, and was discussed with some warmth and animation, gentlemen contending on the one side that if the choice was made without each branch having a negative on the other (i.e., in their legislative capacity) the choice would not be constitutional. On the other side it was urged, that if, as expressed in the 4th section of the Federal Constitution "the times, places, and manner of holding elections for Senators and Representatives, shall be prescribed in each State by the Legislature thereof," that then undoubtedly any mode that the legislature might prescribe would be agreeably to the Federal Constitution, and therefore right. It was said, too, by gentlemen on this side the question, that gentlemen had contended that the Congress would be the judge of the constitutionality of the choice, and that they had a right to prescribe in what manner—whether by ballot, or hand vote—by a majority or plurality—and at what time the choice shall be made. If this is true, said they, and the authority therefore is derived from the 4th section, then undoubtedly the same section gives the legislature the same authority. This being admitted, and the usual practice of choosing members of Congress being by joint ballot, it was their opinion that such a mode would not only be proper and constitutional, but was in fact the only mode in which it could be effected. With respect to our own state constitution, in which the legislature is defined to be the two branches of the General Court, *acting on each other by a negative*, it was contended, that this definition did not extend to elections, but to acts, etc., and that if it did, the revisionary power of the Supreme Executive would be necessary to completing the choice, as it is in the completion of laws. These arguments were combatted by the other side with much close and argumentative reasoning, in which Mr. March said, that if the two branches of the General Court, convened in one room, were in fact the legislature, and in that capacity ought to act in the organization of the general government, he could not conceive what apology could be made for the conduct of the two branches, in acting *separately* on the subject, for ten days before, as undoubtedly they ought to have acted in a convention of both houses. If, said he, we ought to choose the Senators by joint ballot, we ought to prescribe the mode, time, and place of the elections in a joint assembly, and that the one mode was as plain, as fair, and as constitutional as the other.

(A variety of other observations on both sides the question, came from gentlemen during the discussion, and we do not give the above as a report of the debate, but merely a hasty sketch for a specimen.)

On the question being taken, to nonconcur the Senate, in this particular, and to adhere to the vote of the House, to have the choice by joint ballot of both houses, it was carried—yeas 148—nays 44. During the debate it was moved, by Mr. Widgery, that the Speaker be requested to deliver his opinion on the subject in debate, and he accordingly indulged the House therewith. His Honor appeared to be in favor of the opinion, that it was not necessary to a constitutional choice, that the legislature in the election should act in their concurrent capacity, but concluded with saying that he conceived that any *manner* the legislature might prescribe would be constitutional. He, however, wished that some mode of compromise might be adopted by the two branches. (The principal speakers were Dr. Jarvis, Mr. Ames, Mr. Gore, Mr. March, Mr. Widgery, and Mr. Bowdoin.)

The subject of organization committed to a joint committee.

1. *Massachusetts Centinel,* 22 November. With the exception of the final sentence, this newspaper report summarizes the House debates on Wednesday morning.

2. Although the *Centinel* report says "Electors," it is clearly an error. The legislative journals, as well as the remainder of the *Centinel* report, make it clear that the House was debating the mode of electing Senators, not Electors.

Final Joint Committee Report, Wednesday, A.M., 19 November

The Joint Committee Report of 4 November contained eight "propositions," which the Senate accepted without change and sent them to the House. The House debated and amended the report from 5 to 13 November and sent it to the Senate. The Senate took up the report, as amended by the House, on Tuesday, 18 November. It refused to concur in certain House amendments, proposed others, and returned the report to the House on the same day. On Wednesday morning, 19 November, the House accepted the Senate amendments, except for the Senate version of Article Three concerning the election of Senators, and returned the report. The Senate in turn refused to accept the House version of Article Three. This article was thus dropped from the report as finally agreed upon by the two houses by Wednesday noon, 19 November.

The document printed below combines the original report of 4 November and the House and Senate amendments and substitute articles, and indicates the action taken by each house. Certain actions of the two houses are recorded in their journals, but some of the most important ones are not. The latter are included in messages sent back and forth between the two houses and signed by the President of the Senate, Samuel Phillips, Jr., and the Speaker of the House, Theodore Sedgwick. These messages were added to the manuscript containing the original committee report of 4 November. In addition, four important amendments (House "Paper A" and "Paper B" and Senate "Paper C" and "Paper D") were written on separate sheets of paper which were sent back and forth with the original manuscript of 4 November and its appended messages. This manuscript and the slips of paper are in Miscellaneous Resolves, 1788, Chapter 49, M-Ar.

By Wednesday noon, 19 November, the way was thus cleared for the appointment of a new joint committee to prepare election resolutions based on those sections of the report upon which the two houses could agree (see House and Senate Proceedings, Wednesday, P.M., printed below).

[The Report]

Article One

[Committee Report, 4 November] That the Electors be chosen by the two houses of the General Court, by joint ballot [Expunged by House, 10 November; by Senate, 18 November].

[House Substitute, 10 November ("Paper A")] That when the inhabitants of the several towns and districts qualified to vote for Representatives for the general government shall be assembled for that purpose, they shall also give in their votes for some one person an inhabitant of the district in which such town or district respectively may be, for an Elector of the President and Vice President; or if such district is to choose two Electors the votes shall be given in accordingly. And a list of the votes so given in as aforesaid, shall by the selectmen of the several towns and districts, or the major part of them, be transmitted to the secretary's office, on or before the first Tuesday in January next, and, on the next day the General Court then in session, shall examine the returns, and from the three who shall be found to have the greatest number of votes in their respective districts, the two houses assembled in one room, shall by joint ballot choose one, who shall be considered the Elector for the district to which he belongs, observing also to double the number of candidates in those districts which are to choose more than one Elector, and that provision be made in a bill accordingly [Rejected by Senate, 18 November].

[Senate Substitute, 18 November ("Paper D")] That when the inhabitants of the several towns and districts qualified to vote for Representatives for the general government shall be assembled for that purpose, they shall also give in their votes for two persons who are inhabitants of the district in which such town or district may be as candidates for an Elector of the President and Vice President of the United States, and a list of the votes so given in as aforesaid, shall by the selectmen of the several towns and districts, or the major part of them be transmitted to the secretary's office on or before the first Monday in January next, and on the Wednesday following the General Court then in session, shall examine the returns, and from the two who shall be found to have the greatest number of votes in each district[———] members of the [two] houses assembled in one room shall by joint ballot elect one who shall be considered a[s] the Elector for the district to which he belongs, and in case it should so happen that more than two persons voted for as Electors should have an equal[ity?] of votes among the highest voted for, then the members of the two hous[es] as aforesaid shall out of such number choose the Elector.

And if in any case the aforesaid returns shall not be received from a district at the secretary's office on or before the first Monday in January, the members of the two houses of the legislature shall on the first Wednesday of January appoint some person who is an inhabitant of such district, for an Elector of the President and Vice President.

That the members of the two houses of the General Court shall in manner as aforesaid appoint at large two Electors for the President and Vice President not voted for by the districts as aforesaid [Accepted by House, 19 November].

Article Two

[Committee Report, 4 November] That the Electors meet on the first Wednesday of February, in the town of Boston, for the purpose of voting for President and Vice President, and for their time and travel receive the same compensation as members of the [state] Senate are entitled to [Approved without amendment by House and Senate].

Article Three

[Committee Report, 4 November] That the Senators be chosen by the two houses of the legislature, each having a negative upon the other [Rejected by House, 7 November].

[House Amendment, 7 November] That the Senators be chosen by the two houses of the legislature, by joint ballot in one room assembled [Rejected by Senate, 18 November].

[Senate Substitute, 18 November ("Paper C")] That the Senators be chosen by the two houses of the legislature, each having a negative upon the other. That each house of assembly in their separate capacity vote for Senators, the votes being collected by their committees, they shall repair into one lobby, count and sort the votes of each house separately, and in case any person shall have a majority of votes in each house, the committees aforesaid shall severally declare to each house by whom they were chosen, the choice [several illegible words] [——]tion [——]reof shall be given in manner aforesaid and each house continue to proceed in the same manner until two Senators shall be chosen by a majority of votes in each house [Rejected by House, 19 November].

Article Four

[Committee Report, 4 November] That the commonwealth be divided into eight districts, the inhabitants of each of which shall be authorized to choose one Representative [Approved without amendment by House and Senate].

Article Five

[Committee Report, 4 November] That each district be formed in such manner as to comprehend one eighth part of the polls in the commonwealth, as nearly as may be, without dividing counties [Approved without amendment by House].

[Senate Amendment, 18 November] That each district be formed in such manner as to comprehend one eighth part of the polls in the commonwealth as nearly as may be, without dividing counties, or connecting counties very remote from each other [Accepted by House, 19 November].

Article Six

[Committee Report, 4 November] That the county of Suffolk form one district; the county of Essex, one; the county of Middlesex, one; the county of Hampshire and Berkshire, one; the county of Plymouth and Barnstable, one; the counties of York, Cumberland, and Lincoln, one; the counties of Bristol, Dukes County, and Nantucket, one; the county of Worcester, one [Approved without amendment by House and Senate].

Article Seven

[Committee Report, 4 November] That precepts issue to the towns in the several districts, to vote on the ——— day of ———, for their respective Representatives, and to return lists of the votes to the Supreme Executive, on or before the ——— day of ———; and if any of the districts shall not have given a majority of votes to any one candidate, the Supreme Executive shall issue new precepts to such district for the choice of a Representative out of the two highest candidates first voted for, and that a majority of votes in this last instance constitute a choice; but in case the two candidates shall have an equal number of votes, the senators and representatives in the state legislature from such district shall determine which of the persons so voted for shall be the Representative.

[House Substitute, 10 November ("Paper B")] That the selectmen of the several towns and other places incorporated in this commonwealth shall ——— days before the ——— day of next issue their warrants to convene the inhabitants qualified by the constitution to vote in their respective towns and other places incorporated for a representative in the state legislature, at that time to assemble and vote for a Representative of the people of this state in Congress, at which meeting the selectmen shall preside, and a fair record shall in open town meeting be made by the town clerk, or in his absence by such person as the selectmen shall for that purpose appoint, of the names of persons voted for, and the number of votes for each, and a declaration thereof shall be made by the selectmen in the same meeting. A copy of which record, within ——— days thereafter certified by the selectmen and attested by the clerk, shall by them be transmitted to the office of a register of deeds within the district to which they respectively belong.

That the registers of deeds to whom copies of the said votes shall be transmitted, shall record the same in a book by them severally to be specially kept for that purpose and they shall count the said votes returned as aforesaid, and if it shall appear that any person shall have a majority of all the votes, in such case the register shall transmit within ——— days thereafter to the secretary's office, an account of the names of all the persons voted for in the respective towns and other places incorporated, and which the Secretary shall lay before the Governor and Council, and His Excellency the Governor shall make a certificate under the Seal of the Commonwealth of the election of the person so chosen to be one of the Representatives of the people of this state.

That if it shall appear, upon the said votes being so counted by any register as aforesaid, that no person hath had a majority of votes, the said register in every such case, shall within ——— days give notice thereof to the selectmen of the several towns and other places incorporated within the district, to which such register belongs and shall therewith transmit the names of all the persons voted for and the number of votes for each, and the said selectmen shall thereupon within ——— days thereafter issue their precepts as aforesaid for the voters as aforesaid, to assemble and vote in their respective towns, and other places incorporated within ——— days after issuing said precepts, and when so assembled the same proceedings shall be had in recording, declaring, and returning the votes as above specified, and the said register shall again examine and record the returns in manner as is aforesaid, and he shall thereupon make return of the state of votes, specifying the towns and other incorporated places, and the names of the persons voted for, and the number for each in the respective towns to the secretary's office, and on the second process as above pointed out, the person having the greatest number of votes shall be the Representative of the people of this commonwealth, from such district, and shall receive a certificate from the Governor as aforesaid. But if in the second time of voting two or more persons who have the greatest number of votes shall have an equal number the same proceedings shall be repeated, with this only difference, that information shall be communicated in manner above expressed of the names of the persons who have an equal number of votes as aforesaid, and so until some one person shall have a greater number of votes than any other, whereupon all proceedings in such election shall be transmitted to the secretary's office, and all other above pointed out, performed as aforesaid[1] [Rejected by Senate, 18 November].

[Senate Amendment, 18 November] That the selectmen of the towns and districts in the several districts described in this report cause the inhabitants thereof duly qualified, to assemble on the ——— day of ——— to vote for their respective Representatives, such Representative being an inhabitant of the district for which he may be chosen and return lists of the votes to the secretary's office, on or before the ——— day of ———; and if any of the districts shall not have given a majority of votes to any one candidate, the Supreme Executive shall issue precepts to such district for the choice of a Representative out of the two highest candidates first voted for, and that a majority of votes in this last instance, constitute a choice; returns thereof to be made as aforesaid, and in case there should be an equality of votes for the two candidates then voted for, another precept shall issue from the Supreme Executive as aforesaid and so [thus?] until one of the candidates shall have a majority of v[otes] [Accepted by House, 19 November].

Article Eight

[Committee Report, 4 November] That one Elector be chosen out of each district entitled to elect a Representative, and that the two remaining Electors be chosen in any part of the state [Expunged by House, 10 November; by Senate, 18 November].

1. Immediately beneath this substitute article there is the following, which is partially crossed out and evidently was not intended to be a part of the article:

"The subcommittee are further of opinion that all frauds in conducting this business and all neglects should be severely punished, and that provision should be made for a reasonable recompense to the registers."

House and Senate Proceedings, Wednesday, P.M., 19 November

The Senate

Met according to adjournment.

Ordered, that Caleb Strong and Thomas Dawes, Esqr., with such as the honorable House may join, be a committee to bring into a resolve for carrying into effect, those parts of the report for organizing the federal government, in which the two houses have concurred.

Sent down for concurrence.

The House

[The House received the Senate message.]

Read and concurred and Mr. Gore, Mr. Ames, and Mr. Lyman were joined.

Ordered, that Mr. Ives, Dr. Jarvis, and Mr. Wedgery be a committee on the part of the House to confer with such committee as the honorable Senate may appoint on the subject matter of the difference between the houses on the said report [i.e., the election of Senators].[1]

Sent up for concurrence.

The Senate

[The Senate received the House message.]

Read and concurred. Ebe[ne]zer Brooks, Benjamin Goodhue, and Tristram Dalton, Esqr., are appointed on the part of the Senate.

. . . .

Received resolve for organizing the federal government, as reported by a committee of both houses.

Read and accepted with amendments.

Sent down for concurrence.[2]

In Senate, November 19, 1788.[3]

Read and accepted with amendments at A, B, D, E, F, G, H, and I, and resolved accordingly.

Sent down for concurrence.

[s] Saml. Phillips, Jr., President

1. In the Wednesday morning session William Widgery proposed that the House seek a compromise with the Senate on the election of Senators (see Newspaper Report of House Proceedings, Wednesday, A.M., printed above). For the House compromise and its rejection by the Senate, see House and Senate Proceedings, Thursday, P.M., 20 November, printed below.

2. Immediately after this entry in the Senate Journals is this entry: "Came up concurred with amendments. Concurred." The entry is misplaced because the House did not act on the Senate amendments until Thursday afternoon, 20 November.

3. This message to the House is not in the Senate Journals but is written on the manuscript of the resolutions immediately after the conclusion of the last resolution. The Senate amendments were written on a separate sheet of paper and lettered from "A" through "L" and keyed to letters which the Senate inserted in the manuscript of the resolutions. They are printed below as part of the Massachusetts Election Resolutions, 20 November.

House Proceedings, Thursday, A.M., 20 November

[The House received the Joint Committee Resolutions of 19 November with the Senate's proposed changes.]

Read and a motion was made and seconded that in the clause providing for the choice of Representatives the words "an inhabitant of such district" be stricken out, and the question being put passed in the negative.[1] It was then moved and seconded that the districts (for choosing Representatives) be so altered that the counties of Plymouth and Bristol form one district, the counties of Barnstable and Berkshire one district, and the counties of Nantucket and Duke's County be annexed to Suffolk; and that the county of Hampshire form one district. And the question being put was determined in the negative.[2] A motion was then made and seconded that this vote be reconsidered, and the question of reconsideration being required to be taken by yeas and nays, they were found to be as follows, viz.,

Yeas: [81]

Thomas Clarke	David Smead
Nathaniel Bayley	Nehemiah Stebbins
Moses Richardson, Jr.	John Goldsbury
Israel Hutchinson	Isaac Pepper
Christopher Sargent	Reuben Slaten
Edward Barns	Hezekiah Newcomb
Abner Sanderson	John Jennings
Parker Varnum	William Ward
Samuel Lyman	William Stebbins
Benjamin Ely	Elijah Hayes
Phinehas Stebbins	Jacob Bradbury
Samuel Henshaw	Samuel Nasson
Benjamin Sheldon	Jeremiah Emery
Enoch White	Daniel Forbes
Daniel Cooley	Jeremiah Learned
Benjamin Eastman	Samuel Robinson
William Bodman	Seth Washburn
Samuel Fowler	James Hathaway
John Bardwell	Asaph Sherman
Consider Arms	Joseph Wright
Joseph Browning	Stephen Maynard
Asa Fisk	John Fuller
Ezekiel Kellogg, Jr.	Josiah Whitney
Benj. Bonney	Luke Drury
Adam Clark	Peter Woodbury
David Shaw	John Warren
Moses Severance	John Black
Ebenezer Jones	Jonas Temple
Justus Dwight	Edmund Phinney
Hugh McClellan	William Wedgery
Edward Giles	Samuel Perly
Samuel Thrall	James Cargill

Samuel Thompson
Solomon Stanley
Jacob Ludwig
John Ashley, Jr.
Thomas Ives
Ebenezer Peirce
Daniel Taylor
Thompson J. Skinner
Ephraim Fitch

Ezekiel Hearick
John Picket, Jr.
Nathaniel Bishop
Thomas Lusk
John Hurlbut
Reuben Hinman
Ebenezer Jenkins
Denison Robinson

Nays: [100]

Oliver Wendell
Jonathan Mason
Charles Jarvis
Thomas Dawes, Jr.
Thomas Russell
Christopher Gore
William Heath
James Bowdoin, Jr.
Joseph Blake
Ebenezer Thayer
Theophilus Cushing
Fisher Ames
Aaron Holbrook
Thomas Mann
John Goddard
Seth Kingsbury
Richard Manning
Ebenezer Beckford
William Vans
William Pickman
Francis Cabot
John Choate
John Heard
Ebenezer March
William Coombs
Jonathan Marsh
Jonathan Glover
Samuel Sewall
John Carnes
Thomas Mighill
Nathaniel Marsh
Peter Russell
Ebenr. Carlton
Stephen Dana
Jeduthan Willington
Timothy Winn
Abraham Fuller
Edward Farmer

Joseph Simonds
John Minot
Daniel Whitney
William Rice
William Wait
Isaac Jones
Thomas Brook
Walter McFarland
Zacheus Wright
Jonathan Wood
Benjamin Morse
Daniel Adams
Samuel Park
Thomas Noyes
Chambers Russell
William Brown
Samuel Reid
Joseph Curtis
Thomas Davis
Joseph Tolman
Elisha Mitchell
Benjamin Thomas
Abraham Holmes
Francis Shurtliff
Samuel Goold
Ebenezer Washburn
Jacob Smith, Jr.
Lemuel Curtis
Shearjashub Bourne
David Thatcher
David Nye
Nathaniel Leonard
Frederick Drown
John Bishop
James Luther, Jr.
David Willcox
John Crane
Elisha May

Sylvester Richmond	Benjamin Joslyn
Jail Hathway	Isaac Harrington
Abiel Mitchell	Joshua Harding, Jr.
John Pratt	David Wilder
Walter Spooner	Samuel Wilder
William Davis	Moses Hale
John Swett	David Stearns
Mark Adams	Benjamin Richardson
Joseph Hubbard	Joseph Noyes
Samuel Scamman	William Thompson
Timothy Paine	Samuel Calef
Michael Newhall	Daniel Cony

So the question was determined in the negative.
Adjourned to 3 o'clock P.M.

1. On 8 November, a motion had been made in the House to amend the fourth article of the Joint Committee Report of 4 November to require that Representatives be inhabitants of the districts in which they were elected. The motion "Passed in the negative." The issue was not raised again until 18 November, when the Senate included the residence requirement in its amendment to Article Seven of the original report. This was the amendment accepted by the House.

There was very little comment by men who opposed the division of the state into districts and the requirement that Representatives be inhabitants of the districts they represented. One was Nathaniel W. Appleton, who wrote that "the division of the state into districts and the confining the choice of a candidate to his own district, is, in my opinion, contrary to the true spirit of the Constitution, which aims at being as *national* as possible in the choice of Representatives to the new Congress. This measure was carried, I imagine, by the influence of those members in the House who were candidates [———] the birth and imagined that their influence was such in their respective counties, as to secure them an election, [b]ut if chosen at large, their influence would be lost" (to Noah Webster, Boston, 30 November, RC, Webster Collection, NN). Another was Christopher Gore, who, after failing in his campaign to elect his friend Rufus King to either the Senate or the House of Representatives, declared that King would have been elected in the Suffolk District if it had not been for the "unconstitutional restriction of the resolve of the General Court" requiring Representatives to be inhabitants of the districts they represented (Gore to King, 21 December, printed below in The Election in Suffolk District).

2. For previous attempts in the House to alter the districts as agreed upon in the Joint Committee Report of 4 November, see the House Proceedings, 7, 8, 11, 12, 13 November, and the newspaper reports on House Proceedings, 7 and 8 November, all printed above.

House and Senate Proceedings, Thursday, P.M., 20 November

The House

The House proceeded to consider the report of the committee appointed to bring in a resolve providing for the choice of federal Electors and Representatives with the proposed amendments thereon and after debate,

Voted, that the House of Representatives shall originate the choice of two Senators for the government of the United States, and send up to the Senate the names of two persons to be by them concurred in said choice, and in case the

Senate do not concur, the House shall then proceed to choose again and shall continue to proceed in the same manner until the two houses do agree.

Sent up for concurrence.

The House then concurred in the proposed amendment of the honorable Senate in the said resolve, excepting at G and H as to which the House nonconcurred the honorable Senate.

Sent up for concurrence.

In the House of Representatives November 20, 1788[1]

Read and concurred excepting as to the proposed amendments at G and H and as to them the House nonconcur.

Sent up for concurrence.

[s] Theodore Sedgwick, Speaker

The Senate

[The Senate received the House compromise proposal for the election of Senators.]

Read and nonconcurred.[2]

[The Senate received the House concurrence in all but two of the proposed Senate amendments to the Joint Committee Resolutions of 19 November.]

In the Senate November 20, 1788[3]

Read and concurred.

[s] Saml. Phillips, Jr., President

Approved.

[s] John Hancock

1. This message to the Senate is not in the House Journals but is written on the manuscript of the resolutions immediately after the Senate message to the House of the previous day (Miscellaneous Resolves, 1788, Chapter 49, M-Ar).

2. Since the two houses could not agree, the Massachusetts Election Resolutions of 20 November contain no mention of the election of Senators.

3. This item is not in the Senate Journals but is written immediately after the House message cited in note 1, as is Governor John Hancock's signature. What appears to be the Senate concurrence is in the Senate Journals for 19 November.

For the resolutions as agreed to by the two houses, including the Senate's amendments and the House's action thereon, see The Massachusetts Election Resolutions, 20 November, printed below.

Newspaper Report of House Proceedings on Thursday, 20 November[1]

The joint committee appointed yesterday reported, and the discussion of the subject of organization again took up much time; but on the question to pass the resolution respecting the choice of Electors and Representatives being put,

General Whitney said, that as the resolve under consideration was but a partial one, and as it did not appear the Senate would concur with the House, or the House with the Senate, respecting the manner of choosing Senators, and that therefore the plan could not be at present completed, he moved, *that the consideration of the whole subject be referred to the next session of the General Court.* This was seconded by Mr. Wedgery.

This motion created much surprise in the House, and occasioned many pointed animadversions from several gentlemen. Among them Mr. Henshaw moved, to make the matter *complete*, and to *effect the whole design*, that it be referred to the third Tuesday of May next—(*A general smile*).

Mr. Breck said, as he was sure the gentleman who first moved for the reference, must be joking, he wished the question might be put.

Mr. Whitney and Mr. Widgery said they were serious in the matter. This drew from Dr. Coney, Mr. Breck, Mr. Bowdoin, and Mr. Choate some very pointed remarks in which they reprobated the measure in the strongest terms.

Mr. Widgery in support of the motion said, rather than only *half-do* the business, he would wait until the whole could be finished, which he did not see there was any likelihood of the present session. No one, he said, would want to go to sea in half a ship, but would rather wait until they could build a whole one. For this reason he was in favor of the motion. (It is, however, but just to observe, that Messrs. Whitney and Widgery both repeatedly declared that they wished a speedy organization of the new government, if it could be done complete.)

The agitation into which the House was thrown by this motion subsided, as did the motion itself on Mr. Lyman's rising and moving a conciliatory plan by which, in the choice of Senators, the House should choose two and send them up to the Senate for concurrence. If the Senate did not concur, then the House to choose again, and so on, until the choice should be completed. This motion obtained, and was sent up to the honorable Senate. After which the resolve in debate passed.

1. *Massachusetts Centinel,* 22 November.

Herald of Freedom, 20 November

Our legislature have not yet been able to agree upon a mode of electing Senators. Each branch is extremely tenacious of its authority. As there can be no point of mutual concession, but either the House or the Senate must completely concede to the other, we are fearful that the difficulty will not easily be removed. A correspondent laments that so many embarrassments appear in organizing the new government, to retard the progress of the business. It is not however the work of a moment, to bring into operation a Constitution which is to protect the rights and secure the glory of the vast empire of united America.

The Massachusetts Election Resolutions, 20 November

There is no evidence to explain why Massachusetts was the only state to provide for the first federal elections with a set of resolutions rather than a formal act of legislation. The Joint Committee Resolutions of Wednesday afternoon, 19 November, as finally agreed upon by the two houses on Thursday afternoon, 20 November, and which became the Massachusetts Election Resolutions, are transcribed from the manuscript of the resolutions in Miscellaneous Resolves, 1788,

Chapter 49, M-Ar. We have placed the seven Senate amendments and one deletion in brackets in the text of the Joint Committee Resolutions, and have lined out the deletion, which the House agreed to, and the two amendments which the House rejected.

The six pages of the manuscript resolutions conclude with the Senate message of 19 November proposing amendments, the House message of 20 November concurring in all the amendments except "at G & H," the final Senate concurrence, and the Governor's signature. The manuscript of the Joint Committee Resolutions was folded and endorsed: "Resolve for Organizing the Federal Government Nov. 19th 1788." The endorsement was followed by the notation: "Copied for the Press."

The copy was sent to Thomas Adams and John Nourse, publishers of the *Independent Chronicle,* who were also "Printers to the Honorable General Court." They published the Massachusetts Election Resolutions as a broadside, which was headed: "Commonwealth of Massachusetts" and on the next line: "In Senate, November 19, 1788." By giving a prominent place to the date 19 November, the printers repeated the error of the endorser of the Election Resolutions and presumably of the clerk who copied the resolutions for the press. However, the broadside also includes in smaller type near the bottom of the sheet the House action dated 20 November. After the end of the session on 24 November, the resolutions were published in *Resolves of the General Court . . .* [29 October–24 November] (Boston, 1788), 52–54, under the title: "Resolve for organizing the Federal Government, November 19, 1788."

The Election Resolutions received widespread newspaper attention (see, for example, the *Massachusetts Centinel,* 22 November; Portsmouth *New Hampshire Gazette,* 26 November; Providence *United States Chronicle,* 27 November; New York *Daily Advertiser,* 2 December; Hartford *Connecticut Courant,* 8 December; Philadelphia *Pennsylvania Packet,* 9 December; and Baltimore *Maryland Journal,* 16 December).

The legislature revised the Election Resolutions of 20 November with respect to the election of the two Electors at large on 6 January 1789 (see House and Senate Proceedings, 6 January 1789, printed below in The Election of Presidential Electors). The votes cast for Representatives on 18 December, the recording of the votes by the Governor and Council, and additional election resolutions are printed below in The Official Results of the First Election, 5-10 January 1789.

[The Resolutions] [1]

Commonwealth of Massachusetts

In Senate November 19 1788

Resolved

That the Commonwealth be divided into eight districts for the purpose of choosing eight persons to represent the people thereof in the Congress of the United States—Each district to choose one representative who shall be an inhabitant of such district—and that the districts be as follows—*viz*—

The County of Suffolk be one district
The County of Essex one district
The County of Middlesex one district
The Counties of Hampshire & Berkshire one district

The Counties of Plymouth & Barnstable one district
The Counties of York, Cumberland & Lincoln one District
The Counties of Bristol Duke's County & Nantucket one district
The County of Worcester one district
And be it further Resolved

That the Selectmen of the respective Towns & Districts before described [Insertion: shall in manner as the law directs for calling town meetings] cause the inhabitants thereof, duly qualified, to vote for representatives to the General Court of this Commonwealth, to assemble on Thursday the eighteenth day of December next, to give in their votes for their respective Representatives to the Selectmen who shall preside at such meeting—And the Selectmen, or the major part of them shall, in open town meeting, sort and count the votes, and form a list of the persons voted for, with the number of votes for each person against his name, [Deletion: and shall cause the Town Clerk to make a fair record of the same in the Town Books], and shall make a public declaration thereof in the said meeting—and shall in the presence of the inhabitants, seal up *copies* of the said list, and transmit the same to the office of the Secretary of the Commonwealth, on or before the first monday of Jany. next [Insertion: And the Clerk of each town & district, shall make [and] fairly transcribe in the Records thereof the list aforesaid] and the Secretary shall lay the same before his Excellency, the Governor—[Insertion: and the Council] And in case of an election for any district by a majority of all the votes returned his Excellency the Governor is hereby requested forthwith to transmit to the person so chosen a Certificate thereof—And in case no person shall have a majority of votes, the Governor is hereby requested to cause precepts to issue [Insertion: accompanied with a certificate of the names of the two persons who had the greatest number of votes in the first return] to the Selectmen of the several towns & districts within the district for which no person shall have been chosen as aforesaid to assemble the inhabitants of their respective towns and districts, qualified as aforesaid, on a day in such precept to be appointed, to give in their votes [Insertion: for one of the persons named in the said Certificate] [2] for a Representative [Insertion: & in case two or more persons who have the greatest number of Votes shall have an equal number, then the Governor is requested to Certify the names of such persons to the Selectmen as aforesaid—], and the like proceedings shall be had thereon, as are herein before directed, and the Selectmen shall make return thereof in manner as aforesaid to the Secretary's office on or before a day in such precept to be prescribed—and the Secretary shall lay the same before the Governor—[Insertion: *and Council*] And in case any person shall have a majority as aforesaid, the Governor is requested forthwith to transmit to the person so chosen a Certificate thereof And in case no person shall have a majority of votes, the Governor is requested to issue like precepts as often as the case may require.

And be it further Resolved,

That when the Inhabitants of the several Towns & Districts qualified as aforesaid shall be assembled on the said eighteenth day of December next, they shall also give in their votes for two persons who shall be inhabitants of the district in which such Town or District may be, as Candidates for an Elector of the President and Vice President of the United States—And a list of the votes so given in as aforesaid, Shall, by the Selectmen of the several Towns & Districts, or the major part of them be transmitted to the Secretary's office on or before the first monday in January next—and on the Wednesday next following, the General Court then in session shall examine the said Returns, and from the two who shall be found to have the greatest number of votes in each district, the members of the two houses assembled in one room shall by joint ballot elect one who shall be the Elector for the district to which he belongs—and in case it should so happen, that more than two persons voted for as Electors should have an equality of votes among the highest voted for, then the members of the two houses as aforesaid shall out of such number choose the Elector

And if in any case the aforesaid Returns from a district shall not be received at the Secretary's office on or before the first monday in January next, the members of the two houses of the Legislature shall on the first wednesday of January next appoint some person, being an inhabitant of such district for an Elector of the President and Vice President—

And be it further Resolved

That the members of the two houses of the General Court shall in manner as aforesaid appoint at large, two Electors for the President and Vice President, not voted for by the districts as aforesaid—

And be it further Resolved

That the said Electors be and they are hereby directed to meet on the first Wednesday of February next at ten o'clock in the forenoon at the State House in the Town of Boston for the purpose of voting by ballot for two persons for President and Vice President of the United States agreably to the Constitution of said United States, and that for their Travel and Attendance, they shall receive the same compensation as members of the [state] Senate are entitled to—

1. (LT), Miscellaneous Resolves, 1788, Chapter 49, M-Ar.
2. If the House had accepted this amendment and the one following, there could have been only one runoff election in any district. There was at first some confusion because the House did not reject the amendment immediately preceding the two rejected amendments, the amendment which required the Governor to name the two men receiving the highest number of votes in the preceding election when issuing precepts for runoff elections. However, the newspapers explained that the voters could vote for anyone they chose despite the precepts (see, for example, the *Herald of Freedom*, 29 December), and the voters did so.

The Election of United States Senators, 21, 22, 24 November

By 21 November, at least eight men had been "nominated" for the United States Senate in newspaper articles or private correspondence, but only one of them, John Adams, had refused to be considered for a Senate seat, and only one, Caleb Strong, was elected.

The Massachusetts House and Senate could not agree on how to elect Senators. The House proposed to elect them by joint ballot, as had been done in electing members of the Confederation Congress. According to George Minot, House Speaker Theodore Sedgwick worked hard for the joint ballot because the larger numbers in the House would favor his candidacy (Minot Journal, November, printed below). The Senate proposed that each house vote separately and that as soon as a candidate obtained a majority of the votes in each house, he would be elected. At the last moment, the House proposed a compromise: the House would elect two men and send their names to the Senate, and if the Senate rejected one or both House nominees, the House would send up a new name or names. The Senate refused to accept the House plan, with the result that the Massachusetts Election Resolutions of 20 November contained no provision for the election of Senators. On 21 November, the House persisted in its "compromise" plan and nominated two men. The Senate approved one choice (Caleb Strong), rejected Charles Jarvis, and selected a candidate of its own. The House after repeatedly rejecting the Senate's nominees finally yielded and accepted Tristram Dalton. With the exception of Charles Jarvis, whom the Senate rejected on three separate occasions before he withdrew, neither house seemed to have fixed on a single candidate as a second Senator.

The documents that have been located do not provide much evidence as to the motives involved in the Senate contest. However, the election stirred up much animosity among Federalist leaders, and Theophilus Parsons of Newburyport appears to have played a key role; but the documents do not indicate what Parsons did that so angered Theodore Sedgwick and other disappointed candidates, and there is little evidence of the nature of the "lies" told about Rufus King. Also, aside from the personalities involved, it is clear that each house was jealous of its own prerogatives, and leaders in each branch of the legislature insisted that their house elect the Senators.

The documents printed below range chronologically from John Adams's letter of 2 November refusing to be considered for a Senate seat through the credentials issued to Caleb Strong and Tristram Dalton on 10 February 1789.

John Adams to Theophilus Parsons, Braintree, 2 November [1]

From the conversation that passed between you and me, when I had the pleasure to see you for a few moments at this place, I am apprehensive that you may think of me for a Senator, as I find that some other gentlemen have done and continue to do.

You know very well how ungracious and odious the nonacceptance of an appointment by election is, and therefore let me beg of you, not to expose me to the necessity of incurring the censure of the public and the obloquy of individuals by so unpopular a measure.

I have long revolved in an anxious mind the duties of the man and the citizen, and without entering into details, at present, the result of all my reflections on the place of a Senator in the new government is an unchangeable determination to refuse it.

1. FC, Adams Papers, MHi. Parsons, who represented Newburyport in the House in 1788, was one of the leading lawyers in the state. He was the leader of what was known as the Essex Junto, and he played a key role in securing ratification of the Constitution by Massachusetts and was later chief justice of the state.

Boston Gazette, 3 November

The gentlemen almost universally talked of as federal Senators are the Honorable John and Samuel Adams and the Honorable Francis Dana, esquires. These are all highly meritorious, and equally entitled to the first honors of the government. The distinguished rank the two first of these gentlemen have sustained in the course of the Revolution; their unshaken attachment to the liberties of the people and the honor of government, their long tried fidelity, their uninterrupted friendship, and above all, the respect and affection they have invariably discovered to the citizens of this state in particular, and the United States in general, have placed them in the first rank of American patriots. The republican principles of the last of the three are equally unsuspected. It was this honorable gentleman who introduced among the amendments proposed by the Convention that one, which limits the power of direct taxation in the federal legislature till it was preceded by a formal requisition on the states, and then to be exercised upon them which were delinquent.[1] By this important provision, a host of continental officers in the several states and towns will be prevented. The honorable judge is a decided friend of amendments and therefore a suitable person for this important office. The public will, no doubt, felicitate itself on the prospect of success which two of these gentlemen have, and on the little chance there is, of any other candidate obtaining this high honor. Notwithstanding the dark intrigues of an active and interested party of unprincipled *seekers,* whose existence and vanity depend on the success of their nefarious attempts, to insert in the new government none but their own connections.

1. The amendment referred to was among those submitted by Governor John Hancock rather than by Dana (Convention, *Debates,* 80).

Massachusetts Centinel, 5 November

The gentlemen, whom the *interest* of this commonwealth, and the great concerns of the United States would lead all true Federalists to wish may be chosen federal Senators, are the Hon. Caleb Strong, and Hon. Rufus King, esquires.[1] This will be properly balancing the *landed* and *commercial* interests. These gentlemen possess characters unrivalled for republican principles and abilities, great from nature, and matured by the fullest experience in national affairs. Their reputations are unsullied, and the services rendered by them to their country are engraven on the heart of every son of Massachusetts. There are other characters perhaps equally deserving, but few that we can rationally hope will have equal weight and influence in the federal legislature.

1. On 16 November Henry Van Schaack reported from Pittsfield that "the candidates for a seat in the Senate are Caleb Strong, Judge [Francis] Dana, Samuel Adams, Theodore Sedgwick, and Rufus King. Who will succeed it is difficult to determine. The two former it is expected will be chosen" (to Peter Van Schaack, RC, Van Schaack Special Manuscript Collection, NNC). Another portion of this letter relating to candidates for the Vice Presidency is printed in Chapter XIV.

Theodore Sedgwick to Mrs. Theodore Sedgwick, Boston, 9 November (excerpt)[1]

It is at present impossible to determine when the General Court will adjourn, none of the great business having as yet been attended to, so as to be completed, but there seems to be a general determination to be at home at Thanksgiving. I hope it will be possible.

With regard to the important subject you mention, your tenderness, delicacy, and generosity are such as might be expected from you and from almost no one else. Among the many distinguished characters, it is impos[sible] with any degree of certainty to determine where the choice of the majority will fall. If the partiality of my friends consider me as an object on whom to devolve so important a trust, their delicacy is extreme and nothing but their silence induces me to suppose this is the case. But let what will take place, be assured, best beloved of my soul, that I will never continue to exercise an office which shall separate me from my family. My resolution on this subject is decided, and I do now most solemnly pledge you my faith for the fulfillment of this declaration. My own happiness out of the question which must be sacrificed to a separation, the duty I owe my children, and more particularly you, my love, will forever you [———] [———] assured keep me steady to my [———] already have suffered enough to [———] my country.[2]

1. RC, Sedgwick Papers, MHi.
2. Despite Sedgwick's professions to his wife, documents printed below indicate that he was bitter because he was not elected United States Senator. Furthermore, he waged five election campaigns before he was elected to the House of Representatives from the Hampshire-Berkshire District.

House and Senate Proceedings, Friday, 21 November

The House, A.M.

The House assigned 12 o'clock this day for coming to the choice of two Senators to represent this commonwealth in the Senate of the United States.

. . . .

The House, P.M.

The House proceeded by ballot to the choice of two Senators to represent this state in the Senate of the United States for a term to commence on the first Wednesday of March next, according to the Constitution of the said states, and the Hon. Caleb Strong, Esquire, and Charles Jarvis, Esquire, were chosen.

Sent up for concurrence by a committee of five members.

The Senate, P.M.

[The Senate received the House vote for Caleb Strong and Charles Jarvis.]

Read and concurred with an amendment: delete Charles Jarvis, Esqr., and ins[ert] Honble. John Lowell, Esqr.

Sent down for concurrence.

The House, P.M.

[The House received the Senate message rejecting Charles Jarvis and proposing John Lowell.]

Voted, that the House will assign a time for coming to the choice of a Senator.

The House then assigned the present time for that purpose. The House then proceeded to the choice of a Senator as aforesaid by ballot, and Charles Jarvis, Esquire, was chosen.

Ordered, that the vote of Senate be entered upon as follows, viz.: Read and nonconcurred and the House adhere to their own vote.

Sent up.

Newspaper Report of House Proceedings on Friday, 21 November[1]

Twelve o'clock, being the time assigned for the House coming to the choice of two persons to represent this commonwealth in the Senate of the United States, a committee was appointed to collect, sort, and count the votes for the same—who reported that the whole number of votes was 201—101 making a choice, that the Hon. Caleb Strong, Esquire, had 125 votes, and was chosen.

(The other persons voted for were the Hon. Mr. [Theodore] Sedgwick, who had 67, Dr. [Charles] Jarvis 79, Mr. [John] Lowell 59, Mr. [Samuel] Holten 39, Mr. [Nathaniel] Gorham 23.)

The committee then proceeded to collect the votes for one Senator, who reported that the whole number of votes were 204—103 making a choice—that Charles Jarvis, Esquire, had 113, and was chosen.

A committee, consisting of Mr. Henshaw, Mr. Dawes, Mr. Heath, Mr. Spooner, and Mr. Bourne was then chosen to carry to the honorable Senate the above choice for concurrence.

A message was received from the honorable Senate concurring in the choice of the Hon. Caleb Strong (who had 27 of 29 votes), nonconcurring Dr. J[arvis] and proposing for the concurrence of the House, the Hon. John Lowell, Esq.

The House again proceeded to give in their votes for one Senator when the committee appointed for that purpose reported, that the whole number of votes was 185—93 making a choice—that Charles Jarvis, Esq., had 108, and was rechosen by the House. The choice is not yet completed.

1. *Massachusetts Centinel,* 22 November.

House and Senate Proceedings, Saturday, 22 November

The Senate, A.M.

[The Senate received the House message adhering to its choice of Charles Jarvis for Senator.]

Read again and reconsidered, and instead of the Hon. John Lowell, Esqr., insert Hon. Azor Orne, Esqr.

Sent down for concurrence.[1]

The House, A.M.

[The House received the Senate's vote for Azor Orne.]

The House then proceeded by ballot to the choice of a Senator to represent this state in the Senate of the United States, and Charles Jarvis, Esquire, was chosen.

Ordered, that the following entry be made on the vote: Read again and nonconcurred and the House again adhere to their own vote.

Sent up.

The Senate, P.M.

[The Senate received the House's third vote for Charles Jarvis.]

The Senate again reconsidered their vote and instead of Honorable Azor Orne, Esquire, insert Honorable Tristram Dalton, Esquire.

Sent down for concurrence.[2]

The House, P.M.

Read and a motion was made and seconded that the further consideration of the choice of a Senator to represent this state in the Senate of the United States be referred to the next setting of the General Court, and the yeas and nays being required they were found to be as follows, viz.,

Yeas: [70]

Charles Jarvis	John Jennings
Thomas Russell	Thomas Davis
William Heath	Nathl. Leonard
Aaron Holbrook	Frederick Drown
Moses Richardson, Jr.	John Bishop
Peter Osgood, Jr.	David Willcox
Thomas Mighill	John Crane
John Minot	Jail Hathway
Isaac Jones	Abiel Mitchell
Walter McFarland	Samuel Nasson
Abner Sanderson	Jeremiah Emery
Benjamin Morse	Daniel Forbes
Daniel Adams	Samuel Robinson
Samuel Reid	Jonathan Woodbury
Benjamin Ely	Seth Washburn
Phinehas Stebbins	James Hathway
Daniel Cooley	Asaph Sherman
Benjamin Eastman	Joseph Wright
Josiah Allis	Benjamin Joslyn
William Bodman	Stephen Maynard
Consider Arms	Isaac Davis
Asa Fisk	Isaac Harrington
Adam Clark	Josiah Whitney
David Shaw	Joshua Harding, Jr.
Justis Dwight	Luke Drury
Silas Fowler	Peter Woodbury
Nehemiah Stebbins	Stephen Holden
John Goldsbury	Ezekiel Knowlton
Isaac Pepper	John Black
Reuben Slaten	Jonas Temple

Edmund Phinney
William Wedgery
Samuel Perly
Samuel Thompson
Daniel Cony

Thomas Ives
John Picket, Jr.
Thomas Lusk
John Hurlbut
Denison Robinson

Nays: [78]

Oliver Wendall
Samuel Breck
Jonathan Mason
Thomas Dawes, Jr.
Christopher Gore
Thomas Clarke
Joseph Blake
Ebenezer Thayer
Theophilus Cushing
Fisher Ames
John Goddard
Seth Kingsbury
John Choate
John Heard
Ebenezer March
Theophilus Parsons
William Coombs
Jonathan Marsh
Jonathan Glover
Samuel Sewall
John Carnes
Larkin Thorndike
Israel Thorndike
Joseph March
Nathl. Marsh
William Pearson
Peter Russell
Stephen Dana
Jeduthan Willington
Amos Bond
Abraham Fuller
James Bancroft
Edward Barns
Daniel Whitney
William Rice
Thomas Brook
Parker Varnum
Samuel Park
Joseph Curtis

Benjamin Sheldon
Enoch White
Samuel Fowler
John Bardwell
Joshua Shaw
Oliver Smith
Hugh McClellan
David Smead
William Stebbins
Joseph Tolman
Elisha Mitchell
Benjamin Thomas
Samuel Goold
Jacob Smith, Jr.
Lemuel Curtis
Shearjashub Bourne
David Thatcher
Walter Spooner
William Davis
John Swett
David Wilder
Park Holland
Samuel Wilder
Benjamin Richardson
Joseph Noyes
John Fox
William Tompson
Samuel Calef
Ebenezer Whittier
John Stinson
James Cargill
Solomon Stanley
John Ashley, Jr.
Ebenezer Peirce
Daniel Taylor
Tompson J. Skinner
Nathaniel Bishop
Reuben Hinman
Ebenezer Jenkins

So the question was determined in the negative and the House then proceeded by ballot to the choice of a Senator to represent this state in the Senate of the United States and the Hon. Nathan Dane, Esqr., was chosen.

The following entry was then made on the vote, viz.: Read and nonconcurred and the House reconsider their original vote so far as to insert the Hon. Nathan Dane, Esqr., instead of Charles Jarvis, Esqr.[3]

Sent up for concurrence.

1. This entry is not in the Senate Journals for 22 November but is inserted in the Journals for 21 November. See Miscellaneous Legislative Documents, Senate Files, M-Ar, for the Senate message to the House containing the above vote. The message is headed "In Senate Nov. 22 1788." The message is contained in a document which is endorsed "Choice of Senators in the 1st Congress 1788." The document contains all the messages signed by Speaker Theodore Sedgwick and President of the Senate Samuel Phillips, Jr., reporting the actions of each house concerning the election of Senators on 21, 22, and 24 November.

2. This entry, like the one referred to in note 1 above, is inserted in the Senate Journals for 21 November. However, this action was taken the afternoon of the 22nd (see Newspaper Report of House and Senate Proceedings on 22 November, printed below).

3. For Charles Jarvis's speech withdrawing from the contest, see Newspaper Report of House Proceedings on 22 November, printed immediately below.

Newspaper Report of House and Senate Proceedings on Saturday, 22 November [1]

A variety of public and private business was this day completed.

A message was received from the honorable Senate, on the subject of the election of Senators of the United States, in which it appeared, that they non-concurred the choice of Dr. [Charles] Jarvis, and sent down for concurrence, the Hon. Azor Orne, Esq. The House then again proceeded to ballot for one Senator, when the Hon. Mr. Orne was nonconcurred, and Charles Jarvis, Esquire, a third time elected by the House, and sent up.

In the afternoon, the Senate sent another message to the House, in which it appeared, that they had again nonconcurred Dr. Jarvis, and sent down the Hon. Tristram Dalton, which being read,

Dr. Jarvis rose, and requested the indulgence of the House a few moments. He hoped to be excused, if he could not do justice to his feelings on the occasion, on account of a severe inflammation in his breast, with which he had some time been affected. The Doctor spoke in a low voice—and was called on to raise it but he declared it impossible, that he would with pleasure do it if he could, but if he could, he was convinced, that it was wholly out of his power, by any strength of language, or force of expression, to communicate an adequate idea of the deep emotions of gratitude which he felt, for the uniform and manly support he had so often received from a large and respectable majority of the House. Their suffrages, he said, did him the highest honor—and the sensations they impressed on his mind would only terminate with his life. This pleasure, he said, was heightened by the consciousness of their having been altogether unsolicited on his part. If this is not the case, said he, let a single instance be produced to the contrary. It was now his duty, he said, to make his warmest acknowledgments to his friends on the occasion, and to request them no longer to protract a contest, which, perhaps, might not speedily be terminated. In the present state of the country, just recovering from the distresses of a long and cruel war, and oppressed with the weight of those public exactions, which the necessity of the times has occasioned, every mark of economy, the Doctor said, became of consequence. The expense of the present opposition to the wishes of the House has already been considerable, and he wished it might not be augmented.[2] Therefore, he most cheerfully resigned his pretension and hoped that some other person might be found who would be reciprocally agreeable. For himself, he said, he was fully satisfied with the zeal, and constancy of attachment, which had been displayed in his favor and he hoped that it might be one day in his power to convince the House, by more than words, that he was not insensible of the honor they had done him.

Previous to the question for coming to the choice, at the present time, being put, a motion was made for referring it to the next session of the General Court. The late period of the session, the absence of a number of the members, and its being unimportant whether the Senators were chosen at this session, or the next, were the reasons assigned for referring. These were answered by gentlemen on the other side and the question of reference was determined by yeas and nays— yeas 69—nays 79, so it passed in the negative.[3] On which the House proceeded to ballot for a Senator and on the first ballot, the committee reported, that the whole number of votes were 156—79 making a choice, that the Hon. Nathan Dane had 74, the Hon. Tristram Dalton 71, and that no one was chosen. In the second ballot, the whole number was 145—73 making a choice. The Hon. Nathan Dane, Esq., having 74 votes, was chosen by the House, and sent up to the Senate. The House then adjourned.

1. *Massachusetts Centinel*, 26 November.

2. A correspondent in the *Massachusetts Centinel* on 29 November asked if the opposition to the Senate did not create as much expense as opposition to the House, and he praised the Senate for supporting its dignity and "the constitutional rights of the people." For another short essay supporting the Senate in the election dispute, see "Constitutionalis," *Herald of Freedom* (supplement), [24] November.

3. The vote on the roll call was 78 nays and 70 ayes.

House and Senate Proceedings, Monday, 24 November

The House, A.M.

Mr. Parsons was charged with a message to enquire of the honorable Senate whether they had passed upon the vote of the House for electing the Hon. Nathan Dane, Esqr., a Senator to represent this state in the Senate of the United States.

The Senate, A.M.

Mr. Parsons came up with a message from the honorable House to request the Senate to inform them, whether they have passed upon the choice by the House of the Honble. Nathan Dane, Esq., [as?] a federal Senator.

On the vote for the choice of Senators, the honorable House [of Representatives] proposed to insert Honble. Nathan Dane, Esqr., in the room of Charles Jarvis, Esqr. The Senate read and nonconcurred that vote, and adhered to their own vote, in the choice of Honble. Tristram Dalton, Esqr.

Sent down for concurrence.

The House, A.M.

[The House received the Senate vote adhering to Tristram Dalton.]

A motion was made and seconded that the further consideration of the choice of a Senator to represent this state in the Senate of the United States be referred to the next setting of the General Court, and the question being put passed in the negative. The House then proceeded by ballot to the choice of a Senator as aforementioned and the Hon. Tristram Dalton, Esquire, was chosen.

The following entry was then made on the vote of the honorable Senate: Read and concurred.

The Senate, A.M.

Came up concurred [i.e., the House vote for Dalton].

The Senate, P.M.

Ordered, that the Secretary notify the Honble. Caleb Strong and Tristram Dalton, esquires, that they have been elected Senators to represent this state in the Senate of the United States for a term to commence on the first Wednesday of March next, according to the Constitution of said states.

Sent down for concurrence.

The House, P.M.

The Hon. J. B. Varnum, Esqr., brought down an order of Senate of this day directing the Secretary to notify the Hon. Caleb Strong and Tristram Dalton, esquires, of their being chosen Senators to represent them in the Senate of the United States.

. . . .

Read and concurred.

The Senate, P.M.

Came up concurred.

Newspaper Report of House Proceedings on Monday, 24 November[1]

A message from the honorable Senate was received, nonconcurring the choice of Mr. [Nathan] Dane, and again sending down Mr. [Tristram] Dalton. On which, after another motion for referring it to the next session was discussed, and lost, the House proceeded to the choice; and on the second ballot, the committee raised for that purpose reported, the whole number of votes to be 145—73 making a choice—that the Hon. Tristram Dalton, Esq., had 78, and was chosen a Senator to represent this commonwealth in the Congress of the United States.[2]

After this, a joint committee was raised to wait on His Excellency the Governor, to request His Excellency to grant a recess to the General Court this evening, and to convene them again the last Wednesday of December next.

At 6 o'clock, the Secretary came down to the House, and said, I am directed by His Excellency the Governor to inform the honorable House, that His Excellency has given his assent to the following acts: . . . . The Secretary then said, it is His Excellency's pleasure, by and with the advice and consent of the Council, and at the request of the General Court, that this Court be prorogued to the 31st day of December next, then to meet in this place—and this Court is prorogued accordingly.

(The Printer has thus far given a sketch of the proceedings of the General Court, the present session. The organization of the general government and the trial of the Sheriff of Worcester County[3] were subjects, he conceived, important to the public; and thinking it to be his duty to report an account of the proceedings thereon, most readily undertook the task. And, if he may judge from the avidity with which his brethren in this and the neighboring states have copied the sketches he has from time to time given, he must think that they have not been deemed less important by the public. With respect to them he can say, that however deficient some may be, he has been governed by the strictest impartiality.)[4]

1. *Massachusetts Centinel*, 26 November.

2. Massachusetts' choice of Senators was widely reported outside the state (see, for example, the Hartford *American Mercury*, 1 December; Providence *United States Chronicle*, 4 December; Philadelphia *Independent Gazetteer*, 8 December; Baltimore *Maryland Journal*, 16 December; and Edenton *State Gazette of North Carolina*, 1 January 1789).

A false report that James Bowdoin rather than Tristram Dalton was elected also gained wide currency (see, for example, the Philadelphia *Pennsylvania Mercury*, 2 December; *Carlisle Gazette*, 10 December; Richmond *Virginia Independent Chronicle*, 17 December; and *State Gazette of North Carolina*, 18 December).

3. The Massachusetts newspapers, and newspapers in other states, reported the trial of Sheriff William Greenleaf of Worcester County at least as fully as they did the debate on the Election Resolutions and the election of Senators. Greenleaf was impeached by the House of Representatives for misconduct, which included pocketing public funds and making dishonest reports. The trial before the Senate, sitting as the "High Court for the Trial of Impeachments," began on 5 November and concluded on 18 November with Greenleaf's removal from office. And judging from the newspaper reports of debates, the legislature spent at least as much time debating Governor Hancock's refusal to appoint Lieutenant Governor Benjamin Lincoln to the command of Castle William as it did debating the Election Resolutions.

4. Benjamin Russell's pride was justified, for when newspapers in and out of the state reported the debates, they copied them from the *Massachusetts Centinel*.

Commentaries on the Election of Senators, 22 November 1788— 29 January 1789

The only public comments on the election of Senators are newspaper reports naming the men elected. Most of the few private commentaries concern the role of Theophilus Parsons, a member of the House from Newburyport in Essex County. Parsons and his supporters failed in their efforts to elect Nathan Dane and to prevent the election of Tristram Dalton. At the same time, they destroyed any hopes Theodore Sedgwick and Rufus King had of being elected. Whatever Parsons did created bitterness among Federalist leaders, including those in Essex County, and had its impact later in the election of the United States Representative in Essex District (see headnotes to the first and second elections in Essex District, printed below).

Jeremy Belknap to Benjamin Rush, Boston, 22 November (excerpt)[1]

Our General Court have adopted a mode of choosing Senators for the new Congress by the 2 houses voting separately, the one as a negative on the other. Yesterday they proceeded to the experiment. The lower house balloted and sent up 2 gentlemen, one of whom, Mr. [Caleb] Strong, was accepted, the other, Dr. [Charles] Jarvis, was not. The lower house again sent up Jarvis. The Senate again nonconcurred. The Senate sent down Mr. [John] Lowell. The House then nonconcurred—thus each being inflexible. It is said today that both these gentlemen will be dropped and they will probably unite in Colonel [Azor] Orne of Marblehead. Strong was a member of the late Federal Convention. A worthy man and living in the country will properly represent the agricultural part of the state; the other will represent the mercantile interest.

"There is a generation (says Solomon) who are wise in their own eyes." Is not this the generation of *seekers* and are they not at this day a very large body? Ought we not to beware of them? The Senate in our state is justly accounted the bulwark of the Constitution. They have hitherto been *well chosen* and have acted nobly. You will see in the papers an account of a solemn trial of a sheriff and his dismission from office by this body. This sheriff is a brother-in-law to the G[overno]r.[2]

Christopher Gore to Rufus King, Boston, 23 November[3]

On Friday the House chose two Senators, Mr. [Caleb] Strong and Mr. [Charles] Jarvis. The Senate concurred the former, and negatived the latter, sending to the House [John] Lowell. The House negatived Lowell and returned Jarvis. Senate nonconcurred Jarvis and returned [Azor] Orne. The House again sent up Jarvis; Senate nonconcurred and sent down [Tristram] Dalton. The House chose [Nathan] Dane by a majority of one, and thus the matter rests. Whether the Senate will agree to Dane, or adhere to their own vote, is uncertain. The monstrous lies told by your Essex friends pervaded every quarter of the House, and the envy of these people had much greater weight than I could have supposed.[4] My dear friend, I must pray you not to suffer these things to estrange you from Massachusetts. Unless very interesting objects render your residence in New York necessary, think seriously of returning to the state of your nativity. [Theodore] Sedgwick is sore as man can be. He feels and acknowledges to me the error of his conduct.[5]

Christopher Gore to Rufus King, Boston, 26 November (excerpt)[6]

In my last[7] I informed you that the Senate had sent to the House Mr. [Tristram] Dalton as Senator—that the House nonconcurred and sent up [Nathan] Dane. On Monday morning, notwithstanding the influence of Phillips,[8] who exerted himself most warmly for D[ane], the Senate nonconcurred and repeated Dalton; and with much trouble, owing mostly to the Essex members, we carried Dalton, who is now the Senator. Soon after your departure, I was convinced, that my wishes could not be gratified. The various falsehoods industriously propagated, and oppositely turned to the prejudices of those to whom they were applied, so powerfully operated, as to leave nothing but defeat in the hazard. Deeply mortified are the partisans of P[9] and his coadjutors. Dane was exalted as one, who, through every opposition of proffered favors, on the one side, and cruel persecution on the other, perseveringly pursued the defaulters of public money and the domineering aristocrats of our dear country. As a friend to the Constitution, supported by the uniform assertions of General [Henry] Knox and other firm Federalists, and a letter from Mr. Dane, indicative of these sentiments, was shown to those who wished well to the Constitution, but these things did not prevail. Among other things whispered against one of the candidates, was added that Mr. Dane would have succeeded in his wish of appointing Mr. [Jonathan?] Jackson a commissioner, for settling the Continental accounts, had it not been for the external influence of that gentleman in the election in Congress. This I knew not, till after the choice. I enquired of Mr. [Samuel A.] Otis, whether this was in any degree founded. He replied, that my mentioning it was the first insinuation of the kind he ever heard, and that he believed no influence could have secured this gentleman the place of commissioner.[10]

Mrs. Richard Cranch to Mrs. John Adams, Braintree, 30 November (excerpt)[11]

You will see by the papers what a contest there has been between the House and Senate—the *stubborn* Senate. But such plotting and caballing indoors and out is a scandal to our state. I foresee that some of our late popular characters will sink into disgrace. The man who dares to pluck the mask from the face of the dissembling villain will be feared but must not expect to be beloved but by the virtuous few. He who with honesty will not be so much hurt by the ingratitude of those whose interests he has greatly served as one whose motive was merely the applause of the multitude because he acted from a better principle. He will, like the being he has imitated, rejoice in the good he has [occasioned?] to others altho they may not see the hand from which it came.[12]

Journal of George R. Minot, November[13]

The session of the General Court in this month rose to a boisterous height, and terminated with the usual effects of political storms; that is, it embittered old friends, who had separated in the subdivisions of party, with each other; an evil which too often attends the pursuit of politics. Several things were worthy of remembrance.

In settling the elections for the federal government, Mr. [Theodore] Sedgwick was extremely mortified in not being chosen a Senator. He averred that he came forward only on the strength of a declaration of Mr. C[aleb] Strong that he would not serve; and he considered Mr. Strong's pursuit of the office afterwards as a great breach of faith. Mr. S[edgwic]k labored hard to bring about the mode of electing by joint ballot of both houses, in which case the *numbers* of the lower house would have operated greatly in his favor; but the Senate preserved their negative, which enraged many of the representatives to a high degree, especially when they came repeatedly to negative them in the choice of Dr. [Charles] Jarvis. Mr. [Theophilus] Parsons obtained such a character as a cunning man in the course of the elections as very much affected his influence in the House. Mr. Sedgwick, though in sentiment with him in almost every measure before, became now so disgusted with him as scarcely to name him with moderation. In short all the Federalists had joined unanimously enough in erecting the new political fabric, but when it became a question who should occupy its commodious apartments, they displayed the various divisions of particular interests.

Mrs. John Adams to John Quincy Adams, Jamaica, New York, 13 December (excerpt)[14]

I have only seen one Newspaper from our State Since I came here, and that Mr. George Storer sent me last week. It containd the choice of Senators. I was glad to see our Senate act with proper spirit and dignity. Virginia, you will see by the papers, is lighting up a fire. The Gv [Governor] and assembly of N[ew] York tis said will blow the coals. Col. [William] Duer dined here last week. it was his opinion that there would not be any congress this winter. a few members only were come.

Christopher Gore to Rufus King, Boston, 29 January (excerpt)[15]

I have seen and conversed with Mr. [Jonathan] Jackson on the subject of [Theophilus] Parsons' communication to Mr. [Tristram] Dalton. Mr. Jackson begs me to assure you that he has not the least reason to believe this assertion of P. to be true; that he has now, and always has had the greatest confidence in your honor and friendship; and that it is not in the power of P. in the smallest degree to shake that confidence.[16]

Mr. [Theodore] Sedgwick, of whom I asked the reason why he should express himself in the manner he did respecting your being in this town, declares, that he said what passed on this subject to General [Henry] Knox as a mutual friend, who might communicate to you, not his sentiments, but the opinion of illiberal men; and that he had frequently endeavored to say the same thing to you personally, but could not bring his mind to state such uncandid observations to a friend for whom he entertained so high a respect. And this he desires me to communicate to you.

1. RC, Rush Papers, PPL. The letter is undated, but it was evidently written on Saturday, the 22nd.

2. For information on the trial and removal of Sheriff William Greenleaf of Worcester County, see Newspaper Report of House Proceedings on 24 November, n. 3, printed above.

3. RC, King Papers, NHi.

4. None of the documents located indicate what "lies" were told by the representatives from Essex County. King did not receive a single vote for Senator, according to the Newspaper Report of House Proceedings on 21 November, printed above.

5. There is no evidence as to the nature of Sedgwick's "error."

6. RC, King Papers, NHi. Printed: King, *Life*, I, 346—47. Another part of this letter is printed below in The Election in Suffolk District, 18 December.

7. 23 November, printed above.

8. This was probably Samuel Phillips, Jr., president of the Senate.

9. The word "Parsons," in another hand, is written on the margin of the manuscript.

10. On 8 May 1788, Congress elected two commissioners to settle Continental accounts. There is no evidence that Nathan Dane supported Jonathan Jackson or that King, who was no longer a member of Congress, had any influence. Dane, in fact, nominated Benjamin Walker, who was one of the two men elected (JCC, XXXIV, 148).

11. RC, Adams Papers, MHi. Mary Cranch was the older sister of Abigail Adams. Mrs. Adams was visiting relatives in New York at the time.

12. On the same day, Nathaniel Gorham wrote to Henry Knox from a different point of view: "The close of the business relative to the Senators you must ere this have seen in the newspapers. Considering the jumble it wound up very well. Everything perfectly quiet and peaceable at present" (Charlestown, RC, Knox Papers, MHi).

13. George R. Minot Papers, MHi. Minot had been clerk of the House of Representatives since 1781 and had served as the secretary of the state Convention which ratified the Constitution. His journal is undated, but we have placed it at the end of November since he summarizes the events of that month.

14. RC (LT), Adams Papers, MHi.

15. RC, King Papers, NHi. Printed: King, *Life*, I, 349–50.

16. See Gore to King, 26 November, printed above.

Secretary John Avery, Jr., to Caleb Strong, Boston, 24 November[1]

In pursuance of the direction of the General Court, I have the honor of informing you, that you have been elected by the Legislature, a Senator to represent this State in the Senate of the United States for a term, to commence on the first Wednesday of March next, according to the Constitution of the said States.

1. RC (LT), Stephen C. Strong Collection of Caleb Strong Manuscripts, MNF. A similar letter was sent to Tristram Dalton. For their replies, see Dalton to Avery, 24 December, and Strong to Avery, 12 January 1789, both printed below.

Tristram Dalton to Secretary John Avery, Jr., Newburyport, 24 December[1]

I duly received your official information of my having been "elected by the Legislature a Senator to represent this State in the Senate of the United States for a term to commence on the first Wednesday of March next according to the Constitution of the Said States."[2]

Be pleased to acquaint the honorable legislature, that I am deeply impressed with a sense of the very high honor they have been pleased to confer on me, in an appointment to so important a station; that accepting of this their election, I shall devote my time and services, totally, to the discharge of the arduous duties thereof; that the true interest and real liberties of the people of *this* and the United States shall be the dearest objects of my attention, and to promote and secure them, as far as may be in my power, my greatest happiness.

1. RC, Miscellaneous Legislative Documents, Senate Files, M-Ar. The Senate received Dalton's letter on 5 January 1789 and transmitted it to the House of Representatives the same day.

2. See Avery to Caleb Strong, 24 November, printed above.

Tristram Dalton to Caleb Strong, Newburyport, 9 January 1789 (excerpt)[1]

Will you be so kind as to obtain a proper certificate or commission of our appointment to the federal Senate—![2]

An order of the two houses requesting the Governor to grant a commission under the Seal of the Government [met?] my idea.

In whatever form you take it, permit me to mention the propriety of inclosing it under a cover directed to either of us at New York, and of sending this packet to the care of our friend [Nathaniel] Gorham or [Samuel A.] Otis, requesting by a line his retaining it until one of us shall arrive and calls for it. As there is no expense of postage it may go by post. This might prevent a detention by an accident that might *possibly* happen to whomsoever of us took charge of the instrument. Your determination on this matter please to advise me.

. . . .

I am pleased with the event of your choice of Electors.

1. RC, Thompson Collection, CtHC.

2. See Senate and House Proceedings, 7 and 9 February, and Credentials of the Massachusetts Senators, 10 February, printed below.

Caleb Strong to Secretary John Avery, Jr., Boston, 12 January[1]

I have received your letter informing that I am elected by the legislature a Senator to represent this state in the Senate of the United States for a term to commence on the first Wednesday of March next according to the Constitution of the United States.

I must request you, sir, to inform the honorable legislature that I feel myself under great obligations for the honor done me by this appointment, and that I shall endeavor to deserve their confidence by an assiduous attention to the public interest and a faithful discharge of the duties of the office to which I have been elected.

1. RC, Miscellaneous Legislative Documents, Senate Files, M-Ar. The state Senate received Strong's letter on 13 January and transmitted it to the House of Representatives the same day.

House and Senate Proceedings, Saturday, 7 February

The Senate, A.M.

Resolve requesting the Governor to issue credentials to the gentlemen who have been or may hereafter be chosen Senators and Representatives, to represent this commonwealth in the federal government.

Commonwealth of Massachusetts: In Senate 7th of February 1789[1]

Resolved, that His Excellency the Governor be and he hereby is requested, to make out proper credentials, under the Seal of this Commonwealth, to the Honble. Caleb Strong and Tristram Dalton, esquires, elected by the legislature as Senators to represent this state in the Senate of the United States, and to each of the persons who have been or hereafter shall be duly elected to represent the people of this state in the House of Representatives of the United States, expressing in such credentials the offices to which they have been or shall be respectively chosen; and the Secretary, having countersigned the said credentials, is hereby directed to transmit the same with an attested copy of this resolve, to the persons [A] *which* have been or shall be elected as aforesaid. [B][2]

Sent down for concurrence.

The House

The Hon. N. Wells, Esqr., brought down a resolve of Senate of this day requesting the Governor to deliver credentials to the persons who are or may be chosen Senators or Representatives for this commonwealth in Congress.

1. The Senate resolve is not in the Senate Journals but is in Miscellaneous Resolves, 1788, Chapter 85, M-Ar.
2. The letters "A" and "B" were added to the text of the Senate resolve by the House on 9 February, and these letters were keyed to two amendments to the original resolve (see House Proceedings, 9 February, printed immediately below).

House and Senate Proceedings, Monday, A.M., 9 February

The House

Resolve of Senate of the 7th instant requesting the Governor to make out proper credentials for the Senators and Representatives in Congress.

Read and concurred with amendments.

Sent up for concurrence.

[The House Journals stop at this point. The House entered its message to the Senate on the manuscript of the Senate resolution of 7 February. It reads: "In the House of Representatives, February 9, 1789. Read and concurred with amendments as on the paper accompanying. Sent up for concurrence. Wm. Heath, Speaker Pro Tem." The "paper accompanying" includes, in addition to the amendments, the form of credentials prepared by the House as printed below.]

At A dele[te] "*which*" and insert "*who.*"

At B insert the following:

And the credentials for a Senator may be in the form following:

Commonwealth of Massachusetts[1]

To all people to whom these presents shall come, greeting:

[SEAL]   Know ye that ——— Esq. on the ——— day of ——— in the year of Our Lord one thousand seven hundred and eighty ——— was chosen *by our legislature a Senator to represent us* in the Congress of the United States of America for the term by the Constitution for the said United States expressed to commence on the first Wednesday in March next, at the time and *place* and in the manner of holding elections prescribed by our legislature agreeably to the powers therein vested by the Constitution aforesaid. Given under our Seal. Witness: J[ohn] H[ancock], Esq. our Governor and Commander in Chief at Boston the ——— day of ——— in the year of Our Lord one thousand seven hundred and eighty nine.

By His Excellency's command.

J[ohn] A[very] Secretary.

And the credentials for a Representative may be of the same form—having only for the words *"by our legislature a Senator to represent us"* substituting the following *"by the people of this state legally qualified therefor a Representative to represent them"* and for the word *"place"* substituting the word *"places."*

The Senate

[Senate action on the 9th is recorded in the Journals for the 7th and reads: "Came up concurred with amendments. Read and concurred." The following record of Senate action, with the signatures of the President of the Senate and Governor Hancock, is written on the manuscript of the Senate resolution of 7 February immediately after the House message of 9 February transmitting the amendments and form of credentials.]

In Senate February 9. 1789—

Read and concurred.

[s] Saml. Phillips, junr. President

Approved   Approved by the [Governor?]

[s] John Hancock   February 10. 1789—[2]

1. (LT), Miscellaneous Resolves, 1788, Chapter 85, M-Ar. The House added the letters "A" and "B" to the original Senate resolution of 7 February, but the amendments were written on a separate sheet of paper attached to the Senate resolution.

2. The Senate action and the Governor's signature are in Miscellaneous Resolves, 1788, Chapter 85, M-Ar. The Senate Journals only record the following: "Read and concurred."

Credentials of the Massachusetts Senators, 10 February[1]

Commonwealth of Massachusetts
        [SEAL]
      [s] John Hancock

To all People to whom these presents shall come. . . . Greeting

Know ye that the Honble. Tristram Dalton[2] esqr. on the twenty fourth day of November, in the year of our LORD One thousand seven hundred & eighty eight was chosen by our Legislature a Senator to represent us in the Congress of the United States of America for the term by the Constitution for the said United States expressed to commence on the first Wednesday in March next, at the time & place & in the manner of holding elections prescribed by our Legislature agreeably to the powers therein vested by the Constitution aforesaid.

Given under our Seal. Witness His Excellency John Hancock Esqr. our Governor & Commander in Chief at Boston the tenth day of February, in the year of Our LORD One thousand seven hundred & eighty nine—

By His Excellency's Command—

[s] John Avery jun Secretary—

1. (LT), RG 46, DNA.

2. The name of Caleb Strong was substituted for Tristram Dalton in the other copy of the credentials for the Massachusetts Senators.

The Election of Presidential Electors, 5-7 January 1789

The Massachusetts Election Resolutions of 20 November 1788 provided that on 18 December, when the voters cast their votes for Representatives in each district, they should also vote for two men as presidential Electors. The votes were to be sent to the Secretary of the Commonwealth by Monday, 5 January, and on 7 January the legislature in joint session would elect one of the two men receiving the highest number of votes in each district. The legislature would then elect two Electors from the state at large from among men who had not received votes as Electors in any district.

When the votes were returned to the Secretary, it was revealed that more than 220 men had received votes, including virtually every Federalist leader in the state. The Federalist-controlled legislature therefore hurriedly passed a resolution on 6 January declaring that anyone not disqualified by the Constitution "shall be considered as eligible for an Elector at large, any resolve to the contrary notwithstanding" (see House and Senate Proceedings, 6 January, printed below). It is worth noting that in four districts—Suffolk, Essex, Plymouth-Barnstable, and Bristol-Dukes-Nantucket—the legislature chose the runner-up rather than the candidate with the largest popular vote.

An Elector, Massachusetts Centinel, 3 December 1788[1]

If it has been considered as important, that the greatest circumspection should be observed in the election of federal Representatives, how much more so ought it to be displayed in the choice of the Electors of President and Vice President of the United States—persons with whom are to be intrusted the highest concerns and interests of the continent. Many persons are spoken of as candidates for this important appointment, in this district, but the two in whom the town and country interests appear most to unite are the Hon. Jabez Fisher, Esq., of Franklin, and the Hon. Caleb Davis, Esq., of Boston.

The Federalism, patriotism, and experience in public affairs of the above gentlemen are such, as to inspire the fullest confidence that their votes will be given for such characters as will answer the just expectation of every friend to the happiness and union of this Federal Republic.

1. This item was dated Milton, 1 December.

An Elector to the Printer, Massachusetts Centinel, 6 December

In your last, I was pleased to see a nomination, as candidates for Electors of President and Vice President of the United States, of two persons of unimpeachable characters. It had howe[ver] been previously agreed upon, by a number of persons, to vote for the Hon. James Bowdoin, Esquire, and the Hon. Jabez Fisher, Esquire, and as unanimity appears to be the wish of the Federalists in both town and country, it is hoped that either the above list or the one published by you on Wednesday [3 December, printed immediately above] will be promoted, and the other dropped.[1]

1. The above item was dated Roxbury, 5 December. In the same issue the *Centinel* reported a "correspondent" as saying that Thomas Dawes and Jabez Fisher "stand foremost" among the candidates in Suffolk County. On 17 December the *Centinel* printed an item from "An Elector" saying that his town would vote to a man for Jabez Fisher and Caleb Davis. When the votes were counted, Fisher had 801 votes and Davis 585. The legislature chose Davis on 7 January 1789.

Henry Jackson to Henry Knox, Boston, 21 December (excerpt)[1]

From the appearance of the persons that will be chosen Electors, if I can form any judgment, I should doubt whether Mr. H[ancock] will be elected V[ice] P[resident]; but this, a better opinion can be formed after the General Court have made their election from those chosen by the people. Governor Hancock is and has been confined to his chamber ever since you left us. I call on him as usual. He very particularly inquires after you. I always tell him you desire to be remembered to him and that in a very respectful manner.[2]

1. RC, Knox Papers, MHi. Jackson, a native of Massachusetts and a close friend of Knox, had commanded Massachusetts troops throughout the Revolution. Unemployed after the war, Jackson was appointed by Knox to raise Federal troops in 1786, ostensibly to be used against the western Indians, but in fact to help suppress Shays's Rebellion. However, Jackson could not raise the money, for Massachusetts merchants and other wealthy men provided funds for state troops commanded by General Benjamin Lincoln.

2. Other portions of this letter are printed below in the elections of Representatives in Suffolk, Bristol-Dukes-Nantucket, and Middlesex districts, 18 December.

Benjamin Lincoln to George Washington, Boston, 4 January 1789 (excerpt)[1]

I mentioned in my last[2] that our Senators were chosen. This commonwealth has been divided into eight districts, each having a right to choose one Representative to the general government. Each town was directed to return the name of two persons for Electors of President and Vice President from the two highest in each district. The General Court are to choose one. This will make eight and two are to be chosen by the Court at large in the state.

. . . .

By the returns of gentlemen for Electors of President and Vice President we [cannot?] have a bad set. Indeed, we might have a good one. What we call good here are gentlemen who love the Constitution and who will vote for ——— President and Mr. J[ohn] A[dam]s Vice President. The other candidate [John Hancock] could not act if he was elected. His want of health is such as to prevent his attending to the duties of so important a station. He has not been abroad but a very few times for two months past and is now confined to his chamber and it is quite uncertain whether he will be able or not to see the General Court which met here on Wednesday last.

1. RC, Washington Papers, DLC. Other portions of this letter are printed below in the second elections of Representatives in Middlesex and Worcester districts, 29 January.

2. 20 December, printed below in The Election in Suffolk District, 18 December.

The Popular Vote for Presidential Electors, 6 January

In accordance with the Massachusetts Election Resolutions of 20 November, the votes for presidential Electors were sent to John Avery, Jr., secretary of the commonwealth. He prepared lists of returns for each district. The lists include the names of the towns in each district that returned votes, the name of each man who received votes, and the total vote for each man. These lists were submitted to the legislature on 6 January 1789.

While more than 220 men received votes, in most districts a relatively small number of men received most of the votes. In the following tables, which are based on the original manuscript returns (M-Ar), we have given the names of the men who received scattered votes (i.e., less than 100) at the end of the table for each district, with the number of votes received placed in parentheses after the name of each man.

Suffolk District

Hon. Jabez Fisher	801
Hon. Caleb Davis	585
Hon. Thomas Dawes	132
Scattered among 18 candidates	280

Hon. James Bowdoin (46); His Honor Benjamin Lincoln (43); Hon. William Heath, Esq. (39); Hon. Cotton Tufts (36); Stephen Metcalf, Esq. (31); Dr. Charles Jarvis (23); Hon. Oliver Wendell, Esq. (21); Dr. John Metcalf (10); John Winthrop, Esq. (8); Hon. Richard Cranch (6); Hon. Samuel Adams (5); Hon. Fisher Ames, Esq. (4); Hon. James Humphreys (2); Lemuel Kollock, Esq. (2); Nathaniel Bailey, Esq. (1); Captain Norton Brailsford (1); John Lowell, Esq. (1); Captain Elias Parkman (1)

Essex District

Hon. George Cabot	955
Hon. Samuel Phillips, Jr.	676
Hon. Jonathan Titcomb	323
Hon. Azor Orne, Esq.	184
Hon. Samuel Holten	155
Hon. Benjamin Goodhue	100
Scattered among 18 candidates	93

Samuel Phillips, Esq. (30); Hon. Benjamin Greenleaf (14); Hon. John Pickering, Esq. (11); John Choate, Esq. (8); Jonathan Gardner, Esq. (7); Hon. Jonathan Jackson (5); Dr. Thomas Kitteridge (4); Hon. Nathan Dane, Esq. (2); Hon. Israel Hutchinson (2); Dr. Daniel Killiam (2); Mr. Aaron Cheever (1); Timothy Dexter (1); Mr. Samuel Fowler (1); Nathan Goodale, Esq. (1); Jonathan Greenleaf, Esq. (1);

Hon. Theophilus Parsons, Esq. (1); Nathaniel P. Sargent, Esq. (1); Mr. Squire Shove (1)

Middlesex District

Hon. Francis Dana	572
Hon. John Brooks	338
Hon. Nathaniel Gorham, Esq.	333
Hon. Eleazer Brooks	267
Hon. Oliver Prescott	259
Hon. Joseph B. Varnum, Esq.	182
Scattered among 21 candidates	436

William Winthrop, Esq. (87); Hon. Elbridge Gerry, Esq. (78); Joseph Hosmer, Esq. (66); Ebenezer Bridge, Esq. (46); Loammi Baldwin, Esq. (30); Dr. Marshall Spring (28); James Winthrop, Esq. (24); Abraham Fuller, Esq. (19); Joseph Curtis, Esq. (18); Hon. James Russell, Esq. (17); Walter McFarland, Esq. (7); Hon. John Pitts (7); General Benjamin Brown (1); Francis Faulkner, Esq. (1); William Hull, Esq. (1); Duncan Ingraham, Esq. (1); Mr. Aaron Johnson (1); Joseph Lee, Esq. (1); Chambers Russell, Esq. (1); Parker Varnum, Esq. (1); Captain Asahal Wheeler (1)

Hampshire-Berkshire District

Samuel Henshaw, Esq.	614
Hon. Elijah Dwight	509
Samuel Lyman, Esq.	473
Thompson J. Skinner, Esq.	455
Samuel Fowler, Esq.	200
Hon. John Hastings	160
Hon. William Whiting	114
Scattered among 39 candidates	1031

Thomas Ives, Esq. (96); Theodore Sedgwick, Esq. (92); David Smead, Esq. (91); Oliver Phelps, Esq. (79); William Bodman, Esq. (66); Simeon Strong, Esq. (64); William Williams, Esq. (61); General William Shepard (59); Hon. John Bliss (46); Reuben Hinman, Esq. (46); Hugh McClallen (36); William Walker, Esq. (30); Hon. Noah Goodman, Esq. (28); Ebenezer Mattoon, Esq. (28); Ephraim Fitch, Esq. (26); John Bacon, Esq. (22); Captain Phineas Stebbins (19); Joshua Henshaw, Esq. (18); Eleazer Porter, Esq. (17); Captain Reuben Munn (16); Hon. John Ashley, Esq. (15); Timothy Robinson, Esq. (13); Woodbridge Little, Esq. (12); Thomas Lusk, Esq. (11); Jonathan Hale, Esq. (7); Justin Ely, Esq. (6); John Williams, Esq. (5); Ebenezer Pierce, Esq. (4); Lieutenant Ely Parsons (3); Dr. Ebenezer Hunt (2); Captain Joshua Shaw (2); Captain Oliver Smith (2); Hon. Jahleel Woodbridge (2); John Worthington, Esq. (2); Mr. James Coe (1); William Lyman, Esq. (1); General [Warham] Parks (1); Elisha Porter, Esq. (1); William Pynchon, Esq. (1)

Plymouth-Barnstable District

Dr. Samuel Savage	373

Hon. William Sever   319
Scattered among 16 candidates   292

> Nathan Cushing, Esq. (92); Joshua Thomas, Esq. (61); Shearjashub Bourne, Esq. (55); Hon. Solomon Freeman (32); Hon. William Cushing (17); Daniel Howard, Esq. (12); Mr. Thomas Davis (6); James Warren, Esq. (4); John Gray, Esq. (3); Captain Francis Shurtliff (3); Dr. Samuel Freeman (2); Hon. Joseph Cushing (1); Samuel Jackson (1); George Partridge, Esq. (1); Captain Joseph Smith (1); David Thacher (1)

York-Cumberland-Lincoln District

Hon. David Sewall   231
Daniel Cony, Esq.   213
Hon. Nathaniel Wells, Esq.   196
Hon. Josiah Thacher, Esq.   168
William Widgery, Esq.   157
Hon. William Lithgow, Jr., Esq.   107
Scattered among 25 candidates   494

> Samuel Thompson, Esq. (69); Samuel Nasson, Esq. (43); Peleg Wadsworth, Esq. (43); Stephen Longfellow (37); Edmund Phinney, Esq. (37); Henry Dearborn, Esq. (35); Dummer Sewall, Esq. (34); Hon. Thomas Rice (29); William Gorham, Esq. (24); Lieutenant William Cunningham (22); Thomas Cutts, Esq. (22); Tristram Jordon, Esq. (20); Enoch Ilsley (16); Hon. George Thacher (16); Ichabod Goodwin, Esq. (12); Joseph Noyes, Esq. (10); Joshua Bailey Osgood, Esq. (7); Hon. John Frost (6); Hon. John Lewis (5); Lieutenant James Purrington (2); James Carr (1); Edward Cutts, Esq. (1); Daniel Davis, Esq. (1); Mr. John Fox (1); John Swett, Esq. (1)

Bristol-Dukes-Nantucket District

Elisha May, Esq.   437
Hon. Walter Spooner, Esq.   357
Samuel Tobey, Esq.   332
Holder Slocum   300
Phanuel Bishop   295
Hon. David Cobb, Esq.   162
Scattered among 9 candidates   119

> James Athearn, Esq. (53); John Worth, Esq. (34); Beriah Norton, Esq. (13); George Leonard, Esq. (12); Hon. William Bailies (2); Cornelius Dunham (2); Jerathmeel Bowen, Esq. (1); Daniel Leonard, Esq. (1); Zaphaniah Leonard, Esq. (1)

Worcester District

Hon. Moses Gill   340
Hon. Abel Wilder   335
Hon. John Sprague   281
Hon. Timothy Paine   191
Hon. Artemas Ward   176
Hon. Samuel Baker   163

Amos Singletary, Esq.	154
Hon. Jonathan Warner	144
Martin Kinsley	135
Hon. Peter Penniman	123
Timothy Fuller	104
Scattered among 31 candidates	703

Samuel Willard (91); John Fessenden, Esq. (71); Hon. Jonathan Grout (69); Samuel Curtis, Esq. (65); Seth Washburn, Esq. (55); Henry Bromfield, Esq. (41); Captain John Black (32); Captain Jeremiah Learned (30); John Taylor, Esq. (30); Levi Lincoln, Esq. (25); Daniel Clark, Esq. (24); Captain Stephen Maynard (24); Major David Wilder (23); Joseph Allen, Esq. (20); Caleb Ammidown (16); Hon. Joseph Dorr (14); Samuel Crosby, Esq. (12); Timothy Newell, Esq. (12); Colonel Samuel Denny (10); Benjamin Heywood, Esq. [10?]; Andrew Peters, Esq. (9); Josiah Whitney, Esq. (6); Ebenezer Larned, Esq. (3); Josiah Whiting, Esq. (3); Captain Park Holland (2); David Bigelow (1); Seth Newton (1); Joseph Read, Esq. (1); Joseph Stone (1); Mr. David Taylor (1); Joseph Wheeler, Esq. (1)

House and Senate Proceedings, Tuesday, 6 January

The Senate, A.M.

Ordered, that Eben. Bridge and Jona. Grout, Esqr., with such as the honorable House may join, be a committee to consider and report such measures as shall appear necessary to be adopted by the legislature, previous to its proceeding to the appointment of Electors of President and Vice President of the United States, agreeably to their resolve of November 20. 1788.

Sent down for concurrence.

The House, A.M.

Read and concurred and Mr. Heath, Mr. Dawes, and Mr. Russell of Boston were joined.

The Senate, P.M.

Ordered, that the Secretary lay before the General Court, the returns from the several towns and plantations within this commonwealth of votes for candidates for Electors of President and Vice President of the United States, if he has entered them in a book. If he has not, to lay them before the General Court, as soon as he shall have entered them.

Sent down for concurrence.

The House, P.M.

Read and concurred.

The Senate, P.M.

Report of committee appointed to consider what is proper to be done previous to the appointment of Electors of President and Vice President of the United States.

Read and accepted with an amendment at A.
Sent down for concurrence.

[Committee Report] [1]

The committee of both houses appointed "to consider and report such measures as shall appear necessary to be adopted by the legislature previously to its proceeding to the appointment of Electors of President and Vice President of the United States agreeably to their resolve of November 20. 1788"—ask permission to report, as the opinion of the said committee that tomorrow after the General Court shall have examined the returns made by the selectmen of the several towns and districts, within this commonwealth, of the votes given for candidates for Electors of President and Vice President of the United States, the members of the two ho[uses] assembled in one room shall proceed by joint ballot to make choice of the Electors aforesaid for the several districts *separately*, beginning with the District of Suffolk and proceeding in the order in which the districts are mentioned in the said resolve of the General Court of the 20th. day of November last; and then proceed to appoint two Electors at large [A] *And every citizen of this commonwealth, who shall not have been appointed an Elector for some district, and is not disqualified by the Constitution of the United States, shall be considered as eligible for an Elector at large*—which is submitted.

January 6. 1789.   [s] Ebenr. Bridge per order

The House, P.M.

[The House received the committee report with the Senate amendment.]
Read and nonconcurred [in the amendment] and the report of the committee is accepted.
Sent up for concurrence.

The Senate, P.M.

Came up nonconcurred and the report is accepted.
Concurred.

The House, P.M.

A resolve that every citizen of this commonwealth who shall not have been appointed an Elector of the President and Vice President of the United States, for some district, and is not disqualified by the Constitution of the United States, shall be considered as eligible for an Elector at large, any resolve to the contrary notwithstanding.[2]
Read and passed.
Sent up for concurrence.

The Senate, P.M.

[The Senate received the House resolve.]
Read and concurred.[3]
The Secretary laid upon the table, the returns from the several towns and plantations within this commonwealth, of votes for candidates, for Electors of President and Vice President of the United States.

Committed to Joseph Hosmer and Benj. Goodhue, Esqr., with such as the honorable House may join, to examine and report.

Sent down for concurrence.

The House, P.M.

Read and concurred and Mr. Gill, Mr. Paine, and Mr. Heath were joined.

1. This committee report is not entered in the Senate Journals but is in Miscellaneous Legislative Documents, Senate Files, M-Ar. Also written on the report are the Senate amendment "A," the House rejection of the amendment, and the Senate concurrence in the rejection.

2. This House resolve is virtually the same as the Senate amendment to the committee report that the House had just rejected. There is no explanation for this, except that perhaps the House was asserting its prerogatives.

On 7 January the *Massachusetts Centinel* explained that this resolve "was necessary, as by the resolve for putting the general government into operation, the legislature are to appoint at large two Electors of President etc. not voted for by the several districts which, as there are upwards of two hundred persons voted for, as Electors, would have confined the legislature to very narrow limits." The voting returns (printed above) indicate that over 220 men received votes. The *Salem Mercury* on 6 January reported that in Worcester County alone over forty men received votes. On 8 January the *Massachusetts Spy* reported that "there were *only* between forty and fifty candidates voted for! Behold how good and how pleasant it is for brethren to dwell together in unity!"

3. This sentence is not in the Senate Journals, but it is in Miscellaneous Resolves, 1788, Chapter 10, M-Ar. The Senate approval of the House resolve is written on the manuscript containing the resolve and the Governor's signature of approval.

Report of the Joint Committee Appointed to Examine Returns of Votes for Electors, Wednesday, A.M., 7 January[1]

Commonwealth of Massachusetts

The committee of both houses appointed to examine the returns of the several towns and plantations within the commonwealth of the votes for candidates for Electors of President and Vice President of the United States report that they have examined said returns and find that the following persons, having had the highest number of votes, are returned as candidates for Electors, viz.:

	Votes
For the District of Suffolk:	
The Honorable Jabez Fisher, Esq.	801
The Honorable Caleb Davis, Esq.	585
For the District of Essex:	
The Honorable Samuel Philips, Jr., Esq.	676
The Hon. George Cabot, Esq.	955
For the District of Middlesex:	
The Hon. Francis Dana, Esq.	572
The John Brooks, Esq.	338

For the District of Hampshire and Berkshire:
                 The Hon. Elijah Dwight, Esq.   509
                 Saml. Henshaw, Esq.   614

For the District of Plymouth and Barnstable:
                 Hon. William Sever, Esq.   319
                 Dr. Saml. Savage   373

For the District of York, Cumberland, and Lincoln:
                 The Hon. David Sewal, Esq.   231
                 Dr. Daniel Coney   213

For the District of Bristol, Dukes County, and Nantucket:
                 Hon. Walter Spooner, Esq.   357
                 Hon. Elisha May, Esq.   437

For the District of Worcester:
                 Hon. Moses Gill, Esq.   340
                 Hon. Abel Wilder, Esq.   335

All which is submitted.[2]

[s] Joseph Hosmer, per order.

January 7. 1789—

1. Miscellaneous Legislative Documents, Senate Files, M-Ar. On the reverse of the manuscript of this report is a record of House and Senate approval (see House and Senate Proceedings, 7 January, printed immediately below).

2. The names of the final candidates for presidential Electors were printed as a news item in the *Massachusetts Centinel* the same day.

House and Senate Proceedings, Wednesday, 7 January

The Senate, A.M.

Report of committee appointed to examine the returns from the several towns and plantations within this commonwealth of votes for candidates for Electors of President and Vice President of the United States.

Read and accepted.

Sent down for concurrence.

The House, A.M.

[The House received the Senate message.]

Read and concurred.

Mr. Fuller was charged with a message to inform the honorable Senate that the House proposed coming to the choice of Electors of President and Vice President of the United States this morning at 11 o'clock and that the usual seats would be assigned for their members. Leave was given to put up a nomination list for the two Electors to be chosen at large.

The Senate, A.M.

[The Senate received the House message.]

Benja. Goodhue, Esqr., was charged with a message to the honorable House, to inform them, that the Senate agreed to their proposal.

The House, A.M.

The Hon. B. Goodhue, Esqr., came down and said that he was directed by the Senate to inform this House that the Senate agreed to the proposal of coming to the choice of Electors aforementioned, at 11 o'clock this forenoon.

The House and Senate, A.M.

Mr. Dawes was charged with a message to the honorable Senate to inform them that the House were ready to proceed to the choice of Electors of President and Vice President of the United States, according to assignment. Whereupon the members of the two houses assembled together in one room and proceeded to the choice by joint ballot and the following persons were chosen for the following districts, viz.:

Suffolk: Hon. Caleb Davis, Esqr.; Essex: Hon. Samuel Phillips, Jr., Esqr.; Middlesex: Hon. Francis Dana, Esqr.; Hampshire and Berkshire: Samuel Henshaw, Esqr.; Plymouth and Barnstable: Hon. William Seaver, Esqr.; York, Cumberland, and Lincoln: Hon. David Sewall, Esqr.; Dukes County, Bristol, and Nantucket: Hon. Walter Spooner, Esqr.; Worcester: Hon. Moses Gill, Esqr.; At large: Hon. William Cushing, Esqr., and Hon. William Shepard, Esqr.

The houses then separated.[1]

The Senate, A.M.

Ordered, that the Secretary notify the Honble. Caleb Davis, Esqr., Saml. Phillips, Jr., Francis Dana, Esqr., Saml. Henshaw, Esqr., Honble. William Seaver, David Sewell, Walter Spooner, Moses Gill, William Cushing, and William Shephard, esquires, that they have been chosen Electors of President and Vice President of the United States, agreeably to the Constitution thereof and of the time and place of their meeting.

Sent down for concurrence.

The House, P.M.

[The House received the Senate message.]
Read and concurred.[2]

1. The report of the joint session of the Massachusetts legislature is from the House Journals. A slightly different version is in the Senate Journals.

The Federalists were pleased with the choice of Electors. Henry Jackson wrote to Henry Knox "the above elections [for Electors] are highly pleasing to the Federalists . . ." (Boston, 7 January, RC, Knox Papers, MHi). Similar sentiments were expressed by Christopher Gore to Andrew Craigie: "These Electors are firm Federalists and will, unquestionably, vote for George Washington and John Adams" (Boston, 7 January, RC, Craigie Papers, MWA). In a letter to his wife, Theodore Sedgwick also anticipated that the Massachusetts Electors would vote for Washington and Adams (Boston, 9 January, RC, Sedgwick Papers, MHi).

On 14 January, the *Massachusetts Centinel*, after listing the names of the Electors, commented: "We cannot but congratulate the state, and indeed the Union, on this truly Federal appointment. They are men eminent for their abilities and integrity, and all now sustain very important offices under the commonwealth. Three of them are judges of the Supreme Judicial Court, three judges of the Court of Common Pleas, and five of them were members of this state's Convention and voted for the ratification of the Constitution."

2. The formal order prepared by the Senate and House, and signed by the President of the Senate and Speaker of the House, is printed immediately below.

House and Senate Order to Secretary John Avery, Jr., 7 January[1]

Commonwealth of Massachusetts
In Senate Jany. 7—1789
    Ordered, that the Secretary notify
The Honble. Caleb Davis
          Saml. Phillips Jr &
          Francis Dana Esqrs
          Saml. Henshaw Esqr
The Honble. William Seaver
          David Sewell
          Walter Spooner
          Moses Gill
          William Cushing &
          William Shephard Esquires, that they have been chosen Electors of
President & Vice President of the United States, agreably to the Constitution
thereof, and of the time & place of their meeting—
    Sent down for concurrence
    [s] Saml. Phillips junr. Presidt—
In the House of Representatives Janry 7 1789
    Read and concurred.
    [s] Theodore Sedgwick, Spkr.

1. (LT), Miscellaneous Resolves, 1788, Chapter 10, M-Ar. Secretary John Avery sent attested copies to the Electors, and on 4 February an attested copy was sent by David Sewall, one of the Electors, to George Thacher, a Massachusetts member of Congress in New York.

Secretary John Avery, Jr., to Caleb Davis, Boston, 7 January[1]

Agreeably to the directions of the two branches of the Legislature, I have the honor of informing you, that you have been this day elected as an Elector of President & Vice President of the United States, agreably to the Constitution thereof;—and in pursuance of a resolution of the General Court passed the 20th of November last you are to meet on the first Wednesday of February next at 10 o'Clock in the forenoon at the State House in the Town of Boston for the purposes aforesaid.

1. RC (LT), Davis Papers, MHi. A similar letter was sent to Samuel Henshaw (Boston, 7 January, RC, MSS L, VI, no. 3b, Boston Athenaeum), and presumably the other eight Electors also received copies.

Aristides to the Printers, Independent Chronicle, 8 January

By inserting the following observations, you will give a new proof of the independence of your paper, and oblige a constant reader.

To the Hon. William Cushing, David Sewall, and Francis Dana, esquires, judges of the Supreme Judicial Court.

Gentlemen, you were yesterday chosen to an office "under the authority of this Commonwealth," in a manner no less honorable to yourselves, than in a high degree complimentary to the discernment and integrity of that body in which your election originated. Your honor and fidelity, as well as your qualifications in most respects to fill well with dignity the important station to which you have been appointed, is not to be disputed. Those who know you best are thoroughly convinced that the good of the community at large, as well as the true interest of this state in particular, will be the clear and decided objects which will govern your conduct as Electors of the President and Vice President for the United States. It is not therefore your judgment or integrity that I presume to question; but I confess, gentlemen, I have some doubts as to the constitutionality of your election. Having been led to form a favorable opinion of the views of the present legislature, I was surprised that not a single member of this honorable assembly should have suggested a single doubt upon this subject, especially when it appears to me, gentlemen, that the constitution of this government is so directly in the way of your appointment. To convince you that I am not without some grounds for my opinion, I beg leave to solicit your attention to the 2d article of the 6th chapter, under the head of oaths and incompatibility; it there appears "That no Governour, Lieutenant-Governour, or Judge of the Supreme Judicial Court, shall hold any other office or place under the authority of this Commonwealth, except such as by this Constitution they are admitted to hold, saving that the Judges of the said Court, may hold the office of Justices of the Peace throughout the State; nor shall they hold any other place or office, or receive any pension or salary from any other State or government, or power whatever."

I wish, gentlemen, that this difficulty might be fairly removed, and if it cannot be, exhibit a new proof of your virtue and independence, by refusing the acceptance of any place, which (as it appears to me) you cannot hold, but in direct violation of that constitution of government, which you have sworn to preserve from violation.[1]

1. Justice William Cushing of the Supreme Judicial Court wrote a reply to "Aristides" in which he argued that it was constitutional for judges to serve as Electors. See draft in Cushing's hand, endorsed: "On the Consistency of ye Judges being appointed Electors, (among others) of the president & Vicepresid with the state Conston." (Cushing Papers, MHi). Cushing apparently did not publish this document. For a public reply to "Aristides," see the item in the *Independent Chronicle*, 29 January, printed immediately below.

To the Printers, Independent Chronicle, 29 January

If you receive no answer to Aristides, before this comes to hand, please to insert this. Your correspondent lives at a distance from the press, and therefore frequently receives not your *Chronicle* until five or six days after the publication of it, and but seldom has a direct opportunity of conveying anything to your office. Yours, etc.

If Aristides had learned the A, B, C, of our [state] constitution, would he not have been able to read it better, or more understandingly? Or could it appear to him to stand in the way of the appointment of the judges of the Supreme Judicial Court to be Electors of the President and Vice President of the United States? Would he not have seen, that all the offices and places the constitution speaks of, relative to this commonwealth, belong to the three departments of power, viz.: legislative, executive, and judicial, which are therein clearly defined and distinctly held up to view? And if the question was put to him, to which of these departments of power does these office or place of an Elector belong? Would he not be able to answer, "to neither of them?" If so, must he not now acknowledge, that he had no other grounds for his opinion "that the constitution of this government stands directly in the way of their appointment," but his ignorance of the A, B, C, of the constitution? The Governor and several of the judges of the Supreme Judicial Court were chosen to be delegates in the late state Convention, to consider, etc., the Federal Constitution, and the Governor was appointed president, and one of the judges vice president, of said Convention; and might not Aristides as well have said, that the constitution stood as directly in the way of those appointments, as of this to be Electors, the business of whose appointment may, and it is likely will, be performed, for the first instance, in a single day, viz., the first Wednesday of February next?

Votes of the Massachusetts Presidential Electors, 4 February[1]

Commonwealth of Massachusetts

This certifies that we the underwritten being duly chosen Electors of the President & Vice President of the United States of America in behalf of the Commonwealth of Massachusetts, convened at the Senate Chamber in Boston on the first wednesday of February instant for the purpose aforesaid, did thereupon Vote by ballot for the said President and Vice President, pursuant to the Federal Constitution, & the resolution of the Congress for that purpose made. And that upon counting the votes so given in, there were Ten votes for the honorable George Washington of Virginia, late Commander of the American Forces; and Ten votes for the honorable John Adams of Braintree in this Commonwealth, late Minister Plenipotentiary of the United States at the Court of Great Britain.

In testimony whereof WE the said Electors have hereunto set our hands this first Wednesday of February 1789, being the fourth day of the same month.

[Signed:]

Caleb Davis
Saml. Phillips junr.
Fra Dana
Samuel Henshaw
Wm Sever
David Sewall
Walter Spooner

The President of the Senate
of the United States of
America

Moses Gill
Wm Cushing
Wm Shepard

1. (LT), RG 46, DNA.

David Sewall to George Thacher, Boston, 4 February[1]

As you are a member of the present, and also of the new Congress, the votes of the Massachusetts Electors are transmitted under cover to your care, as they do not know of any officer as Secretary of Congress, not doubting of your care and attention to deliver them in seasonably to the President of the Senate. Upon the receipt of this package you are desired to acknowledge the same by letter to Caleb Davis, Esqr., the Elector for the County of Suffolk.

Duplicates are made out and will be forwarded by Mr. [Fisher] Ames or some other safe hand.[2]

P.S. To satisfy you, the votes are unanimously for G. W——n and J. A——s.[3]

1. RC, Chamberlain Collection, MB. The cover of the letter was addressed to "Honorable George Thatcher, Esqr., Member of Congress New York." In addition to sending the votes of the Electors, Sewall enclosed copies of the Massachusetts Election Resolutions, 20 November (printed above); the order of the House and Senate to John Avery to notify the Electors of their election (printed above); and a certificate signed by John Hancock stating that as Secretary, the acts and attestations of John Avery should have full faith and credit "both in Court & without."
2. This sentence was written after Sewall's signature. The duplicates were sent, for there is another set in RG 46, DNA, including a duplicate of the votes of the Electors with their signatures.
3. This P.S. was written at the bottom of the page.

Massachusetts Centinel, 7 February

On Wednesday last, at 11 o'clock, agreeably to the resolutions of Congress, and of the legislature of this commonwealth, the gentlemen appointed Electors of President and Vice President of the United States met at the Senate Chamber, and having appointed the Hon. William Cushing, Esq., chairman, gave in their votes, unanimously, for His Excellency Geo. Washington, Esq., and the Hon. John Adams, Esq., as President and Vice President of the United States.

As a circumstance which adds to the repeated traits of genuine Federalism in Massachusetts, we can inform the public, that notwithstanding the honorable gentlemen appointed Electors reside in different parts of the state, and some of them were much indisposed in health, the whole ten appeared on the floor of the Senate, within 16 minutes of the time appointed for their meeting; that there was not a word spoken, except in the choice of a chairman; that each gentleman came prepared with his votes; and that the issue was, that they were unanimous in one opinion. If any thing can express the wishes of the people, it must be this. And if any thing can induce our illustrious Fabius and Lycurgus, once more to burden themselves with the cares of their country, it must be, because they see it to be the unanimous wish of that country that they should.

The Election of United States Representatives, 18 December 1788–
6 January 1789

The Massachusetts Election Resolutions of 20 November 1788 divided the state into eight districts, with elections to be held on 18 December. The candidates had to be inhabitants of their respective districts and receive a majority of the votes cast to be elected. The votes were to be returned to the Secretary of the Commonwealth on or before 5 January 1789 and then laid before the Governor and Council. The Governor was requested to issue certificates of election to the successful candidates.

Four candidates received majorities in the election on 18 December: Fisher Ames in Suffolk, George Partridge in Plymouth-Barnstable, George Thacher in York-Cumberland-Lincoln (Maine), and George Leonard in Bristol-Dukes-Nantucket districts. No candidate received a majority in Essex, Middlesex, Worcester, and Hampshire-Berkshire; therefore, new elections were required in those districts.

More than 100 men received votes for Representative on 18 December, although in most districts the contest was among only a few men. Despite the number of men voted for, the voter turnout was low. Writers in the Boston newspapers deplored the lack of voter response as compared to the state elections in the spring of 1788, but aside from voter indifference, bad weather also seems to have been a factor (see The Election in Suffolk District). However, voter turnout increased in the districts where further elections were required; the vote in Worcester District, for example, almost doubled between the election on 18 December and the third and final election on 2 March 1789.

The newspaper and other documentary material concerning the elections varies enormously in kind and in quantity. The Boston newspapers published a host of items about the election in Suffolk District and about the second election in Middlesex District. At the other extreme, the Portland, Me., *Cumberland Gazette* did not print a single item about the election in Maine prior to 18 December, and only a few letters written after the election give any hint as to the issues involved.

The documents for each district for the elections on 18 December are placed in a sequence determined in part by the order in which the districts appear in the Election Resolutions of 20 November and in part by the number of elections required before a Representative received the required majority of the votes cast. That order is as follows: (1) Suffolk District; (2) Plymouth-Barnstable District; (3) York-Cumberland-Lincoln District (Maine); (4) Bristol-Dukes-Nantucket District; (5) Essex District (two elections); (6) Middlesex District (two elections); (7) Worcester District (three elections); (8) Hampshire-Berkshire District (five elections).

The voting returns for the elections on 18 December in all eight districts are printed below in The Official Results of the First Election, 5-10 January 1789. For the documents and the votes in those districts that required additional elections before Representatives were chosen, see The Continuation and Completion of the Election of Representatives, 6 January–26 May 1789, printed below.

The official credentials for United States Representatives were adopted by the General Court on 7 February. They are a variant of the form of credentials adopted for United States Senators on the same day (see The Election of United States Senators, printed above).

The Election in Suffolk District, 18 December

The Boston newspapers paid little attention to candidates for the House of Representatives prior to the election of Senators, except for the publication of items concerning the qualifications of men who should be elected to Congress. Letter writers did mention that various men were talked of, but there is little evidence of concerted effort on the behalf of any candidate. However, the newspapers began nominating candidates as soon as the Senators had been elected. By 4 December five men had been nominated, and three of them had withdrawn. This left Samuel A. Otis and Fisher Ames as the only candidates, at least according to the newspapers.

The *Boston Gazette* gave a new turn to the campaign on 8 December by renewing the demand for amendments to the Constitution, by nominating Samuel Adams, and by raising the issue of Samuel A. Otis's bankruptcy. Two days later the *Massachusetts Centinel*, which had supported Otis, joined in the attack upon him, and Federalist leaders soon switched their support from Otis to Fisher Ames as the candidate who might be able to defeat Adams. In the week before the election on 18 December, the *Massachusetts Centinel* and the *Herald of Freedom* denounced Antifederalists and amendments and assured the voters that Adams was unsuitable, whatever his past services might have been. The *Boston Gazette* and the *Independent Chronicle* praised Adams at length and supported amendments.

Some idea of the intensity of feeling during the campaign is indicated in the following account by Samuel Adams's grandson: "About this time an anonymous letter was thrown over his garden wall, warning Mr. Adams against the intentions of certain parties who were watching him, and unless he changed his political course, were determined to assassinate him. The writer professed to be actuated by personal esteem for Mr. Adams and by friendship for his late son; and added that the intelligence was given at his own personal peril. On the back of the missive, in Mr. Adams's handwriting, is the following: 'This letter was found this morning in my yard, and immediately brought to me by my servant'; and then follow some contemptuous observations revealing a spark of the old Revolutionary fire. He concludes that little is to be feared from secret conspirators, who, if they really intended to assail him, dared only to do so in the dark. Neither the informant nor the conspirators were ever again heard from" (William V. Wells, *Life and Public Services of Samuel Adams* . . . [3 vols., Boston, 1866], III, 281-82, n. 1).

The bitterness aroused during the campaign did not subside after the election, at least among some of Adams's supporters and opponents (see "Bostoniensis," *Boston Gazette*, 29 December; "Northend," *Herald of Freedom*, 1 January 1789; and James Sullivan to Richard Henry Lee, 11 April, all printed below).

The voters of Suffolk District cast 1,613 votes. Fisher Ames, the winner, received 818; Samuel Adams 521; and 274 votes were scattered among thirteen other candidates, including Samuel A. Otis, Dr. Charles Jarvis, and Benjamin Austin, Jr. On 31 December the *Massachusetts Centinel* reported that there were 9,417 voters in Suffolk District; and in Boston, where 1,500 had voted in the state elections in the spring, only 900 voted for Representative. Thus, despite all the newspaper furor, less than 20 percent of the voters turned out. Although the newspapers reported that weather conditions were severe on election day, the publishers nevertheless chided the voters for the poor turnout (see the post-election newspaper comments, 20 December 1788—1 January 1789, printed below).

Christopher Gore to Rufus King, Boston, 26 November (excerpt)[1]

[John] Lowell, [Thomas] Dawes, and [Samuel A.] Otis are the predominating candidates for this district. I think the choice, of one of the first two, is most likely, and the middle man the most prob[able?] tho great exertions will be made for all. I say nothing about your future residence—of this you alone can determine the propriety. Everything that envy can suggest will be brought forward to detract from your reputation in this country, and if you should conclude to remain in New York, it will be urged as an argument of duplicity on your part. But I wish you, my friend, not to feel influenced by any conduct of mine in the late politics, to elect this as the place of your residence. I say this much because I know it will be urged on you as an argument for removing from New York. My conduct and reputation cannot suffer from any insinuations of such vile partisans as oppose you while I am present, and I earnestly desire that you would suffer such arguments to have no force on your mind, in opposition to your true interests as they shall be impartially weighed by yourself.

1. RC, King Papers, NHi. Printed: King, *Life,* I, 346-47. Another portion of this letter is printed above in The Election of United States Senators.

Independent Chronicle, 28 November

The indispensable necessity of some commercial character to represent this town in Congress could never be doubted. The welfare and happiness of the mechanics, and of all the middling classes of people, are deeply interested in this choice. The expedience, however, of this measure is more remarkably conspicuous, when we consider that we have no member in the federal Senate; and this will be the only metropolis in the Union in this destitute situation. The inhabitants, therefore, of this town will undoubtedly unite with their brethren in the country, in giving their votes for the Hon. Samuel Allyne Otis, Esq., the present member of Congress, to represent the District of Suffolk.

An Elector to the Printer, Massachusetts Centinel, 29 November

Agreeably to the laudable plan which you have adopted, in times past, of handing to the public the names of suitable persons to fill the important stations of representatives, etc., etc., you are requested to insert those of the following gentlemen, who are publicly mentioned as candidates for the interesting appointment of federal Representative for Suffolk District, viz., Hon. John Lowell, Esq.; Hon. Samuel A. Otis, Esq.; Charles Jarvis, Esq.; Thomas Dawes, Jr., Esq.

Thomas Dawes, Jr., to the Printer, 1 December[1]

I observed my name in Saturday's *Centinel* among the candidates for the ensuing election. If any of my friends in the county really intend voting for me,

I wish to save them that trouble, it being necessary for me to pursue my private profession, and to disencumber it, as soon as possible, of public engagements. I hope no unfavorable construction will be put upon this publication, as a transfer of the votes now possibly intended for me (*however few*) may be of consequence in completing a majority for some other gentleman in the first instance, and without the great expense of a second trial.[2]

1. *Boston Gazette*, 1 December.
2. On 4 December the *Herald of Freedom* printed the following: "A correspondent *laments* the distressed state of this county, as Mr. D[awes] has publicly declared that he will not go to Congress. What shall we do? Who shall we get?"

Massachusetts Centinel, 3 December

As it is essential, that the people should be unanimous as possible in the election of federal Representatives, we inform, that of the four gentlemen mentioned in our last as candidates for this district, Mr. [John] Lowell,[1] Dr. [Charles] Jarvis,[2] and Mr. [Thomas] Dawes, Jr., have been heard to declare that they could not, if they were chosen, accept of the appointment. The candidate, therefore, now is the Hon. Samuel Allyne Otis, Esquire.[3]

1. Evidently it had been assumed that Lowell would be elected and that he would serve. As late as 30 November Henry Jackson in Boston assured Henry Knox that "our friend Mr. Lowell will go if he is chosen, and it is generally thought he will be the man" (RC, Knox Papers, MHi). John Adams reported that it was "generally supposed" that "Mr. Lowell will be Rep[resentative] for the District of Suffolk" (to Abigail Adams, Braintree, 2 December, RC, Adams Papers, MHi).
2. The *Independent Chronicle* reported on 4 December that Jarvis had withdrawn, "owing to the urgency of his professional avocations."
3. For an attack on the *Centinel* and on newspaper "nominations," see "Suffolk," *Herald of Freedom*, 8 December, printed below.

To the Printers, Independent Chronicle, 4 December[1]

In this and the neighboring towns, Fisher Ames, Esq., who is a gentleman of acknowledged abilities, and unimpeachable integrity, is much talked of as a Representative for the District of Suffolk, and as by the *Centinel* of this day, the number of candidates is reduced to one, we think it but fair play to announce to the public the determination of a respectable number in this part of the county to honor Mr. Ames with their suffrages.

1. This item was dated Medfield, 3 December.

Suffolk, Herald of Freedom, 8 December

The peculiar method lately taken with respect to Representatives for our federal government is certainly very curious. In the first place, a number of names are mentioned as candidates, as if the whole county had met and determined on those gentlemen, or as if the whole county were to be guided by a number of lazy scribblers in R[ussel]l's printing office.[1] In the next paper, one of the candidates comes forth in a formal manner, and declares he cannot go to Congress, and that he is determined to disencumber himself of all public concerns. In a few days after, the *Centinel* declares there is only one candidate for the whole county. Certainly, Messrs. Printers, this method of proceeding is not only affronting to the independent electors of the county, but derogatory to the government, as if this important station in our federal system was already become too contemptible for acceptance. The mode, however, of publishing certain names may serve (*in future*) to bring forth some individuals who would not otherwise have been thought of, and give them an opportunity to publish to the world their own consequence. This may truly be called a *little trick* of maneuvering, and unworthy the character of a great man.

1. Benjamin Russell, publisher of the *Massachusetts Centinel*.

Boston Gazette, 8 December

This issue of the *Boston Gazette* changed the direction of the campaign in Suffolk District. The Boston newspapers had published many articles for and against amendments between late August and early November, but almost none since then (for items supporting amendments, printed above, see the *Independent Chronicle*, 28 August, 11 September, and 30 October; the *Boston Gazette*, 1 September, 3 November; the *Massachusetts Spy*, 2 October. For items opposing amendments, printed above, see the *Massachusetts Centinel*, 27, 30 August, 3, 6 September, 1 October, and one item which the *Boston Gazette* printed, when challenged to do so, on 8 September). By publishing an essay by "E" in this issue, and by setting most of it in italic type, the *Gazette* revived the issue of amendments only ten days before the election.

The *Gazette* also nominated a new candidate. Until the 8th, only Federalists had been nominated by the newspapers. Now the *Gazette* named Samuel Adams, the man the Federalists feared more than any other. Similar paragraphs naming Adams appeared in the *Herald of Freedom* on the 8th and in the *Massachusetts Centinel* on the 10th, but both newspapers opposed him. A correspondent in the *Gazette* on the 8th also suggested William Heath, but he was virtually ignored thereafter, except that the *Massachusetts Centinel* on the 10th questioned his abilities as a general and a legislator, and the next day the *Herald of Freedom* charged that he had written the paragraph nominating himself.

Samuel Adams was clearly the *Gazette*'s candidate, and the candidate of the *Independent Chronicle* as well. The *Gazette* had nominated Samuel Adams and Elbridge Gerry for the Senate on 25 August (printed above) and on 3 November had nominated him again, along with John Adams and Francis Dana (printed above in The Election of United States Senators).

A third item in this issue of the *Gazette* destroyed the candidacy of Samuel A. Otis within a few days. Otis had become a bankrupt in 1785. Now, in the midst of a column of miscellaneous news, a "correspondent" asked if a bankrupt should represent the state in Congress (Otis had been elected to the Confederation Congress in June 1787 and again in June 1788). Two days later the *Massachusetts Centinel*, which on 3 December had declared Otis the only candidate, published a long attack on him (10 December, printed below) and many of his supporters soon deserted him.

E on the Need for Amendments

As the choice of federal Representatives is soon to take place, it is essentially necessary for the good of the Union, that those men be chosen who are most likely to promote the general desire of the people at large—men who are of the persuasion that amendments to the new proposed Constitution are absolutely requisite and necessary to secure the freedom, security, and perfect confidence of every individual throughout the Union. That amendments are necessary you are requested to submit the following to the candid observation of your readers.

To the FREEMEN of MASSACHUSETTS: Friends and Countrymen! A fellow citizen, who is impressed with real anxiety at the approaching crisis of our public affairs, begs leave to address a few words to you. Whilst the enterprising and ambitious are pressing forward to the harvest of office and emolument which they promise themselves under the new Constitution, he freely resigns all hopes of private advantage from the government, and feels no other interest than that which every citizen ought to feel in the misfortunes or prosperity of his country. He expects no benefit from the administration of public affairs but that which every individual will share in common with himself; he fears no misfortunes but those which will equally affect every member of the community. With these views and motives, which are alike interesting to every good citizen, he flatters himself he shall be heard with attention.

Liberty was the avowed object of the late glorious Revolution in search of which we waded with patience and resolution through all the horrors of a civil war; and the constitutions of the several states were framed with admirable wisdom, according to the best models, and upon the noblest principles of civil liberty. One only defect remained. The general government of the continent, under the late Articles of Confederation, was too feeble to secure the safety of the people. Its defects were evident; and yet, as if by a studied contrivance, they were suffered to remain, with hardly an attempt to remedy them until the public affairs of the continent had sunk into utter imbecility and ruin. The cry, at length, for a new form of continental government, became loud and universal.

A continental convention was called, the hopes of the people were raised to the highest pitch of expectation, and the sun never beheld a more glorious opportunity of establishing a happy form of government. Nothing short of the most glaring defects could have excited any shadow of opposition. But it is to be feared some selfish and artful men amongst us were but too willing to avail themselves of so favorable an opportunity of consulting the profit and power of the future governors of the continent, at the expense of the liberties of the people. Whether, however, it was the effect of accident or design, most glaring defects appear in the Constitution which they have proposed to the people. These defects have been freely stated by writers in the public papers throughout the continent, as well as in the debates of the several state conventions. Indeed many of these defects seem now to be generally acknowledged, even by those men who, there is too much reason to fear, would still wish to evade their amendment and to retain them in the system. Some of these defects are very glaring and important; others, perhaps, in the heat of contention have been exaggerated. One or two of the most considerable, I shall attempt briefly to lay before you.

The future Congress, if the new Constitution be not amended, will be vested with unlimited powers; the state governments, which have been founded on the most excellent constitutions in the world, will crumble into ruin, or dwindle into shadows; and, in their stead, an enormous, unwieldly government will be erected, which must speedily fall to pieces by its own weight, and leave us to the wretched alternative of anarchy or tyranny; whereas by a due temperature, the continental government may be clothed with all necessary powers for the management of foreign affairs, and leave the state governments in the possession of such powers as will enable them to regulate our internal concerns which a continental government can never effectually reach. It is just as absurd to suppose that the general government of the whole empire can regulate the internal police of the several states, as to believe that the several states could regulate our foreign trade, and protect us in our intercourse with foreign nations. The latter we have already tried without success; the former will be found equally impracticable.

Another defect in the Federal Constitution is equally alarming. No security is provided for the rights of individuals; no bill of rights is framed nor is any privilege of freemen secured from the invasion of the governors. Trust me, my fellow citizens! We shall not be more powerful or more respected abroad, for being liable to oppression at home; but on the contrary, the freest states have ever been the most powerful. Yet with us no barriers will remain against slavery, under the new continental government, if it be not amended. The state governments by the express terms of the Constitution can afford no protection to their citizens, and not even a single right is defined or stipulated, which the subject may appeal to against the will and pleasure of the moment.

These circumstances and others of a like tendency have excited great opposition, but the absolute necessity of a continental government of some sort has silenced the opposition of those, who were dissatisfied with the present Constitution, first in the Continental Convention, and afterwards in most of the conventions of the states. The wiser, if not the major, part of the Continental Convention would have produced to us a much better form of continental union, had it been in their power, but they preferred this to none; and in the different states, the wisest and best of the people have acquiesced in the scheme of adopting it in its present form, from the hope of obtaining those amendments which the Constitution itself provides for the attaining, provided two-thirds of Congress, or two-thirds of the state legislatures, shall concur in requiring them. Without such a clause of obtaining amendments, there is little doubt but a majority of the freemen of America would have spurned at the idea of subjecting themselves to the other terms of the new Constitution; with this clause of obtaining amendments, it has become the duty of good citizens to make a beginning with the Constitution as it is, confiding in the hope of obtaining all essential amendments in a constitutional mode. In this mode which is provided, it is certainly more eligible to reform the Constitution than by any violent or irregular opposition to attempt to overthrow it. We must have a continental government, or we are an undone people. At the same time we ought to preserve our liberties, if possible, so far as they may consist with our essential protection. If those two points can be attained, and this extensive continent held together, in the course of a few years, we may, at once, be the greatest and happiest people on earth.

Samuel Adams Nominated for the House of Representatives

As many gentlemen have been held out to the public as candidates for Representatives in the federal court, you are requested by a number of our correspondents to propose the Honorable Samuel Adams, Esquire, who, if not the first, was among the first, who proposed the first American Congress, and who has been proved, approved, and found faithful, and whose abilities cannot be called in question.

His friends (and they are the friends of the people) intend to vote for him; and it is not to be doubted, that he will obtain a full vote throughout the District of Suffolk.

Shall a Bankrupt Represent the State?

Shall a *Bankrupt of no distinguished abilities* represent this State in the Federal Convention? *asks a correspondent.—He then apostrophizes,* Oh Massachusetts! where are thy Hampden's, thy Chatham's, thy rising Patriots, thy illustrious Worthies? Are they all fled! all gone to receive the rewards of their virtuous actions in the realms of bliss!—I hope there are some left more capable than Mr. O[tis].

Suffolk, Massachusetts Centinel, 10 December

If there is propriety in holding up to public view such candidates for public offices as are agreeable to the wishes or interests of the proposer, I conceive there can be no impropriety in pointing out disqualifications.

In casting an eye on the election made in other states—when I see men of the first abilities, rank, and character chosen in some parts of the continent, and contrast them with some of the candidates held up in the public papers of Massachusetts, it is not without pain for the honor of my country.

Some of these candidates, we are told, have declined the intended honor. But who is the man left, by a kind of newspaper-necessity, upon our hands? Is he a man of abilities compared with such as will be chosen by other counties, or by other states? Is he a man of property? Is he a man of integrity? These are serious questions, and such as ought, for the honor of the individual, to be secluded from the observation of the public. But in the name of everything that is dear and valuable in society, to what a pitch of degeneracy have we arrived? Shall the friends of one man propose him for the most important offices in government, when they know him to be deficient in the great essentials? And shall the whole community be silent? Shall not one honest man come forth and declare the truth? Yes, my fellow citizens, there is among you one man, who has nothing to hope or to fear—to gain or to suffer by the elections—and he tells you in plain words that a b[ankrupt] ought never to represent the County of Suffolk.[1]

(The writer of the foregoing, must excuse the omission made in it—"he might say it, but we dare not.")[2]

1. This article and the paragraph in the *Boston Gazette* on 8 December provoked immediate replies. The next day, 11 December, the *Herald of Freedom* published an article by "Z" (printed below) and three paragraphs "from correspondents" attacking Otis's detractors. The *Independent Chronicle* also published a defense of Otis by "Justice" on the 11th, but the *Chronicle*'s candidate was clearly Samuel Adams (see "Prudence," *Independent Chronicle*, 11 December, printed below).

2. This insertion by the publisher was printed in italic type.

Z, Herald of Freedom, 11 December

The Hon. Mr. [Samuel A.] Otis, surmounting the usual obstacles to the advancement of merit and abilities, will doubtless have the honor to represent this district in the general government. These obstacles have proceeded from the malice of a gentleman who, in so gallant a manner, lately disencumbered himself, as Sancho did, when he was first offered the government of an island,[1] or they have proceeded from a mere disappointed lawyer, the celebrated *recanter*,[2] who so modestly asserted that "his country would never be at peace, till Hancock and Adams were hung"—the very late advocate of two of the most in[famous?] causes that were ever introduced into a court of justice; even by the most brazen impudent v[illai]n, or the more secret, atrocious one. This latter character, who will be nothing but a senator or a judge, has been the most fortunate politician of his age. How happy would it have been for his former compatriot, the renowned Jonathan Sewall, had the good people of Newburyport, or any other place, compelled him to sign and publish a recantation of his dangerous sentiments. He would not have had occasion in that case, to upbraid the former associate of his apostacy and infidelity, which the other justified by very good pleas of necessity and compulsion, and the convenient one of an apparent change only. Had he likewise have recanted, we should have the benefit of his abilities in the federal, legislative, or judicial branch. The ebulations of this recanter against the present honorable candidate, will, we trust, have no influence upon the well-informed electors of Suffolk District; for it cannot be supposed, that on these occasions he can lay aside that habit of abusing the name of Otis, which he acquired with "Philalethes," when they were jointly in the pay of his patron, Governor [Thomas] Hutchinson, for that and other laudable purposes.[3]

1. The reference is evidently to Thomas Dawes, Jr., who announced that he was not a candidate (*Boston Gazette*, 1 December, printed above).

2. The reference is evidently to John Lowell. Originally from Newburyport, he had moved to Boston in 1776 and was one of its most prominent lawyers by 1788. While in Newburyport he had denounced the Otises and Adamses at the time of the Stamp Act, had opposed nonimportation in 1768, and in 1774 had signed the address to Governor Thomas Hutchinson before he left for England. A few months later he had publicly apologized in the *Essex Gazette* for signing the address to Hutchinson.

3. In addition to "Z" the *Herald of Freedom* printed three items "from correspondents" defending Otis and attacking his detractors. They are printed immediately below. On 15 December, the printers of the *Herald of Freedom* declared that they were of no party, but that they would not print an attack on Samuel A. Otis and Harrison Gray Otis unless the man who had handed it in would identify himself.

From Correspondents, Herald of Freedom, 11 December

If misfortune is a crime, says a correspondent, a scurrilous paragraphist in last Monday's *Gazette* has sufficient foundation for his abuse of the Hon. Mr. O[tis]. But if a man of honor and integrity, a man of sense, and a staunch friend to the freedom and welfare of his country is, in common with others, subject to the frowns of adversity, surely the wretch who would attempt to brand with infamy the unfortunate, merits the "universal hiss, the sound of public scorn." No illiberal abuse, continues our correspondent, can ever prejudice the independent citizens of Massachusetts against a candidate deserving of their suffrages; but, with unanimity will they elect a man to represent them, whose ambition will be to promote their interest and prosperity, and watch their liberties with a jealous eye.

The malignant abuse of wretches, some of whom are under the deepest obligations to the family of the gentleman whom they endeavor to wound, can produce no other effect than to excite the indignation of his fellow citizens.

A correspondent observes, it is too late for the envenomed pen of slander to cast a shade upon the integrity of a worthy citizen. His townsmen have already borne evidence in his favor. He has been deputed by the legislature to represent the commonwealth in Congress. How pitiful then is the objection to his eligibility to represent a district?

In answer to the infamous and libellous publication in Edes's *Gazette* of scandals, another correspondent, no way interested, would enquire: What Hampden or Chatham have done more for their country, than the venerable father and brother of the gentleman alluded to? And where were these scribblers, in the year 1776, when this very gentleman was first chosen to represent this town?

Prudence to the Freemen of the County of Suffolk, Independent Chronicle, 11 December

By the act of the last session, you are called upon in the course of the present month, in your respective towns, to determine upon a gentleman to represent you in the new Congress. Though very little has yet been said, I conceive it to be a subject of great consequence both to you and your posterity. To choose with propriety, you must have recourse to those principles upon which all societies are founded, and remember however free the government, and however well administered, the passions of the human heart are all displayed in its execution. The prerogatives of the President, and the rights of the Senate, at the future court of America, will be as much the subject of discussion as the privileges of the people. Many individuals, also, will be striving to place themselves in that situation where they may ride both secure and steady at the expense of others, and unless the people at large in the first instance provide a *centinel* for themselves, to guard against undue encroachments, few of their own accord will be found to do this duty for them. It will therefore be necessary that a complete, fair, and unequivocal representation be obtained, and that the democratical branch consist of men who have been tried and found faithful, of persons who have had experience in more dangerous seasons, and who have executed with success and fidelity commissions of importance in more perilous times. You are not now called to choose a Senator, or a President, but a man to personate yourselves; to act in your stead, and to be present to speak for you; to make known your wants; to state your inability; and to keep at a distance the pressure of too heavy burdens. He must be a man capable of watching at all seasons, and spending his time and talents in your services. His head and heart must be wholly devoted to you: the qualities of the one sufficient to keep him upright, and of the other to screen you from the insidious propositions of the artful and the smooth, oily speeches of the ambitious. He must not himself be a seeker and do your business for the sake of a maintenance, for he will be frequently exposed to temptation and often times his influence and vote so much wanted as to command at market a greater price than you can pay him. If these observations are pertinent, if age, experience, integrity, ability, and firmness ought to form a part of the character of the man upon whom you bestow your suffrages, give me leave to turn your attention to that tried patriot, I mean the Honorable Samuel Adams, and to offer him as a candidate to fill that important post. It is but too true, that a prophet is without honor in his own country, but there is scarce another spot in the globe where the actions of this great and good man are not celebrated. From youth to manhood, and from thence to old age, he has been a decided friend to the rights of mankind. Whenever he has promised, he hath never deceived, and I now challenge the greatest among his enemies (if real enemies can be found to this gentleman in America) to step forward and point either to the conduct or the moment wherein he has once deviated from that steady attachment for the people of this country. So early as 1760 he distinguished himself for his opposition to Great Britain, and in the cabinet took a very active part against the King's governors, [Francis] Bernard and [Thomas] Hutchinson.

His pen was always conspicuous in those famous controversies between the General Assembly and those gentlemen, and with a few others, and but a few to support him, he beat them from the field. As the opposition became more serious, his abilities and perseverance became more brilliant, and in almost every important assembly from that day to the present, he has been not only a member, but in it a man of attention and business. America in her darkest periods ever found him forward and near the helm, and for her sake, he with cheerfulness for seven years served her with a halter about his neck. Naked he went into her employ, and naked he came out of it. Can we then, my fellow citizens, hesitate again to trust our most important concerns in such hands. Can it be possible, that after having spent a life of fifty years in promoting our freedom and welfare, that this period of it can be reserved to betray us. It cannot be. It is not in human nature. Let us then one and all unite in giving our suffrages to this our respectable fellow citizen. Let us manifest to the world that we do not neglect faithful servants, because of their uprightness, and employ others for their flattery and professions. Let not the sin of ingratitude stain our country, and by our conduct let us not drive from our employ men that are independent, that will think, and act for themselves. The town of Boston in general will vote for him, and if our country brethren will join them, it will prevent the trouble and expense of a second choice, and give general satisfaction.[1]

1. In this issue, the *Chronicle* also printed essays by "Marcus" and "A Countryman," as well as four brief paragraphs by "correspondents," all of them recounting Adams's service during the Revolution and recommending his election.

Harrison Gray Otis to the Printer, 13 December[1]

Many of my friends have informed me, that pains have been taken to propagate an opinion, of my being the author of a piece in the *Herald* of Thursday, signed "Z." Although I am persuaded this suspicion does not exist with those who know my sentiments of the characters designated in that performance—yet, under all circumstances, there is a peculiar propriety in my assuring the friends of those gentlemen, that I know not, nor have any [ra]tional ground to conjecture, who may have been the writer of that, or any other invective against any individual.

The gentleman who is more directly pointed at has ever been my patron and friend; and whatever may naturally be my wish respecting the issue of the present controversy, I have no other inducement to give my name to the public, but the apprehension of being exposed to the charge of ingratitude.[2] Previous to the publication alluded to, I had no reason [t]o think the abovementioned gentlemen oppose[d] to my father, and, in any event, am willing t[o] rest my honor upon the proof of any personal virulence having proceeded from my lips or pen or from those of any other person with my knowledge.

1. *Massachusetts Centinel*, 13 December. This issue of the *Centinel* also included the following paragraph: "We have the fullest authority to assure the public that the piece in Thursday's *Herald*, under the signature of Z, as well as every other piece and paragraph relative to the approaching election of Representative, have been written and inserted without the consent or privity of the gentleman principally concerned [Samuel A. Otis] and that he has uniformly requested his most intimate friends to refrain from addressing the public in any instance upon his subject. For the truth of the above we have liberty to pledge the honor of the gentleman, and that he never had the least suspicion that Mr. L[owell], Mr. D[awes], or any of their friends had so far departed from their characters as to insert the malignant paragraphs that have appeared against him."
2. Harrison Gray Otis, the son of Samuel A. Otis, had studied law with John Lowell.

Constitutionalist, Massachusetts Centinel, 13 December

I have attended to the several recommendations of the Hon. Mr. A[dams], as a candidate for *federal Representative* for this district, and could not but observe the *total silence* of the different writers (if there was indeed *more than one*) upon the *great*, and *essential*, requisite of FEDERALISM.

We are *over*, and *over*, and *over* again, informed of facts, that every person has for *years* been fully acquainted with, but as to the GRAND INQUIRY, which every *Federalist*, every friend to our *excellent Federal Constitution*, and to the SOLID UNION of the states, would make, viz., is he *now* a firm, decided Federalist? No satisfaction can be obtained from any of his advocates.

It will readily be granted, that this gentleman merits highly of his country, for his firmness and intrepidity, in the hour of danger; that he *has been* steady, consistent, and persevering; that he *was* a distinguished patriot of '75, etc. But what of all this? What was the state of facts in '87? And how is it in '88? How is he affected as to the new Constitution? What are his ideas of trade and commerce? Are they matter of great importance in *his* estimation? Or were *they* ever considered so by *him*? Have these subjects ever employed his attention? Or is he any ways qualified to advocate these important points, which are justly considered as of the *first* consequence to this commercial commonwealth? What are his acquirements upon the great subject of finance? Has he ever attended to system of revenue, or matters that have a complicated reference to the sources from which a revenue must be drawn, to support the government, discharge the debts, or establish the credit of this rising republic? In short, has he of *late* discovered that *attachment* to the new system, on which all our hopes as people are founded, which can rationally promise *his* support to that system? If these questions can be fairly answered in the affirmative by his advocates, he is a suitable person to represent this *commercial district* in the federal government; if they *cannot*, unless the people see through a different medium from what they did, twelve months since, no misplaced, misconceived ideas of gratitude will lead them to an election which may produce a complete disappointment of all that they hope and expect from the operation of the federal government.

Edward H. Robbins to Theodore Sedgwick, Boston, 14 December (excerpt)[1]

I received the necessary papers in season. With respect to our election we are in a dreadful situation. S[amuel] Adams has all his *myrmidons* to support him and they are numerous; Mr. [Samuel A.] Otis a considerable party. We are pushing brother [Fisher] Ames and shall make some figure, at least prevent a choice. I always deprecated the mode of election and now see the evils of it.

1. RC, Sedgwick Papers, MHi. Robbins, a Milton lawyer and justice of the peace for Suffolk County in 1788, was evidently a close associate of Sedgwick and other Federalist leaders. He later served as speaker of the House (1793-1802) and lieutenant governor (1802-1807).

Christopher Gore to Rufus King, Boston, 14 December (excerpt)[1]

Suffolk will, as you suggest, be much divided. [Samuel] Adams, [Samuel A.] Otis, [Fisher] Ames, and [William] Heath and James Bowdoin, Jr., will be voted for, and it is probable, that at the first meeting no choice will be made, tho many fear that S. Adams will be elected. A week hence we shall know more of this matter. At present we are in a very sorry condition.

1. RC, King Papers, NHi. Printed: King, *Life*, I, 347.

Consistency to the Free Electors, Herald of Freedom, 15 December

The day approaches, my fellow citizens, upon which you are either to confirm your uniform professions of love to your country, and of your attachment to the blessings of good government, or to exhibit a melancholy and fatal instance of the utter instability of popular sentiment. If you, my friends, allow your reason to operate, unwarped by the influence of your passions and affections, you must be convinced that upon the unanimity of your suffrages in favor of a Federal candidate, depends not only the prosperity, but the peace and salvation of this Union. This commonwealth was among the foremost of the states to ratify the present Constitution; and, unaided by the influence of this metropolis, this great and interesting event would not probably have happened. With what anxiety did you, my friends, throng the galleries of the honorable Convention! What fear and agitation did you experience concerning the event! Have you forgotten how sincerely and how justly you considered that all your hearts held dear, your liberties, lives, and fortunes, the revival of commerce, the encouragement of manufactures, the welfare and honor of the republic, depended upon the issue of their debates! Do you not recollect the indignation and chagrin which affected every bosom, upon the appearance of a bigoted opposition, arising from the pride and obstinacy of some, and from the mischievous policy of others! If these suggestions remind you of the ideas and principles which you then entertained, let me entreat you to consult your dignity and happiness, by a consistent and patriotic conduct, by the deputation of a man to serve you, whose Federalism is unsuspected, and whose commercial abilities may be equal to his station, and to your purposes. Upon this measure, I may venture to assert, the happiness of this continent depends. In the ancient dominion of Virginia, popular art and intrigue have gained the ascendant, and their delegation [Senators] principally consists of men [Richard Henry Lee and William Grayson] who are warm advocates for *a new convention*, or at least for *numerous amendments*. From several other states a similar deputation may be expected. This party consists of men who are conspicuous; and who, having espoused the Antifederal cause, must rise or fall by its success. Their pride cannot suffer them to recede. It is notorious that great efforts will be attempted in favor of a new convention. The *sanguine Virginians* declare it openly. And if these efforts are successful, the Union will be immediately involved in anarchy, uproar, and civil war! Massachusetts must, as she has ever done, hold the balance. The men of true and Federal principles throughout the continent depend upon a delegation of calm and steady adherents to the Constitution, from this commonwealth. We have reason to fear they may be disappointed; and all the promised advantages of this system will in that case vanish like a dream. Three or four of our districts will probably elect Antifederal men. From Bristol, Worcester, and even from the upper counties [i.e., Maine] much is to be feared. And should the delegate from this district, supported by the influence which he will naturally acquire, be even lukewarm in the cause, the Federal scale will kick the beam; a thousand systems of amendments will arise; and God only knows what fate will attend this once happy country. I conjure you, therefore, my friends, to consider the importance of the approaching crisis. If a man who *was* professedly Antifederal, and who is remarkable for the obstinacy of his temper, appears a candidate, will you think upon him a moment! If he declares he has changed his opinions, will you believe him?

Or if you believe him, can you approve his motives, or confide that he will not alter his sentiments whenever interest shall prompt? No my friends! Such a man may have great merit, and may be entitled to an honorable provision at home; but if trusted abroad, persevering, disappointed and ambitious, connected with the warmest Antifederalists in all the states, he will pull down the pillars of the government in attempting to prop it, and expire in the ruins.

Brutus to the Printers, Herald of Freedom, 15 December

By inserting the following observations in the *Herald*, you will further evince that impartiality, which you have hitherto maintained.

The press (in my humble opinion) ought never to be made the partial vehicle of party productions, and whenever it is devoted to any particular class, it may reasonably be supposed that the impartial will withdraw their patronage from it.

The late compositions of malice and slander which have flowed through the channel of the *Independent Chronicle* induced me to relate a few serious and striking truths, respecting that party to which the *Chronicle* is devoted [Samuel Adams], and send them to the printers of it, for publication. They refused, however, to lay them before the public; and the same day, on which (did they act impartially) the production I sent them ought to have appeared, their paper was nearly filled up with encomiums upon one of the heads of that party, which it has ever been their aim and object to support. It is, however, the last time I shall ever give them an opportunity to evince their attachment to their own cause, and the reason I request this to be made known, is, that others may take the hint.[1]

1. On 18 December, the publishers of the *Independent Chronicle* replied that they were not obliged to publish an article "which the real author is either afraid or ashamed to acknowledge" as his own. "Brutus's" piece was, they said, an "unequaled" specimen of "abuse and scurrility."

From a Correspondent, Herald of Freedom, 15 December

As Fisher Ames, Esq., of Dedham is the person whom it is certain the Federal electors of Suffolk District out of town will vote for, it is hoped, that all in town who wish to unite in a Federal character—altho intended to give their votes for Mr. [Rufus] King, Mr. [Samuel A.] Otis, Mr. [Samuel] Adams, or any other gentleman, on this principle, will now give their votes for Mr. Ames. Freemen! Federalists! *on your* unanimity *depends the* SALVATION OF OUR COUNTRY!

Boston Gazette, 15 December

This was the last issue of the *Gazette* before the election. It contained several items supporting Samuel Adams, items warning the voters of Middlesex and Essex districts about suggested candidates in those districts, and attacks on the *Massachusetts Centinel*, the *Herald of Freedom*, and Samuel A. Otis. "An Elector,"

"Belisarius," "A Mechanic," and an item from an "unknown correspondent" are printed below.

An Elector

The independent electors of the County of Suffolk I presume cannot hesitate a moment in their choice of a Representative for the federal government, when they are informed, that the Hon. Samuel Adams, Esquire, stands a candidate for their suffrages. The enemies of this patriot without doubt will be busy to deceive the county (as they were at the time of choosing lieutenant governor) by propagating, *that he will not be supported in this town*; and, *that he is determined not to go, if chosen*. But these suggestions, the public may be assured, are FALSE; as a number of respectable characters (being persuaded of his willingness to serve in this station) have already met, and unanimously determined to exert their whole influence for this gentleman; and provided the county will give him their support, it is not doubted that he will be chosen by a large and respectable majority of INDEPENDENT ELECTORS.

The freeholders of this county should be actuated with a laudable *pride* with respect to their representation; they should consider their own weight in the national scale, with respect to the proportion of TAXES they will be subject to. They should therefore be careful to have a Representative whose character is well established as to his integrity and patriotism; whose *influence* is in proportion to the great interest delegated to him. If we are not careful to secure to ourselves a Representative whose *opinion* will be considered of some weight, there is great danger that this county may be over-rated, provided a direct tax should be required.

For these reasons, the electors of this county, as they regard their *interest*, should be attentive to introduce a man who is well acquainted with their circumstances; and who, from *long practice* in public affairs, will be able to defeat (however subtle) those measures, which may prove injurious to them in their operations.

No man can doubt the attachment of Mr. Adams to the liberties of this country. But he is now represented by some, as opposed to the present Constitution; this is an unfair measure taken by his enemies, as he was warm in the support of it in the [Massachusetts] Convention, as the debates will show.

The friends to America it is not doubted will despise the INFAMOUS ARTS now practiced by those, who were enemies to this country, when Mr. Adams was its friend, to *the hazard of his life*. It is presumed that [Thomas] Hutchinson, [Francis] Bernard, and the whole group of TORIES, if they *now* had a voice in our election, would use their influence against this great and good man.

Mr. Adams was in our first Congress previous to the war. He then became acquainted with many of those leading characters, who probably will compose the present government. HE KNOWS THEM, and THEY KNOW HIM. They are conversant with each other's politics. Such a body of men, meeting in our first Congress, will give decision to the public business; *as they are only to begin where they before left off*.

But on the contrary, suppose we send a young man, whose system of politics is not yet matured, and who has to form his connections with the several members; will not these necessary preliminaries rather retard the accomplishment of those great national objects which ought to claim the immediate attention of Congress?

If therefore the people of this county mean to support their respectability, and secure themselves against even the attempt of imposition, let us unite in the choice of Mr. Adams, whose *venerable name* will give importance to the county, whose *exertions* will add energy to government, and whose *prudence* will guarantee the rights and liberties not only of his constituents, but of the people of the whole confederation.

Belisarius

If the writers in the *Chronicle* of Thursday have omitted to do justice to the Federalism of Mr. [Samuel] Adams, as is asserted in the *Centinel* of Saturday,[1] they have indeed been guilty of an omission, which, in my opinion, should by all means be corrected. It is in this point, that the virtue of this venerable patriot is unquestionably the most resplendent, as it was perhaps chiefly owing to his exertions, at a period when the intended union of America was compared to a "rope of sand," that this great and important object was so happily accomplished. If the Revolution was then effected by our union, can there exist a suspicion, that so true, uniform, and active a friend to his country would fail in his efforts to perpetuate that blessing which the wisdom of his counsels has produced. The Federalism of this consistent republican is not the offspring of the moment, played off for the purpose of party and deception. It originated in the hour of peril, and has been confirmed in his mind by the experience of its benefits. It has not been an occasional existence, blown into action to secure the comforts of a sinecure, or the emoluments of an office. The Federalism of this incorruptible statesman has grown into vigor, by a solid conviction that the honor, liberty, and happiness of his country depend, no less on the union, than on the purity of its councils. Who then will question the Federalism of Mr. Adams; or if he dare, from what suspicious source will he derive his evidence. Surmise and calumny, in the moment of cool reflection, will not be considered as arguments, by a people who are not to be warped in their attachment by the subtlety of party insinuations, or the malice of personal resentment. In the present moment it would be a disgrace to Mr. Adams, if he had not SOME enemies, and their exertions to injure him are but proofs of his virtue.

This sterling patriot, this genuine Federalist, has not only been distinguished for his consistency in '75, but in every subsequent year those who know him best are satisfied that he has been equally deserving. When a number of questions, therefore, are proposed to impeach his consistency, or his patriotism, the answers will be as satisfactory, as his merit is conspicuous, or even as his warmest friends can desire. On commerce, and on finance, as well as on the principles of government, and the views of party, his knowledge is profound and his integrity unsuspected. He is of course, then, the very person to represent this commercial district. Nor, my countrymen, do you believe that he is not acquainted with these subjects. A knowledge of the commercial interests of this commonwealth is no way connected with the little art of driving a bargain, or tricking an unhappy widow of the hard earnings of an honest employment. Mr. Adams acquired his mercantile information in a respectable counting house, as he obtained his political information in the same school which produced that effulgent constellation of patriots who projected our independence. But after all, where is the mystery?

The great objects of the new government are as clear as our necessities and sufferings can make them. Agriculture, manufactures, and commerce, the restoration of public faith and private credit, economy in our public expenditures, together with the greatest caution and frugality in the creation of offices and the annexment of salaries, are among the great and leading points, which will no doubt first attract the attention and engage the wisdom of the federal legislature. In the order of things, relief in our difficulties will precede every attempt to meliorate the new system, so as to prevent the probability of abuse in its administration, by adding such amendments as the concurring opinions of a whole continent have in a manner agreed to be necessary to confirm the wavering, and to conciliate its opponents. Our public faith, the honor of the state, and our reputation for consistency depend upon something being done, agreeably to the form of our own ratification. To such amendments Mr. Adams is not opposed. If he was, he would indeed be what his enemies represent him; and what, if there is not a want of charity in the observation, I verily believe many of them are. Freemen of the county, citizens of Boston, let us not then hesitate. Let us once more trust him, whom we have so often trusted. Let it never be said, that the man shall want your support and assistance, in that country which has been saved by his wisdom.

A Mechanic

As the *Centinel*[2] has made a great outcry for a merchant to represent the District of Suffolk in the federal House of Representatives, I would ask the profound writers in that paper:

What business there will be for a merchant to do at Congress? Will his counting house, stores, vessels, and wharves be wanted there? Will he be wanted to negotiate bills of exchange? Will he be wanted there to barter any one article of commerce for another? Or, will he be wanted to buy and sell places under government? If he will not be wanted for any of those purposes, he will not be wanted at all; for merchandise and government are, and ought to be, distinct branches of science.

A Correspondent

In last Monday's paper I observed the Honorable Samuel Adams proposed as a candidate for a federal Representative for the District of Suffolk.[3] It has always been a disgrace to our country that certain characters, who were the first promoters of the Revolution, have been neglected. Mr. A. was early in the cause of liberty; he was one of those patriots, who, at the risk of their lives, stood forth in the defense of their country, and burst the shackles of tyranny. He has been rewarded with the esteem of all virtuous men; but the mere regard of individuals is not sufficient. He should be supported by a grateful country; a country, which, were it not for a few patriots, would now be galled with the fetters of slavery. Early in the year 1775, Mr. A. distinguished himself among a band of worthies, some of whom now hold the first offices in the commonwealth. His friends in the country, as well as many independent citizens in this town (who consider him as one of those to whom we owe our liberty), are determined to give him their suffrages; and who, from patriotic motives, choose to be represented by a venerable republican and able statesman, rather than by a man

****

(The remainder we think prudent not to publish. *Our unknown correspondent may* report *it if he pleases.*)

1. See "Prudence," *Independent Chronicle*, 11 December, and "Constitutionalist," *Massachusetts Centinel*, 13 December, both printed above.
2. See "Constitutionalist," *Massachusetts Centinel*, 13 December, printed above.
3. *Boston Gazette*, 8 December, printed above.

Boston Meeting Supports Samuel Adams, Tuesday Evening, 16 December[1]

You are desired to make known to the public, that a caucus was held last evening, consisting of above one hundred respectable tradesmen, merchants, and other gentlemen, who unanimously agreed to give their votes and use their influence for the Hon. Samuel Adams, Esq., as a Representative in the Congress of the United States, and the Hon. Thomas Dawes, Esq., [and] Hon. Jabez Fisher, Esq., as candidates for Electors for Suffolk District.

1. *Massachusetts Centinel*, 17 December.

Boston Meeting Supports Fisher Ames, Tuesday Evening, 16 December[1]

At a meeting of a numerous body of Federalists, held in this town, it was unanimously determined to support the election of Fisher Ames, Esquire, as a Representative for Suffolk District, in the federal legislature; also, the Hon. Jabez Fisher, Esq., [and] the Hon. Caleb Davis, Esq., as candidates for Elector of President and Vice President; and this determination was founded, not only upon the abilities and Federalism of the above gentlemen; but from *authentic information*, that our brethren, who are Federal, through the county, would give their suffrages for the same Federal characters.

1. *Massachusetts Centinel*, 17 December. On 18 December (election day) the *Independent Chronicle* reported that "about one hundred and fifty Federalists" attended the meeting. However, "Civis" in the same issue of the *Chronicle* denied that there had been a meeting to support Ames. "Civis" is printed immediately below.

Civis to the Citizens of Suffolk, Independent Chronicle, 18 December

The flagrant imposition attempted to be imposed on you, by a paragraph in yesterday's *Centinel*, is too glaring and evident not to be detected. It is there asserted, that "At a meeting of a numerous body of Federalists held in this town, they determined to support the election of Fisher Ames, Esq." The public may be assured, that the whole of the aforesaid information is an abominable falsehood, and is only held out to deceive; there having been no such meeting of the friends of Mr. Ames. This scandalous attempt at deception, together with another under the signature of Mentor, in the same paper,[1] are probably the production of an inveterate *Tory*, who superintended the compilation of yesterday's *Centinel*, until late on Tuesday evening, with intention to preclude every thing therefrom favorable to the Hon. Samuel Adams, Esq., who highly merits your support. This inveterate *Tory*, is no other than a *nephew* of the late Governor [Thomas] H[utchinso]n and breathes the same pestiferous sentiments of high-handed power and arbitrary authority, as did his infamous uncle.[2] Therefore, my fellow citizens, I hope you will not be led away by false, delusive, and base detraction; but one and all who wish well to your country, give in your votes for the Hon. Samuel Adams, Esq., for Representative, and for the Hon. Thomas Dawes, and the Hon. Jabez Fisher, esquires, as candidates for Electors for the District of Suffolk.

1. "Mentor" is printed below among the items in the *Massachusetts Centinel* for 17 December.
2. We have not been able to identify the person referred to.

Massachusetts Centinel, 17 December

This issue the day before the election of Representatives contained several items attacking Antifederalists and Samuel Adams and supporting Fisher Ames, and one item suggesting that Adams was not an enemy of commerce and a violent stickler for amendments. The publisher had also received several other items: "It is with pain that we are obliged to omit 'an Old Whig'—'Federalissimo'—'Justice'—and two pieces signed 'an Elector.' The first in favor of the election of Mr. Adams, the other four in favor of that of Mr. Ames. Our previous engagements to the writers of the pieces inserted hinder their appearance. Several other articles omitted."

Printed below are "Good Old '75," "An Elector to the Federal Mechanics of This Town," "A Federal Mechanic," "Mentor," and several paragraphs "from correspondents" which appeared in the miscellaneous news column under the heading: "Boston, Wednesday, 17 December." These paragraphs might well have been an "editorial" by the Federalist publisher, Benjamin Russell.

Good Old '75

The Antifederalists of the *Southern, Middle,* and *Eastern states* are severally actuated by very *different* ideas, none of them very honorary to the parties.

Those in the *Southern States* entertain an extreme jealousy of the power and population of their brethren to the eastward. They cannot entertain the idea with any degree of patience, that we should have the carrying trade, because, they say, it will operate as a monopoly to the increasing of our wealth at their expense, while it builds up our marine, and enlarges our maritime consequence. Having failed of defeating the Constitution in the first instance, they now mean to attack it by *"amendments,"* and by doing away the exceptionable clauses, or those which may eventually benefit us, leave their trade open to the whole world. There is too much reason to suppose, that their delegation to the new government will consist principally of characters disaffected to the Eastern States. This narrow policy is seen through, by the Federalists, and is despised and opposed by the best men among them.

The Antifederalists of *New York* have never lost sight of the *original* motives of their opposition to the federal system. Any system of national government whatever, which would place them upon *equal terms* with the other states, would be just as obstinately opposed—for let confusion, poverty, and distress prevail through all the Union beside, they would not be affected thereby, while they could, as they undoubtedly would, pursue their present line of conduct—enriching themselves at the expense of their neighbors; that state, therefore, will very probably be represented by a majority of Antifederal characters, or which is the same, by sticklers for amendments, for *delay, embarrassment,* and *procrastination* to the operation of the new government constitute their ultimate object.

The Antifederalists of *Massachusetts* to a man are insurgents, whose element is confusion, without which they must sink into their "primitive nothingness."

The amendmentites pretend to be anxiously concerned for a more perfect security of the liberties of the people, but from the known characters of many of them it is evident, this is mere pretence, and is only a steppingstone to popularity—and should we be so unfortunate as to send a proportion of such men, to represent us in the federal government, they would in all probability join issue with the two descriptions before mentioned, and while they thought they were carrying their point, in raising barriers to the freedom of the country, they would be made tools of, to effect the purposes of the Southern Antifederalists, in the overthrow of the federal government.

From these considerations, it is evident, that our safety can only consist, in electing true Federalists, a term as fully understood at the *present* day, as Whig or Tory was in Good Old '75.

An Elector to the Federal Mechanics of This Town

Gentlemen, having, by your *timely* and *seasonable* interposition on the 7th January last,[1] been a principal means, under Providence, of effecting the RATIFICATION of the new Constitution, which you *then* justly considered as the last hope of your FAMILIES, your TRADE, and your COUNTRY—it now remains for you to finish your labors, by giving your votes for a man who is known to be a *firm, decided* FEDERALIST; a man, who has given *full evidence,* through *every stage* of the business, of his being *heartily* engaged in the cause, who realizes the absolute importance of a national government; a man, who has given proof of his abilities to *defend* and *support* the principles of the new Constitution, against that FORMIDABLE ANTIFEDERAL INTEREST, which will, in all probability, constitute a considerable part of the new Congress, whose object will be, *from the beginning*, to set everything afloat by pretended amendments and alterations. From the abilities of such a man, as I hope we shall choose, we may rationally expect, that a government will be established, for these states, which will lay a foundation on which every *order* and *profession* of men may rest, with a full confidence, that the labors of their hands will prove sufficient for them, that their trade and commerce will be placed on a SOLID BASIS, that every one may sit securely under his *own vine and own fig tree*, having neither *insurgents, mobs, Antifederalists, paper money,* or *tender laws,* to make him afraid.

Every one of you can recollect, with what pleasure you listened to the debates of the late Convention, and how the words of that truly independent, learned, and ingenious Federalist, Fisher Ames, Esquire, "dropped upon you as the rain upon the thirsty ground," and how "his speech distilled like the dew."

A real friend to the best interests of the town, its peace and prosperity, begs leave therefore to recommend this truly deserving character, to your particular attention. He is now in the prime and vigor of his abilities, of the same age with the Hon. Mr. [Samuel] Adams, when *he* was placed at the head of the opposition to British measures. This gentleman will concenter in his favor, by the best intelligence from all parts of the county, a decided majority of Federal votes, and his friends in the country are fully acquainted with the determination of the Federalists of this metropolis, to support his election. Let us therefore act as men of consistency at this important juncture, and not put the Constitution, and all our prospects under it, TO HAZARD, by giving a single vote to an uncertain character.

A Federal Mechanic

Having read "Marcus," "Prudence," and "Justice" in the *Independent Chronicle*,[2] directing to the person whom *they* would wish to be chosen to represent this district in the general government— as a tradesman of the town of Boston, my business, and the occasions of my family, with the want of ability, forbids me to enter deeply into such inquiries. I beg leave, however, to observe that my opinion is the same now, as it was on the 7th January last, when the tradesmen met, previous to the meeting of the Convention, viz., "That the form of government now adopted by eleven of the states, is well calculated to secure the liberties, protect the property, and guard the rights of the subject." This was then the opinion of all the tradesmen and mechanics of this town. It was also the opinion of all Federal men, and His Excellency General Washington to a friend in Fredericksburg observes, that

"All the opposition to this government is addressed more to the passions, than to the reasons of people; and if another Federal Convention is attempted, the probability is that the sentiment of the members will be more *discordant*. Then let us not attempt to mend the present before it is tried. We need not the gifts of prophecy to foretell that if we lose the present Constitution the next will be sealed in blood."[3]

Should the tradesmen of this place be so unfortunate and so unwise, as to give their suffrages to a person who is an enemy to the Federal Constitution, or who will go to work immediately to make alterations and amendments, or who is known to be ONE IN SENTIMENT with those Antifederal characters, which will be sent to Congress from some of the *Southern States*; it is my opinion that my brethren, the mechanics of this town, will be miserably disappointed in all that they expect from the new Constitution.

I hope, therefore, that we shall support our Federal character, and consistency, by giving our suffrages for a decided Federalist.

Mentor to Fellow Electors

Tomorrow you are to exercise the noble and exclusive privilege of freemen. On this all-important occasion, when you are to give *death* or *operation* to a form of government from which we reasonably expect the richest advantages, the strictest scrutiny should be made of the qualifications of the several candidates, and should bestow the honor of your suffrages on him who most deserves them. What should be the governing motives of our choice? Shall the plea of *necessity* have any force? Will the inhabitants of this district be represented by a man who has no qualification but his poverty? No. Surely they will not subject themselves to the hazard of having their commerce, their fishery, their manufactures, bartered for the vile exchange of Southern gold, and thus throw away the happiness which is now within their reach. Will they elect a man of at least *suspected Federalism*; for no other reason than because he *has been* of service to the country? Will they intrust their liberty, their property, their lives, to the protection of a man whose mysterious carriage renders him dangerous, and whose judgment age has impaired? No, surely the electors of Suffolk will shun the dire consequences of mean duplicity, and avoid the effects of an almost heretical obstinacy. On whom then shall we fix our choice? Happy am I to say there is one candidate, who has not sought the appointment; a gentleman admired for his talents, loved for his patriotism, and respected for his integrity; a gentleman to whose unremitted exertions we are greatly indebted for the adoption of our valuable Constitution; whose persuasive eloquence and sound political judgment are celebrated throughout the continent; and in whose character the vigilance of envy hath not found a flaw. The public are well aware, that the gentleman here intended is Fisher Ames, Esq., of Dedham.

Citizens unite—and by your unanimous choice of this worthy candidate, evince to the world the independence of your election, and the Federalism of your principles.

From Correspondents

Since it has been ascertained that the citizens of this federal metropolis are in favor of a fair trial of the Constitution previous to amendments, the *junto*, to suit their plans to the *popular opinion*, now *shamelessly* assert, that those who are known to be decidedly *against* the Constitution are in favor of a previous trial. But, until within *two or three days*, those who were opposed to previous amendments have been abused with every opprobrious epithet.

The people of this *federal* metropolis cannot have forgotten with what *anxiety* they waited through the *long* session of the Convention, to hear from the Hon. Mr. A[dams's] voice in support of the Constitution. And when at the *close* of the session, he did *come out*, what a CONSTERNATION they were then thrown into, by the extraordinary propositions he *then* brought forward.[4] Truly "the die" with respect to the RATIFICATION, "spun doubtful."

If this gentleman really possesses all that Federalism and love to his country, which his advocates pretend, how can they reconcile his *silence* at so interesting a period with an independent noble spirit of patriotism—especially when it is known that much was expected from his age and abilities.

The *consistency* of the junto is strikingly exemplified in their eulogium upon *some* deserving characters of 1775, and that torrent of abuse which they pour out upon others *equally deserving*. But it is remarkable, that the *same spirit* which actuates the *Antifederalists* at the *southward*, is predominant in the *scurrilities* of their coadjutors at the eastward. Not a *veteran* of 1775, even General Washington himself, has escaped the gall and venom of these harpies.

In Edes's paper of Monday last, the Antifederalists have fairly "*let the cat out of the bag*" as the saying is. Hear their whole plan in this precious Antifederal paragraph, viz., "Mr. Adams was in our first Congress, *previous* to the war, he then became acquainted with many of those leading characters, who will probably compose the present government. HE KNOWS THEM, AND THEY KNOW HIM. They are conversant with each other's politics. Such a body of men, meeting in our first Congress, will give decision to the public business; AS THEY ARE ONLY TO BEGIN, WHERE THEY BEFORE LEFT OFF."[5] That is, in plain English, by first deciding upon the NEW CONSTITUTION, which it is very generally believed, the amendment stickler would very soon *annihilate*, and then *"begin where they left off,"* that is, with that wretched *sand-rope*, the OLD CONFEDERATION. FEDERALISTS! If this does not open your eyes, it is because judicial blindness hath fallen upon you.

1. This refers to a meeting of tradesmen in Boston on the evening of 7 January 1788 prior to the meeting of the Massachusetts Convention. The meeting adopted five resolutions supporting the Constitution. The widely reprinted resolutions were published first in the *Massachusetts Gazette*, 8 January.

2. "Marcus," "Prudence," and "Justice" appeared in the *Independent Chronicle*, 11 December. "Prudence" is printed above.

3. The quoted portion is an inaccurate version of a letter Washington wrote to Charles Carter, 14 December 1787, which was printed in several newspapers in 1788, although Washington did not intend that it should be (to Benjamin Lincoln, 31 January 1788, Fitzpatrick, XXIX, 396).

The phrase "sealed in blood" used by "A Federal Mechanic" was not in Washington's letter or the newspaper version of it. However, on 7 November 1787 the Elizabethtown *New Jersey Journal* printed a speech Washington was supposed to have given on the last day of the Constitutional Convention. According to the newspaper, Washington said that if the proposed Constitution were rejected *"the next will be drawn in blood!"* This item was reprinted at least thirty-seven times, the *Massachusetts Centinel* printing it on 24 November 1787.

4. On 31 January 1788, Adams recommended to the Massachusetts Convention that the state make its ratification of the Constitution conditional upon the passage of amendments (Convention, *Debates*, 225-27).

5. See "An Elector," *Boston Gazette*, 15 December, printed above.

Election Day Appeals, 18 December

Two Boston newspapers, the Federalist *Herald of Freedom* and the Antifederalist *Independent Chronicle*, published on election day. Both were filled with last-minute appeals to voters. The *Herald* printed three lengthy essays (two favoring Fisher Ames and one Samuel Adams) and three shorter paragraphs (two for Ames, one for Adams). The *Independent Chronicle* printed thirteen election items, all but one favoring Adams. A selection from these election day appeals is printed below.

Marcus, Herald of Freedom

It is asserted, by gentlemen who are respected for their integrity and uprightness, that the Hon. Mr. A[dams] has written several letters to the southward, for no other purpose, than to vilify the character of the great and immortal Washington, and thereby to hinder his election as our chief and father.[1] If this, my fellow citizens, is true, and concurring circumstances has justified the belief, ought we a moment to hesitate in withdrawing our aid from this suspicious, Antifederal character? Surely no, and the Federal mechanics of this town, who have, by their patriotism and consistency of conduct, rendered this common-wealth respected in every part of the world, it is hoped, will show, by giving their suffrages to another man, their detestation and abhorrence of such in-gratitude and baseness. The name of Washington is grateful in our ears, and the sound will harmonize until time shall cease. The whole continent will unite in placing this venerated patriot at their head. In this district, it is wished, and believed, that the patriotic citizens will further evince their Federalism and good sense, by placing in the federal government, as a Representative for the County of Suffolk, Fisher Ames, Esquire, whose patriotism and integrity are unimpeach-able, whose FEDERALISM has been shown and celebrated, and whose talents in the science of legislation are great and extensive. In trusting this gentleman we shall be secure, and future generations, while experiencing the wisdom of our elections, will offer up orisons to our memory, for keeping secure, and trans-mitting to them those blessings to which ourselves were born.

Jeroboam to the Printers, Herald of Freedom

By giving the following a place in your impartial paper you will oblige a correspondent.

Anticipation for the *Chronicle* of this day.

Huzza for *Chronicle* authenticity.

Vive le *Chronicle*.

Last night, at half past 10 o'clock, an express arrived at the secretary's of the caucus ho[use?] with the important news, that delegates from 57 towns in the county of Suffolk met at Stoughton, and unanimously agreed to give their suf-frages for the old Federal patriot, S[amuel] A[dams], Esq. This we aver to be as TRUE as any thing yet told on our side, this or last year.

N.B. If some folks say, there are but 30 towns in this county, we as usual say they lie.

We pledge the authenticity of this paper, that there will be at least SEVEN VOTES for the Hon. Mr. A[dams] in this town, to one against him. Every *honest* man will vote for him, and none but rogues will vote against him.

Mr. A[dams] is a decided Federalist. He spoke in the Convention every day in favor of the Constitution, has never done or said any thing against it, and is wholly against amendments. Mr. [Fisher] Ames is a boy. Nobody will vote for him, and this is truth, or the court *Chronicle* tells—what to be sure, it never does—a whapper.

As for Mr. Ames, we repeat it again, he won't obtain a vote. All his friends are for Mr. A[dams], besides Mr. A[dams] is in the prime of life, and Mr. Ames is an old man.

Common Sense, Independent Chronicle

If one were to form a judgment from the *Centinel* of yesterday, there appears a fatality in the great business of election. By holding up a new candidate every day, there will be a division of votes, and the first efforts for a choice will be to no purpose. The friends to good government have long since determined to give their votes to Mr. [Samuel] Adams; and it is not in the power of any writer, by descanting on the abilities of any other man in the county, to change their purpose. Mr. [Fisher] Ames, we with pleasure acknowledge, is a man of agreeable, amiable manners; is possessed of abilities and information; and in time, we doubt not, will make a good legislator. But we have already in Mr. Adams what Mr. Ames may be in some future day. Besides it is too late to propose Mr. Ames. The citizens of Boston do not make up their minds suddenly. They have long thought on Mr. Adams and determined him to be the man. They have long experienced his abilities and his integrity; they have invariably found him attached to good government; and they know that the dignity of his character will have an influence in Congress upon some younger politicians, who upon first taking the reins, may be disposed to ride the people too hard. In this old and steady patriot, they are sure of sending an upright man, above temptation, and who scorns a bribe. *He is the poor man's friend*, and *if he has a prejudice in his politics, it leans to the rights and privileges of the common people.*

It has been said he is old and Antifederal. My fellow citizens, be not deceived; his age and experience are the very qualifications you want. *His influence caused the Constitution to be adopted in this state*, and if he fails to give it his support for a fair trial, remember it will be the first time he ever failed you. In forty years he has never deceived you; in times of more consequence than the present, he has proved true; and for his own sake as well as yours, he will not now forfeit your good opinion.

By an inflexible adherence to the liberties of the people at large, he has made a few enemies, who have improved upon slander in their frequent attempts to alienate your affections from this old servant. But he is above their reproaches, and worthy your confidence.

From Correspondents, Independent Chronicle

Is it remarkable, says a correspondent, that every old Tory should be opposed to Mr. Adams? Not at all. He was the cause of the Revolution!

The spirits of [Joseph] Warren and the Whigs of '75 wait with impatience the result of this day's meeting, and the ghost of [Thomas] Hutchinson will view with malignant pleasure the instability of human affairs, if Tory influence, and Tory connections, prevail against the venerable Adams in the town of Boston.

A correspondent observes, that some of us know Fisher Ames, Esq., as a *pretty speaker*; but the WORLD knows the Hon. Samuel Adams, Esq., as a PATRIOT, and STATESMAN.

The enemies of the Hon. Samuel Adams, Esq., have objected to his ignorance of commerce. They are therefore going to give you a lawyer!

Bostonians! The inhabitants of the country towns are willing to honor this town with a Representative for the district. Will you reject the honor?

Antifederalism has been objected to Mr. Adams. His enemies might as well have objected to his republicanism. One is just as false as the other.

Aristides, surnamed the *just*, was banished by the people he had saved. Cato was persecuted by his countrymen in Rome; but these were times when liberty was not thoroughly understood and before the benefits of even the art of printing was thought of. But neither of these would be so extraordinary, as that the Hon. Samuel Adams should be neglected and borne down by a party in that town, the inhabitants of which he had preserved from massacre and rapine. Bostonians, where are ye?

If ever there was a great and good man persecuted and reviled, Mr. Adams has been the man, but it has not been by the tradesmen of Boston. They know his worth, and it is to be hoped will honor him with their suffrages.

1. No such letters have been located.

Samuel A. Otis to John Adams, Boston, 18 December (excerpt)[1]

I flattered myself my friends would have supported my election for the District of Suffolk but I am disappointed.[2] But long disciplined in the school of adversity, disappointment sits the lighter upon my mind; especially, as I rather viewed this an object whereby I might gain subsistence rather than gratify my vanity. I think, sir, I shall hardly be disappointed in my expectations that you will be elected Vice President, in which situation you will have it in your power to assist me in the attainment of another object. The clerk of the Senate or of the House would give me subsistence, for "I want but little." And I have reason to think Mr. [Charles] Thomsen will decline the secretary's department. If I fail in both these, I think I could discharge the office of collector of excise, naval officer, or the active offices at home or abroad, for I am a citizen of the world.

1. RC, Adams Papers, MHi. Otis wrote similar letters seeking an appointive post to James Madison (New York, 4 February 1789, RC, Madison Papers, DLC) and to Paine Wingate (New York, 20 January 1789, RC, Gratz Collection, PHi).
2. Otis was not alone in commenting on his abandonment by the Federalists late in the campaign. See, for example, the *Herald of Freedom*, 29 December: "How fluctuating are human prospects! Only one week before the late election, Mr. Otis was almost the only gentleman talked of as a federal Representative. In a few days such an entire revolution is effected, that he is pushed behind the curtain and has scarcely a single advocate to espouse his cause."

Benjamin Lincoln to George Washington, Boston, 20 December (excerpt)[1]

Last Thursday our votes were given in for Representatives and for Electors of President and Vice President. Mr. [Fisher] Ames is probably chosen for this district. He was an active member in our Convention and has always distinguished himself as an honest good man. I can hardly guess who will represent any of the other districts, excepting the western one which I think will be represented by Mr. [Theodore] Sedgwick. The majority however I am confident will be good members. There were great exertions made for Mr. Samuel Adams. He would probably have carried the vote, could the people have been persuaded that he was in heart a Federalist. Our Senators are Federal indeed: Mr. [Caleb] Strong and Mr. [Tristram] Dalton.

By one of the enclosed papers Your Excellency will learn some of the exertions which have been made for Mr. Adams, and by the other how far in many towns they succe[ed]ed. In about one week we shall be able to determine more fully wh[o] will represent us and who will be our Electors. As soon as these events shall take place I will do myself the pleasure of communicating such things as may be worthy you[r] notice.

1. RC, Washington Papers, DLC.

Massachusetts Centinel, 20 December

Thursday last was the day appointed by the legislature, for the freemen of this state, to give in their votes for persons to represent this commonwealth, in the Congress of the United States. The following are the most authentic accounts of the votes given in we have received.

Suffolk District:

Towns	Mr. [Fisher] Ames,	Mr. [Samuel] Adams,	Lost votes[1]
Boston,	445	439	17
Roxbury,	45	5	18
Dorchester,	41	3	0
Milton,	16	3	12
Hingham,	28	1	0

Middlesex: Charlestown, Hon. Mr. [Joseph B.] Varnum, 45; Hon. Mr. [Elbridge] Gerry, 25. Woburn, Loammi Baldwin, Esq., 43; Hon. Mr. Gerry, 7.

Essex: Andover, Hon. Mr. [Nathan] Dane, 104. Marblehead, Hon. Jonathan Jackson, 88; Hon. Mr. [Benjamin] Goodhue, 5.

Salem, we hear, a majority for Mr. Jackson.

The votes for Electors of President and Vice President were: in Boston, Hon. Jabez Fisher, 369; Hon. Caleb Davis, 369. Roxbury, Mr. Fisher, 58; Mr. Davis, 22. Hingham, for Messrs. Fisher and Davis. In Essex District: in Marblehead, unanimous for Hon. Azor Orne, and Hon. George Cabot. Danvers, [Jonathan] Titcomb and Cabot. Andover, Hon. S[amuel] Phillips, Jr. and Mr. Cabot. Cambridge, Hon. Mr. [Francis] Dana, 75; Hon. E[leazer] Brooks, 44.[2]

The elections in the country have, in general, been very thinly attended—owing in some measure to the late fall of snow, making the passing bad.[3]

1. By "lost" votes the *Centinel* evidently meant the votes scattered among candidates in Suffolk District other than Ames and Adams.

2. The above account is typical of the scattered returns published by the Boston newspapers during the rest of the month. No attempt has been made to correct the errors in the vote returns given in this article. For the correct totals, see The Official Results of the First Election, 5-10 January 1789, printed below, and The Popular Vote for Presidential Electors, 6 January 1789, printed above.

3. Eight inches of snow fell the day before the election (William Heath Diary, 18 December, MHi). The snow and resulting bad roads hindered the voter turnout and the collection of voting returns afterwards. On Wednesday, 31 December, the *Massachusetts Centinel* reported: "We have not been able to obtain a single return from this district since our last (27

December) owing to the badness of the roads." The publisher promised a "true statement" of the returns in the next issue (Saturday, 3 January 1789).

Christopher Gore to Rufus King, Boston, 21 December (excerpt)[1]

The election in Suffolk is clearly for [Fisher] Ames. [Samuel] Adams has been distanced even in Boston. In the country he had very few votes. The people of the county and, I believe I may say with perfect truth, those who voted for Ames in this town even to a man had determined to vote for Mr. K[ing] till the warrant for summoning the inhabitants to vote for a Representative had issued, when it appeared that the selectmen, adopting the unconstitutional restriction of the resolve of the General Court, directed the votes to be given for a man, who was an inhabitant of the county of Suffolk.[2] This very explicit restriction operated so powerfully on the timid and uninformed, who were too indolent to read the Constitution for themselves, or if informed, were afraid that an opposition to the resolve would be injurious, joined to a much larger number, who were afraid that nonresidence in one candidate would throw many votes in favor of another, who was abhorred for his Antifederalism, obliged the Feds to relinquish their candidate, and run for Ames—who is strictly Federal, an honorable man and, in the estimation of his friends, wants nothing but age and experience to render him a very able supporter of his country's rights. I ought to say in justice to Ames that he was very desirous that Mr. K[ing] should be elected in preference to himself, and to this purpose did use all his influence till he was convinced that it would not avail. Mr. [Samuel A.] Otis very cheerfully offered to give up his pretensions if the election of Mr. K[ing] could thereby be secured.

1. RC, King Papers, NHi. Printed: King, *Life*, I, 348. Another portion of this letter is printed below in The First Election in Essex District.
2. The Massachusetts Election Resolutions specified that "each district [was] to choose one Representative, who shall be an inhabitant of such district . . ." (Massachusetts Election Resolutions, 20 November, printed above).

Henry Jackson to Henry Knox, Boston, 21 December (excerpt)[1]

Last Thursday was the day appointed by the state for the choice of federal Representatives. In this county there is no doubt but Fisher Ames, Esqr., of Dedham will be chosen by a very large majority. The friends of Mr. S[amuel] A[dams] in this town are exceedingly disappointed as great exertions were made for him. The doctor took the lead, but all would not do. The *Feds* are highly gratified in the election of Mr. Ames.

1. RC, Knox Papers, MHi.

Herald of Freedom, 22 December

A correspondent observes, that the friends of the Hon. Mr. [Samuel] Adams were mistaken in propagating the idea that all the true friends of that venerable patriot would give him their votes for Representative to the new Congress. Many, many of that worthy gentleman's best friends did not, for various reasons, bestow on him their suffrages: some, from the idea that he would not accept of the office; others, that the duties of it would be too great for his age and infirmities to bear; and some, from a supposition, that his abilities were too much wanted at home. So that those who plume themselves upon what they term the declension of Mr. Adams's popularity, are certainly in the wrong. While the Americans remain sensible of the blessings of independence, the name of Adams will continue to be revered.

An American, Massachusetts Centinel, 24 December

It is an observation, the truth of which the experience of ages has verified, that the supineness of the people, and their inattention to the sacred right of election, have laid the foundation for the loss of public liberty.

The friends of the Federal Constitution in this district have discovered an unpardonable negligence in the late election of Representatives, and of candidates for Electors for the general government.

In this federal metropolis the election of our own domestic officers brought together last spring 1500 voters, but of so small importance is the organization of the federal government considered, on which we have more depending than upon any former occasion, that the votes in the latter case amounted to only 900.

Boston! how art thou depreciating thyself in the view of thy proud rivals at the southward! Truly if more attention is not paid by the citizens to the great cause of Federalism, to thy rights as electors, if thy apparent numbers are suffered to be diminished by thy negligence and inattention, thou mayest fancy thyself to be of some importance, but thy neighbors will consider thee as verging to the low scale of an insignificant fishing town.

To an European how will it sound, that in Philadelphia, New York, and Baltimore, the votes in each amount to 2000 and upwards on this important occasion, while those of what they have considered as the capital of America show but about half the number. Surely they will think our glory is departed.

Herald of Freedom, 25 December

The recent conduct of the freemen of this commonwealth, says a correspondent, does not evince that ardor for liberty and privileges which the representatives of the different towns have ever held up to view, as actuating the people whom they had the honor to represent. According to the present statement of votes given in, it does not appear that more than half the citizens of this state have paid proper attention to the darling privilege of choosing their own rulers. Lethargy is not becoming the spirit of a free and independent people.

The severity of the weather, says a correspondent, has been assigned by some, as a reason, why so few of the freemen in this state have attended the late town meeting for the choice of federal Representatives and Electors. How surprising that a matter so trivial [to be?] put in competition with the object in view, [———] as has been evinced. The chilling frosts of winter are but trifling compared to the consequences which will result from choosing men to govern us, who are unworthy of our trust and confidence. Wherever a choice should not take place, FREEMEN think of these things.

Bostoniensis, Boston Gazette, 29 December

Having been absent from America for several years past, and having lately returned to the place of my nativity, I am astonished to observe the fickleness of my countrymen. Before my departure the free citizens felt an honest pride in noticing the Honorable Samuel Adams as one of the saviors of their country; they also regarded him as the sheet anchor of their future hope. His long-tried integrity and disinterested patriotism had gained him their entire confidence; his meritorious services had filled the minds of every friend to the liberties of America with respect and veneration for his character. Impressed with the same ideas, I travelled through several countries of Europe and was delighted to hear his eulogium pronounced by every foreigner who had occasion to speak of American affairs; they would often dwell with rapture on his resplendent virtues, as calculated to emancipate a great people from the jaws of oppression, and to legislate for them as free citizens of a republic. They did not forget the merits of other American patriots who with him had rescued their country from the heavy hand of tyranny; but none among them was more particularly distinguished than this American Cato. Filled with the idea of the dignity of his character, at the late election for a federal Representative, I was astonished to hear a name mentioned as a candidate opposed to him which I did not know. I began to accuse my own memory of forgetfulness, and immediately recapitulated in my mind the names of all the Massachusetts worthies, but did not recollect the name of [Fisher] Ames among them. However on enquiry, I was informed that he was son to the almanac maker: that he had been educated for the bar, and was just entering into practice; that he was called a pretty speaker, but had never been without the limits of the state, and hardly ever beyond those of the country village of his nativity. What was my surprise at the contrast! And what were my feelings and mortification when I found that this man of yesterday obtained a majority of votes of the enlightened citizens of Boston! I exclaimed with the poet, "Something must be rotten in the State of Denmark."[1]

1. This entire article was set in italic type. Ralph V. Harlow, *Samuel Adams* ... (New York, 1923), 344, suggests that Benjamin Edes, publisher of the *Gazette*, was the author but offers no evidence.

Fisher Ames's father, Dr. Nathaniel Ames of Dedham, began publishing *Ames' Almanac* in 1729. After his death in 1764 the *Almanac* was carried on until 1775 by his son and namesake, Dr. Nathaniel Ames, who was such a bitter political opponent of the Federalists that he refused to attend Fisher Ames's funeral in 1808.

On 31 December the *Massachusetts Centinel* published a long defense of Ames by "Candidus" and also told its readers: "We are authorized to say that Mr. S. ADAMS, alluding to a late paper, wishes never again to see his own merit, if he is thought to have any, held up to the prejudice of any virtuous man. If A.B. has merit, why the inquiry, what his father was, especially if he also bore the character of an honest man?" For the most vigorous attack on "Bostoniensis," see "Northend," *Herald of Freedom*, 1 January, printed immediately below.

Northend, Herald of Freedom, 1 January 1789

So, the *"staunch old Whigs,"* as the Antifederalists and the amendment sticklers call themselves, have at last openly appeared in their true colors. In Edes's last Monday's *Gazette*, they rail at a great rate against a worthy young patriot, because his father was possessed of abilities sufficient to make an almanac, which the whole junto with all their [*acquirements?*] are not able to do; no, not even able to make a right calculation for a *political almanac*. This, however, is to be considered, that perhaps they mean to have *amendments* to all their productions, and of course, we must suspend our judgment till the work is finished, which possibly may not be till nearly the *end of the year*, and then their *almanac* will be what they are striving to make the Federal Constitution—of no use. To prove that their calculations are not right, it need only be observed, that they have been raising a hue and cry, that the [liber]ties of the people will be swallowed up, and republicanism soon be extinct; that men in power will [form?] distinctions, and set themselves up for the "better sort," and "well born"—mind this: "well born." Now these mighty advocates for equality and republicanism are crying out against a man, because his father was an almanac maker. Ha! Ha! Ha!—well done, poor junto. You have now fairly turned your insides out and discovered the rottenness of your bones; silence now is your last resort—to that, retreat and avoid, if you can, the "universal hiss, the sound of public scorn."

James Sullivan to Richard Henry Lee, Boston, 11 April (excerpt)[1]

Your arrival in Congress gives great satisfaction to the old revolutionists of this state. While I presume to congratulate you on the subject, I wish to indulge myself the pleasure of mentioning the success of the supporters of your old friend and compatriot the Hon. Samuel Adams. He has been exceedingly maltreated, or you would have now had him by the hand in Senate of the United States; but the votes in our late election, a sample whereof is exhibited in the [*Boston*] *Gazette* inclosed, will evince how much he lives in the esteem of his fellow citizens.[2]

We have a very uneasy party in this commonwealth, composed of the seekers of emolument under government, and of the old antirevolutionists. They hate democracy on different principles; the former because it is ever unfriendly to the [two lines illegible].

The imprudence of this party was the sad cause of the disgrace of our people in the year 1786. The measures their influence obtained produced that uneasiness which ended in an insurrection. They now pant for a rebellion because they think it would end in a standing army and finally produce a monarchy. But our people are disposed to live quietly, and when Congress shall pay a proper attention to the amendments proposed to the general Constitution, all will be easy; unless a particular partiality is shown by the general government to those who have affected to be the champions of it. Our people have good sense enough to know, that anarchy must end in despotism. They have all property, and they want laws and government to support and protect it. They feel as freemen, and they act in that character. However they may be despised and scandalized by men who cannot gain their confidence, they will cheerfully support a good government.

1. RC, Lee Papers, PPAmP. Sullivan, a prominent lawyer, had represented Boston in the General Court in 1788 and was appointed to a judgeship by Governor Hancock that year. Although he supported the ratification of the Constitution in newspaper essays, he wanted amendments and later became a Republican. For Sullivan's role in Elbridge Gerry's election to the House of Representatives, see The Second Election in Middlesex District, 29 January, printed below.

2. In the state elections on 6 April, Adams was elected lieutenant governor over the incumbent, Benjamin Lincoln, and received 55 percent of the votes cast.

The Election in Plymouth-Barnstable District, 18 December 1788

There was almost no opposition to George Partridge in the Plymouth-Barnstable District, although long after the election was over it was reported that the Antifederalists had talked of running a man of scandalous character (*Herald of Freedom*, 24 February, printed below). The *Independent Chronicle* reported on 11 December that Partridge was "in nomination," and a few days later Edward H. Robbins reported to Theodore Sedgwick that he would "undoubtedly" be elected (Boston, 14 December, RC, Sedgwick Papers, MHi). Partridge, sheriff of Plymouth County, 1777-1812, and member of Congress, 1779-1782 and 1783-1785, received 501 of the 554 votes cast. After the election a "gentleman of the cloth" reported that the "formerly Antifederal town of Sandwich" had "become regenerate" and voted unanimously for Partridge (*Herald of Freedom*, 29 December).

The only problem was whether Partridge could retain his post as sheriff of Plymouth County and accept a seat in Congress, as he had done in 1779-1782 and 1783-1785. He received a certificate from Governor Hancock on 10 January notifying him of his election. Partridge wrote three letters to the Governor. In the first, which he apparently did not send, he refused the appointment. He accepted in the two following letters but explained that he would not take the seat if he had to give up his post as sheriff (12, 20 January, 23 February, printed below).

The issue of whether or not a state officeholder could retain a state post and still serve in Congress had been and would be raised in other states. On 12 February Governor Hancock asked his Council for advice about Partridge and about George Leonard, judge of probate in Bristol County, who had been elected to Congress from the Bristol-Dukes-Nantucket District.

The Council replied in writing the same day that it was "inexpedient" for a man to hold the office of judge of probate and a seat in Congress, but that it did not find anything in the state constitution which prevented a sheriff from also being a member of Congress. The Council advised, however, that it would be inexpedient to introduce the practice of sheriffs' being absent for long periods, although Partridge "may at present be indulged" and take a seat in Congress "consistently with the safety of that county" (Council Proceedings, Thursday, 12 February, M-Ar).

The next day Governor Hancock sent the Council's written reply to the legislature and asked for its advice (13 February, Miscellaneous Legislative Documents, House Files, M-Ar). The two houses appointed a joint committee which wrote a report that was approved and sent to the Governor on Monday, 16 February.

The legislature declared that if George Leonard continued to hold the office of judge of probate and also took a seat in Congress, any future legislature would address the Governor authorizing him and the Council to appoint another person judge of probate in Bristol County. But the legislature refused to give advice about George Partridge. It pointed out that sheriffs served during the pleasure of the governor, and (with the advice of his Council) were removable by him at any time. Sheriffs were not removable in any other way except through impeachment by the House and a trial before and conviction by the Senate. Therefore the House and Senate declared that intervention by the legislature was "neither necessary or proper; and from the conduct and advice of your Council, they see no reason to doubt the wisdom of that constitutional provision" (House and Senate Proceedings, 13, 14, 16 February).

George Partridge to Governor John Hancock, Duxbury, 12 January 1789[1]

I yesterday received a certificate, signed by Your Excellency, purporting that I was elected to represent the District of Plymouth and Barnstable in the Congress of the United States.

I sensibly feel the unmerited honor done me by my fellow citizens, in committing into my hands so important a trust, and wish it was in my power to accept it but such are my engagements in business as sheriff of the County of Plymouth, in connection with an ill state of health, as render it indispensably necessary for me (in justice to the public and myself) to decline an acceptance of that appointment in full confidence that some gentleman will be elected whose abilities will enable him to render more important services to his country than is in my power to do.

1. ALS, Charles Roberts Autograph Collection, Haverford College, Haverford, Pa. The cover of this letter is addressed to the Governor, but it is doubtful that Partridge sent it. See his letter to Hancock written in Boston on 20 January, printed immediately below.

George Partridge to Governor John Hancock, Boston, 20 January[1]

On the 10th instant I received a certificate signed by Your Excellency, purporting that I was elected to represent the District of Plymouth and Barnstable in the Congress of the United States.

I am sensible of the unmerited honor done me by my fellow citizens, in committing into my hands so important a trust, but my business as sheriff of the

County of Plymouth, in addition to an ill state of health, have occasioned me to doubt of the propriety of my accepting it. However, wishing to serve my country in any business to which they may judge me competent, I have concluded to accept this appointment. But nevertheless, if it appears to Your Excellency and the honorable Council that this commission is inconsistent with the duties which I owe to my county as sheriff, I will resign it with pleasure, in the fullest confidence that some other person will be elected to represent [this?] district, whose abilities will enable him to do better service for his country than I can pretend to.

1. RC, Emmet Collection, no. 540, NN. On the envelope of this letter is the following endorsement: "Letter from the Hon. George Partridge, Esq. referring to the consideration of the Govr. & Council whether his Appointment as a Representative to the federal Congress was inconsistent with the duties of his Office as Sheriff. Jany 21: 1789 referred for Consideration."

George Partridge to Governor John Hancock, Duxbury, 23 February[1]

When I was last at Boston I did myself the honor of addressing a letter to Your Excellency, signifying my willingness to accept a seat in Congress agreeably to my appointment, provided the Governor and Council were of opinion that I might do it consistently with my hold[ing] my sheriff's commission. I have heard that Your Excellency has advised on the matter, but I have not been informed of the issue.[2] As the time is now at hand when I ought to be at New York if I go at all, I hope Your Excellency will excuse my troubling you with a second letter, the design of which is, that I may be informed whither I am at liberty to take a seat in Congress while I continue in the office of a sheriff.

I should have been more early and particular in my application for leave of absence, but that in the year 1779 when I [urged?] to the then General Court the business of my sheriff's office, as a reason why I ought not to accept a seat in Congress, it was considered by that General Court as an insufficient reason, and I was directed to proceed. I have also been three years in Congress since our [state] constitution was formed, but never heard that any objections were made.

However, I shall most freely resign my seat in Congress, if my continuing in it is considered incompatible with the commission which I hold as sheriff of Plymouth County; and of this I hope to be informed by Your Excellency's order.

1. RC, Fogg Autograph Collection, MeHi.
2. See headnote above for the advice which Governor Hancock received from the Council on 12 February and from the legislature on 16 February.

An Abashment, Herald of Freedom, 24 February

A man of about fifty years of age, an inhabitant of B[ridgewate]r, in the county of Plymouth, who has a large family of children, who looks with contempt and with the greatest abhorrence on *sterility*, and esteems *concubinage* as a sacred privilege, was lately accused of copulation—with a young girl of about

17 years old, who is now pregnant. He, among the ANTIES, was talked of for a Representative to Congress, for that district. His abilities now recommend him to fill some important office in the Egyptian government, where "polygamy and concubinage were allowed, except to priests." So *he* is not excluded.

The Election in York-Cumberland-Lincoln District (Maine), 18 December 1788

Thomas B. Wait, publisher of the Portland, Me., *Cumberland Gazette*, was a personal friend of George Thacher, the man who won the election. Wait complained in his election-day issue that "for want of news we must publish nonsense, and do from necessity that which printers in the metropolis have done from choice." This statement was followed by an anti-Catholic poem reprinted from the Boston *Herald of Freedom* of 8 December. Elsewhere in the paper there was another poem prefaced by the remark: "More Boston nonsense published from necessity." The *Cumberland Gazette* thus provides no information as to the issues, if any, prior to the election. However, letters written to Thacher after the election (printed below) indicate that Thacher's religious views might have been an issue, and certainly would be an issue in coming elections.

Thacher had moved to Maine from Massachusetts in 1782 and was a resident of Biddeford. Since 1787 he had been a member of the Confederation Congress in New York. He was a Deist and hence in the eyes of the orthodox he had little or no religion. It is quite possible that he was the author of a series of articles in the *Cumberland Gazette* signed "Crazy Jonathan" (see Wait to Thacher, 14 March, printed below). Among other things, "Crazy Jonathan" argued for secular rather than religious education. In Number 12 he declared: "Let mystical nonsense be banished—let reason be the guide, and nature and revelation be the subject of enquiry ..." (*Cumberland Gazette*, 18 December 1788). And unlike many contemporaries, "Crazy Jonathan" argued that a man's religion or lack of it should have nothing to do with politics. In Number 14, in the *Cumberland Gazette* on 15 January 1789, "Crazy Jonathan" set out to prove that religion was "a bad criterion" of fitness for public office, and concluded by declaring that "even Atheists, or such as are by very religious people deemed Atheists, have demonstrated that they are governed by principles of integrity, and love of truth, as firmly as any of those celebrated martyrs, who with their blood have witnessed a belief of the Christian religion." Even if Thacher was not the author of "Crazy Jonathan," some of the letters printed below indicate that his friends thought that his religious beliefs would alienate Maine voters.

Only 948 voters out of a total population of over 90,000 voted in the first federal election in Maine. Thacher received 588 votes. His two leading opponents, Josiah Thacher, justice of the Court of Common Pleas in Cumberland County, and Nathaniel Wells, justice of the Court of Common Pleas in York County, received 255 votes between them, with 105 votes scattered among ten other candidates. Thacher was in Maine during the election but was back in Boston early in January 1789 preparing to go on to New York (to Mrs. Thacher, Boston, 11 January, RC, Thacher Papers, MHi). He received his credentials after he arrived in New York (Secretary John Avery to Thacher, Boston, 11 February, RC, Thacher Papers, MB).

Daniel Cony to George Thacher, Hallowell, 12 March 1789[1]

Your favor of the 8th ulto. was received at Boston two days before I left that place, and as it contained the latest advice therein, several extracts were taken from it, and published in the Boston and Portland papers. I was solicited to let the whole letter be published, but as it contained sentiments which are not yet generally admitted, was matter of the opinions considering your *public station*, twas not the best time to enter into a *field* of theological sentiments or disquisitions, which generally has been accompanied by the most frantic enthusiasts, and virulent bigots who (to use a chemical phrase) abound with vitriolic acids with a certain proportion of *aqua regia* and such like ingredients; but I hope the time is fast hastening when such acrimonious miscreants and malcontents of society will give place to the rational, the liberal, and the god-like—and that philosophy, [———] [———] and liberality of sentiment will overspread America and the whole [———] [———] of the globe, when the lion and the kid shall have sweet intercourse together, but no more at present on this [score?].

The result of President Washington and Vice President Adams being elected has diffused universal joy in this quarter [———] [———] for even a single cur have as yet [———] to move their tongue by way of dislike.

Dr. Obediah Williams, a gentleman in this quarter, contributed largely towards your election, by uniting the votes or rather the voters in several towns above Hallowell up Kennebec River. Could wish (if agreeable) to have you introduce a correspondence with him, as I think twill be agreeable to him, and at the same time open a new channel of information and communication from the federal legislature to the margin and interior part of the Kennebec. Superscription: "Obediah Williams Esquire [in Putborough?]."

I lodged at your house as I came from Boston. Your lady was at York on a visit but Mr. [Silas] Lee and the girls were at home. So we passed away a winter's evening in reading your letters, talking about *politics, lunatics, sheep tics*, and *bed tics*, with a number of other clever things.

Do, sir, give us a line, I mean a letter upon tics of some sort, or something else as often as time will permit, that is as often as you have time to spare. We want to know how you venerable Congress lads go on. You know [———] [———] [———] folks in the eastward for politics. They tell us near a month was spent last year in agreeing or rather disagreeing where the new Congress should meet. Something like our General Court's spending a fortnight to determine whether General [Benjamin] Lincoln should have £300 or £160 but good by, perhaps a little more next time about a *post* or something else that we expect at Kennebec.[2]

1. RC, Thacher Papers, MB. This letter is illegible in several places and partly so in others. Dr. Cony represented Hallowell in the Massachusetts House of Representatives. On 6 November 1788 he had made an eloquent speech on behalf of the popular election of presidential Electors (printed above in The Passage of the Massachusetts Election Resolutions).

2. In the margin following the close of the letter, Cony wrote: "Confounded bad pen and Ink."

Thomas B. Wait to George Thacher, Portland, 14 March[1]

How could you charge T. B. W. with "abusing" the man whom his soul loveth? How could you talk of *drawing* a *letter* from one, who has long since *freely given* you his *heart*?

Simple Simon,[2] as you suggest, may possibly be "a *seed*" etc., and if so, I thank God it was not *planted*, least it might have *taken root, sprang up,* and filled our *oriental orchard of literature* with insipid, tasteless, and worthless *fruit.*

Plain Reason[3] belongs to the same *class*; and by the great *botanist*, Lineus himself, would have been *ranked with the same order* and *laid on the same shelf* with S. Simon.

As a *subject of Massachusetts* I must remonstrate against your proceedings. Am I to be arraigned, found guilty, condemned, etc., by a court sitting in the city of *New York*, without a hearing too, either by myself or my attorney? Should you here plead the *Federal Constitution*, it will but confirm me in my former *Antifederalism.*[4]

I have this day planted one *seed of originality*, under the signature of *Leonidas.*[5] May it vegetate, spring up, and bear fruit abundantly! The writer has not seen Crazy Jonathan, and declares himself unacquainted with Jonathan's sentiments with respect to the qualifications of Representatives.

In my last I told you that I had something of importance to communicate. I have, my friend; but this pen, and this paper, are but vile interpreters of the language of one's heart. I would give nine pounds ten shillings for an half hour's personal interview; but ten pounds ten will not purchase it—and so Messieurs pen and paper, I implore your assistance most humbly.

The Hon. Dummer Sewall, Esq., of Bath, on his way home from Court, did me the honor of a visit—spent two long hours and dined with me. We talked of religion, politics, and politicians—news, newspapers, and newspaper writers. Among the latter he mentioned C[raz]y J[onatha]n, then the reputed author, his abilities, his religious sentiments, his morals, his conduct in public and in private life.

It seems he has discoursed with Judge [Nathaniel] W[ell]s (who, by the by, is one of your implacable enemies), with Judge [Josiah] T[hache]r, with Judge [David] Sewall,[6] and others, not one of whom, as I can learn, say a syllable in your favor. You are said to be a man of no religion—*your integrity in your profession is called in question.* You are said to be unprincipled, light, frothy and even boyish in your conduct and conversation, in private and public life—at home, among your friends and acquaintance, and while at New York, and to such a degree, that it was feared the credit of the state which you represented would suffer, and your constituents disgraced, by giving their suffrages to a character so undeserving. You are said to have written letters to the W[i]dg[er]ies, the N[asso]ns, the C[on]ys etc. etc.[7] for no other purpose than to secure a future election, while gentlemen of character and ability were totally neglected by you; that persons of the former character were every day stepping about the floor of the [Massachusetts] House—with information fresh from New York, while gentlemen of the latter description knew nothing but what N[asso]n and W[idger]y pleased to tell them, etc. etc. etc.

I will not write another word—my heart bleeds a stream.

Yours for ever—and ever—and ever.

1. RC, Wait Papers, MHi.

2. See the *Cumberland Gazette*, 21 and 29 January.

3. Not found.

4. This paragraph might possibly be a reference to the campaign to separate Maine from Massachusetts, in which Wait was one of the leaders.

5. "Leonidas" No. 1, in the *Cumberland Gazette*, 19 March, declared that no matter how good a man might be, or how sincerely he worshipped his Maker, "he can never be equal to the duties of a legislator" without a knowledge of history, of the principles by which mankind has been governed in the past, and a close and accurate attention to the effect of climate and other causes, both moral and physical, on national character. "Leonidas" said that he did not mean to insinuate that religion and virtue were unnecessary: "he who is a traitor to his God will never be true to his country—but only that religion and virtue do not alone constitute a political character, and that education is absolutely necessary."

6. The references are probably to Nathaniel Wells, justice of the Court of Common Pleas, York County; Josiah Thacher, justice of the Court of Common Pleas, Cumberland County (both of whom were beaten by Thacher in the election); and Judge David Sewall of the Massachusetts Supreme Judicial Court.

7. The references are probably to William Widgery, Samuel Nasson, and Dr. Daniel Cony. Widgery and Nasson had voted against ratification of the Constitution in the Massachusetts Convention, and all three men were representatives from Maine in the Massachusetts House of Representatives in 1788.

Ezra Ripley to George Thacher, Concord, 30 March (excerpt)[1]

Far be it from me, to think of you as your free conversation hath led some to think of you. Not long since, I heard you called a Deist, and represented as paying no regard to religion. Whether you will thank or censure me, I leave; but I undertook to clear you of the charge of infidelity, and to maintain, that you were not only a believer in religion, but in revealed religion.

1. RC, Chamberlain Collection, MB. Ripley was minister of a church in Concord from 1778 until at least 1833.

Samuel Nasson to George Thacher, Sanford, 16 June (excerpt)[1]

I will inform you I was lately told to my face if I had not strove so hard for your election I might have been in the [Massachusetts] Senate. I called for an explanation and was then answered that if I had done the same for Mr. [Nathaniel] Wells then he would [have] been at Congress and his friends would have exerted themselves in my interest and I undoubtedly would have had a seat in the Senate. My answer was that I had done my duty and if any election depended upon my selling my conscience, that is, if that was the way to gain a seat, and if others took that way to gain one, then I thought the post of honor was a private station to which I cheerfully retired and hope there to remain forever.

1. RC, Thacher Papers, MSaE. Nasson was elected to the Massachusetts House of Representatives from Sanford in 1787 and 1788, and he represented the town in the Massachusetts Convention, where he voted against ratification of the Constitution. As early as 25 March 1789, Jeremiah Hill in Biddeford wrote to Thacher that "our friend Nason is (as they tell

me) maneuvering for a seat in the Senate of this commonwealth at the next election. However, I don't think that his political abilities will make many proselytes in this part of the county" (RC, Thacher Papers, MB).

Samuel Nasson to George Thacher, Sanford, 9 July (excerpt)[1]

It is a good saying of an author that I have read that a man should have some sincere friend or great enemy or both, for by one or the other he will find out his faults, and I think in some measure his perfections if he has any, for where his enemies give credit and his friends praise he may think he was right. A foe may stab and by that means open some imposthume that might without vent prove his ruin. However you have had, I am sure, so many instances of my feeble efforts to help you that you cannot suspect me of being your enemy. And I am sure, if I know my own heart, I am your sincere friend. Then suffer me to tell you in a few words what is now spreading in this county. You know that I am in friendship with almost all the reverend clergy in this county or at least they pretend friendship for me, although it may be for nothing more than they can turn it to advantage that when they travel they may know where to call for a dinner or lodging. This much for the prologue.

Now for the play that is acting. They praise your President to me for all his virtues but none more than for his attendance on public worship; for this they almost adore him and I join with them and could almost fill a volume with his virtues; but why should I attempt to paint the sun. I stop—and again come to the point. I now get my share of their tongues or at least their slander (for after saying how good the great Washington is for his regard to their order and, say they, this is the most essential matter; without this there cannot be any government). It is otherways with your Mr. G. Thatcher. He never goes to meeting more than twice in one year; nay, he opposed having a chaplain. This you know is horrid, for then down comes their Dagon. We shall lose our influence among the lower class if the Congress don't fall down and worship and pay due regards to our great men etc.

I suppose you have done wrong, for I think if there was not any [future?] estate it would be best to maintain good order among mankind, but true religion I know consists in loving our Maker supremely and our neighbor as ourselves. This is a short description of a good man. But then say they, a public confession of religion show[s] to the world our religion and sets an example before the Lord on orders and then they can depend upon us because our principles are right.

If you don't reform, and the honorable deacon can learn to screw up his teeth as he can his mouth, I shall fear for [you] at another election—but this only by the by.

Do you attend prayers or do you not? Do you ever go to worship or do you [tarry?] at home and study law or politics, or what is worse spend your time in drinking wine? I think you have time enough for such business for I find you do not work very hard, only four hours in twenty-four. Therefore I think you may afford to worship on Sunday.

If you don't reform it will be against you, for they say that you slight or pretend to slight all revealed religion. [It] is only pretense, I hope. For a gentleman of learning to say that he believes nothing of what the vulgar call religion is forever to lay himself in the way of being lashed by the rev[erends], and you know that in these parts they can down with a man if he is twenty-four feet high. Therefore attend prayers and also call at the church on Sundays at least one in four weeks if you mean to live and not die. Pardon my boldness, for I before told you that it was good for a man to have some open friends and I will venture to say that your friends have not informed you that death was in the pot. And I am also sure that your enemies have not [been] informed that by that manner they intend your ruin.

1. RC, Thacher Papers, MSaE. The letter contains no punctuation whatever, and capital letters are used indiscriminately. We have provided punctuation and removed the random capitals.

The Election in Bristol-Dukes-Nantucket District, 18 December 1788

The election was a three-way contest, with fewer scattered votes than in any other district except Essex. The candidates were all well-known men in Bristol County. David Cobb was a doctor who had been an officer in Henry Jackson's regiment during the War for Independence and an aide to George Washington toward the end of the war. He was appointed a justice of the Court of Common Pleas in Bristol County in 1784 and major general of the militia in 1785. In 1786 he defied the mobs that attempted to close the court at Taunton. Phanuel Bishop had been a leader of the convention movement in Bristol County that tried to close the courts. He was elected to the state Senate in 1787 but was denied a seat because the voters had spelled his first name in various ways. Bishop attended the state Convention and voted against ratification of the Constitution. In 1788 he was elected to the state Senate as an Antifederalist. George Leonard was a member of a family long important in Bristol County. He held various offices in the county for years before 1776 and was appointed judge of probate in the county in 1785 and justice of the Court of Common Pleas in 1787.

Leonard was elected, but some questioned whether he could retain his seat as probate judge and still serve in the House of Representatives. The Council and the legislature advised Governor Hancock that Leonard should be replaced if he served in Congress (see Headnote: The Election in Plymouth-Barnstable District, printed above). However, Leonard took his seat in Congress and seems to have retained his judgeships.

Henry Knox to David Cobb, Boston, 20 November[1]

Our friend Harry[2] had stated to me your situation and prospects.

I have considered the matter in all the points of view in which it has presented itself to my mind, and the result is most decidedly that if the people should think proper to choose you the Representative to the general government that you ought to accept as well for your own interest as to promote the good of your country. I pray you therefore to make no further hesitation.

I am unhappy that I have not had the pleasure of embracing you. I shall depart in a few days and shall be glad to hear from you in New York.

1. RC, Cobb Papers, MHi.

2. Presumably this was Henry Jackson, who wrote to Knox on 30 November: "as to Cobb, the matter is determined and he will be the man without doubt. I intend to set out tomorrow or next day and pay him a visit, and if he has any doubts to remove them" (Boston, RC, Knox Papers, MHi). On 6 December Jackson again wrote to Knox that the weather had been so bad that he had not been able to go to Taunton but that "Cobb will be the man for the district" (Boston, RC, Knox Papers, MHi).

Taunton, Providence Gazette, 13 December[1]

The General Court having ordered Thursday the 18th inst. for the choice of gentlemen to represent the eight divisions of our commonwealth, I think it the bounden duty of every real friend to the peace and prosperity of the nation at large, to impress on your minds the consequence of fixing on a proper person to fill the important office. Give me leave, gentlemen, to assure you, that of all the momentous concerns which have been transacted from the time of the Revolution to the present period, this is the most weighty. By the conduct of the first session of the new Congress, the people will receive a bias that will be attended with the most beneficial or pernicious consequences to the whole Union. A strong and powerful opposition hath been made, in the most respectable states, to many parts of the new Constitution, and that resistance founded on patriotic principles. As it will therefore behoove our legislators, at their first outset, to act not only with firmness, but also with particular prudence in their resolves, it is highly expedient, my friends, to choose men of abilities, learning, and experience, that are independent in their principles and fortune. That we, therefore, may do our part, gentlemen, I take the liberty to recommend to your attention the Hon. George Leonard, Esq., judge of probate for the County of Bristol, whose knowledge in politics and jurisprudence stand confessed, and his ample landed possessions will render him watchful of the interests of the *farmer* and *mechanic*; for let us never lose sight of this perpetual truth, that on *them* the prosperity and happiness of America must ever depend. And I am sorry to observe, that the Southern and Middle states, as far as their nomination hath extended, have chosen a *majority* of commercial gentlemen to represent them in Congress, whose views, however upright, may be too intent on that fantastic lady *commerce*; who, although she is of high importance to the consequence of small states, ought to be considered, in regard to our immense empire, in a distant point of view.

1. The full title of this "letter," dated 8 December, was "To the Electors of a Federal Representative for the Counties of Bristol, Dukes and Nantucket." Rhode Island newspapers circulated in the adjacent counties of Massachusetts, and "Taunton" requested the publisher of the *Providence Gazette* to print the piece as a service to his "subscribers in the commonwealth of Massachusetts."

Extract of a Letter from a Gentleman at Norton, Massachusetts, 18 December[1]

This day being appointed for the choice of a federal Representative for this district, the votes were unanimous for the Hon. George Leonard, Esq.; a circumstance not only highly flattering to the honorable gentleman, who is a native of this town, and hath ever been a resident among us, but is a proof of the good sense and politeness of his townsmen. From every appearance he will have a majority of votes in our district, and we hope he will ultimately be appointed to go to Congress, being from his abilities, experience, and independence, beyond contradiction, the most proper person we can fix on at this truly important period.

1. Providence *United States Chronicle*, 25 December. The first mention that Leonard was a candidate is in a letter from Edward H. Robbins in Boston to Theodore Sedgwick on 14 December: "The Bristol elections will be carried in favor of Colonel Leonard, a gentleman of good disposition, but an inefficient politician" (RC, Sedgwick Papers, MHi).

Henry Jackson to Henry Knox, Boston, 21 December (excerpt)[1]

Our friend D[avid] Cobb might have been chosen for the district in which he lives by a large majority, but declined and they turned their attention to a Mr. [George] Leonard the Feds, and the Antis to Mr. [Phanuel] Bishop. But the district will be divided between the three abovementioned and no one will be chosen in the first instance. I have paid a visit to Taunton. David desires to be particular remembered to you. In the second trial if he should be elected he will not hesitate in going.

1. RC, Knox Papers, MHi. Another part of this letter is printed in The First Election in Middlesex District, 18 December. On the 28th Jackson wrote Knox that Cobb would have been chosen if he had not declined "in the first instance" (Boston, RC, Knox Papers, MHi), and on 11 January Jackson reported to Knox that Cobb "has no one to blame but himself" and of that "he is convinced, and is exceedingly mortified at his own conduct" (Boston, RC, Knox Papers, MHi).

Essex Journal, 24 December

A striking instance of the rapid progress of Federal principles was seen at Attleborough on the 18th inst. at the election of a Representative for the federal government.
Candidates:
Hon. Geo. Leonard, Esq.   88 votes.
Hon. Phan. Bishop, Esq.   12.
By the above votes, it appears, that Attleborough is now more than 7 to 1 Federal; whereas in April, 1787, said Phanuel Bishop had a majority of votes in said town for [state] senator.

The First Election in Essex District, 18 December

The Essex Federalists had fallen out with one another over the election of United States Senators, and the bitterness among them affected the election of a Representative in the district (see Christopher Gore to Rufus King, 21 December, printed below). As early as 14 December, Edward H. Robbins reported to Theodore Sedgwick (who was himself involved in a closely contested race in Hampshire-Berkshire District) that Essex, like Middlesex, was "cut up into a number of small parties and the event of either very uncertain" (Boston, RC, Sedgwick Papers, MHi).

Apparently before the General Court had adjourned, some of the leaders in Essex had agreed on Nathan Dane as their choice for Representative. In a letter to Rufus King, Christopher Gore reported: "The *knowing ones* of Essex are the people that support Dane. Before the adjournment of the General Court they had a meeting and agreed to give their influence in favor of Dane" (Boston, 14 December, RC, King Papers, NHi). Dane, a lawyer from Beverly, had served in the state legislature and was a member of Congress, 1785-1788. He had opposed the Constitution and did not win election to the state Convention in January 1788. He ran a poor third on 18 December and was not a serious contender in the second election in Essex District on 29 January 1789.

Benjamin Goodhue of Salem, a Federalist, had been a merchant during the Revolution and a member of the state Senate from Essex County since 1784. Samuel Holten of Danvers, a doctor who had given up medicine for politics by 1775, had served in the state legislature and Congress for several years. He was elected to the state Convention as an Antifederalist but soon left the Convention because of ill health.

A principal issue in the campaign seems to have been a pamphlet by Jonathan Jackson of Newburyport stating an extreme Federalist position. *Thomas's Massachusetts Spy* on 14 August advertised the pamphlet as being published "this day," and Jackson was soon recognized as the author (see Peter Thacher to Jackson, Boston, 30 October, RC, Jackson Papers, MHi). *Thoughts Upon the Political Situation of the United States of America* ... (Worcester, 1788) "By a Native of Boston" denounced "numerous assemblies," rotation in office, frequent elections, the idea that the voice of the people was the voice of God, and declared that ordinary people in large groups were as incapable of electing public officials as they were of holding office themselves. Jackson proposed that a constable be appointed for every group of 100 voters, that the voters be divided into "squads" of ten who would meet only to elect one of their number to attend a meeting of ten men representing the hundred voters. These in turn would elect one of their number to attend meetings representing a thousand voters, and so on. Jackson was not specific, but apparently representatives of representatives several times removed from the original "squads" of ten voters would elect men to govern the state.

A letter of William Eustis to Jackson in reaction to Jackson's pamphlet and Jackson's reply (both printed below) provide a unique view of some of the political thinking of the times.

Newspaper Nominations for Essex District, 6-13 December

Between 6 and 13 December the Boston and Salem newspapers named the four principal candidates in the first Essex election: Nathan Dane, Benjamin Goodhue, Samuel Holten, and Jonathan Jackson. These items are printed below.

Massachusetts Centinel, 6 December

In Essex County we learn, that the Hon. Nathan Dane, Esq., it is probable, will be elected a federal Representative.

Salem Mercury, 9 December

I observed in the *Centinel* of the 6th instant, it was supposed the Hon. N[athan] Dane would be elected Representative to Congress for Essex District. It may not be amiss to inform the freemen of this county, that a very respectable number of the electors are determined to give their suffrages for the Hon. Benjamin Goodhue.

An Elector, Salem Mercury, 9 December

From the many characters in the county of Essex deserving the highest public trust and confidence, the suffrages of the citizens thereof will undoubtedly be greatly divided, at the approaching election, unless some one of those characters is in some measure previously agreed on as the object of their choice. And perhaps no candidate has been more frequently or more deservedly mentioned, or will more completely unite the votes of the electors, than the Hon. Benjamin Goodhue, who for several years has had the united suffrages of this county as a senator. His virtues as a man, his integrity, abilities, and experience as a statesman, and the zeal and fidelity with which he has long served the public— strongly recommend him to the notice of the independent electors of Essex, when they shall give in their suffrages for a person to represent them in the new Congress of the United States.

Salem Mercury, 9 December

A correspondent observes, that by the resolutions of the General Court, it appears, that the county of Essex are to elect one person to represent them in Congress, therefore takes the liberty to mention the Hon. Samuel Holten, Esq., as a suitable person. His long and faithful service, together with his general knowledge of our national affairs, at this time, he thinks, cannot but engage the attention of the electors for the county of Essex.

Massachusetts Centinel, 13 December

As the real friends of our country must feel solicitous to have the elections of the coming week issue in the choice of men of the *most unquestionable merit*, to represent us in the federal legislature, it is with great pleasure, we learn from the county of Essex, that in that district, the Hon. Jonathan Jackson, Esq., is in nomination among the foremost candidates.

William Eustis to Jonathan Jackson, Boston, 6 December[1]

If I had contented myself with the many beauties of sentiment and style to be found in the pamphlet of which we have conversed, instead of opposing my own opinion to any part of it; or if I had paid the writer the just compliment of having thought more and better on the subject than I had or could do, it would have discovered that wisdom which everybody is sometimes without. Having had the indiscretion to object to one part of the system, it now becomes me to spend no time in eulogium on the others, but to give the reasons of my dissent in the best manner I am capable of.

When I object to the mode of election proposed by our author I beg leave to lay down one or two leading principles to which his assent will be necessary. The first is that whenever the people divest themselves of power and place it in other hands for their government, it should be given with a sparing hand. Or in other words they should look well to it that they grant no powers but such as are absolutely necessary to obtain the end they have in view; it being forever the nature of man to abuse this power. And secondly the happiness of the many is secured in proportion as this power is retained or reverts into their own hands. I have long believed in the often quoted sentiment of Lord Bolingbroke that there is a certain quantum of ethereal spirit diffused among mankind, and that it is monopolized by a few. This sentiment caught my belief in early life; but the history of the human heart from that time to this has invariably taught me that the few thus favored of Heaven are disposed to avail themselves of their superior advantage, and that unless they are well guarded and restrained they will tyrannize over the many. I agree with the writer that our assemblies are too numerous, and should rejoice in seeing the good sense and information of the commonwealth concentrated in a smaller focus.

The word liberty has been in everybody's mouth for these ten years. It was made the stalking horse of a great revolution and perhaps not one in a thousand has troubled himself about its meaning. It conveys different ideas in different situations and countries. To the peasant in France and to the insurgent in Berkshire its implication is very different; and perhaps both are wide of the mark. To the rational American it implies the exercise of certain rights or duties in person, property, and government: a right to property which he has earned, personal security, and to be governed by laws and rulers of his own making. And if in addition to these, the fervor of a warm and enlightened imagination should place a thousand other fancied attendants upon this celestial goddess, the happiness of her votary is thereby extended and society suffers no injury.

In order to prepare us for the new system of election our writer tells us that "the people should never be brought together in large bodies but under a ruler." When we suspect that we are near a ditch or some bad place in walking, we naturally look about us and take heed to our steps. So when we think error near us in reasoning we should examine well the ground about us and be sure of every step we make.

I have reconnoitered this sentence and with due submission I must say it appears in at least a questionable shape.

In Europe large bodies of the people have frequently assembled and perhaps as frequently they have done mischief. In America the same has happened; but it was generally malice prepense, the mischief was hatched at home and they came abroad to execute it. When they have assembled for the quiet purposes of choosing representatives and conducting their town or parish business, I have seldom seen or known of disorder, never of violence. It is true they choose a ruler to regulate their proceedings; business over, the ruler is dethroned and goes home like the rest.

"But in large bodies the people are acted upon and cajoled by a few." This is true, ever has been, and ever will be. The question then is whether it [is] more dangerous for the people to be acted upon with their own eyes open, with the eyes of all the citizens open too, in public meeting, where everybody sees and hears, where the sources of light and knowledge are open and near them; or to be acted upon at home, alone and in the dark?

Besides, I apprehend, much information is gained by the intercourse which a public meeting affords. A man sees the weakness of his own opinion and judgment by having it contrasted with a better. It is by attrition that metals are polished and why not opinions? Each one gathers the opinion of his neighbor at home and on the way to the meeting; and when there the opinions of all are put forth, from which it is uncharitable to imagine that the worst will be selected. Some will be bribed, bought; but a whole people will never sell themselves.

At home and by tens they can be practiced upon. How often do we wish to close a bargain with one man before he can see another, because the other will give him such information as will prevent it? So the people not seeing each other will be forever making bad bargains, for want of knowing better. If the demagogue (destitute of abilities) has address enough to mislead and misinform the people when the eyes of all their understandings are open at once, how much more easy will it be for him to manage them separately and individually? If their united powers cannot detect him, they will not be able to do it separately. There is another reason why I would have them vote together in their own proper persons and not by proxy. Admitting that there is an equal or greater chance of being duped in this way than the other, inasmuch as each individual acts and determines, or determines and acts for himself, if wrong is done him, it is no small consolation that he has done it himself. He will brook that from himself which he would not take from the hands of another; and by all the wrong he suffers he will lay up a determination to keep a better lookout in future.

By assembling in towns or parishes, the inferior or poorer citizens come forward once in a year before their superior or rich neighbors to exercise in common with them this great right of freemen. They are upon the footing of a perfect equality; and the idea of this equality operates as a safeguard to the poor. Having exercised this right publicly, in the presence of all the people for ages, who will ever dare to dispute it or set it aside? There is also a conscious pride attending the public exertion of this right, which very pride enters perhaps into our idea of liberty; while the courtesy and other little sacrifices made by the candidate in order to obtain the suffrages of his fellow citizens prove checks upon his conduct in office. He has made these little concessions in presence of many witnesses, and the recollection that he is to appear again at the same tribunal on the next year will rise constantly to his recollection when any measure is proposed which he knows will be disagreeable to the people.

It is said that "in the scheme proposed, the attendance of every voter is made indispensable." I do not see that this is more feasible in the election by tens than by hundreds or thousands. If coercion is used, and if men are to be *forced* to exercise an act of freedom, the freedom of such act is certainly destroyed. I am rather of opinion that a sense of its importance to their happiness must keep alive the business of election; and it is not to be feared from the present disposition that the people will neglect the exercise of this or any other right. On ordinary occasions there will always be a number who will not attend the business of elections. It is because they trust to others, and believe that the public affairs will go on well enough without them. Some it is true neglect from pride, from a contempt of the measures carrying on, from disappointment that their particular plans cannot be made to succeed; but whenever the people conceive that any important object is at stake, the meetings are crowded and everyone will give in his vote.

On the whole, however imperfectly I am able to support my opinion by method and argument, I must think that the scheme of election by tens, and so on by sublimation, would draw out from the people an aristocracy which would be hateful to them; with which they would never be satisfied.

Admitting, for argument's sake, that this mode of election was best in theory, that it could be proved to demonstration preferable to the mode now in use, I ask is there a disposition in the Americans, would it be expedient for them to adopt it at the present time? It must after all reasoning be determined by experiment. And is it safe for the people of the United States to make this important experiment? I apprehend not. "To catch the manners living as they rise" should be the object equally of the moralist and politician. I acknowledge that it is frequently necessary to hold out more than you expect to obtain, to exact too much in order to acquire what is right; and so far as this proposal is intended as a balance for the excess of republicanism which threatens the ruin of our country, so far it is good. Indeed when I view it as a dangerous experiment, and one inapplicable and unadvisable for the citizens of America, it is with diffidence of my own judgment, and attended with a consciousness of my want of acquaintance with political science.

Everyone is willing however to pay a compliment to his own sentiment, however weak or ill grounded; nor can I close this observation without doing myself the justice to add that I *think* more strongly on this subject than I can *express* and that if some conviction does not attend what I have written, it is because of my inability to arrange and systematize ideas.

To the world, or to almost any other gentleman than the one I am addressing, this would savor of the grossest vanity. With you, sir, I am in no danger of such an imputation. You will probably peruse what is written and give it to the flame of fire or cover it in the embers of oblivion. In either alternative the writer will acquiesce, provided you will continue him in your esteem and friendship.

1. RC, Jackson Papers, MHi. Eustis was a Boston doctor who was elected to the legislature from that city in 1789 and was elected to Congress in 1800 as a supporter of Jefferson. He became secretary of war in 1807 and served until forced to resign at the end of 1812. He was elected governor of Massachusetts as a Democrat in 1823 and died in office in 1825.

Jonathan Jackson to William Eustis, Newburyport, December[1]

Your very obliging communication dated in this month I received some days since. The good sense and candor in which it is conceived would almost conciliate one to the sentiments it contains if those it stands opposed to were capable of demonstration. Political science is a ground that but a few if any of us in this country have passed over with much attention, and I am of opinion this knowledge has scarcely [got?] beyond its infancy among the Europeans. The subjects of it when theoretically proposed are seldom if ever such as can be demonstrated; and when reasoning from the successful practice of one country we urge the adoption of like institutions in another, the most sagacious can seldom compare minutely the relative situations of the two countries, or comprehend in either the great variety of circumstances which serve to distinguish them, and the finer and more delicate parts in the natural organization of each which, though not obvious to our gross perceptions, may be essential to the constitution of each and yet be different in both.

Where speculative men in the same country have turned their attention in any degree to trace the science of politics and have endeavored to adapt to the state of their own times the maxims they may think that they have established, it is to be expected that different men with the same zeal to investigate the truth will in many respects form different opinions; as the notices we take in from youth to manhood and even mature age are so very various, and upon these in a great degree depend our reasonings and conclusions upon most subjects.

That an excess of republicanism, or what has obtained that name, though perhaps it might more properly be styled *unchecked democracy*, has threatened the ruin of our country, and has almost effected it, we have both, I believe, been some time agreed in; that the proposed scheme of refinement or sublimation, in which we do not agree, would effect what both of us wish and cure the evil, can only be determined by actual experiment; that the rejection of such a scheme would immediately follow the proposal of it, if made to the present people of the United States, *and properly explained to them*, can only remain a matter of opinion till the trial was actually made. The innovations proposed within the last eighteen months in this country, and the so general adoption of them among the people, give us a very respectable opinion of their good sense in the aggregate. Yet we have had sufficient evidence through our whole Revolution to believe that the common people of this country, like those of most others, very imperfectly comprehend what best tends to their political happiness. The author of the sentiments which have led us to some disquisitions on these subjects, if I know his disposition, has a very sincere one to promote the political happiness of his countrymen; but I suspect like the physician who wishes to make a radical cure, he more studiously sought for an effectual remedy, than to consult what would be palatable or pleasing to the present taste.[2] A remark may here come in pertinently enough: "that this is not to catch the manners living as they rise." I shall not object to the justness of it, for nothing is more true in a country so free as this than that public measures must be conformed to public opinions and sentiments, for if the public mind is not previously prepared for the measures you would propose, the success of them will be very uncertain. The late [Lieutenant] Governor [Thomas] Cushing has at different times remarked to me, when we were about reforming our constitution of government in this state, which you know was several times attempted before it was effected, that the wisest way to do this was by degrees, as necessity and the public conviction called for alterations, and that reforms thus introduced would be more thoroughly kept up to, as well as the public tranquility be better preserved. The remark, whether originally his own or another's, has struck me as that of a politician of some experience; and could we rationally expect always to have *honest and skillful pilots* at *helm*, we might be as well be done troubling our heads about these matters and leave all to them. For though upon paper we might not appear to have so perfect a constitution and so systematical, yet as far as we had one, if it was always kept up to and upon new exigencies or alterations of circumstances easy judicious reforms were made and the government well administered according to its professed principles, our political happiness might at least be equal to what it now is. The universal experience of mankind testifies that those at helm are neither always the most knowing nor the best disposed of any in the community. We therefore very justly choose to prescribe them rules of action. But are we not too tenacious of power, and like the dog in the manger growlingly forbid others to use that we cannot use ourselves—though perhaps others might use it for our benefit? We learned from our British ancestors to be jealous of all rulers, and perhaps have not yet distinguished the difference between those who rule by prescription and inheritance, and those whom we create; and whom we can destroy when we please. The difference it must be acknowledged is immense. The hypothesis of Lord Bolingbroke that a certain quantity of ethereal spirit is diffused among mankind and that this is possessed only by a few, is at least ingenious. Perhaps it would be as just to say that of the class of mankind who are born with good capacities, but a very few of them meet with such a lucky concurrence of circumstances from youth to riper age so to inform and improve them as to set them supereminently above their brethren; and that it is only these, when we take an accurate survey of mankind, who attract our attention and admiration. But if I remember right even Bolingbroke allows among these few a small number of them to be of the well disposed, or possessed of the true ethereal spirit. It might be acknowledged the scheme of sublimation so warmly contended for by our author goes upon the supposition of Bolingbroke that with the precious metal much dross and inferior stuff are intermixed which can do no service in the higher operations of government, but will always be a clog and impediment to the constancy and accuracy which such operations require. Therefore, by some refinement it is proposed to separate that inferior part after it has served its use in the first operation, but still always to recur to it then, as it is an essential part and is most thoroughly incorporated with the whole mass. For indeed it makes the greater part of it, and the little and the great vulgar together forming the bulk of mankind.

Are not the two leading principles laid down in the early part of your letter stated, my good sir, rather too much in the spirit of republican jealousy? Can the people by themselves exercise the functions of government? If not, must they not deputize somebody to do it for them? Which is most rational: to depute so many that no hope can be formed of their doing it well, or only such a number as may be sufficient to know all the people can wish, or require with reason? Which is most rational: to devolve the trust upon any who present without any tolerable means of judging of their qualifications, or by creating responsibility in all who are concerned in devolving the trust, to endeavor to obtain the favorite few of Bolingbroke at least in the higher departments of the government, presuming on the favorable side of human nature that among them will be some of the well disposed who can always go far in keeping the rest to their duty when they are small in number and men of thorough information? If it be granted that the people must depute others to act for them, it appears to me absurd not to give them all the powers which it is probable will be wanted in the exercise of a thorough administration. To be parsimonious in such a case is expecting the end to be obtained without the necessary means, and by not allowing them enough we shall tempt our governors to encroachment and usurpation; and this with a plausible pretense for the public good, and at first perhaps honestly meant so it would not be difficult to point out some stretching of this kind in the present existing Congress beyond the limits prescribed them by the Confederation. I cannot subscribe to the first part of your second position that the happiness of the many is secured in proportion as power is retained in their hands, for I believe it absolutely necessary that full powers should be imparted to a few that the happiness of the many may be secured. I am decidedly in favor of "this delegated power's reverting often enough into the hands of the many" to secure their control over the few, and to learn these a thorough dependence upon their fellow citizens for creation and support, but I profess myself as real a republican as any of you, though charged with aristocratical principles, and am willing to try the system in any shape that will promise us good government. There is a latitude for such a variety of opinion that scarcely two speculatists will take up the subject with the same view, or reason upon it from like notices imbibed. It must be granted that it is strongly in the disposition of man to abuse power when placed in his hands, as also to avail himself of superior advantages when possessed of them, to the prejudice of his fellow men. To provide against this evil, a well-constructed government must be organized with different bodies for different departments and with reciprocal checks upon as well as mutual assistances to each other. In this machinery some modern schemes of government appear to have the advantage of any ancient ones. It must be granted when reasoning *a priori* (I believe the logicians call it) to establish such checks we may sometimes err, or if not that, the wit and ingenuity of man are probably at different periods so nearly equal that those who follow may be ingenious enough to break through or leap over the barriers prescribed by the constitution mongers of the former age and plead necessity for so doing. But distinct from all checks marked out by constitutions on paper, we have one that I believe has by some kind or other among the people of every country—that is public opinion, or what is called [their?] [———] or mode of thinking—to which the administrators of every government must in a great degree conform. The check last mentioned must in this country for many years to come have a peculiar force from the spirit with which it has been exercised for many years past. The right, everywhere tacitly acknowledged and in some states expressly reserved, freely to declare and publish our opinions upon public measures and the conductors of them, if exercised with half the freedom which our presses permit and give a great facility in doing, will serve to keep public men very generally to their duty, after our institutions have pointed out expressly "whose *watch and ward it is*," or where the responsibility lies, for without this there is no knowing the point of attack. Are not the present people of this country inclinable enough to political enquiries, and public investigations to deter those at helm from practicing any undue arts to impose upon the people or infringe their rights? But after recognizing the genius of the people of this country from its early settlement, and recurring to the spirit with which the late Revolution was begun and in some respects carried out, when at the same time we view them in the singular instance of a whole people with arms in their hands and for such well instructed in the use of them, what idea can be more chimerical than that the despotism of the few, while we in the gross keep clear of confusion, shall advance upon us without our notice and without the power to restrain it in its early approaches— and this with the simple apparatus by which a paper war is carried on, and not by that more hazardous as well as more inhuman one the sword. The late dissents concerning the new Constitution are sufficient to evince no want of political combatants, some of whom can sound even false alarms where real ones are wanting. The word liberty, it is true, has been much abused and little understood in this country as well as all others. There is not, I believe, such a mighty difference between different countries in the actual enjoyment of it as some men are apt to imagine. "A rational man however, whether American or any other, would in making up his mind upon this subject wish to have his property and such personal rights as he can exercise in social life secured to him by known established laws," and in this country I conceive he need be abridged of few or no such rights which are conducive to his political happiness. I am rather of Mr. De Lolme's opinion that it is not necessary for this nor always conducive to it that these laws should be of his own making, nor made by rulers immediately chosen by himself. Do consult De Lolme upon the Constitution of England if you have him or find it among your friends—4th edition and page 53 and from page 240 to 290 or further if you please.[3] He may convince you perhaps that the same end may sometimes be better obtained otherwise. I am an advocate for the people's exercising all the powers they can manage to advantage for themselves, but I have long been of the opinion this can only be the appointment on the first instance, and by small parties, of those who shall again by one or more refinements appoint the managers of their public concerns; and had they once got habituated to this mode of appointment, I am apt to think they might be as pleased in the exercise of it, as they now are in their general meetings. They certainly ought to be if more good to them politically considered was the result of it. Human opinion is frequently founded upon such prejudice, and often subject to so much caprice it is impossible to say that my argument or persuasion could ever lead the people to adopt a plan like the one proposed, or if some superior power visible or invisible should force them into it, that they would ever view it but with an hateful eye. All seem to agree that few in fact are the real managers in every government. This plan proposes drawing forth these few according to established forms in which more discretion it is presumed will be exercised in their choice, and they authoritatively impowered and no others, and by being few easily watched and made responsible. Aristocracy is a term that has never been well defined and is, I believe, but little understood by most of us. For my part I have no idea that it can be applied to any set of men who are chosen at stated periods by the people and again return to private life and into the common mass. Let them be chosen immediately by the people or mediately by two or three removes, as many of our officers have always been, and whether their continuance is for one year or even seven—if it be fixed. National pride is a good engine for the common people of every country to play with, though my friend Dr. [Richard] Price condemns the indulgence of it. We will grant him that a good Christian or philosopher ought to be above it, but "if the votaries to freedom in this country, after it was once well established, could find a thousand fancied attendants upon the goddess, we should have no business to quarrel with them." I am sensible that enthusiasm of some kind or other is the chief pabulum upon which the human mind has been fed, perhaps from the days of father Adam. I wish therefore that every American might be inspired with an high opinion of his peculiarly happy situation in a political view. I wish to see such institutions take effect that everyone nearly in proportion to his abilities will take some part or other in support of the system, and this with the bulk must be by their industry and attachment to good government, which I hope may be so well braced and kept up that everyone shall think it, and with reason, the best that any country was ever blessed with. A wise administration with our present expected institutions might in a few years effect this to a great degree, and it ought to be one of their chief objects to inspire the people with a reverence for their constitution and laws.

Our author has said that "the people should never be brought together in large bodies but under a leader." This proposition is at least plainly expressed. There appears to be nothing ambiguous in the terms. I will grant you it is boldly expressed, but I believe with no latent design. It is true, or it is not, or perhaps with those who shall violently take its opposite sides it will always remain as matter of opinion. To me it appears self evident and therefore harder to explain perhaps than to defend. I never saw a crowd convened but they must have some object in view, or they would create to themselves one, and too often a mischievous one. I never saw a multitude assembled but some few must direct their motions either by appointment or tacit acknowledgment. You allow "that the people in large bodies are always acted upon and cajoled by a few, ever have been, and ever will be." Then why bring them together in large bodies? Your answer is "that they may be acted upon with the eyes of all the citizens open, in public meeting, where the sources of light and knowledge are open and near them, and much information is to be obtained"; this, if they could be made sensible of it, would be the punishment of Tantalus if still they are to be cajoled and imposed upon. If the speeches commonly made at our meetings were intended to have the propriety of the measures to be proffered as being the best, or the fitness of the candidate to be proposed in preference to all others, or if those harangues were found to be given by men the best disposed and with the most honest designs, I will grant you "it would be uncharitable to imagine the people would always select the worst opinions." But you and I must know it is not thus the people are commonly dealt with. A popular harangue needs but a few words and those declaratory of attachment to the people's liberties and all is carried—*fas aut nefas*. How different does a man conduct when he is haranguing a town meeting, or when talking outside of it to a small knot of his fellow citizens. In the one case he addresses himself chiefly to their passions, in the other he must convince them by reason and argument or most commonly fail in his purpose. There must be certainly something discouraging in these meetings or they would not be so thinly attended. The elections of the present month, though without comparison of more importance than any we have had these ten years, prove that in some view or other the people consider them of little import; and "from the wrongs they suffer a better look out in future" is not to be expected. "Some it may be true neglect from pride, or from disappointment that their plans cannot be made to succeed," and many perhaps, and among them some of the best, "from a contempt of the measures carrying on." But "the meetings *we find* are not always crowded, when an important object is at stake and when everyone *ought* to give in his vote." And to him who does convene "the consolation must be small, that he has done himself wrong," if by a different arrangement right could have been done him. I will grant you that opinions are matured by collision "as metals are polished by attrition." We shall only differ here in the application of the means by which this is effected among the people. It has been advanced, and I believe it, that not more than one in ten, take mankind as they arise in any community, have any opinion upon public affairs or give themselves the trouble to think about them. It had been supposed that men when gathered in multitudes are much less apt to decide with judgment than the same men when separated in small parties. It has been presumed that ten men can pitch upon the most capable one among them of their next neighbors to speak or act for them; and this, I honestly think, though perhaps it ought not to be spoken loud, is as much as in the first concoction mankind in the gross are capable of doing. It has been said and I believe it, that ten men proceeding from the squads of tens will carry from the hundred at large more information than the hundred when together could afford each other. They will collect from these little parties they issue from more opinions and these will undergo more collision than among the hundred if together, for men can only when in small bodies deliberate with any precision.

I find it is considered as an infringement of liberty to oblige the citizens without distinction or discrimination to assemble when delegating to others the trust of their important affairs. As a republican I am proud of this austerity, if it ought to be considered such, when the real good of the whole requires they should meet. The advantages proposed by it are not only by obliging everyone in some degree to take an active part to avail ourselves of the discretion of the whole community, but by everyone's having acted a part they are deprived of the opportunity of finding fault so much as now with public appointments and public measures. Besides, the equality of the whole community is recognized in a truly republican sense when all are put upon the same footing and called and obliged to exercise equal rights. The governor and his coachman may meet in the same squad if they are next neighbors and each revert to their condition as men and freemen—and further than this the equality of nature does not exist. But it is a burden, say you, for the whole community to attend. To many, life is a burden, but we are obliged to support it, and if it be a duty we owe the public and our own interest requires it, constraint is proper if the object cannot otherwise be obtained. It is true coercion must at first be used to bring them together but after that they are to vote as they please. Their freedom in this case is not destroyed, they are only obliged to use it for the good of the whole; only it is more feasible for next neighbors to meet together in parties of tens than for hundreds to meet because then the circle is enlarged, and still more if thousands meet together. And it surely is economy for ten men afterwards to do the business of the hundred, and so again ten for the thousand than that the hundred or thousand should be collected. And granting it shall be better done, which I confess is begging the question, for nothing perhaps but actual experiment can determine it; ought we to hesitate, but if it promises much is it not worth the trial? We have had abundant proof for many years "that a sense of the importance to their happiness of it has not been sufficient to keep the people alive to the business of elections," and the history of other countries besides our own may convince us that this negligence and inattention is strongly fixed in the disposition of the common people. And upon critical examination we shall find that the people in every community who *voluntarily* busy themselves about public affairs are in general the flashy and vainly conceited who may be denominated the empty skulls, and a few men of artifice and deep design. I am suspicious the main drift of our author's scheme of refinement is to counteract as far as possible the natural propensities just mentioned to be existing in every community—to excite the attention of all in the first instance, and to select finally the best materials for public use whenever in the common operation for want of critical enquiry they are passed by, and meaner or more improper ones are made use of. "Though a whole people will never voluntarily sell themselves," yet the mass of mankind are too easily imposed upon, and are often betrayed by those who have their confidence. Low cunning is a quality much more common than genuine patriotism.

The new system of election, as you term it, must be taken together, and if the principles upon which it is founded are defensible, ingenious men may make it more practicable perhaps as well as more palatable to some persons than it now appears. It is because "the people cannot or never do unite their powers to detect" that it is proposed to select those who will obtain information and practice more vigilance. The objection "that the tens at home can be practiced upon alone and in the dark" disappears when we recollect that the proposed elections are immediately to follow each other. The demagogue with or without abilities cannot make his application when he does not know whom to make it to; and if he did, time is not allowed him to see the persons whose influence and suffrages are necessary to his appointment.

I have replied to your letter, my good sir, without method or form; as upon perusal of it now and again different parts have struck me, and you will have much repetition of the same sentiments every now and then I suspicion. This reply would have been sooner finished and forwarded to you had not several avocations intervened since my receiving it. I pretend not to style, for I know not what it is and have grown too old to learn. Possessed of your easy manner, fewer sheets might have contained the same sentiments. Convinced of your candor, and partiality to the writer, they are now submitted to your perusal, and to dispose of them as you please without exposing the weakness of the writer of them.

1. FC, Jackson Papers, MHi.
2. The reference is probably to the first volume of John Adams's *A Defence of the Constitutions of Government of the United States of America*, published in London in 1787 and reprinted in the United States in the same year. Jackson had quoted at length from Adams's work in his pamphlet.
3. In his pamphlet Jackson frequently cited Jean Louis de Lolme, *The Constitution of England* . . . . The first English edition was printed in London in 1775.

Boston Gazette, 15 December

A correspondent would caution the Electors of ESSEX to guard against a Candidate [Jonathan Jackson], who has in a late pamphlet, *strongly recommended the establishment of a small Body of permanent regular Forces as a military example for the Militia*; whose political tenets are, "*That the People should* NEVER *be brought together for elections, but in small numbers.*" *That the people are incapable of deliberating and deciding on* their own *political concerns; who highly recommends a* "STATE PAPER" *under the guidance of certain men; and declares that this establishment "would give more true information, than a Representative from every Town in the State, with the Town-Clerk to attend him.*" If these are thy Federal Politicks, oh America, woeful is thy condition![1]

1. This item also appeared in the *Herald of Freedom* on the same day.

Robert Hooper to Samuel Holten, Marblehead, 16 December[1]

Yours of the 15th inst. just received; in answer say I have always given you my vote for public life when my friends in town were not candidates, but I find now that the principal inhabitants propose Colonel [Azor] Orne, who is my very good friend, and intimate acquaintance, and by what I have understood his conduct in public life has been very much approved of.

I am now confined with a light touch of the gout, though fear a visit of it will soon take place, but if I should be able to go out it will be expected by all my friends that I give my townsman and friend the preference.

1. "Samuel Holten Correspondence: From the Originals in the Possession of Mrs. John H. Kimball," Danvers Historical Society *Historical Collections*, XX, 55. Hooper was reputed to be one of the richest merchants in New England before the Revolution. During the war he was a Loyalist. He was the father-in-law of Senator-elect Tristram Dalton, and died insolvent in 1790.

Salem Mercury, 16 December

We are requested to hold up to the notice of the electors of Essex, by inserting the following letter, a worthy and respectable character, as a candidate for the office of federal Representative.

Newburyport, December 11, 1788
Dear Sir: I received yours yesterday by the Rev. Mr. ******, and am highly gratified to see you so mindful of the approaching elections.

With respect to a suitable candidate for this district, it will be agreed to by all, that the man, whose character is not formed on the solid basis of moral virtue, is undeserving the public confidence. But, as honest intentions *alone* will not avail in works of GREAT CONTRIVANCE, a federal legislator, in addition to the most perfect integrity of heart, ought to possess a cool head, and a sound judgment, a good general acquaintance with all those subjects, on which he may be called to deliberate; and if he be a Representative of this county, he ought to be well versed in commerce, in all its *principles, relations*, and *effects*. He ought to discern clearly in what manner agriculture, commerce, and manufactures mutually affect each other, and the necessity of giving to each of them that support which is essential to the prosperity of all. And he ought *especially* to possess a degree of personal independence, and firmness of spirit, sufficient to resist the attacks of unprincipled or mistaken factions, and sufficient to enable him to *decide* with promptness on all measures, *in such a manner* as in his opinion will most promote the interest of the nation, and the real happiness of the people. If the character of a suitable person for a federal Representative is fairly delineated thus far, I know you must feel anxious to see that office filled by the Hon. Jonathan Jackson, Esq., a man, who is acknowledged to possess, in a most eminent degree, every qualification which I have described, and of whom it is emphatically said, by all who know him, that *"he will dare to be honest in the most trying times."*

P.S. If unequivocal proofs of Mr. Jackson's patriotism are required, it may be remembered, that at the commencement of the late contest, at the hazard of his fortune, and at the expense of many valuable friendships, he stood forth a *manly* and *decided advocate of the people*; and, thro every period of the Revolution, exhibited abundant evidence of uniform attachment to the cause of rational liberty.

From a Correspondent, Salem Mercury, 16 December

Next Thursday, the freemen of the county of Essex will be assembled for the most important election, perhaps, which they were ever called on to make—viz., to choose a person as a Representative in the first Congress under the new Constitution; and to choose two persons as candidates for the office of Elector, for Essex District, of a President and Vice President of the United States. May the independent electors of Essex prove themselves worthy of the privileges they possess, by giving their votes for such men as would do justice to this large and respectable district!

From present appearances, it is probable the votes of this district will not be very unequally divided between four several candidates—the Hon. Samuel Holten, the Hon. Benjamin Goodhue, the Hon. Jonathan Jackson, and the Hon. Nathan Dane.

While we regret the improbability of a choice of Representative on Thursday next, we cannot but feel great satisfaction, that the votes are likely to be divided by men, each of whom would do honor (for the public have long experienced their patriotism and abilities) to the office for which they are candidates. And it cannot be doubted, that the good sense of the electors will easily lead them to unite, at a second meeting at least, in one of the most promising candidates.

Christopher Gore to Rufus King, Boston, 21 December (excerpt)[1]

In Essex there is no probability of an election. [Jonathan] Jackson had all the votes in Marblehead, 99; 77 in Beverly; [Nathan] Dane 30; [Benjamin] Goodhue 198 [in Beverly]; in Salem, Jackson 8, Dane 1. I have not heard from Newburyport, or Haverhill. Andover gave all for Dane. The wise men of Essex are at variance. They say every thing bad of P[arsons]; impute to him corrupt motives and deceitful conduct.[2] At [Tristram] Dalton's senatorial honors they are mortified beyond measure.[3]

1. RC, King Papers, NHi. Several of the votes reported by Gore are inaccurate.
2. The reference is evidently to Theophilus Parsons, an Essex County member of the General Court, who during the election of Senators, according to George R. Minot, "obtained such a character as a cunning man . . . as very much affected his influence in the House" (see Minot Journal, November, printed above in The Election of United States Senators).
3. See Gore to King, 26 November (printed above in The Election of United States Senators).

The First Election in Middlesex District, 18 December

The Boston newspapers concentrated on the election in Suffolk District and paid little attention to the elections in other districts prior to 18 December. There are only a few scattered references to the Middlesex election. A few of the men who received votes were mentioned in the newspapers or in private correspondence, and it is evident that the Federalists had difficulty deciding upon a candidate who would accept if elected, a difficulty that continued in the second election in the district.

The required majority of the 1,473 votes cast was 737, and no candidate received that number. Nathaniel Gorham led with 536, Elbridge Gerry was second with 384, Joseph B. Varnum received 254, and John Brooks 106. The remaining 193 votes were scattered among eleven candidates.

The following are the few items that have been located that comment on the first election in Middlesex.

Henry Jackson to Henry Knox, Boston, 30 November (excerpt)[1]

[John] Brooks has given up the idea of offering himself as a candidate—being satisfied he will stand no chance with those that intend to make interest for it, which will be either your *friend* or his influence will be exerted for another person.

Henry Jackson to Henry Knox, Boston, 6 December (excerpt)[2]

S[amuel] A. Otis for this [Suffolk], and Mr. [Joseph B.] Varnum for Middlesex. Mr. [Nathaniel] G[orha]m will not go if chosen. Our friend [John] B[rooks] is talked of but I am afraid he will not be the man.

Massachusetts Centinel, 13 December

In Middlesex the electors appear to be asleep.

Boston Gazette, 15 December

The electors of Middlesex would do well to guard against a certain candidate, who is strongly recommended by ONE whose prospects depend on some lucrative appointment, which he thinks to obtain, provided he can introduce some of his own tools into the federal government.[3]

Federalist, Massachusetts Centinel, 17 December

If integrity, uprightness, and diligence in office; if real Federalism, true Republicanism, and substantial property are qualities requisite for federal Representatives to possess—the characters of the Hon. William Heath, Esq., in Suffolk, and Hon. J[oseph] B. Varnum, Esq., in Middlesex, will meet with the approbation of the free electors in those districts. That the present generation may always have their eyes on the faithful of the land, and that our posterity to the latest ages may distinguish, by their suffrages, the wise, the virtuous, and the inflexible patriots of their country, is the hearty prayer of an honest FEDERALIST.

Henry Jackson to Henry Knox, Boston, 21 December (excerpt)[4]

Middlesex: there will be no choice. They have a number of candidates, as [Joseph B.] Varnum, General [Eleazar] Brooks of Lincoln, Mr. [Elbridge]

Gerry, Mr. J[ames] Winthrop, General [William] Hull, General J[ohn] Brooks, and some others. Mr. [Nathaniel] Gorham has given all his influence for Mr. Varnum.

1. RC, Knox Papers, MHi.
2. RC, Knox Papers, MHi.
3. There is no evidence as to who this "certain candidate" was. This item was also printed the same day in the *Herald of Freedom.*
4. RC, Knox Papers, MHi.

The First Election in Worcester District, 18 December

Two newspapers, the *Massachusetts Spy* and the *American Herald*, were published in the town of Worcester. These papers published a great deal of news about events in other states and about candidates for the Presidency and Vice Presidency, but they published remarkably little about the election in Worcester District. Thus, between 4 and 18 December, they published only four election items; three of them named candidates and one argued for the need of amendments to the new Constitution.

It was evident before the elections were completed in Worcester District that a candidate who did not support amendments to the Constitution had no chance of winning. The three leading candidates in the three Worcester District elections were Jonathan Grout, Timothy Paine, and Artemas Ward. Grout, a local leader during the Revolution, had voted against ratification of the Constitution and in 1788 was a member of the legislature. Paine, a prominent officeholder in the county for two decades before the Revolution, had been appointed to the Royal Council in 1774. Unlike most "mandamus councillors," he did not become a Loyalist. By 1788 he had regained much of his influence in the town of Worcester. Ward had been appointed commanding general of Massachusetts troops after Lexington and Concord, and he remained in charge until George Washington was appointed commander-in-chief of the Continental Army in July 1775. The popular Ward resigned his commission in April 1776 and returned to state politics.

The past records of these three men did not become a public issue until shortly before the third and final election (see The Third Election in Worcester District, 2 March 1789, printed below). In the first election Grout received more votes than Paine, but not a majority; Ward finished third; and 376 votes were scattered among sixteen other candidates in the district.

A True Federalist to the Free Electors of the County of Worcester, American Herald, 4 December

We have now arrived to a critical period of our political existence; and we are soon to determine (and we must determine for ourselves) whether we are to be a free, happy people under our government or not; whether the new system has been sent directly from Heaven, as has been represented, and is, in its nature, perfect; or, whether it would *possibly* admit of some amendments; whether the *balance* of government is fixed on its proper basis; and whether the powers delegated are properly *checked,* etc. These are questions important for us to determine; and as the time for electing a federal Representative and Electors for this district is at hand, we shall naturally form our choice according as we determine upon the questions above.

It is hoped, however, that every person will have an opinion of his own upon the subject, and act accordingly, now the system is in embryo; and all depends upon the first impressions. In fact, the great and ultimate question is, shall we preserve our *republican government,* or shall we suffer it to degenerate into a *baleful aristocracy?* Upon the determination of this one question, depends our political salvation and happiness; and much therefore depends on our first impressions. It is therefore wished, that those who are better qualified for the task would give information of such characters as they suppose would be well calculated for the present important exigencies of our political affairs.

The following characters have already been recommended, viz., the Hon. Artemas Ward, Esq.; the Hon. Jonathan Grout, Esq.; the Hon. Timothy Paine, Esq.; Martin Kingsley, Esq.; John Sprague, Esq.; Dr. Samuel Williard.

A Friend to the County, Massachusetts Spy, 4 December[1]

This county, as a district for that purpose, is called upon to make choice of a gentleman for one of the Representatives of this commonwealth in the Congress of the United States. The time for a choice is near at hand. I do not know of a person more likely to give general satisfaction than the Hon. Timothy Paine, Esq. If the county at large should think as I do, they will not fail to give their votes for that gentleman.

1. This item was dated Lancaster, 1 December.

Nathaniel Paine to William Paine, 14 December (excerpt)[1]

We are all as well as usual, much taken up with our approaching election for the Representative of the District of Worcester. The probable candidates are our father [Timothy Paine] and Colonel [Jonathan] Grout.

1. RC, William Paine Papers, MWA.

A Federalist of Worcester County, Massachusetts Spy, 18 December[1]

This county, as a district for that purpose, is called upon to make choice of a gentleman for one of the Representatives of this commonwealth in the Congress of the United States. The time for a choice is near at hand. I do not know of a person more likely to give general satisfaction than the Hon. Jonathan Grout, Esq. If the county at large should think so, as well as I, they will be fond to give their votes for that gentleman.

1. This item was dated 26 November.

T. W., Massachusetts Spy, 18 December[1]

As it must be the wish of every real friend to his country, in this county, to have the citizens thereof united in the choice of a suitable person to represent them in the federal Congress, I take the liberty to name the Hon. Moses Gill, Esq., whose undisputed integrity, useful knowledge, and long experience in governmental matters, together with his early and uniform attachment to the interests of his country, justly entitle him (in my opinion) to the suffrages of a truly Federal people.

1. This item was dated Lancaster, 8 December.

The First Election in Hampshire-Berkshire District, 18 December

The first election in the district was in part a reflection of the rivalry between Hampshire and Berkshire counties. Berkshire was the less populous county, but four of the six candidates who received the most votes—Theodore Sedgwick, William Whiting, Thompson J. Skinner, and William Williams—were residents of the county. The two Hampshire candidates were Samuel Lyman and John Worthington.

The first election did not reflect the fact that the two counties were centers of agrarian discontent and of support for Shays's Rebellion. Nor did it reflect the fact that in the state Convention the Hampshire delegates voted 32 to 19 and the Berkshire delegates voted 16 to 6 against ratification of the Constitution. Only Whiting was regarded as a Shaysite and an Antifederalist, while the other five men were Federalists, and two of these—Worthington and Williams—had been virtual if not actual Loyalists during the Revolution.

The issue of amendments to the Constitution was not raised during the first election in the district, but it became so important in the ensuing elections that Theodore Sedgwick, who opposed amendments, publicly promised to support them before the fifth election, which he won.

The voters cast 2,251 votes in the first election. The six leading candidates received 2,027 votes, with 224 scattered among sixteen other men. Sedgwick received 801 votes, 325 short of the required majority of 1,126. Within a few days after the election it was known in the district that there would be another election.

A Friend to All Parties to the Good People of the Counties of Hampshire and Berkshire, Hampshire Gazette, 3 December

You will soon be called upon to elect your Representative to the federal government, and altho it is common on the approach of such occasions for the votaries of party to step forward with a bigoted recommendation of particular favorites, yet the author of this scroll hopes he shall not expose himself to a similar imputation, by throwing out a few ideas, of the propriety of which you are the sole judges.

It is obvious, that if ever there was a time, when the presumption of inculcating candor and impartiality might be palliated by the particular circumstances that attended it, the present is one of them. It is a new era in the privileges of Americans. The theatre is novel, the audience extensive, the parts interesting and difficult, and it therefore behooves us to place upon it our best and most experienced actors.

At the ensuing election therefore, we must approach the altar of liberty, with pure minds and holy passions. We ought not to profane the worship of that sacred goddess, by mingling in our prayers the imprecations of party, but rather let the simple and honest fervor of our devotion display to the world a sincerity untinged with the idolatry of faction, and uncorrupted with the fanaticism of popular prejudice. In fine (to continue the figure) let the whole of our political creed breathe the pure language of unanimity and candor, unadulterated with the rude dialect of party. But, perhaps an apology is necessary for the introduction of sentiments that amount to no more than a caution against the exercise of feelings that are now merged in the interest of the republic. The time is past when the *ignis fatuus* of licentious freedom dazzled the eyes and misled the feet of our honest countrymen, when the tide of political passion flowed in with an irresistible violence upon our land, and threatened to sweep away the monuments of liberty and independence. Thanks be to God that the tree of liberty hath lived through that intemperate winter, and that our mild government, like the genial sun, is now unlocking its secret springs of vegetative vigor.

After these observations, I shall venture to propose, as a candidate for the ensuing election, the Honorable Theodore Sedgwick, Esquire. This gentleman had many votes for the senatorship in the late session of our General Court; and whatever were the circumstances that concurred to render his appointment impracticable, it by no means becomes us to utter the language of discontent. We have already the happiness in this part of the country, of boasting the appointment of a great, good, and faithful man [Caleb Strong] to the office of a federal Senator. All therefore that we can now do (and it is certainly what we ought to do) is to confer a secondary honor upon a man, who perhaps merited a greater.

In this gentleman may be found whatever enters into the composition of a wise magistrate, an useful citizen, and an honest man. In his political capacity, he has ever been eminent for an ability to suspend the scale of judgment with a delicate and impartial hand; and with this ability his counsels are equally distant from the crude and hasty decisions of a partial enquirer, and the doubtful vibrations of an undetermined statesman. Whatever talents are necessary to reconcile the interests of contending parties, to soften the edge of animosity, and to subdue the obstinacy of prejudice, without violating the feelings of humanity by a prideful conquest, are possessed by this gentleman in a very high degree. He never invaded the freedom of your choice, by the cringing servility of a sycophant or the disgustful importunity of a petulant ambition. He never rioted upon the spoils of a plundered admiration, or mocked your independence and your virtue, by the degenerated essays of venality and corruption; yet fame hath courted him, and the tributary compliment of political promotion, uncalled for, and undemanded, hath been repeatedly paid to his merit, with a public cordiality.

I am well aware of an objection that will be made to this gentleman, derived from his profession [lawyer], but it will be made by those who are accustomed to skim the surface of things and that only. The distinction of profession in the federal government will be in no way important; and unless we suppose that this in particular must of necessity be joined to an evil disposition, an objection of this kind will be nothing but vapor. We have indeed reason to be thankful that the clamor upon this subject is dying away, and that it is no longer the fountain of feuds and contentions. We have entombed this *spirit of faction*, and the *laus republica* will ere long sing· an eternal *requiem* to its *masses*.

Let us therefore concenter our wishes in this gentleman, and not suffer to pass unimproved, the coming occasion of showing both our patriotism and our gratitude, by bestowing our suffrages upon a man whose real merit and external circumstance all conspire to prefer him into the service of the state.[1]

1. An excerpt from this item was printed in the *Herald of Freedom*, 11 December, and the New York *Daily Advertiser*, 20 December.

On 10 December the *Hampshire Gazette* printed an article by "Yeoman," who said he was initially given "much pain" by the above item for fear it would injure Sedgwick's chances. However, he reported that he was glad to find that virtually all classes were united behind Sedgwick. A different view was taken by "Monitor" in the *Gazette* on 17 December (printed below), who attacked newspaper "nominations" and who implied that Hampshire County voters should vote for a man from their own county.

Samuel Henshaw to Henry Van Schaack, Northampton, 5 December (excerpt)[1]

I must beseech you to use your influence, in Berkshire, that our friend [Theodore] Sedgwick may be chosen to represent our district in Congress. We have had, here, a large and respectable meeting of gentlemen, and were unanimous for Mr. Sedgwick; and have wrote letters to our friends in all parts of this county, and to some in yours, to make every exertion in his favor. If Berkshire don't join us, they ought to be cursed.

1. RC, Van Schaack Scrapbook, Newberry Library, Chicago. Printed: Van Schaack, *Memoirs*, 159-60. Van Schaack, a member of a New York Loyalist family, was banished from that state and settled in Pittsfield, where he became a friend of Sedgwick.

Theodore Sedgwick to Henry Van Schaack, Stockbridge, 10 December (excerpt)[1]

It is not the wish of Colonel [Thomas] Dwight to be a Representative in the federal government, nor is there the least probability he will have any considerable number of votes. The Devil is in the Federalists if they divide. Who can have endeavored the division in Lanesborough?[2] Could any good man comprehend the votes? I certainly would wish at this time to retire, but I will never desert the service as long as it remains severe.

1. RC, Washburn Papers, MHi.
2. In the election on 18 December, Lanesborough's votes were almost evenly divided between Thompson J. Skinner and Sedgwick. See The Official Results of the First Election, 5-10 January 1789, printed below.

Hampshire Chronicle, 10 December

A correspondent informs us, that the Hon. John Worthington, Esq., is an eligible candidate for the important office of federal Representative for this district. The knowledge which this gentleman has of the landed interest of his fellow citizens, his literary talents, and republican character, entitle him to the suffrages of the independent freeholders of the counties of Hampshire and Berkshire.[1]

1. A report was circulated that Samuel Lyman or his supporters inserted this paragraph to draw votes away from Theodore Sedgwick. Later, Sedgwick and Lyman had a personal altercation about it (see Sedgwick to Thomas Dwight, 23 January, printed below in The Second Election in Hampshire-Berkshire District).

Monitor, Hampshire Gazette, 17 December

When I look back upon the late glorious Revolution—when I take a retrospective view of the noble, manly, and united exertions of every true American, for the extirpation of tyranny, and the establishment of a free government, the general satisfaction that apparently prevailed among the people of this commonwealth at the establishment of the Constitution, and the joy that diffused itself through every breast and appeared in every countenance at the close of hostilities and settlement of the peace; I say, when I reflect upon those events and their then promising consequences, to stop here, a recollection of them would excite in me the most agreeable sensations. But when I consider the failure of public virtue, and the want of a republican principle, so apparent, it fills me with pain and anxiety to see the face of our political affairs so changed. And as we are soon to be called upon to give in our votes for a Representative for the District of Hampshire and Berkshire, I hope I shall be excused for offering something to the public on so important a subject. It is of great importance to look out for the best man that can be found among us—one who has, from the beginning of our contest with Britain, proved himself a steady friend to his country, who hath the interest of the public at heart; one who will not be governed by selfish motives; one who feels for the people under their present burthens; one who is a friend to government, and good order; and one who has an honest heart and a sound mind. On the other hand, we ought to guard against those who are unfriendly to a republican government, to shun giving our votes for those who have used their influence to make the law very expensive, and who have used unjustifiable measures to get themselves into office. I should not have been so particular in my observations, had it not been for the publications in your two last papers, setting up a gentleman in the county of Berkshire [Theodore Sedgwick] as a candidate for a Representative,[1] which practice, I think very unjustifiable; especially among a free people. Are we, my countrymen, to be governed in our elections by the influence of designing men? Do good men want the assistance of newspaper writers to get into office? How far is such a practice consistent with the freedom of a republican government?* Let us guard against such influence. Let us act like freemen, and stand fast in the support of those rights and privileges which have cost us so much blood and treasure. Let us give our votes free from prejudice; not because the gentleman hath been voted for a

Senator in the federal government, not because he is a lawyer, but because we think he is the best man. Shall the county of Hampshire give up the privilege of a Representative, when we are an eighth part of the commonwealth, because the General Court have seen fit to annex the county of Berkshire with us? Shall fifty thousand souls be unrepresented in the federal court, when by the Constitution thirty thousand gives a Representative? If we have not a single man in the county of Hampshire, not to say, who might be highly complimented, but of ability, real merit, and patriotism, then let us by all means give up our just right of choosing a Representative in this county, and go to Berkshire for one.

The subject of election is important: let us therefore set out well, hoping that by the blessing of a kind Providence, the federal government may be made a permanent blessing to the people.

*I question whether the proposed candidate, if he is a man of feeling, would thank the late writers for lavishing encomiums upon him, and taking so much pains to establish his character by fulsome panegyrics—for he must not be insensible that it has the appearance that his character needed such support, in as much as he is so generally known. But perhaps the gentleman may forgive these writers the injury they may have done his character in thus overacting, by imputing it to their good intentions in his favor. It is to be hoped that the free citizens of Hampshire are not so much like children as to be dictated in their choice implicitly by newspaper writers, and feel themselves under obligation to give in their suffrages for a man barely because he is set up by them as a candidate.

1. See "A Friend to All Parties," *Hampshire Gazette*, 3 December, printed above. For a reply to "Monitor," see "A Friend to All Parties," *Hampshire Gazette*, 25 February, printed below in The Third Election in Hampshire-Berkshire District.

Henry Van Schaack to Theodore Sedgwick, Pittsfield, 20 December (excerpt)[1]

I have the pleasure to acquaint you that after the votes were sorted and counted last Thursday the town clerk announced that Your Honor had 38 votes and [William] Whiting only 15. This looks well. Permit me to tell you that you have many warm and sincere friends in this town; make much of them I beg of you. At Richmond I hear you had nearly all the votes. How have the lower towns acted? I fear to the northward things have not gone on so well. From what I can learn Partridgefield and Windsor have run upon [Thompson J.] Skinner. How comes this?

1. RC, Sedgwick Papers, MHi.

Samuel Henshaw to Theodore Sedgwick, Northampton, 23 December (excerpt)[1]

Your friends here have made every exertion in your favor but there will not be a choice this time, I think. However, I am confident we shall succeed in the next attempt, if your friends in Berkshire are awake.

It is said, and I firmly believe it, that a certain clergyman, I think his name is Taylor, of Deerfield,[2] has essentially injured your reputation and interest, among many good, but weak, Christians, by reporting that you are a Deist. If this should extort a smile of contempt at the illiberal and bigoted priest, yet it will not do to rest here, for the report has had a baneful influence, and it will increase, unless some measures are speedily taken to counteract it. The Reverend Zealot! has made a journey through this town to Westfield and the towns around exhorting people not to build up Anti-Christ, not to vote for a Deist, etc., etc., etc. In Westfield and Southampton, I am told, he had much influence. Captain Lem Pomeroy conversed with him on the subject, and will tell you all about it.

1. RC, Sedgwick Papers, MHi.
2. The Reverend John Taylor became a minister in Deerfield in February 1787 and held his post until 1807.

The Official Results of the First Election, 5-10 January 1789

The election returns for the election on 18 December 1788 are placed under the date 5 January, the date upon which the returns were to be in the hands of the Secretary of the Commonwealth. The Secretary recorded the returns on separate charts for each district. These charts, the originals of which are in the Massachusetts Archives (Massachusetts Abstract of Votes for Members of Congress, 1788), list the names of all the towns in each district, the names of all the men who received votes, and indicate the votes each man received in each town that voted.

We have reproduced these charts as literally as possible with the following changes and additions: (1) we have corrected the vote totals where the original charts or the totals given in the Council Proceedings are in error; (2) we have given the modern spelling of town names; (3) where town names have been changed, we have placed the present-day name of the town in brackets following the eighteenth-century name wherever we have been able to identify the changes.

The Election Resolutions of 20 November directed the Secretary to lay the voting returns before the Governor and Council. The Governor and Council recorded the results of the first election on 6 January (printed below).

On 6 January Governor John Hancock also issued precepts for a second election in Essex, Middlesex, Worcester, and Hampshire-Berkshire districts. Evidently the Election Resolutions of 20 November were regarded as the precepts for the election on 18 December. However, as soon as it was learned that no Representatives had been elected in four districts, printed precepts were prepared. These precepts set the date for the next election and the date upon which the votes were to be returned to the Secretary of the Commonwealth. Blank spaces were left in the printed forms to be filled in with the names of the districts, the names of the towns in each district, and the names of the two candidates receiving the highest number of votes. Only a few of these precepts have been located. The precept sent to the selectmen of the town of Northampton for the second election in Hampshire-Berkshire District on 29 January is printed below as an example. There were some minor variations in format but no essential differences in content in the printed precepts for later elections.

To ensure prompt return of the votes, the General Court adopted additional election resolutions on 10 January (printed below).

Official Election Returns, 5 January 1789

SUFFOLK DISTRICT, 18 DECEMBER

Town	Hon. Samuel Adams, Esq.	Fisher Ames, Esq.	Hon. Samuel A. Otis, Esq.	Hon. James Bowdoin, Esq.	Hon. William Heath, Esq.	John Read, Esq.	Thomas Dawes, Esq.	Hon. Benjamin Austin, Jr., Esq.	Charles Jarvis, Esq.	Hon. John Lowell, Esq.	Hon. Richard Cranch, Esq.	Hon. Benjamin Lincoln, Esq.	Hon. John Adams, Esq.	Hon. Oliver Wendell, Esq.	James Bowdoin, Jr., Esq.
Boston	439	445	15	2											
Roxbury	5	45	3		14	1									
Dorchester	3	41													
Milton	1	16	1												12
Braintree		43													
Weymouth	20										4				
Hingham	1	28													
Cohasset															
Dedham	8	20	1		1										
Medfield		6	32												
Stoughton		17						43					1		
Bellingham		8			6										
Medway									24	8					
Wrentham		34			4										
Brookline		6	17												
Needham	2	26													
Walpole	13	23								2					
Chelsea	12													7	
Hull															
Franklin		29	1		3				21	1		18			
Foxborough	13	4					3								
Dover		1											29		
Sharon	4	26													
Totals	521	818	70	2	28	1	3	43	45	11	4	18	30	7	12

Votes cast: 1613
Majority required: 807

PLYMOUTH-BARNSTABLE DISTRICT, 18 DECEMBER

Town	Hon. George Partridge, Esq.	Hon. James Warren, Esq.	Mr. Thomas Davis	Mr. William Hall Jackson	Hon. William Cushing	Hon. Nathaniel Cushing	John Gray, Esq.	Joshua Thomas, Esq.	Dr. Samuel Savage
Plymouth	50	25	2	1					
Scituate	20								
Duxbury	13								
Marshfield						12			
Bridgewater	46								
Middleborough	37							1	
Rochester	24								
Plympton	20	3	1		1	1	1	3	
Pembroke	20								
Kingston	27								
Abington	44								
Hanover	27				1				
Halifax	17								
Wareham	7								
Barnstable	25								1
Sandwich	50								
Yarmouth	33								
Eastham									
Harwich									
Wellfleet									
Falmouth	41								
Truro									
Chatham									
Provincetown									
Totals	501	28	3	1	2	13	1	4	1

Votes cast: 554
Majority required: 278

YORK-CUMBERLAND-LINCOLN DISTRICT, 18 DECEMBER

Town	Hon. George Thacher, Esq.	Hon. Josiah Thacher, Esq.	Hon. Nathaniel Wells, Esq.	Hon. William Lithgow, Esq.	Hon. Samuel [Weder?]spoon, Esq.	Hon. David Sewall, Esq.	Thomas Cutts	Hon. Dummer Sewall	John Fox	Hon. William Gorham, Esq.	Daniel Cony, Esq.	Thomas Rice, Esq.	Joshua B. Osgood, Esq.
York	33		19										
Kittery	30												
Wells	18		2			5							
Berwick					7				4				
Arundel													
[Kennebunkport]	1		10				15						
Biddeford	8		10										
Pepperellborough													
[Saco]	16	8											
Lebanon													
Sanford	26		5										
Fryeburg	1	1	1										5
Coxhall	1		10		1								
Massabeseck													
[Waterboro]													
Limerick					11								
Brownfield													
Littlefalls													
Shapleigh	31												
Parsonfield													
Little Ossipee													
Washington													
Francisborough													
Portland	23	28	3										
Falmouth													
North Yarmouth	2	14	12										
Scarborough	2	24											
Brunswick													

(Table continued on following pages)

YORK-CUMBERLAND-LINCOLN DISTRICT, 18 DECEMBER *(continued)*

Town	Hon. George Thacher, Esq.	Hon. Josiah Thacher, Esq.	Hon. Nathaniel Wells, Esq.	Hon. William Lithgow, Esq.	Hon. Samuel [Weder?] spoon, Esq.	Hon. David Sewall, Esq.	Thomas Cutts	Hon. Dummer Sewall	John Fox	Hon. William Gorham, Esq.	Daniel Cony, Esq.	Thomas Rice, Esq.	Joshua B. Osgood, Esq.
Harpswell	10												
Cape Elizabeth													
Gorham		35											
Windham		8											
New Gloucester	22	1											
Buxton	8	14	1										
Gray													
Standish	2	22			3								
Royalsborough [Durham]													
Raymondstown [Raymond]													
Sylvester													
Bridgton													
Shepardston													
Otisfield													
Pownalborough [Pownal] [1]	26												
Georgetown	22												
Newcastle	61												
Woolwich													
Waldoboro													
Topsham	2	13				2							
Winslow	9				1								
Bowdoinham													
Boothbay													
Bristol													
Vassalboro	32					2						1	
Edgecomb	4			20									
Hallowell [Augusta]	74										16		
St. George													
Warren													
Thomaston													

(Table continued on following page)

YORK-CUMBERLAND-LINCOLN DISTRICT, 18 DECEMBER *(continued)*

Town	Hon. George Thacher, Esq.	Hon. Josiah Thacher, Esq.	Hon. Nathaniel Wells, Esq.	Hon. William Lithgow, Esq.	Hon. Samuel [Weder?] spoon, Esq.	Hon. David Sewall, Esq.	Thomas Cutts	Hon. Dummer Sewall	John Fox	Hon. William Gorham, Esq.	Daniel Cony, Esq.	Thomas Rice, Esq.	Joshua B. Osgood, Esq.
Bath	3	14											
Winthrop	51												
Lewiston													
Ballston													
Walpole													
Wales													
Green										12			
Canaan	35												
[Pittstown?]													
Medumcook													
Norridgewock	35												
Sterlington													
[Union]													
Belfast													
Machias													
Totals	588	182	73	23	21	3	20	0	4	12	16	1	5

Votes cast: 948
Majority required: 475

1. Later, in the nineteenth century, Pownal was divided into three towns: Wiscasset, Dresden, and New Milford.

BRISTOL-DUKES-NANTUCKET DISTRICT,
18 DECEMBER

Town	Hon. George Leonard, Esq.	David Cobb, Esq.	Hon. Phanuel Bishop, Esq.	William Rotch	Mr. Paul Sanford
Taunton	47	97	40		
Rehoboth	111		169		
Swansea	11		102		
Dartmouth	6	1	8		
Norton	89				
Mansfield	20	34			
Attleboro	91		12		1
Dighton	51				
Freetown	37				
Raynham	3	41			
Easton	15	2	11		
Berkley	30				
New Bedford	17	28			
Westport	38				
Edgartown		38			
Chilmark				22	
Tisbury					
Sherburn					
[Nantucket]	144				
Totals	710	241	342	22	1

Votes cast: 1316
Majority required: 659

ESSEX DISTRICT, 18 DECEMBER

Town	Hon. Samuel Holten, Esq.	Hon. Benjamin Goodhue, Esq.	Hon. Nathan Dane, Esq.	John Jackson, Esq.	Hon. Jonathan Jackson, Esq.	Hon. Samuel Phillips, Jr., Esq.	Hon. George Cabot, Esq.	Jonathan Titcomb, Esq.
Salem	1	198	2		8			
Danvers	36	31						
Ipswich	27	13	24		37	1	1	
Newbury		12	45		13			
Newburyport		38	1		153	1		2
Marblehead		5			88			
Lynn		23	1		3			
Lynnfield		17	2					
Andover			104	1				
Beverly	1		30		77			
Salisbury	2	38						
Haverhill	1		61			8		
Gloucester	46	108						
Topsfield	26	5	4					
Amesbury	20				4			
Bradford		48						
Methuen	23	4	2					
Boxford		23	2					
Wenham								
Manchester	4	4			8			
Middleton								
Rowley	15		17					
Totals	202	567	295	1	391	10	1	2

Votes cast: 1469
Majority required: 735

MIDDLESEX DISTRICT, 18 DECEMBER

Town	Hon. Joseph B. Varnum, Esq.	Hon. Elbridge Gerry, Esq.	Hon. Francis Dana, Esq.	Hon. Eleazer Brooks, Esq.	Loammi Baldwin, Esq.	John Brooks, Esq.	James Winthrop, Esq.	Hon. Nathaniel Gorham, Esq.	Samuel Dexter, Jr., Esq.	Hon. Ebenezer Bridge, Esq.	William Winthrop, Esq.	William Hull, Esq.	Hon. Joseph Hosmer, Esq.	Parker Varnum, Esq.	Hon. Oliver Prescott, Esq.
Cambridge	37	3		1		1	28				1				
Charlestown	49	25	2	1											
Watertown		24		3		13									
Woburn	1	7			43										
Concord	4							76	1						
Newton		11				11		20				1			
Reading	6	10						39							
Marlborough		25				4		39							
Billerica		1		1				37							
Framingham						1		50							
Lexington		6	1					27							
Chelmsford															
Sherborn		1				29		1							
Sudbury		16	3					13							
Malden	3					1		6		17					
Weston		20				26									
Medford	2	1		11									16		
Hopkinton		10						33							
Westford	20	21				4									
Waltham		24				12									
Stow								31							
Boxborough								21							
Groton		18				1	16	3							

(Table continued on following page)

MIDDLESEX DISTRICT, 18 DECEMBER *(continued)*

Town	Hon. Joseph B. Varnum, Esq.	Hon. Elbridge Gerry, Esq.	Hon. Francis Dana, Esq.	Hon. Eleazer Brooks, Esq.	Loammi Baldwin, Esq.	John Brooks, Esq.	James Winthrop, Esq.	Hon. Nathaniel Gorham, Esq.	Samuel Dexter, Jr., Esq.	Hon. Ebenezer Bridge, Esq.	William Winthrop, Esq.	William Hull, Esq.	Hon. Joseph Hosmer, Esq.	Parker Varnum, Esq.	Hon. Oliver Prescott, Esq.
Shirley		24													
Pepperell							1	27							
Townsend								21							8
Dracut	51	1		1		1		2						2	
Bedford	31	1													
Holliston		9						25							
Acton	2	16						27							
Carlisle	10	8						3					2		
Dunstable		7	2					8							
Lincoln	15			18											
Wilmington															
Tewksbury	20	3					5			1					
Littleton		15						9							
Ashby		30						2							
Stoneham	3	12											7		
Natick		16				2									
East Sudbury		19						16							
Totals	254	384	8	36	43	106	50	536	1	18	1	17	9	2	8

Votes cast: 1473
Majority required: 737

WORCESTER DISTRICT, 18 DECEMBER

Town	Hon. Artemas Ward, Esq.	Hon. John Sprague, Esq.	Hon. Timothy Paine, Esq.	Captain Stephen Maynard	Hon. Jonathan Grout, Esq.	Hon. Abel Wilder, Esq.	Hon. Samuel Parker, Esq.	Rev. Ebenezer Chaplin	Captain Jeremiah Learned	Dr. Samuel Willard	Hon. Moses Gill, Esq.	Martin Kinsley, Esq.	Dr. John Taylor	Mr. Simon Houghton	Hon. Seth Washburn, Esq.	Daniel Grosvenor	Jonathan Warner, Esq.	Peter Penniman	Ebenezer Learned
Worcester	1		46		25	3					11								
Lancaster			41		14														
Mendon		12	1																
Brookfield	50	7			37														
Oxford			41		2														
Charlton	1	1	21		8														
Sutton			79																
Leicester		2	2								38								
Spencer			18		34														
Rutland		2	24		33														
Paxton																			
Oakham	1	4			23														
Barre	10	3	6		33	1				4									
Hubbardston					47														
New Braintree			12		23							10					1		
Southborough			6		2										9	1			
Westborough	9	1	10		17														
Northborough	18				1	1													
Shrewsbury	30	2			33							2							
Lunenburg	5		17		11	4					2						3		
Fitchburg			1			37											1		
Uxbridge		1	13		26														

	C1	C2	C3	C4	C5	C6	C7	C8	C9	C10	C11	C12	C13	C14	C15	C16	C17
Harvard			13		5			18									1
Dudley		16	2		21												
Bolton	15		4		2	1								2			
Upton																	
Sturbridge			26		38						1						
Leominster	13		37		1						3						
Hardwick		8			31												1
Holden	6		21		21						12				1		
Western																	
[Warren]			24		1												
Douglas																	
Grafton	2	4	11		49												
Petersham			12		41												
Royalston	6		2		2		1									31	
Westminster																	
Templeton			19		13	9											
Princeton			1		19						53						
Ashburnham	12		10		5							1				3	
Winchendon	16		1		20	6										1	
Northbridge																	
Ward																	
[Auburn]	3					2		21	2	3							
Athol	30				16						16						
Milford																	
Sterling	21		21									1					
Berlin	12		7	3													
Gardner	5				16												
Boylston	18		5		13						2						
Gerry																	
[Phillipston]	9		9		9												
Totals	284	63	561	3	665	71	19	22	2	7	110	24	2	9	1	39	1
																1	1

Votes cast: 1886
Majority required: 944

619

HAMPSHIRE-BERKSHIRE DISTRICT, 18 DECEMBER

Town	Hon. Theodore Sedgwick	John Worthington, Esq.	Hon. Thompson J. Skinner	Hon. Elijah Dwight	Samuel Henshaw, Esq.	Hon. John Bacon	William Whiting, Esq.	William Williams, Esq.	Dr. Ebenezer Hunt	Samuel Lyman, Esq.	Hon. Oliver Phelps	Nathaniel Kingsley	Samuel Fowler, Esq.	Timothy Robinson	Hon. John Hastings	Simeon Strong	Ebenezer Mattoon, Esq.	William Lyman, Esq.	Hon. Israel Williams, Esq.	Moses Bliss, Esq.	Nehemiah [Rockin?]	Mr. Samuel Field
Springfield	45			3						9												
Longmeadow	4	37								5												
West Springfield	6	2					101			9	1		1			1						
Wilbraham	11									23												
Northampton	59							78														
Southampton	30										32											
Hadley	25						1	1		2												
South Hadley																						
Amherst	5							5														
Granby										38												
Hatfield										27												
Whately																						
Williamsburg																						
Westfield	28						23	3			1		16									
Deerfield	25		8					12														
Greenfield	19							1		5										1		
Shelburne	13							20												1		

620

Town						
Conway						
Sunderland						
Montague						
Northfield						
Brimfield	37					
South Brimfield [Wales]	7					
Monson	9					
Pelham	37	27				
Greenwich	30					
Blandford						
Palmer	1	16				
Granville	28	1	13	3	7	2
New Salem	40					
Belchertown	21	41				
Colrain	25					
Ware	12	7				
Warwick	26					
Bernardston	8	16	1			
Chester						
Charlemont	5	8				
Ashfield						
Worthington	12					
Shutesbury	20	2	1			
Chesterfield	11	15	2	1		
Goshen						
Southwick	5	24	1	1		

[Table continued on following pages]

HAMPSHIRE-BERKSHIRE DISTRICT, 18 DECEMBER *(continued)*

Town	Hon. Theodore Sedgwick	John Worthington, Esq.	Hon. Thompson J. Skinner	Hon. Elijah Dwight	Samuel Henshaw, Esq.	Hon. John Bacon	William Whiting, Esq.	William Williams, Esq.	Dr. Ebenezer Hunt	Samuel Lyman, Esq.	Hon. Oliver Phelps	Nathaniel Kingsley	Samuel Fowler, Esq.	Timothy Robinson	Hon. John Hastings	Simeon Strong	Ebenezer Mattoon, Esq.	William Lyman, Esq.	Hon. Israel Williams, Esq.	Moses Bliss, Esq.	Nehemiah [Rockin?]	Mr. Samuel Field
Norwich [Huntington]	23																					
Ludlow						7	5	35														
Leverett																						
Westhampton	32					17																
Montgomery																						
Plantation No. 7 [Hawley]																						
Cummington																						
Wendell	19															3						
Orange																						
Holland	10								26													
Leyden																						
Rowe	16																					
Heath																						
Easthampton																						
Sheffield	34					29																
Great Barrington	28	2			14														11			

Town																					
Stockbridge	49						39	15														
Pittsfield	38						13	5														
Richmond	33						2	29														
Lenox	2		38																			
Lanesborough	27		28																			
Williamstown	2		45					16														
Adams			39																			
Egremont													1									
Becket	18						15	18														
West Stockbridge	1		1							1												
Dalton																						
Alford	8						1	16														
New Ashford			15																			
New Marlborough	15						15	8														
Tyringham	5																					
Loudon [Otis]																						
Windsor			48																			
Partridgefield																						
[Peru]			12			1																
Hancock																						
Lee																						
Buckland	12	3		10																		
Sandisfield	1					7		28														
Totals	801	165	233	15	0	93	302	196	5	330	50	1	21	7	2	6	1	7	11	2	1	2

Votes cast: 2251

Majority required: 1126

Governor and Council Record the Votes in the First Elections, Tuesday, 6 January[1]

The Governor and Council upon examination of the returns from the several districts in this commonwealth for Representatives to represent the people thereof in the Congress of the United States find them to stand as follows, viz.

District comprehending the County of Suffolk. Number of voters, 1613; [to] make a choice, 807. Fisher Ames, Esq., had 818 and is chosen.

District comprehending the County of Essex. Number of voters, 1469; [to] make a choice, 735. Hon. Benjamin Goodhue, 567; Jonathan Jackson, Esq., 391. Candidates.

District comprehending the County of Middlesex. Number of voters, 1473; [to] make a choice, 737. Hon. Nathaniel Gorham, 536; Elbridge Gerry, Esq., 384. Candidates.

District comprehending the counties of Hampshire and Berkshire. Number of voters, 2251; [to] make a choice, 1126.[2] Hon. Theodore Sedgwick, Esq., 801; Samuel Lyman, Esq., 330. Candidates.

District comprehending the counties of Plymouth and Barnstable. Number of voters, 554; [to] make a choice, 278. Hon. George Partridge, Esq., has 501 and is chosen.

District comprehending the counties of York, Cumberland and Lincoln. Number of voters, 948; [to] make a choice, 475. Hon. George Thacher, Esq., has 588, and is chosen.

District comprehending the counties of Bristol, Dukes County, and Nantucket. Number of voters, 1316; [to] make a choice, 659. Hon. George Leonard, Esq., has 710, and is chosen.

District comprehending the County of Worcester. Number of voters, 1886; [to] make a choice, 944. Hon. Timothy Paine, 561; Jonathan Grout, Esq., 665. Candidates.

1. Council Records, XXX, 432–33, M-Ar.
2. The vote totals recorded in the Council Records for Hampshire-Berkshire District are incorrect and have been corrected here.

Precept for the Second Election, Hampshire-Berkshire District, 6 January[1]

Commonwealth of Massachusetts.

These are in the name of the Commonwealth of Massachusetts, to will and require you, forthwith, in manner as the law directs for calling Town-Meetings, to cause the freeholders and other inhabitants of the town of *Northampton* duly qualified to vote for Representatives to the General Court of this Commonwealth, to assemble on Thursday the twenty-ninth of January current, to give in their votes for a Representative, who shall be an inhabitant of the district of *Hampshire & Berkshire* to represent the said district in the Congress of the United States of America, to the Selectmen who shall preside at said Meeting, and the Selectmen or the major part of them, shall in open Town-Meeting, sort and count the votes, and form a list of the persons voted for, with the number of votes for each person against his name, and shall make a publick declaration thereof, in the said Meeting, and shall in the presence of the inhabitants, seal up copies of said list, which list they shall transmit to the office of the Secretary of the Commonwealth, on or before the seventh day of February next.

Given at the Council-Chamber in Boston, this Sixth day of January, in the year of our Lord, one thousand seven hundred and eighty-nine, and in the thirteenth year of the Independence of the United States of America.

John Hancock.

By His Excellency's command.

[s] *John Avery junr Secy*

To the Selectmen of the Town of *Northampton* in the District of *Hampshire & Berkshire*.. Greeting.

These certify, that the returns from the several towns within the district of Hampshire & Berkshire respecting the choice of a Representative, to represent the people thereof, in the Congress of the United States, have been examined agreeably to the resolution of the General Court, passed the twentieth of November 1788, by which it appears, that

The Hon. *Theodore Sedgwick Esq & Samuel Lyman Esq*

have had the greatest number of votes in the returns from the said district, in which no person has been chosen.

John Hancock.

[SEAL]   By His Excellency's command.

[s] *John Avery junr Secy*

1. Broadside (LT), Rare Book Division, NN. This document is an example of the printed forms sent to the sheriffs of each county for delivery to the selectmen of each town. The italicized portions above indicate the handwritten insertions in the blank spaces left in the printed forms. We have therefore not reproduced the italicized type in the original forms.

Voters were not restricted to voting for the two men listed as receiving the highest number of votes (see Massachusetts Elections Resolutions, 20 November, printed above). As early as 29 December, the *Herald of Freedom* explained that in case runoff elections were necessary, the voters should "not be misled by a false idea that their suffrages must be confined to the two highest candidates. One moment's attention to the Resolve of the General Court will rectify this mistake, which has been propagated by ignorant or designing men."

Additional Election Resolutions, 10 January[1]

Commonwealth of Massachusetts

In the House of Representatives Jany 8 1789

Whereas further Provision is necessary for compleating the Election of persons to represent the People of this Commonwealth in the Congress of the United States—

Resolved, that the Selectmen of the several Towns & Districts to whom the Governor has issued or shall hereafter issue his Precepts for calling a Meeting of the Inhabitants thereof to give in their Votes for a Representative in the Congress of the United States, shall within four days after such meeting return a list of such Votes to the Sheriff of the County in which the said towns & districts respectively lie, or otherwise shall make return of such Votes into the Secretary's Office, on or before the day prescribed therefor in the said Precept—And it shall likewise be the duty of every Sheriff, seasonably to deliver all precepts which are or shall be issued by the Governor with advice of Council for compleating the election of Representatives in the Congress of the United States, & may be delivered to him to be dispersed, to the Selectmen to whom they are severally directed—and also to make return of the list of Votes to him committed into the Secretary's Office, on or before the day prescribed therefor in the said Precept, and every Sheriff who shall refuse or neglect to perform the duty which is herein required of him, shall for every offence forfeit & pay a sum not exceeding One hundred pounds, or less than three pounds—And it is further Resolved, that if any Selectmen or Town Clerk shall refuse or neglect to perform the duty required of them by this Resolve, & the Resolve of this Court for organizing the Foederal Government, passed in November last, they shall for each & every Offence severally forfeit and pay a sum not exceeding twenty pounds nor less than three pounds—And it shall be the duty of the Attorney General to sue for and recover all such fines & forfeitures as shall be incurred by a breach of this Resolve, to the use of this Commonwealth—And the Secretary is hereby directed to cause the foregoing Resolve to be published in the Districts in which Elections are not compleated, as soon as may be.

1. (LT), Miscellaneous Resolves, 1788, Chapter 17, M-Ar. The House appointed a committee on 7 January "to bring in a resolution for obliging selectmen to return the votes of the several towns for Representatives for the Government of the United States." The next day the committee brought in a resolution "providing penalties for neglect in Selectmen and Sheriffs on returning the votes for Representatives." The resolution was read, passed, and sent to the Senate. The Senate made some verbal changes in the House resolution and sent a new draft to the House on 9 January. The House accepted the Senate's version the next day, which is the version printed here.

The Continuation and Completion of the Election of Representatives, 6 January–27 May 1789

On 6 January 1789 the Governor and Council recorded the votes for the first election on 18 December and the fact that no candidate had received a majority in Essex, Middlesex, Worcester, and Hampshire-Berkshire districts. On 6 January, therefore, Governor John Hancock issued precepts for a second election to be held in the four districts on 29 January, with the votes to be returned to the Secretary of the Commonwealth by 7 February.

On 9 February the Governor and Council recorded the votes for the second election and confirmed the election of Benjamin Goodhue in Essex District and Elbridge Gerry in Middlesex District. On the same day Governor Hancock issued precepts for a third election in Worcester and Hampshire-Berkshire districts on 2 March, with the votes to be returned to the Secretary by 14 March. Jonathan Grout was elected in Worcester District in the third election, but no candidate received a majority in Hampshire-Berkshire District.

Although no precept for the fourth election in Hampshire-Berkshire District has been located, Governor Hancock apparently issued it on 16 March, the day he and the Council recorded the votes for the third election. The election was held on 30 March and the votes were to be returned to the Secretary by 9 April. Again, no candidate received a majority and Governor Hancock issued a precept for the fifth election on 10 April, the day he and the Council recorded the votes for the fourth election. The fifth election was held on 11 May, and on 27 May the Governor and Council recorded the election of Theodore Sedgwick.

The documents for these elections are arranged in the following order: The Second Election in Essex District; The Second Election in Middlesex District; The Second Election in Worcester District; The Second Election in Hampshire-Berkshire District; The Third Election in Worcester District; The Third Election in Hampshire-Berkshire District; The Fourth Election in Hampshire-Berkshire District; The Fifth Election in Hampshire-Berkshire District.

The voting returns for each election are placed with the documents for each district under the date they were to be deposited with the Secretary of the Commonwealth. Those dates are 7 February for the second election, 14 March for the third election, 9 April for the fourth election, and 26 May for the fifth election.

The Second Election in Essex District, 29 January

The second election in Essex District was a two-way contest between Benjamin Goodhue of Salem, who received the most votes in the first election, and Jonathan Jackson of Newburyport, who finished second. Nathan Dane and Samuel Holten, who placed third and fourth respectively, either dropped out of their own accord or were abandoned by their supporters. They were mentioned only once during the second campaign, when a newspaper noted that they, too, received votes in the first election. Since Goodhue and Jackson were both Federalists, the contest in the second election was in part a struggle between the towns of Salem and Newburyport. Tristram Dalton of Newburyport had been elected one of the United States Senators from Massachusetts, and supporters of Goodhue thus had an argument in favor of a Salem candidate, which probably seemed plausible to some voters.

More than town rivalry was involved, however. The dissension among Essex Federalists over the election of United States Senators, and in particular the role of Theophilus Parsons, continued to divide county politics. Parsons, who had opposed both Tristram Dalton and Rufus King for Senator, apparently told Dalton that King had prevented the appointment of Jackson as a commissioner to settle Continental accounts (see Commentaries on the Election of United States Senators, 22 November 1788—29 January 1789, printed above). During the second campaign for Representative in Essex District, Jackson reported that people said he was without property. He was so embittered that in the state elections in May he joined forces with the Antifederalists in a futile attempt to prevent the reelection of Parsons to the state legislature (Michael Hodge to Benjamin Goodhue, Newburyport, 7 May, RC, Goodhue Papers, NNS).

Jonathan Jackson to Oliver Wendell, Newburyport, 11 January (excerpt)[1]

If Prentice has received any money from Asa Powers or any others, do desire him to send it by you, unless you are going to Albany etc. This want of money is a sad thing. I wish I could help you to some in your present straits, but if those fellows Howe and Osgood don't soon come with theirs, my own credit will suffer and my family, too, I am afraid. Still I am not without friends, nor without property—if real estate may pass as such—having enough to qualify me for the first magistracy here. But some folks whom you see almost every day have tried to propagate in some parts of this county that I am without property. I believe that I can still compare with any of my brother candidates. This electioneering has grown a vile business. Let us not any more reproach Great Britain for their practices; they are more open and manly. When we next meet, put me in mind to show you Dr. [William] Eustis' letter and my answer.[2] I think the choice of Electors for President etc. is good. The election of a Representative in this district is at present very undetermined.

1. RC, Hugh Upham Clark Collection, Arlington, Va. The letter was written to the "Honble. Judge Wendell." The recipient was evidently Oliver Wendell, Jackson's brother-in-law, who was one of the "Justices of the Peace throughout the Commonwealth" in 1788.
2. See Eustis to Jackson, 6 December, and Jackson to Eustis, December, printed above in The First Election in Essex District.

Herald of Freedom, 16 January

From the diversity of opinions no choice of a Representative to the federal Congress has taken place in this district. Charity, says a correspondent, [induces?] the belief that all the freemen were actuated by [good?] motives in the bestowment of their suffrages; and it is hoped that they will see the necessity of uniting in their votes, in order that a man may be introduced to office who is every way adequate to the performance of the important duty which must fall to the share of a federal Representative to perform. Let us look through our district, and examine the characters of such as are candidates for the office before mentioned; and after scrutinizing them, let any unprejudiced elector say, whether there is a man more suitable to represent this district in the new Congress, than the Hon. Jonathan Jackson, Esq., a man whose integrity and abilities have heretofore recommended him to the notice of his fellow citizens. In this gentleman may we all unite. His conduct will doubtless be such as to justify our choice, and do honor to those whose suffrages may appoint him their delegate.[1]

1. The article was dated Newburyport, 8 January. See also the *Essex Journal*, 21 January, for a similar item in Jackson's behalf.

Massachusetts Centinel, 17 January

An Essex correspondent wishes right ideas may be had respecting the ensuing election. Messrs. [Benjamin] Goodhue and [Jonathan] Jackson have been published as the candidates.[1] He however informs, that Mr. [Nathan] Dane had 295, and Dr. [Samuel] Holten 182 votes, and are also candidates.[2]

1. This refers to the election precepts issued by Governor Hancock calling a second election in Essex District. The Massachusetts Election Resolutions of 20 November (printed above) required the Governor in issuing precepts for runoff elections to publish the names of the two men receiving the highest number of votes in the preceding election—in this case, Goodhue and Jackson. No precept for Essex District has been located, but for the form, see the election precept issued for Northampton, 6 January, printed above in The Official Results of the First Election, 5—10 January 1789.

2. Samuel Holten received 202 votes.

Middlesex Essex, Herald of Freedom, 20 January (excerpt)[1]

It appears to me, you *"Boston folks are full of notions."* Is it not a little curious you should recommend in your papers the Hon. J[onathan] J[ackson], Esq., as a proper person for a federal Representative for Essex?[2] Is not this the man that was copartner with a certain merchant, distinguished for his *contemptible opinion of the people*? Has not this same J[ackson] drank deep of the political sentiments of "S.H." [Stephen Higginson]? Did he not lately remove from the capital to Newburyport in hopes of obtaining some office? Is he not the author of an infamous pamphlet[3] lately published, wherein the ax is laid at the root of the tree, *to deprive the people of all their liberties*? Do you think *the people* will give their suffrages for one, who looks upon them with such contempt as is exhibited in this book? No! May the man and his book be treated with the contempt they deserve. To recommend such characters is very alarming. *Some* of you in town, assisted by all the old Tories and refugees coming in among you, may have influence enough to obtain a majority, *a very small majority* of votes for similar characters, but pray let us alone. We mean to support such men as will *stand up for the people*, and maintain their liberties. Such a man is the Hon. Benjamin Goodhue, Esq. This gentleman will undoubtedly obtain a large majority of votes for Essex District.[4]

1. This item was preceded by a brief paragraph addressed to the printer of the *Herald*: "Some folks say you are [———] partial in your publications; to convince them of the contrary, publish the following copy of a letter from an honest mechanic in the country, to his friend in town—and you will oblige many of your readers, in particular your correspondent W."

2. See the *Herald of Freedom*, 16 January, printed above.

3. See headnote to The First Election in Essex District, 18 December, printed above.

4. The remainder of the article dealt with the election in Middlesex District and is printed below in The Second Election in Middlesex District. For replies to "Middlesex Essex," see "A Federalist," *Herald of Freedom*, 23 January, and "An Elector of Essex," *Essex Journal*, 28 January, printed below.

An Observer, Independent Chronicle, 22 January (excerpt)

In Essex the people are divided between a number of candidates. The Hon. Benjamin Goodhue, Esq., and Hon. Samuel Holten, Esq., appear to be the idols of their respective parties. The latter of these gentlemen has, from the beginning, been practiced in public and national affairs, and his acknowledged abilities, and acquaintance with the general principles of politics and legislation, gave him great advantage, and were of much benefit to the state. The former has not been to Congress, but has for several years been a member of the General Court, and is supposed to be well acquainted with the principles of commerce. He will be supported chiefly by the maritime towns, while his rival will be the favorite of the landed interest. In the other districts which have not yet come to a choice, the landed property predominates; all the persons in nomination are of this description.[1]

1. Other excerpts from this item, headed "The Present State of Parties," are printed below in the sections on the second elections in Middlesex, Worcester, and Hampshire-Berkshire districts. In the first portion of the article, "An Observer" contends that there was general agreement that the Constitution needed to be amended.

A Federalist, Herald of Freedom, 23 January

When the sluices of detraction are once opened, it is impossible to tell who will not become subject to defamation from the pen of slander, and who will escape the envenomed shafts of malice, which are hurled indiscriminately among all orders, ranks and characters. Tis true, the man of integrity, whose conscience vindicates his conduct, and whose heart tells him he is treading the path of rectitude, may hope to escape the rude blast of scurrility and move secure from the attacks of the veiled defamer; but it is equally true, that he who sets out to promote the interest of a party, or exalt the leaders of a junto, pays no regard to decency, to virtue or even common honesty, and will level an attack against an unblemished character, equally as soon as against one of the most vile. An instance of this may be seen in the *Herald* of the 20th inst. There the Hon. J[onathan] J[ackson] is most scandalously reviled by a poltroon who is not deserving the title of a rational being.[1] Instead of the production alluded to being the composition of an *"honest mechanic in the country,"* I venture to assert it to be the mere vent of a despairing wretch, who trembles for the fate of amendments, which are the offspring of Antifederalism. Mr. Jackson is revered and beloved wherever he is known. Amiable in the private and honest and upright in the public walks of life, his abilities are inferior to few among us, and his patriotism and love of his country indubitably established on a firm foundation. These things are well known to the free electors of Essex, and it cannot be doubted but they will so far show their attachment to merit, and firm Federalism, as to unanimously bestow their suffrages in favor of the Hon. Jonathan Jackson, Esq., as a Federal delegate from that district to the new Congress.

1. See "Middlesex Essex," *Herald of Freedom*, 20 January, printed above.

A Federal Elector, Salem Mercury, 27 January[1]

It is certainly of the greatest consequence to this district, that it should have a Representative in Congress, who is acquainted with the principles of commerce, and, more especially, who thoroughly understands the value and importance of the fisheries—that nursery of seamen and source of wealth. The towns of Salem, Marblehead, Beverly, Manchester, Gloucester, Ipswich, and Newburyport, which more immediately depend on this branch of business, will therefore, no doubt, exert themselves to effect the choice of the Hon. Benjamin Goodhue to that office, he being the only candidate concerned in it (or, I believe, in any species of navigation) and who *experimentally* knows its importance. However persons less interested in it might be influenced, *this* gentleman could never consent to a treaty with Great Britain, or any other nation, which would relinquish our right to the fisheries, without consenting to a sacrifice of the means of his own prosperity—a measure which we were in great hazard of being adopted as the price of the late treaty of peace.[2]

Nor can the respectable yeomanry of the district be less interested in the choice of Mr. Goodhue. The value of their estates depends greatly on the success of our navigation. And, besides, Mr. Goodhue is known to possess a just respect for the landed interest, and to be ever ready to allow it that weight in the scale of public measures, which all thorough politicians acknowledge it deserves.

We do not find, Messrs. Printers, in making the comparison desired in your last, between Mr. [Jonathan] Jackson and Mr. Goodhue, that the latter suffers thereby in any one point.[3] Both are esteemed for their many private and public virtues, and it is an honor to the district that such worthy characters are likely to divide its votes. But, allowing them to be equally deserving, does not Newburyport afford one member of Congress (Mr. [Tristram] Dalton), and shall not this part of the district, also, have the same privilege, that the interests of the whole district may be represented? *Other* considerations balancing, *this* ought to turn the scale.

We see, then, that the interests of our trade, our fisheries, and our lands may be safely trusted to Mr. Goodhue, who has so faithfully supported them in our General Court, many years; and, certainly, candor and fair dealing will allow this part of the district to furnish a Representative, as another part affords a Senator.

. . . .

N.B. In the late returns of votes for federal Representative,

Mr. Goodhue had	569
Mr. Jackson	390
Which gives Mr. Goodhue an excess of	179

1. This item was dated Salem, 24 January.
2. For another essay supporting Goodhue on similar grounds, see "An Elector to the Inhabitants of Salem," *Salem Mercury*, 27 January.
3. This refers to a brief, unsigned paragraph dated Newburyport, 8 January, in the *Salem Mercury* of 20 January, which urged voters to "examine the characters of such as are candidates" and to support Jackson.

An Elector of Essex, Essex Journal, 28 January

In the last week's *Herald* an insignificant writer has had the effrontery to prostitute the name of this county, and that of Middlesex, at once; to stamp a value on the contemptible labors of his pen.[1] That he is not the *honest mechanic of Lynn*, whom his friend W. would represent him, is fully proved out of his own mouth. To every impartial reader he will appear to have [but?] slender claims to *honesty*, or any other quality usually found [allied?] to it. Nothing in his work shines so illustrious as his rancorous spite against the federal government of America—his impotent [nuance?] against some of the most respectable characters, and his singular arrogance in presuming to dictate to two of the principal counties in the commonwealth, what men they must elect to represent them in the national assembly, and whom they must reject. With the affront he has dared to offer to Middlesex I shall not interfere—that respectable county does not want citizens of her own to chastise his insolence; but as a freeman of the county of Essex, I resent the insults of the first part of its piece, while I despise the spirit with which they are offered.

For the person and character of Mr. [Benjamin] Goodhue I entertain proper esteem; nor would I wish to derogate a tittle from the honors due to him. But when he is to be obtruded on me in preference to Mr. [Jonathan] Jackson, as a federal Representative, I think his own judgment will approve my resentment.

Mr. Jackson pledged his life and fortune in his country's cause by the most open and decisive conduct, both in his own town and in the public councils of the state, at that early *crisis which tried men's souls*, when men of more selfish cunning, and less patriotism, hid themselves in the privacy of retirement. His fellow citizens in Newburyport will not soon forget the wisdom and firmness, with which he forwarded their exertions in the years 1775, 1776, and 1777. Nor can his compatriots in the Provincial Congress and General Court, in that period, ever lose the impressions made by some of his speeches on the most trying occasions. They know that among the number who composed their body, none studied harder, none wrote or labored more, and none rendered more effectual service to his distressed country than Mr. Jackson. In all the storms of state, which turned so many of his contemporaries aside, he steered the course of an able statesman, and a fixed patriot. His principles were unshaken and his conduct uniform. Offices of profit or honor he never courted, and not a little of his own estate was freely spent in his country's service. A liberal education, improved by a long course of diligent study, has furnished him with qualifications fit for any trust the public has to repose. His knowledge in all the interests of this nation, acquired by the closest attention while a member of Congress, has been greatly enlarged by his tour of Europe. His acquaintance with the commercial and landed interest of his country renders him worthy of the suffrages and confidence of both; and without disparagement, I will venture to affirm, that among the candidates that have been his competitors on this occasion, there is not one possessed of so many things desirable in a federal Representative, and those mixed with so few of a contrary nature.

Of this we need no better proof than the miserable shifts to which the scribbler is reduced, who undertakes to traduce him. It is evident he has racked his invention, and raked up all he could think a matter of slander. And let us see the mouse which this laboring mountain has brought forth! Why, all his mighty crimes are reduced to these three. He was a partner in trade with a certain merchant, who had a contemptible opinion of some people.[2] He quitted Boston when his business no longer required his stay there, and returned to his former place of abode, where lay his estate, and where his family connections and friends chiefly dwelt. To these charges common sense requires no answers. The public will be at no loss to conclude that if the spirit which retails them could have found matters of more weight against Mr. J., it would not have failed to allege them.

As to his being the author of an obnoxious pamphlet on politics, I presume it is a matter as much a secret to this writer, as to me. If he means that, lately published under the signature of *A native of Boston*,[3] since the author is not announced, neither we, nor the public have a right to say who he is; but this I will venture to affirm, that whoever he be, the best judges will pronounce him a man of sense, well versed in the politics both of Europe and America, and a [———] [———] to the liberty and union of those states. It is a work of which no genius among us need blush to be reputed the author; and I doubt not I shall have the concurrence of the body of the electors in the county of Essex, when I declare for myself, that if I knew the author of that pamphlet, and knew no other objections to his character, I should not scruple to give him my suffrage for a seat in the national legislature; merely on the evidence it gives of enlarged acquaintance with matters of state, impartial views of the interest of this country, and warm attachment to its glory and happiness.

1. See "Middlesex Essex," *Herald of Freedom*, 20 January, printed above.
2. Stephen Higginson.
3. For Jackson's pamphlet, see the headnote to The First Election in Essex District, 18 December, printed above.

Diary of Benjamin Goodhue, Thursday, 29 January[1]

I was elected by a majority of two-thirds of Essex District their Representative in Congress under government.

1. Copy, Extracts from the Diary of Benjamin Goodhue, NNS.

Jonathan Jackson to Oliver Wendell, Newburyport, 5 February (excerpt)[1]

I hope that Mr. Lawrence will be returned by next week and bring me some money from Prentice or at the least a letter mentioning what prospect he has of collecting any. Do send the money that may come by Mr. Parsons, March, or any safe hand or in bank bills by letter, for I cannot move without it. The last month has been the most embarrassed or rather the most mortifying, for want of that *unum necessarium*, of any I ever yet experienced; and the tide, I hope, is at its lowest ebb. Without money, character abused, election lost, cold weather and some comfortables wanting is a gloomy picture. Still I will not despair, for I flatter myself that upon the whole my *reputation* has mended by the scrutiny. And if Washington and Adams are to be the men, as tonight we hear is determined in this state, the general weal, I augur, will be well managed and the whole thrive if I must sink—which I do not yet intend to.

1. RC, Hugh Upham Clark Collection, Arlington, Va. The manuscript contains only the salutation "Dear Sir" to indicate the recipient. However, "To Oliver Wendell Fort Hill Boston" is written on the margin in another hand.

Official Election Returns, 7 February

ESSEX DISTRICT, 29 JANUARY

Town	Hon. Benjamin Goodhue, Esq.	Hon. Jonathan Jackson, Esq.	Hon. Nathan Dane, Esq.	Hon. Samuel Holten, Esq.	Dr. Daniel Killham
Salem	529	8			
Danvers	95				
Newbury	63	5			
Newburyport	19	174			
Beverly	47	80			
Ipswich	71	12		1	
Marblehead	3	421	1		
Gloucester	218				
Lynn	38				
Lynnfield	27				
Andover	106				
Rowley	32				
Topsfield	40				3
Haverhill	64	2			
Salisbury	22				
Amesbury	9	6			
Boxford	20				
Bradford	40				
Methuen	25			2	

(Table continued on following page)

ESSEX DISTRICT, 29 JANUARY *(continued)*

Town	Hon. Benjamin Goodhue, Esq.	Hon. Jonathan Jackson, Esq.	Hon. Nathan Dane, Esq.	Hon. Samuel Holten, Esq.	Dr. Daniel Killham
Wenham					
Manchester	4	16			
Middleton					
Totals	1472	724	1	3	3

Votes cast: 2203
Majority required: 1102

Governor and Council Record the Votes in the Second Election in Essex District, Monday, 9 February[1]

The Governor and Council upon the examination of the returns from the district[s] of Essex, Middlesex, Worcester, Hampshire and Berkshire, who did not on the first election make choice of Representatives to represent them in the Congress of the United States, found them to stand as follows, viz.

District of Essex. Number of voters, 2203; [to] make a choice, 1102. Hon. Benjamin Goodhue, Esq., had 1472 and is chosen.

1. Council Records, XXXI, 8, M-Ar.

The Second Election in Middlesex District, 29 January

The campaign for the second election got underway before the votes for the first election were recorded officially on 6 January 1789. The Boston newspapers, which virtually ignored Middlesex District before 18 December, thereafter devoted almost as much space to it as they had to the Suffolk election. The central issue, as far as the Boston newspapers were concerned, was the candidacy of Elbridge Gerry and the fact that he supported amendments to the Constitution.

The Federalists, according to the newspapers, had great difficulty in deciding which of several candidates would run or, if elected, which ones would serve. The Antifederalists had difficulty of another sort: most of them evidently supported Gerry, who insisted that he was not a candidate. Gerry, however, never said flatly that he would not accept if elected, although Federalist newspaper writers insisted that he had done so.

Gerry won overwhelmingly, receiving more than three times the votes given the nearest contender, Joseph B. Varnum, and more than five times the votes cast for William Hull, whom the Boston newspapers finally settled upon as *the* Federalist candidate.

Adolphus, Independent Chronicle, 1 January

Fellow Citizens.

There is an over-ruling Providence in all things, and the mercies of Heaven, and the kind superintendency of the Most High, are always observable in the affairs of our free, rising, and happy country. Here religious and political freedom are to flourish, and the machinations of wicked, and ambitious men, or the temporary follies of anarchy, can never prevail against them.

The reasons of my addressing you at this time is, because you have *happily, yet*, the election of the Representative for your county before you. I say *happily*, because the tumult of the ambitious; the overbearing of the proud, aristocratical gentry, who think the yeomanry of the country unfit, totally unfit, to have any part in the government; and the many idle and worthless minions, who expect an unearned living from the industry of the people, have long borne down the sacred freedom of elections, and nearly distracted the people with abuse, and misrepresentation. But the hour of cool consideration has arrived, and your ears will be open to truth, and your hearts capable of conviction.

The Honorable Elbridge Gerry, of Cambridge, stands very high on the list of votes which is returned from your county, but he is objected to as an Antifederalist, and therefore said to be unfit to represent you in Congress. You will give me your candid attention while I examine this objection, having first given a description of the political character of the man.

In the year 1774, Mr. Gerry, being as he now is, a man of generous fortune, and a liberal education, he had no place to seek, no debts to pay, or avoid, nor any post to wish for. He embraced the cause of his country, and risked his life, and fortune, from the purest principles of patriotism, and the most ardent, and disinterested love to his fellow citizens. Those who were with him in the Provincial Congress, and in the General Court, in the years 1774, 1775, and 1776, are witnesses to his unshaken firmness, and distinguished abilities. Take not the word of an unknown writer for this; there is not a town in your county which has not many witnesses on this head—*ask them*. From the year 1777 he has been constantly employed in public, and generally in the Congress of the United States, and no day has passed without exhibiting the highest proofs of his zeal for, and ability in, the interest of the states in general, and this state in particular. And it is well known that no man possessed more entirely the confidence of the people than he did, until October 1787.

We will now inquire by what fault of his, he has in any degree lost this confidence; and should it appear, that it was by *honesty, united with an ardent love for the liberty, and political happiness of his fellow citizens, you will certainly restore him.*

He was a member from this state, appointed to meet in a general Convention, to *revise the Confederation*. When that body met, they, instead of a revision of the Confederation, agreed upon a new form of government for the United States. Whether this was within their commission, or whether that was a good, or bad form of government, we have now no authority to decide; it is adopted by more than nine states, and is to be carried into force, and execution. Mr. Gerry did not approve of it. He had honor and integrity enough, to declare his sentiments. He foresaw undoubtedly, from divers circumstances peculiar to that crisis, that he should lose a share of his popularity, but he knew that an honest man like a light substance overwhelmed by a flood would finally rise on the surface of the public opinion. But how was he criminal in holding an opinion, that the system was an imperfect one? His worst enemies never dared to charge him with a wish to avoid or overthrow government. The objection to his being your Representative is, that he will boldly attempt to procure amendments to this Constitution, and you may feel yourselves assured that if you choose him, he will exert himself for that purpose. But then they say, if he would do this, he is an Antifederalist, and is not to be trusted. Let us examine this, and see with what face some of them can bring it as an accusation.

In the county of Middlesex, there were seventeen members in the [state] Convention in favor of ratifying the Constitution, and twenty-five against it; of the county of Worcester there were seven members for it, and forty-three against it; in the whole Convention, there were one hundred and eighty-seven for, and one hundred and sixty-eight against it, although it was proposed with such amendments as essentially altered it for the better. We might suppose that on such a division as this, one might decently utter an opinion in favor of amendments, without being liable to such torrents of abuse, as have been retailed in the paper called the [Massachusetts] Centinel, and of which Governor [George] Clinton, Governor [Edmund] Randolph, Governor [John] Hancock, and others of the first patriots in the country have in some measure been the objects.

When Governor Hancock proposed the amendments in Convention, the Honorable S[amuel] Adams said "a proposal of this sort coming from Massachusetts, from her importance, will have its weight. It appears to me that such a measure will have the most salutary effect throughout the Union. I apprehend, sir, that these states will be influenced by the proposition."[1] But who will mind him? He is a son of liberty! Young Mr. [James] Bowdoin [Jr.] said that "he could not but express his approbation of the propositions made by His Excellency."[2] He added, "Your Excellency's propositions, are calculated to quiet the apprehensions of gentlemen, lest Congress should exercise an unreasonable control over the state legislatives, with regard to the times, places and manner of holding elections, which by the 4th section of the first article, are prescribed, etc. I have had my fears lest this control should infringe the freedom of elections, which ought ever to be held sacred."[3] The Honorable Judge [Increase] Sumner said "that the probability was very great, that if the amendments proposed were recommended by this Convention, that they would, on the first meeting of Congress, be adopted by the general government."[4] The Honorable Judge [Francis] Dana proposed and carried a very important article in the proposal for amendments, respecting a requisition on the states, before Congress assessed a tax upon them, and said that "the proposal contained the amendments generally wished for" and that "if they were recommended to be adopted by the Convention it was very probable that two-thirds of Congress would concur in proposing them."[5] The Hon. Mr. [Caleb] Strong went into a particular discussion of the several amendments recommended in the proposition submitted by His Excellency, each of which he considered with much attention. He anticipated the good effects it must have in conciliating the various sentiments of gentlemen upon the subject, and expressed his firm belief that if it was recommended by the Convention, IT WOULD BE INSERTED IN THE CONSTITUTION; Mr. [Theophilus] Parsons, Colonel [Azor] Orne, Hon. Mr. [William] Phillips, and others spoke in favor of the proposition as a conciliatory measure, *and the probability of the amendments being adopted.*"[6] Doctor [Charles] Jarvis said, "there has scarcely been an instance where the influence of Massachusetts has not been felt, and acknowledged in the Union. In such a case her voice will be heard, sir, and I am fully in sentiment if the *amendments* are not engrafted on the Constitution, it will be our own fault."[7] Mr. [Fisher] Ames observed, "that the mode of obtaining amendments is pointed out in the Constitution itself; if, however, there was an irregularity in the proceeding, the General Court would not delay to confirm it."[8] Mr. [Charles] Turner said "in my judgment there is a rational probability, a moral certainty, that the proposed amendments will meet the approbation of the several states in the Union."[9]

It would be too much to detail all that was said in favor of amendments; what I have mentioned is taken from the printed proceedings of the Convention, where much more remains of the same tenor.

Finally, the Convention adopted the form of government, by a small majority, with the most solemn injunctions upon the Representatives of the commonwealth in Congress, to exert their influence to obtain the proposed alterations, and amendments.

Were these men sincere, or were they jesting with the people? If they were honest, and sincere, why should there be an objection to Mr. Gerry because he is in favor of these amendments and alterations? These men, or some of them, at least, spoke their sentiments, but there are others who having obtained a vote for a ratification, now laugh at amendments, and revile everyone who is in favor of them; but you my fellow citizens know your friends. Your eyes are now opened by the perfidy and duplicity of men, who are too lazy to dig, and are ashamed to beg. But Mr. Gerry loves the people too well to participate in wealth arising from their misery, and so you are not to vote for him.

There is neither policy or propriety in this violent opposition to amendments. Three-quarters of the people in this commonwealth expect them to be attempted. The general assemblies of Virginia, and the Convention of New York, two very important states, have written circular letters in favor of them. The two Northern States, and one of the Southern, have ratified the Constitution by a small majority, and on the express stipulation of exertions for alterations. Six other states have adopted it, generally by small majorities, but all in consideration, that there could be amendments made. North Carolina and Rhode Island have rejected it. In this situation, is it wise to make such a violent opposition to the sense and understanding of so large a majority?[10]

1. See Convention, *Debates*, 226–27.

2. Ibid., 228.

3. These remarks were made by Samuel Adams in a speech that followed the one by James Bowdoin, Jr. Ibid., 233–34.

4. Ibid., 240.

5. Ibid., 241.
6. Ibid., 243.
7. Ibid., 256.
8. Ibid., 258.
9. Ibid., 274.
10. For another item supporting Gerry on 1 January, see the *Herald of Freedom*. For answers to "Adolphus" see "Cambridge" and "An Elector," *Massachusetts Centinel*, 7 and 10 January, printed below.

James Sullivan to Elbridge Gerry, Boston, 2 January[1]

I have your favor of this day, and for the reasons I shall mention shall defer applying to the printers as you direct until I hear further from you.

That you are a candidate for Representative in the county of Middlesex is very true, and it is no less certain that you will be elected unless you take pains to prevent it. The whole county (nearly) will be for you.

I conceive that you will do your country a great injury by withdrawing yourself at this crisis. There are a number who are wickedly deceiving the people but their day is nearly over. Should they not meet a speedy check they will involve the county in civil wars and bloody controversies. Perhaps this might cure the people of their credulous follies, but you know, sir, that when matters arrive at this dangerous extreme we know not where they will stop. Perhaps such a controversy may be made the excuse for establishing the tyranny which was begun by excuse of the late insurrections. We who saw each other in '75 will appear very awkward under the feet of a tyrant. Should you now decline to serve your country I think you may [———] a great while if you should live to repent of it. The ambitions and wishes of your friends and party have a claim upon you and it shall not be given over without further orders. Let us have the pleasure of beating those madmen in elections if you refuse afterwards. Please to render our compliments agreeable to Mrs. Gerry and [Hugh?] Thompson and believe me to be your friend.

1. RC?, Gerry Papers, DLC. The letter was dated 2 January 1788 but was obviously written in 1789.

Benjamin Lincoln to George Washington, Boston, 4 January (excerpt)[1]

In Middlesex Mr. [Elbridge] Gerry stands high, perhaps the highest, and Mr. [Nathaniel] Gorham next. Mr. Gorham suggested to his friends that he would not accept the appointment or probably he would have been elected. [John] Brooks[2] and [William] Hull are put up. One or the other will be pushed the next attempt.

1. RC, Washington Papers, DLC.
2. On the same day Henry Jackson reported to Henry Knox: "If our friend Brooks will go, it's only for him to say so. He can be chosen in that district" (Boston, RC, Knox Papers, MHi). Brooks's candidacy soon ended, for the *Massachusetts Centinel* announced on 7 January that Brooks would not serve if elected and urged all his supporters to vote for William Hull.

A Moderate Man of Middlesex, Boston Gazette, 5 January

Several late papers have propagated a report that James Winthrop, Esq., is the probable successor to the professorship vacated by Mr. [Samuel] Williams. I have not heard any one express a doubt of the propriety of such an appointment, and the public voice proclaims his qualifications for such an office. But all that are acquainted with him know, that his talents are not confined within the limits of mathematical studies. He has on several occasions been eminently serviceable in preserving the public tranquility; and that he has a large share of the confidence of the people, in this district, is evident from the unsolicited votes which several towns have bestowed upon him for their federal Representative, and the pleasure manifested by the inhabitants of many other towns, on account of such a nomination, and their declared intention of supporting it. It is therefore not improbable that he may be called to exercise his abilities to greater extent than in the Chapel of the University.[1]

1. This seems to have been the only newspaper item written in behalf of James Winthrop, an Antifederalist, who received 82 votes in the second Middlesex election. Winthrop, who had once been librarian of Harvard, did not succeed Williams in the Hollis Professorship of Mathematics and Natural Philosophy.

Cambridge to the Printer, Massachusetts Centinel, 7 January

Although it is confessed on all hands, that in point of ability, and argument, the junto are much inferior, it must be acknowledged, that in point of candor, they beat all—nay, even beggar candor itself. An instance of it we had retailed from the paper, called the *Chronicle*, on Thursday, where one Mr. Adolphus[1] complains bitterly of the abuse, which, he says, has been levelled at the "sticklers for amendments" in the papers. Yes, sir, this very Adolphus, I repeat it, complains of abuse, in the very piece which contains the following liberal and candid paragraph:

"The reason of my addressing you at this time" says this votary to candor, "is because you have happily, yet, the election of a Representative for your county before you. I say *happily*, because the tumult of the AMBITIOUS, the OVERBEARING of the PROUD, ARISTOCRATICAL GENTRY, who think the yeomanry of the country unfit, TOTALLY UNFIT to have any, *any part* in *the government*, and the many IDLE and WORTHLESS MINIONS, who expect an *unearned living* from the *industry of the people*, have LONG BORN[E] DOWN THE FREEDOM OF ELECTIONS, and *nearly distracted* the people with ABUSE and MISREPRESENTATION."

Here, Mr. Russell, is the very quintessence of liberality—untinctured by even the shadow of abuse. Writers of this cast, say they cannot abuse—and, indeed, "if they be measured rightly," I am of their opinion.

It must be confessed, however, that Governor [George] Clinton has, by the Federalists, been called, a "stickler for previous amendments"—but nothing else. Compare this with the above specimen, and how *intolerably "abusive"* it appears.

Now, though these candid gentlemen of the junto may, in the goodness of their hearts, call a man, "nearsighted"—"low born"—"son of an almanac

maker"[2]—"seeker"—"one too lazy to dig, and to beg ashamed"—"minion, etc.,"
yet, Falstaff-like, they aver it is no abuse—"no abuse, Hal"—nothing but *argument*; and, therefore, when *"amendment sticklers,"* or Antifederalists, are retorted on them, they raise a hue and cry, and the whole *posse* are set to work to bespatter and traduce the appellator—as if the name of *amendmentite* was disgraceful and opprobrious.

Though Mr. Adolphus so strenuously recommends Mr. [Elbridge] Gerry as a person who will exert himself to procure amendments; yet it is conjectured, that a great majority of the electors in this district are firmly of the opinion, that the Hon. John Brooks, Esq.,[3] is by far a better man to represent them in the Congress of the United States, and for executing a Constitution of government which has been ratified by the people, than him.

Where Mr. Gerry is best known, it is said, he has the smallest number of votes. Now, I do not aver this to be the truth, but this I can say, that although a resident, he had but three votes out of seventy-one in the town of Cambridge.

1. See the *Independent Chronicle*, 1 January, printed above.
2. See "Bostoniensis," *Boston Gazette*, 29 December 1788, printed above in The Election in Suffolk District.
3. This issue of the *Centinel* also contained an item stating that Brooks would not accept if elected and urging his supporters to give their votes to William Hull. For similar difficulties concerning Nathaniel Gorham and Hull, see "An Elector" and "Middlesex" in the *Centinel*, 10 January, printed below.

Samuel Dexter to Elbridge Gerry, Weston, 8 January[1]

I know not whether you would accept of a seat in Congress; but am certain many in the state wished you might be elected a Senator, and now are very desirous you may be one of the Representatives. A number of this town gave their suffrages for you, at the meeting on the 18th of December last, several of whom were induced to vote by my assuring them that you did not wish to annihilate the new Constitution for the United States, as they had heard, but only to amend it, as proposed; that I had had opportunity, in some measure, to become acquainted with your political principles, and would engage for your being in favor of such a government as, while it would be sufficiently energetic, would also effectually preserve the liberties of the people. If you will favor me with only three lines upon the subject it shall be made no ill use of. *Sat verbum.*[2]

P.S. I only want to be able to say—I have seen a letter from Mr. G,[3] in which were sentiments similar to those I assured you he entertained respecting the Constitution, when we met last time to choose a Rep[resentative].

1. RC, Gerry Papers, MHi. Dexter was a member of the Massachusetts House of Representatives in 1789. After Gerry refused to run for reelection in 1792, Dexter was elected as a Federalist from Middlesex District.
2. See Gerry's reply, 12 January, printed below.
3. This was probably Nathaniel Gorham, who received the most votes in the first Middlesex election on 18 December.

An Elector, Massachusetts Centinel, 10 January

If Adolphus[1] meant to be a real friend to Mr. [Elbridge] Gerry, he would have injured him less, if he had embraced the good policy which his other friends have more wisely found expedient, and have considered his political character like the old emission money, as dead and buried, and its friends out of mourning. He would then have saved him the fresh opprobrium that his publication must carry to every mind that knows the character of Mr. G. And I am mistaken if it gains anything on examination.

It is extraordinary enough, that since Mr. G's conduct and principles have been so publicly traced, and found to be in professed enmity to the new Constitution, that so many voters in the county of Middlesex could be found to support his interest, and especially when opposed to so honest and able a man as Mr. [Nathaniel] Gorham.[2] But it is much more extraordinary that anyone should come forward to the bar of a public chronicle, and tell the electors of Middlesex that Mr. Gerry must be their man—that Mr. Gerry with "a generous fortune early embraced the cause of his country; with no debts to pay or avoid; nor any post to wish for"—"that he risked his life and fortune from the purest principles of patriotism, and the most disinterested love to his fellow citizens."

This farrago would have sounded well enough in 1775 or 1776, when enthusiasm sanctified the extravagant pretensions of every hypocrite, and when no man dared to act or think different from the current principles of the times. Such language might yet find attention in Bedlam, and if it serves to exercise the imagination, or please the fancy of Adolphus, it still has its uses. But the man has more understanding than to suppose that a single elector in the county of Middlesex has faith enough to swallow such a dose, and it is a phenomenon in human understanding, if Adolphus himself believes one single article of it. "Mr. Gerry," he says, "did not approve of the Constitution, and had honor and integrity enough to declare his sentiments—that he foresaw that he should lose a share of his popularity, but, he knew that an honest man would finally rise on the surface of public opinion."

If we may judge of Mr. G's apprehension of the unpopularity of his conduct, by his pompous letter to the General Court, announcing his approach to their capital, and the exercise of his commission,[3] and by the frequent seditious publications of his advocates, we must differ in opinion from Adolphus. And I believe that three-fourths of Massachusetts are fully satisfied that his opposition to the Constitution originated in a calculation of popularity, the success of which may have then appeared quite problematical to small calculators; and in the drooping state of his character, it was the best chance he could hope for to recover himself. But alas it failed him.

Adolphus holds out, "that the objection to Mr. Gerry as a Representative is, that he would be for amendments." It is happy for the country, and I dare say for the county of Middlesex, that such sophistry is too feeble to deceive common sense. What sort of amendments would Mr. Gerry aim at? Where would they terminate? I answer that he would probably pursue amendments until nothing of the original was left. But admitting that he embraces the same system of amendments that so many of our worthiest characters have countenanced, what then? Would any man trust an infant as readily in the power of a domesticated tiger, as he would with a lamb? There can be no necessity to trust what has been dangerous, and may again be so. It is much more rational and prudent to trust the man who has before conducted aright, than to take a hazard with one that has conducted oppositely. For the honor, safety, and welfare of the commonwealth, that so much depend on the energetic execution of the new government, it is most devoutly to be wished, that no Antifederal clog will find admission in it, and that the free electors of Middlesex will unite their voices for a Federal character—a man of unquestioned honor and integrity—a man that dares appeal to his native town and county for his public and private character. Such a man is Mr. Gorham.[4]

1. See the *Independent Chronicle*, 1 January, printed above.

2. This issue of the *Centinel*, like that of the 7th, which urged the voters to support both John Brooks and William Hull, must have confused the voters. The *Centinel* now urged support for Nathaniel Gorham (although the *Independent Chronicle* had announced on the 8th that he would not accept election) and again urged the voters to support William Hull. Actually, it had been known privately since early December that Gorham would not run (Henry Jackson to Henry Knox, 6 December, printed above).

3. For Gerry's letter to the General Court, 18 October 1787, see Max Farrand, ed., *The Records of the Federal Convention of 1787* (rev. ed., 4 vols., New Haven, Conn., 1937), III, 128—29.

4. When Gerry received a copy of the *Centinel* with the above piece by "An Elector," he at once wrote a letter to publisher Benjamin Russell demanding the name of the author (Cambridge, 13 January, ADS, Gerry Papers, MHi). He also wrote an address "To the Public" (ALS, Benjamin Franklin Collection, CtY), in which he defended his record and attacked "An Elector" as "a base calumniator, who without decency or veracity wishes to reduce to *his level* everyone who differs from his extravagant notions of politics." It would appear that Gerry did not send either the letter or the address to the *Centinel*. At least there is no reference to either item in the *Centinel* or in the other Boston newspapers. His more temperate address to the electors of Middlesex District was published in the *Independent Chronicle* on 22 January (printed below).

Middlesex, Massachusetts Centinel, 10 January[1]

As a majority of our votes have been given to Federal characters, it is evident your general determination is to be represented by a Federalist. The misfortune is that in being divided with respect to the man, our object has been lost. The Antifederalists have discovered more policy by bestowing *all their votes on one man*. And unless we follow their example in this instance, there is every probability that they will succeed, while we are disappointed.

Unite therefore at the next election. Let all our votes be bestowed on one man, and let that man be Brigadier General William Hull. We will thus defeat the designs of the enemies to the new Constitution, and have the satisfaction of being represented by an able and upright Federalist.

1. This article was addressed "To the Electors of the County of Middlesex" and dated 8 January.

Henry Jackson to Henry Knox, Boston, 11 January (excerpt)[1]

... Middlesex would certainly and without the least doubt choose our friend *General J*[ohn] *Brooks* but he positively declines going, and it is not in the power of any of his friends to alter his mind. Mr. [Joseph B.] *Varnum* will not be chosen for the district, as he is disliked by both parties. It will therefore lay between General [William] *Hull* and Mr. [Elbridge] Gerry. The Fed[eral] interest is, and will be in favor of our friend Hull. Altho Mr. [Nathaniel] Gorham gave out publicly and in the most positive manner before he set out for New York that he would not accept if chosen, yet *the Antis* and friends to Mr. Gerry are holding Mr. Gorham up as a candidate, by which means the *Feds* will be divided between him and Hull, and by that plan Mr. Gerry may possibly gain a majority. If Mr. Gorham is of the same opinion as when he talked with me on the subject, I think it would be best he should make it known, as I find some of *his friends* say he will accept if chosen. If he has altered his mind from what he told me, I will engage Brooks, Hull, and other interest in his favor, and I believe there is no doubt but he will carry all before him, against any interest Mr. Gerry may be able to make. If he still declines, get him to write his friends in favor of Hull.[2]

1. RC, Knox Papers, MHi. The next day Samuel Breck wrote to Knox: "Our mutual friend Jackson has undoubtedly made you acquainted with our federal elections, and which, I presume, are highly pleasing. No *Anties* yet, nor will there be more than *one* [Elbridge Gerry] and his influence very small! The Governor in his message urges amendments, but the committee of the two houses will not *echo* this sentiment" (Boston, 12 January, RC, Knox Papers, MHi).

2. There is no direct evidence to support Jackson's charge that Gerry's supporters were engaging in such tactics. However, see note to "A Countryman," *Boston Gazette,* 26 January, printed below.

Elbridge Gerry to Samuel Dexter, Cambridge, 12 January[1]

I was absent when your letter of the 8th was left at my house, in answer to which I can only inform you, that I am now as I ever have been since the commencement of our independence anxious for an efficient federal government, with every power for promoting the welfare and sufficient *checks* for securing the liberties of the people. The *latter* is what I have contended for, and those who wish to prey on the people by means of a corrupt government are loading me and everyone else who opposes them with anathemas for urging amendments. I consider myself bound by the voice of a majority whether in favor of the Constitution as it now stands or of amendments, but wish not for a seat in the federal legislature and make this communication for your own satisfaction and not to answer any purpose of electioneering. I am no ways concerned at the invectives against myself, for the authors know themselves incapable of supporting it, and the people will in due time be able to determine who are the *real* friends of their liberty.[2]

1. FC, Sang Collection, ICarbS. Although there is no address, the letter is evidently a reply to Samuel Dexter, who asked Gerry for a statement concerning his candidacy (see Dexter to Gerry, 8 January, printed above).

2. For Gerry's public statement defending his record but denying that he is a candidate, see his address "to the Electors of Middlesex," 22 January, printed below.

A Middlesex Elector, Independent Chronicle, 15 January

As the Hon. Mr. [Nathaniel] Gorham, and the Hon. J[ohn] Brooks have respectively declared to their friends, that they could not accept of the office of federal Representative for this district, it is probable, that the votes designed for these gentlemen will be given for William Hull, Esquire.

It is hoped, that the district will *generally* unite in the choice of this gentleman. The man who, in the early part of the late war, took a decided part in his country's cause, who *endured so many hardships, and braved so many dangers*, till we were safely led to independence and peace, will naturally exhibit the same assiduity and zeal, in the cabinet, for the rights and prosperity of his country. None, who knew him, will doubt, that he has that *extensive information*, and *those political abilities*, which a federal Representative should possess.

His particular attachment to *agriculture* and *domestic manufactures*, and his long *known aversion to that system of land tax*, which has involved this state in difficulty and distress, will recommend him to the *virtuous and enlightened yeomanry of Middlesex*. Even the *friends to amendments* would do well to give their votes for a gentleman, who, from his tried patriotism and natural condescension to the *well meant* prejudices of others, would cheerfully exert himself in the national legislature for every alteration in the Federal Constitution, which *impartial enquiry and experience* should point out, as promotive of the general harmony and safety.

The high place, which he has long held in the *private friendship* of General Washington, and his *effectual recommendation* of Mr. Hull to Congress at the commencement of the peace, as the most suitable person to execute, with dignity, fidelity, and address, the *important commission* of *demanding* from the British government the execution of the treaty by an evacuation and delivery of the forts on the lakes, the property of the United States—must be *an additional recommendation*, to *all who love the Political Savior of their country*.[1]

1. For further short items supporting Hull, see the paragraph in the *Herald of Freedom*, 20 January; "extract of a letter" and "A Plain Farmer" in the *Herald*, 23 January; and "Candidus" in the *Massachusetts Centinel*, 24 January.

X to the Electors of Middlesex, Herald of Freedom, 16 January

I am a plain farmer, and meddle but little with politics. When the new Constitution was proposed, I liked it, and from that time to this, have always given my vote for such men as I thought were willing it should have a fair trial. A majority of the electors of Middlesex are, so far as we can judge by the returns of the votes, of the same mind with myself; and the reason we did not carry our choice was not because we were not a majority, but because our votes, though all aimed at the same great object, were scattered on different men. This is a great pity; and to prevent a repetition of this misfortune, I have taken pains to inquire into the nature of the business, both for my own satisfaction and that of my neighbors, and upon the whole I find, that those who mean to destroy the new Constitution ought to vote for Mr. [Elbridge] Gerry. All who are in debt and wish for paper money, all who are for tender acts, all Shayites and such, ought to vote for Mr. Gerry. This is settled. Then the question comes, who are honest men to vote for? The last time, some voted for Mr. [Nathaniel] Gorham, some for General [William] Hull, some for Mr. [Joseph B.] Varnum, and some for General [John] Brooks; all honest, good men; but neither of them had votes enough to make a choice. Now in order not to be balked again, let us join and put all our votes upon one of these four. But the question is, which shall it be. One says one, and another says t'other, but what I say is this: Mr. Gorham is in Congress already; he has been there a good while, and I think long enough; besides, Mr. Gorham has said he could not go if he was chosen; General Brooks says plumply, he won't go; Mr. Varnum is a good senator, and we want him at home; so that there is but one thing left, and that is to choose General Hull. He has always been a good whig, and he has done a good deal for the county in the fighting way. He is a man of good learning, and an honest man; he is the brigadier of the country, and pretty well known; and by what I can find out, he will be the man. But, my friends, if we do not unite in this man, the chance is, they will carry Mr. Gerry, and then fare you well poor Middlesex.[1]

1. For replies to this essay, see "Middlesex Essex," *Herald of Freedom*, 20 January, printed immediately below, and "Marcellus," *Herald of Freedom*, 23 January.

Middlesex Essex, Herald of Freedom, 20 January (excerpt)[1]

A crabbed X. writer in the last *Herald*[2] has the impudence to tell the electors of Middlesex, that "all who are in debt, and wish for paper money, all who are for tender acts, all Shayites, and such, ought to vote for Mr. [Elbridge] Gerry." No! no! sir, you may, if you please, inform this same X, he is mistaken. Honest good men mean to support Mr. Gerry, and by what I can find out, the electors of Middlesex do not intend to vote for any *self-created nobleman*. Neither do they intend to vote for Mr. [Nathaniel] Gorham, for as X. says (and sometimes these people speak the truth, though perhaps undesignedly) "he is in Congress already; he has been there a good while, and I think long enough." Neither do they mean to vote for a mere dependent tool of any man's—such as [Joseph B.] V[arnum]. No! no! my good friend, the *honorable yeomanry, the true republicans, the old whigs, and the friends of the people*, in Middlesex, are determined to give their votes, and use their influence for the Hon. Elbridge Gerry, Esq., for a federal Representative. They can trust their liberty and property in his hands. He has been an *old tried servant of the people*, and has proved faithful in times of the greatest danger, and therefore no doubt he will be sent to Congress again.

1. The first half of this essay discusses the election in Essex District and is printed above in The Second Election in Essex District.
2. See "X to the Electors of Middlesex," *Herald of Freedom*, 16 January, printed immediately above. On 23 January, the *Herald* published "Marcellus," another and longer essay that defended Gerry's integrity and praised his long service to the people.

Elbridge Gerry to the Electors of Middlesex, 22 January[1]

Friends and Fellow Citizens,

It appearing by your suffrages that I am one of your candidates for a federal Representative, give me leave for this evidence of your confidence, to express my warmest acknowledgments, but at the same time to request, that such of you as may again be disposed to honor me with your votes will turn your attention to some other candidate, for although I have been long honored with the confidence of my countrymen, and am conscious that a real regard to their political happiness has been the sole motive of my conduct, yet circumstanced as I am, to me an election would by no means be agreeable. Since however, my name is again, without any effort or inclination of my own, brought into public view, I embrace this opportunity to explain that conduct for which I have been treated with so much invective and abuse.

When the question on the Constitution was put in the Federal Convention, conceiving myself to be in a land of liberty, where the privilege of deliberating and voting with freedom would in the fullest extent be firmly supported, I voted against the Constitution, it being in my mind, in many instances, *defective*. Had my opinion been founded in error, it would have been but an error in judgment, for the fabricated falsehoods against me have been frequently and fully exposed. But five states having ratified the Constitution in the fullest expectation of amendments, and two having rejected it, no one can I think deny, that my opinion on this subject has been confirmed by the proceedings of a majority of the Union. An attempt has been made by means of *invective*, which must be condemned by this, and by every respectable community, to impair or destroy the privilege mentioned; a privilege, which no good citizen will ever permit to die in his hands, and which the good sense of the community will undoubtedly protect as one of the great pillars of a free state.[2]

Some have endeavored to hold me up as an enemy to the Constitution, than which, nothing is more remote from the truth. Since the commencement of the Revolution, I have been ever solicitous for an efficient federal government, conceiving that without it, we must be a divided, an unhappy people. A government too democratical have I ever deprecated, but wished for one that should possess every power requisite for the welfare of the Union, and at the same time be so balanced, as to secure the *governed* from the rapacity and domination of lawless and insolent ambition. To an unconditional ratification of the Constitution was I therefore opposed, because thereby every necessary amendment would be rendered precarious. But as the system is adopted, I am clearly of opinion, that every citizen of the ratifying states is in duty bound to support it, and that an opposition to a due administration of it would not only be unjustifiable, but highly criminal.

Amendments, every citizen has still a right to urge, without exciting a spirit of persecution, which is unnecessary in a good, and never gains proselytes in a bad cause. Every friend to a vigorous government must, as I conceive, be desirous of such amendments, as will remove the just apprehensions of the people, and secure their confidence in, and affection for, the new government. For to defeat amendments of this description, must be in effect, to defeat the Constitution itself. But when the question on amendments shall have received a constitutional decision, I shall cheerfully acquiesce in it, and, in any event, shall be happy to promote the true interest of the respectable county of Middlesex, of this commonwealth, and of the United States.

The part which I have had to act, and the uncandid treatment which I have received in this matter, will I trust justify me in being thus explicit; for I am conscious, that every part of my political conduct has had for its object, the public welfare.[3]

1. *Independent Chronicle*, 22 January. This copy of the letter is undated. We have given it the date it first appeared in the newspapers.

2. For an example of the "invective" which outraged Gerry, see "An Elector," *Massachusetts Centinel*, 10 January, printed above, and note 4 thereto.

3. On the same day the *Chronicle* published Gerry's address it published an "extract" of a letter from the county of Middlesex. The author said he had "made inquiry," and that although Gerry "feels himself wounded in the treatment he has received respecting the general government," he was a zealous supporter of an efficient government but wanted amendments "in the way the Constitution has provided. Should the people call him to represent them ... he will accept the appointment."

Federalist newspapers argued that he would not accept. On 23 January a "correspondent" in the *Herald of Freedom* "admires the ingenuity and frankness of Mr. Gerry in declining to accept a seat in the federal legislature; this explicit mode of acting is highly commendable, and of the utmost service in popular elections. The electors of Middlesex will now unanimously turn their attention to the Honorable William Hull, Esquire."

On 24 January the *Massachusetts Centinel* printed an item dated Cambridge, 22 January, which stated: "Mr. Gerry observing, in an 'extract of a letter from the county of Middlesex,' inserted in the *Chronicle* of this day, an assertion that 'should the people call him to represent them' in Congress 'he would accept the appointment,' is in justice to himself obliged to declare, that he has not now, neither has he ever had such an intention, much less, has he directly or indirectly expressed it to any person whatever; and that the writer of the letter must have been misinformed on the subject."

In the same issue the *Centinel* publisher, Benjamin Russell, deleted several paragraphs from a long anti-Gerry essay by "An Elector," noting that "The Hon. Mr. Gerry having declined the election for Middlesex County, we trust the writer of the above will excuse our omitting the pointed observations on his public and private character, which were contained in the paragraphs where the asterisks are inserted." The note was set in italics.

Farther afield, the Philadelphia *Federal Gazette* on 2 February, after reporting Gerry's address, commented that his real reason for withdrawing was that "he well knew that the people would not elect him, on account of his Antifederal principles."

An Observer, Independent Chronicle, 22 January (excerpt)

In Middlesex, the Hon. Elbridge Gerry, Esq., whose abilities have been long in public exercise, is supported by a strong party, consisting of those who were at first opposed to the Constitution, and of some of the more zealous friends to amendments. The moderate men who adhere to the amendments, but wish if possible to save the system, and are an extensive and influential party, are in favor of James Winthrop, Esq., whose abilities, moderation, and candor, they have been long acquainted with, and whose integrity and republicanism have secured him many friends. Those who are against any amendments at all will vote for General [William] Hull, whose military merit is conspicuous.[1]

1. The remainder of this essay, headed "The Present State of Parties," assesses the merits of candidates in Essex, Worcester, and Hampshire-Berkshire districts. Additional portions of this essay are printed in the sections dealing with those districts. In the first portion of the article "An Observer" contends that there was general agreement that the Constitution needed to be amended.

Countryman, Boston Gazette, 26 January

I Think it is likely the minds of the voters of Middlesex are nearly settled in their determination who to chuse for Representatives to the Federal Congress; and as that excellent man the Hon. N[athaniel] G[orham] Esq; is so tired of a political life, that he is determined not to go again for nobody—without a better birth (and I don't wonder at it) it is therefore needless to vote for him.—The Hon. Generals Brooks are both good men, but they don't chuse to go, it is therefore best not to lose votes for them.—Several other gentlemen have been talk'd of—such as the Hon. B. V[arnum] Esq; and others.—Now I think Mr. B V. might suit very well, because Mr. G[orha]m says he will be a very good man, one that would answer his purpose right well—but these odd country folks, strange creatures, will not believe all he says for all so good a man as he is.—And there is that Anti Shays man. I don't know what's his name, [Elbridge] GERRY, I believe he might do very well, some folks think, if he was not such an honest kind of a man; and besides, he has been so long in public life, that he knows how to do, and how to talk, and how to figure, and how to write, as well as any of the great ones that was with him in Congress. But this is the thing Mr. Printer—it was whisper'd to me to'ther day, and I want every body to know it—they say he will not say what all the rest of the great folks say, if he thinks they are not right—Now one such a man to be in office, ev'ry body knows, what a plague it must be to be hindered and questioned about ten thousand things that ev'ry body should not know. And I'll tell you another thing, but you must not tell ev'ry body on't—he's not a lawyer—Now, I say, if you tell that, and neighbour Tatler knows that I said so, he'll carry the story to Boston to'morrow, and ev'ry body will call me antifed, paper money, Shayite, and all such terrible hard names I shall not know what to say.—Now, I say, Mess. Printers, seeing this Mr. G[err]y is such an honest knowing man, and no lawyer, and it is well known he has always been a uniform, honest, faithful, able servant to the people, to chuse him, will not be acting as the great folks (some of them) would have us—Is there any body so foolish?

Therefore let us all unite in giving Mr. General [William] Hull our votes—he they say is a *toping fed*—a brave General, and one of your great Cincinnatick-men, and above all a Lawyer; and as the lower town folks are going to send one, and some of them say they are the best men to go, because they were appointed to expound the law to the people, and as they live in a decent, modest, temperate kind of life—not extravagantly spending their little earnings, they will be likely to set good examples before the people, and be moderate in their own salaries, because the poor people are to pay them for their abilities, for finding out such deep great learned words and things that nobody else can find out:—and besides, if we are good and kind to them now, they will be kind to us bye and bye, and tell us how to have our deeds drawn so as to save our lands for less than one half the land is worth.[1]

1. This issue of the *Gazette*, three days before the election, also contained three other articles which might be an indication of the tactics of Gerry's supporters discussed in Henry Jackson's letter to Henry Knox, 11 January, printed above. One item by "Lucius" urged votes for Joseph B. Varnum (who had received almost no newspaper support), while another article by "Charlestown" attacked lawyers in public office, and Varnum in particular. A third article by "An Old Soldier" said the voters should support William Hull. "Countryman," printed above, also says that the voters will vote for Hull, but the nature of the recommendation was not designed to win votes for him, but for Gerry. It should be remembered that the *Gazette* had nominated Gerry and Samuel Adams for the Senate as early as August 1788.

Laco, Herald of Freedom, 27 January

Enough! Enough! Good Heavens Enough!

It seems as if the Devil himself had got into the scribblers of the present day. They have tired out the patience of the public, with their reiterated harangues about economy, profligacy, salaries, electioneering, reviling and defaming public and private characters, tending to render our government contemptible on the one hand—and wounding the peace and happiness of individuals on the other. Ye who are tools of a party, desist awhile, grant a momentary respite, for the sake of yours and your patrons' reputation. Ye who are the ruthless defamers of private characters desist, for charity's sake. It is high time to blunt the stiletto which is reeking with tears, drawn from the eye of wounded humanity. Shall there be no check to the overflowing torrent of scurrility? Is the [ground?] too defective to be repaired? If it is, for heaven's sake let us set about making a new one. To our eternal disgrace, our rulers are bambooz[le]d as if they were the greatest scoundrels in creation, and are painted by the pen of infamy, blacker than a chimney sweeper's soot-boy. Are we civilized freemen? If we are, in the name of common sense let us conduct as such, and not be guilty of actions which would cast a shade on the ancient Goths and Vandals. If our rulers are guilty, summon them before the tribunal of justice, a tribunal which regards not the gaudy glitter of external appearance, but treats guilty majesty with the same rigor as the meanest offending individual. This would be the proper mode of procedure; and then those who best rule over us would either stand acquitted in the eyes of the people, or their guilt would be justly exposed. With respect to private characters, let them alone while they remain veiled in the private walks of life. But if they should step forward as candidates for public offices, ere you attempt to point out blemishes in them, be at first indisputably assured that you have just grounds for your assertion. Otherwise you may expose the innocent to public scandal, and hold up the guiltless as a mark for every unprincipled tool to shoot at. In short, let me conclude with this best of rules: "do unto others as you would they should do unto you."[1]

1. The above appeal had no effect, of course. "An Independent Man" in the same issue of the *Herald* (printed immediately below) continued the argument on behalf of Elbridge Gerry, and the next day (the day before the election) the *Massachusetts Centinel* printed an item by "Middlesex" (printed below) denouncing Gerry because he was not a friend of George Washington.

An Independent Man, Herald of Freedom, 27 January[1]

The address of Mr. [Elbridge] Gerry to the electors of Middlesex[2] holds up to view, those principles of freedom and moderation, and that independence of character, which deserves our applause and must eventually command it. The motives of his opposition to some parts of the new Constitution, whatever pains have been taken to render them disgraceful to him personally, and to the cause of liberty in general, have been, I had almost said, *universally* known, to be disinterested. The intrepidity, and perhaps temper, which have been discovered in that opposition, are characteristic of the man, but by no means argue that implacable hatred to the cause of FEDERALISM which his enemies endeavor to establish. The writer of this paper is a friend to a firm, efficient, federal government, and may in some points differ from Mr. G[erry]. But he has known that gentleman for many years; and though they may differ in some articles of their political creed, he is not for abandoning a man, for a single error of judgment, who was foremost to emancipate this country from a dependence on Britain, and who has manifested upon every occasion, unless perhaps in the instance before us, not only a zeal for liberty and the best interests of the people, but the most anxious solicitude to give every possible force to a federal government; and this zeal and solicitude determined his election to the Convention at Philadelphia. In the mode of exerting that force he may differ from others; but it cannot from thence be inferred, that he is an enemy to the government itself. Mr. Gerry's friends, of whom I am not afraid to profess myself one, did not stand in need of a declaration from his own mouth, "that *every* citizen of the ratifying states (a strong expression to include himself) is bound to support the Constitution; that when the question on amendments shall have received a constitutional decision, he shall cheerfully acquiesce in it; and that he has ever been solicitous for an efficient federal government, conceiving that without it, we should be a divided and unhappy people." This evidence was to them unnecessary, and they who would wish to know must have been satisfied in these particulars, with a little pains, for his labors have been unwearied and notorious during many years, to perfect a national system of vigorous government, to pervade and control every part of the United States; to establish justice; give energy to the laws; and encourage commerce and agriculture. It has been said, that being an enemy to the Constitution, he is an improper person to be intrusted with the administration of it. If this were true in the latitude contended for, the observation would be just. But it is first assumed that he is an enemy to the Constitution *at large*; for if the objection has any meaning, it is *that*, because no man thinks that instrument *all perfect*; and we then infer, that this would be *ovem committere lupo*, to give to the wolf the custody of the fold. The assumption is unfair, not being founded in truth and fact, and the inference must fall, of course, to the ground. It is also objected that he is a friend to amendments. To real amendments no man will object; but in what mode, under what form, and within what period will he endanger the immediate operation of the general government, by unseasonable attempts for amendments? This is what some good men fear; but they who affirm this, do not know Mr. G[erry], or the principles of his conduct. He venerates the Constitution in general, and is for a fair trial of it under its present form; and so far is he from desiring some alterations in it, which his enemies attribute to him, that he is the last man in America who would give in to them, because such alterations in his opinion would destroy the energy of the system. But it does not require the spirit of prophecy to predict that it is not from such men as a Gerry or Lee, that the new government is in danger. Better reasoning than any I have yet seen is necessary to convince me that these men, the constant tenor of whose lives has been to brace up the government, and give force and vigor to the laws, should, without reason, sacrifice their ancient, deep rooted habits and principles, and involve us at once in anarchy, or, which is the same thing, carry us back to that weak, disgraceful form (or any resemblance of it) of governing by recommendatory resolves, from which we have just escaped. The real enemies of the Constitution are its over zealous, imprudent friends, men who have great expectations from and under it, the most of whom will be greatly disappointed. A spirit of conciliation ought to be encouraged, and the friends of good order and government combined together, whatever their differences may be in speculative points. We are peaceable at present, but storms in our hemisphere suddenly and unexpectedly arise, which level all things with the dust. We then need the assistance of good men of all parties, if men who are friends to justice and a steady administration of government can be said to be of different parties. So far from wishing that the general government may be administered by none but its enthusiastic admirers, so far from believing that this will conciliate affection or give weight to it, it would be wiser in us to imitate the conduct of King William, after the revolution, when parties run high through the nation. He came at one time very near losing the confidence of the people, which would have cost him his throne, by attempting from ill advice to humble and crush the supporters of monarchy and the hereditary succession, and by including in that number every man who was an enemy to changes of government. But he regained that confidence by embracing and trusting those very men, and was ably supported by them in the most trying times of his reign. Men do not readily change their principles or habits. They who from nature or education love order and good government, however averse they may be to the introduction or form of a new one, become its ablest supporters after it is once established, unless borne down by ill usage and oppression.

1. Portions of the original article are unreadable. The editors have supplied the missing material from a reprinting in the *New York Morning Post*, 6 February.

2. See "Gerry to the Electors of Middlesex," 22 January, printed above.

Middlesex, Massachusetts Centinel, 28 January[1]

It is strikingly strange, after Mr. [Elbridge] Gerry has so plainly and repeatedly declared, he would not accept the appointment of federal Representative, that the advocates for alterations should still continue to give the *lie* to those declarations, by foisting his name into every page of every paper, as being still a candidate; and can only be accounted for in that *want of faith in each other*, which distinguish men engaged in a bad cause.

If even Mr. G[erry] was still a candidate, can it be supposed that the free electors of Middlesex would give him their suffrages. I think it cannot. They, almost to a man, wish, that a WASHINGTON should be called to sustain the important and weighty office of President of the United States; and to induce him to *accept* of that trust, they know, there ought to be a prospect to him of meeting persons in the legislature of the United States, in whom he can place confidence; and whose attachment to a system, which he thinks the best that can be formed for the United States, at the present juncture, he will not doubt. Mr. Gerry has once opposed what WASHINGTON thought for the good of his country—and the electors of Middlesex still think he may ever be opposed to any measure, which his wisdom shall recommend, as necessary for the peace, happiness, and prosperity of a country, for which he hath fought, and endured all the hardships of a perilous warfare. They know WASHINGTON; he has resided among them. Their hearts have beat with rapture, when they have dwelt on his virtues; they loved, and they still love him; and they think it will be imposing upon that good man a disagreeable task, thus, *in the evening of his days*, to associate him with men, whose opinions and measures will be at perpetual variance with his. This consideration, if there were no others—but which there are many, will induce the electors of this district not to vote for Mr. G[erry]. Their suffrages, it is expected, will be bestowed on a deserving man—and such is William Hull, Esquire—who, notwithstanding all what has been said by malevolent writers to his prejudice, is the farmer's friend; the manufacturer's supporter; a cool, determined Republican; and a landholder of the county of MIDDLESEX.

1. The article was dated Concord, 26 January.

Jonathan Glover to Elbridge Gerry, Boston, 2 February (excerpt)[1]

From the best accounts that I can collect you are made choice of as a Representative for the county of Middlesex, and I do [assure?] you it gives great satisfaction to many of your good friends in the house. I have not conversed with any person but is rejoiced to hear you are like to get the vote.

I have now, sir, to beg and entreat you will not refuse. [———] it should turn out to be so.

1. RC, Gerry-Townsend Papers, NN. The letter is signed "Jon Glover" and is endorsed as being from "Colo Glover." Hence it was probably written by Jonathan Glover of Marblehead rather than by General John Glover of the same town. A P.S. to the letter reads: "You'd please to Excuse the ritting this Letter as my Ink frose in the pen & I am very Cold."

Official Election Returns, 7 February

MIDDLESEX DISTRICT, 29 JANUARY

Town	Hon. Elbridge Gerry, Esq.	Hon. Joseph Varnum, Esq.	William Hull, Esq.	James Winthrop, Esq.	Hon. Ebenezer Bridge, Esq.	Hon. Eleazer Brooks, Esq.	Loammi Baldwin, Esq.	Hon. Francis Dana, Esq.	Hon. Nathaniel Gorham, Esq	Hon. Abraham Fuller, Esq.	James Russell, Esq.
Cambridge	41	30	2	40							1
Charlestown	72	23	19	2							
Watertown	45	2	14								
Woburn	70	8									
Concord	20	51	17	1							
Newton	36		33							2	
Reading	18	27	3								
Marlborough	71		12								
Billerica	29	28	1	1	9						
Framingham	19	6	7						2		
Lexington	25		12	3							
Chelmsford	21	13			21						
Sherborn	19		2		12		3				
Sudbury	16	2	12								
Malden	6	21									
Weston	41	8	12								
Medford	13	1	24								
Hopkinton	42		1								
Westford	65	3		5	4						
Stow	1	25	4					1			
Boxborough		18	1								
Groton	35		3								
Shirley	29										
Pepperell	20		7		19						
Waltham	17	9	8								
Townsend	63										
Dracut		58									
Bedford											
Holliston	26	4									
Acton	34		3	10		5					
Dunstable	17										
Lincoln	12	19	2								
Wilmington	51							6			

(Table continued on following page)

MIDDLESEX DISTRICT, 29 JANUARY *(continued)*

Town	Hon. Elbridge Gerry, Esq.	Hon. Joseph Varnum, Esq.	William Hull, Esq.	James Winthrop, Esq.	Hon. Ebenezer Bridge, Esq.	Hon. Eleazer Brooks, Esq.	Loammi Baldwin, Esq.	Hon. Francis Dana, Esq.	Hon. Nathaniel Gorham, Esq.	Hon. Abraham Fuller, Esq.	James Russell, Esq.
Tewksbury	34	4		1	1						
Littleton	19		4								
Ashby	37										
Natick	14	5	2								
Carlisle	16				5						
Stoneham	23	1							2		
East Sudbury	23										
Totals	1140	366	205	82	52	5	9	1	4	2	1

Votes cast: 1867
Majority required: 934

**Governor and Council Record the Votes in the Second Election
in Middlesex District, Monday, 9 February**[1]

The Governor and Council upon the examination of the returns from the
district[s] of Essex, Middlesex, Worcester, Hampshire and Berkshire, who did
not on the first election make choice of Representatives to represent them in the
Congress of the United States, found them to stand as follows, viz.
. . . .
District of Middlesex. Number of voters, 1867; [to] make a choice, 934. Hon.
Elbridge Gerry, Esq., had 1140 and is chosen.

1. Council Records, XXXI, 8, M-Ar.

Elbridge Gerry to Samuel R. Gerry, Cambridge, 14 February (excerpt)[1]

I must go to Congress or render this state so disagreeable to me as to oblige
me to leave it, for I will not live in a place where I can have no friendship for
the inhabitants or they for me. The people will not hear of my declining; neither
will my friends who say in Boston as well as in this county I shall sacrifice them,
by refusing the office. It is extremely painful to me to accept; no other under-
taking could be half so disagreeable; and what is more extraordinary, some of the
high Federalists have been urging me to go.[2]

1. RC, Gerry Papers, MHi. Samuel Gerry was Elbridge Gerry's brother.

2. Henry Jackson was one of the "high Federalists" who talked to Gerry. He wrote to Henry Knox: "Mr. E. Gerry is chosen and will go on to Congress. I have had some conversation with him on the subject. I believe he will make a good member" (Boston, 15 February, RC, Knox Papers, MHi).

For what other "high Federalists" said about Gerry and for what he thought of them, see James Warren to Gerry, 3 March, and Gerry's reply, 22 March, both printed below.

Massachusetts Centinel, 14 February

A correspondent really hopes, that the Hon. Mr. [Elbridge] Gerry will accept the appointment of one of the Representatives in Congress of the people of this state, as he is convinced that there has not been one person as yet chosen, who will more firmly support the Constitution of the United States, or whose exertions will be greater for the *active* operation of the powers under it.

Elbridge Gerry to James Warren, Cambridge, 15 February[1]

I suspect you will consider me as manifesting a disposition to change my principles, or of a want of resolution to adhere to them, when I tell you it is probable I shall go to Congress. Indeed if this be your opinion, you will alter it when I assure you, of all political events in which I have been interested, my election I consider as most unfortunate to myself. I had not, during its pendency, the most remote idea of acceptance, but thought of it with horror.

I now think the measure one of all others that threatens destruction to my peace, interest, and welfare, and yet such has been the torrent of abuse against me, that no person here will listen to my declining; my best friends say they shall be sacrificed by my refusal, and that I myself shall be considered as an obstinate opposer of the government, which is an opinion that has recently been much circulated.

Should I decline then, I am to be considered as a nonjuror in Great Britain, or an Irish Catholic; and sooner than so live, I would quit the continent. In accepting, I see nothing but two years of extreme *disagreeables*. To gratify my friends, and to avoid the consequences menaced, I have selected a certain positive evil; whether it be the least of the two, I am yet to learn.

1. James T. Austin, *The Life of Elbridge Gerry* . . . (2 vols., Boston, 1828-1829), II, 95-96.

Samuel Osgood to Elbridge Gerry, New York, 19 February[1]

It gives me great pleasure to find that your countrymen have emerged from obscurity and mist.

Whether you accept or whether you do not the event is very flattering and I can assure you it has great effect here. The Federalists are courting favor by false pretenses, saying that they are now openly for amendments, that they never liked the Constitution, that it was a matter of the highest expediency, but they will now be very happy to join with the cool and rational Antifederalists. But, *latet Anguis in Herba*.

I am mortified at seeing your letter to Mr. Otis in which you say there are weighty objections against your accepting of the appointment. Mr. Thompson also informs me he has no encouragement from you.[2]

So far as I can learn the sense of parties this way it is, I assure you, that you should accept.

Your conduct has been irreproachable and bore the test. Your last address to the electors of Middlesex[3] is considered here as not courting a choice and also as not refusing it. Some indeed go so far as to say it was well calculated to procure an appointment.

I know very well if you should utterly decline it will be endeavored to be made to appear that you have sported with the electors, which I am sure you never would.

I consider the first Congress as a second convention. It is evident they must do some acts relative to amendments which will bear hard upon the Convention that framed the Constitution, some of the members of which never ought to be forgotten, if forgiven.

I may with sincerity tell you that if you accept and come forward, I have well-founded reasons for expecting a very different government as well as administration of it [from?] what it will be if you do not. It will be a crisis. It now lies with you more than any one man in the United States to bring it to a happy issue. If you refuse and things should go very badly, you must permit me to be a witness against you. I very well know the scurrilous, shameful abuse you have met with, but the victory is all on your side. And as you fairly and openly espouse and avow genuine republican principles, is it not a necessary concomitant of those principles that the voice of the people ought to be yielded to? A true Republican never ought to be so offended with the people as to forsake them or withdraw from their service. Such governments are at times, and always will be, tumultuous. The only way to render them good for anything is for the cool and rational part of the society to adhere together, and always be ready to afford all the assistance they can in preserving peace and good order. I do not carry my principles so far, however, as to deny any person the rights and privilege of refusing to serve his country when he is well persuaded he has good reason for such refusal, and the person alone is the proper judge for himself in such case.

My ardent desire is that you may accept of the appointment for the reasons I have mentioned.

As to myself whether in office or out,[4] I shall be resigned. Had not the same unprincipled wretches who have persecuted you, touched me, as the Devil did Job, I should have retired before this time. But I have now nothing to hope or fear.

Be pleased to make Mrs. Osgood's compliments and my own acceptable to Mrs. Gerry and her sisters, and give me leave to flatter myself, for I really do, and cannot rid myself of the idea, that I shall have the pleasure of making my compliments to you personally in this place.

1. RC, Sang Collection, ICarbS.
2. No letter to "Mr. Otis" or "Mr. Thompson" has been located.

3. See "Gerry to the Electors of Middlesex," 22 January, printed above.

4. Osgood had been a member of Congress from Massachusetts, 1781-1784, and was a member of the Board of Treasury, 1785-1789. He had opposed the Constitution, but President Washington appointed him Postmaster General in 1789.

James Sullivan to Elbridge Gerry, Boston, 21 February[1]

I inclose you the articles you obliged me with the perusal of. I hope to see them in another form as soon as the public good will admit of.

I have made the alteration you requested me to make in the letter you sent to the Governor. It will appear in next week's paper, the *Chronicle*,[2] also the production you gave me.

I wish you a happy and prosperous journey. I have confidence in you, that while you endeavor to support the honor and dignity of the United States and to give force and efficacy to their government, you will hold yourself obliged to contend for that freedom and political happiness which our dear countrymen by their arms and public sacrifices have so dearly purchased. We must never forget that the exertions of the body of our countrymen saved their intrepid and virtuous leaders from ignominy and perdition. Give our best regards to Mrs. Gerry and the Miss Tompsons. God bless and preserve you my dear sir.

1. RC, Gerry Papers, MHi.
2. See Gerry to Governor John Hancock, 26 February, printed immediately below.

Elbridge Gerry to Governor John Hancock, 26 February[1]

Copy of a LETTER from the Honorable ELBRIDGE GERRY, Esq., to His Excellency the GOVERNOR.

Sir,

I have received a commission from Your Excellency, for the office of a federal Representative, and am deeply impressed with this honorable testimony of the electors of Middlesex, after I had repeatedly informed them of my declining the appointment. This, however, has placed me in a situation, which of all others I wished to avoid, being hereby reduced to the disagreeable alternative of disappointing my fellow citizens, who have thus conferred on me their suffrages, or of filling a place which the most cogent reasons had urged me to decline. Under these circumstances, in the present critical state of public affairs, I have preferred the latter, being determined to sacrifice every personal consideration to an acceptance of the office, that, desirous as I am of the establishment of a federal government, no act of mine may have the least aspect of impeding it. But this I do in full confidence of the candor and firm support of my constituents; for the body politic, after the late ferment, is not unlike a patient recovering from an acute disease, the feelings of both being so exceedingly delicate as to make it very difficult for their friends to please them, and without giving general satisfaction, any office to me would be extremely painful. It is to be hoped that these inconveniences will be soon removed by an adoption of such measures as will terminate dissensions, and restore harmony to the community; and when this is accomplished, there is no reason to doubt that we shall all have the completion of our wishes, an energetic, and, at the same time, a free system of federal government.

I have the honor to be, sir, with the greatest respect, your most obedient, and very humble servant.

E. GERRY.

1. *Independent Chronicle*, 26 February. This copy of the letter is undated. We have given it the date it first appeared in the newspapers. For a public comment on Gerry's letter, see the *New York Daily Gazette*, 10 March, printed below.

John Bacon to Elbridge Gerry, Stockbridge, 26 February[1]

I most sincerely congratulate you on your election to a seat in the Congress of the United States. This event, whatever relish you may have contracted for private life, must, I conceive, be attended with circumstances, in some respects, grateful to you, as well as to your numerous friends. In their gratification at least, you will be, in some measure, gratified.

Your election seems to have brought a gloom over the minds of some particular characters, not altogether unlike to that which befell a certain Naman mentioned in ancient story, on the promotion of one whose ruin he had sought, and, as he vainly imagined, with full assurance of success. These gentlemen, I believe, in the present case, begin to adopt the logic of Naman's lady.

Those men who have been base enough to stab, and strive to disgrace, my honorable friend, will now, I doubt not, have meanness enough to fawn upon, and court, the man who is equally above the reach of flattery and malice.

Altho I do not imagine that Mr. Gerry, or any other individual, can effect everything, I must, nevertheless, consider your election as bearing a favorable aspect on the operation of our new government. It will check the sanguine views of our violent Constitutionalists, and add strength and importance to the sober friends of liberty and government. Next Monday is the day appointed for a third attempt to choose a Representative for this district [Hampshire-Berkshire]. I think it is most likely no choice will be made at this time.

1. RC, Sang Collection, ICarbS. Bacon, a one-time minister who had been fired as pastor of Old South Church in Boston in 1775, moved to Stockbridge, where he became a farmer and a leading political figure. He was a justice of the Court of Common Pleas and represented Stockbridge in the state House of Representatives and Berkshire County in the state Senate several times. He became a Republican in the 1790s.

James Warren to Elbridge Gerry, Plymouth, 3 March (excerpt)[1]

Your Antifederal sins will never be forgiven by a party who, while they wish you to support their system, are malignant enough to represent you as puerile and unsteady in your own, that is, they report that you was greatly elated with your election, and had become the highest Federal in the country. All this and much more would be too contemptible to be mentioned for any other purpose than to show the temper of the party. I often reflect on your situation, and think where you will fix your confidence. A man that has been used to act with the old patriots will feel a defect in modern sentiments and modern views which even considerable abilities will not supply the place of.

1. RC, Chamberlain Collection, MB. Printed: Gardiner, *Warren-Gerry Letters*, 216-18.

New York Daily Gazette, 10 March

Mr. Gerry's late letter to Governor Hancock,[1] says a correspondent, reflects the brightest honor on his political, as well as moral, character. His fellow citizens, fully apprised of his sentiments in the late General Convention, which were opposed to the new system, were so convinced of his abilities and integrity, as to elect him one of their federal Representatives; and that statesman, whose patriotism has induced him to comply with their wishes in opposition to his private opinion, has accepted the office. It may therefore be presumed, that his judgment, uninfluenced by an enthusiastic prepossession in favor of the new government, will enable him clearly to discern its benefits and defects. The proof of moderation, which he has already exhibited, is a pledge of his future equanimity; and the Union, as well as his more immediate constituents, ought to exult in the possession of this truly illustrious patriot.[2]

1. See Elbridge Gerry to Governor John Hancock, 26 February, printed above.

2. This article was reprinted at least five times, including the *Herald of Freedom*, 20 March; *Massachusetts Centinel*, 21 March; and *American Herald*, 26 March.

Elbridge Gerry to James Warren, New York, 22 March (excerpt)[1]

I have had so much of politics as to feel an aversion to them, and should be happy to bid a final adieu to them, more especially to legislatures, whether state or federal, as a measure that would most contribute to my own and my family's happiness; and therefore I fear not any mortification from my enemies, but from my friends. I experience it, by their urging me to places which are neither pleasant, lucrative, or honorable. These measures of the *latter* have put me in trammels; and had I declined them, the consequences must have been injurious to *them* as well as to myself, by giving an opportunity to my enemies to represent me as an enemy to a federal government, and to reproach my friends for supporting my election when I would not attend Congress to procure those amendments which I had so warmly urged. Whilst I only thought that there was a probability of such consequences from my declining the appointment, I was determined on that line of conduct; but when I found from all quarters that my resolution had actually produced that effect, I found that I must either leave the state in order to seek a more agreeable place of residence, which I could not do without giving away a great part of my real property, or submit to a temporary mortification in order to counteract the malignity of inveterate foes and therefore I concluded on the latter, altho I think it not very probable that I shall continue in the office till the expiration of my commission.

. . . .

I want much to have the anecdotes you hint at, but the delay of them will not make me less cautious, for there are very few to whom I shall commit myself. Notwithstanding the scurrility which I have experienced, I cannot but be highly diverted at the arts or folly, for I know not which is the true cause, of the Federalists in representing me as being *elated* with my late appointment, when I consider it truly, or at least the acceptance of it, as an act of the highest injustice to myself. A Federalist I always was, but not in their sense of the word, for I abhor now as much as ever the corrupt parts of the Constitution, but am bound in honor to support a government ratified by the majority until it can be amended, for to oppose it would be to sow the seeds of a civil war and to lay the foundation of a military tyranny. I shall however be a *spectator* till I can form some adequate idea of *men* and *measures*.

1. RC, Gerry Papers, DLC. Printed: Gardiner, *Warren-Gerry Letters*, 219-20.

John Tracey to Josiah Harmar, Pittsburgh, 31 March (excerpt)[1]

I find that Mr. Elbridge Gerry is elected a member of Congress for the County of Middlesex, State of Massachusetts. This is a gentleman of the first abilities. He has ever been as far as our constitution [Articles of Confederation] would admit a member of Congress, was of the grand Federal Convention at Philadelphia, *and a very great enemy to the new Constitution*. I am afraid that the Massachusetts election will prove Anti.

1. RC, Harmar Collection, MiU-C. Harmar was in charge of federal army operations on the Ohio frontier from 1785 to 1790.

John Wendell to Elbridge Gerry, Portsmouth, 22 May (excerpt)[1]

I was sensibly affected when I found your friends had chosen you to a seat in Congress; [it?] discovered such an attachment to your integrity, as must do you honor with all honest men. Your manly deportment and your letter to Governor Hancock made my heart glow with gratitude to you, for accepting the appointment. For altho I could not join in sentiments with you to reject the proposed plan laid before you for adoption, in total, yet I readily wished to see some amendments take place, and which indeed must, or aristocracy will be the event, instead of republicanism. How far we may be disappointed, time alone must discover.

1. RC, Gerry Papers, MHi. Wendell, who had been born in Boston and graduated from Harvard, was a Portsmouth, N.H., lawyer and land owner.

The Second Election in Worcester District, 29 January

The two Worcester newspapers paid no more attention to the second election than they had to the first. Between 18 December 1788 and 29 January 1789 the *American Herald* ignored the election entirely. The *Massachusetts Spy* did so, too, except for the issue of 22 January, seven days before the election. In the longest of the four items pertaining to it, "An Old Man" pled for the election of a Representative who could stand up in the forthcoming battle with the delegates from the Southern States. He implied that both Timothy Paine and Jonathan Grout were good men, although he did not choose between them. Two items recommended that the voters unite behind Paine to prevent the need of a third election, while the fourth suggested that since the district was divided between Paine and Grout, the voters should support Major Martin Kinsley of Hardwick.

The Boston newspapers also ignored the election, except for the *Independent Chronicle*.

In the second election Timothy Paine ran ahead of Jonathan Grout, but he did not receive a majority, while Artemas Ward ran a poor third. There were only 27 votes scattered among eight other candidates.

Benjamin Lincoln to George Washington, Boston, 4 January (excerpt)[1]

Worcester are very much divided. The struggle there finally will be, I think, between Mr. [Timothy] Paine who was one of the mandamus councillors, a gentleman of abilities and a good Federalist, and a Colonel [Jonathan] Grout of a different character. We can, I think, promise ourselves that six and perhaps seven of the eight Representatives will be firmly attached to the Constitution.

1. RC, Washington Papers, DLC.

An Observer, Independent Chronicle, 22 January (excerpt)[1]

In Worcester, the parties run very high, but rather from affection to their leaders, than from any essential difference of opinion, for in order to have any votes, a man must be known to be in favor of the amendments. The Hon. Timothy Paine, Esq., is respectable for his abilities, his integrity, and moderation. His rival, the Hon. Jonathan Grout, Esq., is also confessed to have the same good qualities, and perhaps of the two is rather more attached to the system which, considering the people collectively as sovereign, admits of the separate rights of the local governments, both the general and local governments being upon this plan, only different delegations from the same authority for the special purposes of their appointment.

1. Other portions of this essay, headed "The Present State of Parties," assess the merits of candidates in Middlesex, Essex and Hampshire-Berkshire districts, and are printed in the sections relating to those districts.

To the Printer, Massachusetts Spy, 22 January

A number of your customers wish you to insert in your paper, that as this district is again called on to vote for a Representative to the Congress to meet in New York in March next, and as it is necessary we should unite in a man, and the district seems now to be divided between Mr. [Jonathan] Grout and Mr. [Timothy] Paine, it is wished the district would join and give their votes to some other person in whom the district would be more united. Major Martin Kinsley[1] is proposed, and it is hoped will be chosen, and thereby prevent the trouble and loss of time which another meeting must occasion.

1. Kinsley had sympathized with those who engaged in Shays's Rebellion and lost his commission as a major of militia because he had done so. However, supporters of the Rebellion remained in control of Hardwick, Kinsley's home town, and elected him town treasurer from 1787 to 1792 and representative to the General Court, 1787-1788, 1790-1792, 1794-1796.

A Voter to the Printer, Massachusetts Spy, 22 January

You are requested to inform the respectable voters in this district, that the Honorable Timothy Paine, Esq., by the returns made to the honorable executive of this commonwealth, stand as a candidate for a Representative to the new Congress; and as he is a gentleman well known to be every way qualified for that office, it is agreed on by a very respectable part of the inhabitants of this district, to give him their votes on the 29th inst. By uniting in him we shall undoubtedly have a choice, otherwise in all probability the business will be to do over again.

A Voter for Worcester District, Massachusetts Spy, 22 January

To the voters for a federal Representative, in Worcester District, particularly those who voted for the Hon. Timothy Paine, Artemas Ward, Moses Gill, and John Sprague, esquires.

Gentlemen: For want of unanimity in the choice of a gentleman to represent this district in the Congress of the United States, our votes were lost, at the late election; we are therefore again called on for that purpose. It is supposed that no person who gave his vote for either of the above gentlemen, but would be willing either of them were chosen. But as the Hon. Timothy Paine has the highest number of votes among the names above-mentioned,[1] it is hoped that on the twenty-ninth inst. you will unanimously vote for him, and thereby make a choice, and prevent the district the expense and trouble of another meeting. I am, gentlemen, your humble servant.

1. Paine had the greatest number of votes among the men named above, but Jonathan Grout received more votes on 18 December.

An Old Man, Massachusetts Spy, 22 January[1]

Every patriot must have been alarmed at the smallness of the number of votes returned into the secretary's office for Representatives to the Congress of the United States. The privilege to choose the men with whom our lives and properties are to be entrusted will not be trifled with by those who realize its worth. In this district, as well as in some others, there will be an opportunity on the 29th instant, by a more general attendance, to correct the late error; and it is wished that all might be roused to a just sense of the magnitude of the object before them. In point of numbers, and natural resources, few of the districts which will be represented in Congress exceed this. For fertility of soil, and a numerous, industrious, and enterprising yeomanry; for the conveniences of life in time of peace; and for a brave soldiery and the means of their support in times of war, the county of Worcester stands high in the estimation of every person of information, through the Union. And every individual must feel his honor and reputation concerned in the ensuing election, for the man delegated will be considered as a representation of the political knowledge, and the dignity, of the county; and by him will our discernment and general acquaintance with the sciences of government be determined.

To the character of the county, every honest man will add the welfare of his country. A man who to good purpose might represent a town or a county in our state government may be very unsuitable to fill a seat in the Congress of the United States. He may be acquainted with the state of the yeomanry in the county, and be able to defend their rights in all cases of competition between the landed and mercantile interest of this commonwealth; but in Congress the scene will be entirely changed. Land taxation will not be adopted until all other sources fail; and there can never be a competition between this and other parts of the state. The contention of interest in Congress will be between the Southern and Northern states. The Southern part of the Union is unfavorably situated for shipping and sailors. Their endeavor will be to establish such commercial regulations as will subject our navigation to their interest. This must materially effect our produce, already much too low. For a Representative, then, we ought to select a man of sound judgment and unshaken integrity, of long experience and allowed dignity; a man not only acquainted with the farming interest, but with the general principles of legislation, that he may be qualified to enter the lists with the Representatives of the Southern States, men of sagacity and address and practiced in all the arts of politicans. They have such and on this occasion they will certainly delegate them. Let us look for the man whose age and reputation will add force and influence to his arguments; a man who, while at Congress, will have the fewest avocations, and whose attention and time will not be taken up by the pursuit of private gain. Though there may be many gentlemen in the district who would answer the above description, yet the candidates who in the last trial had the highest number of votes, and whose names are returned by the Supreme Executive, seem to be the men nominated by the people, from whom they are now to choose. Attempts in favor of any other can subserve no better purpose than to cause the county fruitless expense. Both these candidates are known to be in favor of the amendments proposed by our Convention. I have no disposition to traduce the character of either. In great national concerns personality ought to be kept as far as possible out of sight.

In a transaction in which the interest of all are inseparably blended, local prejudice and party distinction must be buried. The enquiry is not, which is the man whom we delight to honor, but which is the man who will serve us best. And permit me to beg every man, before he gives his suffrage, to ask himself this question: in case my most valued property was at hazard, and it was necessary for me to call in the assistance of a man of integrity, judgment, and wisdom, in which of those gentlemen could I place the most confidence? To whose fidelity, prudence, and care should I trust the management of my important private concerns? The answer to this question will probably lead to the man, to whom the rights and property of the people may the most safely be committed, who will do the most honor to the county, and the best transact the business of the public.

1. This item was dated Sutton, 17 January.

Official Election Returns, 7 February

WORCESTER DISTRICT, 29 JANUARY

Town	Hon. Artemas Ward, Esq.	Hon. Timothy Paine, Esq.	Hon. Jonathan Grout, Esq.	Hon. Abel Wilder, Esq.	Hon. Moses Gill, Esq.	Hon. Jonathan Warner, Esq.	Hon. Seth Washburn	Hon. John Sprague, Esq.	Martin Kinsley, Esq.	Jeremiah Learned	Rev. Ebenezer Chaplin
Worcester	15	67	40								
Lancaster	5	48	7								
Mendon											
Brookfield	41	38	91								
Oxford		34	4								
Charlton		53	6								
Sutton		61	8	1							
Leicester	17	16	3	1							
Spencer		17	34								
Rutland		36	49								
Oakham	1	3	25					1			
Paxton	7	9	4								
Barre	15	12	45						1		
Hubbardston			65								

(Table continued on following pages)

WORCESTER DISTRICT, 29 JANUARY *(continued)*

Town	Hon. Artemas Ward, Esq.	Hon. Timothy Paine, Esq.	Hon. Jonathan Grout, Esq.	Hon. Abel Wilder, Esq.	Hon. Moses Gill, Esq.	Hon. Jonathan Warner, Esq.	Hon. Seth Washburn	Hon. John Sprague, Esq.	Martin Kinsley, Esq.	Jeremiah Learned	Rev. Ebenezer Chaplin
New Braintree		17	43								
Southborough		9	12				1				
Westborough		17	20								
Northborough		17									
Shrewsbury	45	2	46					1			
Lunenburg	33	15	22								
Fitchburg	12	10	1	5							
Uxbridge		11	28								
Harvard		21	18								
Dudley		24	24								
Bolton		32									
Upton		18	29								
Sturbridge		33	15								
Leominster	7	49	9								
Hardwick		22	17								
Holden		21	8						1		
Western [Warren]		22	2								
Douglas		23									
Grafton	1	8	49		1						
Petersham		20	37								
Royalston	1	1	44				1				
Westminster	3	37	14								
Templeton		28	8								
Princeton		49	25								
Ashburnham	4	24					4				
Winchendon		21	29								
Northbridge		25	1								
Ward [Auburn]	3	2	13					1		7	1
Athol	21		12								
Milford		13	5								
Sterling	11	29	4								
Berlin											

(Table continued on following page)

WORCESTER DISTRICT, 29 JANUARY *(continued)*

Town	Hon. Artemas Ward, Esq.	Hon. Timothy Paine, Esq.	Hon. Jonathan Grout, Esq.	Hon. Abel Wilder, Esq.	Hon. Moses Gill, Esq.	Hon. Jonathan Warner, Esq.	Hon. Seth Washburn	Hon. John Sprague, Esq.	Martin Kinsley, Esq.	Jeremiah Learned	Rev. Ebenezer Chaplin
Gardner		4	15								
Boylston	16	7	12								
Gerry											
[Phillipston]		15	13								
Totals	258	1040	956	5	3	5	1	3	2	7	1

Votes cast: 2281
Majority required: 1141

Governor and Council Record the Votes in the Second Election in Worcester District, Monday, 9 February[1]

The Governor and Council upon the examination of the returns from the district[s] of Essex, Middlesex, Worcester, Hampshire and Berkshire, who did not on the first election make choice of Representatives to represent them in the Congress of the United States, found them to stand as follows, viz.

. . . .

District of Worcester. Number of voters, 2281; [to] make a choice, 1141. Hon. Timothy Paine and Jonathan Grout, esquires, candidates. No choice.

1. Council Records, XXXI, 9, M-Ar.

The Second Election in Hampshire-Berkshire District, 29 January

As far as the newspapers were concerned, the only two candidates in the second election were Theodore Sedgwick and Samuel Lyman, although William Whiting and William Williams received more votes than they did in the first election. Furthermore, the issue of amendments to the constitution was apparently of growing concern, for a writer in a Boston newspaper on 22 January reported that a "great majority" in the west was in favor of amendments.

Rumors were spread by word of mouth about both Sedgwick and Lyman. Among the charges against Sedgwick were that he was opposed to amendments and that he was a public defaulter. This last charge did not appear in a newspaper until 25 March, just before the fourth election, when it was vigorously denied.

Sedgwick and his supporters accused Lyman and his followers of nominating John Worthington prior to the first election in order to draw votes away from

Sedgwick. Lyman denied this charge personally to Sedgwick, and Sedgwick's treatment of him continued to be an issue in the following elections.

In the voting on 29 January only ten men received votes, contrasted to twenty-two men in the election on 18 December. William Williams, who received 196 votes on 18 December, received 221 on 29 January; and William Whiting, who received 302 votes in December, received 578 in January. Thompson J. Skinner received the same number of votes as before, 233, while Worthington received none.

The most dramatic shift was in the votes for Sedgwick and Lyman. Sedgwick dropped from 801 votes in December to 716 in January, while Lyman's vote increased from 330 to 717, one more than for Sedgwick. Both totals were far short of the required majority of 1,257 out of a total vote of 2,513.

A Friend to Real Merit, Hampshire Chronicle, 21 January

Gentlemen: By late intelligence from our honorable General Court, we find there is no choice of federal Representative by the people of this district. How unhappy for ourselves that we could not have been more firmly united in the first attempt for that important purpose. Many of us have undoubtedly been ignorant of the qualifications of the gentleman whom I shall now take the liberty to recommend to your suffrages, and who will be most likely to give general satisfaction to men of every order in the community. His character as a politician is inferior to but few, and whenever honored with a public station, his views have always terminated in the best good of his constituents. He is a substantial Federalist, but not from motives of *selfishness*; cool and deliberate when engaged in controversies which require penetration and discernment. He has never been reproached with rashness, when called on to give his voice for or against any measure which has immediately concerned the landed or any other property of his fellow citizens. This, gentlemen, is the character we want, and which ought to fill the important and honorable office of federal Representative. Let us then ONE and ALL firmly determine to support the interest of that worthy and respectable inhabitant, Samuel Lyman, Esq., who, in consequence of the abilities which nature and a collegiate education have given him, is ably capacitated to assert and maintain the prerogatives of a free and independent people. His knowledge of agriculture is extensive; and he is generally known, by his own example, to be the farmer's friend, an encourager of commerce and the manufactures of his own country. We shall then, by giving him our votes, faithfully discharge a part of that duty which we owe to a faithful, honest and upright character.[1]

1. This item was addressed "To the Independent Electors of Federal Representative in the counties of Hampshire and Berkshire." During the campaign for the third election in the district, it was rumored that Lyman had written this paragraph himself, a charge denied by the printer of the *Hampshire Chronicle* on 18 February (printed below in The Third Election in Hampshire-Berkshire District).

Hampshire Gazette, 21 January

There were 2201 votes returned from this district into the secretary's office, for a federal Representative. The Hon. Theodore Sedgwick, Esq., had 801, Samuel Lyman, Esq., had 330—and these two gentlemen, having the highest number of votes, are sent out to the people in the precept for calling another meeting. No other person had 300 votes—so greatly were the people divided. *"By uniting we stand, by dividing we fall."*

There being no choice made of a federal Representative for this district, Thursday the 29th inst. is appointed by His Excellency the Governor, for the meeting of the several towns, to make choice of a gentleman to represent them in the new Congress of the United States.

An Observer, Independent Chronicle, 22 January (excerpt)[1]

In the upper division, they have been much agitated by parties, and at present there seems to be little probability of their settling into a calm state, unless an union should take place in favor of the Hon. Theodore Sedgwick, Esq., whose fidelity and abilities have rendered him respectable, while his principles are equally removed from tyranny on one hand, and from licentiousness on the other.

The great body of the community is certainly in favor of amendments, and will not knowingly vote for anybody who is against them. They have been much alarmed at the bold claims of those who openly assert, that the amendments were proposed only as an expedient to procure a majority, and that the rights of mankind are not originally equal. These things, being published here so frequently as they have been, have much lessened the influence of this town [Boston] upon the country, where an high value is set upon constitutional liberty, by a people who cannot bear to be contradicted upon principles which they hold sacred.

1. This is an excerpt from a longer article that discusses the need for amendments and analyzes the political situation in several other districts. Additional excerpts are printed above in the sections on the second elections in Essex, Middlesex, and Worcester districts.

Theodore Sedgwick to Thomas Dwight, Boston, 23 January[1]

I am informed that a very strange report is circulating in your county respecting a supposed fracas between your representative [Samuel Lyman] and myself. Permit me, while the House is sitting, for I have this moment information that the bearer is going out of town, to state the material facts which have come to my knowledge in this subject.

On my way to this town I met Mr. L[yman] at Worcester. He immediately entered into a conversation relative to the election, and soon observed that it had been said that he or some of his friends had procured the insertion of the paragraph in your paper respecting Colonel [John] Worthington.[2] Mr. [Samuel] Henshaw and Captain [Lemuel] Pomeroy were present.[3] No answer was made.

After some hesitation he proceeded in these words: "whoever [———] such a suggestion is a god damned liar." After a moment he in an angry tone demanded of me to be informed whether I had ever received information of that purport. His question put in that manner, I declined answering. He then moderated his voice, and said "as your friend I beg you to answer my question." I did in the affirmative. He then most solemnly, and with oaths of execration, declared that there was not the least foundation for such a suggestion, upon which I declared myself satisfied. I thought nothing further on the subject, until I was, some days after the poll was closed, informed that Mr. L. conceived himself abused by my suspicion. The next was from Mr. L. that he had heard such report was circulating, that it did not originate from him, that he had not the most distant idea of ill treatment. This declaration he has voluntarily, and I believe more than fifty times, without any application on my part, declared, and never has failed to add that it is his sincere wish that I may be elected, and that the only reason why he should permit himself to be considered as a candidate was the importunity of his friends. These declarations he is constantly repeating not only to myself but to every Federal member belonging to our district. How far these declarations are the result of sincerity, it is not in my power to determine.[4] Perhaps you may from this anecdote. On the way down a ludicrous description was given by myself of the Amherst member under the character of D. C.[5] This he faithfully reported to him. Of this I have all the evidence resulting from his own confession. I should not have given you this trouble, had not Colonel [Simeon] Learned and Mr. [Joshua] Danforth from Pittsfield this morning told me that my conduct with regard to Mr. L. was exceedingly misrepresented, and that it was a subject of general conversation on the road.[6]

1. RC?, Gratz Collection, PHi. Dwight's reply, 1 February, is printed below. Dwight was a prominent Springfield leader who had married a daughter of John Worthington. Dwight and Sedgwick's wife were cousins. He sat in the state legislature on several occasions and was a member of Congress, 1803-1805.

2. A paragraph in the *Hampshire Chronicle* on 10 December, only eight days before the first election, nominated Worthington for Representative from the Hampshire-Berkshire District (printed above). Presumably Lyman was accused of nominating Worthington to draw votes from Sedgwick. Worthington received 165 votes in the first election, but these votes, if they had been given to Sedgwick, would not have affected the outcome of that election.

3. Henshaw and Pomeroy were members of the General Court in 1788-1789, representing Northampton and Southampton, respectively.

4. Fisher Ames also doubted Lyman's declarations. He commented that "L[yman] will not give up—and seems to trust his chance, altho he thinks it a very hazardous one. If mischief ensues from his pretensions how will the respectable people, who now very justly esteem him, consider his conduct and motives. I am almost sick of reason—for when ambition or temper are up, it will not do its office. It shines, however, as the Negro said the sun does, 'in broad daylight when nobody need him' " (from Ames, Dedham, 18 January, RC?, Gratz Collection, PHi). The recipient of this letter is unknown, although from the context it is clear that Ames was writing to a friend in Springfield.

5. Amherst's representative to the General Court in 1788-1789 was Daniel Cooley. Sedgwick implies that Lyman told Cooley of Sedgwick's "ludicrous" description in order to win Cooley's support in the election. For whatever reason, Cooley later campaigned for Lyman (see the *Hampshire Gazette*, 29 April, printed below).

6. Sedgwick's conduct toward Lyman continued to be a campaign issue throughout the remaining elections in Hampshire-Berkshire District (see, for example, "Junius, Jr.," *Berkshire Chronicle*, 1 May, printed below).

Theodore Sedgwick to Mrs. Theodore Sedgwick, Boston, 27 January (excerpt)[1]

I hope your fears least I should continue in public life will not create any considerable pain. Believe me, my love, your wishes on this subject perfectly coincide with my own. It is impossible to suppose that a majority of the district can be in favor of a man, who has never disguised his political opinions and on no occasion [courted?] their vices. This is, I believe, my character. As it respects the public my most ardent desire is that men of wisdom and virtue may direct our councils and that I may participate not in the means but in the effects.

My own opinion on the event of the election coincides with that of every other person who desires me to serve on this occasion. They are loath to give me up but yet they nearly despair.

1. RC, Sedgwick Papers, MHi.

Thomas Dwight to Theodore Sedgwick, Springfield, 1 February (excerpt)[1]

I have received your esteemed favor of the 23d ult.[2] and was happy to find in it your own account of a fracas between you and Mr. [Samuel] L[yman] which has been misrepresented here by *his* friends with uncommon assiduity. Mr. L's own letters have contributed in no small degree to convince the people that your conduct towards him has been not cavalier only but insulting and abusive, and however some few of your friends here might doubt the truth of many of their circulating reports, yet for a long time it was not in their power to contradict such reports, from the want of a candid detail of facts. Indeed, before I received your letter, the people had wrought themselves into such a passionate resentment on the occasion that all reasoning on the subject would be idly spent. You will discover by our votes in this town how mighty the conversions. The spirit of insurgency and Antifederalism, which has for a long time before slumbered, was thoroughly awakened and joined in the general phrenzy, on this occasion.[3] It is true the dead were not raised, but the halt, the lame, the *blind*, and many *creeping things* were summoned and did in fact hobble together and give their suffrages for Mr. L. But among the number of his votaries there were undeniably many worthy good men who believe Mr. L has been abused by you, and *therefore* give him their votes. They will, I am sure, sooner or later discover their error. There are a few *very singular* people who cannot view Mr. L's conduct thro the same medium as the multitude. Among this few, there are certainly some whose good opinion he has hitherto highly valued. *Their* sentiments of him are now changed, and he will in the end find it out. You know my local situation as well as family connections with Mr. L.[4] I would not have a personal quarrel with him if I could avoid it, and therefore wish you not to make use of any assertions of mine as I can't conceive they can be of any service to you at present. There will soon be a time when the views and means of that gentleman will be better understood and acknowledged, even by those who are now his advocates. I shall not however go so far to prevent an altercation between Mr. L and myself as to dissimulate with him should he urge me to conversation on the subject.

It is the general opinion here that no choice will be made in this district by the second election. In the lower part of this county Mr. Lyman has almost all the votes. [William] Whiting has again exerted himself, but will not, I believe, gain much ground.

Every new election discovers, to *us honest* Hampshire and Berkshire men, some new arts to acquire popular opinion and cajole the people out of their reason as well as their votes. Precedents in the county of Suffolk are pled in justification of any expedients to get a person elected to office, so that a man will soon (without the imputation of indelicacy) be able to hawk himself in the highways, as an excellent candidate for the highest promotion, with as much freedom and vociferation as your market men now cry codfish and lobsters.

1. RC, Sedgwick Papers, MHi.
2. Printed above.
3. In the second election in Springfield, Lyman received 112 votes and Sedgwick only 14, whereas in the first election, Sedgwick carried the town against Lyman, 45 to 9.
4. Samuel Lyman's mother-in-law was a Dwight, but we have not been able to determine her relationship to Thomas Dwight.

Theodore Sedgwick to Benjamin Lincoln, Stockbridge, 6 February (excerpt)[1]

Nothing could have been more injudicious than the manner provided for the election of Representatives. In this district no election will, I presume, this time be made. Never at any time hath the rancor of party been more virulent. With regard to myself there is no character which is odious and detestable that has not been given me, excepting that it has not been said that I am a whoremaster. Mean, servile, and fawning to great men (pray have you observed it?); proud, haughty, and imperious to those in lower stations; a public peculator[2] and a private usurer; and above all things opposed to any amendments.[3] These are some of the few things which are proclaimed of your friend in every Antifederal meeting thro the district. It is added by way of completing my character that in all my public conduct I have betrayed the landed interest and have basely attempted to sacrifice its most important interests to commercial advantages. It would have given me pleasure would my friends have permitted me to retire from the public theater. The natural warmth and the habitual independence of my temper render me totally unfit to be a principal actor in such a scene. It is impracticable to disguise my feelings, and it is impossible for me to give the smile of approbation to the wretch whom my judgment has determine[d] to be a rascal.

It would be happy could the progress of this business be for the present suspended. The spirit of party would probably in a degree subside.

1. RC, Lincoln Papers, MHi.
2. The charge that Sedgwick was a public defaulter did not appear in the newspapers until "A Friend to the People" vigorously denied the charge (*Hampshire Chronicle*, 25 March, printed below).
3. Sedgwick was finally forced to make a public statement declaring that he was for amendments to the Constitution (see Sedgwick to Samuel Henshaw, 6 April, in the *Hampshire Gazette*, 6 May, printed below).

Official Election Returns, 7 February

HAMPSHIRE-BERKSHIRE DISTRICT, 29 JANUARY

Town	Hon. Theodore Sedgwick	Samuel Lyman, Esq.	William Williams, Esq.	Hon. Noah Goodman	William Whiting	Hon. Oliver Phelps	Hon. Thompson J. Skinner	[Eldred?] Lewis	John Bacon, Esq.	Thomas Lyman
Springfield	14	112	1							
Longmeadow	8	37								
West Springfield	3	81			31					
Wilbraham	4	26								
Northampton	78		18							1
Southampton	47									
Hadley	15	3	7							
South Hadley	2	24			6	1				
Amherst	5	1	42							
Granby		30								
Hatfield	17	1	23							
Whately										
Williamsburg										
Westfield	23	2	5		34					
Deerfield	18		15							
Greenfield	4	10	24							
Shelburne	8	33								
Conway										
Sunderland	12	2								
Montague	3		2							
Northfield	17									
Brimfield	29	1								
South Brimfield [Wales]										
Monson	2	43								
Pelham										
Greenwich		28								
Blandford					24					
Palmer		23								
Granville	3	21			20					
New Salem										
Belchertown	37	36								
Colrain	8	9	13							
Ware	3	25								
Warwick	1	12								

(Table continued on following pages)

HAMPSHIRE-BERKSHIRE DISTRICT, 29 JANUARY (continued)

Town	Hon. Theodore Sedgwick	Samuel Lyman, Esq.	William Williams, Esq.	Hon. Noah Goodman	William Whiting	Hon. Oliver Phelps	Hon. Thompson J. Skinner	[Eldred?] Lewis	John Bacon, Esq.	Thomas Lyman
Bernardston	2	28								
Chester										
Chesterfield										
Charlemont	3		11							
Ashfield			22							
Worthington	12									
Shutesbury										
Goshen										
Southwick	5				30					
Norwich [Huntington]	18	3								
Ludlow		32								
Leverett	1		20							
Montgomery	1	16								
Westhampton	22		11							
Cummington	7	3								
Buckland										
Middlefield										
Wendell										
Orange	8	3								
Holland										
Leyden		26								
Rowe		10								
Heath										
Easthampton	3	9	6							
Plantation No. 7 [Hawley]										
Sheffield	37				63					
Great Barrington	33				49					
Stockbridge	41	1	1						22	
Pittsfield	27				31			1		
Richmond	24	20								9
Lenox	3	1			34		39			
Lanesborough	79						48			
Adams										
Egremont					26					

(Table continued on following page)

HAMPSHIRE-BERKSHIRE DISTRICT, 29 JANUARY *(continued)*

Town	Hon. Theodore Sedgwick	Samuel Lyman, Esq.	William Williams, Esq.	Hon. Noah Goodman	William Whiting	Hon. Oliver Phelps	Hon. Thompson J. Skinner	[Eldred?] Lewis	John Bacon, Esq.	Thomas Lyman
Becket										
West Stockbridge	6				16				6	
Dalton										
Alford										
New Ashford	1						16			
Williamstown	4				34		71			
New Marlborough										
Tyringham	12				39					
Loudon [Otis]										
Windsor							56			
Partridgefield [Peru]					33		3			
Washington										
Hancock										
Lee	6	2			88				2	
Sandisfield		3			26					
Mount Washington										
Totals	716	717	221	6	578	1	233	1	39	1

Votes cast: 2513
Majority required: 1257

Governor and Council Record the Votes in the Second Election in Hampshire-Berkshire District, Monday, 9 February[1]

The Governor and Council upon the examination of the returns from the district[s] of Essex, Middlesex, Worcester, Hampshire and Berkshire, who did not on the first election make choice of Representatives to represent them in the Congress of the United States, found them to stand as follows, viz.

. . . .

District of Hampshire and Berkshire. Number of voters, 2513; [to] make a choice, 1257. Hon. Theodore Sedgwick, Esq., and Samuel Lyman, Esq., candidates. No choice.

1. Council Records, XXXI, 8, M-Ar.

The Third Election in Worcester District, 2 March

When the votes for the second election were recorded on 7 February, no candidate had a majority. Governor Hancock issued a precept on 9 February calling for a third election on 2 March, with the votes to be returned to the Secretary of the Commonwealth by 14 March.

As in the two previous elections, the two Worcester newspapers, with one exception, printed nothing until their last issues before the election on 2 March. The exception consisted of two items (one of which supported Timothy Paine) in the *Massachusetts Spy* on 19 February. Then on 26 February the *Massachusetts Spy* published five articles. Two of them supported Jonathan Grout, one supported Artemas Ward, one backed Timothy Paine, and the fifth did not mention any names. On the same day the *American Herald* published four items. One supported Grout, one opposed Paine because he had been a mandamus councillor, and the other two items urged that he be elected. The issue of Paine's appointment as a mandamus councillor by the British government in 1774 had been brought up for the first time by the Boston *Independent Chronicle*, 12 February, and not by the Worcester newspapers.

Despite the ambivalence of the newspapers, there was a considerable increase of interest, for the vote almost doubled over the first election on 18 December 1788: from 1,886 to 3,484. Grout was elected Representative by a decisive majority. Artemas Ward, who ran a poor third in each of the three elections, finally defeated Grout in the election to the second Congress in 1791. Paine was elected to the state House of Representatives in 1789.

Independent Chronicle, 12 February

A correspondent observes, that it is very extraordinary that the county of Worcester should give their suffrages for a federal Representative, to a *quondam mandamus councillor,* a man who has uniformly been opposed to a republican government and is possessed of no extraordinary qualifications to serve them in that capacity. *Tell it not in Gath!*

Lancaster to the Respectable Citizens of the District of Worcester, Massachusetts Spy, 19 February

As there appears to be no choice of a person, in your district, to represent you in the federal assembly, it behooves you to attend to the next election. The Hon. Mr. [Timothy] Paine and the Hon. Mr. [Jonathan] Grout are still the highest candidates; each of them have their zealous friends. The Hon. Mr. [Artemas] Ward has had a number of votes; but the number given has, by no means, been equal to the votes given for Messrs. Paine and Grout. It seems almost reduced to a certainty, that either Mr. Grout or Mr. Paine will be eventually chosen. They are characters that are generally known, both of them having been long in the county. Mr. Paine's acquaintance in the county has been more diffuse than Mr. Grout's, having held a number of respectable offices, by which the generality of the people have a knowledge of him. However, it may be necessary to delineate the characters of both—in short it has become necessary. No man in the district doubts, but what Mr. Paine sincerely wishes for an efficient government, a government adequate to the purposes of protecting each individual in the full and ample enjoyment of all his rights; and there is no doubt, but what Mr. Paine will be a warm advocate for the proposed amendments. That he is a friend to the substantial yeomanry of the district, is equally true. The integrity of his heart, and the great purity of his morals, have never been questioned. He early received a liberal education, and has always been esteemed a man of real substantial abilities, though not of the most splendid kind. Yet he is possessed of that kind of knowledge, which really will always render him extremely useful in public assemblies. No man distinguishes the right from the wrong readier than he. The great use that has been made of him, as a referee and an arbitrator, in this as well as in other counties, demonstrates that he is esteemed for his abilities and impartiality. He is a man of large landed property, and which lands are in the commonwealth of Massachusetts, and mostly in your district, consequently he is a proper person to represent the yeomanry of your district; and, added to this, his easy circumstances, and leisure, will admit his constant attendance on the federal court. I shall not say anything to the disadvantage of Mr. Grout. I mean to state facts simply. Grout's advantages, in the early part of life, were by no means equal to Mr. Paine's. No one will deny that Mr. Grout is a man of good natural capacity; but to say that he is a man of real science would be doubted, as would also, by many, his having abilities every way adequate to represent the great and important District of Worcester, in addition to which, his property is not in this commonwealth. All his real estate, except a small farm at Petersham, is supposed to lie in Vermont and New Hampshire. I do not mean to represent him as avaricious; but every man who knows him, knows that he is extremely attached to the management of his estates in Vermont and New Hampshire, and is constantly in one or the other of those governments, excepting the short time he is in the legislature of Massachusetts. Consider, my friends, which is the properest person of the two, and give your votes as your good sense shall direct. Put away all little foolish prejudices, and elect such a man as you will not be ashamed of hereafter, who is able and willing to assert and support your dearest rights and privileges—whether he is named Paine, Grout, Ward, or [Martin] Kinsly.[1]

1. For a reply see "Politicus," *Massachusetts Spy*, 26 February, printed below.

Massachusetts Spy, 19 February

The second day of March next is appointed by the legislature for the election of a Representative for this district. Unity of sentiment is earnestly recommended on this important occasion—and it is hoped the yeomanry of Worcester District will no longer suffer themselves to be divided and distracted by a baneful and pernicious party spirit, which is industriously fomented, not only by the open and professed enemies of our country, who still hold up their favorite maxim *"divide and rule,"* but also by insidious, pretended friends, who seek only their *own* emolument, without being, in the least, warmed by that patriotic flame, that pure emanation of the divine spirit of liberty, which glowed in the bosoms of all virtuous Americans, pervaded our councils, rendered our arms victorious, and, through innumerable dangers and difficulties, supported and inspired us in accomplishing the late glorious Revolution. Arouse, fellow citizens! Shake off your shameful lethargy!—and, by uniting in the choice of a person to represent you in the ensuing Continental Congress—a person who, to a thorough knowledge of the landed and commercial interests of this extensive district, joins a liberality of sentiment, inflexible integrity, and patriotic virtue, which render him fully capable of honorably representing you in that august body. Convince the world that you are not unworthy the invaluable blessings you enjoy, and that you will transmit them undiminished, unimpaired, to a grateful and admiring posterity!

Newspaper Support for Jonathan Grout, 26 February

In their last issues on 26 February before the third election on 2 March, each of the Worcester newspapers printed items supporting both Timothy Paine and Jonathan Grout. The three items following support Grout.

Politicus to the Printer, Massachusetts Spy

I have observed, in the course of our electioneering in this district, a number of pieces published in favor of the Hon. Mr. Paine, as being the most suitable person to represent us in the federal government, and only one short piece in favor of the Hon. Mr. Grout; and that one was on the very day of election, and consequently the district at large had no knowledge of it until it was too late to receive any advantage from it.[1] I, however, am not disposed to suspect any partiality in the matter; but only request you will be so obliging as to insert the following tribute of justice to Mr. Grout, as competitor with Mr. Paine, and leave it to the good sense of the people, in this important affair, after hearing all that has been said in favor of both candidates, to act for themselves.

The important period will now speedily arrive in which you, my fellow electors, will have an invaluable price put into your hands; and, I pray God, you may have hearts to make a proper improvement of it to your own present honor and advantage, as well as to the heart-felt satisfaction of the unborn descendants of those patriots and heroes who bravely stepped forth in the day of our common danger and distress, in support of our heaven-born rights and privileges, which were wantonly infringed on by a despotic British administration. This, my friends, is the important crisis, in which you are bound, by every tie of justice and gratitude, to bestow your suffrages on a man who has uniformly exerted his influence and abilities in favor of a republican government and universal liberty; in preference to one who was early in favor of a British administration. Is it possible, as you are now just emerging from the distresses of a horrid war, in which you have made unparalleled exertions to secure your independence, that you should trust it in the hands of any man, or body of men, which has thought, that that independence would prove your greatest curse? I have no doubt of Mr. Paine's integrity in this matter. He had a right to enjoy his sentiment. It was a mere matter of opinion, and so is the preference in point of election. It is observed in your last *Spy*, by a writer under the signature of Lancaster, *"that Mr. Paine's acquaintance in the county has been more diffuse than Mr. Grout's; having held a number of respectable offices, etc."* I believe Mr. Paine held the office of clerk of the Court of Common Pleas, and of the Sessions, by which means he had an opportunity to get acquainted with the sheriffs and lawyers of the county. If this is what was meant by his acquaintance being *"more diffuse,"* I believe it must be granted. I think he was likewise clerk of probate and register of deeds, by which he must have been acquainted with the business of filing and recording deeds, and minuting defaults; and, pray, what is all this knowledge (though useful in its place) towards qualifying a man for a national Representative? The author further observes, that "all his real estate, except a *small farm* at Petersham, is *supposed* to be in Vermont and New Hampshire." I *suppose*, however, that his *small* farm at Petersham is much larger than Mr. Paine's *large* one at Worcester, besides several other *small* ones which he owns in various parts of the county; and can his owning real estate in other parts of the United States be an objection to his being a Representative of the United States? I think, on the contrary, it is a circumstance highly in his favor. Mr. Grout has had a very liberal education, though not a collegiate one. He has been much, and for a long time, improved in public life; has an extensive knowledge of mankind, and acquaintance with the world; is well versed in geography; and acquainted with the relative situations and interest of the several states in the Union. He has uniformly expressed himself in favor of supporting the Constitution, since the adoption, though in favor of amendments. In fine, I believe his character, as a citizen, a friend, or a patriot, stands unimpeached. And, I think, the good people of the county cannot bestow their suffrages on a more deserving character.

Worcester District to the Free Electors of the County of Worcester,
American Herald

On Monday, the 2d day of March next, you will be, a third time, called upon, to give in your votes for a Representative to the federal Congress. There is the greatest necessity of a strict attendance on that day, and it is of the highest importance, that every man, who is a voter, should appear, and give in his vote for a Representative. The man, who will finally be chosen, will be either the PATRON, the FRIEND, and the GUARDIAN of your lives, liberties, and properties; or, he MAY be your SOVEREIGN, or your TYRANT. Do, my friends, consider the consequences. A few month[s] ago, there was scarcely a man among you, but that would have paid the most scrupulous attention to an affair of such consequence. The first object in the choice of a Representative should be to choose one, who will carefully guard your lives, liberties, and properties. Your lives depend, in a great measure, upon the security of your liberties; your liberties depend, more essentially, upon the security of your properties; and your properties depend, ultimately, upon good and wholesome laws, made for the protection of your landed interest.

The Hon. Mr. Grout and Hon. Mr. Paine are held forth as candidates; one of the two, in all probability, will be chosen. But as a choice is yet to be made (I will speak with candor) Mr. Grout is, I think, by far the most suitable man of the two, and my reasons are as follow: the man, who represents so much landed property as this county contains, ought himself to be [a] large landholder. Mr. Grout is the owner of a much greater landed interest in this county, than Mr. Paine. Mr. Grout also possesses a large landed interest in other states, which he has acquired by his superior knowledge in landed property, all which sufficiently demonstrate that he is a suitable person to represent the yeomanry of this county. Again, as to his experience: from the first infringement of American liberty by the hand of British tyrants, Mr. Grout has boldly advocated the independence of America, and has particularly been the friend and guardian of the rights of this country. He has been a member of the legislature almost every year since our rights were first invaded by foreign and domestic foes; and, he has therefore had a greater opportunity of being acquainted with our laws and government; and what is still more in his favor, his uprightness and integrity have never yet been warped from the rights of humanity. Again, he has long possessed the confidence and the trust of his countrymen, which he has never betrayed; and it is sufficiently known, that his abilities for that office are every way adequate to the importance of the station. Mr. Paine, it is well known, has been extremely attached to the British administration, and has therefore been opposed to the independence of America. His acquaintance with mankind is by no means adequate to Mr. Grout's. Mr. Grout has had occasion to attend the general assemblies in almost every state east of Pennsylvania, to transact business for himself, and others, by which means he has had an opportunity to form a more particular acquaintance with political characters, than the other candidate. Mr. Grout's friends are FIRM, and act from the purest motives, viz.: they vote for him because he has proved himself a friend to this country, and the rights of humanity. Mr. Paine's friends are *zealous* and *fearful*, and act, perhaps, from sinister motives, viz.: they may vote for him because they wish to have laws made that shall abolish equality, and raise *them* and *their sons*, to *honors, titles*, and *dignities*, in conformity to the British government. Think of these things: consider coolly, act deliberately, and choose wisely.

A Correspondent, American Herald

A correspondent observes, that he was lately asked by an honorable gentleman in Boston, who we were likely to choose in the District of Worcester for a federal Representative? And upon being answered, that Mr. Paine had the highest number of votes, exclaimed, "Is it possible, that the people of the county of Worcester, who have been uniformly in favor of a republican government, and have made the greatest exertions in supporting our independence, should, at the very organizing of our federal government, give their suffrages to a man, who has long been [attached?] to a British administration, and was chosen a mandamus councillor, for the purpose of carrying into execution the nefarious designs of that corrupted court."[2]

1. The reference is to a short item in the *Masssachusetts Spy*, 18 December, printed above.

2. After Jonathan Grout had been elected, the *Boston Gazette* on 16 March printed the following: "A correspondent congratulates us on the failure of Timothy Paine, Esq., to obtain an election in the county of Worcester. The independent yeomanry were convinced he had no other qualification for the place in question but his Toryism."

Newspaper Support for Timothy Paine, 26 February

In addition to the following three items in behalf of Paine, the *American Herald* printed an item by "Brookfield" arguing against Grout because of his landholdings outside the state; the *Massachusetts Spy* printed an "extract of a letter from a gentleman in Connecticut" supporting Artemas Ward and an item by "A Landholder" which did not clearly support either Grout or Paine.

A Yeoman of Worcester District, Massachusetts Spy

The candidates for a federal Representative, for this district, appear to be the Hon. Timothy Paine, Artemus Ward, and Jonathan Grout, esquires. I am a plain man, do not like many words, and am not fond of blackening characters. Mr. Paine, at the last choice, had the highest number of votes, Mr. Grout the next highest number, and Mr. Ward the smallest number. Had those who voted for Mr. Ward given their suffrages for Mr. Paine, or Mr. Grout, there would have been a choice. I am now informed that several over-zealous Federalists (who, if the report be true, are not acquainted with the general disposition of the honest yeomanry of this district) are aiming to set up Mr. Ward, and endeavoring by little artifices to get those who have hitherto voted for the other gentlemen, to give Mr. Ward their suffrages at the next choice for a federal Representative. These zealots may be assured their plan will not answer. Many who have heretofore given their votes for Mr. Paine, in order to show their disposition for reconciliation, and put an end to all party disputes, will, if these hot Federalists persist in bringing forward and forcing down Mr. Ward, immediately give their votes to Mr. Grout; as a number of us (and we have all a right to vote for whom we please) had rather have Mr. Grout than Mr. Ward. "Fair play is a jewel"—this is fair warning. If the friends of Mr. Ward will meet us half way, and give their votes for Mr. Paine, we will join them; and in all probability, by that means, we may be so happy as to effect a choice, and prevent farther trouble to the county, and ill will amongst individuals, which is the earnest wish of A YEOMAN of Worcester District.

A Free Elector to the Free Electors of Worcester District, Massachusetts Spy

The ungenerous methods taken by some persons to injure the Hon. Mr. Paine, in your esteem, are truly contemptible, and are evidently the ravings of a party to serve their own purposes. But has one thing been said against his uprightness, his integrity, or his abilities to serve you? No!—the tongue of slander has not yet dared to impeach him in either of these respects. It is evident, from the returns made, that at the late choice, he stood highest in the esteem of the respectable voters in this district. And it is hoped, that on the ensuing day of election, all who wish to promote the peace and tranquility of this district, and are desirous of choosing an able, virtuous Representative will give their attendance, and vote for the Hon. Timothy Paine, Esq., who is known, notwithstanding the breath of slander might insinuate to the contrary, to be a man of true republican principles, and one who will with firmness support our civil and religious rights and privileges.

A Correspondent, American Herald

A correspondent expresses his surprise, that there should be a citizen within this extensive district, who can hesitate a single minute, on which side to cast his vote, for a federal Representative, whether for the Hon. Mr. Paine, or the Hon. Colonel [Jonathan Grout]. Not that either is deficient in point of abilities to manage the great affairs of this mighty empire, but the motives which actuate the men, these are the essential points, one making the interest, the prosperity, and the security of the rights of the great family of this country his ultimate pursuit. Add to all this, that Mr. Paine is a gentleman of the strictest integrity and honor in his private walks of life—not to mention his more exemplary conduct in a moral view while the other honorable gentleman seeks his own emolument and aggrandizement, to the great neglect of the weightier matters of the community.

Official Election Returns, 14 March

WORCESTER DISTRICT, 2 MARCH

Town	Hon. Artemas Ward, Esq.	Hon. Timothy Paine, Esq.	Hon. Jonathan Grout, Esq.	Mr. Ebenezer Davis	Hon. Moses Gill, Esq.	Hon. Timothy [Pain?], Esq.	Simon Houghton	Samuel Baker, Esq.	Martin Kinsley	Mr. Caleb Hitchcock	Rev. Ebenezer Chaplin	Josiah Whitney, Esq.	Mr. William Jones	Dr. Israel Whiton	John Sprague, Esq.	Jonathan Warner, Esq.	Hon. Abel Wilder, Esq.
Worcester	15	62	60														
Lancaster	9	53	19														
Mendon		1	65														
Brookfield	4	42	146								1						
Oxford		52	15														
Charlton		55	46	2													
Sutton		42	111								4						
Leicester	15	15	35														
Spencer		15	79														
Rutland	3	32	72														
Oakham	3	3	61														
Paxton	10	18	21														
Barre	9	27	79							1							
Hubbardston		1	89														
New Braintree		14	62													1	
Southborough		25	20														
Westborough	4	18	42														
Northborough	16	8	3														
Shrewsbury	41	3	70												2		

(Table continued on following page)

WORCESTER DISTRICT, 2 MARCH *(continued)*

Town	Hon. Artemas Ward, Esq.	Hon. Timothy Paine, Esq.	Hon. Jonathan Grout, Esq.	Mr. Ebenezer Davis	Hon. Moses Gill, Esq.	Hon. Timothy [Pain?], Esq.	Simon Houghton	Samuel Baker, Esq.	Martin Kinsley	Mr. Caleb Hitchcock	Rev. Ebenezer Chaplin	Josiah Whitney, Esq.	Mr. William Jones	Dr. Israel Whiton	John Sprague, Esq.	Jonathan Warner, Esq.	Hon. Abel Wilder, Esq.
Lunenburg	11	20	50									1	1				
Fitchburg	10	16	20														
Uxbridge		11	27														
Harvard	15	14	24														
Dudley		33	56														
Bolton	19	17	7				1										
Upton	1	17	38														
Sturbridge																	
Leominster		84															
Hardwick	9	18	89														
Holden	5	32	25														
Western [Warren]		55	17														
Douglas		74	1														
Grafton	4	13	61	1	1												
Petersham		27	105														
Royalston	7	6	89														
Westminster	2	44	30														
Templeton		38	14					1									
Princeton		66	40														
Ashburnham	3	29													1		
Winchendon	1	37	42														
Northbridge		28	19														
Ward [Auburn]	4		48														
Athol																	
Milford	15																
Sterling																	
Berlin	13	13	2														
Gardner		12	22														
Boylston	3	36	23														
Gerry [Phillipston]	5	15	24														1
Totals	256	1241	1968	2	1	1	1	1	1	1	4	1	1	1	2	1	1

Votes cast: 3484
Majority required: 1743

Governor and Council Record the Votes in the Third Election in Worcester District, Monday, 16 March[1]

The Governor and Council on the examination of the returns from the districts of Hampshire and Berkshire and Worcester for Representatives to represent them in the Congress of the United States found them to stand as follows, viz.

. . . .

District of Worcester. Number of voters, 3484; [to] make a choice, 1743. Hon. Jonathan Grout, Esq., had 1968 and is chosen.

1. Council Records, XXXI, 16, M-Ar.

Samuel P. Savage to George Thacher, 31 March (excerpt)[1]

You doubtless know that Mr. [Jonathan] Grout is chosen for Worcester. I would fondly hope he has honesty, sense, and patriotism, for if he has not something excellent within to balance the inharmoniousness of his name, I cannot conceive any person who is blessed with ears would ever vote for him.

1. FC, Savage Papers, MHi. The copy is unsigned, the place of writing is not indicated, and it is addressed to "Mr. Thatcher," who from the context is in Congress. The manuscript is in Savage's handwriting, and he wrote several letters from Weston to George Thacher in Congress.

The Third Election in Hampshire-Berkshire District, 2 March

The Governor and Council recorded the votes for the second election on 9 February. Again, no candidate had a majority, and Governor Hancock issued a precept for a third election on 2 March, with the votes to be returned to the Secretary of the Commonwealth by 14 March.

The only documents located for the third election are in the incomplete runs of the three newspapers published in the two counties. Five of the newspaper items located supported Samuel Lyman and only one supported Theodore Sedgwick. One article was a vitriolic attack on "Monitor" in the *Hampshire Gazette*, 17 December (printed above). "Monitor" had opposed Sedgwick by insisting that Hampshire County with 50,000 people was entitled to a Representative, whereas Berkshire with 30,000 people was not. A writer in the *Berkshire Chronicle* declared that since Berkshire was so divided, the district ought to vote for Thompson J. Skinner.

The rumor campaign against Lyman, among other things, reported that he wrote the article praising himself, "A Friend to Real Merit," in the *Hampshire Chronicle* on 21 January (printed above). The publisher of the *Hampshire Chronicle* denied this categorically on 18 February and urged other newspaper publishers to reprint his denial.

The votes on 2 March were almost double the number cast on 29 January, rising from 2,513 to 4,731. Samuel Lyman's vote more than doubled—from 717 to 1,557; Theodore Sedgwick's from 716 to 1,449. William Whiting, the lone Antifederalist candidate, received 578 votes in the second election and 1,083 in the third. Thompson J. Skinner's votes increased from 233 to 606, while William Williams dropped from 221 to 27.

The required majority of the 4,731 votes cast was 2,366, and since no candidate received that number, a fourth election was necessary.

Massachusetts Centinel, 14 February

A correspondent observes, that as there is no choice of a Representative in the western district, it is expected the electors will at their next meeting unite in Samuel Lyman, Esq., as his character as a legislator stands fair, after several years experience in the General Court. He has been particularly distinguished for his attention to business, his knowledge of the state finances, and his happy talent in reconciling parties, and uniting them in measures for the good of the commonwealth. In short, he is one of those fair, open, honest characters, who never fail to have an influence in public assemblies, and direct it for the public good; therefore the interest of the people must be safe in his hands.[1]

1. This item was reprinted in the *Hampshire Chronicle*, 25 February.

Hampshire Chronicle, 18 February

The printer of the *Hampshire Chronicle* [Ezra W. Weld], having learned from the best authority, that there have been various reports industriously circulated through this district, declaring Samuel Lyman, Esquire, to be the author of a publication which appeared in his paper a few weeks past, holding himself up to the public as a fit candidate for the office of federal Representative,[1] takes this method most respectfully to assure the public, that the said reports are totally groundless. How illiberal, how ungenerous and uncharitable, is such a declaration, when it is well known that this gentleman was at the General Court, sitting in Boston, almost one hundred miles from Springfield, when that publication in his favor was handed to the public! It may further be depended on, that Mr. Lyman was no way influential in the promotion of its publication, and had not even the least knowledge of the existence of such a piece, until a number of days after it was published.

Mr. [William] Butler, printer of the *Hampshire Gazette*, and Mr. [Roger] Storrs, printer of the *Berkshire Chronicle*, are requested to publish the foregoing declaration in their respective papers, that truth may be established, and falsehood detected and exhibited to the public in its proper colors.[2]

1. See "A Friend to Real Merit," *Hampshire Chronicle*, 21 January, printed above in The Second Election in Hampshire-Berkshire District.
2. Both publishers ignored the request.

Hampshire Chronicle, 18 February

A correspondent observes, that it gives him great pain, to see and hear with what assiduity some persons attempt to injure and wound the reputation of Mr. [Samuel] Lyman, who is one of the candidates for a Representative for this district. He certainly is a worthy, a sensible, and an honest man.

These things portend and forebode innumerable evils, which may originate from the nature of free governments; but let us, says the correspondent, be candid and liberal, and not injure either of the gentlemen who are candidates, and whom we esteemed before they were considered as candidates for that important office.

I have heard, says the correspondent, that if Mr. Lyman should be appointed, he would not accept of the appointment, on the account of his having a new farm under cultivation, which requires his immediate care; but I have not the least doubt, but that if he should be honored with the suffrages of his fellow citizens, and be chosen, he would accept of the appointment. And for my part, observes the correspondent, I should be happy if we should be so fortunate as to make so good a choice.

Berkshire Chronicle, 20 February

Extract of a letter from a gentleman in the county of Hampshire, to another in Lanesborough, February 13.

Permit me to recommend to your most vigorous exertions, in the ensuing election for a federal Representative, that able statesman and feeling citizen, Thompson J. Skinner, Esq., of Williamstown, as your district seem to be much divided. He will not only represent the feelings of the people, but can and will do his part to guide and reduce to form the deranged finances of the United States.

A Friend to All Parties to Mr. Monitor, Hampshire Gazette, 25 February

You will pardon me if I rake over the ashes of your publication of December last,[1] upon the subject of electing a Representative for the western counties. Whatever be my motive at this period of time, in animadverting upon so old a performance, and whatever be the cause that hath hitherto preserved you from the ravages consequent on detection, whether a contempt that originated in its insufficiency, or a spirit of mercy too partially indulgent on your generosity and candor, it becomes not you to enquire. My thoughts both of you and your offspring I shall publish to you with decency and freedom. The influence of your principles in general I know not the extent of; but am fully satisfied that the influence of that piece could creep nowhere but into the unenlightened vault of ignorance, or the narrow pen of party prejudice. Your address, however insufficient for the support of the original design, certainly could aspire at no higher an object than to delude the illiterate and flatter the ignoble. You will not therefore be so unjust as to suppose that the fear of your injuring the cause for which I contended, prompts me at this late hour to notice that performance, nor ascribe to me a less honorable motive—viz. an endeavor to spur your audacity, and draw you into an altercation for the pleasure of wounding your feelings. No. I can assure you that my only wish is to furl the veil which hides you from the show of men, and let your real character meet the meridian of the public judgment. And indeed when you plucked that contagious weed from the dreary banks of your Cocytus and transplanted it into this seminary of intelligence, I did not at all fear its poisonous quality on account of the barrenness of the soil on which only its seed could be scattered.

But to elucidate your patriotic intentions, suffer me to recur to one of your sentences in which you ask, "Whether the county of Hampshire shall give up the privilege of a Representative, when it forms an eighth part of the commonwealth, merely because the General Court hath seen fit to annex the county of Berkshire *with* it? Or whether fifty thousand *souls* shall be unrepresented in the federal court, when by the Constitution *thirty thousand* gives a Representative?"

Whether this paragraph be not pregnant with these three qualities, viz. *deceit*, *bigotry*, and *ignorance*, let the public judge. Pray what right hath the county of Hampshire to one federal Senator and two Electors, when the *whole state* can claim but two of the former and ten of the latter? But friendly *Monitor*, when we are so liberally provided for, will you be so *mean*, so *narrow*, so *bigoted*, and so *ungenerous* as to refuse the county of Berkshire one morsel of the political loaf?

I will go one step farther, however, and tell you that if things were otherwise than they are, your insinuation would have no force in it. Our *state* is to be represented and not our counties. Do you suppose that the federal governors will enquire which member is from the county of Hampshire, which from Suffolk, etc.? No—by no means. It will be enough for them to know that there are eight from the state of Massachusetts, and it will be sufficient for us if we do our duty by sending *that number*.

But perhaps you will answer, that the county of Hampshire contains *fifty thousand* inhabitants (not to say souls), and the Constitution allows one for every *thirty thousand*. But is that saying that there shall be one *in* or *out* of every 30,000? No. You are ignorant of the subject on which you pretend to write. The rule is applied generally to states, viz. each state shall send Representatives to the federal court, in proportion to their inhabitants in that ratio. We know not but that these members had better been all chosen out of one county; however, there is most certainly an incidental convenience in selecting them from different parts of the state, and perhaps the General Court have made as just a distribution of this general right as could have been made. Although it is not necessary in the scale of positive right, that either of the western counties, or that any particular county, should have a *state* [i.e., federal] *Representative* taken from it, yet upon that of *peace* and *unity* it is undoubtedly convenient. I hope you will be convinced from these remarks on that paragraph, that in it you discovered the meanness of *deceit*, the narrowness of *bigotry*, and the stupidity of *ignorance*.

But Mr. Monitor, what design but a bad one could you have had in adding those futile observations at the bottom of your piece. If the character of that worthy candidate, who it is conceded must inevitably bear the *palm*, if, I say his character had really been extolled to his prejudice, did it need the additional gall of your pen to aggravate the evil? Here the black peeps thro the white. You question whether that gentleman, "if he is a man of feeling, would thank the late writers for lavishing encomiums upon him taking so much pains to establish his character by fulsome panegyrics." Away with your paltry innovations upon the feelings of humanity. It is not nature, but artificial pride that shrinks from the public recital of excellent qualities and noble actions. You acknowledge yourself destitute, then, of that boldness of spirit which shudders not to invade this *pretended modesty* of nature. But you, my friendly Monitor, may let your mind rest easy on this score; for be assured that upon your own principles your feelings will never be shocked or wounded by the *violence* of *encomium*.

To tell you the truth, I find it difficult in writing to you to restrain my pen from ridicule, and your own conscience, unless it be *tongueless*, must tell you that you deserve it. If Shakespeare was alive, he would tell you with an air of irony that you were born under a fortunate planet. Nay, Mr. Monitor, let me know whether you cannot yourself "*calculate nativities, erect all manner of schemes, make almanacs, tell credulous men their future fortunes, appoint the eclipses of the sun and moon, set Venus and Mercury by the ears, and stir up furious Mars to make a hurly burly in the elements; or whether you cannot wheedle the sour curmudgeon SATURN, into a soft obliging humor, or fret the noble Jupiter to madness by a conjunction with his mortal enemy, and a thousand more astrological wonders.*" Repent, and be forgiven.

1. See "Monitor," *Hampshire Gazette*, 17 December, printed above in The First Election in Hampshire-Berkshire District.

A Yeoman to the Electors of the Western District, Hampshire Gazette, 25 February

No choice has as yet been effected in this district of a federal Representative, although we have the second time been called to offer votes for that purpose, which failure, in a very considerable degree, arises from the almost incredible inattention of the great body of electors. Consequently we are next Monday again called to depute a person with the representative majesty of fifty or sixty thousand inhabitants. In those who will give the smallest opportunity to reflection, the magnitude of the occasion cannot fail to excite the most critical attention. Or must posterity be told that the present generation (after having greatly secured) abandoned the exercise of the inestimable right of election, to the mercy of either the misguided, interested, or wicked, and therefore failed to transmit the blessed inheritance. Forbid it every manly and generous sentiment— may we rather atone for past neglect by generally and faithfully conferring our suffrages on the character best formed to promote and secure the true interest of ourselves and our posterity. From a long inclination to believe we shall now attend, and to the best of our understandings discharge a duty so important, I shall take the liberty to suggest a few considerations respecting the gentlemen who in any degree have presented themselves as objects of our confidence; premising that from the small proportion of votes on each former occasion, William Williams, and Thompson Skinner, esquires, there is little if any prospect of their success, and I am told that they, with their suspected friends, do now wholly relinquish any idea of such an event. I may also add that there is little if any more prospect of effecting the choice of William Whiting, Esquire. Admitting which, a preference will remain to either Theodore Sedgwick, or Samuel Lyman, esquires. I submit therefore to the candid and dispassionate on which side the advantage lies when we draw a comparison, and which of the two last gentlemen is the most suitably entrusted with such important concerns. The plea of abilities urged by the advocates for Mr. Sedgwick is at best but flimsy, for it may at least be doubted whether he possesses so valuable a fund of knowledge to form the statesman, as Mr. Lyman. But of what consequence are abilities, if not united to a suitable regard for the rights of mankind, which at least appears not a probable trait of Mr. Sedgwick's character from deriving his principal support from those who hold, and are expectants to, offices with their connections and dependents—a circumstance alone sufficient to adopt his choice. On the other hand, of what class are those who appear to wish the choice of Mr. Lyman? You will reply, the substantial and considerate citizens and yeomanry of this district. Has he not ever been distinguished for his moderation and conciliatory character, together with a most thoro knowledge of the public finances and returns? On a view of which circumstances, those who have heretofore voted for either Whiting, Williams, or Skinner, with any others, cannot now act more consistently than in voting for that friend to the people, Samuel Lyman, Esquire.

Hampshire Gazette, 25 February

A correspondent observes, that he has just seen the precept from the Governor, calling upon us to make the third trial for a federal Representative, and that Mr. [Theodore] Sedgwick and Mr. [Samuel] Lyman are named in the precept as having the greatest number of votes in our last attempt.

Newspaper electioneering, says our correspondent, is very disagreeable to him, and he detests everything that looks like personal abuse and scandal on the one hand, or fulsome flattery on the other. He will not, therefore, trouble our readers with any observations that can possibly wound the delicate sensibility of either of the candidates, or of any of their partisans. But should there be any voters who are not predetermined how to act, and who wish to promote the best interest of this state, *to them* he would further observe (what is already well known to the members in Congress) that Mr. Sedgwick,[1] while in Congress from this state, made every exertion in the power of human abilities, to have justice done to this state relative to the Penobscot expedition,[2] and respecting those heaps, those mountains, of old Continental bills which were thrown into our treasury, and into the hands of our citizens; and that his manly eloquence, rational arguments, and unabating zeal in the cause of this state and the citizens thereof, had so far worked conviction on the minds of many influential members of Congress, that this important business was in a fair train to be accomplished; and that it is believed, should this gentleman now obtain the suffrages of the district, that he would be able to give the finishing stroke to this interesting affair.

Our correspondent adds, that some members of Congress have observed, that the only fault they ever found in Mr. Sedgwick was a too great attachment to the interests of his constituents. Massachusetts was always his idol—to exalt her character was ever the ardent wish of his soul.

Tis also well known, in and out of Congress, continues our correspondent, that Mr. Sedgwick is a mortal enemy to heavy land taxes, that he has unceasingly pled the cause of the farmer, and represented him as unable to raise money to pay taxes, and at the same time be able to make such improvements in agriculture as are absolutely necessary to advance our national prosperity. These are truths which need no comment. Happy! thrice happy people, to have such a candidate![3]

1. Starting with "Mr. Sedgwick," this essay was closely paraphrased in the *Salem Mercury*, 10 March, under the title: "Of Mr. Sedgwick, Candidate in the Upper District for Federal Representative."

2. In July 1779 Massachusetts sent an expedition against the British post at Penobscot, Me., which was not authorized by the Confederation Congress. The disastrous expedition left the state with a debt of $387,000, which it attempted to have charged to the United States (Ferguson, *Power of the Purse*, 204-5).

3. This essay was reprinted, with a change in the first paragraph from "third trial" to "fifth trial," in the *Hampshire Chronicle*, 29 April. For an attack on this article, see "Curtius," *Hampshire Gazette*, 29 April, printed below in The Fifth Election in Hampshire-Berkshire District.

Hampshire Chronicle, 25 February

A correspondent expresses his surprise, that the public papers have given no account which of the candidates voted for in this district, for Representative, has had the highest number of votes. He thinks the reasons for such a neglect are not obvious, as the Boston newspapers have never failed of giving, at every election, a particular account of the highest number of votes, as returned into the secretary's office. Reports, however, from gentlemen of integrity, say, that Samuel Lyman, Esq., had a small majority at the last election. This is pleasing intelligence, as it is likely he will at the next meeting be chosen to fill that truly important office.[1]

1. Lyman received 717 votes to 716 for Theodore Sedgwick in the second election.

Hampshire Gazette, 4 March

A correspondent informs us that a certain magistrate in the south part of this county, eat up with pious zeal for the honor of the district, has pushed his horses so hard in pursuit of votes for Samuel Lyman, Esquire, thro various parts of both counties, that their marrow-bones are visible at an immense distance, and that tis much to be doubted whether said beasts will live to taste the herbage of the ensuing summer. He went, Hudibras like, with one faithful Sancho, accustomed either to mix liquor or drink it; and in his excursion to the west, enquired for such persons as John Hubbard, and Captain [Roswell] Downing, of Sheffield,[1] gentlemen *of established character, to whom the secrets of the club were to be communicated*; that in a fit of phrenzy, he was left to call on William

Whiting, Esq., to request him to give up his pretentions as a candidate for the district, in favor of Mr. Lyman, who answered him, "I esteem myself as well qualified to serve the district as either of the candidates, and besides, sir, am certain I was chosen the last election day, had the votes given for me been duly returned. I shall therefore keep what I have got, and get what I can." *Help, Lord, for the godly man ceaseth, and the faithful fail among the children of men!*

1. Hubbard was active in Shays's Rebellion and was fined for his participation in it. He represented Sheffield in the General Court, 1789-1791, and perhaps later. Downing was a militia captain during the Revolution, but no evidence has been located to indicate what role he took during the Rebellion.

Official Election Returns, 14 March

HAMPSHIRE-BERKSHIRE DISTRICT, 2 MARCH

Town	Hon. Theodore Sedgwick, Esq.	Samuel Lyman, Esq.	William Whiting	William Williams, Esq.	[---] Clap	Ebenezer Warner	Hon. Thompson J. Skinner, Esq.	John Worthington, Esq.	Jeremiah Hirsh	Hon. John Bacon	Elisha Hunt
Springfield	18	126									
Longmeadow	7	42									
West Springfield	7	84	155								
Wilbraham	11	85									
Northampton	112	17									
Southampton	56	14			1						
Hadley	36	10									
South Hadley	2	45									
Amherst	15	70	4								
Granby		51									
Hatfield	35	11		1							
Whately	16	15		1							
Williamsburg											
Westfield	41	1	74								
Deerfield	37	18									
Greenfield		37									
Shelburne	4	58	18								
Conway	3	88									
Sunderland	24	11		1							

(Table continued on following pages)

HAMPSHIRE-BERKSHIRE DISTRICT, 2 MARCH *(continued)*

Town	Hon. Theodore Sedgwick, Esq.	Samuel Lyman, Esq.	William Whiting	William Williams, Esq.	[———] Clap	Ebenezer Warner	Hon. Thompson J. Skinner, Esq.	John Worthington, Esq.	Jeremiah Hirsh	Hon. John Bacon	Elisha Hunt
Montague	45	1	10								
Northfield											
Brimfield	45	4									
South Brimfield [Wales]	2	31									
Monson	15	43									
Pelham		66	1								
Greenwich											
Blandford	36	9	40					2			
Palmer	1	24	5								
Granville	4	30	61								
New Salem		50									
Belchertown	30	63				1					
Colrain	12	46									
Ware	6	50									
Warwick	10	18									1
Bernardston	1	40		1							
Chester											
Chesterfield	24	5									
Charlemont	4	30		3							
Ashfield											
Worthington	65	4									
Shutesbury		44									
Goshen	5	23						1			
Southwick	29	3	5								
Norwich [Huntington]											
Ludlow		75									
Leverett											
Montgomery											
Westhampton	36	26									
Cummington	1			2				17			
Buckland											
Middlefield	5	40									

(Table continued on following pages)

HAMPSHIRE-BERKSHIRE DISTRICT, 2 MARCH *(continued)*

Town	Hon. Theodore Sedgwick, Esq.	Samuel Lyman, Esq.	William Whiting	William Williams, Esq.	[- - - -] Clap	Ebenezer Warner	Hon. Thompson J. Skinner, Esq.	John Worthington, Esq.	Jeremiah Hirsh	Hon. John Bacon	Elisha Hunt
Wendell	15	4									
Orange	8	4									
Holland											
Leyden											
Rowe											
Heath	19	1									
Easthampton	16	23									
Plantation No. 7 [Hawley]											
Sheffield	71		77						1		
Great Barrington	44		46								
Stockbridge	64	1	21				3				
Pittsfield	50		48								
Richmond	61	2	31							1	
Lenox	7	4	50				56				
Lanesborough	102						126				
Williamstown	6	1	47				105				
Adams	1		1				133				
Egremont	4	2	43								
Becket	33	1	8								
West Stockbridge	10		69				1				
Dalton											
Alford	14		31								
New Ashford	4		2				35				
New Marlborough	53		20								
Tyringham	13		66								
Loudon [Otis]											
Windsor	1						102				
Partridgefield [Peru]	12		1				11				
Washington	12		15								
Hancock											

(Table continued on following page)

HAMPSHIRE-BERKSHIRE DISTRICT, 2 MARCH *(continued)*

Town	Hon. Theodore Sedgwick, Esq.	Samuel Lyman, Esq.	William Whiting	William Williams, Esq.	[----] Clap	Ebenezer Warner	Hon. Thompson J. Skinner, Esq.	John Worthington, Esq.	Jeremiah Hirsh	Hon. John Bacon	Elisha Hunt
Lee	12		100				16			2	
Sandisfield	14	6	39								
Mount Washington	3		13								
Totals	1449	1557	1083	27	1	1	606	2	1	3	1

Votes cast: 4731
Majority required: 2366

Governor and Council Record the Votes in the Third Election in Hampshire-Berkshire District, Monday, 16 March[1]

The Governor and Council on the examination of the returns from the districts of Hampshire and Berkshire and Worcester for Representatives to represent them in the Congress of the United States found them to stand as follows, viz.

District of Hampshire and Berkshire. Number of voters, 4731; [to] make a choice, 2366. Hon. Theodore Sedgwick, Esq., 1449; Samuel Lyman, Esq., 1557. Candidates. No choice.

1. Council Records, XXXI, 16, M-Ar.

The Fourth Election in Hampshire-Berkshire District, 30 March

The Governor and Council recorded the results of the third election on 16 March. Samuel Lyman received 1,557 and Theodore Sedgwick 1,449 votes, but 2,366 was the required majority out of 4,731 votes cast. Furthermore, William Whiting with 1,083 votes and Thompson J. Skinner with 606 remained in the running, while only 36 votes were scattered among seven other men. Skinner's withdrawal shortly before the election on 30 March probably was an advantage for Sedgwick.

During the campaign the newspapers continued the argument begun in previous elections over the respective claims of the two counties to a Representative. Meanwhile, the rumor that Sedgwick was a public defaulter, which had been started prior to the second election on 29 January, became so widespread that Sedgwick's supporters published a public denial in the newspapers.

No precept for the fourth election has been located, but since Governor Hancock had usually issued precepts for the next election on the same day that the votes of the previous election were recorded, he probably issued the precept for the fourth election on 16 March. In any case, the election was called for 30 March, with the votes to be returned to the Secretary of the Commonwealth by 9 April (*Berkshire Chronicle*, 27 March).

If the precept was issued on 16 March, this left only two weeks between that date and the election, an unusually short time as compared to the other elections, and the precept did not reach Northampton in Hampshire County until 25 March, only five days before the election. Sedgwick's supporters charged that the Governor had deliberately allowed so little time in order to aid Samuel Lyman. However, Samuel Henshaw assured Sedgwick that Sheriff Elisha Porter of Hampshire County would see to it that the precepts would be rushed to "such towns as will vote like rational beings." Presumably this precluded delivery to towns which had voted for Samuel Lyman in previous elections. In the case of the town of Greenwich, which voted overwhelmingly for Lyman in the second and fifth elections, a newspaper reported that the precept for the fourth election had been left three miles from the town by "a stranger" and that the town had not held an election because it did not know that one had been called.

Shortly after the results of the election were recorded on 9 April, the Northampton and Springfield newspapers reported that the votes for twenty-one towns had been either detained or had not been returned in time to be counted. The supporters of both Sedgwick and Lyman charged that their candidates had been cheated out of the election. For the documents pertaining to this issue, see The Question of Delayed and Missing Election Returns, 15 April–3 May, printed below.

A Whiting's Man, Hampshire Gazette, 4 March[1]

Three trials we have made to choose a Representative for Congress. I believe, upon enquiry, the last attempt will be found as fruitless as the two first. Only I expect the gentleman for whom I write will rise upon the other gentlemen in the number of his votes. Taking it for granted that there is no choice, I mean to be in season against our fourth attempt. For *electioneering* is now all the fashion. I have seen several pieces in the papers in favor of the Hon. Mr. [Theodore] Sedgwick, and Samuel Lyman, Esq., as if forsooth either of those gentlemen were to be chosen. Is it not very strange that nothing has been published to display the singular talents, abilities, and virtues of the Honorable William Whiting, Esq. It is very extraordinary that in three several elections, the majority of voters in this great district should overlook a gentleman of such undoubted character.

That the county of Berkshire should have the Representative is so fair and reasonable, that it seems to be conceded by the greater part; since four gentlemen have been voted for in that county, and but one in Hampshire. If Hampshire have enjoyed two Electors out of ten, and one Senator out of two in the commonwealth, I think they may well be content and give Berkshire the privilege of a Representative. In the language of the "Yeoman," a polite writer in the *Hampshire Gazette*, "premising that from the small proportion of votes on each former occasion, William Williams, and Thompson Skinner, esquires, there is little if any prospect of their success; and I am told that they with their *suspected* friends do now wholly relinquish any idea of such an event."[2] So, if I comprehend the grammar, these competitors are out of the way. But strange blindness, this very "Yeoman," after presumptuously insinuating that there is little prospect of Mr. Whiting's obtaining the choice, goes on to beg votes for Mr. Lyman.

Now, gentlemen electors, I will fairly canvass the question of qualifications. Which of the gentlemen, Mr. Whiting, Mr. Lyman, or Mr. Sedgwick, are [———] [———] with talents to represent this great district?

And first, of Mr. Lyman. The "Yeoman" praises him for "his moderation and conciliatory character." He adds other things which are only words of cour[——]. He builds his strength upon Mr. Lyman's "*moderation* and conciliatory character." I know very well what [he?] means; he means to persuade us that Mr. Lyman will answer our purpose, and so hook us in, and draw off [our?] votes from Mr. Whiting. But plainly, Mr. "Yeoman," I am a man of fixed sentiments and a fixed plan. I [am?] for none of your pendulums. There is no knowing which way they will swing.

I have other objections to make to Mr. Sedgwick. Even his friends tell about his wisdom, firmness, and influence, what sway he formerly had in Congress, and his hating heavy land taxes and the like. These are the very things you ought to be most afraid of. Now I know the gentleman very well. I know he will follow his own opinion, and as he and Mr. Whiting do not agree in opinions, so I am against him. He will never come into our views, that is certain. Now if Mr. Sedgwick with his influence etc. should get into Congress, he would manage matters so that I believe the people would generally set down contented and easy and would have nothing to do but to mind their own private business, and to live peaceable and quiet lives. Everybody that understands politics knows that it is best to have some bones to pick among the states, and to keep up something of a *hurly-burly* now and then, [or?] the people's jealousy will all go to sleep; and then, gentlemen, when you have such rulers as not to be jealous of them, where are your liberties that you have talked so much about. If we should get a number of such men into Congress, I don't know what would come next. So you see plain enough, that we ought not to give our votes for such a man as Mr. Sedgwick.

Now let us see what is to be said in favor of Mr. Whiting.

1. He is a representative of the County of Berkshire in the Senate of this state. But Mr. Sedgwick, and Mr. Lyman, are only representatives of towns, and therefore our honor is concerned to prefer Mr. Whiting. For our district contains not less than [80,000?] inhabitants—the largest in the state. And the name of the Hon. William Whiting, Esq., will be [a?] mighty credit to the largest district in Massachusetts.

2. Everybody, far and near, knows that the gentleman in whose behalf I plead, when Judge Whiting, notwithstanding his oath, etc., was distinguished for his opposition to government. And how much has he suffered for it; being under bonds, etc.? Ought we not to reward so much uprightness and integrity, honest electors? For consider how every party ought to be represented; and if we send Mr. Whiting, who will say that this noble district is not equally represented.

3. As to abilities, if he has not so much wisdom, as some call it, then surely

he will not be so cunning as to run away with our liberties. You know we ought to be guarded in this spot.

4. As to sobriety, temperance, and other moral virtues, few men can be set in comparison with Mr. Whiting, you know.

5. They tell us about the other gentlemen being attached to the farming interest. It is granted. And is not Mr. Whiting attached to another interest as important as husbandry—to the mercantile interest? The Congress are to have the power of laying duties of impost and excise, but we may conjecture that Mr. Whiting will be against all excises upon rum, and other spirits, as cider, penny-whiskey, etc. And should those articles be loaded with heavy taxes, how could we live? We should be curtailed of our best privileges; we must pay the taxes, and the substantial farmers run away with all the profits; and we and the poor merchants and retailers must starve. Rouse, brethren, if we don't take care in this spot, we had as good be dead as alive—so, all our liberties will be gone at once.

Now some may hope that Mr. Lyman's friends will tire us out, but this will never be, and therefore we pray all of them to join us in the next choice; and when we have an opportunity, we will do them as good a turn, if they won't vote for Mr. Sedgwick. We don't despair of getting some votes from Mr. Sedgwick's friends, but then we expect to worry them [out?] of patience, and then we shall carry it as we have [in?] mind. Those who are for a firm, uniform, and quiet government, and for this end vote for Mr. Sedgwick, we don't expect to gain them. Let them take care of the general good and the landed interest as they call it. We believe that our interest is of more importance than theirs; and we are sure, if others think as they ought, that we shall the very next choice, or if not yet, before summer is out, obtain a decided majority in favor of the Hon. William Whiting, Esq. Some perhaps may think that I have said too much, and that a few hints would have been enough to secure Mr. Whiting the vote; but I always love plain dealing, and I thought I would say so much that nobody could answer my reasons. If I should fail in my zealous attempts for the worthy gentleman, I should have a new and melancholy instance of human ignorance and depravity, and should cry out in the language of the Roman orator,

O tempora! O Mores!

O temperance! O Morality!

Gentlemen electors, permit me to subscribe myself, yours to serve, A WHITING's MAN.

1. This essay was addressed "to the Virtuous Electors of the District of Hampshire and Berkshire." Portions are illegible because the only extant copy of the newspaper is tightly bound. Missing letters have been supplied by the editors. The item was preceded by a Note to the Printer: "You have heretofore published for other parties. If you would now publish this address for me, I should consider it as a fresh proof of your impartiality, and would acknowledge my obligations for the favor. Quere. Is not the subject worthy to be printed in the Springfield and Pittsfield papers, as highly important to the whole district? The author leaves the question to the judgment of the printers." No copy of a reprinting in the *Hampshire Chronicle* or *Berkshire Chronicle* has been located.

For an answer to "A Whiting's Man," see "PQ" in the *Hampshire Gazette*, 18 March, which reiterated that, because of its size, Hampshire County should have the Representative and that Samuel Lyman was the man to vote for.

2. See "Yeoman to the Electors of the Western District," *Hampshire Gazette*, 25 February, printed above in The Third Election in Hampshire-Berkshire District.

Henry Van Schaack to Theodore Sedgwick, Pittsfield, 9 March (excerpt)[1]

I suppose we shall have another meeting, when I am convinced there must and will be a great majority for you. I had an application yesterday from Lanesborough to make against them to put some folks right who, it seems, have departed from the true political faith by wrong insinuations of the artful and designing. I shall make a trial to reform them. Your situation, I know, is a disagreeable one and requires all your fortitude to persevere; but persist you must, be your feelings what they may. I hope our friends in Hampshire will not be worried out by the unaccountable conduct of some of our fellow citizens. Read the enclosed and if you approve of its contents, let it go on by a safe hand.[2] I think when it comes out to the people that you have a great majority of votes, we Federalists shall unite more firmly than we have done and proselyte others who have hitherto gone astray from wrong impressions received from the designing ones. In one word, perseverance in your friends, I think, will bring us to the wished for haven.

1. RC, Sedgwick Papers, MHi.
2. The enclosure has not been located.

Henry Van Schaack to Theodore Sedgwick, Pittsfield, 12 March[1]

I received yours by Dickison last evening with a packet to [Samuel] Henshaw, which by your permission I opened.[2] I do not altogether approve of what was inclosed. My objections, in part, I have stated to our Northampton friend. I presume you will not take it amiss in some instances to let your friend judge for you at so delicate a period as the present.

I do insist upon it that it is your duty, and that it ought to be your inclination, not to yield to the opposition if your friends in the other county will countenance a further struggle. Your friends in Berkshire, I am persuaded, will not desert you at this time. Such as I have seen will undauntedly pursue measures to further the choice of you.

The letter I alluded to in my note to you yesterday by Dickison was sent by my neighbor Welles. I hope it is come to hand. It contained political ideas as well as private business.

Elder Rathbone's[3] coming in has interrupted the thread of my discourse to you and now he is gone. I will tell you that we have had much to say upon our political situation. Methinks I hear you exclaim "What is that to me?" It is something to you as a citizen at large as well as your being held up as a candidate for the western district. He is clearly and decidedly of opinion that you ought to go. He gave flattering reasons to me as your friend why you should be the man, and what is more, I believe he was sincere.* He had been told that you or your friends for you had given up the contest. Captain [Daniel] Sacket[4] of this town had reported that you had declined and that therefore people should unite for [Thompson J.] Skinner. I told the Elder that I would venture to say this was not the case; that such a resolution I conceived would not be taken; that it was an object near the hearts of your friends and other well-wishers to the new government; that you should be elected etc., etc.; and there-fore begged of him that reports of this kind might not influence him to throw away his vote and interest etc., etc. Has any thing been said at Stockbridge to give countenance to Sacket's report? If so it is cursed wrong and highly pro-voking. In most political struggles the difficulties to keep our friends within due bounds is greater than to combat opponents.

*The Elder is now convinced the new Constitution is for the best[5] [this is a marginal note on the blank page of the letter].

[P.S.] Pray inquire for my letter. I presume it must have been left at some [house?]. It is probable I shall see Mr. Welles before I seal this up. Your letter for Northampton I will carry to town this evening to be in the way to get forward.

1. RC, Sedgwick Papers, MHi.
2. The contents of the "packet" are unknown. Sedgwick frequently sent political corres-pondence to Henshaw via Van Schaack. See Van Schaack to Sedgwick, 15-16 March, printed below.
3. Valentine Rathbun, a clothier by trade, had organized a Baptist church in Pittsfield in 1772. During the Revolution he represented the town in the General Court on numerous occasions. He was often called "Elder Rathbun" because of his position in the church.
4. Sacket, who had been a captain in the Massachusetts militia during the Revolution, was fined by the Supreme Judicial Court in April 1787 at Great Barrington for "seditious behavior" during Shays's Rebellion. This session of the court also fined William Whiting for "divers seditious words" (*Norwich Packet*, 26 April 1787, from Northampton, 12 April).
5. Rathbun represented Pittsfield in the state Convention and voted against ratification.

Henry Van Schaack to Theodore Sedgwick, Pittsfield, 15-16 March (excerpt)[1]

This moment, my dear sir, yours of the 14th was handed me on my return from Lanesborough. I feel confident that if your name comes out in the precept as one of the two highest, that a change must take place in the minds of a great number of those who voted for Colonel [Thompson J.] Skinner. It will evidently appear, I trust, that Colonel Skinner is not sufficiently known to be voted for in Hampshire. Why then should his friends wish to hold him up any longer? It is certainly not an eligible situation to be held up as a candidate without any prospect of success. I conceive great hopes in our pursuits to carry you; it will be made manifest to the people that if you are not chosen now, a member from the other county will probably be elected. The idea of having no Representative from Berkshire, I find, alarms many of our people.

Your letter for publication I have not read with attention enough to give an opinion whether it should go to the press. I will read it over again before it is forwarded.[2] In the meantime I bid you be of good cheer. I trust all will yet go well. I cannot agree that the whole mass of the voters for Skinner wish for no government. I am well satisfied it is not the case. I know many well-disposed friends to government have voted for Skinner from good principles, though from wrong impressions made on them by others. I am thoroughly satisfied that a number of people have been made to believe that Colonel Skinner would have a great number of votes in Hampshire. When it comes to be known that he has not, it is more than probable that they will not any longer throw away their votes, but bestow them on a person in this county and who is like to succeed. Who is that person but yourself?

I am much out in my conjectures if the votes from Lanesborough will not be different from what they were the last polling.[3] Here your friends will, as usual, exert themselves. If our friends in Hampshire are not wearied out I shall really flatter myself with success.

. . . .

[16 March]

I wrote you the foregoing scrawl late last night, imagining that I should have no time to say any thing this morning, being determined to go over into Hancock, but the weather is too bad to leave the chimney corner. In the letter proposed to be published you say "Lawyers have ever been objects of *popular* dislike." Would it no[t] do better to express yourself *"objects of dislike to some part of the community"*? "There will also probably appear from experience other defects" etc. Suppose all those sentences were struck out. You begin a paragraph: "Above all things it is important after the ferment and agitations which have taken place to render tranquil the public mind. This country is at present afflicted with evils of an enormous nature." Have you expressed yourself full enough?

After the evils have been enumerated and the remedies you offer for them, you say "This will go far to render him contented, and if one other objected [*sic*] can be effected, I am confident you may with reason expect to see our country great, happy and respectable."

Ought not this object to have been mentioned? Is it not too obscure as it stands?

"That the true characters, public and private, of the candidates should be unknown to the people was to be expected but events have taken place" etc. This whole paragraph is rather in my mind too pointed with respect to others as well as yourself. Perhaps I am wrong. I will think a little more on the subject.

No chance of sending the letter for Northampton on as yet, nor I fear that there will be any opportunity soon.

1. RC, Sedgwick Papers, MHi.
2. No printing of the "letter for publication" (portions of which are quoted in Van Schaack's letter) has been located. It was possibly a version of Sedgwick's letter to Samuel Henshaw, 6 April, in the *Hampshire Gazette*, 6 May (see Theodore Sedgwick and Amendments to the Constitution, 6-30 May, printed below in The Fifth Election in Hampshire-Berkshire District).
3. In the first election in Lanesborough, Skinner received 28 votes and Sedgwick 27; in the second election, Sedgwick received 79 and Skinner 48; and in the third, Skinner received 126 and Sedgwick 102. In the fourth election, after Skinner withdrew, Lanesborough gave 127 votes to Sedgwick.

John Avery, Jr., to George Thacher, Boston, 25 March (excerpt)[1]

The Honorable Mr. [Jonathan] Grout is elected for Worcester District and have sent in his credentials and suppose he is now with you. The District of Hampshire and Berkshire seem to struggle hard in their choice, but am in hopes the next trial will produce a member; indeed I sincerely wish it, as it will save me great trouble. By the way, why can't there be an alteration in this mode when you come upon the subject of amendments, that when there is no choice by the people, for the several legislatures to determine the matter as in the case of Senators, etc., etc.

1. RC, Thacher Papers, MB.

A Friend to the People to the Electors of the Western District, Hampshire Chronicle, 25 March (excerpt)[1]

It will be asked, how is it that a gentleman of these distinguished abilities has so often failed of the suffrages of the electors? The answer is obvious. Respectable characters have their friends, and it is not strange, that in a district so extensive, several gentlemen should be thought worthy of an appointment; and when we have begun to vote for a person, we are not very willing to give him up. Oftentimes party has too much influence in such elections. In party contentions the public interest is forgotten. Prejudices have been raised against Mr. [Theodore] Sedgwick, from his law profession. Pardon me, fellow citizens, when I say (for I am no lawyer) that commonly prejudices against professions are highly injurious; they are narrow prejudices. The calling is useful; and if it has been abused, it is no argument against the calling itself, and much less against the individuals who belong to it. He has been a faithful counsellor to his clients, and therefore as a Representative he will be habitually faithful to his constituents. In my opinion, his law knowledge is a desirable qualification, and will be a safeguard to the public, especially when civil institutions are to be formed for the Union. In fact, law knowledge, intermixed with knowledge of other branches of business, is absolutely necessary. This prejudice has had, no doubt, great influence in impeding his choice. I am the more sorry for it, since I view his eminence in his profession as a flattering circumstance in his favor, and it would be thought so by any of us who wanted his help in a trial of character, privilege, or property.

Men of shining talents are most subject to envy and calumny. Interested persons who aspire at their eminence are ever ready to disseminate among the people jealousies and suspicions, and thus weaken the public confidence, and prevent the improvement of men best able to serve their country. In this respect the public have been abused in the case of the gentleman whose true character I am canvassing. A malicious report, which has had more influence than any thing else upon the conduct of a great part of the electors, is, *that Mr. Sedgwick is a public defaulter, that he owes the public fifteen hundred dollars, out of which he would defraud them.* This calumny, for it is certainly no better, has been whispered about in private circles, and has sought to conceal itself, while it ruined the reputation of the injured person.[2] The report is *wholly,* and in *every part* without foundation; and there is no man of character who dares to pledge himself publicly to support the charge. Secret slander, whispered in corners, is the *hidden dagger,* with which the assassin murders the characters of honest men, and weakens the public confidence of their most tried friends. I say, *no man of character* dare pledge himself to support the imputation upon Mr. Sedgwick, which has done him so much *injury* through the district.

In addition to this *calumny* that has been whispered round the country, *runners* have been employed to carry false intelligence through the district: that Mr. Sedgwick's voters had given him up, and were about to vote for another candidate. I have now five towns in my mind in which Mr. Sedgwick lost a majority, merely in consequence of such false information. And if these *runners* should again attempt to abuse and mislead the electors as they have done before, they may be assured that Mr. Sedgwick's voters have too much regard, not to him, but to themselves and the public, to give up their expectations of honoring and serving the district in the choice of that gentleman to the important trust of a federal Representative. It is not from any prejudice to the other candidates, that the voices of the electors are solicited for Mr. Sedgwick, at the next election. When the freemen view their own interest, and reflect upon the impositions they have suffered from misrepresentation and dark insinuation, they will, I am firmly persuaded, give their suffrages for the person whom I have named, and who has served his country with so much reputation and ability. The electors ought to resent, and they will resent, the self design and intrigue of a few busy agents in imposing upon them false information to *mislead* them, and *malicious slander* to *wean* them from their *faithful friend*. I wish that what I have said upon this subject may be canvassed and brought to the bar of candid examination; if I have misrepresented, I wish to be corrected, but if I have stated to the electors their true interests, I wish to be heard. Yes—for their sakes I wish to be heard.

Do we desire a man to represent us who is attached to us by long residence, by landed property, and who has a *stake* in the government? Do we wish for a man who is able to make laws for the *common good*; to prevent regulations of trade and agriculture injurious to the Northern States? Do we wish for a *statesman*, faithful and skillful, to set at the head of our public affairs? I sincerely believe that we shall not be able to find a man who answers the description so well as Mr. Sedgwick; and should he be chosen, I am persuaded he would never violate his trust, nor disappoint our expectations from him.

1. The *Hampshire Chronicle* of 25 March is missing. This item is taken from the reprint in the *Hampshire Gazette* on 29 April. The *Gazette* prefaced its printing as follows: "The following address was published in the Springfield paper of March 25, and had a very happy effect upon the minds of many of the worthy electors in the district. It is a composition of so much good temper and real sentiment, and is so much approved by the impartial and dispassionate, that we cannot deny ourselves the pleasure of reprinting it for the entertainment of our customers."

2. The charge that Sedgwick was a public defaulter was made at least as early as the second election in the district (see Sedgwick to Benjamin Lincoln, 6 February, printed above). "A Friend to the People" was answered specifically by "Mentor" in the *Hampshire Gazette*, 6 May, after reading the reprint in the *Gazette*. "Mentor" declared that it could be proved by reference to the account books that Sedgwick had received public property worth $14,000 in specie in 1776 and that the account had not been settled. For additional items on the subject, see The Issue of Theodore Sedgwick's Public Accounts, 6-15 May, printed below in The Fifth Election in Hampshire-Berkshire District.

Samuel Henshaw to Theodore Sedgwick, Northampton, 27 March[1]

I have time only to acknowledge the receipt of your favors,[2] but not to answer them, nor to give you my opinion upon either of them. Nothing that you have sent can be published till we have had another trial, and I hope any publication will be needless afterwards. However, should there not be a choice on Monday next, everything that you can wish for shall be done before we make another attempt. Your friends will not forsake you. I wrote [Henry] Van S[chaack] that we should make but one more trial for you, but I did it to rouse him and your other friends in Berkshire who, till now, have not been sufficiently awake. I rejoice that they begin to see and feel as I have done for this long while. I say again your friends here will not leave you.

Your letters did not come to hand until Wednesday afternoon [25 March], nor did I know till that day, that precepts were issued. Had I known that we were called on to meet on Monday next [30 March], [William] Butler's last paper[3] would have held up to view a few stubborn facts, that would have made the Lymanites to tremble, and the Sedgwickites to shout aloud for joy. But not expecting to meet before the first Monday in April, I would not let Butler publish any thing till next week. But our beloved economical Governor has stole a march upon us.[4] It will not, however, answer his purpose. He has been told, I guess, by [James] Sullivan and Bill Lyman[5] who is now with him, that the precepts could not get to the northern part of this county and through Berkshire so as to have the people warned to meet on Monday next, and therefore there would be the highest probability that [Samuel] Lyman would be chosen. But Mr. Governor and his advisers will have their match. Our sheriff [Elisha Porter, of Hadley] is as good a general as any of them, and has taken care to send the precepts *by very safe hands* to such towns as will vote like rational beings. My time has been much employed in writing either for public or private inspection, and will be until the people return to their senses and place my friend where I would he should be.

I sent last week a piece to Van S[chaack] for Pittsfield paper, and had the same published last Wednesday in the Springfield paper.[6] I have heard today that they think it will kill [Samuel] Lyman, and they suppose it came from New York, and was wrote by [Caleb] Strong or [Fisher] Ames. The very circumstance of its being printed in that paper will injure Lyman more than twenty better pieces in Northampton paper would have done. I did not write it. I corrected it, and would have left some things out and added others, but the author was fond of his own child, and I consented that it should appear in its present dress.

It is now almost twelve o'clock at night, and I have several more letters yet to write. I met with a Mr. Kingsley of Becket[7] this evening and took him home with me. He has just gone to bed and left me to write you and others. I have not time to read this. I will write you more and better very soon. Farewell; and know I am unalterably yours.

N.B. We shall try hard for [James] Bowdoin as governor and [Benjamin] Lincoln for lieutenant governor. Join us with all your forces.[8]

1. RC, Sedgwick Papers, MHi.
2. Sedgwick's "recent favors," enclosed in a letter from Sedgwick to Henry Van Schaack on 11 March, have not been located.

3. The *Hampshire Gazette.*

4. See the headnote to The Fourth Election in Hampshire-Berkshire District, printed above.

5. William Lyman was a member of the Massachusetts House from Easthampton in Hampshire County in 1787 and 1788 and the state Senate in 1789 and 1790. He was evidently a follower of Governor Hancock.

6. This is presumably "A Friend to the People to the Electors of the Western District," *Hampshire Chronicle*, 25 March, printed above, which denied that Sedgwick was a public defaulter.

7. This was probably Nathaniel Kingsley, who was one of the founders of Becket, and who represented that town in the Massachusetts House on numerous occasions, including 1787-1789.

8. John Hancock and Samuel Adams were elected governor and lieutenant governor, respectively, on 6 April.

A Correspondent, Berkshire Chronicle, 27 March

On Monday next we are again to give our votes for a Representative for the western district. On the last return the votes stood nearly as follows: for Mr. [Theodore] Sedgwick, 1545; Mr. [Samuel] Lyman, 1460; Mr. [William] Whiting, 1000; Mr. [Thompson J.] Skinner, 600.[1]

It is to be hoped that the electors will endeavor to be a little more united than they have been, especially as the Hon. Mr. Skinner has, within a few days past, made the most pointed assurances to his friends, that he wished them not to consider him as a candidate. A respect is certainly due from the electors in this county, to those in Hampshire, who have thus repeatedly and decidedly demonstrated by the number of their votes, that Mr. Sedgwick or Mr. Lyman ought to be elected. They have a Senator from Hampshire; they ought not to have the Representative also. They are determined still to exert themselves for Mr. Sedgwick; and it will be our own fault if we are unrepresented. I am not for panegyric or calumny. These two gentlemen are men well known; tis as well known that Mr. Sedgwick is a gentleman of the most experience. It is objected, that he is a lawyer; so is Mr. Lyman. And if we are to be represented by a lawyer, we in Berkshire ought to give our votes for Mr. Sedgwick, whom we know, and whose interest is the same as ours, than for Mr. Lyman, whom we do not know, and who has not been an inhabitant of Massachusetts more than six years.

1. Whether deliberately or not, the *Chronicle*'s publisher or the "Correspondent" reversed Sedgwick's and Lyman's votes. On 2 March Sedgwick received 1,449 votes and Lyman 1,557, while Whiting received 1,083 and Skinner 606.

Official Election Returns, 9 April

HAMPSHIRE-BERKSHIRE DISTRICT, 30 MARCH

Town	Hon. Theodore Sedgwick	Samuel Lyman, Esq.	William Whiting	Colonel William Lyman	Thompson J. Skinner	John Bacon, Esq.	Samuel Fowler	William Williams
Springfield	21	127						
Longmeadow	12	55						
West Springfield	13	147						
Wilbraham	9	97						
Northampton	142	18						
Southampton	61	10	1					
Hadley	42	13						
South Hadley	7	45						
Amherst	13	30						
Granby	2	32						
Hatfield	46	13			1			2
Whately	4	12						
Williamsburg	9	24						
Westfield	66	15					31	
Deerfield	38	2						
Greenfield	13	19						
Shelburne	6	55						
Conway								
Sunderland	16	5						
Montague	21							
Northfield	29	1						
Brimfield	37	7						
South Brimfield								
[Wales]	8	42						
Monson	19	70						
Pelham	1	55						
Greenwich								
Blandford	25	15						
Palmer	2	52						
Granville	3	61	15					
New Salem								
Belchertown	49	25						
Colrain	3	20						
Ware	1	44						
Warwick	2	14						

(Table continued on following pages)

HAMPSHIRE-BERKSHIRE DISTRICT, 30 MARCH *(continued)*

Town	Hon. Theodore Sedgwick	Samuel Lyman, Esq.	William Whiting	Colonel William Lyman	Thompson J. Skinner	John Bacon, Esq.	Samuel Fowler	William Williams
Bernardston	9	29						
Chester								
Chesterfield	30							3
Charlemont								
Ashfield								
Worthington								
Shutesbury								
Goshen	14	4						
Southwick	15	10	8	3				
Norwich								
[Huntington]	14	5						
Ludlow		62						
Leverett								
Montgomery								
Westhampton	26	4						
Cummington	9				2			
Buckland								
Middlefield								
Wendell	20	3						
Orange	9	2						
Holland	5	16						
Leyden		12						
Rowe								
Heath								
Easthampton	24	6	1					
Plantation No. 7 [Hawley]								
Sheffield	62	2	59					
Great Barrington	49		35					
Stockbridge	88	3						
Pittsfield	55							11
Richmond	65	20	1					
Lenox	29	7	23		10			
Lanesborough	127							
Williamstown								
Adams								

(Table continued on following page)

HAMPSHIRE-BERKSHIRE DISTRICT, 30 MARCH *(continued)*

Town	Hon. Theodore Sedgwick	Samuel Lyman, Esq.	William Whiting	Colonel William Lyman	Thompson J. Skinner	John Bacon, Esq.	Samuel Fowler	William Williams
Egremont	2		43					
Becket	27	2						
West Stockbridge	17		21					
Dalton	16							
Alford	38		34					
New Ashford								
New Marlborough	31	1	9					
Tyringham	23		61					
Loudon								
[Otis]	3	1	12					
Windsor								
Partridgefield								
[Peru]	19							
Washington	11		14					
Hancock								
Lee	25		37			1		
Sandisfield								
Mount Washington	2		17					
Totals	1584	1314	391	3	13	1	31	16

Votes cast: 3353
Majority required: 1677

Governor and Council Record the Votes in the Fourth Election in Hampshire-Berkshire District, Friday, 10 April[1]

The Governor and Council upon examination of the returns from the district comprehending the counties of Hampshire and Berkshire for Representative to represent the people thereof in the Congress of the United States found them to stand as follows, viz.

Number [of] voters, 3353; [to] make a choice, 1677. Hon. Theodore Sedgwick, Esq., 1584. Samuel Lyman, Esq., 1314. Candidates. No choice.

1. Council Records, XXXI, 28, M-Ar.

The Question of Delayed and Missing Election Returns, 15 April–3 May

The Governor and Council recorded the votes for the fourth election on 10 April. Five days later Samuel Henshaw wrote Theodore Sedgwick that he had heard that Sedgwick would have received a 300-vote majority if all the votes had been returned in time to be counted, and that if the report was true, there had been "some damnation maneuvering."

On 22 April the *Hampshire Chronicle*, which supported Samuel Lyman, reported that twenty towns had not voted or that their votes had been returned too late to be counted. The *Chronicle* stated that it had been informed by "a gentleman of veracity, directly from Boston" that Lyman would have been elected if they had been returned. Later, Secretary John Avery informed George Thacher that one of the candidates would have received a majority, but he did not say who would have won. On 22 April the *Chronicle* implied that the Hampshire and Berkshire county sheriffs were responsible for the delay, and on 29 April a letter in the *Chronicle* charged that the precept for Greenwich, a pro-Lyman town, had been left outside the town, so that no election was held there.

The *Hampshire Gazette*, which supported Sedgwick, reported on 22 April that the votes of twenty towns were missing but, unlike the *Chronicle*, denied that the towns had voted and that there was "neglect or design" in distributing the precepts. However, the *Gazette* agreed with the *Chronicle* that if the votes had been returned, Lyman would have been elected. On 29 April a writer in the *Gazette* denied that Lyman would have won and denounced the articles which charged the sheriffs with misconduct.

Twenty-one towns either did not hold elections or did not return their votes in time. The *Chronicle* did not list Hancock as the *Gazette* did, while the *Gazette* omitted Plantation No. 7 [Hawley], which was on the *Chronicle*'s list. Most of the towns listed were in the northern parts of the two counties, and presumably their isolation had something to do with their failure to hold elections or their delay in returning votes. For example, eleven towns voted in the first election, eleven in the second, twelve in the third, and fifteen in the fifth election. Three of the towns did not return votes in any of the elections, and two of them returned votes only in the fifth election.

Thompson J. Skinner ran ahead of all other candidates in the first three elections in those twenty-one towns. Sedgwick ranked fourth among six candidates in the first election, fifth and last in the second, and third among four leading candidates in the third election. Lyman ranked fifth among six candidates in the first election, third among five in the second, and second among four in the third election. In the fifth election Lyman and Sedgwick were the two principal candidates, and Lyman received 326 votes to 311 for Sedgwick from the fifteen towns whose votes were counted.

The dispute over the election returns continued to be an issue during and after the fifth election.

Samuel Henshaw to Theodore Sedgwick, Northampton, 15 April (excerpt)[1]

I have this moment (10 o'clock A.M.) received your agreeable favor of Monday last[2]—and at the same instant I had news from Boston of the state of votes, viz.: My friend, 1564; [Samuel] Lyman, 1309; [William] Whiting, 391; scattering, 64; [Total] 3328.[3] I am also informed that the day after the poll was closed, you had votes delivered into the secretary's office which, could they have been counted, would have given you a majority of 300. I will not vouch for the truth of this information; but if it is true, there has been some damnation maneuvering, and I shall immediately take proper steps to satisfy myself respecting it. I understand the next attempt is to be on Monday, 11th May. I am glad it is put off so long, because we shall have a fine time to fix matters at our Court.

. . . .

Let your friends be cool, persuasive, and persevering. They must not be too sanguine of success, and they must make people attend town meeting, and when they have voted, see that the votes are returned into the secretary's office in time. I believe there has been some address in this business, and it is time to be guarded in this spot also.

I am persuaded by recent experience that we can do infinitely more by private letters than by newspaper publications. However, I shall have all kinds of weapons in burnishing order, those you have supplied me with among the principal ones, and shall wield those of them that will do the most execution at the time of trial.

Let your friends be very cautious to whom they write, and by whom they send; and let the carrier be charged not to lisp to any person whatever the design of his riding, but let him deliver his letters as tho he knew nothing of their contents.

Your people are surely convinced by this time, that you, or nobody, must go from Berkshire. And, being sensible of this, it seems to me, that it would not be a difficult task to persuade them to unite their suffrages in you. County pride would easily kindle, if a few prudent persons would gently fan the latent sparks, and feed the spreading flame with the oil of friendship. This would blunt the edge, the acrimonious edge, of party rage, and beguile them into the way of life! Lyman's adherents do not despair. They expect to prevail with Whiting's party to join them, and they will make every exertion to effect it. One of his [Lyman's] wiseacres told me yesterday, that the next trial would be in a very busy season, and people would not generally attend; and they meant to avail themselves of this circumstance to get Lyman in. Knowing our danger we must guard against it.

1. RC, Sedgwick Papers, MHi.

2. Sedgwick wrote a letter to Henshaw on 6 April declaring that he supported amendments to the Constitution. Henshaw published the letter in the *Hampshire Gazette* on 6 May (see Theodore Sedgwick and Amendments to the Constitution, printed below in The Fifth Election in Hampshire-Berkshire District).

3. The *Massachusetts Centinel* in Boston published these figures on 11 April.

From a Correspondent, Hampshire Chronicle, 22 April

A gentleman of veracity, directly from Boston, assures us, that twenty towns in this district made no seasonable returns to the secretary's office, of the state of their votes which were given in on the 30th of last month, for the choice of a federal Representative. The names of the towns are, *Conway, New Salem, Chester, Charlemont, Ashfield, Worthington, Shutesbury, Leverett, Montgomery, Buckland, Middlefield, Rowe, Heath, Greenwich,* [Plantation] *No. 7* [Hawley], *Williamstown, Adams, Windsor, Sandisfield,* and *New Ashford*—fifteen in this county, and five in Berkshire. Returns from sundry of the above towns were lodged in the secretary's office some days after the return day; and the gentleman observes, that the Secretary informed him that Mr. [Samuel] Lyman had the greatest number of votes, but that they unfortunately came in too late.

Query. Is the sheriff of the county, or the selectmen of those towns, liable to pay the *fine*?[1]

1. For the fines for delay in delivering returns, see the Additional Election Resolutions, 10 January, printed above in The Official Results of the First Election, 5-10 January. In addition to the above, the *Chronicle* gave the voting returns for the election and a short notice to the effect that it hoped that the twenty towns would return their votes in the next election.

Hampshire Gazette, 22 April

Unfortunately on the return day for the last election of a Representative in this district, the towns of Conway, Greenwich, New Salem, Chester, Charlemont, Ashfield, Worthington, Shutesbury, Leverett, Montgomery, Buckland, Middlefield, Rowe, Heath, Williamstown, Adams, New Ashford, Windsor, Hancock, and Sandisfield sent in no votes; otherwise, we should, most probably, have been rescued from the inconvenience of another meeting; as we may most reasonably presume that the votes of the aforesaid towns would have decided the election in favor of Samuel Lyman [———] he hath had the honor of their suffrages in previous elections. However, be that event as it is, we now [hope?] that no neglect or design in dispersing the precepts may prevent an universal meeting on the eleventh day of May, being the day appointed for giving in the votes, and also making certain and seasonable returns consequent thereon. It is further to be hoped that if any towns, through either design or neglect, shall fail seasonably to receive their precepts, they will nevertheless meet and send in their votes as there can be very little doubt in this case of their reception.

The Public, Hampshire Gazette, 29 April

A good cause needs no falsehood and prevarication to support it. Such means belong to a bad cause. A writer in [the *Hampshire*] *Gazette* of April 22nd has named 20 towns in the district who failed of returning their votes upon the last balloting for a Representative; by which failure he intimates that Samuel Lyman, Esq., lost the majority. This suggestion is designed to give Mr. Lyman consequence with the electors, and stir up and interest a party in his favor. Such artifices have been too much the support of that gentleman's cause. I hope he does not encourage them. Let us examine this pretense. Of these twenty towns, six larger than any remaining six towns, I believe, never in any instance gave Mr.

Lyman a single vote. In four others Mr. [Theodore] Sedgwick has commonly had a majority. One or two of the remainder have been wavering. The rest, being eight or nine towns, have for some reason been engaged for Mr. Lyman. Is it fair play? Does it tend to truth and equity, to say, that had the returns been made from these towns Mr. Lyman would have been chosen? He would have been no nearer to a choice than by the votes as they now stand. But we are told by insinuation, that the precepts were not fairly dispersed. This is a calumny to raise an unjustifiable resentment. With equal ingenuity we are told that returns were not duly made. Did not the sheriff convey to the Secretary all the votes handed to him? If some of the towns failed through distance and shortness of time, if others in the neighborhood of the sheriff who voted for Mr. Lyman sickened at their own conduct and neglected to make returns, who is in fault? Is the sheriff to be slandered? Why need this busy tool of Mr. Lyman be so angry and petulant? What warrant has he in a lordly manner to direct the towns to pursue in future an unlawful conduct, and promise them approbation in it? I wish to have falsehood detected, and that the minds of the people may have a fair scope without prejudice. I have only to add, that should a stranger with whose qualifications I am unacquainted be preferred to my long-tried, faithful servant (which event I do not expect), I should feel myself deeply injured, and should regret the after disappointment of my misjudging friends, the PUBLIC.

Hampshire Chronicle, 29 April

I think it no more than my duty, to inform the District of Hampshire and Berkshire, that at the last call from His Excellency, to come to a choice of a Representative to Congress, the town of Greenwich had not a precept, and did not meet on that day. And I know it to be fact, by the best information, that it was carried by the road which leads to Greenwich, three miles out of the way, on the road to Boston, by a stranger, and by him posted up in the house of Mr. Benjamin Howe. Mr. Howe did not know the man. This account I have from Mr. Howe's brother, and I leave the public to judge whether there was design in it or not. I also heard of one town more which had no precept.[1]

1. This letter to the printer was dated "Greenwich, April 9, 1789."

John Avery, Jr., to George Thacher, Boston, 3 May (excerpt)[1]

As you observe, they have a high contest in the counties of Berkshire and Hampshire about a representation. However, I hope they will settle the matter this time, being the fifth trial. They would have made a choice the last time had all the votes arrived in time. I have a great respect for both the gentlemen and shall heartily acquiesce in the choice of either of them.

1. RC, Chamberlain Collection, MB.

The Fifth Election in Hampshire-Berkshire District, 11 May

Prior to the fifth election on 11 May, the newspapers debated most of the issues that had been raised in previous campaigns. The charge that Theodore Sedgwick was a public defaulter was argued at great length. Apparently Samuel Lyman was also charged with questionable financial practices, for the charge was publicly denied by a Springfield tavern keeper. Newspapers continued to print arguments about the candidates' abuse of one another. Some writers continued to argue that Berkshire County was entitled to a Representative since United States Senator Caleb Strong was from Hampshire County. There were also hints that Lyman would have won the fourth election if the precepts had not been held back from pro-Lyman towns.

The issue of amendments to the Constitution apparently became so important that Samuel Henshaw, Sedgwick's manager in Hampshire County, published a letter on 6 May, written by Sedgwick on 6 April, declaring that he favored amendments, opposed heavy land taxes, and would support assumption of state debts by the federal government.

On 6 May, in their last issues before the election on 11 May, the *Hampshire Gazette* and the *Hampshire Chronicle* each printed six election pieces. Four of those in the *Gazette* supported Sedgwick; the other two were attacks upon him. Four of the items in the *Chronicle* attacked Sedgwick, a fifth defended a "caucus" at Northampton which supported Sedgwick, while the sixth was a satirical attack on the caucus. Half of the pieces published on 6 May concerned the charge that Sedgwick was a public defaulter. Both newspapers published a letter written by Oliver Phelps about Sedgwick's role as a purchasing agent during the Revolution. The *Gazette* claimed that the letter proved that Sedgwick was innocent, while the *Chronicle* insisted that it proved him guilty.

Additional newspaper items not printed below include "a correspondent" in the *Hampshire Chronicle*, 22 April, who urged the people to vote; "The Independent Reflector" and "An Old Farmer" in the *Hampshire Gazette*, 29 April, who took no partisan positions but urged people to vote for a man who would see that the Massachusetts war debts were assumed by the federal government; "G" in the *Hampshire Gazette*, 6 May, who argued that Berkshire should have a Representative and who deplored the abuse of all the candidates; "Mentor" in the *Hampshire Gazette*, 6 May, who criticized the terrible abuse of Samuel Lyman by Sedgwick's supporters and insisted that Sedgwick was a public defaulter; and "Curtius" in the *Hampshire Gazette*, 13 May.

The implication that there had been fraud in the issuing of precepts and in the return of votes in the fourth election, and that the sheriff of Hampshire County was responsible, possibly led to the publication of a notice in the *Hampshire Chronicle* on 29 April that Sheriff Elisha Porter would receive the votes at his office in Hadley from Monday, 11 May, through Saturday, 16 May. Sedgwick won the election, but again there were charges that the election had been "stolen" from Lyman by holding back the votes of pro-Lyman towns (see The Question of Delayed and Missing Election Returns, 27-30 May, printed below).

Hampshire Chronicle, 8 April

A correspondent, in the upper part of this county, observes, that he has heretofore uniformly voted for Mr. [Theodore] Sedgwick, for a Representative to the Congress, but that he has, within a few days past, determined not to vote for him again; not because he has any thing against him personally, but because, says the correspondent, I know Mr. Sedgwick's friends have unjustly abused Mr. [Samuel] Lyman in the Northampton papers; and that they have made use of unjust arts against him, by reporting things to his disadvantage, which I know are false. I have, says the correspondent, been three years well acquainted with him at Court; and I know he is an honest and sensible man, and that he has great influence at Court, and that in many important matters he has come forward when the parties were very high, and has united them when it was almost impossible for anybody to propose any new plan without risking his character. And another thing, says the correspondent, why I have altered my mind is, because I was the other day in company with a number who have supported Mr. Sedgwick, and they were talking about [state] senators—said they should have been glad to have appointed Mr. Lyman, if he had not been the means of preventing the choice of Mr. Sedgwick as a Representative to Congress, but that they would now prevent Mr. Lyman's being chosen senator,[1] if possible. Indeed, says the correspondent, I have seen and heard so much I am perfectly sick of it. I think it is cruel and abusive, to treat any man as some of them have treated Mr. Lyman.

1. Lyman was elected a state senator on 6 April.

Zenas Parsons to the Printer, Hampshire Chronicle, 15 April[1]

The other day, for want of proper information, I was a little dissatisfied with respect to Mr. [Samuel] Lyman's conduct, relative to a specie order, which he bought of me, and for which he gave me eighteen shillings on the pound, but I am now fully satisfied, that his conduct was both just and honest; and I do not know, that there is now any complaint, among any of his constituents, but what his treatment of them has been just, honest, and honorable; and I had no idea, that the report of my uneasiness would have spread, as I find it has, by the publication in last week's Northampton paper.[2]

1. The letter was dated Springfield, 6 April. It was followed by a request that the printers in Northampton and Pittsfield publish the "certificate." It was published in the *Hampshire Gazette* on 15 April. Parsons was a long-time innkeeper in Springfield.
2. The *Hampshire Gazette* for 1 April has not been located.

An Impartial Observer, Hampshire Gazette, 22 April

While the several parties in the district are endeavoring to raise to the important office of a Representative of 80,000 people, each their own creature, a friend to good order and peace, society and good neighborhood, cannot but lament the folly of a large number of the people, who suffer themselves to be influenced by men who are governed by party prejudice and party interest; who, having no lawful business of their own, are forever walking "to and fro in the earth, and up and down it," like their father the *Devil*, to disturb the peace of communities, and set all by the ears; who delight in nothing but anarchy and confusion; who, in order to effect their nefarious designs, drive about from day to day, through town to town, and from country to country; who are not deterred from their grand object, either by hedges or ditches, storms or tempests; even Hell is disturbed by their restless dispositions. They solicit their father to preside in their councils, and when they have, in combination with Hell, brewed all the mischief that is possible for such miscreants to invent, their president, after assigning to each their duty, adjourns their meeting sine die. But while they are executing his orders, he strokes his grisly beard, and laughs in his sleeve, when he reflects upon the immensity of the harvest he shall soon gather in; and, like Dives in the Gospel, says to his soul, "Soul, thou hast many goods laid up for thee, take thy ease, eat, drink, and be merry."

It is well known that two of the three candidates have exerted their whole strength, stretched every nerve, and it is feared have brought an incurable consumption upon their purses, in order to effect their own election, and, it is a fact, have worn a coat of as many colors, as that of ancient Joseph. But what would appear to be beyond any man's belief is, that a MINISTER[1] has drove the quill in their cause, and, what is more incredible, has with his brother runners gone from town to town *devil-like*, prejudicing the minds of men against the remaining candidate, because he had a personal quarrel with him. Very different this conduct from the precepts of his divine Lord and Master, who commands his followers to love their enemies, do good to them who hate them, and pray for those that despitefully use or persecute them. But the prospect brightens upon us. The scales begin to fall from the eyes of the electors; and they are convinced of the folly of spending so much time to gratify the pride or vanity of any man; and they are also convinced of the justice of a Representative being chosen from the county of Berkshire, and who he shall be, was sufficiently pointed out at the first election; for it is a truth, that Mr. [Theodore] Sedgwick was then chosen by the people, but owing to the negligence of a number of the towns, the votes were not returned to the Governor within the limited time. Free electors! should it so happen that you are again called upon to vote for a Representative, act your own judgment; act like freemen; let every man be persuaded in his own mind, but spurn with contempt the man who shall offer to influence your conduct in a case of so great importance to the district. Should this be the case, that every elector, regardless of the insinuations and misrepresentations of artful and designing men, votes for the person who he is conscious would do the most good to the district and state, I have not the least doubt in my own mind, but that Mr. Sedgwick will be the man.[2]

1. This possibly refers to the Reverend John Taylor of Deerfield. See Samuel Henshaw to Theodore Sedgwick, 23 December, printed above in The First Election in Hampshire-Berkshire District.

2. On 6 May this item was reprinted by the *Hampshire Chronicle* and introduced by "An Independent Elector": "You are requested by a number of your customers, to publish the following address, which most decently graced the Northampton paper of the 22d of last

month, in favor of the Hon. Mr. Sedgwick. This pretty piece of composition is only a modest specimen of the brilliant wit, and of the manly, noble, and generous publications, which have too often appeared in that IMPARTIAL paper, in favor of that honorable gentleman." At the conclusion of the item, the *Chronicle*'s correspondent added this commentary: "Fellow citizens: What impiety! What defamation, scandal, and abuse! Will you be called miscreants, and be charged with having formed a league and a combination with Hell—and not resent it? Reverend sir, whoever thou art, shall you be thus publicly insulted and abused; and shall the gentlemen, whom we have honored with our suffrages, be charged with duplicity and bribery; and shall we ourselves be charged with being corrupted and bribed—and shall we not resent it? Certainly we will resent it."

An Elector, Hampshire Gazette, 22 April

As the election of a federal Representative for the western district is to be on the 11th of May next, and as there have been many imputations cast on the two candidates—the friends of Mr. [Theodore] Sedgwick charge Mr. [Samuel] Lyman with being a false double dealing man; also the friends of Mr. Lyman charge Mr. Sedgwick with being a public defaulter, etc.—now as neither of these charges have been proved or disproved to the satisfaction of the public, and as they or either of them will have an opportunity before the election, I wish them to embrace it.[1]

1. Most of this item was set in italics.

Curtius, Hampshire Gazette, 29 April

After such a multiplicity of endeavors to influence the public mind in the election of a federal Representative for this district, no apology will, I presume, be expected at this time, for enquiring whether the motives urged for some and against others who have presented themselves as candidates have been fair and generous. For if it appears on examination, that the advantages of electing any particular character are mere illusive phantoms of overheated imaginations, we shall undoubtedly spurn them from us with the utmost disdain. How far this is the case, I submit to your determination, on a review of the inducements held forth.

And first, what is really more deceptive than the pretended claim of some, that justice and equity both require that the Representative should be taken from the county of Berkshire, and that because we have a Senator chosen from this county, we are to gratify their prejudices in the choice of a Representative—however unreasonable. Such a right is certainly too unfounded to deserve the smallest serious notice. For if local and personal motives are to have any weight, each town would do well to earnestly contend the privilege of sending one of their number. It seems to me that we ought ever to consider the person most actuated by local and personal motives, the least worthy of our confidence.

And then the ghosts of the Penobscot expedition, and the old Continental money are introduced as questions most probably to be agitated by the new Congress, as likely enough they may with others of far more importance, and perhaps far better understood by many persons in the community than Mr. [Theodore] Sedgwick.

But the finishing touch to the picture declares the very great partiality of Mr. Sedgwick to the farmer and yeomanry, and his heightened aversion to the land [taxes] and odious poll taxes.[1] Incredible effrontery to our understandings. Have we ever on any former occasion known either him or any of his zealous partisans discover any such disinterestedness? And have not their pursuits always centered in the vortex of self-interest; and I may add, that there is reason to fear if he should now be chosen, that he would be more solicitous to please the aristocratic faction, composed of the designing, crafty office-hunters, than to give dignity and respectability to the great body of the people. I might proceed to supply the shades to the portrait which they have left, but forbear from an abhorrence to personalities, which public safety may not at present require, and pass to the agreeable enquiries of whom we shall choose to represent the district, to which the suffrages do proclaim Samuel Lyman, Esquire, who it is believed was really chosen, if an unaccountable neglect or design had not prevented the seasonable return of votes of twenty towns on the return day, but is charged with speculating and trimming between two opposites—a full proof of the want of proper accusation, when recourse is had to such pitiful subterfuge, for it is the property of exalted and philosophic understandings, raised above the low mist of narrow prejudices, to draw forth truth from the violence of party zeal like the spark from the collision of flints.

There cannot be a greater pledge of his ability and integrity expected, than the unmerited obloquy and abuse with which he constantly has been treated by the faction before suggested, composed of characters not famed for their patriotism and public spirit. It is the highest characteristic of virtue, that it is obnoxious to vice. Under these considerations, we cannot hesitate to determine whether we choose to risk the operation of the flowing zeal of Theodore Sedgwick, Esq., or experience the benign influences of the candid and enlightened understanding of Samuel Lyman, Esq. I submit to your determination.

1. See the item in the *Hampshire Gazette*, 25 February, printed above in The Third Election in Hampshire-Berkshire District. In the same issue of the *Gazette* in which "Curtius" was printed, "An Old Farmer," in a long essay addressed "To the Electors of the Western District," implied that Sedgwick (although he was not specifically mentioned) was the man who should be sent to Congress precisely because he would vote in favor of the measures outlined in the *Gazette* article of 25 February: "give your votes for the man . . . who will be most likely to stand up in a firm and manly manner to have the Penobscot affair, which now lies on us of this state solely, become a continental affair; to have justice done us with regard to that great part of the army which we raised and supported; and also with regard to the great quantities of paper money which are among us . . . ."

Extract of a Letter from a Gentleman in Berkshire, Hampshire Gazette, 29 April

By publishing the following extract of a letter from a gentleman in Berkshire to his friend in this town, you will oblige, Yours, etc.

Nothing has more completely unmasked the designs of the aristocratic faction, than their deep laid attempt to displace from the chair of government our present worthy Governor,[1] whose uniform patriotism and distinguished disinterestedness must ever command the attachment and gratitude of all; except the avenues of their understandings are closed by the blindest bigotry and prejudice, or only open to a black design on the equal liberties and rights of mankind. I also find the same faction thus leagued against our worthy Chief Magistrate, practicing every deception to obtain the election of Theodore Sedgwick, Esq., federal Representative—mounting their arrogance to such a pitch as though they came into the world for no other purpose than to watch and govern the motions of others. I am therefore resolved to defeat, if possible, his election (of which I think there is little or no prospect), as from their plotting I am confident no good can be expected; and republican caution might very justly suspect a fatal stab aimed at the vitals of liberty. I shall consequently support the election of Samuel Lyman, Esq., whom I think a man of a fair, candid, unbiased mind, accompanied with good sense and information; and I think from the violent abuse attempted against him, the conclusion is natural that he is a man of integrity and a true friend to liberty.

1. The state elections for governor, lieutenant governor, and senators were held on 6 April. John Hancock was reelected governor by an overwhelming majority, over former Governor James Bowdoin.

Hampshire Gazette, 29 April

LIKE TO HAVE BEEN LOST, on Sunday the 19th inst., the sage politician, and mighty orator—sometimes styled poor D.C.[1] As the most trivial circumstances attendant on *great personages* have sometimes been known to engage the feelings of the public, and particularly so when objects of great moment are by their influence and exertions to be effected—it may not be displeasing to the inhabitants of this district to hear how nigh they came to the loss of a man, who has at every period exerted his various and well-known talents for the choice of a *people's man* to represent us. The seemingly bitter circumstances were as follows: D.C., who by the way is no slouch at his trade, found that the state of his politics required his immediate presence at a neighboring town, in order that the common people, who everybody knows *are incapable of judging for themselves*, might not throw away their votes at the ensuing election of federal Representative. But as great statesmen had rather veil in mystery or falsehood the drift of their purposes, than expose them to vulgar apprehension—so our political sage thought fit upon this occasion to amuse common understandings with a rumor, that he was bound for a place very wide from that which he really intended to visit, that his business was quite in the line of common life, and that he should speedily return. However, after he had been absent a longer time than he had proposed, whether from obstinacy or inattention to his councils was of no consequence to his particular friends, their fertile imaginations pictured a thousand misfortunes which might befall a man of his talents and consequence. And when they heard that he really had not been at the place which he had proposed to them, their former anxiety was changed into frantic rage. Some fell monster had seized him; some political adversary had cast him into a pit, as the only means left to withstand his *measures*. But how easy is it for men of such profound talents to effect things, which to common understandings are perfectly astonishing. Our hero, if I may so call him, was not hurt or even touched. But at a time when more than a hundred people were in search of him in swamps, ditches, pits, and inaccessible caverns, he had the consummate skill by a route quite unexpected, to get home almost unobserved. "Ye little stars hide your diminished heads." Now gentlemen, if you will not enlist under this man's banners and hear to his counsels, you deserve to be all hanged for fools. But should you mind him, as I trust you will, we may have a man to represent us who will hear every man's grievance, and particular tale of woe—and who will, no doubt, promise them all immediate relief.

1. Presumably Daniel Cooley, representative of Amherst to the General Court. See Theodore Sedgwick to Thomas Dwight, 23 January, printed above in The Second Election in Hampshire-Berkshire District.

Junius, Jr., to the Printer, Berkshire Chronicle, 1 May

One good turn deserves another. Your impartiality is called on for the insertion of the following.[1]

To Junius. Sir: The federal electors of the county of Berkshire have a high sense of the abuses which Mr. [Theodore] S[edgwick] has received from Mr. [Samuel] L[yman], and will certainly enter deeply into the spirit of the quarrel, in avenging his wrongs.

Be assured, sir, it is with a becoming indignation they reflect upon the notorious effrontery of Mr. L——, in his incredible assertion that Mr. S—— had "most egregiously abused him."[2]

Can they forbear execrating his name, when they consider that, not contented, like the modest Mr. S——, and his more modest adherents, to leave the electors to the discretionary disposal of their suffrages, Mr. L—— and his friends "spare no pains to effect his election!"—that, little short of blasphemy, he has even been left to speak disrespectfully of the immaculate character of Mr. S——! They can never be sufficiently grateful to the good *Junius* for rousing them from their "lethargy," by his *thumping* "truths"—for his refreshing their memories of what many might perhaps have nearly forgotten, respecting Mr. S——'s *good qualifications,* and particularly his having "long possessed the confidence of the people!"

Could the sagacious Junius harbor a dubious thought whether those suffrages which have formerly been ranked under the class of "scattering votes," would now be concentrated to his wish, to the prejudice and confusion of the *"base"* L——?

Remember, Junius, to whom you are addressing yourself—remember the electors of Berkshire are men of republican principles—that they *know how to prize liberty*—that they are *too sensible* of the *republican spirit* of Mr. S——; have seen *too much* of his lenity, moderation, and goodness; and are under *too great obligations* to him, to think of prostituting their suffrages upon any other. They have heard of men who glory in the oppression of the poor, and make it their primary aim to aggrandize themselves thereby. They have been told of those who wish to reduce their free government to a system of despotism; and place their *summum bonum* in that state of society, where the support of the laborious class of its members depends on, and is constituted by, the daily wages of a *"sheep's head and pluck."* How shall they be assured that this is not the character of "this said Mr. L——," about whom the hairbrained electors of Hampshire make such a pother? And shall they run the important risk, while the mild, the meek, the moderate, the compassionate, the beneficent Mr. S—— is holden up to their view?

Tell your master, Junius, in the paroxysm of his fever, to fear nothing; that he may rest assured there will be no more "scattering votes"; that though true it is, that, mad with the notion of liberty, the electors *will vote as they please*, fixed in a habit of *looking up to him*, and reminded of his having "long possessed" their "confidence," he will *not be forgotten*. Some, indeed, there are, who are not totally inflexible; suggest therefore the expediency of his active exertions; send him abroad to shake them by the hand, bow, smile, and play with their buttons; and, believe me, he has nothing to fear. If any, however, should hang back, and prove refractory, up and give them another sly touch in the *Chronicle*, and the day is your own. Huzza! for S—— and Republicanism!

1. This satirical attack on Sedgwick is apparently a reply to an item in the *Berkshire Chronicle*, 17 April. The issue of the 17th is mutilated so that only a portion of the item is readable. It declares that Sedgwick had long enjoyed the confidence of the people and charges that Samuel Lyman told stories to injure Sedgwick which Lyman knew to be "as false as the tongue that uttered them."
2. See Sedgwick to Thomas Dwight, 23 January, printed above in The Second Election in Hampshire-Berkshire District.

The People, Hampshire Gazette, 6 May

It is the privilege of the freemen in this district to give in their votes for gentlemen to fill public offices, as they shall be directed by their own judgment. Whoever calls them a faction, for giving their votes to any particular gentleman most agreeable to them, must possess an uncommon stock of impudence. In the last *Gazette* an acrimonious writer reproaches the freemen for using their essential privilege. The writer we mean is the author of the piece signed "Curtius," and of the pretended extract of a letter from a gentleman in Berkshire.[1] Both those productions are, from their style and temper, the works of the same author. Is it not very singular for a person to complain that the freemen did not universally give their votes for the present worthy Governor, when the last year he himself used every exertion to displace him and introduce Mr. [Elbridge] Gerry. It is quite a blunder for him to set a Berkshire man to complain of this, when the Governor had almost all the votes in that county, where Mr. [Theodore] Sedgwick had also a great majority as federal Representative. He talks of the gentlemen who have been honored by the suffrages of the freemen as *presenting themselves candidates for an election*. We say Mr. Sedgwick never *presented himself a candidate for election*. He was solicited into that situation by the substantial characters of the district. He insinuates, that Mr. [Samuel] Lyman would have been chosen, had not the votes of twenty towns through some designed neglect, failed of reaching in season the public office.[2] The public may be assured that soon after the time for counting the votes, the generality of the unreturned votes did reach the office; and two letters from two members of the Council who counted the votes certify, one of them that by those votes, Mr. Sedgwick was chosen by a clear majority. The other letter states that he had a majority of two hundred votes. But this is now nothing to the purpose, only to detect falsehood. We must try again. Those who have voted for Mr. Sedgwick are no faction. They are quiet, substantial yeomen of two large counties. They are able to give a satisfactory reason for their preference of him. We have no controversy with Samuel Lyman, Esquire. We wish him prosperity in the proper line of his business. We think Mr. Sedgwick better qualified for service in the government of the United States. Mr. Sedgwick, and those who vote for him are accused of avarice and ambition. Modest charge upon a free enlightened people! But we are not surprised at it. It is accounted for upon the same principles that influence lewd women to call the virtuous part of their sex prostitutes. If this writer is an office hunter, as we shrewdly suspect him to be, he will doubtless succeed better by the influence of a kinsman, than by the influence of Mr. Sedgwick, who will never wittingly employ it in favor of a person who is not a man of merit. He labors to lay the ghosts of the Penobscot expedition, and of the old Continental money. But he can never succeed while the substantial citizens groan under those and other heavy and unequal burdens. They will be wise enough to choose a man of influence who will be most able to obtain justice for the commonwealth, and distribute public expenses equally. True, these burdens are nothing to men in ruined circumstances, who live in taste and fashion upon the property of their creditors. But they are weighty considerations and will be felt so to be by men of honesty and property. We are sure that this writer appears in his compositions with the eagerness of a party man, who expects some personal advantage from the choice of Samuel Lyman, Esq. He would not have reviled honest characters, belabored the freemen, and made such palpable misrepresentations, were he not a *self seeker*. Beware of self seekers who dare misrepresent public facts, and call good people hard names. We say nothing against Mr. Lyman; wish him God speed in his proper sphere. We vote for Mr. Sedgwick; we are not ashamed of it. We are acquainted with him. He is no stranger to our interests. His real estate lies in this government. He is interested in our welfare. We think him a very sensible, candid gentleman—a statesman of deep experience, versed in the school of public business. Above all we think him a downright, plain, honest man. We wish not to be reviled for our thoughts by the angry Curtius. We wish to act with the integrity and dignity of freemen, who would stand well in their own consciences, and serve our country by our patriotism.[3]

1. Both items were in the *Hampshire Gazette*, 29 April, and are printed above.

2. See The Question of Delayed and Missing Election Returns, 15 April–3 May, printed above in The Fourth Election in Hampshire-Berkshire District.

3. "Curtius" replied to this item in the *Hampshire Gazette*, 13 May.

Hampshire County to the Electors of the County of Hampshire, Hampshire Gazette, 6 May

As your paper, Mr. Printer, is an impartial one, I presume you will not refuse a place to a piece, though opposite to your own party, or to the majority of those pieces which have lately appeared in your paper.

The public are once more called upon to give their votes for a federal Representative. We seem to be pretty much disposed to vote for either Mr. [Samuel] Lyman or Mr. [Theodore] Sedgwick, and very considerable efforts have been made for each of them. I have the honor of some acquaintance with both the gentlemen, and I hope I shall not trespass too much upon the time of your readers, if I offer some observations upon their different characters through the medium of your paper.

Mr. Lyman is a man who is possessed of a soft, easy manner of behavior, which wins the good will of the company he is in equal to any man I ever saw. He has no such thing as haughtiness and pride about him, but he will be familiar with anybody. He was bred to the practice of the law, and knows how to manage a dispute, if he pleases, as well as any man in the county. Tis true he is not one of your noisy folks who seem as if they would carry all before them. He speaks but little, but tis to the purpose; and when he has been but a *proper time* in Congress, I doubt not will make as good a figure as those who appear superior to him at first. But I cannot help going back to his sweet disposition, so soft, so clever, and so gentle. Tis really charming to hear him in conversation. He engages the love of all who are present, both men and women; and I never saw his countenance change in my life, but tis always exactly the same, equally smooth, good-natured, and smiling—not ruffled by passion and anger, as other people's are I could mention. What man so able as this to carry a point in a large assembly? Besides, has not this man been abused before his face and behind his back, merely because he was like to carry the vote against his rival? Where were Mr. Sedgwick's feelings, where was his tenderness when he could load with reproaches this gentleman? To be sure, Mr. Sedgwick found he was mistaken, and that some enemy to him, and a cunning friend to Mr. Lyman, had raised the report on purpose to produce a quarrel for Mr. Lyman's advantage, unknown to either of them—but he might, I should think, have enquired this out before. Tis a poor recompense to Mr. Lyman for him to acknowledge his mistake now; surely something more is due; and I think the people of this county show their kind disposition to take part with the injured.

As to Mr. Sedgwick, I do not want to injure his reputation, though I suppose I could not if I would. He is a gentleman of some abilities and some experience, but surely not worth all this fuss that is made about it. Is there a man in this county equal to Mr. Sedgwick, and must we go to the county of Berkshire for a Representative? *Oh! tell it not in Gath.* It has never been my misfortune to employ Mr. Sedgwick to assist me at the Supreme Court but once, and then indeed I paid him so well that I was resolved rather to trust my own tongue next time, and the judges of the court. However, he may be a good man for all this. I don't say this to hurt him, but only to show the man. But if any man denies he loves money, he knows but little of him—and he would never go to Congress if he had not provided a young man to take care of his office in his absence and do the common business. But let me ask the people, did they ever know a man in the practice of the law who did not mind more his own interest than that of his friends. The gentlemen of this profession are not in the highest esteem among us—and pity it would be if they were, for it would be the first time they ever were in any country. And though Mr. Lyman was a lawyer, and a good one too (although he did not speak much), yet he is no longer one, and I am sure the people of this county who know him, know he is preferable to any lawyer in the state.

I have heard a great deal about Mr. Sedgwick being a grand speaker, and what a figure he makes; but for my part I own I never could see anything very extraordinary in him besides a great fat belly, and a great loud voice; or as we say, "*all talk and no cider*." This is not the man for me, nor do I think him equal to Mr. Lyman in conversation, or that he would be at Congress after some little time—but however I will not take upon me to run him down, for no man detests more than I do, these newspaper scandals. Let me conclude with recommending, in one word, Samuel Lyman, Esq., as the most proper and able man to represent this district in Congress.

From a Correspondent, Hampshire Chronicle, 6 May

Freemen, attend! Next Monday is the day appointed for you to exercise the privilege which you all hold dear, that of choosing your own Representative to the first grand federal Congress. Forget not to assemble yourselves together; let not this important period pass unimproved, but show yourselves worthy of being styled freemen. Let all those who wish this district to be represented in such a manner as to promote the interest of individuals, and the welfare of the community, join heart and hand in giving their suffrages in favor of Samuel Lyman, Esq. This man is consistent in his conduct; is not governed, like some others, by caprice and folly; and has the public good always present to his view.

The Northampton Caucus, Hampshire Chronicle, 6 May

A Correspondent

I am informed, that last week, a number of gentlemen held what they called a *caucus*, at Northampton, in order to digest some well-concerted plan, so as to insure the election of Mr. [Theodore] Sedgwick. They say that Mr. [Samuel] Lyman is exceedingly popular, and that there is great danger of his election, unless they exert themselves to the utmost. Accordingly a majority of them agreed to do every thing in their power to accomplish Mr. Sedgwick's election. A certain gentleman of large and goodly port, who, previous to the last election, wrote addresses to be read in the town meetings, and who actually did procure sundry persons to attempt to read them, but they unfortunately met with the resentment and just indignation of the independent electors, and had to make a most precipitate retreat, in fearful apprehension of a violent attack in the rear; this gentleman, I say, declared he would leave no stone unturned. Another gentleman, ever true and faithful to his trust, declared that he was afraid the precepts would this time all get to Lyman's towns, and that the votes would all be returned. Another gentleman, much noted for his great integrity and high notions of honor, declared that for his part, he would not hesitate a moment at publishing a few lies about Lyman, if thereby the election of Mr. Sedgwick could be secured. A fourth gentleman, a man of candor, observed that for his part, he did not care a fig who is chosen, whether Sedgwick or Lyman, were it not for one reason, and that was, that he had heretofore voted for Sedgwick, and that he did not like to be beat. A fifth gentleman observed, that there was no danger of being beat, if Sedgwick's friends would exert themselves as they ought—for, said he, we can go, or send runners to almost any of the insurgent [i.e., Shaysite] towns, and bring over a great many to vote for Sedgwick, by making them believe that he is in favor of scaling down the public securities; and that it is in *his* power alone, and not within the power or abilities of any other man, to get rid of the whole of the debt, incurred in consequence of the failure of the Penobscot expedition; and that he can, by a kind of magic (I suppose by looking bold and speaking loud), turn all those mountains of old Continental money which we have in the treasury, into mountains of silver and gold. This fifth gentleman is an old fox; he is one of the children of this world, and is exceeding wise in his generation—for he further observed, that Sedgwick would run a pretty good chance this time, because the meeting will be in a very busy season; and that it would be almost impossible for the farmers to meet so generally on that day, as they have heretofore done; and that the old farmers, Lyman's friends, are almost tired out. Let us exert ourselves, said he, and the day is our own.

Fellow citizens: Shall we be treated thus, and not resent it? The electors ought to resent, and they will resent the self design and intrigue of a few busy agents in imposing upon them false information to mislead them, and malicious slander to wean them from their faithful friend.[1]

A Friend to Truth

Attempts have been industriously made to misrepresent a meeting had at Northampton the last week, consisting indiscriminately of all the different parties in the county, as well as the several juries belonging to the court. It was then unanimously agreed, that to put an end to the divisions which have heretofore subsisted in this district, concerning the election of a federal Representative, they would unite in the choice of the Hon. Theodore Sedgwick, Esq., at the ensuing election. It is therefore hoped that the good people of this district will not be deluded by any misrepresentations of that fact, but cordially unite in favor of that gentleman.

1. This paragraph was set largely in italic type.

The Issue of Theodore Sedgwick's Public Accounts, 6-15 May

Theodore Sedgwick had been a purchasing agent for the Continental Army in the Northern Department from 1775 to 1778. The charge that he had never settled his accounts and was therefore a "public defaulter" was made before the second election (see Sedgwick to Benjamin Lincoln, 6 February, printed above in The Second Election in Hampshire-Berkshire District), but notice of the charge did not appear in the newspapers until shortly before the fourth election (see "A Friend to the People," *Hampshire Chronicle*, 25 March, printed above). On 22 April "An Elector" in the *Hampshire Gazette* (printed above) asked for proof or disproof of the charges.

On 6 May both the *Hampshire Gazette* and the *Hampshire Chronicle* published a letter written by Oliver Phelps dated Granville, 24 April. Phelps had been connected with the Commissary Department during the Revolution. Printed below are

Phelps's letter as it appeared in the *Chronicle*, 6 May, an item which appeared immediately following the letter in the *Chronicle*, and the item written by "A," who sent the letter to the *Gazette*. These are followed by "A Farmer" in the *Chronicle*, 6 May, and by letters from Joseph Lyman to Theodore Sedgwick, 8 May, and Joseph Savage to George Thacher, 15 May.

A Constant Customer, Hampshire Chronicle, 6 May

Mr. Weld, You are desired to give the following certificate a place in your paper—of which the candid may judge for themselves; it needs no comment of mine. Yours, A CONSTANT CUSTOMER.

[Oliver Phelps's Letter]

"I had the pleasure to receive your favor, in which you request me to give you information, whether there is any foundation for the report which is industriously circulated, that Mr. [Theodore] Sedgwick is a public defaulter. I shall with pleasure give you every information in my power on this subject. The facts are these: Early in the late war, by order of Joseph Trumbull, Esq., then commissary general, I employed Mr. Sedgwick to superintend purchases in the county of Berkshire, and in the state of New York. His purchases were very considerable. Some time in the year 1778, Mr. Sedgwick called on me to settle his account. He then closed his account of purchases, *and accounted for all the monies he had received of me.* He then produced me vouchers for the *delivery of the articles* contained in his account of purchases; but on examining those vouchers, I found that numbers of them were not from proper officers, being only receipts of his agents, which would not answer me as vouchers to charge the United States. Under these circumstances, that my accounts with him might be finally closed, I took *his receipt* to the United States; he engaging that the necessary vouchers should be procured. And in a settlement of *my accounts* with the public, *I lodged this receipt* with the commissioner for settling the accounts of the United States.

"In JUSTICE to Mr. Sedgwick, I must say, it did not appear, that there was *the least neglect in him*, but in those he was *obliged* to employ under him, in the negotiation of his business; and that in the progress of it, *he conducted himself with* HONOR, FIDELITY, *and to the public* ADVANTAGE. I am, in haste, your obedient humble servant, OLIVER PHELPS."

For the Hampshire Chronicle

Mr. Weld, Mr. Phelps's *letter proves beyond all doubt or contradiction, that Mr.* Sedgwick *is a* PUBLIC DEFAULTER—*and the books of the Federal Treasury fully demonstrate that he has not produced those receipts which he engaged to, even after the expiration of* thirteen years!

A to the Printer, Hampshire Gazette, 6 May

If Mr. Butler will be so obliging as to publish in his impartial paper the foregoing letter, he will disseminate truth, and oblige his *readers*, who have been anxious to discover the truth or falsehood of the report alluded to. *They* now can have no reasonable doubt in the matter, since the honorable gentleman who employed Mr. Sedgwick has thus declared, under his hand,* that HE *accounted* *for all the money he received, and "conducted himself with honor, and fidelity, and to the public advantage."* Is this being a public defaulter? No answer, or comment is necessary. "Let him who hath sinned, sin no more."

*If any person is so uncharitable as to suppose the letter to be fictitious, and inserted as a sheer electioneering piece, he is desired to call at this [printing] office, where the original is left on purpose to confound the wisdom of this world.

A Farmer to the Printer, Hampshire Chronicle, 6 May

I recollect a little piece in the Northampton paper, of the 22d of last month, from one of Mr. [William] Butler's customers, requesting information relative to the report of the Hon. Mr. [Theodore] Sedgwick's being a public defaulter.[1] This customer of his certainly ought to be gratified. And I recollect a piece, under the signature of *A Friend to the People*, in your paper of the 25th of last March, in favor of choosing the Hon. Mr. Sedgwick, to represent this state in the Congress of the United States.[2] This piece is well written, but very lengthy, and exceedingly labored. I shall pass over this long and tedious piece, and make two or three strictures upon it. I observed in it sundry unjust and ungenerous insinuations and allusions; however, a disposition of this kind is perfectly natural and congenial to a party spirit; and since that spirit, at present, is raging and epidemical, charity, and an indulgence to the infirmities of human nature, induce me not to animadvert with severity upon it.

That publication, and that highly finished encomium, should not have been noticed by me, in this public manner, had I not been constrained to do it, from principles and considerations of a public and private nature. Shall I see a fellow citizen charged with giving credit and currency to a report, which is said to be, wholly and in every part, without foundation? Shall I hear him charged with the crime of falsely and maliciously originating a report, to injure and blast the reputation of another fellow citizen? Shall I hear him publicly challenged to come forward, and adduce evidence of the truth of that report, and yet remain silent? Or shall I see him borne down under an accumulating load of defamation, scandal, and abuse, and have it in my power, and yet not exonerate and relieve him? Or shall I advise him to put on charity that endureth all things, and bow down with more than Christian patience, and be pressed to death? Certainly I will not, for it would be inconsistent with every sentiment, and with every principle of religion and honor.

This terrible REPORT, which is said to have done more mischief than all other reports put together, and which is compared *to the hidden dagger, with which the assassin murders the characters of honest men*, is this, *That the Hon. Mr. Sedgwick is a public defaulter, that he owes the public fifteen hundred dollars, out of which he would defraud them.* A most uncharitable inference! What! a man of honor and vast property, *and one who has an interest in his own state*, cheat the public out of fifteen hundred dollars? Certainly it cannot be. This report I know is false, for *plain dealing and prompt honesty, without disguise, are his known characteristics*. Therefore he cannot be a public defaulter, in the sum of fifteen hundred dollars; and if he was, he certainly would not cheat the public out of this sum, for he is an honest man, and able to pay it. THE FACT IS, he is a public defaulter, in the sum of FOURTEEN THOUSAND

DOLLARS, in specie, for public property received in the year 1776, and for which he has not yet accounted, although thirteen years have elapsed, and although frequently called upon by the commissioner appointed by Congress, to audit and settle accounts of this nature. Mr. Sedgwick stands charged upon the books of the Federal Treasury, for the following articles, received in the year 1776, when the late Mr. [Joseph] Trumbull, of Connecticut, was commissary general, viz.:

For two thousand, two hundred and sixty-one hundred and one quarter of flour; seven thousand, four hundred and six and an half bushels of wheat; four barrels of beef; two barrels of pork; and three thousand, one hundred and ninety-six flour casks.

In testimony of the truth of this statement and declaration, I pledge my sacred honor; and if this declaration is not true, I do hereby direct and authorize the Printer, to deliver up and publish my name, and I will then most voluntarily and cheerfully submit to all the stings and arrows of infamy. Why this long delay! Why not have settled this account months and years ago, and not have been haunted by this malicious report, this hidden dagger, covered over with the rust of thirteen years, that now comes forth, like a malignant foe, and threatens to thwart and disappoint him in his career of ambition!

Pardon me, it is with reluctance I have made this declaration; and I should not have made it, had I not known that Mr. [Samuel] Lyman had been exceedingly abused by false reports, and by ungenerous, false, and unmanly publications in newspapers; and had it not been for the imprudence or indiscretion of the author of that long labored piece above referred to. He calls on every man who dares come forward and support the charge, and he virtually tells all men that they believe a lie, who believe that awful and malicious report, and that they are malicious liars who propagate it. He was either ignorant of the truth of this report, or he was a bold fellow indeed. He however thought it would answer his purpose, to be positive and impudent. The challenge being made so late, he knew it was impossible to return an answer before the then next election day.

Mr. Printer, I will trouble you no more. Any gentlemen who wish for further information of this subject may apply to Mr. [Jonathan] Burral, commissioner of accounts, at his office in New York.[3] There they may have complete and full evidence, that the report is wholly, and in every part, *built on good and solid foundation.*

Joseph Lyman to Theodore Sedgwick, Hatfield, 8 May[4]

I was disappointed in not seeing you at Hatfield the last term. You must compensate me by future visits when they lie in your power. I have seen a piece signed, "A Farmer" in the Springfield paper May 6, 1789[5] accepting the challenge made by the "Friend to the People"[6] charging you with being a defaulter to the public of the amount of £14,000 in specie—a pretty round sum if you have still to pay it. This charge ought not to blow over in silence, whether your election for federal Representative be made good or not. I wish, if the liberty is not disagreeable, to be resolved in sundry questions as soon as you can send me the answers. I observe, by the way, that the charge is that you are a defaulter in that sum and cannot be brought to a settlement by the Commissioner, after repeated endeavors for 13 years etc. Now my enquiries are:

1. What are we to understand by a public defaulter in law or politics? Is he a defaulter who stands charged with a debt or he who upon settlement cannot account or make payment?

2. Is the matter of fact truly stated, that you are charged with £14,000 upon the treasury books?

3. Has the Commissioner often called for a settlement and been evaded in his applications?

4. What evidences have you that the public property committed to you was disposed of according to the design of the entrustment?

5. Are the vouchers of your agents of that nature as to prevent every imprudent pretense of a collusion between the principal and his accomplices?

6. Why has this account lain so long unsettled?

7. Is the public in any danger from the delay or does the danger arise solely to yourself?

8. What said Mr. [Nathan] Dane in this matter in his conversation to Mr. [Samuel?] Lyman?

These are a number of plain questions. I ask them, not for curiosity, but to be able to vindicate an honest man, as I believe him to be, to silence malicious scribblers and serve the public. I wish you to enter into the merits of these questions and to give me such information and advice as you think may be serviceable. If not agreeable I must ask your pardon for venturing into your business. You see what the squib after Mr. [Oliver] Phelps's letter[7] suggests. These busy folks ought to be reprehended and I feel it in my heart to administer them a little wholesome discipline. I think if your choice should now obtain, as I hope and rather believe it will, if your people in Berkshire exert themselves, yet this imputation upon a public representative ought to be wiped off and the calumniator detected or otherwise your usefulness may be obstructed.

I am in great haste and must beg you to excuse this imperfect production. If you can guess at my meaning you will have it in your power to satisfy your affectionate friend and humble servant.

Joseph Savage to George Thacher, Springfield, 15 May (excerpt)[8]

We have been able to collect the votes of 24 towns. Mr. [Theodore] Sedgwick has only twelve votes more than Mr. [Samuel] Lyman. But it's generally believed Mr. Lyman will obtain the election. However it's not certain who will be chose.

The report of Mr. S—— being a public defaulter will certainly have its dire effect, as Mr. Lyman's friends have not been backward in spreading the report.

1. See "An Elector," *Hampshire Gazette*, 22 April, printed above.

2. Printed above in The Fourth Election in Hampshire-Berkshire District.

3. In 1786 the Confederation Congress elected Burrall to settle the accounts of the Quartermaster and Commissary departments of the Continental Army. He was reelected in 1787 and 1788.

4. RC, Sedgwick Papers, MHi. Lyman was pastor of the Congregational church at Hatfield from 1772 until his death in 1828. If Sedgwick replied, the reply has not been located.

5. *Hampshire Chronicle*, 6 May, printed above.

6. *Hampshire Chronicle*, 25 March, printed above in The Fourth Election in Hampshire-Berkshire District.

7. See "For the Hampshire Chronicle," printed above.

8. RC, Thacher Papers, MB.

Theodore Sedgwick and Amendments to the Constitution, 6-30 May

On 6 April Theodore Sedgwick wrote a letter to Samuel Henshaw, ostensibly answering a letter from Henshaw dated 25 March. In his letter Sedgwick declares that he had always been a "zealous advocate" of amendments to the Constitution, but states that the letter was not for publication because it would look like "electioneering," a business in which he was "not versed." On 6 May, five days before the fifth election, it was published in the *Hampshire Gazette* with an introduction evidently written by Henshaw.

Early in March Sedgwick had sent "a packet" for publication to Henry Van Schaack and Samuel Henshaw, but Henshaw received the material too late for publication before the fourth election on 30 March (see Van Schaack to Sedgwick, 12 and 15-16 March, and Henshaw to Sedgwick, 27 March, printed above in The Fourth Election in Hampshire-Berkshire District). It is possible that the letter printed below is a version of the material sent to Henshaw in March.

The first public response was by "Curtius" in the *Hampshire Gazette*, 13 May, two days after the election. "Curtius" had attacked Sedgwick in the *Gazette* on 29 April (printed above) and "The People" replied in the *Gazette* on 6 May (printed above) that Sedgwick had never "presented himself" as a candidate. On the 13th "Curtius" declared that Sedgwick's letter in the *Gazette* proved that Sedgwick had indeed "presented" himself as a candidate.

The letter was also the subject of controversy in the Boston newspapers. On 28 May, in the same issue that it reported that Sedgwick had won the election "by a majority of seven votes," the *Independent Chronicle* printed excerpts from Sedgwick's letter, preceded by sarcastic comments. "Amator Justitiae" responded in the *Massachusetts Centinel* on 30 May with an appeal to have the letter published in full.

Sedgwick's letter is printed below as it appeared in the *Hampshire Gazette*, with an introduction which is evidently by Samuel Henshaw, although it is unsigned. The original manuscript of the letter (RC, Houghton Autograph Collection, MH) has been compared with the printed version. There are several minor differences between the two but no substantive changes. The letter is followed by the item from the *Independent Chronicle* on 28 May and the response in the *Massachusetts Centinel* on 30 May.

Theodore Sedgwick to Samuel Henshaw, Hampshire Gazette, 6 May

[Henshaw's Introduction]

On the 25th of last month [March], I wrote to Mr. Sedgwick, and suggested a number of things for his consideration, and received the following answer. It is wrote so judiciously, and discovers such an affection for the people—such an ardent desire to advance their prosperity, that I cannot refrain from sending it to you for publication. For I am convinced that if the people knew his sentiments and wished their own political happiness, they would give him their suffrages for a federal Representative. I cannot however but ask his pardon for publishing a private letter with his name to it. And when I assure him, as I now do, that my only motive in doing it is to undeceive many virtuous electors, who have been imposed upon by insidious men, he will forgive me. The letter is as follows, viz.:

[Sedgwick's Letter]

Stockbridge, April 6th, 1789.

"My Dear Sir,

In your obliging letter of the 25th ult. you are pleased to observe, '*that many people in this district have several objections to my being a Representative in the national government.*' I thank you for that frankness and friendship which you discover in naming the objections, and for your candor and delicacy in observing upon them; and shall endeavor to give you the satisfaction required.

"You say, '*that the primary objection to me is, that I have not publicly declared my sentiments in favor of amending the national Constitution of government, and that, therefore, the people conclude that I am against any amendments at all.*' I am not, my dear sir, answerable for such conclusions. They may be drawn with equal propriety against the objectors themselves, and against every person in the district who has not publicly declared himself to be of different sentiments. My friends and acquaintance know; and all with whom I have had the pleasure of conversing on the subject know, that I have been, and now am, a zealous advocate for many amendments.[1] Before the Constitution was ratified by this state, I did every thing in my power to forward its adoption; because I then thought, and do now think, that the happiness, the permanent happiness of the people would be established by it—not the happiness of any professional order of men, nor of the rich and great—but of the bulk of citizens, of the various artisans and innumerable yeomanry of the country. Sure I was, and am, in my own mind, that if the government could begin to operate on the leading principles of the Constitution, the farmer, the manufacturer, and the laboring poor would soon reap vast advantages from the efficiency of our national Union. But I never once dreamed but what the Constitution would be *perfected* agreeably to the provision in the 5th Article. And those amendments which will render it more perfect, more congenial to the sentiments and feelings of the PEOPLE *who are to live under it, and to support it,* can never meet with successful opposition from any quarter. But, my friend, we must guard against amendments that will be partial or local in their operation. Should amendments of this kind, which are proposed by some of the states, be adopted, the most essential advantages of a commercial nature would be lost to Massachusetts.

"You mention, '*that the people are groaning under the weight of public taxes, and that they imagine I do not feel for them.*' This, my dear sir, gives me pain! Is it possible that a people who have often experienced the humanity of my heart—who have often seen and heard me declare my abhorrence of heavy land taxes—is it possible for that people to believe that I do not feel, exquisitely feel, for them under any of their burdens whatever? I hope not. They essentially injure me if they do. To lessen land taxes and to enable government to raise a revenue from other sources has been the wish of my heart and the employment of my head for years past; and to effect this desirable object the several state debts should be assumed by the general government, at least so far as they were contracted to effect our independence. And this, I think, can be done on principles of equality. Indeed I cannot conceive it possible that equal justice can be done to each state without this assumption. And in my mind, it is impossible that any other measure should so effectually and lastingly cement our national Union. We should then truly be one people bearing an equal burden, sharing an equal benefit, and having an equal prospect. And this, more than any thing else, would annihilate local prejudices, give liberality of sentiment, and lead us to embrace with united affection, the whole continent of America.

"You very justly observe, '*that Massachusetts has greatly suffered on account of the Penobscot expedition, the old paper money,*' etc. and you wish for a remedy—and so does every friend to this state, and every friend to equal justice. But, my dear sir, can you think of any one so equal, so just, and so easily to be effected as the one abovementioned? Who can say, that the whole public debt, which was contracted solely in consequence of the Revolution, ought not to be borne equally by the states according to their respective abilities? The idea is acknowledged to be just in speculation; but the difficulty lies, it is said, in reducing it to practice. That there are difficulties in the way, no one will deny; and what great national measure is unattended with difficulties? This, I dare say, will not involve Congress in greater perplexities than any other business of equal magnitude. And I am persuaded, from my personal acquaintance with many of the gentlemen who compose that august assembly, that they will not be diverted from the path of duty through fear of encountering difficulties in their progress. Men of so much knowledge, so much virtue and patriotism, never can set easy and see *one part* of the community groaning under a heavy state tax, raised on purpose to discharge a debt that was contracted to carry on the war, while *another part* have no such tax to pay, or if any, but a trifle; and because their local situation, or something else, did not *necessitate* them to contract such a debt for *the general good*.

"But I shall trespass upon your patience. I will only observe, that should Congress take the whole debt upon themselves, and should agriculture, arts, manufactures and commerce be duly encouraged by them, we must soon become a great and happy people. Their attention to these subjects would render tranquil the public mind—would strengthen the hands and encourage the hearts of the great body of the people. The industrious husbandman would then be stimulated to rural improvements, and would make *the wilderness blossom and bud, and fill the face of the world with fruit*. And (commerce being duly regulated) he would find a ready market for all his surplusage produce. And this above all things would increase population and give life and vigor to agriculture. Indeed, my dear sir, I hope to see the day when that class of virtuous citizens, who till the ground for the pleasure and support of animal life, will be more encouraged, because they are more beneficial than any other order of men in the community.

"Thus, my friend, I have given you a few of my sentiments, in much haste, on the subject of your letter. But this is not making *a public declaration*. And pardon me, my dear sir, for telling you I never could do that, for it would look like electioneering—a business in which I am not versed.[2] If the good people of the district should see fit to choose me, I shall unceasingly endeavor to advance *their* happiness. If they now let me retire to the private walks of life, after having faithfully served them for many years, they will add to my personal ease and domestic felicity.

"I am, my dear sir, with much affection, your obliged humble servant,
"THEODORE SEDGWICK."

Independent Chronicle, 28 May
Mess'rs. Adams and Nourse, Please to publish the following extract of a letter to a friend, from the Hon. Theodore Sedgwick, which was published in the *Hamp-*

shire Gazette, of the 6th inst. and said to be inserted at his desire, and you will greatly oblige many of your customers; and the public at large will be presented with a true and genuine specimen of modern electioneering, and will see how suddenly a man may be converted from high Federalism to low Antifederalism. Charity however presumes that this sudden conversion was in consequence of the powerful operation of a sublime patriotic principle.

"You say, 'that the primary objection to me is, that I have not publicly declared my sentiments in favor of amending the national Constitution of government, and that, therefore, the people conclude that I am against any amendments at all.' I am not, my dear sir, answerable for such conclusions. They may be drawn with equal propriety against the objectors themselves, and against every person in the district who has not publicly declared himself to be of different sentiments. My friends and acquaintance know, and all with whom I have had the pleasure of conversing on the subject, know, that I have been, and now am, a zealous advocate for many amendments." [3]

Amator Justitiae to the Printer, Massachusetts Centinel, 30 May

In the *Chronicle* of Thursday [28 May], a malevolent and uncandid writer endeavors, by a false statement of facts, to injure the reputation for consistency of the Hon. Mr. [Theodore] Sedgwick, by the publication of a partial extract of a letter written by that gentleman, but which never was intended by him to be published. That the public may not be imposed on, I wish you to publish the letter entire, and the introduction to it, as it appeared in the Northampton paper [*Hampshire Gazette*, 6 May]. [4]

1. Sedgwick had in fact opposed amendments (see Sedgwick to Benjamin Lincoln, 23 September 1788, printed above in From the Adjournment to the Reconvening of the General Court, 20 June—29 October 1788).

2. The documents printed above indicate that Sedgwick had electioneered for office for months.

3. This item, according to Samuel Henshaw, "staggered many of your firm friends" (to Sedgwick, 14 June, printed below).

4. This item was followed in the *Centinel* by Sedgwick's letter as it appeared in the *Hampshire Gazette*, 6 May.

Theodore Sedgwick to Samuel Henshaw, Stockbridge, 15 May[1]

The result of the election is, in this county, for Sedgwick 954, [Samuel] Lyman 376, and for [John] Bacon, [William] Whiting etc. 108. My friends in this town had a meeting last evening to deliberate on the course necessary now to be pursued. I was not present; but have this morning been informed of the result. They determined to make it absolutely certain that all the federal majorities of votes shall be delivered in season, and seem pretty confident this will insure a choice. Of this I am far from being of the same opinion, because as far as our information extends, the votes in Hampshire are more unfavorable than at the last trial. This however I do not suggest to them because I would not wish to dampen their ardor, and also because, by the course they have pointed out, success is not altogether improbable.[2] Mr. Hunt, whose goodness has induced him to undertake the negotiation of this business, will explain to you the several steps proposed to be pursued in the progress of it. Should your opinion concur with that of the gentlemen here, as I am induced to believe it will, I shall have pretty sanguine expectations of a happy issue to this untoward affair.

It was absolutely necessary to see your sheriff [Elisha Porter] before he went to Boston (which we are informed will be on Monday), to know what votes remained unreturned. My friends here will cheerfully discharge any expense which may be incurred in procuring the votes of the delinquent towns.

The exertions the Shaysites have made are unparalleled on any former occasion. Within the three last days more than thirty expresses were sent into every town, urging the people to make a last effort for the preservation of their liberties. And on Sunday the true begotten son of the redoubted Luke Day circulated a very considerable number of the Springfield papers of the 6th of May in which the certificate of O[liver] Phelps was taken out and the blank occasioned thereby filled with other matter.[3] This is a more infamous fraud than I have ever known put in practice in any election, and yet I presume neither this nor anything else will undeceive those poor deluded animals who support the despicable wretch who has so long given us trouble. Present my affect[ionate] regards to Mr. Hunt, and accept my sincere gratulations that the good people of Northampton have done themselves the honor of electing my friend [Henshaw] their representative.[4] I absolutely refused to go to the General Court and I am sorry to add *Bacon is chosen.* [5]

1. RC, Miscellaneous Bound Manuscripts, XVII, MHi.

2. What "course" Sedgwick's friends in Stockbridge proposed to take is unknown.

3. *Hampshire Chronicle*, 6 May. Luke Day of West Springfield was one of the leaders in Shays's Rebellion. No copy of the altered newspaper has been located.

4. Samuel Henshaw was elected to the state House of Representatives from Northampton in the spring election.

5. John Bacon, an opponent of Sedgwick, was elected to the state House of Representatives from Stockbridge in the spring election.

Official Election Returns, 26 May

HAMPSHIRE-BERKSHIRE DISTRICT, 11 MAY

Town	Hon. Theodore Sedgwick, Esq.	Samuel Lyman, Esq.	Simeon Strong, Esq.	Hon. Thompson J. Skinner	Hon. John Worthington, Esq.	William Whiting	Samuel Henshaw, Esq.	Colonel William Lyman	Joel Smith	Lieutenant Ichabod [Crittenden?]	John Bacon
Springfield	20	137									
Longmeadow	14	56	1								

(Table continued on following pages)

HAMPSHIRE-BERKSHIRE DISTRICT, 11 MAY *(continued)*

Town	Hon. Theodore Sedgwick, Esq.	Samuel Lyman, Esq.	Simeon Strong, Esq.	Hon. Thompson J. Skinner	Hon. John Worthington, Esq.	William Whiting	Samuel Henshaw, Esq.	Colonel William Lyman	Joel Smith	Lieutenant Ichabod [Crittenden?]	John Bacon
West Springfield	18	177				1					
Wilbraham	11	132									
Northampton	123	11					1	1			
Southampton	65	22									
Hadley	49	8									
South Hadley	21	15									
Amherst	32	56			1						
Granby	7	29	1								
Hatfield	40	7							1		
Whately	31	2									
Williamsburg											
Westfield	78	42									
Deerfield	41	8									
Greenfield	14	51									
Shelburne											
Conway											
Sunderland											
Montague	33	5									
Northfield	31										
Brimfield	69										
South Brimfield											
[Wales]	9	14									
Monson	26	68									
Pelham	2	62									
Greenwich	6	78									
Blandford	43	40									
Palmer											
Granville	7	64									
New Salem	9	51									
Belchertown	44	55									
Colrain	23	4									
Ware	6	45									
Warwick	15	39									
Bernardston	12	25									
Chester											

(Table continued on following pages)

HAMPSHIRE-BERKSHIRE DISTRICT, 11 MAY *(continued)*

Town	Hon. Theodore Sedgwick, Esq.	Samuel Lyman, Esq.	Simeon Strong, Esq.	Hon. Thompson J. Skinner	Hon. John Worthington, Esq.	William Whiting	Samuel Henshaw, Esq.	Colonel William Lyman	Joel Smith	Lieutenant Ichabod [Crittenden?]	John Bacon
Chesterfield	27	16									
Charlemont	4	5									
Ashfield											
Worthington	78	1									
Shutesbury		60									
Goshen	14										
Southwick											
Norwich [Huntington]											
Ludlow		64									
Leverett	11	40									
Montgomery	4	7									
Westhampton	31	18									
Cummington	40	1		1							
Buckland	10										
Middlefield	3	40									
Wendell	13	3									
Orange	11	15									
Holland	10										
Leyden		85									
Rowe	9	4									
Heath	11										
Easthampton	15	9									
Plantation No. 7 [Hawley]											
Plainfield											
Sheffield	70	81									
Great Barrington	44	25					2				
Stockbridge	107										35
Pittsfield	64	11									
Richmond	72	19									
Lenox	34	39					2				9
Lanesborough	100	2									
Williamstown	105	37		3							

(Table continued on following page)

HAMPSHIRE-BERKSHIRE DISTRICT, 11 MAY *(continued)*

Town	Hon. Theodore Sedgwick, Esq.	Samuel Lyman, Esq.	Simeon Strong, Esq.	Hon. Thompson J. Skinner	Hon. John Worthington, Esq.	William Whiting	Samuel Henshaw, Esq.	Colonel William Lyman	Joel Smith	Lieutenant Ichabod [Crittenden?]	John Bacon
Adams	32	2		1							
Egremont											
Becket	27	4									
West Stockbridge	14	3									8
Dalton	9	3									
Alford											
New Ashford											
New Marlborough	66	13				1					
Tyringham	39	30									2
Loudon											
[Otis]	13	3								1	
Windsor	29	1		5							
Partridgefield											
[Peru]	16	1		1	2						
Washington											
Hancock	23	1									
Lee											
Sandisfield											
Mount Washington	2	12				1					
Totals	2056	1958	2	11	1	9	1	1	1	1	54

Votes cast: 4095
Majority required: 2048

Governor and Council Record the Votes in the Fifth Election in Hampshire-Berkshire District, Wednesday, 27 May[1]

The Governor and Council upon examination of the returns from the District of Hampshire and Berkshire for Representative to represent them in the Congress of the United States found them to stand as follows, viz.

Number of voters, 4095; makes a choice, 2048. Hon. Theodore Sedgwick, Esq., has 2056 and is chosen.

1. Council Records, XXXI, 40, M-Ar.

The Question of Missing or Delayed Election Returns, 27 May–6 June

The votes of seventeen towns were not returned, or were not returned in time to be counted in the fifth election. As in the fourth election, Samuel Lyman's supporters believed that Theodore Sedgwick's men were responsible and that Lyman had been cheated of the election. Sedgwick's supporters, on the other hand, insisted that he was the choice of the majority of those who voted in all five elections.

Barring the discovery of the missing returns, or other evidence aside from such assertions, the only evidence to evaluate the charges is the votes cast in the previous elections. Only seven of the seventeen towns whose votes were not returned in the fifth election voted in the first election. Sedgwick received 51, William Whiting 44, and 110 votes were scattered among nine other candidates. This was the only election in which Sedgwick received a plurality of votes in these towns.

Ten of the seventeen towns voted in the second election. Whiting received 170, Lyman 66, and Sedgwick 50, with 40 votes scattered among three others. Eleven of the seventeen towns voted in the third election. Whiting received 240 votes, Lyman 192, and Sedgwick 121, with 72 votes for three others. Ten of the seventeen towns voted in the fourth election. Lyman received 151 votes and Sedgwick nosed out Whiting for second place by two votes, 138 to 136. Four votes were divided between two other men.

Lyman's followers said that the seventeen towns whose votes were not returned in the fifth election were "Lyman towns," although Whiting had received the most votes in the second and third elections. Whatever they were, they were not "Sedgwick towns." In the second election, five candidates received a total of 276 votes to 45 for Sedgwick, and in the third election five candidates received a total of 504 votes to 121 for Sedgwick. In the fourth election Lyman and Whiting together received 276 votes to 45 for Sedgwick, with two other men receiving a total of 4 votes.

It is unknown whether or not Whiting formally withdrew from the race before the fifth election, but he received a total of only nine votes in the entire district. It would seem unlikely that virtually all of his supporters in the seventeen missing towns would have voted for Sedgwick instead of Lyman.

Massachusetts Centinel, 27 May

Last evening, at nine o'clock, the Hon. Theodore Sedgwick, Esq., had a majority of seven of all the votes returned for national Representative for the upper district. If no more votes were returned before twelve o'clock, he is chosen.

James Sullivan to Elbridge Gerry, Boston, 28 May (excerpt)[1]

[Theodore] Sedgwick has seven votes more than the other candidates but if there had not been am an [sic] agreement somewhere in keeping back the votes of seventeen towns, [Samuel] Lyman would have been clearly chosen.

Independent Chronicle, 28 May

The Hon. Theodore Sedgwick, Esq., is chosen federal Representative for the upper district, by a majority of seven votes. Tuesday last the time expired for receiving returns. Fourteen towns, we hear, have not returned their votes.

Massachusetts Centinel, 30 May

A correspondent observes, that he is happy to learn, by the returns from the upper district, that they have at length completed the election of a federal Representative, and the gentleman declared to have been elected is a man of acknowledged abilities. Though it is singular that the true sense of the district has not been known; but either for a want of attention, or by means of *too much attention*, in the returning officers, the votes of a number of towns which were in favor of Mr. [Samuel] Lyman have at every election been detained. At the last trial, I think there were seventeen towns not returned, a[t] the one preceding that, twenty-one.[2] Had the last votes been properly returned, Mr. Lyman would have been elected, if there had been any choice of either; and Mr. [Theodore] Sedgwick, by the votes actually returned, is chosen by a majority of seven. I have no comment to make on the characters of the two gentlemen, as they are both unquestionably established to be good; but shall only observe, that if we mean to secure "the freedom of elections" in this state, the laws annexing a severe penalty for a neglect of duty in returning officers ought to be scrupulously put in execution—otherwise it may, and will, be in the power of an intriguing minority to carry an election against a majority of honest and undesigning electors.[3]

Candidus, Massachusetts Centinel, 30 May

Various reports have been spread respecting the election in the upper district. And as some suspicions have been entertained on the subject, which a just statement may remove, I shall beg your indulgence to a few observations.

Owing to a great diversity of sentiment in that district, the people were not able to effect a choice until a *fifth* trial. The eyes of the district appeared to be fixed on the Hon. Theodore Sedgwick, Esq., of Berkshire, and Samuel Lyman, Esq., of Hampshire. But Mr. Sedgwick had, besides prepossessions, to combat a predilection which many of the people of Hampshire had, for choosing a person belonging to their own county. Besides this, there were two other candidates in Berkshire County, so that the majority he obtained was as great as could be expected.

It is thought that in the fourth choice, Mr. S. would have been chosen, had all the votes been returned; and some idea may be formed of the wishes of the people being more in his favor than any other of the candidates, by showing the number of votes for him, and Mr. L. at each time of voting.

At the *first* time, the whole number of votes returned being 2201, Mr. Sedgwick had 801, and Mr. Lyman 330.

At the *second*, the whole number was 2513—and Mr. S. had 716, and Mr. L. 717.

At the *third* choice, the whole number being 4731—Mr. S. had 1449, and Mr. L. 1557.

At the *fourth*, the whole number being 3328—Mr. S. had 1564, and Mr. L. 1309.

At the *fifth*, the whole number being 4095—Mr. S. had 2056, and Mr. L. 1958.

This being a true account, it appears, that in the *second* choice, Mr. Lyman had a plurality of but *one* vote, in the *third* but of 108, and at each time wanted above 800 votes to make a choice; while Mr. Sedgwick, at the *first* choice had 471 more than Mr. Lyman, at the *fourth* 255, and in the last 98.

This unequivocally shows that Mr. Sedgwick is the man best liked in the upper district, and proves that the reports of tricking, etc., in his friends to be without foundation.

Independent Chronicle, 4 June

The following towns in the upper district made no returns of votes for a Representative to the general government at the last time of returning votes, viz. *Williamsburg, Shelburne, Conway, Sunderland, Palmer, Chester, Ashfield, Southwick, Norwich,* [Plantation] *No. 7, Plainfield, Egremont, Alford, New Ashford, Washington, Lee, Sandisfield.*[4]

Massachusetts Centinel, 6 June

The votes of one of the towns in the upper district, which was not returned in the secretary's office, in season, has since arrived—in which *two-thirds* are for the Hon. Mr. [Theodore] Sedgwick.

1. RC, Sang Collection, ICarbS.
2. See The Question of Missing and Delayed Election Returns, 15 April–3 May, printed above in The Fourth Election in Hampshire-Berkshire District.
3. The above item was reprinted in the *Hampshire Chronicle*, 10 June.
4. Ibid.

Henry Jackson to Henry Knox, Boston, 31 May (excerpt)[1]

Mr. [Theodore] Sedgwick is elected a federal Representative for the western district. He will without delay take his seat in Congress. This choice gives pleasure to all *Feds* and he certainly will add respectability to our representation.

1. RC, Knox Papers, MHi.

Samuel Henshaw to Theodore Sedgwick, Boston, 2 June[1]

I most heartily congratulate you and my country on your recent appointment. Your friends in Boston also greatly rejoice. Be cool, be calm, and answer their raised expectations. Say nothing about [Samuel] Lyman. The victory is yours—that is enough for the present. You know some people think you are rather sudden—that you are apt to speak before you sufficiently deliberate. I would therefore advise you (and I would not advise you, if I did not love you) not to speak much in Congress, and never but on great questions. Let the little folks do the little business.

If it should be in your power with the assistance of your connections to get me back to Boston in my old station, I will return. All your brethren know my character and my much greater experience in revenue affairs than any other man in this state. You may consult Mr. [Caleb] Strong and Mr. [Elbridge] Gerry particularly, but don't let them, nor anybody else know I wrote you on the subject. But let them know, that you are sure from conversation you have had with me on the subject, that I would accept of an eligible appointment in the revenue department, and immediately return to Boston.

Burn this, I beseech you, as soon as you have read it.

Thomas Melville, Esqr., is now naval officer for the Port of Boston. There can be no better officer in that department.

I will write you next week. Let me hear from you immediately. I am in infinite haste. God bless you.

1. RC, Sedgwick Papers, MHi.

Samuel Henshaw to Theodore Sedgwick, Boston, 14 June[1]

I have had the pleasure of hearing that you left Berkshire on Tuesday last on your way to Congress, escorted in high style by the noble Federalists in your vicinity. I rejoice at their honoring, not only my friend, but themselves also. [Samuel] Lyman and his friends, I am told, lay your success to me—say I have out-generalled them, and fairly too. Lyman told me himself, that tho I had done everything for you, yet he should always esteem me, and would do everything in his power to serve me at all times, because he was certain I had never abused him, and had conducted thro the whole exactly as I told him I would. I am much obliged to them all for their candor, and shall be stimulated to double my diligence, if possible, on any future occasion.

Is your letter to me known in New York? There was a partial, ill-natured extract from it printed by [Thomas] Adams and [John] Nourse immediately after your choice, which staggered many of your firm friends. But our friend [Benjamin] Russell printed the whole letter in his next *Centinel* which not only took of[f] the ill impressions made by printing the extract but raised you higher than ever in the opinion of those whose esteem you value.[2] But I would not have you broach (too suddenly and violently) those sentiments in Congress. For I guess there must be considerable private management before it will do to say much openly on the subject. Could Congress be prevailed with to assume the whole debt contracted to carry on the war, it would immortalize them in this state.

In consequence of a letter I received from Mr. [Fisher] Ames, I have wrote him relating to this subject. Consult him—and consult Mr. [Elbridge] Gerry. I advise you to take pains to be on good terms with Mr. Gerry. I am sure you won't find a better man—a better friend.

About ten days since, I wrote you inclosed to Mr. [Caleb] Strong. I wrote you also on Monday last. The letter arrived at the post office on Thursday last. If you have not received it, pray enquire after it. I shall be greatly disappointed, if I don't hear from you this week, and I beg you to write me your mind fully and freely on the subject of my last,[3] and first too. I should not have had a thought of coming forward as a candidate for office had not my friends here— friends to the federal government—urged me into it. They say much, very much depends on getting into office, the revenue office especially. Characters who by their past conduct have obtained the confidence and esteem of the people, and who know how to soothe and palliate the irritable and choleric, instead of insulting and exasperating them with those haughty airs—that insolence of office, which too often accompany men in such stations. In fact they have been importunate. And I have been silly enough to come *forward*, and soon expect to have the mortification to go *backward* again!

But if there is no prospect of my success, I hope my few friends to whom I have wrote on the subject will, in mercy to my feelings, bury the whole in oblivion.

I thank you, my dear sir, for the friendship you discover in wishing that I might be your successor in the chair.[4]

I will only observe that I have the pleasure to believe that my not being there is owing entirely to my own exertions to prevent it. My lungs are not adequate to the labors of the chair.

In my opinion we never had a worse [state] House of Representatives. I thank God that we have a federal government.

I have had the honor to move an address to the President. The address is reported to the Senate. It is not so sublime and sentimental as I could wish, but it is as good as ought to be expected from such a mixed medley as compose our General Court.

When you honor me with any letters after the reception of this, direct them to be left at the post office in Springfield. For I shall be at home next week.

Fare well, and be as happy as I wish you—more you need not ask.

1. RC, Sedgwick Papers, MHi.
2. See Theodore Sedgwick and Amendments to the Constitution, 6-30 May, printed above.
3. 2 June, printed above.
4. Speaker of the Massachusetts House of Representatives.

Jeremiah Hill to George Thacher, Biddeford, 14 June (excerpt)[1]

Please to give my kind love to my good friend [Theodore] Sedgwick if he has arrived at the federal seat. I think by this time he must have arrived to one of the first seats in the apostolic order, as he has been purified at least *five times*.

1. RC, Thacher Papers, MB.

Thomas Dwight to Theodore Sedgwick, Springfield, 19 June (excerpt)[1]

Several fortuitous circumstances have prevented my offering you more early congratulations on your appointment to Congress. You will gratify me highly in believing that no one can experience a more heartfelt satisfaction in the event than your friend—altho personal attachment may be, in me, the greater source of such feelings, yet I am not without vanity enough to believe that some part of the pleasure is derived from the consideration of public good, and had your competitor arisen to office upon the disgraceful means used for the purpose of his election, I should have pitied even his own dupes and should have felt it as the triumph of vice over virtue. But I desire to thank God for the joy I feel, that the position is so happily reversed.

1. RC, Sedgwick Papers, MHi.

Theodore Sedgwick to Ephraim Williams, New York, 19 June (excerpt)[1]

I am as yet hardly warm in my place, and yet I find that the violent opposition which was made to my election and the length of the contest have been at least advantageous to the personal distinction with which I am treated.

1. RC, Sedgwick Papers, MHi. The recipient of this letter was probably the Ephraim Williams who represented West Stockbridge in the Massachusetts House, 1787-1788, and was Sedgwick's law partner. In the 1790s he was an unsuccessful Federalist candidate for Representative, Berkshire District.

Theodore Sedgwick to Mrs. Theodore Sedgwick, New York, 5 July[1]

I am surprised, my dearest [———] love, that at the time of writing your letter by Mr. [William?] Whiting you had received none of mine.

Believe me, kindest of women, that, this is not the [———] of life, most agreeable to my inclination, but is most painful and disagreeable. You, my love, will know the progress of inducements which brought me here, and I have the vanity to believe my feeble aid in the important business in which I am engaged will not be altogether without effect. My children are dear to my heart and I love the companion of my life as I love my own soul. From your own tender sensibility you will then judge my pain in the separation. To deny my compliance, with the earnest solicitations of my friends, was impossible, and it was equally so not to wish them success after the vile and wicked arts which were used to defeat my election. But I look forward with pleasure to the time when I shall again be restored to the bosom of my family and to your affectionate arms.

I have the pleasure to inform you that Mrs. [Beem?] is returned, and that the threatening symptoms of her lovely daughter are much abated. Her fever and cough have left her and she will, I hope in a little time, be perfectly restored to health.

As yet I am at the house of a Mrs. [Deniscomb?] with a number of the delegation of our state, but the place is not agreeable to me; the people are not very cleanly nor very obliging. At present it does not appear unlikely that I shall be at home by the beginning of September. As to Mr. Douglas I have told him it will not be in my power to make him any payment until the fall. I shall write him on the subject.

Yesterday there was much noise, confusion, and drinking on the occasion of celebrating the 4th of July. These are scenes, you know, not agreeable to me. To avoid them I proposed to ten other gentlemen a ramble on Long Island, which took place, so that I can't give a particular history of the transactions.

1. RC, Sedgwick Papers, MHi.

Henry Van Schaack to Theodore Sedgwick, Pittsfield, 5 July (excerpt)[1]

How could you be so thoughtless as to take [Great] Barrington in your rout[e] down to Congress. A day or two ago, I was seriously asked whether I did not think it was done to insult [William] Whiting. I replied that I was positive you never had him in your mind and that your going down that way was to accommodate the friends who accompanied you from the lower parts of the county. I am sure that I am right.

1. RC, Sedgwick Papers, MHi.

Thomas Dwight to Theodore Sedgwick, Springfield, 9 July 1789 (excerpt)[1]

Our papers have acquainted you with the proceedings of our General Court. The [state] House is said to be a more indifferent one taken collectively than ever sat before. Is this possible? If we may form an opinion of the tree by its fruit, the appointment of Wm. Lyman to the [state] Senate and some other creations will easily discover to us the political complexion of our rulers. I desire to thank God, it is not in their power to make paper money or to take many other disgraceful measures, which we should undoubtedly be obliged to submit to but for that sovereign balm the Federal Constitution.

The noise of election in this district is for the most part subsided. The disappointed party console themselves (with the idea) that [Samuel] Lyman was fairly chosen by the people and would have had his votes duly returned but for the *damned Sedgwickinian tricks*. As we have carried our point, we can bear imputations of this kind without resorting to blows.

1. RC, Sedgwick Papers, MHi.

MASSACHUSETTS CANDIDATES

Adams, Samuel (1722-1803), Candidate for Representative, Suffolk District

Born in Boston, the son of Samuel Adams, a Boston brewer and merchant active in local politics, Adams graduated from Harvard in 1740. After briefly studying law and serving in a countinghouse, he entered his father's business, which he inherited in 1748. Adams had no talent for, nor interest in, business, and most of the estate soon vanished. His interest was in politics, and in 1756 he was elected one of Boston's tax collectors and was reelected annually until 1764. In 1765 he was elected a Boston representative in the House of Representatives, and the next year he became clerk of the House. In that strategic position, which he held until the last session of the colonial legislature in 1774, he was a major leader of the opposition to British policies and to the royal governors and their allies. At the same time he was one of the most important figures in the Boston town meeting, an organizer of popular political groups, and a leading newspaper writer.

He was elected to the First Continental Congress in 1774, was an early advocate of independence, and signed the Declaration of Independence. He served in Congress until 1781. He was a member of the Massachusetts constitutional convention in 1779-1780, but for a time his political influence was destroyed by his one-time protégé, John Hancock. Adams was elected to the state Senate, 1780-1788, and was president of the Senate, 1787-1788. In 1789 he and Hancock were reconciled, and Adams was elected lieutenant governor. Upon Hancock's death in 1793, Adams became governor. He retired as governor in 1797 because of ill health.

Adams opposed the Constitution of 1787, although he finally voted to ratify it because of pressure from the Boston artisans and because the state Convention agreed to propose amendments. However, Adams opposed any encroachment by the central government upon the power of the states and opposed the Federalist Party throughout the remainder of his political career.

Ames, Fisher (1758-1808), Elected Representative, Suffolk District

Born in Dedham, the son of Nathaniel Ames, an innkeeper, astronomer, physician, and almanac maker, Ames graduated from Harvard in 1774. He studied law and was admitted to the Suffolk County bar in 1781. He represented Dedham in the Massachusetts Convention and voted to ratify the Constitution. In April 1788 he was elected to the state House of Representatives from Dedham.

Ames served in the first four federal Congresses but declined reelection in 1796. He was an ardent Federalist and supported Hamilton's economic policies, the Jay Treaty, and the Alien and Sedition acts. Ames wanted the country purged of "Jacobinism" and the influence of the French Revolution. He foresaw anarchy as the result of the democratic movement and the election of Thomas Jefferson as President. His last public office was as a member of the governor's Council, 1799-1801.

Bishop, Phanuel (1739-1812), Candidate for Representative, Bristol-Dukes-Nantucket District

Bishop was born in Rehoboth, Bristol County. Little is known of his early life. He was a leader of the convention movement in Bristol County during the 1780s and sympathized with Shays's Rebellion. He was elected to the state Senate in 1787 but was denied a seat because the voters had spelled his first name in various ways on their ballots. He was then elected to the House in June 1787 and was a delegate to the Massachusetts Convention, where he was an Antifederalist leader and voted against ratification of the Constitution. He continued to oppose the Constitution during the February 1788 session of the legislature. Bishop was elected to the state Senate as an Antifederalist in 1788 and served until 1791. He returned to the state House of Representatives in 1792 and served almost every year thereafter until the end of the decade. In 1799 he was elected to the United States House of Representatives and served until 1807.

Brooks, John (1752-1825), Candidate for Representative and for Elector, Middlesex District

Born in Medford, the son of a farmer, Brooks studied medicine and began to practice in Reading in 1773. In January 1776 he became a major in the Continental Army, saw action in several campaigns, was promoted to colonel, and served on the staff of Baron Von Steuben. In the winter of 1782-1783, he was one of the three officers at Newburgh, New York, who presented a petition outlining the officers' grievances to Congress and was implicated in the Newburgh "plot." He resumed medical practice at Medford after the war. Governor James Bowdoin appointed him a major general of the Middlesex militia during Shays's Rebellion.

He was state representative from Medford in 1785 and 1786. As a Medford delegate in the state Convention, he voted to ratify the Constitution. He was elected to the state Senate from Middlesex County in 1791 and was appointed federal marshal for Massachusetts the same year. He served as a brigadier general in the regular army during the "quasi-war" with France.

Brooks was adjutant general of the state and a member of the governor's Council, 1812-1816. He was elected governor in 1816 and was reelected by substantial majorities over Republican opponents in succeeding elections until 1823, when he refused to run again.

Cabot, George (1752-1823) Candidate for Elector, Essex District

Born in Salem, the son of a merchant, Cabot entered Harvard in 1766 but withdrew in 1768 and went to sea. In 1777 he entered the family firm, which owned at least forty vessels during the Revolution and profited from privateering.

Cabot was active in Essex County politics. He served in the 1780 convention that drafted the state constitution. In 1783 he was an Essex County senator. Cabot became director of the Massachusetts Bank in 1784 and was an active promoter of the Essex bridge and the Beverly cotton manufactory. He was elected to the Annapolis Convention in 1786 but did not attend. As a Beverly delegate to the state Convention, he voted to ratify the Constitution. In 1791 he was elected to the United States Senate in Tristram Dalton's place and served until he resigned in June 1796. In the Senate Cabot supported Hamilton's economic policies and was a director of the Bank of the United States (1791-1793).

In 1796 Cabot moved to Boston. In 1803 he became president of the Boston branch of the Bank of the United States and in 1809 became president of the Boston Marine Insurance Company. He was president of the Hartford Convention in 1814, his last public activity.

Cobb, David (1748-1830), Candidate for Representative, Bristol-Dukes-Nantucket District

Born in Attleboro, Bristol County, the son of an iron manufacturer, Cobb graduated from Harvard in 1766, studied medicine in Boston, and began practice in Taunton.

Cobb was active in Revolutionary politics. He was secretary of the Bristol County convention in 1774 and was a member of the first provincial congress. During the war he was promoted from surgeon of a Massachusetts regiment to colonel and also served on George Washington's staff. He was appointed a brevet brigadier general at the end of the war.

Cobb was appointed a judge of the Court of Common Pleas in Bristol County in 1784 and served until 1796. He opposed Shays's Rebellion; raised a militia force in September 1786 to protect the Taunton court; and raised troops to serve in western Massachusetts, but they saw no action.

He was elected to the Massachusetts House in 1789 and was speaker, 1789-1793. Cobb was a Federalist congressman from 1793 to 1795 and continued to be active in state politics after moving to Maine in the 1790s. He was a member of the state Senate, 1800-1805, served on the governor's Council on several occasions, was lieutenant governor in 1809, and was a member of the Board of Military Defense in 1812. His last public office was that of chief justice of the Hancock County court, in Maine.

Cony, Daniel (1752-1842), Candidate for Elector, York-Cumberland-Lincoln District

Born in Stoughton, Suffolk County, Cony studied medicine with a physician in Marlborough. He became a militia lieutenant in Tewksbury at the outbreak of the Revolution and served at Boston, 1775-1776, and at Saratoga, 1777.

In 1778, Cony left the army and moved to Hallowell (later Augusta), Maine. He was the Hallowell town clerk, 1785-1787. In 1786 he was elected to the Massachusetts House and to the first of several Maine conventions to consider separation from Massachusetts. For the next twelve years he served as representative, as senator, or as member of the governor's Council. During this period he was also a special justice of the Court of Common Pleas and a justice of the peace and of the quorum. He was a presidential Elector in 1792, and, upon the creation of Kennebec County, Maine, in 1799, Cony was appointed a judge of the Court of Common Pleas, a position he held for twelve years. In 1804 he became judge of probate in the same county and held the post until 1823. In 1819 he was an Augusta delegate to the Maine constitutional convention. He retired from active political and judicial life in 1823.

Cushing, William (1732-1810), Presidential Elector, At-Large

Born in Scituate, Plymouth County, Cushing graduated from Harvard in 1751. He taught school in Roxbury, studied law, and was admitted to the bar in 1755. He practiced in Scituate until the creation of Lincoln County, Maine, in 1760. Cushing obtained the posts of judge of probate and register of deeds for the new county. He was the only lawyer in the county for twelve years. In 1772 he returned to Massachusetts and succeeded his father as a judge of the Superior Court.

At the outbreak of the Revolution, Cushing was the only judge of the court to retain his post. He became a member of the newly created state Supreme Judicial Court, and from 1777 to 1789 he was chief justice. He was one of the targets of a mob that attempted to prevent the sitting of the court in Springfield in September 1786.

Cushing was a member of the Massachusetts convention of 1779-1780, which drafted the state's first constitution. He was also a Boston delegate to and vice president of the Massachusetts Convention in 1788 and voted to ratify the Constitution.

Cushing was the first associate justice appointed to the United States Supreme Court. During his twenty-one years on the Court he served briefly as acting chief justice during John Jay's diplomatic mission to England in 1794 and for a short period after the Senate rejected John Rutledge's nomination as chief justice in December 1795. After his appointment to the Court, Cushing made only one entry into the political arena: in 1794 he was the unsuccessful Federalist candidate for governor of Massachusetts against Samuel Adams.

Dalton, Tristram (1738-1817), Elected Senator

Born in Newbury, Essex County, the son of a sea captain, merchant, and land owner, Dalton graduated from Harvard in 1755. He read law and then went into business with his father. He was a member of the provincial congress in 1774. In 1776, and from 1782 to 1786, Dalton represented Newburyport in the legislature. In 1783 he was elected speaker of the House but declined to serve again in 1784. He was an Essex County senator, 1786-1789. Dalton was elected to the Annapolis Convention in 1786 but did not attend. As a Newbury delegate to the state Convention in 1788, he voted to ratify the Constitution.

He drew the two-year term as United States Senator and was not reelected. He sold his Massachusetts holdings to speculate in Washington, D.C., lands. However, he lost most of his household possessions and was nearly bankrupted by the collapse of the speculative boom in Washington lots. President John Adams appointed him to the Board of Commissioners in Washington. After Adams's presidency, Dalton returned to Massachusetts, where he was surveyor of the Port of Boston from 1814 until his death.

Dana, Francis (1743-1811), Presidential Elector, Middlesex District, and Candidate for Senator

Born in Charlestown but reared in Boston, Dana graduated from Harvard in 1762. He studied law with his uncle and was admitted to the bar in 1767. Dana at first sought reconciliation with Great Britain and sailed for England shortly after Lexington and Concord. He returned in April 1776, convinced that reconciliation was impossible.

Dana was a member of the Massachusetts Council from 1776 to 1780. In December 1776 he was elected to the Continental Congress but did not attend until November 1777. He left Congress in August 1778 and refused reelection in June 1779.

In 1779, when John Adams was appointed minister plenipotentiary to negotiate peace with Great Britain, Dana went with him as secretary. In 1780 Congress appointed Dana the first United States minister to Russia. During his stay in Russia, August 1781—September 1783, he accomplished little because Russia refused to recognize the independence of the United States.

Dana returned to Boston in 1783. He served briefly in Congress in 1784 before Governor John Hancock appointed him an associate justice of the Supreme Judicial Court in 1785. He was chief justice from 1791 to 1806.

In 1786 Dana was elected to the Annapolis Convention and in 1787 to the Constitutional Convention but did not attend either because of ill health. He was a Cambridge delegate to the state Convention in 1788 and voted to ratify the Constitution.

President Adams appointed him to serve on a mission to France in 1797, but again ill health prevented him from going.

Dane, Nathan (1752-1835), Candidate for Representative, Essex District, and for Senator

Born in Ipswich, the son of a farmer, Dane graduated from Harvard in 1778. He read law in Salem, taught school in Beverly, and was admitted to the bar in 1782. From 1782 to 1786 he represented Beverly in the legislature. He was elected to the Confederation Congress in 1785, 1786, and 1787 and played an important role in drafting the Ordinance of 1787. He opposed the Constitution in Congress and was defeated for election to the Massachusetts Convention.

In September 1788 Dane retired from the Confederation Congress to practice law in Beverly. He was elected a state senator from Essex County in 1790 and was reelected in 1793. He was appointed a judge of the Court of Common Pleas of Essex County in 1793 but resigned. He was reelected annually to the state Senate from 1793 to 1798.

Dane was appointed a commissioner to revise the laws of the commonwealth in 1795 and, periodically, to revise the statutes. The result of his work was the publication of a nine-volume compilation entitled *General Abridgment and Digest of American Law* . . . (1823-1829).

Dane was a presidential Elector in 1812. In 1814 he was a delegate to the Hartford Convention, where he attempted to restrain the more extreme Federalists. Increasing deafness kept him from filling his last public appointment as a Beverly delegate to the state constitutional convention of 1820.

Davis, Caleb (1738-1797), Presidential Elector, Suffolk District

Born in Woodstock, Connecticut, the son of an innkeeper who later moved to Brookline, Massachusetts, Davis was associated with his uncle in a commercial venture by 1759 and later became a ship owner. At the beginning of the Revolution he took an active part in Boston politics. During the war he was appointed "agent of the state of Massachusetts." From 1776 to 1788, when he resigned, Davis was a Boston member of the Massachusetts House. In 1780 he was the first speaker of the House under the Constitution of 1780. He was elected a Suffolk County senator in 1783 but preferred to serve in the House. As a Boston delegate to the Massachusetts Convention, Davis voted to ratify the Constitution.

Dawes, Thomas, Jr. (1757-1825), Candidate for Representative, Suffolk District

Born in Boston, the son of an architect and prominent revolutionary leader, Thomas Dawes, Dawes graduated from Harvard in 1777. He studied law with John Lowell and was admitted to the Suffolk County bar in 1780. He was a member of the Massachusetts constitutional convention of 1779-1780. In 1788 he was a Boston delegate to the Massachusetts Convention and voted to ratify the Constitution. In 1790 he was appointed judge of probate for Suffolk County and in 1792 judge of the Supreme Judicial Court, a post he held until 1802. In 1803 he was appointed judge of the Boston municipal court and served until 1823. From 1823 until his death, Dawes was again judge of probate in Suffolk County. In 1820 he was a delegate to the Massachusetts constitutional convention.

Dwight, Elijah (1740-1794), Candidate for Elector, Hampshire-Berkshire District

Born in Brookfield, Worcester County, Dwight had moved to Great Barrington, Berkshire County, by 1761. He was appointed clerk of the courts and register of probate for the county in 1761 and held both offices until 1781. Dwight was town clerk from 1764 to 1770 and was town treasurer for several years after 1768 and again from 1782 to 1790. Dwight was neutral during the War for Independence.

He was elected Great Barrington's representative in 1785 and was a state senator from Berkshire County, 1786-1793. He represented Great Barrington in the state Convention in 1788 and voted to ratify the Constitution.

He was a justice of the peace from 1765 onward and, from 1783 until his death, was a judge of the Court of Common Pleas in Berkshire County. He was the only judge of the court in 1786 who refused to accede to the demands of a Shaysite mob.

Fisher, Jabez (1717-1806), Candidate for Elector, Suffolk District

Born in Wrentham (later Franklin), Fisher represented Wrentham in the provincial assemblies on several occasions prior to the Revolution. He was a member of the first three provincial congresses and was elected to the Council, which acted as the executive of the state and the upper house of the legislature, 1775-1780. He represented Franklin in the Massachusetts Convention in 1788 and voted to ratify the Constitution. He also represented Franklin in the General Court, 1786-1787 and 1798-1799. Among his judicial positions were those of justice of the peace and of the quorum in Suffolk County.

Gerry, Elbridge (1744-1814), Elected Representative, Middlesex District

Born in Marblehead, Essex County, the son of an English-born merchant, Gerry graduated from Harvard in 1762 and joined his father and brothers in the mercantile business. He was elected to the General Court in 1772 and 1773. In 1774 he was a member of the committee of correspondence and of the Essex County convention. He was a delegate to the first and second provincial congresses, where he was a member of the committee of safety and chairman of the committee of supply.

An early ally of Samuel Adams, he was elected to the Second Continental Congress to break the deadlock in the Massachusetts delegation, and he signed the Declaration of Independence. In July 1780 Gerry left Congress after a dispute over personal privilege, and although he was regularly reelected, Gerry refused to attend its sessions until 1783. He served in Congress from 1783 to 1785, and in 1786 he moved from Marblehead to Cambridge, Middlesex County.

Gerry refused to attend the Annapolis Convention in 1786. As a delegate to the Constitutional Convention in 1787, he took an active part in the debates but refused to sign the Constitution. He sent a lengthy protest to the General Court in October 1787, outlining his objections, and he joined forces with the Antifederalists. He was not elected to the Massachusetts Convention but was assigned a seat to provide information. He left the Convention after he was prevented from speaking.

Gerry supported both amendments to the Constitution and Hamilton's financial program in the first Congress and became a stockholder in the Bank of the United States. He was elected to the second Congress but refused to run for the third. He was a Federalist Elector in 1796. The next year President John Adams appointed him, John Marshall, and Charles Cotesworth Pinckney to what became known as the "X.Y.Z. Mission." Gerry's sympathy for France and his independent behavior in France alienated the other commissioners.

After his return to the United States, the Republicans ran him for governor of Massachusetts four years in a row (1800-1803), but he refused to run in 1804 because the Federalist candidate had beaten him by increasing margins each year. He was a presidential Elector in 1804 and voted for Thomas Jefferson.

After another period of political inactivity, Gerry ran against Federalist Christopher Gore for governor in 1810. Gerry won and was reelected in 1811. After his defeat by Federalist Caleb Strong in 1812, the Republicans nominated him for Vice President on the ticket with James Madison. Gerry died in Washington, D.C., while serving as Vice President.

Gill, Moses (1734-1800), Presidential Elector, Worcester District

Born in Charlestown, Gill was trained as a merchant in Boston. Shortly before the Revolutionary War, he moved to Princeton, Worcester County, where he became a judge of the Court of Common Pleas in 1775. He was elected to the Council each year from 1775 to 1780 and to the governor's Council from 1780 until 1795, when he was elected lieutenant governor. He served in the post until 1799, when he became acting governor. He was serving in that capacity when he died.

Goodhue, Benjamin (1748-1814), Elected Representative, Essex District

Born in Salem, the son of a merchant, Goodhue graduated from Harvard in 1766. He became a merchant in Philadelphia, but by the end of 1776 he was back in Salem importing supplies for American troops and buying land in New Hampshire.

He was a member of the state constitutional convention, 1779-1780; a Salem representative in the legislature, 1780-1782; and an Essex County senator, 1783-1784 and 1785-1789. He was elected to the first, second, and third Congresses, where he supported most Federalist programs.

He was elected to the United States Senate to succeed George Cabot, who resigned in June 1796. Goodhue resigned in 1800 because of his wife's ill health and because of the dispute between President John Adams and Goodhue's friend Timothy Pickering.

Gorham, Nathaniel (1738-1796), Candidate for Representative, Middlesex District, and for Senator

Born in Charlestown, Gorham was apprenticed to a New London, Connecticut, merchant from 1753 to 1759 and then returned to Charlestown as a merchant. He was a member of the colonial legislature, 1771-1774; delegate to the provincial congresses, 1774-1775; member of the Board of War, 1778-1781; delegate to the state constitutional convention, 1779-1780; member of the state Senate, 1780-1781; and member of the state House, 1781-1787. Gorham was speaker of the House, 1781-1782 and 1785. He also served on the governor's Council, 1788-1789.

He was elected to the Confederation Congress and served there, 1782-1783 and 1785-1787. He was elected to the Constitutional Convention and took an active part in the debates. He represented Charlestown in the state Convention and voted to ratify the Constitution. Among the judicial offices he held was judge of the Court of Common Pleas in Middlesex County.

In 1788 Gorham and Oliver Phelps bought six million acres of land in western New York which that state had ceded to Massachusetts (the Phelps-Gorham Purchase). The partners were unable to meet their payments, and Gorham became a bankrupt.

Grout, Jonathan (1737-1807), Elected Representative, Worcester District

Born in Lunenberg, Worcester County, Grout served in the French and Indian War. He studied law and began practice in Petersham. Beginning in 1771, he was elected at least twenty-five times to offices in Petersham: moderator, town clerk, selectman, assessor, and chairman of numerous special committees. He was captain of the local militia company during the Revolution. He was elected to the provincial congress in 1775 and was state representative from Petersham in 1781 and 1784. In 1787 he was elected to both the House and the Senate but was denied a seat in the Senate when Samuel Adams, president of the Senate, broke a tie by voting against him. The next year he was elected to the Senate from Worcester County.

Grout sympathized with Shays's Rebellion, although there is no evidence that he took an active part. Elected to the state Convention, he voted against ratification of the Constitution. He was defeated for reelection to the second Congress by Artemas Ward. In 1803 he moved to Lunenberg, Vermont, and died in Dover, New Hampshire, while attending court there.

Henshaw, Samuel (1744-1809), Presidential Elector, Hampshire-Berkshire District

Born in Milton, Suffolk County, Henshaw graduated from Harvard in 1773. He trained as a minister and then studied law. He represented Milton in the state constitutional convention, 1779-1780, and the state House of Representatives, 1780. Sometime before 1788 he moved to Northampton, Hampshire County, and represented that town in the House, 1788-1790. He was also a justice of the peace and of the quorum in 1788.

During the election to the United States House of Representatives in 1788-1789, Henshaw was Theodore Sedgwick's "campaign manager" in Hampshire County but did not receive an expected reward of a job with the new government. He was appointed a judge of probate in 1797 and later was a judge of the Court of Common Pleas in Hampshire County.

Holten, Samuel (1738-1816), Candidate for Representative, Essex District, and for Senator

Born in a part of Salem that became Danvers, Holten was forced by ill health to give up college. He studied medicine with a local doctor; practiced at Gloucester, 1756-1758; and then returned to Danvers. Danvers elected him to the legislature in 1768. By 1775 he had abandoned medicine for politics, and for the next forty years he was almost constantly in public office.

He was a member of Revolutionary committees of correspondence, represented Danvers in the Essex County convention in 1774, and was a delegate from Danvers to the provincial congress, 1774-1775. In 1778 he was elected to the Continental Congress, and he served there almost continuously until 1787. He signed the Articles of Confederation and opposed the Constitution. He was elected to the Massachusetts Convention of 1788 but was forced to leave because of ill health.

Thereafter he served at various times as a state representative, state senator, and member of the governor's Council. He was elected to the third Congress (1793-1795). His last public office was as judge of probate in Essex County, a position he held from 1796 to 1815.

Jackson, Jonathan (1743-1810), Candidate for Representative, Essex District

Born in Boston, son of a merchant and manufacturer, Jackson graduated from Harvard in 1761. The following year he became a clerk in a Newburyport countinghouse. By 1766 he was an independent merchant and later formed partnerships with other Newburyport merchants. He was a delegate to the Essex County convention and the provincial congress in 1775. In 1777 he was a member of the state House of Representatives and of the Board of War.

In July 1782 he and John Lowell were elected to the Confederation Congress, but Jackson only served four months. Soon after his return to Newburyport, he formed a partnership with Stephen Higginson. In 1783 he was appointed a justice of the peace for Essex County. Shortly thereafter he made an unsuccessful business trip to England and three years later an equally unsuccessful trip to the West Indies. He dissolved his partnership with Higginson and turned his attention to strengthening the central government. He wrote *Thoughts on the Political Situation of the United States* . . . (Worcester, 1788), a statement of the extreme Federalist position. Jackson was elected to the state Senate from Essex County in 1789 and was appointed a United States marshal for the District of Massachusetts; he served until 1791, when he was appointed inspector of the revenue for the Northern District. Six years later he was appointed supervisor of excise offices in the same district. After the latter office was abolished in 1802, Jackson was treasurer of Massachusetts until 1805. In 1803 he became the first president of the Boston Bank and was appointed treasurer of Harvard in 1807.

Jarvis, Charles (1748-1807), Candidate for Representative, Suffolk District, and for Senator

Born in Boston, the son of a merchant, Jarvis graduated from Harvard in 1766. After serving medical apprenticeships in Boston and London, he returned to Boston in 1769 to practice medicine.

Jarvis was a prominent local officeholder during the Revolution. He was a delegate to the state constitutional convention in 1779-1780 and was a Boston delegate to the Massachusetts Convention, where he voted to ratify the Constitution. In 1789 he was elected to the Massachusetts House and appointed justice of the peace for Suffolk County. In 1790 Jarvis joined Samuel Adams in supporting Benjamin Austin, Jr., for Congress against incumbent Fisher Ames. In 1794 Jarvis ran against Ames on an anti-British, anti-administration platform and lost. However, Jarvis retained his seat in the state House of Representatives until he retired in 1797 because of ill health. In April 1801 President Thomas Jefferson appointed him physician and surgeon at the Marine Hospital in Charlestown.

King, Rufus (1755-1827), Candidate for Senator

Born in Scarborough, Cumberland County, Maine, the son of a merchant and farmer, King graduated from Harvard in 1777. He studied law with Theophilus Parsons of Newburyport, was admitted to the bar in 1780, and began practice in Newburyport. He was elected to the legislature in 1783, 1784, and 1785. From 1784 to 1787 he was a delegate to the Confederation Congress. King, who favored a strong central government, was a delegate to the Constitutional Convention. He was a Newburyport delegate in the Massachusetts Convention and voted to ratify the Constitution. In 1788 he moved permanently to New York City after his friends failed to secure his election to either the United States Senate or House of Representatives from Massachusetts. [For King's political career in New York, see Chapter XIII, The First Federal Elections in New York.]

Leonard, George (1729-1819), Elected Representative, Bristol-Dukes-Nantucket District

Born in Norton, Bristol County, the son of the owner of an iron works, Leonard graduated from Harvard in 1748. He studied law and was admitted to the bar in 1750. In 1748 he was appointed register of probate for Bristol County and held that position to the beginning of the Revolution. Leonard succeeded his father as Norton town clerk in 1751 and was elected selectman (with his father) in 1753. He later served as town moderator and treasurer. He was appointed a justice of the peace in 1754 and justice of the peace and the quorum in 1762. He served four terms in the Massachusetts House, 1764-1768, where he initially supported the policies of Governor Thomas Hutchinson. In 1770 Leonard was elected to the Council and was a member until 1774.

In 1785 he was appointed judge of probate, and from 1787 to 1804 he was a justice and later chief justice of the Bristol County Court of Common Pleas. After serving in the first Congress, 1789-1791, he was a member of the state

Senate, 1792-1794. He was elected to the fourth Congress (1795-1797), defeating incumbent David Cobb. From 1801 to 1803 he was a member of the state legislature.

Lowell, John (1743-1802), Candidate for Representative, Suffolk District, and for Senator

Born in Newbury (later Newburyport), Essex County, the son of a minister, Lowell graduated from Harvard in 1760, studied law in Boston, and began practice in 1763. He returned to Newburyport and served as a selectman in 1771-1772, 1774, and 1776. In 1774 he signed a petition to Governor Thomas Hutchinson expressing regret at his departure from the colony and an address welcoming Governor Thomas Gage. Lowell later publicly recanted, and his standing seems to have been unimpaired. In April 1776 he was elected to the Essex County convention and in May 1776 to the legislature.

In 1777 he moved to Boston and opened a law office. The following year he represented Boston in the House. He helped draft the state constitution in 1779-1780. In 1780-1781 Lowell was a member of the House and in 1782 and 1783 was a delegate to the Confederation Congress. He was senator from Essex County in 1784-1785 and a Suffolk County senator in 1785-1787. Lowell was a judge of the Federal District Court of Massachusetts from 1789 to 1801, when the outgoing Adams administration appointed him chief justice of the First United States Circuit Court (Massachusetts, New Hampshire, and Rhode Island). After the Jefferson administration abolished the circuit courts, Lowell returned to private practice.

Lyman, Samuel (1749-1802), Candidate for Representative, Hampshire-Berkshire District

Born in Goshen, Connecticut, and graduated from Yale in 1770, Lyman studied law in Litchfield, was admitted to the bar, and commenced practice in Hartford. He moved to Springfield, Massachusetts, around 1784. He was a member of the Massachusetts House, 1786-1789, and the state Senate, 1790-1793. He opposed Shays's Rebellion and called the insurgents a "pack of villains." He was elected to the fourth, fifth, and sixth Congresses, serving from March 1795 until his resignation in January 1801. He was also one of the justices of the Court of Common Pleas in Hampshire County from 1791 to 1800.

May, Elisha (1738?-1811), Candidate for Elector, Bristol-Dukes-Nantucket District

Born probably in Swansea, Bristol County, May was a member of the provincial congress in 1775. He was a captain in the militia at the beginning of the Revolutionary War and fought in several engagements around New York in 1776. He was Attleboro's representative in the General Court, 1778-1782, 1784-1785,

1788-1789, 1791-1792, 1793-1799, and 1800-1802. He represented the town in the Massachusetts Convention in 1788 and voted to ratify the Constitution. When he was not a member of the House, he was a state senator from Bristol County.

Orne, Azor (1731-1796), Candidate for Senator

Born in Marblehead, Essex County, the son of a merchant and politician, Orne was active in both business and politics. He was appointed justice of the peace in 1767; special judge of the Court of Common Pleas in 1775; and Marblehead selectman in 1760-1762, 1765-1768, 1771-1774, 1781-1783, 1787-1789, and 1793.

Orne was active in revolutionary affairs. As early as 1771 he was chairman of a town committee to consider the Boston circular letter and was chairman of a committee of correspondence. He declined election to the Continental Congress in 1774 but attended the Essex County conventions in 1774-1775 and the Massachusetts provincial congress in 1775. He was a colonel in the Essex County militia and also served on the state committee of safety. Orne was elected to represent Marblehead in the legislature in 1773, 1775-1777, 1785, and 1787. He was a delegate to the state constitutional convention in 1779-1780. A Marblehead delegate in the Massachusetts Convention, he voted to ratify the Constitution. He was a presidential Elector in 1792.

Otis, Samuel A. (1740-1814), Candidate for Representative, Suffolk District

Born in Barnstable, the son of Colonel James Otis and the brother of James Otis and Mercy (Otis) Warren, Otis graduated from Harvard in 1759, read law with his brother James, and became a Boston merchant. He was elected a Boston representative to the legislature in May 1776. In October he was appointed to the Board of War and was president of it in 1777. He was appointed an agent to collect clothing for the Continental Army, and in 1779 he became deputy quartermaster general.

He continued to be active in Boston affairs. He was a justice of the peace in Suffolk County and was a Boston delegate to the constitutional convention in 1779-1780. Boston elected him regularly to the House, beginning in 1781. He was on the board of directors of the Massachusetts Bank but was bankrupted when the bank failed in 1785. Otis was elected to the Confederation Congress, 1787-1788, and was elected secretary of the United States Senate in 1789. He served in that office until his death.

Paine, Timothy (1730-1793), Candidate for Representative, Worcester District

Born in Bristol and reared by his stepfather, John Chandler of Worcester, Paine graduated from Harvard in 1748. He was elected to numerous Worcester offices: assessor, clerk, selectman, and moderator. In 1750 he was appointed clerk of courts; in 1755, justice of the peace; in 1757, register of probate; and in 1765, register of deeds. In 1755 he was elected to the first of six terms in the Massachusetts House and was a member of the Council from 1763 to 1769. In August 1774 he was appointed a mandamus councillor by the British Crown. He accepted the appointment and as a result had to flee to Malden in 1775. However, he was not forced to leave the country. In 1785 Paine was elected moderator of the Worcester town meeting. He was elected to the legislature in 1788 and served two years.

Partridge, George (1740-1828), Elected Representative, Plymouth-Barnstable District

Born in Duxbury, Plymouth County, where he kept a boarding school while preparing for college, Partridge graduated from Harvard in 1762. After graduation, he taught school in Kingston and studied theology. By 1770 he had returned to schoolteaching in Duxbury. In 1773 he began taking an active part in town meetings. He was chosen a militia captain in 1774 and a delegate to the legislature. He was an active member of the Plymouth County convention and a delegate to the three provincial congresses in 1774-1775. In 1775 he was appointed a justice of the peace in the county and major, later colonel, of the first Plymouth County regiment. Partridge was a member of the legislature, 1775-1779, and was appointed sheriff of Plymouth County in 1777, an office he held (except for one year) until 1812.

He was a delegate to the Continental and Confederation congresses, 1779-1782 and 1783-1785. As Duxbury's delegate in the state Convention, he voted to ratify the Constitution. After a stagecoach accident involving Partridge and Elbridge Gerry, Partridge retired from the first Congress in August 1790. He was defeated for election to the second Congress by Shearjashub Bourne of Barnstable. He was a presidential Elector in 1792. After his retirement as sheriff, he served five more terms as Duxbury representative in the Massachusetts House.

Phillips, Samuel, Jr. (1752-1802), Presidential Elector, Essex District

Born in Andover, the son of a merchant, Phillips graduated from Harvard in 1771. In 1773 he succeeded his father as town clerk and treasurer. In 1774 he was chairman of a town committee that drafted a protest against British policies. In 1775 he represented Andover in the provincial congress. He was also an Andover delegate to the state convention in 1779-1780 and a member of the committee that wrote the state constitution. In 1780 he was elected senator from Essex County and served without interruption until 1800. Phillips was president of the Senate for fifteen years. In April 1801 he was elected lieutenant governor on the Federalist ticket and held that office at the time of his death.

Savage, Samuel (1748-1831), Candidate for Elector, Plymouth-Barnstable District

Born in Boston, the son of Samuel Phillips Savage, Savage graduated from Harvard in 1766. He taught at the Lincoln school, 1768-1771, and the Weston school thereafter. Savage studied medicine with Dr. Benjamin Church and established a practice in Barnstable in 1773. He was appointed a justice of the Barnstable County Court of Common Pleas in 1782, a justice of the peace in 1790, and a justice of the quorum in 1815.

Sedgwick, Theodore (1746-1813), Elected Representative, Hampshire-Berkshire District

Born in West Hartford, Connecticut, the son of a merchant, Sedgwick entered Yale in 1761 but was expelled before graduation. However, Yale gave him a degree in 1772, retroactive to 1765. In 1810 Harvard gave him an honorary degree, also retroactive to 1765.

Sedgwick moved to Great Barrington, Massachusetts, after his expulsion from Yale, studied law, and was admitted to the Berkshire County bar in 1766. He practiced for a time at Sheffield. He was clerk of the Berkshire County convention in 1774. He opposed independence prior to May 1776 but was active in Revolutionary affairs thereafter. He was military secretary to Brigadier General John Thomas during the northern campaign in 1776. In 1776-1777 he was purchasing agent for the Continental Army in the northern theater.

Sedgwick was elected to the Massachusetts House in 1780, 1782-1783, 1787-1788, and was speaker in 1788. From 1784 to 1786 he was a state senator. Sedgwick was a delegate to the Confederation Congress, 1785-1786 and 1788. Because of his opposition to Shays's Rebellion, his life and property were threatened. He represented Stockbridge in the Massachusetts Convention and voted to ratify the Constitution.

He was a member of the first four Congresses, 1789-1796, and in June 1796, after the resignation of Caleb Strong, Sedgwick was elected to the United States Senate. When his term expired in 1799, he returned to the House and was speaker of the sixth Congress. He retired in March 1801 after the Republican victory in the national elections. Returning to Massachusetts, Sedgwick was appointed a justice of the Supreme Judicial Court.

Sever, William (1729-1809), Presidential Elector, Plymouth-Barnstable District

Born in Kingston, Plymouth County, Sever graduated from Harvard in 1745. Following graduation, he entered his father's mercantile business. He represented Kingston in the lower house of the legislature in 1754 and 1766-1769. He was elected to the Council in 1769 and served throughout the Revolution as the senior member. He was a member of the provincial congress, 1775, and the Kingston committee of correspondence, 1774-1775. From 1775 to 1780 he was

"President of Massachusetts" (alternately with James Bowdoin and James Warren) and exercised many of the executive duties given the governor after 1780. He served two terms as a Plymouth County senator, and from 1776 to his death he was a justice of the Plymouth County Court of Common Pleas. In 1788, as a Kingston delegate to the Massachusetts Convention, he voted to ratify the Constitution. A Federalist, Sever was a presidential Elector on four occasions. He also served as a justice of the peace and of the quorum and judge of probate for several years. In 1804 he became the first president of the Plymouth Bank.

Sewall, David (1735-1825), Presidential Elector, York-Cumberland-Lincoln District

Born in York, Maine, and graduated from Harvard in 1755, Sewall studied law in Portsmouth, New Hampshire, and began practice in York in 1759. In 1766 he was appointed register of probate and was appointed a justice of the peace the following year. He was elected to the York County convention in 1774.

After the war began, he was reappointed a register of probate and served to 1781 and again, 1791-1795; he was also a notary public and a justice of the peace and of the quorum. In 1776-1777 he was a member of the Council. In 1777 he was elected to the supreme court of Massachusetts and served until 1789, when President Washington appointed him judge of the United States Court for the District of Maine. He retired from the court in 1818. He also served for fourteen years as president of the Board of Overseers of Bowdoin College.

Shepard, William (1737-1817), Presidential Elector, At-Large

Born in Westfield, Hampshire County, the son of a tanner, Shepard served in the French and Indian War and rose to the rank of captain. He served throughout the War for Independence as an officer of the Continental Army.

In 1785 and 1786 he was a member of the Massachusetts House. In the latter year he was appointed a major general in charge of the Hampshire County militia. He was charged with keeping the court open in Springfield during the height of Shays's Rebellion, and his forces repelled the attack on the Springfield arsenal in January 1787. He was a presidential Elector in 1792, was elected to the governor's Council that year, and served for five years. He was elected to three terms in the federal House of Representatives (1797-1803).

Skinner, Thompson J. (1752-1809), Candidate for Representative, Hampshire-Berkshire District

Born in Salisbury, Essex County, the son of a minister, Skinner came to Williamstown, Berkshire County, around 1775 and served a brief apprenticeship as a carpenter and joiner. He served in the militia during the Revolution and rose to the rank of captain.

From 1781 to 1785 he was state representative from Williamstown, and from 1785 to 1787 he was a Berkshire County senator. In 1788 he represented Williamstown in the state Convention and voted to ratify the Constitution. From 1788 to 1807 he was a judge of the Court of Common Pleas for Berkshire County. From 1789 to 1796 he again served as a state senator. He was a presidential Elector in 1792. In 1796 he was elected to Congress as a Republican in place of Theodore Sedgwick, who resigned to take Caleb Strong's seat in the United States Senate. Skinner was reelected to the fifth Congress and served until March 1799. He was a state representative in 1799 and 1800.

President Jefferson appointed him a United States marshal for the District of Massachusetts. He was elected to the eighth Congress and served until he resigned in August 1804. He served as treasurer of Williams College intermittently after 1793 and was treasurer of the state in 1806 and 1807. He was accused of taking public monies to pay debts incurred while speculating in Georgia lands and was forced from office.

Spooner, Walter (1720-1803), Presidential Elector, Bristol-Dukes-Nantucket District

His birthplace is unknown, but by 1739 Spooner was living in Dartmouth, Bristol County. He was a Dartmouth selectman for thirteen consecutive years beginning in 1759, and from time to time thereafter. He was elected to the General Court in 1761 and reelected until 1770. In 1769 his election to the Council was vetoed by Governor Francis Bernard. The next year he was admitted to the Council, and he was a royal and state councillor for seventeen years. He was a delegate to the Massachusetts constitutional convention of 1779-1780. In March 1781 Governor John Hancock appointed Spooner chief justice of the Court of Common Pleas of Bristol County, a position he held for over ten years. In 1788 Spooner was one of the New Bedford delegates to the Massachusetts Convention and voted to ratify the Constitution. He was also a presidential Elector in 1792 and 1800.

Strong, Caleb (1745-1819), Elected Senator

Born in Northampton, Hampshire County, the son of a tanner and militia officer, Strong graduated from Harvard in 1764. He preached briefly after graduation, then studied law with Joseph Hawley, and was admitted to the bar in 1772. He was elected a selectman of Northampton that year. From 1774 through the Revolution he was a member of the town's committee of safety. In 1775 he was appointed register of probate and a justice of the peace for Hampshire County.

After the outbreak of the Revolution, he served for twenty-four consecutive years as Hampshire County attorney. He was elected to the Massachusetts House in 1776 and was a Northampton delegate to the constitutional convention of 1779-1780, where he was a member of the drafting committee. He was a member of Council in 1780 and was elected state senator that year and served, with one brief break, until 1789. He was offered a seat on the Supreme Judicial Court

759

but refused it because the salary was inadequate. He was a delegate to the Constitutional Convention but left before the Constitution was completed. Strong was an important Federalist leader in the Massachusetts Convention of 1788.

He was one of the administration leaders in the federal Senate. He was active in framing the Judiciary Act of 1789. He won reelection in 1793 but resigned in 1796. In 1800 he was the reluctant Federalist candidate for governor against Elbridge Gerry and won in a close race. He was reelected governor each year until James Sullivan defeated him in 1807. He refused the Federalist nomination in 1808, but was elected in 1812 as war with Great Britain drew near. He refused to furnish state militia for federal service at the beginning of the war, and his action was sustained by the governor's Council and the Supreme Judicial Court. Throughout the War of 1812 Strong refused to cooperate in the national war effort. After successive reelections to the governor's office during the war, he refused reelection in 1816 and retired.

Thacher, George (1754-1824), Elected Representative, York-Cumberland-Lincoln District

Born in Yarmouth, Barnstable County, George Thacher graduated from Harvard in 1776 and studied law with Shearjashub Bourne of Barnstable. Thacher moved to Biddeford, York County, Maine, in 1782 to practice law.

He was elected to the Confederation Congress in 1787. He served in the first six Congresses under the Constitution, 1789-1801; and supported the assumption of state debts, antislavery measures, and the Alien and Sedition laws. He was appointed associate justice of the Massachusetts Supreme Judicial Court in 1801, an office he held until just prior to his death. When Maine became a separate state in 1820, Thacher moved to Newburyport, Massachusetts, in order to continue in his judicial office. He returned to Biddeford shortly before his death.

Thacher, Josiah (1733-1799), Candidate for Representative, York-Cumberland-Lincoln District

Born in Lebanon, Connecticut, Josiah Thacher graduated from the College of New Jersey. He was ordained a minister in Gorham, Maine, in 1767 but was dismissed from the church there in 1781 as a result of a religious controversy. He turned to politics, was appointed a justice of the peace, and held that office for many years. He represented Gorham in the Massachusetts legislature for eleven years, was a senator from Cumberland County for a number of years, and served as a judge of the Court of Common Pleas in the county from 1784 until he died.

Varnum, Joseph B. (1751-1821), Candidate for Representative, Middlesex District

Born in Dracut, and largely self-taught, Varnum was a farmer most of his life. In 1770 he was elected a militia captain in Dracut, was replaced in 1774, was reinstated in 1776, and served in that capacity to 1787.

Varnum represented Dracut in the Massachusetts House, 1780-1785, and Middlesex County in the state Senate, 1786-1795. He helped suppress Shays's Rebellion. An Antifederalist in the Massachusetts Convention of 1788, he voted to ratify the Constitution after a bill of rights was recommended.

He was a candidate for the second and third Congresses and won election to the fourth Congress, defeating Federalist Samuel Dexter by eleven votes in a contest marked by charges of vote fraud in Varnum's home town. After his initial election Varnum was reelected to the next seven Congresses (March 1795 to March 1811). A stalwart Republican, he was Speaker of the House during the tenth and eleventh Congresses. He was elected to the United States Senate and served from March 1811 to March 1817. He was one of the strongest supporters of President Madison's policies. In 1813 he was president pro tempore of the Senate and acting Vice President after the death of Elbridge Gerry. Varnum was defeated for governor in 1813. He was a state senator, 1817-1821, and was a delegate to the state constitutional convention in 1820.

Ward, Artemas (1727-1800), Candidate for Representative, Worcester District

Born in Shrewsbury, the son of the founder of the town, Ward graduated from Harvard in 1748. He taught school in Groton and then opened a general store in Shrewsbury in 1750. He held various town offices: assessor, clerk, moderator, selectman, and treasurer. He also served on several occasions in the colonial legislature and was an officer in the French and Indian War. Governor Francis Bernard cancelled Ward's military commission in 1766 because of his opposition to British policies.

He was appointed a judge of the Worcester County Court of Common Pleas in 1762 and became chief justice in 1775. Governor Bernard vetoed his appointment to the Council in 1768 and 1769, but Governor Thomas Hutchinson approved Ward's election in 1770, and he served until 1774. Ward played a prominent role in the early revolutionary struggle—as a member of the Worcester County convention in 1774, member of the first and second provincial congresses, and commander of provincial forces around Boston from 20 April to 17 June 1775. Ward was appointed second in command to General Washington on 17 June. He resigned on 22 March 1776 but continued to serve in the Continental Army until 20 March 1777.

Ward resumed his political career and served on the Council, 1777-1780. He was a delegate to the Continental Congress in 1780 and 1781. He was a representative in the General Court from 1782 to 1787 except for one year. Ward was elected to the second and third Congresses (1791-1795). In 1798 he resigned from the Court of Common Pleas because of ill health.

Wells, Nathaniel (1740-1816), Candidate for Representative, York-Cumberland-Lincoln District

Born in Wells, York County, Maine, the son of a prominent local politician, Wells graduated from Harvard in 1760. For several years he was a schoolmaster in Wells. In 1770 he was elected a selectman and in 1773 was a member of the committee of correspondence. In 1774 he was named a York County justice of the peace, was reappointed in 1776, and was promoted to the quorum in 1778. In 1776 Wells succeeded his father as town clerk, and in 1780 he took his father's place as deacon of the church. In 1779-1780 he was a member of the Massachusetts constitutional convention. He was elected to the state Senate in 1782 and served for fifteen years. In 1786 he was appointed a justice in the York County Court of Common Pleas and was chief justice of the court from 1799 to 1811. A delegate from Wells in the state Convention, he voted to ratify the Constitution. He was elected to the governor's Council in 1794 and 1800-1801. Wells was elected a state representative in 1802, 1804, and 1812.

Whiting, William (1730-1792), Candidate for Representative, Hampshire-Berkshire District

Born in Bozrah, Connecticut, the son of a militia colonel, Whiting studied medicine in Colchester and began practice in Hartford. By 1765 he was living in Great Barrington, Berkshire County, Massachusetts. He practiced medicine and was active in local politics. He was a delegate to the Berkshire convention of 1774 and served in the three provincial congresses, 1774-1775. He had been appointed a justice of the peace before the war and was one of the few men who continued to hold court during the war. He represented Great Barrington in the legislature in 1781, and from 1781 to 1787 he was chief justice of the Berkshire County Court of Common Pleas. In 1786 he signed a paper at the request of the insurgents agreeing not to hold court until their grievances were redressed. In 1787 the Supreme Judicial Court sentenced him to seven months in jail and fined him 100 pounds for "divers seditious words, and publishing an inflammatory libel."

Wilder, Abel (1741-1792), Candidate for Elector, Worcester District

Born in Leominster, Wilder was living in Winchendon by 1762 and was the first town clerk. He served in all the prominent town offices during his political career. From 1779 until his death he represented Winchendon in either the House or Senate except for one or two years when the town was unrepresented. He was a member of the state constitutional convention in 1779-1780. During Shays's Rebellion he supported the state government, while the majority of the people in the town favored the insurgents.

Williams, William (1734-1808), Candidate for Representative, Hampshire-Berkshire District

Born in Hatfield, Hampshire County, the son of Israel Williams, one of the "River Gods" of the Connecticut Valley, Williams graduated from Yale in 1754, studied law, and was admitted to the bar. Before 1774 he was clerk of the Hampshire County court. He opposed the Revolution and was forced to leave Hatfield. He settled in the Ashuelet Equivalent, which became Dalton, Berkshire County, in 1784. Williams was the first town clerk and one of the first selectmen. He was elected to the state Senate in 1797 and 1799-1800. For several years he was a deacon of the local Congregational church and was a trustee of Williams College from 1793 until his death.

Worthington, John (1719-1800), Candidate for Representative, Hampshire-Berkshire District

Born in Springfield, Hampshire County, Worthington graduated from Yale in 1740. After two years as a tutor at Yale, he studied law at Suffield, Connecticut, was admitted to the bar, and began practice in Springfield in 1744. He attended the Albany Congress in 1754. He became a prominent lawyer and land owner in western Massachusetts and frequently represented Springfield in the provincial legislature. From 1767 to 1769 he was a member of the Council. In 1774 he was appointed a mandamus councillor, but a mob forced him to renounce the appointment. He stayed in Springfield and gradually recovered some of the influence he had lost during the Revolution.

CHAPTER VI

The Elections
in New Hampshire

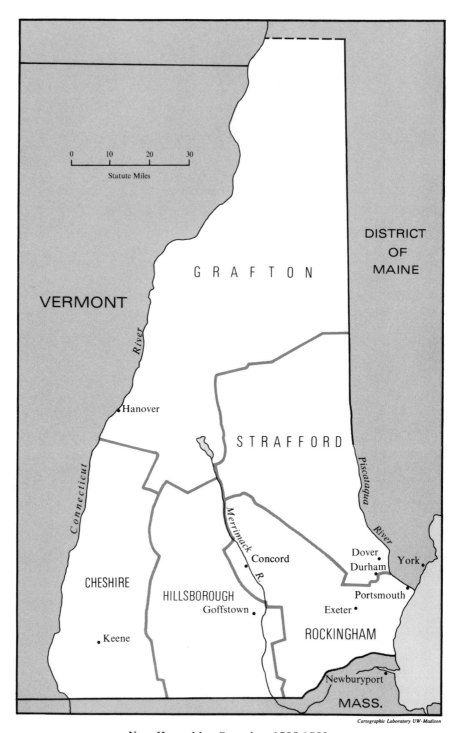

New Hampshire Counties, 1788-1789

INTRODUCTION

American independence freed New Hampshire from British control, but perhaps of equal importance to many people of New Hampshire, from the control of the Wentworth family oligarchy. It had ruled the colony ever since 1741 when Benning Wentworth was appointed governor. Wentworth had solid support in England, where he cultivated such allies as the merchant and lobbyist John Thomlinson and, through him, the Duke of Newcastle, who distributed colonial patronage. Within the colony Wentworth built up his power by control of land grants, by the use of patronage and public contracts, and by his selective enforcement of the laws regulating the cutting of mast timber—one of the colony's principal exports. Wentworth and his supporters dominated the government and reduced their occasional opponents to impotence or self-serving conformity.

Wentworth held the office of governor from 1741 to 1767, longer than any other governor in the British colonies, and was succeeded by his nephew, John. As governor, John Wentworth spent eight years watching the steady erosion of British authority and the authority of himself and his family. A Loyalist, he fled from the colony in 1775.

Revolutionary congresses took control, and by the beginning of 1776 a new government had been created. At the end of 1775 the fourth provincial congress, acting on advice from the Continental Congress to establish a government that would best "produce the happiness of the people," adopted rules for the election of the fifth congress, which would create a new government. The colonial requirement that voters own land worth £50 was abolished, and all taxpayers were given the vote. The requirement that representatives in the legislature own land worth £300 was reduced to £200. In addition, the fourth congress provided for "equal representation." Colonial representation had been by towns, but only 36 of approximately 150 towns in the colony were represented in the last colonial assembly, and two-thirds of the representatives came from an area within ten miles of Portsmouth. The congress decided that each town with 100 freeholders should have one representative, with an additional representative for each additional 100 freeholders. Towns with fewer than 100 were to combine and elect a representative jointly.

In January 1776 the fifth congress adopted a brief constitution, declared itself a legislature, elected an upper house, and gave the legislature the power to elect local officials. The property qualifications for voting and officeholding and the basis of representation were not mentioned in the constitution but were apparently taken for granted by the new self-proclaimed legislature. This temporary constitution shifted the center of legislative power from the Portsmouth area to the Merrimack Valley, but it aroused the antagonism of the smaller towns, particularly those along the Connecticut River in the western part of the state. They insisted that representation be by towns, and they demanded the right to elect local officials and abolition of the property qualification for officeholding.

Many of the western towns refused to combine to elect representatives and send them to the legislature. Some of the towns threatened to secede; talked of a new state; and twice, although briefly, became a part of Vermont. Meanwhile, the western towns came to insist, like those in western Massachusetts, that only a constitutional convention could write a constitution and that it must be approved by the voters before it could go into effect.

While delegates from the Portsmouth area, which had lost its monopoly of the legislature, and the new leaders from the towns lying between the seacoast area and the Connecticut Valley continued to struggle with one another for office and over policies, they united to oppose the demands of the far western towns for more democratic government. Nevertheless, these leaders were forced to yield, to call a constitutional convention, and to submit the results to the voters. The voters turned down two proposed constitutions, and it was not until 1784 that the voters agreed to accept a constitution.

Although eastern leaders failed to create a powerful executive in the constitution, they did maintain the principle of "equal representation." The constitution provided that every town with 150 white adult male taxpayers should elect one representative, plus another for each additional 300 taxpayers. Towns with less than the minimum were merged into districts that contained at least 150 taxpayers, with each such district to elect one representative.

The second major dispute in New Hampshire after 1776 between the Portsmouth area and the remainder of the state—that over economic policy—was more difficult to compromise, and it threatened the state with serious disorder in the years preceding the first federal elections. New Hampshire, like the rest of New England, suffered from a postwar depression after 1783. By 1785 there were demands throughout the state for the same kind of relief measures that discontented farmers were seeking in neighboring Massachusetts: for a legal tender paper currency issue or, at the very least, one that would be accepted for taxes; for a reduction or outright suspension of taxes; for a lowering of court costs and legal fees; and for an easing of the laws providing for the collection of private debts. The chief opposition to such demands came from the merchant community in general and from the Portsmouth merchants in particular.

In 1785 John Langdon, a Portsmouth merchant, was president of the state. He had been elected by the legislature that year, when none of the four candidates for the office received a majority of the popular vote. To many people, Langdon's economic policies seemed to favor the interests of the Portsmouth merchant community over the welfare of the rest of the state, and he certainly showed little sympathy for the demands of the interior towns.

In 1786 the leading rivals for the presidency were Langdon and John Sullivan (who had finished third in 1785). Sullivan appealed to the interior towns, intimating that he would support legislation favoring debtors, oppose merchant-oriented legislation, and favor a paper currency issue funded by a land bank.

Despite his campaign hints, President Sullivan did little to relieve debtors or advance a paper money issue, and the Assembly's relief measures were piecemeal and ineffective. In the fall of 1786 there was a brief outburst of violence similar to Shays's Rebellion in Massachusetts. County conventions had begun meeting in the spring to lay their grievances before the Assembly and to petition for relief. The first convention met at Concord in June, and several more met during the summer and fall. On 20 September an armed mob surrounded the legislature then meeting at Exeter and demanded, according to eyewitness William Plumer, a paper money issue; the cancellation of debts and taxes; the elimination of inferior courts; a reduction of fees and government salaries; and, most frightening of all, "an equal distribution of property." The next day the local militia dispersed the mob with little trouble. Although the violence was local and easily contained, the discontent grew in intensity, and by 1787 many people had lost confidence in the ability or willingness of the government to deal with their problems and redress their grievances.

Thus, many people were in a state of unrest and uncertainty in January 1788 when the voters were asked to elect delegates to a convention to consider the proposed Federal Constitution. The Portsmouth merchant community and most of the state's lawyers looked to the Constitution as the solution for most if not all of New Hampshire's problems: to a national government that on the one hand would promote trade and on the other would prohibit dangerous economic experiments such as legal tender paper currency and the suspension of debt collections. Most of the state's important political leaders supported ratification, including both of the major rivals for the state's presidency, John Langdon and John Sullivan. However, contemporary observers agreed that probably a majority of the New Hampshire voters were opposed to the new Constitution at the beginning of the debate over ratification. Since much of the population was demanding debtor relief legislation and paper currency issues, a constitution that flatly prohibited both held little appeal for them.

When the New Hampshire Convention convened on 13 February 1788, President John Sullivan estimated that seven of every ten delegates opposed ratification, but the Federalists in the Convention had an advantage their opponents lacked: leadership. Many of the state's most prominent Federalists were at the Convention, including John Sullivan, Josiah Bartlett, and John Langdon. Joshua Atherton, a lawyer from Amherst, led the opposition to ratification on the Convention floor. Atherton was a capable and tireless debater, but he lacked the political experience of Langdon and the military reputation of Sullivan. In fact, Atherton had once been arrested as a suspected Tory, and he had refused to take an oath of allegiance to the government of New Hampshire until 1779. Nathaniel Peabody, who did have considerable political experience and who had served on the powerful Committee of Safety during the Revolution, was strongly opposed to ratification, but he had not been elected a delegate to the Convention. However, he was present and active outside the Convention.

Nevertheless, Federalist leaders concluded that they still did not have the votes necessary to ratify, in part because several delegates known to favor the Constitution were flatly forbidden by instructions from their constituents to vote for ratification. Therefore, the Federalists decided to adjourn rather than risk a defeat. On 22 February they secured adjournment until June by a vote of 56 to 51. They hoped that ratification by other states and changes in instructions to Convention delegates would give them enough votes to ratify. Their strategy succeeded. By the time the Convention met again, eight states had ratified, which gave the New Hampshire Convention the opportunity to become the ninth state to ratify and thus enable the Confederation Congress to put the Constitution into effect. When the Convention reassembled in June, enough delegates were won over with a promise of subsequent amendments to the Constitution and a bill of rights to make ratification possible by a narrow margin. On 21 June the New Hampshire Convention ratified by a vote of 57 to 47.

Some disappointed Antifederalists like Joshua Atherton considered the possibility of winning back through the first federal elections what they had lost at the Convention. If enough Antifederalists could be elected to the first Congress, they reasoned, perhaps the amendments the Federalists had promised could be more substantive, and the new Constitution rendered tolerable, if not wholly desirable. In the elections, however, they were defeated more decisively than they had been at the Convention.

On 5 November the New Hampshire legislature met in special session to draft an election law and to elect two United States Senators. John Langdon (who had been elected president in the spring of 1788) was chosen Senator on 11 November. The next day, the House proposed to balance the delegation by electing Antifederalist Nathaniel Peabody. The Senate balked and nominated Josiah Bartlett, a Federalist; and the House concurred. Bartlett ultimately refused to serve, and on 3 January 1789 the legislature chose another Federalist, Paine Wingate, to replace him.

The New Hampshire election law passed on 12 November set Monday, 15 December, as election day. Voters were to choose five presidential Electors and three federal Representatives, with candidates for both offices running at-large rather than in districts. Any candidate for presidential Elector who received more than one-tenth of the popular vote and any candidate for Representative who received more than one-sixth of the popular vote would be elected. The law provided different plans for filling the two offices in the event that no candidate received enough votes on 15 December. Vacancies among the Electors were to be filled by the legislature from among the leading candidates, while vacancies among the Representatives were to be filled by another popular election to be held in February 1789.

These precautions proved prudent, for no candidate for Elector or Representative received enough votes on 15 December to be elected. New Hampshire's five presidential Electors were eventually chosen by the legislature from among the ten leading candidates, but only after a long dispute between the House and Senate over whether they should vote separately or jointly. The Senate insisted on maintaining its independence and refused to merge the votes of its twelve members with those of the much more numerous House. Near midnight on 7 February, the House gave up its insistence on a joint ballot; and Benjamin Bellows, John Pickering, Ebenezer Thompson, John Sullivan, and John Parker were chosen Electors.

New Hampshire's second election for Representatives was held on 2 February and was limited by law to the six candidates who received the most votes in the first election: Benjamin West, Samuel Livermore, Paine Wingate, Abiel Foster, John Sullivan, and Nicholas Gilman. However, by election day there were only four active candidates left. Paine Wingate had been elected to the United States Senate on 3 January, and John Sullivan had let it be known that he would not accept election. West, Livermore, and Gilman were elected; but West refused to serve. In a third election on 22 June, Abiel Foster was chosen to replace him.

New Hampshire's congressional delegation was entirely Federalist. The election results confirmed the judgment of Antifederalist Joshua Atherton who wrote to Antifederalist John Lamb in New York on 23 February 1789 that the public's attitude toward the new Constitution seemed to be "it is adopted, let us try it."

NOTE ON SOURCES

The legislative records of New Hampshire consist of the manuscript journals of the House of Representatives and the Senate; manuscript Council records; and the original manuscript acts, all in the New Hampshire State Archives. In addition to the legislative journals, loose papers such as messages between the House and the Senate are filed under the category "State Records (Document Series of 1901)," also in the New Hampshire State Archives. Although the records are relatively complete, they are sometimes more cryptic than similar records in other states. The manuscript journals of the House and Senate, for example, often do not indicate the first and second readings of bills which later became laws. And as is the case in most states at the time, the official records provide little more than a framework for understanding the elections. Critical detail concerning the politics of the elections must be supplied from other sources.

Contemporary manuscript material relating to the elections in New Hampshire is extremely sparse. The John Lamb Papers in the New-York Historical Society are among the most useful for Antifederalist opinion, for they contain Joshua Atherton's letters to Lamb. An important source for legislative proceedings is the retrospective manuscript autobiography of William Plumer in the Library of Congress. The portions dealing with the elections were written in 1826, long after the events described, and the work is sometimes unreliable concerning details. Nevertheless, the autobiography contains information about the election of Senators and presidential Electors which cannot be found in any other source.

Also important are the manuscript town records at the New Hampshire Historical Society and the transcripts of town records at the New Hampshire State Library. These sources record the proceedings of numerous town meetings during the period and contain in many cases the votes cast by the towns for presidential Electors and Representatives in the several elections in 1788 and 1789. The manuscript town records and transcripts are not complete but can be supplemented by several published town histories.

With manuscript sources so limited, the contemporary newspapers are vitally important sources of information. Four were published in New Hampshire during the elections: two in Portsmouth and one each in Exeter and Keene. By far the most useful for information about the elections is the Portsmouth *New Hampshire Spy*, published semi-weekly by George J. Osborne, which became *Osborne's New Hampshire Spy* with the issue of 6 March 1789. There are less complete runs extant of the three remaining papers, all of which were weeklies. John Melcher published the Portsmouth *New Hampshire Gazette, and the General Advertiser;* John Lamson and Henry Ranlet the Exeter *Freeman's Oracle: or, New Hampshire Advertiser*; and James D. Griffith the Keene *New Hampshire Recorder, and the Weekly Advertiser.* William Hoyt published *The Essex Journal and New Hampshire Packet* in Newburyport, Massachusetts, but, as indicated by its name, the newspaper also circulated in New Hampshire and contains much useful information about events in that state.

New Hampshire's political history from the late colonial years through the early national period is surveyed in two books which supplement one another. These are Richard F. Upton, *Revolutionary New Hampshire: An Account of the Social and Political Forces Underlying the Transition from Royal Province to American Commonwealth* (Hanover, N.H., 1936; rev. ed., Port Washington, N.Y., 1970), and Jere R. Daniell, *Experiment in Republicanism: New Hampshire Politics and the American Revolution, 1741-1794* (Cambridge, Mass., 1970). Political alignments in the state prior to ratification of the Constitution are discussed in Jackson T. Main, *Political Parties Before the Constitution* (Chapel

Hill, N.C., 1973), and the ratification struggle in the state is covered briefly in Robert A. Rutland, *The Ordeal of the Constitution: The Antifederalists and the Ratification Struggle of 1787-1788* (Norman, Okla., 1966). In addition, there is useful background material in William B. Weeden, *Economic and Social History of New England, 1620-1789* (2 vols., Boston, 1890) and in several published biographies of the state's leading politicians, including Charles P. Whittemore's *A General of the Revolution: John Sullivan of New Hampshire* (New York, 1961) and Lawrence S. Mayo's *John Langdon of New Hampshire* (Concord, N.H., 1937).

NEW HAMPSHIRE CHRONOLOGY, 1788-1789

1788

10 October	President John Langdon calls special session of the General Court for 5 November to prepare for first federal elections.
5 November	General Court assembles at Concord.
6 November	House and Senate begin debate on plan for elections.
7 November	House and Senate appoint joint committee to prepare law for election of Representatives and Electors.
10 November	Election law read third time and passed by House.
11 November	House nominates John Langdon and Nathaniel Peabody for United States Senate.
12 November	Senate accepts John Langdon, nominates Josiah Bartlett, rejects Nathaniel Peabody, and passes election law. House accepts Josiah Bartlett.
13 November	General Court adjourns to 24 December.
15 December	First election for Representatives and Electors; no candidate receives sufficient votes for election.
24 December	General Court reassembles.
27 December	Josiah Bartlett refuses to serve as Senator.
31 December	General Court opens and counts vote returns for Representatives and Electors.

1789

1 January	General Court appoints committee to recount votes for Representatives; House nominates Paine Wingate to replace Josiah Bartlett as Senator.
2 January	Joint committee reports that no candidate for Representative received sufficient votes for election; names of six leading candidates ordered sent to towns for second election on 2 February; General Court counts votes for Electors.
3 January	Senate concurs in Paine Wingate's nomination for Senator; joint committee appointed to recount returns for Electors.

6 January	Joint committee reports no candidate for Elector received enough votes for election; House moves to choose Electors by joint ballot; Senate insists on separate votes in each house.
7 January	Benjamin Bellows, John Pickering, Ebenezer Thompson, John Sullivan, and John Parker elected Electors by separate vote of both houses.
22 January	John Langdon sends resignation as president to General Court; John Pickering named to fill remainder of term.
2 February	Second election for Representatives: Benjamin West, Nicholas Gilman, and Samuel Livermore elected.
4 February	New Hampshire Electors cast five votes for George Washington and five for John Adams.
6 February	President and Council issue John Langdon credentials as United States Senator.
7 February	Supplementary election law for filling vacancies in congressional delegation by death or resignation read third time and passed by both houses; General Court adjourns to 26 May.
13 February	President and Council issue Paine Wingate credentials as United States Senator.
20 February	President and Council count votes for Representatives.
21 February	President and Council certify election of Benjamin West, Samuel Livermore, and Nicholas Gilman.
2 March	Election for state representatives, senators, and president held.
16 May	*New Hampshire Spy* reports Benjamin West had declined election as Representative.
20 May	President and Council call special election to replace Benjamin West as Representative.
6 June	General Court counts votes in state election; no candidate for president received a majority of votes. John Sullivan elected president of state by General Court.
22 June	Special election for Representative to replace Benjamin West; Abiel Foster elected.
15 July	President and Council count votes for United States Representative.
16 July	President and Council certify Abiel Foster's election.

THE DOCUMENTS

New Hampshire Gazette, 31 July 1788

To Be Given Away,

SEVERAL important and high stations, in the new government. No persons need offer themselves as candidates for them, unless they can be well recommended, for tried abilities, strict honour and integrity, and *unshaken federalism.* Inquire of *"The People."*

Information having been given that *some persons* have *offered* some of these stations as being in *their* gift, the world are assured that such persons were in no wise empowered to make the offer.

Wanted,

A *Reasonable Pretext for ratifying the Constitution.* Apply to No. 46, Poughkeepsie.

Lost.

By a flaming patriot in Virginia, all his *Pretensions to Consistancy*—They were dropt at Richmond, wrapped up in an *"Address of the Minority."*[1]

Wanted to Purchase,

Blank Recantations of antifederal sentiments—Those of a good form will receive any price. Inquire of two would-be candidates for seats in the Federal Government, in two adjacent counties.[2]

WANTED,

By the Federalists—*the ratification of North Carolina and New-York.*

By the antis—*eye sight.*

By the R.I. majority—*anarchy.*

By the minority—*a separation.*

And by America in general—*the speedy operation of the new government.* *July 22.*

---

1. The "flaming patriot" was probably George Mason. On the final day of the Virginia Convention, he suggested that the minority meet and prepare "an address to reconcile the minds of their constituents to the new plan of government." The meeting was held, and Mason presented an address which was not well received. One observer thought it tended "to irritate rather than quiet the public mind." Mason withdrew the address, and the meeting broke up without taking any action. See "A Spectator of the Meeting," Richmond *Virginia Independent Chronicle*, 9 July, which was reprinted in the *New Hampshire Spy* on 26 July.

2. Possibly this refers to Joshua Atherton of Hillsborough County and Nathaniel Peabody of Rockingham County, both prominent New Hampshire Antifederalists.

From a Correspondent, New Hampshire Spy, 23 August

Whilst the new Constitution is advancing shortly to be put into action, and these states are soon to be called to the election of the important officers, who are to guide our public affairs; every man must exult in the opportunity of giving his vote, that shall testify his zeal for the public good, as well as his gratitude to those worthy citizens, whose tried abilities and steady patriotism entitle them to a place in the public confidence. Whilst a Washington and a Hancock are selected by many, New Hampshire must be proud also that she has a [John] Sullivan, whose patriotism, heroism, and virtuous struggles in her civil, military, commercial, agricultural, and manufacturing concerns have been unremitted for her best good, and making her honored and respected in the world. And whilst our allies in Europe, and friends in the world at large, and this continent in particular, wish his important assistance in regulating our national concerns, those who have formerly sat with him in the general Congress, those who have served with and under him during the late war—who shared with him in all the toils, and hardships of the campaign, and the dangers as well as the applause of battle and victory—mean to unite their virtuous endeavors to call him into public station. There is no doubt but the affection and gratitude of his fellow citizens will cause them also to unite with one voice, in electing him into a seat in the great Senate of these states.

New Hampshire Gazette, 28 August

The station at the head of our Superior Court, the dignity with which he has presided there, and the many proofs of real learning and abilities, which our worthy citizen, the Hon. Samuel Livermore, Esq., has for many years exhibited, through the late contest with Great Britain, both in the legislature of the state and great Congress of America, present him to his countrymen as worthy a station in the new government. It will be no disparagement to many valuable characters there, to say that none excelled this deserving man, in the late Convention of this state, in zeal, arguments, and influence, to lead to its adoption, which caused such general joy, through the continent. His line of life has furnished him with every requisite to fit him for the science of legislation, whereby he will afford much benefit to the community and honor to the states, should he be distinguished in the expected election, as one of the Senate of the new government.[1]

1. For a reply see "A Friend to the People," *Freeman's Oracle*, 1 November, printed below.

Proclamation by President John Langdon, 10 October[1]

State *of* New-Hampshire.

Whereas matters of Importance render it necessary that the General Court of said State should be called together at an earlier day than that to which it stands adjourned:—[2]

I HAVE therefore thought fit, by and with the ADVICE of COUNCIL, to convene the same at *CONCORD*, on *WEDNESDAY*, the *FIFTH* day of *NOVEMBER* next:—and the Members thereof, and all other persons concerned, are hereby directed to take notice and govern themselves accordingly.

GIVEN at the COUNCIL-CHAMBER in *Portsmouth*, this Tenth Day of *October*, Anno Domini, One Thousand, Seven Hundred and Eighty-eight, and of the Sovereignty and Independence of the United States of AMERICA the Thirteenth.

JOHN LANGDON.

By his Excellency's Command,
   JOSEPH PEARSON, *Secr'y.*

1. (LT). The text of the proclamation is from the *New Hampshire Spy*, 14 October. It was printed in the *New Hampshire Gazette*, 16 October.

2. The next regular meeting of the legislature had been scheduled for 24 December. The special session was called in response to the election ordinance adopted by Congress on 13 September, which Nicholas Gilman sent to Langdon on the day it passed (RC, State Papers Relating to the Revolution, II [1785-1789], Nh-Ar).

A Friend to the People, Freeman's Oracle, 1 November

I took notice, not long since, of a piece in your paper, marking out the abilities of the Honorable Chief Justice [Samuel] Livermore, of this state, and conclu[ded?] by recommending him as a suitable person for a Senator in Congress under the new government.[1] I agree with him in sentiment, that the abilities of the gentleman are great, and I will venture to say further, that I do not think we have a gentleman in this state that will grace the bench equal to him. The aged and experienced lawyer[s] look to him as their superior in science; the young admire his knowledge and abilities. They consider him as the essence of law—not like the young practitioner who appears with his abridgments, but like an old sage carries the whole code of laws with him. In short, the wisdom of the Council was most excellently marked out in the appointment of the gentlemen, as justices on the superior bench, added to their extraordinary natural abilities and acquirements.

There is the lawyer, the physician, the farmer, and the merchant.[2] Besides their law and knowledge they have an idea of the nature of almost every cause that comes before them. Upon these principles and many others I do not wish to see them separated. It is an old and good saying, *"of two evils choose the least."* Therefore, I think those gentlemen who have really considered the matter well would not wish to see the Honorable Chief Justice removed from the seat he is now placed upon; for he presides with great dignity. The innocent courts his smiles, and the guilty fears his frowns.

If any gentleman thinks the office deserves greater emoluments placed to it, I shall have no objection; for I have wished to see the salaries of the justices of the Superior Court raised, so that not only the office but the emoluments should be respectable.

I beg leave further to differ from your correspondent to say, I do not think His Honor the Chief Justice is a suitable person to represent us in Congress at this time as a Senator. I do not wish to hurt his feelings, for I love and respect his abilities, but the call of my country is more extensive than my feelings for a bosom friend. The amendments to the new Constitution is the most important object we are looking for, at the settling of the new Congress. *Vox populi, est vox Dei*—the voice of the people cry aloud for it. Every gentleman has a right to give his own sentiments, and His Honor the Chief Justice delivered his in the

Convention with a great degree of firmness, *"that the Constitution was now complete without any amendments."* If so, why should we send him to Congress to be an instrument to withhold from us the amendments so ardently wished for, and at the same time deprive us of a gentleman on the superior bench that time will scarce ever replace? Were I to recommend any person for the office of Senator, I should be careful to avoid any character who had a hand in framing the Constitution, as it is, in some measure, a child of their own making. Consequently, they would wish to support it at any rate. Witness the expression of a respectable character in the late Convention, viz., *"that the Constitution was now complete; the amendments would not take place in five hundred years."*[3] On the other hand, I should avoid those who wish to destroy the whole. But take the middle path and choose some gentleman who wishes well to the whole community, and whose acquaintance and extensive knowledge will be serviceable in bringing about the amendments.

1. See the *New Hampshire Gazette*, 28 August, printed above.
2. Besides Livermore, the members of the Superior Court were Josiah Bartlett ("the physician"); Woodbury Langdon, brother of President John Langdon ("the merchant"); and John Dudley (presumably "the farmer").
3. The "respectable character" was probably John Langdon, who attended both the Constitutional Convention and the New Hampshire Convention, and who supported the Constitution. A reply to this article in the *Freeman's Oracle* on 8 November (printed below) suggests that Langdon was the man referred to.

House Proceedings, Wednesday, 5 November[1]

The House met in consequence of a proclamation issued by His Excellency the President for that purpose, and adjourned to 9 o'clock tomorrow morning.[2]

1. MS Journals, Nh-Ar. Unless otherwise indicated, the New Hampshire House and Senate proceedings are transcribed from the manuscript journals of the two houses and hereafter will be cited by date only.
2. The proclamation, dated 10 October, is printed above. The Senate also met briefly on the 5th and adjourned to the following day.

President John Langdon's Message to the House and Senate, 5 November[1]

The United States, in Congress assembled, having by their ordinance of the 13th of September last[2] determined the time for choosing Electors, as well as the time of their meeting, and the place for commencing proceedings under the federal government; which appearing of great importance to the citizens of this state, I have thought fit, by the unanimous advice of Council, to convene you at an earlier day than that to which you were adjourned, that you might have full opportunity for arranging this important business in such way as should be advantageous to the state.

I most sincerely wished to have avoided the great expense of calling a special session of the General Court, but the way and manner of choosing the Electors under the new government being left to the legislature of each state to determine, and the time from the adjournment of the General Court to the meeting of the new Congress, not giving sufficient opportunity for the choice of Representatives, made it necessary.

Gentlemen, I shall not point out any mode of proceeding in the choice of Senators, Electors, or Representatives under the new government, but you will permit me to observe, that it is of the greatest importance to this as well as the other states, that these offices should be filled by gentlemen of abilities and integrity, who shall be well acquainted with the different objects which the national government may have in view, and who have the confidence of the people. For however the federal government may be well calculated to promote the happiness of the United States, yet it will require ALL the exertions of the most able and upright men, to form the first arrangements, as on these will greatly depend our future happiness and tranquility.

Gentlemen, as you are called together specially for the election of Senators, and making the necessary arrangements for the choice of Electors and Representatives under the Federal Constitution, I suppose the session will be short; but should you determine to take up the business of the year in general, the public papers received during the recess of the Court shall be laid before you; and I shall be happy in making any communications that may tend to the general welfare of the state.

1. The message (which is dated "Council Chamber, Concord, 5 November") is from the *New Hampshire Spy*, 14 November. Both the House and Senate received it on 6 November, although the text does not appear in the journals of either house.

2. Printed, Chapter II.

House and Senate Proceedings, Thursday, 6 November

The House, A.M.

Voted, that Mr. Sullivan, Mr. Peabody, Mr. Green, Mr. Smith, and Mr. Simpson with such of the honorable Senate as they may join be a committee to take under consideration the several matters contained in His Excellency's message this day received and report thereon.

Sent up by Mr. Wm. Peabody.

The Senate

A vote [of the House] for a committee to join a committee of the Senate, to consider of His Excellency's message and report thereon was brought up, read and concurred. Mr. Toppan, Mr. Long, and Mr. Smith joined.

The House, A.M.

The committee to consider of the matters contained in His Excellency's message reported (in part) that there be a conference of both houses as soon as convenient, to consider upon the best method of carrying into effect the resolve of Congress relative to the new Constitution.

Signed, Christopher Toppan, for the committee.

Which report being read and considered, voted, that it be received and accepted and that the conference be held in the Assembly Chamber if the honorable Senate see fit.

Sent up by Mr. Barrett.

The Senate

A vote to accept the report of the committee on His Excellency's message, who reported in part that a conference be held in the Assembly Chamber if the Senate see fit, was brought up, read and concurred.

The House and Senate, P.M.[1]

The honorable Senate and House being met in the Assembly Chamber, agreeably to a vote of this day, proceeding in debating on the best method of carrying into effect the resolves of Congress relative to the new Constitution, and after a considerable time spent thereon, the honorable Senate withdrew.

The House then adjourned to 9 o'clock tomorrow morning.

1. The proceedings of the joint session are from the House Journals.

Newspaper Report of House and Senate Proceedings on Thursday, 6 November[1]

[Both houses received the President's message printed above.]

The House then requested a conference with the Senate, on the necessary steps to be taken with respect to the Constitution of the United States; which being agreed to, the Senate came down, at three o'clock, P.M., to the representative's chamber.

His Excellency President Langdon then opened the debate with some observations on the necessary business of the session, and on the manner of choosing Electors which he recommended to be done by the legislature.

General [John] Sullivan favored the opinion, that the Electors should be chosen by *the people*, and that the Representatives of the United States should be chosen out of such districts as should be marked out by the legislature, etc.

After a great variety of observations being made by many of the members of Senate and House, on the mode of choosing Electors and Representatives, the conference ended, and the Senate withdrew.

A committee was then appointed by the Senate and House to bring in a bill to regulate the manner of choosing Senators, Electors, and Representatives.[2]

1. *New Hampshire Spy*, 14 November.
2. The joint committee to draft an election law was elected on 7 November, not on the 6th. The committee was charged with drafting a law providing for the election of Representatives and presidential Electors but not United States Senators. See House and Senate Proceedings, 7 November, printed below.

House and Senate Proceedings, Friday, 7 November

The House, A.M.

Voted, that Mr. Sullivan, Mr. Barrett, Mr. Peabody, Mr. Parker, Mr. Plummer, Mr. Smith, and Mr. Freeman with such of the honorable Senate as they shall join be a committee to report in what manner the Representatives to the general Congress, and Electors for a President of the United States, shall be appointed.

Sent up by Mr. Storer.

The Senate

A vote for a committee to join a committee of the Senate to report in what manner the Representatives to the general Congress and the Electors for a President of the United States shall be appointed, was brought up, read and concurred. Mr. Toppan, Mr. Long, Mr. Smith, Mr. Webster, Mr. Bell, and Mr. Worcester joined.

Friend to Amendments, Freeman's Oracle, 8 November

I am but a plain simple man, but call myself an honest one—and therefore hope for the indulgence of the public tho I shall cut no figure in print. I am one of those who had objections to the new Constitution and wished for amendments. I don't think so badly of it as I did at first, but I think it wants mending. So I believe do most of those who voted for it. But I cannot fall in with the notions of the *friend to the people*[1] in your last with regard to the unfitness of our worthy President [John Langdon] and Chief Justice [Samuel Livermore] for Senator in the new Congress. As to the latter I know he holds an office of importance and fills it as nicely as a man can do, for I have been on the jury and heard him talk as glibly as ever I heard a minister read a sermon in the pulpit without having a word writ. But if there is another office of greater importance that he is better qualified to fill than any other man, it seems to me good policy would not oppose his being hoisted into it. And such an office is that for which he is a candidate. This writer says that amendments to the new Constitution *is the most important object to be looked at in settling the new Congress.* In this I cannot agree with him. I think there is a number of much greater importance, but will mention only two of them, viz., the *establishing a system of revenue and revenue laws*—which will require the very wisest heads we have among us—and the *appointment of a number of very important officers*—which will demand not only an extensive acquaintance with characters but the most disinterested views. The only objection to His Excellency's having a seat in the Senate is his having assisted in making the Constitution, and his declaring in Convention, as well as the Chief Justice, that *it was already complete.* Supposing that should continue to be their opinion after they get to Congress, I don't believe they will be against the people's trying to amend it, because they would not injure it if they did not succeed; and if the people should really amend it, I would stake a yoke of oxen, that those gentlemen would acknowledge it better for it. But I am no stickler for these particular characters. We have other men, I hope, fit to go to Congress or anywhere else. There is the late President [John Sullivan?] and Judge [Josiah]

Bartlet and several more, fit for any business however important and difficult. I only mean to show that those two gentlemen, supposing they have the other qualifications for congressmen, ought not to be set aside for their attachment to the Constitution in its present form. The business that must be done by the first Congress requires longer heads and honester hearts than we can find united in the same person among the opposers of the Constitution, I am afraid. I must here speak freely, Messieurs Printers, tho perhaps I may give offense. I opposed the Constitution in my own mind from my first reading it, without knowing whether others of better judgment liked it or not. As I am but a plain man with no other education than what I picked up by my own industry, I thought I would keep my thoughts to myself and wait to see how it was relished by others. In this state I soon found out who and who were of a side; and what I knew of the characters of all the leaders of the opposition served to make me shut my mouth the closer, for really I did not like the company I must have kept had I publicly acknowledged my dislike to the Constitution. I have also endeavored to inform myself of the characters of the two parties in the neighboring states with pretty good success. By this enquiry I have discovered that almost every man of abilities and established reputation is in favor of the Constitution, and that its opposers consist principally of *honest uninformed yeomanry* like myself, headed by men of shattered fortunes, blasted reputations or inveterate tories—or in other words *men who had something to gain by living under a bad government, or something to lose by the establishment of a good one.* If there is in some of the neighboring states here and there a man of good abilities, a fair reputation, and a clear estate in the opposition, I believe it will be found that he is more famed for his obstinacy than candor. In short it must be confessed that in New England we have but a very small number of men who would not equally disgrace the states and the Antifederal Party were they sent to Congress. If then *the friend to the people* would exclude all those who are friendly to this Constitution as it is, or enemies to any good one at all, from a seat in Congress, I fear we shall be poorly represented at best; for as to such men as he describes, *men whose acquaintance and extensive knowledge may be serviceable in bringing about amendments*, it is a lamentable truth that they are not to be found among that part of us who wish for a good government. If there are any such, for God's sake let them discover themselves and rid us of the disgrace we now lie under. In a word, my honest brethren in the opposition, as the Federalists have got all the men of character and abilities among them, and as we have none in our number who would not disgrace us by their want of knowledge or principle (I mean not even except myself), I don't see but we must, for our own honor and that of our state, join with the other party in giving our voices for Federal members and leave the rest to Providence. They shall certainly have the influence of one honest and unfeigned Friend to Amendments.

1. See "A Friend to the People," *Freeman's Oracle*, 1 November, printed above.

House Proceedings, Monday, P.M., 10 November

An act for carrying into effect an ordinance of Congress of the 13th of September last relative to the Constitution of the United States was read a third time and passed to be enacted,[1] which vote was determined by yeas and nays and were as follows, viz.,

Yeas [60]

Gains	Cummings
Sheafe	Taylor
Odlin	Dole
Runnels	Wm. Page
McMurphy	Wm. Peabody
Blanchard	O. Parker
March	Abbott
Leavitt	Rand
Jos. Dow	Smith
Brown	Duncan
Wiggin	Wallace
B. Clough	Gove
Wheeler	Storey
Rogers	Jackman
Bartlett	Flanders
Clark	Weare
Hilliard	Shepherd
Jere. Clough	A. Parker
Drew	Chamberlain
N. Peabody	Temple
Jere. Dow	Smith
Gilmore[2]	Allen
Butler	Lane
Palmer	Morse
Badger	Tainter
Brackett	Winch
Gilman	Burnam
Hoit	Powers
Austin	Hutchens
Page	Simpson

Nays [17]

Hale	Copland
Plummer	Brown
Sullivan	Freeman
Emerson	Hough
Barrett	Franklin
Cragin	Patterson
Wm. Page[3]	Young
Chase	Eames
Frink	

60 Yeas.
17 Nays.

1. The *New Hampshire Spy* reported on 14 November: "On Monday, the 10th inst. the election bill was reported, and the debates upon the same was the chief business of the day." The election law is printed below under the date 12 November, the day on which it was read a third time and passed by the Senate.

2. The printed journals of the House (*A Journal of the Proceedings of the Honorable House of Representatives of the State of New-Hampshire...* [Portsmouth, 1788]) omitted Gilmore's name and reported the total "yea" vote as 59.

3. Two men named William Page were members of the House. Usually the clerk identified one of the men as "Colonel Page," but on this roll call he did not do so.

The Election of United States Senators, 10-12 November

The House and Senate Journals and the New Hampshire election law do not mention the election of Senators. Furthermore, the House Journals do not record some of the actions taken by the House. Apparently the two houses agreed to follow the procedure they had used in electing members of the Confederation Congress: nomination by one house and approval by the other. However, it is possible to reconstruct the approximate order of events in the election of the two Senators from newspaper accounts and William Plumer's autobiography.

The House Journals for the 10th do not record the fact, but the Journals on the 11th state that on the preceding day the House resolved to elect Senators on the morning of the 11th. The only actions recorded in the House Journals on the 11th are the following: (1) John Langdon's election "by a majority of ballots"; (2) the motion that he be appointed Senator; and (3) the roll call vote on the motion. However, the Journals for the 12th record that Nathaniel Peabody was "named by a majority of ballots" on the 11th. This is confirmed by a newspaper report which stated that immediately after the ballot for Langdon on the 11th, the House balloted a second time and elected Nathaniel Peabody over Samuel Livermore by a vote of 39 to 37. The newspaper reported that the question was then called on whether Langdon, who had been "nominated by ballot, ... should be appointed a Senator," and that this action was followed immediately by a similar action confirming Peabody's nomination.

Years later, William Plumer remembered the events in a different order. He said that he insisted that the vote electing Langdon should be put in writing and sent to the Senate immediately after the ballot for Langdon, and that when the House agreed, he demanded the roll call which nominated Langdon, 60 votes to 3. Plumer recalled that after the roll call for Langdon and after Peabody was elected by ballot, he called for the same procedure and made a speech against Peabody. Whatever happened on the afternoon of the 11th, the roll call on the motion to nominate Peabody was the first order of business on the morning of the 12th.

On the same morning, the Senate's first order of business was to approve the nomination of John Langdon. Immediately thereafter the Senate nominated Josiah Bartlett and sent the message to the House. According to the newspaper report, the House did not act on the Senate's nomination of Bartlett until after it had sent Peabody's nomination to the Senate and the Senate had rejected it. The House then accepted Bartlett's nomination during the afternoon session.

On 27 December Josiah Bartlett notified President Langdon that he could not accept election as Senator, and on 3 January 1789 the legislature elected Paine

Wingate in Bartlett's place. Wingate accepted the election on 6 January, but Langdon did not resign as president of the state until 22 January.

House Proceedings, Tuesday, P.M., 11 November

Whereas this House on the tenth instant determined on this day at ten o'clock A.M. they would appoint Senators to represent this state in the Congress of the United States and as they have this day proceeded to ballot, it appeared on counting the ballots that His Excellency John Langdon, Esq., was named by a majority of ballots.

Therefore voted, that he be and hereby is appointed a Senator on the part of this state to the Congress of the United States. Upon which vote the yeas and nays were called and are as follows, viz.,

Yeas [60]

Gains	Abbott
Hale	Cragin
Sheafe	Smith
Blanchard	Duncan
Leavitt	Wallace
Jos. Dow	Gove
Brown	Darling
Wiggin	Storey
Wheeler	Jackman
Plummer	Weare
Rogers	Wm. Page
Bartlett	Shepherd
Clark	Temple
Drew	Smith
Jere. Dow	Allen
Butler	Chase
Sullivan	Lane
Rand	Frink
Palmer	Copland
Brackett	Morse
Gilman	Tainter
Hoyt	Winch
D. Page	Brown
Cummings	Burnam
Taylor	Powers
Dole	Freeman
Page	Hough
Emerson	Franklin
O. Parker	Young
Barrett	Eames

Nays [3]

B. Clough   Flanders
Austin

60 Yeas.
3 Nays.

[The House sent a message dated 11 November, signed by Speaker Thomas Bartlett, notifying the Senate of Langdon's nomination. The message to the Senate is not in the House Journals but on a loose paper filed in State Records (Document Series of 1901), Nh-Ar.]

Adjourned to 9 o'clock tomorrow morning.

House and Senate Proceedings, Wednesday, 12 November

The Senate, A.M.[1]

A vote that His Excellency John Langdon, Esq., be and hereby is appointed a Senator on the part of this state to the Congress of the United States, was brought up, read, and concurred.

A vote that the Hon. Josiah Bartlett, Esq., be and hereby is appointed a Senator on the part of this state to the Congress of the United States was sent down for concurrence.[2]

The House, A.M.

Whereas this House on the 10th instant determined that on the morrow at 10 o'clock A.M. they would proceed to appoint Senators to represent this state in the Congress of the United States and whereas they then proceeded to ballot, it appeared on counting the ballots that Nathanael Peabody, Esq., was named by a majority of ballots.

Therefore voted, that he be and hereby is appointed a Senator on the part of this state to the Congress of the United States. Upon which vote the yeas and nays were called and are as follows, viz.,

Yeas [40]

Odlin	Palmer
Runnels	Badger
McMurphy	Brackett
Leavitt	Austin
Brown	D. Page
B. Clough	Cummings
Wheeler	Taylor
Jenness	Dole
Hilliard	Wm. Page
Jere. Clough	Wm. Peabody
Drew	Wallace
Green	Gove
Jere. Dow	Darling
Butler	Flanders

Weare	Winch
A. Parker	Burnam
Chamberlain	Franklin
M. Smith	Hutchens
Frink	Simpson
Tainter	Young

Nays [36]

Gains	Cragin
Hale	Jere. Smith
Sheafe	Duncan
Blanchard	Storey
Jos. Dow	Jackman
Wiggin	Wm. Page
Plummer	Shepherd
Rogers	Temple
Bartlett	Allen
Clark	Chase
Sullivan	Lane
Gilman	Copland
Hoit	Morse
Emerson	Brown
O. Parker	Powers
Barrett	Freeman
Abbott	Hough
Rand	Eames

40 Yeas.
36 Nays.

So it was determined.
Sent up by Mr. Smith.[3]

The Senate

A vote appointing Nathl. Peabody, Esq., a Senator on the part of this state to the Congress of the United States, was brought up and read. On a motion made and seconded that the yeas and nays be taken, they were as follows: the Hon. John Pickering, nay; Pierce Long, nay; Christo. Toppan, nay; John Bell, nay; Ebenr. Smith, yea; John Waldron, nay; Robt. Wallace, nay;[4] Ebenr. Webster, yea; Amos Shepard, nay; Moses Chase, nay; Francis Worcester, nay.

So it was nonconcurred.

The House, P.M.

Information having been given this House that the vote appointing Nathanael Peabody, Esq., a Senator was nonconcurred, and the following vote, having been previously sent from the honorable Senate for concurrence, was taken under consideration.

On a motion made in Senate, voted, that the Hon. Josiah Bartlett, Esq., be and hereby is appointed a Senator on the part of this state to the Congress of the United States. On concurrence of which vote the yeas and nays were called for and are as follows, viz.,

Yeas [60]

Gains	Dole
Hale	Wm. Page
Sheafe	Emerson
Odlin	Wm. Peabody
McMurphy	O. Parker
Blanchard	Barrett
March	Abbott
Leavitt	Rand
Jos. Dow	Cragin
Brown	Jere. Smith
Wiggin	Duncan
Wheeler	Wallace
Plummer	Gove
Rogers	Darling
Bartlett	Storey
Jenness	Jackman
Clark	Weare
Hilliard	Shepherd
Jere. Clough	A. Parker
Drew	Allen
Green	Chase
Jere. Dow	Lane
Butler	Frink
Palmer	Copland
Brackett	Morse
Gilman	Brown
Hoit	Hutchens
Page	Eames
Cummings	Freeman
Taylor	Powers

Nays [16]

Runnels	Temple
Clough	Smith
N. Peabody	Tainter
Sullivan	Winch
Badger	Hough
Austin	Simpson
Colonel Wm. Page	Young
Chamberlain	Burnam

60 Yeas.[5]
16 Nays.

So it was concurred.
Sent up by Mr. Temple.[6]

1. Although the Senate Journals do not distinguish between morning and afternoon sessions, the approval of Langdon and the nomination of Bartlett were the first orders of business on the 12th. Furthermore, the House learned of the Senate's nomination of Bartlett before its roll-call vote on Peabody's nomination that morning.

2. The Senate message to the House is in State Records (Document Series of 1901), Nh-Ar.

3. The House message to the Senate is in State Records (Document Series of 1901), Nh-Ar.

4. The printed journals of the Senate (*A Journal of the Proceedings of the Honorable Senate . . . Holden at Concord on Wednesday November 5th, 1788* [Portsmouth, 1788]) record Wallace as voting "yea."

5. The printed journals reported 61 yeas.

6. The next day the House and Senate directed the Secretary of State, Joseph Pearson, to notify John Langdon and Josiah Bartlett of their election and to request them to return an answer to the legislature at the next session. That afternoon, 13 November, President Langdon adjourned the legislature to meet again on 24 December. Bartlett refused the appointment (to President Langdon, 27 December, printed below). The legislature elected Paine Wingate on 3 January (House and Senate Proceedings, 1-3 January 1789, printed below). Wingate accepted the post on 6 January (to President Langdon, printed below), and Langdon resigned as president of New Hampshire and accepted his appointment on 22 January (House and Senate Proceedings, 22 January, printed below).

Newspaper Report of House and Senate Proceedings on Tuesday and Wednesday, 11 and 12 November[1]

On Tuesday, the *important* business of choosing SENATORS for Congress came on. His Excellency President [John] Langdon was first named, by ballot. After which, upon the second ballot, the numbers were for

General [Nathaniel] Peabody, 39
Judge [Samuel] Livermore, 37

The yeas and nays were then called for upon the question, that as His Excellency President Langdon was nominated by ballot, whether he should be appointed a Senator to the Congress of the United States, which was confirmed by a very large majority of yeas.

The like question was then put with respect to General Peabody, whether he should be appointed a Senator, upon which question the yeas and nays were as follow:

[Omitted here is the roll-call vote as given in the House Journals on 12 November.]

The vote appointing General Peabody a Senator in the Congress of the United States was sent up to the Senate, which vote they nonconcurred, the yeas and nays being as follow:

[Omitted here is the Senate vote rejecting Peabody's nomination as given in the Senate Journals on 12 November.]

On Wednesday, previous to the yeas and nays being called for on General Peabody's election, the Senate nominated Judge Bartlett as a Senator; which vote was not considered by the House, until the vote for General Peabody was sent up and nonconcurred; after which Judge Bartlett's appointment was concurred by a large majority.[2]

1. *New Hampshire Spy*, 14 November.
2. The elections of Langdon and Bartlett were reported widely throughout the states. See, for example, the Boston *Herald of Freedom*, 20 November; Hartford *Connecticut Courant*, 24 November; New York *Independent Journal*, 26 November; *Newport Herald*, 27 November; Philadelphia *Federal Gazette*, 1 December; Baltimore *Maryland Journal*, 9 December; and Fredericksburg *Virginia Herald*, 11 December.

William Plumer's Account of the Election of Senators, 11-12 November[1]

At the November session we were required to elect two Senators to Congress. John Langdon, then president of the state, was elected without opposition; but in electing the other Senator we were much divided. Samuel Livermore and Nathaniel Peabody were the principal candidates. The former was a Federalist, and the latter an Antifederalist; but the members did not in the election all vote according to their political creed—other considerations governed some of them. John Taylor Gilman, who was then treasurer and a zealous Federalist, used the whole weight of his influence, and it was considerable, in support of Peabody. I was in favor of Livermore, and decidedly opposed to Peabody, whom I knew was an artful, cunning, intriguing man, destitute of moral principle, and an inmate with infamous characters. I thought his election would reflect disgrace on the state, and I opposed him from principle.

The mode of electing Senators in the houses was by ballot, and as I heard Peabody was to be a candidate before he was publicly announced, I early resolved to have the names of those who voted for and against him entered on the journals, that it might appear who was responsible for his appointment. To effect this was a delicate and difficult task, for it was considered by many that the design of electing by ballot was to conceal from the candidates and the world for whom they voted, so as to leave each elector at perfect freedom to act according to his own unbiased judgment. As soon as Mr. Langdon was declared elected, I observed to the House that it was necessary that a written vote should be formed and passed appointing him a Senator, and sent to the other branch of the legislature for their concurrence; to this all consented. I then presented such a vote, the form of which was agreed to, and I moved that the question should be decided by yeas and nays. It was objected that such a mode was subversive of the principle of balloting. I replied, the balloting ought to be considered only as the *nomination* of a candidate for the Senate; and if we did not pass the vote then offered, Mr. Langdon could not be appointed, for the other branch of our legislature could not concur [in] his appointment until after our vote is sent to them. That I thought no man was worthy of being a representative, who sought to conceal his official conduct from his constituents, under the veil of a *secret ballot*. And as the choice of a Senator to Congress, for six years, was an important act of the legislature; and the [New Hampshire] constitution having explicitly provided that "upon motion made by *any one member*, the yeas and nays upon *any question* shall be entered upon the journal," I could not abandon my right of demanding them in this case. The yeas and nays were taken, and were for Mr. Langdon yeas sixty, nays three. As soon as Peabody was declared elected by ballot, the same course was adopted. On that question I made a speech to the House, in which I investigated his character and conduct in life, and contrasted it with that of the other candidate. The ayes were forty, and the nays thirty-six; but the Senate unanimously nonconcurred [in] the vote; appointed Josiah Bartlet Senator to Congress, to which the House agreed.

1. MS, Autobiography of William Plumer, Plumer Papers, DLC. The portion of the autobiography printed here was written in 1826. Plumer, a Federalist, represented Epping in the legislature in 1788.

The New Hampshire Election Law, 12 November[1]

State of New Hampshire

In the Year of Our Lord One thousand Seven hundred and eighty eight

[SEAL]   An act for carrying into effect an Ordinenance of Congress of the 13th Sept. last—relative to the Constitution of the United States

Be it enacted by the Senate and House of Representatives in General Court convened that the Inhabitants of the several towns & parishes plantations & places unincorporated in this State who are qualified to vote for state representatives shall assemble in their respective towns parishes or places on the third monday of December next to elect by ballot three persons having the qualifications required by the Constitution of the united States to represent this State in Congress—and the Selectmen of the several towns parishes & places aforesaid shall give fifteen days notice of the design of sd. meeting & shall during the Choice of Representatives preside at such meetings impartially and shall receive the votes of all the Inhabitants of such towns parishes & places present & qualified as aforesaid and shall sort and count the same in the meeting and in the presence of the town Clerk who shall make a fair record in presence of the Select men & in open meeting of the name of every person voted for and the number of votes against his name and a fair Copy of this record shall be attested by the Select men and Town Clerk and shall be sealed up and directed to the Secretary of this State with a Superscription expressing the purport thereof, and returned into the Secretary Office on or before the last Wednesday of December next who shall lay the same as soon as may be before the Senate & House of Representatives to be by them examined and in Case there shall appear to be any or the full number returned elected by a majority of Votes he or they so chosen shall be declared elected[2]—but in Case there shall not be any or the whole number elected the General Court shall make out a list of such persons as have the highest Number of Votes equal to double the number of Representatives wanting and if in completing such list it shall so happen that two or more persons voted for shall have an equal number of Votes the names of such Persons shall be put into a Box and the Secretary shall draw the Number wanting to complete such list. And the names of the persons contained in such list shall be transmitted to the Selectmen of the several towns parishes and places aforesaid who shall thereupon warn a meeting to be holden on the first monday of February next giving at least eight days notice & the Inhabitants of each Town qualified as aforesaid shall out of such list give in their votes for the number of Representatives wanting   And the Selectmen and the town Clerk as aforesaid shall cause a record of the number of Votes against each mans name in such list to be made & a Copy thereof attested in manner aforesaid to be transmitted to the Secretary's Office on or before the 20th. of the same February   And such Votes shall be examined by the President and Council for the time being or by such of them whose names are not contained in such list—And in Case it shall appear to the General Court that the names of a major part of the Council are on such list then the same shall be examined and counted by a Committee chosen by the General Court for that purpose   And such number of the Candidates equal to the number of Representatives wanting as shall have the highest number of Votes Shall be declared elected—And in Case it Shall so happen by reason of an equality of Votes a Choice of the whole number or any part of the Representatives wanting cannot be declared the names of such Candidates shall be put into a Box and the Secretary shall draw out the number wanting   And the person or persons so drawn shall be declared elected   And the members chosen and declared as aforesaid shall be the Representatives of the State of New Hampshire in the Congress of the United States for the Term of two years from the first Wednesday of March next—: And the Secretary Shall as soon as may be notify them of their appointment—And each of the Representatives Shall have a Certificate of their election under the Seal of the State Signed by the President and countersign'd by the Secretary—

And be it further enacted by the Authority aforesaid that the Inhabitants of the several towns & parishes plantations And places unincorporated qualified as aforesaid shall on the third monday of December next in town meeting assembled give in their votes for five persons Inhabitants of this State who shall not be Continental Senators Representatives or persons holding offices of profit or trust under the united States to be the electors for this State which Votes shall be taken recorded sealed and transmitted to the Secretary's Office at the same time and in like manner as Votes for Representatives to the Congress of the United States as is by this Act required   And the Secretary shall lay such Votes before the General Court to be counted and examined in the same manner as Votes for the representatives   And the persons having a majority of Votes[3] shall on the first wednesday of January next be duly Appointed & declared elected   And in Case it Shall so happen that the whole or any part of the number of electors are not chosen by the people then the General Court shall take a number of names out of the Candidates who have the highest number of Votes equal to double the number of electors wanting from which the Senate and House shall in such way and manner as may be by them agreed on proceed to appoint the Electors wanting—who shall be declared the Electors of this State for the President & vice Presidt of the Unitd States And notified to attend their duty as such—

And be it further enacted by the Authority aforesaid that if a Vacancy Shall happen in either of said Cases they shall be filled up in manner Aforesaid—

And be it further enacted by the Authority aforesaid that it shall be the duty of the town Clerks in the several Towns parishes and places in this State to Cause the last mentioned Votes for Representatives to be returned into the Secretary's Office before the said twentieth of Feby. or delivered to the Sheriffs of their respective Counties on or before the 15th. day of said month whose duty it Shall be to cause the same to be lodged in the Secretary's Office on or before the sd. 20 Feby. And the respective Sheriffs & Town Clerks shall be liable to the same pains and penalties for neglect of duty in this respect as they are by law in the Case of the Votes for President and Senators of this State

State of \
New hamps ∫

In the house of Represtives—Novr. 10th 1788

The foregoing Bill have been read a third time voted that it pass to be enacted

Sent up for Conccu—

[s] Thos. Bartlett   Speaker

In Senate Novr 12th—1788   The foregoing bill having been read a third time voted that the same be enacted

[s] John Langdon, President

1. (LT), Original Manuscript Acts, XI, Nh-Ar. For the distribution of the law throughout the state, see House and Senate Proceedings, 13 November, printed immediately below.

2. The language of the law is confusing at this point. Since three Representatives were to be elected at-large simultaneously, "majority of votes" did not mean a majority of the *total* popular vote. That is, a candidate must receive one more vote than one-sixth of the total vote cast to be elected.

3. As with Representatives, "majority of votes" did not mean a majority of the total number of votes cast. Since there were five Electors, a "majority" meant that to be elected, a candidate must receive one more vote than one-tenth of the total vote cast (see The Controversy over the Final Selection of Presidential Electors, 6-7 January 1789, printed below).

House and Senate Proceedings, Thursday, 13 November

The House, A.M.

Voted, that Mr. Odlin, Mr. Badger, Mr. Smith, Mr. A. Parker, and Mr. Young, with such of the honorable Senate as they may join, be a committee to consider in what manner the act for carrying into effect the ordinance of Congress of the 18th [13th]. of September last shall be printed and dispersed to the several towns and places in this state.

Sent up by Mr. Hoit.

The Senate

A vote for a committee to join a committee of the Senate to consider in what manner the act for carrying into effect the ordinance of Congress of September last shall be printed and dispersed to the several towns and places in this state was brought up, read and concurred. Mr. Webster and Mr. Bell joined.

The House, A.M.

The committee for considering in what manner the act for carrying into effect the ordinance of Congress of the 13th of September last [shall be printed and dispersed] reported, that the Secretary be ordered immediately to procure as many printed copies of the said act as may be sufficient for each town and parish and that the same be forwarded by express as soon as may be to the sheriffs of the several counties with a special direction to transmit them to the selectmen of the several towns and parishes within their respective counties. Signed, Christopher Toppan, for the committee.

Which report being read and considered, voted, that it be received and accepted.

The Senate

[The Senate accepted the above report.] [1]

1. The printed copies of the election law sent to the towns served as election warrants. That sent to Lebanon, for example, is endorsed "Warrant for a Representative to Congress 1788" (DLC).

Most towns balloted only once for Representatives, with each voter entitled to cast three votes. The exceptions were the towns of New Chester (the name was later changed to Hill) in Grafton County and Surry in Cheshire County. Both towns held three separate ballots, one for each Representative. At least one town (New Chester) did not hold its election on the appointed day. When the town meeting assembled on 15 December, it appeared to "those few that were assembled which was but eight in number that it would be best to adjourn the meeting and accordingly the meeting was adjourned until Wednesday the seventeenth . . ." (The Town Record Transcripts for Hill [II, 94-95], and Surry [I, 152], Nh).

Freeman's Oracle, 15 November

We have the pleasure to inform the public that the legislature have made choice of His Excellency John Langdon, and the Honorable Josiah Bartlett, esquires, to represent this state in the Senate of the United States under the new Constitution, and congratulate our customers on the appointment of gentlemen so well calculated to do honor to their constituents, and to promote the political happiness of the Union.

A Voice in the Air, New Hampshire Spy, 28 November

By inserting the following queries in your very useful paper, you will oblige an enquirer after truth and knowledge.

Quere. Whether those parts of the constitution of this state, which disqualified persons from being elected to the offices of president, senators, representatives, members of Congress, etc., are still in force?

Quere. Whether the new form of government, by leaving each state to form its own constitution, and laws for the support of their own religion, and disclaiming any power of trying such members as they may send to Congress, by a religious test, releases the inhabitants of either state from the obligations they have entered into with each other, by the constitution which they have adopted?

Quere. Whether the framers of the constitution of New Hampshire meant by the words *Protestant religion*, [1] to designate those denominations of Christians who protest against the errors of the Romish church, or whether they meant to render eligible, *Atheists, Deists, Infidels,* and *protestors against* ALL *religion,* and them only?

Quere. Whether by the laws of the state now in force, a person for denying the Trinity, or speaking against the scriptures of the Old and New Testament, is not liable to a severe and infamous punishment?

Quere. Whether it would not be disgraceful, as well as unconstitutional, to elect a man [to] high office, who, [under the la] ws of the state, is sub[ject to] [2] persons who *deny the Scriptures, and openly ridicule the Christian system?*[3]

1. The New Hampshire Constitution of 1784 required that the president of the state, state senators, state representatives, members of the Council, and delegates to Congress be of the Protestant religion (Thorpe, IV, 2458-67).

2. At this point, the original article is mutilated and several lines are missing from the page. The bracketed words are conjectural.

3. It is not clear to whom this essay refers. It may be a criticism of Josiah Bartlett, who was a Deist, although he kept his Deism private (see William Plumer's biographical sketch of Bartlett in N.H. *State Papers*, XXIII, 824-29). On the other hand, the phrasing of the final paragraph of the article—"*would* it not be disgraceful ... *to* elect a man"—suggests that the author was concerned about an impending election rather than a past one. The article is, therefore, more likely an attack on Nathaniel Peabody. A skeptic in religion and an Antifederalist in politics, Peabody had been defeated for the United States Senate (see House and Senate Proceedings, 12 November, printed above), and he was being mentioned as a candidate for the House of Representatives (*New Hampshire Spy*, 5 December, printed below).

Warrant for Town Meeting, Warren, Grafton County, 29 November[1]

This is to Notify & warn all the Legal Inhabitants of Warren qullified [*sic*] by law to Vote for State Representatives to meet at the house of Joshua Copp in said Warren on monday the fifteenth day of December Next at one Oclock afternoon to act on the following purposes (Viz)

Firstly to choose a moderator to govern said meeting

Secondly to Elect three persons having the quallifications required by the Constitution of the United States to represent this State in Congress

Thirdly to give in their votes for five persons Inhabitants of this State to be the Electors of said State for the President & Vice President of the United States.

Warren 29th. of November 1788   Joshua Copp   } Selectmen for
                                          Ephraim True } Warren

1. Transcript of Warren Town Records (LT), II, 65-66, Nh. The Warren call to election is printed as an example of the type of notice that was issued by selectmen throughout the state.

New Hampshire Spy, 2 December[1]

The "*loaves and the fishes,*" are all the cry in Boston, but the citizens of New Hampshire (or Portsmouth if you please) have no need of either. Consequently, we do not learn that the *seekers* here are very numerous; though it is said, perhaps with some truth, that there are some who would gladly partake of *a small slice.*

The Hon. Pierse Long,[2] Paine Wingate, and Benjamin West, esquires, are mentioned as characters deserving the suffrages of the patriotic and virtuous freemen of New Hampshire for federal Representatives. In these characters the commercial, agricultural, and civil interests of the state are so happily blended, as to excite the warmest exertions for their election.

1. No copy of the 2 December *Spy* has been located. The paragraphs printed here are from separate reprintings. Both paragraphs were datelined "Portsmouth, 2 December." The first appeared in the Boston *Massachusetts Centinel*, 10 December, and the second in the Portland, Me., *Cumberland Gazette*, 11 December.

2. Long, a Portsmouth merchant, served in the Confederation Congress (1784-1786) and in the New Hampshire Convention, where he voted to ratify the Constitution. From June 1788 until his death in April 1789, Long was a Rockingham County senator.

New Hampshire Spy, 5 December

Among other candidates for federal Representatives (says a correspondent from the country), the following gentlemen will, in all probability, command a majority of votes, viz., Hon. Nathaniel Peabody, Paine Wingate, and Simeon Olcott,[1] esquires.

We hear, that the inhabitants of one of the principal towns in this state have requested to know of his late Excellency, President [John] Sullivan, whether it was his desire to be elected one of the Representatives from this state, in the new Congress of the United States; assuring him, that if it was, their exertions should not be wanting to effect his election.[2]

1. Olcott, a Connecticut-born lawyer, established a practice in Charlestown, Cheshire County, N.H., before the Revolution. From 1784 to 1790 he was chief justice of the Cheshire County Court of Common Pleas. From 1790 to 1795 he was a justice on the New Hampshire Superior Court and from 1795 to 1801 chief justice of the court. A Federalist, Olcott filled the unexpired term of Samuel Livermore as a federal Senator from 1801 to 1805.

2. For a reply, see the *New Hampshire Spy*, 12 December, printed below.

Y.Z. to the Printer, New Hampshire Spy, 9 December

In proposing to the public John Parker, Esq., as a suitable person for an Elector, you will meet the wishes of many of your readers. The candor and integrity of this gentleman are so universally acknowledged, that, to insure him the suffrages of the citizens of this state, it need only be known that he is a *candidate*.

From a Correspondent, New Hampshire Spy, 9 December[1]

On Monday next our fellow citizens are to assemble, for the choice of three suitable persons, to serve as Representatives from this state in the Congress of the United States. In the above choice, we doubt not, our fellow citizens will be actuated by the purest motives; and, by their choice, evince to the world, that they are not the *dupes* of *party*, the *slaves* of *men*, nor the *echo* of the *self-created* GREAT. The LO! HERE'S! will undoubtedly be busy—mind them not; and know, that those who now crouch with the *duplicity* of *spaniel dogs*, for your suffrages, will turn *wolves*, when possessed of them.

1. This item is mutilated in the only copy of the 9 December *Spy* that has been located. Missing words are supplied from a reprint in the New York *Independent Journal*, 24 December.

New Hampshire Spy, 12 December

The *New Hampshire Spy* published on Friday, 12 December, was the last issue before election day and was crowded with election articles. Page 3, for example, contained nothing but election news, printed under a large headline that read "ELECTIONEERING." All of the election items published in the *Spy* on 12 December are printed below in the order in which they appeared.

Report on John Sullivan's Candidacy[1]

We have the best authority for asserting, that his late Excellency President Sullivan does not crave the suffrages of his fellow citizens as federal Representative, and that he has formally acquainted several towns (who have requested to know his mind upon the subject) that his intention was not to serve the state in that capacity, and that any votes given for him would be thrown away.

From a Correspondent

> *Hark! hark! my friends, the hydra junto roars,*
> *Ambition's surges lash* Hantonia's *shores:*
> *Repel their force: be firm in Virtue's cause:*
> *Support your rights: revere your* sacred laws.
> *In men of merit see your rights secure,*
> But turn! O! turn! from men of minds impure!

The great qualification of a legislator is *honesty*, and in the establishment of that, *a good character* is the great outline. The maxim, laid down by some writers, is a most dangerous one, *that a bad man in private life may be a good man in a public capacity.* The idea is contrary to reason; for the mind being the source of good and evil, where *infamy* dwells, the *villain* must exist, and, therefore, can only be screened by *hypocrisy.*[2]

Notice from the Printer[3]

The production of a *little* correspondent, received last evening, burlesquing several eminent characters, reminds us of the following scrap, which may serve to represent his affected *importance*, in trifling with characters, in our opinion, infinitely beyond his reach:

> "*His rod he drew, made of a sturdy oak,*
> *His line a* cable, *which in storms ne'er broke;*
> *His hook he baited with a dragon's tail,*
> *And sat upon a rock, and bobb'd for whale.*"

*Publicus to the Virtuous, Sensible and Judicious Freeholders
of the State of New Hampshire*[4]

The time is nigh at hand, when we are to give our suffrages for our representation in the national assembly of these United States. Never has any period presented itself to our view, through the long series of our troubles, more interesting than the present. Ability, integrity, and all the assemblage of heroic virtues were never more required than at *this day*! We have (and we trust), with views benevolent to ourselves and posterity, broken down the barriers of civil government, engaged in a defensive, but victorious war; of course, have been obliged to erect temporary establishments of civil policy for our protection, suitable to the exigencies of our affairs, and such as the minds of men would then bear, but perhaps defective in those essential points, which are to give consistency and energy to legislation, so as to embrace the general interest of the Union. Upon this retrospect has the wisdom of these states erected the Grand Federal CONSTITUTION, to unite in sentiment, and one uniform government, the various views and interests of the whole, and thereby give a spring to every national effort. In this view the Federal Constitution may be justly considered, with some few exceptions, a model of refinement in government and police, second to none; containing the great and essential rights of men, and those proper balances, and operative checks, between its several departments, that are so evidently necessary in a free constitution. To carry into effect, the salutary purposes of this liberal and beneficent Constitution; to amend its defects, and to give to each part of the Union its just rights; to frame laws consentaneous to its genius and principle; to form a nice symmetrical and harmonious system, demands the exertions of the honest heart, the soundest principles, and the profoundest abilities. On whom, then, my virtuous friends, will you fix your attention on this all-important occasion? Consider whom you can trust in these momentous affairs of state. Forgive my vanity if I should attempt to direct your choice, and put a negative on those equivocal characters that are held up as deserving attention. Will you choose the man who, in his public and private transactions, put on the garb of Jesuitism; whose creed is skepticism; who will vibrate, right or wrong, from one doctrine to another, and cannot be fixed at any given point; who openly avows, that mankind ought to be made use of, as the tools of a man's profession, for his profit and emolument; * * * * * * * * * * * * * *;[5] whose enmity is deep rooted against our most excellent *Federal Constitution*, because it is just; and whose principles, in a moral view, are disgraceful to a Christian age, and tend to destroy every social and political obligation? Would *this* be the *man* of your choice, *if any such there be*? No!--leave him to himself. Let justice haunt him without, and conscience goad him within, until repentance has completed the good work of reformation.[6] Or will you, my friends, attempt to foster with your smiles a character which has any *congeniality* with the *former*; a man who never acts with an open and liberal mind; who, with a [sl?]y, feigned gravity of countenance, when he wishes to develop your designs, and worm out the secrets of the heart, will a[sk] : *"What is the matter?"--"How is a[ll] this?"--"Let us know the secret of the affair!"--"I never heard a lisp of the matter!"--"Pray, can you give me any information about it?"* and the like, when, at the same time, the very thing about which his inquiries are made is minutely known to himself; though, with an affected gravity, he can roundly assert he knows nothing of the matter; * * * * * *;[7] a man who never yet was heard to give one pleasing encomium on the beauty and symmetry of that goodly edifice, so much admired by the republican and patriot; in short, the man who possesses countless disqualifying properties for such an important station? Should it be attempted, by advocates for such characters as before depicted (if any such there be), to form a union of interest, and thereby erect a *junto* to play into each other's hands at a future day; should they join hand in hand, and strengthen themselves for this purpose, as *Simeon* and *Levi* of old, then let the indignation of the just burn against them. Let their schemes be withered, and by a timely and well-directed opposition, let their hopes be blasted.

When I see our public papers announcing the pretensions of several worthy characters for high office, I am almost ready to accuse the public with criminal neglect, in suppressing the names of other distinguished patriots. Has the watchful guardian of our state slumbered? What demon of sloth has enervated our minds? Are there not characters yet unnamed of which New Hampshire can boast; why are they slipped aside? Are not the names of a [John] Sullivan, or a [John] Pickering, grateful to our ears?

> "Why should other *names* be sounded *more* than *theirs*?
> *Write* them *together; theirs* stand as *fair* in *name;*
> Sound them; they *become* the *mouth* as *well;*
> *Weigh* them; *they* are as *heavy.*"

Have not these patriots early distinguished themselves in their country's cause? Who headed the hardy veterans of New Hampshire? a Sullivan. Who called the first assembly of delegates of New Hampshire, and gave the royal cause a deadly blow? a Pickering! Have not their integrity and ability been witnessed in the Senate and the forum? Their steady, uniform conduct in support of the common cause, their unwearied endeavors in rearing the pillars of the federal structure, demand of every virtuous citizen their suffrages and support; that these patriots will proceed, if they are chosen, remains not a doubt. Men of true worth will not shrink from their duty when the calls of their country are importunate. Attend, ye well wishers to order and government; come forth, gird yourselves with strength, and be strong; divest yourselves, ye inhabitants of New Hampshire, of all party views and local attachments; act virtuously and ye will act nobly; let the general interest of the state and Union at large call forth your most animated exertions to support and elect such characters for our representation, who are known to be steady to their trust, inflexible to the allurements of power and obstinately just.

To the Printer

Among the several tickets for federal Representatives, which you have mentioned in the *Spy*, I have not observed one, which, from the disposition of the people to *a general coalition*, I think the most likely to succeed. I mean that for Woodbury Langdon,[8] Nath'l. Peabody, and Benjamin West, esquires. This ticket is founded on principles of reciprocal *accession*, and is calculated to embrace all parties. As there are two classes, one for, and one against amendments, an attempt to force a ticket composed entirely of gentlemen from either class would have a direct tendency to destroy that confidence and mutual goodwill, which, in the commencement of the new government, is so essential to ensure success. If a large number of respectable citizens yet wish for amendments, they undoubtedly are entitled to have their proposals duly discussed in the federal legislature; but if the Representatives consist of those only who are decidedly against any amendments, such a discussion will never, probably, take place. Therefore, to remove all complaints, and to give satisfaction, and a fair chance, even to those that differ from us in sentiment, prudence and good policy will dictate an adoption of the foregoing, or a similar ticket. Mr. Langdon, being intended as the representative of commerce, and his influence and abilities, in that line, being universally acknowledged, *he* probably will have the general suffrage in his favor.

Federal Electors

Attend to your interests, ye citizens of New Hampshire! Act nobly for yourselves and posterity, and be happy.

UNITE in choosing the following gentlemen for your Electors of a PRESIDENT and VICE PRESIDENT of the United States: Hon. John Parker, John Pickering, Joseph Cilley, Nath'l Folsom, and Timothy Walker,[9] esquires.

To the Printer

By inserting in your paper the following list of gentlemen, for ELECTORS of the President and Vice President of the United States, you will much oblige a customer: Hon. Judge [John] Dudley; John Pickering, Esq.; Christ'r Toppan, Esq.; Judge [John] Calfe, General [Thomas?] Bartlett.[10]

As the above gentlemen are of unexceptionable characters, and live within a small distance of each other, so that they may be convened without much expense, it is generally thought they will be chosen.

Patrick O'Fleming to Dear George

Why all this bust'ling, this noise & this pother?
Each paddy is trying to screw in his brother.
(The *fishes* how plump, the *loaves* how they rise,
How charming they swell to political eyes;
Than cake, more alluring, from wedding red hot,
Or pudding, fresh smoking, from family pot)
By my shout they are mad, they are blind, and can't see,
Or by St. Patrick's cap they'd all vote for me.

1. This paragraph appeared without heading or signature. Despite this report, Sullivan finished among the top six vote-getters in the first round of the elections (see House Proceedings, 2 January 1789, printed below).

2. When this piece was reprinted in the Boston *Massachusetts Centinel*, 20 December, it was preceded by this comment: "Electioneering is not endemic to Massachusetts; that it rages in New Hampshire will be seen by the following lines from a Portsmouth paper."

3. This notice appeared in brackets and without heading or signature. It is evidently by the *Spy*'s publisher, George J. Osborne.

4. The article was dated: "Dover, December 9, 1788."

5. The asterisks appear in the article as it was originally printed in the *Spy*. Presumably they represent material deleted by publisher George J. Osborne.

6. This attack was probably directed against Nathaniel Peabody, an Antifederalist and a religious skeptic. The *Spy* of 5 December (printed above) had identified Peabody as a leading candidate for Congress. The remainder of the paragraph may refer to Joshua Atherton, who

led the opposition to ratification in the New Hampshire Convention. Although no newspaper mention of Atherton as a candidate has been located, he finished seventh in the popular voting on 15 December, just ahead of Peabody (see Partial Returns for the First Election of Representatives, 2 January, printed below).

7. The asterisks are in the article as published in the *Spy*.

8. Langdon was a Portsmouth merchant and brother of Senator-elect John Langdon. He opposed independence and went to England during the early stages of the Revolution. He returned in 1777, served in the Continental Congress in 1779-1780, refused reelection to Congress, and was appointed a justice of the New Hampshire Superior Court in 1785. The General Court impeached him for neglect of duty in 1790, and he was allowed to resign in 1791.

9. Walker, a Concord merchant and politician, served for many years on the Rockingham County Court of Common Pleas. He later became a Democratic-Republican, but during the ratification struggle he was reputed to have kept several Antifederalist delegates occupied at dinner while the Federalists passed a crucial vote in the state Convention.

10. Toppan, a Hampton merchant and politician, represented his town in the New Hampshire Convention and voted in favor of ratification. He represented Hampton on several occasions in the House and was a Rockingham County senator from 1788 to 1790 and perhaps later.

Calfe was born in Massachusetts but lived most of his life in Hampstead, N.H. He represented his town in the state Convention, served as clerk, and voted for ratification. For twenty-five years he was clerk of the House.

Bartlett, a Nottingham politician, was Speaker of the House from 1787 to 1790. He represented his town in the New Hampshire Convention and voted for ratification. From 1790 until his death in 1805 he was a justice of the Rockingham County Court of Common Pleas.

The Election of United States Representatives and Presidential Electors, 15 December

The election law of 12 November provided that the state's three Representatives be chosen at-large; therefore, each voter was entitled to vote for three men. To be elected, a candidate needed one vote more than one-sixth of the total number of votes cast.

The *New Hampshire Spy* reported returns for Portsmouth and Northill on 16 December, and the *Freeman's Oracle* reported returns for Exeter on 20 December. The returns were tabulated officially by the legislature on 2 January 1789 and showed that no candidate had received enough votes to be elected, that is, 2,563 of the 15,377 votes cast. Hence a runoff election was required among the six leading candidates: Benjamin West, Samuel Livermore, Paine Wingate, Abiel Foster, John Sullivan, and Nicholas Gilman.

For the election returns located, see Partial Returns for the First Election of Representatives, 2 January; and for the House report naming the six candidates receiving the highest number of votes, see House Proceedings, 2 January, both printed below. See also The Second Election of Representatives, 2 February, printed below.

The election law of 12 November provided for the election of five presidential Electors at-large. To be elected, a candidate needed one vote more than one-tenth of the total popular vote. Final returns were tabulated by the legislature on 6 January 1789, and as with the election of Representatives, no candidate received enough votes to be elected, that is, at least 2,015 of the 20,142 votes cast. The law provided that in such cases, Electors would be chosen from among the leading ten candidates by the House and Senate "in such way and manner as may be by them agreed on."

For the election returns located, see Partial Returns for Presidential Electors, 6 January, and for the House report naming the ten candidates receiving the highest number of votes, see House Proceedings, 6 January, both printed below. For the election of Electors by the legislature, see The Controversy over the Election of Presidential Electors, 6-7 January, printed below.

New Hampshire Spy, 16 December (excerpt)

It is to be lamented, that in matters of such general consequence, our fellow citizens should be so *inattentive* to their true interests. At the above meeting[1] not more than one quarter of the inhabitants, qualified by law to vote, attended.

From the general complexion of affairs, it is very difficult to conjecture, whether there will be a choice, by the people of this state, of federal Representatives.[2] To *"divide and conquer"* is the maxim of *some*, while *others* are dozing away their privileges in sloth and supineness. *"Men and brethren, these things ought not to be so."*

1. This paragraph was preceded by a report of the 15 December Portsmouth town meeting that voted for Representatives and Electors.

2. On 26 December, the *Spy* reported: "So divided have the people of this state been in their choice of federal Representatives, that every idea of a choice by the people must be entirely given up." A rephrased version of this item appeared in the Boston *Massachusetts Centinel*, 3 January 1789. For a reaction, see the *Freeman's Oracle*, 13 January (printed below).

Senate Proceedings, Saturday, 27 December[1]

A vote that the Secretary be desired to open, file, and make out a list of the names of those gentlemen voted for as Representatives to Congress, also of Electors, and to lay the same before the Court for examination was sent down for concurrence.

1. On 13 November, President John Langdon adjourned the General Court to 24 December. On the 24th, Langdon prepared a long opening message to the legislators, noting that "the last session of the General Court was mostly taken up in making the necessary arrangements on the part of this state, for carrying into effect the federal government; of course, the general public business of the year has been put off until this time. It is therefore now necessary that the great and important objects of the state should be taken into consideration" (Langdon's message is in the *New Hampshire Gazette*, 7 January 1789). But Josiah Bartlett's refusal to serve as Senator and the failure of any candidate for Representative or Elector to obtain enough votes to win election made the elections a major focus of this session of the legislature as well.

Josiah Bartlett to President John Langdon, Kingston, 27 December[1]

I have received a letter from the Secretary informing me that the legislature at their last session at Concord did me the honor to appoint me a Senator to the Congress of the United States and requested an answer at their next now present session.

In answer to which I must inform Your Excellency and the legislature, that I am sorry to find that the circumstances of my family and my own precarious state of health will not permit me to accept of the appointment, as I am convinced that I should not be able to give that punctual attendance that the importance of the business requires. I have and shall ever retain a grateful sense of the honor and confidence reposed in me by the legislature in their appointing me to a trust so honorable and important and nothing but the want of health in myself and family would induce me to decline the business, as I now do.

1. RC, Fogg Autograph Collection, MeHi. The letter does not indicate the place from which it was written, but an unsigned copy (including some minor variations in wording) in the Bartlett Collection, Nh, is dated "Kingston, Decr., 29th, 1788."

House and Senate Proceedings, Wednesday, 31 December

The House, A.M.

Voted, that this afternoon be assigned for opening and counting the votes for Representatives and Electors which have been received from the several towns and places in this state.

Sent up by Mr. Young.

The Senate

A vote, that this afternoon be assigned for opening and counting the votes for Representatives and Electors was brought up, read and concurred.

The House and Senate, P.M.[1]

Both branches having met together agreeably to the above vote, the Secretary laid before the Senate and House of Representatives the votes returned for Representatives to Congress to be by them examined; which being done, the Senate retired to their chamber.

1. The record of the joint session is from the Senate Journals. On 6 January 1789, the *New Hampshire Spy* noted that "this business took up the time of both branches until 9 o'clock . . . ."

House and Senate Proceedings, Thursday, 1 January 1789

The House, A.M.

Voted, that Mr. Sheafe, Mr. Gilman, Mr. Smith, Mr. Page, and Mr. Freeman, with such of the honorable Senate as they may join, be a committee to reexamine and cast the votes returned for the choice of Representatives for the Congress of the United States.

Sent up by Mr. Temple.

The Senate

A vote for a committee to join a committee of the Senate, to reexamine and cast the votes returned for Representatives to Congress was brought up, read and concurred. Mr. Toppan and Mr. Shepard [joined].

The House, P.M.

Whereas this House on this day determined that at three o'clock, P.M., they would appoint a Senator to represent this state in the Congress of the United States and as they have proceeded to ballot it appeared on counting the ballots that the Hon. Payne Wingate, Esq., was named by a majority of ballots. Therefore, voted, that he be and he hereby is appointed a Senator on the part of this state to the Congress of the United States. Upon which vote the yeas and nays were called and are as follows, viz.,

Yeas [58]

Gains	Wm. Peabody
Hale	O. Parker
Odlin	Rand
McMurphy	Wallace
March	Gove
Leavitt	Darling
Jos. Dow	Storey
Brown	Jackman
Wiggin	Flanders
B. Clough	Weare
Wheeler	Shepherd
Rogers	Belding
Jenness	Gaskill
Clark	A. Parker
Hilliard	Chamberlain
Drew	Allen
Jere. Clough	Lane
Green[1]	Frink
Fifield	Reed
N. Peabody	Copland
Jere. Dow	Morse
Gilmore	Tainter
Badger	Winch
Pierce	J. Brown
Cummings	Powers
Taylor	Franklin
Dole	Patterson
Wm. Page	Simpson
Emerson	Hutchens

Nays [26]

Sheafe	Barrett
Runnels	Abbott
Blanchard	Cragin
Plummer	J. Smith
Bartlett	Duncan
Torr	Colonel Wm. Page
Sullivan	Richardson
Palmer	Temple
Brackett	Burnam
Gilman	Freeman
Hoit	Hough
Austin	Young
D. Page	Eames

58 Yeas————26 Nays.

So it passed in the affirmative.

Sent up by Mr. Odlin.

1. Green is recorded voting "yea" in the manuscript House Journals, but his name is not included in the roll call in the printed journals (*A Journal of the Proceedings of the Honorable House of Representatives ... begun and holden at Exeter, December 24th, 1788 ...* [Portsmouth, N.H., 1789]). For the Senate's concurrence in the election of Wingate, see House and Senate Proceedings, 3 January, printed below.

Newspaper Report of House Proceedings on Thursday, 1 January[1]

The Honorable Judge [Josiah] Bartlett having declined to accept of his appointment as a Senator of the United States, and having notified the President of the same, His Excellency, by a message to the House, informed them thereof. In consequence whereof, they appointed this day at three o'clock, P.M., for the choice of a Senator to represent this state in the Senate of the United States.

Previous to their entering upon the choice, some queries were proposed relative to the mode to be pursued in the choice. Whether, after balloting, any member should not call for the yeas and nays. This was said to be constitutional, and a liberty which no member of the House could be deprived of. It was objected to by some, as it would have a tendency of procrastinating the business, without producing any essential service. These observations took up a considerable time, when the House proceeded to the choice of a Senator; and the ballots being counted, it appeared, that the Honorable Paine Wingate, Esq., was named by a large majority.

[*This gentleman lately represented this state in the Congress of the United States, and is said to be a staunch Federalist.*][2]

1. *New Hampshire Spy*, 6 January.
2. The brackets are in the article. The *New Hampshire Spy* apparently sent a reporter to cover events in the legislature from 26 December to 2 January, a practice sufficiently novel that it justified a special notice set in italics on 6 January to call attention to it: "The

foregoing sketches are handed to our readers, not as matter for criticism, but information. The end aimed at was their gratification. An assurance of having effected that purpose will be sufficient to obliterate every idea of extra trouble (not to say expense) in obtaining them, and prompt us to persevere in such pursuits as may insure their patronage and esteem."

Partial Returns for the First Election of Representatives, 2 January

There is no complete tabulation of the votes for Representatives on 15 December 1788. The tables printed here are incomplete, since the returns on which they are based account for only 70 percent of the total popular vote recorded by the legislature. Each table lists the votes of the towns, county by county, for the twelve leading candidates. The tabulation for each county is followed by a paragraph listing the names of those who received fewer votes in that county.

Returns for the following towns are from the manuscript town records at the New Hampshire Historical Society: Dublin, Orford, Nottingham, Nottingham West, Mason, Salisbury, Stratham, Hampstead, New Market, Newton, Windham, Greenland, Danville, Londonderry, and Pembroke. The returns for Northill are from the *New Hampshire Spy* of 16 December. Derryfield returns are printed in George W. Browne, ed., "Early Records of the Town of Derryfield, now Manchester, N.H., 1782-1800," Manchester Historical Association *Collections*, IX (1906), 176-77. Returns for all other towns listed in the tables are from the transcripts of town records in the New Hampshire State Library. In this and the succeeding tables we have given the modern spelling of town names. Where town names have changed, we have placed the present-day name of the town in brackets following the eighteenth-century name wherever we have been able to identify the changes.

CHESHIRE COUNTY, PARTIAL RETURNS

Town	Benjamin West	Samuel Livermore	Paine Wingate	Abiel Foster	John Sullivan	Nicholas Gilman	Joshua Atherton	Nathaniel Peabody	Pierse Long	Benjamin Bellows	Moses Dow	Woodbury Langdon
Langdon	14			2	12	13				1		
Jaffrey			28			28					28	
Dublin	20		16	2	19	3	2					
Cornish	71	71			71							
Chesterfield	2	7	8		2					1		
Stoddard			17									
Rindge				11						20		
Plainfield	36	38										
Packersfield [Nelson]				39		39						
Newport	12	45			41					27	5	
Marlborough	2	2	18		2		18	18				
Lempster			26	26								
Swanzey	5	22			22					31		
Winchester	34	39	36									
Westmoreland	32	32		32								
Washington	37		36				25					
Surry	29	1				32				1		
Charlestown	33	30	3		30							
Totals	327	287	188	112	199	115	45	18	0	81	33	0

Others receiving votes: John Calfe (7), Elisha Payne (82), John Pickering (88), Simeon Olcott (17), Peter Green (1), Lemuel Holmes (3), Beza Woodward (2), Samuel Denny (13), Joseph T. Gilman (20), John T. Gilman (11), Thomas Brimmer (1), Thomas Bartlett (29), Benjamin More (1), William Harwell (1), Enoch Hale (1)

GRAFTON COUNTY, PARTIAL RETURNS

Town	Benjamin West	Samuel Livermore	Paine Wingate	Abiel Foster	John Sullivan	Nicholas Gilman	Joshua Atherton	Nathaniel Peabody	Pierse Long	Benjamin Bellows	Moses Dow	Woodbury Langdon
Thornton	33	33	33									
Piermont			36					35		11	23	
Orford		21	48			46		33				
Lebanon	17	22			20					29	3	
Lancaster		8	1							8		
Haverhill	31	31	17					21			27	
Hanover	11	19	3									
Cockermouth [Groton and Hebron]	23	26		27								
Bridgewater		21	19	2				3				
New Chester [Hill]		19	28					1				
Totals	115	200	185	29	20	46	0	93	0	48	53	0

Others receiving votes: Elisha Payne (50), John Pickering (2), Simeon Olcott (29), Beza Woodward (7), Christopher Toppan (1), Nathaniel Fulmer (1)

HILLSBOROUGH COUNTY, PARTIAL RETURNS

Town	Benjamin West	Samuel Livermore	Paine Wingate	Abiel Foster	John Sullivan	Nicholas Gilman	Joshua Atherton	Nathaniel Peabody	Pierse Long	Benjamin Bellows	Moses Dow	Woodbury Langdon
Dunstable [Nashua]	33	18		3	11	9	25					2
Henniker	7							28		35		19
Amherst	58		72	68	5	28	66	3	1	1	42	
Hancock		36			31					35		
Goffstown			46				50	58			1	
Francestown				19							19	21
Fishersfield [Newbury]												
Dunbarton	26	5		24			4			1		1
Boscawen	1	4	22	23			23	26			18	
Bedford	26			33			1					
Nottingham West [Hudson]	66	67				1	67					
Mason	41	43		40								
Weare	22		19	19			3	3				
Warner				23				23				
Salisbury	2	1	1	29	30		3	1				
Peterborough	34		29		29		5				5	
New Ipswich	66	54		65								
New Boston		5	26		5		26	1			25	
Lyndeborough		7	24	4	2				3	36	31	
Hopkinton	2		57	65								
Hollis	31	29		41	19	15	6			1		
Derryfield [Manchester]	1	7								15		
Hillsborough	32	1		24	21	1	9	6		1		
Totals	448	277	296	480	153	54	288	149	4	125	141	43

Others receiving votes: Timothy Farrar (194), John Pickering (24), Simeon Olcott (2), Ebenezer Webster (7), Archibald McMurphy (2), Christopher Toppan (13), John Bell (13), James Underwood (13), Joshua Wentworth (23), Samuel Dana (33), Bezalel Woodward (21), John Shepherd (3), Joseph Meriam (4), Ephraim Adams (4), Peter Green (23), Judge Woodward (26), Ebenezer Smith (1), Francis Worcester (1), John Stevins (1), Robert Means (9)

ROCKINGHAM COUNTY, PARTIAL RETURNS

Town	Benjamin West	Samuel Livermore	Paine Wingate	Abiel Foster	John Sullivan	Nicholas Gilman	Joshua Atherton	Nathaniel Peabody	Pierse Long	Benjamin Bellows	Moses Dow	Woodbury Langdon
Portsmouth	89	36	52		13	6		4	109	1		44
East Kingston			31	31							31	
Sandown		17	17	17								
Seabrook	24		24						24			
Stratham	10	53	64		8	2			59			
Brentwood	34		42									
Poplin												
[Fremont]	28	30	28				2					
Canterbury	37	4	26	42			18					
Chester	40		84	83	3	3		1			1	
Hampstead			31	12				20	25			
Rye	20	2			7	16		1	24			8
Newmarket	2	55	60						27			53
Salem			15	11		12	4	9		15		2
Deerfield	40	59	63	2	8		5	10	4			
Epping		31	31				6		37			
Nottingham	50	52		3		47			3			
Northill												
[North Hampton]	54	11	56						30			22
Chichester			14		14			14				
Newton												
Pelham	7		12		4	7					11	
Bow		6	16				17	14		2		
Greenland	1		30	1	7				29			28
Windham			13		13	13						
Plaistow	10		14	12			11	21	9			
Hawke												
[Danville]			2	4						3	8	
Kensington	38	9	51		39			6	5			
Londonderry												
[Derry]	32	26	29	3	9	37	2	71	3	30	3	5
Candia			26	13	1	27		1				
Concord	45	28	125	7			65	64	26			
Pembroke	6	1		27			3	6		4		
Totals	567	420	956	268	126	170	133	242	414	55	54	162

(Continued on following page)

ROCKINGHAM COUNTY, PARTIAL RETURNS *(continued)*

Others receiving votes: John Calfe (81), John Pickering (24), Simeon Olcott (98), George Gains (1), James Sheafe (1), Daniel Ring (1), Jonathan Dow (8), Ebenezer Thompson (2), Samuel Sherburne (62), Peter Green (16), C[——] Thomson (3), Thomas Cogswill (13), Joshua Wentworth (53), Thomas Bartlett (3), Oliver Peabody (1), John Dudley (22), Amos Shepherd (12), Nathaniel Folsom (12), Samuel Sumter (9), Timothy Walker (45), Jeremiah Gilman (2), Christopher Toppan (17), James McGregore (44), Archibald McMurphy (2), John Bell (16), John Prentice (3), Stephen Pharrar (3), Amos Cogswell (3), Daniel Bing (1), Jno Stevens (4), Daniel Emison (1), Colonel Webster (1), Samuel Dunell (1), Jno Hall (1)

STRAFFORD COUNTY, PARTIAL RETURNS

Town	Benjamin West	Samuel Livermore	Paine Wingate	Abiel Foster	John Sullivan	Nicholas Gilman	Joshua Atherton	Nathaniel Peabody	Pierse Long	Benjamin Bellows	Moses Dow	Woodbury Langdon
Dover		107	10			90		21	1	80		
Conway		3	7	13	4		7	3				
Wakefield		20	17		19				1		14	
Tamworth		23				23						
Rochester	37	50	33	3	3		14	1			12	
Meredith		26					11	20				
Somersworth	9	17	5			7				1		12
Middleton					20		21					
Madbury	19	5				5						
Lee	36	36			52							
Durham	20	29				29						
Totals	121	316	72	16	98	154	53	45	3	80	26	12

Others receiving votes: John Pickering (11), Thomas Bartlett (8), Ebenezer Smith (38), William Hooper (25), Joseph Badger (2), Joshua Wentworth (2), Christopher Toppan (1)

STATE-WIDE PARTIAL RETURNS

Benjamin West	1,578	Joshua Atherton	519
Samuel Livermore	1,500	Nathaniel Peabody	547
Paine Wingate	1,697	Pierse Long	421
Abiel Foster	905	Benjamin Bellows	389
John Sullivan	596	Moses Dow	307
Nicholas Gilman	539	Woodbury Langdon	217

House and Senate Proceedings, Friday, 2 January

The House, A.M.

The committee appointed to reexamine and cast the votes returned for Representatives to the Congress of the United States reported that they have carefully examined the returns and find the whole number of votes returned from the several towns and places to be fifteen thousand three hundred and seventy seven;[1] that two thousand, five hundred and sixty-three votes are necessary to make choice;[2] that no candidate has that number; that the six candidates who have the highest number of votes are as follows:

The Hon. Benjamin West, Esq.	2374.
The Hon. Samuel Livermore, Esq.	2245.
The Hon. Payne Wingate, Esq.	2054.
The Hon. Abiel Foster, Esq.	1236.
The Hon. John Sullivan, Esq.	1058.
The Hon. Nicholas Gilman, Esq.	861.

Signed, Christopher Toppan, for the committee.

Which report being read and considered, voted, that it be received and accepted and that the Secretary be desired to procure a sufficient number of copies of the foregoing list and disperse them to the several towns and places in this state in the same manner as he was directed to send out the last act.[3]

Sent up by Mr. Rogers.

The Senate

A vote to accept the report of the committee appointed to reexamine and cast the votes for Representatives was brought up, read, and concurred.

The House and Senate, A.M.[4]

The honorable Senate and House, being met in the Assembly Chamber, proceeded to examine the returns of votes for Electors, and after proceeding to examine those from a number of towns the honorable Senate withdrew and the House adjourned to 3 o'clock P.M.

The House and Senate, P.M.

The honorable Senate and House being again met in the Assembly Chamber proceeded to examine the remainder of the returns for Electors and formed a list of the same after which the honorable Senate withdrew and the House adjourned to 9 o'clock tomorrow morning.

1. The printed journals give 15,337 as the total number of votes cast. But both the manuscript journals and copies of the report the legislature ordered published and distributed give the total as 15,377. A copy of the printed report is in the Chase Collection, NhD.

2. New Hampshire's election law directed each voter to cast ballots for three Representatives. To win election, a candidate needed one vote more than one-sixth of the total votes cast. See the Election Law, 12 November, printed above.

3. The committee's report was printed, and the broadside circulated throughout the state. It ended: "N.B. That since the acceptance of the above report, the Honorable Paine Wingate, Esquire, one of the above named candidates, has been chosen a Senator to the Congress of the United States, and has accepted that office."

4. The events of both the morning and afternoon joint sessions are from the House Journals.

House and Senate Proceedings, Saturday, 3 January

The Senate

A vote appointing Paine Wingate, Esq., a Senator on the part of this state to Congress was brought up, read, and concurred.[1]

. . . .

A vote that Mr. Wallace and Mr. Shepard, with such as the House may join, be a committee to reexamine and cast the votes for Electors and report thereon as soon as may be, was sent down for concurrence.

The House

A vote came down from the honorable Senate for concurrence appointing Mr. Wallace and Mr. Shepherd a committee to reexamine and count the votes for Electors and report thereon as soon as may be, which was read and concurred, and Mr. March, Mr. Green, Mr. Emerson, Mr. Richardson, and Mr. Pierce joined. Sent up by Mr. Hilliard.

1. News of Wingate's election was published widely in the newspapers. See, for example, the *New Hampshire Spy*, 6 January; *Salem Mercury*, 13 January; Providence *United States Chronicle*, 15 January; Philadelphia *Pennsylvania Packet*, 22 January; New York *Daily Advertiser*, 26 January; Baltimore *Maryland Gazette*, 27 January; Richmond *Virginia Independent Chronicle*, 4 February; and Edenton *State Gazette of North Carolina*, 19 February. A false report that Samuel Livermore had been chosen in Bartlett's place appeared in four Massachusetts newspapers between 10 and 15 January, beginning with the Boston *Massachusetts Centinel*, but a series of retractions quickly followed.

Elisha Payne to Jonathan Freeman, Lebanon, 5 January (excerpt)[1]

I was as much surprised in reading your nomination of candidates for Representatives to find the name of a certain gentleman[2] wanting as I was when you gave me an account of the progress he made at the other sessions. He, together with his advocate, I think must feel the agreeable sensation of mortification in their turn as well as others. Wish you may be directed in all your proceedings with wisdom and prudence.

1. RC, Freeman Papers, NhHi. In January 1789, Payne, who had represented Lebanon in the state Senate in 1787 and 1788, was out of office; and Freeman was at Exeter representing Hanover in the House. The letter may have been forwarded to William Simpson, a state representative from Orford and a member of the Council. The letter is endorsed on the reverse side "Colo. Simpson." All three men had attended the New Hampshire Convention and had voted to ratify the Constitution.
2. This may refer to Nathaniel Peabody. On 12 November, the New Hampshire House supported him for federal Senator, 40 to 36, although the state Senate refused to concur; and he missed being nominated for Congress in the state's initial election for Representatives on 15 December by less than 100 votes (see House Proceedings, 2 January, n. 2, printed above). Thus Freeman could reasonably have been "much surprised" at Peabody's failure. If in fact Peabody was the "certain gentleman," then "his advocate" probably refers to John Taylor Gilman (see William Plumer's Account of the Election of Senators, 11-12 November, printed above).

Paine Wingate to President John Langdon, Stratham, 6 January[1]

I have received, from the Secretary of the State official notice, that I am appointed a Senator on the part of this state to the Congress of the United States. This renewed instance of the confidence and favorable opinion of the honorable the General Court, in placing me in so important and distinguished a station, does me the highest honor, and merits my most grateful acknowledgments. With diffidence I accept the trust, and permit me to assure Your Excellency and the honorable the legislature, that however unequal to the duties of the office, yet my constant zeal and my utmost attention and exertions shall be afforded to serve the interest of the United States, and of this state in particular, so long as I shall have the honor of continuing in that station.

1. RC, Fogg Autograph Collection, MeHi.

Partial Returns for Presidential Electors, 6 January

The table printed here was compiled from the same sources as the Partial Returns for the First Election of Representatives, 2 January (printed above). The local returns for Electors that have been located account for only 62 percent of the popular vote. The table below gives the partial returns for the candidates in each of the counties and the final returns as recorded by the legislature on 6 January. The number of towns for which returns have been located is indicated in parentheses after the name of each county. Following the table are the votes, county by county, giving the names of other men who received fewer votes than the ten leading candidates.

PARTIAL RETURNS, BY COUNTY

Candidate	Cheshire (17 towns)	Grafton (8 towns)	Hillsborough (23 towns)	Rockingham (26 towns)	Strafford (10 towns)	Partial Returns	Final Returns
Benjamin Bellows	293	50	291	270	105	1,009	1,759
John Pickering	156	60	239	419	50	924	1,364
Ebenezer Thompson	166	0	285	199	42	692	1,063
John Sullivan	102	44	13	250	152	561	872
John Parker	0	0	24	399	104	527	851
John Dudley	0	60	98	223	20	401	718
Joshua Wentworth	69	96	35	74	45	319	667
Nathaniel Folsom	9	0	0	281	93	383	589
Ebenezer Smith	67	35	164	57	43	366	543
Joseph Cilley	33	0	39	138	136	346	528

Others receiving votes:

Cheshire County: Timothy Farrar (85), Robert Wallace (52), Moses Dow (83), Timothy Walker (27), Amos Shepard (12), Nicholas Gilman (43), Pierse Long (123), Jonathan Freeman (44), Thomas Bartlett (23), Elisha Payne (140), Moses Chase (98), Mathew Thornton (90), Simeon Olcott (54), Samuel Livermore (49), Benjamin West (36), Joseph Badger (41), Robert Means (57), John Bell (1), Ebenezer Webster (29), Peter Green (11), Daniel Emerson (1), Joshua Bailey (22), Francis Blood (47), John Prentice (74), William Page (15), John Bellows (18), Bezaliel Woodward (53), Samuel Hunt (2), Josiah Richardson (33), John Taylor Gilman (16), Joseph Gilman (12).

Strafford County: Robert Wallace (25), Christopher Toppan (16), Moses Dow (4), Amos Shepard (24), Thomas Bartlett (24), Nathaniel Peabody (16), Paine Wingate (2), Mathew Thornton (19), George Reede (54), Simeon Olcott (10), Samuel Livermore (35), Francis Worcester (23), Joseph Badger (40), George Gains (1), Peter Green (14), Abiel Foster (2), John Waldron (23), Francis Blood (23), Theophilus Daine (62), Oliver Peabody (2), David Coffers (20), Daniel Ridge (21), John B. Hanson (18), David Copp (16), Samuel Hale (19), Dr. Cutter (1), Daniel Beardy (1).

Hillsborough County: Timothy Farrar (254), Robert Wallace (152), Christopher Toppan (14), Moses Dow (73), Woodbury Langdon (60), Cyrus Baldwin (44), Samuel Dana (81), Timothy Walker (10), Amos Shepard (43), Nicholas Gilman (54), Pierse Long (2), Jonathan Freeman (35), Joshua Atherton (18), William Simpson (25), Paine Wingate (2), Elisha Payne (31), Moses Chase (13), Archibald McMurphy (71), Mathew Thornton (65), Simeon Olcott (3), Samuel Livermore (15), John Calfe (83), Benjamin West (3), Francis Worcester (92), Joseph Badger

(Continued on following page)

PARTIAL RETURNS, BY COUNTY *(continued)*

(41), Robert Means (89), George Gains (78), John Bell (65), Henry Gerritt (30), Ebenezer Webster (59), Peter Green (82), John Wilkins (2), Abiel Foster (70), John Waldron (6), John Gove (36), Moses Nichols (3), Daniel Emerson (13), Jacob Abbott (26), Robert Megrager (10), Benjamin Pierce (7), [———] Penneman (3), Joshua Bailey (62), James Gipson (13), James Hosley (28), Charles Barrett (22), John Duncan (5), Archibald McHumphrey (5), Timothy Taylor (1), Nathaniel Peabody (5), John Stark (12).

Rockingham County: Timothy Farrar (32), Robert Wallace (160), Christopher Toppan (152), Moses Dow (64), Woodbury Langdon (37), Timothy Walker (157), Amos Shepard (5), Nicholas Gilman (11), Pierse Long (1), Thomas Bartlett (77), Nathaniel Peabody (107), Joshua Atherton (41), William Simpson (68), Paine Wingate (6), Elisha Payne (5), Moses Chase (51), Archibald McMurphy (23), Mathew Thornton (67), George Reede (13), Simeon Olcott (4), Samuel Livermore (139), John Calfe (137), Benjamin West (47), Francis Worcester (31), Moses Badger (52), Robert Means (54), George Gains (8), John Bell (96), Ebenezer Webster (7), Peter Green (75), Abiel Foster (100), John Waldron (43), John Duncan (5), Nathaniel Rogers (36), Daniel Bing (8), Thomas Odhoine (5), Francis Blood (7), John Sherburne (3), James MacGregore (22), James Sheafe (3), Isaac Thom (3), William Weeks (6), Enoc Stevens (7), John Prentice (42), John Bellows (6), Bezaliel Woodward (18), John Taylor Gilman (1), Samuel Sherburne (1), Dudley Odlin (17), Philip White (37), T[———] Adams (2), Daniel Runnells (3), Major McConnell (5), Reverend Flagg (1), Reverend Buchmaster (6), Reverend McClintock (6), Reverend Merrill (6), John Dinsmoor (1), James Betton (3), James Gilmore (5), [———] Golvan (2), John Bradley (1), John McClary (58), Ephraim Robinson (44), Moses Leavitt (1), Jonathan Dow (21), John McClury (52), Nathaniel Emerson (23), Robert Wilson (4), Moses Baker (2).

Grafton County: Timothy Farrar (33), Christopher Toppan (29), Moses Dow (5), Woodbury Langdon (47), Timothy Walker (25), Pierse Long (33), Nathaniel Peabody (12), William Simpson (36), Elisha Payne (13), Moses Chase (10), Simeon Olcott (12), Samuel Livermore (7), Benjamin West (9), Francis Worcester (54), Joseph Badger (38), Robert Means (34), George Gains (2), Peter Green (1), Abiel Foster (54), Enoc Stevens (1), Bezaliel Woodward (27), Samuel Sherburne (53), Dudley Odlin (36), Nathaniel Adams (49), Charles Johnston (29), Francis Smith (1), Jeremiah Smith (2), Philip White (16), Samuel Chase (19), Teukel Suliven (17), Esq. Mueser (17), Richard Bailtite (17), Aaron Kingsman (17), Eliza Welade (17).

The Controversy Over the Final Selection of Presidential Electors, 6-7 January

When the votes for Electors were tabulated in the legislature on 6 January, no candidate had enough votes to be elected. The law provided that in such a case the Electors should be chosen from among the top ten candidates by the two houses of the legislature "in such a way and manner as may be by them agreed on" (Election Law, 12 November, printed above). The House proposed that the Senate and House meet in joint session, but the Senate insisted upon voting separately.

The legislators were working against a deadline, since the congressional Election Ordinance of 13 September (printed, Chapter II) required that Electors be chosen on 7 January. Various attempts at compromise failed during the debates on 7 January, and the state ran the risk of not playing any part in the first presidential election. The deadlock continued until shortly before midnight when the House, reluctantly and under protest, gave in to the Senate.

No correspondence dealing with the dispute has been located, but the bare outlines indicated by the legislative journals for 6 and 7 January (printed below) can be filled in from two other sources. The *New Hampshire Spy* sent a reporter to observe the debates, and the paper published an account of what went on in its 13 January issue (printed below). Finally, the selection from William Plumer's autobiography (printed below) contains important detail about the dispute.

House and Senate Proceedings, Tuesday, 6 January

The House, A.M.

The committee for reexamining and counting the votes for Electors reported that they have examined and cast the same and find the whole to amount to twenty thousand one hundred and forty-two, and it appears there is no one chose, and the ten highest numbers are as follows: General [Benjamin] Bellows, 1759; Hon. Jno. Pickering, 1364; E[benezer] Thompson, Esq., 1063; General [John] Sullivan, 872; John Parker, Esq., 851; Judge [John] Dudley, 718; Colonel [Joshua] Wentworth, 667; General [Nathaniel] Folsome, 589; Colonel [Ebenezer] Smith, 543; General [Joseph] Cilley, 528. Signed, Robert Wallace, for the committee.

Whereupon voted, that the honorable Senate and House in one room assembled proceed by joint ballot tomorrow morning at ten o'clock to appoint Electors agreeably to an act for that purpose.

Sent up by Mr. Hough.

The Senate

A vote that the honorable Senate and House in one room assembled proceed by joint ballot tomorrow morning at 10 o'clock to appoint Electors agreeably to an act for that purpose, was brought up, read, and nonconcurred.

House and Senate Proceedings, Wednesday, 7 January

The Senate

A vote that the Senate and the honorable House of Representatives proceed as soon as may be to the choice of Electors in the separate branches was sent down for concurrence.

The House, P.M.

Voted, that the Senate and the honorable House of Representatives proceed as soon as may be to the choice of Electors in their separate branches; which vote was read and nonconcurred.

Voted, that Mr. Sullivan, Mr. Rogers, Mr. Plummer, Mr. Duncan, Mr. Page, Mr. Gove, Mr. A. Parker, Mr. Simpson, and Mr. Gilman, with such of the honorable Senate as they may join, be a committee to consider what method is most proper to be taken for the appointment of Electors and report thereon.

Sent up by Mr. Flanders.

The Senate

A vote for a committee to join a committee of the Senate to consider what method is most proper to be taken for the appointment of Electors and report to this House, was brought up, read, and concurred. Mr. Pickering, Mr. Smith, Mr. Toppan, Mr. Wallace, and Mr. Waldron joined.

A vote that General Benjamin Bellows, Esq., be and hereby is appointed one of the Electors of this state for the choice of the President and Vice President of the United States, was sent down for concurrence.

A vote that the Hon. John Pickering, Esq., be and hereby is appointed one of the Electors of this state for the choice of the President and Vice President of the United States, was sent down for concurrence.

A vote that the Hon. Ebenr. Thompson, Esq., be and hereby is appointed one of the Electors of this state for the choice of the President and Vice President of the United States, was sent down for concurrence.

A vote that the Hon. John Sullivan, Esq., be and hereby is appointed one of the Electors of this state for the choice of the President and Vice President of the United States, was sent down for concurrence.

A vote that the Hon. John Parker, Esq., be and hereby is appointed one of the Electors of this state for the choice of the President and Vice President of the United States, was sent down for concurrence.

The House, P.M.

The committee to consider what method is most proper to be taken for the appointment of Electors reported that the Electors be chosen in the separate branches of the legislature. Signed, John Pickering, for the committee.

Which report being read and considered, motion was made for receiving and accepting said report; on which motion the yeas and nays were called, and are as follows, viz.,

Yeas [29]

Gains	Gilman
Hale	Hoit
Sheafe	Pierce
Odlin	Abbott
March	Rand
Jos. Dow	Wallace
Emerson	Storey
E. Brown	Weare
Wiggin	Shepherd
Wheeler	Richardson
Plummer	Frink
Rogers	Morse
Bartlett	Brown
Duncan	Hough
Torr	

Nays [42]

McMurphy	Cragin
Blanchard	Gove
Jenness	Darling
Clark	Flanders
Green	Colonel Wm. Page
N. Peabody	Gaskill
Butler	A. Parker
Sullivan	Chamberlain
Brackett[1]	Temple
B. Clough	Smith
Hilliard	Allen
Drew	Chase
Palmer	Lane
Badger	Reed
D. Page	Winch
Cummings	Powers
Taylor	Freeman
Dole	Franklin
Wm. Peabody	Simpson
O. Parker	Young
Barrett	Eames

29 Yeas————42 Nays.

So it passed in the negative.

Voted, that Mr. Sheafe, Mr. Torr, Mr. Taylor, Mr. Frink, and Mr. Freeman, with such five of the honorable Senate as they may join, be a committee to nominate and report to this House out of the ten highest numbers voted for and returned as Electors of President for the United States the names of five persons who shall be considered as Electors for this state.

Sent up by Mr. Gains.

The Senate

A vote for a committee to join a committee of the Senate to nominate and report to the House, out of the ten highest numbers voted for and returned as Electors of President for the United States, the names of five persons who shall be considered as Elector[s] for this state, was brought up, read and concurred, with this amendment: that Mr. Toppan, Mr. Wallace, Mr. Webster, Mr. Chase, and Mr. Waldron be joined and that said committee report five persons out of the nomination list for Electors to be laid before the General Court for their concurrence.

Sent down for concurrence.

The House, P.M.

The foregoing vote [of the House] was returned by the honorable Senate for the following amendment: that Mr. Toppan, Mr. Wallace, Mr. Webster, Mr. Chase, and Mr. Waldron be joined and that said committee report five persons out of the nomination list for Electors to be laid before the General Court for their concurrence. On which amendment the yeas and nays were called and are as follows, viz.,

Yeas [29]

Gains	Wm. Page
Hale	Emerson
Sheafe	Abbott
March	Rand
Jos. Dow	Duncan
E. Brown	Wallace
Wiggin	Storey
Plummer	Shepherd
Rogers	Richardson
Bartlett	Frink
Hilliard	Morse
Torr	Tainter
Gilman	Brown
Hoit	Hough
Pierce	

Nays [42]

Odlin	O. Parker
Runnels	Barrett
McMurphy	Cragin
Clough	Smith
Wheeler	Gove
Rogers	Darling
Jenness	Flanders
Clark	Colonel Wm. Page
Green	Gaskill
N. Peabody	A. Parker
Jere. Dow	Chamberlain
Butler	Temple
Sullivan	Smith
Palmer	Allen
Badger	Lane
Brackett	Reed
D. Page	Winch
Cummings	Freeman
Taylor	Simpson
Dole	Young
Wm. Peabody	Eames

29 Yeas————42 Nays.

Voted, that the names of ten persons who have the highest number of votes as Electors for a President of the United States be put into a box and that the Secretary and Clerk of the House, under the inspection of two members of each branch, draw out the names of five persons who shall be considered as Electors for this state.

Sent up by Mr. Peabody.

The Senate

A vote that the names of ten persons who have the highest number of votes as Electors for a President of the United States be put into a box and the Secretary and Clerk of the House under the inspection of two members of each branch draw out the names of five persons who shall be considered as Electors for this state, was brought up, read, and nonconcurred.

The House, P.M.

The honorable Senate gave information that the foregoing [House] vote was nonconcurred.

Motion was then made that a vote be passed in the following words:

Whereas several votes of the honorable Senate now lies before the House appointing five persons as Electors of this state, voted, that the House proceed to consider and concur or nonconcur the said votes, at the same time solemnly protesting against the said mode of choice and declaring that in the opinion of this House the present mode of appointing Electors ought not to be considered as establishing a precedent, or drawn into example, or insisted upon as a rule in any future appointment of Electors. On which motion a division was called for as follows, viz.,

Whereas several votes of the honorable Senate now lies before the House appointing five persons as Electors of this state, voted, that the House proceed to consider and concur or nonconcur the said votes. On which division of said motion the yeas and nays were called and are [as] follows, viz.,

Yeas [35]

Gains	Barrett
Hale	Rand
Sheafe	Cragin
March	Smith
Jos. Dow	Duncan
E. Brown	Wallace
Wiggin	Storey
Plummer	Shepherd
Rogers	Richardson
Bartlett	Temple
Jere. Clough	Chase
Torr	Frink
Sullivan	Morse
Gilman	Tainter
Hoit	Brown
Pierce	Hough
Taylor	Eames
Emerson	

Nays [42]

Odlin	Jenness
Runnels	Clark
McMurphy	N. Peabody
B. Clough	Jere. Dow

Butler	Colonel Wm. Page
Palmer	Gaskill
Badger	A. Parker
Brackett	Chamberlain
D. Page	Smith
Cummings	Allen
Dole	Lane
Wm. Page	Reed
Wm. Peabody	Winch
Gove	Freeman
Darling	Simpson
Flanders	Young

35 Yeas————————32 Nays.

So it passed in the affirmative.

Proceeded to consider the remainder of said motion, which was in the following words: At the same time solemnly declaring that in the opinion of this House the present mode of appointing Electors ought not to be considered as establishing a precedent, or drawn into example, or insisted upon as a rule in any future appointment of Electors. On which the yeas and nays were called and are as follows, viz.,

Yeas [46]

Gains	Emerson
Sheafe	Wm. Peabody
Odlin	Barrett
Runnels	Rand
March	Cragin
Jos. Dow	Smith
Brown	Duncan
Wiggin	Wallace
B. Clough	Storey
Plummer	Colonel Wm. Page
Rogers	Shepherd
Bartlett	Richardson
Clark	Gaskill
Butler	Chamberlain
Torr	Temple
Sullivan	Chase
Palmer	Frink
Badger	Morse
Brackett	Tainter
Hoit	Brown
Pierce	Freeman
D. Page	Hough
Taylor	Eames

Nays [11]

Hale	M. Smith
Jenness	Allen
N. Peabody	Lane
Gilman	Reed
Wm. Page	Young
Gove	

46 Yeas—————————11 Nays.

So it passed in the affirmative.

Votes came down from the honorable Senate for concurrence appointing the Hon. Benjamin Bellows, John Pickering, Ebenezer Thompson, John Sullivan, and John Parker, esquires, Electors for this state. Which votes were read and motion made to concur [in] the same, on which motion the yeas and nays were taken, and are as follows, viz.,

Yeas [40]

Gains	Barrett
Hale	Rand
Sheafe	Cragin
March	Smith
Jos. Dow	Duncan
Brown	Wallace
Wiggin	Storey
Plummer	Colonel Wm. Page
Rogers	Shepherd
Bartlett	Richardson
Clark	Temple
Jere. Dow	Chase
Torr	Frink
Brackett	Morse
Gilman	Tainter
Hoit	Brown
Pierce	Freeman
D. Page	Hough
Taylor	Young
Emerson	Eames

Nays [19]

Runnels	Wm. Peabody
McMurphy	Gove
B. Clough	Gaskill
Jenness	Chamberlain
Green	Smith
N. Peabody	Allen
Butler	Lane
Palmer	Read
Badger	Winch
Page	

40 Yeas———————19 Nays.

So they were concurred.[2]
Sent up by Mr. Frink.
Adjourned to 9 o'clock tomorrow morning.

The Senate

Adjourned till tomorrow 9 o'clock A.M.

1. The manuscript journals of the House list "Mr. Brackett" voting "nay," while the printed journals do not indicate that Brackett voted. They do list "Mr. Bartlett" in both the yea *and* nay columns. Since the manuscript journals show that Bartlett voted "yea," the printer probably erred in substituting his name for Brackett's in the nay column of the printed journals.

2. Reports of the election of New Hampshire presidential Electors appeared in the Boston *Independent Chronicle*, 15 January; Hartford *Connecticut Courant*, 26 January; *New Hampshire Recorder*, 27 January; Providence *United States Chronicle*, 29 January; Philadelphia *Pennsylvania Packet*, 2 February; and Baltimore *Maryland Gazette*, 6 February.

Newspaper Report of House and Senate Proceedings on Wednesday, 7 January[1]

Owing to a disagreement between the two branches of the legislature, relative to the mode to be pursued in the choice of Electors, the business was procrastinated until near 12 o'clock at night, before an agreement took place. The Senate insisting upon holding their right of a negative upon the choice of the House; and the House, equally tenacious of their privileges, insisting, that in the present instance, the Senate had no right of controlling the choice of the House; but, that in choosing Electors, both branches should join, and proceed to the choice by joint ballot. A contrary step, it was considered by the House, would be establishing a dangerous precedent, an adherence to which might, at some future period, fatally affect the privileges of the people, of whom the House considered themselves as fathers and guardians. The observations made by the members of the Senate, relative to their prerogative, were pertinent, manly, and firm—as were those of the House—ingenious, deep, and well digested. The legislative contest, however, terminated in the lower branch's acceding to the proposal of the upper, and the choice was happily effected. What rendered the above circumstance more delicate, and greatly heightened the anxiety of the spectators, was a knowledge, that if a compromise did not take place before the close of the day, New Hampshire would lose the honor of giving her suffrages for a President and Vice President of the United States, and thereby be prevented from paying that tribute which her citizens owe to the great American Fabius.

1. *New Hampshire Spy*, 13 January.

Autobiography of William Plumer (excerpt)[1]

Town meetings were held on this winter for the first time for the choice of Electors of President and Vice President of the United States; but the candidates were so numerous that no one was elected. The law in that case provided that the legislature should from the ten persons having the highest number of votes elect five; but a question arose upon the mode of completing the election. The House contended that the two branches should meet in convention, and by joint ballot complete the election; but the Senate insisted that each house should vote separately, and each have a negative upon the other. After much altercation and debate, a joint committee was appointed, by votes in the separate branches, to consider and report upon the subject. Of this committee I was a member; we reported in favor of the two houses acting separately. The Senate accepted the report, but the House rejected it, ayes 29, nays 42. I thought the Senate was right, and the House wrong. I considered the appointment a legislative act, and that the House had no authority to compel the Senate to a joint ballot without their previous consent; that the House being more numerous, if the Senate came into convention, every Elector might be appointed against the will of all the senators, and the voice and responsibility of the Senate be destroyed. I therefore opposed the plan adopted by the House. It was necessary that the Electors should be chosen on or before the 7th of January. The legislature sat very late in the evening of that day after repeated attempts, but in vain, to obtain a vote for a separate ballot; at eleven o'clock at night I discovered that the leaders of opposition in the House were determined, if they could not induce the Senate to meet in convention, they would themselves yield. I was apprehensive the Senate, some of the members not being of the sternest stuff, would recede; I therefore went privately to the Senate door, and informed Colonel [Christopher] Tappan, a senator, of the fact, and urged him not to submit to the claim of the House. The Senate soon after sent us a vote appointing the five Electors, accompanied with a committee of five of their members, informing us that the Senate had resolved in no event to consent to a joint ballot. After they retired, much altercation ensued, but just before midnight we concurred [in] the appointments, ayes 40, nays 19. General [John] Sullivan then requested the Speaker, that as *I knew the way to the Senate chamber*, I might be appointed to inform that body of our vote; I was accordingly requested, with two other members, to deliver the message. I thanked the House for the appointment, and assured them that it gave me great pleasure to think my conduct had in any degree contributed to the preservation of the right, and independence of the two branches of the legislature. I delivered the message without delay, to the great satisfaction of the Senate. Those Electors afterwards voted for George Washington to be President, and John Adams Vice President.

1. MS, Autobiography of William Plumer, Plumer Papers, DLC.

House and Senate Proceedings, Thursday, 8 January

The House, A.M.

Voted, that the Electors within this state for a President and Vice President of the United States meet at Exeter on the day appointed by the resolve of Congress for that purpose.

Sent up by Mr. Chamberlain.

The Senate

A vote that the Electors within this state for President and Vice President of the United States meet at Exeter on the day appointed by the resolve of Congress for that purpose was brought up, read, and concurred.

New Hampshire Recorder, 13 January (excerpt)

Our informant[1] further adds, that General [John] Sullivan has signified his intention of resigning the office of federal Representative, should he be elected.

1. The publisher identified him as a "Gentleman from Exeter." The informant also reported that William Gardner was chosen state treasurer after John Calfe declined the post and that the legislature had chosen five Electors.

Freeman's Oracle, 13 January

A citizen of New Hampshire enquires of the editor of the *Massachusetts Centinel* [Benjamin Russell] by what authority he published, in his paper of the 3d instant, that unqualified falsehood announced in the words following—*"There is not the most distant prospect of federal Representatives in New Hampshire"*—and takes occasion to inform him there is not one opposer of the new system in the nomination, notwithstanding the utmost efforts of the leaders of the party,[1] and that it is the general opinion of this state that it will be wise in the people to make alterations in their national government *only* when experience shall have dictated the necessity of the measure and pointed to such reforms as bid fairest to preserve their rights, their tranquility, and their happiness.

1. The "Citizen of New Hampshire" misread the Boston *Massachusetts Centinel* report. Russell's paper was merely reporting that the vote in New Hampshire was so scattered that no *national* Representatives would be chosen at all in the first round of elections. Also, Russell was only rephrasing an observation made in the *New Hampshire Spy* on 26 December (see *New Hampshire Spy*, 16 December, n. 2).

House and Senate Proceedings, Thursday, 22 January

The House, A.M.

The Secretary came down from the honorable Senate with the following letter from His Excellency:

Gentlemen of the Senate and gentlemen of the House of Representatives:

As the time is near at hand when I shall set out for New York to attend my duty in the Senate of the United States, you will permit me to express the great obligation I feel myself under to my fellow countrymen for the many marks of confidence and respect they have from time to time been pleased to show me. And the honorable Senate and House of Representatives in particular will please to accept my most grateful thanks for their kind attention during my administration.

With my mind deeply impressed with gratitude to my country, I now resign my office of chief magistrate.

The prosperity of New Hampshire will ever lay near my heart, and my constant endeavors shall be to promote her happiness, and that we may all enjoy true liberty, peace, and safety is the most ardent wish of, gentlemen, your most obliged, obedient, and humble servant, John Langdon.[1]

Voted, that Mr. Sheafe, Mr. N. Peabody, Mr. Page, Mr. Simpson, and Mr. Smith, with such of the honorable Senate as they may join, be a committee to consider of a letter from His Excellency the President, this day received and report thereon.

Sent up by Mr. O. Parker.

The Senate

A vote for a committee to join a committee of the Senate to take under consideration a letter from His Excellency the President and report thereon was brought up, read, and concurred. Mr. Toppan and Mr. Shepard joined.[2]

1. Langdon's letter was dated Exeter, 22 January.
2. For the reply to Langdon's letter, see House and Senate Proceedings, 24 January, printed below.

Warrant for Town Meeting, Warren, Grafton County, 23 January[1]

This is to notify & warn all the Legal inhabitants of Warren quallified by Law to vote for State Representitives to meet at the house of Joshua Copp in said Warren on monday the second day of February next at one oclock in the afternoon to act on the following purposes (viz)

1st To choose a moderator to govern said meeting

2nd To Elect three persons having the qualifications required by the constitution of the united States to Represent this State in Congress.

3rd To see where the Town shall think most proper to hold the Annual meeting.

Warren January 23rd. 1789

Joshua Copp } Selectmen for
Ephraim True } Warren

1. Transcript of Warren Town Records (LT), II, 66, Nh. The warrant is printed as an example of the warrants issued by selectmen throughout the state.

House and Senate Proceedings, Saturday, 24 January

The Senate

The committee on His Excellency's letter this day received[1] beg leave to report the following answer:

May it please Your Excellency,

The Senate and House of Representatives having been honored with your letter of this day containing a resignation of the office of chief magistrate beg leave to assure Your Excellency that they most sensibly realize the loss they sustain by Your Excellency's leaving the chair of state in which you were placed by the free suffrages of your fellow citizens.

The regret which they cannot but feel on this occasion is greatly alleviated when they reflect on the agreeable prospect they have of Your Excellency's service in the important office to which you have been appointed in the new government. When they consider Your Excellency's abilities, commercial knowledge, and experience in the various concerns of the state and review your conduct in the many and important offices you have sustained with reputation to yourself and entire approbation of your fellow citizens, they are led to entertain the most flattering hopes that Your Excellency's future services may be eminently useful to this state.

The legislature sincerely thank Your Excellency for the many and repeated proofs they have had of your attention to them and unremitted endeavors to promote the welfare of the state.

They are happy that the office which Your Excellency has resigned is filled for the present by a gentleman of whose abilities and integrity they have the most unequivocal proofs.[2]

With the most ardent wishes for your personal happiness and welfare, they most cordially unite with Your Excellency in praying that the citizens of this state may long enjoy the blessings of true liberty and good government.[3]

Which is submitted by Christopher Toppan, for the committee.

The report of the committee on His Excellency's letter having been read, voted, that it be received and accepted and that Mr. Toppan and Mr. Smith be a committee, with such of the honorable House as they may join, to present the same to His Excellency John Langdon, Esq., was sent down.

The House

[The House received the Senate's message to the President and its vote to appoint a committee to present it.] Which report and vote was read and concurred, and Mr. Gains, Mr. Hale, and Mr. Sheafe joined.

The committee having presented the foregoing, His Excellency was pleased to return them the following answer:

Gentlemen: I return you my most sincere thanks for the friendly and polite manner in which you have been pleased to communicate the vote, together with the report of the committee from both branches of the legislature of this state.

I assure you, gentlemen, I shall ever consider this public testimony of the approbation of my past conduct by that honorable and respectable body as [one] of the happiest circumstances of my life. Words are wanting to express my feelings. I can only repeat the great obligations I am under to my country.

I also am happy when I reflect that the chair of government is now filled by a gentleman whose great abilities and firm integrity render him an ornament to his country; that his administration may be honorable and the people happy under it is the sincere wish of, gentlemen, your most obedient servant, John Langdon.[4]

1. The phrases "this day received" and (in the paragraph following) "this day" refer to 22 January, the day on which Langdon's letter was received by both houses and the day on which the joint committee was appointed to draft a reply. See House and Senate Proceedings, 22 January, printed above.

2. This refers to John Pickering, who automatically became acting president of the state following Langdon's resignation. The Constitution of 1784 provided that "Whenever the chair of the president shall be vacant, by reason of his death, absence from the state, or otherwise, the senior senator for the time being, shall, during such vacancy, have and exercise all the powers and authorities which by this constitution the president is vested with when personally present" (Thorpe, IV, 2,465).

3. On 27 January, a correspondent in the *New Hampshire Spy* commented on Langdon's resignation in similar terms: "The regret (says a correspondent) every good citizen feels on the resignation of His Excellency, President Langdon, is in some respect alleviated by the reflection, that His Excellency will find an ampler field for the exercise of his distinguished talents, in the Senate of the United States, and that he is succeeded in office by a gentleman of acknowledged abilities, independent judgment, and illustrious merit."

4. Although Langdon's reply was dated "Portsmouth, Janr. 26th," it was nevertheless incorporated in the journals of the 24th.

New Hampshire Spy, 27 January

It must afford much satisfaction to the citizens of this state when they reflect, that although some opposition was at first made to the new system of government, owing in part to its principles not being properly known, and fully investigated, the proceedings of this state have hitherto been perfectly Federal. Our Senators are Federal—strictly so—and our Representatives cannot but be so, the probability is, that out of the nomination list, the following gentlemen will, almost unanimously, be elected, Hon. Samuel Livermore, Esq.; Benjamin West, Esq.; Nicholas Gilman, Esq. The two former gentlemen were of this state's Convention. The first warmly advocated the new system, and both voted in favor of its adoption. Mr. Gilman lately represented this state in the Congress of the United States, and added to his Federalism, which is unquestionable, is said to possess many shining, political virtues. With such props, Hantonia still may rise; her drooping commerce may once more revive, agriculture be encouraged, arts flourish and be protected, and the voice of complaint and discord no more be heard in the land,

> But Heav'n-born peace and liberty shall join;
> Embrace all ranks—in ev'ry order shine;
> Blaze in the cabinet—in the forum rise,
> And reign the glory of the Western skies.

Tobias Lear to John Langdon, Mount Vernon, 31 January (excerpt)[1]

We were pleased [to] see your name as a Senator from New Hampshire. Judge [Josiah] Bartlett, I presume, is attached to the government, which will give New Hampshire a Federal voice in one branch of Congress—though it is a matter of concern to see, by the late papers, that there was no prospect of a Federal representation from that state.[2]

1. Copy, William Whipple Papers, DLC. Lear was George Washington's personal secretary. Similarly, on 1 December, William Jackson wrote Langdon from Philadelphia that his elec-

tion was "an event on which every Federalist of our city felicitates himself" ([A. L. Elwyn, ed.], *Letters by Washington, Adams, Jefferson, and Others, Written During and After the Revolution, to John Langdon, New Hampshire* [Philadelphia, 1880], 89).

    2. See the *Freeman's Oracle*, 13 January, printed above.

The Second Election of Representatives, 2 February

    On 2 February, Benjamin West, Samuel Livermore, and Nicholas Gilman were elected Representatives from New Hampshire. The *New Hampshire Spy* accurately predicted the result before the election, and the *New Hampshire Gazette* followed with the same prediction on 4 February. However, Benjamin West refused to serve, and the state was forced to call a special election in order to replace him (see The Resignation of Benjamin West and the Calling of a Special Election for a Representative, 16-20 May, printed below).

    For the election returns located, see Partial Returns for the Second Election of Representatives, 21 February; and for the official tabulation of the votes, see Proceedings of the President and Council, 21 February, both printed below.

House and Senate Proceedings, Monday, 2 February

The House, A.M.

    Whereas the members of the General Court by reason of the present session cannot attend the meetings in their respective towns for choosing Representatives this day to be holden,

    Therefore resolved, that the members of the General Court may give in their votes for Representatives to the Congress of the United States this afternoon at this place and that they be sorted, counted, and certified by the President and any two of the Council, any law to the contrary notwithstanding.

    Sent up by Mr. Brown.

The Senate

    A resolve that the members of the General Court may give in their votes for Representatives to the Congress of the United States this afternoon at this place and that they be sorted, counted, and certified by the President, and any two of the Council, any law to the contrary notwithstanding, was brought up, read, and concurred.

Proceedings of Goffstown Town Meeting, 2 February[1]

    At a Legal meeting of the Inhabitants of the Town of Goffstown holden at the Meeting house in Goffstown on the first Monday of Feby 1789—

    Vote for Representatives in Congress—Nobody——00000

    A true Copy attest Moses Little Town Clerk P.T.

                                  John Butterfield } Selectmen of
                                  Philip Clement   } Goffstown

Instead of voting for individuals the Inhabitants of Goffstown passed the following votes vizt

1st Voted not to bring any Votes for Representatives

2dly Voted that it is the *scence* of this meeting that there are but three persons sent to the people to chuse out of—And that the other three (if voted for) the votes must be lost—as Mr [Paine] Wingate is appointed a Senator—Mr [John] Sullivan (as we hear) absolutely declines accepting (if chosen)[2] and Mr [Nicholas] Gilman is supposed to be a half pay Officer[3] And that none but Children can be brot to beleive that Hobson's choice was very considerable when he was to have that or none—All which we the abovenamed Clerk & Selectmen Humbly *submitt* to your Honors consideration

> Moses Little Town Clerk P.T.
> John Butterfield ⎱ Selectmen of
> Philip Clement ⎰ Goffstown[4]

1. MS copy of Goffstown return (LT), Miscellaneous Collection, Box 10, MHi. The copy is endorsed: "This is Copied verbatim & literatim from Goffstown return—If tis worth your reading accept it from your yours. O.P——."

2. See *New Hampshire Recorder*, 13 January, printed above.

3. Gilman served as adjutant of the Third New Hampshire Regiment in the Continental Army during the Revolution. The Goffstown meeting apparently believed that he was receiving a half-pay pension in 1789, that the pension made him a federal officeholder, and that it automatically disqualified him from sitting in Congress. Article I, Section 7, of the Constitution provides that "no person holding any Office under the United States, shall be a Member of either House during his Continuance in Office."

4. The town of Dunstable (whose name was later changed to Nashua) at first also refused to vote for Representatives because "one of these Gentlemen which are returned in the precept of the second day of January last was Elected a Senator in the proposed Congress of the United States   The Minority Not withstanding claimed their Right of Suffrage where on the Ballots were again called for and there was brought in for Benja. West, Esqr. 8; Saml. Livermore, Esqr. 8; Nicholas Gilman, Esqr. 8" (Transcript of Nashua Town Records, III, 721-22, Nh).

House and Senate Proceedings, Tuesday, 3 February

The Senate

A vote that Mr. Long and Mr. Wentworth be a committee, with such of the honorable House as they may join, to consider and report how the elections of the Senators for this state to the Congress of the United States shall be certified and the Senators commissioned, was sent down for concurrence.

The House, P.M.

A vote came down from the honorable Senate for concurrence appointing Mr. Long and Mr. Wentworth a committee, with such of the honorable House as they may join, to consider and report how the election for the Senators for this state to the Congress of the United States shall be certified and the Senators commissioned, was read and concurred and Mr. Richardson, Mr. Pierce, and Mr. Sheafe joined.

Sent up by Mr. Chamberlain.

The Senate

A vote that Mr. Toppan and Mr. Wentworth, with such as the honorable House may join, be a committee to consider and report how the vacancy of any person or persons, who may be chosen federal Representatives, declining the trust, shall be filled, was sent down for concurrence.

The House, P.M.

A vote came down from the honorable Senate for concurrence appointing Mr. Toppan and Mr. Wentworth, with such of the honorable House as they may join, a committee to consider and report how the vacancy of any person or persons who may be chosen federal Representatives declining the trust shall be filled, was read and concurred and Mr. N. Peabody, Mr. Green, and Mr. Gains joined.

Sent up by Mr. Darling.

Adjourned to 9 o'clock tomorrow morning.

New Hampshire Spy, 3 February

In nothing, says a correspondent, are we so inconsistent with ourselves as in panting after enjoyments, which we imagine would certainly confer happiness, if attained. Yet we generally find these objects of our wishes incapable, when possessed, of affording the blessings we expected; or we neglect to cultivate them. In nothing can this be better exemplified [than by an] [1] anxious solicitude for the [preservation of that liberty] to which freedom of election, [and] government by the representatives of our choice, is deemed absolutely essential. How do the vassals of Europe pant for this darling prerogative! Through what deluges of blood have Americans waded to secure their first privilege of free citizens! And yet (shameful to behold) how many of them suffer it to lie dormant and how few exercise their boasted right! How will every foreigner be struck with astonishment, when he hears we are so lost to a sense of freedom, that not more than a fourth, in some instances not a tenth, of us think worthwhile to assist in the choice of legislators, etc., and this too on the most important occasions. Oh, Americans, why do you thus prove yourselves unworthy of freedom?

1. Several words are obliterated by ink. Words in brackets are conjectural.

Votes of the New Hampshire Presidential Electors, 4 February [1]

State of New Hampshire

We the Subscribers being appointed by the Legislature of this State Electors of two persons for President of the United States met at Exeter in said State on Wednesday the fourth Day of February AD 1789 agreeably to resolve of Congress and Act of this State and Voted by Ballot for two persons for said Office and upon counting the Votes it appeared there were five Votes for His Excellency George Washington Esqr and five for the Honble John Adams Esqr of the Massachusetts for President of the United States and we hereby Certify the same accordingly—Given under our Hands at Exeter the Day and Year aforesaid—

	Benja. Bellows
	John Pickering
[Signed:]	Jno Sullivan
	Ebenezer Thompson
	Jno Parker

1. (LT), RG 46, DNA.

House and Senate Proceedings, Wednesday, 4 February

The House, A.M.

The committee who were appointed to consider how the elections of Senators to the Congress of the United States shall be certified, etc., reported that each of them should be furnished with a commission signed by His Excellency the President and countersigned by the Secretary, and that the Executive be desired to take order accordingly. Signed, Pierce Long, for the committee.

Which report being read and considered, voted, that it be received and accepted.

Sent up by Mr. Parker.

The Senate

A vote that each of the Senators to Congress should be furnished with a commission signed by His Excellency and countersigned by the Secretary and that the Executive be desired to take order accordingly, was brought up, read, and concurred.

John Langdon's Commission as United States Senator, 6 February[1]

The State of New-Hampshire

To the Honorable John Langdon Esquire . . . . Greeting.

Whereas the Legislature of this State at their Session at Concord in November last, Reposing special Confidence in your Fidelity Integrity and Ability, did make choice of you as a Senator for this State to the Congress of the United-States to be convened at New-York on the first Wednesday of March next—In Pursuance of which Choice and a Subsequent Order of the Legislature aforesaid—You are hereby constituted and declared a Senator, on the part of this State, of the Congress of the United States—

To have and to hold the Office of a Senator of the Congress of the United-States with all the Powers Rights and Privileges to the same appertaining for and during the term of Six Years from the said first Day of March next agreeably to the Federal Constitution—

In Testimony whereof We have caused the Seal of our said State to be hereunto affixed Witness His Excellency John Pickering Esquire the President of our State at Exeter the Sixth Day of February in the Year of our Lord One Thousand Seven Hundred and Eighty Nine and of American Independence the Thirteenth—

By His Excellency's Command
by and with Advice of Council.   [SEAL]   [s] John Pickering
   [s] Joseph Pearson Secy

1. (LT), RG 46, DNA. A similar commission was issued to Paine Wingate on 13 February (RG 46, DNA).

House and Senate Proceedings, Saturday, 7 February

The Senate

An act in addition to an act for carrying into effect an ordinance of Congress of the 13 of September 1788 relative to the Constitution of the United States passed 12th of November last, having been read a third time, voted, that the same be enacted.

The House

An act in addition to an act for carrying into effect an ordinance of Congress of the 13th of September 1788 relative to the Constitution of the United States passed the 12th of November last, was read a third time and passed to be enacted.

Sent up by Mr. Brown and Mr. Copland.[1]

1. Later on the same day the President, with the consent of both houses, adjourned the legislature until Tuesday, 26 May.

The New Hampshire Supplementary Election Law, 7 February[1]

State of New Hampshire

In the year of our Lord One thousand seven hundred and eighty nine.—

[SEAL]   An Act in addition to an Act for carrying into effect an Ordinance of Congress of the thirteenth of September 1788 relative to the Constitution of the United States passed the 12th of November last—

Whereas it is necessary that some further Provision should be made for filling up vacancies that may happen in the representation of this State to the Congress of the United States

Therefore

Be it enacted by the Senate and House of Representatives in General Court convened That all vacancies of Representatives to Congress that shall happen by death resignation or other wise shall be filled up in manner following to wit— Upon Notice of any such Vacancy the President for the time being by & with the advice of Council shall issue Precepts to the Select Men of the several Towns & parishes plantations & places unincorporated in this State requiring them to warn the Inhabitants of their respective Towns parishes plantations & places to meet on a certain day in said Precept to be mentioned to vote for a Representative or Representatives to fill up such Vacancy And such meetings shall be notified warned & governed And the Votes received sorted counted certified & returned in the same manner as the said Act directs by a certain day in said Precept to be mentioned And the Secretary shall lay said Votes before the President & Council at their first meeting after the same shall have been returned as aforesaid to be by them examined And if a choice by a majority of Votes shall have been made the same shall be declared and the Person or Persons so chosen shall be notified of their appointment in the manner said Act directs—But if no such Choice shall be made by the People then the said President and Council shall issue a new Precept which shall contain a number of names out of the Candidates voted for, who have the highest number of Votes—equal to double the number wanting—in which Precept the said Select men shall be required (on a certain day in said Precept to be mentioned) to assemble the Inhabitants of their respective Towns parishes plantations and places to give in their Votes out of the Number so returned by the President and Council for the Representatives wanting which Votes shall be returned at the time and in the manner as shall be directed in said Precept and the Persons having the greatest number of Votes shall be declared elected as aforesaid

And the respective Sheriffs and Town Clerks shall be liable to the same Penalties for neglect of the duties injoined on them in pursuance of this Act as they are in said Act—

In the house of Representatives Feby 7th 1789

The foregoing Bill having been read a third Time Voted that it pass to be enacted.

Sent up for Concr

[s] Thos. Bartlett Speaker

In Senate the same day, this bill was read a third time voted that the same be enacted

[s] John Pickering President

1. (LT), Original Manuscript Acts, XI, Nh-Ar. The document is endorsed on the reverse side, "Copied for the press—*Recorded.*"

Proceedings of the President and Council, Friday, 20 February[1]

Present: His Excellency John Pickering, Esq., President; the Hon. Ebenr. Smith, Peter Green, Robt. Wallace, Josiah Richardson, and William Simpson, esquires.

Proceeded to open and enter the returns for the Representatives of the federal government.

Adjourned till tomorrow.

1. Council Records, II, 66, Nh-Ar. The Council records for this period are printed in N.H. *State Papers*, XXI, 739-75.

Partial Returns for the Second Election of Representatives, 21 February

The voting returns for the second election on 2 February, as for the first election on 15 December 1788, are incomplete. The town returns located account for only 68 percent of the popular vote recorded by the Governor and Council. And, although the election law of 12 November limited the election to the six candidates who received the highest number of votes in the first election, there were a few scattered votes for other men.

Returns for the following towns are from the manuscript town records at the New Hampshire Historical Society: Stratham, Hampstead, New Market, Pembroke, Londonderry, Nottingham, Greenland, Windham, Danville, Durham, Francestown, Amherst, Mason, Dublin, and Cockermouth. Derryfield returns are printed in George W. Browne, ed., "Early Records of the Town of Derryfield, now Manchester, N.H., 1782-1800," Manchester Historical Association *Collections*, IX (1906), 179. Returns for all other towns listed in the tables are from the transcripts of town records in the New Hampshire State Library.

CHESHIRE COUNTY, PARTIAL RETURNS

Town	Benjamin West	Samuel Livermore	Paine Wingate	Abiel Foster	John Sullivan	Nicholas Gilman
Langdon	10	10		1	9	
New Grantham [Grantham]	10			10		10
Dublin	25	23		5		22
Claremont	15	16		1		16
Chesterfield	11			11		11
Charlestown	31	31			1	30
Unity	15	15		15		
Stoddard	16			16		16
Rindge	32			32		32
Packersfield [Nelson]	20	1		21		21
Marlborough	22	4		18		22
Lempster	7			7		7
Winchester	17	16				13
Westmoreland	29	29		28	1	
Washington	17	15		15		
Surry	28	28				28
Totals	305	188	0	180	11	228

GRAFTON COUNTY, PARTIAL RETURNS

Town	Benjamin West	Samuel Livermore	Paine Wingate	Abiel Foster	John Sullivan	Nicholas Gilman
Warren	16	16		16		
Piermont	10	9		10		
Lebanon	23	23		23		
Haverhill	11	11		11		
Cockermouth [Groton and Hebron]	13	13		13		
Bridgewater	28	22		16		
New Chester [Hill]	10	8		10		1
Totals	111	102	0	99	0	1

HILLSBOROUGH COUNTY, PARTIAL RETURNS

Town	Benjamin West	Samuel Livermore	Paine Wingate	Abiel Foster	John Sullivan	Nicholas Gilman
Derryfield [Manchester]	9			9		9
Hancock	27	27		26		
Francestown	15			15		15
Dunbarton	38	38		38		
Amherst	28	21	4	17	3	15
Mason	25	25		25		
Weare	12	12		12		
Peterborough	14	14				14
Dunstable [Nashua]	8	8				8
New Ipswich	42	42		15		30
New Boston	16	15		14	5	
Lyndeborough	38	38		38		
Hopkinton	52	6		52		47
Hollis	42	20		40		24
Totals	366	266	4	301	8	162

ROCKINGHAM COUNTY, PARTIAL RETURNS

Town	Benjamin West	Samuel Livermore	Paine Wingate	Abiel Foster	John Sullivan	Nicholas Gilman
Portsmouth	94	100		17		96
East Kingston	15	15		15		
Sandown	12			12		12
Seabrook	13			13		13
Stratham	22	19		28		6
Brentwood	54	54				54
Poplin						
[Fremont]	14	14		13		1
Canterbury	33	20		48		3
Chester	47	48		49		3
Hampstead	16			16		16
Rye	36	36		22		13
Newmarket	77	77				77
Salem	14	9		14	1	7
Deerfield	25	25		25		
Concord	84	41		82		44
Pembroke	27	26		27		1
Kensington	40	40		13		27
Londonderry						
[Derry]	46	36		34	35	38
Candia		2		15	1	16
Epping	40	40		3		37
Nottingham	64	64		3		61
Chichester	12	12		12		
Pittsfield			22			
Greenland	24	23		10	15	
Windham	19	11		8	5	11
Plaistow	6	7		1		7
Hawke						
[Danville]	13			13		13
Totals	847	719	22	493	57	556

STRAFFORD COUNTY, PARTIAL RETURNS

Town	Benjamin West	Samuel Livermore	Paine Wingate	Abiel Foster	John Sullivan	Nicholas Gilman
Dover	58	58		16	1	49
Conway	17	17		15	2	
Wakefield	15	15		13		2
Tamworth	11	11				11
Somersworth	15	15				15
Madbury		18	18			16
Lee	19	19		19		
Durham	50	50				50
Totals	185	203	18	63	3	143

STATE-WIDE PARTIAL RETURNS

Benjamin West	1,814
Samuel Livermore	1,478
Paine Wingate	44
Abiel Foster	1,136
John Sullivan	79
Nicholas Gilman	1,090

Proceedings of the President and Council, Saturday, 21 February[1]

Present as yesterday.

Proceeded to enter the remainder of the returns for Representatives of the federal government, and upon casting up said returns, we find that the Honorable Benjamin West, Esq., had 2733, the Hon. Judge Livermore had 2166, the Hon. Nicholas Gilman had 1619, the Hon. Abiel Foster 1612, the Hon. John Sullivan had 154, and the Hon. Paine Wingate had 4.[2] By which it appears that the Hon. Benja. West, Samuel Livermore, and Nicholas Gilman, esquires, are chosen to represent this state in Congress.[3]

[Signed:] John Pickering, President; Ebenr. Smith, Peter Green, Robert Wallace, William Simpson, Josiah Richardson, councillors.

1. Council Records, II, 66-67, Nh-Ar.

2. This figure is in error. Town vote returns indicate that Wingate received at least 44 votes (see Partial Returns for the Second Election of Representatives, 21 February, printed above).

3. Results of the election were widely reported throughout the states. For example, see the *New Hampshire Spy*, 24 February; *Boston Gazette*, 2 March; Hartford *Connecticut*

Courant, 9 March; Philadelphia *Pennsylvania Mercury,* 10 March; Baltimore *Maryland Gazette,* 13 March; and Richmond *Virginia Independent Chronicle,* 18 March. The *Massachusetts Magazine* of February 1789 commented that New Hampshire's choice "evinced her attachment to the general Constitution."

Joshua Atherton to John Lamb, Amherst, 23 February[1]

It is with every sentiment of respect, that I acknowledge the honor of your favor of the 27th. December last, together with the agreeable commission therein assigned me. To have rendered any service to so distinguished a patriot and ornament of his country as Governor [George] Clinton, to have put it more in the power of his great abilities to secure to the United States freedom and happiness, to have placed him as one of the principal directors of the scene in so interesting a period would indeed have been rendering a service highly honorable to myself, and of the utmost importance to our tottering country.

Of the event of elections in New Hampshire I need not inform you. They terminated under the direction of the Federalists (as the abettors of the new system *modestly* call themselves) and I suppose very much to their satisfaction. This was inevitable.

It would be unentertaining to you to be informed by what means the Federalists (if I after them may use so improper a term) have eventually brought about their own measures, notwithstanding they seemed throughout the course of the whole transactions, to have been on the brink of failure. In our General Assembly, [where for a] long time there was a decided majority against the new system, opposition has ceased—and the language is "It is adopted, let us try it." No slaves could speak a language more agreeable to their masters. And the unavailing measure of choosing a committee to consider the address of New York relative to a new convention for the purpose of amendments was all the Assembly of New Hampshire found leisure to do.

Not to descend too far into particulars, it is very obvious, that a kind of aristocratical influence throughout the states buoys up and carries forward a system of government wherein all the solid foundations of liberty are (strange to relate) totally forgotten. To carry on the farce the Federalists have taken the liberty to step onto the ground of their opponents, and, clothing themselves with their armor, talk high of amendments—and by a kind of duplicity, often successful if not discovered, are taking possession of the political citadel under the style of friends.

You, sir, live in the very focus of the maze of collected wisdom from the body of our political system, and will discover how the planets move. Happy should I be, to owe to your goodness (so far as is compatible with propriety and your convenience) the earliest information of the real characteristics of this new collection of satellites. Will they prove by their ordinances that they have the general liberty firmly at heart? Will they establish the common law for the rule of the judicial department? Or will they canonize the civil law, that imperceptible, but sure engine of political slavery? Will they unequivocally guard us against the oppression of standing armies? Will they separate with inviolable boundaries the legislative, the executive, and the judicial departments? Will they make us a free and happy people? Or in other words, that I may sum up the whole in one sentence, will they make the real liberty of the citizens, the immediate object of all legislation? If they should be so happy as to speedily determine upon amendments, will they take it upon themselves to do it? Their authority seems much better suited to the calling a convention for the purpose.

Before I conclude, it may not be improper to add by way of apology, that New York, Virginia, and other states having gone so fully into the detail of amendments, the strokes of abler hands ha[ve] rendered the lines of my feeble pen unnecessary.

1. RC, Lamb Papers, NHi. The letter was endorsed to "John Lamb, Esqr. Chairman of the Federal Republican Comtee. for the City of New York, &c." Lamb was a New York Antifederalist who corresponded with other Antifederalists around the country in order to coordinate opposition to the Constitution and, in November 1788, to secure the election of George Clinton as Vice President under the new Constitution (see Chapter XIV).

New Hampshire Spy, 10 March[1]

This state, after having been for some time past engaged in her federal elections, has lately completed them—and in the choice she has made has evinced her attachment to the general Constitution. Engaged in organizing her militia, which is by far the best disciplined in the United States, and encouraging the domestic arts, she enjoys a tranquility, which, while it must be highly advantageous to her citizens, adds greatly to her reputation.

1. This item, dated "Portsmouth, March 10," is taken from a reprint in the *New York Daily Gazette* of 23 March. It evidently first appeared in the *New Hampshire Spy* on 10 March, but only a mutilated copy of that issue remains.

Samuel Livermore to President John Pickering, Concord, 20 April[1]

I have the honor to receive your commission certifying my appointment as a Representative to Congress. Permit me through Your Excellency to express my grateful sense of the honor done me by my fellow citizens in electing me to this important office, and to assure them of my warmest attachment to their service.

Sickness has detained me till this time but I am now on my journey to New York.[2]

If I did not conceive it to be of importance to proceed immediately there, I should have given myself the pleasure to visit my friends in Portsmouth and to have taken part of the circuit of the Superior Court in my way.[3]

1. RC, Emmet Collection, NN.
2. On 6 March, the *New Hampshire Spy* reported that Livermore was suffering from "gout in his stomach," and that his recovery "was a circumstance rather to be wished than expected...."
3. At the time of his election to Congress, Livermore was chief justice of New Hampshire, and his nonattendance at court became a political issue. On 17 June, a joint legislative committee reported that Livermore's election to Congress was "incompatible with the office of chief justice of this state," and recommended that "the legislature should address the

Executive to remove him from that office." The House and Senate concurred in the report, and on 19 June both houses recommended to President John Sullivan that he remove Livermore "from the seat of chief justice of the Superior Court of Judicature, he having accepted a seat in Congress which is incompatible with the office of chief justice of this state" (House and Senate Journals, 17, 19 June). Although New Hampshire had no law that specifically forbade one man holding both offices, Livermore did resign in 1790.

The Resignation of Benjamin West and the Calling of a Special Election for a Representative, 16-20 May

The election of 2 February did not complete New Hampshire's delegation to the first Congress because Benjamin West refused to serve. The exact date of his resignation is not known. West had refused elective office several times previously, and some members of the legislature may have learned of his intention to refuse a seat in Congress almost as soon as he was elected. On 3 February, the day after he was elected, a joint legislative committee was appointed to "consider how the vacancy of any person or persons who may be chosen federal Representatives declining their trust shall be filled" (House and Senate Proceedings, 3 February, printed above). On the other hand, the *New Hampshire Spy* reported as late as 27 March that West was on his way to New York to take his seat.

West may have resigned, then, at any time following his election. No newspaper report of his decision has been found prior to that in the *New Hampshire Spy* on 16 May (printed below). It is a brief item announcing James Sheafe as a candidate to replace West. The article's phrasing implies that West's resignation had been reported earlier—perhaps in a supplement to the 9 May issue of the *Spy* which has not been located.

It is not clear why West was twice a candidate only to resign after his election, or why his decision was not made public until May. "Senex," writing in the *New Hampshire Spy* on 19 May (printed below), charged it was a case of "ridiculous vanity, in having it to tell ... that [he] ... refused the highest offices in the state." Perhaps West's Federalism explains his silence. He was unquestionably the most popular Federalist candidate for the House of Representatives, finishing first in the popular balloting in both the December and February elections. His name on the ballot in December almost certainly deprived Antifederalist Joshua Atherton (who finished seventh in the voting) from a place on the second election ballot in February. Whatever his reasons may have been, his resignation forced the state to hold a third election on 22 June in order to complete its delegation to the first Congress.

For the election returns located, see Partial Returns for the Special Election to Replace Benjamin West, 15 July; and for the official tabulation of the votes, see the Proceedings of the Governor and Council, 16 July, both printed below.

New Hampshire Spy, 16 May

Mr. West having declined his appointment as a Representative from this state to the Congress of the United States, the public index points toward Colonel James Sheafe, of this town, and seems to say *"thou art the man."*

Senex, New Hampshire Spy, 19 May

In unfolding the pages of history, we often meet with examples of the most illustrious men seeking for public offices, and by every honorable means seeking occasions to do their country good, esteeming it their greatest glory, and then only the noblest employed, when their lives were devoted to the public service. How shall we compare these testimonies of ancient and modern patriotism with each other, without exhibiting strong and humiliating proofs of the degeneracy of the latter! The reflection would be melancholy were a comparative view of the subject to apply to the present age in general. This application, it is happy for us, cannot be made, but in a partial manner only; and here we have to go no farther for an example of dissimilarity of manners than the limits of our own state, and this in the person of one of our federal Representatives, who declined a seat in the representative body of Congress, notwithstanding he was honored by a distinguished majority of votes given him by the free citizens of this state, in two successive efforts. When a gentleman proposes himself as a candidate to an office, where the whole people have to assemble to elect him, it is highly indelicate to reject their favors, after a compliance with his wishes; but what must we think of him, who will thus suffer his friends and fellow citizens, to collect twice upon the same occasion (including thereby a twofold honor) by which a prodigious expense of time and trouble must be the consequence, and then to decline a predilection in his favor. Must we not think he is egregiously deficient in point of politeness? Nay, would not every man who had given such a person a vote feel hurt upon his refusal? Although this is not precisely the case of Mr. W——, yet in effect it is the same. When a candidate knows he will be voted into office (as in our popular elections, and by the current of the papers, it is almost impossible he should not know), he is not legally bound to acquaint his friends in a public manner, that there are certain reasons which induce him to decline an acceptance of their suffrages; yet he may do it consistent with the strictest propriety, and it is indecent to neglect, if this is his intention. But when this candidate must be convinced that there existed a moral certainty of being elected, in a second balloting, it then either becomes his indispensable obligation to give such public notice, or in default thereof, he must be considered as tacitly proposing himself; and in the latter case it is his duty, and ought to be his inclination, to accept an appointment made under these circumstances. Had there been substantial reasons for Mr. W——'s resignation, the public ought to have known them, by which no disagreeable impressions would have been made on the public mind. Inattention in this respect also is a fresh cause of disgust; a conduct so irreconcilable appears paradoxical to those whose ears have been deafened with the praises of Mr. W——. These reflections are not intended to awaken, in this gentleman, a sense of impropriety—his own feelings must have anticipated it—but to show him, that however keenly he may criminate himself, the people have equal consciousness of the magnitude of his fault; as the same inconveniences ever attended on popular elections must again be repeated, which is an additional aggravation of the evil complained of, the following method is proposed to prevent in future, the effects of this nature: that when it is generally concluded in a county that one or more will have a majority of votes, within that district, the selectmen of the town in which he or they reside would at their discretion acquaint the people in the public prints whether such choice will be acceptable. This will frustrate the design of artful men, who to raise themselves or friends falsely propagate that this or that candidate will not accept if chosen. It will inform the people in other counties with some certainty, who are eligible, and give them an opportunity to examine their pretensions; and lastly, it will deprive those who wish to gratify their ridiculous vanity, in having it to tell, and to be said, that they refused the highest offices in the state—when that infinite deal of trouble and expense occurring to their friends and countrymen ought to make them blush. Should any error in the judgment of selectmen happen, with respect to information, no detriment can arise, as the end will be attained; namely, who will accept—not, who will be chosen.

Proceedings of the President and Council, Wednesday, 20 May[1]

Present as yesterday.[2]

. . . .

His Excellency the President asked the advice of Council whether writs of election should issue now, to fill the vacancy in the representation from this state to Congress, the Hon. Mr. West declining his appointment, or whether it would be most advisable to postpone the issuing such writs till the next session of the General Court?[3]

Whereupon the Council advise that writs of election issue immediately. Advised by [signed:] Peter Green, Josiah Richardson, William Simpson, Robert Wallace, Ebenr. Smith. Which [writs] were issued accordingly in the following words, viz.,

State of New Hampshire—

To the Selectmen of [town name] Greeting
In the name of said State, you are required to warn the Inhabitants of said [town name] who are qualified to vote for State Representatives, to meet at some convenient place therein, on the 22d day of June next, to elect by ballot some person having the qualifications required by the Constitution of the united States; to represent this State in Congress, in the room of the Honorable Benjamin West who has declined his appointment, giving fifteen days notice of the design of said meeting: And you are hereby further required, during the choice of said Representative, to preside in said meeting impartially, and receive the votes of said Inhabitants, qualified as aforesaid, and to sort and count the same in said meeting, in the presents of the Town Clerk, who shall make a fair record in your presence and in open meeting of the name of every person voted for, and the number of votes against his name, and a fair copy of such Record attested by you and the Town Clerk, you are directed to seal up and direct to the Secretary of this State, with a Superscription of the purport thereof. And cause the same to be returned to the Sheriff of your County, on or before the thirtieth day of said June, who is required to return the same into the Secretarys Office, on or before the sixth day of July next as the laws in such case made and provided, direct. Hereof fail not.

Witness John Pickering, Esq——, President of our said State, at Portsmouth, the twentieth day of May Anno Domini 1789—[4]

John Pickering

1. Council Records, II, 73-75, Nh-Ar.

2. The Council Journals for 19 May read "Present as yesterday." The Journals for 18 May record the following present: President John Pickering, Peter Green, Ebenezer Smith, Josiah Richardson, William Simpson, and Robert Wallace.

3. The legislature was not scheduled to reconvene until Tuesday, 26 May.

4. (LT). The election writs were published in Portsmouth by George J. Osborne and distributed throughout the state. One of the printed writs (for Hanover in Grafton County) is in the Chase Collection, NhD.

New Hampshire Spy, 19 May

A correspondent observes, that the lower house of Congress seems to abound with able speakers from the Southern States, but the voice of New Hampshire is not heard amongst them. This surely does not proceed from a deficiency of talents; for the abilities of our Representatives are truly respectable. But a gentleman without the powers of elocution, in a popular assembly, is like a figurante on the stage: he serves to fill up the number, and count one; this is the extent of his influence. His abilities are like gold in the center of the earth, of no value, because it can never be brought into use.[1]

1. This complaint was later made part of a campaign appeal for John Sullivan. See the *New Hampshire Spy*, 6 June, printed below.

New Hampshire Spy, 23 May

His Excellency President [John] Pickering, with advice of Council, has issued precepts to the several towns in this state, requiring them to assemble on the 22d day of June next, for the purpose of electing by ballot some person having the qualifications required by the Constitution of the United States, to represent this state in Congress, in the room of the Hon. Benjamin West, who has *declined* his appointment. The returns are to be made into the secretary's office on or before the 6th day of July next.

At the above meeting the selectmen will preside in order to receive, sort, and count the votes. *They are required to preside impartially*.

Warrant for Town Meeting, Warren, Grafton County, 5 June[1]

This is to notify & warn all the Inhabitants of Warren quallified by Law to vote for state Representitives to meet at the house of Ensn. Moses Copp in said Warren on monday the twenty second day of june Instant at four Oclock P.M. for the following purposes (viz)

1stly To choose a Moderator to govern said meeting

2ndly To elect by ballot some person having the quallifications required by Congress (in the room of the Honourable Benjamin West who has declined his appointment) to Represent this state.

Warren june 5th 1789

Samuel Knight ⎫ Select men
Nathl. Knight ⎭ for Warren

1. Transcript of Warren Town Records (LT), II, 71, Nh. The Warren call to election is printed as an example of the type issued by selectmen throughout the state.

New Hampshire Spy, 6 June

In the choice of a Representative for Congress, a correspondent observes, that the public interest would be greatly served by the choice of that tried patriot and friend to our liberties, General [John] Sullivan. No man can be more safely intrusted with the administration of a government than him who has risked his life to establish it. His principles are known to be truly republican and friendly to the interests of the people. And in point of eloquence (a talent so necessary to give weight and importance in a popular assembly, and the want of which is objected to in other candidates) he is acknowledged to excel.[1] He would meet the Southern members on equal ground in this field, from which New Hampshire seems to be excluded. He would not only be able silently to judge for himself but to convey his sentiments to others—a talent, without which, a man and the state he represents, in such an assembly, would be cipherized. Many in his day doubtless possessed equal judgment and abilities with Cicero, but it was by his eloquence that the conspiracy of Catiline was defeated, and the commonwealth preserved from ruin. The same observation will apply to more modern times. Had Pitt been dumb, the English would never have reached such a pitch of eminence. Had the advocates for the new Constitution, in our Convention, been silent, it certainly never would have been adopted.

From the debates of Congress it appears the Southern States have elected distinguished orators; let us show that New Hampshire is not without her speakers, and elect Sullivan for our Representative.

1. See the *New Hampshire Spy*, 19 May, printed above.

Freeman's Oracle, 9 June

A correspondent observes that the virtuous citizens of the state of New Hampshire must feel a particular pleasure at the prospect of the Hon. Nathaniel Peabody's recovery from his late illness; that in all probability he will attend the General Court next week; that this annunciation must be the more pleasing since so many of our respectable citizens are unanimous for the choice of this truly wise, and worthy patriot to represent them in the Grand Congress of the United States of America.

New Hampshire Spy, 13 June

Colonel James Sheafe, we are informed, declines proposing himself as a candidate to represent this state in the Congress of the United States.

Colonel Samuel Sherburne, Jr., is mentioned as a candidate for the vacant seat in our federal representation. The Hon. Mr. [Abiel] Foster is also mentioned.

This last gentleman stood next highest to the gentlemen elected to that important station, has been a member of Congress, and is now one of the judges of the Court of Common Pleas for the County of Rockingham.[1]

1. On 20 June, the Boston *Massachusetts Centinel* reported that a Mr. "Parker" was also being "held up in New Hampshire" as a candidate. Presumably this referred to John Parker, sheriff of Rockingham County and a presidential Elector. However, no New Hampshire source mentions Parker as a candidate, and his name does not appear among those who received votes in the election (see Partial Returns for the Special Election to Replace Benjamin West, 15 July, printed below).

J to the Independent Citizens of the State of New Hampshire, New Hampshire Recorder, 18 June[1]

By the refusal of the Hon. Mr. [Benjamin] West, to accept a seat in the federal House of Representatives, you are again called upon, to give your suffrages for a person to fill that important office; that th[e]re should be a full and able representation of this state, is a matter of the first consequence. On the landed interest, and the improvements in husbandry, the prosperity and happiness of this state must in a great measure depend; to find a man who is not only possessed of an extensive knowledge in general, but in particular of this great branch of business (the others being already represented) is the wish of all; and as such a one I would beg leave to recommend to your consideration, the Honorable Judge [Samuel] Dana of Amherst.[2]

1. The article was dated "June 15, 1789, County of Hillsborough."
2. Elsewhere in this issue the *Recorder* noted that "it is currently reported in the eastern part of this state, that the Hon. Samuel Dana will be elected federal Representative instead of the Hon. Mr. West, who has resigned."

Dana, who was born in Massachusetts, had been a minister there until the beginning of the Revolution. He was suspected of being a Tory and was forced to leave his home state. He moved to Amherst, studied law with Joshua Atherton, and opened practice in Amherst. He was an Antifederalist in politics and was judge of probate in Hillsborough County from 1789 to 1792.

Partial Returns for the Special Election to Replace Benjamin West, 15 July

On 22 June, Abiel Foster was chosen to replace Benjamin West (who had resigned) as one of New Hampshire's congressmen. The tables printed below are incomplete and represent only 69 percent of the popular vote. Returns from the following towns are from the manuscript town records at the New Hampshire Historical Society: Stratham, Hampstead, New Market, Pembroke, Newington, Londonderry, Dublin, Deering, Amherst, Mason, Boscawen, Barrington, and Durham. Returns for all other towns listed in the tables are from the transcripts of town records in the New Hampshire State Library.

CHESHIRE COUNTY, PARTIAL RETURNS

Town	Abiel Foster	Samuel Sherburne	James Sheafe	Elisha Payne
Gilsum				32
Dublin	17			
Claremont				
Chesterfield				
Charlestown				2
Rindge	20	8		
Plainfield				
Packersfield				
[Nelson]	23			
Marlborough				
Lempster	8			
Swanzey				1
Winchester				21
Westmoreland	23	5		
Washington				18
Surry	28			
Totals	119	13	0	74

Others receiving votes: Simeon Olcott (76), John Pickering (26), Moses Dow (19), John Hubbard (10), Timothy Farrar (5), Samuel Dana (2)

GRAFTON COUNTY, PARTIAL RETURNS

Town	Abiel Foster	Samuel Sherburne	James Sheafe	Elisha Payne
Warren	5			
Lebanon				53
Landoff				
Bridgewater	7			
Totals	12	0	0	53

Others receiving votes: John Pickering (13), Nathaniel Peabody (2), Benjamin Bellows (1), Simeon Olcott (1)

HILLSBOROUGH COUNTY, PARTIAL RETURNS

Town	Abiel Foster	Samuel Sherburne	James Sheafe	Elisha Payne
Hancock				
Deering	3			
Dunbarton	21			
Amherst				
Mason	23			
Boscawen	47	23		
Warner	52			
New Ipswich	41	13		
New Boston		16		
Lyndeborough	24			
Hillsborough				
Hollis				
Totals	211	52	0	0

Others receiving votes: Joshua Atherton (70), Benjamin Bellows (46), Benjamin West (27), Samuel Dana (26), John Pickering (13)

ROCKINGHAM COUNTY, PARTIAL RETURNS

Town	Abiel Foster	Samuel Sherburne	James Sheafe	Elisha Payne
Portsmouth	1	114	59	
East Kingston	13			
Sandown	11			
Seabrook	22			
Stratham	27	7	1	
Poplin				
[Fremont]	9			
Canterbury	18			
Chester	52			
Hampstead	26			
Rye		44		
New Market	4	6	41	

(Table continued on following page)

ROCKINGHAM COUNTY, PARTIAL RETURNS *(continued)*

Town	Abiel Foster	Samuel Sherburne	James Sheafe	Elisha Payne
Salem	21	1		
Deerfield	47	7		
Concord	42	50		
Pembroke	16			
Epping	41	5		
Newington		7	13	
Londonderry [Derry]	4	34		
Candia	29			
Brentwood	9			
Totals	392	275	114	0

Others receiving votes: Nathaniel Peabody (43), Joshua Atherton (18), Nathaniel Rogers (1), Charles Henzell (1), Joseph Whipple (1), James MacGregor (1)

STRAFFORD COUNTY, PARTIAL RETURNS

Town	Abiel Foster	Samuel Sherburne	James Sheafe	Elisha Payne
Dover	37	56		
Barrington		7	18	
Wakefield	19			
Tamworth	9			
Rochester		10	37	
Somersworth	13	5		
New Durham				
Middleton				
Lee		19		
Gilmantown	21			
Effingham				
Durham	2	18		
Totals	101	115	55	0

(Continued on following page)

STRAFFORD COUNTY, PARTIAL RETURNS *(continued)*

Others receiving votes: Woodbury Langdon (22), Nathaniel Peabody (19), John Pickering (10), John Waldron (2)

STATE-WIDE PARTIAL RETURNS

Abiel Foster	835
Samuel Sherburne	455
James Sheafe	169
Elisha Payne	127

Proceedings of the President and Council, Wednesday, 15 July[1]

Present: His Excellency John Sullivan, Esq., President; the Hon. John Pickering, Icabod Rollins, and Charles Barret, esquires.

Proceeded to open and enter the returns for a Representative of the federal government in the room of Mr. [Benjamin] West, who had declined accepting.

Adjourned till tomorrow morning, 9 o'clock.

1. Council Records, II, 81, Nh-Ar.

Proceedings of the President and Council, Thursday, 16 July[1]

Present as yesterday—with the addition of Jona. Freeman, Esq.

Upon examining and counting the votes for a Representative to Congress it appeared that the whole number of votes returned was 3094, of which the Hon. Abiel Foster had 1804, being a majority of the whole. He therefore is declared to be duly elected a Representative for this state to the Congress of the United States.

[Signed:] Jno. Sullivan, President; John Pickering, Ichad. Rollins, Charles Barrett, councillors.[2]

1. Council Records, II, 81, Nh-Ar.
2. The results were widely reported throughout the states. See, for example, the *New Hampshire Spy*, 18 July; Boston *Massachusetts Centinel*, 22 July; New York *Gazette of the United States*, 25 July; Hartford *American Mercury*, 27 July; *Newport Mercury*, 29 July; Philadelphia *Pennsylvania Packet*, 30 July; and Baltimore *Maryland Gazette*, 31 July.

Abiel Foster to President John Sullivan, Canterbury, 22 July[1]

I was yesterday favored with a line from Mr. Secretary [Joseph] Pierson, enclosing Your Excellency's commission, appointing me a Representative for New Hampshire, to the Congress of the United States.

I must beg the favor of Your Excellency to communicate to my fellow citizens my most respectful thanks for the honor they have conferred on me by their free suffrages in the present instance. This call to represent them in the federal legislature, and assist in arranging, and carrying into effect, the new government, I consider as an high and distinguishing mark of their confidence, and at the same time, as a flattering circumstance, that my past services in a public line has met with their candid and favorable reception. I beg leave to assure Your Excellency, and my fellow citizens, of my warmest wishes for the prosperity of this state, and the Union at large; that nothing could afford me greater satisfaction, than to perceive all those public blessings and benefits result from the new Constitution of government, which have been hoped for, and predicted by the most sanguine advocates for its adoption; and that nothing within the limits of my abilities shall be wanting in the station I am called to fill, to give it those happy effects.

I cannot, however, on the present occasion refrain (through Your Excellency) from suggesting to my constituents the necessity of general virtue in the citizens, even under the best constituted, and best administered governments, in order that those governments may become the means of public happiness and prosperity; and of expressing my wish, that this northern part of the Union may excel in those private and domestic good qualities, which form the surest basis of national freedom and felicity.

As I conceive, sir, that my call to serve out of the state will interfere with the due discharge of the duties of my station in the Court of Common Pleas, I therefore avail myself of the present occasion, to offer to Your Excellency my resignation of that office, and of returning my sincere thanks to the state and county for the candor with which my services in that station have been received.

I shall lose no time in preparing for my journey, and shall repair in a few days to the discharge of the duties of my appointment.

1. RC, Independence National Historical Park MS Collection, Philadelphia.

John Wendell to Elbridge Gerry, Portsmouth, 23 July (excerpt)[1]

I join with you in wishing never to see oppressive measures take place, but hope we shall always have a power to remove the oppressors, and of exercising our own thoughts on any system of government. Yet the present mode of elections is dilatory, partial, and dangerous to the Union. *Entre nous*, a late Mr. [Benjamin] West was chosen by the people of this state at large as a federal Representative, who, it was said, would serve but he declined, and the people were ordered to choose again, who were so displeased, that but 3000 voters assembled again in the whole state, and any person of the least address or interest might have been elected. Judge [Abiel] F[oster] is a good honest working member of society, and so are others of our Representatives, but they do not seem to be speakers or men of argument. They may be voters, and that only. We have some good men who would make a fine figure in Congress, but like myself carefully avoid the quicksands of popularity and of elections to places in church or state. I have seen so many instances of ingratitude towards gentlemen who have exerted themselves to serve the people that I don't know which to admire most at, the ingratitude of the one or the promptitude of the other.

1. RC, Sang Collection, ICarbS. Wendell was a Portsmouth lawyer.

New Hampshire Gazette, 23 July 1789

Last week the President and Council met at the State House in this town, for the purpose of examining the returns for a Representative to Congress, when they found the whole number returned amounted to 3094—1548 making a choice. The Honorable Abiel Foster, Esq., having 1804, was chosen. This choice completes the organization of the federal government by the ratifying states.[1]

1. New York had completed the election of Senators on 16 July, the same day that the New Hampshire Council declared Abiel Foster elected Representative.

NEW HAMPSHIRE CANDIDATES

Atherton, Joshua (1737-1809), Candidate for Representative

Born in Harvard, Worcester County, Massachusetts, the son of a blacksmith and local politician, Atherton graduated from Harvard in 1762, read law in Worcester and Lancaster, and was admitted to the Worcester County bar in 1765. He moved to Litchfield, Hillsborough County, New Hampshire, that year and to Amherst in 1773. He was appointed a justice of the peace and register of probate in 1771. Atherton lost his provincial offices in 1776 because he refused to sign a loyalty oath to the Revolutionary government. In August 1777 he was arrested as a "disaffected person," but in January 1779 he swore allegiance to the state and resumed the practice of law.

Atherton prospered as a lawyer and a politician. He played an active role in the state constitutional convention which drafted the constitution adopted in 1784. He represented Amherst at the state Convention in 1788, where he led Antifederalist opposition to ratification. He was a delegate to the state constitutional convention in 1791 and 1792, and a state senator in 1792 and 1793. He was appointed attorney general of the state in 1793 and held the office until 1801. Although he was initially an Antifederalist, he soon became a strong Federalist. He supported the Jay Treaty in 1795, and President John Adams appointed him a federal tax commissioner for Hillsborough County in 1798.

Bartlett, Josiah (1729-1795), Elected Senator

Born in Amesbury, Essex County, Massachusetts, Bartlett studied medicine there and then moved to Kingston, Rockingham County, New Hampshire, in 1750. He represented Kingston in the provincial assembly from 1765 until the Revolution, served as a justice of the peace from 1767 to 1775 and as a lieutenant colonel of the militia from 1770 until 1775. Bartlett was active in the Revolution. He was a member of the New Hampshire committee of correspondence in 1774 and a delegate to the Continental Congress from 1774 until 1779, although he did not attend in 1774 and 1777. He signed the Declaration of Independence and the Articles of Confederation.

In 1779 he refused reelection to Congress and was appointed chief justice of the Court of Common Pleas for Rockingham County. In 1782 he became an associate justice of the state Superior Court and in 1788 was named chief justice. He retired from the bench in 1790. Bartlett represented Kingston in the state Convention of 1788 and voted to ratify the Constitution. The legislature elected him a United States Senator that year, but he declined the appointment. He was president of the state from 1790 to 1792 and was elected governor under the new state constitution in 1793, but poor health forced his retirement the next year.

Bellows, Benjamin (1741?-1802), Presidential Elector

Born in Lunenburg, Worcester County, Massachusetts, Bellows moved to Walpole, Cheshire County, New Hampshire, sometime before the Revolution. He was appointed a lieutenant colonel in the militia in 1768 and a justice of the peace and register of deeds for Cheshire County, positions he held until his death. He represented Walpole in the assembly from time to time and was a member of the Council for several years. He served as a militia colonel during the Revolution and was elected to the Confederation Congress in 1781 and 1782 but declined to serve.

Following the war, Bellows became brigadier general of the militia in 1784 and major general in 1786. He served as a judge of the Court of Common Pleas for Cheshire County from 1784 until he resigned in 1793. Bellows represented Walpole in the state Convention of 1788 and voted to ratify the Constitution. He was a presidential Elector in 1792, 1796, and 1800.

Cilley, Joseph (1734-1799), Candidate for Elector

Born in Nottingham, Rockingham County, Cilley fought in the French and Indian War as a private soldier. By 1774 he was a militia captain. Cilley served in the Continental Army from 1775 to the end of 1780 and rose to the rank of colonel. In 1779 he was appointed a brigadier general of the New Hampshire militia.

After the war, Cilley became a justice of the peace in Rockingham County, a post he held until his death. He was a major general of the state militia by 1786, when he led the forces that quelled the riot at Exeter in September. Cilley became a Jeffersonian Republican in national politics. He was a member of the state Senate in 1790 and 1791, of the state constitutional convention in 1791 and 1792, of the state House in 1792, and of the Council in 1797 and 1798.

Dudley, John (1725-1805), Candidate for Elector

Born in Exeter, Rockingham County, Dudley was a farmer, a laborer, and a grocer in his youth. From 1760 to 1765 he served as a town selectman. In 1766 he moved to Raymond, Rockingham County, and engaged in farming and lumbering. In 1768 he was appointed a justice of the peace. He served in the provincial congress in 1775, in the state legislature intermittently from 1775 to 1784, and was speaker of the House in 1782 and 1783. Dudley was also a member of the New Hampshire Committee of Safety and a justice of the Court of Common Pleas for Rockingham County from 1776 to 1784, when he was appointed a judge of the state Superior Court, a post he held until he resigned in 1797.

Folsom, Nathaniel (1726-1790), Candidate for Elector

Born in Exeter, Rockingham County, Folsom served in the French and Indian War, held several militia positions prior to the Revolution, and conducted a mercantile business at Exeter. He was elected to the First Continental Congress in 1774 and was placed in charge of the New Hampshire militia in 1775. During the war he served in the Council and in the House from time to time. He served in the Continental Congress in 1777 and 1778 and for a brief time in 1779 and 1780.

Foster, Abiel (1735-1806), Elected Representative

Born in Andover, Essex County, Massachusetts, Foster graduated from Harvard in 1756 and in 1761 became a minister in Canterbury, New Hampshire. He resigned in 1779 after a dispute with his congregation. Foster played an active role in the Revolution, serving as a member of the Provincial Congress in 1775, in the state legislature from 1779 to 1783, and in the Confederation Congress from July 1783 to October 1785. In 1784 he became a judge of the Rockingham County Court of Common Pleas and was elected to Congress in 1789. He was defeated in the election to the second Congress, was a member of the state Senate from 1791 to 1794, and was its president in 1793 and 1794. He attended the state constitutional convention in 1791 and 1792 and was reelected to Congress in 1795, where he served until March 1803. He usually supported Federalist policies.

Gilman, Nicholas (1755-1814), Elected Representative

Born in Exeter, Rockingham County, Gilman attended local schools and worked as a clerk in his father's countinghouse. At the beginning of the Revolution he was a captain in the Third New Hampshire Regiment in the Continental Army, became its adjutant in 1776, and served to the end of the war. He was a member of the Confederation Congress from 1786 to 1788 and one of New Hampshire's two delegates to the Constitutional Convention in 1787. He was elected to Congress in the first election and served until March 1797. Although Gilman supported ratification of the Constitution, he later became a Jeffersonian Republican. In 1802 President Jefferson appointed him a commissioner in bankruptcy. He served briefly in the state Senate in 1804 but was elected to the United States Senate the same year and served in the Senate until his death.

Langdon, John (1741-1819), Elected Senator

Langdon, the brother-in-law of John Sullivan, was born in Portsmouth, attended local schools, worked in a countinghouse, went to sea, and became a well-to-do merchant by the beginning of the Revolution. He was a delegate to the Continental Congress in 1775 and 1776, a member of the state legislature from 1775 to 1781, and a judge of the Court of Common Pleas for Rockingham County in 1776 and 1777. During the war, he was continental agent for handling prize cases arising from the capture of British vessels.

Langdon's fortunes prospered during the war, as did his political career. In 1783 he represented New Hampshire in Congress, and in 1784 and 1785 he was a state senator. Langdon was elected President of New Hampshire in 1785 but was defeated by John Sullivan in 1786 and 1787. He was one of two New Hampshire delegates to the Constitutional Convention in 1787 and in 1788 supported ratification in the state Convention, where he represented Portsmouth. He was reelected president in 1788 but resigned early in 1789 after he was elected to the United States Senate.

He served two terms in the Senate. He began as a Federalist and supported Hamilton's national bank and funding system but opposed the assumption of state debts, the Jay Treaty, and the Alien and Sedition laws. By 1801 he was a Jeffersonian Republican and was offered but declined appointment as Secretary of the Navy. He became a prominent Republican Party organizer in New Hampshire, served in the legislature from 1801 to 1805, and was elected governor in 1805. He was reelected continuously until 1811, except in 1809 when his support of Jefferson's embargo made him temporarily unpopular. He retired from politics in 1812.

Livermore, Samuel (1732-1803), Candidate for Senator; Elected Representative

Born in Waltham, Middlesex County, Massachusetts, the son of a farmer, Livermore graduated from the College of New Jersey (Princeton) in 1754, taught school briefly, then began practicing law in Waltham. By 1758 he had moved to Portsmouth, where he continued his law practice. Before the Revolution, he moved to Londonderry, Rockingham County, which he represented in the colonial assembly from 1768 to 1770. He returned to Portsmouth in 1769 when Governor John Wentworth appointed him judge advocate of the Admiralty Court and attorney general of the province. By 1774, however, he was back in Londonderry. Livermore began buying land in Grafton County after 1765, and in 1775 he moved to Holderness, where he owned two-thirds of the township.

Livermore served as attorney general of New Hampshire from 1776 to 1779 and as a member of the assembly in 1779 and 1780. Livermore was also a delegate to Congress from 1780 to 1782 and in 1785, and chief justice of the Superior Court from 1782 to 1790, when he was forced to resign after his election to Congress. He was a member of the New Hampshire Convention and voted for ratification of the Constitution. Livermore served two terms in Congress. In June 1792 he was elected to the United States Senate, where he remained until his resignation in June 1801.

Parker, John (1732-1791), Presidential Elector

Born in Portsmouth, the son of a judge of the Superior Court, Parker was apprenticed in a countinghouse in Kittery, Maine. After his apprenticeship, he served as a master of vessels sailing out of Portsmouth. In 1763 he entered a business partnership which failed after a few years. Governor John Wentworth appointed Parker sheriff of Rockingham County after New Hampshire was divided into counties in 1768. He was reappointed sheriff by the Revolutionary government and served in that post until his death. In 1789 he was appointed federal marshal for the District of New Hampshire.

Peabody, Nathaniel (1741-1833), Candidate for Senator and Representative

Born in Topsfield, Essex County, Massachusetts, the son of a physician, Peabody studied medicine with his father; and about 1761 he began to practice medicine in Atkinson, Rockingham County, New Hampshire. Governor John Wentworth commissioned him a justice of the peace of the county in 1771, a post he resigned at the beginning of the Revolution. During the war he was a member of the Committee of Safety and, for a time, adjutant general of the state militia. He served intermittently in the legislature from 1776 to 1795, and was a member of the state constitutional conventions from 1781 to 1783 and in 1791 and 1792.

Peabody was a leading Antifederalist, although he was not a member of the state Convention which ratified the Constitution. After his retirement from public service in 1795, he spent much of the rest of his life in an unsuccessful effort to pay his debts.

Pickering, John (1737-1805), Presidential Elector

Born at Newington, Rockingham County, Pickering graduated from Harvard in 1761 and began the practice of law at Portsmouth. He served in various town offices and was a member of the provincial congress in 1775. Thereafter he withdrew from public life until 1781, when he was elected to the state constitutional convention. He represented Portsmouth in the legislature from 1783 to 1787 but refused to serve in the Confederation Congress, the Annapolis Convention in 1786, or the Constitutional Convention at Philadelphia in 1787.

Pickering was attorney general of the state in 1786 and 1787 and represented Portsmouth in the state Convention in 1788, where he voted to ratify the Constitution. As senior state senator, he succeeded John Langdon as president of the state in 1789 after the latter was elected United States Senator. He became chief justice of the state Superior Court in 1790 and held the post until 1795, when he was appointed judge of the United States District Court in New Hampshire. Increasing mental instability and drunkenness led to his impeachment by the United States House of Representatives and his removal after conviction by the Senate in 1804.

Sheafe, James (1755-1829), Candidate for Representative

Born in Portsmouth, the son of a merchant, Sheafe graduated from Harvard in 1774. He was a Loyalist during the Revolution but remained in the state. After the war he served at various times in the state legislature. Sheafe was nominated for United States Representative in the spring of 1789 after Benjamin West refused to serve, but he ran third in the election in June. A Federalist, he was elected to the sixth Congress and served from March 1799 to March 1801, when he was elected to the United States Senate, where he served until he resigned in June 1802. He ran for governor of New Hampshire in 1816 but was defeated.

Sherburne, [John] Samuel (1757-1830), Candidate for Representative

Born in Portsmouth, Sherburne graduated from Dartmouth in 1776, failed to achieve success as a merchant, and then lost a leg in the campaign in Rhode Island in 1778. He studied law with John Pickering and began practice at Portsmouth after the war. He was appointed United States district attorney for New Hampshire in 1789 and held the post until 1793 while serving simultaneously in the state legislature. He was elected to the United States House of Representatives in 1793 and again in 1795. After serving in the state legislature in 1801, he was reappointed United States district attorney for New Hampshire in 1802. Sherburne was one of the men instrumental in the impeachment of Judge John Pickering by the United States House of Representatives and in his conviction by the Senate in 1804. Sherburne succeeded Pickering as United States district judge for New Hampshire and held the post until his death.

Smith, Ebenezer (1734-1807), Candidate for Elector

Born in Exeter, Rockingham County, Smith became the largest landowner in and the founder of what became the town of Meredith in 1768. He served as town clerk, selectman, and justice of the peace; and during the Revolution he was a member of the legislature and a colonel of militia. After the war he was a member of and president of the Senate, judge of the county court, and judge of probate. He was a delegate to the New Hampshire Convention but was not recorded as voting in the second session, which ratified the Constitution.

Sullivan, John (1740-1795), Candidate for Representative; Presidential Elector

Born in Strafford County, the son of immigrants from Ireland, Sullivan was educated by his schoolteacher father and studied law with Samuel Livermore in Portsmouth. He began to practice law at Durham in 1763 and in 1772 was appointed a major in the militia by Governor John Wentworth. In 1774 he was elected to the first provincial congress, to the committee of safety, and to the First Continental Congress. He led the forces that captured the fort at the entrance to Portsmouth harbor in December 1774 and returned to the Second Continental Congress in May 1775. Congress appointed him a brigadier general of the Continental Army in June 1775 and promoted him to major general in August 1776, shortly before he was captured by the British at the Battle of Long Island. After his exchange for a captured British general, he was active in the military campaigns in 1776 and 1777, although there was mounting opposition to him in Congress. His most successful military venture was his campaign against the Iroquois Indians in New York in 1779, after which he resigned because of ill health.

He served in Congress in 1780 and 1781 and was attorney general of New Hampshire from 1782 to 1786, when he was elected president of the state. He was reelected president in 1787 but was defeated by his brother-in-law, John Langdon, in 1788. Sullivan was chairman of the New Hampshire Convention which ratified the Constitution in 1788, and in 1789 he was again elected president of the state. In September 1789 President Washington appointed Sullivan judge of the United States District Court for New Hampshire, a post he held until his death.

Thompson, Ebenezer (1737-1802), Presidential Elector

Born in Durham, Strafford County, Thompson studied and practiced medicine for a time before abandoning it for politics. He was a Durham selectman from 1765 to 1775 and town clerk for eighteen years. He represented the town in the legislature from 1766 to 1774 and was in the provincial congresses after 1774. He was secretary of the state from 1775 to 1786 and a member of the Council and of the Committee of Safety until 1781. He was twice elected to the Continental Congress but refused to serve.

From 1783 to 1787 he was clerk of the Strafford County Court of Common Pleas and was appointed judge of that court in 1787, a post he held until 1795, when he was appointed a judge of the state Superior Court. He resigned the next year and was reappointed judge of the Strafford County Court, a post he held until his death. He was a presidential Elector in 1792, 1796, and 1800.

Wentworth, Joshua (1742-1809), Candidate for Elector

Born in Portsmouth, probably, Wentworth was a distant relative of Governor John Wentworth. He was a successful Portsmouth merchant before the Revolution. He became colonel of the First New Hampshire Regiment in 1776 and during the war served as a purchasing agent for the Board of War and as a naval agent in charge of prize cases. He was a member of the state Senate from 1785 to 1789, received the second highest number of votes for the presidency of the state in 1790, and in 1791 was appointed to a federal position in New Hampshire by President Washington.

West, Benjamin (1746-1817), Elected Representative; Refused to Serve

Born in Rochester, Plymouth County, Massachusetts, the son of a minister, West graduated from Harvard in 1768. He taught school for two years, studied divinity and preached for a few months, and then studied law. He moved to Charlestown, Cheshire County, New Hampshire, where he formed a law partnership with Simeon Olcott, the county judge of probate. He went to South Carolina in 1777, where he saw military service and was captured. He returned to Charlestown, New Hampshire, in 1780 and was admitted to practice law before the Superior Court. He refused to serve in the Confederation Congress in 1781 and refused an appointment as attorney general of the state in 1786. He was a delegate from Charlestown to the New Hampshire Convention in 1788 and voted to ratify the Constitution.

West received the highest number of votes for United States Representative in the first election on 15 December 1788, although no candidate received enough votes to be elected. West also received the highest number of votes in the second election on 2 February and was declared elected. Some time thereafter he refused to serve, thereby requiring a special election on 22 June 1789, before New Hampshire could complete its election of Representatives. West declined an appointment as judge of probate for Cheshire County in 1802 but served as a presidential Elector in 1808 and 1812 and was a delegate to the Hartford Convention in 1814.

Wingate, Paine (1739-1838), Candidate for Representative; Elected Senator

Born in Amesbury, Essex County, Massachusetts, the son of a minister, Wingate graduated from Harvard in 1759. He was ordained pastor of the Congregational church in Hampton Falls, Rockingham County, New Hampshire, in 1763 but was dismissed from the post at his request in 1771 after a dispute with his congregation. He was a member of the provincial congress in 1775, and in 1776 he moved to Stratham in Rockingham County, where he became a farmer. He opposed the Revolution but was elected to the state constitutional convention in 1781 and to the legislature in 1783. He was a member of the Confederation Congress in 1788. In the drawing for senatorial terms, he drew four years and thus served until 1793, when he was elected to the House of Representatives, where he served one term. He was elected to the state legislature in 1795. In 1798 he was appointed a judge of the state Superior Court and served until 1809, when he retired.

Index

There are five major subdivisions within the index, corresponding to the five major sections which constitute this volume. Subjects pertaining to the Confederation Congress and the first federal elections and to the first federal elections in Massachusetts, New Hampshire, Pennsylvania, and South Carolina are indexed in detail under those headings. Many of the same subjects also appear as entries in the main body of the index, but those entries normally list only page numbers. Thus "Federalists" is indexed in detail in each of the subdivisions, while the main index entry, "FEDERALISTS," brings together the page numbers for the volume as a whole. Cross-references to the entries in the main index are set in capital letters. Cross-references to the entries within each of the five major subdivisions are set in capital and lower-case letters.

The entries for the names of individuals are limited to those who played important roles in legislatures, to serious candidates for office during the first federal elections, and to those who wrote letters and other documents or received letters concerning the elections. The abbreviation "id." following the name of an individual indicates the page or pages wherein the individual is identified.

Omitted from the index are the hundreds of names of individuals appearing in roll-call votes, and the names of individuals who received only scattered votes in the first federal elections or who are mentioned incidentally.

KENTUCKY: allotted two Representatives after Census of 1790, xxiv; petitions for statehood, 11-12, 33; opposition to Constitution, 12; statehood opposed by Eastern States, 33; "Spanish Conspiracy" in, 34n

KING, RUFUS (Mass.): id., 448n, 753; as candidate for Representative, 447-48, 506n, 545, 555, 557, 571; as candidate for Senator, 448n, 455, 472, 506n, 512, 513, 521, 522, 522-23, 524, 627
Letter from, 23
Letters to, 26n, 209-10, 447-48, 448, 455-56, 506n, 522, 522-23, 524, 545, 555, 571, 586, 599

KINSLEY, MARTIN (Mass.): id., 663n; votes for as Elector, 534; as candidate for Representative, 602, 663, 677; votes for as Representative, 618-19, 665-67, 682-83

KNOX, HENRY (Mass.): id., 28n; mentioned, 524; arranges to send news of New Hampshire ratification to New York Convention, 23; lends support to Nathan Dane candidacy for Senate, 523
Letters from, 27-28, 38n, 448, 583-84
Letters to, 38, 63n, 64, 67, 79n, 80, 82n, 88, 524n, 530, 538n, 546n, 571, 584n, 585, 585n, 600, 600-601, 639n, 644, 644n, 656n, 738

KNOX, LUCY [Mrs. Henry] (Mass.)
Letter from, 67

KNOX, WILLIAM (Mass.): id., 64n
Letters from, 63n, 64, 67, 79n, 80, 82n, 88

LAMB, JOHN (N.Y.): id., 840n
Letters to, 79n, 770, 839-40

LANCASTER. See PENNSYLVANIA: cities and towns; PENNSYLVANIA: counties; PENNSYLVANIA: Lancaster Conference

LANE, SAMUEL (N.H.): id., 26n
Letters to, 26, 53

LANGDON, JOHN (N.H.): id., 855-56; mentioned, 768, 769, 770, 801n; transmits news of New Hampshire ratification of Constitution, 24, 25; urges prompt passage of U.S. Election Ordinance, 122n; proclamation and message to General Court on U.S. Election Ordinance, 775-76, 777-78, 779; as candidate for Senator, 777, 777n, 780;

elected Senator, 783-84, 784-85, 788, 789, 793, 832-33; resigns as New Hampshire president to take Senate seat, 825-26, 826-27, 828n; congratulated on election as Senator, 828, 828-29n
Letters from, 25, 122n
Letters to, 30, 44, 122, 129, 802, 813, 828, 828-29n

LANGDON, WOODBURY (N.H.): id., 777n, 800n; mentioned, 776; as candidate for Representative, 798-99; votes for as Representative, 806-10, 850; votes for as Elector, 814-15

LANSING, ABRAHAM G. (N.Y.): id., 25n
Letter to, 24-25

LAURENS, HENRY (S.C.): id., 222; mentioned, 176, 209; elected Elector, 202, 203, 212; casts Electoral vote, 211

LEAR, TOBIAS (N.H.): id., 828n; and news of New Hampshire ratification, 24
Letter from, 828

LEE, ARTHUR (Va.): id., 377n; mentioned, 177, 258n
Letter from, 377

LEE, HENRY (Va.): on location of federal capital, 51n, 55, 82, 134-35
Letters from, 82, 134-35
Letter to, 369-70

LEE, RICHARD HENRY (Va.), 258n; proposes amendments to Constitution, 3, 14; elected Senator, 16; election as Senator criticized, 556; congratulated on election as Senator, 574
Letters to, 15, 82, 574-75

LEONARD, GEORGE (Mass.): id., 583, 753-54; mentioned, 543; votes for as Elector, 533; and issue of dual office-holding, 575-76, 583; as candidate for Representative, 583, 584, 585; votes for as Representative, 584-85, 614; elected Representative, 624

LEWIS, MORGAN (N.Y.): id., 127n
Letter from, 126-27

LEWIS, WILLIAM (Pa.), 285, 286, 288n, 313; speech in Assembly supporting at-large election of Representatives, 283-84

L'HOMMEDIEU, EZRA (N.Y.): and agreement of New York congressional delegates on federal capital, 81-82

LINCOLN, BENJAMIN (Mass.): id., 57n; mentioned, 521n, 579; and Shays's Rebellion, 436; elected lieutenant gov-

DESIGNED BY IRVING PERKINS
COMPOSED BY FOCUS/TYPOGRAPHERS, ST. LOUIS, MISSOURI
MANUFACTURED BY MALLOY LITHOGRAPHING, INC., ANN ARBOR, MICHIGAN
TEXT AND DISPLAY LINES ARE SET IN BASKERVILLE

Library of Congress Cataloging in Publication Data
Main entry under title:
The Documentary history of the first Federal elections,
1788-1790.
Bibliography: p. xix-xxi.
Includes index.
1. Elections—United States—History—Sources.
2. United States—Politics and government—1789—1797—
Sources. I. Jensen, Merrill, 1905- II. Becker, Robert A., 1943-
JK171.A1D6   329'.023'7303   74-5903
ISBN 0-299-06690-8